OPERATION CHINA

"The author is a pioneer in the search for China's unreached peoples. This book is a brilliant work of research on the spiritual frontiers of China.... For all who have discovered that China's millions are precious to God, this book is a gold mine!"
— **Jim Ziervogel,** *Senior Research Fellow, Institute of Chinese Studies*

"Carefully researched and brilliantly presented, this book will wake up those who think the Great Commission is virtually completed and bless those who want to see it completed. This book is a spiritual pacemaker, getting our hearts to beat in time with God's."
— **Michael O'Rear,** *President, Global Mapping International*

"A helpful resource as we mobilize people to pray for China and reach these groups. The color photos help to give a greater vision and appreciation for the unreached peoples."
— **Paul Eshleman,** *President, The Jesus Film Project*

"A remarkable, graphic visualization of the urgent reality of the unreached peoples."
— **Dr. Ralph Winter,** *Founder, U. S. Center for World Mission*

"*Operation China* is an essential tool for prayer, strategy and action."
— **Tony Lambert,** *Director for Research, China Ministries, OMF International*

"The most significant new contribution to missions research in 20 years."
— **Dr. David Barrett,** *President, Global Evangelization Movement*

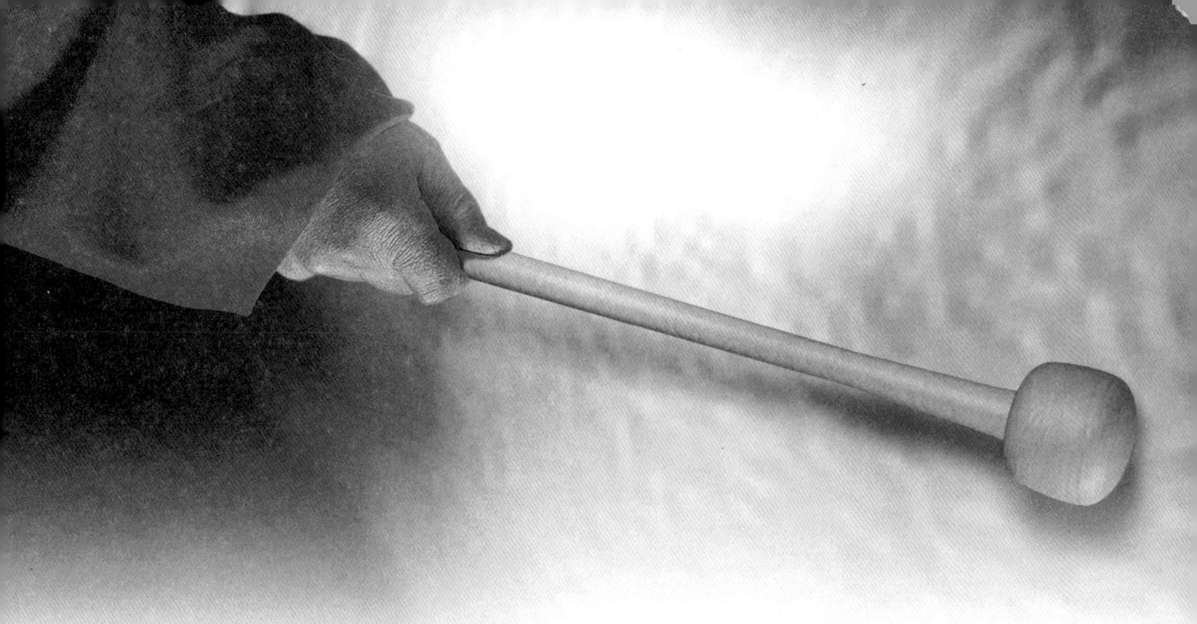

OPERATION CHINA

Introducing all the Peoples of China

PAUL HATTAWAY

William Carey Library
Pasadena, California

piquant

First edition 2000
05 04 03 02 01 00 7 6 5 4 3 2 1
ISBN 0-9535757-5-6

Published by Piquant
PO Box 83, Carlisle, CA3 9GR, United Kingdom
E-mail: info@piquant.net
Website: www.piquant.net

Copublished by William Carey Library
Po Box 40129, Pasadena, CA 91114, USA
Tel.: +1(626)798-0819
Website: www.wclbooks.com

ISBN 0-87808-351-0

A catalogue record of this book is available in the UK from the British Library and in the USA from the Library of Congress.

Cover photographs (clockwise):
Amdo woman from Xiahe, Gansu [Paul Hattaway];
Eastern Hmu boy from Kaili, Guizhou [*Miao Messenger*];
Ami man from Fujian Province [Paul Hattaway];
Western Lipo woman from Dayao, Yunnan [Jamin Pelkey];
Chinese Gong [Martyn Hollingworth]

Cover design by Sam Hill

Designed and produced for the publisher by
Gazelle Creative Productions, Mill Hill, London NW7 3SA.

Printed and bound in Singapore.

For Little Lek and Big D

How shall God's name be hallowed by them? His kingdom come among them? His will be done by them? His Name, His attributes, they have never heard; His kingdom is not proclaimed among them. His will is not made known to them. Do you believe that each unit of these millions has a precious soul, and that there is no other Name under heaven given to men by which they must be saved except that of Jesus? Do you believe that He alone is the door of the sheepfold? He is the Way, the Truth and the Life? that no man comes to the Father but through Him? If so, think of the state of these unsaved ones and solemnly examine yourself in the sight of God to see whether you are doing your utmost to make Him known to them.

Shall not the eternal interests of one-fifth of our race stir up the deepest sympathies of our nature with the most strenuous effort of our Blood-bought powers; shall not the low wail of helpless misery arising from one-half of the heathen world pierce our sluggish ear and rouse us, spirit, soul and body, to one mighty, continued, unconquerable effort for China's salvation; that strong in God's strength and in the power of His might, we may snatch the prey from the hand of the mighty; that we may pluck these brands from the everlasting burning, and rescue these captives from the thralldom of sin and Satan; to grace the triumph of our Sovereign King, and to shine forth forever as stars in His diadem.

J. Hudson Taylor
Founder of the China Inland Mission

Contents

Foreword

China remains one of the biggest challenges for world evangelization for the Church of the Lord Jesus Christ as we enter the twenty-first century. We all marvel at the millions of Chinese who have come to Christ over the past twenty years, but this fact obscures a vital truth that this turning to God is not happening for every part of China nor for all its constituent peoples. Paul Hattaway's remarkable research into the peoples of China has been shedding more light on the areas of need.

Many who know something of China have heard of some of China's significant minority peoples — such as the Tibetans, Mongolians and the Uygur — or have perhaps read about the pioneering work of J.O. Fraser and Isobel Kuhn among the Lisu in Southwest China. Few realize that there are more than 100 million people in over 450 distinct minorities, for their 7% share of the population seems so small in comparison to China's huge population of 1,262,000,000 (in 2000).

China recognizes these minority peoples but classifies them all in 55 "official nationalities," an administrative simplification. In this striking book, however, the variety of Chinese peoples and their spiritual needs are vividly displayed as never before.

I have relied much on the information in *Operation China* during compilation of the section on China for the latest edition of *Operation World*, due to be published in 2001.

May this unique book go a long way to focus prayer on the need for the gospel among these peoples.

Patrick Johnstone
Author of *Operation World*
WEC International, England

Miao Messenger

Miao Messenger

Acknowledgments

In a sense, this book has taken a decade to research and write. During this time numerous people have assisted in one way or another. Like a massive jigsaw, *Operation China* slowly took shape, piece by piece.

A number of people have made key contributions to this project. I greatly appreciate their help in seeing this book through to completion.

If it were not for the vision and wisdom of Dr. David Barrett, and his team of coworkers at the Global Evangelization Movement in Richmond, Virginia, this book would never have been birthed. His enthusiasm to see this information published encouraged me immensely.

I thank Dwayne Graybill who traveled many tough miles to gather priceless information and take superb photographs of some of China's "hidden" peoples. Dwayne once traveled for five weeks by train and bus into the heart of Xinjiang to get the photographs used for the Muslim groups in *Operation China*. I also thank Dwayne for his help — much of it unglamorous work behind the scenes — which enabled me to concentrate on research and writing.

I thank Jab who faithfully and methodically proofread the entire manuscript and, in the process, gained a heart of compassion for China's peoples. Thanks too to Joyce Renick for her thorough copy-editing.

In addition, I want to express my appreciation for Mike O'Rear, Warren Lawrence, Loren Muehlius, and Bruce Hanson of Global Mapping International in Colorado. With patience and understanding they taught me how to draw the maps used in the Profiles. (All the maps used in this book were created using the Atlas GIS 3.0 program.)

I am grateful to Dr. Ralph Winter, and Ben Sells, Dwight Baker, and Jim Ziervogel at the U.S. Center for World Mission in Pasadena, California, who share my vision for the evangelization of all the peoples of China, and whose interest has greatly motivated the publication of *Operation China*.

Part of the way in which God brought this project to completion was to bring me in contact with Pieter and Elria Kwant of Piquant Publishing. Because they do not see publishing merely as a job but rather as their ministry to the Lord, they caught the vision for China's people and had the expertise and perseverance to see the book through to completion. Warm thanks to the Gazelle Creative team at Angus Hudson who coped with the demanding production process, and to Patrick Johnstone for his encouraging Foreword.

I appreciate Jamin Pelkey for contributing his leading research into the numerous ethnic branches of the Yi nationality; and Michael Johnson, for graciously helping with the Miao and Hmong sections.

A heartfelt thanks is due to the many fellow travelers and friends who shared with me hundreds of long trips on Chinese airplanes, trains, buses, boats, hovercrafts, donkeycarts, and tractors, and who walked sometimes for days over remote mountain ranges so that another little-known tribe could be brought to the attention of the Body of Christ for the first time. I cannot remember all who shared China with me over the years, but some who come to mind include Jeff and Kendra McAffee, Eric Davidson, Keith Kline, and Midge Conner. I thank them not only for being there but also for the laughter and fun we enjoyed in some of the strangest and most remote places on earth.

To my wonderful vivacious wife, Joy,... Thank you for your patience and understanding. This book could never have come close to completion if it were not for your involvement and encouragement.

It was Keith K who first introduced me to the fascinating world of China's minorities. I thank him for his vision and example of a single-minded, uncompromising commitment to see God's kingdom come among the forgotten people groups of China.

Thanks to each photographer who contributed to the 704 original photographs in this book. Their names appear throughout the text alongside the photographs which so greatly enhance this project.

To the Chinese house church believers: Thank you for showing me what it means to be a true Christian by your lives of love, dedication, faith, joy, and incredible commitment to your loving Savior. As I travel around the world people often ask me, "What is the most beautiful thing you have seen?" They expect me to answer: "The Grand Canyon," or "The Himalayas," but these days I simply tell them, "The most beautiful thing I have ever seen is the Chinese Church." May God bless your efforts to reach every single group profiled in this book!

Finally, no acknowledgments can be complete without mention of Jesus Christ, the unseen helper who never failed to amaze me with the way in which he turned up information, books, articles, and the right people at just the right time. I wrote with a strong awareness and confidence that he was overseeing the whole project because of his love and concern for the peoples of China whom he created and longs to know intimately.

May God use the information in *Operation China* to call many people to pray for and go to the hidden and forgotten peoples of China with the glorious gospel message. When this age ends, may there be people from "every tribe and language and nation" in China worshiping around the throne of the Lamb who was slain that they may live forevermore.

Paul Hattaway
Chiang Mai, Thailand

Abbreviations

AMO — Asian Minorities Outreach
ANU — Australian National University
CASS — Chinese Academy of Social Sciences
CCRC — Chinese Church Research Center
CIM — China Inland Mission
CMA — Christian Missionary Alliance
COM — Center for Oriental Ministries
CPLMR — China Prayer Letter and Ministry Report
DAWN — Discipling a Whole Nation
EDCL — Encyclopedic Dictionary of Chinese Linguistics
FEBC — Far East Broadcasting Company
GEM — Global Evangelization Movement
GPD — Global Prayer Digest
HRAF — Human Relations Area Files
KMT — Kuomintang
LAC — Language Atlas of China
n.d. — no date
NIV — New International Version
NT — New Testament of the Bible
OMF — Overseas Missionary Fellowship
OT — Old Testament of the Bible
OW — Operation World
ROPAL — Registry of Peoples and Languages
SIL — Summer Institute of Linguistics
SPCK — Society for Promoting Christian Knowledge
STEDT — Sino-Tibetan Etymological Dictionary and Thesaurus
TEAM — The Evangelical Alliance Mission
TSPM — Three-Self Patriotic Movement
TWR — Trans World Radio
UBS — United Bible Society
USCWM — United States Center for World Mission
YASS — Yunnan Academy of Social Sciences
YWAM — Youth With a Mission
YWAM COM — Youth With a Mission Center for Oriental Ministries

Operation China is Paul Hattaway's fifth ethnographic book.

Although the author has made every effort to ensure the information in this book is accurate and up to date at the time of going to press, ethnographic research of this kind requires constant fresh input. Readers who are knowledgeable about a certain people group in China or who have found a new group, or those with additional or updated information, corrections, or suggestions are warmly invited to contact Paul Hattaway at Asian Minorities Outreach in Chiang Mai, Thailand (see the information page at the end of *Operation China*). Of particular interest is all information regarding the state of Christianity among China's people groups. Christian workers from within China are also welcome to contact Paul. He undertakes to treat the identity of every person who wishes to remain anonymous as strictly confidential.

At present *Operation China* is being translated for publication in Chinese, at the request of church leaders inside China who desire to learn about and plant churches among every unreached people group in their country. AMO has set up a fund to cover the cost of this project. If you would like to contribute to the funding of the Chinese *Operation China*, please send donations, by cheque, to Asian Minorities Outreach at any of the addresses listed in the back. All contributions will be receipted. All U.S. donations are tax-deductible.

Introduction

The Hidden China

For centuries the outside world has yearned to understand the mysterious land of China. Since the late 1970s — when China again opened her doors to foreign trade and tourism — thousands of visitors have flocked into the Middle Kingdom, sampling her sumptuous food, photographing her scenic beauty, and experiencing her bustling marketplaces.

People around the world conjure up several key images when they think of China — the Great Wall, the Forbidden City of Beijing, the canals of Suzhou, or the spectacular karst peaks of Guilin.

Few, however, have been fortunate enough to experience the "hidden" China which possesses a side so dramatically colorful and enticing, they are surprised to find it even exists. Woven into the fabric of the largest population on earth is the rich thread of China's ethnic minorities — numbering more than 100 million people — lost, largely, amid the vast population of 1.2 billion Han Chinese.

Operation China introduces the reader to these hidden minority peoples, to groups and cultures as diverse as the pale, blue-eyed Muslims of Xinjiang and the tribal people of the jungles of Yunnan with their intricately embroidered costumes; the Tibetans in the west, proud of their fascinating heritage, and the nomadic hunter tribes, related to the Eskimos, in the extreme northeast of this vast country. Although numerically the minorities of China account for only 6.7% of China's population, they inhabit 62.5% of China's territory.[1]

Changing Fortunes

The name the Chinese use for their country is *Zhong Guo*, or "The Middle Kingdom." For more than a thousand years the Chinese have believed theirs is the cradle of civilization, the culture at the centre of all human existence. This attitude surfaced frequently when foreign powers attempted to enter into trade relations with China. When a British delegation, led by Lord Macartney, applied for permission to trade with the Chinese in 1793, Emperor Qianlong promptly dismissed the delegation, informing the British monarch that

> The Celestial Empire, ruling all within the four seas, simply concentrates on carrying out the affairs of government properly, and does not value rare and precious things. Now you, O King, have presented various objects to the throne, and mindful of your loyalty in presenting offerings from afar, we have specially ordered the Yamen to receive them.... Nevertheless, we have never valued ingenious articles, nor do we have the slightest need of your country's manufactures.

Ignoring the power of the emerging British Empire, the Emperor added:

> I do not forget the lonely remoteness of your island, cut off from the world by intervening wastes of sea, nor do I disregard your inexcusable ignorances of the ways of the Celestial Empire... My capital is the hub and center about which all quarters of the globe revolve... Tremblingly obey and show no negligence.[2]

By the beginning of the twentieth century, however, the Chinese felt great shame as a nation. Parts of their country had been divided up and were controlled by foreign powers — the Japanese, British, Dutch, Spanish, French, Portuguese, Russians, and others had seized strategic ports and regions for their own benefit. The Chinese economy was in tatters, and the countryside was practically ruled by warlords and gangsters.

On 1 October 1949 Chairman Mao ascended to the podium before one million spectators in Beijing's Tiananmen Square and triumphantly declared the founding of the People's Republic of China. The humiliated Chinese people sensed in the founding of the People's Republic that a new dawn had arrived.

China's reaction was to close the door to foreigners for the best part of the next 30 years. The 1920s had been a "high water mark of the missionary enterprise in China."[3] More than 10,000 missionaries were scattered throughout the region. Now these Christian missionaries were ordered to leave. Many of the departing missionaries lamented the future of the church in China, believing it too young and weak to withstand the ferocity of a totalitarian regime. History, however, has proven that, far from being overcome by persecution, the Chinese church found a maturity and boldness in their faith that they probably would never have experienced in other circumstances. The Chinese church today has a testimony similar to that of the Israelites in Egypt: "The more they were oppressed, the more they multiplied and spread."[4]

The Communist government brought a mixture of fortune to China's minority peoples. The nation's new leaders reacted mercilessly and violently towards the Tibetans and Uygurs, not tolerating even the slightest suggestion of claims to independence by these two people groups. It soon became clear that what the law stated and how it was applied were two different things. China's law states:

> If any worker of the government unlawfully deprives the citizens of their rights of lawful religious freedom, or violates the customs and practices of any minority nationality, he may be sentenced to imprisonment or compulsory labor for up to two years.[5]

The 1931 Constitution of the Jiangxi Soviet had even gone so far as to declare

> the right of self-determination of the national minorities in China, the right to complete separation from China, and to the formation of an independent state for each minority nationality. All Mongolians, Tibetans, Miao, Yao, Koreans and others living on the territory of China shall enjoy full right to self-determination.... The Soviet regime must encourage the development of the national cultures and the national languages of these people.[6]

The reality has proved to be in stark contrast to these bold declarations. In *My Land and My People* the Dalai Lama in 1962 listed some of the atrocities inflicted on the Tibetan people:

> Tens of thousands of our people have been killed, not only in military actions, but individually and deliberately. They have been killed without trial.... Fundamentally they have been killed because they would not renounce their religion. They have not only been shot, but beaten to death, crucified, burned alive, drowned, vivisected, starved, strangled, hanged, scalded, buried alive, disemboweled and beheaded. These killings have been done in public. Men and women have been killed while their own families were forced to watch, and small children have even been forced to shoot their parents.[7]

Yet for some of the smaller groups, the new regime meant an end to centuries of exploitation by greedy landlords and slave-owners. It also meant, for some, they were officially allowed "to exist" for the first time ever. The small Kucong tribe, inhabiting a mountainous jungle in the extreme southwest of the country, had lived in dire poverty for centuries, and were on the brink of extinction:

> The Kucong cultivated the land by the traditional "slash and burn" method.... To clear the brush, only three hatchets were available in the whole village.... Their clothing was plantain leaves, in which they also wrapped their babes.... In their nakedness the Kucong dared not to go out, so they placed their rattan, animal hides and meats by the wayside and hid in the bushes waiting for a prospective barterer. Then they would call out: "Take these. Leave in exchange clothes and salt." Only when the takers were far away would the Kucongs emerge from the bushes and collect whatever had been left for them.[8]

Sun Yatsen in the 1920s considered China to consist of only five nationalities. The Kuomintang government simply denied the existence of ethnic minorities, regarding them erroneously as branches of the Han nationality. The original flag of the Republic of China displayed five colors, representing five people groups: Han, Manchu, Mongolian, Tibetan, and Uygur.

Centuries of hostility and prejudice between the Han Chinese and the minority peoples was poignantly illustrated by the Chinese use of the character for "dog" after the name of a tribe. This was officially banned by the government of the young People's Republic in favor of the use of the character for "nationality." Each officially recognized minority group was allowed a representative at the National Party Congress in Beijing. More recently, health and education benefits have been given to minority peoples. Only those of minority groups who live in urban areas are subject to China's one-child policy. Most minority families are allowed two children, while those living in remote regions are allowed three. Some of these small gestures of goodwill have been appreciated by the people. The Miao, for example, who use an abundance of silver in their traditional costume, are allowed to purchase silver at a much cheaper rate than other Chinese citizens. As Ralph Covell notes, "Efforts are being made to remove tensions that have existed for centuries between Han Chinese and minority nationalities living in the same or nearby areas."[9]

Origins

Today there are hundreds of distinct ethnic groups scattered throughout China's territory. Linguistically, their languages are as diverse as Persian, Turkish, Malayo-Polynesian, Burmese, and Siberian. This ethnic composition is a result of thousands of years of history. As one author notes:

> In 1500 BC there was no China, and there were no Chinese. The area that is now China was then inhabited by a great number of tribes with different cultures. Though the majority of them belonged to one or another branch of the Mongoloid race, other races were represented. There was no great man who created the first Chinese empire; it grew out of a long, slow process of assimilation and integration over centuries.[10]

Many groups and peoples migrated across the continent, some fleeing from persecution, others because of famine, and still others searching for a land where they might live in peace. Some people groups who appeared at different times in history can no longer be traced, having been assimilated into the vast Han Chinese race in the same way "stomach juices will treat a steak."[11]

Prior to the 1950s little was known about China's minority peoples. Chinese scholars did little or no research. The lack of motivation and the practical and geographical barriers kept many minorities hidden from the outside world. French Catholic missionary Paul Vial, who worked among the Sani and Axi peoples in Yunnan between 1880 and 1930, vividly described his frustrating observations of Chinese prejudice against minority peoples:

> All siniologists are legion... to travel through the labyrinth of Chinese literature: I would prefer to travel on foot, and gather the information myself.... The Chinese observe foreigners, Miao, Lolo, or Europeans only through the magnifying glass of their immense conceit, and all objects have the appearance of a grotesque caricature which seems reality to them.[12]

Such attitudes contributed to the lack of knowledge about China's minority peoples, and in the 1840s British Consul F.S.A. Bourne lamented:

> There is probably no family of the human race... of which so little is accurately known as the non-Chinese races of Southern China. This is in great measure due to the perfect maze of senseless names, taken from the Chinese, in which the subject is involved. In the *Topography of the Yunnan Province* (1836 edition) there is a catalogue of 141 classes of aborigines, each with a separate name and illustration, without any attempt to arrive at a broader classification.[13]

The majority of the early missionaries did not progress past the Chinese coastal areas, where they worked faithfully and valiantly among the Han Chinese, sowing the seeds for the great revival still in progress. Of course, there was mission activity among some of the larger and better-known minority groups such as the Tibetans, Miao, and Mongolians. Although some brave and faith-filled souls ventured to extremely remote border areas to proclaim the gospel among groups such as the Lisu, Lahu, Wa, and Jingpo, however, the lack of research before the arrival of Communist rule, and the ensuing antireligious fervor which still continues today, meant that the smaller ethnolinguistic people groups of China have remained hidden from the Christian world and, therefore, from prayer, awareness, and efforts to evangelize them.

In the 1950s, motivated by the need to extend its rule to all corners of the nation, the government commenced massive communication projects. Millions of miles of railways and roads were constructed across the length and breadth of China. Minority villages that required an arduous two-week horse ride through dangerous bandit-filled mountains in the 1940s were now a short flight and bus ride away from a provincial capital.

Perhaps most important of all, Mandarin became the national language, used in all schools throughout the nation. Minority tribesmen from remote locations, who previously on their irregular visits to the marketplaces only looked askance at the Han Chinese, could now communicate with their Han neighbours. Accurate information about the smaller people groups of China became easier to obtain to benefit the advance of the gospel among them. It should also be noted that in recent decades the Chinese authorities have adopted a better approach to the minorities, taking a genuine interest in their lives, culture, and welfare and generally no longer viewing them with the flippant arrogance that once prevailed.

How Many Groups Are There?

Early writers were aware of a large number of different tribes and peoples in China but had no means of conducting ongoing research or gathering further information, or biographical data. Most of them simply offered a list of names and locations to the interested world. In 1942 the anthropologist Wolfgram Eberhard

> drawing from Chinese sources reaching over a period of two thousand years... compiled the names, and the cultural and geographical data of eight hundred "alien" or marginal peoples.[14]

The Christian world marveled at the results of a 1944 survey by missionary John Kuhn, who documented 100 tribes in Yunnan Province alone. Kuhn wrote:

> Everywhere we kept finding tribes, many of whom we had never heard of, until our hearts were thrilled. On December 23 we tabulated the one-hundredth tribe! One hundred tribes in Yunnan! And two-thirds of these had never had a gospel witness.[15]

When a new constitution in the early 1950s declared China to be "a unitary, multi-national socialist state,"[16] leaders from China's minority groups were invited to come forward, register their groups with the government, and be considered for official recognition. The results, first released in 1953, were staggering. Over 400 groups submitted their names; more than 260 of them were located in Yunnan Province alone.[17] In *Operation China* the author has researched and profiled a total of 234 ethnic groups in Yunnan, of which 200 groups are primarily located in this province, and 34 groups are primarily located in another part of China but have communities also within Yunnan.

The long history of suspicion at best, and utter contempt at worst, with which the Han Chinese have viewed the minority tribes and nationalities was epitomized in an ominous statement by Sun Yatsen:

> The name "Republic of Five Nationalities" exists only because there exists a certain racial distinction which distorts the meaning of a single republic. We must facilitate the dying out of all the names of individual peoples inhabiting China.[18]

The unique contribution of *Operation China* is linked to what the Chinese authorities did with these 400 groups from across China. Obviously not willing to deal with so many different tribes and groups, the new communist government began to artificially trim the list down to manageable proportions.

In 1956, 16 teams with a total of more than 1,000 people were established by the government and sent across China to investigate the claims of the 400 groups who had applied for recognition. "The members included linguists, archaeologists, historians, economists, and experts in literature and the arts."[19] The teams "collected a large body of data and presented their views on the classification of minority languages. These form most of the language information used today on China's minorities."[20] The researchers rejected most of the 400 names, claiming that

> Some were different names referring to the same group of people, some were different branch names of one ethnic family, some were place names of the areas where the minority groups lived and some were Chinese transliterations of a group of people.[21]

While there is no doubt that this is true in part, even a casual researcher of China's ethnic composition will soon realize that there exist many groups in China today which defy their official classification.

By 1964 the government had managed to reduce the number of groups on their list to only 183.[22] Dismayed at being rejected, many minority groups applied again in the late 1960s, including over 80 groups representing 900,000 people in Guizhou Province alone.[23]

With the central government feeling uncomfortable at the prospect of dealing with so many collective needs, and with administrators in Beijing no doubt feeling unwilling to welcome hundreds of new representatives — Deputies to the National Party Congress — the scholars were sent back to work. From their revised list of 183, they squeezed together dozens of groups into broad ethnic classifications, grouping together tribes who in many cases shared no historical kinship and could not understand a word of each others' languages. In this way in 1976 the State Council of the People's Republic finally arrived at a total of just 51 selected "minority nationalities" in China. Since then four more groups have been added to arrive at the current total of 55 officially recognized minorities. The State Nationalities Affairs Commission now "considers the work of identifying nationalities virtually complete and is unlikely to accept any of the outstanding claims."[24]

Martin Heijdra of Princeton University further explains how,

> most ethnic self-designations were brought under one or another of these official "nationalities," and only in Guizhou did much identification work remain unfinished. Subsequent harsher policies against the nationalities resulted in practically freezing this list, and what little subsequent work on minorities was undertaken was considered too secret to be published. The original list of four hundred-odd "basic" designations has not been published, and even in the much freer period since the 1980s the actual policies leading up to decisions on actual nationality identification are closed to Western inspection. This has resulted in a common conception that all classification work has been finished, and even that all languages and ethnic groups have already been identified. This is not the case, however, and there are still many insufficiently investigated groups in, for instance, Tibet, Yunnan, and Hainan, where the groups in question are provisionally already classified under other groups, as well as in Guizhou, where many groups have never been classified at all.[25]

This has created a curious situation. One source states that at present there are only 21 officially recognized minorities living in Yunnan Province, but these 21 groups have 138 ethnic names, with an additional 157 ethnic names given to them by neighboring peoples.[26] The small Lopi people group who live on the Yunnan-Sichuan border have been officially included as part of the large Yi minority group, but "they think of the Yi as mountain barbarians and have no wish to be associated with them; they are both puzzled and bitter that they have not won recognition as a separate nationality."[27]

The Eastern Lipo people of northern Yunnan were also officially assigned to the Yi nationality, even though their language is much more closely related to Lisu than Yi. This official classification horrified the Eastern Lipo, who had been slaves to the Eastern Nasu (another Yi group) for centuries. Eastern Lipo leaders petitioned the government saying they did not care what minority group they were assigned to, as long as it was not the Yi. The government ignored their pleas until recently. The illogical classification of the Eastern Lipo today embodies all that is wrong with their approach: On a national level the Eastern Lipo continue to be classified as Yi people; on the district, county, and prefecture administrative levels, however, the Eastern Lipo are now counted as Lisu! If any lesson is to be learned from the example of the Eastern Lipo, it is that a people group's self-identity is crucially important.

The Nosu people of northern Yunnan and southern Sichuan, who are considered a branch of the Yi nationality, consist of "44 subgroups with different self-designations and obscure dialects."[28] The eight million Yi people, rather than being a cohesive ethnolinguistic people group, are a collection of 120 smaller groups from diverse cultural and historical backgrounds. Many speak mutually unintelligible languages. One source even goes as far as to divide the Yi into 485 clans — with each clan occupying a distinct territory![29]

There can be no excuse for the official trend, for even as long as a century ago, scholars were calling for the various branches of the Yi to be recognized as distinct entities. In 1906 Sir Reginald F. Johnston wrote:

> I venture to express a doubt whether we should gain much by classifying under one such designation a number of peoples who, whatever their origin, have been so long separated from one another that they refuse to acknowledge any mutual connection, and to some extent have different customs and speak different languages.[30]

One ethnographer, who has researched the Yi, recently wrote:

> If the "Yi" had a mutual and continuous history, perhaps this would lend some credence to their common classification, yet even here one is hard-pressed to find similarities or continuity. The official stance on the origin of the "Yi" usually states they were descendants from the Qiang who migrated south from Qinghai and Gansu 2,000 to 3,000 years ago. While this is plausible and even probable in many cases, it does not follow, therefore, that this nationality has remained one homogeneous people group some 2,000 years later.... How long have the "Yi" been in existence? The answer is clear: "they never were."[31]

Many outsiders view the nine million Miao as one people group, but from a linguistic viewpoint they "consist of 30-40 mutually unintelligible dialects [i.e.

languages]."[32] These languages are not merely slight variations of a common language but, as Joakim Enwall explains,

> In Europe various languages may be mutually comprehensible to a large extent, like Swedish and Norwegian, or Spanish and Portuguese. In China dialects are usually not mutually comprehensible, and in many cases speakers of various sub-dialects have difficulty in understanding each other.[33]

In addition to the Yi, many distinct ethnolinguistic peoples have been artifically grouped together in the Tibetan, Miao, Hani, Zhuang, Yao, Dai, and Mongolian nationalities. Even Chinese scholars have admitted that the true number of distinct ethnic groups in China is staggeringly high. Among the Yao minority, for example,

> There are thought to be as many as 300 such different appellations... making research and classification ethnically an impossible task... [the different Yao groups] are probably not of the same ethnic stock.[34]

Reaction to the rejection of official status has been violent in some locations. The Deng, a numerically small minority group living in southeast Tibet, have even "threatened secession from China if they were not officially recognized as a nationality.... The Tibetan authorities strongly oppose such a move, arguing that it would split the Tibetan nationality."[35]

To form the Ewenki minority, the Solon and the Yakut were combined.[36] Even the relatively small Pumi minority of Yunnan, comprising less than 40,000 people, is a collection of several tribes, each speaking their own language.[37] Most of the 55 official minorities in China have been created by a similar artificial fusion of smaller groups.

Furthermore, 748,380 people in the 1990 census were not assigned a minority group because they did not fit into any of the established categories.[38] Guizhou Province contained 737,464 unclassified people, while there were 6,172 in Yunnan, 3,022 in Tibet, and 1,722 on Hainan Island.[39] Most of these people are members of small, distinct tribes. The 1982 census listed 817,810 people in unclassified communities, but one Chinese source stated that "the actual number is higher."[40] This probably indicates that a number of groups had already been provisionally placed or marked for placement in existing nationalities.

Although this book draws on a large reservoir of information available at the time of going to print, new information is continually becoming available and there will probably be a need to update the information in future. The highly respected *Ethnologue*, which describes more than 6,000 languages in the world, in its 1992 edition listed 168 "living languages" within China, but an extra 37 languages had been "discovered" in China by the time the 1996 edition was published. As anthropologists and linguists begin to conduct studies in more remote mountainous areas of southwest China, it can be expected that dozens more tribes and languages will come to light, especially among the artificially constructed Yi, Hani, Yao, Tibetan, and Miao nationalities.

The Christian Perspective

What should be the Christian response to the official Chinese classification of 55 minorities in China? Does it matter?

Christ's command to "go and make disciples of all nations"[41] is brought into focus with the word "nation." It is translated from the Greek word *ethnos*, from which is derived the English word "ethnic." The book of Revelation describes the worshipers around the throne of God as those who have been purchased by the blood of Christ and who come from "every tribe and language and nation."[42]

If the ultimate aim of God is to redeem individuals from among every ethnic and linguistic representation of humankind on the earth, then everything must be done to learn who those people are so that the church may do everything in their power to see them won for Christ. This appears to be of such importance in the Scriptures that the final sign of the imminent Second Coming of Christ is linked to the completion of this task: "And this gospel of the Kingdom will be preached in the whole world as a testimony to all nations (*ethnae*), and then the end will come."[43]

Since the gradual opening up of China in the 1980s, numerous Christian workers and ministries have commenced work there. That has coincided with a world-wide movement in missions, focusing on ministry to unreached people groups. The AD2000 Movement has been at the forefront of this mission emphasis, with thousands rallying around their statement of purpose: "A Church for Every People and the gospel for Every Person by the Year 2000." In response to this emphasis, many ministries in China have wished to focus their energy on the minority groups.

However, people interested in China's ethnic groups will be hard pressed to find information on the approximately 350 "missing" groups — ones that have disappeared since the 1953 study. Few details of the original list of 400 names have ever been released by the Chinese authorities, and there is generally little information available for Chinese students beyond what supports the official 55 minorities. Missionaries and Christian researchers in the West are similarly obliged to support the official classification of the minorities for lack of research done prior to the expulsion of missionaries from China almost 50 years ago. In addition, a stream of books, articles, and studies from both inside China and abroad continue to promote the official classifications.

Operation China contains information on approximately 300 people groups that have never before appeared on Christian mission ethnolinguistic lists. More than just a dry list of names, these 300 groups are made up of precious, unique individuals who need to be reached with the gospel of Jesus Christ.

Some may argue that it is not important from a missiological perspective to classify groups ethnolinguistically. They explain that the gospel can penetrate into each people group cluster once indigenous believers are mobilized to spread the gospel. In China this has proven to be a false assumption. For instance, observers have noted that the Yi nationality contains an estimated 200,000 Christians. Many would immediately classify them as a "reached" group, but this is not the case:

> People have the impression that these groups should be able to effectively evangelize the other members of the Yi.... However, upon closer inspection it is found that almost all of the Yi Christians are among the Eastern Nasu and Eastern Lipo.... The other 100 or so Yi groups are totally unreached.... They live as far as 1,000 km [620 miles] away from the center of Yi Christianity. But, even if the Eastern Nasu and Eastern Lipo Christians should decide to travel and share the gospel with other Yi groups, they would find it a cross-cultural experience. They would have to learn a new language, in many cases with hardly a single word the same as in their mother tongue, and they will have to learn new customs and a new culture.... Far better if we view all these people groups as separate gospel targets to begin with.[44]

History confirms the truth of this finding among the Yi. In the mid-1940s James Broomhall of the China Inland Mission tried to mobilize Yi Christians from Yunnan to evangelize the Nosu in Sichuan: "They found it very difficult to adjust to the differences in language, culture, and general lifestyle and soon returned to their homes."[45]

Until All Are Reached

The term "unreached people group" has been around in mission circles recently. However, it is not always clear what the criteria are to determine whether a group should be classified as "reached" or "unreached." Many Western Christians claim immunity from involvement in mission activity by saying, "Why should I travel to the other side of the world when there are unreached people right here in my town?" While it is true that there are lost people in every community of the world, the difference is that in places like China there are whole races of people who have never had the opportunity to hear the gospel. Not only are these lost individuals but they are lost ethnic representations of humankind.

The 1982 Lausanne Conference on World Evangelization defined an unreached people group as:

> A people group among which there is no indigenous community of believing Christians with adequate numbers and resources to evangelize their people group without requiring outside (cross cultural) assistance.... Therefore a group is considered reached if it has a viable, indigenous, self-producing church movement in its midst. This means a people group has strong churches pastored by their own people using their own language, and these churches are actively evangelizing their people and planting daughter churches.[46]

The AD2000 Movement defined the difference between "reached" and "unreached" by saying a group may be considered statistically reached if it contains more than 5% adherents to any form of Christianity, including 2% adherents to evangelical Christianity. Using this guideline, of the 490 groups we have profiled in this book, a mere 52 groups could be considered reached. Although the revival of Christianity in eastern and southeastern China has resulted in millions of conversions among the Han Chinese, most of western and northern China remains in complete spiritual darkness without a glimmer of gospel light.

Many of the profiled people groups have no known believers in their midst. Some could be considered completely unevangelized — that is, 100% of the population has never yet heard anything of the gospel and is unaware of the Person of Jesus Christ.

China's more than 400 unreached people groups are in desperate and urgent need of a "people movement" to Christ which is defined by missionary statesman Donald McGavran as

> the joint decision of a number of individuals — whether five or five hundred — all from the same people, which enables them to become Christians without social dislocation, while remaining in full contact with their non-Christian relatives, thus enabling other groups of that people, across the years, after suitable instruction, to come to similar decisions and form Christian churches made up exclusively of members of that people.[47]

It is the author's hope that readers will gain a burden for the condition of China's unreached peoples and, through *Operation China*, will gain a searing realization that they truly are precious in God's sight; that many Christians may be spurred on to pray for and give their time, talents, energy, resources, and lives to do whatever is necessary for all China's peoples to have access to the saving grace and the indwelling life of Jesus Christ. To echo French explorer Vicomte d'Ollone, who spent years traveling through remote minority areas in China during the early twentieth century:

> The non-Chinese races of China form a whole world in themselves; long study, and ample research on the spot, will still be necessary before it issues from the obscurity into which its downfall has plunged it. We shall be only too happy if the results of our efforts succeed in attracting the attention of the general and special publics, and provoke the searching inquiry which the subject demands.[48]

Methodology and Terminology

This book contains one-page Profiles of 490 distinct ethnolinguistic people groups in China. They are arranged in alphabetical order, from the Achang to the Zuoke. Each Profile also has a date. This is to help readers who wish to pray daily, or to read the book in bite-size chunks, to complete the whole book over a period of one year. Because the number of groups in the book exceeds the number of days in a year, two consecutive smaller groups are sometimes given the same date. Where this happens, it is indicated by an arrow ➤ following the date. Each Profile consists of seven general categories: Location, Identity, Language, History, Customs, Religion, and Christianity.

Group Names

In China a particular people group is often known by several different names. When selecting the name for each group, the group's autonym, or self-name, has been used as far as possible. The exception to this rule is when a group has become so well known by a certain name that it would be counter-productive to present the group by their autonym. For example, more than seven million Tujia people call themselves *Bizika*, but *Tujia* has been used to refer to this people for many centuries. The official Dongxiang people in Gansu Province call themselves *Santa*, but it was not considered helpful to include them by a name, little-known outside the inner circle of the people themselves. Moreover, it is probably a religious term rather than an ethnic name.

When attempting to define ethnicity in China, the author found that the Chinese name used for a group often confuses the issue. Among the various ethnic branches of the Yi, for example, many ethnolinguistically distinct groups have been given the same nickname by the Chinese. The Chinese apply the term *Bai Yi* (White Yi) to the Gepo, Nasu, Luoluo, Lipo, Gaisu, Lopi, Nosu, and others. *Hong Yi* (Red Yi) is similarly applied to the Naisu, Nisu, Aluo, Gese, Luowu, Michi, and others. Because of this, autonyms are preferred and Chinese terms have been avoided.

In most other cases involving one of the smaller, more obscure people groups the self-name is used. If a group is profiled because a distinct language is spoken, the language name is listed after the ethnic name, e.g. *De'ang, Pale* or *Ewenki, Solon*. The same applies to a group that is classified by geographical considerations such as a location, e.g. *Achang, Husa*, or direction, e.g. *Dong, Northern*. The Index of Alternate Names in the back of the book lists approximately 2,800 alternate names and spellings for the 490 groups profiled in *Operation China*.

Qualifications for Inclusion

The following definition of a "people group" was made in 1982 by a group of mission leaders:

> A significantly large ethnic or sociological grouping of individuals who perceive themselves to have a common affinity for one another because of their shared language, religion, ethnicity, residence, occupation, class or caste, situation, etc. or combinations of these. For evangelistic purposes, it is the largest group within which the gospel can spread as a church-planting movement without encountering barriers of understanding or acceptance.[1]

Missiologist Lawrence Radcliffe poignantly stated, "Ethnic identity is not so much in the blood as it is in the head (or in the heart) of the subject, or the observer."[2]

Using these criteria, 490 distinct ethnolinguistic people groups are profiled in *Operation China*. It is believed that this book is the first ever attempt to profile *all* the peoples in China. Information has been gathered from literature both inside China and abroad. In addition, the author has made more than 100 journeys into China over a ten-year period, conducting on-site field research and taking the majority of the photographs that appear here.

This study is limited to the people groups of the People's Republic of China and does not include information on the dozen or more tribes in Taiwan. The exclusion of Taiwan's people is in no way a political statement by the author. Quite simply, the bulk of ethnographic and linguistic information available in China does not include Taiwan.

The majority of groups profiled in this book do not appear in official Chinese literature. Because China is a Communist country, all forms of media are tightly controlled by the central government. Most important documents on China's unofficial people groups are classified as *neibu*, or "restricted material," publications intended for internal use. Although at a national level it is almost impossible to find information on the unofficial ethnic groups, there is often abundant information available in China at local county, district, and prefecture levels for those who know how to obtain it. As Joakim Enwall notes:

> These publications are never for sale, are not available in ordinary libraries and are not listed in official bibliographies. They are simply not intended for outsiders, especially not foreigners, and are not supposed to be taken out of China.[3]

Because of the *neibu* restrictions, most research into the smaller tribes and minority groups remains unobtainable. And, because information is unavailable, these groups are not considered "to exist."

More than 64 pages of notes are included in the back of *Operation China* — the author sought to provide as much documentation and corroborating evidence for the existence of groups as possible. An extensive bibliography, listing the titles of more than 1,000 books and articles, will help both students and missionaries to find more information about a particular group. Some groups in the book, however, have been included, based on the results of field-work by the author, though no independent documentation has been cited. The reader needs to understand that *Operation China* presents a considerable amount of brand-new material on the ethnography and anthropology of China.

Population

Population figures in China are notoriously difficult to obtain. The most recent, documented population figures for each group are used. In each Profile, a shaded box contains three population figures. The first figure is the most recent, documented figure available. Often this comes from the 1990 census, the 1987 *Language Atlas of China*, the 1991 *Encyclopedic Dictionary of Chinese Linguistics (Zhongguo Yuyanxue Dacidian)*, or some other ethnolinguistic source. The source is listed in the Overview section of each Profile. There sometimes appears to be a discrepancy between figures listed as Population in China and those listed in the Overview section as Population Source. This mostly results from the fact that the official figure in the Overview section includes distinct ethnic groups who have been profiled separately in *Operation China*, while the figure given as Population in China excludes them. An endnote explains the situation in these cases. In addition, population estimates for the years 2000 and 2010 are provided. It is important to note that the figures for each group refer only to that group's population within China. Many groups have members living in neighboring countries. This additional information is also included in the Overview section.

As a result of the hand-over of Hong Kong to China in 1997 — and that of Macau in 1999 — the populations of ethnic groups living in Hong Kong and Macau have been incorporated in the Profiles.

Population Estimates

Population estimates for people groups in China may be more difficult to calculate than for any other country in the world. There are numerous political, religious, and demographic considerations unique to China. For example, China's one-child policy is applied inconsistently throughout the nation. The Han Chinese are allowed only one child per couple. This has resulted in a population growth of only 1.3% per year, the lowest growth rate in Asia.[4] On the other hand, the minority groups are generally allowed two children per couple. In some thinly populated farming areas, such as Tibet and Inner Mongolia, couples are allowed three children, and in many minority areas the policies are not enforced at all; families with six, eight, or even ten children are not uncommon. For centuries the minorities have viewed children as a valuable labor asset. As a result, the biological growth of minorities in China averages 2.9% per year.[5] In some minority groups — such as the Tibetans and Mongolians — religion affects their population growth. The Buddhist populations, for instance, have increased at a considerably lower rate than non-Buddhist groups as a result of thousands of men joining the Buddhist monkhood every year and taking a vow of celibacy.

To obtain population estimates for the years 2000 and 2010 for each group, the difference between the figures recorded in the 1982 census and the 1990 census for each official nationality was analyzed and the annual growth calculated. However, where any particular group increased by more than 2.9% over the period from 1982 to 1990, that figure was ignored and considered to reflect reclassification and other artificial adjustments rather than biological growth. The Gelao minority is the most extreme example of non-biological growth. In the 1982 census they numbered 53,800 people. By the 1990 census, however, the government listed a figure of 438,000 Gelao, an eightfold increase over eight years! Special medical and educational benefits, plus an allowance of two children per couple, suddenly meant that it was advantageous to be a member of a minority. As a result, thousands of people in this part of China traced their genealogies back to find Gelao ancestry and were granted minority status. In cases such as the Gelao, the year 2000 population was calculated using a 2.9% annual growth between 1990 and 2000 to arrive at 565,000 Gelao by 2000, and the same rate between 2000 and 2010 to arrive at 728,900 Gelao by 2010.

Identity

Each tribe or people group in China has been placed under a *minzu* (nationality) by the Chinese authorities. Information has been provided about how each group is officially classified. Many groups are unhappy about the *minzu* to which they have been assigned. In addition to the hundreds of distinct branches of the 55 official minority nationalities, more than 20 Han Chinese language groups are profiled in *Operation China*. Although all Han Chinese view themselves as members of the same race, there is no doubt that from a missiological point of view they should be targeted as separate linguistic entities. As Robert Ramsey points out:

> What makes Chinese different is the number and complexity of [its] dialects. In order to classify this enormous linguistic body as a single language, a very large number of links are required to connect all of its many varieties of speech — more, probably, than for any other single language on earth. The interconnections between its dialects are in fact as complicated as those which connect a family of languages. Romance languages, such as French, Spanish, Portuguese, and Italian, are linked to each other just about as closely as the Chinese dialects are.... From a linguistic point of view, the Chinese "dialects" could be considered different languages, just as French and Italian are.[6]

Where available, information is given regarding how groups view themselves, the name they use for themselves, and what neighboring people call them. In several cases — such as the Rao people of Guizhou and the Lami people of Yunnan — members of the same minority group living in different locations have been placed under different nationalities. The 1990 census included a category of *Undetermined Minorities* — containing almost 750,000 people belonging to groups not yet assigned a nationality.

Language

The linguistic affiliation of each group is provided. In most cases, this information comes from Grime's *Ethnologue: Languages of the World*. Linguists have researched the relationship between different languages and dialects, providing valuable information which can indicate linguistic intelligibility and reveal something of the historical relationship between groups. In China today, all languages fall into seven main linguistic families: Sino-Tibetan; Daic; Austronesian; Austro-Asiatic; Indo-European; Hmong-Mien (Miao-Yao); and Altaic. Within each family there may be several major subdivisions. The Altaic family, for example, contains the Mongolian languages, the Turkic languages, and the Tungus languages. Within the Turkic group are languages such as Uygur, Kazak, Kirgiz, Tuerke, Salar, and Uzbek. Uygur further breaks down into several mutually unintelligible varieties. Literacy rates are also listed in the Overview section for each of the 55 official minorities. These figures come from data collected in the 1982 Chinese census.

Scholars have long disagreed about how they should define a language. The point when a variation of a language becomes so different that it should be viewed as a distinct language is often blurred. This, in part, has led to conflicting statistics being presented to the Christian world. For years Ralph Winter, founder of the U.S. Center for World Mission, has put forward the number 24,000 as the total number of people groups in the world. On the other hand David Barrett, leader of the Global Evangelization Movement and editor of the *World Christian Encyclopedia*, lists 8,990 ethnolinguistic people groups.[7] Patrick Johnstone, the British researcher and author of *Operation World*, states, "All distinct ethnolinguistic groups with a sufficient distinctiveness within each nation for which church planting may be necessary total 12,017."[8]

Ralph Winter helped to explain the apparent discrepancies in these figures. He says:

> It is clear in [Barrett's] table that his listing is almost identical to the number of languages which in his opinion need [Bible] translations. Now let's see where that leads us. Wycliffe Bible Translators, for example, go into South Sudan and count how many languages there are into which the Bible must be translated, and presented in printed form, in order to reach everybody in that area. Wycliffe's answer is 50 distinct translations. What does "50" mean in this instance? Does it mean 50 groups of people? Certainly not, if we are speaking of unreached peoples, because in many cases quite alien groups can read the same translation.
>
> How do I know this? Gospel Recordings also goes into South Sudan and counts the number of languages. Their personnel, however, come up with 130. Why? Because they put the gospel in cassette form, and those cassettes represent a more embarrassingly precise language communication than does the written language. Different authors for different reasons, and different organizations for different purposes, are counting different things.[9]

Languages vs. Dialects

In simple terms, if two people cannot understand each other's speech, this book considers that they speak different languages. If two people are able to communicate with each other in their mother tongues, even though with some difficulty, this book considers them to be speaking dialects of the same language. When considering groups for inclusion in this book on linguistic grounds, the author was primarily concerned with mutually intelligible speech. To put it simply, if two groups cannot understand each other, they are viewed as separate groups. From the Christian perspective, this is vital in determining how far the gospel can spread from one people to another before it encounters linguistic barriers which impede the spread of Christianity. The matter of languages vs. dialects is particularly confusing because the Chinese authorities have a very broad definition of the term "language." Much of the confusion has resulted from the mistranslation of Chinese terms into English. The Chinese have five major linguistic categories[10] (see Table). From this it can be seen that many of the "dialects" and "subdialects" described by the Chinese are in fact mutually unintelligible languages according to Western understanding.

Chinese term:		***English term used to render the Chinese:***	***How it corresponds in a Western context:***
yuyan	语言	language	language family
fangyan	方言	dialect	language
cifangyan	次方言	subdialect	dialect group
tuyu	土语	vernacular	dialect
fangyin or	方音	local variety	subdialect
difanghua	地方话		

On the question of languages spoken in China among the officially recognized nationalities, one scholar has noted: "The equation of one language with one nationality was adhered to in almost all cases (except for some well-established exceptions), thereby relegating sometimes very disparate languages among one nationality to 'dialects.'"[11] The Miao nationality, for example, are considered speakers of one "language" (*yuyan*) by the Chinese. In actual fact they speak 30 to 40 mutually unintelligible languages.[12] In many cases tribes and people groups who were combined into the same nationality by the Chinese cannot understand a word of the others' languages. The Yugur nationality in Gansu Province is comprised of one group who speak a Mongolian language and another who speak a completely different language belonging to the Turkic linguistic family. The Yi nationality in southwest China speak at least 40 distinct languages and more than 100 dialects.

History

A brief account of each group's history is given. In some cases there is sufficient documentation available to determine particular historical roots. The history of other groups is shrouded in uncertainty, especially groups with no written script to record their past.

Customs

A brief description of each group's culture and customs is provided. Where possible, the names of major festivals and other significant cultural facts that contribute to a group's ethnicity are included.

Religion

The religious affiliations of each group are listed. In the Overview section all significant religions for a group are listed in descending order, starting with the belief system considered the most prevalent within that group. Most groups in China fall into the following major religious classifications:

No Religion: The majority of the Han Chinese people in China today could be accurately portrayed as nonreligious. After half a century of strict Communist rule, millions of people have forsaken all outward religious beliefs. A number of minority groups too, especially those more assimilated to Chinese culture, are nonreligious. In China the general trend is toward secularism and away from religion. Among many minorities in southern China, people over the age of 50 still observe religious rituals, but few youths — who have been educated in atheistic schools — have any interest in religion and most view it as superstition.

Animism: Most of the minority groups in southern China are animists. Although it is not an organized religion — it does not have temples, monasteries, or a priesthood — animism still has a hold over the hearts and minds of millions of people. Animists believe nature consists of spirits that must be appeased. They offer regular sacrifices to these spirits to procure their blessings. They believe trees, rivers, mountains, animals, their homes, doors, and even large rocks have spirits living in them. In some cases, whole animistic communities are enslaved to evil spirits. Strictly speaking the people do not worship the spirits, but they feel the need to offer sacrifices continually to keep the spirits from afflicting their families and communities.

Polytheism: Polytheism literally means "many gods." It is similar to animism but differs in that polytheists may have temples, altars, and idols; it is generally more "visible" than animism.

Ancestor Worship: Ancestor worship is practiced to some degree by almost all communities and people groups in China. It is often combined with animistic and polytheistic rituals, although among a few groups it could accurately be described as the dominant religion. Adherents to ancestor worship believe they are responsible for the well-being of the souls of their ancestors. Ancestral altars are kept in the main room of the home where regular offerings of food and drink are made. Incense is frequently burned. In many communities the eldest son is responsible for taking care of the soul of his father. For this reason no effort is spared to procure a son; without one, the father's soul will be lost forever. This belief has contributed to the widespread favoring of boys over girls in China, exacerbated by the government's one-child policy.

Daoism: Daoism (or Taoism) is the only true homegrown Chinese religion. Much of Chinese folkreligion is sometimes considered part of Daoism. The founder of Daoism was a mystical figure known as Laozi, who is believed to have been born around 600 BC. At the center of Daoism is the following concept of Dao:

> Dao cannot be perceived because it exceeds senses, thoughts and imagination; it can be known only through mystical insight which cannot be expressed with words. Dao is the way of the universe, the driving power in nature, the order behind all life, the spirit which cannot be exhausted.[13]

Shamanism: Shamanism shares many similarities with animism and polytheism but differs with the inclusion of shamans, mediums, or diviners, who serve the community as a link between the spirit world and the material world. They regularly enter trances to determine the will of the spirits in an important matter. They determine auspicious dates for weddings, funerals, or other important events. In many communities, shamans also act as counselors, healers, and judges. In some areas the shamans have abused their power and trapped whole villages in poverty, subject to their wishes. People must pay a large fee for their services. Shamans may insist on the sacrifice of valuable livestock, possibly causing famine and forcing a family into debt for generations. Shamanism is generally dying out in most parts of China, although it is experiencing a revival among the minorities in the northeast of the country. The Mongols and Tibetans also practice forms of shamanism, with an overlay of outward adherence to Tibetan Buddhism. Buddhist lamas often double as shamans in these areas.

Buddhism: Buddhism, which came to China from India, flourished throughout China between the third and sixth centuries AD. It gained such sweeping acceptance that several Chinese emperors, threatened by its power, persecuted Buddhist monks and destroyed temples. There are two main sects of Buddhism in China:

(a) Mahayana Buddhism: Mahayana means "greater vehicle." It is practiced in Japan, Korea, and Vietnam, in addition to China. This sect believes the fate of individuals is linked to the fate of others. Mahayana Buddhism "is replete with innumerable heavens, hells and descriptions of *nirvana*. Prayers are addressed to the Buddha and combined with elaborate ritual."[14]

(b) Theravada Buddhism: Theravada, or "doctrine of the elders," is the sect of Buddhism practiced in Thailand, Myanmar, Laos, Cambodia, and Sri Lanka, as well as in several minority groups in China's Yunnan Province. It is also known as Hinayana Buddhism or "lesser vehicle." Most Theravada Buddhists reject the term Hinayana, however, claiming it has derogatory connotations. Theravada Buddhism "holds that the path to *nirvana* is an individual pursuit. It centers on monks and nuns who make the search for *nirvana* a full-time profession."[15]

Tibetan Buddhism: Tibetan Buddhism should be considered a distinct religion. When Buddhism arrived in Tibet around AD 600, it was added to the ancient religion of Bon, already entrenched in the hearts of Tibetans for centuries. Bon was characterized by the worship of demons, ghosts, and fearsome and wrathful deities who demanded regular animal and even human sacrifices. Tibetan Buddhism — also called Tantric Buddhism and Lamaism — today retains many of the features of Bon. In many Tibetan locations, especially in Gansu and Qinghai provinces, Bon has experienced a resurgence in recent years. Unlike Tibetan Buddhist monks, Bon monks are allowed to marry. Their temples and pagodas are circled in a counter-clockwise direction; Buddhist temples are circled clockwise.

Islam: There are more than 20 million Muslims in China, belonging to two main Islamic sects. The vast majority of China's Muslims belong to the Sunni sect. It was introduced to China peacefully by Central Asian traders and merchants starting in the eighth century. Muslims were heavily persecuted in China during the Cultural Revolution (1966-76), but in recent years thousands of mosques have been reopened, often with Saudi oil money. Several people groups in China, including the Purik and Tajik, adhere to Shi'ite (or Shi'a) Islam. Shi'ite Muslims do not have mosques but meet every week in homes for prayer and reading of the Qur'an.

Christianity: At least 50 million Christians live throughout China, especially in the eastern provinces. Some claim there are 90 million or more Christians in China. Christianity was first introduced to China by Nestorian missionaries in AD 635. By the time the Communist government came to power in 1949, there were less than one million Protestants in China. In the 50 years since, Christianity has experienced a massive boom, possibly unparalleled in world history. Today about 80% of China's Christians are Protestants, meeting in government-sanctioned churches belonging to the Three-Self Patriotic Movement and in tens of thousands of unregistered house churches. Approximately eight million people in China are Catholics, concentrated in the eastern and southern provinces. The Chinese authorities strongly discourage contact with the Vatican and have severely persecuted some Catholic communities who sought to establish relationships with foreign organizations loyal to the Pope.[16]

Other Religions: There are numerous other religions in China that do not fall under any of our main categories:

Confucianism: Although more a philosophy than a religion, it has contributed to the character and worldview of almost every community in China. Confucius was born in Shandong Province around 551 BC.

> Confucian codes of conduct... became inextricably bound up in Chinese society. Women obey and defer to men, younger brothers to elder brothers, sons to fathers. Respect flows upwards, from young to old. Age is venerated because it gives... dignity and worth.[17]

Statues of Confucius and other great philosophers are seen throughout China today and are venerated in many places.

Judaism: Although now extinct, Judaism flourished in China for more than 1,000 years. The remnant of a Jewish community still exists in Kaifeng, Henan Province — see the You Tai Profile — but there are no longer any functioning synagogues in China.

Dongbaism: This was the traditional religion of the Naxi people in Yunnan Province. There are still several *Dongbas* (religious clerics) operating today. The Naxi have their own code of ethics and a religious book, but Dongbaism is largely a dead religion.

Hero worship: The Jino people of Yunnan Province worship a complex array of spirits. One of their most honored is Kong Ming, a former Chinese war hero (AD 200). The Jino claim they were originally soldiers in Kong Ming's battalion who were commanded to stay behind in southern China to rule the region. The Yao, Bunu, She, and some Miao groups in southern China worship Pan Hu, a mythical half-dog, half-dragon they believe to be their forefather.

There are numerous other local beliefs across China, such as the Xibe people's worship of Xilimama, the god of Tranquility, and Haierkan, the god who protects livestock. Groups with such localized deities have usually been categorized as polytheists.

Christianity

In each Profile estimates of the Status of Evangelization are provided. Over the years numerous words and phrases have been used to describe the state of Christianity, including "evangelical Christians," "born-again Christians," "Protestants," "baptized Christians," "true believers," "Bible-believing Christians," and "Spirit-filled Christians." Such definitions are not practical in China. It has been the author's approach to portray the level of awareness of Christ among each group rather than attempt to determine the spiritual merits of their form of Christianity. In *Operation China*, Christians are simply defined as those who make a profession of faith, regardless of their particular set of doctrines or methods. The children of believing parents are also included in the figures. The assumption for the inclusion of children when measuring Christianity is that in Asian societies it is common for the family unit to adhere to one religion. It is unheard of, for example, for a family to consist of Muslim parents with Buddhist children, or for Christian parents to have animist children. Overall, the author acknowledges that only God knows the true number of people who have appropriated Christ's salvation. The aim is to present estimates that show the degree of penetration the gospel has made among China's peoples. As the reader will discover, numerous groups have never heard of Christ or known a Christian believer in their midst.

Status of Evangelization Graphs

Each Profile includes an easy-to-use graph which shows estimates of the Status of Evangelization among each group. This graph is intended to provide the reader with a quick visual impression of the awareness of the gospel in each group. Estimates take into consideration factors such as the history of mission work among a people group; the proximity of other Christian communities; reports of and interviews with people who know the group or geographical region where the group is located; data gathered personally by the author during more than 100 trips to China over a ten-year period; the linguistic variety present in each group — e.g., how many people understand Mandarin; interaction with other communities — do the young people go to cities for work and education; and geographical isolation — many mountainous regions in western China are unable to receive shortwave Christian radio broadcasts.

Each graph lists the following three percentages:

A = the percentage of people in that group who have never heard the gospel or the name of Christ, people who are completely unaware of Christianity.

B = the percentage of people in that group who have been evangelized but have not yet become Christians. This does not necessarily reflect the percentage of people who have received a thorough presentation of the gospel but rather the percentage of people estimated to be aware of the existence of Christ. Many people in China have become aware of Christianity through gospel radio broadcasts produced by ministries such as the Far East Broadcasting Company (FEBC) and Trans World Radio (TWR). Daily or weekly messages are recorded in more than a dozen languages outside China and then broadcast into China via shortwave radio.

C = the percentage of people in that group who adhere to any form of Christianity. This indicates the total percentage of people who profess to be Christians, regardless of their denomination or adherence to any particular creed or doctrine. This figure does not necessarily portray the true number of people in a living relationship with Christ.

Note: Decimal points have been rounded up to the next percentage point. Only those groups without any known churches or believers appear on the graph at 0% Christianity. This helps readers identify quickly which groups are completely untouched by the gospel and without any Christian witness.

Maps

Each Profile contains a map. The geographical extent of each group is blackened, while a small inset map of China shows the reader which provinces the members of the group inhabit.

Overview Data

On each Profile an Overview of each particular group is provided. Sixteen fields of information are listed:

Countries: The names of all countries where that group is found are listed in descending order of population size.

Pronunciation: A simple guide for each syllable helps the reader learn how to pronounce the group's name.

Other Names: All other names the group is known by, are listed, with alternate spellings. An additional Index of approximately 2,800 alternate names appears as an Appendix in *Operation China*.

Population Source: The figure used as population base for the group is listed, followed by the date and source from which it was quoted. This figure sometimes appears to be in conflict with the figure quoted as Population in China because it may include population groups that have been profiled separately in *Operation China*. An endnote explains the situation in these cases. The figure for all members of the group living in other countries is also provided.

Location: The location of each group includes provinces, prefectures, counties, districts, townships, and in some cases, village names.

Status: The official classification of each group, as determined by the Chinese authorities, falls into one of four main categories:

An official minority of China: There are 55 officially recognized minority nationalities in China in addition to the majority Han Chinese.

Officially included under... : Most of the Profiles are of groups that have not been granted their own status but have been combined with similar groups to form an acknowledged nationality.

Counted in the census as an Undetermined Minority: More than 740,000 individuals did not fit into any of the government's existing classifications in the 1990 census and were placed in a general category of *Undetermined Minorities*.

Unidentified: The official classification of a small number of groups is unknown. In some cases it is possible that groups in remote border areas were not counted at all in the Chinese census.

Language: The genetic affiliation of each language includes language families and all corresponding branches.

Literacy: These figures, taken from the 1982 census, are only available for China's 55 officially recognized minorities.

Dialects: Where available, all dialects spoken by a group are listed.

Religion: The main religious adherence of each group is given, followed in descending order by all significant religious beliefs present among the group.

Christians: The total number of professing Christians for each group is listed, and the source noted.

Scripture: All available translations of the Bible, New Testament, or books of the Bible (portions) are listed, including the year dates of their publication. Where orthographies used in the past are now obsolete, or the Scriptures are only available or understood by members of the group living in countries outside China, or they are no longer in print, this information has been added in parenthesis or as endnotes.

Jesus *Film:* This category indicates whether the *Jesus* film (a powerful visual portrayal of the Gospel of Luke distributed by Campus Crusade for Christ) has been translated into the language spoken by the group. Currently the film is available in about 30 languages in China, but plans are in progress for many more translation projects in the future.

Gospel Recordings: The Christian ministry Gospel Recordings has produced recordings in more than 150 languages in China. Most of them are short, 10-15 minute Gospel messages, including testimonies, songs, and outlines of the life of Christ, in each native tongue. This tool is especially valuable among tribal groups where there is a high rate of illiteracy. The Gospel Recordings' catalogue number is also provided, where available. Some new recordings had not yet been consigned a catalogue number at the time of *Operation China* going to print.

Christian Broadcasting: If gospel radio broadcasts are available in a group's language, details are given, including the ministry responsible for the broadcasting — Far East Broadcasting Company (FEBC), or Trans World Radio (TWR).

ROPAL code: ROPAL stands for the Registry of Peoples and Languages. It is used by Christian researchers to identify and classify the world's people groups, languages, and dialects.

The 56 Official Nationalities of China

Classification by Population (projected for the year 2000)

HAN CHINESE* 汉族	**1,149,538,850**
Han Chinese, Mandarin	783,300,200
Han Chinese, Wu	81,947,000
Han Chinese, Cantonese	59,125,600
Han Chinese, Jin	53,423,000
Han Chinese, Gan	36,554,000
Han Chinese, Xiang	36,064,000
Han Chinese, Min Nan	31,728,100
Hakka	31,309,000
Han Chinese, Min Dong	8,797,900
Han Chinese, Hainanese	5,143,600
Han Chinese, Dan	4,296,600
Han Chinese, Huizhou	3,647,300
Han Chinese, Puxian	2,633,700
Han Chinese, Min Bei	2,561,300
Subei	2,494,500
Han Chinese, Pinghua	2,338,000
Han Chinese, Shaozhou	935,200
Han Chinese, Shaojiang	870,900
Han Chinese, Min Zhong	798,400
Lingao	641,700
Chuanlan	324,800
Han Chinese, Waxiang	319,500
Han Chinese, Hui'an	155,800
Cun	79,100
Linghua	22,300
Indonesian	8,830
Japanese	5,700
Shenzhou**	4,050
Liujia**	4,050
Hakka, Hainan Island	2,070
Han Chinese, Xunpu	1,040
Fuma	860
You Tai	750

* Note: The government has officially counted part of some minority groups as Han Chinese. These multiple classifications include the Pingdi (see *Yao*) and the Nanjingren (see *Bai*).
** Prior to 1985 the Shenzhou and Liujia were classified as *Undetermined Minorities*.

ZHUANG 壮族	**18,525,600***
Zhuang, Northern	11,568,000
Zhuang, Southern	4,203,900
Giay	273,700
Nung	137,200
Tho	134,000
Cao Lan	40,270
E	34,700
Yongchun	13,400
Dianbao	11,000
Pusha	5,490
Tulao	4,140
Buyang	3,450

* Note: The overall population figure for the Zhuang does not match the total populations of our sub-groups. This is because the figures for each group profiled in this book are drawn from various linguistic and anthropological sources, while the overall minority population total is based simply on the 1990 official Chinese census. When linguistic sources are used, often the figure given is for the number of speakers of a certain language, which may be less than the total number of people within the ethnic group.

MANCHU 满族	**12,676,070**
Manchu	12,666,700
Lu*	4,560
Saman	2,580
Kyakala	2,230

* Note: The Lu of Guizhou were classified as Manchu in 1985; previously they were included in a list of *Undetermined Minorities*.

HUI 回族	**10,685,070**
Hui	10,676,500
Utsat	6,570
Keji	2,000

MIAO 苗族	**9,543,400***
Hmu, Northern	1,612,500
Ghao-Xong, Western	1,057,800
Hmu, Southern	645,000
Hua Miao	596,700
Miao, Enshi	516,000
Hmu, Eastern	451,500
A-Hmao	387,000
Hmong Shuad	264,500
Aoka	252,200
Hmong Leng	248,600
Hmong Daw	232,700
Laba**	228,300
Miao, Chuan	150,900
Miao, Guiyang (Northern)	108,300
Ghao-Xong, Eastern	103,200
Ge	102,500
Gha-Mu	91,300
Miao, Guiyang (Southwestern)	90,300
Miao, Huishui (Northern)	90,300
Miao, Luobohe	77,400
Miao, Mashan (Central)	76,100
Mjuniang	75,600
Miao, Huishui (Southwestern)	72,200
Horned Miao	63,480
Hmong Bua	52,900
Miao, Huishui (Central)	51,600
Miao, Lupanshui	51,600
Miao, Mashan (Northern)	45,150
Hmong Njua	42,300
Miao, Guiyang (Southern)	18,650
Miao, Huishui (Eastern)	18,050
Miao, Mashan (Western)	18,050
Changshu Miao	15,870
Hmong Dlex Nchab	15,870
Miao, Baishi	12,900
Miao, Mashan (Southern)	12,900

Qanu	11,450
Miao, Guiyang (Northwestern)	7,610
Sanqiao***	5,140
Miao, Guiyang (South-Central)	4,560
Hmong Vron	4,460
Hmong Dou	3,350
Hmong Be	1,050

* Note: The overall population figure for the Miao does not match the total populations of our sub-groups. This is because the figures for each group profiled in this book are drawn from various linguistic and anthropological sources, while the overall minority population total is based simply on the 1990 official Chinese census. When linguistic sources are used, often the figure given is for the number of speakers of a certain language, which may be less than the total number of people within the ethnic group. The Kim Mun on China's Mainland have been classified as Yao, but on Hainan Island they have been classified Miao, for example.
** Note: The Laba were classified under Miao in 1985; previously they were included in a list of *Undetermined Minorities*.
*** Some Sanqiao are classified under Dong and others under Miao. Prior to 1985 they were classified as an *Undetermined Minority*.

UYGUR 维吾尔族	**9,136,080**
Uygur	9,041,200
Uygur, Yutian	53,900
Uygur, Lop Nur	33,500
Ainu	6,570
Keriya	660
Uygur, Takilmakan	250

YI* 彝族	**8,258,325**
Nosu, Shengzha	1,024,400
Laluo, Mishaba	579,400
Nosu, Yinuo	512,200
Nosu, Xiaoliangshan	439,400
Nasu, Eastern	413,500
Nisu, Jianshui	370,200
Luoluopo, Central	353,400
Nasu, Panxian	290,100
Nasu, Wusa	248,500
Nosu, Shuixi	234,800
Poluo	232,700
Nasu, Western	215,300
Nosu, Butuo	210,200
Nisu, Yuanyang	204,200
Nisu, Xinping	197,300
Luoluopo, Western	193,300
Suodi	189,200
Lipo, Western	146,400
Sani	105,600
Nasu, Southern	104,800
Lami**	100,400
Lipo, Eastern***	90,200
Nosu, Tianba	84,080
Xiangtang	82,400
Axi	78,100
Limin****	76,100
Nosu, Mangbu	66,800
Gepo, Eastern	64,000
Azhe	58,950
Muji	53,300
Naisu	49,200
Wumeng	39,250
Lalu, Xinping	38,950
Lalu, Yangliu	37,900
Naluo	37,600
Luoluopo, Southeastern	36,700
A Che	36,200
Gaisu, Southern	35,900
Tusu	31,750
Gaiji	30,750
Jiasou	30,750
Laluo, Jiantou	30,750
Xijima	30,700
Limi	29,700
Michi	29,700
Puwa	29,700
Niesu, Central	28,700
Samei	28,200
Sanie	25,900
Aluo	25,100
Awu, Southeastern	24,900
Mili	23,750
Digao	22,850
Luowu	22,550
Bai Yi	22,500
Pula	20,300
Lawu	19,950
Mengwu	18,650
Nasu, Jinghong	18,450
Boka	18,350
Guopu	16,920
Enipu	16,400
Lesu	15,170
Lopi	15,060
Xiqi	13,630
Ati	12,900
Gesu	12,430
Gese	12,300
Naruo	12,200
Naru	11,790
Daizhan	11,650
Qiangyi	10,250
Asahei	8,610
Samadu, Western	7,650
Neisu, Xiao Hei	7,580
Talu	7,150
Adu	7,080
Chesu	6,670
Gepo, Western	6,650
Labapo	6,560
Laowu	6,450
Neisu, Da Hei	6,450
Zuoke	6,450
Depo	6,275
Lagou	6,150
Laka	6,150
Aling	5,740
Alu	5,640
Mixisu	5,120
Popei	5,120
Tushu	5,120
Liwu	4,300
Gouzou	4,100
Lalu, Xuzhang	4,100
Awu, Northern	3,590
Tagu	3,590
Ani	3,070

Wopu	3,070
Apu	2,560
Eka	2,560
Lati	2,050
Minglang	1,530
Muzi	1,530
Liude	1,430
Long	1,360
Naza	1,330
Tanglang	1,040
Ta'er	1,025
Azong	1,020
Gaisu, Western	1,020
Micha	1,020
Xiuba	970
Doupo	615
Samadu, Eastern	615
Ayizi	580
Guaigun	410
Pubiao	385
Pengzi	255
Suan	255

*Note: The Nanjingren of Guizhou were previously classified as an *Undetermined Minority*. In 1987 most were reclassified as Bai, but individuals were given the choice of being classified under Bai, Gelao, Yi, or Han Chinese. The exact number of Nanjingren who are classified as Yi remains uncertain.
** The majority of Lami have been counted under the Yi nationality, but some members of the same ethnic group have been officially classified under Hani.
*** The Eastern Lipo are counted as part of the Yi on the national level, but are classified as Lisu on the district, county and prefecture levels.
**** The Limin were officially included under Yi in 1985; previously they were included in a list of *Undetermined Minorities*.

TUJIA 土家族	**7,358,340**
Tujia	7,353,300
Mozhihei	5,040

MONGOL 蒙古族	**6,299,670**
Mongol	5,811,400
Torgut	146,000
Buriat	98,900
Oirat	91,300
Mongol, Khalka	51,800
Sogwo Arig	37,000
Mongol, Sichuan	27,100
Mongol, Alxa	21,700
Mongol, Yunnan	6,890
Tuva	3,260
Olot	2,400
Mongol, Khamnigan	1,920

TIBETAN 藏族	**5,659,520***
Khampa, Eastern	1,245,200
Tibetan, Central	741,000
Amdo, Hbrogpa	700,900
Tibetan, Gtsang	595,700
Khampa, Western	205,200
Jiarong, Situ	161,550
Amdo, Rongmahbrogpa	146,800
Amdo, Rongba	127,000
Golog	127,600
Khampa, Northern	118,400
Tibetan, Jone	100,200
Tibetan, Deqen	95,750
Amdo, Rtahu	78,800
Tibetan, Nghari	49,900
Ergong	48,800
Chrame	39,000
Tibetan, Zhugqu	38,300
Ersu	27,850
Minyak	20,900
Zhaba	20,900
Groma	14,920
Jiarong, Chabao	14,170
Baima	13,700
Xiangcheng	11,160
Guiqiong	9,760
Queyu	8,460
Namuyi	6,950
Kyerung	6,820
Jiarong, Sidabao	5,580
Jiarong, Guanyingqiao	5,110
Hdzanggur	4,370
Jiarong, Shangzhai	4,090
Yonzhi	3,270
Tibetan, Boyu	3,260
Shixing	2,780
Ladakhi	2,720
Lahuli, Tinan	2,450
Bolozi**	2,110
Manyak	1,880
Lhomi	1,350
Menia	1,250
Luzu	1,040
Sherpa	910
Purik	650

* Note: The overall population figure for the Tibetans does not match the total populations of our sub-groups. This is because the figures for each group profiled in this book are drawn from various linguistic and anthropological sources, while the overall minority population total is based simply on the 1990 official Chinese census. When linguistic sources are used, often the figure given is for the number of speakers of a certain language, which may be less than the total number of people within the ethnic group.
** The listing of Bolozi under Tibetan is tentative. They may have been officially counted under Qiang.

BOUYEI 布依族	**3,207,340**
Bouyei	3,176,200
Mo	18,550
Rao*	9,890
Ai-Cham	2,700

* Note: The Rao of Duyun County have been classified under Bouyei, while the Rao in Majiang have been classified as Yao. Both Rao groups were previously classified as *Undetermined Minorities*.

DONG* 侗族	**3,086,030**
Dong, Southern	1,910,200
Dong, Northern	1,170,700
Xialusi**	3,080
Diao**	2,050

* Note: Some of the Sanqiao ethnic group have been classified as Dong but most as Miao. Prior to 1985 they were classified as an *Undetermined Minority*.

** Prior to 1985 the Xialusi and Diao were classified as *Undetermined Minorities*.

YAO* 瑶族	**2,763,120**
Pingdi**	1,116,000
Iu Mien	980,400
Bunu	324,500
Kim Mun***	258,000
Dongnu	233,800
Iu Mien, Hunan	167,700
Biao-Jiao Mien	50,400
Nunu	48,600
Baheng, Sanjiang	41,200
Zaomin	35,700
Ban Yao	27,900
Biao Mien	25,800
Iu Mien, Changping	25,800
Baonuo	25,080
Beidalao	19,350
Younuo	17,900
Bunuo	17,050
Lakkia	15,200
Ao Biao	12,900
Biao Mien, Shikou	10,320
Wunai	9,360
Baheng, Liping	5,160
Changpao****	5,140
Iu Mien, Luoxiang	3,870
Youmai****	2,055
Kiong Nai	1,890
Numao	1,745
Yerong	510
Beidongnuo	370

* Note: The Rao of Duyun County have been classified under Bouyei, while the Rao in Majiang have been classified as Yao. Both Rao groups were previously classified as *Undetermined Minorities*.
** About half of the Pingdi people have been officially counted as Yao and half as Han Chinese. Because of this, the total population of the Yao groups listed here is greater than the main Yao figure at the top.
*** The Kim Mun living on Mainland China are counted as Yao, but those living on Hainan Island have been officially counted as part of the Miao nationality, even though they speak exactly the same language as the Kim Mun on the Mainland.
**** Prior to 1985 the Changpao and Youmai were classified as *Undetermined Minorities*.

KOREAN 朝鲜族	**2,130,000**
Korean	2,130,000

BAI 白族	**2,067,400**
Bai	1,915,200
Nanjingren*	121,700
Bei	22,900
Qixingmin**	4,560
Longjia***	3,040

* Note: The Nanjingren of Guizhou were previously classified as an *Undetermined Minority*. In 1987 most were reclassified as Bai, but individuals were given the choice of being classified under Bai, Gelao, Yi, or Han Chinese. The exact number of Nanjingren who are classified as Bai remains uncertain.
** Before 1985 the Qixingmin were included in an official list of *Undetermined Minorities*.
*** Before 1987 the Longjia were included in an official list of *Undetermined Minorities*.

HANI 哈尼族	**1,566,690**
Hani	614,500
Akha	194,600
Baihong	194,600
Biyo	122,900
Haoni	122,900
Kado	122,900
Woni	110,300
Lami	100,400
Enu	20,920
Yiche	19,460
Neisu	16,700
Sansu	13,370
Duota	11,900
Budo	10,580
Bisu	7,380
Meng	4,090
Pana	4,090
Muda	2,090

DAI 傣族	**1,552,260**
Tai Lu	614,300
Tai Mao	318,500
Hongjin Tai	170,500
Tai Nua	135,600
Tai Pong*	89,500
Huayao Tai	70,000
Han Tai	55,500
Ya	50,700
Tai Dam	34,700
Tai Kao	11,350
Paxi	1,110
Shan	500

* Note: Most Tai Pong people have been officially classified under the Dai nationality, but some have been included under Zhuang.

LI 黎族	**1,433,000***
Li, Ha	537,000
Li, Qi	245,100
Li, Jiamao	71,600
Li, Bendi	60,600
Li, Meifu	41,300

* Note: The overall population figure for the Li does not match the total populations of our subgroups. This is because the figures for each group profiled in this book are drawn from various linguistic and anthropological sources, while the overall minority population total is based simply on the 1990 official Chinese census. When linguistic sources are used, often the figure given is for the number of speakers of a certain language, which may be less than the total number of people within the ethnic group.

KAZAK 哈萨克族	**1,422,249**
Kazak	1,419,300
Kazak, Qinghai	2,890
Teleut	59

SHE 畲族	**868,500**
She	813,200
Ga Mong*	54,000

Xi*	1,300

* Note: The Ga Mong and the Xi were counted as part of the Miao nationality until 1997.

LISU* 傈僳族	**717,240**
Lisu	715,100
Lemo	2,140

* The Eastern Lipo are counted as part of the Yi on the national level, but are classified as Lisu on the district, county and prefecture levels. If they are reclassified as Lisu in the proposed national census of 2000, the overall population of Lisu will increase considerably.

GELAO* 仡佬族	**576,080**
Gelao	565,000
Gao	2,750
Hagei	2,340
Yizi**	2,280
A'ou	2,060
Duoluo	1,650

* Note: The Nanjingren of Guizhou were previously classified as an *Undetermined Minority*. In 1987 most were reclassified as Bai, but individuals were given the choice of being classified under Bai, Gelao, Yi, or Han Chinese. The exact number of Nanjingren who are classified as Gelao remains uncertain.
** The Yizi have been classified as Gelao since 1985; previously they were included in a list of *Undetermined Minorities*.

LAHU 拉祜族	**543,800**
Lahu	489,400
Kucong	40,400
Laopang	14,000

DONGXIANG 东乡族	**482,300**
Dongxiang	482,300

SHUI 水族	**439,200**
Shui	430,000
Shui, Yunnan	9,200

WA 佤族	**429,020**
Wa	299,600
Kawa	73,300
Lawa	55,000
Ben	1,120

NAXI 纳西族	**323,295**
Naxi	271,300
Mosuo	46,000
Naxi, Northern	2,690
Naju	1,550
Naheng	1,240
Malimasa	515

QIANG 羌族	**266,900***
Qiang, Yadu	29,650
Qiang, Jiaochang	24,500
Qiang, Heihu	20,640
Qiang, Mianchi	20,250
Qiang, Sanlong	19,350
Qiang, Luhua	18,060
Qiang, Mawo	15,480
Qiang, Cimulin	12,600
Ming	11,700
Qiang, Dajishan	9,540
Qiang, Taoping	6,320
Qiang, Longxi	4,250

* Note: The overall population figure for the Qiang does not match the total populations of our sub-groups. This is because the figures for each group profiled in this book are drawn from various linguistic and anthropological sources, while the overall minority population total is based simply on the 1990 official Chinese census. When linguistic sources are used, often the figure given is for the number of speakers of a certain language, which may be less than the total number of people within the ethnic group.

TU 土族	**242,050**
Tu	199,800
Mongour	39,800
Wutun	2,450

XIBE 锡箔族	**222,900**
Xibe	180,500
Xibe, Western	42,400

MULAO* 仫老族	**205,500**
Mulao	205,500

* Note: In 1993, 2,800 Mulao Jia were included in the official Mulao nationality. The remainder of Mulao Jia (approximately 28,000) are still included in the list of *Undetermined Minorities*.

KIRGIZ 柯而克孜族	**182,800**
Kirgiz	178,800
Akto Turkmen	2,460
Khakas	1,540

DAUR 达斡尔族	**156,310**
Daur	149,600
Daur, Western	5,630
Bogol	1,080

JINGPO 景颇族	**145,681**
Zaiwa	90,300
Jingpo	25,800
Maru	23,900
Bela	3,700
Lashi	1,950
Hkauri	31

SALAR 撒拉族	**113,100**
Salar	113,100

BULANG 布朗族	**104,940**
Bulang	79,850
Puman	16,520
Angku	7,000
Kong Ge	1,450
Samtao	120

MAONAN 毛南族	**100,300**
Maonan	51,600
Yanghuang	48,700

TAJIK 塔吉克族	**43,230**
Tajik, Sarikoli	33,300

Tajik, Wakhi	9,930
MONBA 门巴族	**41,440**
Monba, Cona	34,850
Monba, Medog	6,590
PUMI 普米族	**37,900**
Pumi	37,900
ACHANG 阿昌族	**35,898**
Achang	29,300
Achang, Husa	6,450
Xiandao	148
NU 怒族	**33,500**
Nu	26,200
Zauzou	2,970
Ayi	2,210
Lama	1,060
Tuwo	1,060
EWENKI 鄂温克族	**31,424**
Ewenki, Solon	27,150
Yakut	2,190
Ewenki, Tungus	2,060
Ongkor	24
JING 京族	**24,400**
Jing	24,400
JINO 基诺族	**23,210**
Jino	21,950
Jino, Buyuan	1,260
DE'ANG 德昂族	**20,410**
De'ang, Pale	8,260
De'ang, Shwe	5,970
De'ang, Rumai	4,640
Riang	1,540
UZBEK 乌兹别克族	**17,470**
Uzbek	17,470
RUSSIAN 俄罗斯族	**17,400**
Russian	17,400
BONAN 保安族	**16,090**
Bonan	10,590
Bonan, Tongren	5,500
YUGUR 裕固族	**14,680**
Yugur, Saragh	9,870
Yugur, Enger	4,810
LHOBA* 珞巴族	**13,422**
Lhoba, Yidu	8,350
Lhoba, Bogar	3,580
Adi	1,070
Puroik	340
Miguba	82

*Note: Although the 1990 census listed only 2,312 Lhoba people, several linguistic surveys report their numbers to be considerably higher.

OROQEN 鄂伦春族	**8,980**
Oroqen	8,980
DERUNG 度龙族	**7,390**
Derung	6,850
Rawang	540
TATAR 塔塔而族	**5,970**
Tatar	5,970
HEZHEN 赫哲族	**5,470**
Hezhen	5,470
GAOSHAN 高山族	**3,730**
Ami	1,930
Bunun	1,290
Paiwan	510

Groups Counted in the 1990 Census as an 'Undetermined Minority'

Chuanqing	761,000
Mulao Jia*	30,400
Cai	25,800
Palyu	12,030
Deng, Geman	11,000
Deng, Darang	8,260
Za	2,640
Hu	1,460
Khmu	1,420
Manmet	1,310
Sanda	1,110
Ake	1,000
Bit	640
Mang	440

* Note: In 1993, 2,800 Mulao Jia were reclassified in the official Mulao nationality. The remainder of the Mulao Jia have stayed on the list of *Undetermined Minorities.*

Groups With an Unknown Official Classification

Bugan	3,350
Vietnamese	2,110
Bunan	1,680
Kemei	1,260
Kuan	1,260
Nubra	520
Thami	460
Tuerke	189
Chin, Asho	167

Achang 阿昌

Location: Approximately 30,000 Achang inhabit an area along the Yunnan-Myanmar border near the Chinese town of Ruili. The Achang share the southern end of the Gaoligong Mountains with about a dozen other colorful ethnic groups. An additional 1,700 Achang live in Myanmar's Shan State where they are mainly employed as seasonal laborers.[1]

Identity: The Achang are one of 55 minorities officially recognized by China. In Myanmar the Achang, traditionally known as *Mongsha*, are culturally and historically linked to the Shan. There is speculation that the Achang were originally Zaiwa who moved east to their present location.

Language: The Achang language — which has four tones — is related to the Phun, Maru, Lashi, and Zaiwa languages. It also appears to be influenced by Shan which is part of the Tai linguistic family. The Achang minority include speakers of three mutually unintelligible dialects.[2] Longchuan is the most distinct, using many Tai Mao loanwords.[3] The Lianghe and the Luxi dialects, on the other hand, contain many Chinese words.[4] In addition, Achang also has some Burmese loanwords.

History: The Achang have a rich heritage of singing ballads and telling folk tales to each other. These stories are the main way Achang culture and history are passed down to children. The Achang claim to have once lived in a matriarchal society in northwestern Yunnan. After the Achang migrated to their present location, they began to rely more on farming and less on hunting to feed themselves. During the Ming and Qing dynasties (1368–1911), the Achang were ruled by hereditary chiefs.

Customs: Achang women wear colorful skirts and wrap dark cloth high upon their heads. Traditionally, unmarried women tie their pigtails together on top of their heads. During an Achang funeral, a cloth ribbon, 10 to 20 meters (11 to 22 yds.) long, is attached to the coffin. A Buddhist monk is hired to walk in front of the procession holding the ribbon, which signifies the monk leading the soul of the deceased to the afterworld.[5]

Dwayne Graybill

Religion: Although they are nominally Theravada Buddhist, the older generation of Achang exhibit many traits of polytheism and animism in their religious rituals and everyday lives. Most Achang homes have posters of deities and demons pasted on their walls. However, there are also some Christians in nearly every Achang village in China.[6] The present generation, having been educated in atheistic schools, are gradually forsaking the religious practices of their parents.

Christianity: A 1989 report commented that the Achang had "at least one known Christian."[7] The situation appears to have improved rapidly; by 1992 the same source reported there was a church in nearly every Achang village in China.[8] A strong, vibrant church also exists directly across the border among the Jingpo (Kachin), as well as among the Achang of Myanmar. Members of the new Achang church are often invited for training in northern Myanmar. The Achang New Testament was completed in 1992, using a script that was invented specifically for the Achang in Myanmar.

Population in China:
22,708 (1990)
29,300 (2000)
37,800 (2010)
Location: Yunnan
Religion: Polytheism
Christians: 2,000

Overview of the Achang

Countries: China, Myanmar

Pronunciation: "Ah-tsung"

Other Names: Achung, Atsang, Acang, Ahchan, Mongsha, Maingtha, Ngacang, Ngatsang, Ngachang, Ngac'ang, Ngochang, A-ch'ang, Achan, Mongsa

Population Source: 27,708 (1990 census);[9] 20,441 (1982 census); 12,032 (1964 census); 1,700 in Myanmar (1983)

Location: *W Yunnan:* Dehong Dai Prefecture[10]

Status: An official minority of China

Language: Sino-Tibetan, Tibeto-Burman, Burmese-Lolo, Burmish, Northern Burmish

Dialects (3): Longchuan, Luxi, Lianghe

Literacy: 39%

Religion: Polytheism, Theravada Buddhism, Daoism, Animism, Ancestor Worship, Christianity

Christians: 2,000

Scripture: New Testament 1992

***Jesus* film:** None

Gospel Recordings: Ngochang #04370

Christian Broadcasting: None

ROPAL code: ACN00

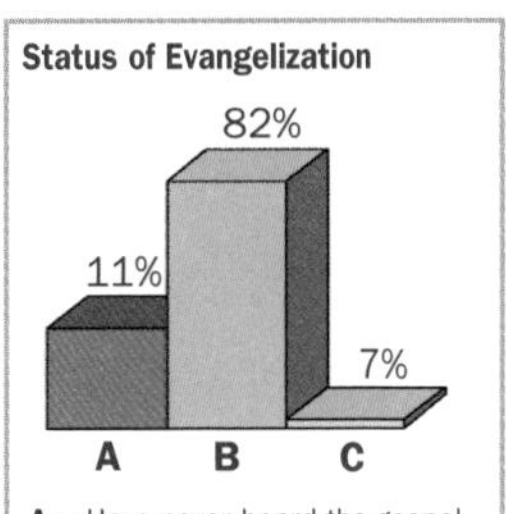

Achang, Husa 阿昌 (户撒)

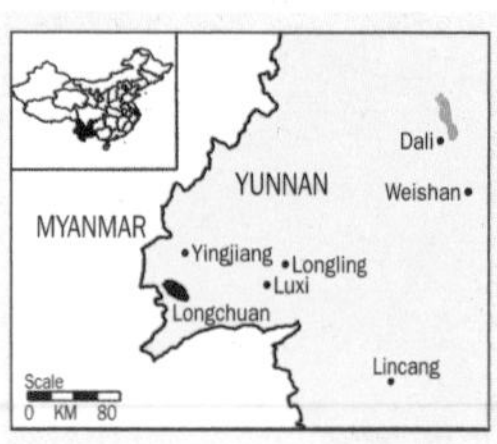

Population in China:
5,000 (1990)
6,450 (2000)
8,320 (2010)
Location: Yunnan
Religion: Buddhism
Christians: 100

Overview of the Husa Achang

Countries: China

Pronunciation: "Ah-tsung-Hoo-sa"

Other Names:

Population Source:
5,000 (1990 AMO);
Out of a total Achang population of 27,708 (1990 census)

Location: *W Yunnan:* Husa District of Longchuan County in the Dehong Dai Autonomous Prefecture

Status:
Officially included under Achang

Language: Sino-Tibetan, Tibeto-Burman, Burmese-Lolo, Burmish, Northern Burmish

Dialects: 0

Religion: Theravada Buddhism, Daoism, Animism, Ancestor Worship, No Religion, Christianity

Christians: 100

Scripture: None

***Jesus* film:** None

Gospel Recordings: None

Christian Broadcasting: None

ROPAL code: ACN01

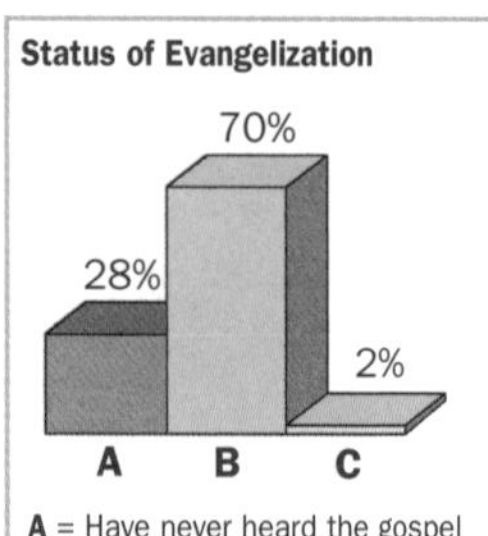

A = Have never heard the gospel
B = Were evangelized but did not become Christians
C = Are adherents to any form of Christianity

Location: Approximately 6,000 Husa Achang live in the Husa District of Longchuan County in Yunnan Province. Longchuan forms part of the Dehong Prefecture, which borders Myanmar.

Identity: Additional members of the Achang minority live in the Husa region, but this study refers only to that branch of Achang which claims to be descended from Chinese soldiers stationed in the region during the Ming Dynasty (1368–1644). As one writer notes, "They differ from Achang people elsewhere in their customs and religious beliefs."[1] The Husa Achang claim to be distinct; in the 1950s they lodged an unsuccessful application with the government to be recognized as a separate nationality.

Language: The Achang in Husa speak a language distinct from other Achang people. Their speech — which has four tones — has more Chinese influence than other Achang varieties. While the Achang groups in China do not possess their own written script, many are literate in either the Chinese or Tai Mao scripts or both. Dai Mao is the trade language throughout most of the Dehong Prefecture.

History: The Husa Achang have a common affinity for each other because of their historical roots. "The Achang of Husa are said to be descended from Achang women who married Han Chinese soldiers serving in the Ming army who were left behind to farm and garrison this area after three successful campaigns against the rebellious clan of Si in 1448."[2] After more than five centuries, the Husa Achang still consider themselves ethnically separate and possess numerous cultural and religious observances that are not found among other Achang. Husa is also the site of a famous Qing Dynasty tomb from the late nineteenth century.

Customs: The military background of the Husa Achang is probably the reason for their great skill in making knives, daggers, and swords. The Husa woodcutting knife is famous all over southwest China. The swords they make are similar in design to those used in the Imperial Court of China around the year 1388.[3] The sword is reputed to be "so pliable that it can wind around your finger, and so sharp that it cuts iron like mud."[4]

Religion: The historical origins of the Husa Achang have also provided them with religious practices distinct from other Achang people. For instance, "quite a few Achang homes in Husa contain a memorial tablet of the Confucian type... evidence of Han Chinese cultural influence."[5] Some Husa Achang practice a mixture of Theravada Buddhism and Daoism, while many of the current atheism-educated generation are nonreligious.

Christianity: There are a small number of Christians among the Husa Achang. Surrounded by strong Jingpo churches, most Achang in Husa are aware of the gospel. The Kachin church in nearby northern Myanmar offers Bible training to believers from the Achang region.

Paul Hattaway

A Che 阿车

Jamin Pelkey

Location: Approximately 35,000 A Che people predominantly live in Shuangbai (23,000) and Yimen (11,100) counties in the eastern part of Yunnan Province's Chuxiong Prefecture. Other A Che villages spill over into Lufeng and Eshan counties in Yuxi Prefecture. Most of the A Che in Shuangbai County are extremely isolated. In Yuxi Prefecture, on the other hand, some A Che villages are a mere five kilometers (three mi.) from Yimen City.

Identity: Despite the similarities in their names, the A Che are not the same as the Azhe people, another Yi subgroup located in Yunnan Province. The Azhe live in Mile and Yimen counties farther to the east and speak a different Southeastern Yi dialect. Because of their inclusion in the artificially constructed Yi nationality (made up of more than 100 distinct groups), the A Che are mostly unknown to outsiders. However, they were mentioned in the 1953 national census of China.[1] The A Che do not believe they are related to other Yi groups, in much the same way many of the numerous Native American tribes in the United States do not consider themselves historically, culturally, or ethnically related to each other.

Language: The A Che language is one of many that forms the Southern Yi branch of the Tibeto-Burman language family. Most A Che are illiterate, although compulsory education in the last few decades has allowed some A Che youth to gain knowledge in reading and writing Chinese characters. The Yi pictographic orthography used in southern Sichuan is not known among the A Che.

History: Despite their marked present-day linguistic differences, the A Che and the Azhe share similar origins. They say they migrated south to Jianshui County during the Sui and Tang dynasties (581–907). They were enlisted in the armies of the Luodian Kingdom. After settling in Jianshui for a time, some crossed the mountains into Yimen and Shuangbai counties where they gradually evolved to become the A Che.[2]

Customs: There are two important festivals unique to the A Che of Shuangbai County. The Open Street Festival is held every eighth day of the first lunar month in Damaidi District, and the Dragon Worship Festival is held on the second day of the second lunar month in Fadian Community of Yulong District.

Religion: The A Che are polytheists. In the past, they claim they were closer to the gods, but then their line of communication with the Creator was broken. Therefore, they are now unable to enter heaven.

Christianity: Hidden away in some of the most remote areas of southwest China, the A Che are known to few outsiders. As a result, they are a completely unreached and unevangelized people. They have also never appeared in mission lists of people groups. The vast Chuxiong Prefecture experiences very little Christian witness. Added to the difficult task of reaching this group is the A Che's inability to read or speak Chinese. Evangelists to the A Che face a daunting communication challenge.

Population in China:
35,300 (1999)
36,200 (2000)
45,400 (2010)
Location: Yunnan
Religion: Polytheism
Christians: None Known

Overview of the A Che

Countries: China
Pronunciation: "Ah-Cheh"
Other Names: A-Che
Population Source: 35,300 (1999 J. Pelkey); Out of a total Yi population of 6,572,173 (1990 census)
Location: *Yunnan:* Shaungbai (23,000), Yimen (11,100), Lufeng (500), Eshan (500), and Zhenyuan (200) counties
Status: Officially included under Yi
Language: Sino-Tibetan, Tibeto-Burman, Burmese-Lolo, Lolo, Northern Lolo, Yi, Southern Yi
Dialects: 0
Religion: Polytheism, Animism
Christians: None known
Scripture: None
***Jesus* film:** None
Gospel Recordings: Yi: Ache
Christian Broadcasting: None
ROPAL code: None

Status of Evangelization

A = Have never heard the gospel
B = Were evangelized but did not become Christians
C = Are adherents to any form of Christianity

Adi 阿地

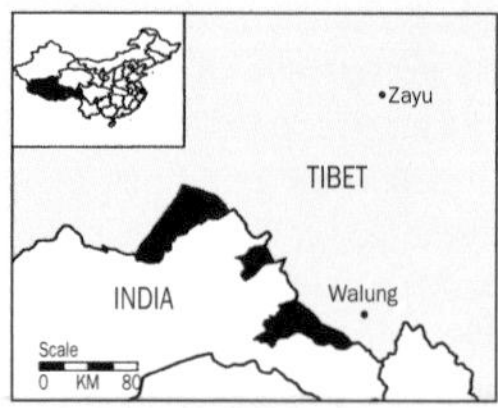

Population in China:
1,000 (1995)
1,070 (2000)
1,230 (2010)
Location: Tibet
Religion: Shamanism
Christians: None Known

Overview of the Adi

Countries: India, China

Pronunciation: "Ah-dee"

Other Names: Miri, Abor, Arbor, Abor-Miri

Population Source: 1,000 (1995 AMO); 482,489 in India, consisting of 122,489 Adi (1981 census) and 360,000 Miri (1989 USCWM)

Location: *SW Tibet:* Along the border with Arunachal Pradesh, India

Status: Probably officially included under Lhoba

Language: Sino-Tibetan, Tibeto-Burman, Baric, Mirish

Dialects (2): Adi, Miri

Religion: Shamanism, Tibetan Buddhism, Polytheism

Christians: None known

Scripture: New Testament 1988; Portions 1932

***Jesus* film:** None

Gospel Recordings: Available in 4 dialects: Adi #04147; Adi Gallong #02409; Adi Padam #02410; Adi Padam-Miri #02251

Christian Broadcasting: None

ROPAL code: ADI00

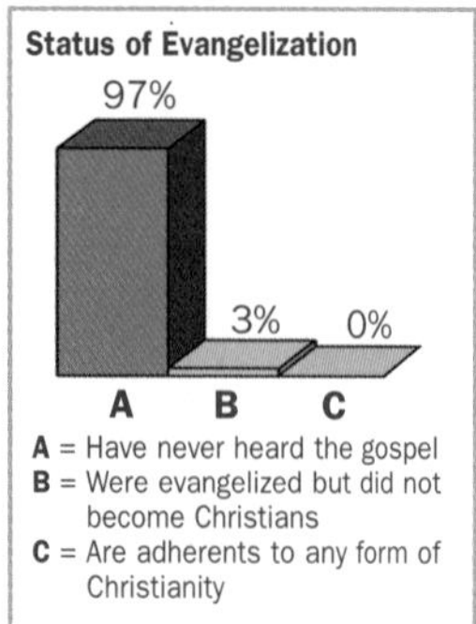

Dwayne Graybill

Location: The great majority of Adi live in India, with 482,000 occupying the north hills of the Assam Valley between Bhutan and the Burili River. Approximately 300,000 Adi live on Majuli Island — the world's largest river island — which lies in the mighty Brahmaputra River. There are no more than 1,000 Adi inside China, although some publications have claimed as many as 61,000 live there.[1] Living in remote valleys near the juncture of India, Bhutan, and Tibet, the Adi experience less severe winters than people living on the Tibetan Plateau. The Adi inhabit a beautiful, forested region which abounds with mountain strawberries, hemp, irises, azaleas and rhododendrons. Medog County still contains many Bengali tigers as well as 40 species of other rare, protected animals.[2]

Identity: The Adi do not appear in Chinese government publications. It is likely that they have been officially counted as part of the Lhoba nationality, who have a similar language and live in the same region. In India, *Adi* is a general name given for a collection of as many as 15 tribes or subgroups, including the Ramo, Bokar, Bori, and Shimong.[3]

Language: The Adi language is part of the Baric branch of the Tibeto-Burman family. Most sources list Adi and Miri as two dialects of the same language, while other scholars describe them as two distinct, mutually unintelligible languages.[4]

History: After the Communist takeover of Tibet in the 1950s, the Indian military went on full alert. In the following decades, several border skirmishes between the two giant nations took place, particularly at the opposite ends of the Himalayan Range. Those Adi who are now located in China did not migrate there, but found themselves technically in Tibet as the result of the redrawing of international boundaries after these conflicts. The Adi are perhaps the most remote people in China, with no roads at all in the region.

Customs: Expression by dance is an important part of the Adi culture. Religious and war dances use aggressive movements to relate the violent history of the Adi against other tribes in northeast India.[5] Adi women are renowned throughout northern India as expert weavers.

Religion: The Adi in Tibet are an isolated people who follow an ancient form of shamanism. Acting as mediums between the Adi and the spirit world, shamans often fall into demonic trances while communicating with the spirits. In India, some Adi have converted to Hinduism. Some Adi in Tibet outwardly adhere to Tibetan Buddhism more to please their aggressive Tibetan neighbors than from sincere, heartfelt conviction.

Christianity: There are reports of existing churches among the Adi in India, largely due to the work of the Baptist General Conference. Locked in by massive mountains, few Adi in China have ever heard the gospel. Adi territory is rugged and off-limits to foreigners: It is inaccessible from the Chinese side. The Adi in both India and China remain an unreached people in desperate need of attention from the global Body of Christ. The conversion of the Adi would likely impact dozens of smaller, related peoples throughout this ethnically diverse area.

Adu 阿笃

Population in China:
5,643 (1990)
7,080 (2000)
8,880 (2010)
Location: Yunnan
Religion: Animism
Christians: None Known

Overview of the Adu

Countries: China

Pronunciation: "Ah-doo"

Other Names:

Population Source: 5,643 (1990 *Huaning Xian Minzu Zhi*); Out of a total Yi population of 6,572,173 (1990 census)

Location: *Yunnan:* Yuxi Prefecture: Huaning and Chengjiang counties

Status: Officially included under Yi

Language: Chinese, Mandarin

Dialects: 0

Religion: Animism, No religion, Ancestor Worship

Christians: None known

Scripture: None

***Jesus* film:** None

Gospel Recordings: Yi: Adu

Christian Broadcasting: None

ROPAL code: None

Location: More than 6,500 Adu people live in central Yunnan Province in southwest China. Approximately 3,500 live in Huaning County within Yuxi Prefecture. Their village names in Huaning are Songzichang, Xinzhai, Keju, and Chengmentong. There are many additional villages in the Lufeng District. An official Chinese report also lists 2,025 Adu people in the mountains of Haikou District in Chengjiang County, in the northern tip of Yuxi Prefecture.[1]

Identity: The Adu are an interesting people group, in that they have been officially included in the Yi nationality but speak a form of Yunnan Chinese.

Language: It is unclear whether the Adu were originally a tribe of Yi who moved to their present location and lost the use of their mother tongue as they were assimilated to the Chinese language, or if they were an early Chinese group who were influenced by minority languages that prevailed in the area they inhabited. Either way, it appears the Adu language contains a mixture of characteristics that are both Yi and Chinese in nature. The Chinese report the Adu language to be close to the dialect spoken in the Dajie District of Jiangchuan County. Adu is also said to be the same as the *Zijun* dialect of Kunming.[2]

History: Yunnan has witnessed numerous ethnic migrations. Hemmed in by huge mountains that separate it from its Southeast Asian neighbors, Yunnan has witnessed a massive fusion and scattering of people groups. The Yi have splintered into dozens of ethnic components, of which the Adu are just one. As clans and tribes moved away they formed their own communities and gradually forgot their relationship to the larger group. After centuries of isolation these different groups have developed their own identity, customs, and languages.

Customs: Marriage customs are simple among the Adu. In the past, parents were responsible for arranging their children's partners, but today most Adu youth choose their partners. The custom of paying a dowry, or bride price, has also lessened in recent decades. These days it is essential to own certain material possessions for a young Adu man to be considered attractive to a woman. These include a color TV, stereo, motorbike, sewing machine, refrigerator, and washing machine.

Religion: The majority of Adu under the age of 40 are nonreligious. At most they observe customs relating to ancestor worship, and they may clean their ancestors' graves once a year. Most elderly Adu, however, retain their animistic practices and rituals, including worship of the spirits of trees, mountains, dragons, and rivers. The animism of the Adu is certain to diminish as time passes.

Christianity: There are no known Christians among the Adu. Few members of this small tribe have ever been exposed to the gospel. The Christian organization Gospel Recordings traveled to the Adu in 1999 and produced the first ever gospel message in the Adu language. It is hoped Christians will use this resource to take the gospel to the Adu for the first time.

Jamin Pelkey

A-Hmao 阿贸

Location: A 1995 Chinese study listed a 1990 figure of 300,000 A-Hmao people in southern China.[1] They live in the mountains of northwest Guizhou Province and adjacent areas of northeast Yunnan. A group of A-Hmao live in Wuding and Luquan counties in northern Yunnan Province, having migrated there in the 1830s.[2] A small number also live in the Panzhihua area in southern Sichuan.

Identity:[3] The A-Hmao are one of "close to a hundred distinctive subgroups of Miao in China alone, each speaking a slightly different dialect and maintaining its own traditional customs."[4] These people call themselves A-Hmao. The Chinese and foreigners have traditionally called them *Da Hua Miao* (Big Flowery Miao). The "Big Flowery Miao" (A-Hmao) speak a completely different language from the "Small Flowery Miao" (Gha-Mu) who also live in Guizhou.

Language: The Chinese officially label A-Hmao the Diandongbei (Northeast Yunnan) dialect of Miao. It is one of the "30–40 different Miao languages in China."[5]

History: For centuries the A-Hmao lived in dire slavery to the Nosu Yi. The Nosu bullied the A-Hmao by seizing their land, taking slaves, and imposing unfair taxes on them. Nosu landowners customarily used the back of an A-Hmao slave to mount their horses. As recently as 80 years ago, the A-Hmao still practiced cannibalism. Samuel Pollard recorded in his diary, "After a fight, the warriors who are killed on either side are opened and their hearts removed... these are cooked and eaten."[6]

Customs: Before their mass conversion to Christianity, the A-Hmao were ensnared by a complex system of evil spirits they called *bidlang*. The people's immorality was "so bad that they could hardly be worse.... There are no decent women among the Big Flowery Miao [A-Hmao]."[7]

Michael Johnson

Religion: When missionary Samuel Pollard first arrived in 1904, he found the A-Hmao trapped in slavery to the Nosu and overwhelmed with poverty. Together with Francis Dymond he converted them to Christianity, invented an alphabet for their language, and taught them to read and write.[8] Although a severe famine in 1918 left many A-Hmao believers "disenchanted with Christianity,"[9] Pollard baptized 10,000 A-Hmao believers, and before the mission was expelled from China, 80,000 had turned to Christ. Some estimate that as many as 80% of the A-Hmao today are Christians.[10]

Christianity: After the departure of the missionaries, the A-Hmao church stayed steadfast to Christ, despite sinister plots during the Cultural Revolution aimed at destroying their faith.[11] During the 1940s the church experienced "a very serious process of retrogression and decay, which if not soon arrested will... bring us back to our starting point again."[12] The A-Hmao New Testament was printed in 1917; 50,000 copies were reprinted and sold out between 1983 and 1988.[13] In 1974 many A-Hmao believers were massacred by Chinese troops when they secretly met for prayer in a cave at Xinglongchang.[14] Instead of destroying the church, the massacre caused a doubling in the number of Christians over a short time.[15]

Population in China:
300,000 (1990)
387,000 (2000)
499,200 (2010)
Location: Guizhou, Yunnan, Sichuan
Religion: Christianity
Christians: 200,000

Overview of the A-Hmao

Countries: China
Pronunciation: "Ahc-Maow"
Other Names: Big Flowery Miao, Hmong: Northeastern Dian, Hwa Miao, Hua Miao, Diandongbei Miao, Variegated Miao, Great Flowery Miao, Northeast Yunnan Miao, Ta Hua Miao, Flowery Miao, Dahua Bei, Da Hua Miao
Population Source:
300,000 (1995 Wang Fushi – 1990 figure);
200,000 (1985 Wang Fushi – 1982 figure);
Out of a total Miao population of 7,398,035 (1990 census)
Location: *Guizhou:* Weining, Shuicheng, Pu'an, Zhenning, Ziyun, and Hezhang counties; *Yunnan:* Wuding, Luquan, Fumin, Xundian, Anning and Lufeng; *S Sichuan:* Panzhihua area
Status:
Officially included under Miao
Language: Hmong-Mien, Hmongic, Western Hmong, Farwestern Hmong
Dialects: 0
Religion: Christianity, Animism, No Religion
Christians: 200,000
Scripture: New Testament 1917; Portions 1905
***Jesus* film:** None
Gospel Recordings:
Flowery Hmong #00104
Christian Broadcasting: None
ROPAL code: HMD00

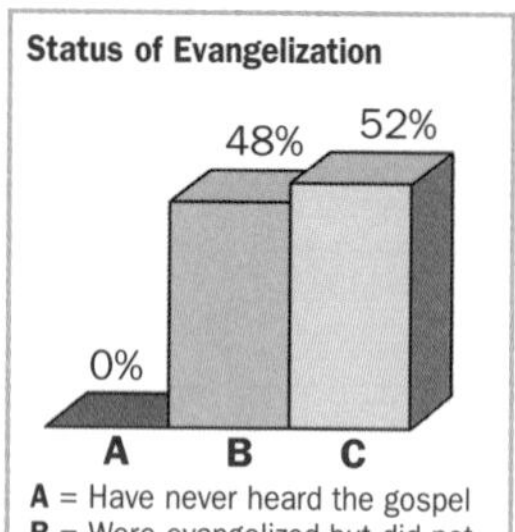

Ai-Cham 唉查么

Population in China:
2,300 (1986)
2,700 (2000)
3,370 (2010)
Location: Guizhou
Religion: Polytheism
Christians: None Known

Overview of the Ai-Cham

Countries: China

Pronunciation: "Eye-chum"

Other Names: Jiamuhua, Jinhua, Atsam

Population Source: 2,300 (1996 B. Grimes – 1986 figure); Out of a total Bouyei population of 2,545,059 (1990 census)

Location: *S Guizhou:* Libo County: 13 villages near Di'e and Boyao townships

Status: Officially included under Bouyei

Language: Daic, Kam-Sui

Dialects (2): Di'e, Boyao

Religion: Polytheism, Animism, Ancestor Worship

Christians: None known

Scripture: None

***Jesus* film:** None

Gospel Recordings: None

Christian Broadcasting: None

ROPAL code: AIH00

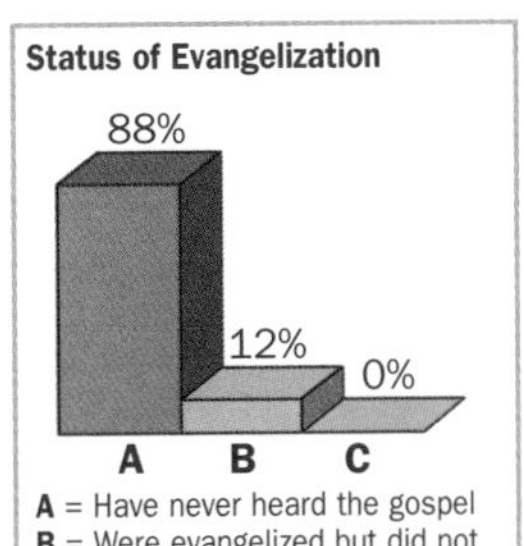

A = Have never heard the gospel
B = Were evangelized but did not become Christians
C = Are adherents to any form of Christianity

Paul Hattaway

Location: Approximately 2,300 Ai-Cham people inhabit 13 isolated villages in southern Guizhou Province, near the Bouyei and the Baonuo people.[1] Hidden away among the never-ending range of mountains and the gushing rivers of Guizhou, the majority of Ai-Cham are concentrated near the towns of Di'e and Boyao in Libo County.

Identity: The Ai-Cham have been erroneously counted as part of the Bouyei nationality in China. The Ai-Cham believe themselves to be a separate ethnic group and are unwilling to be identified as part of the Bouyei. Whereas Bouyei is a Northern Tai language, Ai-Cham is part of the Dong-Shui branch of the Tai language family. The Ai-Cham were probably counted as Bouyei by Chinese researchers because most of them are able to speak Bouyei, which is the local trade language.

Language: The two Ai-Cham dialects, Di'e and Boyao, have phonological differences but are largely intelligible.[2] Ai-Cham — which is also known as Jiamuhua — is similar to the Mo language. There are six tones in the Ai-Cham language. Because the Ai-Cham possess no written orthography, Chinese is used as the literary language.

History: The Ai-Cham find themselves sandwiched between giant ethnic groups, including the Zhuang to the south, the Bouyei to the north, and more recently the Han Chinese who have migrated into southern Guizhou in large numbers since the 1950s. It is possible the Ai-Cham were originally a group of Dong or Shui who long ago moved south to their present location. The historical roots of the Ai-Cham remain uncertain.

Customs: The Chinese have long had this famous description of Guizhou: "There are not three days of sun, not three measures of flat land, and the people do not have three coins." This saying proves true today: Guizhou is still one of the poorest and least developed of China's provinces. Despite abundant rainfall, the inhabitants are cursed by poor harvests due to poor returns from the rocky ground.

Religion: The Ai-Cham are primarily polytheists. They worship a multiplicity of gods, ghosts, and spirit beings. They believe all of nature has a soul, including mountains, rivers, trees, and even large rocks. The Ai-Cham also worship their ancestors and put plates of food out several times a year for the souls of their deceased family members. In the past shamans held positions of great power among the Ai-Cham, but their influence was diminished during the antireligion campaigns of the Cultural Revolution between 1966 and 1976.

Christianity: The Ai-Cham are an unreached people group without a gospel witness. Few have any knowledge of Christ. Prior to the 1950s there were both Protestant and Catholic missionaries in southern Guizhou, although there is no record of any workers who specifically targeted the Ai-Cham. The Protestant efforts met with little success, but a small number of Catholic churches were established in some Bouyei villages. There are no Scriptures or recordings available in the Ai-Cham language to aid in their evangelization.

Ainu 艾努

Dwayne Graybill

Location: The Ainu, who number approximately 6,500 people, live scattered over a wide area of northwest China. The Ainu inhabit the six counties of Hetian, Luopu, Moyu, Shache, Yingjisha, and Shulekuche, near the famous ancient city of Kashgar.[1] Kashgar, a giant oasis 1,290 meters (4,230 ft.) above sea level, is almost totally inhabited by Uygur, Uzbek, Tajik, and Kirgiz Muslims.

Identity: For reasons that are unclear, the majority of Uygur despise the Ainu and call them Abdal, which means "beggar".[2] The Uygur refuse to intermarry with the Ainu, who are linguistically, culturally, and socially a distinct people group.

Language: The Ainu language has the same grammar as Uygur, but in addition, as much as one-third of the Ainu vocabulary consists of Persian words.[3] In fact, some scholars label Ainu as an Iranian (Persian) language.[4] The Ainu speak their language at home but must use Uygur to communicate with outsiders. The Ainu in China are not related to the identically named Ainu of Japan and Russia.

History: The history of the Ainu is shrouded in uncertainty. Why they came to be hated by their fellow Muslims is a mystery. Their Persian language suggests they probably originated in Central Asia long ago. Kashgar is one of the most isolated cities in China. To reach Kashgar from Beijing once required two years' travel by camel. It is located more than 3,000 kilometers (1,850 mi.) from Beijing and is even a grueling three-day bus journey from Urumqi, the capital of the Xinjiang Uygur Autonomous Region. Kashgar today has more in common with nearby Pakistan than with the rest of China.

Customs: Most Ainu lead simple lives, herding sheep and goats. Some Ainu men in recent years have been forced to travel to other large cities in Xinjiang to seek employment in industry and construction.

Religion: The Ainu are Muslims of the Sunni sect; they worship in mosques scattered throughout their villages. They have been described as a "caste of circumcisers."[5] Few Ainu have ever studied Arabic, so even the religious leaders of their communities are unable to read the Qur'an.

Christianity: Although no trace of Christianity remains in Kashgar today, it was once a church center for much of Central Asia. Kashgar was the appointed seat of a Nestorian metropolitan bishop in the thirteenth century.[6] When the intrepid explorer Marco Polo visited Kashgar at the time, he noted that it contained "Turks who are Nestorian Christians who have churches of their own, and they are mixed and dwell with the inhabitants as the Jews in these parts live with Christians."[7] Today, Kashgar is a stronghold of Islam, and the Ainu have no knowledge of the gospel message. Only a handful have been evangelized, primarily as a result of listening to the recently begun weekly gospel radio broadcasts in the Uygur language. Being a despised people, the Ainu eagerly desire the acceptance of their Uygur neighbors, an acceptance that makes the practice of Islam a prerequisite and the acceptance of Christianity unlikely.

Population in China:
5,000 (1988)
6,570 (2000)
8,290 (2010)
Location: Xinjiang
Religion: Islam
Christians: None Known

Overview of the Ainu

Countries: China
Pronunciation: "Eye-noo"
Other Names: Aynu, Aini, Abdal
Population Source: 5,000 (1992 B. Grimes – 1988 figure); Out of a total Uygur population of 7,214,431 (1990 census)
Location: *Xinjiang:* Kashgar area: Yengixar Town, Hanalik and Paynap villages; Hoban area: Gewoz Village; And in parts of Hetian, Luopu, Moyu, Shache, Yingjisha, and Shulekuche counties in southern Xinjiang
Status: Officially included under Uygur
Language: Altaic, Turkic, Eastern Turkic
Dialects: 0
Religion: Sunni Islam
Christians: None known
Scripture: None
***Jesus* film:** None
Gospel Recordings: None
Christian Broadcasting: None
ROPAL code: AIB00

Status of Evangelization

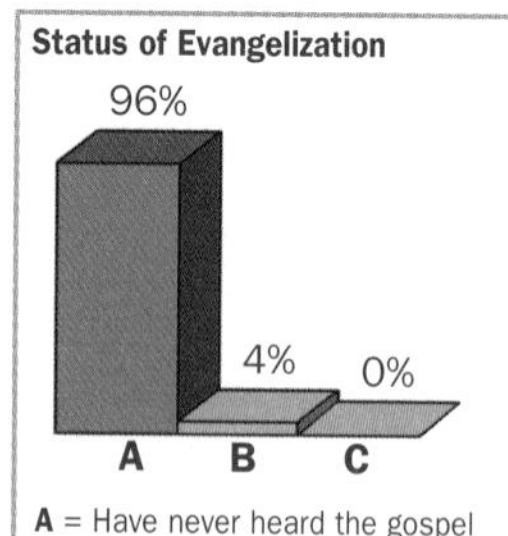

A = Have never heard the gospel
B = Were evangelized but did not become Christians
C = Are adherents to any form of Christianity

Ake 阿克

Location: A 1985 publication reported the Ake to have a population of "not more than 1,000 people."[1] In 1996 researcher Dwayne Graybill counted 900 Ake, including 95 families living in three villages of Menghai County with additional Ake living in Jinghong County.[2] Both counties are located in Xishuangbanna Prefecture, the most ethnically diverse region in all of China. Small numbers of Ake also live in Laos, Myanmar, and northern Thailand.

Identity: Not to be confused with the large Akha group who live in the same area of China, the Ake are a small, distinct tribe. The Chinese in 1985 listed the Ake in a list of groups "yet to be identified and classified."[3] More than ten years later this situation remains the same. The Ake were also included on a list of groups which "need further investigation."[4] The Ake view themselves as totally different from all other minorities even though their genealogies show they were once related to the Akha.[5]

Language: The Ake language is a member of the Bi-Ka branch of Tibeto-Burman, related to Biyo, Kado, and Enu.[6] The Ake claim to have once possessed a written script prior to their migration from Mintang, an area in central Yunnan Province, to their present location in southern Yunnan.

History: The Ake claim a history going back at least 20 generations. The names on the Ake ancestral tree are handed down orally from generation to generation. Until recently, slash-and-burn agricultural techniques were common practice among the Ake; they relocated their villages every few years after exhausting the land. Malaria often had free rein among the Ake, decimating their population and causing havoc to entire communities.

Customs: The Ake lived in a very isolated society until recently. They kept records and reminders by carving notches on wood, tying knots on rope, or counting beans. Ake frequently intermarry with other minorities, a practice which has kept their population low. Marriages are only allowed to take place between January and April each year. Ake are frequently seen selling pans and brooms at the marketplace. Those who remain in the villages grow rice, tea, and sugarcane.

Religion: When asked what they believe, most Ake will say they do not have a religion. In practice, the majority worship their ancestors. They also attempt to live at peace with nature and the spirits which they believe control their communities. An increasing number of Ake youth are becoming atheists and do not feel the need to continue the practices of their parents.

Dwayne Graybill

Christianity: Few Ake have ever heard the gospel, and they did not comprehend the meaning of the word when asked if they had ever heard the name of Christ. Despite their ignorance, the Ake appear quite receptive to Christianity. The nearest Christian communities to the Ake are among the Tai Lu and Han in Jinghong, but up to this point the church there has not reached out to the Ake. Most mission agencies and research ministries have never heard of the Ake, and little prayer has ever gone up to the throne of God on behalf of this completely unevangelized and needy people group.[7]

Population in China:
900 (1996)
1,000 (2000)
1,290 (2010)
Location: Yunnan
Religion: Ancestor Worship
Christians: None Known

Overview of the Ake

Countries: Laos, China, Myanmar, Thailand

Pronunciation: "Ah-ker"

Other Names: A-ke, Akeu, A-k'o, Ako, Akui, Keu

Population Source: 900 (1996 D. Graybill); 2,000 in Laos (1995 L. Chazee); Also in Myanmar and Thailand

Location: *SW Yunnan:* Xishuangbanna: Menghai, and Jinghong counties; Also in Myanmar and Thailand

Status: Counted in census as an *Undetermined Minority*

Language: Sino-Tibetan, Tibeto-Burman, Burmese-Lolo, Southern Lolo, Akha, Hani, Bi-Ka

Dialects: 0

Religion: Ancestor Worship, Animism, No Religion

Christians: None known

Scripture: None

***Jesus* film:** None

Gospel Recordings: None

Christian Broadcasting: None

ROPAL code: None

Status of Evangelization

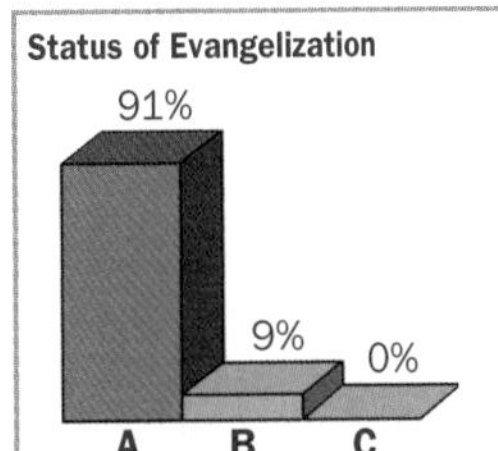

A = Have never heard the gospel
B = Were evangelized but did not become Christians
C = Are adherents to any form of Christianity

Akha 阿卡

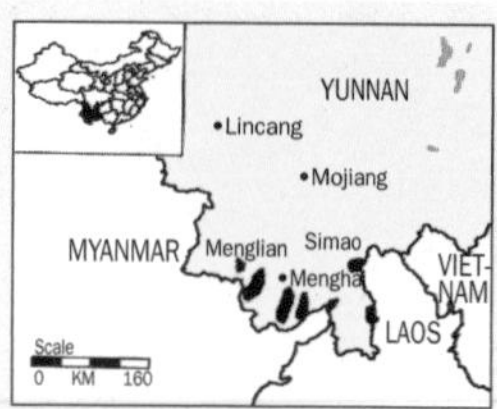

Population in China:
150,000 (1987)
194,600 (2000)
239,200 (2010)
Location: Yunnan
Religion: Animism
Christians: 600

Overview of the Akha

Countries: Myanmar, China, Laos, Thailand, Vietnam

Pronunciation: "Ah-kar"

Other Names: Aini, Aka, Ko, Ekaw, Kaw, Ahka, Khako, Ekwa, Ikho, Ikor, Ak'a, Yani, Jeu-g'oe, Guoke

Population Source:
150,000 in China (1987 D. Bradley);
200,000 in Myanmar (1991 United Bible Society);
66,108 in Laos (1995 census);
25,000 in Thailand (1993 P. Johnstone);
Also in Vietnam

Location: *SW Yunnan:* Xishuangbanna Dai Prefecture

Status: Officially included under Hani

Language: Sino-Tibetan, Tibeto-Burman, Burmese-Lolo, Lolo, Southern Lolo, Akha, Hani, Ha-Ya

Dialects (2): Gelanghe, and an unknown dialect

Religion: Animism, Theravada Buddhism

Christians: 600

Scripture: New Testament 1968; Portions 1939; The script is not understood in China.

***Jesus* film:** Available

Gospel Recordings: Akha #00529

Christian Broadcasting: Available (FEBC)

ROPAL code: AKA00

Status of Evangelization

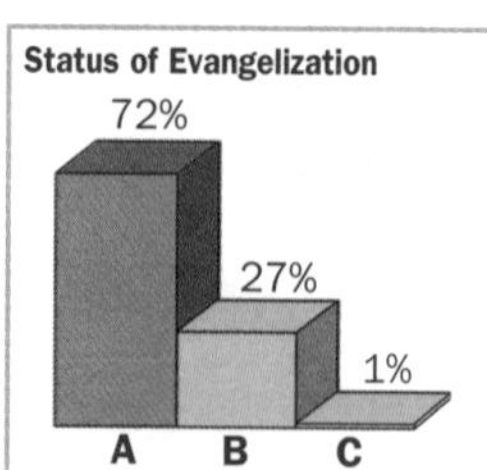

A = Have never heard the gospel
B = Were evangelized but did not become Christians
C = Are adherents to any form of Christianity

Location: Approximately 400,000 Akha are scattered throughout Asia. About 150,000 of these are located in southern China's Yunnan Province. Today the majority of Akha live in Myanmar, Laos, Vietnam, and Thailand. In China the Akha primarily inhabit Xishuangbanna Prefecture, which has a lazy, slow-paced feel.[1] The prefecture is home to approximately 30 ethnic groups, of which the Akha are one of the most visible.

Identity: The colorful Akha — called Aini by the Chinese — have their historical origins in southern China. The government considers them part of the Hani nationality, which is a collection of more than a dozen distinct ethnic groups. The Akha themselves consist of "five distinct branches,"[2] and possess their own unique customs, culture, language, and dress.

Language: The Akha language — which has five tones — is part of the Tibeto-Burman language family. All Akha children can speak their language, which is taught in some primary schools. The Akha have a legend of a lost book that was written on buffalo skin by the Creator. On a long journey the Akha got hungry and ate the book, and ever since they have been without a written language.[3]

History: Most scholars agree that the Akha were originally of Tibetan origin.[4] The Akha have a detailed creation epic poem. Long recitations, committed to memory and handed down from parents to children, are essential for continuing the Akha culture. Among the Akha it is important for a man to be able to memorize his complete genealogy right back to the first man, Sm Mi O. To be unable to do so is considered a disgrace. The Akha genealogy now covers more than 60 generations.[5]

Customs: Despite being some of the poorest people in southern China, Akha women have a striking appearance. They wear heavily decorated headdresses and skirts. Made from beaten silver, Indian rupee coins, fur, beads, and feathered tassels, the Akha headdress is removed only for the purpose of cleaning and washing their hair.

Religion: The Akha's religious philosophy, *Akhazang* (Akha-way), permeates every aspect of their lives and social structure. "Akhazang is a social and spiritual code that guides day-to-day living such as house-building, rice-planting and relationships with one another and with other nationalities."[6] The Akha believe in a supreme deity named Apoe Miyeh. They are also careful to appease the "Lord of Land and Water" who they believe is the spiritual ruler of each locality where they live.

Christianity: In Myanmar and Thailand the Akha have responded in large numbers to the gospel, with as many as 60,000 Akha Christians reported in Myanmar alone.[7] In China, however, only 500 to 600 Akha have believed. In recent years one evangelist has planted 16 house churches.[8] Missionaries first targeted the Akha in the 1910s but had little visible success. Recently, Akha believers from Myanmar have reached out to their cousins in China. The New Testament has been translated into Akha by missionaries in Myanmar, but the Akha in China cannot read the Roman script.

Paul Hattaway

Akto Turkmen 阿克哦土而克

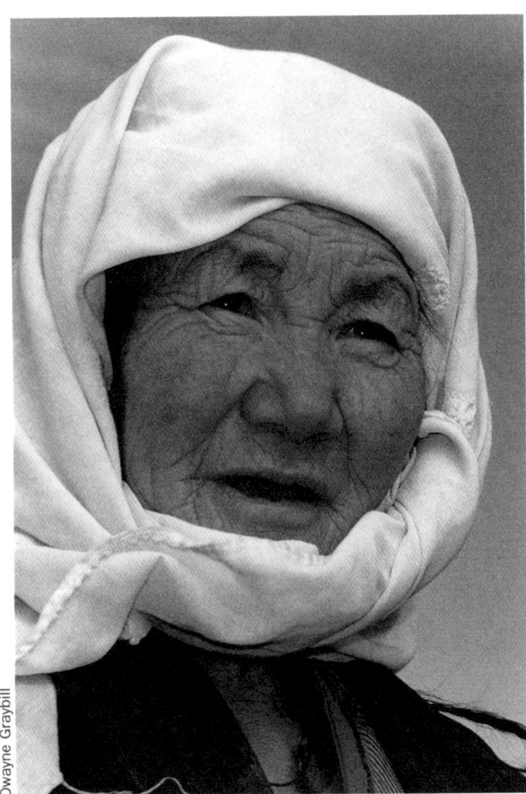

Dwayne Graybill

Location: A 1992 study listed 2,000 speakers of the Akto Turkmen language in China.[1] They live in two large villages, Kosarap and Oytak, south of Kashgar in the Xinjiang Uygur Autonomous Region. Little has changed in the area since Marco Polo described Kashgar 700 years ago: "The inhabitants live by trade and industry. They have very fine orchards and vineyards and flourishing estates. Cotton grows here in plenty, besides flax and hemp. The soil is fruitful and productive of all the means of life. This country is the starting-point from which many merchants set out to market their wares all over the world.... The inhabitants have a language all of their own."[2]

Identity: Although the Akto Turkmen are considered part of the Kirgiz nationality, their language and customs are more closely related to that of the Uygur. They claim originally they came from Samarkand, which lies in present-day Uzbekistan. The Akto Turkmen are a unique ethnolinguistic group. Their customs and physical features are also distinct from all other groups in Xinjiang.

Language: Some linguists describe Akto Turkmen as a dialect of the Turkic Uygur language, but the Akto Turkmen vocabulary is interspersed with approximately 500 words that are seldom used in standard Uygur.[3]

History: The history of the Akto Turkmen is uncertain. They claim to have migrated long ago from Samarkand to their present location in China. The Akto region is a part of China that has been rocked with conflict. In April 1990 an "armed counter revolutionary rebellion" occurred in Baren Township of Akto County. "There were over twenty deaths, mainly of members of Islamic minorities. Later in 1990... fifty mosques were closed down and the construction of 153 others was halted."[4]

Customs: These people are skilled shepherds and goatherds despite the harsh landscape where they must raise their animals. Their clothing, food, and housing all reflect their seminomadic, pastoral lifestyle. The diet of the Akto Turkmen consists mainly of animal by-products, complemented with cabbage, potatoes, and onions. They store their butter in dried sheep or cattle stomachs.

Religion: The Akto Turkmen are Sunni Muslims who observe both Uygur and Kirgiz religious festivals, along with some rituals they have retained from their pre-Islamic religion of shamanism. Most Akto Turkmen can read the modified Arabic script used by their Uygur neighbors.

Christianity: No record exists of any mission work being conducted among the small but proud Akto Turkmen people group. They are strongly bound to their Islamic beliefs, which form their ethnic identity, and to their own ancient form of shamanism and black magic. Few Akto Turkmen have had the opportunity to hear the gospel and intelligently respond to the claims of Christ. Probably the best opportunity for the Akto Turkmen to hear about Christ is through the Uygur gospel radio broadcasts that have aired in the region for the past several years.

Population in China:
2,000 (1992)
2,460 (2000)
3,180 (2010)
Location: Xinjiang
Religion: Islam
Christians: None Known

Overview of the Akto Turkmen

Countries: China

Pronunciation: "Ahk-toe-Turk-men"

Other Names: Akto

Population Source:
2,000 (1992 B. Grimes);
Out of a total Kirgiz population of 141,549 (1990 census)

Location: *SW Xinjiang:* Kosarap and Oytak villages in Akto County, south of Kashgar

Status:
Officially included under Kirgiz

Language:
Altaic, Turkic, Eastern Turkic

Dialects: 0

Religion: Sunni Islam, Shamanism

Christians: None known

Scripture: None

***Jesus* film:** None

Gospel Recordings: None

Christian Broadcasting: None

ROPAL code: None

Status of Evangelization

A = Have never heard the gospel
B = Were evangelized but did not become Christians
C = Are adherents to any form of Christianity

Aling 阿灵

Population in China:
5,600 (1999)
5,740 (2000)
7,200 (2010)
Location: Yunnan
Religion: Animism
Christians: None Known

Overview of the Aling

Countries: China

Pronunciation: "Ah-ling"

Other Names: Alingpo, Gan Yi, Yiqing, Yiqin

Population Source: 5,600 (1999 J. Pelkey); Out of a total Yi population of 6,572,173 (1990 census)

Location: *Yunnan:* Shizong (3,000), Luliang (2,400), and Shilin (200) counties

Status: Officially included under Yi

Language: Sino-Tibetan, Tibeto-Burman, Burmese-Lolo, Lolo, Northern Lolo, Yi, Eastern Yi

Dialects: 0

Religion: Animism, Ancestor Worship, No Religion

Christians: None known

Scripture: None

***Jesus* film:** None

Gospel Recordings: None

Christian Broadcasting: None

ROPAL code: None

Status of Evangelization

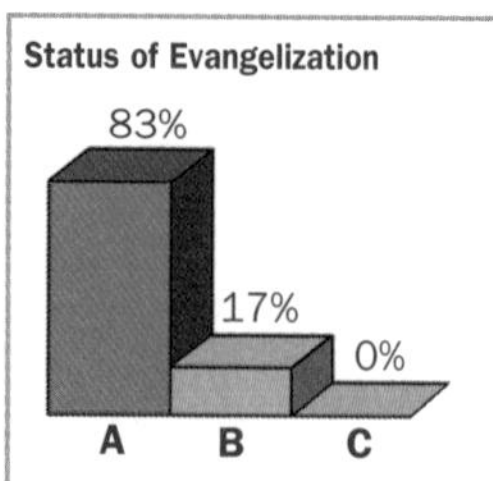

A = Have never heard the gospel
B = Were evangelized but did not become Christians
C = Are adherents to any form of Christianity

YWAM COM

Location: A total of 5,600 ethnic Aling people live in Yunnan Province, China. The majority inhabit the villages of Yimai, Faze, Chezhai, Musheluo, Yinie, Qianjia, Shugandian, and Dashao within Shizong County. Some 2,400 Aling dwell in the Longhai Mountains of Luliang County, while just a few hundred more inhabit villages within the Guishan, Zhuqing, and Dake districts of Shilin County (formerly called Lunan County). In Shilin, the largest Aling concentration is found in Yumeidu Village of the Guishan District.[1]

Identity: The Aling are one of many subgroups of the Yi nationality in southern China. They view themselves as a distinct people group with their own history and language. The Han Chinese call the Aling different names in different locations. In Luliang County they refer to the Aling as *Gan Yi* (Sweet Yi). In Shizong County they call them *Gan Yi* (Dry Yi) (Here a different Chinese character for *Gan* is used). In Shilin County the Aling are known as the *Yiqin* or *Yiqing*.

Language: The Aling language falls into the Eastern Yi group of Tibeto-Burman languages. It contains some similarities with Da Hei Neisu and Xiao Hei Neisu.

History: Very little is known about the history of the Aling. Few people have ever heard of them. They no longer wear any traditional clothing that might visually distinguish them from other groups.

Customs: The Aling is one of many groups in the area who celebrate the annual Torch Festival. According to one visitor, "The first two days of the festival were fairly rough and ready, but on the third day the girls had a chance to compete against one another in the beauty contest. The scene for this event was a leveled piece of ground on a mountain slope. Early in the morning, the slope was already crowded with girls carrying their yellow oilcloth umbrellas, looking from a distance like so many yellow blossoms on the grassland. I heard that girls from counties all around had set off for this contest two or three days before, making their way across mountains and rivers. The girls gathered together, formed circles and began a dance called *duoluohe*. The panel of judges consisted of elderly villagers. They shuttled about amidst the dancers trying to find suitable candidates. The first criterion was that she should be a Yi girl living in the countryside. The other criteria was simple: an oval face and a tall, slim figure."[2]

Religion: Although many Aling no longer consider themselves to be religious, traditionally the Aling were animists, worshiping a host of spirits and protective deities.

Christianity: The gospel has made no impact at all among the unreached Aling people group. They have never been targeted by missionaries or church planters. A 1922 mission report issued a challenge for workers to give their lives to reach the Yi, a challenge which still stands true today: "These aborigines are tall, strong, brave, keen, and clever, and some of them are extraordinarily anxious that missionaries should go and teach them. Whoever takes up this work needs to be courageous and to have plenty of grit. Such a one would become an uncrowned king."[3]

Alu 阿鲁

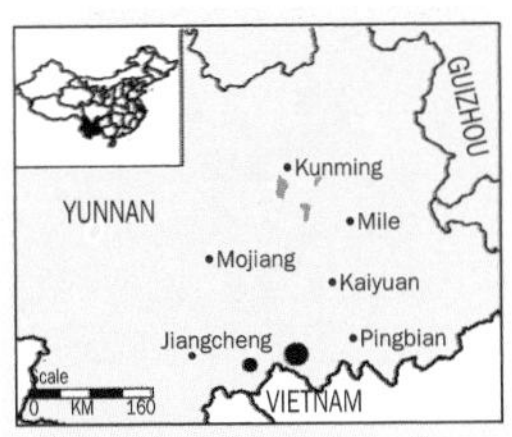

Population in China:
5,500 (1999)
5,640 (2000)
7,050 (2010)
Location: Yunnan
Religion: Polytheism
Christians: None Known

Overview of the Alu

Countries:
China, Laos, possibly Vietnam

Pronunciation: "Ah-loo"

Other Names: Alupo, Luwu, Luowu

Population Source:
5,500 (1999 J. Pelkey);
Out of a total Yi population of 6,572,173 (1990 census);
1,407 in Laos (1999 AMO);
Possibly also in Vietnam

Location: *S Yunnan:* Laojizhai District of Jinping County (4,400); Huangcaoling District of Yuanyang County (600); and Jiangcheng County (500) of Simao Prefecture

Status:
Officially included under Yi

Language: Sino-Tibetan, Tibeto-Burman, Burmese-Lolo, Lolo, Northern Lolo, Yi, Southern Yi

Dialects: 0

Religion: Polytheism, Animism, Ancestor Worship

Christians: None known

Scripture: None

***Jesus* film:** None

Gospel Recordings: None

Christian Broadcasting: None

ROPAL code: None

Status of Evangelization

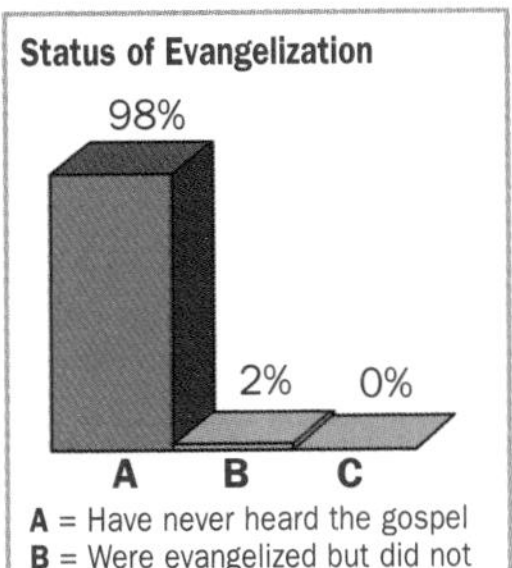

A = Have never heard the gospel
B = Were evangelized but did not become Christians
C = Are adherents to any form of Christianity

Location: A total of 5,500 Alu people live in southern Yunnan Province. They live in the Hama Community of Huangcaoling District in Yuanyang County and in the adjoining western part of Laojizhai District in Jinping County.[1] There is also a people group who call themselves Alu living in Jiangcheng County of Simao Prefecture. An additional 1,407 Alu live in northern Laos where they are officially labelled Lolo.

Identity: Because of their extreme geographic isolation, the Alu are not well known. They have little contact with the outside world. The Alu have been placed under the official Yi nationality in China, even though they speak their own distinct language and possess their own unique customs and style of dress. They are also known as *Luwu* and *Luowu*.

Language: Alu is believed to be a part of the Southern Yi linguistic group. Most Alu women and children are only able to speak their own language and do not know any Chinese. Little else is known about the Alu language.

History: During the Tang and Song dynasties (581–1276), the various Yi groups in southern China were known by the Chinese as the "Seven tribes of Wuman." They were part of a much larger Tibeto-Burman group. According to Chinese records, the Wuman started to migrate southward into Yunnan during the second century BC and gradually splintered into the numerous different tribes and clans that make up the Yi nationality today.[2]

Customs: Most Alu families live in packed-dirt homes with flat roofs. They use the flat roofs as a place to dry grain. Alu homes usually have three large rooms. The central room is used as a living room, dining room, and an animistic worship center. The other two rooms serve as a kitchen and a bedroom. In some areas, the Alu slap water buffalo manure on the sides of their homes and leave it to dry in the sun. The dried manure is later used for fuel and also for insulation from the weather in the winter. Among other things, the Alu are known for their home-brewed whiskey. During special occasions and festivals it is not uncommon to see the entire community of Alu people, including small children, completely drunk. Alcoholism has a strong hold on the Alu and contributes to a short life expectancy among them.

Religion: The Alu are animists and polytheists and, as a result, feel the need to appease many gods and ward off many forms of evil. On the first day of the year two chickens are sacrificed at every path of entrance into a village. They pray to a dragon spirit, asking it to not allow demons to enter the village in the coming year.

Christianity: The Alu are a totally unreached people group. Yuanyang County, where the majority of Alu live, counts about 2,000 believers among the Yuanyang Nisu. These believers live some distance away from the Alu, however, and have not attempted to take the gospel to them at this stage. Chinese evangelists visited the Alu in March 2000, but reported, "The Alu couldn't speak Mandarin and didn't want to listen to the gospel."

Jamin Pelkey

Aluo 阿罗

Location: Approximately 25,000 members of the Aluo tribe inhabit two counties in Yunnan Province. The majority of Aluo communities are in Shizong and Luliang counties, east of Kunming.

Identity: The Aluo have been officially included as part of the Yi nationality by the Chinese authorities. They are one of more than 100 subgroups of Yi in Yunnan Province. Aluo is the self-name of this group. Neighboring peoples generally call them *Hong Yi* (Red Yi) because of the predominant color of their clothing. Since the name *Aluo* is taken from a Yi hero, some other groups in Yunnan may also identify themselves by that name, including the Eastern Nasu in Wuding County.

Language: The Aluo language is part of the Southeastern Yi branch, related to Yi languages such as Sani, Axi, and Puwa.[1] Aluo is relatively uniform within itself. Speakers from Aluo villages in different locations have little problem understanding each other.

Jamin Pelkey

History: The Aluo believe their race was founded by the legendary *Ah-luo*. They have taken their name from this hero, who was reputed to have possessed superhuman strength. "During his life, according to tribal mythology, there were nine suns and eight moons in the sky, the heat from which caused immense suffering on Earth. Ah-luo shot down all but one sun and moon, making human life possible."[2] In another story, Ah-luo is credited with single-handedly killing evil monsters that caused great human misery. After their death at Ah-luo's hand, the ghosts of the monsters appealed to Yama, the King of Hell, to avenge them. "After his own death, Yama turned Ah-luo's limbs into the Luo grove and his heart into what is now called the Luo Holy Stone."[3]

Customs: Once every 12 years, in the Year of the Horse, the Aluo celebrate the Paying Tribute to Ah-luo Festival. It takes place at a site where Ah-luo is believed to have become deified as a god. The venue is made up of 144 small pine trees and 80 small fir trees which form a path leading to the entrance. The 144 pine trees signify the 12 months in a year, multiplied by the 12 years that have elapsed since the last festival.

Religion: A visitor to the Ah-luo Festival related his experiences: "After passing through the arch, I saw the sacrificial altar.... A container holding one hectoliter of grain... symbolized the sacrifices to Ah-luo each year for the past twelve years. On the flat roof of the altar sat an oval pebble, a symbol of the reincarnated body of Ah-luo.... The main altar was presided over by an old shaman who was wearing a special sacrificial costume and chanting prayers from the Sutra scripture. Beside the main altar were eleven smaller altars where eleven other shamans led prayers."[4]

Christianity: There are no known Christians among the Aluo people today. Shizong and Luliang counties received little mission work prior to 1949, and few people there today are aware of the gospel. The Aluo's identity as a people is wrapped up in their reverence of Ah-luo, making it very difficult for them to break free and believe in Christ.

GUIZHOU
•Dongchuan
YUNNAN
•Wuding
•Yao'an
•Kunming
•Luliang
•Shizong
•Chuxiong
•Mile
Scale
0 KM 80

Population in China:
20,000 (1990)
25,100 (2000)
31,500 (2010)
Location: Yunnan
Religion: Polytheism
Christians: None Known

Overview of the Aluo

Countries: China

Pronunciation: "Ah-luoh"

Other Names: Aluopuo, Ah-luo, Hongyi, Red Yi, Ouluo

Population Source:
20,000 (1990 AMO);
Out of a total Yi population of 6,572,173 (1990 census)

Location: *E Yunnan:* Shizong and Luliang counties

Status:
Officially included under Yi

Language: Sino-Tibetan, Tibeto-Burman, Burmese-Lolo, Lolo, Northern Lolo, Yi, Southeastern Yi

Dialects: 0

Religion: Polytheism, Animism, Shamanism, Ancestor Worship

Christians: None known

Scripture: None

***Jesus* film:** None

Gospel Recordings: None

Christian Broadcasting: None

ROPAL code: None

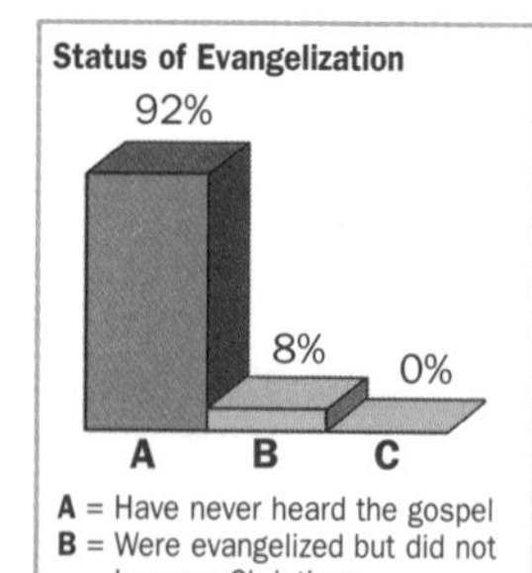

Amdo, Hbrogpa 安多, 玻巴

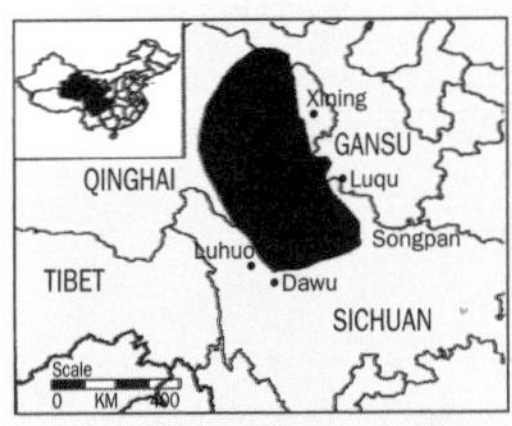

Population in China:
448,500 (1987)
583,700 (2000)
719,200 (2010)
Location:
Qinghai, Gansu, Sichuan
Religion: Tibetan Buddhism
Christians: 100

Overview of the Hbrogpa Amdo

Countries: China

Pronunciation: "Druk-pah-Ahm-doe"

Other Names: Brogpa, Amde, Anduo, Ngambo

Population Source: 538,500 (1987 *LAC*);[1] Out of a total Tibetan population of 4,593,330 (1990 census)

Location: *E Qinghai; N Sichuan; SW Gansu*[2]

Status: Officially included under Tibetan

Language: Sino-Tibetan, Tibeto-Burman, Bodic, Bodish, Tibetan, Northern Tibetan

Dialects: 15

Religion: Tibetan Buddhism, Bon

Christians: 100

Scripture: Tibetan Bible 1948; New Testament 1885; Portions 1862

***Jesus* film:** Available

Gospel Recordings: Amdo #00182 Zang, Anduo

Christian Broadcasting: None

ROPAL code: ADX01

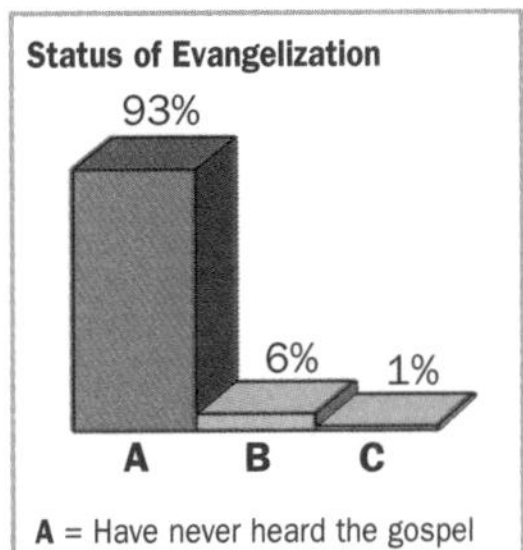

Paul Hattaway

Location: More than 550,000 speakers of the Hbrogpa Amdo language live in a vast, sparsely populated area. The majority are located in eastern Qinghai Province, as far north as the Qinghai-Gansu border. Significant numbers also live in southwest Gansu Province and in adjacent parts of northern Sichuan. The Hbrogpa region ranges from Qinghai Lake in the north — which at 4,000 square kilometers (1,560 sq. mi.) is the largest lake in China — to the town of Songpan in Sichuan in the south. Songpan, encircled by a wall built in 1379, once housed 10,000 families.[3] The Amdo region was incorporated into the Chinese empire in the early 1700s.

Identity: Hbrogpa, which means "nomad" or "herder" in Tibetan, is the largest of four main Amdo languages. These in turn have been counted as part of the Tibetan nationality in China. "Within these groups are many subgroups, each speaking its own language and living in different areas."[4]

Language: Amdo is very different from other varieties of Tibetan. Within Amdo there are four mutually unintelligible languages, of which Hbrogpa is the largest.[5] Various sources mention 15 unnamed dialects within Hbrogpa.[6]

History: Horrendous clashes with the Chinese have resulted in massive loss of Amdo Tibetan life. The Dalai Lama listed 49,049 deaths from battles within the Amdo regions before 1983, in addition to 121,982 deaths from starvation.[7]

Customs: Most Amdo are seminomadic herders of sheep, yaks, and goats. They move to new pastures whenever their animals have made good use of the land.

Religion: Although the vast majority of Amdo are Tibetan Buddhists, in recent years there has been a revival of interest in the pre-Buddhist religion of Bon.[8]

Christianity: Several mission agencies worked in the Amdo area prior to 1949. At least five small churches consisting of Amdo Tibetans remain today.[9] One report optimistically estimates as many as 10,000 Tibetan believers near Hezuo.[10] Approximately 200 Tibetan believers attend a church in Lintan County in southern Gansu, but they are Jone Tibetans, not Amdo.[11] Cecil Pohill of the China Inland Mission started a mission station in Xining in 1888. Later he "opened up Songpan as a center for Tibetan work."[12] In 1922 it was reported, "The confidence of the people has to a great extent been achieved, and not a few have an intelligent knowledge of the way of salvation."[13] In 1986, "A few Christian households in Gansu Province gathered to worship during a Chinese New Year's celebration. Their neighbors, seeking to wipe out Christianity, told them to disperse. The Christians were unwilling to stop their meeting and were severely beaten by the crowd. The next morning the persecutors found their sheep, cows and horses were dying. Their family members also began to die one by one. Realizing that the wrath of God had fallen upon them, they pleaded with those who believed in Jesus to pray. The Lord heard the believers' prayers, and the sick and dying were healed. As a result, over a hundred Amdo Tibetans turned to the Lord!"[14]

Amdo, Rongba 安多,容巴

Paul Hattaway

Location: A 1987 report listed 97,600 speakers of the Rongba Amdo language living in eastern Qinghai Province.[1] In many locations in the region the towns are inhabited by Han Chinese and Muslims, while the Rongba Amdo lead nomadic lives in the countryside. The Rongba Amdo primarily live in Hualong, which is an autonomous county of the Hui Muslims; and in Xunhua County, partly administered by members of the Salar minority. The Tibetan population in China has been kept comparatively low by disease and infanticide. Modern health and hygiene practices have caused the death rate for Tibetans to fall from 28 people per 1,000 in 1951 to 9 per 1,000 in 1990.

Identity: The Rongba Amdo are part of the Tibetan nationality. The name Rongba means "farmer" in Tibetan.[2] When the Communists took over all of Tibet in the 1950s, thousands of Tibetans were butchered. The official Chinese version of these events is markedly different. "This rebellion accelerated the destruction of Tibet's reactionary forces and brought Tibet onto the bright, democratic, and socialist road sooner than expected."[3]

Language: The Rongba Amdo language has two dialects and contains more Chinese loanwords than any other Tibetan language in China. Rongba is only partially intelligible with the three other Amdo languages; however, all Tibetans use the same written script.

History: For centuries the Amdo roamed the borderlands of the Tibetan-Chinese world. Their menacing reputation struck fear into all who dared to venture, unwelcomed, into their realm.

Customs: The Rongba Amdo are largely unconcerned about the outside world. They celebrate the Tibetan New Year in February, according to the Tibetan lunar calendar. In the past, celebrations commenced the moment the peach tree blossomed. It is a time for relatives to get together and celebrate the past year's events.

Religion: The Rongba Amdo adhere to Tibetan Buddhism, also known as Tantric Buddhism. "Tantra's most striking feature is its technique of occult visualization. The tantric master gives each student a deity which the student has to visualize. These deities, most of which appear in wrathful or monstrous forms, are supposed to be able to help the student achieve liberation. As the student visualizes, he tries to become what he sees, and in fact some Tibetan Buddhists claim to be able to actually materialize demons in front of them."[4]

Christianity: There are about ten known Christians among the Rongba Amdo today. They have historically proven to be a difficult group to penetrate with the gospel. The criteria used in the 1920s for missionaries among Tibetan peoples still applies to would-be laborers today: "In sending out missionaries for work among the Tibetans, candidates with a strong constitution should be chosen, as missionary work in Tibet is more strenuous than in most places. Missionaries that are afraid to expose themselves to hardship and even danger should not be sent to Tibet."[5]

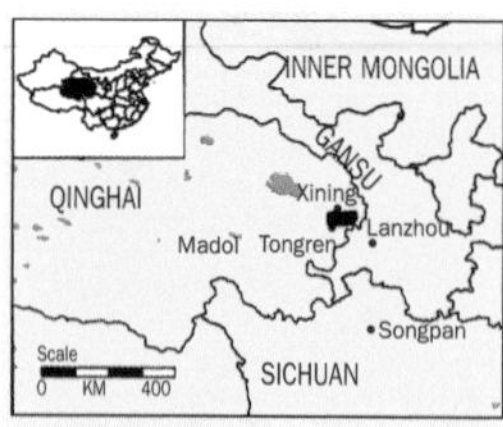

Population in China:
97,600 (1987)
127,000 (2000)
156,500 (2010)
Location: Qinghai
Religion: Tibetan Buddhism
Christians: 10

Overview of the Rongba Amdo

Countries: China
Pronunciation: "Rong-wah-Ahm-doe"
Other Names: Rongba, Rongpa
Population Source: 97,600 (1987 *LAC*); Out of a total Tibetan population of 4,593,330 (1990 census)
Location: *E Qinghai*: Hualong Hui and Xunhua Salar counties, and as far north as Ledu
Status: Officially included under Tibetan
Language: Sino-Tibetan, Tibeto-Burman, Bodic, Bodish, Tibetan, Northern Tibetan
Dialects: 2
Religion: Tibetan Buddhism, Bon
Christians: 10
Scripture: Tibetan Bible 1948; New Testament 1885; Portions 1862
***Jesus* film:** None
Gospel Recordings: None
Christian Broadcasting: None
ROPAL code: ADX02

Status of Evangelization

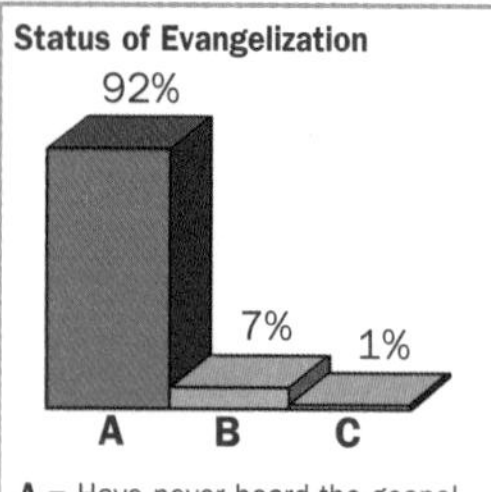

A = Have never heard the gospel
B = Were evangelized but did not become Christians
C = Are adherents to any form of Christianity

Amdo, Rongmahbrogpa 安多，容马玻巴

Location: A 1987 linguistic survey of China listed 112,800 speakers of the Rongmahbrogpa Tibetan language.[1] The main center of the Rongmahbrogpa is the picturesque town of Xiahe in southwest Gansu Province. The language is also spoken in and around Tongren County in neighboring eastern Qinghai Province.

Identity: Although ethnically and culturally the Rongmahbrogpa belong to the Tibetan nationality, they speak a language that is distinct from other Tibetan varieties. The name Rongmahbrogpa is a combination of the Tibetan words *Rongba* (villager or farmer) and *Brogpa* (nomad or herder).

Language: Rongmahbrogpa — which contains "two or more dialects"[2] — is part of the Northern Bodic branch of Tibetan languages. Although they may not understand each other's speech, all Tibetans use the same written script. Tibetans from different areas can often be seen exchanging notes to communicate.

History: The Labrang Monastery in Xiahe was built by E'ang-zongzhe in 1709. Presently it houses about 1,700 monks, drawn from Qinghai, Sichuan, Gansu, and Inner Mongolia. The Amdo and the Hui Muslims have had numerous violent clashes in the past. In 1919 the Hui sacked the Labrang Monastery, burned to death hundreds of monks, and dumped their corpses on the temple grounds. In 1929 Joseph Rock witnessed the carnage of one battle in Xiahe: "154 Tibetan heads were strung about the walls of the Moslem garrison like a garland of flowers. Heads of young girls and children decorated posts in front of barracks. The Moslem riders galloped about the town, each with 10 or 15 human heads tied to his saddle."[3]

Customs: The Tibetan prayer wheel, or *manichorkor*, can be turned by hot air, hand, wind, or water. As it spins, the scroll contained in the cylinder is believed to release prayers to the heavens.

Paul Hattaway

Religion: Outwardly the Amdo are Tibetan Buddhists, but the ancient Bon religion has experienced growth in recent years. Bon was characterized by shamans, whose job was to "present the sacrifices, appease the spirits with magic, heal the sick, and even control the weather. The shaman specialized in a kind of ecstatic trance that let him travel to the spirit world and serve as a medium for the ghosts of the dead. In addition to the shamans there were also magicians and healers who had the power to control gods, demons, and locality spirits."[4]

Christianity: The Christian & Missionary Alliance church opened a mission base in the town of Xiahe in the early 1920s. They made little progress against the Buddhist stronghold. One wrote, "The main difficulties as they appear to me are: The food question. The food of the Tibetans is such that for a foreigner it is very hard to partake of, and still harder to digest... yet the itinerating missionary in this district has to eat it, for if he does not, he greatly offends his host and gets no opportunity to preach the Gospel."[5] The *Jesus* film was translated into Amdo in 1998.

Population in China:
112,800 (1987)
146,800 (2000)
180,800 (2010)
Location: Gansu, Qinghai
Religion: Tibetan Buddhism
Christians: 20

Overview of the Rongmahbrogpa Amdo

Countries: China

Pronunciation: "Rung-ma-Druk-pah-Ahm-doe"

Other Names: Amde, Labrang Amdo, Rongbabrogpa

Population Source: 112,800 (1987 *LAC*); Out of a total Tibetan population of 4,593,330 (1990 census)

Location: *SW Gansu:* Xiahe County; *E Qinghai:* Tongren County

Status: Officially included under Tibetan

Language: Sino-Tibetan, Tibeto-Burman, Bodic, Bodish, Tibetan, Northern Tibetan

Dialects: 2

Religion: Tibetan Buddhism, Bon

Christians: 20

Scripture: Tibetan Bible 1948; New Testament 1885; Portions 1862

***Jesus* film:** Available

Gospel Recordings: None

Christian Broadcasting: None

ROPAL code: ADX03

Status of Evangelization

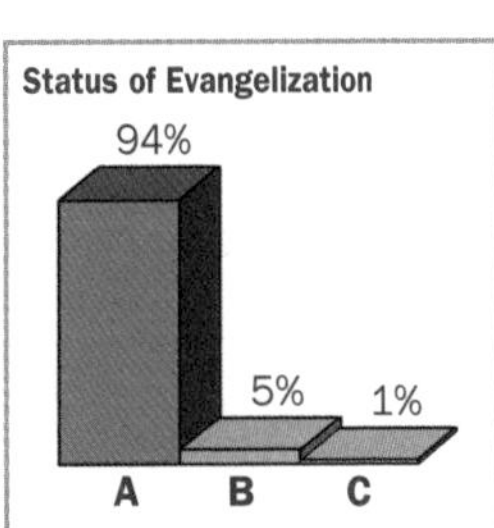

A = Have never heard the gospel
B = Were evangelized but did not become Christians
C = Are adherents to any form of Christianity

Amdo, Rtahu 安多，他户

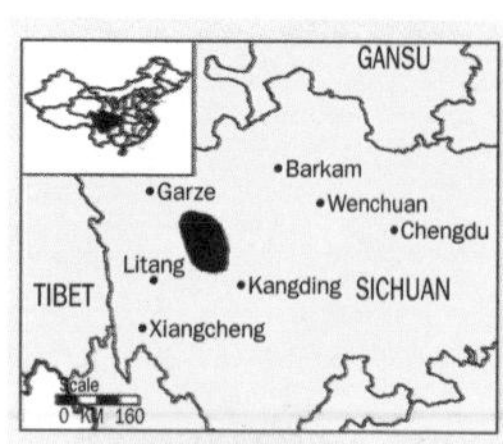

Population in China:
60,600 (1987)
78,800 (2000)
97,100 (2010)
Location: Sichuan
Religion: Tibetan Buddhism
Christians: None Known

Overview of the Rtahu Amdo

Countries: China

Pronunciation: "Ta-hoo-Ahm-doe"

Other Names: Tahu

Population Source:
60,600 (1987 *LAC*);
Out of a total Tibetan population of 4,593,330 (1990 census)

Location: *N Sichuan:* Garze Prefecture: Dawu and Luhuo counties

Status:
Officially included under Tibetan

Language: Sino-Tibetan, Tibeto-Burman, Bodic, Bodish, Tibetan, Northern Tibetan

Dialects (2): Braghgo, Tahu

Religion: Tibetan Buddhism, Polytheism

Christians: None known

Scripture: Tibetan Bible 1948; New Testament 1885; Portions 1862

***Jesus* film:** None

Gospel Recordings: None

Christian Broadcasting: None

ROPAL code: ADX04

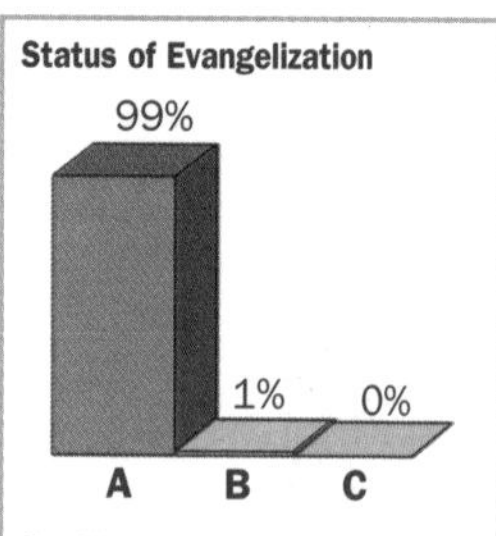

Location: Approximately 70,000 Tibetans in northwest Sichuan Province speak the Rtahu Amdo language. They live primarily on grasslands along the banks of the turbulent Xianshui River in Dawu and Luhuo counties. These two counties form part of the huge Garze Tibetan Autonomous Prefecture which is home primarily to the fierce Khampa Tibetans.

Identity: Of the four Amdo languages, the Rtahu language is used in the most southern part. Linguists have identified Rtahu as a variety of Amdo, but the Rtahu claim to culturally belong to the Khampa Tibetans. They have been officially counted as members of the Tibetan nationality in China — which numbered almost 4.6 million people in the 1990 census.

Language: The Rtahu language seems to be transitional between Amdo and Khampa Tibetan; these two are reported to have about 70% lexical similarity.[1] The Rtahu language contains two dialects: Braghgo and Tahu.[2]

History: Padmasambhava, a Tibetan sage, gave the following prophecy in the eighth century: "When the iron bird flies and horses run on wheels, the Tibetan people will be scattered like ants across the world and the Dharma will come to the land of the Red Man."[3] In October 1950 the Chinese army invaded Tibet from Sichuan. Another garrison moved southward from Xinjiang into western Tibet. Tenzin Gyatso, the 14th Dalai Lama — who himself is an Amdo Tibetan — fled into India. From his base in Dharamsala, northern India, the Dalai Lama has continued to lobby for the liberation of his people.

Customs: Between 1913 and 1950 Tibet tried to assert its authority as a separate nation, with its own flag, passports, and currency. Tibetan passports were only accepted as legal documents by Great Britain, India, and the United States. A Tibetan stamp was printed in India in 1910, bearing the image of the Dalai Lama. "These were rejected by the Tibetans.... The Dalai Lama could not be placed on a stamp as it might get trodden underfoot, which would bring dishonor to him. Besides, who was going to strike his head with a great metal franking hammer?"[4]

Religion: All Rtahu Amdo Tibetans are fervent Tibetan Buddhists. No more than a handful have ever heard of the existence of Jesus Christ.

Christianity: In the past, some mission agencies considered working among the Tibetans but found excuses easier than the hardships the workers would have had to endure. In 1922, Dr. A. Reeve Heber of the Moravian Mission in Ladakh was challenged to expand his work into Tibet. He responded, "When once the country has been opened to the missionaries, I do not think that we are in a very good position to enter it from any of our present stations.... It is almost entirely inhabited by nomads among whom it would be very difficult to work."[5]

Paul Hattaway

Ami 阿美

Paul Hattaway

Location: The Ami are the largest of the tribes in Taiwan, with a population of more than 130,000. In Mainland China, approximately 1,500 Ami live in small villages in southern Fujian Province. Many have settled in Beijing and Shanghai municipalities.

Identity: In China, the Ami were considered too small by the government to be recognized as an official minority group. Along with the Bunun and Paiwan tribes, they were grouped together under the official banner of *Gaoshan*, a generic Chinese name which simply means "high mountains". The Ami believe they are descended from the god Abokurayan and from the goddess Taribrayan who produced so many children that the Ami had to move from Orchid Island to the Taiwan mainland.[1]

Language: Although all three Gaoshan tribes in Fujian Province speak languages from the Austronesian language family, they cannot understand each other and must use Chinese to communicate. Many elderly Ami in Taiwan speak Japanese.

History: The Ami, who "seem to be composed of several more or less unrelated ethnic elements,"[2] say their ancestors came from an overseas island called Sanasai or Vasai. Some scholars have speculated these islands are today's Caroline Islands in the Pacific Ocean.[3] Small pockets of Ami migrated across the Taiwan Strait to China at least a century ago. Between 1946 and 1949, about 100 Ami men were forcibly enlisted in the Kuomintang forces during the civil war in China. When the KMT lost to the Communists, most stayed in Fujian and formed Ami communities.[4]

Customs: Many Ami villages have a matrilineal clan system, with the grandmother acting as the head of the household. Some Ami believe men should only eat male fish and women should only eat female fish. They believe a woman who eats a male fish might fall sick or die.[5] It is common practice for an Ami husband to live with his wife and mother-in-law after the marriage. "If the wife later finds that the marriage has turned sour, she will put the man's sword and trunk in front of the courtyard, which will make the man depart without complaint."[6]

Religion: The Ami in Fujian are polytheists. Their worship includes paying homage to Maadidil (the god of Fire), Tsidar (the Sun god), Botal (the Moon god), Malataw (the god of Heaven), Makosem (the god of Rain), and Laladay (the god of Water).

Christianity: The Ami are an unreached group in China, despite the presence of a strong Ami church in Taiwan. As many as half of the 130,000 Ami in Taiwan claim to be Christians. There were only 100 Ami believers in Taiwan by 1945,[7] but 80 churches by 1955.[8] Recently the Presbyterians alone claimed a total of 20,989 Ami believers meeting in 138 churches.[9] The Ami Overseas Mission sent four families to Borneo in 1968.[10] Today there are Ami missionaries in Malaysia, the Philippines, Indonesia, and Papua New Guinea. Teams of Ami Christians from Taiwan have ministered in China but not as yet to their own people.[11] The Ami in Taiwan have the entire Bible in their language, but it is not available in China.

Population in China:
1,500 (1990)
1,930 (2000)
2,500 (2010)
Location: Fujian
Religion: Polytheism
Christians: None Known

Overview of the Ami

Countries: Taiwan, China

Pronunciation: "Ah-mee"

Other Names: Amis, Amia, Tagkah, Pangtsah, Bakurat, Lamsihoan, Maran, Sabari, Tanah, Pagcah

Population Source: 1,500 (1990 AMO); Out of a total Gaoshan population of 2,909 (1990 census); 130,000 in Taiwan (1986 TEAM)

Location: *S Fujian:* Near Zhangzhou City; Many Ami live in *Beijing* and *Shanghai* municipalities, and other cities.

Status: Officially included under Gaoshan

Language: Austronesian, Formosan, Paiwanic

Dialects (5): In Taiwan: Central, Southern, Northern, Tavalong-Vataan, Chengkung-Kwanshan

Religion: Polytheism, Animism, Ancestor Worship

Christians: None known in China

Scripture: Bible, New Testament 1972; Portions 1957; Available in Taiwan only

***Jesus* film:** None

Gospel Recordings: Amis #01989

Christian Broadcasting: None

ROPAL code: ALV00

Status of Evangelization

A	B	C
82%	18%	0%

A = Have never heard the gospel
B = Were evangelized but did not become Christians
C = Are adherents to any form of Christianity

Angku 昂库

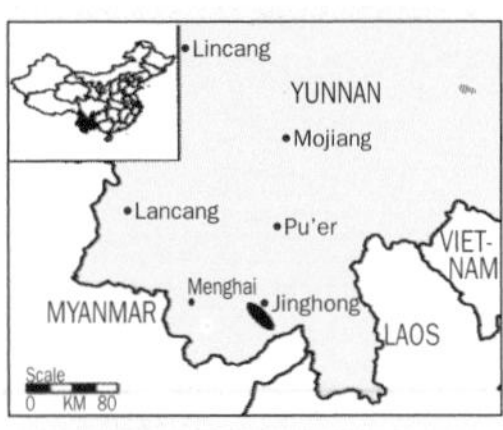

Population in China:
6,113 (1995)
7,000 (2000)
9,030 (2010)
Location: Yunnan
Religion: Buddhism
Christians: None Known

Overview of the Angku

Countries: Myanmar, China, Laos, possibly Thailand

Pronunciation: "Ung-ku"

Other Names: Kiorr, Con

Population Source:
6,113 (1995 GEM);
Out of a total Bulang population of 82,280 (1990 census);
2,359 Kiorr in Laos (1985 F. Proschan)

Location: *SW Yunnan:* The Angku inhabit the western banks of the Lancang (Mekong) River in Xishuangbanna Dai Prefecture

Status:
Officially included under Bulang

Language: Austro-Asiatic, Mon-Khmer, Northern Mon-Khmer, Palaungic-Khmuic, Palaungic, Western Palaungic, Angkuic

Dialects (4):
Angku, Kiorr, Amok, Pou Ma

Religion:
Theravada Buddhism, Animism

Christians: None known

Scripture: None

***Jesus* film:** None

Gospel Recordings: None

Christian Broadcasting: None

ROPAL code: ANG00

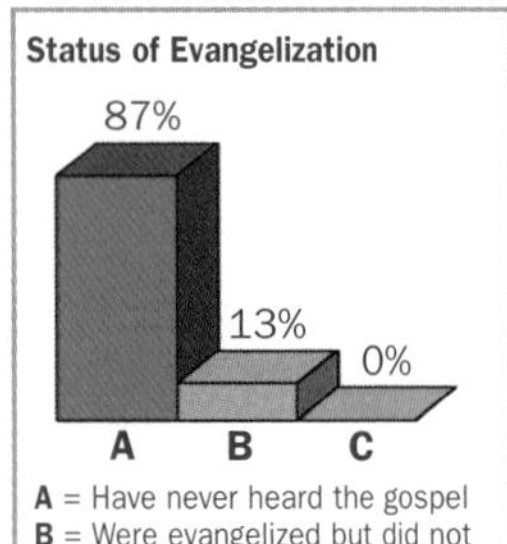

Dwayne Graybill

Location: Approximately 6,000 Angku people inhabit six villages in southern Yunnan Province.[1] Several thousand Angku speakers live in Laos, Myanmar, and possibly Thailand. The Angku in Yunnan are located on the western banks of the Lancang (Mekong) River in Xishuangbanna Prefecture. The mighty Mekong flows south from Yunnan through the countries of Laos, Myanmar, Thailand, and finally spills out into the ocean in southern Vietnam. More than 2,500 Kiorr, listed as a dialect of Angku, live in northern Laos.[2]

Identity: The term *Angkuic* is used by linguists as a generic term to describe many Palaungic languages, but there are also people who speak a specific language by that name. In China the government has officially counted the Angku as members of the Bulang nationality, but the Angku language is not intelligible with Bulang.

Language: Angku is a Mon-Khmer language that is distinct and inherently unintelligible with the other Mon-Khmer languages in the province such as Wa, Bulang, and De'ang. Angku is possibly the same language as Puman. There are four Angku dialects, some of which may also qualify as distinct languages.[3]

History: The Angku, in addition to the Wa, Bulang, and De'ang minorities, were originally part of a large Austro-Asiatic group that occupied much of Yunnan before the Dai and Yi people arrived. "They were driven out of their habitats by the invaders, dispersed and split into the isolated groups they are today."[4] The Angku in countries outside China used the Mekong River to migrate away from the oppression of their Dai and Han landlords.

Customs: Most Angku women are fond of chewing betel nut which blackens their teeth and gums. Stained teeth are considered a mark of beauty among Angku women. Since the betel juice only stains temporarily, some women use black dye to artificially stain their teeth. Body tattooing was common among the Angku in the past but now is rarely practiced.

Religion: The Angku, like their Bulang counterparts, are staunch followers of Theravada (also known as *Hinayana*, "Lesser Vehicle") Buddhism. Angku life revolves around the local temple. Traditionally all Angku boys become novice monks and live in the temple until they are 12 years old. The Angku obey the three tenets of Buddhism: practicing self-discipline, teaching, and discussing doctrine. Buddhist temples are found in most Angku villages.

Christianity: Few Angku have ever been exposed to the gospel. Their villages are away from the mainstream of travelers; therefore, it takes a specific effort to make contact with the Angku. So far the few Christian workers who have labored in the region have preferred to target the larger minorities, leaving the Angku without any witness or church. The nearest Christian community to the Angku are the approximately 1,500 Tai Lu and Han Chinese Christians living in Jinghong. There are no Scriptures or ministry tools available in the Angku language.

Ani 阿尼

Population in China:
3,000 (1999)
3,070 (2000)
3,860 (2010)
Location: Yunnan
Religion: Ancestor Worship
Christians: None Known

Overview of the Ani

Countries: China

Pronunciation: "Ah-nee"

Other Names: Ani Aza, Azar, Anipo, Aza, Pula

Population Source:
3,000 (1999 J. Pelkey);
Out of a total Yi population of 6,572,173 (1990 census)

Location: *Yunnan:* Yanggai District of Kaiyuan County in Honghe Prefecture

Status:
Officially included under Yi

Language: Sino-Tibetan, Tibeto-Burman, Burmese-Lolo, Lolo, Northern Lolo, Yi, Southeastern Yi

Dialects: 0

Religion: Ancestor Worship, Animism, No Religion

Christians: None known

Scripture: None

***Jesus* film:** None

Gospel Recordings: None

Christian Broadcasting: None

ROPAL code: None

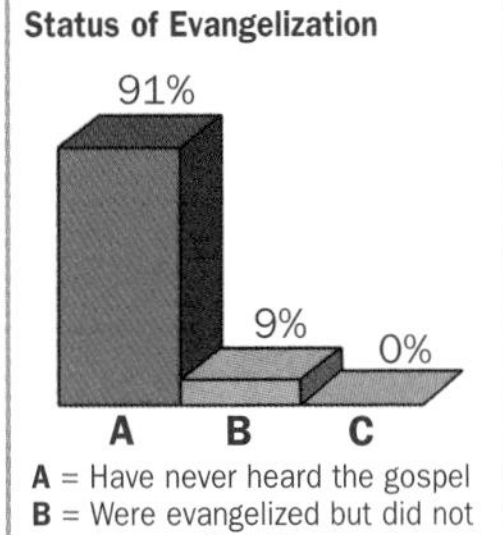

Location: Approximately 3,000 people belonging to the Ani tribe live in one small area of southwest China. All Ani live within the Zongshe, Masangqing, Qibudi, and other surrounding villages in the Yanggai District of Kaiyuan County in Yunnan Province's Honghe Prefecture.

Identity: The Ani are one of five ethnic groups in Kaiyuan County who have been grouped together and labeled the Aza by the Chinese. One publication, the *Kaiyuan Xian Zhi* (Annals of Kaiyuan County) states, "Based on linguistic and cultural differences, the Aza can be divided into five groups."[1] Despite their claims of self-identity, the Ani and the other four groups called *Aza* have been included under the official Yi nationality by the Chinese authorities.

Language: The little-known Ani people speak their own unique dialect within the Southeastern Yi linguistic group. It is related to, yet mutually unintelligible with, other Southeastern Yi varieties such as Puwa, Axi, and Sani. Most Ani are bilingual in Yunnanese Chinese. They also use the Chinese script for reading and writing.

History: Today the Ani are being rapidly assimilated to the Han Chinese culture and language, but in the past the forefathers of today's Yi groups had many unique customs that shocked visitors. When Marco Polo passed through Yi areas in the thirteenth century, he recorded, "When [the people] fall in with any stranger in want of a lodging they are all eager to take him in. And as soon as he has taken up his quarters the master of the house goes forth, telling him to consider everything at his disposal, and after saying so he proceeds to his vineyards or his fields, and comes back no more until the stranger has departed. The latter abides in the caitiff's house, be it three days or be it four, enjoying himself with the fellow's wife or daughter or sister, or whatsoever woman of the family it best likes him; and as long as he abides there he leaves his hat or some other token hanging at the door, to let the master of the house know that he is still there. As long as the wretched fellow sees that token, he must not go in. And such is the custom over all that province."[2]

Customs: Today there are few customs remaining among the Ani that could be considered traditional. However, until about 50 years ago an Ani son made wooden figures of his dead father and mother which were kept in the roof hatch until the son's death. They were then taken out and burned by the grandson.

Religion: Although they mostly ignore him, the Ani believe in a Creator. Today, most practice simple ancestor worship and believe in spirits that can cause disease if ceremonies are not held to placate them.

Christianity: Catholic and Protestant mission work in Kaiyuan County prior to 1949 failed to impact the Ani people. Although Catholic work began in the late 1800s, the first Protestant missionary in Kaiyuan was an American who came in 1914. He established three "Gospel halls." Five years after he came, he had won only eight people to Christ, but by 1934 there were 60 Han Chinese believers.[3]

Jamin Pelkey

Ao Biao 奥标

Dwayne Graybill

Location: More than 12,000 Ao Biao people inhabit the Dayaoshan (Big Yao Mountains) of Jinxiu County in the central part of the Guangxi Zhuang Autonomous Region.[1] The Ao Biao are not located in any other part of China.

Identity: The Ao Biao have been officially included under the Yao nationality in China. *Ao Biao* is their autonym. The Chinese call them *Ao Yao*, which means "Yao of the plateau". They are one of five different branches of Yao people in the Dayao Mountains, "all speaking different languages and each having its own peculiar customs and living habits."[2] Each group firmly believes it is ethnically and historically distinct from the others. The Ao Biao do not like to intermarry with other Yao people.

Language: The Ao Biao language belongs to what is loosely labeled the *Hmong-Mien* language family. Chinese scholar Fei Xiaotong, who visited the area over a period of 50 years, documents five distinct Yao languages, including Ao Biao, spoken by the inhabitants of the Dayaoshan.[3] People from the different Yao groups are forced to speak Chinese in order to communicate with each other.

History: The Ao Biao share the belief of many Yao groups that they are descended from the dragon-dog Pan Hu. The Ao Biao claim to be one of the original inhabitants of the mountains, having migrated from Guizhou via Bai Se and Nanning.[4] The Ao Biao possess most of the best land in the mountains. They live in brick and wood homes in villages concentrated near the rivers. By the time the Iu Mien and Kim Mun groups arrived in the region, they were forbidden to own land and had to live in bamboo sheds. In addition, they were forced to pay rent and render manual labor to the Ao Biao and to the other groups already established in the area.[5]

Customs: The Ao Biao have a legend about a great flood that destroyed the earth long ago, and about the repopulation of the earth. In part, it states: "All the people in the world have been drowned by the flood.... We brother and sister got married. After being true husband and wife for a few years, on the seventh morning the flower entered her body."[6]

Religion: The Ao Biao are one of the few minorities of China who adhere to the religion of Daoism. Fearsome pictures of Daoist deities are posted on the walls and doors of most of their homes. Gruesome religious masks are used in their ceremonies and festivals. The Ao Biao also worship their ancestors, believing any action that goes against centuries of tradition will insult the spirits of their forefathers. Each year the Ao Biao participate in the Pan Hu Festival, an occasion of great significance in the community. The Ao Biao dress in their best traditional clothing for the ceremony. Here the youth have an opportunity to meet prospective partners.

Christianity: The Ao Biao are a relatively unreached people group, although in 1996 the first known penetration of the gospel among them occurred. A Hong Kong-based ministry won approximately 30 Ao Biao and Iu Mien believers to Christ in Jinxiu County.

Population in China:
10,000 (1990)
12,900 (2000)
16,600 (2010)
Location: Guangxi
Religion: Daoism
Christians: 15

Overview of the Ao Biao

Countries: China

Pronunciation: "Aow-Beeow"

Other Names: Au Byau, Ao, Au, Ao Yao

Population Source: 10,000 (1990 AMO); Out of a total Yao population of 2,134,013 (1990 census)

Location: *Guangxi:* Jinxiu Yao Autonomous County

Status: Officially included under Yao

Language: Hmong-Mien, Mienic

Dialects: 0

Religion: Daoism, Polytheism, Animism, Ancestor Worship

Christians: 15

Scripture: None

***Jesus* film:** None

Gospel Recordings: None

Christian Broadcasting: None

ROPAL code: BJE01

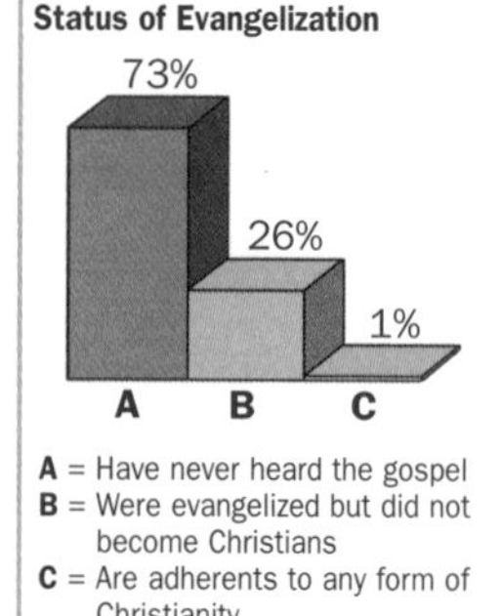

Aoka 奥卡

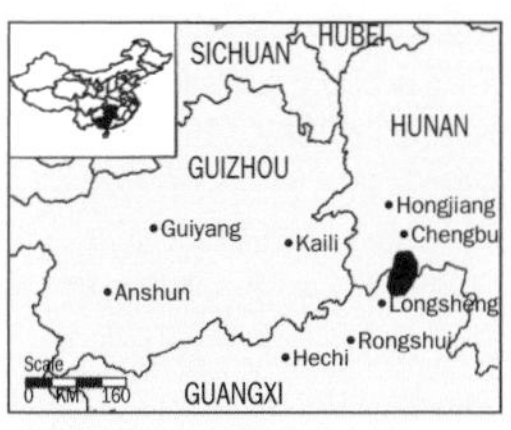

Population in China:
200,000 (1991)
252,200 (2000)
325,300 (2010)
Location: Hunan, Guangxi
Religion: Animism
Christians: 200

Overview of the Aoka

Countries: China

Pronunciation: "Aow-kha"

Other Names:
Mao, Maojia, Qingyi Miao

Population Source:
200,000 (1991 *EDCL*);
Out of a total Miao population of 7,398,035 (1990 census)

Location:
SW Hunan: Chengbu County;
NE Guangxi: Ziyun District of Longsheng County

Status:
Officially included under Miao

Language: Chinese, Qingyi

Dialects: 0

Religion: Animism, Ancestor Worship, Christianity

Christians: 200

Scripture: None

***Jesus* film:** None

Gospel Recordings: None

Christian Broadcasting: None

ROPAL code: None

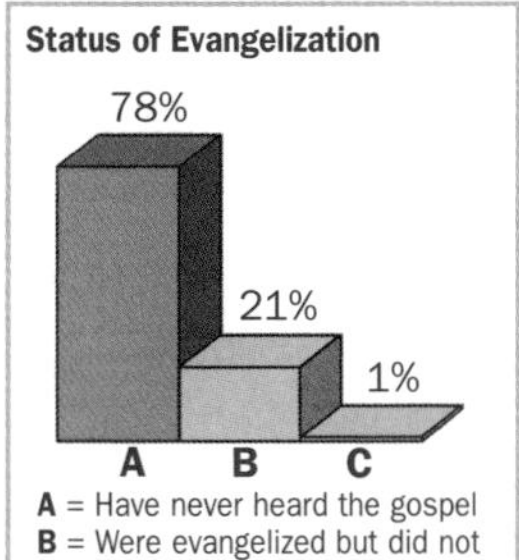

Paul Hattaway

Location: The 1991 *Encyclopedic Dictionary of Chinese Linguistics* lists 200,000 Aoka people who speak the Maojia language, also known as *Qingyi Miao*.[1] They are located in the mountains of Chengbu County in southwestern Hunan Province; and also in the Ziyun District of Longsheng County in the northeastern part of the Guangxi Zhuang Autonomous Region.

Identity: Although they are officially part of the Miao nationality, the Aoka speak a unique Chinese language — a fact they apparently refuse to accept. When linguists visited them and told them that they spoke a form of Chinese, "they claimed that they spoke Miao, because their speech was very different from that of the surrounding Chinese population, and because they wore Miao clothes instead of Chinese clothes."[2]

Language: The Aoka's language — which has seven tones — has been classified as a distinct Chinese language. "In pronunciation, vocabulary and grammar it is close to Chinese."[3] It is not, however, intelligible with any other Chinese varieties in China. After many centuries of contact between the two groups, the Aoka appear to have combined their original Miao tongue with Chinese.

History: In the aftermath of Chinese wars against them, the ancestors of the Aoka were launched into an era of migration. Tired of being harassed, they fled across mountain ranges in hope of finding an isolated place where they could be left alone to live their lives. Many of the ethnic groups now known as the Hmu also traveled into Hunan and Guangxi.[4] They may be the ancestors of the Aoka. After centuries of living beside the all-powerful Han Chinese, the Aoka have lost their language and are being speedily assimilated to the Han Chinese language and culture.

Customs: Aoka communities work together as one to design and build homes for each other. During a crisis, all the people come together to find a solution. In many villages, the Aoka believe the stove is the center of their home and they are afraid to offend the "spirit of the stove". They are forbidden to place their feet or shoes on the stove, and at night they must remove all pots and pans from it: not to do so is believed to bring a curse to the family.

Religion: Some Aoka believe there was once a ladder connecting heaven to the earth. A long time ago the ladder was broken and no people have been able to visit heaven since. Today the majority of Aoka are animists, living under the influence of demons and evil spirits. Many have also adopted the ancestor worship belief systems of their Han Chinese neighbors.

Christianity: More than three-quarters of Aoka people have yet to hear the gospel for the first time. No widespread mission effort was undertaken in their area before missionaries were expelled from China in the early 1950s. There are few Miao or Han Chinese Christian communities in that part of China today. Hunan remains one of the most unreached provinces in China. Although they have their own spoken language, the Aoka use the Chinese script for writing. Few Aoka, however, are literate enough to read the Chinese Bible or other evangelistic literature.

A'ou 阿欧

Paul Hattaway

Location: With a population of approximately 2,000 speakers, the A'ou ethnic group inhabits three counties in the north central part of Guizhou Province in southern China. They are concentrated in the Longjiazhai District of Zhijin County; in the Shawo, Lannigou, and Xinkaitian districts of Qianxi County; and in and around the town of Pudi in Dafang County.[1] The number of people who identify themselves by the ethnic name A'ou may be substantially higher than the total number who can still speak the language.

Identity: Although they have been officially counted as part of the Gelao nationality in China, the A'ou have their own ethnic identity and speak a language not mutually intelligible with any of the other Gelao varieties.

Language: A'ou is part of the Kadai branch of the Tai language family. The Gelao languages seem to be a complicated mixture of many different languages. This is shown by a linguistic study which found one Gelao language to have 45% lexical similarity with Southern Zhuang and Dai, 40% with Dong, 36% with Lati, 32% with Pubiao, 29% with Buyang, 27% to 40% with Li, 24% with Northern Zhuang, 22% with Lakkia, 10% to 15% with Hmong, and 5% to 15% with Lu Mien.[2] The reason Gelao is related to so many different widespread languages today may be because it was once the *lingua franca* (common speech) for many peoples. It absorbed characteristics which remain today. Ironically, the Gelao languages are now in danger of extinction as vast numbers of Gelao have been assimilated by the Han Chinese.

History: The ancestors of the A'ou have lived in Guizhou Province since time immemorial. Jacob Lee explains, "Some 2,000 years ago, many tribes lived in this southwestern part of China, each with its own ruler and territory. The Gelao, known in ancient times as the Liao, were one of the largest tribes and they called their country the Yelang Kingdom. During the Han Dynasty (206 BC – AD 220), the imperial court sent armies to conquer the southwest, and then the king of Yelang submitted peacefully by the persuasion of the dispatched ambassadors. Subsequently, most of the tribal rulers were defeated, leaving only the king of Yelang still in control of his territory."[3]

Customs: Most A'ou are hardworking farmers who earn a meager income cultivating rice from the poor Guizhou soil. As a result, many youth have moved to the cities in recent years in search of work.

Religion: Most A'ou do not consider themselves religious, although they do honor their ancestors; many elderly people still make sacrifices to various spirits and gods.

Christianity: There are no known Christians among the A'ou today. Catholic workers targeted the Gelao in other parts of Guizhou in the late 1800s, but no mission work specifically among the A'ou has ever been recorded. With a small population and living in a remote location, groups like the A'ou are often overlooked when Christian ministries plan their evangelism and church-planting strategies.

Population in China:
1,500 (1987)
2,060 (2000)
2,650 (2010)
Location: Guizhou
Religion: Ancestor Worship
Christians: None Known

Overview of the A'ou

Countries: China

Pronunciation: "Ah-ow"

Other Names: A'ou Gelao

Population Source: 1,500 (1987 Zheng Guo-qiao); Out of a total Gelao population of 437,997 (1990 census)

Location: *Guizhou:* Zhijin, Qianxi, and Dafang counties

Status: Officially included under Gelao

Language: Daic, Kadai, Lati-Kelao

Dialects: 0

Religion: Ancestor Worship, Animism, No Religion

Christians: None known

Scripture: None

***Jesus* film:** None

Gospel Recordings: None

Christian Broadcasting: None

ROPAL code: KKF02

Status of Evangelization

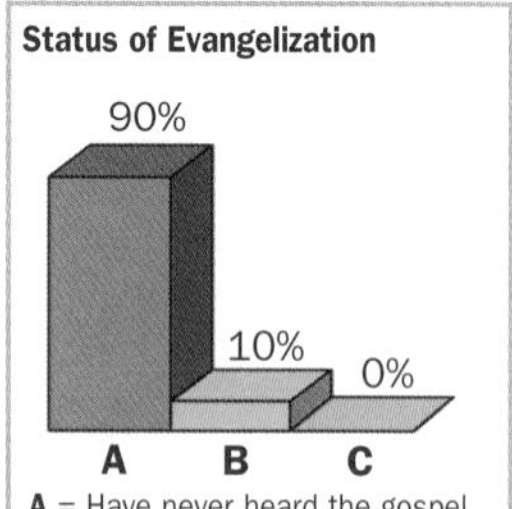

A = Have never heard the gospel
B = Were evangelized but did not become Christians
C = Are adherents to any form of Christianity

Apu 阿普

Location: Approximately 2,500 Apu people were counted in a recent study of the peoples of Honghe Prefecture in Yunnan Province.[1] They live in one small area: the western part of Maandi District within Jinping County. They may also spill across the border into northern Vietnam.

Identity: The Apu were only "discovered" in the past few years. Apart from the fact that they have been officially included as part of the Yi nationality by the Chinese government, little is known about the Apu.

Language: The Apu language has never been studied. It is part of the Lolo (Yi) branch of the Tibeto-Burman language family, but its genetic affiliation remains unclassified.

History: The Apu are one of 120 distinct tribes and groups of Yi in China that have been officially combined into the Yi nationality. This great number of groups is the result of war, migrations, and the threat of slavery over the course of many centuries. Conflict has caused small groups like the Apu to leave their homes and move away to more peaceful settings. After being isolated for generations, the Apu developed their own customs, identity, and dialect.

Customs: Yi groups in China celebrate weddings in various ways. An observer recounted how one ceremony took place "on a day chosen in consultation with a shaman for its auspiciousness as determined by its conjunction with the couple's birthdates and those of their parents. The men of the groom's party are greeted by the women of the bride's family, first with witty remarks, then with buckets of water; their faces may be smeared with pepper and soot, and some girls even physically attack them. Once the ice has been broken, the pig and other ingredients for the marriage feast are prepared. After the feast, the bride is taken to the groom's home, with much weeping and protestation. For three to five days the bride remains at the groom's parents' home, during which time the groom and bride are separated. The bride then returns to her parents' home for a 'waiting-at-home-period' that may last for one or two years or until she is pregnant. During this time, the bride takes lovers — often cousins — and the groom must not only bring presents if he wishes to have sexual intercourse with her but must usually use force to do so. This is a probationary period, which allows both parties to reconsider the match and allows the woman to prove her childbearing abilities."[2]

Jamin Pelkey

Religion: The Apu worship a host of spirits that they believe control the life of their communities. Among these spirits the Dragon god is held in great honor.

Christianity: The Apu are a people group in dire need of the gospel. Alcoholism and sexual immorality have affected the Apu so that few adults do not live in bondage to one or both of these. Although many Hmong and Iu Mien living in Jinping County have come to faith in Christ in recent years through gospel radio broadcasts in their languages, they live some distance away from the Apu and have little contact with them. There are no Scriptures, recordings, or gospel radio programs presently available in a language the Apu readily comprehend.

Population in China:
2,500 (1999)
2,560 (2000)
3,210 (2010)
Location: Yunnan
Religion: Polytheism
Christians: None Known

Overview of the Apu

Countries: China, possibly Vietnam

Pronunciation: "Ah-poo"

Other Names:

Population Source: 2,500 (1999 J. Pelkey); Out of a total Yi population of 6,572,173 (1990 census)

Location: *S Yunnan:* Maandi District in Jinping County, Honghe Prefecture; Possibly also in Vietnam

Status: Officially included under Yi

Language: Sino-Tibetan, Tibeto-Burman, Burmese-Lolo, Lolo, Northern Lolo, Yi, Unclassified

Dialects: 0

Religion: Polytheism, Animism, Ancestor Worship

Christians: None known

Scripture: None

***Jesus* film:** None

Gospel Recordings: None

Christian Broadcasting: None

ROPAL code: None

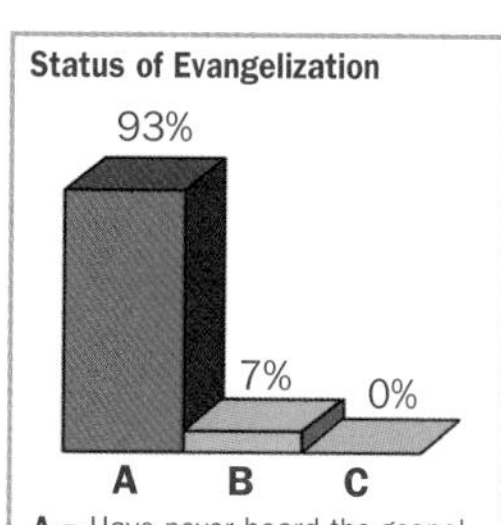

A = Have never heard the gospel
B = Were evangelized but did not become Christians
C = Are adherents to any form of Christianity

Asahei 阿洒黑

Population in China:
8,400 (1999)
8,610 (2000)
10,800 (2010)
Location: Yunnan
Religion: Ancestor Worship
Christians: None Known

Overview of the Asahei

Countries: China

Pronunciation: "Ah-sa-hay"

Other Names: Asahei Aza, Azar, Asaheipo, Pula

Population Source:
8,400 (1999 J. Pelkey);
Out of a total Yi population of 6,572,173 (1990 census)

Location: *Yunnan:* North central Kaiyuan County in Honghe Prefecture

Status:
Officially included under Yi

Language: Sino-Tibetan, Tibeto-Burman, Burmese-Lolo, Lolo, Northern Lolo, Yi, Southeastern Yi

Dialects: 0

Religion: Ancestor Worship, Animism, No Religion

Christians: None known

Scripture: None

***Jesus* film:** None

Gospel Recordings: None

Christian Broadcasting: None

ROPAL code: None

Location: A total of 8,400 Asahei people live in the north central part of Kaiyuan County in China's Yunnan Province. They inhabit the Jiufang and Hongshiyan villages of Lebaidao District and Chongmen Village of Mazheshao District.

Identity: The Asahei are not granted status as a minority group in China. They are one of five tribes the Chinese collectively call Aza, although the name is not used by any of the five groups themselves.[1] The Aza, in turn, have been combined with approximately 120 different ethnolinguistic groups to form the large Yi nationality. Many of the groups within the Yi do not acknowledge kinship, and the linguistic diversity among many groups is so great that they are often forced to speak Chinese in order to communicate. One source from the early 1900s even divided the Yi into 485 clans! — "with each clan occupying a distinct territory."[2]

Language: The Asahei language has yet to be studied in any detail, but it is a unique dialect within the Southeastern Yi group of languages. Since some Asahei children are no longer taught to speak their native tongue, the language may soon become extinct.

History: Although today the Asahei and other Yi appear to live in relative peace and harmony with other groups, in the past they were known as an incredibly violent people. One observer remarked how "Clan feuds seem to have been endemic.... They are caused by arguments over women, insults... murder, theft (especially of slaves or horses), and defaulting on a debt; but, as elsewhere, the reasons for most feuds were long forgotten, and each clan had traditional enemies. Battles or war could be averted if the offenders paid an indemnity in silver or horses, or, if the offending clan were poor and no loss of life was involved, the wrong-doer might go on horseback (wearing a silk dress with a mirror in his hair and raw beef in his mouth) to apologize and to offer wine and beef to the offended party."[3]

Customs: Today many customs and ceremonies among the Asahei are becoming extinct. Until recently they played traditional bamboo musical instruments and carried pouches which contained charms such as boar's teeth, tiger claws, bear claws, and prayers written by the shaman to guide their lives and bring good luck and prosperity.

Religion: Ancestor worship is the predominant religion among the Asahei today. Many Asahei under the age of 40 are nonreligious and participate in the rituals of their parents only with reluctance.

Christianity: There has never been a single known Christian church among the Asahei. French Catholic missionary Paul Vial, who worked among the related Axi and Sani peoples, found that he was accepted because the Yi believed they were also of Caucasian descent. Vial wrote, "The Lolo is convinced that we belong to the same race as him; and this conviction draws him all the closer to us, as he hates the Chinese race. 'Since we are of the same race, it is natural,' he says, 'that we be of the same religion.' And so he hopes to live in the safety of the protective shadow of our influence."[4]

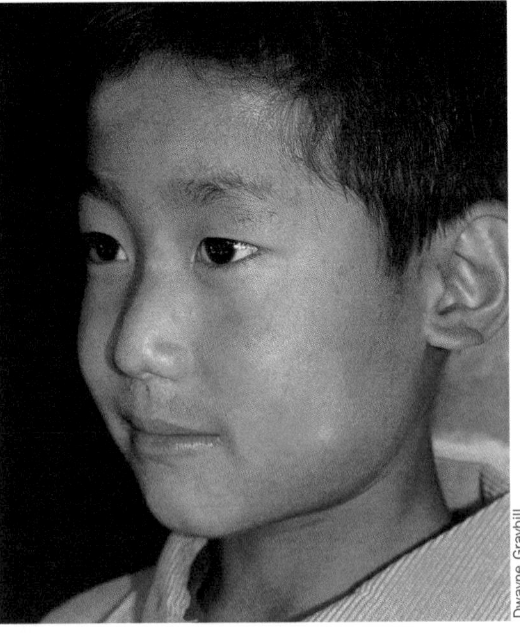
Dwayne Graybill

Ati 阿梯

Jamin Pelkey

Location: In 1999 it was estimated that 12,600 Ati people lived in parts of central Yunnan Province in southwest China. The Ati have lived with a shrouded identity for centuries, known only to those who live close enough for direct contact. The majority live in Huaning County, situated south of Kunming City. Smaller numbers also live in neighboring Jianshui County.[1]

Identity: The Ati are one of dozens of distinct tribes and ethnolinguistic groups the Chinese authorities combined to form the official Yi nationality. There are 120 distinct subgroups of Yi in China. The Ati are only distantly related to other Yi groups in the area, such as the Axi, Adu, Long, Xiqi, and Sani.

Language: The Ati language has recently been found to be part of the Southeastern Yi language family.[2] Because they live in counties dominated by the Han Chinese, most Ati also speak Mandarin Chinese. This does not include the elderly or the women and children in more remote locations.

History: Several hundred years ago, tribes like the Ati lived relatively uninterrupted lives in the hills of central Yunnan. The Han Chinese then flooded the area in massive waves of migration, especially over the last 150 years. Today groups like the Ati, swamped amid the sea of Han Chinese, are barely noticeable to outsiders. As the Han grew in numbers and influence, they forced the Ati off the best land and into the mountains. The Ati were forced to move in order to retain their own customs and ethnicity. Those who stayed in the rural areas were soon absorbed culturally and linguistically.

Customs: The Ati share many cultural traits with the Adu, Long, and Xiqi groups who also inhabit Huaning County and speak Yi languages. The Ati live in two-story wooden homes that are built as a safeguard against intruders and wild animals. Most Ati are engaged in agriculture, but in recent years many youth have ventured into the cities and towns of Yunnan looking for work. Those fortunate enough to gain employment send most of their income home to support their families.

Religion: The Ati are ardent animists and polytheists. In particular they revere and worship the Dragon god. Most Ati villages have a "dragon tree" set aside for this purpose. The antireligion and antisuperstition campaigns of the Cultural Revolution (1966–1976) caused many Ati rituals to cease. As government opposition has eased, the Ati have slowly revived their former beliefs.

Christianity: A Chinese government survey in 1989 found there to be 23 Christians among the Yi in Huaxi District of Huaning County.[3] These are probably people from the Ati tribe. Little mission work was done in this part of Yunnan Province, although some Catholic endeavors may have resulted in the small amount of fruit that remains today. Despite the presence of these few families of believers, most Ati are completely unaware of the gospel. No Scriptures or recordings have been translated into the Ati language.

Population in China:
12,600 (1999)
12,900 (2000)
16,200 (2010)
Location: Yunnan
Religion: Polytheism
Christians: 30

Overview of the Ati

Countries: China
Pronunciation: "Ah-tee"
Other Names:
Population Source: 12,600 (1999 J. Pelkey); Out of a total Yi population of 6,572,173 (1990 census)
Location: *Yunnan:* Huaning and Jianshui counties
Status: Officially included under Yi
Language: Sino-Tibetan, Tibeto-Burman, Burmese-Lolo, Lolo, Northern Lolo, Yi, Southeastern Yi
Dialects: 0
Religion: Polytheism, Animism, No Religion, Christianity
Christians: 30
Scripture: None
***Jesus* film:** None
Gospel Recordings: None
Christian Broadcasting: None
ROPAL code: None

Status of Evangelization

	A	B	C
%	83%	16%	1%

A = Have never heard the gospel
B = Were evangelized but did not become Christians
C = Are adherents to any form of Christianity

Awu, Northern 阿乌(北)

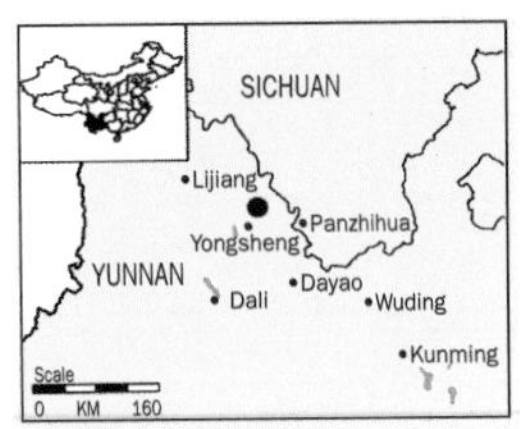

Population in China:
3,500 (1999)
3,590 (2000)
4,500 (2010)
Location: Yunnan
Religion: Polytheism
Christians: None Known

Overview of the Northern Awu

Countries: China

Pronunciation: "Ah-woo"

Other Names: Awupu, Awuzhe, Xiangtan

Population Source: 3,500 (1999 J. Pelkey); Out of a total Yi population of 6,572,173 (1990 census)

Location: *N Yunnan:* Yongsheng County

Status: Officially included under Yi

Language: Sino-Tibetan, Tibeto-Burman, Burmese-Lolo, Lolo, Northern Lolo, Yi, Northern Yi

Dialects: 0

Religion: Polytheism, Animism, Ancestor Worship

Christians: None known

Scripture: None

***Jesus* film:** None

Gospel Recordings: None

Christian Broadcasting: None

ROPAL code: None

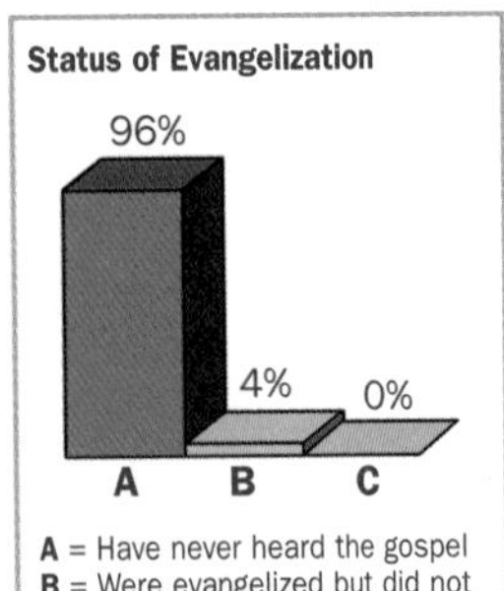

A = Have never heard the gospel
B = Were evangelized but did not become Christians
C = Are adherents to any form of Christianity

Paul Hattaway

Location: Numbering just 3,500 people, the Northern Awu inhabit the Peiyuan, Shuiping, and Yongle communities within the Da'an District of Yongsheng County in northern Yunnan Province. Yongsheng is the only area known to be inhabited by the Northern Awu.

Identity: Although the Northern Awu share the same autonym as the Southeastern Awu, the two groups speak vastly differing languages and live separated by more than 200 miles of rugged mountains. The Northern Awu have been officially included under the Yi nationality by the Chinese government, even though they possess their own customs, ethnicity, and language.

Language: The Northern Awu are so named because they speak a language from the Northern Yi branch of the Tibeto-Burman language family. It is related to other Northern Yi varieties in the area such as Xiaoliangshan Nosu, Talu, Liwu, Tagu, and Naza. Many people are surprised to learn of the great linguistic diversity found among minority peoples in southern China. Even the various groups of the Yi nationality, for example, "are widely diverse in their language and in their customs and habits... [many Yi languages] are mutually unintelligible and indeed more different from each other than are the various Han Chinese dialects such as Mandarin, Min, and Cantonese."[1]

History: The Northern Awu have lived in their remote part of Yunnan Province for many centuries. They may have been former slaves of the Xiaoliangshan Nosu, who dominated the lives of people in the area until slave trade was finally abolished in the late 1950s.

Customs: Numerous festivals are celebrated by the Yi peoples of northern Yunnan. The Northern Awu participate in many of them, including the Garment Competition which involves the women's embroidery skills. All the women are dressed in their finest attire, which causes the hillsides to come alive with color. Later, there is singing and dancing, and special competitions are held. This festival affords young people a chance to meet prospective partners. It also allows older participants a time to relax from their work and to catch up with their friends and relatives from other areas.

Religion: The Northern Awu believe in a host of spirits and deities which must be appeased in order to bring peace and prosperity to their communities. They also believe the human soul lives on after death and travels back to the abode of ancestors.

Christianity: Little Christian activity has ever taken place in Yongsheng County. The remote mountains and former threat of slavery combined to keep evangelists and missionaries away from the area. As a result, the Northern Awu are an unreached and unevangelized people group with no access to the gospel and no contact with Christians.

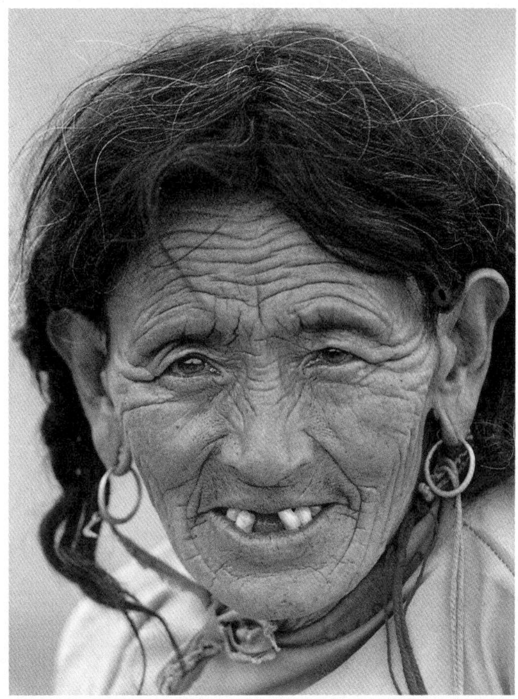

2

1

3

1. The 400,000 unreached *Akha* in China and Southeast Asia wear spectacular traditional dress. [Paul Hattaway]
2. An old *Amdo* Tibetan woman, northern Sichuan. [Paul Hattaway]
3. The polytheistic *Achang* live on both sides of the China-Myanmar border. [Dwayne Graybill]

4

5

6

7

4. An *Amdo* nomad boy and his yak, Sangke Grasslands, Gansu. [Paul Hattaway]
5. An *Amdo* girl dressed in her festival-best, Xiahe, Gansu. [Paul Hattaway]
6. A woman from the small *Ake* ethnic group, Mengyuan, Yunnan. [Dwayne Graybill]
7. An *Hbrogpa Amdo* nomad girl, near Zoige, Sichuan. [Paul Hattaway]

8

9

10

8. More than 78,000 *Axi* live in the mountains of central Yunnan Province. [International Mission Board]
9. Although there are thousands of Christian *Akha* living in Myanmar and Thailand, the 190,000 *Akha* in China remain an unreached people group. [Paul Hattaway]
10. Two *Bei* friends, Lijiang, Yunnan. [Paul Hattaway]

11. Approximately two million *Bai* live in and around the ancient city of Dali in Yunnan. Dali has been continuously inhabited for more than 3,000 years and was the capital of the former Nanzhao Kingdom.
[Paul Hattaway]

Awu, Southeastern 阿乌(东南)

Population in China:
24,300 (1999)
24,900 (2000)
31,200 (2010)
Location: Yunnan
Religion: Polytheism
Christians: 600

Overview of the Southeastern Awu

Countries: China

Pronunciation: "Ah-woo"

Other Names: Lawu, Luopuo, Awupuo, Mengwu, A-wou

Population Source: 24,300 (1999 J. Pelkey); Out of a total Yi population of 6,572,173 (1990 census)

Status: Officially included under Yi

Location: *Yunnan:* Mile (10,900), Luxi (8,000), Shizong (5,000), and Luoping (400) counties

Language: Sino-Tibetan, Tibeto-Burman, Burmese-Lolo, Lolo, Northern Lolo, Yi, Southeastern Yi

Dialects: 0

Religion: Polytheism, Animism, Ancestor Worship, Christianity

Christians: 600

Scripture: None

***Jesus* film:** None

Gospel Recordings: None

Christian Broadcasting: None

ROPAL code: YIE03

Status of Evangelization

	A	B	C
%	67%	30%	3%

A = Have never heard the gospel
B = Were evangelized but did not become Christians
C = Are adherents to any form of Christianity

Location: Approximately 24,000 members of the Southeastern Awu ethnic group live in communities across a widespread area of southeastern Yunnan Province. Awu villages are located in parts of Mile (8,710 Awu people in 1984),[1] Luxi (8,000), Shizong (5,000), and Luoping (400) counties.

Identity: The Southeastern Awu are part of the official Yi nationality in China. Neighboring people groups call them a variety of names, including Lawu and Mengwu. The Southeastern Awu speak a language completely different from the Northern Awu.

Language: Awu is one of numerous languages and dialects that make up the Southeastern Yi branch of Tibeto-Burman. The Northern Awu speak a Northern Yi language.

History: The Southeastern Awu entered Honghe Prefecture from Shizong and Luoping during the Ming Dynasty (1368–1644).[2] The ancestors of the Awu are thought to have originally been part of the ancient Luowu tribe.

Customs: The Southeastern Awu living in Chuxiong Prefecture engage in a number of festivals and celebrations throughout the year. Some are shared with other Yi groups. On the eighth day of the second month of the lunar calendar, the people living in the mountainous areas of Chuxong celebrate the Cattle Festival. The people wrap their cows' horns with flowers and place flowers above the cattle stall. They sing, dance, and pay homage to the mountain god. Other celebrations throughout the year include the Third Month Fair, when people gather in the marketplace and play games; and the New Rice Festival, when people taste the freshly harvested rice and sing and dance. All gatherings are opportunities for the Awu to meet with friends and relatives, catch up on events, and trade with one another.

Religion: The majority of Southeastern Awu practice a mixture of animism, polytheism, and ancestor worship. On the second day of the second lunar month, the Awu of Mile County worship the White Dragon god.

Christianity: Before 1949 Catholic missionaries established a church among the Southeastern Awu at Sunong Village in Dongshan District of Mile County. The number of Awu believers at one time numbered 94. In 1901 a church building was constructed in Aying Village of Xiangyang District in the eastern part of Luxi County. This church is still active today. By 1949 there were 132 Awu families professing faith in Christ in eastern Luxi. According to an official source there are presently 300 Awu believers in Luxi County.[3] There may be many more Catholic believers among the Southeastern Awu in neighboring counties, although some reports suggest their faith has become extremely syncretistic since the departure of the missionaries almost 50 years ago. Idol worship and animistic rituals are practiced by many professing Christians, even inside the church buildings.

Jamin Pelkey

Axi 阿细

Location: More than 78,000 Axi live in Yunnan Province. The majority live in Mile County of Honghe Prefecture where 59,014 were reported in 1984.[1] Others live near the Stone Forest in Shilin (formerly Lunan) County. About 300 Axi live in eastern Huaning County of Yuxi Prefecture and 1,200 in Luxi County. For centuries the Axi have lived in peaceful communities, separated from other groups in the area.

Identity: The Axi people in Shilin County are closely related to the Sani. The Sani chose to live at the base of the Qui Mountains and therefore are more assimilated to Chinese culture.[2] Seeing this, the Axi have chosen to remain hidden in the hills and retain their own identity. The Axi possess their own traditions, language, and style of dress.

Language: The Axi language — which has 35 consonants, 15 vowels, and 4 tones — is distinct from the speech of all surrounding peoples. It is described as being "genetically closer to Lisu and Hani than... to other Yi languages."[3] An Axi orthography was created by the government in 1986, but few Axi have been educated past primary school level and are able to use it.

History: The Axi claim to have originated in a place called Azhede in northwestern Sichuan many centuries ago.[4] They are famous for their unique dance, the *Axi Tiaoyue*. It is a dance depicting a terrible fire long ago on the mountain where the Axi live. It burned for nine days and nine nights. The ground became so hot that the Axi had to hop up and down on one leg to avoid being burned. After the fire was extinguished, the Axi people played flutes and *sanxians* (a plucked instrument) to celebrate the victory. They hop around on one leg, imitating their fire-fighting heroics.[5]

International Mission Board

Customs: The *Axi Tiaoyue* is now famous throughout China. A troupe of 50 Axi dancers have performed it all over the country. In 1993 the troupe traveled to Europe where they performed in Portugal, France, and Germany. The Axi also participate in the Torch Festival which takes place at the Stone Forest every year.[6]

Religion: The Axi believe demons will afflict them should someone in their village upset the spiritual harmony. Chickens and other animals are immediately sacrificed in an attempt to placate the demons and prevent them from causing further harm. A festival is held in the third lunar month in which the Axi strip down to their loincloths, paint their bodies, wear grotesque masks, and run around the hillsides. This enactment represents the time when the Fire god was drawn out of a pool of water.[7]

Christianity: French Catholic missionary Père Alfred Liétard spearheaded work among the Axi beginning in the 1880s.[8] Later, Paul Vial continued the work, heading a team of priests dedicated in reaching out to the Axi, Sani, and some other Yi groups in the area. Vial wrote, "These sweet, honest, naive, and likeable faces have conquered me."[9] In 1948 Vial listed 1,500 Axi converts in seven churches.[10] Today, mostly elderly Axi believers remain in the Shilin and Mile areas. Despite these Catholics, most Axi have yet to hear the gospel for the first time.

Population in China:
76,200 (1999)
78,100 (2000)
98,100 (2010)
Location: Yunnan
Religion: Polytheism
Christians: 2,000

Overview of the Axi

Countries: China

Pronunciation: "Ah-shee"

Other Names: Axipu, Ashi, A-chi, A-hi, Ahi, Asci, Axipo, Aoxi, A-hsi, Axibo

Population Source: 76,200 (1999 J. Pelkey); Out of a total Yi population of 6,572,173 (1990 census)

Location: *Yunnan:* Mile (73,900), Shilin (800), Huaning (300), Luxi (1,200), and Yiliang (45) counties; Also in Kunming Municipality

Status: Officially included under Yi

Language: Sino-Tibetan, Tibeto-Burman, Burmese-Lolo, Lolo, Northern Lolo, Yi, Southeastern Yi

Dialects: 0

Religion: Polytheism, Animism, Christianity

Christians: 2,000

Scripture: None

***Jesus* film:** None

Gospel Recordings: Axi #04806

Christian Broadcasting: None

ROPAL code: YIE02

Status of Evangelization

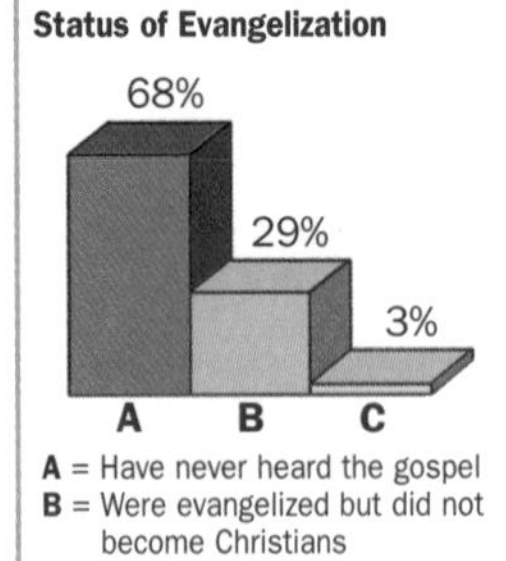

A = Have never heard the gospel
B = Were evangelized but did not become Christians
C = Are adherents to any form of Christianity

Ayi 阿夷

Population in China:
2,000 (1995)
2,210 (2000)
2,680 (2010)
Location: Yunnan
Religion: Christianity
Christians: 1,300

Overview of the Ayi

Countries: China

Pronunciation: "Ah-yee"

Other Names:

Population Source:
2,000 (1995 AMO);
Out of a total Nu population of 27,123 (1990 census)

Location: *NW Yunnan:* Fugong and Gongshan counties

Status:
Officially included under Nu

Language: Sino-Tibetan, Tibeto-Burman, Unclassified

Dialects: 0

Religion: Christianity, Polytheism, Animism

Christians: 1,300

Scripture: None

***Jesus* film:** None

Gospel Recordings: None

Christian Broadcasting: None

ROPAL code: AYX00

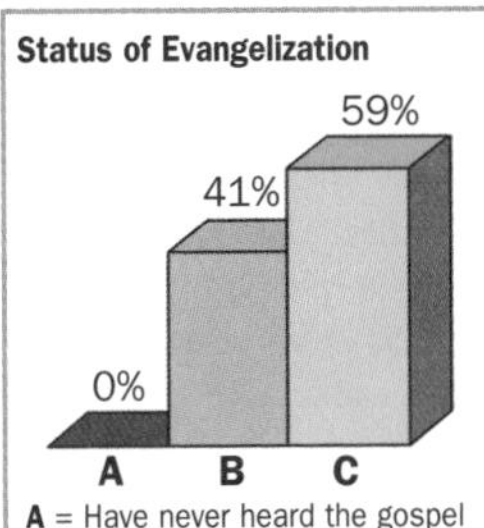

Dwayne Graybill

Location: Approximately 2,000 people speak the Ayi language, out of a total of 27,000 in the Nu nationality. Other Nu subgroups in China include the Lama and Zauzou. The Ayi live in parts of Fugong and Gongshan counties in Nujiang Prefecture.[1] They inhabit the remote mountains of northwest Yunnan near the Myanmar border. Although the region is off-limits to foreign travelers, it is one of the most Christianized areas in China. Most of the remainder of the Nu minority live farther north of the Ayi. The Ayi area is rich in mineral deposits. Dense virgin pine trees and fir forests cover the high mountain slopes.

Identity: Although the Ayi are included as part of the official Nu nationality, they possess their own distinct customs and speak a language mutually unintelligible with other Nu varieties. The Ayi culture shares many similarities with the Lisu.

Language: The exact affiliation of the Ayi language has yet to be determined, except that it is part of the Tibeto-Burman language family. The Ayi language consists of four tones and has borrowed words from the Chinese, Tibetan, Lisu, Bai, and Burmese languages.[2]

History: The Ayi have historically been viewed by outsiders as more culturally backward than the Bai, Naxi, or Han Chinese people farther to the east. In the eighth century the Ayi came under the control of the Nanzhao Kingdom centered in Dali. During the Yuan and Ming dynasties the area was controlled by a Naxi headman. In 1907 the Ayi joined an uprising in protest against the British who had entered China from Burma.[3] Alcoholism has long been a curse on the Ayi people. Often in villages, all the people, including children, were addicted, but since the arrival of Christianity the problem has subsided.

Customs: The Ayi live by subsistence farming. Their major crops are maize, buckwheat, barley, potatoes, yams, beans, and corn. They supplement farming by hunting with crossbows. Those who live near the rivers fish from two-man flat boats. Ayi society has traditionally been monogamous, although some wealthy landlords kept extra wives and concubines. The youngest son among the Ayi inherits the family property.

Religion: It is estimated that more than 50% of the Ayi are professing Christians. A recent report stated, "Fugong County, which is in China's northwestern Yunnan Province, has so many Christians that it is known as 'Christ County'. Ninety percent of the people there are believers. The Christians report that authorities, impressed by the falling crime rate, are actually encouraging people to believe."[4]

Christianity: The Ayi have received a vibrant Christian witness from strong evangelistic churches among the nearby Lisu and Nu. Most Ayi attend mixed-nationality churches where Lisu is the language used in worship. Many Protestant and Catholic missionaries lived in this part of China prior to the 1950s which has resulted in strong churches today among the Lisu, Bai, Nu, and Derung minorities. The New Testament is available in the Nu language based on a dialect in Myanmar, but it is not known to what extent the Ayi can understand it.

Ayizi 阿夷子

Paul Hattaway

Location: In 1986 a total of 426 Ayizi people lived in Shilin County (formerly known as Lunan County) in Yunnan Province. The village with the largest concentration of Ayizi is Aimailongcun Village in Beidacun District. Some Ayizi people also live in other villages of Beidacun and Banqiao districts.[1] Shilin County, home of the famous Stone Forest, is also the center of the Sani people, a different Yi subgroup.

Identity: The Ayizi have been officially counted as part of the Yi nationality in China. Although they were a distinct ethnic group with a proud history until about 50 years ago, today many of the Ayizi have been culturally and linguistically assimilated by the Han Chinese. Within one or two generations the Ayizi may cease to exist as a distinct people. One writer explains, "Paradoxically, what the Chinese before 1950 could not accomplish by force, they are now accomplishing as a by-product of a quite different goal, all the while encouraging respect for minority differences: the Yi minorities are becoming ever more assimilated into national political, economic, social, and cultural institutions. The Yi, formerly known as 'iron peas' because they could not be assimilated, are joining the stew."[2]

Language: The Ayizi, who are also known as the *Ge*, speak a little-studied language that is on the verge of extinction. It is only spoken by a handful of elderly speakers. It is uncertain which branch of the Yi group the Ayizi language belongs to. Shilin County contains both Eastern Yi and Southeastern Yi varieties.

History: Little is known about the origins of the Ayizi, although it is believed they are fairly recent arrivals in the Shilin area — perhaps only about 200 years ago.

Customs: The traditional dress formerly worn by Ayizi women has also been lost. Today the Ayizi celebrate Han Chinese festivals. Perhaps the only minority festival they still observe is the Torch Festival which is held in the Stone Forest every year.

Religion: Spirit worship and ancestor worship is practiced by most elderly Ayizi, while the younger generation are nonreligious and consider their parents' beliefs to be foolish superstition.

Christianity: There are no known Christians among the Ayizi today, although there was extensive Catholic missionary work in the area prior to 1949. The gospel has not always been gladly received by the Yi in China. In 1910, writing of a related group, Samuel Pollard stated, "We met a Yi in the path. He was most unfriendly towards us. He said, 'We hate Pollard, because he has come into our midst and has destroyed the efficacy of our idols'. Two years ago in this village the Yi landlord oppressed the Miao dreadfully for becoming Christian. They were fined 103 taels of silver, their rents were increased, some were tied up by their hair and others by their hands under their knees — then he beat them and shouted, 'Call on your Jesus to save you? What can Jesus do for you? What can the teacher do for you?' And here they are still believing; we had a crowded house at night with some of the children standing on my bed. Eleven of them were baptized."[3]

Population in China:
426 (1986)
580 (2000)
720 (2010)
Location: Yunnan
Religion: Animism
Christians: None Known

Overview of the Ayizi

Countries: China

Pronunciation: "Ah-yee-zee"

Other Names: Ge

Population Source: 426 (1999 J. Pelkey – 1986 figure); Out of a total Yi population of 6,572,173 (1990 census)

Location: *Yunnan:* Shilin County

Status: Officially included under Yi

Language: Sino-Tibetan, Tibeto-Burman, Burmese-Lolo, Lolo, Northern Lolo, Yi, Unclassified

Dialects: 0

Religion: Animism, Ancestor Worship, No Religion

Christians: None known

Scripture: None

***Jesus* film:** None

Gospel Recordings: None

Christian Broadcasting: None

ROPAL code: None

Status of Evangelization

A = Have never heard the gospel
B = Were evangelized but did not become Christians
C = Are adherents to any form of Christianity

Azhe 阿哲

Location: A 1999 study placed 57,500 Azhe people in central Yunnan Province.[1] A 1984 figure listed 36,447 in Mile County,[2] while 7,200 live in Huaning County of Yuxi Prefecture. Others live in Kaiyuan (4,600) and Jianshui (200) counties. The Azhe typically live in flat-roofed, earthen homes.

Identity: In 1960 the Azhe were officially placed in the Yi nationality. The Azhe, however, refuse to intermarry with other peoples and are culturally and linguistically different from their neighbors. The Azhe are not the same ethnolinguistic group as the A Che people farther to the west, who speak a language from the Southern Yi branch.

Language: In ancient times, the Azhe language had a written script called *Baimawen* or "Shaman's Script". In Xunjiian District of Mile County, an ancient rock painting was recently discovered, representing the earliest form of *Baimawen*. It has been translated as "'Braving the scorching sun of March, we got here on horseback'. In its earliest form, *Baimawen* looked much like Egyptian hieroglyphics; as it developed, this Azhe writing system was used primarily by shamans for incantations and medicinal purposes."[3]

History: The Azhe say they originated in northern Yunnan. They migrated south to Jianshui during the Sui and Tang dynasties (581–907). At that time they were giving military assistance to the Luodian Kingdom. Later, the people separated. Some went back to Yimen and Shuangbai counties where today they are the A Che people.[4] Despite their shared origins, the languages and customs of the Azhe and A Che today differ remarkably.

T.C. Thomas

Customs: The Azhe celebrate the annual Torch Festival. On the first day of the festival, many weddings take place. On the second day, the men sacrifice an ox at the foot of the sacred village tree.

Religion: After sacrificing an ox during the Torch Festival, the Azhe "engage in much chanting to invoke spirits. Having finished the chanting the men take the heart of the ox and boil it together with a rooster in order to appease the god of the Mountain. The meat from the ox is divided among all the men who participated in the sacrifice, and the ox bones are dispersed evenly to each family of the village. No one works during the Azhe Torch Festival and every night of the festival the youth engage in dancing, singing, and courtship."[5] The Azhe hold many holidays centered in animism and polytheism. On the 14th day of the tenth lunar month, the whole village goes to a sacred mountain. They slaughter a cow and two chickens in hope of appeasing a mountain god whom they believe to be in charge of their welfare.

Christianity: There is one known Catholic meeting point among the Azhe, situated in Mile County. French Catholic missionaries worked extensively in the region in the first half of the twentieth century. Today, however, most Azhe are completely unaware of the gospel or the name of Christ, having been cut off from outside influence for generations. In the early part of this century the Sani people, located to the north, were reported to have more than 7,000 Catholics, but there is no evidence of Sani outreach to the Azhe who have a different language and culture.

GUIZHOU
Kunming
YUNNAN
Mile
Huaning
Qiubei
GUANGXI
Kaiyuan
Jinping
Pingbian
Scale
0 KM 160
VIETNAM

Population in China:
57,500 (1999)
58,950 (2000)
74,000 (2010)
Location: Yunnan
Religion: Polytheism
Christians: 100

Overview of the Azhe

Countries: China

Pronunciation: "Ah-jeh"

Other Names: Ajia, Arjie, Azhepuo, A-djay, A-gie, Axhebo, Aozhe, Huami Yi

Population Source: 57,500 (1999 J. Pelkey); Out of a total Yi population of 6,572,173 (1990 census)

Location: *Yunnan:* Mile (36,447), Huaning (7,200), Kaiyuan (4,600), and Jianshui (200) counties

Status: Officially included under Yi

Language: Sino-Tibetan, Tibeto-Burman, Burmese-Lolo, Lolo, Northern Lolo, Yi, Southeastern Yi

Dialects: 0

Religion: Polytheism, Animism, Ancestor Worship, Christianity

Christians: 100

Scripture: None

***Jesus* film:** None

Gospel Recordings: Yi: Azhe

Christian Broadcasting: None

ROPAL code: YIE04

A = Have never heard the gospel
B = Were evangelized but did not become Christians
C = Are adherents to any form of Christianity

Azong 阿宗

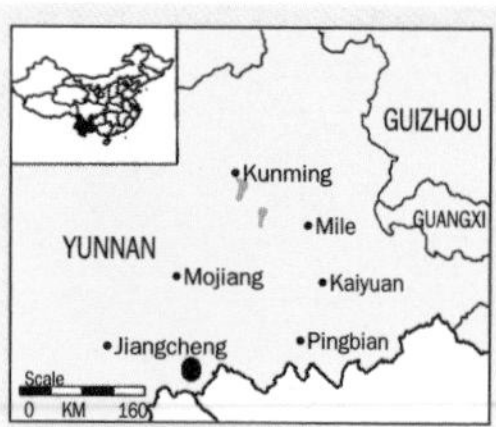

Population in China:
1,000 (1999)
1,020 (2000)
1,280 (2010)
Location: Yunnan
Religion: Ancestor Worship
Christians: None Known

Overview of the Azong

Countries: China

Pronunciation: "Ah-zong"

Other Names:

Population Source:
1,000 (1999 J. Pelkey);
Out of a total Yi population of 6,572,173 (1990 census)

Location: *S Yunnan:* Jiangcheng County in Simao Prefecture

Status:
Officially included under Yi

Language: Sino-Tibetan, Tibeto-Burman, Burmese-Lolo, Lolo, Northern Lolo, Yi, Southern Yi

Dialects: 0

Religion:
Ancestor Worship, Animism

Christians: None known

Scripture: None

***Jesus* film:** None

Gospel Recordings: None

Christian Broadcasting: None

ROPAL code: None

Status of Evangelization

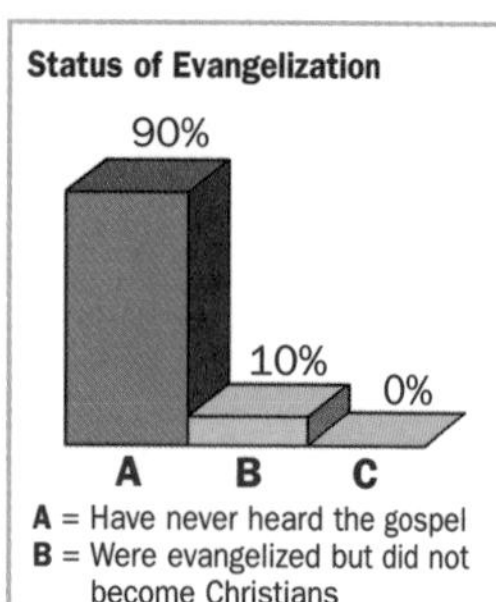

A = Have never heard the gospel
B = Were evangelized but did not become Christians
C = Are adherents to any form of Christianity

Location: According to Jamin Pelkey, 1,000 people belonging to the Azong ethnic group live in Jiangcheng County within Simao Prefecture of southern Yunnan Province.[1] Other people groups included in the official Yi nationality who live in Jiangcheng County are the Xiangtang, Yuanyang Nisu, Alu, and Laowu. The area is hilly and lush, with abundant rainfall. Many of the ethnic groups in the region spill over into neighboring Vietnam and Laos.

Identity: The Azong are one of 120 different subgroups of the officially recognized Yi nationality in China. One ethnographer, who has researched the Yi, wrote, "If the 'Yi' had a mutual and continuous history, perhaps this would lend some credence to their common classification, yet even here one is hard-pressed to find similarities or continuity. The official stance on the origin of the 'Yi' usually states they were descendants from the Qiang who migrated south from Qinghai and Gansu 2,000 to 3,000 years ago. While this is plausible and even probable in many cases, it does not follow, therefore, that this nationality has remained one homogeneous people group some 2,000 years later.... How long have the 'Yi' been in existence? The answer is clear: 'they never were'."[2]

Language: The Azong language is believed to be a part of the Southern Yi group of languages, although no research has been conducted to confirm this. It is possible they speak a Western Yi language as do the Xiangtang who also live in Jiangcheng County.

History: When Marco Polo passed through the Yi areas of "Caindu" in the late thirteenth century, he recounted some of the unique sexual practices of the people at the time: "I must tell you of a custom that they have in this country regarding their women. No man considers himself wronged if a foreigner, or any other man, dishonor his wife, or daughter, or sister, or any woman of his family, but on the contrary he deems such intercourse a piece of good fortune. And they say that it brings the favor of their gods and idols, and great increase of temporal prosperity."[3]

Customs: Until recent years, when burial has been gradually phased out in favor of cremation by the central government, the Azong placed silver in the mouths of their dead. The body was buried in a favorable place with the name of the deceased written on the headstone. The oldest son was required to use the blood from his own finger to write the names of his parents on a wooden tablet, using Yi characters.

Religion: These tablets were then kept for three generations and used in ancestral rites, before they were burned. Ancestor worship mixed with animism remain the major religious beliefs among the Azong.

Christianity: Although there are about 2,000 Christians among the "Yi" in Jiangcheng County, all of them are believed to be from among the Yuanyang Nisu group. There are no known Christians among the Azong. The languages of the Azong and Yuanyang Nisu are divergent enough to make mutual communication impossible. This has created a barrier to the spread of the gospel between different ethnic groups in this part of the country.

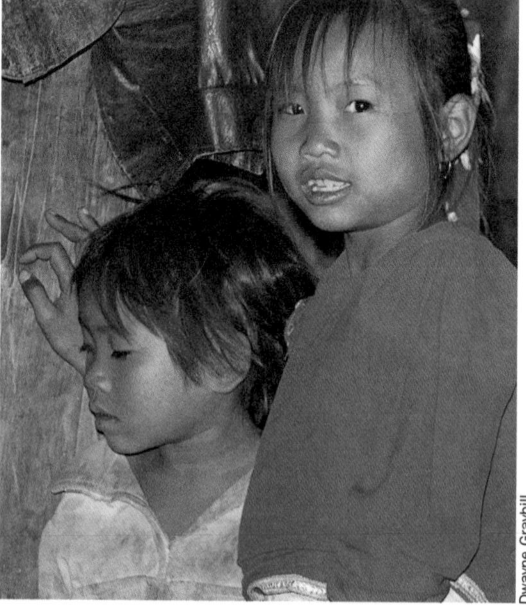

Dwayne Graybill

Baheng, Liping 巴哼(黎平)

Paul Hattaway

Location: Chinese scholars in the 1990s discovered that Baheng speakers in southern Guizhou and northern Guangxi divided into two distinct language groups.[1] The larger group was labeled *Baheng, Sanjiang*, while this smaller group (4,000 people) was named *Baheng, Liping* after the county which they primarily inhabit in Guizhou Province. Liping is home to several minorities, including the Mjuniang and the Dong.[2]

Identity: The Liping Baheng have been counted by the Chinese authorities as one of more than ten Bunu groups. *Bunu* is a generic term, simply meaning "us people." The various groups of Bunu do not consider themselves related to each other and are dispersed over a vast geographical area. The Bunu were not granted status as its own *minzu* (nationality) in China but were included as part of the Yao nationality.

Language: Baheng forms its own branch of the Miao (Hmongic) language family. The Liping Baheng language contains many influences from Dong, which is a Tai based language. It is likely that the language of the Baheng in Liping diverged from the Baheng elsewhere as the result of many centuries of prolonged contact with the Dong.

History: The Baheng consider themselves descended from eight ancient clans. Their name in Chinese, *Ba Xing* (Eight Clans), reflects this.

Customs: The women like to wear much jewelry, including large earrings and necklaces. In the past, a new husband was required to live in his in-law's house for 12 years. After six years, however, he was able to take his wife and build his own home if her family gave their consent. This custom has not been strictly observed in recent years, although most men still move to their wife's village after the wedding.

Religion: Ancestor worship is the primary religion among the Baheng and is the driving force behind many customs and prohibitions in their society. The Baheng believe that only sons can conduct ancestral rites. Boys are therefore highly sought after, especially since the implementation of China's strict family-planning laws. In recent years, a growing number of Baheng women have aborted baby girls, since not having a son means that the souls of the parents may be lost in hell forever. The Baheng also observe many ancient animistic rituals relating to their practise of agriculture. They pray for the soul of the rice after planting, to ensure a successful crop. They have also been known to place drawings of corn, rice, or vegetables next to an altar in a bid to seek the blessings of the spirits.

Christianity: The Liping Baheng are a colorful, friendly people, but few have ever had the opportunity to hear that Christ died for them. They remain a completely unreached people group without a single known Christian in their midst. Unfortunately, no Scriptures or gospel recordings exist in a language the Baheng can easily understand.

Population in China:
4,000 (1990)
5,160 (2000)
6,650 (2010)
Location: Guizhou
Religion: Ancestor Worship
Christians: None Known

Overview of the Liping Baheng

Countries: China

Pronunciation: "Lee-ping-Ba-heng"

Other Names: Pa Hng, Baxing Yao, Eight Clan Yao

Population Source: 4,000 (1995 Wang Fushi – 1990 census); Out of a total Yao population of 2,134,013 (1990 census)

Location:
SE Guizhou: Liping County

Status:
Officially included under Yao

Language:
Hmong-Mien, Hmongic, Bahengic

Dialects: 0

Religion: Ancestor Worship, Animism, Polytheism

Christians: None known

Scripture: None

***Jesus* film:** None

Gospel Recordings: None

Christian Broadcasting: None

ROPAL code: None

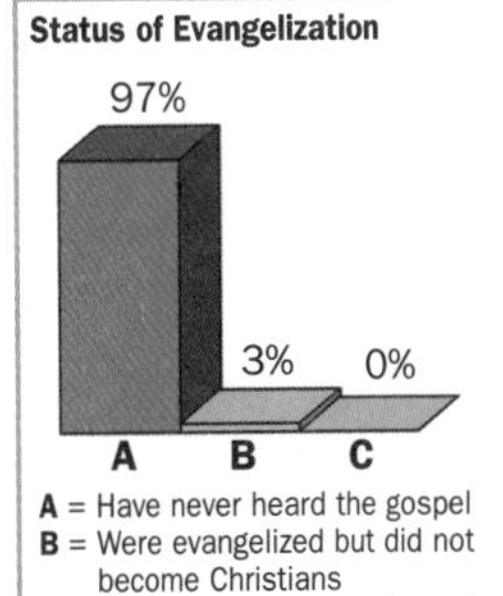

Baheng, Sanjiang 巴哼(三江)

Population in China:
32,000 (1987)
41,200 (2000)
53,200 (2010)
Location: Guizhou, Guangxi
Religion: Ancestor Worship
Christians: None Known

Overview of the Sanjiang Baheng

Countries: China, Vietnam

Pronunciation: "Sahn-jung-Ba-heng"

Other Names: Bunu: Baheng, Pa Hng, Pa Then, Tong, Meo Lai, Ma Pa Seng, Pawu, Pa Ngng, Paheng, Bahengmai, Baxing Yao, Eight Clan Yao

Population Source: 32,000 (1987 D. Bradley); Out of a total Yao population of 2,134,013 (1990 census); 3,700 in Vietnam (1991 census)

Location: *SE Guizhou:* Congjiang and Rongjiang counties; *NE Guangxi:* Sanjiang, Longsheng, Rong'an, and Lingui counties

Status: Officially included under Yao

Language: Hmong-Mien, Hmongic, Bahengic

Dialects: 0

Religion: Ancestor Worship, Animism, Polytheism

Christians: None known

Scripture: None

***Jesus* film:** None

Gospel Recordings: None

Christian Broadcasting: None

ROPAL code: PHA01

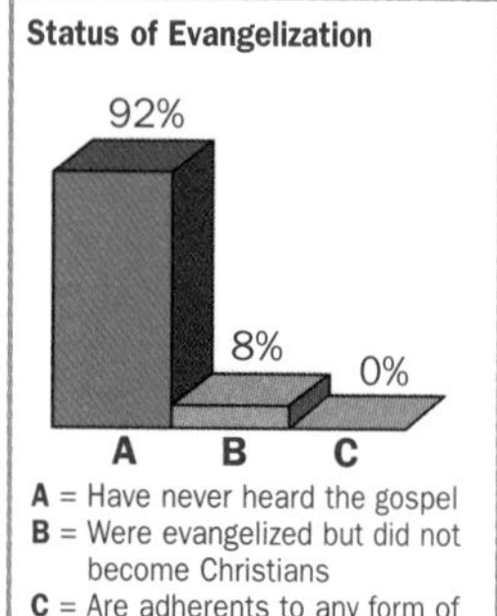

Paul Hattaway

Location: More than 30,000 Baheng live in four counties (Sanjiang, Longsheng, Rong'an, and Lingui) in northeast Guangxi; and in Rongjiang and Congjiang counties in adjacent areas of Guizhou Province. Some 3,700 Baheng also live in northern Vietnam, where they are known as the *Pa Then.*

Identity: The Baheng have been officially included as part of the Bunu group within the Yao nationality in China. In Vietnam the authorities have granted the *Pa Then* status as one of their 53 official minority groups.

Language: The main Baheng group speak a language distinct from the Baheng in Liping County of Guizhou. The Baheng (Pa Then) in Vietnam are thought to have migrated from China in the late 1700s or early 1800s. After two centuries of separation and influence from other languages, their speech now differs from that of their counterparts in China.

History: The Baheng in some locations believe a frog created the heavens and the earth. After a time of living in perfect contentment, man destroyed the harmony of his peaceful existence by killing the frog. "The frog's dying curse was to divide the world into a realm for humans and a realm for spirits. Before that time, mankind did not know sickness, and when a person would die, he would rise again from the dead on the 13th day. After the curse, this no longer happened."[1]

Customs: The Baheng live in communities according to family clans. Marriage is forbidden within each clan. A Baheng man must not have sexual relations with any woman of his clan. This taboo is strictly enforced. Baheng children are told horror stories of what will happen if they break this taboo. This prohibition stands for people of the same family name, even if they live in different provinces and have never previously met. After the birth of a child, the placenta is placed under the floorboards of the house. At the end of the person's life, he must make a journey back to the spiritual village of his ancestors. The dead person's soul must stop to pick up the placenta, which is believed to help the spirits identify who the person is.

Religion: The Baheng believe a person has 12 souls. "When a body is placed in a coffin, it is sprinkled with 12 measures of grilled rice, and 12 sandstone bowls are put in along with the rice."[2] Each Baheng home contains an ancestral altar. The Baheng believe the spirits of their ancestors are fed by placing rice and meat out on the table for them. The male head of the household calls on the spirits of his ancestors to come and share in the feast and to protect his family from sickness and injury.

Christianity: This tribe has rarely been targeted with the gospel and are an unevangelized people group. Their intricate rituals of ancestor worship create barriers that prevent them from embracing the gospel, yet they are still considered by some to be "ripe unto harvest." Most simply have never had the chance to hear.

Bai 

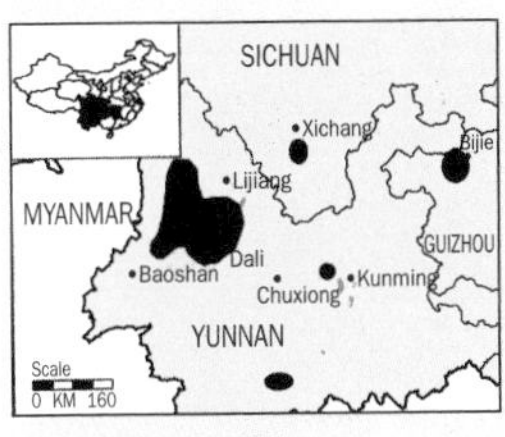

Population in China:
1,442,627 (1990)
1,915,200 (2000)
2,470,600 (2010)
Location: Yunnan, Sichuan, Guizhou, Hunan
Religion: Buddhism
Christians: 50,000

Overview of the Bai

Countries: China

Pronunciation: "Bai"

Other Names: Pai, Minchia, Minkia, Dali, Labbu, Nama, Leme, Baini, Baizi, Baihuo

Population Source:
1,594,827 (1990 census);[1]
1,132,010 (1982 census)

Location: *Yunnan:* Dali Bai Prefecture (1,276,000); Kunming Municipality, Yuanjiang, Lijiang, and Lanping counties;
Guizhou: (122,000);
S Sichuan: Xichang County;
Hunan: Sangzhi County

Status:
An official minority of China

Language:[2] Sino-Tibetan, Tibeto-Burman, Burmese-Lolo, Burmish, Lolo, Minchia

Dialects (4): Dali, Jianchuan, Lanbi, Bijiang

Literacy: 59%

Religion: Mahayana Buddhism, Polytheism, Daoism, Christianity

Christians: 50,000

Scripture: None

***Jesus* film:** None

Gospel Recordings:
Bai: Dali #04699

Christian Broadcasting: None

ROPAL code: PIQ00

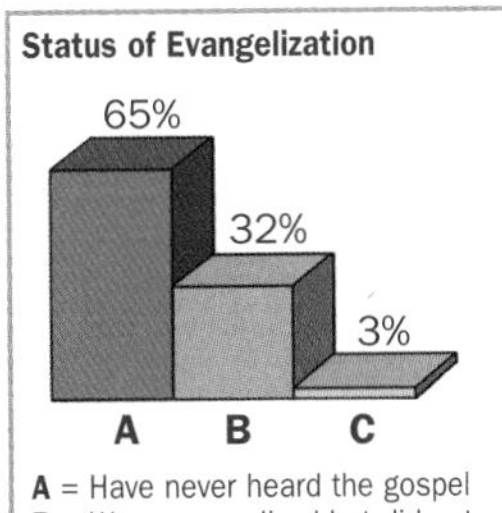

A = Have never heard the gospel
B = Were evangelized but did not become Christians
C = Are adherents to any form of Christianity

Location: More than 1.5 million Bai were counted in the 1990 Chinese census. Yunnan was devastated by the plague, which began in Dali and lasted from 1812 to 1903. The population of Yunnan was reduced from eight million to three million, and the population of the Bai was severely cut. The Bai live primarily in the Dali Prefecture in central Yunnan. Dali has been continuously inhabited for 3,000 years. More than 120,000 Bai are located in Guizhou Province.[3] Smaller numbers of Bai also live in Sichuan and Hunan provinces.[4]

Identity: The Bai are one of the most heavily Sinicized of China's 55 official minorities. Although the Chinese acknowledge two separate branches of Bai — the Lemo and Nama[5] — the Bai scarcely qualify as an ethnic minority. "During the 1940s... the Bai people denied their non-Chinese origin and would show offense if regarded as a minority."[6] Various experts have commented, "The Bai like to be called Chinese."[7] "The Bai nationality as an ethnic label was unknown to the Bai themselves until late 1958,"[8] and were"not quite a minority, but not quite Chinese either."[9]

Language: In the eighth century the Bai possessed their own script, *Baiwen*, which expressed Bai words by means of Chinese characters. This script is now extinct. Sixty percent of Bai vocabulary is Chinese.[10] There are four Bai dialects, all of which "could be separate languages."[11]

History: The Bai partly established the powerful, far-reaching Nanzhao Kingdom which was centered south of Dali. The kingdom grew so strong that they were able to defeat the Tang armies in the mid-700s. The kingdom flourished for 400 years until it collapsed in the tenth century and was replaced by the Kingdom of Dali. Dali, in turn, lasted until AD 1252 when it was overrun and destroyed by the all-conquering Mongol armies.

Customs: During the 30 centuries the Bai have inhabited Dali, they have gradually been assimilated to Chinese culture. Dali has always been famous for its prolific supply of marble, which gave the people their name (*Bai* means "white" in Chinese). Some of the marble used in the great Taj Mahal of India was obtained in Dali and transported over the Himalayas. A survey conducted in 1987 showed Dali Prefecture, mainly due to inbreeding, had 150,000 mentally and physically disabled inhabitants, including dwarfs.[12]

Religion: The Bai are followers of Mahayana Buddhism, unlike other Buddhist groups in Yunnan such as the Tai Lu, Tai Mao, Wa, De'ang, and Bulang who are Theravada Buddhists.

Christianity: George Clarke of the China Inland Mission was the first missionary to the Bai, arriving in 1881. Recent estimates of Bai Christians include figures of 20,000,[13] 30,000,[14] and 50,000.[15] Most of the Bai believers live in rural areas in the mountains and in Fugong County to the west.[16] Most Bai, however, have yet to receive an intelligible gospel witness. The words of John Kuhn 50 years ago remain true today, "No wide-spread work of evangelization will ever be done among them until the message is taken to them in the Minchia [Bai] tongue."[17]

Paul Hattaway

Baihong 白宏

Location: The Baihong "have a larger population" among the various Hani subgroups in China.[1] The Baihong live over a widespread area between Mojiang and Yuanjiang counties in southern Yunnan Province. Almost 200,000 Baihong live in villages that are "situated halfway up the mountain, shrouded by clouds and mists. Their houses are made of earthen walls and thatched roofs sloping down on four sides."[2]

Identity: The Baihong are one of many people groups combined by the government to form the official Hani nationality in China. The Baihong were formerly named *Mahei* — which is the name they are still listed under in most mission publications today.[3]

Language: Baihong is one of at least five different Hani languages in Mojiang (Ink River) County alone.[4] One visitor to the region "learned that there were around 14 different Hani dialect groups in just one area."[5] Most of these dialects are mutually unintelligible. Linguist David Bradley places the Baihong language in the Hao-Bai branch of the Tibeto-Burman language family and notes that fewer than 80,000 Baihong are still able to speak their language.[6]

History: The Baihong belong to a large historical group who are thought to have migrated from the Tibetan Plateau about 2,500 years ago. Legend says the ancestors of the Baihong, at that time numbering 7,000 households, "once lived on a vast fertile plain away in the east where the sun rises."[7] The importance of preceding generations of Baihong is recognized by their saying, "With a strand of hair from each ancestor, one would have to hold nine handfuls of hair."[8]

Dwayne Graybill

Customs: One visitor to the Baihong noted, "The dress of the women here is quite an unusual style. I saw a Baihong woman wearing short, tight pants and attached to her back was a piece of blue cloth about one foot long decorated with silver balls. As she moved, the cloth waved in the air, looking, when seen from a distance, for all the world like a tiny funny tail."[9] They call this "armor." If armor is not worn by a Baihong woman she is considered indecent.

Religion: Because all Baihong youth have been educated in atheistic schools, most are not religious. Traditionally, however, the Baihong were animists. They believe spirits dwell in trees, water, mountains, and the sky. They believe that some of these spirits guard their villages, while others are bad spirits that bring disease and suffering. This has led to a complex set of superstitions and beliefs among the Baihong. For example, they are careful not to strike their hands together while washing because they do not want to offend the spirit of the water.

Christianity: Some Baihong have heard the gospel from the neighboring Kado and Biyo, whose languages are related to the Baihong. As a result, there are some Baihong Christians today. Other Baihong who live in remote communities have yet to be visited by evangelists. The believers among the Baihong have at times encountered severe persecution from the local authorities, who are eager to arrest the spread of Christianity in their areas. Gospel recordings were recently produced in the Baihong language for the first time.

Population in China:
150,000 (1987)
194,600 (2000)
239,200 (2010)
Location: Yunnan
Religion: Animism
Christians: 5,000

Overview of the Baihong

Countries: China

Pronunciation: "Bai-hong"

Other Names: Mahei, Mahe, Mabe, Pai-hung, Buku, Boo Koo

Population Source: 150,000 (1987 AMO); Out of a total Hani population of 1,253,952 (1990 census)

Location: *S Yunnan:* Between Mojiang County in Honghe Prefecture and Yuanjiang County in Yuxi Prefecture

Status: Officially included under Hani

Language: Sino-Tibetan, Tibeto-Burman, Burmese-Lolo, Southern Lolo, Akha, Hao-Bai

Dialects (3): Mahei, Eshan, Woni

Religion: Animism, Polytheism, Christianity, No Religion

Christians: 5,000

Scripture: None

***Jesus* film:** None

Gospel Recordings: Hani: Bukong #04853

Christian Broadcasting: None

ROPAL code: HOW01 (Baihong); MJA00 (Mahei)

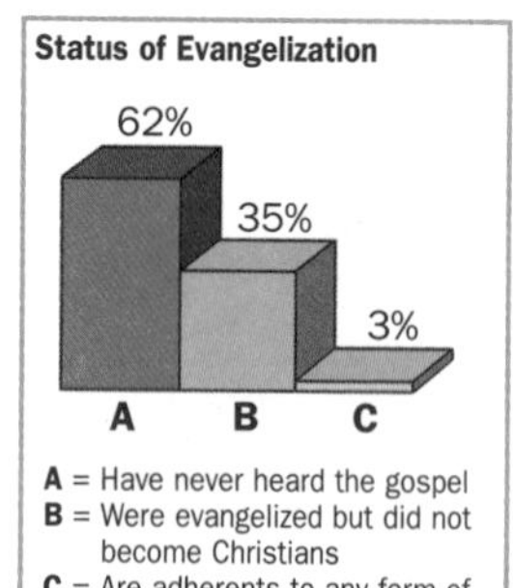

Baima 白马

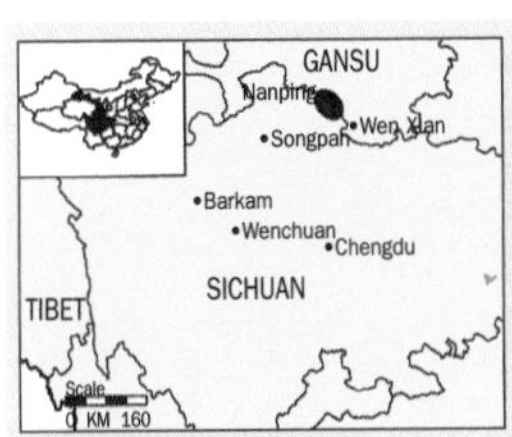

Population in China:
10,000 (1984)
13,700 (2000)
16,900 (2010)
Location: Gansu, Sichuan
Religion: Animism
Christians: None Known

Overview of the Baima

Countries: China

Pronunciation: "Bai-ma"

Other Names: Di, White Horse Tibetans, Pe, Pingwu Tibetans

Population Source:
10,000 (1984 Wong How-Man); Out of a total Tibetan population of 4,593,330 (1990 census)

Location:
SW Gansu: Wenxian County along the Baimajiang Valley, 25km southwest of Wenxian Township; *N Sichuan:* Nanping, Pingwu, and Wenchuan counties

Status:
Officially included under Tibetan

Language: Sino-Tibetan, Tibeto-Burman, Bodic, Unclassified

Dialects: 0

Religion: Animism, Shamanism

Christians: None known

Scripture: None

***Jesus* film:** None

Gospel Recordings: None

Christian Broadcasting: None

ROPAL code: BQH00

Status of Evangelization

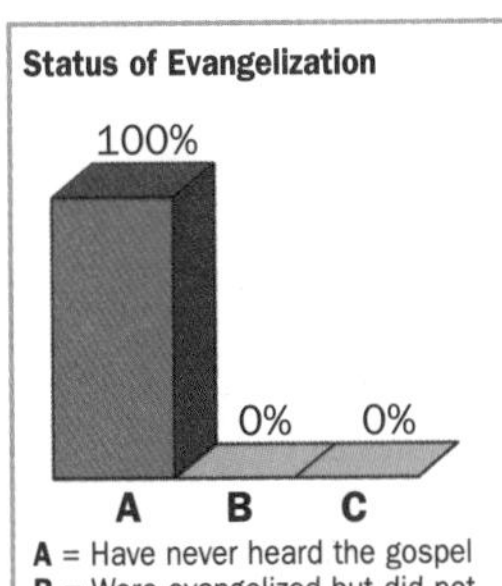

A = Have never heard the gospel
B = Were evangelized but did not become Christians
C = Are adherents to any form of Christianity

Midge Conner

Location: Approximately 13,700 Baima people live in 14 villages along the Baima (White Horse) Valley, on both sides of the Sichuan-Gansu provincial border. Several recent publications have claimed a Baima population of 110,000, but such a high figure is incorrect.[1] Baima villages are accessible from the town of Wenxian in Gansu Province — 32 kilometers (20 mi.) away.

Identity: The Baima have been counted as part of the Tibetan nationality, but they are clearly a distinct ethnic group who have little to do with Tibetans. They speak their own language, wear their own distinct dress, proudly maintain their own traditions and culture; and perhaps most conclusively of all, they have never been followers of Tibetan Buddhism.

Language: The Baima language — which has four tones — is an unclassified member of the Bodic linguistic group. It borrows words from both the Chinese and Tibetan languages. One linguist describes Baima as containing "certain lexical characteristics of the ancient Tibetan language."[2]

History: The Baima claim to be descendants of the ancient Di tribe. Chinese records from AD 551 mention that "The Di... are also called Baima."[3] One historian states, "The Baima tribe was the largest tribe of the Di nationality, which lived in Gansu, Sichuan and Shaanxi during the Three Kingdoms Period (AD 220–265)."[4] During the Western Zhou Dynasty (1100–771 BC), considerable numbers of Han Chinese migrated to Gansu to live in mixed communities with the Di.[5] Other groups over the course of history — including one Miao clan more than 2,000 years ago — were banished to the remote mountains where the Baima live today. They may have contributed to the current ethnic makeup of the people groups in the region.[6]

Customs: Before marriage Baima youth are allowed to be sexually active, but once married, fidelity is stressed and divorce is considered a disgrace. After they are married, Baima women wear fishbone necklaces and hats made of goatskin and chicken feathers. The Baima live near the home of China's giant pandas.[7]

Religion: The Baima regard *Lord White Horse* as the greatest of all gods. Baima tombs are topped with small colorful flags, nine flags for a deceased male and seven for a female. It is said that these flags will lead the souls of the dead into heaven. The Baima also regard the rooster as one of their protective gods. They say that at one time enemy troops were preparing to attack a Baima village in the middle of the night. A rooster crowed loudly and woke up the villagers who were then able to repel the attack.[8]

Christianity: The Baima have never been exposed to the gospel. Their cultural, linguistic, and geographic isolation has blocked them off from the rest of the world. Even Chinese gospel radio broadcasts are unable to penetrate the high remote mountains. It is possible that not one individual among them has ever heard the gospel. The Baima are a good choice for a church or agency wanting to focus on a 100% untouched tribe.

Jamin Pelkey

Location: Approximately 20,000 Bai Yi (White Yi) live along the Sichuan-Yunnan border, especially around the town of Panzhihua.

Identity: The Bai Yi are the former slaves of the fearsome Nosu tribe. In the 1950s they were freed by the Communists and the yoke of slavery was broken. Thousands of people who had been enslaved for decades were relocated to the southern Sichuan area. It is important to note this Profile only refers to those slaves who banded together to form their own communities after their liberation, and not to the lower class of Yi also formerly known as the *White Yi*. These latter White Yi have seen their low status gradually vanish. Today they are virtually indistinguishable from the *Black Yi*, the former ruling class. The Bai Yi speak a different language from the many other groups called "Bai Yi" in southern China.

Language: The Bai Yi speak a mixed language containing words from both the Chinese and Yi languages.

History: Until the 1950s, Nosu tribesmen regularly raided Chinese villages and seized the inhabitants to use them for slave labor. The Bai Yi, many of whom are a Yi-Han ethnic mix, are the descendants of these slaves. Samuel Clarke was one of the first to document their plight in 1911: "It is not uncommon to meet Chinese slaves, boys and girls, in Nosu families. They have either been kidnapped and sold, or their parents, unable to nourish them, have bartered them in exchange for food.... The masters have absolute control over them.... The girl slave he marries to other men's male slaves. The lot of these unfortunate people is hard beyond description. Being looked upon as of little more value than the cattle they tend... the cruel beatings and tortures they have endured have completely broken their spirit, and now they seem unable to exist apart from their masters. Very seldom will any of them try to escape, for no one will give them shelter, and the punishment awarded to a recaptured slave is so severe as to intimidate the most daring.... These poor creatures are born in slavery, married in slavery, and die in slavery."[1]

Customs: The Bai Yi could scarcely believe it when they were liberated from the grip of the Nosu. One former slave explained, "In the beginning... everyone was skeptical and refused to believe the *ganbu's* [cadre's] promises to end slavery. But then a few who dared to run away from their masters were protected by the *ganbu* and allowed to start new lives. Word got around, and eventually we all became free."[2]

Religion: The Bai Yi contain a mixture of polytheists, animists, and atheists.

Christianity: In the past a few Nosu slave owners who became Christians "changed their slaves into tenants, thus showing the way to the solution of this difficult problem."[3] Missionaries were barred from speaking to the slaves and saw no hope for their conversion. One wrote, "Of the Nosu there are some believers.... Of the serfs — well, what chance has a slave, anyway."[4] There are presently only a handful of known Bai Yi believers.

Population in China:
20,000 (1995)
22,500 (2000)
28,300 (2010)
Location: Sichuan, Yunnan
Religion: Polytheism
Christians: 10

Overview of the Bai Yi

Countries: China

Pronunciation: "Bai-Yee"

Other Names: White Yi, Baiyi

Population Source: 20,000 (1995 AMO); Out of a total Yi population of 6,572,173 (1990 census)

Location: *S Sichuan:* Liangshan Prefecture, near Panzhihua; *N Yunnan*

Status: Officially included under Yi

Language: Sino-Tibetan, Tibeto-Burman, Burmese-Lolo, Lolo, Northern Lolo, Yi, Northern Yi

Dialects: 0

Religion: Polytheism, Animism, Ancestor Worship, No Religion

Christians: 10

Scripture: None

***Jesus* film:** None

Gospel Recordings: None

Christian Broadcasting: None

ROPAL code: None

Status of Evangelization

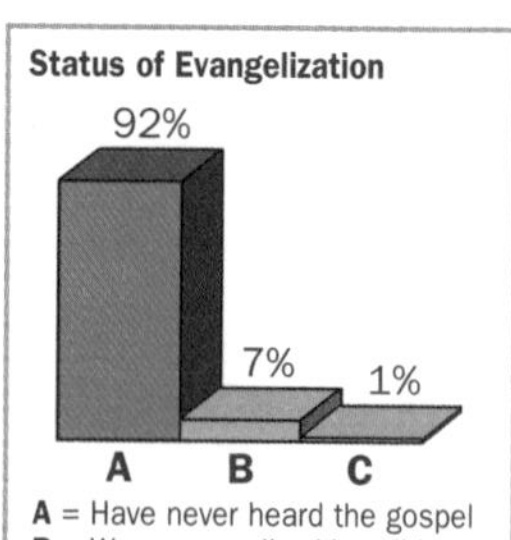

A = Have never heard the gospel
B = Were evangelized but did not become Christians
C = Are adherents to any form of Christianity

Ban Yao 办瑶

Location: Approximately 30,000 Ban Yao live in southwest China. The Ban Yao are the smallest of the three Yao groups (totaling 154,700) located in Yunnan Province.[1] The Ban Yao live in the extreme southeastern arm of Yunnan and in adjacent areas of southwest Guangxi. They are noted for living at the top of verdant mountains throughout the area. Being a people who stubbornly keep to themselves and resist all pressure to change, they do not often appear in the market towns on the plain.

Identity: The Ban Yao are officially considered part of the large Yao minority group. Although they recognize historical kinship with the Yao peoples, the Ban Yao now have their own customs, dress, and language. They are unable to use their own language to communicate with other Yao groups in Yunnan, and must speak Chinese to communicate.

Language: Little research has been conducted into the Ban Yao language to see how it relates to other members of the Hmong-Mien linguistic family. The Ban Yao live in scattered communities, and so dialect variation is likely.

History: Military campaigns were waged by the Chinese during the Hong Wu (1368–1398) and the Jia Qing (1522–1566) periods of the Ming Dynasty, causing the Ban Yao to migrate to their present location. The campaigns were often launched because the Yao refused to pay taxes. They claimed that they were once granted Imperial privilege to avoid taxes from generation to generation, a fact clearly enshrined in their special document, *The King Ping's Charter*, or *The Register for Crossing the Mountains.*

Paul Hattaway

Customs: Until recently, a young Ban Yao man wishing to take a wife had to pay a price for her. Betrothal was therefore little more than a negotiation of the bride-price. The price was divided into three different levels, 72, 60, and 48 ounces of silver, depending on the beauty and health of the young woman.[2] The young woman's parents kept their daughter until the price had been paid in full, in case the young man might refuse to pay after having "received the goods." Some Ban Yao share communal family homes with many of their relatives. The oldest living male is considered the head of the household.

Religion: The Ban Yao are primarily worshipers of nature and the spirits that they believe control it. They believe demons dwell inside large mountains, and the fate of people's lives is linked to whether the spirits are pleased with them or not.

Christianity: There are no known Christians among the Ban Yao, although about 20% are aware of the gospel through the witness of the small number of Hmong and Han believers who live in Funing County. Evangelization of the Ban Yao is difficult because of their isolation and independent mind-set. They are relatively closed to change; decisions are made at a community level, not individually. No Scriptures exist for the Ban Yao because they do not possess a written language. The Ban Yao have lived and died for centuries without knowledge of Christ.

Population in China:
25,000 (1996)
27,900 (2000)
36,000 (2010)
Location: Yunnan, Guangxi
Religion: Animism
Christians: None Known

Overview of the Ban Yao

Countries: China
Pronunciation: "Bahn-Yaow"
Other Names: Ban, Ban Mien
Population Source:
25,000 (1996 AMO);
Out of a total Yao population of 2,134,013 (1990 census)
Location:
SE Yunnan: Funing County;
SW Guangxi: Napo County
Status:
Officially included under Yao
Language: Hmong-Mien, Mienic
Dialects: 0
Religion: Animism, Polytheism, Ancestor Worship
Christians: None known
Scripture: None
***Jesus* film:** None
Gospel Recordings: None
Christian Broadcasting: None
ROPAL code: None

Status of Evangelization

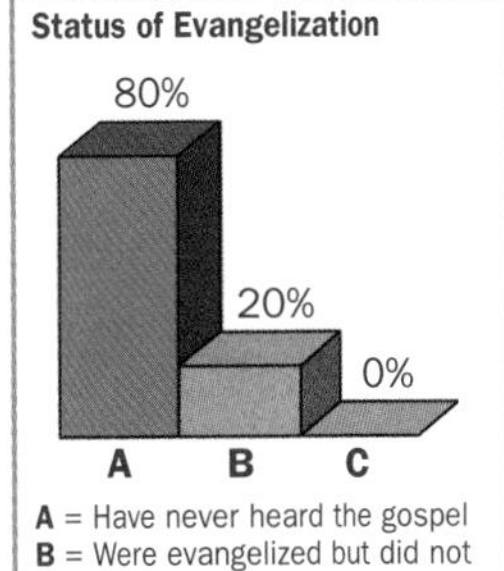

A = Have never heard the gospel
B = Were evangelized but did not become Christians
C = Are adherents to any form of Christianity

Baonuo 保诺

Population in China:
16,476 (1982)
25,080 (2000)
32,350 (2010)
Location: Guizhou, Guangxi
Religion: Polytheism
Christians: 20

Overview of the Baonuo

Countries: China

Pronunciation: "Baow-nuoh"

Other Names: Baiku, Baiku Yao, White Pants Yao, Na Klao, Nao Gelao, Nao Klao,White Trouser Yao, Pou Nuo

Population Source: 16,476 (1982 census); Out of a total Yao population of 2,134,013 (1990 census)

Location: *SE Guizhou:* Yaoshan Township of Libo County; *N Guangxi:* Nandan, Hechi, and Tian'e counties

Status: Officially included under Yao

Language: Hmong-Mien, Hmongic, Bunuic, Naoklao

Dialects: 0

Religion: Polytheism, Animism, Ancestor Worship, Christianity

Christians: 20

Scripture: None

***Jesus* film:** None

Gospel Recordings: Yao: Bai Ku

Christian Broadcasting: None

ROPAL code: BWX04

Status of Evangelization

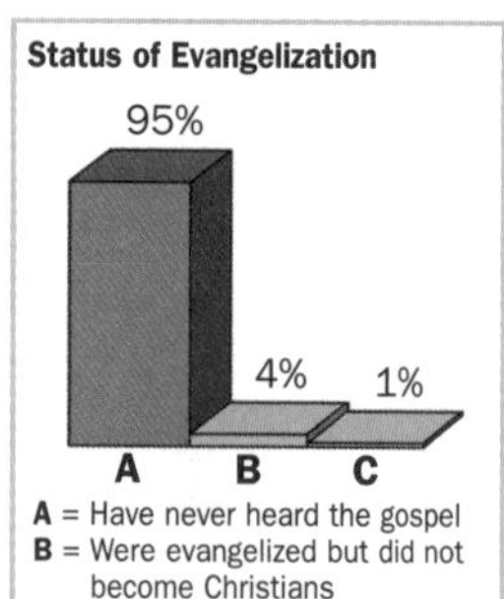

A = Have never heard the gospel
B = Were evangelized but did not become Christians
C = Are adherents to any form of Christianity

Location: The Baonuo are the largest Yao group in Guizhou Province. More than 10,000 are located in Libo County in the southern part of the province. Guizhou contained a total of 19,400 Yao people in 1990.[1] In addition, about 10,000 Baonuo inhabit the mountains of Nandan, Hechi, and Tian'e counties in the northern part of the Guangxi Zhuang Autonomous Region.

Identity: The Baonuo are commonly called *Baiku Yao* (White Pants Yao) by the Chinese. They are so named because the men wear white trousers. Far from being different merely because of their clothing, however, the Baonuo also possess their own ethnicity and speak their own distinct language.

Language: The Chinese officially classify Baonuo as a dialect of the Bunu language, but it is mutually unintelligible with any of the other Bunu varieties. The majority of Baonuo can only speak their own language and do not understand Chinese.

History: The Baonuo have this fascinating account of why they wear their distinctive clothing: A tribal headman once sent troops to attack the Baonuo's villages, intending to exterminate them. The Baonuo king led his troops out in battle to resist the invasion. "The headman's armies were stronger and drove the Baiku [Baonuo] back into the mountains. The king himself was severely wounded. Being trapped in the mountains with no escape, an old villager pointed out a path on the cliff which led down the mountains. When the king heard this he was overjoyed, and happily slapped his knees. His two bleeding hands left five-fingered bloody hand-prints on both his trouser legs. While breaking through the enemy troops, his trouser legs below the knees were torn to shreds. The king eventually died from his wounds, but the Baiku [Baonuo] commemorate him by wearing knee-length trousers with bloody hand-prints sewn in with red yarn."[2]

Customs: On the back of Baonuo women's blouses are square patterns representing King Pan's agreement with the Chinese to release the Yao from having to pay tax. The Baonuo say they were once cannibals. When someone died, they cut the corpse up and ate it. Since the suggestion of a small boy named Laga, who could not bear to see his own mother eaten, the Baonuo have killed a bull instead.[3]

Religion: At funerals the Baonuo hold a traditional bull-beheading ceremony. "Thirty or more brass drums are hung from a frame. The Baiku [Baonuo] consider their brass drums sacred. They are normally hidden away except for special occasions. An offering of wine, meat, rice and water is performed by the head of the family.... After the drum beating a large water buffalo is beheaded, with four or five strokes of sharp knives."[4]

Christianity: The Baonuo are an isolated and primitive people, most of whom have never heard of the name of Jesus, although a small number have believed in Christ in recent years. The Baonuo live in extremely remote villages and are terrified of outsiders. Several foreigners who visited a Baonuo village in the mid-1980s, without prior notice, were stoned to death.[5] Baonuo gospel recordings were first produced in 1999.

Yao Update

Bei 备

Paul Hattaway

Location: Approximately 23,000 people who identify themselves as *Bei* live in Lijiang County in the north central part of Yunnan Province. Lijiang County — home to as many as 26 different tribes[1] — is in a picturesque location with the 5,490-meter (18,000 ft.) Jade Dragon Snow Mountain towering above the Lijiang plain. There were a total of 36,494 members of the Bai nationality in Lijiang County according to the 1990 census.

Identity: Despite sharing an identical historic background with the Bai, those living in Lijiang now sternly insist on being called Bei and have designed a different ethnic dress. Why the Bei are so eager to separate their identity from the Bai is uncertain; but there is no doubt that they view themselves as distinct. One missiologist has said, "Ethnic identity is not so much *in the blood* as it is *in the head* (or *in the heart*) of the subject, or the observer."[2]

Language: The Bei speak a dialect that differs from the standard Bai dialects spoken in Dali Prefecture. Bei — which is a part of the Yi branch of Tibeto-Burman — may be the same as the Jianchuan dialect of Bai.

History: The Bei were a part of the Bai minority group who migrated north about 250 years ago.[3] As late arrivals in the Lijiang area, the Bei were forced to take the worst land on the mountains and to do backbreaking work as manual laborers. The plight of the Bei improved after the Communist victory, when land was redistributed equally to all the inhabitants of Lijiang, regardless of historic ownership. Bei women can often be seen in the busy market in Lijiang, dressed in red and blue sleeveless jackets, topped with a blue and white headdress.

Customs: The Bei are a family-oriented people. Marriages are monogamous and the men lead the families. Their diets are simple, consisting of rice, vegetables, and grain. Bei women do much of the heavy work, hauling baskets of stone attached by a strap to their foreheads. One Western writer who lived among the Bei in the 1940s claimed that among all the peoples of Yunnan they were "closest to Chinese, having adopted the Celestial Civilization almost in its entirety."[4] Many Bei youth today find the Han Chinese culture attractive. Many speak only Mandarin and are not interested in following the customs and religious beliefs of their forefathers.

Religion: The Bei worship Daoist as well as Buddhist deities, although there have never been community temples or an organized religious priesthood among them. The Bei appear to use "whatever works," according to their felt needs.

Christianity: Few Bei have any understanding of the gospel or the Person of Christ. There are a few Naxi believers in Lijiang, but they have yet to reach out to their own people, let alone other groups in the area. In recent years, teams of foreigners have blanketed the Lijiang area with Chinese gospel literature and cassettes; however, apart from scattering some spiritual seed, this seems to have been of little use to people who have no background to or comprehension of Christianity. There are no Scriptures or recordings available in the Bei language.

Population in China:
20,000 (1995)
22,900 (2000)
29,500 (2010)
Location: Yunnan
Religion: Polytheism
Christians: 10

Overview of the Bei

Countries: China
Pronunciation: "Bay"
Other Names: Bai: Lijiang
Population Source: 20,000 (1995 AMO); Out of a total Bai population of 1,594,827 (1990 census)
Location: *Yunnan:* Lijiang County
Status: Officially included under Bai
Language: Sino-Tibetan, Tibeto-Burman, Burmic, Burmese-Lolo, Lolo, Minchia
Dialects: 0
Religion: Polytheism, Animism, Ancestor Worship, No Religion, Buddhism
Christians: 10
Scripture: None
***Jesus* film:** None
Gospel Recordings: None
Christian Broadcasting: None
ROPAL code: None

Beidalao 北大老

Population in China:
15,000 (1990)
19,350 (2000)
24,900 (2010)
Location: Guangxi
Religion: Polytheism
Christians: None Known

Overview of the Beidalao

Countries: China

Pronunciation: "Bay-dah-laow"

Other Names:

Population Source: 15,000 (1995 Wang Fushi – 1990 census);
Out of a total Yao population of 2,134,013 (1990 census)

Location: *N Guangxi:* Rong'an and Rongshui counties

Status:
Officially included under Yao

Language:
Hmong-Mien, Hmongic, Bunuic

Dialects: 0

Religion: Polytheism, Animism, Ancestor Worship

Christians: None known

Scripture: None

***Jesus* film:** None

Gospel Recordings: None

Christian Broadcasting: None

ROPAL code: BWI00

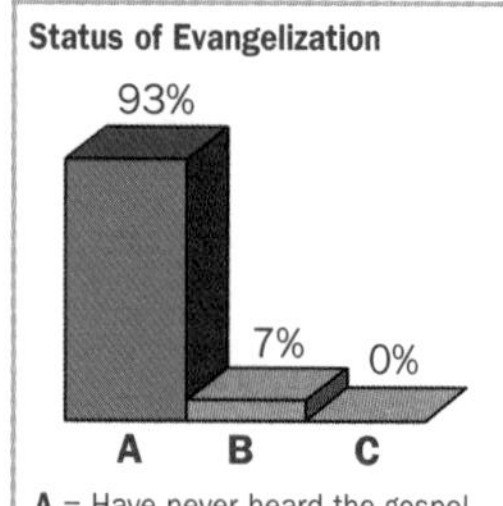

Paul Hattaway

Location: Chinese linguist Wang Fushi (a specialist in the Hmong-Mien languages) listed a 1990 population of 15,000 Beidalao people in southern China.[1] The Beidalao inhabit parts of Rong'an and Rongshui counties in the northern part of the Guangxi Zhuang Autonomous Region. Rong'an and Rongshui are heavily populated by Miao, Dong, Zhuang, and Han Chinese people.

Identity: The Beidalao have only recently been acknowledged by Chinese experts as a subgroup of the Yao minority.[2] They were not noted in the 1982 census, when many of the smaller groups in China registered their names with the authorities. The Beidalao are one of 11 groups of Bunu people in southern China. The Bunu were then included under the Yao nationality by the authorities. Linguist Robert Ramsey explains the complications caused by this classification, "*Yao* is one of the most confused ethnic classifications in China. The many groups known by that name are scattered widely and have been influenced by many diverse peoples; there is very little in all of their cultures that is invariably and unmistakably the same. The 'Yao' call themselves by more than twenty different names."[3]

Language: The Beidalao language has yet to be studied in depth, although the fact that the Chinese have recently added this group as a new "branch" of the Yao implies that they consider them linguistically distinct enough to be a separate group. The Beidalao language is part of the Bunuic branch of the Miao (Hmongic) language family. Because of their ethnically diverse location, it is likely that the Beidalao language has absorbed influences from neighboring languages such as Miao and Dong.

History: Various scholars have speculated on the historical origins of the Yao and Miao peoples (including the Beidalao) who now live scattered across southern China and Southeast Asia. Egon Von Eickstedt has theorized that the Miao-Yao peoples and the Yi were originally part of the same Caucasian group in Central Asia, before they were driven from their homelands by drought in the first millennium BC. After living on the Tibetan Plateau for a time, they were compelled to move again to the empty lands in the south.[4]

Customs: The Beidalao have lost the use of their own customs, and have replaced them with numerous customs and ceremonies borrowed from the peoples alongside whom they have lived for centuries. Even their clothing reflects the Dong and Miao who live in the Rongshui County area.

Religion: Animism and polytheism are the major religions among the Beidalao. They also worship their "close" ancestors to the third or fourth generation. "Distant" ancestors (i.e., more than four generations) are not worshiped regularly but are included at annual ceremonies.

Christianity: The exact status of Christianity among the Beidalao needs to be clarified, but there are very few Christians of any kind in the areas where they live. Mission work prior to 1949 only scratched the surface in northern Guangxi before foreigners were forced to leave China.

Beidongnuo 被动诺

Population in China:
244 (1982)
370 (2000)
480 (2010)
Location: Guizhou
Religion: Polytheism
Christians: None Known

Overview of the Beidongnuo

Countries: China

Pronunciation: "Bay-dong-nuoh"

Other Names: Pei-Tong-Nuo, Changsha Yao, Long Shirt Yao

Population Source:
244 (1982 census);
Out of a total Yao population of 2,134,013 (1990 census)

Location: *S Guizhou:* Libo County

Status:
Officially included under Yao

Language: Hmong-Mien, Hmongic, Bunuic, Naogelao

Dialects: 0

Religion: Polytheism, Animism, Daoism, Ancestor Worship

Christians: None known

Scripture: None

***Jesus* film:** None

Gospel Recordings: None

Christian Broadcasting: None

ROPAL code: None

Status of Evangelization

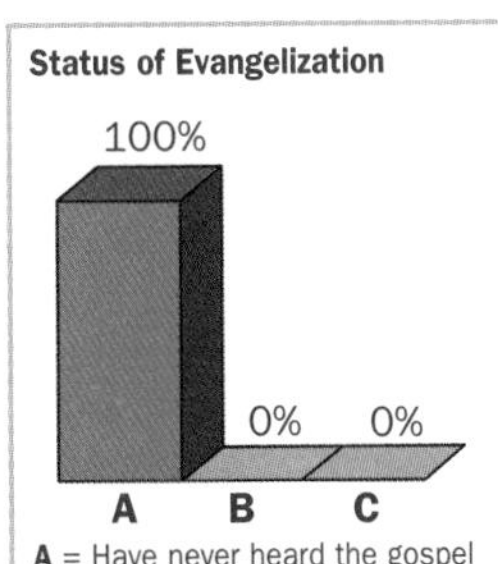

A = Have never heard the gospel
B = Were evangelized but did not become Christians
C = Are adherents to any form of Christianity

Location: When the 1982 Chinese census was conducted, people were asked to name their ethnic group and language. Two hundred and forty-four people answered that they belonged to the Beidongnuo ethnic group. The later 1990 census did not include this question, as people were told to list the official *minzu* that had been assigned to them by the government. The Beidongnuo live in one or two villages in the mountains of Libo County in the southernmost tip of Guizhou Province.[1] Libo is close to the Guizhou-Guangxi provincial border.

Identity: Although they were initially noted in the 1982 census, the Beidongnuo were not granted status as a separate people group. They have since been buried under several artificially constructed layers. Chinese scholars came in and found that the Beidongnuo speak the same language as the Numao, another ethnic group living in Libo County. The Numao (now including the Beidongnuo) were then counted as one of 11 groups of Bunu people. Finally, the Bunu were placed under the Yao nationality, one of China's 55 official minority groups. Because of the government's methods, very few people have ever heard of the Beidongnuo. Even local people in Libo County are not familiar with their name. Although the Beidongnuo may speak the same language as the Numao, they claim they are a different people group and are upset by the government's official classification.

Language: The Beidongnuo language is part of the Naogelao branch of the Bunuic group. Bunuic is part of the Miao (Hmong) language family, distantly related to Miao languages in western Guizhou, Sichuan and Yunnan provinces. Most Beidongnuo women and children cannot speak any Chinese. Most men however, especially those under the age of 40, can speak the local Chinese dialect.

History: The Beidongnuo are believed to have migrated to their present location at least 300 years ago. The remote mountains of Libo County are home to several small unofficial groups including the Mo and the Numao.

Customs: The few Chinese people in the area who are aware of the existence of the Beidongnuo people call them by the nickname *Changsha Yao*, meaning "long shirt Yao." Terms that reflect the clothing of minority groups are commonly given by the Han. The nearby Numao people, for example, are commonly known as the *Heiku* (Black Trouser) Yao.

Religion: The Beidongnuo are polytheistic animists. They worship numerous spirits and deities. Their religious ceremonies also include rituals borrowed from Daoism, including elements of ancestral worship.

Christianity: The tiny Beidongnuo people group have absolutely no knowledge of the gospel or of the existence of Christianity. They are a people who have been effectively hidden away from the outside world for centuries. Pre-1949 missionaries in Dushan (to the north) once listed the *Pei Tong Nuo* as one of the groups in the region, but no outreach was ever undertaken to reach them.

Yao Update

Bela 波拉

Location: Linguist Jerold A. Edmonson estimated a 1992 population of "2,000 to 3,000" Bela in China.[1] Some Bela may also be located across the border in the northern part of Myanmar. Situated near China's western border with Myanmar, the Bela live in Luxi, Yingjiang, and Lianghe counties in Dehong Prefecture — especially Santaishan Township in Luxi County.[2] The Bela live among verdant hills in an area that is experiencing an economic boom because of cross-border trade with Myanmar.

Identity: The Bela have been officially included as part of the Jingpo nationality in China. They wear Jingpo clothing and live among the Jingpo yet consider themselves to be a distinct people. The Bela also speak their own language. According to one researcher, Bela may have been the name used prior to 1949, but the people now call themselves *Laku*.[3]

Language: There are four tones in the Bela language, which is a member of the Yi (Lolo) branch of the Tibeto-Burman linguistic family. Bela is unintelligible with other Jingpo languages and contains loanwords from Chinese, Burmese, Jingpo, and Tai Mao. Bela is not a written language, although the various Jingpo groups have a tale about a script that long ago was given to their ancestors by the *Great Spirit*. It was written on leaves. One day the leaves got wet and were spread out in the sun to dry. When the people were not watching, a buffalo came and ate it. Ever since that time they have been without the Word of God.[4]

Paul Hattaway

History: A large number of people moved into the Dehong area in the sixteenth century, followed by an influx of refugees in 1885 when the British army launched a campaign in the north of Burma.[5] In the past, the Bela were part of a slave system headed by hereditary nobles called *shanguan*. The slaves were not permitted any personal freedom and were forced to work. Slaves were given the family name of their masters. Some managed to escape and formed their own communities in the remote mountains.

Customs: The Bela area is abundant in wild herbs, rubber, tea, coffee, and cotton crops. Most Bela homes are two-level bamboo structures. Bela men were traditionally great hunters when the now extinct leopards, bears, and tigers roamed the forests. The Bela are hard-working agriculturists, usually found tending their long-grain rice fields.

Religion: Although most Bela are aware of the gospel of Christ through the witness of the many strong churches among the neighboring Maru, Lashi, and Jingpo communities, the majority of Bela remain polytheists and animists.

Christianity: In 1986 there were 3,549 baptized Jingpo Christians reported in Dehong, meeting in 71 churches.[6] Approximately 500 of these believers are Bela. J. N. Cushing, in 1876, was the first missionary to work in the China-Myanmar border area. By the time all foreigners were expelled from China in the early 1950s there were numerous churches, medical clinics, and orphanages in the region.

MYANMAR · Tengchong · Baoshan · Dali · YUNNAN · Yingjiang · Luxi · Longling · Longchuan · Lincang · Scale 0 KM 80

Population in China:
3,000 (1992)
3,700 (2000)
4,760 (2010)
Location: Yunnan
Religion: Animism
Christians: 500

Overview of the Bela

Countries: China, possibly Myanmar

Pronunciation: "Bay-la"

Other Names: Pela, Pala, Bola, Polo, Bula, Laku, Pola

Population Source: 2,000 to 3,000 (1992 J. Edmonson); Out of a total Jingpo population of 119,209 (1990 census)

Location: *W Yunnan:* Santaishan Town of Luxi County in Dehong Prefecture; Also in Yingjiang and Lianghe counties

Status: Officially included under Jingpo

Language: Sino-Tibetan, Tibeto-Burman, Burmese-Lolo, Lolo, Unclassified

Dialects: 0

Religion: Animism, Polytheism, Christianity

Christians: 500

Scripture: None

***Jesus* film:** None

Gospel Recordings: None

Christian Broadcasting: None

ROPAL code: BEQ00

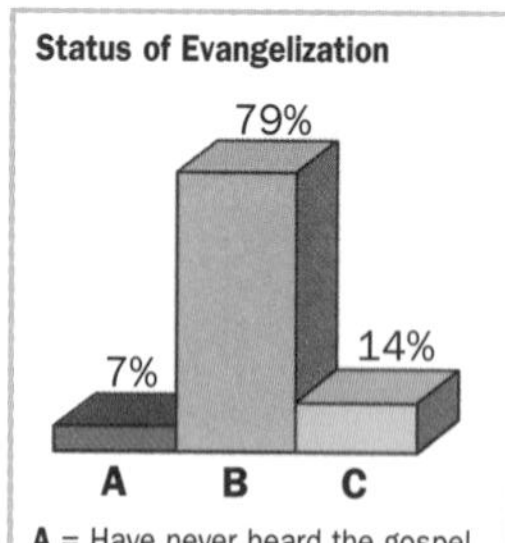

Ben 本人

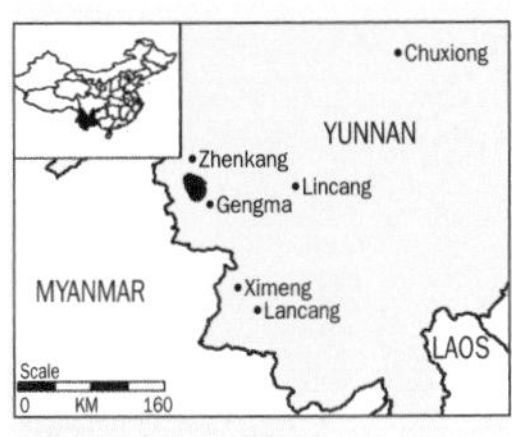

Population in China:
1,000 (1995)
1,120 (2000)
1,360 (2010)
Location: Yunnan
Religion: Animism
Christians: None Known

Overview of the Ben

Countries:
China, possibly Myanmar

Pronunciation: "Ben"

Other Names: Ben Ren

Population Source:
1,000 (1995 AMO);
Out of a total Wa population of 351,974 (1990 census)

Location: *W Yunnan:* Zhenkang and Gengma counties

Status:
Officially included under Wa

Language: Austro-Asiatic, Mon-Khmer, Unclassified

Dialects: 0

Religion: Animism, Theravada Buddhism

Christians: None known

Scripture: None

***Jesus* film:** None

Gospel Recordings: None

Christian Broadcasting: None

ROPAL code: None

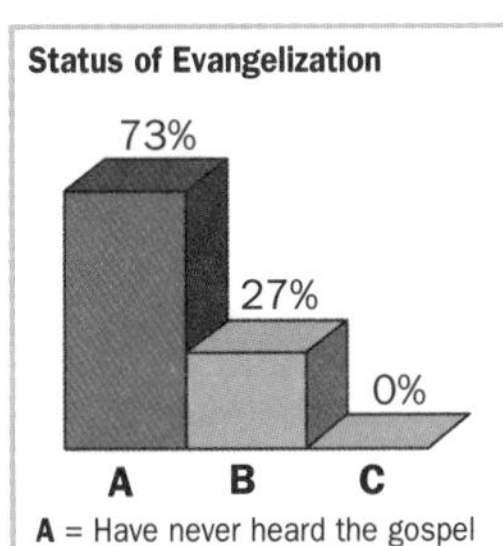

Paul Hattaway

Location: The Ben are a small group, numbering approximately 1,100 people in several villages within Zhenkang and Gengma counties in western Yunnan Province. They live alongside the Wa and Lahu minority groups.

Identity: Although the Ben are a distinct people group, since the 1950s they have been officially counted as part of the Wa nationality. The Ben are not happy with this classification and unsuccessfully applied to be recognized as a distinct minority. Missionary John Kuhn was the first to document the existence of the Ben in 1945, describing them as "a Burmese tribe."[1] The *Ethnologue* describes the Ben as an unidentified group living near the Achang.[2] Another scholar lists the Ben as one of many small groups in China "which need further investigation."[3] The name *Ben* may simply mean "indigenous people."[4]

Language: No extensive research has been conducted into the Ben language. Based on the fact that they have been included under the Wa nationality, it is likely they speak a language from the Mon-Khmer linguistic family — distinct from other Mon-Khmer languages such as De'ang, Wa, and Bulang.

History: The Ben are one of several fragments of the original Mon-Khmer group many centuries ago. One author notes, "The Austro-Asiatics, including the Wa and Palaung [De'ang], spread over Yunnan before the arrival of the Dai and Yi. They were driven out of their original habitat by invaders, dispersed and split into the isolated groups which they are today."[5] Originally the forests where the Ben live were occupied by bears, deer, and wild pigs, but they have now been largely hunted to extinction. Today most Ben grow rice and vegetables.

Customs: The Ben live in a region abundant with natural resources such as coal, copper, iron, lead, and graphite. Young Ben men and women are free to choose their own partners. After the sun sets, a young man will go to the home of the young woman he desires and play musical instruments to win her favor. A few generations ago marriages were arranged by parents, which often led to misery for Ben youngsters. The Ben knew little of hygiene until recently. In 1956 bars of soap were first sold in the district. Many dissatisfied customers returned to the shop demanding a refund, complaining about the soap's awful taste![6]

Religion: The Ben are animists, although they also have traces of Theravada Buddhism from the influence of neighboring groups. Ben funerals are scheduled on Buddhist holy days. The funeral procession is headed by a Buddhist monk who walks at the front of the people and holds a long piece of white cloth tied to the coffin. The Ben believe the monk is leading the soul of the dead person into the next life.[7]

Christianity: There are no known Christians or churches among the Ben; however, many of the neighboring Wa have converted to Christianity. There are no Scriptures available to the Ben who, though numerically small, are an unreached people in desperate need of Christ.

Biao-Jiao Mien 标交敏

Paul Hattaway

Location: Biao-Jiao Mien is a distinct Yao language described as "spoken by about 40,000 people"[1] in an area straddling the Guangxi-Hunan provincial border. The majority of Biao-Jiao Mien are found in Quanzhou and Guanyang counties in northeast Guangxi, as well as in Shuangpai, Lingling, and Daoxian counties in southern Hunan.

Identity: Officially considered part of the large Yao nationality in China, the Biao-Jiao Mien group is not the same as the Biao Mien — another Yao group which has been profiled separately in this book.

Language: A Yao script based on the Roman alphabet was introduced by the government in 1983 but has never caught on in the hearts of the Biao-Jiao people, due in part to the lackluster efforts of schools to teach the script. Also, the linguistic diversity between the dozens of different Yao languages and dialects does not enable a common script to be used over a widespread area. Some sources list Ao Biao as a dialect of Biao-Jiao Mien.

History: The Biao-Jiao Mien migrated to their present locations in Guangxi and Hunan at least several hundred years ago. They found the best land had already been taken and were forced to locate near the summits of mountains. Although most Yao people acknowledge some historical affinity with each other, there are ethnic tensions between some of the groups. Some groups like the Biao-Jiao Mien have little to do with other Yao groups and would never consider intermarriage with them.

Customs: The Biao-Jiao Mien are extremely poor people. Some families have walked off their farms in recent years to join the mass of unemployed workers seeking jobs in China's major cities. The Biao-Jiao Mien construct their villages on flat land near river banks. Their homes are built with brick and wood. Most villages contain 20 to 50 households.

Religion: The Biao-Jiao Mien are one of a small number of non-Han Chinese peoples in China who predominantly adhere to Daoism. Daoism, called *Dao-Jiao* in Chinese, is the only true "home-grown" religion of China. Founded around 604 BC by a mystical figure named *Laozi*, Daoism is a belief that spiritual power is the force of the universe and the order behind all life.

Christianity: The Biao-Jiao Mien, and all other Yao groups in China, are unreached and unevangelized. There are no Scriptures available in a language that the Biao-Jiao Mien can comprehend. The situation in Guangxi seems to have remained unchanged since the 1920s, when one observer lamented, "If we draw a line across the map... we will find by far the greater half of the province, has, as yet, no established Christian work. In these neglected regions there are 58 cities, 700 market towns, and over 17,000 villages, all teeming with human lives for whom no effort whatever is being put forth. The great majority of the inhabitants of these unoccupied sections are aborigines."[2]

Population in China:
40,000 (1991)
50,400 (2000)
65,000 (2010)
Location: Guangxi, Hunan
Religion: Daoism
Christians: None Known

Overview of the Biao-Jiao Mien

Countries: China

Pronunciation: "Beeaow-Jeeow-Mee-en"

Other Names: Biao Chao, Dongshan Yao

Population Source: 40,000 (1991 Pan Chenqiang); Out of a total Yao population of 2,134,013 (1990 census)

Location: *NE Guangxi:* Quanzhou and Guanyang counties; *S Hunan:* Lingling, Shuangpai, and Daoxian counties

Status: Officially included under Yao

Language: Hmong-Mien, Mienic, Biao-Jiao

Dialects: 0

Religion: Daoism, Animism, Polytheism

Christians: None known

Scripture: None

***Jesus* film:** None

Gospel Recordings: None

Christian Broadcasting: None

ROPAL code: BJE00

Status of Evangelization

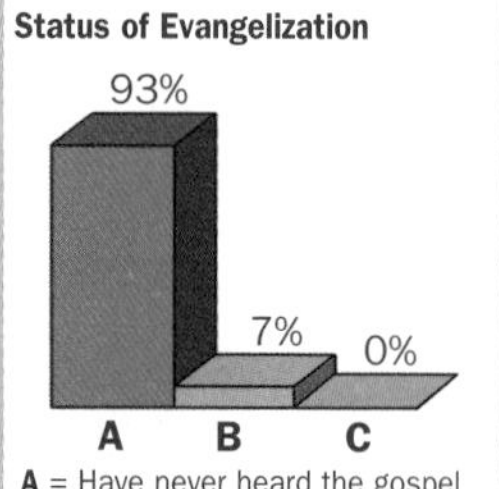

A = Have never heard the gospel
B = Were evangelized but did not become Christians
C = Are adherents to any form of Christianity

Biao Mien 标敏

Location: In 1993 the 21,500 Biao Mien were located in southern China.[1] Lush mountains and rushing waterfalls throughout Ruyuan County in northern Guangdong Province decorate the home of the Biao Mien. Geographically, they are one of the closest minority groups to the cities of Hong Kong and Guangzhou. Numerous other Yao, or Mien, groups are scattered throughout Laos, Vietnam, and Thailand, but the Biao Mien language is only spoken in China.

Identity: Although the Biao Mien are part of the large Yao nationality in China, they speak their own distinct language which is not understood by other Yao groups. This Profile deals only with the Biao Mien language group in northern Guangdong Province. Another group in neighboring Guangxi Province, also called *Biao Mien*, has been included in this book under their alternate name, *Biao-Jiao Mien.*

Language: Various linguists have classified the Yao languages of China in different ways. Pan Chengqian describes Biao Mien as one of four main Yao languages in China.[2] The *Encyclopedic Dictionary of Chinese Linguistics* lists Biao Mien as a dialect of a larger Biao-Jiao Mien group.[3] The *Ethnologue* lists Biao Mien and Biao-Jiao Mien as separate languages.[4] There are 36 consonants in Biao Mien, compared to as few as 18 in other Yao languages.[5]

History: For many centuries, the Biao Mien and other Yao groups have been skilled hunters. The famous Chinese poet Du Fu (712–770) noted that, "the Moyaos shoot wild geese with bows made from mulberry trees."[6] Biao Mien hunters trek for days at a time into the hills and river valleys to track wild pigs, oxen, and deer. In some locations these animals have been hunted to near extinction, and a growing number of Biao Mien have become farmers. Rice cultivation is assisted by the region's abundant rainfall.

Paul Hattaway

Customs: The Biao Mien practice a festival known as *fangniuchulan* (let the cattle out of the stable). For three days every year, starting with the Lantern Festival on the 15th day of the first lunar month, young Biao Mien men and women sing ballads to each other on hill slopes or under trees in order to select their prospective spouses. Young couples who have caught each other's eye sing romantic ballads to each other.

Religion: The Biao Mien adhere to a mixture of religious elements. Daoist, animist, Buddhist, and polytheistic influences can be clearly seen in their rituals. Many of the younger generation of Biao Mien now consider themselves nonreligious and do not participate in any of their parents' rituals.

Christianity: There are only a handful of known Christians among the Biao Mien today. Minimal past mission activity in the region has resulted in very little awareness of the gospel among the Biao Mien today. There is an emerging church among the neighboring Zaomin, but they have not yet conducted outreach to the other groups in the mountains of northern Guangdong Province.

Population in China:
21,500 (1993)
25,800 (2000)
33,300 (2010)
Location: Guangdong
Religion: Daoism
Christians: 20

Overview of the Biao Mien

Countries: China

Pronunciation: "Bee-aow-Mee-en"

Other Names: Biaomin, Jiaogongmian, Biao Mon, Biaoman, Chao Kong Men

Population Source: 21,500 (1996 B. Grimes – 1993 figure); Out of a total Yao population of 2,134,013 (1990 census)

Location: *N Guangdong:* Ruyuan County

Status: Officially included under Yao

Language: Hmong-Mien, Mienic, Mian-Jin

Dialects: 0

Religion: Daoism, Animism, Polytheism, Buddhism

Christians: 20

Scripture: None

***Jesus* film:** None

Gospel Recordings: None

Christian Broadcasting: None

ROPAL code: BMT00; BJE02

Status of Evangelization

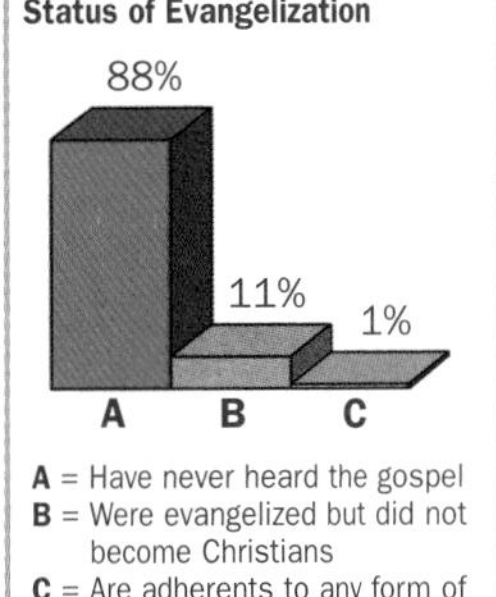

A = Have never heard the gospel
B = Were evangelized but did not become Christians
C = Are adherents to any form of Christianity

Biao Mien, Shikou 标敏(适口)

Population in China:
8,000 (1990)
10,320 (2000)
13,300 (2010)
Location: Guangxi
Religion: Daoism
Christians: None Known

Overview of the Shikou Biao Mien

Countries: China

Pronunciation: "Shee-ko-Beeaow-Jeeaow-Mee-en"

Other Names: Shikou Yao

Population Source: 8,000 (1995 Wang Fushi – 1990 figure); Out of a total Yao population of 2,134,013 (1990 census)

Location: *NE Guangxi:* Gongcheng County

Status: Officially included under Yao

Language: Hmong-Mien, Mienic, Biao-Jiao

Dialects: 0

Religion: Daoism, Animism, Polytheism

Christians: None known

Scripture: None

***Jesus* film:** None

Gospel Recordings: None

Christian Broadcasting: None

ROPAL code: None

Status of Evangelization

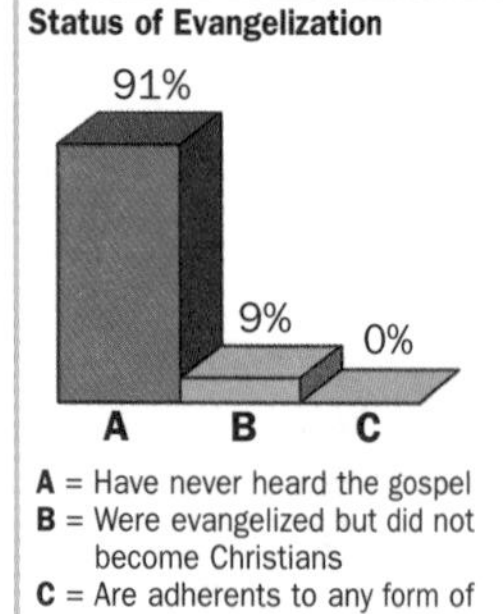

A = Have never heard the gospel
B = Were evangelized but did not become Christians
C = Are adherents to any form of Christianity

Location: More than 10,000 people speaking the Shikou Biao Mien language live in Gongcheng County of the Guangxi Zhuang Autonomous Region. The area is southeast of the large city of Guilin, famous for centuries for its tourist attractions.

Identity: The Shikou Biao Mien are one of 29 groups profiled in this book who comprise the officially constructed Yao nationality in China.

Language: The Shikou language of Biao Mien was recently declared to be a separate language by Chinese scholars. Previously it was classified as a dialect of Biao Mien. The Biao-Jiao Mien language (spoken farther north) is closely related. Most Shikou Biao Mien are bilingual in Chinese, though few apart from the most educated are able to read. Very few minority people in this part of the country have ever attended high school.

History: The various branches of the Yao in China have long been viewed as stubborn and rebellious by the Chinese. The Han viewed tribal groups in two categories: "raw" and "cooked," according to their level of assimilation. The Yao invariably qualified as "raw" people who refused to conform to Chinese culture or rule. Rebellions by the Yao were first mentioned during the reign of the Song Emperor Renzong (1023–1064). "One occurred in Guangdong in 1035, another in Hunan in 1043. There is mention of a rebellion in the Guangzhou region in 1281.... Then there was the famous 1832 Yao rebellion in Hunan, in which the Yao, reacting to theft of cattle and grain by members of the Triad Society, organized an uprising that took several months and armies from three provinces to squelch."[1] Many Yao uprisings occurred because of the Yao's refusal to pay taxes. In many ways the Chinese authorities gave up trying to "civilize" the Yao. Even today many communities, including the Shikou Biao Mien speakers, view outsiders with great suspicion and mistrust.

Customs: The Biao Mien in Shikou share many common cultural traits with other Yao groups in southern China, including the Iu Mien. They are hardworking agriculturists, who live in two-story wooden houses located near the summits of high mountains in extremely remote areas. Few Shikou Biao Mien are seen in the townships except on market days when they come down to buy and sell.

Religion: Daoism (formerly spelled Taoism) is the major religious adherence among the Shikou Biao Mien. They have village priests who officiate at organized festivals. The priests chant from sacred Daoist manuals written in Chinese. These priests also act as intermediaries between the people and the spirit world.

Christianity: There is no known Christian presence among the Shikou Biao Mien. Their remote location and isolated mind-set have prevented them from being exposed to the gospel of Jesus Christ. They remain an unreached people group without hope, in this life or eternity to come.

Paul Hattaway

Bisu 比苏

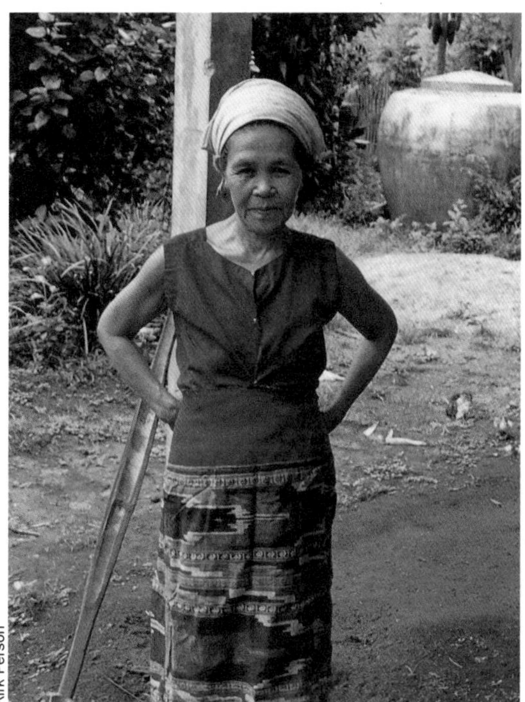

Kirk Person

Location: Seven thousand Bisu live in the southern tip of Yunnan Province. Approximately 1,000 Bisu also inhabit two villages near Chiang Rai in northern Thailand. The Bisu in China live in eight large villages in three different counties of Xishuangbanna Prefecture, including Mengzhe Village of Menghai County; Zhutang, Laba, Donglang, and Fubang villages of Lancang County; and Jingxin, Fuyan, and Nanya villages of Menglian County. A few are also found in Ximeng County. The Bisu are neighbors of the Lahu, Hani, and Dai minority groups.

Identity: The Bisu have been included as part of the Hani nationality in China, yet they firmly hold to their own identity, wear their own distinct dress, and speak their own language. The Bisu in Menghai County are called *Laopin* or *Pin*, while those in Lancang and Menglian call themselves *Laomian*. This suggests possible ethnolinguistic differences between the two areas.

Language: The Bisu language — which has three tones — is part of the Tibeto-Burman language family and is closely related to the Mpi, Pyen, and Phunoi languages spoken in Laos and Myanmar. Bisu is reported to have 36% lexical similarity with Hani, 32% with Lahu and 31% similarity with Lisu.[1] Among some Bisu communities there are dialect differences. Some Bisu use Dai loanwords while the Bisu living in other areas have adopted many Lahu loanwords.

History: The Bisu share a common history with a larger group of related peoples, including the Mpi, Phunoi, and Pyen in the adjoining areas of Laos and Myanmar. Bisu history has been one of harassment and persecution at the hands of neighboring groups. The 1,000 Bisu in northern Thailand migrated south along the Mekong River from either Yunnan or Laos earlier this century, encountering hostile peoples wherever they went. Today the Bisu are despised by both the Chinese and Thai majorities who call them a host of derogatory names.

Customs: Most aspects of Bisu village life revolve around their zealous appeasement of evil spirits. No sacrifice is spared in an effort to keep peace with the demanding demons. This traps the Bisu in dire poverty, as numerous valuable livestock are wasted in needless sacrifices.

Religion: Few groups seem to be so serious in their devotion and so bound in their fear of evil spirits as the Bisu. Every part of the Bisu culture includes spirit appeasement. The Bisu desire to live at peace and believe that ignoring the demons' demands will result in suffering, sickness, and disaster.

Christianity: Few attempts have been made to take the gospel to the Bisu, despite the presence of Lahu and Wa Christians in the vicinity. There are a small number of believers in Menglian County,[2] including a few Bisu, but the majority have absolutely no awareness of the gospel. In Thailand the Bisu have recently invited a Christian family to live in their village and to invent a written script for their language. The handful of Bisu who have embraced Christianity have invariably experienced severe persecution from other Bisu in their communities.[3]

Population in China:
6,000 (1991)
7,380 (2000)
9,260 (2010)
Location: Yunnan
Religion: Animism
Christians: 20

Overview of the Bisu

Countries: China, Thailand, possibly Myanmar

Pronunciation: "Bee-soo"

Other Names: Mbisu, Misu, Mibisu, Mbi, Laopin, Pin, Laomian

Population Source:
6,000 (1991 Li Yongsui);
Out of a total Hani population of 1,253,952 (1990 census);
Less than 1,000 in Thailand (1987 E. Purnell);
Possibly also in Myanmar

Location: *SW Yunnan:* Menghai, Lancang, Menglian, and Ximeng counties

Status:
Officially included under Hani

Language: Sino-Tibetan, Tibeto-Burman, Burmese-Lolo, Lolo, Southern Lolo, Phunoi

Dialects (3): Phadaeng, Tako, Huai Chomphu

Religion: Animism, Polytheism

Christians: 20

Scripture: None

***Jesus* film:** None

Gospel Recordings: None

Christian Broadcasting: None

ROPAL code: BII00

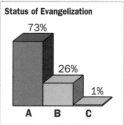

Status of Evangelization

A	B	C
73%	26%	1%

A = Have never heard the gospel
B = Were evangelized but did not become Christians
C = Are adherents to any form of Christianity

Bit 必定

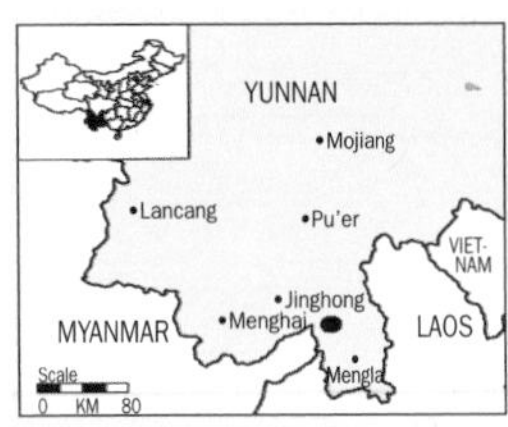

Population in China:
500 (1990)
640 (2000)
830 (2010)
Location: Yunnan
Religion: Animism
Christians: None Known

Overview of the Bit

Countries: Laos, China

Pronunciation: "Bit"

Other Names: Khabit, Phsing, Phsin, Buxin, Buxia, Buxinhua, Bid

Population Source: 500 (1990 J.-O. Svantesson); 1,509 in Laos (1995 census)

Location: *S Yunnan:* Mengla County in Xishuangbanna Prefecture

Status: The Bit are officially included under Khmu, who were counted as an *Undetermined Minority.*

Language: Austro-Asiatic, Mon-Khmer, Northern Mon-Khmer, Khmuic, Khao

Dialects: 0

Religion: Animism, Theravada Buddhism, Ancestor Worship

Christians: None known

Scripture: None

***Jesus* film:** None

Gospel Recordings: None

Christian Broadcasting: None

ROPAL code: BGK00 (Bit); BXT00 (Buxin)

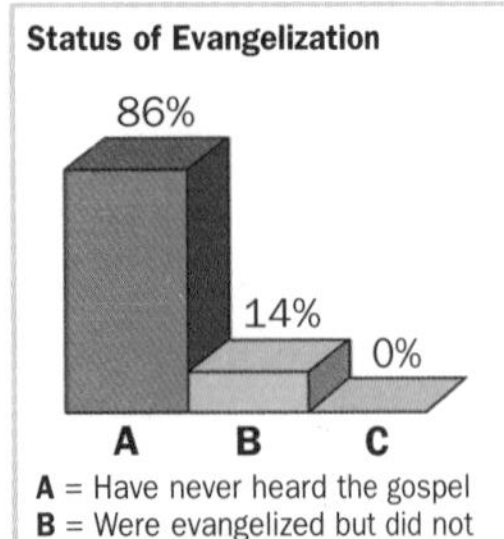

A = Have never heard the gospel
B = Were evangelized but did not become Christians
C = Are adherents to any form of Christianity

Dwayne Graybill

History: The Bit have ethnic relatives in both Laos and Vietnam, yet their language is distinct from the Khmu whom they are counted part of in China. The Khmu claim to be the original inhabitants of Laos, living there before they were driven from the best land by Lao invaders from China during the twelfth and thirteenth centuries.[3]

Customs: Funerals are elaborate affairs for the Bit. The deceased are buried in the mountains. A funeral house is constructed over the grave and is filled with the person's personal items such as a rice basket, drink pipe, bowls, and chopsticks. At the front of the grave a four-to-five-meter (13–16 ft.) pole is erected. A wooden bird and a shirt belonging to the deceased's wife or husband is attached to the top of the pole.

Location: In 1990 just 500 members of the Bit ethnic group were reportedly living in two villages in southern Yunnan province.[1] Approximately three times that number inhabit the forests of northern Laos. The Bit are located within Mengla County in the Xishuangbanna Dai Autonomous Prefecture.

Identity: The identity of the Bit — who are called Buxin by the Chinese — is a complicated matter. The Chinese officially view the Bit as part of the Khmu, but the Khmu do not belong to any of China's official nationalities. They were included in a list of *Undetermined Minorities* in the 1990 national census. In Laos, the Bit were counted separately in the national census of 1995.

Language: The Bit language belongs to the Mon-Khmer linguistic family, although scholars disagree on whether it is part of the Khmuic or Palaungic branch.[2] Bit is related to the Khmu language of Laos and Khao of Vietnam. In Vietnam, where the Khao are better known as *Khang*, they are one of 53 official minorities. The Bit language, which is nontonal, does not have its own orthography. Few older people can speak Chinese, but most people under the age of 40 are bilingual, having been educated in Mandarin.

Religion: The Bit practice a mixture of Theravada Buddhism and animism. They believe a person has five souls. After death, one soul remains in the house; one goes to the fields; one settles in the foot of the tree that was felled to make the coffin; one lives in the funeral home; and the last remaining soul flies to the sky.[4] Missionary William Clifton Dodd, who visited the Mengla area during the first three decades of the twentieth century, described the loose ties the inhabitants of the region feel to the Buddhist religion: "Buddhism presents a well organized front; and although we have yet to hear of any great mass movement of Buddhists into Christianity; yet it is true that Buddhism furnishes many preparations for Christianity. It includes a spirit of religious toleration. Its temples and monastery grounds are hospitable inns. In our tours of evangelistic itineration we habitually sleep in these temples, preach under the nose of the big Buddha, and sing our Christian songs in his ears. Often the abbot and the monks courteously join us in these services."[5]

Christianity: There are no Christian believers among the Bit in China or Laos, although there are many Christians among the related Khmu of northern Laos.

Biyo 碧约

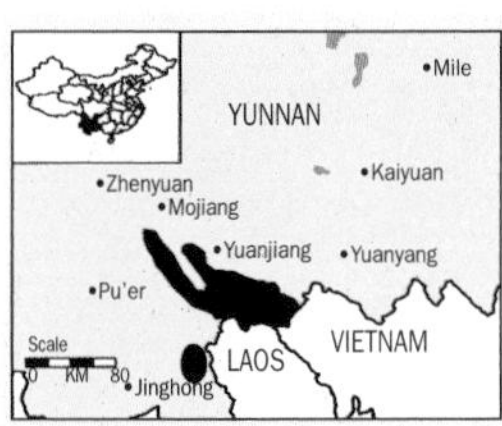

Population in China:
100,000 (1990)
122,900 (2000)
151,000 (2010)
Location: Yunnan
Religion: Animism
Christians: 10,000

Overview of the Biyo

Countries: China, Laos

Pronunciation: "Bee-o"

Other Names: Bio, Biyao, Biyue, Pi-o, Bi, Pi-yueh, Bee Yo

Population Source:
100,000 (1990 J.-O. Svantesson); Out of a total Hani population of 1,253,952 (1990 census); Also in Laos

Location: *S Yunnan:* Mojiang, Jiangcheng, Zhenyuan, and Jingdong counties, and in Xishuangbanna Prefecture

Status:
Officially included under Hani

Language: Sino-Tibetan, Tibeto-Burman, Burmese-Lolo, Lolo, Southern Lolo, Akha, Hani, Bi-Ka

Dialects: 0

Religion: Animism, No Religion, Christianity

Christians: 10,000

Scripture: None

***Jesus* film:** None

Gospel Recordings: None

Christian Broadcasting: None

ROPAL code: BYO00

Status of Evangelization

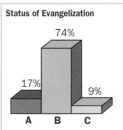

A	B	C
17%	74%	9%

A = Have never heard the gospel
B = Were evangelized but did not become Christians
C = Are adherents to any form of Christianity

Location: Linguist Jan-Olof Svantesson listed a 1990 population of 100,000 Biyo in Yunnan Province.[1] This figure is expected to grow to more than 120,000 by the year 2000. Scattered over a wide area of central and southern Yunnan, the Biyo range as far south as Jinghong County. The majority are located in Mojiang, Jiangcheng, Zhenyuan, and Jingdong counties. All of these areas have recently opened to foreign travelers. A few Biyo are also reported in Laos.[2]

Identity: The Biyo are officially included as part of the Hani nationality. The Hani are a collection of many distinct ethnolinguistic groups. Most Biyo now speak only Mandarin and wear Han clothing. Only Biyo in the mountains and older women in the towns still keep their own ethnicity. A severe racial conflict in the 1960s between the Biyo and Han meant the Biyo "have been so frightened that they dare not go out in their distinctive dress."[3]

Language: The Biyo language is related to Akha and the other Hani languages, but it is distinct and mutually unintelligible with most of them. There are "14 different Hani dialect groups in one area alone."[4] Kado is the closest language to Biyo. In many locations the two groups live beside each other, and many churches contain both Biyo and Kado in their congregations. Biyo has no written script.[5]

History: Originally part of the great Hani-Akha group, the Biyo broke off centuries ago and migrated from western Yunnan to the southern part of the province where they still live today.

Customs: The traditional Biyo women's dress was described as a "dark coat reaching nearly to the knees, open in front with a separate piece of cloth fastened across the breasts.... The skirt consists of one piece of stuff put on round the waist and just tucked in to fasten it. The turban has a long piece of square cloth which is thrown back from the front over the top of the head."[6]

Religion: Most Biyo are either animists or nonreligious, although a significant church is present among the Biyo. The majority of Biyo are aware of Christ.

Christianity: There are approximately 10,000 Biyo Christians who meet in churches with believers from other people groups. Services are conducted in Mandarin. The gospel first came to the Biyo just before Communism in 1949, brought by Danish Assemblies of God missionary Axel Jansen, whose Chinese name was Yan Chung Ren.[7] Bao Zhiyang, a respected Biyo pastor, was also the Communist Party District Deputy. His faithful witness helped the Biyo church survive Communist persecution. It was said, "His word carried ten times more weight than that of the district Party Secretary."[8] The Biyo church even wrote to the central Communist authorities in Beijing, demanding the right to worship freely. Believers often challenged their persecutors by asking, "The district deputy is allowed to keep his faith so why not we?"[9] In 1958 Bao suddenly disappeared and was never seen again, presumably executed.

Dwayne Graybill

Bogol 玻锅炉

Location: The little-known Bogol people live in just one village in the Morindawa Daur Autonomous Banner in the eastern part of Inner Mongolia in northeast China. *Morindawa* is a Mongolian name, from *mori* "horse" and *davaa* "hill."[1] Morindawa — which covers an area of 11,943 square kilometers (4,657 sq. mi.) — is centered in the town of *Nirji* (Prosperous). The region, which has only four frost-free months each year, is watered by the Nonni River and its tributaries: the Gan, Horli, Arong, and Yin.

Identity: The Bogol are the descendants of former slaves of the Daur people. Although they became free in 1908,[2] social and ethnic barriers still exist between the Bogol and Daur. The Daur refuse to intermarry with the Bogol, who have built their own village and developed their own identity. The Bogol do not speak their own distinct language; however, a people group has been defined as "a significantly large ethnic or sociological grouping of individuals who perceive themselves to have a common affinity for one another."[3]

Language: The Bogol speak the local Morindawa dialect of Daur. They do not have their own script, but today most use the Chinese language for writing.

History: In the past the Daur social structure was unique, "being made up of pedigree families, the commoners and the Bogol (reputed to be slaves). The Bogol were comprised from two groups. One group was made up of the descendants of Bardachi who had rebelled against the Qing Dynasty (1644–1911). It ordered that members of the rebelling clan should remain slaves from generation to generation evermore. The second group was made up of the descendants of prisoners-of-war brought in by the Daur army during the Taiping Rebellion. The Daur consider these slaves as members of their own families. They were likely servants. While intermarriage was forbidden, they lacked for nothing in life. In 1908, the slaves of the Daur became free, after which they established a village at the Shiwalt of the Morindawa. Even today intermarriage between the two remains very rare."[4]

Paul Hattaway

Customs: The Bogol observe more Chinese traditions than do the Daur. They enthusiastically celebrate the annual Chinese New Year and Spring festivals.

Religion: The Bogol have a complex collection of gods that must be placated in order to live prosperously. "The Boguol [Bogol] god category includes twenty-four spirits and has two assistants, Keyideng and Maluo. They are represented by a colored painting, his assistants by human figures made of gold foil and by dragon paintings.... They are also represented by wooden images which can reach a height of 11.6 meters [38 feet].... According to old folk tales, when the Daur still lived on the Amur they had only this type of god."[5]

Christianity: Although they were liberated from physical slavery 90 years ago, the Bogol remain in spiritual slavery. Few have ever heard of Jesus Christ or his victory over the powers of darkness that still bind them. There are no known Christians among the Bogol.

RUSSIA
Hailar
Morindawa
MONGOLIA
HEILONGJIANG
Harbin
INNER MONGOLIA
JILIN
Scale 0 KM 400

Population in China:
1,000 (1997)
1,080 (2000)
1,400 (2010)
Location: Inner Mongolia
Religion: Shamanism
Christians: None Known

Overview of the Bogol

Countries: China

Pronunciation: "Bo-gawl"

Other Names: Daur: Bogol, Boguol

Population Source: 1,000 (1997 AMO); Out of a total Daur population of 121,357 (1990 census)

Location: *E Inner Mongolia:* Morindawa Daur Banner

Status: Officially included under Daur

Language: Altaic, Mongolian, Eastern Mongolian, Dagur

Dialects: 0

Religion: Shamanism, Polytheism, No Religion

Christians: None known

Scripture: None

***Jesus* film:** None

Gospel Recordings: None

Christian Broadcasting: None

ROPAL code: None

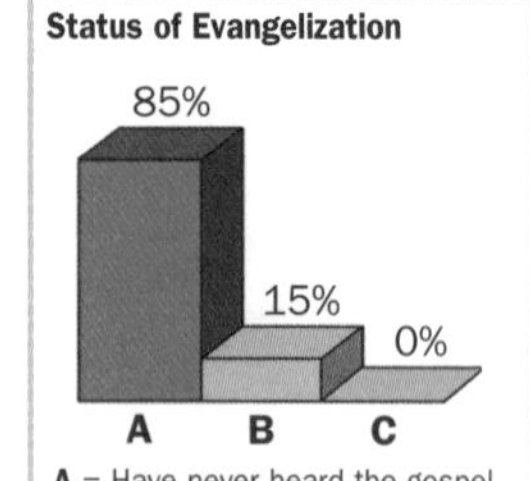

A = Have never heard the gospel
B = Were evangelized but did not become Christians
C = Are adherents to any form of Christianity

Boka 博卡

Population in China:
17,900 (1999)
18,350 (2000)
23,000 (2010)
Location: Yunnan
Religion: Polytheism
Christians: 10

Overview of the Boka

Countries: China

Pronunciation: "Bo-kah"

Other Names: Baka

Population Source:
17,900 (1999 J. Pelkey);
Out of a total Yi population of 6,572,173 (1990 census)

Location: *S Yunnan:* Pingbian County in Honghe Prefecture

Status:
Officially included under Yi

Language: Sino-Tibetan, Tibeto-Burman, Burmese-Lolo, Lolo, Northern Lolo, Yi, Southern Yi

Dialects: 0

Religion: Polytheism, Animism, Ancestor Worship, Christianity

Christians: 10

Scripture: None

***Jesus* film:** None

Gospel Recordings: None

Christian Broadcasting: None

ROPAL code: None

Status of Evangelization

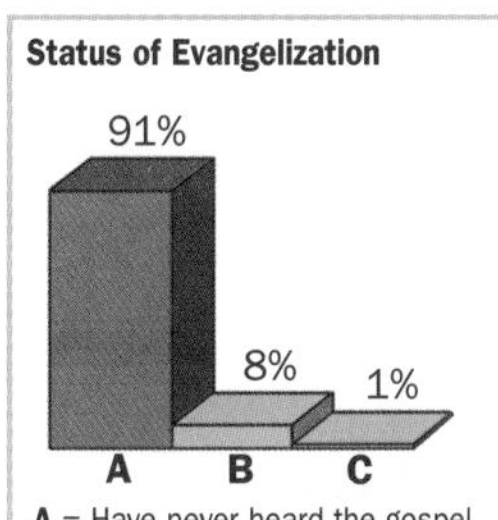

A = Have never heard the gospel
B = Were evangelized but did not become Christians
C = Are adherents to any form of Christianity

Jamin Pelkey

Location: Researcher Jamin Pelkey estimated a 1999 population of 17,900 Boka people in southwest China.[1] They live totally within the Pingbian Miao Autonomous County in Honghe Prefecture of Yunnan Province.

Identity: The Boka are one of more than 100 distinct tribes and people groups that comprise the official Yi nationality in China. The Boka speak their own language which is not mutually intelligible to any of the Yi varieties in the area. They also possess their own unique dress, customs, and festivals.

Language: Boka belongs to the Southern Yi group of Tibeto-Burman. It has only 40% to 50% lexical similarity with Muji and less with Xiuba, two other Southern Yi languages in Pingbian County.[2]

History: The Boka appear to consist of people from more than one historical migration. Most Boka claim to have first arrived in the area after fleeing the chaos of war in Hunan Province more than 1,000 years ago. Their migration route took them through Wenshan Prefecture and into Honghe where they finally settled in Pingbian County. Some Boka people living near Pingbian Township, however, claim to have migrated from Guizhou and Sichuan provinces only about 200 years ago.[3]

Customs: The Boka are skilled at making rice and corn whiskey, which they consume in copious quantities. As soon as a guest enters a Boka home, he or she is offered a bowl of powerful whiskey which the host clasps in two hands as a mark of respect for the guest. To refuse to drink the whiskey is considered a grave insult by the Boka, and a visitor may not be allowed to stay if they cannot offer a good excuse. The Boka have many superstitions relating to preparation of food and eating.

Religion: On certain occasions throughout the year, the polytheistic beliefs of the Boka come to the fore. The Boka set aside the 16th day of the eighth month of the lunar calendar to worship the dragon. Each village has a sacred tree on the outskirts of their village. They believe the tree is home to the spirit of the dragon. The entire village gathers around the tree to offer prayers, incense, and sacrifices. They plead with the dragon to protect them and cause them to prosper in the coming year, and to cause all calamities and disease to stay far from their communities. The Boka living in the northeast corner of Pingbian County "appease the dragon god by placing spicy whiskey on an altar beneath the dragon tree. They then take the whiskey and pour it into a basin in the altar. Having filled the basin they use a hollowed reed and take turns sucking the potent brew from the altar."[4]

Christianity: There are just a few Christians among the unreached Boka people. There are a large number of Catholic Hmong believers in Pingbian County, some of whom have contact and exchanges with believers in France. The only known Yi Christians in Pingbian are about 150 Puwa in Beihe District. They were led to faith in Christ by the Hmong Catholics. The Boka, however, have never been targeted by the gospel. They remain unevangelized and devoid of any Christian witness. There are also no Scriptures or gospel tools available in the Boka language.

Bolozi 玻璃哦子

Paul Hattaway

Location: Between 1,000 and 2,000 Bolozi people live in and around the village of Xiao Heshui, to the west of Songpan in northern Sichuan Province. Smaller numbers live scattered along the Min River as far south as Wenchuan. One early missionary wrote, "In Weizhou [now Wenchuan] most of the people are either Qiang or a mixed race, though there are some... Bolotsze [Bolozi] as well."[1] Another source states, "At Songpan one road goes westward through the Po-lo-tzu [Bolozi] country, one goes northward through the grasslands, and one turns eastward through northern Sichuan."[2]

Identity: The Bolozi may have become a distinct ethnic group as the result of marriage between Tibetans and Qiang people. They were first described by Scottish missionary Thomas Torrance in the 1930s. The Bolozi have been counted as part of either the Tibetan or Qiang nationalities by the Chinese authorities. This classification has caused the Bolozi to be hidden to outsiders. Even among the Bolozi themselves there is a growing tendency to identify themselves as Tibetans. Within a generation or two there may be no remembrance of their distinct ethnic origins.

Language: Little is known about the Bolozi language which may belong to the Qiangic branch of Tibeto-Burman. Most Bolozi men and children are also fluent in Chinese, but many Bolozi women have never been to school and only know their mother tongue.

History: Until the 1960s the Bolozi were renowned for their plundering of other villages. Being a mix of Tibetans and Qiang, the Bolozi were known to have a wild, violent streak. They became the scourge even of other Tibetan communities living in the area. The Bolozi raided communities on horseback, carrying away anything they liked and killing if they so desired. Today they lead a far more peaceable existence, tending to crops and livestock in the green hills of northern Sichuan.

Customs: Bolozi families engage in a wide variety of occupations, which include herding of yaks, sheep, and goats, engaging in agricultural production, and trading with the Tibetans and Han Chinese. Villages in the remote area are watered by fast-flowing rivers. Rickety bridges made of wooden boards and chains are flung across the rivers.

Religion: Tibetan Buddhism has never taken a grip among the Bolozi to the extent that it has among other Tibetan groups. Most are polytheistic animists who try to keep peace with the vindictive spirits they believe control their lives.

Christianity: The Bolozi are virtually untouched by the gospel. There are believed to be just a handful of Han and Qiang Christians in Songpan, the result of pre-1949 missionary efforts. In 1919 there were 543 foreign missionaries working in Sichuan Province,[3] but few ever labored in this remote area in the north of the province. The Church Missionary Society did commence work in Songpan in the 1920s, but no known outreach has ever been conducted to the wild Bolozi people. As a result, the Bolozi today are unreached and unevangelized.

Population in China:
2,000 (1998)
2,110 (2000)
2,720 (2010)
Location: Sichuan
Religion: Polytheism
Christians: None Known

Overview of the Bolozi

Countries: China
Pronunciation: "Boh-luo-tzi"
Other Names: Bolotse, Bolotsze, Po-lo-tzu
Population Source: 1,000 to 2,000 (1998 AMO)
Location: *N Sichuan:* Xiao Heshui village west of Songpan; A few are scattered as far south as Wenchuan Township
Status: Probably officially included under either Tibetan or Qiang
Language: Sino-Tibetan, Tibeto-Burman, Burmese-Lolo, Lolo, Unclassified (possibly Qiangic)
Dialects: 0
Religion: Polytheism, Tibetan Buddhism
Christians: None known
Scripture: None
***Jesus* film:** None
Gospel Recordings: None
Christian Broadcasting: None
ROPAL code: None

Status of Evangelization

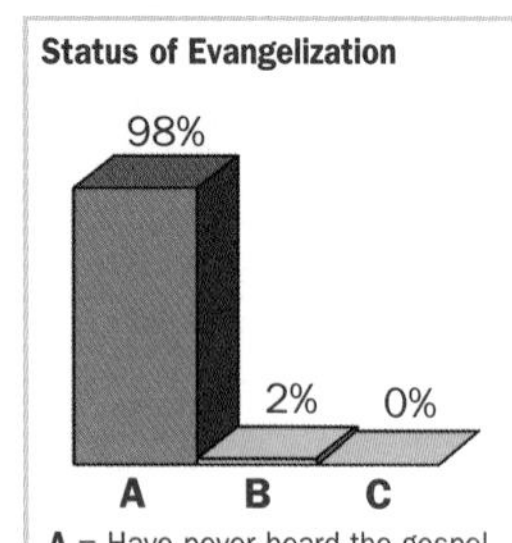

A = Have never heard the gospel
B = Were evangelized but did not become Christians
C = Are adherents to any form of Christianity

12. A *Baihong* lady in traditional dress, Yuanjiang, Yunnan. [Paul Hattaway]
13. The back of a *Baonou* woman's jacket. This pattern is said to represent the Baonou's agreement with the Chinese which would release them from paying taxes for all generations, Libo, Guizhou. [*Yao Update*]
14. More than 10,000 *Biyo* have become Christians since 1949, Mojiang, Yunnan. [Dwayne Graybill]
15. Approximately 25,000 *Biao Mien* live in isolated communities within the mountains of northern Guangdong. [Paul Hattaway]

16

17

18

16. The 194,000 *Baihong* in central Yunnan were formerly known as the *Mahei*. [Paul Hattaway]

17–18. Because of their extreme geographical isolation, few people are aware of the existence of the *Baima* — also known as the *White Horse Tibetans*, Baima Valley, Gansu-Sichuan border. [both by Midge Conner]

19–22. The *Bouyei* people, who number three million, are one of the largest minority groups in southern China. They speak a language related to Thai. Only about one tenth of one percent of the Bouyei profess to follow Christ. [all by Paul Hattaway]

23

24

26

25

27

23. More than 500,000 *Buriat* live in the three countries of Russia, Mongolia, and China. [Paul Hattaway]
24. A *Bonan* beauty, Jishishan, Gansu. [Paul Hattaway]
25. A *Bulang* woman, Xishuangbanna, Yunnan. [Dwayne Graybill]
26. The *Bonan* are the descendants of thirteenth-century Mongolian troops stationed in the Gansu-Qinghai border areas. [Midge Conner]
27. A *Buriat* woman, Hulunbuir, Inner Mongolia. [Midge Conner]

Bonan 保安

Location: Approximately 10,000 Bonan inhabit areas of southwest Gansu Province. In addition, 4,000 members of the Tu minority speak Bonan as their first language.[1] The Bonan occupy several townships and villages in Jishishan County. The Jishi Mountains have long been an effective defense against approaching armies. For centuries the Bonan have lived on the edge of both Tibetan and Chinese civilizations.

Identity: The Bonan are the eighth smallest of China's 55 official minorities. After decades of intermarriage with other peoples such as the Hui, Han, and Tu, a distinct people group formed who came to call themselves *Bonan*, which means "I protect you." This name refers to their long history as the soldiers and protectors of the people in the area.

Language: The Bonan speak a Mongol language, altered from their original Mongol tongue by 700 years of isolation. Today, Bonan is more similar to the Dongxiang and Tu languages than to modern Mongolian. A 1960 study of 3,000 words found that approximately 50% of the Bonan vocabulary were loanwords from other languages.[2]

History: During the Mongolian world empire, large numbers of people from Central Asia were mixed together and sent to China as troops and administrators. These garrisons settled down after the collapse of the empire and gradually formed into their own people groups. It is believed the Bonan were originally Mongol troops sent to their present location on the edge of Chinese territory to act as watch guards against the fierce Tibetans. In 1862 religious friction between Muslim Bonan and those who had embraced Tibetan Buddhism caused the two groups to split.[3] These religious disputes and a quarrel over water rights caused the Muslim Bonan to move east to their present location in Gansu.[4]

Dwayne Graybill

Customs: The Bonan are renowned for their famous *Bonan knife*. It is a skillfully made knife with engraved ox-horn handles. Profits from sales of the knife, along with farming and logging, are the main sources of income for the Bonan. The Bonan send the pick of their young people to study at the Northwest Nationalities Institute in the city of Lanzhou.

Religion: The majority of Bonan are Sunni Muslims. They worship in their own mosques and no longer consider the Tibetan Buddhist Bonan to be their brothers. The Bonan are linguistically related to the Dongxiang Muslims in the area and live downstream from the Muslim Salar people of Xunhua. First converted to Islam by Muhammed Amin in 1750, Xunhua County contained 73 mosques in the early 1980s.[5]

Christianity: The Bonan are an unreached people group. There has never been a Bonan church nor a single known Bonan believer. Missionaries worked among the neighboring Salar until the 1950s, but no church was established.[6] Little has changed since the 1920s when a plea went unheeded for workers to the Muslims in Gansu, "to give their whole time to each of these tribes."[7]

INNER MONGOLIA
GANSU
QINGHAI
Xining
Lanzhou
Linxia
Luqu
Min Xian
SICHUAN
Scale 0 KM 400

Population in China:
8,212 (1990)
10,590 (2000)
13,650 (2010)
Location: Gansu
Religion: Islam
Christians: None Known

Overview of the Bonan

Countries: China

Pronunciation: "Bo-nahn"

Other Names: Bao'an, Paoan, Paongan, Baonan

Population Source:
8,212 (1990 AMO);
Out of a total Bonan population of 12,212 (1990 census);
9,027 (1982 census);
5,125 (1964 census);
4,957 (1953 census)

Location: *SW Gansu:* Dadun, Ganhetan and Meipo villages of Dahejia Township, and in Gaoli Village of Liuji Township in Jishishan County

Status:
An official minority of China

Language: Altaic, Mongolian, Eastern Mongolian, Mongour

Literacy: 24%

Dialects (3):
Jishishan, Genhetan, Dadun

Religion: Sunni Islam

Christians: None known

Scripture: None

***Jesus* film:** None

Gospel Recordings: None

Christian Broadcasting: None

ROPAL code: PEH00

Status of Evangelization

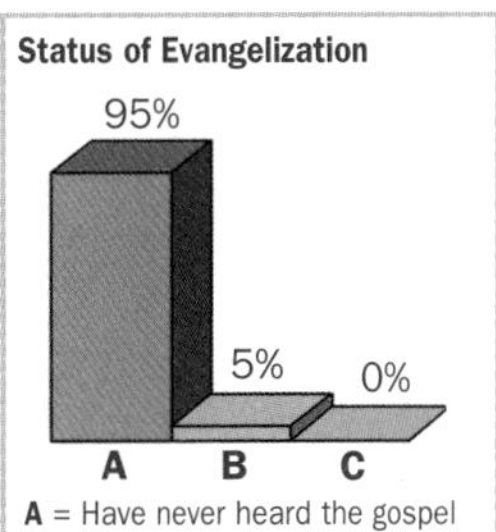

A = Have never heard the gospel
B = Were evangelized but did not become Christians
C = Are adherents to any form of Christianity

Bonan, Tongren 保安(同仁)

Population in China:
4,000 (1987)
5,500 (2000)
7,100 (2010)
Location: Qinghai
Religion: Tibetan Buddhism
Christians: None Known

Overview of the Tongren Bonan

Countries: China

Pronunciation: "Bow-nahn-Tong-ren"

Other Names: Tongren, Buddhist Bonan, Qinghai Bonan

Population Source: 4,000 (1987 *LAC*); Out of a total Bonan population of 12,212 (1990 census)

Location: *S Qinghai:* Tongren County

Status: Officially included under Bonan

Language: Altaic, Mongolian, Eastern Mongolian, Mongour

Dialects (5): Tongren, Nianduhu, Dunmari, Gajiuri, Bao'an Xiazhuang

Religion: Tibetan Buddhism, Bon

Christians: None known

Scripture: None

***Jesus* film:** None

Gospel Recordings: None

Christian Broadcasting: None

ROPAL code: PEH02

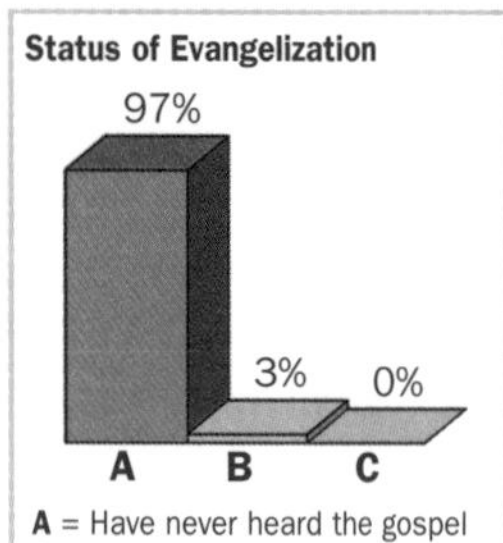

Location: Tongren County, in the eastern part of Qinghai Province, is home to more than 5,000 people of the Bonan nationality. Tongren is a crossroads for many different peoples, including the Salar, Tu, Hui, Amdo Tibetans, and Wutun.

Identity: The Buddhist Bonan in Tongren consider themselves a separate people from the Muslim Bonan in Gansu. Their languages are now also different. Using the definition of a people group as "a significantly large ethnic or sociological grouping of individuals who perceive themselves to have a common affinity for one another,"[1] the Tongren Bonan definitely qualify as a distinct people group.

Language: The Bonan language in Tongren County of Qinghai is distinct from the main body of Bonan across the border in Gansu Province. The Gansu Bonan language has been influenced by Chinese, while Tongren Bonan has been heavily influenced by Tibetan and Tu. Various linguists note that sound structure and grammar also differ between the two areas. While the Tongren Bonan can communicate in their own language with the Tu in Tongren, they cannot with the Tu who live farther north.[2] In addition, a language similar to Tongren Bonan "is spoken by some Han and Hui who had until the 1950s been referred to as the *Tongren Turen* (natives)."[3]

History: The Tongren Bonan are the descendants of Mongolian troops who were stationed in the region during the Mongolian world empire of the thirteenth and fourteenth centuries. After the collapse of Mongol rule in 1368, most soldiers retreated to Mongolia, but a few remained behind. After centuries of intermingling with other nationalities, they became a distinct group called the *Bonan.*

Customs: The Tongren Bonan observe all Tibetan festivals and have culturally become almost indistinguishable from the Tibetans. "Those Bonans who retained their Buddhist faith became strongly acculturated to their neighbors... as a result, only a small number of persons remain in Tongren who from an ethno-linguistic point of view can still be considered Bonan."[4]

Religion: The Tongren Bonan are Tibetan Buddhists. In the early nineteenth century, a portion of the Bonan converted to Islam. This caused deep friction among the two Bonan groups. The Muslim Bonan were forced to migrate into Gansu Province where they remain to this day.

Christianity: The first foreign missionaries among the Tongren Bonan were workers affiliated with the Christian & Missionary Alliance. They commenced work in Bao'an Township around 1910. Despite being in the Bonan neighborhood, the missionaries' primary target were the Tibetans, not the Bonan. By 1922 the mission was closed due to lack of workers.[5] It opened again, but after years of slow and unfruitful progress the work gravitated towards the more receptive Han Chinese.[6] Today, there are no known Christians among the Tongren Bonan.

Dwayne Graybill

Bouyei 布依

Paul Hattaway

Location: The Bouyei are the tenth largest of China's minorities, numbering approximately three million people. In Vietnam, 38,000 members of the *Giay* minority and 1,420 in the *Bo Y* minority speak the same language as the Bouyei in China.[1] The Bouyei inhabit the rolling hills in the southern part of Guizhou Province.[2] Bouyei villages are often located near streams and rivers.

Identity: It appears that the official division between the Bouyei and Zhuang in China is defined by provincial borders. The Northern Tai-speaking groups in Guangxi are labeled *Zhuang*, and those in Guizhou, *Bouyei*.[3] Until one generation ago, the Bouyei were more commonly known as the *Chungchia*, a name meaning "people in the middle."[4] A 1945 study of the Bouyei revealed they were "divided into five distinct tribes."[5] An early missionary described the Bouyei in very unflattering terms: "Crafty, lying, and dishonest... every Bouyei is [reputed to be] a thief, and from what we know of them we should not deny the charge."[6]

Language: Bouyei — which has eight tones — is a Northern Tai language, similar (and in some places identical) to Northern Zhuang. There are three Bouyei dialects in China, although as many as 40 dialects have been incorrectly reported in the past.[7] In 1995 the Chinese government decided to discontinue education in the Bouyei language, and now all schooling is conducted in Chinese.[8] Only 12% of the Bouyei have attended high school — one of the lowest rates among the 55 official minorities in China.[9]

History: The Bouyei are one of the ancient peoples of Guizhou, having inhabited the province for more than 2,000 years. Thousands of Bouyei were burned at the stake during the Nanlang Rebellion in 1797. The horrific persecution forced many Bouyei to flee into Vietnam.

Customs: When a Bouyei woman is in the process of giving birth, a tree branch is placed across the door to prevent intruders from entering. An altar to the spirits is erected to ensure the delivery goes smoothly. After the birth, the placenta is buried under the bed.[10]

Religion: The Bouyei are polytheists. They also practice an ancient form of exorcism called *nuo*. "A family will hire a shaman... to cast out demons of illness or bad fortune. Ceremonies include climbing knife ladders, walking on fire or glass, and other activities to demonstrate the power of the spirits."[11]

Christianity: Catholic missionaries have worked among the Bouyei for 200 years. Many were martyred for their witness. The CIM missionary J. F. Braumton arrived in Guiyang in 1877. A mission station was opened in Dushan in 1895, but "the time of the missionaries was entirely given up to work among the Chinese."[12] A recent estimate places the number of Bouyei Christians at 24,000,[13] but missionaries among the Bouyei claim there to be no more than 5,000.[14] In 1985 there were nine Catholic churches in the Qianxinan Prefecture.[15] Recently, several mission agencies have commenced church-planting efforts among the Bouyei, but few converts have been won so far.

Population in China:
2,545,059 (1990)
3,176,200 (2000)
3,963,900 (2010)
Location:
Guizhou, Yunnan, Sichuan
Religion: Polytheism
Christians: 5,000

Overview of the Bouyei

Countries: China, Vietnam
Pronunciation: "Boo-yee"
Other Names: Buyi, Pu-i, Po-ai, Pui, Puyi, Bo-i, Buzhong, Buman, Buyayi, Chung-chia, Zhongjia, Bui, Buyui, Pu-Jui, Pujai, Puyoi, Shuihu, Quinjiang, Dioi, Kui, Kuei
Population Source:
2,545,059 (1990 census);
2,122,389 (1982 census);
1,348,055 (1964 census);
1,420 in Vietnam (1991)
Location: *S & SW Guizhou:* On the Yunnan-Guizhou Plateau: Qiannan and Qianxinan Bouyei-Miao prefectures;
E Yunnan: Luoping, Fuyuan, and Shizhong counties;
S Sichuan: Ningnan and Huidong counties
Status:
An official minority of China
Language: Daic, Tai, Northern Tai
Dialects (3):
Qiannan, Qianzhong, Qianxi
Literacy: 46%
Religion: Polytheism, Animism, Buddhism, Christianity
Christians: 5,000
Scripture: Portions 1904[16]
***Jesus* film:** None
Gospel Recordings:
Bouyei: Guizhou #04832
Christian Broadcasting: None
ROPAL code: PCC00

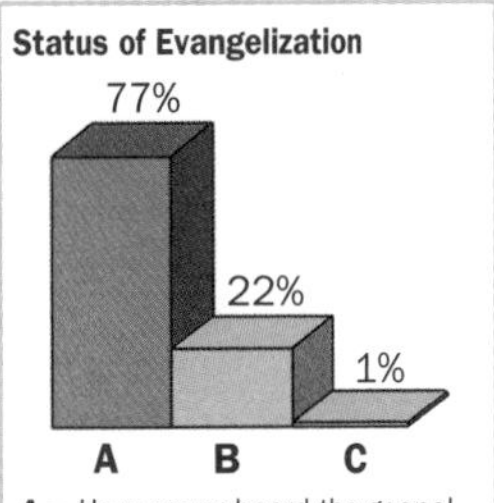

Budo 布度

Population in China:
10,000 (1998)
10,580 (2000)
13,650 (2010)
Location: Yunnan
Religion: Animism
Christians: 2,000

Overview of the Budo

Countries: China, possibly in Laos

Pronunciation: "Boo-doe"

Other Names: Budu, Putu, Pudo, Butu, Bu Dou, Pudu, Buko

Population Source:
10,000 (1998 AMO);
Out of a total Hani population of 1,253,952 (1990 census);
Possibly "Pu Ko" in Laos

Location: *S Yunnan:* Mojiang County in Honghe Prefecture and Yuanjiang and Xinping counties in Yuxi Prefecture

Status:
Officially included under Hani

Language: Sino-Tibetan, Tibeto-Burman, Burmese-Lolo, Lolo, Southern Lolo, Akha, Hani, Bi-Ka

Dialects: 0

Religion: Animism, Christianity

Christians: 2,000

Scripture: None

***Jesus* film:** None

Gospel Recordings: None

Christian Broadcasting: None

ROPAL code: None

Status of Evangelization

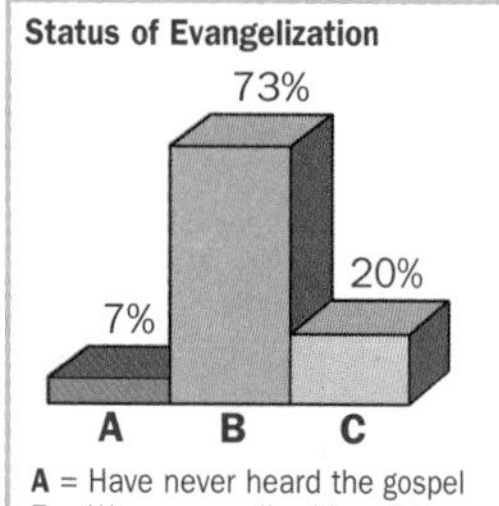

A = Have never heard the gospel
B = Were evangelized but did not become Christians
C = Are adherents to any form of Christianity

Dwayne Graybill

Location: More than 10,000 Budo tribesmen live in the Ailao Mountains, in the Honghe and Yuxi prefectures of southern Yunnan Province.[1] Another source states that the Budo live near the Biyo and Kado people groups.[2] The main areas for the Budo are Mojiang and Yuanjiang counties, while another source also places them in Xinping County farther to the north.[3]

Identity: The Budo are one of 18 distinct subgroups of the Hani nationality profiled in this book. Although there is some measure of linguistic intelligibility between the different Hani groups in the region, each tribe maintains its own ethnicity. Most of the inhabitants of the Honghe-Yuxi area can readily reel off the list of Hani subgroups who live there. Although they acknowledge cultural differences and peculiarities, the Budo are not upset at their inclusion as part of the Hani nationality. They do acknowledge historical kinship with the other groups included in the artificially constructed official classification.

Language: The Budo language is part of the Bi-Ka branch of the Tibeto-Burman family, most closely related to Biyo and Kado. Many Budo under the age of 40, however, are unable to speak their mother tongue.

History: Budo youth find the Han Chinese culture attractive, and few of their customs are being retained. One custom that has survived is the Budo's way of settling an engagement. "The parents of both the girl and boy... walk some distance together, and so long as they meet no animals the engagement can go ahead."[4]

Customs: Most Budo live in simple houses made of plaster or baked mud. Their small, crowded villages usually consist of between 30 and 60 households. Most Budo men are rice farmers who have skillfully built their terraces on mountain and hill slopes on the Ailao Range.

Religion: The majority of Budo today are animists, although there are also a significant number of Christians among them. Many Budo were converted to Christianity by missionaries in the 1930s. H. A. Baker, a Pentecostal missionary who worked in the area in the 1930s and 1940s, wrote, "In another Budo settlement there are a hundred or more real Christians who have long been faithful after several years of severe siftings and persecution. This congregation is made up mostly of young men and women who by their spiritually healthy and live, wide-awake testimony have impressed the Chinese living in surrounding sections. Now former persecution has turned into considerable admiration."[5]

Christianity: Danish Assemblies of God missionaries Axel and Christine Jensen were married in Yunnan in 1928. Jensen — also known as Yan Chung Ren — started work near Mojiang among a host of different tribes including the Nisu, Kado, Biyo, and Budo. The work gained many converts during the 1930s and 1940s.[6] Today there are at least 2,000 believers among the Budo, and all but the most geographically remote have been evangelized and are aware of the gospel. Most Budo Christians today meet in Chinese-language congregations.

Bugan 布干

Population in China:
3,000 (1996)
3,350 (2000)
4,300 (2010)
Location: Yunnan
Religion: Animism
Christians: None Known

Overview of the Bugan

Countries: China

Pronunciation: "Boo-gun"

Other Names: Pukan, Hualo, Huazu

Population Source: 3,000 (1996 J. Edmonson)

Location: *SE Yunnan:* Southern Guangnan and northern Xichou counties; 7 villages: Laowalong, Xinwalong, Jiuping, Shibeipo, Xinzhai, Manlong, and Nala

Status: Unidentified

Language: Austro-Asiatic, Mon-Khmer, Unclassified

Dialects: 0

Religion: Animism, Ancestor Worship, No Religion

Christians: None known

Scripture: None

***Jesus* film:** None

Gospel Recordings: None

Christian Broadcasting: None

ROPAL code: BBH00

Status of Evangelization

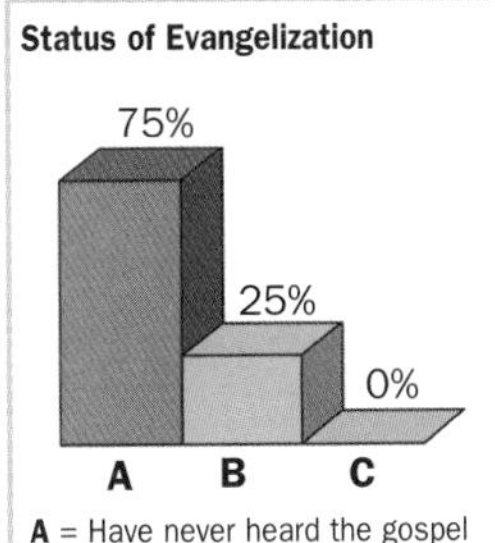

A = Have never heard the gospel
B = Were evangelized but did not become Christians
C = Are adherents to any form of Christianity

Location: More than 3,000 members of the Bugan people group are located in seven villages in the southern part of Guangnan and the northern part of Xichou counties. These counties are in the southeast part of Yunnan Province close to the provincial border with Guangxi and the international border with Vietnam. Four of the seven villages are inhabited solely by Bugan people, while the three other villages are shared with the Han Chinese. Other peoples in the verdant mountain region include the Bunu, Miao, Yao, Southern Zhuang, and Yi nationalities.

Identity: The Bugan were completely unknown until 1996, when Chinese linguist Li Jinfang first documented their existence.[1] It is not known under what minority group, if any, the government categorizes them. The Bugan speak a Mon-Khmer language, but no other source mentions any other Mon-Khmer groups in the southeastern arm of Yunnan.

Language: There are six tones in the Bugan language, but its branch affiliation has yet to be specifically determined within the Mon-Khmer linguistic family. There are no dialect variations reported among the seven Bugan villages.

History: There are many Mon-Khmer languages spoken in China and across Southeast Asia, but the Bugan find themselves alone as a Mon-Khmer people in southeast Yunnan. In the distant past, the various Mon-Khmer groups were part of one large Austro-Asiatic group which was "driven out of their habitats by invaders, dispersed and split into the isolated groups they are today."[2]

Customs: The Bugan live in agriculture-based communities along the rivers and streams in southern China. Most are engaged in rice cultivation. They take full advantage of the land by constructing rice fields that appear to hang from the sides of the mountain slopes. Bugan women and girls spend much time learning to embroider and to make their unique dress, although in recent years many women in the area have begun to wear factory-produced imitations.

Religion: The Bugan do not consider themselves religious, but traces of animism and ancestor worship are prominent in their everyday activities. The Bugan celebrate the Han Chinese festivals, especially the annual Chinese New Year and Spring festivals.

Christianity: There are no known Christian believers among the Bugan, even though small numbers of churches can be found among some of their neighbors. In nearby Guangxi many missionaries labored sacrificially in the past. One committed and love-filled worker was Eleanor Chestnut, a missionary-doctor from Iowa, who often performed free surgery for people in her bathroom. One operation involved the amputation of a coolie's leg. An observer noted, "The surgery was successful, except that the flaps of the skin did not grow together.... Someone noticed that Dr. Chestnut was limping. When asked why, she responded, 'Oh, it's nothing'.... The doctor had taken skin from her own leg for an immediate transplant to the one the nurses called 'a good-for-nothing coolie'."[3]

Dwayne Graybill

Bulang 布郎

Location: Approximately 80,000 Bulang live in southwest China. An additional 1,200 live in Thailand, and between 1,000 and 2,000 in Myanmar. The Bulang live in villages high up on thickly forested mountain slopes. They are located in several counties in Yunnan Province, especially Menghai and Shuangjiang.[1] The Bulang in Thailand call themselves *Khon Doi* which means "mountain people."[2]

Identity: Several smaller ethnolinguistic people groups have been combined by the Chinese to form the official Bulang nationality in China. Other peoples include the Angku, Puman, Kong Ge, and Samtao tribal groups.

Language: The Bulang language has great linguistic variety.[3] One survey found as many as ten dialects spoken in just one Bulang refugee village in Thailand.[4] Only 24,000 (29%) people counted under the Bulang nationality in China can actually speak Bulang; 30,000 (36%) speak Lawa.[5] Two different Roman orthographies exist for the Bulang in China: one is called *to-tham* and is used by the Bulang in Xishuangbanna; the other, *to-lek*, is used in the region between Dehong and Lincang.

History: The Bulang traditionally lived in small clans, according to ancestral affiliations. Each clan possessed its own land and each member of the clan was responsible to work and harvest the crops. If a family moved away from the area, it forfeited its right to own land or reap the benefits from the produce. Each Bulang village has its own cemetery where the dead of each family line are buried. The corpses of those who die from unnatural circumstances are cremated.

Customs: Bulang are renowned as friendly people. The older women love to chew betel nut, which they spit out into the dirt in copious quantities. Betel nut stains their teeth black; this is considered a mark of beauty among the Bulang.

Religion: For centuries the Bulang have been ardent followers of Theravada Buddhism. Most of their villages are located alongside Tai people, who adhere to the same religion. Temples and idols are located throughout their communities. Many Bulang men enter the Buddhist monkhood, which brings great honor to their families. Few Bulang have ever heard of Christ, and few care to seek for anything beyond what they already believe. They strive to observe the Buddhist *Tripitika* (Three Baskets) teaching: practicing self-discipline, preaching, and discussing doctrine. The Bulang believe that right thinking, sacrifices, and self-denial will enable the soul to reach *nirvana*, a state of eternal bliss.

Dwayne Graybill

Christianity: The few evangelistic efforts that have targeted the Bulang have usually been discontinued by mission groups who invariably found a much more willing reception to their message from other groups in the area. Protestant work among the Bulang prior to 1949 resulted in 30 families being converted.[6] Most of them gave up their faith during the oppressive Cultural Revolution, but there are about 50 Bulang Christians remaining in China today. Bulang translation work has begun in Thailand, but the Bulang in China will not be able to understand the script.

Population in China:
61,900 (1990)
79,850 (2000)
103,000 (2010)
Location: Yunnan
Religion: Buddhism
Christians: 50

Overview of the Bulang

Countries: China, Myanmar, Thailand

Pronunciation: "Boo-lang"

Other Names: Blang, Pulang, Pula, Plang, Kala, Kontoi, Bang

Population Source:
82,280 (1990 census);[7]
58,476 (1982 census);
39,411 (1964 census);
1,200 in Thailand (1991);
1,000 to 2,000 in Myanmar (1991)

Location: *SW Yunnan:* Menghai, Zhenkang, Shuangjiang, Lincang, Lancang, and Mojiang counties

Status: An official minority of China

Language: Austro-Asiatic, Mon-Khmer, Northern Mon-Khmer, Palaungic, Western Palaungic, Waic, Bulang

Dialects (2): Phang, Kem Degne

Literacy: 25%

Religion: Theravada Buddhism, Animism

Christians: 50

Scripture: None; Work in progress in Thailand

***Jesus* film:** None

Gospel Recordings: None

Christian Broadcasting: None

ROPAL code: BLR00

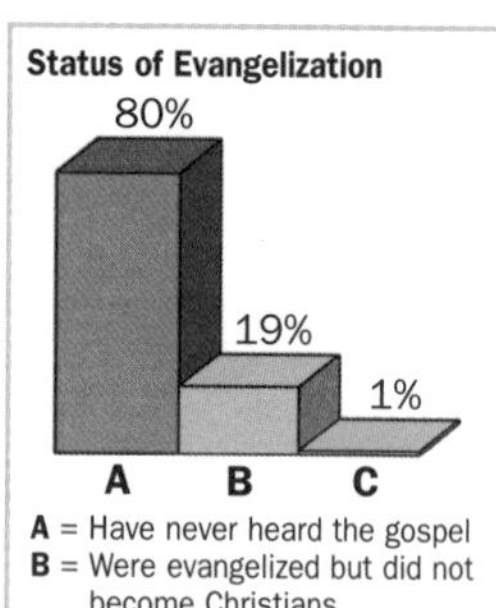

A = Have never heard the gospel
B = Were evangelized but did not become Christians
C = Are adherents to any form of Christianity

Bunan 布难

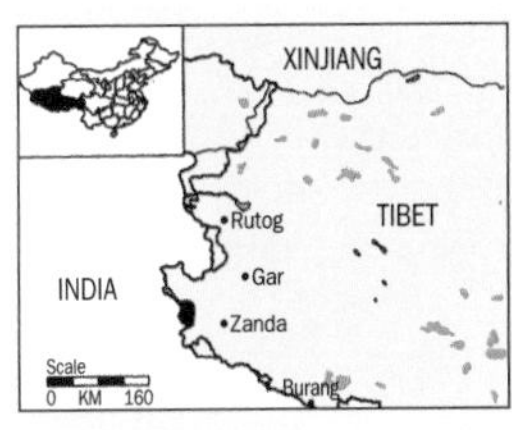

Population in China:
1,467 (1995)
1,680 (2000)
2,160 (2010)
Location: Tibet
Religion: Tibetan Buddhism
Christians: None Known

Overview of the Bunan

Countries: India, China

Pronunciation: "Boo-nun"

Other Names: Gahri, Lahuli of Bunan, Ghara

Population Source: 1,467 (1995 GEM); Also in India; 2,000 in all countries (1972 E. Nida)

Location: *W Tibet:* Border with Jammu and Kashmir, India

Status: Unidentified

Language: Sino-Tibetan, Tibeto-Burman, Bodic, Bodish, Himalayish, Kanauri

Dialects: 0

Religion: Tibetan Buddhism

Christians: None known

Scripture: Portions 1911

***Jesus* film:** None

Gospel Recordings: Lahouli: Bunan #02424

Christian Broadcasting: None

ROPAL code: BFU00

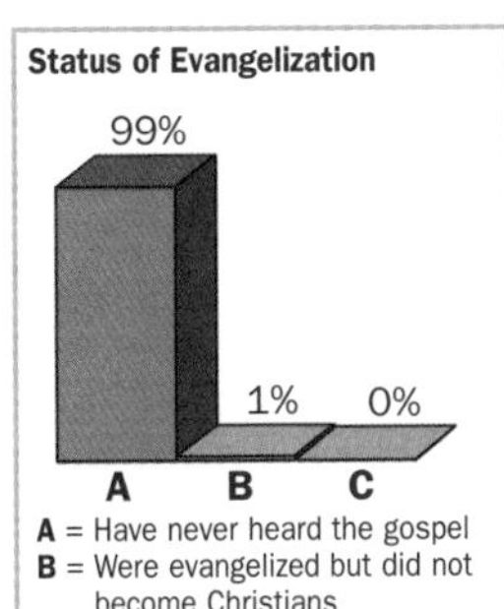

Paul Hattaway

Location: The Global Evangelization Movement listed a 1995 figure of 1,467 Bunan in China.[1] The *Ethnologue* cites a 1972 source (Eugene Nida), stating that a total of 2,000 Bunan live in both India and China.[2] The Bunan inhabit an extremely remote and desolate area of western Tibet along the China-India border. In India, the Bunan live in the lower Bhaga Valley in the northern part of the Himalayan state of Himachal Pradesh. Another source places the Bunan "on the border of western Tibet and Punjab, India."[3] Western Tibet is separated from Xinjiang to the north by the imposing Kunlun Mountains, and in the south Himalayan peaks rise over 7,000 meters (23,000 ft.) above sea level.

Identity: The Bunan are a little-known people group. They are not mentioned in Chinese literature, so it is uncertain how they are officially classified. They may have been included in the Tibetan nationality because of linguistic and religious similarities. The area of China where they live is so remote that it is possible they were not counted at all in the Chinese census.

Language: The Bunan language is a part of the Kanauri arm of the so-called *Himalayish* branch. It is one of a number of different languages located in the linguistically diverse western Himalayan region. Bunan is related to Lahuli Tinan, also spoken in western Tibet. Bunan and Lahuli Tinan share 37% lexical similarity. Bunan is also reported to have up to 34% lexical similarity with varieties of Central Tibetan and 24% with Lhasa Tibetan.[4] In northern India, Bunan is related to the Thebor, Kanam, Lippa, Sumtsu, and Sungnam languages.

History: Numerous small ethnolinguistic peoples live along the Tibetan border with India and Nepal in very sparsely populated locations. China and India had several armed border clashes in the 1950s and 1960s. China has since claimed thousands of square miles of territory from India, including the area inhabited by the Bunan.

Customs: Bunan culture has been heavily influenced by their devotion to Tibetan Buddhism. Their lives are a long struggle against harsh winters. Because very little fruit or vegetables can grow in the Bunan region, their diet is comprised almost entirely of meat, fat, and yak yogurt.

Religion: Many Bunan make annual pilgrimages to Lake Manasarovar and Mt. Kailas — two holy Buddhist sites in western Tibet. The Bunan are trapped in an endless cycle of doing good works, a vain bid to ensure a better reincarnation in the next life.

Christianity: The Bunan's isolated homeland is so remote that few outsiders have ever traveled there. The Indian government, who also claim the territory inhabited by the Bunan, did not find out that the Chinese had built a road there until two years after it was completed.[5] The Bunan in India had parts of the Bible translated into their language by missionaries in 1911, but these have been out of print since 1923. Currently the Christians located closest to the Bunan are the small number of Moravian believers found among the Ladakhi people of northern India.

Bunu 布努

Yao Update

Location: A total of 439,000 Bunu people, scattered throughout Guangxi and Yunnan provinces, were counted in the 1982 Chinese census. Since that time, new information has confirmed that 11 subgroups of the Bunu are distinct ethnolinguistic groups. After subtracting the populations of these 11 groups, there are still more than 300,000 Bunu unaccounted for in China today. This Profile treats those who can no longer speak their mother tongue and those Bunu groups who have yet to be assigned to a subgroup by the Chinese. Bunu villages are customarily built in out-of-the-way places; this results in little contact with the outside world.

Identity: The Bunu were counted separately in the 1982 census before being included under the Yao nationality in China. The name *Bunu* is a generic term, simply meaning "us people."[1]

Language: About 100,000 people, who do not fit into any of the recognized subgroups of Bunu, speak Zhuang as their mother tongue.[2] One linguist notes, "The classification of the Bunu languages and dialects is very complicated. The Bunu people are actually regarded either by themselves and/or by the Chinese as Yao ethnically. However, the languages spoken by the Bunu are actually dialects of Hmong [Miao]."[3]

History: Over many centuries the Bunu were forced to migrate south to their present location. The Chinese and Zhuang often seized Bunu land and slaughtered entire communities.

Customs: Bunu women rule over their families. "If the couple do not get along well, the husband may go back to his own home and the wife may find another man. The husband has no right to claim any property belonging to the wife's family.... In such a marriage arrangement it is the husband who takes orders from his wife."[4]

Religion: The Bunu worship Pan Hu who they believe created the universe. "In ancient times, the world was a chaos, Heaven and earth were still inanimate, with no sun or moon, no Yin and Yang, no day and night. At that time our holy King Pan Hu was first born to the world, he built the heavens and created the earth, he installed mountains and rivers, made the sun, moon and stars, and set up the 10,000 countries and the nine territories."[5] They also have a legend of a great flood which destroyed the earth. At thanksgiving rituals in honor of King Pan, the Bunu still sing: "All the people in the world had been drowned by a flood.... We brother and sister got married... the flower entered her body."[6]

Christianity: The Bunu are one of the largest people groups in China without a single known church. There are believed to be only a small number of scattered Bunu believers. The Bunu's complex ethnolinguistic diversity has kept them from hearing the gospel. "They consist of people from many language groups. Because of these language distinctions, it creates certain difficulties for evangelizing them. This means that different sets of scriptures will need to be translated... different languages of the *Jesus* film translated, and so forth."[7]

Population in China:
165,500 (1982)
324,500 (2000)
418,600 (2010)
Location: Guangxi, Yunnan
Religion: Polytheism
Christians: 100

Overview of the Bunu

Countries: China
Pronunciation: "Boo-noo"
Other Names: Punu
Population Source:
439,000 (1982 census);[8]
Including 11 distinct groups with a combined population of 273,500;
Out of a total Yao population of 2,134,013 (1990 census)
Location: *W Guangxi, SE Yunnan*
Status:
Officially included under Yao
Language:
Hmong-Mien, Hmongic, Bunu
Dialects: 0
Religion: Polytheism, Animism, Daoism, Ancestor Worship
Christians: 100
Scripture: None
***Jesus* film:** None
Gospel Recordings: None
Christian Broadcasting: None
ROPAL code: BWX00

Status of Evangelization

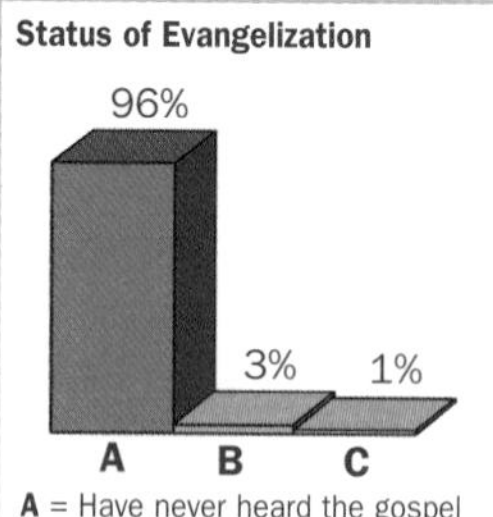

A = Have never heard the gospel
B = Were evangelized but did not become Christians
C = Are adherents to any form of Christianity

Bunun 布嫩

Location: Approximately 1,300 Bunun live in the southern part of Fujian Province on the east coast of China and in Chinese cities. The vast majority of Bunun — more than 34,000 — live in the mountains of central Taiwan.

Identity: The Bunun, the Ami, and the Paiwan are the three tribes which have been combined to form the official Gaoshan (High Mountain) nationality in China.[1]

Language: Bunun is one of 22 Gaoshan languages spoken in Taiwan.[2] All belong to the Austronesian language family. "Bunun oral tradition is particularly rich in animal and hunting stories, reflecting the great importance hunting is to the Bunun economy. Animal stories include not only the transformation of humans into animals, but sexual relations between humans and animals, as well as metamorphosis of animals into humans."[3] The Bunun believe that they once had a written script, "but the ancestors were not careful and the writing fell into the river and floated away, only to be picked up by the plains people."[4]

History: The Bunun believe the human race was started when a gourd fell from heaven. It split open, and the first man and woman emerged. They also have a legend about a great flood long ago. They say it was caused by a snake which blocked up the river until all of the earth was inundated.[5] The Bunun have many theories about their origins. "One is that they originated from a branch of the ancient Yue nationality on mainland China and then mixed with Aborigines from Malaysia and the Ryukyu Islands."[6]

Mike Fioritto

Customs: The Bunun sometimes "practice the extraction of certain front teeth as a sign of social identity as well as adulthood. The Bunun are good singers and often sing when working."[7] When a Bunun dies, that person is buried in a crouching position beneath the hearthstone of the family home. Traditionally, "the body was first wrapped in cloth and placed on an open platform for three years; following this first stage, the bones were removed and buried beneath the house."[8]

Religion: Traditionally the Bunun in Taiwan were polytheists, but today most are Christians. "Bunun oral tradition mentions periodic offerings to the moon, upon which the agricultural calendar is based, but information on the original Bunun religion is too scarce to show clearly to what extent the moon and *dehanin* (heaven) may have been personified. In addition to the male hereditary priesthood, charged with the management of agricultural rituals, the Bunun had male shamans along with female ones. The shamans' concern was sickness and sorcery."[9]

Christianity: In 1946 there were no Christians among the Bunun in Taiwan. By 1959, however, converts numbered 8,881 and had increased to 12,234 by 1969.[10] Today the Presbyterians alone have 14,990 Bunun believers in 76 churches.[11] Hu Wen-chih, who was used by God to win many Bunun to Christ in Taiwan, also translated the New Testament into Bunun in 1973. The Bunun church in Taiwan has sent missionaries out to Japan and Borneo. The Bunun in China, however, have never experienced a revival and cannot read the Bunun Bible that is only available in Taiwan.

Population in China:
1,000 (1990)
1,290 (2000)
1,660 (2010)
Location: Fujian
Religion: Polytheism
Christians: None Known

Overview of the Bunun

Countries: Taiwan, China

Pronunciation: "Boo-non"

Other Names: Bunti, Vonun, Bunan, Bubukun, Vunum, Vunun, Vunung, Bunum

Population Source: 1,000 (1990 AMO); Out of a total Gaoshan population of 2,909 (1990 census); 34,000 in Taiwan (1993 P. Johnstone)

Location: *S Fujian:* Near Zhangzhou; Many Bunun live in *Beijing* and *Shanghai* municipalities and other cities.

Status: Officially included under Gaoshan

Language: Austronesian, Formosan, Paiwanic

Dialects: 0

Religion: Polytheism, Ancestor Worship

Christians: None known

Scripture: New Testament 1973; Portions 1951; Not available in China

***Jesus* film:** None

Gospel Recordings: Bunun #1990

Christian Broadcasting: None

ROPAL code: BNN00

Status of Evangelization

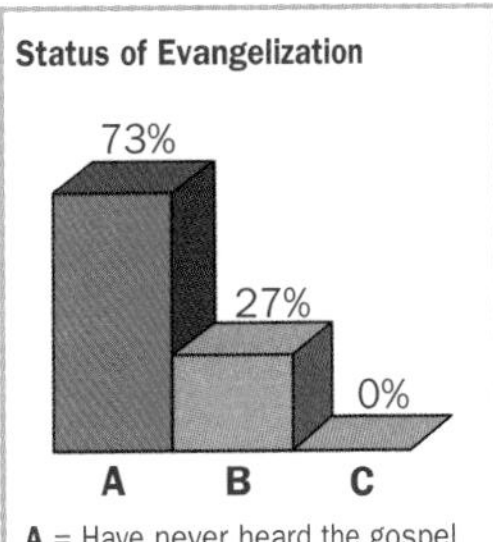

A = Have never heard the gospel
B = Were evangelized but did not become Christians
C = Are adherents to any form of Christianity

Bunuo 布诺

Population in China:
11,211 (1982)
17,050 (2000)
22,000 (2010)
Location: Guangxi
Religion: Polytheism
Christians: None Known

Overview of the Bunuo

Countries: China

Pronunciation: "Boo-nuoh"

Other Names: Pu-No, Beilou Yao, Basket-Carrying Yao

Population Source:
11,211 (1982 census);
Out of a total Yao population of 2,134,013 (1990 census)

Location:
W Guangxi: Du'an County

Status:
Officially included under Yao

Language: Hmong-Mien, Hmongic, Bunuic, Bunu

Dialects: 0

Religion: Polytheism, Animism, Daoism, Ancestor Worship

Christians: None known

Scripture: None

***Jesus* film:** None

Gospel Recordings: None

Christian Broadcasting: None

ROPAL code: BWX03

Status of Evangelization

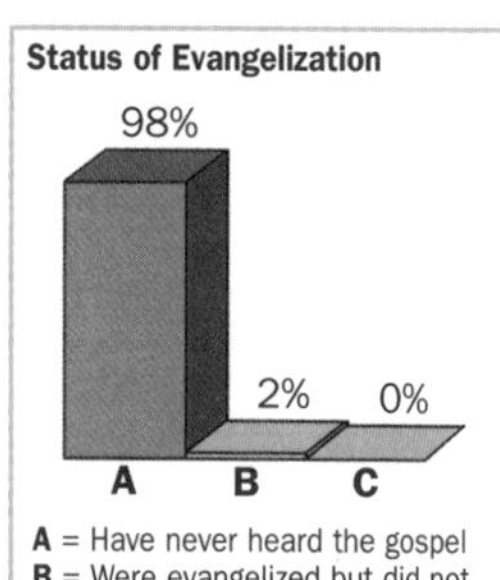

A = Have never heard the gospel
B = Were evangelized but did not become Christians
C = Are adherents to any form of Christianity

Location: Approximately 17,000 Bunuo people live in a small area within Du'an County in the western part of the Guangxi Zhuang Autonomous Region in southern China. Du'an is an isolated mountainous area on the road between Debao and Jingxi townships.

Identity: The Bunuo qualify as a distinct ethnolinguistic people group, but their claims have been ignored by the Chinese authorities who have placed them in the Bunu group, which in turn is officially considered part of the Yao nationality. The Chinese call the Bunuo *Beilou Yao*, which means "basket-carrying Yao." This is also the nickname given to the Dongnu people, but the Dongnu and Bunuo speak separate languages. For centuries the Chinese preferred to ignore the Bunuo: they considered the Bunuo to be ignorant barbarians living in the remote mountains. Not willing to study the ethnolinguistic composition of the Bunuo until recently, the Han gave nicknames like "Beilou Yao" to them in reference to visible attributes they saw on the Bunuo's infrequent trips down from their isolated mountain hideouts.

Language: The Bunuo language is one of 11 varieties of Bunu spoken in China. The languages closest to Bunuo are Dongnu and Nunu. Despite their inclusion in the Yao nationality for cultural reasons, the Bunuo's language is related to Miao. Because of their scant contact with outsiders, few Bunuo are adequately able to read or speak Chinese.

History: Most scholars suggest that the Miao, She, and Yao (including the Bunuo) minority groups today are probably from the same original race. As these peoples split geographically and separated into distinct entities, many of them suffered terrible harassment and persecution from the Chinese and other peoples. Those groups considered particularly violent and rebellious were treated the worst. The 1725 *Guizhou Tongzhi*, a book on the different subgroups of Miao, mentions a group called the *Hei Sheng Miao*. They were described as "a treacherous and aggressive people.... One Miao album assures us that... about half of them were killed and the rest surrendered, while another album reassures the reader that in 1736 they were conquered once and for all."[1]

Customs: The Bunuo have also faced great hostility down through the centuries. This has resulted in them being a very secluded people who distrust outsiders to this day.

Religion: The religious beliefs of the Bunuo include many different rituals borrowed from Daoism and Buddhism. It is not known if the Bunuo worship Pan Hu, as do many other Bunu and Yao groups in Guangxi.

Christianity: The Bunuo are a practically untouched people group, separated from the gospel by geographical, political, cultural, and linguistic barriers. Because they are not officially recognized by the Chinese government, the Bunuo are unknown to both Chinese and Western Christians. There are very few believers of any kind in the part of Guangxi inhabited by the Bunuo.

Paul Hattaway

Buriat 布利亚特

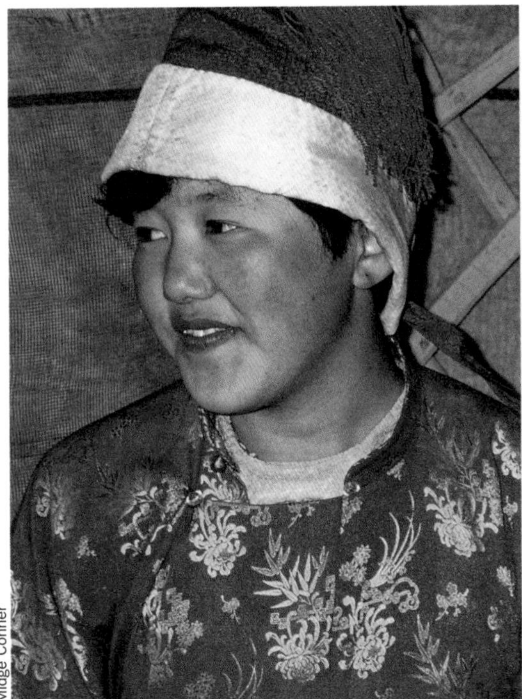
Midge Conner

Location: Sixty-five thousand Buriat in China were noted separately in the 1982 census before being officially included in the Mongolian nationality. The majority of Buriat (420,000) live in the Republic of Buryatia in Russia. An additional 48,000 live in the northeastern part of Mongolia. The Buriat occupy a vast tract of land from the grasslands of the Chinese province of Inner Mongolia to deep inside Siberia. The Buriat in China are a scattered group living in the remote Hulunbuir region of the Inner Mongolia Autonomous Region.

Identity: The Buriat originally consisted of several Mongolian people groups and clans who were recognized as five distinct tribes.[1] The Buriat still share many common traits and customs with the Mongols, but there are many historical and linguistic differences that qualify them as a distinct ethnolinguistic people group.

Language: The Buriat language spoken in China is different from the Buriat in Mongolia and Russia. The Buriat "speak a highly distinctive dialect of Mongolian."[2]

History: The Buriat people claim to be descended from either a gray bull or a white swan.[3] For many generations the Buriat in Russia and Mongolia have been considered different from the mainstream Mongolian group. The Buriat in China are relatively recent arrivals, having migrated from Siberia to Inner Mongolia in 1917.[4]

Customs: The *yokhor* folk dance plays an important role in the lives of the Buriat. Young girls imitate the actions and movements of birds and animals. Most Buriat live in mud and wood houses, although some are still nomads.[5]

Religion: Historically the Buriat have been shamanists and polytheists, allowing mediums to control all interaction between the gods and the Buriat communities. To be a shaman, a person had to be seen to possess *utkha*, a mystical spiritual energy. Early missionary William Swan lamented his team's lack of power to combat the authority of the shamans: "No Christian missionaries, at least none deserving the name, now pretend to the possession of miraculous gifts."[6] There has been a recent revival of shamanism and Tibetan Buddhism among the Buriat. A new religion called *Burkanism* has also appeared among them in recent years.[7]

Christianity: There are no known Christians among the Buriat in China, although small numbers of Buriat Orthodox believers live in Russia. In 1922 missionaries were challenged to work in the Buriat region of China: "It is a well-watered, fertile region.... The domination of Lama priests does not extend to this region."[8] The first Protestant missionaries to the Buriat in Russia were the Stallybrass and Rahmn families who worked in Siberia from 1818 to 1840.[9] They reported the Buriat converts "rejoiced to know that God did not make any distinctions between rich and poor. They had a new identity as people liberated from the bondage of their past life."[10] By 1827 the Old Testament and the four Gospels were translated into Buriat.[11] The script used is now obsolete. A new translation is in progress.

Population in China:
65,000 (1982)
98,900 (2000)
127,600 (2010)
Location: Inner Mongolia
Religion: Shamanism
Christians: None Known

Overview of the Buriat

Countries: Russia, China, Mongolia

Pronunciation: "Boo-ree-aht"

Other Names: Buryat, Northern Mongolian, Buriat-Mongolian, Northeastern Mongolian, Bargu

Population Source: 65,000 (1982 census); Out of a total Mongol population of 4,806,849 (1990 census); 420,000 in Russia (1993 P. Johnstone); 48,000 in Mongolia (1993 P. Johnstone)

Location: *NE Inner Mongolia:* Hulunbuir District near the China-Russia-Mongolia border

Status: Officially included under Mongolian

Language: Altaic, Mongolian, Eastern Mongolian, Oirat-Khalka, Khalkha-Buriat, Buriat

Dialects (4): New Bargu (47,000), Old Bargu (14,000), Khori, Aga

Religion: Shamanism, Tibetan Buddhism

Christians: None known

Scripture: Portions 1827; Work in progress

***Jesus* film:** None

Gospel Recordings: None

Christian Broadcasting: None

ROPAL code: BXU00

Status of Evangelization

	A	B	C
%	87%	13%	0%

A = Have never heard the gospel
B = Were evangelized but did not become Christians
C = Are adherents to any form of Christianity

Buyang 布央

Population in China:
3,000 (1990)
3,450 (2000)
4,000 (2010)
Location: Yunnan
Religion: Ancestor Worship
Christians: None Known

Overview of the Buyang

Countries: China

Pronunciation: "Boo-yung"

Other Names: Burong, Punung, Bunong, Punong, Pulung

Population Source: 2,000 to 3,000 (1990 Liang Min); Out of a total Zhuang population of 15,489,630 (1990 census)

Location: *SE Yunnan:* Wenshan, Guangnan, and Funing counties

Status: Officially included under Zhuang

Language: Daic, Kadai, Bu-Rong

Dialects: 0

Religion: Ancestor Worship, Animism, Polytheism

Christians: None known

Scripture: None

***Jesus* film:** None

Gospel Recordings: None

Christian Broadcasting: None

ROPAL code: BYU00

Status of Evangelization

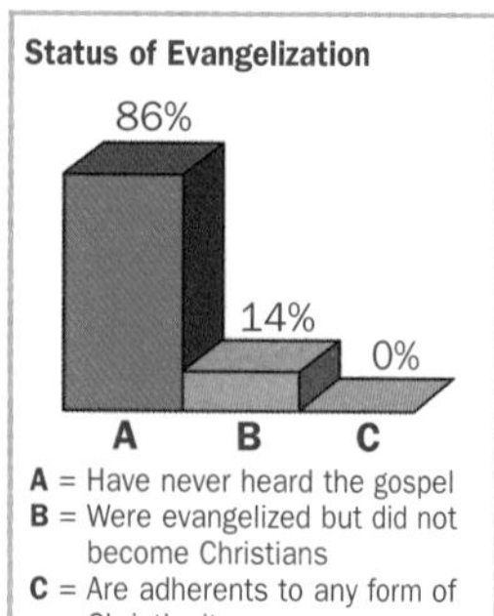

A = Have never heard the gospel
B = Were evangelized but did not become Christians
C = Are adherents to any form of Christianity

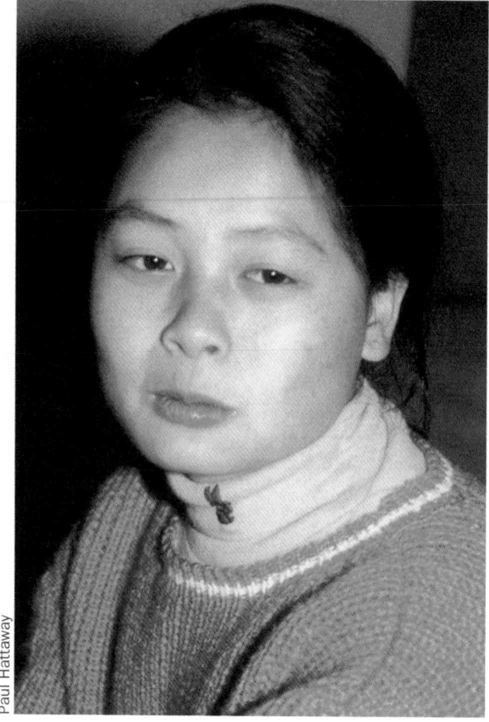

Paul Hattaway

Location: Approximately 3,500 Buyang are spread across a number of different locations in the Wenshan Zhuang-Miao Autonomous Prefecture in the extreme southeast part of Yunnan. The majority live in Funing County, with 300 in Langjia village, 200 in Maguan, 200 in Ecun, 180 in Lagan, 50 near Nongna, 20 at Damen, and 30 to 40 in Jinglong Township. There are also "scattered settlements" in Guangnan County farther to the northwest.[1]

Identity: The Buyang are officially part of China's largest official minority — the Zhuang. As one anthropologist notes, "After 1953 the Buyang were incorporated into the Zhuang."[2] Buyang, however, is a distinct language and is not intelligible with other forms of Zhuang. The Buyang are known by a number of different names. One visitor in the early 1920s stated, "We slept in a village of Tai people, which the Chinese call *Punong*, or *Punung*, or *Pulung*. We heard them called all three of these pretty names."[3]

Language: Buyang is only spoken within their communities. Being a multilinguistic people, the Buyang speak Mandarin to outsiders. Most Buyang between the ages of 15 and 50 are also able to speak Southern Zhuang. About half can also speak Yerong. The Buyang language has six tones and is classified as part of the Kadai family of languages. It is reported to have 38% lexical similarity with Pubiao, 34% with Lati, and 32% with Northern Zhuang.[4] The Buyang do not have a written script.

History: This small tribe speak a language exhibiting influences from many different groups, making it difficult to trace their historical roots. It is known that the Buyang are recent arrivals to their present location. One writer notes, "Due to historical reasons... the Bunong [Buyang] have moved to different places and had different titles but still kept the same characteristics (the same language, customs and traditions)."[5]

Customs: The Buyang practice wet-rice agriculture on terraced hillsides. Other crops include sugarcane, tung oil, and tea. Chinese geckos are also caught and used in traditional Chinese medicine to help people regain vitality.

Religion: The Buyang worship their ancestors, carefully observing rituals that have been designed to ensure that their forefathers are taken care of in the next life. Food is placed in front of altars along with pictures of deceased family members, so the spirits of the dead will not go hungry. The Buyang also burn large amounts of paper money, believing the practice will break any hold of poverty that may have ensnared the dead.

Christianity: Ancestor worship has trapped the Buyang in spiritual bondage, keeping them from accepting any social or religious change. Few Buyang have any awareness of the gospel or the Person of Jesus Christ. All Buyang homes have ancestral altars mounted on the wall of the main room. In the mid-1990s a large revival took place among the Hmong Daw farther south as a result of gospel radio broadcasts in the Miao language, but few Buyang have any contact with the Hmong Daw. No Scriptures or recordings have ever been translated for the Buyang.

Cai 碳家

Population in China:
17,000 (1982)
25,800 (2000)
33,300 (2010)
Location: Guizhou
Religion: Polytheism
Christians: 400

Overview of the Cai

Countries: China

Pronunciation: "Tsai"

Other Names: Caijia, Se-ni, Ma Ah-oh-na, Cai Jia Miao, Song Ren, Man Ni, Awuzi

Population Source: 17,000 (1982 *Minzu Shibie Wenxian Ziliao Huibian*)

Location: *W Guizhou:* Dafang, Zhijin, Nayong, Weining, Bijie, and Qianxi counties

Status: Counted in census as an *Undetermined Minority*

Language: Daic, Tai, Unclassified

Dialects: 0

Religion: Polytheism, Animism, Ancestor Worship, Christianity

Christians: 400

Scripture: None

***Jesus* film:** None

Gospel Recordings: None

Christian Broadcasting: None

ROPAL code: None

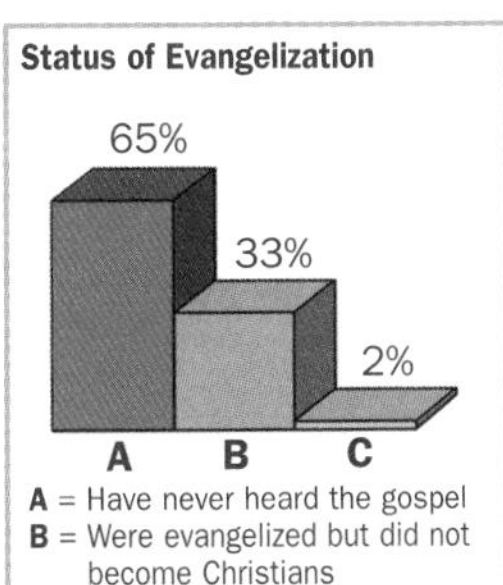

Location: In 1982 a total of 17,000 Cai people inhabited communities in western Guizhou province. They are concentrated in Dafang, Zhijin, Nayong, Weining, Bijie, and Qianxi counties.[1] The Cai live in the vicinity of numerous ethnic groups, including several distinct Yi and Miao groups. The Cai may call themselves *Man Ni*. The Miao call the Cai *Se-ni*; the Yi call them *Ah-oh-ma*, and the Han know them as *Cai Jia Miao*.

Identity: The Cai, who are also known as the Caijia, have never been included as part of any official nationality by the Chinese authorities. In the 1982 census they were placed in a list of *Undetermined Minorities*. The Cai were just one of 80 groups in Guizhou on this list which totaled more than 900,000 people.[2] In 1985 many of these groups were assigned into existing nationalities, but scholars remained baffled by the complexity of the Cai. They remain an unclassified group, although the authorities believe them to be related to the Miao. The Cai consider themselves distinct from all other ethnic groups in the region and strongly insist on being granted their own minority status.

Language: It is believed that the Cai speak a language which is part of the Tai linguistic family, possibly related to Gelao; however, no specific research has ever been conducted to determine their linguistic affiliation.

History: During the Ming Dynasty (1368–1644), when the Cai were a stronger and much larger group than today, they appeared in historical accounts as the *Song Ren*. They are believed to have fragmented into smaller groups over the past 300 years. Today the Lu ethnic group are ethnoculturally close to the Cai. The Cai intermarry with the Lu and consider them to have once been related.

Customs: Dafang, where most Cai live, is renowned across China for its beautiful lacquerware. More than 70 varieties of wild azaleas and rhododendrons also grow in the area. The Cai used to wear clothes made of fur. This can still be seen in some of the more remote Cai villages today. Many Cai are employed as shepherds and goatherds. A sizable number also work in the carpet-making industry.

Religion: Most Cai worship many gods and spirits, although in recent decades an increasing Christian presence has also emerged among them. The polytheistic Cai blow leaves to worship spirits. When a Cai person dies, the people attending the funeral are not permitted to cry or show any remorse. Instead, they walk around the corpse and sing.

Christianity: A conservative estimate places the number of Cai Christians at 400. The true number of believers may be significantly higher. Most Cai Christians heard the gospel from Yi and Miao evangelists who were sent to reach out to them. The northwest Guizhou region was first targeted by missionaries in the late 1800s. A mass people movement to Christ occurred in the early 1900s, especially among the A-Hmao (Big Flowery Miao). Today there are numerous Christian communities in Dafang County, but believers live in dire poverty and have few Bibles.

Paul Hattaway

Cao Lan 草兰

Location: The Global Evangelization Movement listed a 1995 population of 36,677 Cao Lan in China.[1] In addition, more than 114,000 live in northern Vietnam where they are known as *San Chay*. The Cao Lan are located along the Yunnan-Vietnam border in Xichou County. In Vietnam they inhabit the lower Red River area, with communities in seven different provinces: Tuyen Quang, Bac Thai, Ha Bac, Quang Ninh, Yen Bai, Lang Son, and Vinh Phu.

Identity: The Cao Lan are officially considered part of the Zhuang nationality in China. They speak a distinct language — different from other Zhuang varieties — and possess their own set of customs and traditions.

Language: Cao Lan is part of the Central Tai linguistic family. "The Cao Lan, a Sinicized group, consists mainly in various areas of the delta of northern Vietnam; it is also found in smaller numbers in China."[2] It is possible that the Cao Lan language in China is what linguists label the *Yan-Guang* dialect of Southern Zhuang.[3]

History: The Cao Lan in Vietnam migrated from southern China in the first half of the nineteenth century.[4] Cao Lan communities are divided into various family lineages, each clan having their own peculiar customs and their own protective spirit.[5] The Nung and Cao Lan joined with a powerful Hmong army in northern Vietnam in the 1860s. They took possession of large tracts of land and raided Buddhist temples of their gold. The Cao Lan were deceived into following Sioung — the charismatic, self-proclaimed Hmong king.[6]

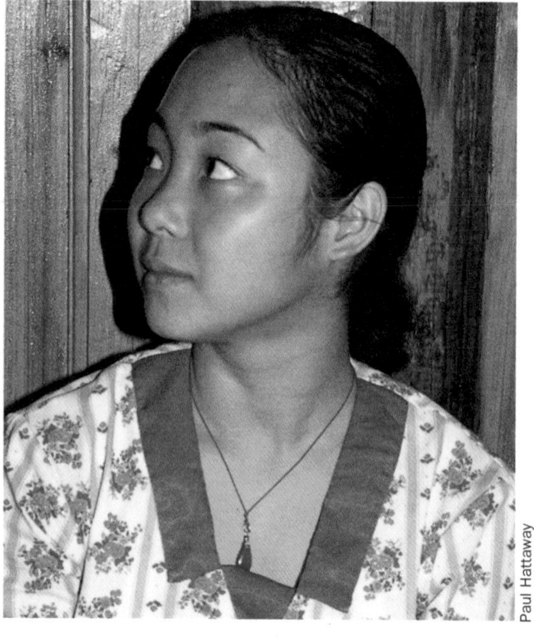

Paul Hattaway

Customs: Strict morality codes are practiced among the rural Cao Lan. Women must observe strict rules and customs. Whenever a woman encounters a man in a social position superior to her husband's, she is required to hide behind bamboo.[7] The Cao Lan were traditionally buried when they died but, due to a lack of land, the government has recently begun demanding that the dead be cremated instead. Traditionally, when the body was placed in the coffin, seven coins were added for a man and nine for a woman. The coins represent the *Khue* star which they believe guides the person's soul to his or her ancestors in the other world.

Religion: Spirit worship takes a major place in the lives of the Cao Lan population. Each branch of the nationality worships a different spirit such as the spirit of the river, the trees, the crops, etc. Elaborate festivals include the playing of castanets, copper bells, drums, cymbals, and wind instruments.

Christianity: In China, as well as in Vietnam, the Cao Lan are unreached with the gospel, although 26 families in Vietnam came to Christ in 1999. Very few have had any exposure to the Christian message and the name of Christ remains unknown. Northern Vietnam and southern China have been Communist strongholds for three generations. There are no Scriptures, gospel recordings, or *Jesus* film currently available in the Cao Lan language, and no Christian ministries or Western mission organizations are known to be targeting them.

Population in China:
36,677 (1995)
40,270 (2000)
48,150 (2010)
Location: Yunnan
Religion: Animism
Christians: None Known

Overview of the Cao Lan

Countries: Vietnam, China

Pronunciation: "Cow-Lahn"

Other Names: Man Cao Lan, San Chay, San Chi, Lan-San Chi, Hon Ban

Population Source:
36,677 (1995 GEM);
Out of a total Zhuang population of 15,489,630 (1990 census);
114,000 in Vietnam (1989 census)

Location:
SE Yunnan: Xichou County

Status:
Officially included under Zhuang

Language: Daic, Tai, Central Tai

Dialects: 0

Religion: Animism, Polytheism, Ancestor Worship

Christians: None known

Scripture: None

***Jesus* film:** None

Gospel Recordings: None

Christian Broadcasting: None

ROPAL code: MLCOO

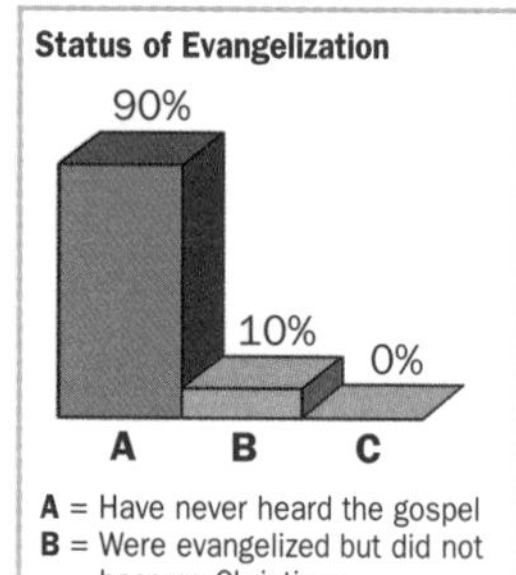

Changpao 长袍

Population in China:
5,000 (1999)
5,140 (2000)
6,630 (2010)
Location: Guizhou
Religion: Animism
Christians: None Known

Overview of the Changpao

Countries: China

Pronunciation: "Chung-paow"

Other Names: Changpao Yao

Population Source:
5,000 (1999 AMO);
Out of a total Yao population of 2,134,013 (1990 census)

Location: *S Guizhou*

Status: Officially included under Yao since 1985;
Previously included in a list of *Undetermined Minorities*

Language:
Hmong-Mien, Unclassified

Dialects: 0

Religion: Animism, Ancestor Worship, Daoism

Christians: None known

Scripture: None

***Jesus* film:** None

Gospel Recordings: None

Christian Broadcasting: None

ROPAL code: None

Status of Evangelization

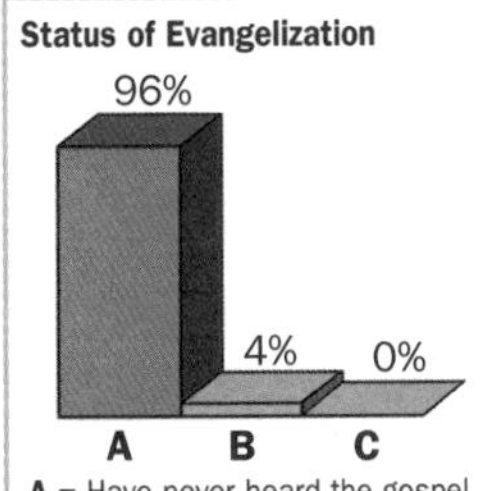

A = Have never heard the gospel
B = Were evangelized but did not become Christians
C = Are adherents to any form of Christianity

Paul Hattaway

Location: Approximately 5,000 members of the Changpao ethnic group live in an unspecified part of southwestern or southern Guizhou Province in southern China.[1] Guizhou "is an intense table-land with a mean altitude of 4,200 feet [1,280 meters]. Deep narrow rivers intersect the table-land which is studded with numerous mountain peaks, some of which, especially in the west, attain an altitude of 8,000 or 9,000 feet [2,440–2,740 meters]."[2]

Identity: When the Chinese sent their teams of experts throughout China to determine the official nationalities, they could not decide which minority group the Changpao were related to. In the 1982 census they were placed in a list of *Undetermined Minorities*. In 1985, possibly at their own insistence, they were reclassified as part of the Yao nationality.[3] The name *Changpao* is Chinese in origin. It is not known what this group calls itself. There is little doubt, however, that from a mission-significant viewpoint the Changpao should be considered a distinct group.

Language: Little is known about the language of the Changpao. Because they were officially considered Yao, it is likely they speak a variety from the Hmong-Mien language family, but whether it is part of the Mienic or Hmongic branch (such as the many Bunu languages in southern China) remains undetermined.

History: The history of the classification of the Changpao began in 1953 when they applied for recognition as a distinct minority group. They appeared on a list as one of 80 groups in Guizhou that remained unclassified. After research, the list of 80 was reduced to only 23 "actual" groups, which included the Changpao. Although they have now been named as part of the Yao, the bureaucratic struggle of the Changpao is indicative of their struggle as a people group to survive against all odds. Poor soil, wars, and famine have combined to keep the Changpao population low over the centuries.

Customs: Culturally, the Changpao share many similarities with the Yao of Guangxi. They may be related to the various Bunu groups, who are linguistically Miao but culturally Yao after countless generations of living near Yao communities.

Religion: Throughout the course of the year, Changpao families observe several ceremonies dedicated to spirit worship and ancestor worship. Daoist priests are also consulted about many important festivities and rituals over which they then preside.

Christianity: Because the location of the Changpao has yet to be specified, nothing is known of the status of Christianity among them. There are no more than a handful of known Yao believers in the whole province, so it is likely that the Changpao are an unreached and largely unevangelized people group. Protestant missionary activity in Guizhou, which commenced when C. H. Judd and J. F. Braumton of the China Inland Mission arrived in 1877, experienced great success among the A-Hmao and Gha-Mu. Few other areas of the province have received a gospel witness.

Changshu Miao 长梳苗

Paul Hattaway

Location: Approximately 15,800 Changshu Miao live along the road between Yangliu and Geli townships in Zhenning County; and as far north as Jichang Township in Anshun County in the western part of Guizhou Province. A new highway has been constructed between Anshun and Guiyang (the provincial capital), reducing the journey to only two hours. The Changshu Miao live in the same area as people from the Bouyei, Chuanqing, and Hmong Shuad ethnic groups.

Identity: Although they have been included as part of the Miao nationality, the Changshu Miao consider themselves to be a unique group and do not consider other Miao groups to be related to them. They generally do not marry outside of their tribe, although this custom is being relaxed in recent years as more youth are traveling to towns and cities in search for jobs. The name *Changshu* Miao is a Chinese word meaning "long comb" Miao. It is uncertain what this group calls itself.

Language: Linguistically, the Changshu Miao speak a variety of Hmong Shuad, which is widely spoken throughout the region. It is a part of the Chuanqiandian (Western) Miao language family.

History: Anshun has been an important trading town in southwest China since the thirteenth century. Merchants from as far away as Burma (Myanmar) frequently came through Anshun. The Chinese described Anshun as "the throat to Yunnan and the belly of Guizhou."[1]

Customs: The Changshu Miao are a distinctively dressed group. "The women wear an ankle length non-pleated white skirt which has about four broad horizontal black bands. The shirt opens in the middle. The hair, along with false hair, is hung on a bamboo comb at least 18 inches long that sticks out horizontally from one side of the head."[2] Every year, on the 12th, 13th, and 14th days of the first lunar month, a Miao festival called *Tiao Hua Chang* is held near Anshun. The people meet at an appointed festival site known as the Flower Ground. It offers a chance for relatives and friends to catch up with each other. Young girls display their finest embroidery and silver jewelry, hoping to capture the attention of a young suitor.

Religion: Most Changshu Miao families are animists. They are a highly superstitious people. Probably because of their prolonged contact with the Chinese, the Changshu Miao also worship their ancestors. Every home has an ancestral altar which is the focal point of attention during festivals and religious events.

Christianity: There are no known Christian believers among the Changshu Miao. It is possible that there are a small number of Catholics among them, as there are several Bouyei and Chinese Catholic churches in the vicinity. There are no Scriptures or audio recordings available in the Changshu Miao language, although most are adequately bilingual in the Guizhou dialect of Chinese.

Population in China:
15,000 (1998)
15,870 (2000)
20,470 (2010)
Location: Guizhou
Religion: Animism
Christians: None Known

Overview of the Changshu Miao

Countries: China
Pronunciation: "Chung-shoo-Meow"
Other Names: Changshu Hmong, Long Comb Miao
Population Source: 15,000 (1998 AMO); Out of a total Miao population of 7,398,035 (1990 census)
Location: *W Guizhou:* Along the road from Yangliu and Geli in Zhenning County to Jichang in Anshun County
Status: Officially included under Miao
Language: Hmong-Mien, Hmongic, Western Hmongic, Han Miao
Dialects: 0
Religion: Animism, Polytheism, Ancestor Worship
Christians: None known
Scripture: None
***Jesus* film:** None
Gospel Recordings: None
Christian Broadcasting: None
ROPAL code: None

Status of Evangelization

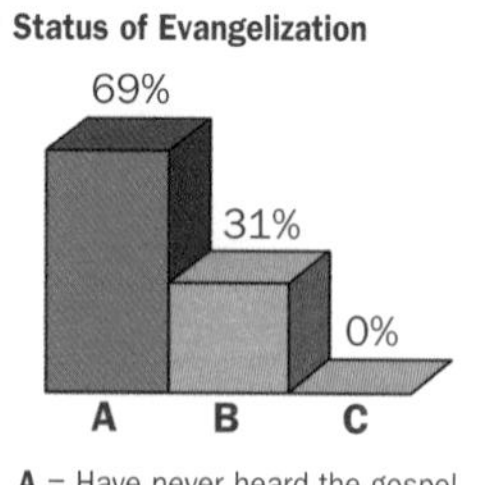

A = Have never heard the gospel
B = Were evangelized but did not become Christians
C = Are adherents to any form of Christianity

Chesu 车苏

Location: Approximately 6,600 members of the Chesu tribe inhabit the southern part of Shuangbai County in Chuxiong Prefecture and the adjacent northern part of Xinping County in Yuxi Prefecture. The Chesu population in Shuangbai actually fell from 2,769 in 1957[1] to 2,528 in 1986.[2] Most Chesu villages are located in remote mountainous areas, deep within forests.

Identity: The existence of the Chesu people has been mentioned in few Chinese publications and never in mission people group lists. The Chesu do not consider themselves part of the Yi nationality. The Han Chinese and other minorities in Chesu areas do not think of the Chesu as Yi either. Local people believe the "Chesu are Chesu, and Yi are Yi... the Chesu speak the Chesu language, and the Yi speak the Yi language," as one elderly man remarked in northern Xinping County.

Language: Although the Chesu claim their language is not a Yi language, preliminary studies suggest it belongs to the Southern Yi language group and is similar to the Lesu language. Few Chesu are able to understand Mandarin Chinese.

History: Originally the Chesu were part of a great Tibeto-Burman race, who were forced to migrate south to their present location under pressure from the advancing Han Chinese, beginning in the fourth century AD. The Han themselves had been forced to move south due to the disrupting influence of the wild barbarian invaders in the north. "Six or seven out of every ten gentry families joined the southward march. In many cases, entire clans including neighbors and servants left their homes and traveled hundreds of miles to establish new homes south of the Yangtze River."[3] One writer notes the result of these massive Han migrations: "As this contact occurred, the non-Han peoples were pushed back by the Han into the mountains, usually much more barren than the fertile river valleys where they had been living."[4]

Jamin Pelkey

Customs: The Chesu people living in Damidi District in Shuangbai County celebrate the annual Body-Wrinkle Dance Festival. It is held on two separate days, on the 24th day of the sixth lunar month and then on the 15th day of the seventh month. Participants dress up in panther costumes and mimic the movements of the panther. The festival remembers the time when large cats roamed the central Yunnan region, terrorizing the local inhabitants.

Religion: The Chesu offer sacrifices to animals such as panthers, bears, and tigers. They believe the spirits of these powerful animals can protect their communities from harm and disease.

Christianity: The Chesu are one of the people groups most untouched by Christianity in China. Few Chesu have ever been evangelized, although in March 2000 a few Chesu came to Christ when visited by Chinese evangelists. The preachers reported the Chesu are very responsive and open, but that ministry to them is difficult because of the lack of Mandarin understood by the Chesu. They live in such remote areas that outsiders have failed in their bid to even locate the Chesu.

Population in China:
6,350 (1998)
6,670 (2000)
8,370 (2010)
Location: Yunnan
Religion: Polytheism
Christians: 20

Overview of the Chesu

Countries: China

Pronunciation: "Cheh-soo"

Other Names: Chesupuo, Sanpuo, Qisu, Qisupuo

Population Source:
6,350 (1998 J. Pelkey);
Out of a total Yi population of 6,572,173 (1990 census)

Location: *Yunnan:* Chuxiong Prefecture: Shuangbai County (2,850); Yuxi Prefecture: Xinping County (3,500)

Status:
Officially included under Yi

Language: Sino-Tibetan, Tibeto-Burman, Burmese-Lolo, Lolo, Northern Lolo, Yi, Southern Yi

Dialects: 0

Religion: Polytheism, Animism, Ancestor Worship, Christianity

Christians: 20

Scripture: None

***Jesus* film:** None

Gospel Recordings: None

Christian Broadcasting: None

ROPAL code: None

Status of Evangelization

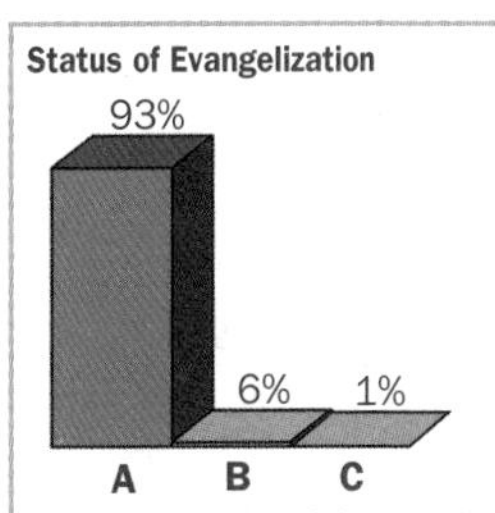

A = Have never heard the gospel
B = Were evangelized but did not become Christians
C = Are adherents to any form of Christianity

Chin, Asho 阿苏痴念

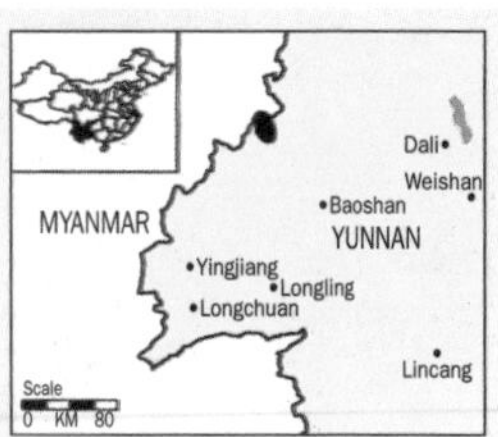

Population in China:
150 (1996)
167 (2000)
215 (2010)
Location: Yunnan
Religion: Animism
Christians: None Known

Overview of the Asho Chin

Countries: Myanmar, Bangladesh, China

Pronunciation: "Chin-Ah-sho"

Other Names: Ashu, Shoa, Kyang, Sho, Qin, Khyang, Khyeng

Population Source: 150 (1996 AMO); 10,000 in Myanmar (1991 United Bible Societies); 1,422 in Bangladesh (1981 census)

Location: *W Yunnan*

Status: Unidentified

Language: Sino-Tibetan, Tibeto-Burman, Baric, Kuki-Naga, Kuki-Chin, Southern Kuki-Chin, Sho

Dialects: 0

Religion: Animism

Christians: None known

Scripture: New Testament 1954; Portions 1921

***Jesus* film:** None

Gospel Recordings: Asho Chin #00401

Christian Broadcasting: Available in Myanmar (FEBC)

ROPAL code: CSH00

Status of Evangelization

	A	B	C
%	71%	29%	0%

A = Have never heard the gospel
B = Were evangelized but did not become Christians
C = Are adherents to any form of Christianity

Location: Between 100 and 200 Asho Chin people live in western Yunnan Province near the China-Myanmar border. One publication states, "There are probably less than 100 in China."[1] Apparently there is some confusion as to whether the Asho Chin are located in China at all. The 1992 *Ethnologue* listed the Asho Chin as being in China, but the 1996 edition states they are not.[2] The Asho Chin who live in Myanmar, however, are aware that they have members of their group living in China.[3] Furthermore, missionary John Kuhn, in his 1945 survey of Yunnan, lists the Asho Chin under the name *Ashu* and places them in "Chiangcheng."[4] More than 10,000 Asho Chin are located along the lowlands of the Irrawaddy River in Myanmar, in addition to 1,422 living in Bangladesh.

Identity: The Asho Chin are part of the great Chin race of Myanmar and India. There are approximately 1.4 million Chin,[5] speaking 19 distinct languages and more than 40 dialects. It is not known in what nationality, if any, the Asho Chin of China have been included by the authorities.

Language: Asho Chin is a member of the Tibeto-Burman language family and is most closely related to Siangbaung Chin. It has no traditional script, although a Romanized script was used by missionaries to translate the Asho Chin Bible.

History: Chin history goes back to the dawn of time. "The Chins have a story of the Tower of Babel to account for the various clans that inhabit the range of hills... and traditions of a deluge are found everywhere."[6] In the past, whole communities of Asho Chin in Myanmar were decimated by malaria. Why this group of Asho Chin migrated from their Myanmar homeland to faraway China is not known.

Customs: The Asho Chin have many customs involving courtship and marriage. "All the marriageable girls have their own rooms where young men come courting at night. If a girl gets pregnant, the parents allow them to marry.... If the girl's family agrees, they may demand five or six pigs or a couple of cows as a dowry."[7]

Religion: Most Asho Chin are animists even though many of the other Chin groups in Myanmar have embraced Christianity. "The people are afraid of evil spirits and of the spirits of their dead ancestors. In order to appease the angry spirits, they offer sacrifices of cows, pigs, buffaloes, goats, dogs or chickens."[8]

Christianity: The status of Christianity among the Asho Chin in China is unknown. In Myanmar they were a completely untouched people group until native evangelists visited them in 1987: "The tribe was isolated from others — accessible only by dugout canoes, since there was not even a footpath or road to their villages.... During the time the missionaries taught.... 76 people invited Jesus into their lives."[9] Gospel radio broadcasts are available in the Asho Chin language, but they are aimed at Myanmar and are probably not received in China.

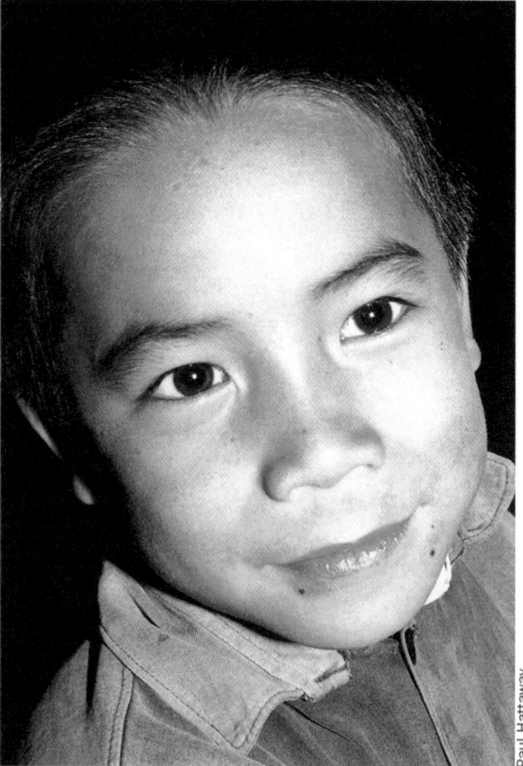
Paul Hattaway

Chrame 差没

Paul Hattaway

Location: A widespread, isolated area of southwest Sichuan Province is home to approximately 39,000 Chrame people. Most are located in and around Muli County, described as "a rich possession. The rivers, especially the Litang, carry gold and produce a considerable revenue."[1] Scattered Chrame communities are found as far west as the Yarlung (Dadu) River at Shimian, 200 kilometers (123 mi.) from Muli and as far north as Wenchuan County.[2] In addition, a small number of Chrame live in the Yongning District of Ninglang County in northern Yunnan Province. The Chrame king once "held sway over a territory of 9,000 square miles — an area slightly larger than Massachusetts."[3]

Identity: Chrame is the self-name of this group.[4] In the past, they were commonly known as *Xifan*, a derogatory Chinese name meaning "barbarians of the west" — a name not only applied to this group but sometimes also used for all Tibetans.[5] The Chrame "are a member of the Tibetan *minzu* [nationality], but feel they have little in common with the Tibetans."[6]

Language: The Chrame language — which has three tones and five dialects — has been labeled by Chinese scholars as a northern variety of Pumi. There is 60% lexical similarity between Chrame and Southern Pumi. When explorer Joseph Rock visited the Chrame in 1924, he noted "the king's knowledge of Tibetan was poor."[7]

History: Muli was formerly a Buddhist monastery town resided over by a king until the 1950s. "The rulers of Muli are said to be of Manchu origin. They were given the sovereignty of the kingdom in perpetuity in recognition of valorous services rendered to Yungcheng, the famous Manchu emperor, who ascended the throne in 1723."[8] In the past the Chrame were often attacked by Nosu raiders from the east. The Chrame king ruled with "absolute spiritual and temporal sway"[9] over his subjects. "The villagers occupy wooden shanties scattered over the hillsides below the town. They are very poor, and live in constant fear of the lama king and his parasitic satellites."[10]

Customs: A 1981 survey of 131 households in Muli found 52% of the marriages engaged in monogamy, 32% practiced *polyandry* (brothers sharing a wife), and 16% practiced *polygamy* (sisters sharing a husband).[11] The king of Muli was fond of feeding visitors "dried legs of mutton and yak cheese... propelled by squirming maggots the size of a man's thumb." Rock's group gave theirs to the beggars, who "fought for it like tigers."[12]

Religion: All Chrame adhere to Tibetan Buddhism. It forms a major part of their ethnic and cultural identity. The Chrame inwardly long for the restoration of their kingdom and their former prestige among the other peoples of the area.

Christianity: The Chrame are one of the most unreached people groups in China. There has never been a single known Chrame church or Christian believer. The Baptist missionaries Dan and Lucy Carr planned to work in Muli in the late 1940s, but they were evacuated from China before they had the opportunity to move there.

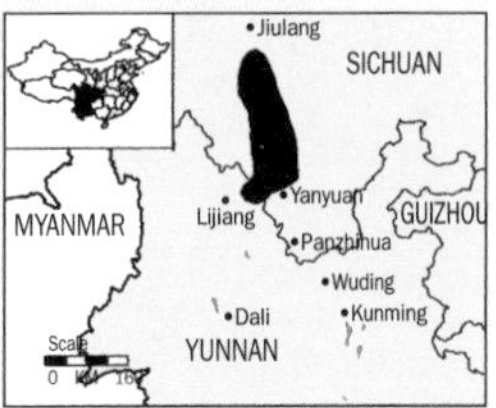

Population in China:
30,000 (1987)
39,000 (2000)
48,100 (2010)
Location: Sichuan, Yunnan
Religion: Tibetan Buddhism
Christians: None Known

Overview of the Chrame

Countries: China
Pronunciation: "Krah-mee"
Other Names: Hsifan, Xifan, Pumi: Northern
Population Source: 30,000 (1987 *LAC*); Out of a total Tibetan population of 4,593,330 (1990 census)
Location: *SW Sichuan:* Muli, Yanyuan; and Jiulong counties; Scattered as far north as Wenchuan County; *N Yunnan:* Ninglang County
Status: Officially included under Tibetan
Language: Sino-Tibetan, Tibeto-Burman, Qiangic, Pumi, Northern Pumi
Dialects: 5
Religion: Tibetan Buddhism, Polytheism
Christians: None known
Scripture: None
***Jesus* film:** None
Gospel Recordings: None
Christian Broadcasting: None
ROPAL code: HSI00 (Xifan); CMY00 (Chrame)

Status of Evangelization

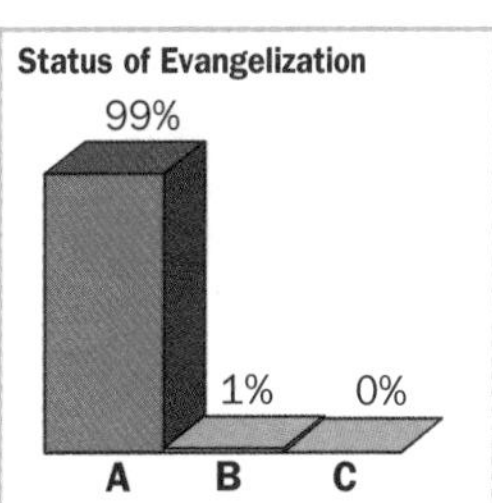

A = Have never heard the gospel
B = Were evangelized but did not become Christians
C = Are adherents to any form of Christianity

Chuanlan 穿兰

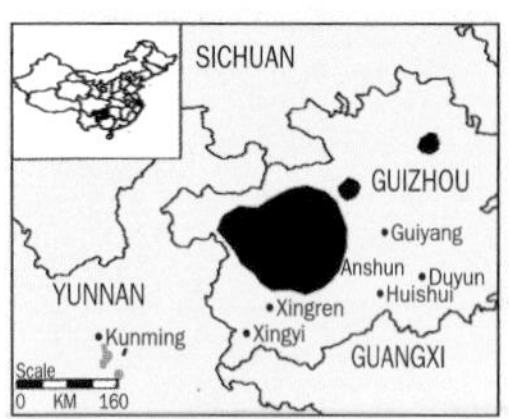

Population in China:
200,000 (1952)
324,800 (2000)
367,000 (2010)
Location: Guizhou
Religion: Ancestor Worship
Christians: 20,000

Overview of the Chuanlan

Countries: China

Pronunciation: "Chooan-lahn"

Other Names: Chuanchun, Ch'uan-chun-tsi, Lao Han, Old Han

Population Source:
More than 200,000 (1952 Fei Xiaotong);
Out of a total Han population of 1,042,482,187 (1990 census)

Location:
W Guizhou: Anshun, Bijie, Weining, and Pingyuan counties

Status: Officially included under Han Chinese

Language:
Chinese, Guizhou dialect

Dialects: 0

Religion: Ancestor Worship, No Religion, Daoism, Christianity, Animism, Buddhism

Christians: 20,000

Scripture: Chinese Bible

***Jesus* film:** None

Gospel Recordings:
Mandarin: Guiyanghua #04574

Christian Broadcasting: None

ROPAL code: None

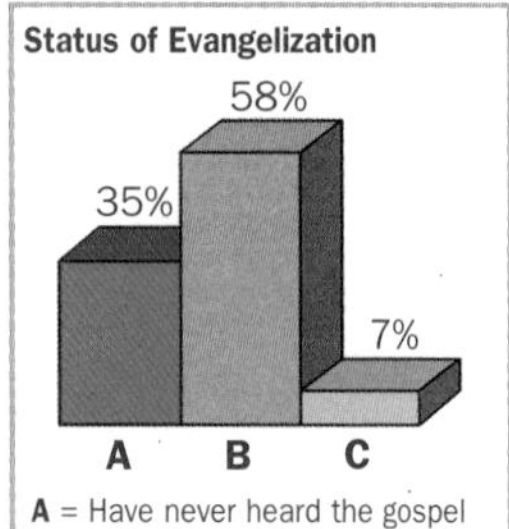

Dwayne Graybill

Location: Approximately 300,000 Chuanlan people are concentrated within Anshun Prefecture in southern China's Guizhou Province. A precise population for the Chuanlan is difficult to obtain. In the early 1950s their population was listed as "more than 200,000,"[1] while a more recent estimate puts their numbers at "several hundred thousand people."[2] Most Chuanlan are located in Anshun, but historically others have lived as far west as Weining County and as far north as Pingyuan.[3] Today Anshun is one of the largest industrial and coal-mining areas of southern China.

Identity: The Chuanlan (Blue-Dressed People) are also known as *Lao Han* (Old Han) by people in Guizhou. In the 1950s the Chuanlan applied for recognition as a separate minority group. Their application was rejected, and they were included as part of the Han Chinese nationality. "Some people of the Han nationality who had migrated into regions inhabited by ethnic minorities in the past, such as the Chuanlan ('the blue-dressed people') in Guizhou, were not recognized as an independent 'nationality'."[4] This upset the Chuanlan who reapplied in the late 1970s, only to be rejected again.

Language: The Chuanlan speak the Guizhou dialect of Chinese as their mother tongue. Many can also speak Bouyei or Miao, depending on their location and the amount of interaction they have had with those groups. Most Chuanlan women and children do not know any Mandarin.

History: The Chuanlan are a Han Chinese group who have remained ethnically, linguistically and socially distinct. The Chinese in Guizhou are divided into the *Lao-han-ren* and *Keh-jia* — that is, the "Original" or "Old Chinese" and the "Immigrants". The "Old Chinese" claimed to have settled in Guizhou in the eighth and ninth centuries AD. A second wave arrived in the fourteenth century. These were soldiers who were left in the area after military campaigns.[5] Many took minority women as wives and formed separate communities.

Customs: Chuanlan women wear distinctive indigo dresses that feature intricate embroidery similar to the Miao. Many Chuanlan customs have been borrowed from the Miao and Bouyei.

Religion: The majority of Chuanlan practice traditional Chinese religions. Elements of ancestor worship, Daoism, Confucianism, Buddhism, and animism are found among them. In addition, there are many atheist Chuanlan who have forsaken all outward appearance of religion because of pressure from the Communist regime.

Christianity: There are many Chuanlan believers in the region. Seventy thousand Christians are reported in Bijie alone,[6] although most of them are Miao and Yi. During the 1930s, the Communists confiscated the two main churches in Bijie and used them for their headquarters. They have now become a revolutionary museum in commemoration of the Communist's Long March.[7] Although they speak a distinct Chinese dialect — for which gospel recordings were recently made — the Chuanlan are able to use the Chinese Bible in their church services.

Chuanqing 穿青

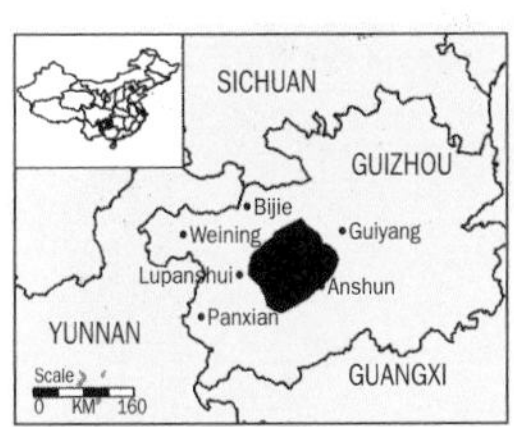

Population in China:
500,000 (1982)
761,000 (2000)
981,600 (2010)
Location: Guizhou
Religion: Ancestor Worship
Christians: 20,000

Overview of the Chuanqing

Countries: China

Pronunciation: "Chooan-ching"

Other Names: Chuangqing, Chuanchun, Lao Han, Pu, Pu Ren, Tun, Fang Teo Ren, Old Han, Sher-tu, Sher-feizu, Da Jiao Ban, Da Xiuzi

Population Source: 400,000 to 500,000 (1982 *Minzu Shibie Wenxian Ziliao Huibian*); "More than 200,000" (1952 Fei Xiaotong)

Location: *Guizhou:* Zhijin, Nayong, Dafang, Shuicheng, Guanling, Qingzhen, Puding, and Luzhi counties

Status: Counted in census as an *Undetermined Minority*

Language: Chinese

Dialects: 0

Religion: Ancestor Worship, No Religion, Daoism, Christianity, Mahayana Buddhism

Christians: 20,000

Scripture: Chinese Bible

***Jesus* film:** None

Gospel Recordings: Mandarin: Guiyanghua #04574

Christian Broadcasting: None

ROPAL code: None

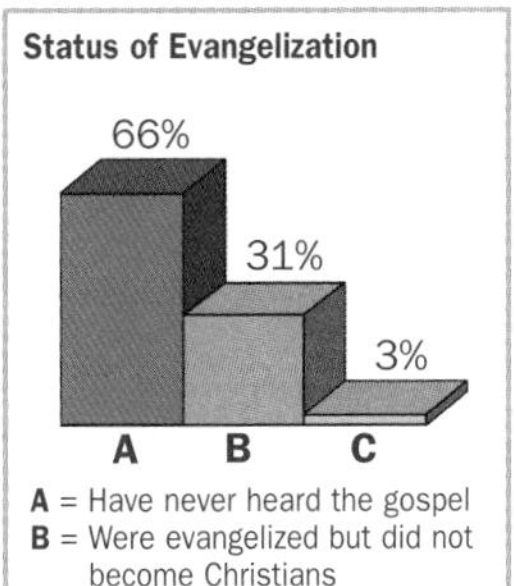

A = Have never heard the gospel
B = Were evangelized but did not become Christians
C = Are adherents to any form of Christianity

Location: A 1982 study listed "between 400,000 to 500,000" Chuanqing (Black-Dressed People), in Guizhou Province.[1] Most are concentrated in Zhijin and Nayong counties, with others in Dafang, Shuicheng, Guanling, Qingzhen, Puding, and Luzhi counties.

Identity: The Chuanqing view themselves as a distinct people group. Although they speak a Chinese language and historically belong to the Han race, the government has placed them in a list of *Undetermined Minorities* in China.[2] In the 1950s their application for full status as a minority group was rejected. The decision was that the Chuanqing were "originally members of the Han nationality," and that their characteristics were "manifestations of the special features of Han in certain regions in an earlier period, not the characteristics of a separate nationality."[3] This upset the Chuanqing, who applied again in the late 1970s. "Encouraged by the political thaw, many groups whose recognition as independent nationalities had been rejected in the fifties re-petitioned for recognition; eighty groups totaling over 900,000 persons petitioned in the province of Guizhou alone, including the Chuanqing."[4] Their application was again rejected.

Language: The Chuanqing speak *Guizhou hua* — the local dialect of Chinese. After many centuries of interaction with the Miao and the Bouyei, the language of the Chuanqing contains many loanwords from those languages.

History: The Chuanqing were formerly known by a variety of names including *Pu Ren*, meaning "garrison people".[5] The Chuanqing (like the Chuanlan) are descended from Chinese soldiers who were sent into Guizhou in the eighth and ninth centuries to quell Miao rebellions. The Chuanqing came from Jiangxi Province and provided forced labor for the army. There were numerous armed clashes between the Chuanqing and Chuanlan. The Chuanqing "clung to their own dialect for generations. The women dressed differently, arranging their hair in three sections. They celebrated separate festivals and followed different marriage customs."[6] Later, many Chuanqing were forced to serve as tenants under the Yi landowners.

Customs: Some of the customs and dress of the Chuanqing are reflected in the various names their neighbors call them. The Yi call them *Sher-tu* or *Sher-feizu*, meaning "white-skinned Han" or "snake-eating Han." Other locals call the Chuanqing *Da Jiao Ban* (Big Foot) and *Da Xiuzi* (Big Sleeves).[7]

Religion: The long history of the Chuanqing is supported by the presence of several ancient religious temples in the Anshun area, including the Wen Miao Confucian temple built in 1368, the Buddhist White Pagoda dating from the Ming Dynasty, and Tian Tai Shan Buddhist Temple built in 1616.

Christianity: There are a number of churches in the Anshun area — mostly Catholic — which contain Chuanqing believers. Catholic missionaries were active in the area in the past, resulting in more than 150,000 Catholics spread throughout Guizhou today.[8]

Dwayne Graybill

Cun 村

Location: More than 79,000 Cun live in the westernmost part of Hainan Island — China's largest island (excluding Taiwan). They inhabit villages in the Sigeng, Xinjie, Hongjiang, and Baoban districts — along the south bank of the Changhua River in northern Dongfang County; and the north bank of the same river in Changjiang County. Hainan is a tropical island with warm temperatures and beautiful beaches. The Chinese authorities have tried to promote Hainan as a tourist haven in recent years. Dozens of five-star hotels have been constructed along the coasts, but to date the tourist influx has fallen far short of the government's unrealistically high expectations.

Identity: The Cun (Village) people have been officially included as part of the Han Chinese nationality by the central government, even though their language is considered a dialect of the Ha Li language. Note that the speakers of the Lingao language in northern Hainan also refer to their language as the "village (Cun) language." Chinese scholars have named that language *Lingao* to avoid confusion.

Language: One linguist has noted, "There are numerous Han Chinese nationality members around Changcheng on the west coast who speak *Cunhua* 'village language' which is one of the four *Ha* dialects of Li."[1] There is some confusion regarding the exact linguistic affiliation of Cun. One respected source classifies it as "Sino-Tibetan, Zhuang-Dong" and describes it as "a separate language that resembles Li."[2] Others have placed Cun in the Li-Laqua branch of the Kadai language family.[3] Cun — which has ten tones — also contains many Chinese loanwords. The majority of Cun are bilingual in the Hainanese dialect of Chinese.

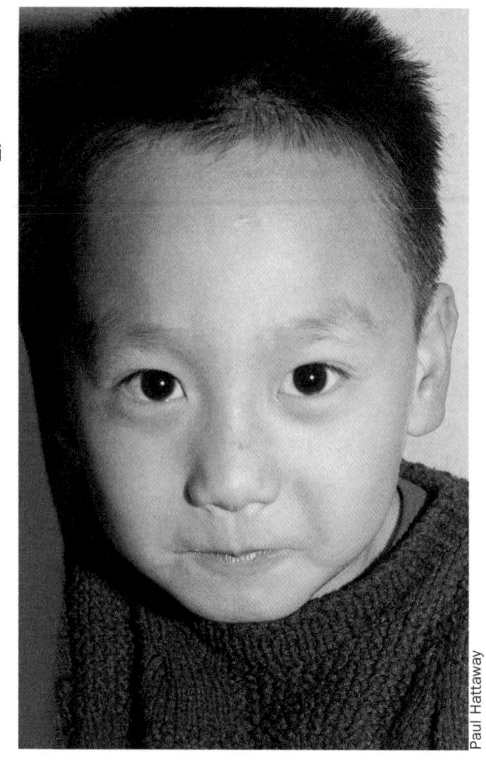

Paul Hattaway

History: The Cun were originally Han Chinese people who migrated to Hainan Island and intermingled with the Li people. After many centuries they developed their own language and ethnic identity.

Customs: The Cun are simple-hearted people. They are extremely poor and do not wear a traditional dress unique to their people. Their main concerns are for the welfare of their families and the annual success of their crops.

Religion: Most Cun are animists, but religion does not take a very important role in their daily lives.

Christianity: Although most Cun live in complete spiritual darkness and neglect, promising signs have occurred in recent years. In 1994 a Hong Kong-based mission gave Bible training to several Cun. When they first came to the course the middle-aged students had never heard of God, but the Holy Spirit found their hearts fertile ground for his Word. After three months the Cun were filled with Christ's peace and love and were desperate to return immediately to their own people to tell them the way to salvation. They did this, and met with immediate success. Many of their family members and fellow villagers were overjoyed to hear the news that Christ died for their sins.[4] By 1998 there were three or four churches among the Cun.

Population in China:
70,000 (1990)
79,100 (2000)
89,400 (2010)
Location: Hainan Island
Religion: Animism
Christians: 200

Overview of the Cun

Countries: China

Pronunciation: "Tswoon"

Other Names: Tsuen, Ngao Fon, Cunhua

Population Source: 70,000 (1990 J.-O. Svantesson); Out of a total Han population of 1,042,482,187 (1990 census)

Location: *W Hainan Island:* Hongjiang and Changjiang counties

Status: Officially included under Han Chinese

Language: Daic, Kadai, Li-Laqua

Dialects: 0

Religion: Animism, No Religion, Christianity

Christians: 200

Scripture: None

***Jesus* film:** None

Gospel Recordings: None

Christian Broadcasting: None

ROPAL code: CUQ00

Status of Evangelization

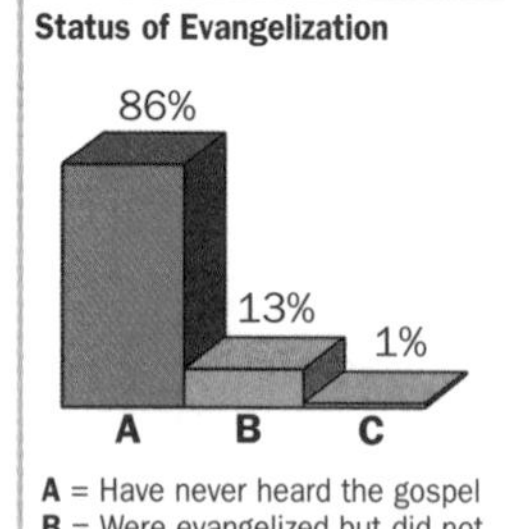

A = Have never heard the gospel
B = Were evangelized but did not become Christians
C = Are adherents to any form of Christianity

Daizhan 帯占

Population in China:
11,400 (1999)
11,650 (2000)
14,600 (2010)
Location: Yunnan
Religion: Animism
Christians: None Known

Overview of the Daizhan

Countries: China

Pronunciation: "Die-zhahn"

Other Names: Daizhan Aza, Azar, Daizhanpo, Pula

Population Source:
11,400 (1999 J. Pelkey);
Out of a total Yi population of 6,572,173 (1990 census)

Location: *Yunnan:* Baige District of Kaiyuan County in the Honghe Prefecture; More are suspected to live in the Ashe District of Yanshan County.

Status:
Officially included under Yi

Language: Sino-Tibetan, Tibeto-Burman, Burmese-Lolo, Lolo, Northern Lolo, Yi, Southeastern Yi

Dialects: 0

Religion: Animism, Ancestor Worship, No Religion

Christians: None known

Scripture: None

***Jesus* film:** None

Gospel Recordings: None

Christian Broadcasting: None

ROPAL code: None

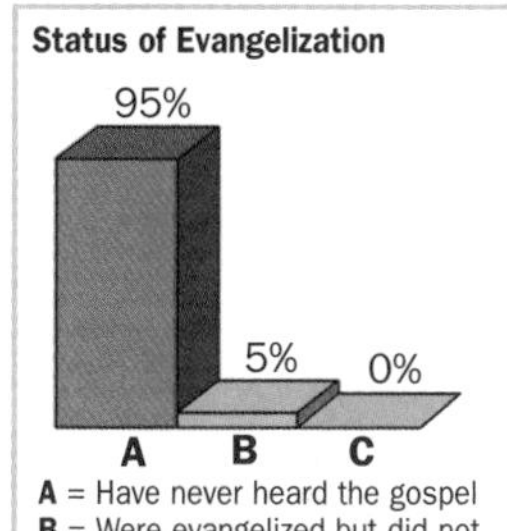

Jamin Pelkey

Location: Approximately 11,600 people belonging to the Daizhan ethnic group inhabit villages in the Baige District of Kaiyuan County in the Honghe Hani-Yi Autonomous Prefecture in Yunnan Province.[1] An unspecified number of Daizhan are believed to live in the adjoining Ashe District of Yanshan County. The Daizhan live in simple houses near streams or some other water source.

Identity: The Daizhan are one of five distinct tribes in Kaiyuan County who have been combined by the Chinese under the name of *Aza*.[2] These five groups, in turn, have been placed under the official Yi nationality. Although they speak many distinct languages and go by dozens of ethnic names, most Yi groups in China have a loose common historical affinity for each other. Many say their ancestors were two brothers, Wusa and Wumeng, who, "like Esau and Jacob, struggled together in the womb of their mother; hence... the wildness of our hearts and our fondness for fighting."[3]

Language: Although many Daizhan people now exclusively speak Chinese, the Daizhan language is still spoken among people over 40 years of age and in villages away from the township of Baige. Daizhan is a Southeastern Yi variety, related to Puwa, Digao, Asahei, Ani, and Labapo.

History: The Daizhan have lived in their present location for more than 300 years. They have gradually been assimilated by the Han Chinese, who have migrated into the area in large numbers over the past century.

Customs: In the past, when a Daizhan couple decided to get married, the groom fixed an auspicious date, assembled flute players, and danced around his sweetheart's home until nightfall. All of a sudden he took the girl in his arms and ran away into the dense forest. Before the girl was accepted as a full-fledged member of her new family, however, she had to kill a chicken. Only then was she considered a full member of the family, never again to live with her parents. One month after they were married, the wife took her new husband to visit her parents. The husband made apologies to his in-laws and brought grain to his father-in-law as a gift of gratitude. Most Daizhan customs like this have now been lost.

Religion: The Daizhan are predominantly animists. They believe a person's soul leaves the body during illness or at death. Red cord is tied around a sick person's arm in a bid to prevent the soul from departing the body.

Christianity: There are no known Christians among the Daizhan. The small amount of mission work done in Kaiyuan targeted the Han Chinese and Miao. Efforts to reach them will best be done by Chinese believers. Mission statesman Roland Allen once said, "Foreigners can never successfully direct the propagation of any faith throughout a whole country. If the faith does not become naturalized and expand among the people by its own vital power, it exercises an alarming and hateful influence, and men fear and shun it as something alien."[4]

Daur 达斡尔

Midge Conner

Location: Approximately 150,000 Daur live in northeastern China. Most are concentrated on both sides of the Nenjiang River in the Morindawa Banner of Inner Mongolia, as well as in several counties in the western part of Heilongjiang Province.[1] A significant number of Daur also live in Russia. A Daur chief named Gantimur led 300 of his people to Russia in 1666.[2] Until this century, their homeland was known to the Russians as *Dauria*. By 1882 Gantimur's descendants in Russia numbered 10,489, most of whom had converted to Russian Orthodox Christianity.[3]

Identity: The Daur are one of the 55 official minority groups in China. In the past they were a larger and more influential group than today. In 1928 there were as many as 300,000 Daur in China.[4] Their numbers have dwindled this century mainly as a result of war, disease, and assimilation to Mongolian or Chinese culture and language.

Language: Most Daur can still speak their language, which has been described as "an aberrant, and in some respects, archaic branch of northern Mongolian."[5] The exceptions are the Daur living in Aihui and Hulan counties who switched to speaking Chinese in the 1930s.[6]

History: The Daur were first mentioned in Chinese records in AD 620. They are thought to be the "remnants of the Chinese garrison left by the Tan tai-tszui (618–626)."[7] A portion of this garrison were committed to fox hunting and were called *dahuli* (those who hunt foxes).[8] The Daur fought against Tsarist Russia and also opposed Japan from 1937 to 1945.

Customs: Daur society is divided into a hierarchical structure. Each group of people with the same family name (*hala*) live in the same group of three or four villages. Each hala is then comprised of several clans (*mokon*) who live in the same village. On his wedding day, a Daur bridegroom must fetch his bride at sunrise and make a present of wine, meat, and pastry to everyone he meets on the way — whether he knows them or not. After the ceremony the Daur enjoy an afternoon of horse races. The sport of field hockey may have been invented by the Daur. They are first mentioned as playing hockey in the *History of the Liao Dynasty* (916–1125).[9]

Religion: For centuries each Daur clan has depended upon shamans. No wedding, burial, long journey, or any other important event was attempted without first consulting the shaman. He, in turn, contacted the spirit realm and announced, for a fee, whether an event should take place or not. Some of the Daur who live alongside Mongolians have embraced Tibetan Buddhism.

Christianity: Until recently the Daur in China were a completely unreached people with no knowledge of the gospel. In the early 1990s missionaries showed the *Jesus* film in Mandarin to the Daur. In a short time, more than 1,000 Daur became Christians. The *Jesus* film is now available in the Daur language. In 1997 the new Daur church faced persecution from the authorities, but the believers stood firm in their faith. The Daur Christians are actively involved in evangelism and have a deep burden to see their whole ethnic group come to Christ.

Population in China:
116,000 (1990)
149,600 (2000)
193,000 (2010)
Location:
Heilongjiang, Inner Mongolia
Religion: Shamanism
Christians: 1,000

Overview of the Daur

Countries: China, Russia
Pronunciation: "Dao-urh"
Other Names: Dagur, Dagour, Dawar, Dawo'er, Tahur, Thauerh, Daghur, Dahur, Daor
Population Source:
121,357 (1990 census);[10]
94,014 (1982 census);
63,394 (1964 census);
Also in Russia
Location: *W Heilongjiang:* Qiqihar (21,748), Fuyu (5,932); Longjiang, Nehe, Nenjiang and Aihu counties;
E Inner Mongolia: Morindawa (26,289), Ewenki (13,929), Elenchun (6,369) counties;
Also Zalantun City (4,810)
Status:
An official minority of China
Language: Altaic, Mongolian, Eastern Mongolian, Daur
Literacy: 81%
Dialects (3):
Bataxan, Hailar, Qiqihar
Religion: Shamanism, Animism, Tibetan Buddhism, Christianity, No Religion
Christians: 1,000
Scripture: None
***Jesus* film:** Available
Gospel Recordings: Daur #04776
Christian Broadcasting: None
ROPAL code: DTA00

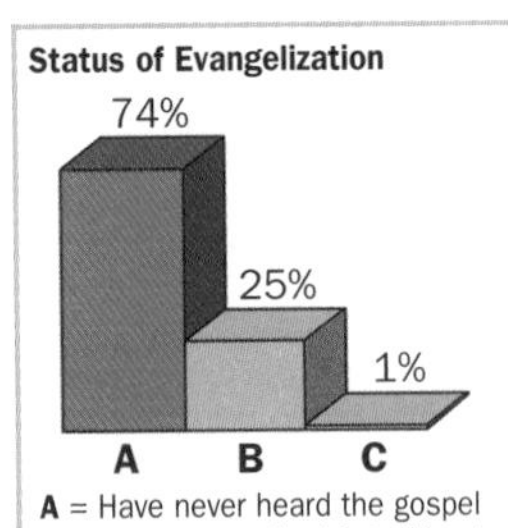

Daur, Western 达斡尔(西)

Location: A total of 4,369 Western Daur were counted in the 1982 Chinese census. They live in the Gurbansher Daur Commune near the city of Tacheng, in the Ili Prefecture of northwest Xinjiang. The region has long been a crossroads for many peoples. In 1936 it was described as "a riot of color... whose community is an amazing mixture of tongues. Here in the winter, old-style Russians in gay *troikas* race to and fro from all-night parties; solemn processions of Mongol lamas parade through the streets on horse-back, and long-robed Chinese and Turki merchants shout and gesticulate in the crowded market places."[1]

Identity: The Daur in Xinjiang are the descendants of a group of Daur troops who were sent from Manchuria in 1763. The Chinese include them under the Daur nationality, despite the fact that their customs are now markedly different from the Daur living on the opposite side of the country.

Language: The Western Daur language, which is related to Mongolian, is taught to some children, but generally the use of the language is declining and is considered to be "seriously endangered."[2] Most adults are reportedly fluent in Daur, but, because of pressure from neighboring peoples, there is widespread multilingualism in Kazak, Uygur, Chinese, and other languages.

History: The Western Daur are related to the Daur in Heilongjiang Province, who came under Chinese control in 1698. During the Qing Dynasty (1644–1911) the Daur were called up for military service a total of 60 times.[3] One assignment in 1763 took a group of Daur soldiers all the way across northern China to Xinjiang. After completing their service, the soldiers decided to stay in the northwest, rather than face the demanding two-year journey back to their homeland.

Midge Conner

Customs: On his wedding day, the groom sets off to fetch the bride the moment the sun rises. "As soon as the bride in her red wedding gown arrives in a car, firecrackers are let off... and the bride's hair is combed with a part in the center. She wears gold, silver or jade earrings, bracelets and rings, and an embroidered tobacco pouch is attached to the front of her dress. She does this because it is the custom with the Daurs to offer each other a cigarette."[4]

Religion: Most Western Daur are polytheists, worshiping five Sky gods. "All humans and animals are believed to have a *sumus*, or spirit, which at the time of death, leaves the body and is presented to Irmu Khan, the lord of the underworld. He decides how each spirit will be reincarnated. Those whose owners have behaved best might become *barkans* (gods) while those with the worst record are condemned to perpetual hell."[5]

Christianity: There has never been a known church among the Western Daur. The recently established Daur church in northeast China, however, has a burden to reach their brothers in the northwest and were planning an evangelistic trip to Xinjiang in 1998.

RUSSIA
•Altay
•Tacheng (Qoqek)
KAZAKSTAN
•Yining (Kuldja)
•Urumqi
•Aksu
XINJIANG
Scale 0 KM 400

Population in China:
4,369 (1982)
5,630 (2000)
7,270 (2010)
Location: Xinjiang
Religion: Polytheism
Christians: None Known

Overview of the Western Daur

Countries: China

Pronunciation: "Dao-urh"

Other Names: Xinjiang Daur, Sinkiang Dagur, Turkestan Dagur

Population Source: 4,369 (1982 census); Out of a total Daur population of 121,357 (1990 census)

Location: *NW Xinjiang:* Gurbansher Daur Commune near Tacheng, in the Ili Kazak Autonomous Prefecture

Status: Officially included under Daur

Language: Altaic, Mongolian, Eastern Mongolian, Daur

Dialects: 0

Religion: Polytheism, Shamanism, Animism, No Religion

Christians: None known

Scripture: None

***Jesus* film:** In progress

Gospel Recordings: None

Christian Broadcasting: None

ROPAL code: None

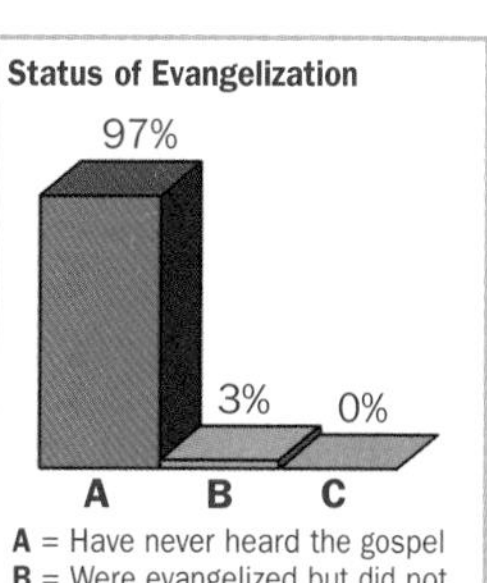

De'ang, Pale 德昂，布蕾

Population in China:
6,000 (1987)
8,260 (2000)
10,650 (2010)
Location: Yunnan
Religion: Buddhism
Christians: 10

Overview of the Pale De'ang

Countries: Myanmar, China, Thailand

Pronunciation: "Deh-ung-Pah-lay"

Other Names: Ngwe Palaung, Silver Palaung, Pale, Palay, Benglong, Bonglung, Bonglong, Penglung, Punglung, Darang, Manton, Nam Hsan, Ta-ang, Bulei, Palaung Pale

Population Source: 6,000 (1987 D. Bradley); Out of a total De'ang population of 15,462 (1990 census); 200,000 to 300,000 in Myanmar; 5,000 in Thailand

Location: *W Yunnan:* Dehong Prefecture: Luxi County

Status: Officially included under De'ang

Language: Austro-Asiatic, Mon-Khmer, Northern Mon-Khmer, Palaungic, Eastern Palaungic, Palaung

Dialects (2): Bulei, Raojin

Religion: Theravada Buddhism, Animism

Christians: 10

Scripture: Work in progress

***Jesus* film:** Available

Gospel Recordings: Pale #03501

Christian Broadcasting: Available (FEBC)

ROPAL code: PCE00

Location: A 1987 survey listed 6,000 speakers of the De'ang Pale language in China.[1] They are located in Luxi County in the western part of Yunnan Province, close to the Myanmar border. The Pale area is just east of the Rumai. In addition, between 200,000 and 300,000 Pale live in northern Myanmar. More than 5,000 also live near Fang in northwest Thailand. They were war refugees from Myanmar in the early 1980s.

Identity: The Pale De'ang are one of four distinct groups that have been combined to form the official De'ang nationality in China. In Myanmar, they are called *Palaung*. Palaung is a Burmese word. The Chinese authorities originally named this minority the *Benglong* — a Chinese transliteration of *Palaung* — but after consultation in 1982 they changed their name to *De'ang*.

Language: De'ang is a member of the Mon-Khmer language family. It is related to Bulang and Wa. Pale is the only one of the four De'ang languages that is not tonal. In Myanmar the Pale language is quite uniform despite its large geographical dispersion.

History: The De'ang were originally part of one great Austro-Asiatic race. It appears the De'ang and Wa shared a common identity in the past but split off from each other when the De'ang embraced Buddhism. The Wa remained animists.

Customs: Most De'ang are employed in agriculture, farming, and logging. Work tasks are assigned according to age and sex. The men perform demanding tasks such as plowing, while the women plant seeds and fetch water. The De'ang have been culturally influenced by their Dai neighbors and celebrate many of the same festivals.

Religion: Many centuries ago the De'ang converted to Theravada Buddhism. Their Buddhist practices are mixed with numerous animistic beliefs and rituals. Shamans, or witch doctors, are powerful figures in De'ang society. No important event is undertaken without first consulting a shaman. He goes into a trance to determine whether or not an event should occur and when the most auspicious date and time would be.

Christianity: The De'ang are considered relatively resistant to Christianity. The majority are trapped in fear of demons and shamans. Few missionaries in the past have tried to reach the De'ang in China. In 1945 work among them was described as "completely virgin soil."[2] A handful of De'ang families in western Yunnan were converted before foreign missionaries were expelled from China in the early 1950s.[3] Today, approximately one out of every thousand De'ang in Myanmar is a Christian. The few minor breakthroughs that have occurred among the Pale De'ang in Myanmar have often resulted in violent persecution and martyrdom.[4] The Pale De'ang are the only one of the four distinct De'ang languages to have gospel radio broadcasts and the *Jesus* film in their language. Although the broadcasts are targeted at Myanmar, it is believed listeners are also able to receive the shortwave signal in China.

Paul Hattaway

De'ang, Rumai 德昂，若买

Midge Conner

Location: More than 4,000 members of the Rumai De'ang group live in Longchuan and Ruili counties, in the farwestern part of China's Yunnan Province.[1] In 1977 more than 135,000 Rumai were reportedly living in Shan State, northern Myanmar.[2]

Identity: The Rumai have been combined with the Pale, Shwe, and Riang groups in China to form the official De'ang nationality. Each group speaks its own language and wears a different style of traditional dress, although all the groups acknowledge a common ancestry.

Language: The Rumai language contains four tones. It has been influenced by the Shan and Tai Mao languages more than the other three De'ang varieties in both China and Myanmar. Rumai is not intelligible with either the Pale or Shwe De'ang languages. Speakers must revert to either Chinese or Tai Mao to communicate with each other.

History: The De'ang claim to be the original inhabitants of northern Myanmar. Historical evidence does little to dispute their assertions. Before they migrated to Myanmar, the ancestors of the De'ang were reportedly settled in communities along the Nujiang River in northwest Yunnan as early as the second century BC.[3] The Chinese claim the De'ang have been living in China continuously for more than two thousand years. Many of the current communities of De'ang in China, however, are almost certainly descended from small groups who migrated back into China earlier this century to escape military campaigns launched by the British against insurgents in northern Burma (Myanmar).

Customs: The Rumai De'ang celebrate many of the festivals of their Tai and Shan neighbors, including *Songkran*, the Water-Splashing Festival which takes place every April. The De'ang have a traditional drum called the *gelengdang* which is made from a hollowed tree trunk. Its ends are covered with ox-hide. Before using it, "it is filled with water through a hole in its body to make the ox-hide and inside of the drum damp so that the desired resonance can be produced."[4]

Religion: Despite their conversion to the Theravada sect of Buddhism many centuries ago, the De'ang retain many of their pre-Buddhist animistic and shamanistic rituals. Many Buddhist monks are also the village witch doctors. They enter trances in order to contact the spirit world. The De'ang believe they should strive to do good works to gain merit for the next life.

Christianity: Like most Theravada Buddhists, the De'ang believe fate predetermines the events of their lives. This results in them having little concern about changing their ways. Their consciences have long been silenced regarding sin. There are no known Christians among the Rumai in either China or Myanmar. There are no Scriptures, gospel recordings, or *Jesus* film available in their language, and no Christian organizations are known to be targeting them.

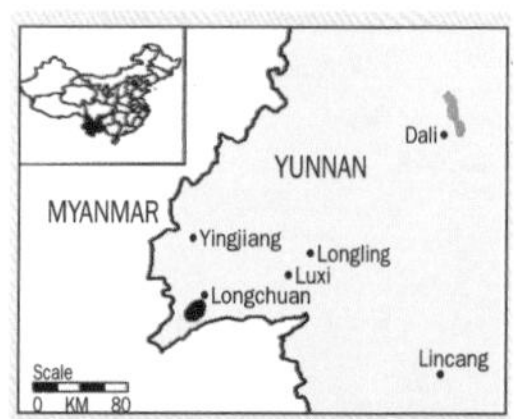

Population in China:
3,600 (1990)
4,640 (2000)
5,990 (2010)
Location: Yunnan
Religion: Buddhism
Christians: None Known

Overview of the Rumai De'ang

Countries: Myanmar, China

Pronunciation: "Deh-ung-Roo-mai"

Other Names: Palaung Rumai, Humai, Ruomai, Rumai

Population Source: 3,600 (1990 J.-O. Svantesson); Out of a total De'ang population of 15,462 (1990 census); 135,400 in Myanmar (1977 Voegelin & Voegelin)

Location: *W Yunnan:* Longchuan and Ruili counties

Status: Officially included under De'ang

Language: Austro-Asiatic, Mon-Khmer, Northern Mon-Khmer, Palaungic, Eastern Palaungic, Palaung

Dialects: 0

Religion: Theravada Buddhism, Animism

Christians: None known

Scripture: None

***Jesus* film:** None

Gospel Recordings: None

Christian Broadcasting: None

ROPAL code: RBB00

Status of Evangelization

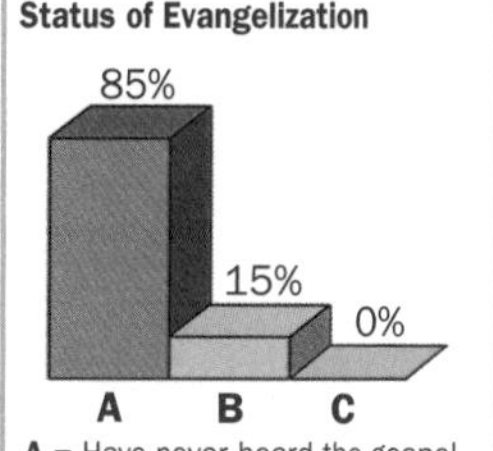

A = Have never heard the gospel
B = Were evangelized but did not become Christians
C = Are adherents to any form of Christianity

De'ang, Shwe 德昂，梁

Population in China:
4,630 (1991)
5,970 (2000)
7,700 (2010)
Location: Yunnan
Religion: Buddhism
Christians: None Known

Overview of the Shwe De'ang

Countries: Myanmar, China

Pronunciation: "Deh-ung-Shway"

Other Names: Palaung Shwe, Golden Palaung, Shwe

Population Source:
4,630 (1991 *EDCL*);
Out of a total De'ang population of 15,462 (1990 census);
150,000 in Myanmar
(1996 B. Grimes – 1982 figure)

Location: *W Yunnan:* Zhenkang and Baoshan counties

Status:
Officially included under De'ang

Language: Austro-Asiatic, Mon-Khmer, Northern Mon-Khmer, Palaungic, Eastern Palaungic, Palaung

Dialects: 0

Religion:
Theravada Buddhism, Animism

Christians: None known

Scripture: None

***Jesus* film:** None

Gospel Recordings:
Palaung #01179

Christian Broadcasting: None

ROPAL code: SWE00

Status of Evangelization

A = Have never heard the gospel
B = Were evangelized but did not become Christians
C = Are adherents to any form of Christianity

Paul Hattaway

Location: A 1991 report stated that 30%, or approximately 4,600 people, out of the total population of the De'ang nationality in China speak the Shwe De'ang language.[1] Their villages are located in parts of Zhenkang and Baoshan counties, in the western part of Yunnan Province near China's border with Myanmar. In addition, more than 150,000 Shwe De'ang live in a widely dispersed area of Shan State in northern Myanmar.[2] The exact population of groups in Myanmar is difficult to estimate. The most recent census was conducted by the British in the 1930s.

Identity: The Shwe De'ang language is officially labeled the *Liang* dialect of De'ang in China. The Chinese do not use the same terms as linguists but refer to the different groups of De'ang as the Red, Black, White, and Flowery De'ang. It is uncertain how these names match the four De'ang languages. In Myanmar, they are known as the *Shwe Palaung*. Their self-name is *De'ang*, which means "rock."

Language: Shwe De'ang is a distinct language. Speakers do share a measure of intelligibility with Pale and Riang, but it is very different from the Rumai language. Shwe has two tones and in some places in Myanmar, three. Most Shwe De'ang can also speak Chinese and Tai Mao.

History: The De'ang believe they were once brothers with the Karen of Myanmar. The two tribes went out hunting with the intent of sharing their food with each other. The Karen caught an elephant, and a huge feast was held for all to enjoy as much meat as they could eat. The De'ang, however, could only manage to catch a porcupine. They skinned it and cooked the small amount of meat for the Karen to eat. The Karen did not mind, as they thought the De'ang had only been able to catch a small animal. But when they finished their meal, they saw the large pile of needles and claimed the De'ang had only given them a small portion of their meat. The two groups have been separated ever since that time, but even today the De'ang long to be reconciled with their Karen brothers. Some De'ang homes in Myanmar have an opening on one side, signifying that the Karen are welcome to return to live with them.[3]

Customs: In the past the De'ang were great hunters, but today most earn their living by growing tea or bamboo.

Religion: Among the De'ang, "two schools of Theravada Buddhism are followed, the Burmese and the Yuan or Shan forms. Daily life is thought to be face to face with the actions of spirits. Ordinary people make a variety of offerings to placate them. Illness is attributed to the actions of evil spirits and the services of a diviner/medical practitioner serves to identify and counteract the proper spirit."[4]

Christianity: There are no known Christians among the Shwe De'ang in China. A tiny percentage of the more than 150,000 in Myanmar have accepted Christ, but they live scattered across a wide area. On the rare occasion of a Shwe De'ang's becoming a Christian, the new believer is usually persecuted and driven from the village.

29

28

30

28. The *Bunu* are a collection of a dozen unreached ethnolinguistic groups scattered throughout the remote mountains of southern China. [Paul Hattaway]

29–30. The *Bulang* minority consists of several distinct ethnic groups, each wearing a unique costume and speaking its own language. [both by Dwayne Graybill]

31. A *Bulang* woman from southern Yunnan Province. [Paul Hattaway]
32. Approximately 150,000 members of the *Daur* minority live in northeast China. [Paul Hattaway]
33. This *Western Daur* woman's ancestors were moved across China to Xinjiang in 1763. [Midge Conner]
34. Most villages of the isolated *Derung* people are several days' walk from the nearest road. [Midge Conner]

35

36

37

38

35. A *De'ang Rumai* woman, who belongs to one of four distinct tribes of China's official De'ang nationality. [Cooperative Baptist Fellowship]

36. The dress of the *De'ang Shwe*, Zhenkang, Yunnan. [Dwayne Graybill]

37–38. The *De'ang Pale* believe they were hatched from a serpent's egg. The many hoops their women wear around their waist resemble a snake's motion when they move. [37 Cooperative Baptist Fellowship; 38 Paul Hattaway]

39

40

41

39. More than three million *Dong* people, speaking two distinct languages, are among China's most poverty-stricken people. [Paul Hattaway]
40. The *Dongxiang* are a Mongolian-speaking Muslim group, Suonaba, Gansu. [Dwayne Graybill]
41. Three lavishly decorated *Ge* ladies, Shi Ban Village, Guizhou. [Paul Hattaway]

Deng, Darang 登, 达让

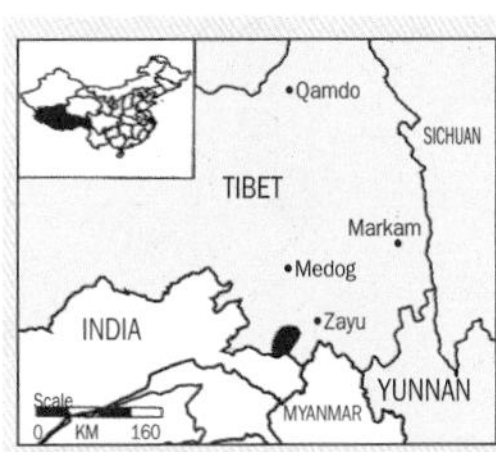

Population in China:
6,000 (1987)
8,260 (2000)
10,650 (2010)
Location: Tibet
Religion: Polytheism
Christians: 10

Overview of the Darang Deng

Countries: China, India, Myanmar

Pronunciation: "Da-rahng-Dung"

Other Names: Tarang Deng, Dalang, Darong, Taraon

Population Source: 6,000 (1987 *LAC*); Also in India (Assam) and Myanmar

Location: *SE Tibet:* Zayu County in the southeastern corner of Tibet

Status: Counted in census as an *Undetermined Minority*

Language: Sino-Tibetan, Tibeto-Burman, Unclassified

Dialects: 8

Religion: Polytheism, Tibetan Buddhism, Animism, Christianity

Christians: 10

Scripture: None

***Jesus* film:** None

Gospel Recordings: None

Christian Broadcasting: None

ROPAL code: DAT00

Status of Evangelization

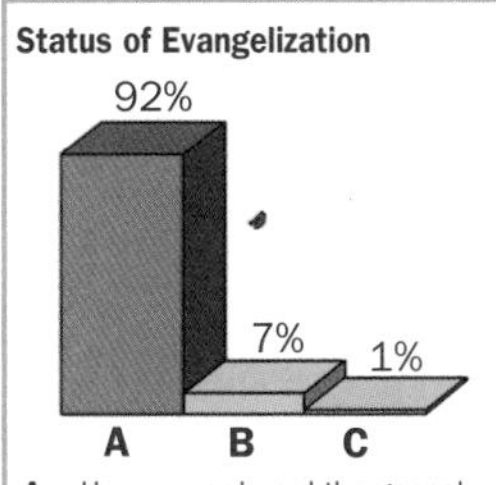

A = Have never heard the gospel
B = Were evangelized but did not become Christians
C = Are adherents to any form of Christianity

Location: Six thousand speakers of the Darang Deng language in China were reported in 1987.[1] The Darang Deng live along the valley of the Dulai River in Zayu (also known as Chayu) County in the southeastern corner of Tibet. The Geman Deng, who speak a different language, live on the tablelands on both sides of the lower reaches of the Zayu River farther to the east of the Darang. Zayu County is off-limits to foreigners. The Deng language is also spoken by people in Assam, India, and the northernmost tip of Myanmar.[2]

Identity: Although the Deng are listed among official statistics for Tibet,[3] they were not counted as part of any nationality in the census. A government publication states, "The Tibetans live alongside the Deng Ren, who have not been identified as a separate ethnic group."[4] The Deng have made strong demands to be recognized as a separate nationality, but their applications have so far been rejected. They have even "threatened secession from China if they were not officially recognized as a nationality.... The Tibetan authorities strongly oppose such a move, arguing that it would split the Tibetan nationality."[5]

Language: There are two separate Deng languages spoken in China: Darang Deng and Geman Deng. The two languages are very different. Darang Deng has four tones and eight dialects that vary considerably from one area to another.[6] Some scholars believe the Deng languages are similar to Jingpo, spoken in western Yunnan Province.[7]

History: Little is known of the Deng people and their origins. It is interesting that the Jingpo minority — who now live in western China and northern Myanmar — claim to have originated in Tibet. Considering the similarities between the two languages, it could be speculated that the Jingpo are descended from the Deng.

Customs: The Deng, who always go barefoot, have their own set of distinctive customs. "It is a common custom for them to swap a few head of cattle and several chickens for a woman as wife. Their dead are cremated, the corpse being burned together with the house he formerly owned."[8]

Religion: The Deng are polytheists. They have been described as a "ghost and deity fearing people."[9] For centuries the Deng have rejected pressure from the Tibetans to convert to Buddhism, although many Deng do outwardly observe Buddhist rituals.

Christianity: Until recently there had never been any known Christians among the Deng in Tibet. When a foreign believer traveled to the Deng, "he and the other foreign tourists helped lead [their Deng tour guide] to Jesus. When he came back a couple of years later he was able to help lead her nuclear family to Jesus."[10] The nearest community of believers is the evangelistic Rawang church in northern Myanmar. The Rawang have sent workers into southern Tibet in recent years, but it is not known if these servants of Christ have traveled as far as the Deng region yet.

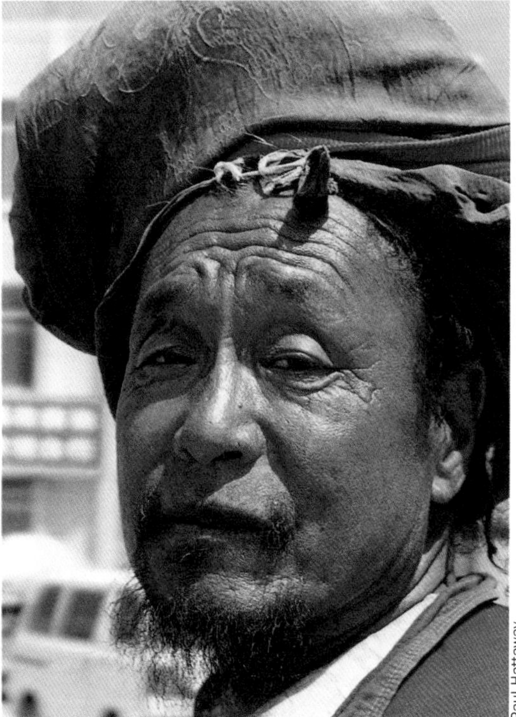

Paul Hattaway

Deng, Geman 登,格曼

Location: Approximately 11,000 speakers of Geman Deng live on the tablelands on both sides of the lower reaches of the Zayu River within Zayu County, in southeastern Tibet. Plenty of rainfall and natural resources provide ideal conditions for their communities. The beautiful Zayu Valley, south of Mount Demula on the Hengduan Range, lies a mere 800 to 1,000 meters (2,600–3,280 ft.) above sea level. "There are vast expanses of woods on the slopes and in the valley itself bananas, water melons and apples grow in profusion together with rice."[1]

Identity: The Geman Deng have not been included as part of any nationality by the Chinese authorities. Instead, they were included in a list of *Undetermined Minorities* which contained 881,838 people at the time of the 1990 census. Neighboring groups may call the Geman Deng *Ah-man.*

Language: Geman Deng — which has four tones and four dialects — is a distinct language from Darang Deng. The difference in language has resulted from the two groups living apart for many centuries. The Deng do not have their own script.

History: Chinese state television has produced a documentary on the Deng, who claim to have lived in their corner of Tibet since the beginning of time. The Deng's recent history has been one of oppression by the Tibetans. Formerly, the Deng were not even allowed to leave their area without permission from the Tibetan lamas.

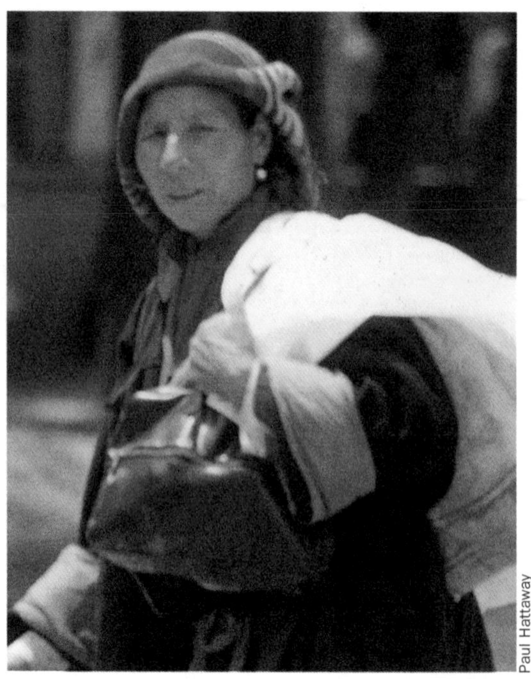
Paul Hattaway

Customs: Deng people with the same name or blood ties live and work together in their villages. Most of the work is done by the Deng women. The women have a striking appearance, including a "silver hair band with engraved flowers over thick hair worn loosely on front of the top of their head. They are fond of big cylinder-shaped earrings with whorl patterns. Their clothes are richly decorated with agate, coral and jade ornaments as well as elaborate boxes of silver or gold in which they keep a copy of the Buddhist scripture. If a woman wears long strips of silver coins on the front of her blouse, she is from a wealthy family and has higher status than other women in the family."[2]

Religion: The Deng fear a variety of ghosts and demons. They believe they are able to temporarily calm the anger of these spirits and so, at appointed times, offer sacrifices of chickens and animals. This killing of valuable livestock has resulted in the Deng being trapped in dire poverty. Deng families often go into heavy debt to pay for the services of a shaman.

Christianity: This group is one of the most difficult peoples in all of China to penetrate with the gospel. Their communities are only accessible by boat or on foot. The Deng have no Scriptures in their language, which does not have its own script. A handful of Geman Deng in Myanmar have been evangelized by the strong Rawang church, but so far there are very few or no believers among them. Most Geman Deng in Tibet are without a witness.

Population in China:
8,000 (1987)
11,000 (2000)
14,200 (2010)
Location: Tibet
Religion: Polytheism
Christians: None Known

Overview of the Geman Deng

Countries: China, India, Myanmar

Pronunciation: "Ah-mun-Dung"

Other Names: Kuman, Kuman Deng, Kaman, Ah-man

Population Source: 8,000 (1987 *LAC*); Also in India (Assam) and Myanmar

Location: *SE Tibet:* The Geman Deng speakers live on the tablelands either side of the lower reaches of the Zayu River, in Zayu County.

Status: Counted in the census as an *Undetermined Minority*

Language: Sino-Tibetan, Tibeto-Burman, Unclassified

Dialects: 4

Religion: Polytheism, Tibetan Buddhism, Animism

Christians: None known

Scripture: None

***Jesus* film:** None

Gospel Recordings: None

Christian Broadcasting: None

ROPAL code: GEN00

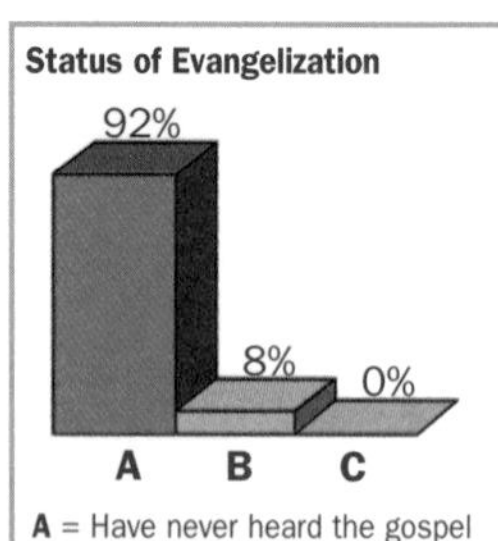

A = Have never heard the gospel
B = Were evangelized but did not become Christians
C = Are adherents to any form of Christianity

Depo 德颇

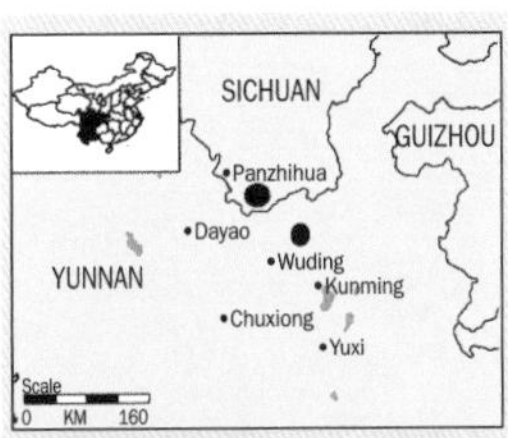

Population in China:
5,000 (1990)
6,275 (2000)
7,870 (2010)
Location: Sichuan, Yunnan
Religion: Chistianity
Christians: 700

Overview of the Depo

Countries: China

Pronunciation: "Deh-po"

Other Names: Adou, Adoupuo, Gan Yi, Bai Yi, White Yi, Baiyizhe

Population Source:
5,000 (1990 AMO);
1,100 in Yunnan (1999 J. Pelkey);
Out of a total Yi population of 6,572,173 (1990 census)

Location:
S Sichuan: Panzhihua area;
N Yunnan: Wuding and Luquan counties

Status:
Officially included under Yi

Language: Sino-Tibetan, Tibeto-Burman, Burmese-Lolo, Lolo, Northern Lolo, Yi, Eastern Yi

Dialects: 0

Religion: Christianity, Animism, No Religion

Christians: 700

Scripture: None

***Jesus* film:** None

Gospel Recordings: None

Christian Broadcasting: None

ROPAL code: None

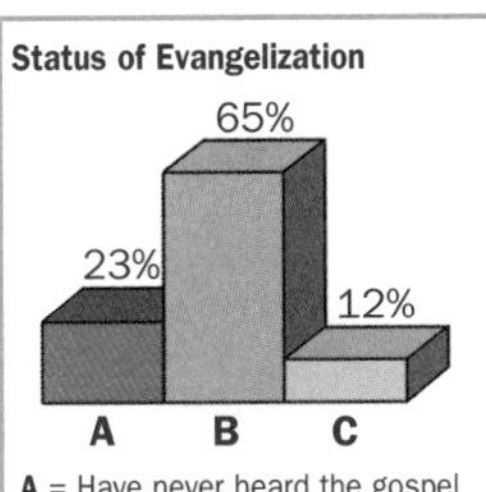

Location: Approximately 6,000 people belonging to the Depo tribe live in the Panzhihua area of southern Sichuan Province, and in Wuding and Luquan counties in northern Yunnan Province. Most Depo villages contain no more than ten families. In the majority of locations the Depo share their villages with members of other ethnic minorities. Wuding County and Luquan County (where only 747 Depo were reported to live in 1957)[1] experienced a massive earthquake in October 1995. Fifty people were killed, 1,000 injured, and 200,000 people were left homeless.

Paul Hattaway

Identity: The Depo also call themselves *Adou* or *Adoupuo*. Neighboring people call them *Gan Yi*, which is not the same as the Eastern Nasu group profiled in *Operation China*. The Eastern Nasu are also commonly called *Gani*. The Chinese character for *Gan Yi* means "sweet Yi," while the character used for the *Gani* means "dry Yi." The Depo have largely been assimilated by the Eastern Nasu.

Language: The Depo language, which may now be identical to Eastern Nasu, is part of the Eastern Yi group of Tibeto-Burman languages. Eastern Yi includes numerous different groups living in Guizhou Province and nearby areas of northeast Yunnan. The Yi groups in northern Yunnan, especially around Wuding, are now so mixed together that specific linguistic information is difficult to obtain.

History: This tribe claims to have been migrating for most of their past. They say they originally lived in the Zhaotong area of northeast Yunnan Province before moving south to Dongchuan. "Some time later they moved again — most of them going to Sichuan, but some of them crossing Luquan to eastern Wuding County."[2] For centuries the Depo have been slaves to the Eastern Nasu. Today, their language and customs are almost identical to their former masters'.

Customs: One of the greatest festivals celebrated by the different Yi groups is the New Rice Festival, which takes place in the eighth month of the lunar calendar every year. The people celebrate the end of the rice harvest by drinking alcohol, singing, and dancing. On three different days in the sixth lunar month the Depo celebrate the Plum Raising Festival. They test the ripeness of their plums and also use the event as an excuse to get drunk, dance, and let their hair down.

Religion: Wuding and Luquan counties, where the Depo live, have been thoroughly evangelized and contain one of the highest concentrations of Christians in all of China. In the past, animals, rivers, trees, and even rocks were worshiped by the Depo. They believed that these natural objects were sources of spiritual power. They also believed that the spirits of animals could "bite" a person, so regular offerings were made to placate them.

Christianity: A relatively high percentage of Depo believe in Christ, especially among those living in the highly evangelized Fawo District of Wuding County in Yunnan Province. The Depo in Sichuan have had less exposure to the gospel.

Derung 度龙

Midge Conner

Location: More than 6,000 members of the Derung nationality live in some of the most isolated terrain in all of China. Ninety percent of the Derung live in the extreme northwestern part of Yunnan Province, along the Dulong River basin in Gongshan County. The Derung region is "highly mountainous and rainfall is abundant. Virgin forests cover the mountain slopes, and wild animals abound."[1] Twenty-one Derung live in Zayu County, Tibet. In addition, the Derung are also found in northern Myanmar.

Identity: The Derung are the fifth smallest of China's 55 official minority groups. Their self-name is *Turung* which the Chinese have transliterated as *Derung*. A visitor in the 1920s described them as "a primitive, harmless jungle people who live in trees like monkeys."[2] The Derung and Nu claim they were once brothers who were separated and forced to live on different sides of the river.

Language: In addition to the ethnic Derung, 5,500 people belonging to the Nu nationality speak Derung as their mother tongue.[3] Derung is one dialect of the larger Rawang group in Myanmar, which contains an astonishing 75 to 100 dialects.[4] Four dialects are reportedly spoken in China.[5] Few Derung are able to speak Chinese. Because they did not have a script, the Derung formerly kept records by carving notches on wood or by tying knots.

History: Before 1949 there were 15 patriarchal clans called *nile* among the Derung. Each nile consisted of several family communes. Each commune possessed its own territory which was marked off by boundaries such as streams and mountain ridges. Each clan was further divided into *ke-eng* — villages where people lived in common long houses. The members of each *ke-eng* regarded themselves as descended from the same ancestor. The Derung gained notoriety for defeating a British military expedition in 1913.

Customs: The Derung are one of the most remote groups in China. There are no roads to their villages, many of which are only accessible by several days' walk over treacherous trails.[6] The Derung wear their hair down to their eyebrows in the front. Until recently, Derung girls tattooed their faces at the onset of puberty with designs according to their respective clans. The dead are buried in hollow logs, except when death is the result of a major disease. Then the corpse is cremated and the ashes disposed of in the river.[7]

Religion: In the past, each Derung clan had its own shaman who directed warfare and healed the sick. Modern health clinics have put the shamans out of business.

Christianity: The first missionary among the Derung was a French Catholic priest in 1907. In 1935 the Morse family came to the Derung area. People from four villages accepted Christ and six churches were built.[8] Through the work of the Morse family, almost the entire Rawang tribe in Myanmar was converted.[9] Today the number of believers among the Derung in China is uncertain. One source states, "Some estimate that there are as many as 5,000 Derung Christians in China (85.97%) while 25% Christian (about 1,450) is estimated by one Western worker close to the situation."[10]

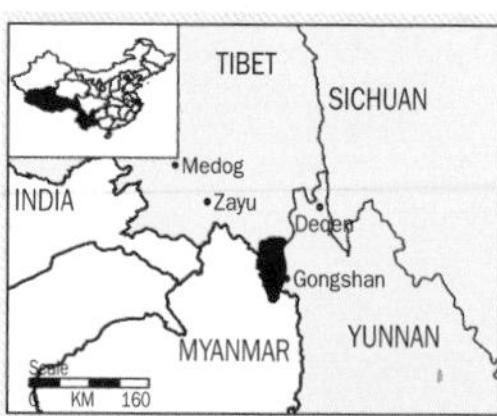

Population in China:
5,316 (1990)
6,850 (2000)
8,840 (2010)
Location: Yunnan, Tibet
Religion: Animism
Christians: 1,450

Overview of the Derung

Countries: Myanmar, China
Pronunciation: "Deh-rohng"
Other Names: Drung, Trung, Tulung, Turung, Dulong, Khanung, Kjutzu, Ch'utzu
Population Source: 5,816 (1990 census);[11] 4,682 (1982 census); 3,090 (1964 census); Also in Myanmar
Location: *NW Yunnan:* 90% live in the Derung River valley, in the Gongshan Derung-Nu County; *SE Tibet:* Zawa in Zayu County
Status: An official minority of China
Language: Sino-Tibetan, Tibeto-Burman, Nungish
Literacy: 38%
Dialects (4): Melam, Metu, Tamalu, Tukiumu
Religion: Animism, Christianity, Polytheism, Shamanism
Christians: 1,450
Scripture: Rawang Bible 1986; New Testament 1974; Portions 1952
***Jesus* film:** None
Gospel Recordings: None
Christian Broadcasting: None
ROPAL code: DUU00

Status of Evangelization

A	B	C
0%	78%	22%

A = Have never heard the gospel
B = Were evangelized but did not become Christians
C = Are adherents to any form of Christianity

Diandao 天保

Location: More than 10,000 Dianbao inhabit part of Funing County in the southeastern corner of Yunnan Province. Funing County is near the juncture where Vietnam, Yunnan, and Guangxi meet. The Funing area is inhabited by Miao, Yao, and Han Chinese people, in addition to other Zhuang language groups.

Identity: The Dianbao are one of many tribes and language groups combined to form the Zhuang nationality in China. The Dianbao did not oppose being officially classified under the Zhuang minority. As one writer explains, "After the establishment of the People's Republic of China, during the stage of the 'recognition of nationalities,' the Zhuangs from different districts agreed, through democratic consultation, that they be regarded as the Zhuang nationality as a whole."[1]

Language: There is disagreement among scholars regarding the classification of the Dianbao language. While some regard it as a distinct variety of the Southern Zhuang language group,[2] others state that it "should not be construed as a meaningful division within the dialect scheme of Zhuang."[3]

History: The Dianbao language suggests they are descended from the great Tai race that splintered into dozens of different tribes over the course of history. Today, Tai (or Thai) peoples are scattered throughout Asia from the northeastern part of India to the Tai-speaking minorities in China such as the Zhuang, Dai, Bouyei, and Li. One historian listed more than 25 different Tai tribes in China.[4] The various Zhuang groups — who first appeared in Hunan during the Song Dynasty (960–1279) — migrated to southwest China in the thirteenth and fourteenth centuries, "under the pressure of the advancing Mongol armies."[5]

Customs: The Dianbao have a rich collection of folk songs and tales that are handed down from one generation to another.[6]

Religion: The majority of Dianbao are animists. They observe a great number of superstitions, especially about eating and how visitors enter their homes.

Paul Hattaway

Christianity: There are no known Christians among the Dianbao today. Few have ever heard the gospel. A missionary near the Dianbao region, Mrs. T. P. Worsnip, described her frustrations at the lack of progress she encountered in the early 1920s: "I am sure that when we can speak the language of these people we will be better able to get into their homes. Even though in many cases they can understand Chinese, the fact that they cannot speak it, and we cannot converse with them in their vernacular, causes them to turn us away and to look upon us with contempt. We have felt this very keenly, especially when we have visited the streets where every house is occupied by aboriginal families. They invariably turn us away. There are many villages surrounding Lungchow [Longzhou] where the women speak only [Zhuang], and in order to give them the witness we must know their language or take a woman who can speak for us."[7]

GUIZHOU
YUNNAN
GUANGXI
•Qiubei
•Guangnan
•Funing
•Napo
•Wenshan
•Pingbian
Scale
0 KM 160
VIETNAM

Population in China:
10,000 (1995)
11,000 (2000)
13,100 (2010)
Location: Yunnan
Religion: Animism
Christians: None Known

Overview of the Dianbao

Countries: China

Pronunciation: "Dee-ahn-bow"

Other Names: Tienpao, Tienpo, Tianpao, Dienbo

Population Source:
10,000 (1995 AMO);
Out of a total Zhuang population of 15,489,630 (1990 census)

Location:
SE Yunnan: Funing County

Status:
Officially included under Zhuang

Language: Daic, Tai, Central Tai

Dialects: 0

Religion: Animism, Polytheism, Ancestor Worship

Christians: None known

Scripture: None

***Jesus* film:** None

Gospel Recordings: None

Christian Broadcasting: None

ROPAL code: TST00

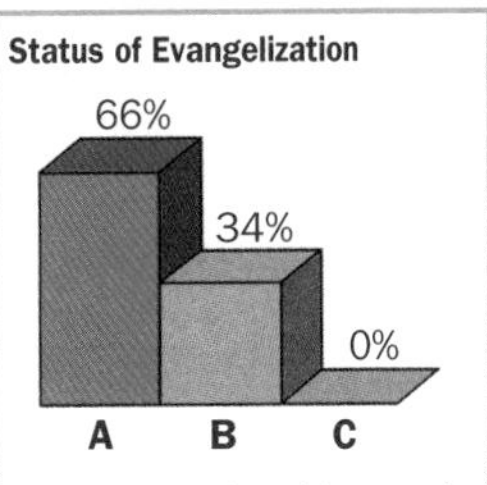

A = Have never heard the gospel
B = Were evangelized but did not become Christians
C = Are adherents to any form of Christianity

Diao 

Population in China:
2,000 (1999)
2,050 (2000)
2,650 (2010)
Location: Guizhou
Religion: Animism
Christians: None Known

Overview of the Diao

Countries: China

Pronunciation: "Dee-ow"

Other Names: Diaozu, Diaoren

Population Source:
2,000 (1999 AMO);
Out of a total Dong population of 2,514,014 (1990 census)

Location: *SE Guizhou*

Status: Officially included under Dong since 1985; Previously included in a list of *Undetermined Minorities*

Language: Unidentified

Dialects: 0

Religion: Animism, Ancestor Worship, Daoism

Christians: None known

Scripture: None

***Jesus* film:** None

Gospel Recordings: None

Christian Broadcasting: None

ROPAL code: None

Status of Evangelization

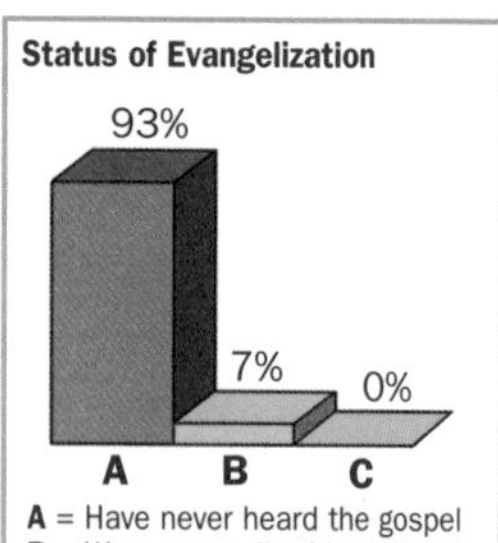

A = Have never heard the gospel
B = Were evangelized but did not become Christians
C = Are adherents to any form of Christianity

Location: More than 2,000 members of the Diao ethnic group live in an unspecified location in the southeastern part of Guizhou Province in southern China. All that is known of the location of the Diao is that they live among the Dong people.[1] The Dong in Guizhou are concentrated in Rongjiang, Congjiang, and Liping counties. The whole of southeast Guizhou is mountainous with abundant rainfall.

Identity: The Diao applied for recognition as a distinct minority group in the 1950s, but their application, along with 90% of the more than 400 groups who applied, was rejected. The official classification of the Diao remained in limbo for more than 30 years. In the 1982 census they were included in a list of *Undetermined Minorities*. After scholars visited them to further investigate their application, the Diao were incorporated into the official Dong nationality in 1985.[2] There appears to have been an official push in the mid-1980s to "tie up the loose ends" of the many minority groups that remained unclassified. Although some groups such as the Diao were assigned to official nationalities, they still regard themselves as distinct from the other people in the group they now find themselves part of. Surrounding peoples in Guizhou continue to call this group *Diao* or *Diaozu*, which means "Diao nationality."

Language: Little is known about the language of the Diao. It is possible that they are either a Chinese-speaking group who have lost the use of their original Dong tongue; or they may have originally been a Han Chinese group who absorbed many aspects of Dong culture and language after having lived alongside the Dong for many centuries. Further research is needed to clarify the situation among the Diao.

History: After the Mongolians took control of China in the thirteenth century, great ethnic upheavals took place in southern China as people groups moved about in all directions seeking to avoid the fierce Mongol armies. At this time many of the small people groups in Guizhou, possibly including the Diao, formed separate identities.

Customs: Among minority peoples in Guizhou, the making of her traditional dress continues to play an important part in a woman's life. Each tribe's dress has its own background story which reflect that group's customs, history, and beliefs. Cultural identity is therefore maintained by the making and wearing of the garments.

Religion: The Diao are animists. They worship the spirit of the bull, which they believe to possess supernatural strength. The Diao participate in the annual Dong bullfights. Some elements of ancestor worship and Daoism are also present among the Diao.

Christianity: It is not known if Christianity has made any impact among the Diao people, but the large Dong nationality among whom they live has received little exposure to the gospel throughout their history. It can safely be assumed that most Diao have no comprehension of the name of Jesus Christ.

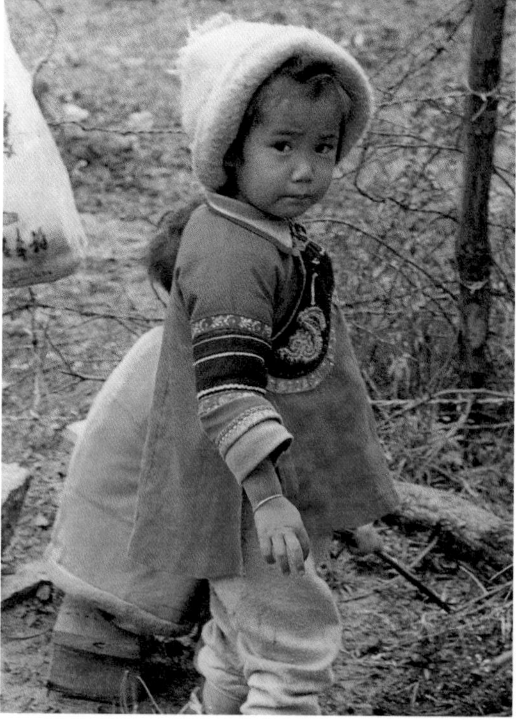

Paul Hattaway

Digao 低高

Jamin Pelkey

Location: A 1999 report listed a population of 22,300 Digao people in China.[1] They mostly live in the Zhongheying District of Kaiyuan County in the central part of Yunnan Province. Smaller numbers of Digao live in the Dazhuang and Lebaidao districts, also within Kaiyuan County; other Digao live in the Pingyuan District of Yanshan County and the Nijiao District of Qiubei County.

Identity: The official classification of the Digao people is somewhat complicated. The Digao are one of five groups in Kaiyuan County that are given the cover name of *Aza*. The 1996 Chinese publication *Kaiyuan Xian Zhi* (The Annals of Kaiyuan County) states, "Based on linguistic and cultural differences, the 'Aza' can be divided into five groups."[2] None of these five groups (which also include the Daizhan, Asahei, Labapo and Ani) calls itself *Aza*. All of these ethnicities have been officially included in the Yi nationality.

Language: The Digao language is part of the Southeastern Yi linguistic affiliation. It is similar to Puwa. Kaiyuan is a predominantly Han Chinese area today, so most Digao people are adequately bilingual in Mandarin.

History: The many Yi groups in China, including the Digao, once lived farther to the north of their present location. When Marco Polo passed through the Yi regions in the thirteenth century, he recorded, "Caindu is a province lying towards the west, and there is only one king in it. The people are Idolaters, subject to the Great Kaan, and they have plenty of towns and villages.... There is a great lake here, in which are found pearls [which are white but not round]. But the Great Kaan will not allow them to be fished, for if people were to take as many as they could find there, the supply would be so vast that pearls would lose their value, and come to be worth nothing."[3] Over the course of many centuries the Yi splintered into numerous ethnolinguistic entities and migrated across a huge area of southern China.

Customs: The typical Digao house is made of wood, bamboo, and mud. Although today the Digao are rapidly being assimilated by the Han Chinese, in the past each village had an entrance with carved images of birds, the sun, or the moon, under which was a wooden guardian eagle which had been blessed by the *bimo* (shaman). Opposite the entrance were goats' horns and chicken feathers remaining from sacrifices. In the northeast corner of the house stood a hearth of three stones, which could never be touched by the feet, as this was believed to bring bad luck.

Religion: Today only the elderly Digao continue to observe the animistic belief in the spirits that marked the identity of their forefathers. Ancestor worship is still strong, however. Annual ceremonies are held to honor the spirits of the Digao's parents.

Christianity: There are no known Christians among the Digao. The Catholics had a small work in Kaiyuan prior to 1949, with one priest, Father Booker, living in the county between 1910 and 1933. He was buried at Lukude. This work resulted in about 2,000 believers among the Hmong, but the various Yi groups were not reached.

Population in China:
22,300 (1999)
22,850 (2000)
28,700 (2010)
Location: Yunnan
Religion: Polytheism
Christians: None Known

Overview of the Digao

Countries: China

Pronunciation: "Dee-gaow"

Other Names: Digao Aza, Azar, Digaopo, Aza

Population Source: 22,300 (1999 J. Pelkey); Out of a total Yi population of 6,572,173 (1990 census)

Location: *Yunnan:* Zhongheying, Dazhuang, and Lebaidao districts of Kaiyuan County in Honghe Prefecture; Also in Yanshan and Qiubei counties

Status: Officially included under Yi

Language: Sino-Tibetan, Tibeto-Burman, Burmese-Lolo, Lolo, Northern Lolo, Yi, Southeastern Yi

Dialects: 0

Religion: Polytheism, Animism, Ancestor Worship, No Religion

Christians: None known

Scripture: None

***Jesus* film:** None

Gospel Recordings: None

Christian Broadcasting: None

ROPAL code: None

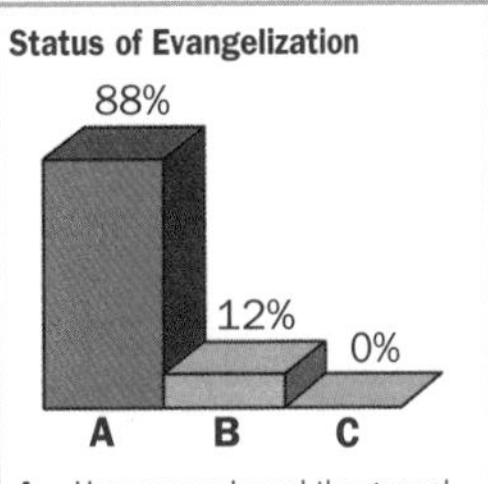

Dong, Northern 侗(北)

Population in China:
907,560 (1990)
1,170,700 (2000)
1,510,200 (2010)
Location:
Guizhou, Hunan, Hubei
Religion: Polytheism
Christians: 600

Overview of the Northern Dong

Countries: China

Pronunciation: "Dong"

Other Names: Kam, Tung, Tungchia, Tungjen, Gam, Tong, Tongkia

Population Source:
907,560 (1990 census);
Out of a total Dong population of 2,514,014 (1990 census)

Location:
SE Guizhou: Tianzhu, Sansui, Jianhe, and Jinping counties;
W Hunan: Xinhuang and Jingzhou counties;
SW Hubei: Enshi County

Status:
Officially included under Dong

Language: Daic, Kam-Sui

Literacy: 55%

Dialects: 3

Religion: Polytheism, Animism, Ancestor Worship

Christians: 600

Scripture: None

***Jesus* film:** None

Gospel Recordings: None

Christian Broadcasting: None

ROPAL code: DOC00

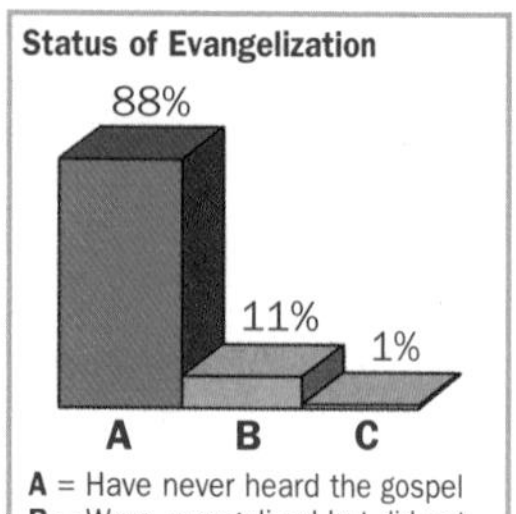

Paul Hattaway

Location: More than one million speakers of the Northern Dong language live in the area of southern China where the provinces of Guizhou and Hunan meet.[1] In addition, a small number live far to the north in Enshi County in southwestern Hubei. In 1990 the Northern Dong amounted to 36% of the total Dong population of 2.54 million.

Identity: Although the Northern and Southern Dong speak different languages, they have been combined to form the official Dong nationality in China. The two groups are also culturally different. The Northern Dong have been assimilated into Chinese culture much more than their southern counterparts. The Dong call themselves *Kam*.

Language: The two Dong languages share 71% cognate vocabulary.[2] Generally more speakers of Northern Dong are bilingual in Chinese than the Southern Dong. Many Northern Dong now speak exclusively Chinese. There are nine tones distinguishable in Northern Dong — the most found in any Tai-related language throughout the world.[3]

History: The Dong were not known by that name until this century. In the past they were part of the ancient Yue race, which dominated southern China. The Dong have many ancient myths and legends about the origin of the world.[4]

Customs: One of the visually striking aspects of a Dong community is the Drum Tower. For centuries, the Dong have used the tower as the rallying point of the community: a place where the village gathers for an emergency, celebrates a wedding, and where young Dong couples sing love songs to each other. One source states that there are more than 30 distinct Dong dialect groups in China, and that marriage is rare between members of the various groups.[5]

Religion: The Dong believe in many gods. They regard certain mountains, trees, stones, and other nonhuman objects as sacred. This is reflected in the Dong custom of planting a fir tree for each newborn baby. A form of black magic, called *Tu*, is practiced by some Dong in remote areas. The Kitchen god is worshiped during the Spring and Fall festivals. A growing number of Dong youth are nonreligious.

Christianity: Although they are considered relatively open to the gospel, the Dong remain one of the most neglected minority groups in China. Today there are an estimated 600 Northern Dong Christians,[6] a meager number considering their large population of more than one million. Most Dong have never heard the gospel. Both Protestant and Catholic missionaries were active among the Dong prior to the introduction of Communism in 1949. Several churches were built, but the gospel never took a firm hold among the Dong. Because the Dong do not have a written script, no Scriptures have been translated into their language. Efforts are underway to produce a Roman script for them. Many Northern Dong could now be reached by Chinese-language media.

Dong, Southern 侗(南)

Population in China:
1,480,750 (1990)
1,910,200 (2000)
2,464,100 (2010)
Location:
Guizhou, Guangxi, Hunan
Religion: Polytheism
Christians: 1,000

Overview of the Southern Dong

Countries: China, Vietnam

Pronunciation: "Dong"

Other Names: Kam, Tung, Tungchia, Tungjen, Gam, Tong, Tongjia

Population Source:
1,480,750 (1990 census);
Out of a total Dong population of 2,514,014 (1990 census);
Also in two villages in Vietnam

Location: The area where *SE Guizhou, W Hunan,* and *N Guangxi* meet

Status:
Officially included under Dong

Language: Daic, Kam-Sui

Literacy: 55%

Dialects: 3

Religion: Polytheism, Animism, Ancestor Worship

Christians: 1,000

Scripture: None

***Jesus* film:** In progress

Gospel Recordings:
Dong: Southern #04831

Christian Broadcasting: None

ROPAL code: KMC00

Status of Evangelization

A = Have never heard the gospel
B = Were evangelized but did not become Christians
C = Are adherents to any form of Christianity

Location: The Southern Dong are the larger of the two Dong language groups in China. Almost 1.5 million speakers of Southern Dong were counted in the 1990 language census, from a total of 2.5 million people in the Dong nationality. The Southern Dong live primarily in the Rongjiang, Jinping, Liping, Zhenyang, and Congjiang counties in Guizhou Province; Longsheng, Sanjiang, and Rongshui counties in northeastern Guangxi; and Tongdao County in Hunan Province. Two villages of Dong are also located in northern Vietnam, although only one individual in Vietnam is still able to speak Dong.

Identity: The Southern Dong speakers are counted as part of the official Dong nationality. The Southern Dong have retained more of their culture and ethnicity than the Northern Dong.

Language: Southern Dong, which is a member of the Daic language family, is related in part to the Zhuang, Maonan, Mulao, and Li languages.[1] A Dong orthography using Roman letters was developed in 1958 but has never gained widespread acceptance among the people. Despite their large population, the Dong have never migrated outside of China. Recent research found just one individual who spoke the Dong language in Vietnam.[2]

History: During the Qin and Han dynasties (221 BC–AD 220) there were numerous tribes scattered across southern China. At that time the ancestors of today's Dong were slaves. The slave society gradually eroded away during the Tang Dynasty (618–907).[3] For countless centuries the Dong have lived alongside Miao and Zhuang people and have absorbed numerous aspects of their culture and language.

Customs: The Dong love to stage bullfights. Every Dong village raises its own bull. "As the bulls lock horns and clash and strain to topple each other, the Dong cheer on their favourite beasts and toast them in fiery *mao tai* [whisky]."[4] A Dong girl is usually taught to weave and embroider at the age of seven. By the age of 12, she starts working on her wedding dress. Marriage usually occurs at the age of 17 or 18. After marriage, a woman lives with her parents until after the birth of the first child. At that time, she is allowed to move into her husband's home.

Religion: The Dong are a highly superstitious people who worship a host of demons and gods. They make annual offerings to the spirits of their village, homes, and crops. Ancestral altars are also found in the main room of most homes.

Christianity: The China Inland Mission commenced work among the Dong around 1910. In the 1930s missionaries from Liuzhou in Guangxi traveled to northern Guangxi and won 80 Southern Dong to Christ near Fuluh Township. In 1998 one ministry led several of this group to Christ. They returned to their village and started a house fellowship of 40 people.[5] Gospel recordings and the *Jesus* film are currently being produced in the Southern Dong language.

Paul Hattaway

Dongnu 东努

Location: The Chinese census of 1982 listed 153,589 speakers of the Dongnu language in southern China. This makes Dongnu the largest language group among the Bunu people, who totaled 439,000 in 1982. The Dongnu inhabit a geographically widespread area across 15 counties in the Guangxi Zhuang Autonomous Region, and as far west as Funing County in southeastern Yunnan Province.

Identity: The official classification of the Dongnu is complicated. Dongnu is one of 12 distinct ethnolinguistic groups within the Bunu group. The Bunu, however, were not granted status as one of China's official minorities but were included as part of the Yao nationality, even though they are comprised of many different ethnic groups and languages. Even most of the Bunu groups, including the Dongnu, do not consider themselves related to other Bunu groups such as the Numao, Baonuo, Wunai and Younou. Because the Chinese government has effectively hidden these people groups, they tend "not to exist." The Dongnu, despite now numbering more than 200,000 people, have never before appeared in any Christian mission lists.

Language: The Dongnu language was originally listed as one of four "dialects" of the Bunao Bunu language by the Chinese, but further research has shown all four qualify as distinct, mutually unintelligible languages.[1] The confusion between dialects and languages is caused by the Chinese term *fangyuan*, which they render as "dialects" but which are considered distinct languages in the Western sense. Dongnu is a language related to Miao and contains eight tones. Other Bunu languages have up to 11 tones. The Dongnu do not have their own orthography; however, some men and educated women can now read Chinese. In addition, many Dongnu now speak Northern Zhuang, having lost the use of their mother tongue.

Dwayne Graybill

History: The Dongnu live in an ethnically complex region. For centuries they have interacted with people from other minority groups such as the Yao, Miao, and Zhuang.

Customs: Dongnu women usually give birth in a hut that has been constructed away from the house. The placenta is saved and buried in a safe place in the forest. The Dongnu believe that when people die they will need to have their placenta in order for their ancestors to recognize them.

Religion: The religious belief system of the Dongnu contains elements of animism, Daoism, and ancestor worship. Ancestors are worshiped down to the fourth generation. It is primarily the job of the oldest son to take care of the ancestral altar.

Christianity: Although they number more than 200,000 people, the Dongnu are without a single known church or Christian believer. Their ethnic, geographic, and linguistic isolation has caused a barrier to the introduction of the gospel. Most mission work in Guangxi prior to 1949 targeted the southern part of the province. Few outsiders have even heard of the Dongnu people. The Dongnu are one of the largest people groups in China without a single known Christian in their midst.

Population in China:
153,589 (1982)
233,800 (2000)
301,500 (2010)
Location: Guangxi, Yunnan
Religion: Polytheism
Christians: None Known

Overview of the Dongnu

Countries: China

Pronunciation: "Dong-noo"

Other Names: Tung-Nu, Beilou Yao, Basket-Carrying Yao

Population Source: 153,589 (1982 census); Out of a total Yao population of 2,134,013 (1990 census)

Location: *Guangxi:* Du'an, Bama, Dahua, Hechi, Yishan, Bose, Debao, Tianyang, Tiandong, Pingguo, Shanglin, Bingyang, Mashan, Long'an, and Laibing counties; *SE Yunnan:* Funing County

Status: Officially included under Yao

Language: Hmong-Mien, Hmongic, Bunuic, Bunu

Dialects: 0

Religion: Polytheism, Animism, Ancestor Worship, Daoism

Christians: None known

Scripture: None

***Jesus* film:** None

Gospel Recordings: None

Christian Broadcasting: None

ROPAL code: BWX01

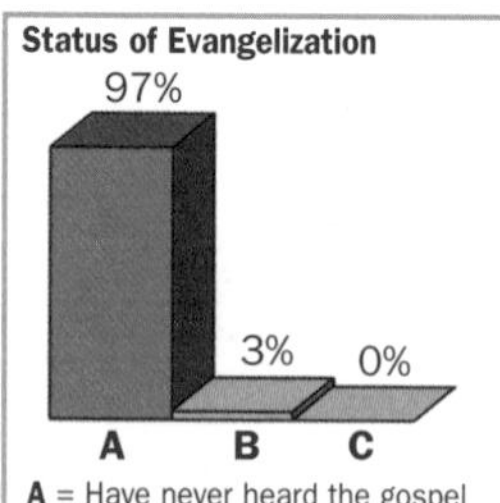

A = Have never heard the gospel
B = Were evangelized but did not become Christians
C = Are adherents to any form of Christianity

Dongxiang 东乡

Population in China:
373,872 (1990)
482,300 (2000)
622,100 (2010)
Location: Gansu, Qinghai, Xinjiang, Ningxia
Religion: Islam
Christians: None Known

Overview of the Dongxiang

Countries: China

Pronunciation: "Dong-shee-ung"

Other Names: Tunghsiang, Santa, Tung, Mongolian Huihui

Population Source:
373,872 (1990 census);
279,397 (1982 census);
147,443 (1964 census);
155,761 (1953 census)

Location: *SW Gansu:* Two-thirds of Dongxiang live in Dongxiang County in the Linxia Hui Prefecture. Smaller numbers live in Hezheng County and Linxia city; a few live in Lanzhou City and Dingxi District. A few Dongxiang also live in *Qinghai*, *Xinjiang*, and *Ningxia*.

Status:
An official minority of China

Language: Altaic, Mongolian, Eastern Mongolian, Mongour

Literacy: 12%

Dialects (3):
Suobana, Wangjiaji, Sijiaji

Religion: Islam

Christians: None known

Scripture: None

***Jesus* film:** None

Gospel Recordings:
Dongxiang #04866

Christian Broadcasting: None

ROPAL code: SCE00

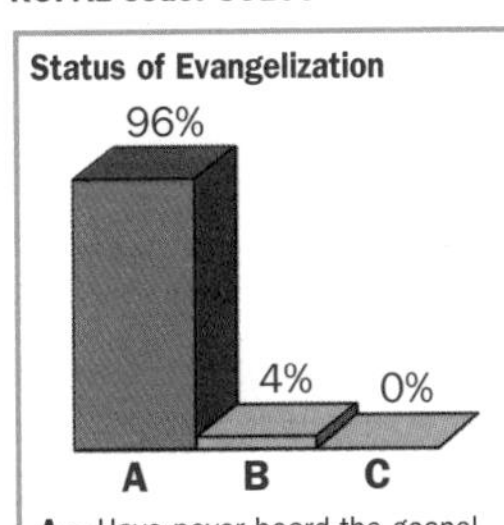

Dwayne Graybill

Location: The majority of the more than 480,000 Dongxiang live in one long, spread-out valley in the southwestern part of Gansu Province. The Dongxiang region is a desolate, arid place with a moon-like landscape, even though it is bordered by the Tao River to the east, the Daxia River to the west, and the Yellow River to the north. Approximately 55,000 Dongxiang also live in the Ili Prefecture in Xinjiang and in parts of Qinghai and Ningxia.[1]

Identity: The Dongxiang are one of China's official minority groups. They were called *Mongolian Huihui* prior to 1949, when their name was changed to the *Dongxiang* (East District) people. They call themselves by the Islamic term *Santa*. Other Muslims in China do not consider the Dongxiang to be a part of the Islamic faith because of their involvement in drug and prostitution rackets. One visitor to the Dongxiang described them as "very mean people, with hard faces."[2]

Language: The Dongxiang speak a Mongolian language. "Quite a few words in the Dongxiang lexicon resemble words of the same meaning in Modern Mongolian, and some are even identical to words presently used in Inner Mongolia. Many other words are close to the Middle Mongolian spoken in the thirteenth and fourteenth centuries."[3] Only 12% of the Dongxiang are literate in Chinese.

History: In the thirteenth century China was subdued by the Mongols. Genghis Khan, in a bid to control the land he had taken over, moved some of his garrisons into China. These soldiers intermarried with local women and gradually developed into their own distinct ethnic group called the Dongxiang.[4] Some place-names seem to support this theory. For example, *Zhayingtan* (Encampment Beach), is said to be the site of an old Dongxiang garrison.[5]

Customs: The Dongxiang are primarily employed as farmers. Their main crops are potatoes, barley, millet, wheat, and corn. They are also renowned across China for producing traditional rugs.

Religion: Not long after the Dongxiang first arrived in China, they were converted to Islam. By 1949, when the Communists took over China, there was one mosque for every 30 Dongxiang homes and one paid Muslim worker for every nine families.[6] Sixty to seventy percent of Dongxiang belong to the Old Sect, which emphasizes worshiping at the tombs of Muslim saints. "The remainder belong to the New Sect, a fundamentalist and reformist group."[7] There were numerous brutal wars between the two Dongxiang sects in the last century.

Christianity: There has never been a single known church or Christian among the Dongxiang. In the 1940s some missionaries briefly visited the Dongxiang area but were unsuccessful in converting anyone to Christ. In 1993 a Hong Kong-based organization conducted mass literature evangelism in the main Dongxiang town.[8] The nearest church to the Dongxiang is a Han Chinese fellowship in Linxia. The Christians there, however, believe "it is impossible to reach the Dongxiang."[9]

Doupo 都泼

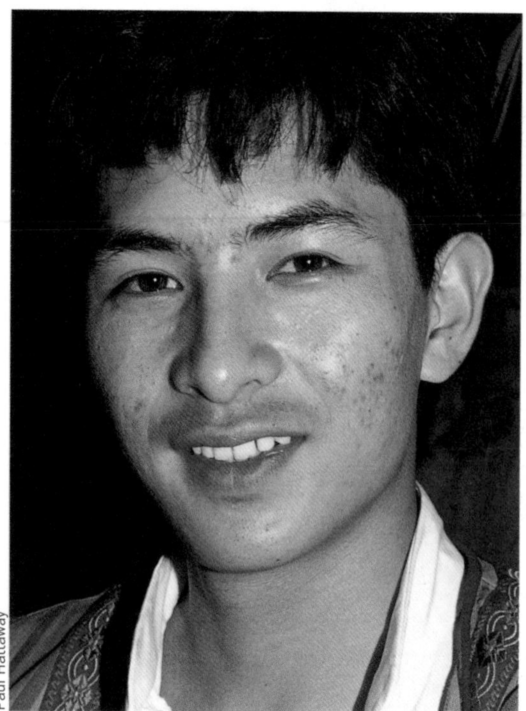
Paul Hattaway

Location: More than 600 Doupo people live in Yunnan Province in southwest China, west of Kunming City. About 400 live in the Mafang Village of Fumin County, while an additional 200 live in the Guanshanchang Village of Qinglong District in Anning County.[1]

Identity: The Doupo appear to have once been the same ethnic and language group as the 6,000 Depo who live in northern Yunnan and southern Sichuan, but since migrating away from the Depo they have developed a slightly different name and identity. Today, they do not consider themselves to be the same as the Depo. Both the Doupo and the Depo have been officially counted as part of the Yi nationality in China.

Language: Doupo is classified as part of the Northern Yi branch of Tibeto-Burman languages. It may be the same as the Eastern Nasu language of northern Yunnan. The Doupo do not possess an orthography.

History: Claiming to have lived in Yunnan Province for only a short time, the Doupo say they migrated to their present location from southern Sichuan Province in 1965. They say that they could not tolerate their lives in Sichuan because of the continual robbing and looting they suffered at the hands of other nationalities there. For centuries the Doupo were enslaved by the Eastern Nasu. Only in the late 1950s did the Communist authorities finally succeed in causing the downfall of the slave system.

Customs: The Doupo are a downtrodden tribe with low self-esteem. After centuries of being oppressed and harassed, a segment of this group finally found the courage to move away from their former masters and start a new life.

Religion: Although many of the younger generation of Doupo do not consider themselves religious, most Doupo over the age of 50 are careful to observe the ways of their ancestors, which consist of ancestor worship and a complex system of spirit worship. Spirits of the water, forest, mountains, and sky are worshiped. In the past the Doupo relied on hunting and appeased the god of the Hunt. To show their reverence, they would take the bones from all the animals they had killed and bury them in a "sacred hole" in the forest. The hunter would then drop to his knees and pray to the god of Hunting for blessing and a rich supply of game. This ritual is no longer practiced by the Doupo.

Christianity: Although there are a number of Christians among the closely related Depo of northern Yunnan, there are no known believers among the two Doupo villages near Kunming. In 1997 Wuding County reported a total of 22,341 Christians, of which 6,218 were "Yi." The county also reported 61 government-sanctioned churches or meeting places, along with Christians in 117 of the county's 127 communities.[2] Despite these impressive figures in Wuding, the Depo living in southern Sichuan have experienced a far lesser level of evangelization. It is from southern Sichuan that the Doupo migrated in 1965. There are no Scriptures, recordings, or other evangelistic material available in the Doupo language.

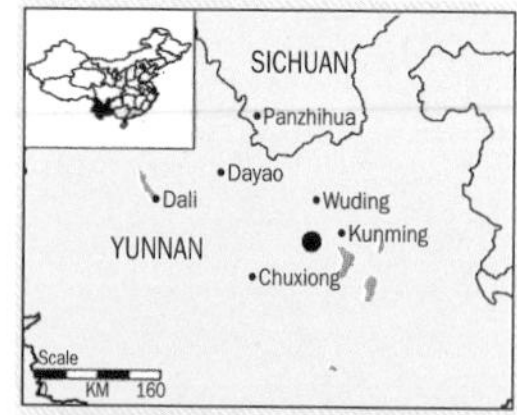

Population in China:
600 (1999)
615 (2000)
770 (2010)
Location: Yunnan
Religion: Polytheism
Christians: None Known

Overview of the Doupo

Countries: China

Pronunciation: "Dow-po"

Other Names: Nisupo, Huang Yi, Yellow Yi

Population Source: 600 (1999 J. Pelkey); Out of a total Yi population of 6,572,173 (1990 census)

Location: *Yunnan:* Fumin (400) and Anning (200) counties

Status: Officially included under Yi

Language: Sino-Tibetan, Tibeto-Burman, Burmese-Lolo, Lolo, Northern Lolo, Yi, Northern Yi

Dialects: 0

Religion: Polytheism, Animism, Ancestor Worship, No Religion

Christians: None known

Scripture: None

***Jesus* film:** None

Gospel Recordings: None

Christian Broadcasting: None

ROPAL code: None

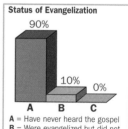

Status of Evangelization

	A	B	C
	90%	10%	0%

A = Have never heard the gospel
B = Were evangelized but did not become Christians
C = Are adherents to any form of Christianity

Duoluo 多罗

Location: In 1987 Chinese linguist Zheng Guo-qiao reported a total of 1,200 speakers of the Duoluo language in southern China. They are located in a spreadout area, including the Agong District of Zhijin County; Xiangyinshao District of Zhenning County; and the Dujiao and Yanjiao districts of Liuzhi City in western Guizhou Province. The Duoluo language is also spoken in Jianshan District of Zunyi County in northern Guizhou, as well as the Sanchong District of Longlin County in the northwestern part of the Guangxi Zhuang Autonomous Region.[1] There may also be ethnic Duoluo people living in eastern Yunnan Province, but they can no longer speak their language and so have not been listed in Chinese sources.

Identity: The Duoluo are one of several distinct ethnolinguistic groups which have been combined to form the official Gelao nationality in China. In 1945 the Gelao were described as being part of the Lao race in China, which included the Mulao and Tulao.[2]

Language: The Duoluo language, though now only spoken by a small number of people, is distinct from all other Gelao varieties in southern China. To show the distinctiveness of these languages, the Duoluo spoken in Longlin County of Guangxi has only 54% lexical similarity with the Gao language spoken in Anshun in Guizhou Province, even though both Duoluo and Gao are considered "Gelao dialects."[3] Missionary Samuel Clarke wrote, "The language of the Keh-lao [Gelao] is quite different from every other spoken in the province."[4] Duoluo has six tones.

History: The Duoluo were once the renowned leaders of the Yelang Kingdom which ruled a large part of southern China. Prior to the advent of Chinese Communism in 1949 many Duoluo practiced child-marriage. "To celebrate the marriage, the bride would walk with her relatives, carrying an umbrella, to the groom's home, where they would live apart from their parents."[5]

Customs: When a Duoluo dies, a colorful funeral procession is staged. "Mourners dance in groups of three, one playing a *lusheng* (reed pipe), one beating a bamboo pole, the third brandishing a sword, and all singing as they dance. In other areas, the mourners sit in front of the coffin while family members of the deceased serve wine in gratitude to them. In some places, a shaman who chooses the time and place of burial recites scriptures at the grave. Animal sacrifice usually accompanies the burial. Trees, rather than stones, mark the grave."[6]

Paul Hattaway

Religion: Animism and ancestor worship are mostly practiced among Duoluo communities in the remote mountains. Most of the Duoluo living near townships have been thoroughly assimilated and have become nonreligious.

Christianity: There is believed to be a small number of Christians among the Duoluo today. Catholic mission work among the different Gelao groups started in the late 1800s. A Catholic church was soon built. Protestant work commenced in the early 1900s. In 1908 the first two Gelao living in the Miao area of "Heo-er-kuan" were baptized.

Population in China:
1,200 (1987)
1,650 (2000)
2,130 (2010)
Location: Guizhou, Guangxi
Religion: Ancestor Worship
Christians: 40

Overview of the Duoluo

Countries: China

Pronunciation: "Duoh-luoh"

Other Names: Duoluo Gelao

Population Source:
1,200 (1987 Zheng Guo-qiao);
Out of a total Gelao population of 437,997 (1990 census)

Location:
Guizhou: Zhijin, Zunyi, and Zhenning counties;
And Luzhi City;
NW Guangxi: Longlin County

Status:
Officially included under Gelao

Language: Daic, Kadai, Lati-Kelao

Dialects: 0

Religion: Ancestor Worship, Animism, No Religion, Christianity, Shamanism

Christians: 40

Scripture: None

***Jesus* film:** None

Gospel Recordings: None

Christian Broadcasting: None

ROPAL code: KKF04

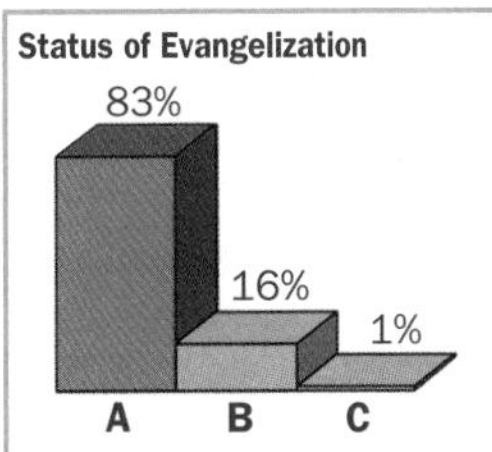

Duota 多它

Population in China:
10,000 (1996)
11,900 (2000)
14,640 (2010)
Location: Yunnan
Religion: Animism
Christians: 300

Overview of the Duota

Countries: China

Pronunciation: "Doo-oh-ta"

Other Names: Dota, Dota Yi, Duoni

Population Source: 10,000 (1996 AMO); Out of a total Hani population of 1,253,952 (1990 census)

Location: *S Yunnan:* Yuanjiang County in Yuxi Prefecture and Mojiang County in Honghe Prefecture

Status: Officially included under Hani

Language: Sino-Tibetan, Tibeto-Burman, Burmese-Lolo, Lolo, Southern Lolo, Akha

Dialects: 0

Religion: Animism, Polytheism, No Religion, Christianity

Christians: 300

Scripture: None

***Jesus* film:** None

Gospel Recordings: Hani: Duguduta #04942

Christian Broadcasting: None

ROPAL code: None

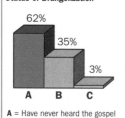

Status of Evangelization

	A	B	C
%	62%	35%	3%

A = Have never heard the gospel
B = Were evangelized but did not become Christians
C = Are adherents to any form of Christianity

Location: More than 11,000 members of the Duota tribe live in Mojiang County in the Honghe Prefecture and in Yuanjiang County in Yuxi Prefecture. Honghe lies in the southern part of Yunnan Province. The Ailao Mountains, which have an average elevation of 1,600 meters (5,250 ft.) above sea level, run through the region and are home to numerous ethnic groups and subgroups.

Identity: The Duota were listed in CIM missionary John Kuhn's 1945 tribal survey of Yunnan Province, entitled *We Found a Hundred Tribes*. Kuhn called them *Dota*. In the 1950s the Chinese authorities included the Duota as part of the Hani nationality. They have always viewed themselves as a distinct tribe and do not believe they are closely related to the 18 groups combined to form the Hani. As one writer explains, "There are many subdivisions of Hanis — Buda, Bukong, Biyo and Duota, among others — and they all have their own traditions and ways of dressing."[1]

Language: The Duota language is part of the Southern Yi language family. Some groups in Honghe Prefecture were classified under the Yi nationality by the Chinese, while others found themselves placed under the Hani nationality. It seems that the criteria used was according to each tribe's linguistic affiliation. Speakers of Northern Lolo languages were included in the Yi minority, while Southern Lolo were placed in the Hani minority. The Duota do not have their own written script. Most members of this tribe, except some of the elderly, are adequately bilingual in Chinese.

History: Records indicate a tribal people known as the Heyis lived south of the Dadu River in the third century BC. Between the fourth and eighth centuries some of them migrated to the Lancang area in western Yunnan before moving east to their present location in Honghe. After living in their own communities for several generations, they developed their own ethnic identities. The Duota are believed to be one of these tribes.

Customs: The main festivals of the Duota fall in June and October. The *Kuzhazha* (Sixth Moon Festival) lasts from three to six days. Duota men and women dress in their finest traditional clothing. Duota men are "bold and unconstrained by nature. Their deep love for life, their hopes for their people, and their wishes for the year ahead are all reflected in their wild dances and the way they dress during the *Kuzhazha*."[2]

Religion: The Duota say they were once in communication with heaven, but after an argument with the gods they were separated from heaven and no longer have access. Today some Duota are animists, but most youth consider themselves nonreligious.

Christianity: There are few churches or Christian communities among the Duota, even though they live near the heavily evangelized Kado and Biyo people groups. Many Duota have some surface knowledge of the gospel, but it has never moved their hearts, probably because the message has always come to them in a language other than their own.

Paul Hattaway

E 鄂

Paul Hattaway

Location: More than 30,000 people in the northern part of the Guangxi Zhuang Autonomous Region speak the E (pronounced "Erh") language. Another study lists a figure of 50,000 E speakers in China.[1] The E inhabit 19 villages in both Rongshui and Luocheng counties. Rongshui is an autonomous county of the Miao people, and Luocheng is an autonomous county of the Mulao nationality. The main population center of the E is in the town of Yongle. The region contains an abundance of beautiful karst hills and rock formations nestled among lush green pastures.

Identity: Although they have been classified as part of the large Zhuang nationality, the E cannot speak Zhuang. The Chinese call them *Wuse*, a derogatory name meaning "five colors." *E* is this group's autonym.

Language: Although few people are aware of the existence of the E people, there has been extensive research conducted into their language.[2] The E speak a Central Tai language which contains characteristics of five neighboring languages: Zhuang, Mulao, Dong, Pinghua Chinese, and Guiliuhua (a variety of Southwestern Mandarin).[3] For this reason the neighboring Chinese call their language *Wusehua* (Five-colored Speech). One linguist states, "Some consider it to be basically a variety of Zhuang that has been heavily influenced by other languages."[4] A vocabulary list of 2,000 E words showed 85% of these were Chinese cognates.[5] Many E are also bilingual in the Tuguai dialect of Cantonese.

History: The north central part of Guangxi has long been a crossroads for many different races. Interaction between Han Chinese and minority people has resulted in the intermixing of ethnic groups such as the Mulao, Maonan, and Zhuang. These groups have many Chinese customs and linguistic influences. On the other hand, the Pinghua Chinese reveal many ethnolinguistic traits of minority groups.

Customs: The E celebrate the traditional Chinese festivals, the most important of which are the Spring Festival and the Chinese New Year.

Religion: Most E are animists, with many aspects of ancestor worship and traditional Chinese religions mixed into their rituals.

Christianity: There are no known Christian fellowships or believers among the 19 E villages in northern Guangxi. The E still await the arrival of the gospel for the first time. Whitfield Guinness, a missionary-doctor who served in China until his death in 1927, summarized the condition of the lost tribes and individuals among whom he worked: "Men and women are toiling without a Bible, without a Sunday, without a prayer, without songs of praise. They have rulers without justice and righteousness; homes without peace; marriage without sanctity; young men and women without ideals and enthusiasm; little children without purity, without innocence; mothers without wisdom or self-control; poverty without relief or sympathy; sickness without skillful help or tender care; sorrow and crime without a remedy; and worst of all, death without Christ."[6]

Population in China:
30,000 (1992)
34,700 (2000)
41,500 (2010)
Location: Guangxi
Religion: Animism
Christians: None Known

Overview of the E

Countries: China

Pronunciation: "Erh"

Other Names: Kjang E, Wuse, Wusehua

Population Source: 30,000 (1992 J.Edmondson); Out of a total Zhuang population of 15,489,630 (1990 census)

Location: *N Guangxi:* Rongshui Miao County and Yongle Township; and 19 villages to the border area of Luocheng County

Status: Officially included under Zhuang

Language: Daic, Tai, Central Tai

Dialects: 0

Religion: Animism, Polytheism, No Religion, Ancestor Worship

Christians: None known

Scripture: None

***Jesus* film:** None

Gospel Recordings: None

Christian Broadcasting: None

ROPAL code: EEE00

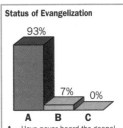

Status of Evangelization

A	B	C
93%	7%	0%

A = Have never heard the gospel
B = Were evangelized but did not become Christians
C = Are adherents to any form of Christianity

Eka 俄卡

March 13

Population in China:
2,500 (1999)
2,560 (2000)
3,210 (2010)
Location: Yunnan
Religion: Polytheism
Christians: 20

Overview of the Eka

Countries: China

Pronunciation: "Ee-kah"

Other Names: Menghuaren

Population Source:
2,500 (1999 J. Pelkey);
Out of a total Yi population of 6,572,173 (1990 census)

Location:
W Yunnan: Shuangjiang County

Status:
Officially included under Yi

Language: Sino-Tibetan, Tibeto-Burman, Burmese-Lolo, Lolo, Northern Lolo, Yi, Western Yi

Dialects: 0

Religion: Polytheism, Animism, Ancestor Worship, Christianity

Christians: 20

Scripture: None

***Jesus* film:** None

Gospel Recordings: None

Christian Broadcasting: None

ROPAL code: None

Status of Evangelization

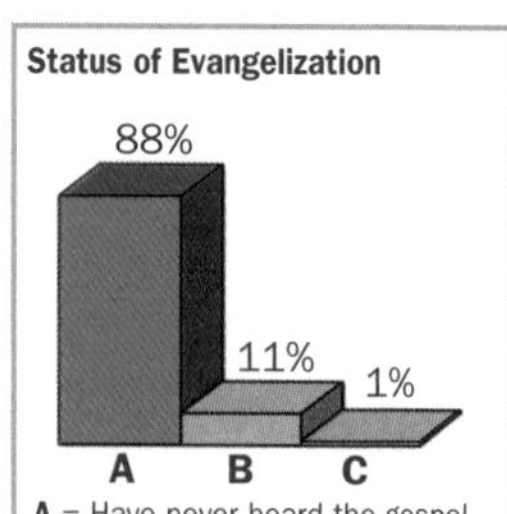

A = Have never heard the gospel
B = Were evangelized but did not become Christians
C = Are adherents to any form of Christianity

Location: With a population of more than 2,500 people, the Eka are the largest Yi group living in Shuangjiang County of Yunnan Province in southwest China.[1] The only other Yi group located in Shuangjiang are the 500 Mishaba Laluo. Shuangjiang is an extremely remote and mountainous area. Many villages are only accessible by foot.

Identity: Eka is one of more than 100 distinct people groups of Yi in Yunnan Province alone, and one of 120 throughout all of China. The Eka formerly possessed a strong cultural identity, but their uniqueness and cohesiveness as a people has eroded over the past century as they have been swamped by Chinese immigrants entering the Shuangjiang area in large numbers.

Language: The Eka language is reportedly part of the Western Yi branch of the Tibeto-Burman family, although most Eka have now lost the use of their mother tongue. Instead, they speak some or all of the Chinese, Lahu, and local Tai languages.

History: The Eka are believed to have moved into the area at least 300 years ago, possibly from areas close to Kunming City. Much of the land was unclaimed at the time, but after the Eka moved onto it and cultivated it, waves of new Chinese entered the area, claimed the land for themselves, and drove the Eka off into the mountains.

Customs: The members of this tribe lead simple lives. They keep pigs, goats, and chickens, as well as grow rice and maize.

Religion: The Eka are polytheists, worshiping many gods and deities. Their beliefs are similar to other tribes in Yunnan. One early visitor, commenting on the beliefs of another Yi group, wrote, "They are, as a matter of fact, pure theists. They have no religious worship properly so called; neither temples, nor priests, nor ceremonies in which the people can participate. But they believe in one God, perfect and omnipotent, and in a magnificent Spirit. After their death the good are called to God and the wicked are tormented by the Demon. But as a rule the dead man has been neither wholly good nor wholly bad; he therefore spends three years in roaming the earth around his home, intervening in events, and the celestial judgment is deferred until the end of that period. That is why the [Yi] keep for three years in their houses, either in a box or under the roof, a kind of effigy of the deceased, made of wood, or hemp, or the root of an orchid, in which magical formulas have fixed the soul of the deceased. On certain anniversaries this figure is brought out and prayers are recited. At the third year's end the figure is thrown away; the soul is judged."[2]

Jamin Pelkey

Christianity: According to one source, there were two Eka believers reported in 1933.[3] These may have come under the influence of missionary work among their Lahu neighbors, hundreds of whom came to Christ in the early part of the twentieth century. There may be as many as 20 Eka Christians today, but most members of this group have yet to receive an intelligible witness of the gospel. Some Eka remain who need to hear the message in their own tongue, but most are now adequately bilingual in Chinese or Lahu for effective evangelization to occur in those languages.

Enipu 厄尼蒲

Population in China:
16,000 (1999)
16,400 (2000)
20,600 (2010)
Location: Yunnan
Religion: Polytheism
Christians: None Known

Overview of the Enipu

Countries: China

Pronunciation: "Uh-nee-poo"

Other Names: Eniba, Enibo

Population Source:
16,000 (1999 J. Pelkey) ;
Out of a total Yi population of 6,572,173 (1990 census)

Location: *Yunnan:* Nanjian (11,000) and Weishan (5,000) counties in Dali Prefecture

Status:
Officially included under Yi

Language: Sino-Tibetan, Tibeto-Burman, Burmese-Lolo, Lolo, Northern Lolo, Yi, Central Yi

Dialects: 0

Religion: Polytheism, Animism, Ancestor Worship

Christians: None known

Scripture: None

***Jesus* film:** None

Gospel Recordings: None

Christian Broadcasting: None

ROPAL code: None

Status of Evangelization

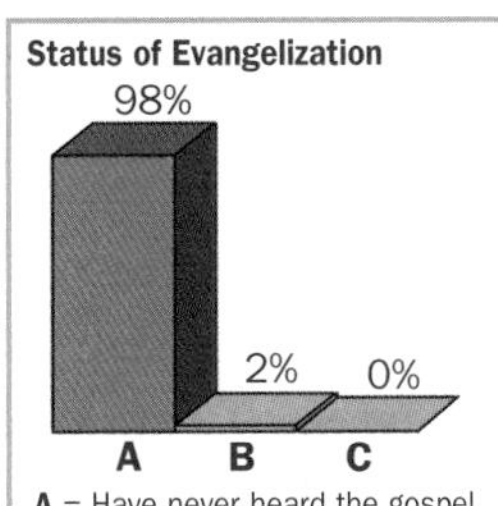

A = Have never heard the gospel
B = Were evangelized but did not become Christians
C = Are adherents to any form of Christianity

Location: More than 16,000 Enipu live in the Dali Prefecture of Yunnan Province. The majority (11,000) live within Nanjian County, while 5,000 inhabit areas in Weishan County.[1] In western Nanjian County the Enipu are dispersed in the Wanubu, Baishajing, and Laojiaku villages of Ximin District; and in Ertaipo Village of Langcang District. In Weishan County they inhabit villages in the Yinchang, Qinghe, Qingmin, and Wuxing communities of Qinghua District.[2]

Identity: The Enipu are one of 120 different ethnic groups in southern China who were combined into the official Yi nationality by the Chinese authorities. French Catholic missionary Père Paul Vial, who worked with two Yi groups, expressed his passion for getting the lesser-known Yi groups recognized and accepted by the Han. Vial wrote, "I love him [the Yi] because he is good, I love him because he is scorned. I would like to have him known for pushing aside the plethora of prejudices that fill books and are unabashedly accepted as proven facts. It seems to me that a missionary who has first of all given eight years of his apostolic life for the salvation of the Chinese, and who has now evangelized the [Yi] for many years, has the right to carry an opinion exempt from ignorance, if not errors of partiality."[3]

Language: Little is known about the Enipu language except that it is a member of the Central Yi linguistic family. Enipu is believed to still be in widespread use.

History: The Enipu claim to have a history of at least 400 years. Their past has been one of struggle against being assimilated by the dominant Han Chinese. As a result, the Enipu moved to extremely remote mountainous locations where they could continue their lives in relative obscurity. The Enipu living in Weishan County moved from Nanjian around 200 years ago.

Customs: Many Yi groups, including the Enipu, do not have written genealogies. They engage in oral competitions, reciting long lists of names. It is a disgrace to make mistakes in one's own genealogy and an insult to do so in another person's.[4] In Enipu culture, the door is considered the most important part of the house. The place of honor at meals is reserved for the person who sits with his back to the wall and his face toward the door.

Religion: The Enipu are a highly superstitious people. "For three years after death they believe the soul of the deceased roams. An effigy of wood, hemp or orchid root, in which magical formulas have fixed the soul, is kept in a box or beneath the roof of the house. At the end of three years the effigy is thrown away, the body is exhumed and burned, and the ashes are placed in an urn and put in a new location."[5]

Christianity: The areas inhabited by the Enipu are practically devoid of any Christian presence. As a result, today there are no known Christians among the Enipu people. They live isolated lives in their mountain communities and have yet to be engaged by any messengers of the gospel. No Scriptures, videos, or gospel audio recordings exist in a language understood by the Enipu.

Jamin Pelkey

Enu 哦怒

Location: More than 20,000 people belonging to a little-known ethnic group, the Enu, live in several counties of southern Yunnan Province. They are spread from Jinggu County in Simao Prefecture as far south as Mengla County in Xishuangbanna Prefecture, near the China-Laos border. The center of the Enu people could be placed at Tayisai District in Mojiang County. In most locations the Enu do not have their own villages; rather, they live in mixed communities with people from other nationalities.

Identity: The Enu, who are officially part of the Hani nationality, are also known as the *Ximeluo* in China. The "Si-mou-lou" were first mentioned in a 1903 survey of Yunnan's ethnic composition.[1] Missionary John Kuhn, in his 1945 tribal survey of Yunnan, listed the "Simoulu" as living at "Ning Erh and Qingku."[2] Qingku is the old spelling for today's Jinggu County, in Simao Prefecture.

Language: Enu is part of the Bi-Ka branch of the Tibeto-Burman language family, related to other Hani languages such as Biyo, Kado, and Ake. A 1986 Chinese linguistic survey studied the Enu.[3] The Enu language seems to consist of two dialects which may be mutually unintelligible. Li Yongsui has given a brief linguistic account of the two varieties, "including comparative phonological notes and a few lexical items."[4]

History: By the 1960s the Enu living near Chinese towns and cities had already begun the gradual process of assimilation. Today, only those living in more remote locations retain their ethnicity and language. The demise of the Enu as a distinct people group may have been a contributing factor in the Chinese government's decision not to grant them status as a separate minority.

Customs: Most Enu live in simple homes constructed of wood and thatched roofs. Most customs and ceremonies of the Enu now closely mirror that of the dominant Han Chinese. Earlier in the twentieth century, however, they still retained many unique customs that reflected their animistic beliefs. In one sacrifice, they spread the hide of a bull over a wooden frame, under which family leaders from feuding sides would drink the bull's blood and take a peace oath. If either party broke this oath, its members would meet the same fate as the slaughtered animal.

Religion: Most Enu people are animists, especially the elderly, who continue to offer prayers and burn incense before spirit and ancestral altars. The younger generation reluctantly continue the practices of their parents out of respect for their forefathers.

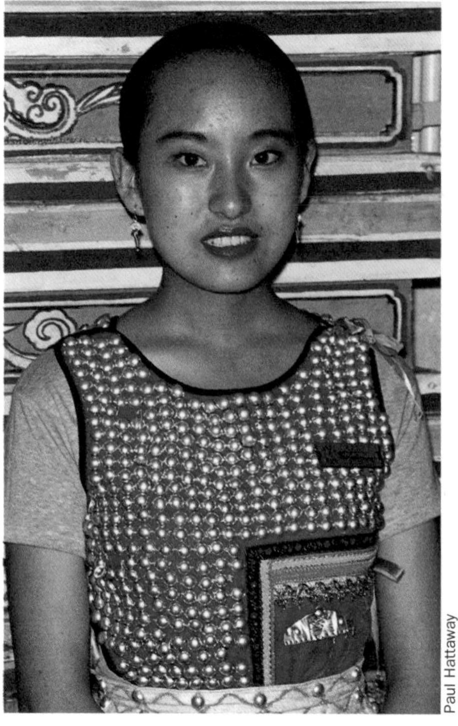

Paul Hattaway

Christianity: There are a small number of scattered Enu Christians, including some who attend a church consisting of people from nine different minority groups in Mengla County near the Laos border.[5] Overall, however, southern Yunnan has been woefully neglected by the scouts of Christianity. Lottie Moon, a Baptist missionary, was disturbed by the lack of interest in China's lost. She bluntly stated, "It is odd that a million Baptists of the south can furnish only three men for all China.... I wonder how these things look in heaven. They certainly look very queer in China."[6]

Kunming
YUNNAN
Lincang
Mojiang
Ximeng
MYANMAR
Simao
VIETNAM
Jinghong
LAOS
Scale
0 KM 160

Population in China:
20,000 (1998)
20,920 (2000)
25,750 (2010)
Location: Yunnan
Religion: Animism
Christians: 600

Overview of the Enu

Countries: China

Pronunciation: "E-noo"

Other Names: Si-mou-lou, Simolu, Similu, Xiumoluo, Ximeluo, Yayisai Enu, O-nu

Population Source:
20,000 (1998 AMO);
Out of a total Hani population of 1,253,952 (1990 census)

Location: *S Yunnan:* Mojiang, Jinggu, and Mengla counties

Status:
Officially included under Hani

Language: Sino-Tibetan, Tibeto-Burman, Burmese-Lolo, Lolo, Southern Lolo, Akha, Hani, Bi-Ka

Dialects: 0

Religion:
Animism, Ancestor Worship

Christians: 600

Scripture: None

***Jesus* film:** None

Gospel Recordings: None

Christian Broadcasting: None

ROPAL code: None

Status of Evangelization

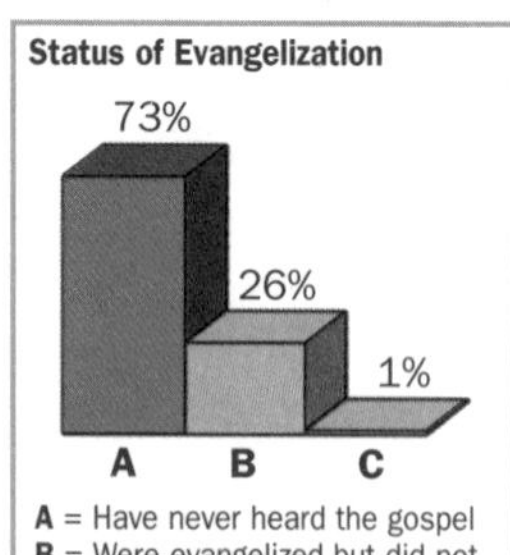

A = Have never heard the gospel
B = Were evangelized but did not become Christians
C = Are adherents to any form of Christianity

Ergong 尔龚

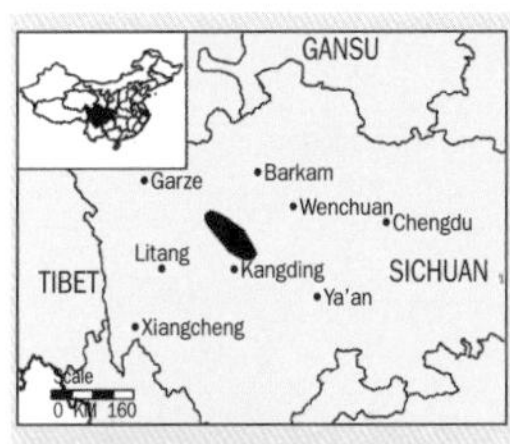

Population in China:
35,000 (1983)
48,800 (2000)
60,100 (2010)
Location: Sichuan
Religion: Tibetan Buddhism
Christians: None Known

Overview of the Ergong

Countries: China

Pronunciation: "Erh-gong"

Other Names: Daofuhua, Bopa, Hor, Horpa, Horu, Hor-ke, Taofu, Pawang, Gesitsa, Bawang Rong-Ke

Population Source: 35,000 (1983 Sun Hongkai); Out of a total Tibetan population of 4,593,330 (1990 census)

Location: *W Sichuan:* Danba, Daofu, Luhuo, and Xinlong counties in the Garze Prefecture; And Jinchuan County of Aba Prefecture in NW Sichuan

Status: Officially included under Tibetan

Language: Sino-Tibetan, Tibeto-Burman, Qiangic, Jiarong, Ergong

Dialects (3): Danba, Daofu, Northern Ergong

Religion: Tibetan Buddhism, Shamanism

Christians: None known

Scripture: None

***Jesus* film:** None

Gospel Recordings: None

Christian Broadcasting: None

ROPAL code: ERO00 (Ergong); HRP00 (Horpa)

Status of Evangelization

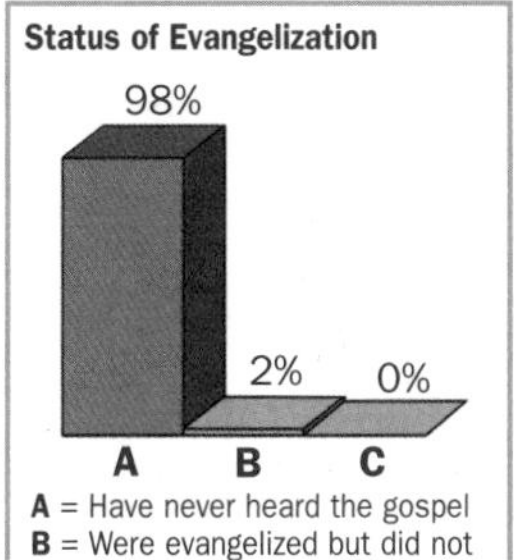

A = Have never heard the gospel
B = Were evangelized but did not become Christians
C = Are adherents to any form of Christianity

Location: Chinese scholar Sun Hongkai in 1983 listed 35,000 Ergong people living in the western part of Sichuan Province.[1] The Ergong inhabit what is now Danba, Daofu, Luhuo, and Xinlong counties of the Garze Prefecture in western Sichuan. They also live in the Guanyinqiao District of Jinchuan County in the Aba Prefecture. All of these areas were formerly part of Kham Province in Tibet. The region where the Ergong live is one of the most remote in the world. Many communities are only accessible by foot. Many of the people in the area, including the Ergong, are nomadic or seminomadic.

Mette Krogh

Identity: Officially the Ergong have been included as part of the Tibetan nationality in China, even though they speak their own distinct language. The Ergong are also widely known as *Hor* or *Horpa.*

Language: The Ergong language, called *Daofuh Hua* by the Chinese, is related to Jiarong in western Sichuan.[2] It is a member of the Qiangic branch of Tibeto-Burman. Ergong, or Horpa, and has been studied by linguists for a surprisingly long time. They were first described by B. H. Hodgson in 1874.[3] One scholar notes that the various Qiangic languages, including Ergong, "are of unusual interest, both synchronically and diachronically. They are characterized by initial consonant clusters comparable in complexity to those of Written Tibetan.... Some languages of the group are tonal, while others are not, providing an ideal terrain for the investigation of the mechanisms of tono-genesis."[4] The Ergong speak their mother tongue within their own communities but use Chinese or Tibetan with outsiders.

History: The great Qiang race was once more populous than today. As they moved into more remote regions along the Tibetan frontier, most Qiang were converted to Tibetan Buddhism and were gradually assimilated to Tibetan culture and customs. Today, minority groups such as the Ergong are an example of those Qiang groups who are still in the transitory stage of assimilation. The Ergong are culturally Tibetan but retain their Qiangic language.

Customs: The customs of the Ergong are similar to Tibetan customs, although massive stone watchtowers called *tianlu* prove their affiliation with the Qiang people. Harsh Sichuan winters give way in May to sunny days when grass and wildflowers bloom throughout the region.

Religion: All Ergong adhere to the Tibetan Buddhist religion. They consider it a priority to visit at least one holy Tibetan site during the course of their lifetime.

Christianity: The Ergong are a completely untouched people group. Few Christians have heard of the Ergong and fewer still have tried to reach them. James O. Fraser, a British missionary who worked among the Lisu in the early part of the twentieth century, often exhorted believers in the Western world to intercede on behalf of the lost in China. Fraser said, "Many of us cannot reach the mission-fields on our feet, but we can reach them on our knees. Solid, lasting missionary work is accomplished by prayer, whether offered in China, India, or the United States."[5]

Ersu 尔苏

Paul Hattaway

Location: A 1983 study listed 20,000 speakers of Ersu living along the lower reaches of the Dadu River, in seven different counties of southern Sichuan Province.[1] The area is also home to members of the Khampa, Nosu, and Chrame people groups. The Dadu River originates at Mount Golog on the Sichuan-Qinghai border and runs a total of 1,155 kilometers (713 mi.) before it empties into the Min River.

Identity: The Ersu are officially part of the Tibetan nationality, but in the 1980s they asked the government to create a new minority, called the *Xifan*, and to include them under it. The authorities declined. The linguist Sun Hongkai says, "Ersu speakers at different localities have different autonyms: those living at Ganluo, Yuexi and Hanyuan call themselves *Ersu*, *Buerzi* or *Ersubuerzi*; those living at Shimian use *Lusu*, and those living at Muli, Jiulong and western Mianning *Lisu*. These different autonyms are dialectal variants of the same word, originally meaning 'white people'."[2]

Language: The Ersu language contains three tones and three dialects, all of which reportedly contain "great differences."[3] The Ersu are noted for their use of an ancient pictographic script. This has baffled and amazed scholars who have speculated on how the Ersu came to possess their unique orthography. One scholar suggests, "Ersu is perhaps an indirect descendant of the extinct Xixia language, spoken in a once-powerful empire in the Tibetan-Chinese-Uighur border regions, finally destroyed by the Mongols in the 13th century. A large literature in Xixia survives, in a logographic writing system invented in the 11th century, with thousands of intricate characters inspired by, but graphically independent of Chinese, the decipherment of which is now well-advanced by Japanese and Russian scholars."[4]

History: Regardless of where the Ersu may have originated, it is known that they have lived in their present location for many centuries. Qiang nomads once ruled western China as far as today's Inner Mongolia. Gradually their kingdoms broke up and they migrated south and west. The present official Qiang nationality in China only represents a fraction of the original Qiang race. Most were assimilated by larger groups long ago.

Customs: Culturally, the Ersu have been swallowed up by the Tibetans. Almost every aspect of their lives reflects their belief in Tibetan Buddhism.

Religion: The Ersu believe they will be reincarnated when they die and will come back to the earth as a person in a higher social position if they have lived a virtuous life. They will come back as an animal if they lived a wicked life. This belief results in the Ersu having little motivation to help the afflicted among them, as suffering is considered the consequence of a person's bad karma.

Christianity: There has never been a known church or Christian among the Ersu. The Border Mission of the Church of Christ in China and the American Baptists worked among the related Jiarong people until 1949, reporting 34 converts in 1934.[5] No outreach, however, was ever undertaken to the Ersu.

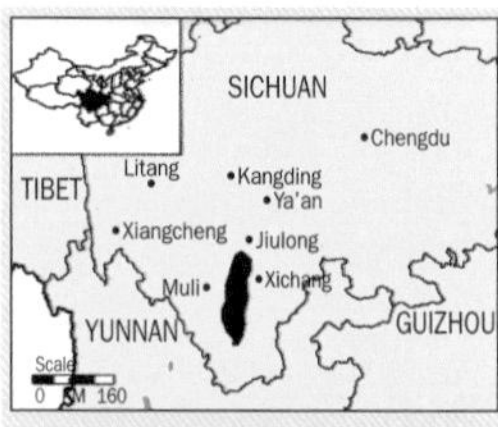

Population in China:
20,000 (1983)
27,850 (2000)
34,350 (2010)
Location: Sichuan
Religion: Tibetan Buddhism
Christians: None Known

Overview of the Ersu

Countries: China
Pronunciation: "Erh-soo"
Other Names: Douxu, Ersu Yi, Tosu, Buerzi, Ersubuerzi, Lusu, Lisu
Population Source: 20,000 (1983 Sun Hongkai); Out of a total Tibetan population of 4,593,330 (1990 census)
Location: *S Sichuan:* Shijin, Yanyuan, Ganluo, Yuexi, Mianning, Muli, and Jiulong counties
Status: Officially included under Tibetan
Language: Sino-Tibetan, Tibeto-Burman, Qiangic, Ersu
Dialects (3): Ersu (Eastern) 13,000, Duoxu (Central) 3,000, Lisu (Western) 4,000
Religion: Tibetan Buddhism
Christians: None known
Scripture: None
***Jesus* film:** None
Gospel Recordings: None
Christian Broadcasting: None
ROPAL code: ERS00

Status of Evangelization

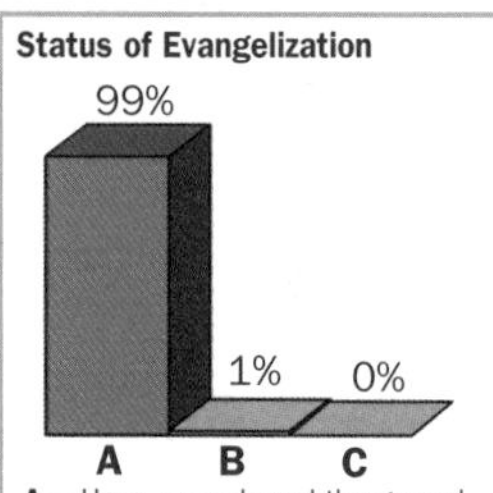

A = Have never heard the gospel
B = Were evangelized but did not become Christians
C = Are adherents to any form of Christianity

Ewenki, Solon 鄂温克，素量

Location: The Solon Ewenki are the largest of the four Ewenki groups in China. They account for approximately 80% of all Ewenki in China,[1] which amounts to more than 21,000 of the total 1990 census figure of 26,300 for the Ewenki nationality. The Ewenki are also found in Russia and Mongolia. They have survived for centuries in the harsh temperatures of north Asian winters. The Solon Ewenki primarily inhabit the Morindawa, Oroqen, and Arong Banners in the eastern part of Inner Mongolia. There they live alongside Mongols, Daur, and Oroqen. It is a beautiful region, with more than 600 lakes and freshwater springs located among the pasture lands and woods of the Greater Hinggan Mountains. A small number of Solon Ewenki also live in Nehe County in Heilongjiang.[2]

Dwayne Graybill

Identity: The name *Ewenki* means "mountain forest people." It was coined by the Russians earlier in this century to describe the nomads in eastern Siberia. The name *Solon* means "those (people) from the upper course of the river."[3]

Language: The Solon Ewenki language is labeled the *Haila'er* dialect of Ewenki by the Chinese. It is mutually unintelligible with the other three Ewenki varieties.[4] The Solon Ewenki are said to be able to understand 70% of the Oroqen language.[5] Many can also speak Daur.

History: The Ewenki are believed to be descended from the Shiwei people who lived in the mountains northeast of Lake Baikal in Siberia. By the early 1600s, groups of Ewenki started to migrate into China, spreading along the tributaries of the lower Amur River.[6]

Customs: Most Solon Ewenki families earn their livelihood by fishing, raising reindeer, and hunting. Many still live in yurts that are easy to assemble and transport from place to place. This is a necessity of life for the Ewenki. Many stay in one place no more than ten days in the summer. In the winter they may move as often as every two days. The Ewenki practice the same burial rites as the Oroqen. Corpses are wrapped in birch bark and hoisted up a tree to decompose naturally.

Religion: The primary religious belief among the Solon Ewenki is shamanism, although some who have been influenced by the Mongolians have adopted the Tibetan Buddhist religion. The Solon Ewenki also worship the spirits of their ancestors. They pray to many gods and deities, asking for success in hunting.

Christianity: Although there are a small number of Ewenki Eastern Orthodox believers in China, they are all among the Tungus Ewenki group in the Chenbaehru region. There are no known Christians or churches among the Solon Ewenki in China. In Russia the Ewenki were forced to convert to Orthodox Christianity in the sixteenth and seventeenth centuries. As a result, by 1862 there were 9,480 registered Ewenki Christians.[7] However, their conversion appears to have been largely superficial. They continued to worship spirits; they also included statues of Jesus among their idols.

Population in China:
21,050 (1990)
27,150 (2000)
35,030 (2010)
Location: Inner Mongolia, Heilongjiang
Religion: Shamanism
Christians: None Known

Overview of the Solon Ewenki

Countries: China, Russia, Mongolia

Pronunciation: "Sor-lon-E-wenk-ee"

Other Names: Evenki, Ewenke, Owenke, Solon, Ewenki, Suolun, Manchurian Solon, Solon Evenki

Population Source: 21,050 (1990 AMO); Out of a total population of 26,315 Ewenki (1990 census); 30,000 in Russia (1993); 2,000 in Mongolia (1982)

Location: *NE Inner Mongolia:* Morindawa, Oroqen, and Arong Banners; *W Heilongjiang:* Nehe and Nenjiang counties

Status: Officially included under Ewenki

Language: Altaic, Tungus, Northern Tungus, Ewenki

Literacy: 81%

Dialects: 0

Religion: Shamanism, Tibetan Buddhism, Ancestor Worship

Christians: None known

Scripture: None

***Jesus* film:** None

Gospel Recordings: Evenki #04697

Christian Broadcasting: None

ROPAL code: EVN00

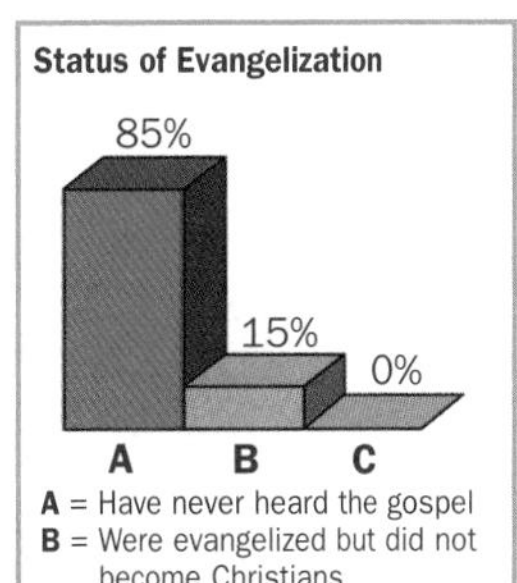

Ewenki, Tungus 鄂温克，吞古

Population in China:
1,600 (1993)
2,060 (2000)
2,660 (2010)
Location: Inner Mongolia
Religion: Shamanism
Christians: 100

Overview of the Tungus Ewenki

Countries: China, Mongolia, Russia

Pronunciation: "Tuun-giss-E-wenk-ee"

Other Names: Tungus, Ewenki: Chenbaehru, Tungus Evenk, Tunguz, Tongoose, Khamnigan, Khamnigan Ewenki, Khamnigan Evenki, Khamnigan Tungus, Horse Tungus, Tonggusi

Population Source: 1,600 (1993 J. Janhunen); Out of a total Ewenki population of 26,315 (1990 census); Also in Mongolia and Russia

Location: *NE Inner Mongolia:* Chenbaehru Banner

Status: Officially included under Ewenki

Language: Altaic, Tungus, Northern Tungus, Ewenki

Dialects: 0

Religion: Shamanism, Tibetan Buddhism, Christianity

Christians: 100

Scripture: None

***Jesus* film:** None

Gospel Recordings: None

Christian Broadcasting: None

ROPAL code: EVN03

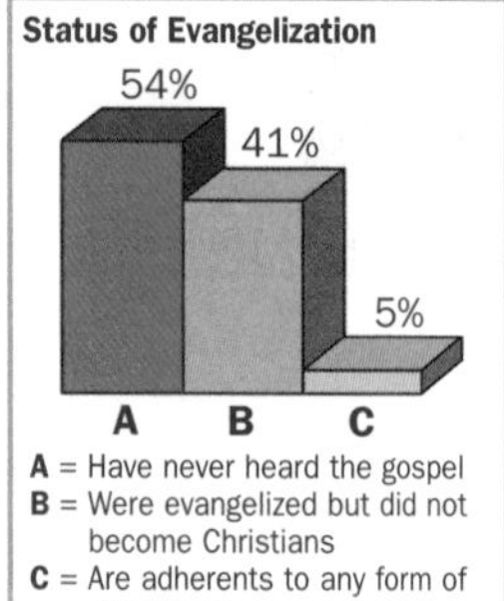

A = Have never heard the gospel
B = Were evangelized but did not become Christians
C = Are adherents to any form of Christianity

Location: Approximately 2,000 Tungus Ewenki live in the northeastern part of the Inner Mongolia Autonomous Region in China.[1] Considering their modest numbers, the Tungus Ewenki inhabit a large area in the Onin-Argun region of the Chenbaehru Banner. Their location is immediately to the south of the Yakut people. The climate in this part of China is severe. Summer is very short, usually lasting no more than eight to ten weeks. The icy winds from Siberia soon start to blow, forcing the Tungus Ewenki inside their yurt-like homes.

Identity: The Tungus Ewenki — also known as the *Khamnigan Ewenki* — are one of four people groups combined to form the official Ewenki nationality in China. Each group speaks a different language and has varying customs. It is believed that the Ewenki were originally tribes or clans in Russia who migrated into China at different times 300 to 400 years ago.

Language: Approximately 1,000 of the 1,600 Tungus Ewenki are able to speak their language.[2] One scholar describes the language as "endangered in China and possibly extinct in Mongolia and Russia."[3] For now, it is still spoken in the homes of two-thirds of Tungus Ewenki children, most of whom can also speak the local variety of Mongolian and Chinese.

History: The forefathers of the Ewenki lived in the forests north and east of Lake Baikal in Siberia and along the upper reaches of the Heilong River. They had a close relationship with the *Northern Shiweis* during the Northern Wei Dynasty (AD 386–534) and the *Ju* tribe at the time of the Tang Dynasty (618–907). "In the mid-1600s, aggression by Tsarist Russia led the Qing government in China to move the Ewenkis to the area around the tributaries of the Nenjiang River in the Hinggan Mountains. In 1732, 1,600 Ewenki soldiers and their dependents were moved to the Hulunbuir grasslands."[4]

Customs: The Tungus Ewenki live in *nimor*, or clans, which are groups of three to ten blood families. Some Tungus Ewenki live deep within the forests. Others have chosen to live on the grasslands where they have been influenced by Mongolian culture.

Religion: Many of the Tungus Ewenki who have experienced prolonged interaction with Mongolians have been converted to Tibetan Buddhism. The remainder practice shamanism, an ancient form of witchcraft and spiritism. The Tungus are also the only Ewenki group in China known to contain Christians.

Christianity: Various sources agree that there are approximately 100 Ewenki Christians in Chenbaehru.[5] The Tungus Ewenki believers are members of the Eastern Orthodox Church. However, "because of the profound influence of Shamanism, they worship the statue of Jesus and other idols together.... Priests of the Eastern Orthodox Church also participate in the religious activities of the Ewenkis."[6] Although the four Gospels were translated into Ewenki in Russia in 1995,[7] the Chinese Ewenki cannot read the script and have no Scriptures available to them.

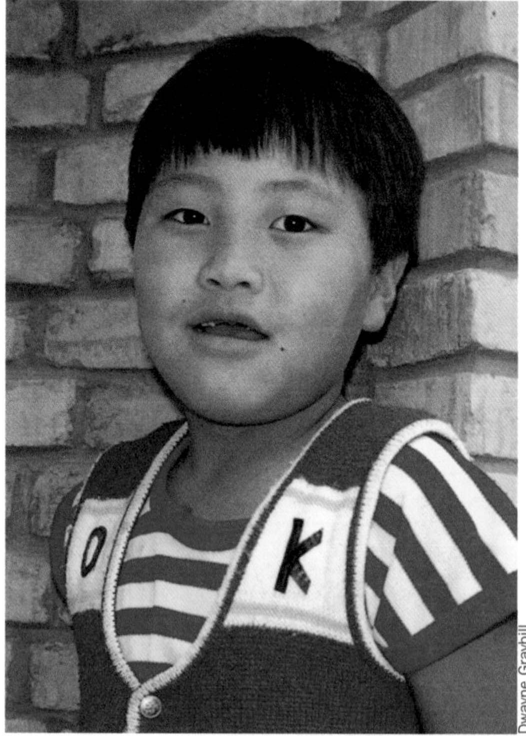
Dwayne Graybill

Fuma 府玛

Paul Hattaway

Location: The Fuma are located in just one village north of the town of Changcheng in the western part of Hainan Island. Changcheng is about 50 kilometers (31 mi.) north of the city of Dongfang (formerly known as Basuo). The Fuma live on the very top of a mountain in the area. As a result of isolation, they have an independent mind-set.

Identity: The Fuma have been officially counted as part of the Han Chinese nationality, even though they speak their own language and hold to their own identity. The Fuma are considered by some to be a subgroup of the Cun, but locals say the Fuma are a distinct people group. *Cun* means "village" and is a generic term applied to Chinese people living in western Hainan who speak languages related to Li.

Language: The Fuma language is part of the Li branch of the Kadai linguistic family. It is closest to the Ha Li language which is spoken by the majority of the Li on Hainan. Fuma is described as a "Li language isolate."[1] Many Fuma also use Ha Li as a common trade language in the area. Some Fuma men are bilingual in Chinese, although most women and children are only able to speak their own language.

History: Hainan Island has witnessed wave after wave of immigrants from the Chinese Mainland over the past 2,000 years. Most settled in the northern part of the island, forcing the original inhabitants of the island, the Li, southward and westward. Today most of northern Hainan is inhabited by Han Chinese and Lingao — members of a mixed race who speak a language resembling Zhuang. In the areas located near the boundaries between Chinese and Li culture, however, a great deal of fusion has taken place. Because of centuries of interaction between the Han and Li, people groups have been formed who are ethnically and historically Han Chinese but speak a Li language. The Fuma fall into this category. In other locations the fusion has occurred the other way around. Ethnic Li people can be found throughout Hainan who can speak only the Chinese language.

Customs: The Fuma have few customs that distinguish them as a people group. They do not wear any traditional dress and are some of the poorest people in all of China. For generations they have struggled to survive in their remote location.

Religion: Most Fuma do not practice an organized religion, although many have a deep reverence and respect for their ancestors.

Christianity: In the mid-1990s a Hong Kong-based mission discovered the Fuma people and commenced evangelistic work among them. They found that the Fuma were sensitive people, willing to embrace God's truth. Several families immediately became Christians. The Fuma fit this 1920s description of China's tribal people: "The children of the hills are much more responsive than the sons of the Han. They are not so proud, not so reserved, not so phlegmatic. Their women and girls are free as are women and girls of Western lands. They are not secluded nor do they bind their feet. They are allowed to meet and to talk with the men, and there is no mock modesty amongst them."[2]

Population in China:
800 (1994)
860 (2000)
970 (2010)
Location: Hainan Island
Religion: No Religion
Christians: 20

Overview of the Fuma

Countries: China

Pronunciation: "Foo-ma"

Other Names: Fu Ma

Population Source:
800 (1994 AMO);
Out of a total Han population of 1,042,482,187 (1990 census)

Location: *W Hainan Island:* North of Changcheng

Status: Officially included under Han Chinese

Language: Daic, Kadai, Li-Laqua

Dialects: 0

Religion: No Religion, Animism, Ancestor Worship, Christianity

Christians: 20

Scripture: None

***Jesus* film:** None

Gospel Recordings: None

Christian Broadcasting: None

ROPAL code: None

Status of Evangelization

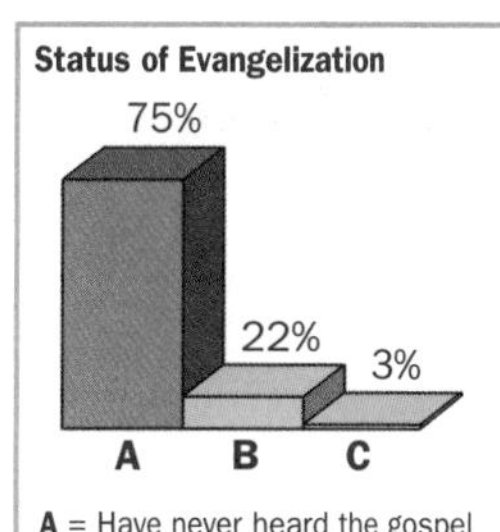

A = Have never heard the gospel
B = Were evangelized but did not become Christians
C = Are adherents to any form of Christianity

Gaiji 改积

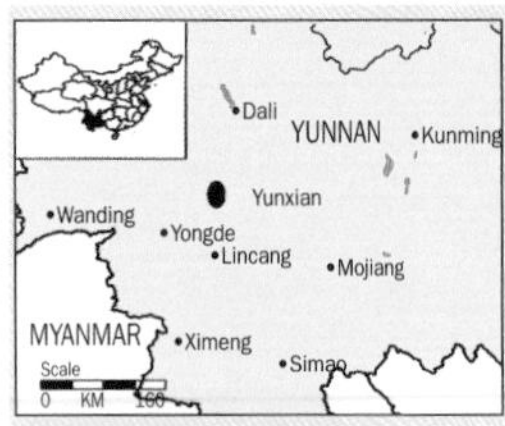

Population in China:
30,000 (1999)
30,750 (2000)
38,600 (2010)
Location: Yunnan
Religion: Polytheism
Christians: None Known

Overview of the Gaiji

Countries: China

Pronunciation: "Gai-jee"

Other Names: Gaijipo, Gaiqipo

Population Source:
30,000 (1999 J. Pelkey);
Out of a total Yi population of 6,572,173 (1990 census)

Location: *Yunnan:* Yunxian County in Lincang Prefecture

Status:
Officially included under Yi

Language: Sino-Tibetan, Tibeto-Burman, Burmese-Lolo, Lolo, Northern Lolo, Yi, Western Yi

Dialects: 0

Religion: Polytheism, Animism, Ancestor Worship

Christians: None known

Scripture: None

***Jesus* film:** None

Gospel Recordings: None

Christian Broadcasting: None

ROPAL code: None

Dwayne Graybill

Location: Approximately 30,000 members of the Gaiji ethnic group reportedly live in the central part of Yunxian County in Yunnan Province. They share the county with many ethnic groups, including the Mishaba Laluo, the Mili, and the Limi. Yunxian County lies within the jurisdiction of the Lincang Prefecture.

Identity: The Gaiji are one of the more assimilated of the 120 ethnic groups that have been combined by the Chinese authorities to form the official Yi nationality. The Gaiji are a little-known people. They have never before appeared on ethnolinguistic lists of China's peoples.

Language: The Gaiji once widely spoke their own language, which was part of the Western Yi group of Tibeto-Burman languages. Today, however, it is reportedly "very near extinction and only spoken by a handful of elderly individuals."[1] In only about 60 years, the entire Gaiji people group has gone from vigorous use of their mother tongue to exclusive use of Chinese.

History: Little is known about the history of the Gaiji people and how they relate to other Yi groups in southern China. Even oral traditions and legends are not handed down to Gaiji children anymore.

Customs: According to one researcher, the Gaiji "retain their folk-dances, certain festivals, and religious beliefs. These, however, along with their bloodline, are the only factors separating them from the pervasive Han culture."[2] Gaiji weddings are traditionally very relaxed. Once a couple decides they are ready for marriage, they choose a day to go farther into the mountains and chop firewood together. The bride "bears the firewood on her back as the two return to the groom's home to meet his parents. The bride then works for the groom's parents for two or three days. After her work is done, the two leave for the home of the bride. At the bride's home the groom engages in conversation with the bride's parents; by and by he leaves with the family water buckets balanced on his shoulders with a bamboo rod. If he is able to return with full buckets and empty them into the household crock without spilling any water he is considered a capable candidate for marriage and knows that he has been accepted by his new in-laws. As soon as the couple returns to the home of the groom's family, the two are considered married."[3]

Religion: Few Gaiji under the age of 30 have any religious beliefs. Most elderly Gaiji retain some vestiges of ancestor worship, Daoism, and animism. In the past, the Gaiji were a very superstitious people, but their beliefs have gradually eroded as have their culture and language.

Christianity: Often when tribal peoples assimilate to Chinese culture and language it affords them a better chance of hearing the gospel, but in the case of the Gaiji this has not occurred because the Chinese living in the Gaiji area, Yunxian County, are also unreached. There may be a very small number of professing Han believers in the county seat, which is the main administrative town, but they are not known to be outward-looking in their faith. The Gaiji remain unreached and untold.

Gaisu, Southern 改苏(南)

Population in China:
35,000 (1999)
35,900 (2000)
45,050 (2010)
Location: Yunnan
Religion: Polytheism
Christians: 100

Overview of the Southern Gaisu

Countries: China

Pronunciation: "Gai-soo"

Other Names: Gaisu Yi, Bailili, Gaisupuo, Bailisu, White Lisu, Luozu, Luoluo, Lolo

Population Source: 35,000 (1999 J. Pelkey); Out of a total Yi population of 6,572,173 (1990 census)

Location: *Yunnan:* Kaiyuan (33,600) and Gejiu (1,400) counties in Honghe Prefecture

Status: Officially included under Yi

Language: Sino-Tibetan, Tibeto-Burman, Burmese-Lolo, Lolo, Northern Lolo, Yi, Southern Yi

Dialects: 0

Religion: Polytheism, Animism, Ancestor Worship, No Religion, Christianity

Christians: 100

Scripture: None

***Jesus* film:** None

Gospel Recordings: None

Christian Broadcasting: None

ROPAL code: None

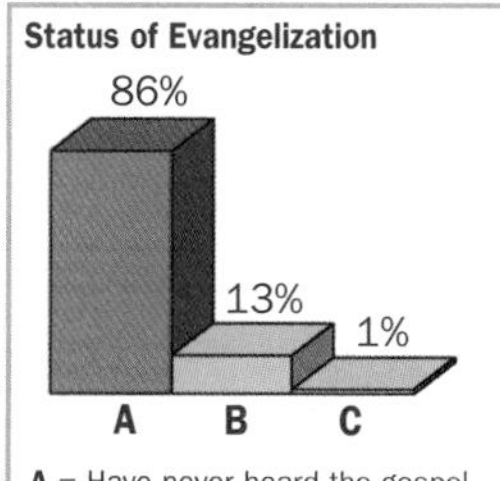

Location: Approximately 35,000 Southern Gaisu live in the eastern half of Kaiyuan County in Honghe Prefecture of Yunnan Province, predominantly in the valleys and on the mountain slopes near Kaiyuan City. About 1,400 Gaisu spill over into Gejiu County.[1]

Identity: The Southern Gaisu are one of approximately 100 Yi subgroups in Yunnan Province. They are not the same as the Western Gaisu who speak a completely different language. Neighboring minority groups have a host of names for the Southern Gaisu, including *Bailili, Bai Lisu* (White Lisu), and *Luozu.* Most Gaisu are highly assimilated to Han Chinese culture and language.

Language: The Southern Gaisu language is part of the Southern Yi linguistic branch. Some scholars have attempted to classify the Yi into six main language subgroups, but this has proved to be far from ideal. Within each language group many distinct languages can be found, all mutually unintelligible with other varieties within that same group.

History: As the various Yi groups splintered into smaller units, they moved southward from their original homeland near the juncture of today's Sichuan, Yunnan, and Guizhou provinces. The Southern Gaisu claim they entered their present location from Luxi and Muli counties to the north of where they now live in Honghe Prefecture.[2]

Customs: The Southern Gaisu observe the Tenth Month Celebration, held to celebrate the end of the harvest season. They sacrifice a pig to honor their ancestors and seek the blessing of the spirits for the upcoming year. They also celebrate the Torch Festival, common among many Yi groups in southern China. The Torch Festival is an occasion for relatives to get together and socialize. Events include bullfighting, wrestling, and singing.

Religion: The Southern Gaisu are polytheists. They worship many deities, ghosts and spirits. Days are set aside for the worship of the spirits. Ancestor worship is also widely practiced by the Southern Gaisu. Food is prepared and placed before pictures of dead family members. The Southern Gaisu observe many superstitions. They believe the manner in which guests eat and the way they leave their plate and chopsticks may bring a curse on the host family. Many of the younger generation are atheists. Most Southern Gaisu have been assimilated to Han Chinese culture.

Christianity: Only a relative handful of Southern Gaisu are Christians. Few missionaries targeted them in the past. Devoted and love-filled laborers are still required today in order for the Gaisu to turn to Christ. Despite their relatively large population size, the Southern Gaisu have no Scriptures or audio recordings available in their language. This has created a barrier to their understanding of the gospel, as evangelists have customarily used written or spoken Chinese to reach them. The Chinese language is considered strange and foreign to many Southern Gaisu.

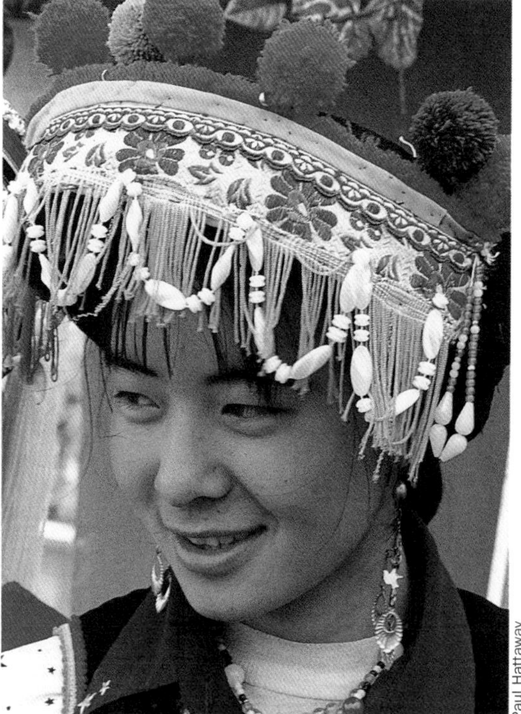
Paul Hattaway

Gaisu, Western 改苏(西)

Location: About 1,000 Western Gaisu live in a few ethnically mixed villages within the northeastern part of Yongde County in western Yunnan Province. The Western Gaisu do not live far away from the China-Myanmar border, although they are not reported to live outside of China. There may be one small group in Myanmar who are related to one of the Yi groups in China, but this remains to be confirmed.

Identity: The Western Gaisu, who are also known as *Luoren*, are not closely related to the Southern Gaisu people of Kaiyuan in Honghe Prefecture. These two groups, despite sharing the same autonym, live a long distance apart, have different histories and customs, and speak completely distinct languages. Both the Southern Gaisu and the Western Gaisu have been officially included under the Yi nationality by the Chinese authorities.

Language: The Western Gaisu language is on the verge of extinction. It is reportedly only spoken today by a few elderly people and is not being taught to children.[1] For now, Western Gaisu is classified as a Western Yi language within the Tibeto-Burman family.

History: The history of the Western Gaisu is very distinct from that of other Yi groups in China. They claim to have originated in Jiangxi Province on China's east coast long ago. They traveled (probably as soldiers) into Yunnan through Chuxiong, where many of them blended with today's Central Luoluopo people. Some of them migrated farther into present-day Yongde County. Judging by this oral history, the Western Gaisu may have originally been Han soldiers who married Yi women and gradually, over the course of many centuries, evolved into a distinct ethnic group of their own.

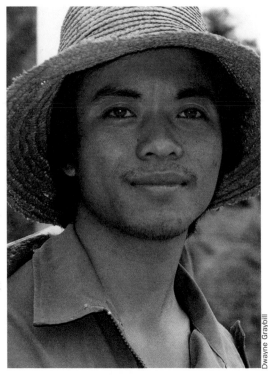

Dwayne Graybill

Customs: Western Gaisu culture strongly mirrors that of their Han Chinese neighbors. Although they once observed their own festivals and ceremonies, and the women proudly wore their own unique style of traditional dress, these have all been lost in the last several decades as the Western Gaisu have rapidly slid toward complete ethnic, cultural, and linguistic assimilation.

Religion: The Western Gaisu worship their ancestors. Rituals are held during which each family cleans off its ancestral altar and spends one or two days making sacrifices, praying, and burning incense to their forefathers. The Western Gaisu believe they are responsible for the spiritual well-being of all those family members who have gone before them.

Christianity: Yongde County has historically received almost no gospel witness. There are a number of Lahu and Wa Christians farther south of Yongde, but few people in the immediate area, and no known Western Gaisu, have ever placed their trust in Jesus Christ. Now that the Western Gaisu language has all but become extinct, this group could be best reached by the use of the Chinese Scriptures and other evangelistic tools.

Dali
YUNNAN
Kunming
Yunxian
Wanding
Yongde
Lincang
Mojiang
MYANMAR
Ximeng
Scale
0 KM 160

Population in China:
1,000 (1999)
1,020 (2000)
1,280 (2010)
Location: Yunnan
Religion: Ancestor Worship
Christians: None Known

Overview of the Western Gaisu

Countries: China

Pronunciation: "Gai-soo"

Other Names: Luoren

Population Source:
1,000 (1999 J. Pelkey);
Out of a total Yi population of 6,572,173 (1990 census)

Location: *W Yunnan:* Northeastern Yongde County

Status:
Officially included under Yi

Language: Sino-Tibetan, Tibeto-Burman, Burmese-Lolo, Lolo, Northern Lolo, Yi, Western Yi

Dialects: 0

Religion:
Ancestor Worship, Animism

Christians: None known

Scripture: None

***Jesus* film:** None

Gospel Recordings: None

Christian Broadcasting: None

ROPAL code: None

Status of Evangelization

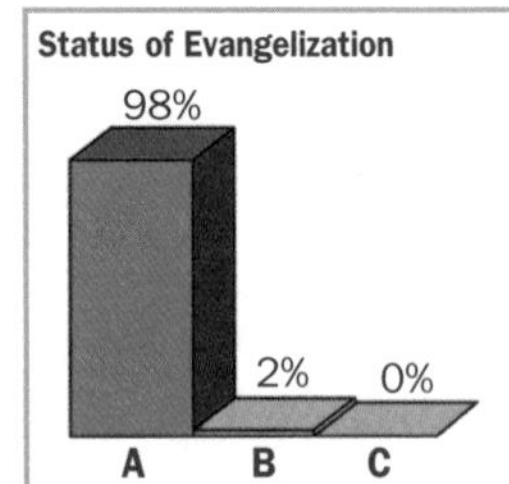

A = Have never heard the gospel
B = Were evangelized but did not become Christians
C = Are adherents to any form of Christianity

Ga Mong 革暮

Population in China:
41,861 (1990)
54,000 (2000)
69,600 (2010)
Location: Guizhou
Religion: Ancestor Worship
Christians: None Known

Overview of the Ga Mong

Countries: China

Pronunciation: "Gah-Mong"

Other Names: Dong Jia, Duck-Raising Miao, Duck-Raising Gedou, Yangya Miao, Yangya Gedou, Dongjiahua, Ge Mong

Population Source: 41,861 (1990 Chen Chao Qui)

Location: *Guizhou:* Kaili, Duyun, Majiang, Longli, and Xiuwen counties

Status: Officially included under She since 1997; Previously included under Miao

Language: Hmong-Mien, Hmongic, Western Hmongic

Dialects: 0

Religion: Ancestor Worship, Polytheism, Animism

Christians: None known

Scripture: None

***Jesus* film:** None

Gospel Recordings: None

Christian Broadcasting: None

ROPAL code: None

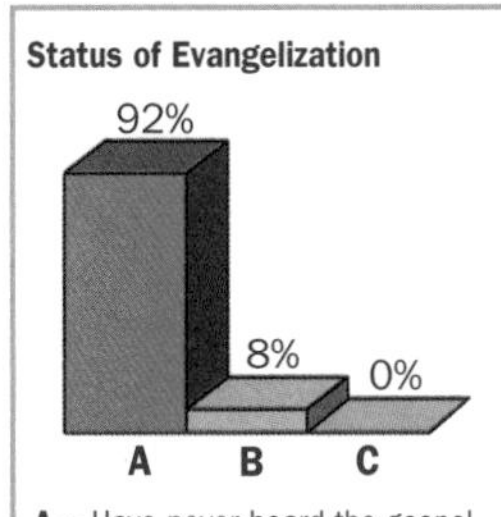

Location: A 1990 government study listed 41,861 Ga Mong people living in Guizhou Province.[1] Their villages are spread out in parts of five counties of central Guizhou. In Duyun County, 2,679 Ga Mong live in 14 villages.[2] The remainder live in parts of Kaili, Majiang, Longli, and Xiuwen counties.

Identity: Until 1997 the Ga Mong had been combined with numerous other groups to form the Miao nationality in China. The Chinese call this group *Dong Jia. Jia* means "family" or "household." The *Dong* Jia are not the same as the large *Dong* people group of eastern Guizhou Province. The Chinese character used for *Dong* Jia is different from that used for the official *Dong* minority. The Ga Mong speak their own language and have their own set of customs and festivals, different from all other peoples in the area. This group calls itself *Ga Mong* or *Ge Mong*. Local Chinese call them *Yangya Miao* which means "duck-raising Miao." In 1997 the government reclassified the Ga Mong into the She nationality, the majority of whom are located in Fujian and Guangdong provinces.[3] The Ga Mong are upset with this change and demand to be given their own status.

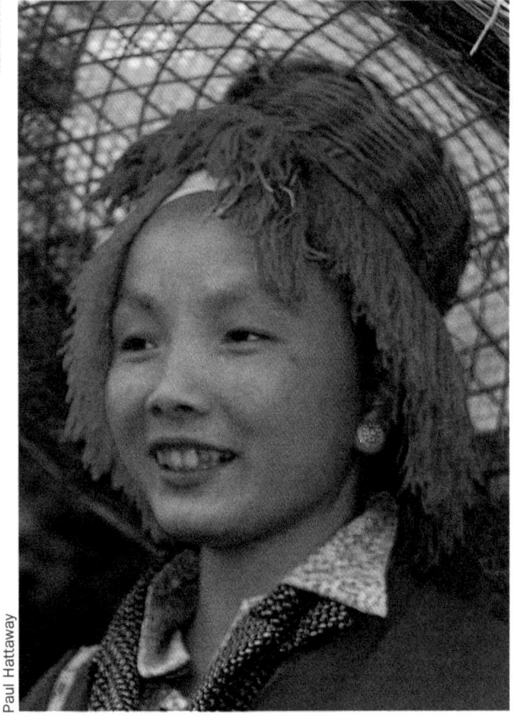
Paul Hattaway

Language: The Ga Mong language "shares many characteristics with Ge."[4] All Ga Mong can speak their language, and they are teaching it to their children. Ga Mong is a member of the Western branch of the Hmong linguistic family, more closely related to the Miao varieties in Yunnan and western Guizhou than those in eastern Guizhou Province where they live.

History: The Ga Mong claim a history dating back as far as the Song Dynasty (AD 960–1279).[5] During the Ming Dynasty (1368–1644), the Ga Mong were a powerful group. They were continually fighting and defending territory. At one stage 13 armed groups of Ga Mong attacked the city of Duyun.[6]

Customs: The Ga Mong celebrate their own set of festivals. Every year on the 18th of October they stage bullfights and cockfights and have a massive communal feast. Prominent family names among the Ga Mong include Wu, Luo, Gin, Ting, Wang, and Yang.[7]

Religion: The primary religious practice among the Ga Mong is ancestor worship. Every home has an ancestral altar. Any action that may offend their ancestors is considered a most serious matter. Bowls of food and drink are placed on the table several times each year, to honor the dead among the family and to ensure they will have enough food in the next life. In one location in Kaili, there was found to be belief in the "heaven-dog religion."[8] This probably refers to the worship of Pan Hu, also practiced by many Yao groups in China.

Christianity: There are no known Christians among the Ga Mong. They live in one of the most spiritually neglected areas of China. Few have ever heard the gospel, and most have never even met a Christian. The nearest believers to the Ga Mong are the handful of small churches among the Northern Hmu and Ge in the Panghai area, east of Kaili.

Gao 稿

Paul Hattaway

Location: According to Chinese linguist Zheng Guo-qiao, 2,000 speakers of a Gelao language called Gao live in Guizhou Province of southern China. They are primarily distributed in Dagouchang District of Pingba County, in Wanzizhai and Heizhai districts of Anshun County, in Wozi District of Puding County, in the Niudong District of Zhijin County, in Dongkou District of Shuicheng County, and in the Longga District of Luzhi City.[1] The Gao live in mountainous areas alongside Miao, Bouyei, Yi, and Han Chinese people.

Identity: Although only 2,000 speakers of this language are reported, the number of people who belong to the Gao ethnic group may be substantially larger than the number of people who can still speak their language. The Gao, who also call themselves *Qau*, *Klao*, and *Klan*, are one of five subgroups of the official Gelao nationality in China.

Language: Chinese sources, which tend to describe many mutually unintelligible languages as "dialects" admit that there are great differences among the varieties of Gelao. One states, "Often Gelao people within the same county cannot understand each other."[2] The Gao language is part of the Kadai branch of the Tai linguistic family. Even though it is a Tai language, Gao bears little resemblance to other Tai languages in southern China such as Zhuang and Bouyei. All Gao are bilingual in Chinese.

History: The different subgroups of the Gelao are usually recognized as the original inhabitants of Guizhou Province by most other minority peoples. Samuel Clarke wrote, "These people claim, and rightly, we believe, to be the real aborigines [original inhabitants] of that region.... Where the Miao and Keh-lao [Gelao] occupy the same district, the Miao allow that the Keh-lao were there before themselves."[3]

Customs: It is likely that most of the Gelao communities across this wide tract of land share few cultural or ethnic traits. Because of many centuries of separation from other groups of Gelao, the Gao have developed their own ethnic identity, customs, and language. Gao women no longer wear traditional dress, except for festivals and special occasions.

Religion: In the past century the Gao have adopted the religious beliefs of their neighbors, especially of the pervasive Han Chinese. The Gao worship their ancestors on several occasions throughout the year. Local spirits — such as the gods of the Water, Forest, Rice Field, and Village — are also appeased by the Gao. Many Gao youth are atheists with no religious persuasion.

Christianity: There are believed to be a small number of Gao Christians in southern China, mixed in with Han Chinese congregations. There is a smattering of believers in most of the areas where the Gao live. Luzhi City, for example, has 470,000 citizens, of which more than 2,800 are Christians who worship in 24 government-sanctioned churches and meeting points. In 1992, "three ministers, including one woman, and 12 elders were ordained at the Luzhi Church to serve Christians in the area. At the same service, 42 new evangelists were also commissioned."[4]

Population in China:
2,000 (1987)
2,750 (2000)
3,550 (2010)
Location: Guizhou
Religion: Ancestor Worship
Christians: 20

Overview of the Gao

Countries: China
Pronunciation: "Gow"
Other Names: Qau, Gao Gelao, Qau Gelao, Klan, Klao, Klau
Population Source: 2,000 (1987 Zheng Guo-qiao); Out of a total Gelao population of 437,997 (1990 census)
Location: *Guizhou:* Pingba, Anshun, Puding, Zhijin, and Shuicheng counties; Also in Luzhi City
Status: Officially included under Gelao
Language: Daic, Kadai, Lati-Kelao
Dialects: 0
Religion: Ancestor Worship, Animism, No Religion, Christianity
Christians: 20
Scripture: None
***Jesus* film:** None
Gospel Recordings: None
Christian Broadcasting: None
ROPAL code: KKF01

Status of Evangelization

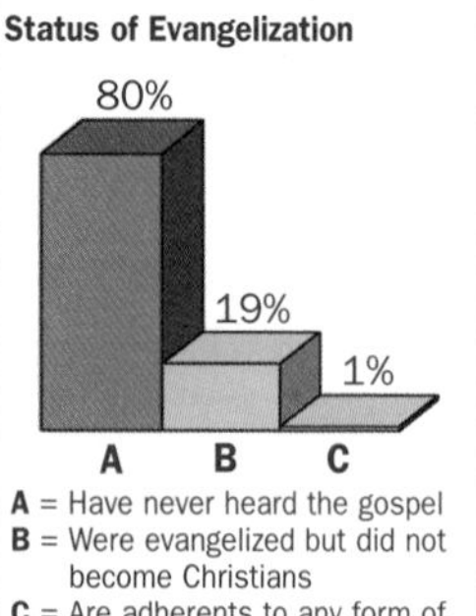

A = Have never heard the gospel
B = Were evangelized but did not become Christians
C = Are adherents to any form of Christianity

Ge 革

Location: A 1984 *National Geographic* article listed a population for the Ge of 70,000.[1] The majority are located in the mountains surrounding Chong'an Township in the central part of Guizhou Province. The largest single community of Ge is in Fengxiang (Maple Fragrance) Village, which contains more than 400 households. Small numbers of Ge are located in several villages southwest of the city of Kaili and in the southern part of Hunan Province.

Identity: The Ge have been counted as part of the large Miao minority group in China — a classification that infuriates them. They believe themselves to be a completely separate people. The Ge wear a unique costume and speak a language unintelligible with that of surrounding communities. They call themselves *Ge Mong*. The Hmu call them *Gedou*; the Xi call them *Gewu*; and the Mulao Jia call them *Gedu*. One unconfirmed report indicated the Ge were granted official status as a minority in 1993.[2]

Language: The Ge language — which has six tones — is a member of the Western Hmongic branch, similar to some Miao varieties spoken in Yunnan.[3] In 1933 missionary M. H. Hutton "reduced the Ge language to writing, using the same spelling principles as for Hmu."[4] A Ge Christian hymn book and catechism were published in 1937; however, one report says the books "were probably never sent to the Ge area."[5] Hutton's script is not used among the Ge today.

History: There are two theories surrounding the origins of the Ge people. Legend has it that many centuries ago a high-ranking Han soldier fell in love with a beautiful Miao girl and desired to marry her. This was an unheard-of disgrace at the time and cost the official his title and position. The couple were forced to move away and live apart from both the Han and Miao. Over time, their descendants formed into the Ge people. The second theory, which is perhaps more realistic, is that the Ge are the remnants of a Western Miao group who originally inhabited an area farther to the west.[6]

Customs: The Ge women's costume is designed to resemble a general's uniform, in remembrance of their progenitor. The Ge are highly skilled makers of batik.

Religion: The Ge practice polytheism and animism. Ancestral altars are also found in most of their homes.

Christianity: China Inland Mission's M. H. Hutton was the only known missionary among the Ge prior to 1949. In a 1935 article he reported, "the best and cheering news of all to us is, one of these new baptized believers is a Keh Deo [Ge] tribesman. It reminds me of the nine years of prayer and work to get an entrance into that tribe and the one soul — now there are six men and I hear their wives and families are interested in the Gospel too."[7] In 1936 Hutton described visiting a Ge Christian service,[8] and in 1937 he reported three Ge families had become Christians.[9] Tragically the Ge Christians ceased to believe once the missionaries were expelled from China. One Ge observer explained, "They believed in the missionaries and not in Jesus."[10] Today there are about 100 Ge Christians in the Chong'an area.

Paul Hattaway

Population in China:
70,000 (1984)
102,500 (2000)
132,200 (2010)
Location: Guizhou, Hunan
Religion: Polytheism
Christians: 100

Overview of the Ge

Countries: China

Pronunciation: "Guh"

Other Names: Ge Jia, Getou, Gedong, Keh Deo, Gedou, Gedou Miao, Huadou (Flowery Root), Keh-teo Miao, Chonganjiang Miao, Hmong: Chonganjiang, Gedang, River Gelao, Flower Gelao, Flower Dou Miao, Gedu, Gewu, Gedoudiu

Population Source: 70,000 (1984 Wong How-Man); Out of a total Miao population of 7,398,035 (1990 census)

Location: *Guizhou:* Fengtang, Chongxin, and Chongren districts of Huangping County; Longchang, Gouchang, Ganba, Longshan, and Bibo districts of Kaili County; *S Hunan*

Status: Officially included under Miao

Language: Hmong-Mien, Hmongic, Western Hmongic

Dialects: 0

Religion: Polytheism, Animism, Daoism, Ancestor Worship, Christianity

Christians: 100

Scripture: Portions 1937

***Jesus* film:** None

Gospel Recordings: Miao: Chang Jiao #04949

Christian Broadcasting: None

ROPAL code: HMJ00

Gelao 仡佬

Population in China:
426,917 (1990)
565,000 (2000)
728,900 (2010)
Location: Guizhou, Yunnan, Guangxi, Hunan, Sichuan, Jiangxi
Religion: Ancestor Worship
Christians: 500

Overview of the Gelao

Countries: China, Vietnam

Pronunciation: "Ger-laow"

Other Names: Gelo, Kelao, Ilao, Khi, Keleo, Chilao, Kehlao, Lao, Thu, Khi, Tulao

Population Source:
437,997 (1990 census);[1]
53,802 (1982 census);
26,852 (1964 census);
6,700 in Vietnam (1984 census)

Location: *SW Guizhou; E Yunnan; NW Guangxi; SW Hunan; Sichuan; Jiangxi*

Status:
An official minority of China

Language: Daic, Kadai, Lati-Kelao

Literacy: 43%

Dialects: Many

Religion: Ancestor Worship, Animism, Polytheism

Christians: 500

Scripture: None

***Jesus* film:** None

Gospel Recordings: None

Christian Broadcasting: None

ROPAL code: KKF00

Status of Evangelization

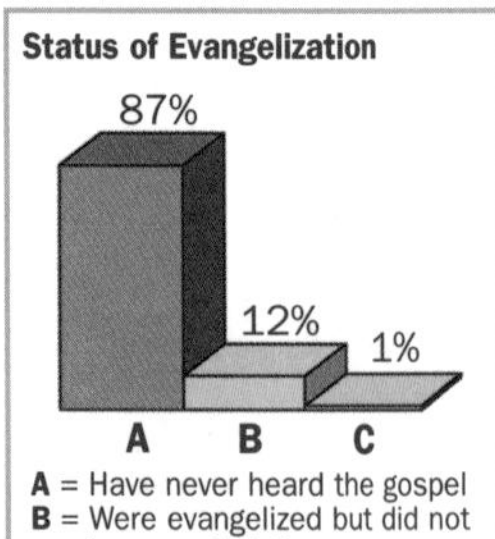

A = Have never heard the gospel
B = Were evangelized but did not become Christians
C = Are adherents to any form of Christianity

Location: The 1982 Chinese census recorded 53,800 Gelao people in China, but by 1990 that figure had dramatically jumped more than eight-fold to 438,000. There are several reasons for this peculiarity.[2] The Gelao are widely scattered across 40 counties in six provinces of southern China. The majority live in western Guizhou Province. Other communities are in Yunnan, Guangxi, Hunan, Sichuan, and Jiangxi provinces.[3] Approximately 7,000 Gelao are also located in northern Vietnam.

Identity: The Gelao, despite their considerable size, are one of the least known of China's official ethnic minorities. *Gelao* means "human beings" as well as "bamboo."[4] Today, most Gelao are culturally indistinguishable from the Chinese. Even back in 1911 one observer wrote, "The Gelao are now nearly extinct; many of them have married into Bouyei and [Chuanlan and Chuanqing] families."[5]

Language: Although the Chinese report that a mere 6,000 individuals (1.4%) are able to speak the Gelao language, "scholars suggest that this is an underestimate, and that perhaps 25,000 (mostly older) can still use some Gelao."[6] One source lists 60,000 speakers of Gelao.[7] This Tai language contains six tones and numerous dialects, some of which differ greatly and should be considered separate languages. The Gao dialect shares only 54% lexical similarity with the Duoluo dialect.[8] The Gao and Duoluo are among the Gelao groups profiled separately in *Operation China.*

History: The Gelao are thought to be descended from the ancient Liao race who established the Yelang Kingdom in Guizhou about 2,000 years ago. A folk tale tells how the king of Yelang was born from bamboo, so the whole group came to be called *Bamboo.*[9] The Gelao are considered the original inhabitants of each region where they live. "Where the Miao and Gelao occupy the same district, the Miao allow that the Gelao were there before themselves."[10]

Customs: The Gelao primarily grow maize, wheat, potatoes, sorghum, millet, tobacco, and tea. "In the past, the Gelao practiced initiation rites for their young men, including tooth-breaking and hair-cutting rituals. The Gelao were once head-hunters and cannibals."[11] Among the *Yaya* (Tooth) Gelao, the custom of breaking the front tooth of a bride was observed until recently.[12]

Religion: The Gelao are primarily ancestor worshipers. "They also worship the gods of giant trees, of mountains, of sky and earth, cows, etc. They have no idols, temples or monasteries, and no systematic religious creeds or organization. But they have a number of primitive superstitions and taboos, which affect every aspect of their lives."[13]

Christianity: Because it is difficult to convey the Gelao as a cohesive people group with a common identity, it is also difficult to gauge the status of Christianity among them. The Gelao were penetrated with the gospel by French Catholic missionaries in the late 1800s, but little fruit from that effort remains today. No Scripture translations have ever been made in the Gelao language.[14]

Paul Hattaway

42 43 44 45

42–45. The Chinese authorities have created an official nationality in Fujian Province called the *Gaoshan*. The Gaoshan — which means "high mountain" — are a collection of three tribes (*Ami*, *Bunun*, and *Paiwan*), each speaking its own language. These four portraits show some of the ethnic dress worn by the various Gaoshan groups in China. [all by Midge Conner]

46

47

48

46–47. *Ghao-Xong* women from western Hunan province. The languages spoken by the Ghao-Xong are perhaps the most divergent of all Miao varieties. [both by *Miao Messenger*]

48. Commonly called *Small Flowery Miao* by others in China, at least 75% of the *Gha-Mu* are Christians; Shuicheng, Guizhou. [Paul Hattaway]

49

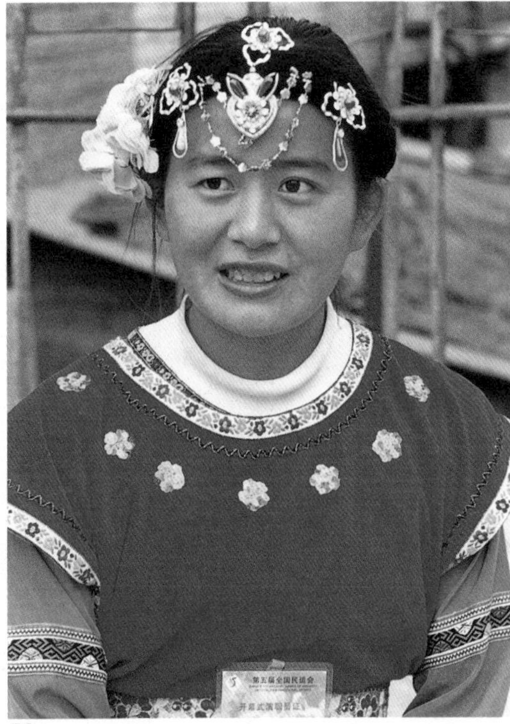
50

51

49. The 127,000 *Golog* belong to one of the most primitive people groups in China. Their name means "those with heads on backwards" in reference to their rebellious nature. [Midge Conner]
50. The *Gelao* are acknowledged by all other tribes in Guizhou as the original inhabitants of the area. [Paul Hattaway]
51. The *Han Chinese* are the largest ethnic group in the world. [Revival Christian Church]

52

53

54

52–54. The *Han Chinese* have a population numbering over one billion people, speaking more than 20 distinct languages and hundreds of dialects. They are the largest ethnic group in the world, and the Mandarin language is spoken by more people than any other. [52 Revival Christian Church; 53 & 54 Paul Hattaway]

Gepo, Eastern 葛泼(东)

Dwayne Graybill

Location: More than 64,000 Eastern Gepo live in the eastern part of Yunnan Province in southwest China.[1] They are distributed in parts of ten different counties. Xundian County, with 23,000 Eastern Gepo, contains the largest concentration of this group.[2]

Identity: Commonly called *Bai Yi* (White Yi) by the Chinese, this people group refers to itself as *Gepo*. Chinese sources further divide the Eastern Gepo — according to their style of headdress — into *Pingtou Yi* (Flathead Yi) and *Jiantou Yi* (Conehead Yi). Nevertheless, both of these groups refer to themselves as *Gepo* and speak the same language.[3] The Eastern Gepo are different from the Depo of northern Yunnan. The Depo also sometimes refer to themselves as *Gepo* or *Gepuo*.

Language: Eastern Gepo is a distinct language within the Eastern Yi linguistic group. It is different from Western Gepo.

History: Before 1949 there seems to have been four classes among the Yi peoples of eastern Yunnan: two lower classes, both called *Gepo*; and two upper classes, both of whom referred to themselves as *Neisu* or *Nasu*. The Gepo "were further separated into Greater and Lesser Gepo as were the Nasu. In their own language, *Gepo* means 'white people'. They were enslaved by the Greater and Lesser Nasu. Many subtle social rules and marriage restrictions that existed between the Greater and Lesser Gepo are all but discarded today."[4]

Customs: The Eastern Gepo are culturally distinct from all other surrounding communities. They are proud of their ethnic identity and prefer to be left alone by outsiders. Many of China's Yi people were decimated by disease in the past. Missionary Samuel Clarke explained the customs of one Yi group that were designed to limit the death toll caused by disease. "When it is known that disease has visited a neighbor's house, a pole seven feet long is erected in a conspicuous place in a thicket some distance from the house.... On the pole an old plow-share is fixed, and it is supposed that when the spirit who controls the disease sees the plow-share he will retire to a distance from these homesteads."[5]

Religion: The Eastern Gepo are polytheists: they worship a multitude of gods and deities. Each year they offer sacrifices of chickens and livestock to the god of the Harvest to ensure a successful crop. The Gepo also carefully observe customs relating to health and hygiene.

Christianity: There are a small number of believers among the Eastern Gepo. The Christians in Huize County, including the Eastern Gepo, have experienced horrific persecution from local authorities in recent years. Land has been confiscated, believers beaten and tortured. One report stated, "The instruments of torture they use include clubs, firewood, ropes, handcuffs and electrically-charged stun-batons. They cuffed and kicked until these instruments broke." Evangelist Cui Chaoshu was "pounded to death with a thick stick, his nose and mouth bleeding profusely."[6]

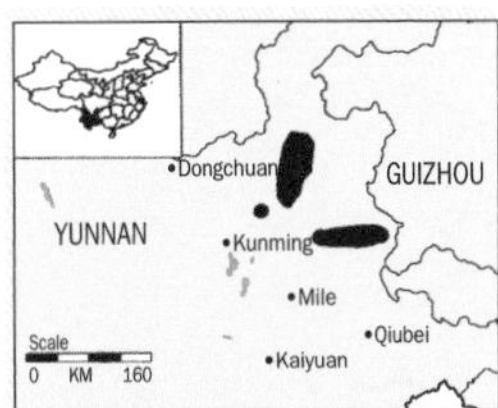

Population in China:
62,400 (1999)
64,000 (2000)
80,300 (2010)
Location: Yunnan
Religion: Polytheism
Christians: 300

Overview of the Eastern Gepo

Countries: China

Pronunciation: "Geh-po"

Other Names: Gepuo, Gepu, Bai Yi, Nasu, Jiantou Yi, Pingtou Yi, Guo, Guopo, Gupu, Guzu, White Yi, Gepo

Population Source:
62,400 (1999 J. Pelkey);
Out of a total Yi population of 6,572,173 (1990 census)

Location: *E Yunnan:* Xundian (23,000), Luxi (12,000), Shizong (9,000), Luoping (5,000), Malong (4,000), Songming (2,200), Huize (2,000), Mile (2,000), Shilin (1,700), and Dongchuan (1,500) counties

Status:
Officially included under Yi

Language: Sino-Tibetan, Tibeto-Burman, Burmese-Lolo, Lolo, Northern Lolo, Yi, Eastern Yi

Dialects: 0

Religion:
Polytheism, Animism, Christianity

Christians: 300

Scripture: None

***Jesus* film:** None

Gospel Recordings: None

Christian Broadcasting: None

ROPAL code: None

Status of Evangelization

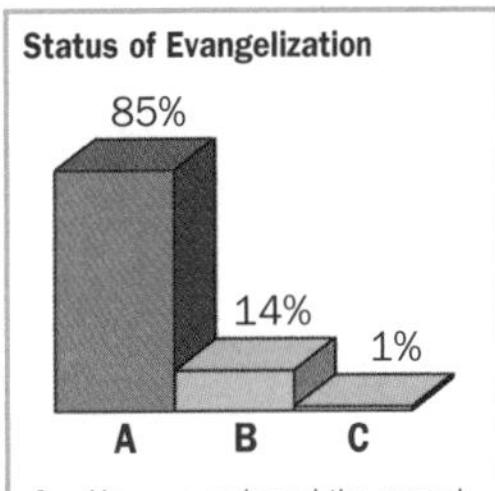

A = Have never heard the gospel
B = Were evangelized but did not become Christians
C = Are adherents to any form of Christianity

Gepo, Western 葛泼(西)

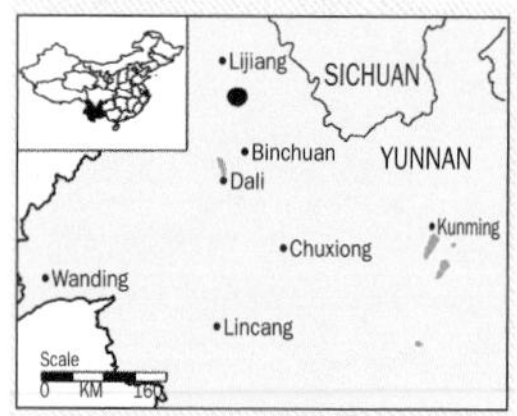

Population in China:
6,500 (1999)
6,650 (2000)
8,350 (2010)
Location: Yunnan
Religion: Polytheism
Christians: None Known

Overview of the Western Gepo

Countries: China

Pronunciation: "Geh-po"

Other Names: Gepo, Baiyiren, Tujia, Luo

Population Source: 6,500 (1999 J. Pelkey); Out of a total Yi population of 6,572,173 (1990 census)

Location: *NW Yunnan:* Heqing County in northern Dali Prefecture

Status: Officially included under Yi

Language: Sino-Tibetan, Tibeto-Burman, Burmese-Lolo, Lolo, Northern Lolo, Yi, Western Yi

Dialects: 0

Religion: Polytheism, Animism, Ancestor Worship

Christians: None known

Scripture: None

***Jesus* film:** None

Gospel Recordings: None

Christian Broadcasting: None

ROPAL code: None

A = Have never heard the gospel
B = Were evangelized but did not become Christians
C = Are adherents to any form of Christianity

Jamin Pelkey

Location: An estimated 6,500 Western Gepo live in many of the villages within the Liuhe District of Heqing County in the northern part of the Dali Bai Autonomous Prefecture.[1] The Western Gepo are located in the northwestern part of Yunnan Province, not far from the main road between the tourist towns of Dali and Lijiang.

Identity: The Western Gepo are one of approximately 120 distinct ethnic groups that have been combined to form the official Yi nationality in China. Although they use the same autonym, *Gepo*, as the Eastern Gepo people farther east in Yunnan Province, the two groups speak widely different languages. Local Chinese people call this group *Baiyiren*, "white-clad people." *Gepo*, in their own language, may mean "white people."

Language: The language spoken by this Gepo group is reportedly part of the Western Yi branch of Tibeto-Burman languages. The only other Yi language spoken in Heqing County is Shengzha Nosu, which is a Northern Yi language. The extra title *Western* has been added to avoid confusion between this group and the Eastern Gepo, who speak an Eastern Yi variety.

History: The history of most of the people groups in northern and western Yunnan has been one of conflict, warfare, and bloodshed. Great battles were waged over land, with smaller groups like the Western Gepo invariably losing out to the stronger and more powerful alliances. As a result, many of the Yi groups in Yunnan have become more pacified than their wild counterparts in Sichuan and the adjoining parts of northern Yunnan.

Customs: The Chinese themselves were often caught up in fighting between the different Yi groups. One traveler, who journeyed through the mountainous area near where the Western Gepo live, wrote, "As one travels further north the Lolos [Yi] become more numerous and more aggressive, until the Chinese are veritably besieged in their valley. We heard of nothing but the exploits of these brigands, who fall upon the valley, kill travelers, and pillage the inhabitants. All the villages are fortified, and posts occupied by peasants armed with pikes, tridents, sabers, and sometimes with indifferent flintlocks, are permanently established along the roadside."[2]

Religion: Today most Western Gepo lead quiet lives as hardworking agriculturists. They enjoy relatively good relations with their neighbors, even with the Nosu who used to force them to do menial labor.

Christianity: The Western Gepo are among the most unreached people groups in northern Yunnan Province. They live in an unevangelized corridor, while many Lisu Christians live farther to the west and the Eastern Lipo and Naluo churches are situated to the east. These believers could potentially be mobilized to take the gospel to the Western Gepo and other unreached peoples in Heqing.

Gese 葛色

Population in China:
12,000 (1999)
12,300 (2000)
15,400 (2010)
Location: Yunnan
Religion: Polytheism
Christians: None Known

Overview of the Gese

Countries: China

Pronunciation: "Geh-seh"

Other Names: Gesu, Bai Yi, White Yi

Population Source: 12,000 (1999 J. Pelkey); Out of a total Yi population of 6,572,173 (1990 census)

Location: *Yunnan:* Lufeng County in Chuxiong Prefecture

Status: Officially included under Yi

Language: Sino-Tibetan, Tibeto-Burman, Burmese-Lolo, Lolo, Northern Lolo, Yi, Eastern Yi

Dialects: 0

Religion: Polytheism, Animism

Christians: None known

Scripture: None

***Jesus* film:** None

Gospel Recordings: Yi: Gese Gaofeng #04977

Christian Broadcasting: None

ROPAL code: None

Location: More than 12,000 people belonging to the Gese tribe live in an isolated part of southwest China. They mainly live in the villages of eastern Tuo'an District and in the villages in the southern part of the Gaofeng District in Lufeng County.

Identity: The Gese (pronounced "Geh-Seh") are one of the dozens of tribes which the Chinese authorities combined to form the official Yi nationality. Jamin Pelkey notes, "Though no Chinese sources firmly attest to this people group's existence, this people refer to themselves as Gese in their own language and think of themselves as different from Naisu."[1] The Gese are not the same as the Gesu or the Gepo — two other Yi tribes in Yunnan Province.

Language: The Gese language is a part of the Eastern Yi group — a collection of loosely affiliated varieties that includes tribes located in Guizhou Province and the Guangxi Zhuang Autonomous Region. The Gese have great difficulty communicating with the members of other Yi groups in Chuxiong Prefecture, many of whom speak languages from the Central Yi and Western Yi language families. Gese may be most closely related to Naisu.

History: A rich oral history recounts the Gese's victory over a terrible plague that struck the people in their region. Their stories may well refer to the Black Plague that decimated Yunnan Province between 1812 and 1903. It is estimated to have reduced the population from eight million to three million.

Customs: Gese women are easily identifiable by their habit of wearing long earrings and black turbans. On the 13th day of the third lunar month the Gese celebrate the Flower Festival. They worship the Medicine King, who they believe saved their race from the plague in the past. According to their folklore, people everywhere were dying. The first sign of impending death was to lose feeling in their arms and legs. The Gese say numerous bodies were being carried out of their villages daily. The people who carried the corpses out also died because of contact with the bodies. The Medicine King set out to find a cure for the plague. He tasted 99 herbs from 99 mountains and drank 99 gulps of water from 99 springs, but none of them provided a cure. Finally he climbed the "Third Month Mountain" in the Gese area and tasted the herbs and drank the water. Immediately, feeling returned to his limbs. He ran down the mountain and told the people, who were also healed when they ate and drank from the mountain.

Religion: The respect the Gese have for the memory of the Medicine King borders on worship. They also appease locality spirits, such as the spirit of the soil, the spirit of the water, and the spirit of the forests.

Christianity: There are no known Christians among the Gese people. Few mission agencies have ever heard of this hidden people who go about their lives in the remote mountains of Lufeng County. The area where the Gese live has historically been devoid of gospel witness, although in recent years it has been rumored that some A-Hmao evangelists have reached out to people there. In 1998 gospel recordings were produced in the Gese language for the first time.

Dwayne Graybill

Gesu 葛苏

Location: The authorities of the Chuxiong Prefecture in Yunnan Province listed a 1957 figure of 6,753 Gesu people.[1] Their population is estimated to have grown to approximately 12,000 today. The Gesu inhabit villages in parts of Dayao and Wuding counties. Both are under the jurisdiction of Chuxiong Prefecture.

Identity: The Gesu have been officially included as part of the Yi nationality in China. In the 1950s the Gesu were one of 260 tribes and people groups in Yunnan Province who applied to be recognized as a separate minority.[2] The Gesu are also called *Gaoshanzu* (High Mountain People) or *Tuzu* (Soil People) by their Han Chinese neighbors. It is possible that these two names represent two different subgroups of Gesu.

Language: The Gesu speak their own distinct language, mutually unintelligible with the speech of all other surrounding communities. Gesu is believed to be a part of the Central Yi linguistic branch, which contains many different varieties. Most Gesu men and children are able to speak Chinese, but most Gesu women are only able to speak their own language.

History: The various branches of the Yi are believed to have descended from the Di and Qiang peoples who migrated south to the Dianchi area in Yunnan and the Qiongdou area of Sichuan in the second century BC.[3] After the Jin Dynasty (AD 265–420), the *Cuan* clan became rulers of the Dianchi region, northeastern Yunnan, and the Honghe River area. These places were later known as the *Cuan area.* Its people became the forerunners of today's various Yi tribes.

Paul Hattaway

Customs: Every year on the eighth day of the second lunar month, the Gesu living near Tanhua Township in Dayao County celebrate the Flower-Decorating Festival.[4] The people get together, worship the mali flower, and have flower decoration competitions. They also sing and dance and generally have a good time with relatives and friends. Because it is usually still quite cold, bonfires are built to give warmth and to roast meat and corn. A similar celebration, called the Festival of the Mali Flower, is held on the same day in Wuding County, although the Wuding version of the festival focuses more on paying respect to the Mali Flower god and on giving the youth a chance to meet prospective partners from other villages.

Religion: In addition to worshiping the Flower god, the Gesu worship the sun, stars, and moon. Perhaps their most-feared deity is the god of the Mountains. They believe large, powerful demons live inside the highest mountains in the area and must be placated to avoid disaster in their communities.

Christianity: No mission agencies have ever included the Gesu on their lists of people groups in China. They are a largely unevangelized and unreached people group. Because their villages are remote and because the Gesu have an independent mind-set, they rarely travel into the towns or have any contact with other tribes. There are no gospel recordings available in the Gesu language.

SICHUAN
GUIZHOU
Panzhihua
Dayao
Wuding
Kunming
Chuxiong
YUNNAN
Yuxi
Kaiyuan
MYANMAR
VIETNAM
LAOS
Scale
0 KM 160

Population in China:
6,753 (1957)
12,430 (2000)
15,600 (2010)
Location: Yunnan
Religion: Polytheism
Christians: None Known

Overview of the Gesu

Countries: China

Pronunciation: "Geh-soo"

Other Names: Gesu Yi, Gaoshanzu, Tu

Population Source: 6,753 (1993 *Chuxiong Yizu Zizhizhou Zhi* — 1957 figure); Out of a total Yi population of 6,572,173 (1990 census)

Location: *N Yunnan:* Dayao and Wuding counties in Chuxiong Prefecture

Status: Officially included under Yi

Language: Sino-Tibetan, Tibeto-Burman, Burmese-Lolo, Lolo, Northern Lolo, Yi, Central Yi

Dialects: 0

Religion: Polytheism, Animism

Christians: None known

Scripture: None

***Jesus* film:** None

Gospel Recordings: None

Christian Broadcasting: None

ROPAL code: None

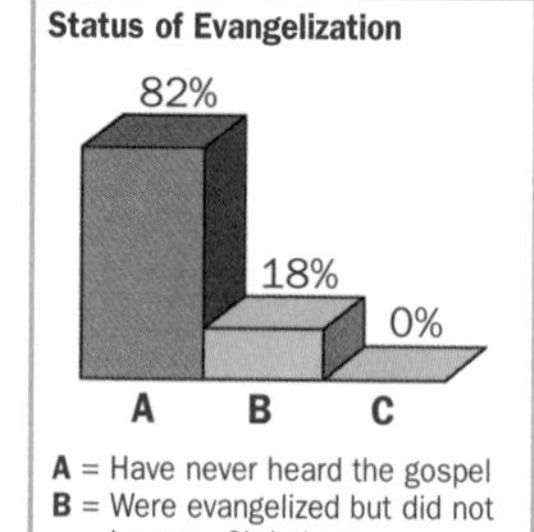

A = Have never heard the gospel
B = Were evangelized but did not become Christians
C = Are adherents to any form of Christianity

Gha-Mu 嘎目

March 27

Population in China:
84,000 (1990)
108,350 (2000)
139,800 (2010)
Location: Guizhou
Religion: Christianity
Christians: 80,000

Overview of the Gha-Mu

Countries: China

Pronunciation: "Ghah-Moo"

Other Names: Small Flowery Miao, Xiao Hua Miao, Hsiao Hwa Miao, Miao: Small Flowery

Population Source:
84,000 (1995 Wang Fushi – 1990 figure);
60,000 (1985 Wang Fushi – 1982 figure);
Out of a total Miao population of 7,398,035 (1990 census)

Location: *W Guizhou:* Shuicheng, Nayong, Zhenning, Guanling and Hezhang counties

Status:
Officially included under Miao

Language: Hmong-Mien, Hmongic, Western Hmongic, Farwestern Hmong, Gha-mu

Dialects: 0

Religion: Christianity, Animism

Christians: 80,000

Scripture: None

***Jesus* film:** None

Gospel Recordings:
Miao: Small Flowery #04793

Christian Broadcasting: None

ROPAL code: None

Status of Evangelization

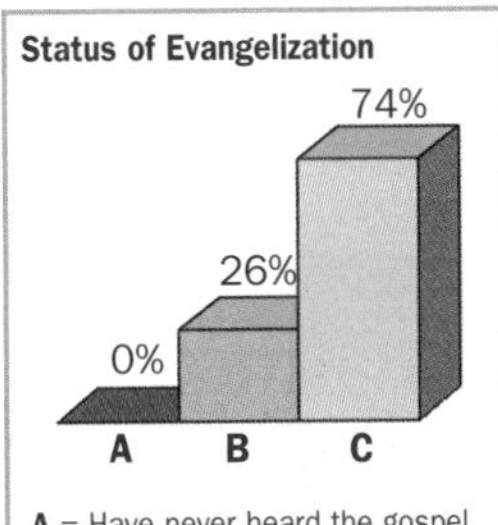

A = Have never heard the gospel
B = Were evangelized but did not become Christians
C = Are adherents to any form of Christianity

Robert Sussland

Location: A 1995 study listed a 1990 population of 84,000 Gha-Mu in China.[1] They are located in Shuicheng, Nayong, Zhenning, Guanling, and Hezhang counties in the western part of Guizhou Province. The main center for the Gha-Mu is Nayong County. The area is cold in the winter, with frequent snowfall and frosts.

Identity: The Gha-Mu are widely known as the *Small Flowery Miao* in Chinese and mission literature. The Small Flowery Miao (Gha-Mu) are not the same people group, nor do they speak the same language, as the Big Flowery Miao (A-Hmao) of Guizhou and Yunnan. The names were given to these groups by the Chinese last century. They do not use the word *flowery* in their autonym, which is *Gha-Mu*, and which may be a cognate for the name *Hmong* used by many Western Miao tribes and peoples. The Gha-Mu have small, complex geometrical shapes embroidered on their clothing around the shoulders and waist.

Language: The Chinese classify the Gha-Mu as a second dialect of the Farwestern Miao group of languages. It is unintelligible with all other Miao varieties in China.

History: There are many flood legends among the Gha-Mu. They believe that when the Thunder god threatened to destroy the earth with a deluge, a man called A-Zie "hollowed out a large gourd for himself, collected a hundred kinds and a thousand sorts of seeds, and put them in a smaller gourd."[2] They believe that from A-Zie came all the peoples of the earth, including the many different branches of today's Miao nationality.

Customs: The Gha-Mu observe the Tiaohuapo Festival each March. "For the marriageable young of both sexes... it is one of their main chances to find a possible spouse. The young men decorate themselves with hats with long pheasant feathers."[3] In the past, bandits raided remote Gha-Mu villages in Nayong County. The Gha-Mu had no weapons with which to defend themselves so they used sticks. Today, to remember their bravery, Gha-Mu maidens perform a Painted Stick Dance during their festivals.[4]

Religion: The Gha-Mu call the spirit world *bi-lao*, a general term "including gods, specters, ghosts, elves, demons, and any other supernatural media. While some bi-lao are kind and act as bodyguards, most are evil and compared to thieves. These malevolent bi-lao are indifferent to human feelings and are continually seeking ways to cause harm to people."[5] Today as many as 80% of the Gha-Mu are reported to have converted to Christianity.[6]

Christianity: The first Protestant missionary to the Gha-Mu was J. R. Adam who commenced work near Anshun in 1899. Just as a breakthrough in the work was starting to occur, a military official and a village headman went through the region, threatening people with death if they joined the "foreign religion." The floodwaters were ready to break, however, and by 1907 the number of believers numbered 1,200. Despite severe persecution in the 1960s and 1970s,[7] the Gha-Mu believers today are a vibrant and effective Christian community of approximately 80,000.[8]

Ghao-Xong, Eastern 高雄(东)

Miao Messenger

Location: Approximately 100,000 speakers of the Eastern Ghao-Xong language are found in China. Western Ghao-Xong is spoken by far greater numbers, claiming close to one million speakers. The Eastern Ghao-Xong inhabit the far northeastern extent of Miao territory in China, near the Xiang (Hunanese) Chinese. They are located in parts of Luxi, Jishou, Guzhang, and Longshan counties in northwest Hunan Province. Most of their villages are on the top of mountains where they are able to maintain their customs in privacy. A Miao proverb states, "Fish swim in water, birds fly in the air, Miao live on the mountains."[1]

Identity: *Ghao-Xong* is the autonym of this group, who have officially been included under the Miao nationality in China. The Ghao-Xong were labeled *Red Miao* by the early missionaries.[2] They have also been called *Huayuan Miao* and *Northern Miao*.

Language: Eastern and Western Ghao-Xong have been combined by linguists to form their own language branch within the Hmongic (Miao) language family.

History: During the Song Dynasty (AD 960–1279) the Ghao-Xong staged 112 wars to save their tribal lands and preserve their way of life.[3] Ralph Covell notes, "The Miao [Ghao-Xong] people in Hunan seem to have been badly oppressed by the Chinese over a long period of time, but remained more independent in spirit than those in Guizhou and Yunnan. This contributed to their reluctance to adopt a new faith."[4]

Customs: For centuries the Ghao-Xong have been "growing mulberries and raising silkworms, spinning and weaving, making paper-cuts and, of course, embroidering."[5] Many Ghao-Xong festivals feature music played on the *suona* horn and on drums.

Religion: The Ghao-Xong have the custom of worshiping Pan Hu, the dragon-dog they claim as their ancestor. Today the Ghao-Xong of Maxiang County in Hunan have a carved stone tablet inscribed "for sacrificing to Great King Pan Hu" and topped by two dragon heads.[6] Certain kinds of trees are also worshiped as deities. In many villages the front door of a family's home is considered a god. The doors in these villages are worshiped annually in a ceremony where a pig is sacrificed and the blood is sprinkled on the doorposts.[7]

Christianity: In the 1920s Father Theopane Maguire of the Catholic Passionist Fathers — based in Brighton, Massachusetts, USA — commenced work among the Ghao-Xong in three counties of Hunan Province. Their work, which was based in Yangshui County, suffered a setback when rebels killed three of the missionaries in 1929. By 1934 they had won 2,500 converts, but no record was made of how many were Ghao-Xong compared to Han Chinese.[8] In 1946 Maguire was forced to concede, "Here are no startling mass conversions, no pilgrimages of the mighty to the feet of the crucified Christ, no peals of thunder to announce the herald of the Great King."[9]

Population in China:
80,000 (1990)
103,200 (2000)
133,100 (2010)
Location: Hunan
Religion: Animism
Christians: 1,000

Overview of the Eastern Ghao-Xong

Countries: China
Pronunciation: "Gaow-Shong"
Other Names: Hmong: Eastern Xiangxi, Red Miao, Meo Do, Hsianghsi Meo, Eastern Xiangxi Miao
Population Source: 80,000 (1995 Wang Fushi – 1990 figure); 70,000 (1985 Wang Fushi – 1982 figure); Out of a total Miao population of 7,398,035 (1990 census)
Location: *NW Hunan:* Luxi, Jishou, Guzhang, and Longshan counties
Status: Officially included under Miao
Language: Hmong-Mien, Hmongic, Northern Hmongic
Dialects: 0
Religion: Animism, Polytheism, Ancestor Worship, Christianity
Christians: 1,000
Scripture: None
***Jesus* film:** None
Gospel Recordings: None
Christian Broadcasting: None
ROPAL code: MUQ00

Status of Evangelization

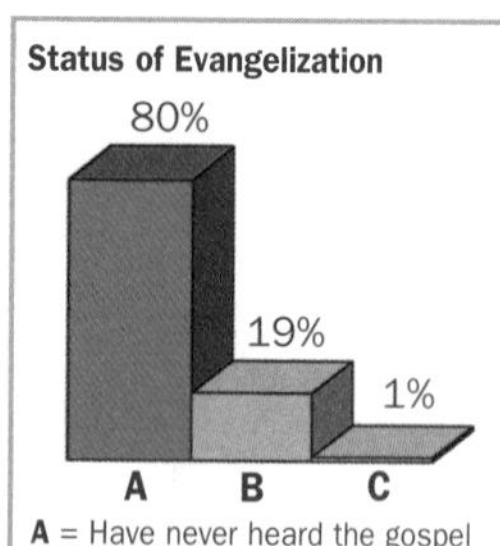

A = Have never heard the gospel
B = Were evangelized but did not become Christians
C = Are adherents to any form of Christianity

Ghao-Xong, Western 高雄(西)

Location: A study based on the 1990 Chinese census listed 820,000 speakers of the Western Ghao-Xong language. Most live in six counties of northwestern Hunan Province.[1] Others are scattered far and wide, from Hubei Province in the north, to Guizhou and Sichuan in the west,[2] and to the Guangxi Zhuang Autonomous Region in the south.

Identity: The Western Ghao-Xong have been called several different names in the past, including *Huayuan Miao, Red Miao*, and *West Hunan Miao*. They are part of the Miao nationality, but they speak a language different from all other Miao groups in China. Their dress and customs are also different. Most Miao in Hunan call themselves *Ghao-Xong*, in contrast to other Miao groups such as the Hmong, Hmu, Gha-Mu, and A-Hmao.

Language: Western Ghao-Xong — which is a member of the Northern Hmongic linguistic family — is divided into two dialects, Chiwei and Layiping. A Roman orthography, introduced by the government, is being taught among the Ghao-Xong.[3]

History: The virtually inaccessible mountains where the provinces of Hunan, Sichuan, and Guizhou meet were the site of countless wars involving the Ghao-Xong. The Qing Emperor Kangxi (1662–1722) issued an edict that "the rules governing them should be different from those enforced elsewhere in China."[4] It took the Chinese 18 years (1855–1872) to crush one rebellion. According to a memorial, "When reaching a Miao village, the government troops slaughtered rebels and those who had surrendered."[5]

Customs: The Ghao-Xong celebrate the Siyueba Festival on the eighth day of the fourth lunar month. "Many centuries ago, there were Miao [Ghao-Xong] people living by the River Longtang at the foot of the Fenghuang Mountains in Western Hunan. No longer able to bear the oppression they suffered under the rule of the Qing Dynasty (1644–1911), they rose in revolt under the leadership of two brothers, Yayi and Yanu.... Yayi was killed in battle. Yanu led the remnants of his forces into safety in Guizhou.... To commemorate their heroes the Miao [Ghao-Xong] people gather to hold a ceremony at which they sing, dance and perform traditional rites."[6]

Miao Messenger

Religion: The Ghao-Xong (along with the She and Yao minorities) worship Pan Hu, the dragon-dog they claim as the forefather of their race. The Pan Hu myth was recorded as early as the fifth century AD in the *Chronicles of the Later Han Dynasty (Hou Han Shui)*.

Christianity: The work of the Catholic Passionist missionaries was hindered by their inability to speak either Ghao-Xong or Chinese fluently. One missiologist remarks, "Little wonder then, that in Hunan there does not appear to be any large-scale turning of the Miao [Ghao-Xong] people to Christ."[7] The western Hunan region was largely neglected by Protestant missionaries prior to 1949. Today, the majority of Ghao-Xong have never heard the gospel. Despite their size, they have no Scriptures, *Jesus* film, or gospel recordings available in their language.

Population in China:
820,000 (1990)
1,057,800 (2000)
1,364,500 (2010)
Location: Hunan, Guizhou, Guangxi, Hubei, Sichuan
Religion: Animism
Christians: 4,000

Overview of the Western Ghao-Xong

Countries: China

Pronunciation: "Gaow-Shong"

Other Names: Hmong: Western Xiangxi, Huayuan Miao, Hsianghsi Miao, West Hunan Miao, Northern Miao, Red Miao, Meo Do, Western West Hunan Miao, Ghao-Xong

Population Source:
820,000 (1995 Wang Fushi – 1990 figure);
700,000 (1985 Wang Fushi – 1982 figure);
Out of a total Miao population of 7,398,035 (1990 census)

Location: *NW Hunan; Guizhou; Guangxi; SW Hubei; SE Sichuan*[8]

Status:
Officially included under Miao

Language: Hmong-Mien, Hmongic, Northern Hmongic

Dialects (2): Chiwei; Layiping

Religion: Animism, Polytheism, Ancestor Worship, Christianity

Christians: 4,000

Scripture: None

***Jesus* film:** None

Gospel Recordings: None

Christian Broadcasting: None

ROPAL code: MMR00

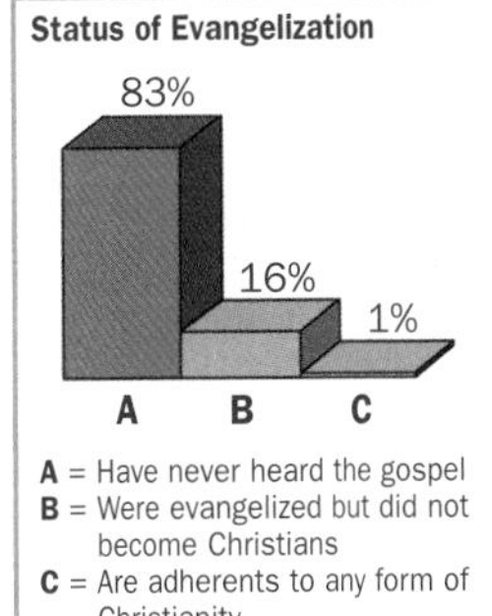

Giay 载

Population in China:
223,000 (1981)
273,700 (2000)
327,300 (2010)
Location: Yunnan, Guangxi
Religion: Ancestor Worship
Christians: 500

Overview of the Giay

Countries: China, Vietnam, Laos, France, USA

Pronunciation: "Zay"

Other Names: Nhang, Niang, Nyang, Giang, Giai, Yay, Dioi, Nhaang, Yai, Dang, Pau Thin, Pu Na, Pu Nam, Cui Chu, Sa, Nong

Population Source: 223,000 (1981 *Pacific Language Atlas*); Out of a total Zhuang population of 15,489,630 (1990 census); 38,000 in Vietnam (1991); 5,000 in Laos (1995 L. Chazee); 100 in France (1992 B. Grimes); 5 in USA (1992 B. Grimes)

Location: *SE Yunnan; SW Guangxi*

Status: Officially included under Zhuang

Language: Daic, Tai, Northern Tai

Dialects: 0

Religion: Ancestor Worship, Animism, Polytheism, Christianity

Christians: 500

Scripture: None

***Jesus* film:** None

Gospel Recordings: None

Christian Broadcasting: None

ROPAL code: NHA00

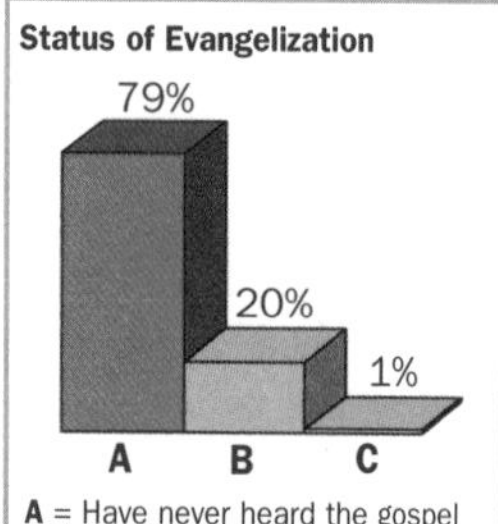

Location: Approximately a quarter of a million Giay (pronounced "Zay") are located in eastern Yunnan and western Guangxi, along the southern Chinese border with Vietnam.[1] The Giay in Vietnam inhabit three provinces of the Red River valley that borders China. Five thousand also live in northern Laos. A few Giay refugee communities have also sprung up in France and southern California.

Identity: In Vietnam, the 38,000 Giay are given official status by the government. In China, the Giay have been combined with many other related groups to make up the huge Zhuang nationality. The Giay, however, speak their own language and possess a distinct historical identity. The Giay are also often referred to as the *Nhang*, which is a name given to them by the Vietnamese.

Language: According to one linguist, the Giay language is the same as Bouyei in China.[2] The Giay in China use a different script from their counterparts in Vietnam.[3]

History: The Giay who now live in Vietnam migrated there from China approximately 200 years ago, "perhaps during the Black and Yellow Flag Wars."[4]

Customs: The traditional dress worn by Giay women included a knee-length skirt, but now the women have begun wearing normal Han Chinese clothing. Giay families are dominated by the males. Wives must obey their husbands, unmarried women must obey their fathers, and widows must obey their sons. Giay women prefer to give birth in a squatting position, in a room where an altar has been erected to ensure that the spirits oversee a favorable birth. The placenta is later buried beneath the woman's bed. When the baby is a month old the parents call for a ceremony to inform the ancestors of the birth and to name the baby.[5] The Giay consult horoscopes to determine the fate of the child.

Religion: The Giay practice ancestor worship. Many are also animists, while some of the current generation of youth are nonreligious, having received an atheistic education under the Communist system. Each Giay village has a "forbidden forest" called a *doong xia* where the biggest tree is considered sacred. Twice a year, worship of the spirit of the village is celebrated at the foot of the tree. Whenever these rituals take place, outsiders and visitors are strictly forbidden to enter the village. Bamboo is cut down and placed at the entrance of the village to bar access to all strangers. Parts of sacrificed animals are then hung from the tree; ears of pigs or buffaloes, chickens' feet, and tufts of animal hair are commonly used.

Christianity: Few Giay have heard that Jesus Christ died for them. They are trapped in superstition and a fear of evil spirits. There are no strong Christian communities near the Giay. The southern tip of China and northern Vietnam are two large unreached regions. A small number of Catholics do live among the Giay in China, and a few believers can be found among the Giay in Vietnam. There are no Scriptures in the Giay language, even though they are one of a relatively small number of groups in China which possesses its own orthography.

Paul Hattaway

Golog 果洛

Midge Conner

Location: The February 1982 *National Geographic* listed a figure of between 80,000 and 90,000 Gologs, living in six counties of the remote Golog Tibetan Prefecture in Qinghai Province.[1] A total of 100,343 people lived in the prefecture in 1953, but by 1964 the population had diminished to only 56,071.[2] Thousands of Golog migrated from the area. Thousands more were either killed in battle or starved to death by the Chinese army. The Golog region is virtually still outside Chinese control. Its extreme isolation was described by a visitor in the late 1920s: "A miserable land it is, of poverty and incredible filth; a land cut off from the modern world, a region which, for uncounted centuries, has had its own forms of government, of religion and social customs; yet a region which knows no railway, no motor car, no radio, or aught of all that science and invention have given the world since Marco Polo's day."[3]

Identity: The Golog are probably the most backward and primitive of all the various branches of the Tibetan race. According to one source, *Golog* means "those with heads on backwards."[4] This name comes from their reputation for being an extremely stubborn and rebellious people.

Language: The Golog language is "largely unintelligible to most Tibetans."[5] There are numerous dialects and local varieties spoken by dozens of different Golog tribes and clans.[6]

History: The Golog are the descendants of Tibetan warriors sent to guard the northern borders. "In the seventh century AD, the Tibetan king dispatched his fiercest warriors, ancestors of the present-day Gologs and neighboring Khampas, to guard the country's mountainous northern frontier against Chinese invasion. When the Tibetan kingdom eventually collapsed, the Gologs stayed in their mountain retreat, defiant of outside authority."[7] A Chinese historian states, "Tibetan tribes from the Upper, Middle and Lower Golog all can trace their roots to Baima.... Baima County is situated on the southeast tip of Qinghai and borders on Sichuan."[8]

Customs: The nomadic Golog wear greasy sheepskins, yak-hide boots, and felt bowler hats, a lasting legacy of the British invasion of Tibet in the early 1900s. Many wild animals inhabit the Golog region, including "blue sheep, gazelles, bears, wolves, and deer."[9]

Religion: All Gologs are Tibetan Buddhists. Many Golog women have 108 braids of hair, considered an auspicious number by Tibetan Buddhists.

Christianity: Few Golog have ever heard of Jesus Christ or his offer of salvation. They have been separated from all outside influence, including Christianity, for centuries. "[Gologs] live here, and other tribes of Tibetans, with whom they quarrel and fight. Yet of these local wars, not even an echo ever reaches the outside world."[10] In the early part of the twentieth century, some missionaries passed through the Golog area and distributed gospel literature, receiving an interested response from one Golog Head Lama.[11] In recent years at least one mission agency has expressed interest in reaching the Gologs.

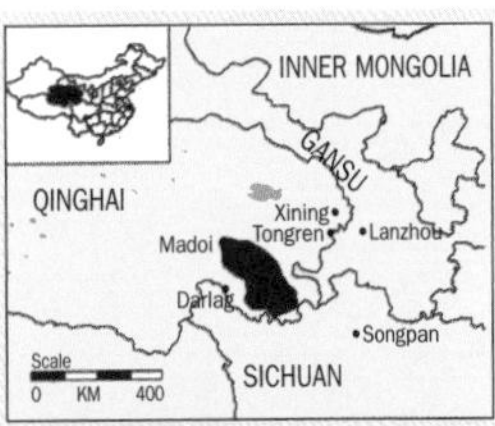

Population in China:
90,000 (1982)
127,600 (2000)
164,600 (2010)
Location: Qinghai
Religion: Tibetan Buddhism
Christians: 10

Overview of the Golog

Countries: China
Pronunciation: "Gor-lok"
Other Names: Ngolok, Mgolog, Golok, Lhardi, Ngura, Amchok, Rimong, Kangsar, Kanggan, Tsokhar, Ngawa, Gatse, Butsang, Shahrang, Jazza
Population Source: 80,000 to 90,000 (1982 G. Rowell);
Out of a total Tibetan population of 4,593,330 (1990 census)
Location: *SE Qinghai:* Golog Tibetan Prefecture: Jizhi, Madoi, Maqen, Gade, Baima, and Darlag counties
Status: Officially included under Tibetan
Language: Sino-Tibetan, Tibeto-Burman, Bodic, Bodish, Tibetan, Northern Tibetan
Dialects: Many
Religion: Tibetan Buddhism, Polytheism
Christians: 10
Scripture: None
***Jesus* film:** None
Gospel Recordings: None
Christian Broadcasting: None
ROPAL code: GOC00

Status of Evangelization

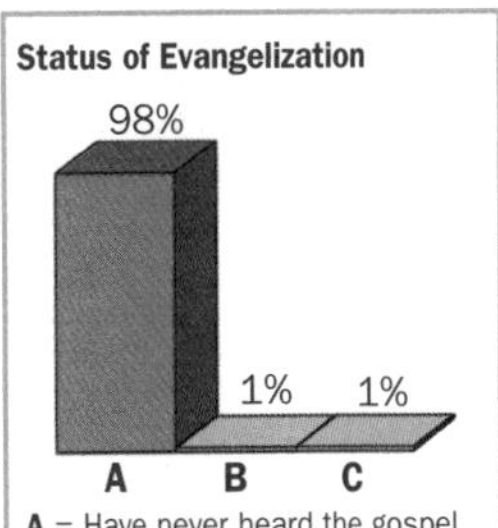

A = Have never heard the gospel
B = Were evangelized but did not become Christians
C = Are adherents to any form of Christianity

Gouzou 构邹

Population in China:
4,000 (1999)
4,100 (2000)
5,150 (2010)
Location: Guizhou
Religion: Polytheism
Christians: 200

Overview of the Gouzou

Countries: China

Pronunciation: "Gow-zo"

Other Names:

Population Source:
4,000 (1999 AMO);
Out of a total Yi population of 6,572,173 (1990 census)

Location:
NW Guizhou: Weining County

Status:
Officially included under Yi

Language: Sino-Tibetan, Tibeto-Burman, Burmese-Lolo, Lolo, Northern Lolo, Yi, Eastern Yi

Dialects: 0

Religion: Polytheism, Animism, Ancestor Worship, Christianity

Christians: 200

Scripture: None

***Jesus* film:** None

Gospel Recordings: None

Christian Broadcasting: None

ROPAL code: None

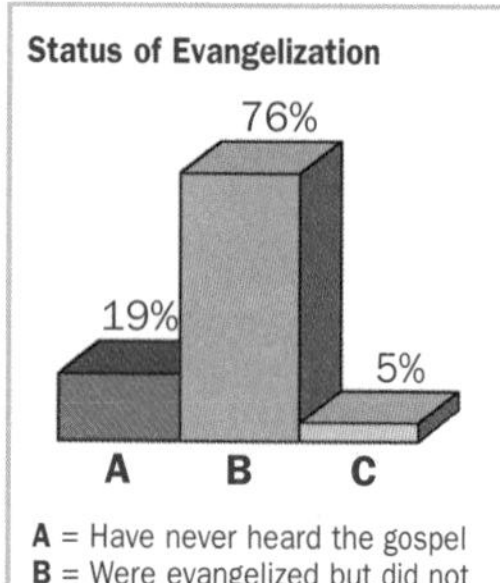

Midge Conner

Location: Approximately 4,000 people belonging to the Gouzou people group live in Weining County in the northwest part of Guizhou Province.[1] The landscape in Weining "is an unimaginable labyrinth of inter-tangled valleys which run in every direction. The soil is formed out of a very soft limestone, which is quickly eroded by running water. A frequent result is that the stream sinks too low, cannot find an escape from the valley it has entered, and finally erodes a subterranean passage and disappears into a cavern."[2]

Identity: The Gouzou are part of the official Yi nationality in China. They are not the same as the *Guopu* people group who inhabit the same area. The various Yi groups in Guizhou Province were considered endangered in the early 1900s. One writer noted, "The unsanitary conditions in which they live — the water they drink is often drawn from stagnant pools fouled by sheep and cattle — and their riotous indulgence in whisky, opium, and other vices, sufficiently account for this.... They are burdened with the thought that their doom as a race is sealed."[3]

Language: Gouzou is part of the Eastern Yi branch of Tibeto-Burman. Some of the Eastern Yi varieties reportedly have only a 50% lexical similarity with each other.[4] It is likely that each of these "dialects" should be viewed as a distinct language.[5]

History: Guizhou may have been the original homeland of all Yi. The Nosu in Sichuan say their two ancestors, Gu Mmu and Cho Li, came from a town called Zzupu in Guizhou. "Even now when a Nosu person dies the relatives chant so that the dead person's spirit will be able to walk back the same way to the original family home in Guizhou."[6] The history of the Yi in Guizhou is one of war and conflict, including numerous clashes with the Hui Muslims.[7]

Customs: Before the introduction of modern medicine, whole Gouzou communities were wiped out by a fever called *Nomatsi*. "No person will stay by the sick-bed to nurse the unfortunate patient. Food and water are placed by the bedside, the sick one is covered with a quilt and left at the mercy of the disease. Since the patient will perspire as the fever progresses, heavy stones are placed upon the quilt that it may not be thrown off.... Many have died from suffocation."[8]

Religion: The polytheistic Gouzou have a flood legend: "A certain man had three sons. He received warning that a flood was about to come upon the earth, and the family discussed how they should save themselves when this calamity came upon them. One suggested an iron cupboard, another a stone one, but the suggestion that they should make a cupboard of wood and store it with food was acted upon."[9] Ancestor worship is also prevalent among the Gouzou. Since the early 1900s, Christianity has made an appearance among them also.

Christianity: Today there is a small church among the Gouzou. One official publication states that as many as half of the overall total of 85,000 Yi people in Weining County follow Christ. The majority of the believers are female and over 30 years old.[10]

Groma 稿麻

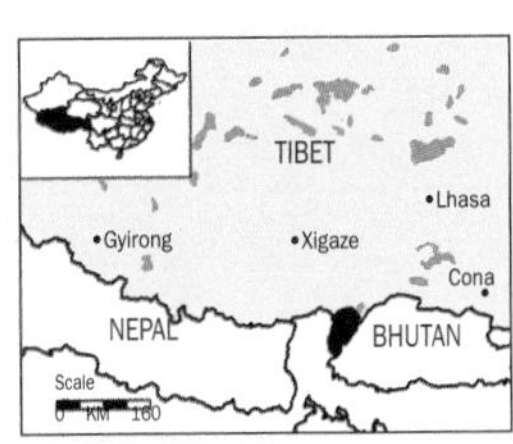

Population in China:
12,840 (1993)
14,920 (2000)
18,390 (2010)
Location: Tibet
Religion: Tibetan Buddhism
Christians: None Known

Overview of the Groma

Countries: India, China

Pronunciation: "Gro-mah"

Other Names: Tromowa, Chomo Tibetan, Chomo, Gromo, Tomo, Zhuomu Tibetan, Chuo-mu Tibetan, Chumbi Tibetan

Population Source: 12,840 (1996 B. Grimes – 1993 figure); 14,000 in India (1995 Joshua Project)

Location: *S Tibet:* Chomo (Yadong) County in Xigaze Prefecture

Status: Probably officially included under Tibetan

Language: Sino-Tibetan, Tibeto-Burman, Bodic, Bodish, Tibetan, Southern Tibetan

Dialects (4): Upper Groma, Lower Groma, Spiti, Tomo

Religion: Tibetan Buddhism, Animism

Christians: None known

Scripture: None

***Jesus* film:** None

Gospel Recordings: None

Christian Broadcasting: None

ROPAL code: GRO00

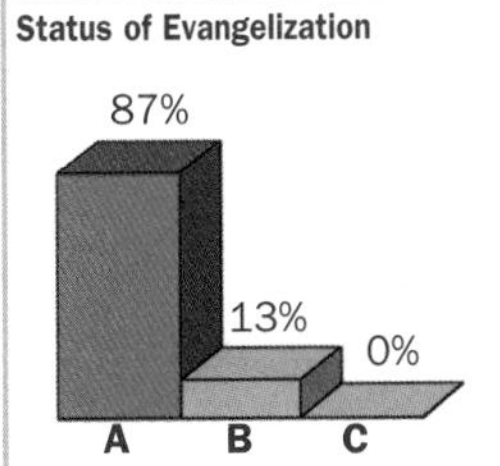

Location: The *Ethnologue* cites a 1993 source stating that there are 12,840 speakers of Groma living in southern Tibet,[1] in the Chambi Valley between Bhutan and the former independent nation of Sikkim — now a state of India. The Chambi Valley is in the middle of the mighty Himalayan range. *Himalaya* means "abode of snow." A French Catholic missionary to Tibet, Monsieur L'Abbé Desgondins, graphically described the region: "Take a piece of paper in your hand. Crumple it up and then open your hand and let it fall out! Nothing is flat — all you have is high points and low depressions — the steep, inaccessible, rugged mountains and the deep valleys."[2] An additional 14,000 Groma are reported to be living on the Indian side of the border.[3]

Identity: Little is known about the Groma. Most anthropological and linguistic sources do not mention them. It is probable that the Groma have been counted as part of the Tibetan nationality in China and may be culturally and ethnically indistinguishable from other Tibetans in the region. The Chinese authorities have included many distinct language groups under the Tibetan nationality, based primarily on their adherence to Tibetan Buddhism.

Language: The Groma language is a member of the Southern Tibetan language branch. It has two dialects, Upper and Lower Groma, with two others, Spiti and Tomo, listed as "possible dialects or related languages."[4]

History: The cornerstone of emerging Tibetan civilization was the Yarlung Valley area, about 80 kilometers (49 mi.) southeast of Lhasa. There, according to tradition, the union of a monkey and a she-devil created the Tibetan race. Around AD 600, the warrior-king Namri Gampo began the work of unifying the clans of Tibet. It was his son, Songtsen Gampo, who consolidated the empire and established Tibet as a military power to be reckoned with. Sikkim was nominally independent — although always under Indian influence — until it was annexed in 1975 and integrated into India. The Bhots from Tibet began entering Sikkim in the thirteenth century. The Nepalese did not come until the nineteenth century, but now they make up 75% of Sikkim's population.[5]

Customs: The Groma lead typical Tibetan lives. They herd yaks, sheep, and goats. Groma women do most of the work. The men often spend their days drinking and gambling with their friends.

Religion: Tibetan Tantric Buddhism dominates the Groma. Pilgrimages to holy sites (such as Mt. Kailas) are often undertaken by devoted pilgrims.

Christianity: There are no known Christians today among the Groma. The little mission work that *has* targeted the area invariably resulted in severe persecution. "Converts did not easily forget the Christian convert who was sewn into a fresh yak skin by merciless shaman priests and placed in the broiling sun until the contraction of the skin squeezed the life out of his frame."[6] In 1997 neighboring Sikkim counted 250 churches, but almost all the believers were ethnic Nepalis. The north district where the Groma live is completely unreached.[7]

Paul Hattaway

Guaigun 乖滚

Location: The Guaigun ethnic group, who number a mere 400 people, live in the southern part of Zhenyuan County in Yunnan Province. In Tianba District, the Guaigun inhabit parts of the following villages: Tianba, Santai, Lianhe, and Minjiang.[1]

Identity: The Guaigun are one of the smallest components of the official Yi nationality in China. Despite their small size, the Guaigun possess ethnic-group identity and believe they are different from all the other peoples surrounding them.

Language: The classification of the Guaigun language is uncertain. The part of Zhenyuan County inhabited by the Guaigun has been classified as both Southern Yi and Southeastern Yi by Chinese sources. For now, Guaigun remains an unclassified member of the Yi branch of Tibeto-Burman.

History: The Guaigun were probably part of a larger group who migrated to Zhenyuan County long ago. Because they do not keep written records, the Guaigun cannot remember their origins. The Guaigun do not inhabit their own villages but share their communities with the Han Chinese and members of other nationalities.

Customs: Many of the customs of the Guaigun mirror those of other Yi groups in southern China. Some cultural rituals have religious overtones, such as where people decide to build a new house. Samuel Clarke, commenting on the Yi earlier this century, wrote, "Houses are built at the foot of a hill, and sacrifices are regularly offered on the hill-side in the fourth month of each year. The exorcist determines which is the most propitious day, and the laird with his people proceed to the appointed place. A limestone rock, with an old tree trunk near, is chosen as an altar, and a sheep and pig are brought forward by the laird."[2]

Dwayne Graybill

Religion: Clarke further explains how the exorcist, "having adjusted his clothes, sits cross-legged before the altar, and begins intoning his incantations in a low muttering voice. The victims are then slain, the blood poured beneath the altar, and a handful of rice and a lump of salt are placed beneath the stone. Some person then gathers a handful of green grass, and the exorcist having finished intoning, the altar is covered and all return to the house. The exorcist twists the grass into a rope which he hangs over the doorway of the house. Then out of a piece of willow a small arrow is made, a bow of corresponding size is cut out of a peach tree, and these are placed on the door-posts. Out of a piece of soft white wood the figure of a man is carved, and this, with two sticks placed cross-wise is fastened to the rope hanging over the doorway.... The exorcist proceeds with his incantations, muttering, 'From now on henceforth and for ever will the evil spirits keep away from this house'."[3]

Christianity: There are no known Christians in the Guaigun villages in Zhenyuan County. Most Guaigun have never heard the gospel, even though there are Hani believers in both Zhenyuan and Mojiang County to the southeast. No Scripture translation or gospel recording has ever been produced in a language easily understood by the Guaigun.

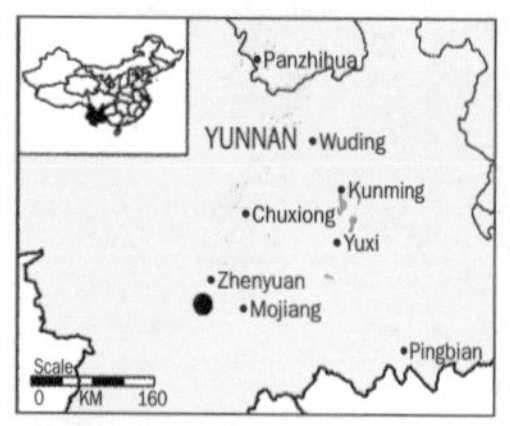

Population in China:
400 (1999)
410 (2000)
510 (2010)
Location: Yunnan
Religion: Polytheism
Christians: None Known

Overview of the Guaigun

Countries: China

Pronunciation: "Gwai-gun"

Other Names:

Population Source:
400 (1999 J. Pelkey);
Out of a total Yi population of 6,572,173 (1990 census)

Location:
Yunnan: Zhenyuan County

Status:
Officially included under Yi

Language: Sino-Tibetan, Tibeto-Burman, Burmese-Lolo, Lolo, Northern Lolo, Yi, Unclassified

Dialects: 0

Religion: Polytheism, Animism, Ancestor Worship

Christians: None known

Scripture: None

***Jesus* film:** None

Gospel Recordings: None

Christian Broadcasting: None

ROPAL code: None

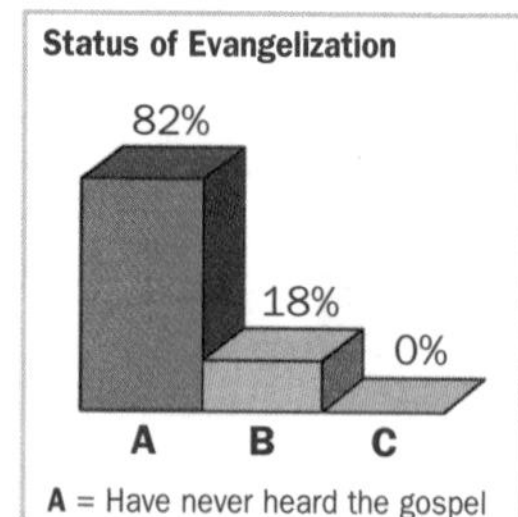

Guiqiong 贵琼

Population in China:
7,000 (1983)
9,760 (2000)
12,020 (2010)
Location: Sichuan
Religion: Tibetan Buddhism
Christians: None Known

Overview of the Guiqiong

Countries: China

Pronunciation: "Gway-chee-ong"

Other Names: Guichong

Population Source:
7,000 (1983 Sun Hongkai);
Out of a total Tibetan population of 4,593,330 (1990 census)

Location: *W Sichuan:* Garze Tibetan Prefecture: On both sides of the Dadu River north from Luding County; Some in Tianquan County

Status:
Officially included under Tibetan

Language: Sino-Tibetan, Tibeto-Burman, Qiangic, Guiqiong

Dialects (4): Duampou

Religion:
Tibetan Buddhism, Shamanism

Christians: None known

Scripture: None

***Jesus* film:** None

Gospel Recordings: None

Christian Broadcasting: None

ROPAL code: GQI00

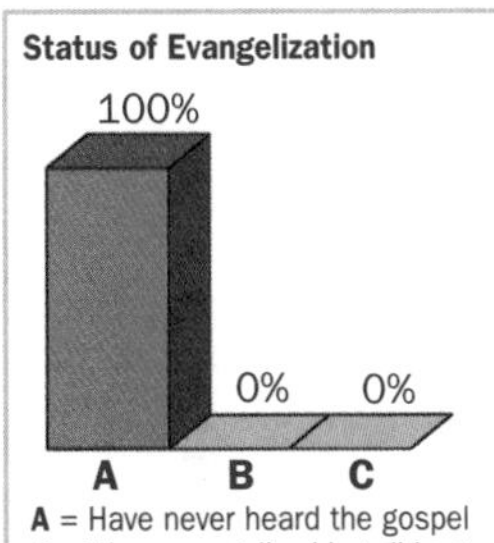

A = Have never heard the gospel
B = Were evangelized but did not become Christians
C = Are adherents to any form of Christianity

Location: A 1983 study listed 7,000 Guiqiong people.[1] They inhabit the tablelands along both banks of the Dadu River, north of Luding County in the Garze Tibetan Autonomous Prefecture in western Sichuan Province. There are also a few Guiqiong located farther to the east in northwestern Tianquan County. The great Dadu River, which surges each summer as the ice fields in the mountains begin to thaw, is the source of life for the Guiqiong. The river cuts a path through the rocky terrain of central Sichuan. As a result, plateaus have formed on both sides of the river.

Paul Hattaway

Identity: The Guiqiong have been included as part of the Tibetan nationality in China. As early as 1930, however, Chinese researchers stated, "The language and customs of the Guiqiong are distinct from those of either the Chinese or Khampa Tibetans. The people here are actually a unique ethnic group."[2]

Language: The Guiqiong language — which has four tones and is part of the Qiangic branch of Tibeto-Burman — is under pressure from the Sichuan dialect of Chinese. In many locations the Guiqiong live in mixed villages alongside much larger Han Chinese communities.[3]

History: The historical border region between the Chinese and Tibetans has witnessed the fusion and assimilation of numerous tribes. The area inhabited by the Guiqiong was formerly part of the province of Xikang. In the 1930s Xikang was a lawless place that few outsiders dared to enter. "Aborigines [minorities] seize and kill members of other nationalities.... In parts of Xikang, abandoned hovels and wasteland due to pillage are common sights. Violent attacks on communities by 'aborigines', as well as government punitive actions against them, cost many tens of thousands of lives."[4]

Customs: One of the main reasons for the extreme violence throughout Xikang in the 1930s and 1940s was the drug trade. Large quantities of opium were manufactured throughout the region until the Communist takeover in the early 1950s. The new government forced the people of western Sichuan to destroy their opium crops. Today most Guiqiong grow maize and barley, while those living near the river or some other source of water grow vegetables.

Religion: The Guiqiong are nominally Tibetan Buddhists, although they retain many aspects of animism and shamanism in their religious beliefs.

Christianity: The Guiqiong have no understanding of the gospel or the name of Jesus Christ. They have been cut off from the message of eternal life for centuries. James O. Fraser described the tenacity needed to reach groups such as the Guiqiong: "Evangelistic work on the mission field is like a man going about in a dark, damp valley with a lighted match in his hand, seeking to ignite anything ignitable... here a shrub, there a tree, here a few sticks, there a heap of leaves take fire and give light and warmth, long after the kindling match and its bearer have passed on. And this is what God wants to see... little patches of fire burning all over the world."[5]

Guopu 果铺

Jamin Pelkey

Location: Approximately 16,900 Guopu (also called *Guoluo*) people live in Weining County in the northwestern part of Guizhou Province and in Yiliang County in the northeastern section of Yunnan Province. They inhabit villages amid the imposing Wumeng Mountains which lie on a northeast-southwest axis along the border between Guizhou and Yunnan. The range averages 2,500 meters (8,200 ft.) above sea level, while its major peak, Xiliang, is at 2,800 meters (9,180 ft.). People living close to Weining Township harvest fish from Lake Caohai. *Caohai* means "grass sea" in Chinese and is so named because of the abundance of reeds along its shores.

Identity: The Guopu are one of 120 distinct groups of the Yi nationality in China. There are three ethnic names of Yi groups in northwest Guizhou Province: Guopu, Guozou, and Guoluo. Although these names all sound similar and may refer to a common ethnic origin, today each name represents a distinct group.

Language: Guopu is an Eastern Yi language within the Tibeto-Burman family.

History: According to some sources, "It was the great Emperor Kang-He who gave the [rulers of Weining] the hereditary government of a number of Lolo [Yi] tribes in 1713. The Emperor Yang Cheng, wishing to consolidate the Chinese suzerainty which until that time had been purely nominal, took up arms against the Lolo in 1727, and crushed them. A great number of them abandoned their country, flying towards the west, crossing the Blue [Yangtze] River, and taking refuge in the wild ranges of Chonolevo and Shama, then covered with forests, to which they set fire."[1]

Customs: In Weining County, "since the slopes are gentle, strip cultivation rather than terracing is the norm, although the strips do tend to follow the natural contours of the land. In season, the ripening crops produce surprisingly vivid slashes of color, the predominant green tinged with contrasting highlights depending on the crop — pink and red for sweet buckwheat, white for bitter buckwheat, for example. The potato plant is visible everywhere, potatoes forming a dietary staple for the peoples of the Wumeng Mountains. Maize is also grown, but the climate and altitude are unfavorable for rice."[2]

Religion: The traditional religion of the Guopu includes worship of the heavens, earth, mountains, rivers, trees, grass, bamboo, rocks, wells and, above all, the spirits of the sun and the moon.

Christianity: Approximately 3,000 Guopu profess Christ as their Lord. The China Inland Mission and the Methodists both had missionaries in Weining County. In 1907 they established the first church in the area. The missionaries soon saw the need to separate their Yi and Miao work. Between 1957 and 1966 the former China Inland Mission churches experienced severe persecution. Because of the government crackdowns against religion, the Yi churches including the Guopu went underground, meeting in secret. In 1988, fifteen Yi churches were reopened.

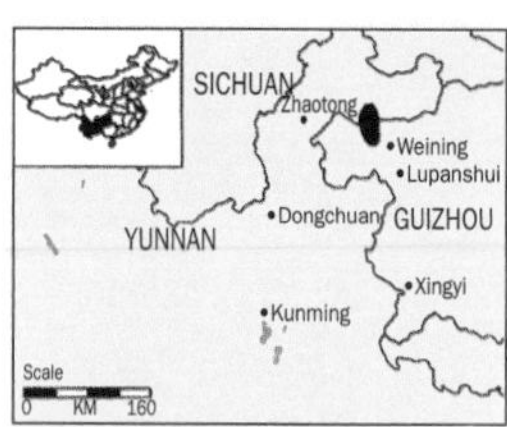

Population in China:
16,500 (1999)
16,920 (2000)
21,200 (2010)
Location: Guizhou, Yunnan
Religion: Polytheism
Christians: 3,000

Overview of the Guopu

Countries: China

Pronunciation: "Guoh-poo"

Other Names: Gan Yi, Dry Yi, Guoluo, Kuo-lo, Guo

Population Source:
16,500 (1999 AMO);
2,000 in Yunnan (1999 J. Pelkey);
Out of a total Yi population of 6,572,173 (1990 census)

Location:
NW Guizhou: Weining County;
NE Yunnan: Yiliang County

Status:
Officially included under Yi

Language: Sino-Tibetan, Tibeto-Burman, Burmese-Lolo, Lolo, Northern Lolo, Yi, Eastern Yi

Dialects: 0

Religion: Polytheism, Animism, Ancestor Worship, Christianity

Christians: 3,000

Scripture: None

***Jesus* film:** None

Gospel Recordings: None

Christian Broadcasting: None

ROPAL code: None

Status of Evangelization

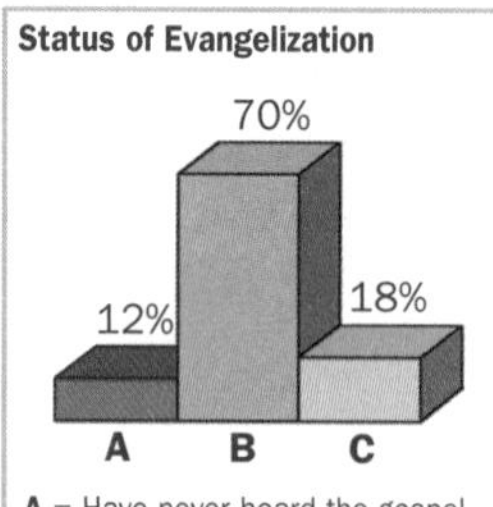

A = Have never heard the gospel
B = Were evangelized but did not become Christians
C = Are adherents to any form of Christianity

Hagei 哈给

Dwayne Graybill

Location: Despite a relatively small population of only 1,700 speakers, the Hagei ethnic group are found in an extraordinarily widespread area of southern China. The majority are found in five counties of northern and western Guizhou Province: including Qinglong District of Zunyi County, Anlang and Taiyang districts of Renhuai County in the north of the province; Maixiang District of Qingzhen County in central Guizhou just west of Guiyang City; Xiangying, and Ma'ao, and Huajiang districts of Zhenning County in western Guizhou. In addition, a small number of Hagei speakers spill over into the Sanchong District of Longlin County in the northwestern arm of the Guangxi Zhuang Autonomous Region.[1]

Identity: The number of people who belong to the Hagei ethnic group is considerably higher than the 1,700 population who can still speak the Hagei language. Almost a century ago, missionaries in Guizhou considered the various branches of Gelao on the verge of extinction. Samuel Clarke wrote, "As far as we know there are now only several hamlets of them in the Anshun Prefecture, which altogether do not number more than two or three hundred families."[2]

Language: In Longlin County of northwestern Guangxi, Hagei speakers live alongside Duoluo speakers, who also belong to the Gelao nationality. The two groups cannot understand each other, however, and must revert to Chinese in order to communicate. Gina Corrigan notes, "Most Gelao speak Chinese as strong local dialects that developed separately, resulting in them not being able to understand each other."[3] Many Hagei can now speak Yi, Bouyei, or Miao better than their own mother tongue.

History: Although they were once the dominant group in the area, the Gelao were subdued by the Chinese and their homelands were taken over during the Yuan Dynasty (1271–1368). Since that time most Gelao have assimilated to Han Chinese culture and language, so that today there is little to distinguish them from their former conquerors.

Customs: The Hagei prefer to construct their homes on the side of a hill or at the foot of a mountain. In their homes, a central kitchen is surrounded by two bedrooms. Many Hagei are extremely poor and live in houses made of mud or bamboo. Maize is the staple food of the Hagei who live in the mountains, while on the plains they eat wheat, rice, millet, and sorghum.

Religion: Apart from ancestor worship, the Hagei are not a particularly religious people.

Christianity: Little is known about the state of Christianity among the Hagei, but most of the areas they inhabit have little Christian presence. The Hagei also spill over into the northwestern part of the Guangxi Zhuang Autonomous Region. The first Protestant missionary to Guangxi was R. H. Graves who arrived in 1862. He reported, "The natives of the province were strongly opposed to a foreigner settling in their midst and met every attempt at entrance with a determined opposition which reached the point of mob violence and bloodshed."[4]

SICHUAN
GUIZHOU
Bijie
Qianxi
Lupanshui
Guiyang
Anshun
Panxian
YUNNAN
GUANGXI
Longlin
Scale
0 KM 160

Population in China:
1,700 (1987)
2,340 (2000)
3,020 (2010)
Location: Guizhou, Guangxi
Religion: Ancestor Worship
Christians: None Known

Overview of the Hagei

Countries: China
Pronunciation: "Ha-gay"
Other Names: Hakei, Hagei Gelao
Population Source:
1,700 (1987 Zheng Guo-qiao);
Out of a total Gelao population of 437,997 (1990 census)
Location: *Guizhou:* Zunyi, Renhuai, Qingzhen, Zhenning, and Pu'an counties;
NW Guangxi: Longlin County
Status:
Officially included under Gelao
Language: Daic, Kadai, Lati-Kelao
Dialects: 0
Religion: Ancestor Worship, Animism, No Religion
Christians: None known
Scripture: None
***Jesus* film:** None
Gospel Recordings: None
Christian Broadcasting: None
ROPAL code: KKF03

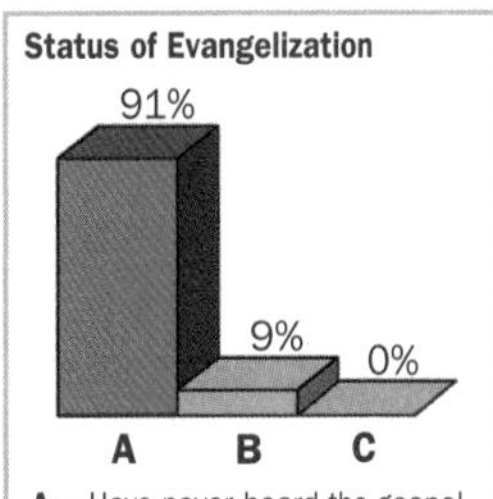

Hakka 客家

Population in China:
25,918,000 (1984)
31,309,000 (2000)
35,379,000 (2010)
Location: Guangdong, Fujian, Jiangxi, Guangxi, Hong Kong, Hunan, Sichuan
Religion: No Religion
Christians: 150,000

Overview of the Hakka

Countries: China, Taiwan, Malaysia, Indonesia, Singapore[1]

Pronunciation: "Hah-kah"

Other Names: Hokka, Kechia, Ke, Kejia, Xinmin, Majia

Population Source: 25,725,000 (1992 B. Grimes – 1984 figure);[2] Out of a total Han population of 1,042,482,187 (1990 census); 2,000,000 in Taiwan (1991); 985,635 in Malaysia; 640,000 in Indonesia (1982); 69,000 in Singapore[3]

Location: *Guangdong; Fujian; Jiangxi; Guangxi; Hong Kong; Hunan; Sichuan*

Status: Officially included under Han Chinese

Language: Chinese, Hakka

Dialects (11): Jiaying, Xinghua, Xinhui, Shaonan, Yuezhong, Huizhou, Yuebei, Tingzhou, Ninglong, Yugui, Tonggu

Religion: No Religion, Animism, Shamanism, Christianity

Christians: 150,000

Scripture: Bible 1916; New Testament 1883; Portions 1860

***Jesus* film:** Available

Gospel Recordings: Hakka #00340

Christian Broadcasting: Available (TWR)

ROPAL code: HAK00

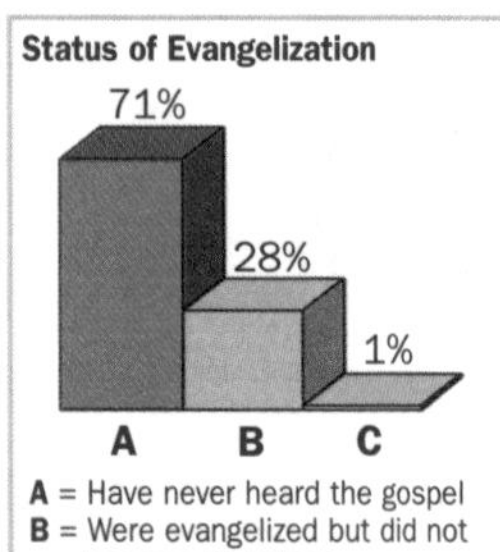

Location: More than 30 million Hakka are located in over 200 cities and counties spread throughout seven provinces and administrative areas of China. An additional two million Hakka live in Taiwan. The Hakka are concentrated in Guangdong, Jiangxi, Guangxi, Fujian, Hong Kong, and Hunan provinces. There are also small numbers in Sichuan and Hunan provinces.[4] In addition, Hakka communities are scattered throughout many nations around the world.

Identity: The Hakka, although proud of their cultural differences, have never claimed to be non-Chinese. Many famous Chinese have been Hakka, including Deng Xiaoping, Lee Kwan Yew, and Hong Xiuquan (the leader of the Taiping Rebellion).

Language: Despite living in geographically scattered communities, the Hakka language is marked with high intelligibility and uniformity between widespread areas. The Hakka are proud of their language and say they would "rather surrender the ancestral land, but never the ancestral speech."[5]

History: There is much speculation concerning the historical roots of the Hakka. Some claim that they were the first Chinese people to arrive in China. Others claim that the Hakka are the descendants of the Xiongnu tribe. This much is agreed upon: At various stages between the fourth and thirteenth centuries AD, large numbers of people were forced to flee their homes in the war-torn Yellow River valley to seek refuge in southern China. These war refugees came to be known as *Kejia* — a Hakka word meaning "strangers" or "guests."[6] When the savage Mongol hordes swept across China in the thirteenth century, many Hakka fled to the south to escape the carnage.[7]

Customs: As part of the careful preservation of their language, when a non-Hakka woman marries into a Hakka family she is required to learn the Hakka language. In the past, many Hakka mothers killed their female babies. "Sooner than sell their daughters into slavery or concubinage, Hakka mothers prefer to kill them soon after birth."[8] The Hakka never practiced foot-binding like other Chinese.

Religion: Since the advent of Communism most Hakka could accurately be described as nonreligious. Aspects of animism and shamanism are found among some of the more remote Hakka locations.

Christianity: Rev. T. H. Hamburg and Rudolf Lechler were the first missionaries sent out by the Basel Mission. They arrived in China in 1846 to commence work among the Hakka. They experienced great success, and by 1922 the Hakka Christians numbered 30,000.[9] Today, most of the estimated 150,000 Hakka Christians in China are located in southern Guangdong.[10] In the 1800s the Taiping leader Chung Wang, a Hakka, pleaded for missionaries to have patience with his people. "You have had the Gospel for upwards of 1,800 years; we only, as it were, eight days. Your knowledge of it ought to be correct and extensive, ours must necessarily be limited and imperfect. You must therefore bear with us for the present, and we will gradually improve.... We are determined to uproot idolatry, and plant Christianity in its place."[11]

Paul Hattaway

Hakka, Hainan Island 客家(海南)

April 5

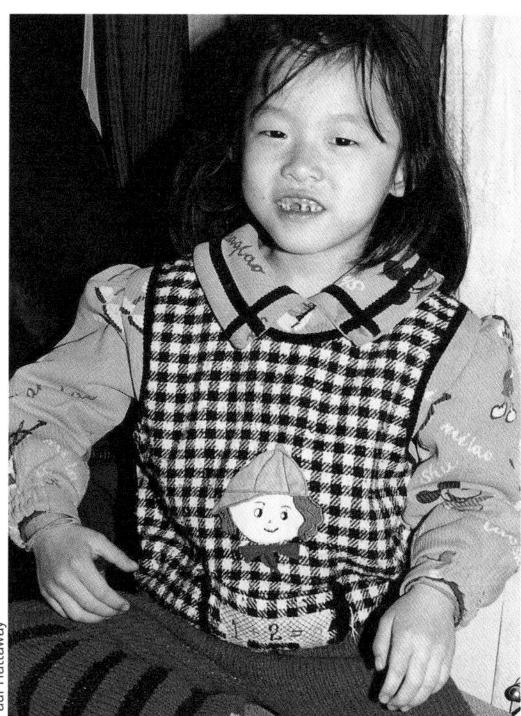

Paul Hattaway

Location: The Hakka of Hainan Island — who speak a language unintelligible with the Hakka on the Chinese Mainland — total approximately 2,000 people in four villages. They live near the man-made Songtao Reservoir in Danzhao County, in the northwestern part of Hainan Island. Hainan was considered part of Guangdong Province until 1988, when it was granted status as a separate province.

Identity: Although considered part of the Han Chinese nationality, the Hakka on Hainan Island speak their own unique language that is unintelligible to speakers of Hainanese Chinese. It is also reported to be distinct from other Hakka varieties in China.[1]

Language: The differences between the Hakka language spoken on Hainan Island and that spoken on the Mainland are probably due to the influence, over many generations, of contact with the speakers of several other languages found on Hainan Island. Some scholars in the past have believed the Hakka language to be related to Japanese.[2] Hideo Matsumoto took blood samples of different Asian races in 1966 and conducted DNA tests. He discovered the Hakka shared many genetic traits with the Japanese and Koreans.

History: It is believed that Hakka communities first migrated to Hainan Island in the aftermath of the Hakka-Cantonese wars in the 1860s. The Hakka were encouraged to migrate to vacant areas by the government. After the Songtao Reservoir was constructed in the 1970s, the Hakka moved to its northern bank and built new communities. Before that time they had lived scattered across various parts of Hainan. "There is evidence that almost as early as 900 AD, wandering farm laborers came by the north and northeastern routes out of Fujian and southern Jiangxi into Guangdong to work for the indolent natives. A census taken of the population of Moichu in the year 976 AD lists 367 such 'guests' and 1,210 'native' residents. A hundred years later the census shows the number of Hakka to have increased to 6,558, while the natives numbered 5,824."[3]

Customs: Some believe the Hakka to have originally been a cross between Chinese soldiers and Ikia women. "They adopted most of the Chinese customs, mingled with the natives, and being bold and enterprising, succeeded in supplanting them."[4]

Religion: The Hakka of Hainan Island practice traditional Chinese religions, especially Daoism and elements of Buddhism. Most of the younger generation are atheists.

Christianity: Without a church or a gospel witness, the Hakka of Hainan Island are a relatively untouched people group. In recent years a powerful church-planting movement among the Hainanese has resulted in more than 550 house churches being formed throughout the island, but this movement has yet to spread to the area inhabited by the Hakka. The Hakka *Jesus* film and Hakka gospel broadcasts are available, but the Hakka on Hainan Island cannot understand them. Because their language is distinct, the Hakka Bible is also of no practical use to them.

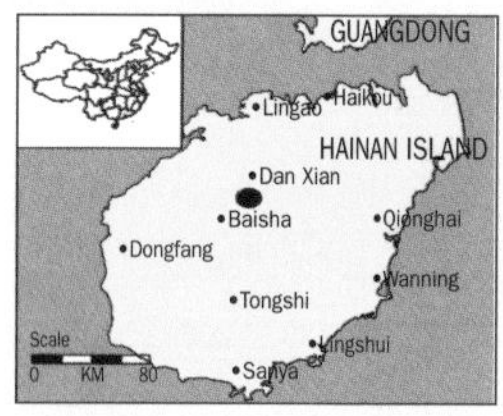

Population in China:
2,000 (1997)
2,070 (2000)
2,340 (2010)
Location: Hainan Island
Religion: Daoism
Christians: None Known

Overview of the Hainan Island Hakka

Countries: China

Pronunciation: "Hah-kah-Hai-nun"

Other Names: Kechia, Ke

Population Source: 2,000 (1997 AMO); Out of a total Han population of 1,042,482,187 (1990 census)

Location: *NW Hainan Island:* Around the Songtao Reservoir in Danzhao County

Status: Officially included under Han Chinese

Language: Chinese, Hakka

Dialects: 0

Religion: Daoism, No Religion, Buddhism

Christians: None known

Scripture: None

***Jesus* film:** None

Gospel Recordings: None

Christian Broadcasting: None

ROPAL code: None

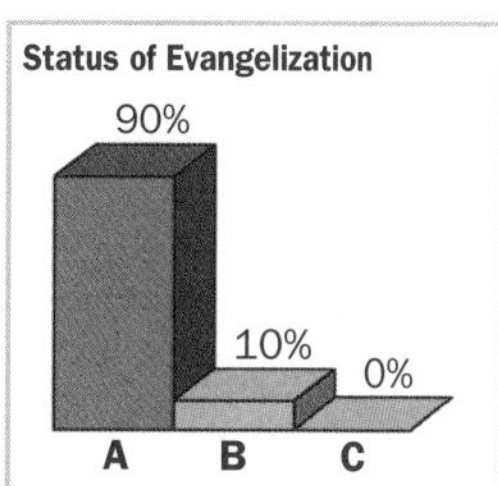

A = Have never heard the gospel
B = Were evangelized but did not become Christians
C = Are adherents to any form of Christianity

Han Chinese, Cantonese 汉，广东话

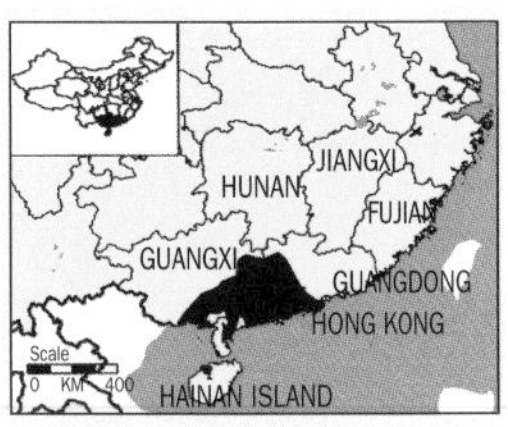

Population in China:
48,945,000 (1984)
59,125,600 (2000)
66,811,900 (2010)
Location: Guangdong, Hong Kong, Hainan Island, Guangxi, Macau
Religion: Daoism
Christians: 1,250,000

Overview of the Cantonese

Countries: China, Malaysia, Vietnam, Canada, Singapore, Indonesia, USA, Brunei, Philippines, Thailand[1]
Pronunciation: "Gwang-dong-Hwa"
Other Names: Cantonese, Yue, Yueh, Guangdong, Punti, Baihua
Population Source: 46,305,000 (1988 B. Grimes – 1984 figure);[2] Out of a total Han population of 1,042,482,187 (1990 census); 748,010 in Malaysia; 500,000 in Vietnam; 400,000 in Canada; 314,000 in Singapore; 180,000 in Indonesia; 180,000 in USA; 29,400 in Thailand[3]
Location: *Guangdong; Hong Kong; Hainan Island; S Guangxi; Macau*
Status: Officially included under Han Chinese
Language: Chinese, Cantonese
Dialects (7): Guangfu, Yongxun, Gaoyang, Siyi, Goulu, Wuhua, Qinlian
Religion: Daoism, Buddhism, No Religion, Christianity
Christians: 1,250,000
Scripture: Bible 1894; New Testament 1877; Portions 1862
***Jesus* film:** Available
Gospel Recordings: Cantonese #00013 Toi Shaan #02097
Christian Broadcasting: Available (FEBC, TWR)
ROPAL code: YUH00

Location: Approximately 60 million Cantonese-speaking Chinese live in southern China. The majority are concentrated in Guangdong Province, radiating out from the capital city of Guangzhou (Canton). More than five and a half million Cantonese also live in the Hong Kong and Macau Special Administrative Regions. Others are located in the southern part of Guangxi and on Hainan Island. In addition, large Cantonese communities are found in many countries around the world.

Paul Hattaway

Identity: Although the Cantonese today proudly consider themselves part of the Han Chinese race, one ethnohistorian has concluded, "The ethnic origins of the ancient Yue people... may have been Tai, but with a sizable Miao-Yao minority in the hills.... The ancient Yue language was definitely not Sinitic.... It is estimated that the population of Guangdong was less than 30 percent Sinitic in 1080."[4]

Language: The more than 30 Han Chinese language groups described in this book are considered by linguists to be mutually unintelligible languages. They are not merely dialects of the same language. Cantonese contains up to nine tones — compared to the national language, Mandarin, which has only four. Although they speak different languages and dialects, all Chinese people in China use the same written script.

History: The large southern city of Guangzhou — which has been continually inhabited for 2,200 years — has always been the center of Cantonese civilization. In the 33rd year of the reign of Emperor Qin Shihuang (214 BC), the Nanhai Prefecture was established in today's Guangzhou. Large numbers of Han flooded into the area.[5] Guangzhou became home to large numbers of foreign merchants in the ninth century until the T'ang emperors lost control of it in AD 878. An Arab traveler reported that "a hundred and twenty thousand Muslims, Jews, Christians and Zoroastrians were slaughtered [in Guangzhou]."[6]

Customs: The Chinese have a saying that to be happy in this life one must be born in Suzhou, live in Guangzhou, and die at Suzhou, "for in the first are the handsomest people, in the second the richest luxuries, and in the third the best coffins."[7]

Religion: Throughout the Communist era the Cantonese have continued to be the most openly religious of all Chinese. Most homes in Guangdong Province have spirit altars. The Cantonese also zealously observe Daoist and Buddhist festivals.

Christianity: In September 1807 Robert Morrison landed in Guangzhou. A new era of Protestant missions began in China. Seven years later he baptized his first convert, "At a stream of water issuing from the foot of a lofty hill, far away from human observation.... May he be the first-fruits of a great harvest."[8] Today there are at least 1.2 million Cantonese Christians in China. Guangdong contains at least 200,000 Protestants[9] and 110,000 Catholics,[10] while heavily evangelized Hong Kong numbers 552,000 Protestants and 312,000 Catholics.[11]

Han Chinese, Dan 汉，单

Population in China:
3,150,000 (1972)
4,296,000 (2000)
4,855,000 (2010)
Location: Guangdong, Guangxi, Hainan Island, Hong Kong, Macau
Religion: Polytheism
Christians: 15,000

Overview of the Dan

Countries: China, Vietnam, Malaysia, Thailand

Pronunciation: "Dan"

Other Names: Tanka, Danjia, Xumin, Soisangyan, Dan, Ngai, Boat People

Population Source: 3,150,000 (1972 E. Anderson); Out of a total Han population of 1,042,482,187 (1990 census); 1,200 in Vietnam (1991 census); Also in Malaysia and Thailand

Location: *Guangdong; Hainan Island; Guangxi; Hong Kong; Macau*

Status: Officially included under Han Chinese

Language: Chinese, Cantonese

Dialects: 0

Religion: Polytheism, Animism, Ancestor Worship, Christianity

Christians: 15,000

Scripture: Bible 1894; New Testament 1877; Portions 1862

***Jesus* film:** Available (Cantonese)

Gospel Recordings: Cantonese #00013

Christian Broadcasting: Available (FEBC, TWR)

ROPAL code: YUH01

Status of Evangelization

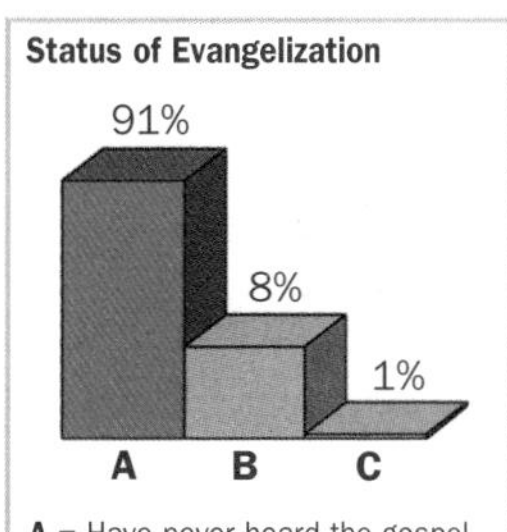

A = Have never heard the gospel
B = Were evangelized but did not become Christians
C = Are adherents to any form of Christianity

Location: A 1972 study listed a population of about three million Dan people, historically known as the "Boat People," living along the coasts of southern China including Guangdong, Guangxi, Hainan Island, and Macau. An additional 150,000 lived on boats in Hong Kong at the time. By the 1980s the number in Hong Kong had diminished to about 50,000.[1] In addition, Dan people have migrated to several countries in Southeast Asia, where they are known by various names, including the official *Ngai* minority in Vietnam.

Identity: The Dan prefer to call themselves *Soisangyan*, a name which means "water-borne people" in their dialect. Although they are officially classified as part of the Han Chinese nationality, most other people in southern China "attest the Dan are not Han Chinese at all, but rather a distinct minority race."[2] Experts now generally agree that although the Dan are ethnolinguistically a Sinitic people, "there is no doubt that they have been discriminated against in the past, officially as well as socially.... It is clear they have developed a strong sense of group identity.... Other Chinese consider them an separate ethnic group.... Such a castelike distinction is more typical of India than of China."[3]

Language: Despite general belief among the Cantonese that the Dan are from a tribal background, linguists have ascertained that the Dan speak the Yuehai dialect of Cantonese.

History: Chinese references to the Dan and their lives as boat people date back at least 800 years. The uniqueness of the Dan was enforced by tales describing how they had short legs, useful only for life at sea. Some stories alleged they had six toes and even a tail. In Hong Kong the status of the Dan has been greatly diminished in recent years since the government has outlawed the practice of living on boats.[4]

Customs: Not surprisingly, all customs of the Dan revolve around their lives on the water. Whole families live on small boats that "seldom if ever touch the shore. Children are born and raised on the boats, and dogs, chickens, and cats move freely from deck to deck. In the old days... little coffin boats carried each [Dan] person to his or her final resting place on land. For some, it was the first time on land as well as the last."[5] The Chinese have a saying that a Dan person "on the water is a veritable dragon, on land is only a miserable worm."[6]

Religion: The Dan developed their own religious beliefs relating to their unique lifestyles. They worship *Tin Hau*, the goddess of fishermen, whose image is carried in floating temples. They also honor the spirit of the fish and sea dragon.

Christianity: Because of their close-knit families and unique, isolated culture, few Dan in China have ever been exposed to the gospel message. Churches have existed among the Dan in Hong Kong for more than 50 years, however, due to the efforts of mission agencies who specifically targeted them and boarded their boats to share the love of Christ. Most Dan can understand standard Cantonese and could be reached using materials in that language.

Paul Hattaway

Han Chinese, Gan 汉, 赣

Location: More than 35 million speakers of Gan Chinese live in Jiangxi Province and the southeastern corner of Hubei Province, including Dachi, Xianning, Jiayu, and Chongyang counties. The Gan account for approximately 3% of all Chinese in China. The greatest concentrations live along the Fuhe River, the lower reaches of the Ganjiang River, and around Poyang Lake. Small numbers of Gan speakers also live in eastern and southwestern Hunan, southern Anhui, and the northwestern part of Fujian Province.

Identity: The Gan Chinese are part of the great Han Chinese nationality — the largest ethnic group in the world. Gan, however, is a distinct language that differs from Mandarin and other Chinese varieties.

Language: The Gan language contains nine dialects. It has only marginal intelligibility with Mandarin and Wu Chinese. Almost all Gan are adequately bilingual in Mandarin Chinese, the national language which is used throughout China for education and in the media.

History: The *Xia Dynasty (2200–1700 BC)*: The Chinese claim 5,000 years of continuous history, beginning with the mythological Xia Dynasty. The very existence of the Xia is doubtful, as archaeological evidence has not been found to support the written accounts of the time. According to legend, the Xia was preceded by three sovereigns. The first sovereign, Fuxi, was thought to be half human and half dragon. His wife, Nugua, is credited with having created humans from clay. Fuxi taught men how to hunt, fish, and farm. The first emperor, Huang Di, is said to have invented the calendar, boats, and pottery. After 500 years, the Xia leaders "became corrupt and were... overthrown by the Shang."[1] Jiangxi, where most Gan live, was incorporated into the Chinese empire at any early date but remained sparsely populated until the eighth century.

Paul Hattaway

Customs: Jiangxi is famous for its abundance of silver. Extensive mining caused the formation of a wealthy ruling class. Today, Jiangxi is one of the most densely populated provinces in China.

Religion: Although the majority of Gan are nonreligious, there has been a revival of Buddhism and Daoism since the relaxing of restrictions on religion in recent years. Zhuangzi (369–286 BC) was an early leader of Daoism. His writings introduced the idea of the unity of opposites, ying and yang. This led to the notion of accepting life without struggle.

Christianity: In 1900 the diabolical Boxer Rebellion broke out across China. Thirty thousand Chinese Catholics and 2,000 Protestants were massacred,[2] as antiforeign and anti-Christian feelings ran hot. The number of Christians in China more than doubled in the six years following the massacres. In 1901 one missionary in Jiangxi reported 20,000 converts.[3] There are an estimated 400,000 Christians among the Gan Chinese today.[4] The *Jesus* film has recently been translated into the Gan language, although most Gan are adequately bilingual in Mandarin.

Population in China:
31,270,000 (1987)
36,554,000 (2000)
41,306,000 (2010)
Location: Jiangxi, Hubei, Hunan, Anhui, Fujian
Religion: No Religion
Christians: 400,000

Overview of the Gan Chinese

Countries: China

Pronunciation: "Gahn"

Other Names: Gan, Kan

Population Source:
31,270,000 (1987 *LAC*);
Out of a total Han population of 1,042,482,187 (1990 census)

Location: *Jiangxi; SE Hubei; Hunan; S Anhui; NW Fujian*

Status: Officially included under Han Chinese

Language: Chinese, Gan

Dialects (9): Changjing, Yiliu, Jicha, Fuguang, Yangyi, Datong, Leizi, Dongsui, Huaiyue

Religion: No Religion, Daoism, Buddhism, Christianity

Christians: 400,000

Scripture: Chinese Bible

***Jesus* film:** Available

Gospel Recordings: None

Christian Broadcasting: None

ROPAL code: KNN00

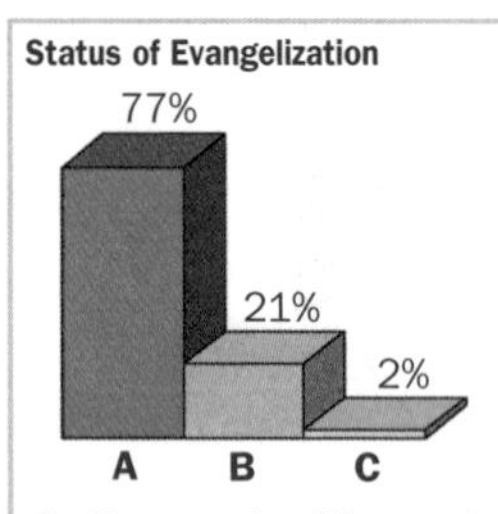

Han Chinese, Hainanese 汉(海南)

Population in China:
4,400,000 (1987)
5,143,600 (2000)
5,812,300 (2010)
Location: Hainan Island
Religion: No Religion
Christians: 92,000

Overview of the Hainanese

Countries: China, Vietnam, Laos

Pronunciation: "Hi-nahn"

Other Names: Chinese: Qiongwen, Qiongwen, Hainan Chinese

Population Source:
4,400,000 (1987 *LAC*);
Out of a total Han population of 1,042,482,187 (1990 census);
Also in Vietnam and Laos

Location: *NE Hainan Island* and along the coastline of most of the island except the northwest

Status: Officially included under Han Chinese

Language: Chinese, Qiongwen

Dialects (5): Fucheng, Wenchang, Wanning, Yaxian, Changgan

Religion: No Religion, Buddhism, Daoism, Christianity

Christians: 92,000

Scripture: None

***Jesus* film:** None

Gospel Recordings: Hainanese #00366

Christian Broadcasting: Available

ROPAL code: CFR04

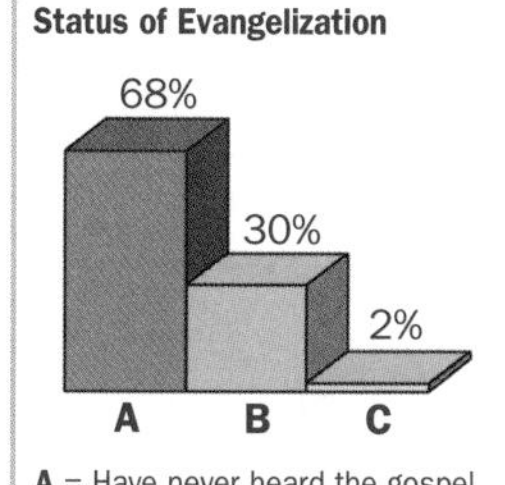

A = Have never heard the gospel
B = Were evangelized but did not become Christians
C = Are adherents to any form of Christianity

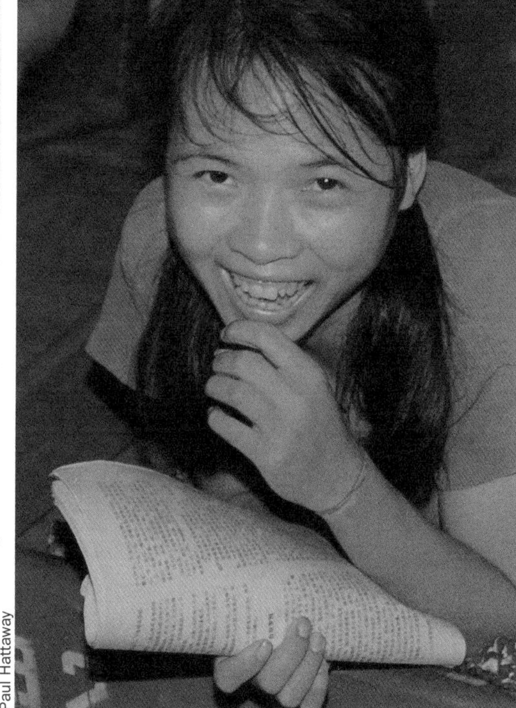

Paul Hattaway

Location: Five million Hainanese Chinese are concentrated in the northeastern parts of China's Hainan (South Sea) Island. They are located along the coast in a clockwise direction, from the northeast all the way to the west of the island.

Identity: Included as part of the Han nationality, the Hainanese are descended from Chinese who migrated from Fujian at various times over the last 15 centuries.

Language: Hainanese is related to the Min Nan language of Fujian. Hainanese "has evolved in unusual directions and is not at all readily understood by other Min Nan peoples."[1] Hainanese is also called *Qiongwen*. Qiongwen is widely spoken throughout 14 counties and cities of Hainan. Most Hainanese are bilingual in Mandarin, while many can also speak Cantonese.

History: *The Shang Dynasty (1700–1100 BC):* The second dynasty in Chinese history was the Shang, which lasted for 600 years. The ruling base at the time was the Yellow River basin in present-day Shanxi, Shaanxi, and Shandong. Archaeological finds from the Shang period have indicated the presence of "a caste of high priests who practiced divination using so-called oracle bones. Associated with ancestor worship and divination are the Shang bronze vessels, the surfaces of which are covered with extraordinarily detailed linear designs."[2] The Shang Dynasty was overthrown around 1100 BC. Chinese have lived on Hainan Island since Madame Xian — a leader of the Yue minority tribes of southern China — pledged allegiance to the Sui Dynasty rulers in the sixth century AD.[3]

Customs: Most Hainanese earn their livelihood from fishing or agriculture. Severe and sudden storms lash the Hainan coastline every summer, causing massive damage to homes and boats. New industry and factories have sprung up on Hainan in the last decade. Significant numbers of Hainanese are employed by the expanding tourist industry which has catered to a growing number of Chinese and foreign tourists since the early 1980s.

Religion: Severe persecution of all religious activity during the Cultural Revolution caused the demise of many traditional Chinese religious practices in the 1960s. Most of the current generation of Hainanese youth are nonreligious.

Christianity: The first mention of Christianity on Hainan was in 1630 when Jesuit priests came from Macau and constructed a chapel in Fucheng Township.[4] The first Protestant missionary on the island was Carl Jeremiassen, a Danish sea captain, who was employed by the Qing government "to hunt down pirates and smugglers." Jeremiassen, however, "changed his mind and his profession upon reaching Hainan in 1881... distributing Bibles with one hand and dispensing medicines with the other."[5] In 1992 there were at least 37,000 Protestants[6] and 3,000 Catholics[7] on Hainan Island, most of whom were Hainanese Chinese. In the six years since then, one church-planting movement has established 550 new house churches with 55,000 new believers on the island.

Han Chinese, Hui'an 汉(惠安)

Paul Hattaway

Location: The majority of the 150,000 Hui'an Chinese live on China's east coast, near the town of Chongwu in Hui'an County. Others are located farther along the Fujian coastline of the Taiwan Strait. One visitor reported, "In the town of Hui'an itself, which is some way inland, one can certainly see these women, but they are more widely scattered. We therefore headed for the Xiaozuo and Dazuo Peninsulas, as here they can be seen in greater concentrations and, as these places are more remote, there is less deviation from the traditional style of dress."[1] Hui'an Chinese are found in larger numbers outside of China. Hui'an Associations exist in the nations of Singapore, Malaysia, Philippines, Myanmar, and Canada.

Identity: Although the Hui'an Chinese officially belong to the Han nationality, many aspects of their culture are unique among the peoples of China. "Visitors coming to Hui'an for the first time often mistake these women for members of a minority nationality. There is some justification for this. Recently, a scholar inferred from their butterfly ornaments and unique customs that they must be a branch of the ancient Yue tribe, the butterfly being the tribe insignia of the Yue. It also seems likely that the customs of tattooing and wrapping their teeth in gold are inherited from the Yue people."[2]

Language: The Hui'an speak the Quanzhang dialect of Min Nan (Hokkien) Chinese. One visitor from northern China expressed frustration at not being able to communicate with the Hui'an, who he said spoke "a local Fujian dialect incomprehensible to me."[3]

History: The Hui'an region was historically inhabited by thousands of merchants from around the world. The elaborate dress of the Hui'an women dates back to the Song Dynasty (960–1279), "when one Li Wenhui, a court official, made a proposal of marriage to a village girl. Notwithstanding her objections, the ceremony went ahead, with the girl bound hand and foot. When the time came for her own daughter to wed, she dressed her in clothes symbolic of her own unhappy marriage. The short loose blouse revealing the midriff represents her dishevelment, the embroidered squares resemble patches and the bands of pattern on sleeve and trouser equate to the rope which bound her."[4]

Customs: For centuries the Hui'an have considered baby girls inferior to boys. They customarily killed girls by drowning them at birth. The Hui'an have a reputation as cunning businessmen. A local expression states the Hui'an will "rob you and then tie you up."

Religion: The majority of Hui'an Chinese are Daoists. Ancestor worship also plays an important role in their lives and beliefs.

Christianity: There are several Catholic, Three-Self, and house churches among the Hui'an Chinese.[5] Although Fujian has one of the largest Christian populations in China, the Hui'an have generally proven more resistant to the gospel than the several other Chinese groups throughout the province.

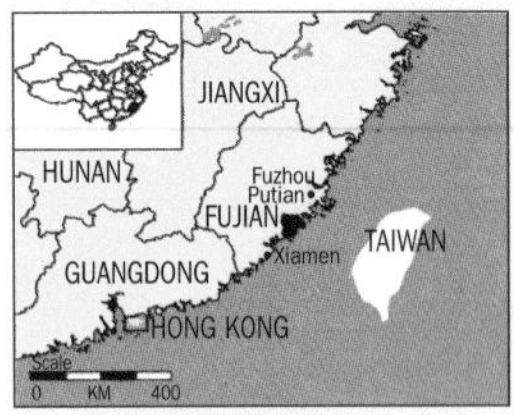

Population in China:
150,000 (1997)
155,800 (2000)
176,100 (2010)
Location: Fujian
Religion: Daoism
Christians: 2,000

Overview of the Hui'an Chinese

Countries: China, Singapore, Malaysia, Philippines, Myanmar, Canada

Pronunciation: "Hway-ahn"

Other Names: Hui'an

Population Source: 150,000 (1997 AMO); Out of a total Han population of 1,042,482,187 (1990 census); 400,000 in Singapore and Malaysia; Also in Philippines, Myanmar, and Canada

Location: *E Fujian:* in and around Chongwu in Hui'an County

Status: Officially included under Han Chinese

Language: Chinese, Min Dong

Dialects: 0

Religion: Daoism, Buddhism, No Religion, Christianity

Christians: 2,000

Scripture: None

***Jesus* film:** None

Gospel Recordings: None

Christian Broadcasting: None

ROPAL code: None

Status of Evangelization

A = Have never heard the gospel
B = Were evangelized but did not become Christians
C = Are adherents to any form of Christianity

Han Chinese, Huizhou 汉(惠州)

Location: A 1987 study listed 3.12 million speakers of the Huizhou Chinese language.[1] The majority are located in the southern part of Anhui Province — in an area previously known as Huizhou Prefecture — on the banks of the Xi'nan River. Since 1912 the city of Huizhou has been known as Shexian. In addition, 800,000 Huizhou live in the northern part of Jiangxi Province, especially in Wuyuan, Yuanling, and Dexing counties. Small numbers also live in Chun'an County of Zhejiang Province. The Huizhou region was badly hit by the Taiping Rebellion and lost as much as half of its population.[2]

Identity: One linguist believes the Huizhou Chinese should be treated "as a separate sublanguage and its speakers as a distinct entity within the mosaic of Sinitic peoples."[3]

Language: Huizhou is unintelligible with other Chinese languages. It is spoken in a widespread geographical area of 25,000 sqare kilometers (9,750 sq. mi.). The five dialects reportedly "differ greatly from each other."[4]

History: *The Western Zhou Dynasty (1100–771 BC):* It is thought that the Western Zhou rulers were a nomadic tribe who based their capital in Hao, near present-day Xian. The Western Zhou Dynasty came to an abrupt end in 771 BC, when barbarian tribes destroyed the capital of Hou. *The Eastern Zhou Dynasty (770–221 BC):* The Chinese consider the Eastern Zhou period as one of the greatest in their long history. During this time the great Chinese philosophers Confucius and Laozi roamed the countryside. Since then, Confucianism, and the Daoist religion founded by Laozi, have left their mark on every generation of Chinese thought and their religions. During this era the "mandate of heaven" was instituted. Political rulers were believed to have gained their position from heaven itself.

Paul Hattaway

Customs: The Huizhou have a reputation as expert merchants and businessmen. A Chinese saying states: "No marketplace is so small there are no Huizhou people." By the sixteenth century, Huizhou merchants "began to assume a major role in the entire national economy [and] soon came to control much of the nation's rice, lumber, and tea trade."[5]

Religion: After taking control of the country, the Communists gradually implemented the atheistic, antireligion policies of Soviet Marxist Vladimir Lenin, who had stated, "Religion is the opium of the people. Religion is a kind of spiritual vodka in which the slaves of capitalism drown their human shape and their claim for any decent human life." But it begs the question whether the Communist system functions merely as a political system, or whether it also has some of the characteristics of a dynamic missionary movement with aspirations for world conquest.

Christianity: Since 1949 Christianity has boomed in the region where the Huizhou live. There are an estimated 120,000 Huizhou believers. The three provinces where Huizhou is spoken contain some of the highest concentrations of Christians in China.

Population in China:
3,120,000 (1987)
3,647,300 (2000)
4,121,400 (2010)
Location: Anhui, Jiangxi, Zhejiang
Religion: No Religion
Christians: 120,000

Overview of the Huizhou Chinese

Countries: China

Pronunciation: "Hway-joe"

Other Names: Chinese: Hui, Wannan, Huichou, Hewichow

Population Source: 3,120,000 (1987 *LAC*); Out of a total Han population of 1,042,482,187 (1990 census)

Location: *S Anhui; N Jiangxi; Zhejiang*

Status: Officially included under Han Chinese

Language: Chinese, Huizhou

Dialects (5): Jishe (850,000), Xiuyi (750,000), Qide (700,000), Yanzhou (700,000), Jingzhou (200,000)

Religion: No Religion, Daoism, Buddhism, Christianity

Christians: 120,000

Scripture: Chinese Bible

***Jesus* film:** None

Gospel Recordings: None

Christian Broadcasting: None

ROPAL code: CZH00

Status of Evangelization

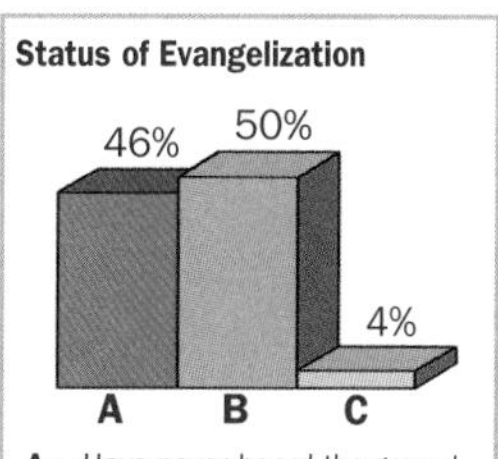

A = Have never heard the gospel
B = Were evangelized but did not become Christians
C = Are adherents to any form of Christianity

Han Chinese, Jin 汉，晋

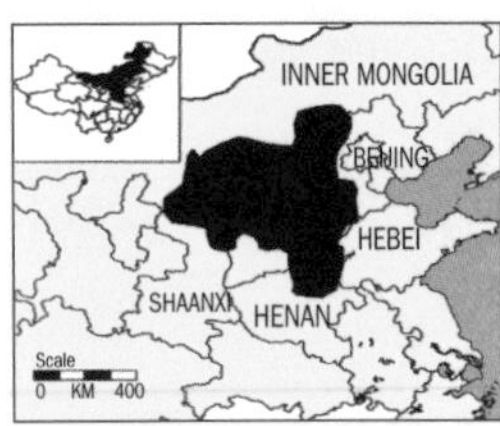

Population in China:
45,700,000 (1987)
53,423,000 (2000)
60,368,000 (2010)
Location: Shanxi, Hebei, Henan, Shaanxi, Inner Mongolia
Religion: No Religion
Christians: 1,200,000

Overview of the Jin Chinese

Countries: China

Pronunciation: "Jin"

Other Names: Jin, Jinyu

Population Source: 45,700,000 (1987 *LAC*); Out of a total Han population of 1,042,482,187 (1990 census)

Location: *Shanxi; Hebei; Henan; Inner Mongolia; Shaanxi*

Status: Officially included under Han Chinese

Language: Chinese, Jin

Dialects (10): Bingzhou, Fenzhou, Xingxi, Shandong, Wutai, Dabao, Zhanghu, Cizhang, Huoji, Zhiyan

Religion: No Religion, Buddhism, Christianity

Christians: 1,200,000

Scripture: Chinese Bible

***Jesus* film:** None

Gospel Recordings: None

Christian Broadcasting: None

ROPAL code: CJY00

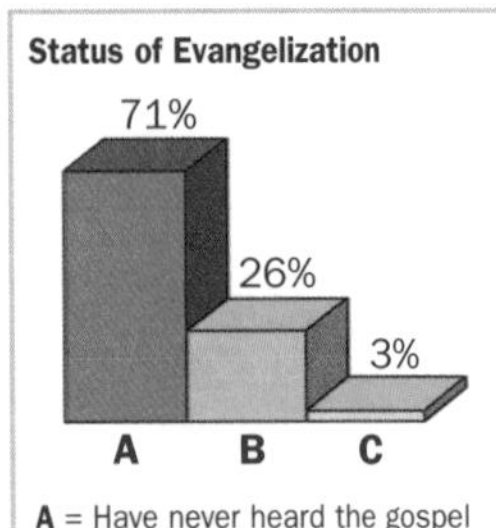

Location: More than 50 million speakers of the Jin Chinese language, called *Jinyu*, inhabit parts of five provinces in northern China: Shanxi (22.3 million speakers by the year 2000), Hebei (10.6 million), areas north of the Yellow River in Henan (9.4 million), Inner Mongolia (8.2 million), and the northern part of Shaanxi (3.2 million). Jin is spoken in a total of 175 cities and counties throughout northern China.[1]

Identity: The Jin were formerly considered part of the *Xibei Guanhua* dialect of Mandarin, but many scholars now consider them a distinct language group.

Language: With all education and media in China using standard Mandarin, the Jin language — which contains ten dialects — is becoming confined to home and social use.

History: *The Qin Dynasty (221–207 BC):* Although it lasted a mere 14 years, the Qin Dynasty constituted the first unified Chinese empire, under Emperor Qin Shihuang. Ascending the throne at the age of 13, Qin is remembered for his ghastly acts of cruelty and torture of innocents. His dynasty left its mark on China in many ways, including the start of nearly 2,000 years of strong, centralized government. China's currency and script were standardized for the first time. The construction of the Great Wall was commenced, and Qin organized the country into provinces through divisions remarkably similar to the provincial boundaries still used today. It was during his brief reign that the 6,000 Terracotta Soldiers were constructed to represent a vigilant army to protect Qin's tomb. *The Han Dynasty (206 BC – AD 220):* The Chinese consider the Han one of the golden periods of their history. For the first time, China extended its borders by military campaigns, bringing China into contact with foreigners.

Customs: The Jin Chinese live in what the Chinese historically viewed as the most backward and far-flung part of China. This has made them a resilient and hardworking people.

Religion: The majority of Jin Chinese are atheists. Shanxi Province has long been a power base of the Communists.

Christianity: Christianity in China is generally believed to have been introduced by the Nestorians around AD 635. However, some scholars believe it may have already been introduced by the Seres around AD 300,[2] or by the Persians in AD 455.[3] Traditionally, some Christians believed that China first received the gospel from St. Thomas, who before his martyrdom reportedly left India and "set sail into China on board of Chinese ships... and landed at a town named Camballe."[4] Today, there are an estimated 1.2 million Jin Chinese believers. Hebei — where more than 10 million Jin speakers live — is the strongest Catholic region in China with more than 800,000 church members.[5] Two-thirds of the population of Shanxi Province are Jin. Recent research indicates there are 200,000 Protestants in Shanxi Province alone.[6]

Paul Hattaway

Han Chinese, Mandarin 汉，普通话

Paul Hattaway

Location: The Han Chinese are the largest ethnic group on earth, and Mandarin is the world's most widely spoken language. More than 780 million Chinese speak Mandarin — known as *Putonghua* meaning "the common speech" — as their mother tongue. Mandarin-speaking Chinese are found all over China but are mostly concentrated in the northern and eastern provinces. Beijing is the unofficial "home" of Mandarin, and the Beijing dialect is the standard used for media and education. Millions of Mandarin speakers are also found in numerous countries around the world.

Identity: The Han Chinese are one of the 56 official nationalities of China. The name China stems from the Qin (Chin) Dynasty of 221–207 BC. The Chinese call their country *Zhongguo*, "The Middle Kingdom."

Language: There is remarkable linguistic uniformity among Mandarin speakers. Chinese from diverse places such as Urumqi in the northwest, Harbin in the northeast, and Kunming in the southwest — thousands of miles apart — are able to understand each other without too much difficulty.

History: *The Wei Dynasty (AD 220–280):* After the collapse of the Han Dynasty, China fell into almost 400 years of crippling war and internal conflict. The country was divided into three kingdoms. The Wei ruled areas north of the Yangtze.

Customs: The Chinese have invented numerous items throughout their long history, including paper and gunpowder.

Religion: The Chinese have been most influenced by Buddhism, Daoism, and Confucianism throughout their history, but since the advent of Communism in 1949 most Chinese could be accurately described as nonreligious.

Christianity: Christianity first made an impact on China in AD 635, when Nestorian Bishop Alopen arrived in China. "Bishop Alopen of the Kingdom of Ta'chin, bringing with him the sutras and images, has come from afar and presented them at our Capital. Having carefully examined the scope of his teaching, we find it to be mysteriously spiritual, and of silent operation. Having observed its principal and most essential points, we reached the conclusion that they cover all that is most important in life.... This Teaching is helpful to all creatures and beneficial to all men. So let it have free course throughout the Empire."[1] By 638 the first church was built in Chang'an, and 21 Persian monks had commenced work in China.[2] By the time missionaries were expelled from China in the 1950s, it is generally agreed there were no more than 750,000 Chinese Protestants across the nation. Since that time, China has experienced one of the greatest revivals in church history, with some eastern provinces experiencing continual growth for more than 30 years. Despite these great developments, hundreds of millions of Han Chinese today have yet to hear the name of Christ. A very wide range of estimates exist for the number of Christians in China today, from a lowest figure of 13.7 million,[3] to widely used but unsupported figures of 90 to 110 million.[4] We believe there are between 40 and 50 million Mandarin-speaking Chinese believers in China today.[5]

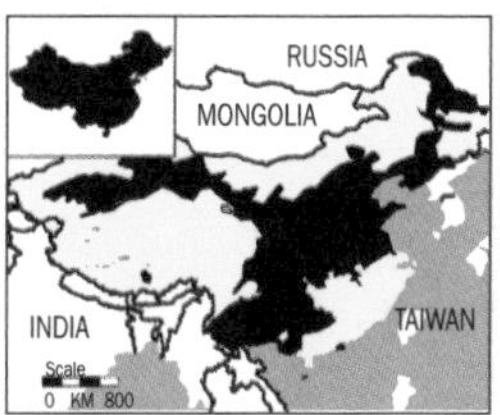

Population in China:
692,188,658 (1990)
783,300,200 (2000)
884,762,200 (2010)
Location: Every Province
Religion: No Religion
Christians: 45,000,000

Overview of the Mandarin Chinese

Countries: China, Taiwan, Malaysia, Singapore, Indonesia, USA, Laos, and dozens of other countries around the world

Pronunciation: "Poo-tong-hwa"

Other Names: Mandarin, Pei, Northern Chinese, Guoyu, Putonghua, Potinhua, Beijinghua, Qotong, Hoton, Guanhua

Population Source: 701,116,436 (1990 census);[6] Out of a total Han population of 1,042,482,187 (1990 census)

Location: Most of China

Status: Officially included under Han Chinese

Language: Chinese, Mandarin

Dialects (62): In 8 main dialect clusters[7]

Religion: No Religion, Daoism, Buddhism, Christianity

Christians: 45,000,000

Scripture: Bible 1874; New Testament 1857; Portions 1864

***Jesus* film:** Available

Gospel Recordings: Mandarin #00037; Yunnanese #00241; Chinese: Sichuan #04837 Chinese: Zhangye; Guiliu

Christian Broadcasting: Available (FEBC, TWR)

ROPAL code: CHN00

Status of Evangelization

A = Have never heard the gospel
B = Were evangelized but did not become Christians
C = Are adherents to any form of Christianity

Han Chinese, Min Bei 汉，闽北

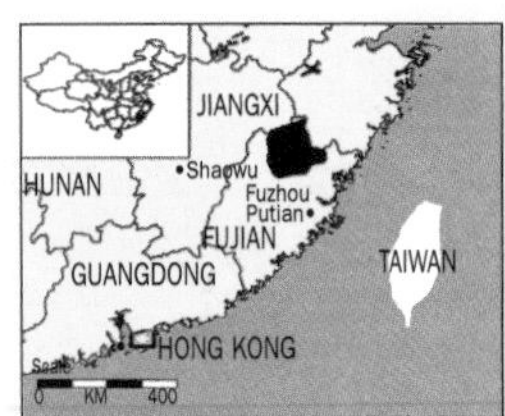

Population in China:
2,191,000 (1987)
2,561,300 (2000)
2,894,200 (2010)
Location: Fujian
Religion: No Religion
Christians: 100,000

Overview of the Min Bei

Countries: China, Malaysia, Brunei, Indonesia

Pronunciation: "Min-Bay"

Other Names: Northern Min, Min Pei

Population Source: 2,191,000 (1987 *LAC*); Out of a total Han population of 1,042,482,187 (1990 census); Also in Malaysia, Brunei and Indonesia

Location: *NE Fujian:* North and south of the Min River including Fuging, Gutian, Fu'an, and Shouning

Status: Officially included under Han Chinese

Language: Chinese, Min Bei

Dialects: 0

Religion: No Religion, Daoism, Christianity

Christians: 100,000

Scripture: Bible 1905; New Testament 1856; Portions 1852

***Jesus* film:** Available

Gospel Recordings: None

Christian Broadcasting: None

ROPAL code: MNP00

Status of Evangelization

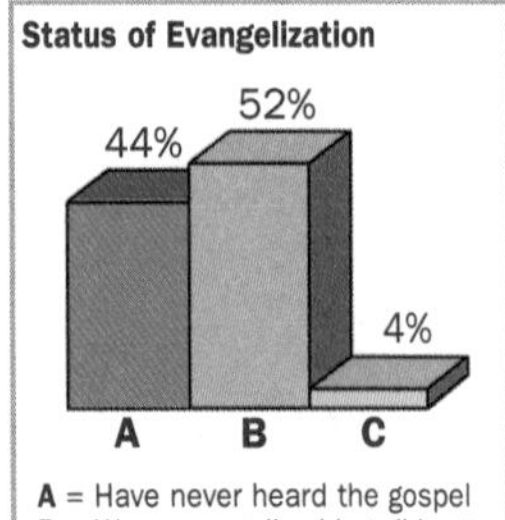

A = Have never heard the gospel
B = Were evangelized but did not become Christians
C = Are adherents to any form of Christianity

Paul Hattaway

Location: A 1987 study listed a population of 2,191,000 Min Bei speakers in China.[1] Other publications have listed a much higher figure of 10.29 million Min Bei,[2] but this figure includes the Min Dong group who have been profiled separately. The Min Bei live in eight cities and counties in the northwestern part of Fujian Province.

Identity: The Min Bei, or Northern Min, are included as part of the Han Chinese nationality by the Chinese authorities.

Language: Min Bei is one of five distinct languages spoken by the Min Chinese in Fujian. Other scholars divide the Min into "nine inherently unintelligible varieties."[3]

History: *The Jin Dynasty (AD 265–420):* The Jin Dynasty was a period of conflict and disunity in China. The Western Jin capital of Luoyang fell to Xiongnu horsemen in AD 306. Xiongnu was a general name given to non-Chinese barbarians to the north and west — the forefathers of the present-day Turks and Mongols. This resulted in "150 years of bloodshed as competing non-Han tribes vied for absolute power."[4] China was once again divided, and the tribes contained within its borders were at enmity.

Customs: The Han Chinese group expanded rapidly as it came into contact with other ethnic groups, conquered them culturally, and assimilated their populations into its own. One historian notes, "In 1500 BC there was no China, and there were no Chinese. The area that is now China was then inhabited by a great number of tribes with different cultures. Though the majority of them belonged to one or another branch of the Mongoloid race, other races were represented. There was no great man who created the first Chinese empire; it grew out of a long, slow process of assimilation and integration over centuries."[5]

Religion: In ancient times the Chinese emperor offered annual sacrifices to Shang Di, the Heavenly Emperor. This has led some to believe the ancient Chinese worshiped the Creator God. The emperor recited: "Of old in the beginning, there was the great chaos, without form and dark. The five elements (planets) had not begun to evolve, nor the sun and moon to shine. In the midst thereof there existed neither form nor sound. You, O spiritual Sovereign, came forth in your presidency, and first did divide the grosser part from the purer. You made heaven; You made earth, You made man. All things with their reproducing power got their being."[6]

Christianity: When Marco Polo arrived in today's Fujian Province, he encountered many Christian communities along the coastal areas. The believers in Fuzhou asked Marco Polo's uncles for advice as to what they should do to gain freedom to worship. They told the Christians to contact the Nestorian Metropolitan in Beijing, "Explain to him your state, that he may come to know you and you may be able freely to keep your religion and rule."[7] The New Testament was translated into the Min Bei language in 1934.[8] The *Jesus* film is also available in Min Bei.

Han Chinese, Min Dong 汉，闽东

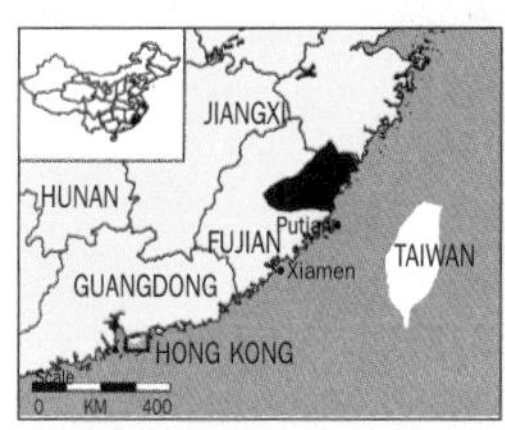

Population in China:
7,526,000 (1987)
8,797,900 (2000)
9,941,600 (2010)
Location: Fujian
Religion: No Religion
Christians: 400,000

Overview of the Min Dong

Countries: China, Indonesia, Singapore, Brunei, Thailand, Malaysia

Pronunciation: "Min-Dong"

Other Names: Min Dong, Eastern Min

Population Source: 7,526,000 (1987 *LAC*); Out of a total Han population of 1,042,482,187 (1990 census); 20,000 in Indonesia (1982); 15,000 in Singapore (1985); 6,000 in Brunei (1979); Also in Thailand and Malaysia

Location: *NE Fujian:* From Fu'an to Fuzhou City

Status: Officially included under Han Chinese

Language: Chinese, Min Dong

Dialects (3): Houguan, Funing, Manhua

Religion: No Religion, Buddhism, Daoism, Christianity

Christians: 400,000

Scripture: Bible 1884; New Testament 1856; Portions 1852

***Jesus* film:** None

Gospel Recordings: Foochow Colloquial Chinese #00113

Christian Broadcasting: None

ROPAL code: CDO00

Status of Evangelization

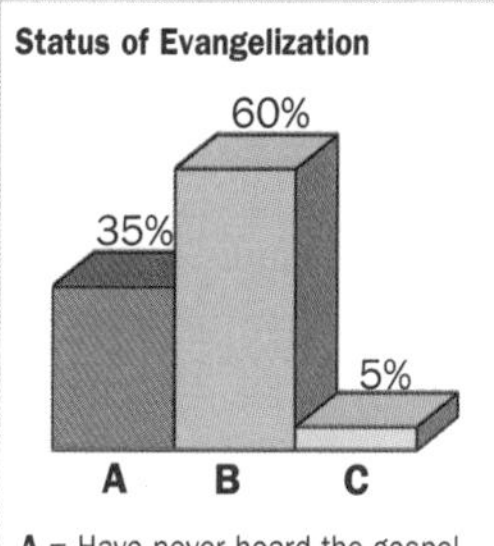

A = Have never heard the gospel
B = Were evangelized but did not become Christians
C = Are adherents to any form of Christianity

Location: More than eight million Han Chinese in Fujian Province speak the Min Dong — or Eastern Min — language. It is spoken by people living in 19 cities and counties of Fujian, ranging from the town of Fu'an in northeastern Fujian to the large city of Fuzhou on the coast. Min Dong speakers are also scattered throughout Southeast Asia.

Identity: The Min Dong are part of the Min group of languages which are distinct from Mandarin and other Chinese varieties.

Language: The different Min vernaculars "seem to incorporate remnants of Sinitic offshoots that predate the Sui-Tang era [AD 589]. They may represent variations as old as the Han Dynasty itself — language forms set in place... during the Jin [AD 265–420]."[1]

History: *The Southern and Northern Dynasties (420–589):* China was reeling under the burden of war and had divided into two ruling kingdoms. Both the southern and northern kingdoms at this time were actually ruled by several different dynasties. In the fifth century the Tuoba tribe defeated all its opposition in the northern kingdom. New rulers solidified authority by introducing a land reform movement. Buddhism, introduced from India, flourished during this period.

Customs: Many Min Dong Chinese living along the coast are fishermen, earning their income from the bounty of the Taiwan Strait.

Religion: In the ancient past the Chinese appear to have had a sense of love, kinship, and filial feeling for Shang Di, the Creator God. Each year the emperor gave the following recitation as he sacrificed at the Temple of Heaven: "You hear us and regard us as a Father. I, your child, dull and unenlightened, am unable to show forth my dutiful feeling. Your sovereign goodness is infinite. As a potter, You have made all living things. Your sovereign goodness is infinite. Great and small are sheltered (by your love). With great kindness You did bear with us, and not withstanding our demerits, do grant us life and prosperity."[2]

Christianity: Generally speaking, the Min Dong have proven more receptive to Christianity than Chinese in other parts of the country. In the thirteenth century Marco Polo came across a large body of believers in Fugiu [now Fuzhou City]. "They had books... found to be the words of the Psalter.... And thus they had in a certain temple of theirs three figures painted, who had been three apostles of the seventy who had gone preaching throughout the world, and they said that those had taught their ancestors in that religion long ago, and that that faith had already been preserved among them for seven hundred years, but for a long time they had been without teaching and so were ignorant of the chief things."[3] Dr. Nathan Site, an American Methodist, arrived in Fujian in 1866. He was the first missionary to Fujian in the modern Protestant era. Today there are at least 400,000 Min Dong believers, including more than 100,000 in Fuqing County alone.[4]

Paul Hattaway

Han Chinese, Min Nan 汉，闽南

Location: The Min Nan language — also called *Hokkien* — is spoken by approximately 30 million people along China's eastern and southern coasts. The majority of Min Nan speakers live in Fujian Province where they inhabit 53 cities and counties. Others are located in Guangdong, Hong Kong, Zhejiang, and Jiangxi.

Identity: The Min Nan, or Southern Min, are the largest Min language group. During the tenth century, the northern part of the Kingdom of Min in Fujian split off to form the Kingdom of Yin. The line between the Min Nan and Min Bei languages today very closely follows the border between those two kingdoms.

Language: The Min Nan language is divided into several related elements. Linguists have traditionally separated the Amoy and Shantou (previously called *Swatow*) dialects as distinct languages. Hainanese is also related to Min Nan. Amoy and Taiwanese are easily intelligible with each other, while Shantou and Amoy "have very difficult intelligibility."[1]

History: *The Sui Dynasty* (AD *589–618):* The Sui Dynasty lasted only 29 years but paved the way for the institutions and laws used by following dynasties. The Tuoba Emperor Yang Jian was known as the *Cultivated Emperor* because of the land reforms undertaken during his reign. It is during his rule that the Grand Canal was constructed — an engineering feat of staggering proportions. Three disastrous military defeats in northern Korea, which cost massive amounts of money and lives, hastened the collapse of Sui rule.

Customs: For the Chinese, having *guanxi* "connections" is very important. Favors are given between willing parties and reciprocated in times of mutual need.

Religion: The Chinese have historically treated Christianity with suspicion. In 1724 Emperor Yungcheng told Jesuit missionaries, "You wish to make the Chinese Christians, and this is what your law demands, I know it very well. But what in that case would become of us? The subjects of your kings! The Christians whom you make recognize no authority but you; in times of trouble they listen to no other voice. I know well enough that there is nothing to fear at present; but when your ships shall be coming by thousands and tens of thousands, then, indeed, we may have some disturbances."[2]

Paul Hattaway

Christianity: A large Christian community existed in Zaitun (now Quanzhou City) in the early 1300s. A Franciscan cathedral was constructed from gifts received from an Armenian woman living in the city.[3] Bishop Andrew of Zaitun wrote in 1326, "We are able to preach freely and unmolested.... Of idolaters a very large number are baptized, but having been baptized they do not walk straight in the path of Christianity."[4] There are more than one million Min Nan believers in China today. In 1933 the Bible was translated into Min Nan. In 1986, 50,000 hymnals were printed, using the characteristic Amoy script, and distributed.[5]

Population in China:
26,265,000 (1984)
31,728,100 (2000)
35,852,800 (2010)
Location: Fujian, Guangdong, Hong Kong, Zhejiang, Jiangxi
Religion: No Religion
Christians: 1,200,000

Overview of the Min Nan

Countries: China, Taiwan, Malaysia, Singapore, Thailand[6]

Pronunciation: "Min-Nahn"

Other Names: Min Nan, Southern Min, Amoy, Hokkien, Hoklo

Population Source: 25,725,000 (1992 B. Grimes – 1984 figure);[7] 14,177,800 in Taiwan; 1,948,581 in Malaysia; 1,170,000 in Singapore; 1,081,920 in Thailand; 700,000 in Indonesia; 493,500 in Philippines; 10,000 in Brunei

Location: *S Fujian; N Guangdong; Hong Kong; S Zhejiang; S Jiangxi*

Status: Officially included under Han Chinese

Language: Chinese, Min Nan

Dialects (8): Fujian, Chaoshan, Hainanese, Zhejiang, Pingyang, Yuhuan, Tongtou, Taishun

Religion: No Religion, Daoism, Buddhism, Ancestor Worship, Christianity

Christians: 1,200,000

Scripture: Bible 1933; New Testament 1896; Portions 1875

***Jesus* film:** Available

Gospel Recordings: Amoy #00185

Christian Broadcasting: Available in Amoy, Swatow (FEBC, TWR)

ROPAL code: CFR00

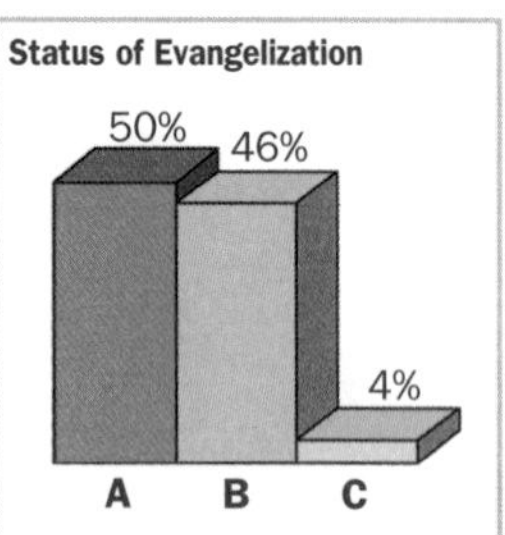

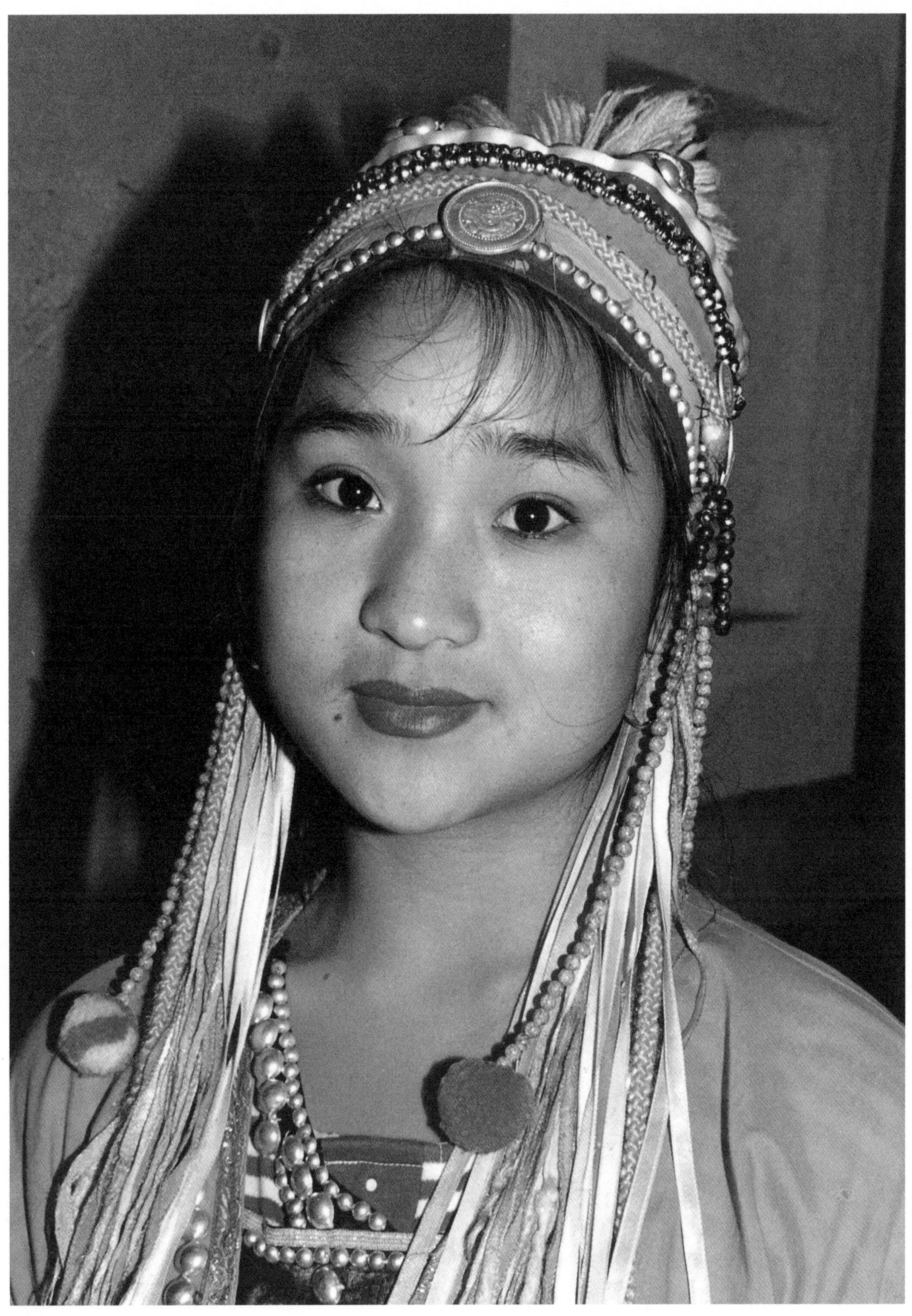

55. More than 1.5 million people belong to the *Hani* nationality, which consists of more than a dozen distinct tribes. [Paul Hattaway]

56

57

58

59

56. The 5,500-strong *Hezhen* minority live in the extreme northeast of China bordering Siberia. In the past they were known as the *Fish Skin Tatars*. All their clothing — and even their shoes — were made from fish skin. [Paul Hattaway]
57. The spectacular dress of the small *Hmong Dou* ethnic group; Bijie, Guizhou. [Michael Johnson]
58. An intricately embroidered apron of the *Hua Miao*. [Michael Johnson]
59. *Horned Miao* women wear as many as 30 layers of skirts and have large wooden horns attached to their heads. [Michael Johnson]

60

61

62

63

60. *Hmong Daw* (*White Miao*) girls, southern Yunnan. [Overseas Missionary Fellowship]
61. *Hmong Daw* lady from Jinping, Yunnan. Thousands of Hmong Daw in both China and Vietnam have turned to Christ in recent years because of gospel radio broadcasts in their language. [*Miao Messenger*]
62. The extraordinary costume of the *Hmong Leng*. It often takes up to ten years work for a girl to complete her dress. [International Mission Board]
63. A *Hmong Njua* girl, southern Yunnan. [Paul Hattaway]

64

65

66

67

64. Three *Hmu* women on the banks of the Qingshui river, Guizhou. [*Miao Messenger*]
65. The 4000 *Hmong Vron* are also known as the *Long Horn Miao*. The women tie wooden horns into their hair. They also wrap large quantities of hair around the horns. The hair comes from dozens of deceased relatives and is passed down through the generations. [Robert Sussland]
66. Even the little ones are arrayed in their best clothing during *Hmu* festivals and special occassions, nothern Guangxi. [both by *Miao Messenger*]
67. *Northern Hmu* woman in ceremonial costume; Shidong, Guizhou. [*Miao Messenger*]

Han Chinese, Min Zhong 汉，闽中

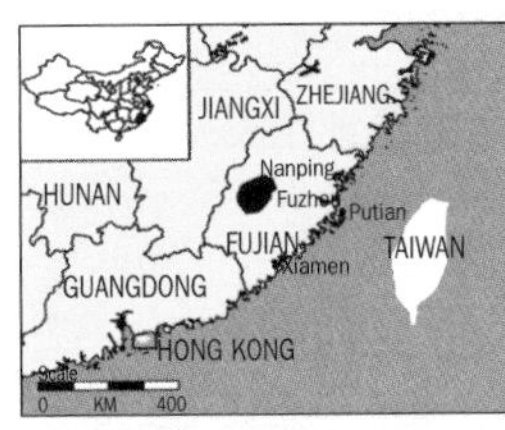

Population in China:
683,000 (1987)
798,400 (2000)
902,200 (2010)
Location: Fujian
Religion: No Religion
Christians: 35,000

Overview of the Min Zhong

Countries: China

Pronunciation: "Min-Jong"

Other Names: Central Min

Population Source:
683,000 (1987 *LAC*);
Out of a total Han population of 1,042,482,187 (1990 census)

Location: *Central Fujian:* Around Yong'an, Sanming, and Shaxian townships

Status: Officially included under Han Chinese

Language: Chinese, Min Zhong

Dialects: 0

Religion: No Religion, Buddhism, Daoism, Christianity

Christians: 35,000

Scripture: None

***Jesus* film:** None

Gospel Recordings: None

Christian Broadcasting: None

ROPAL code: CZO00

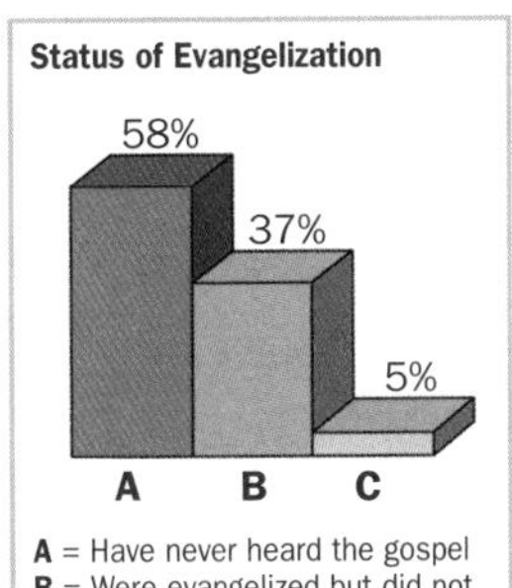

Paul Hattaway

Location: The Min Zhong (or Central Min) numbered 683,000 speakers in 1987, making them one of the smallest of the Chinese language groups in the country. Min Zhong is spoken in the central part of Fujian Province, especially around the towns of Yong'an, Sanming, and Shaxian.

Identity: The Min Zhong are part of the Min group of Chinese languages, all of which are considered part of China's Han nationality.

Language: Fujian has been called "The province of a hundred dialects." Missionary J. E. Walker, after an 1878 trip through Fujian, wrote, "What a Babel of brogues, and dialects there is among those wild mountains! A native can hardly pass the limits of his own village but his speech will betray him.... The tones seem utterly lawless. They shoot up to the sky, then plunge into the bowels of the earth, they stiffen straight out, then double up and twist about; they sing, cry, whine, groan, scold, plead."[1]

History: *The Tang Dynasty (618–907):* The Tang Dynasty is considered the most auspicious and glittering period in history by the Chinese. China was again united, and a strong military extended China's borders to its largest extent: encompassing parts of present-day Central Asia, Russia, Myanmar, Vietnam, Tibet, Nepal, Bhutan, and northern India. For the first time China was divided into 300 prefectures and 1,500 counties, which mirror the present boundaries remarkably closely. Following the collapse of the Tang Dynasty in 907, China again entered into a period of discord and war.

Customs: The Grand Canal, constructed over a period of 1,000 years, linked four of China's major rivers: the Yangtze, Yellow, Huai, and Qiantang. Between Beijing and Hangzhou the canal measured 1,800 kilometers (1,110 mi.). It opened up China's trade and caused the inland provinces to flourish.

Religion: Recently there has been speculation claiming the wise men who visited Bethlehem may have come from China. The Chinese were using the compass 1,000 years before the birth of Christ. Maps have been found from that time which show a clear passage from China to the Mediterranean Sea. Ancient Chinese astrologers discovered a star they called the "King Star." "They believed whenever this star appeared, a king was born. Chinese history says it was at its most brilliant peak during the Han Dynasty [time of Christ]."[2] One of the main astrologers during this period was Liu Shang, who disappeared from China for over two years at the time of Christ's birth.

Christianity: An eighth century Chinese Nestorian church leader claimed the Magi, returning from Bethlehem, had brought the first news of the Savior to China.[3] By the thirteenth century, Christians numbered in the hundreds of thousands throughout China and Mongolia. In 1330 the Nestorians were described as having "very handsome and devoutly ordered churches with crosses and images in honour of God and the saints. They hold sundry offices under the Emperor and have great privileges from him."[4] Today about 5% of Min Zhong Chinese profess to follow Christ.

Han Chinese, Pinghua 汉, 平话

Paul Hattaway

Location: More than two million speakers of Pinghua Chinese inhabit the Guangxi Zhuang Autonomous Region in southern China. They live primarily along the major traffic routes between Lingchuan (north of Guilin) and Nanning in the south, especially those following the railway line. "A northern subgroup (Guibei) can be found extending from Guilin, through Yangshuo and Pingle, to Fuchuan, Zhongshan and Hexian."[1]

Identity: Although the Pinghua Chinese are counted as part of the Han nationality, their language is clearly distinct from all other varieties of Chinese.

Language: Pinghua is divided into two dialects: *Guibei* (Northern) and *Guinan* (Southern). These two dialects "show significant disparities, though there are a few common features."[2] The Northern dialect consists of only five tones, while the Southern dialect contains eight. One early visitor noted, "The dialect that results from this mixture of races is called *Pengwa*. A large proportion of the people... evidently do not speak Cantonese or Mandarin, or at any rate do not speak it freely."[3]

History: *The Song Dynasty (960–1279):* Zhao Kuangyin conquered more than a dozen regional kingdoms and assumed power in 959. The Song period is usually divided into the Northern Song (960–1126) ruled from Kaifeng City in Henan Province; and the Southern Song (1127–1279) which had Hangzhou in present-day Zhejiang as its capital. The northern state had fallen to Tibetan and Mongol kingdoms, who set up their own rule in the north, known as the Western Xia (1038–1227) and Jin (1115–1234) dynasties. The Song rulers were forced to relocate to Hangzhou. During this time, the world first learned about the mysteries and grandeur of China after explorers such as Marco Polo visited there.

Customs: Historical records suggest chopsticks were not always used by the Chinese. In ancient times the Chinese used utensils similar to knives and forks, but after a prolonged period of famine, food was eaten in small pieces, and the use of chopsticks developed.

Religion: The Chinese *Book of History* mentions that at the dawn of Chinese history in the days of Yao and Shuen, 2,200 BC, a terrible inundation was recorded that had once desolated the land. "In their vast extent the waters embrace the mountains and over-top the hills, threatening heaven with their floods."[4] The Chinese have now reduced these accounts to merely a bad flood of the Yellow River.

Christianity: Guangxi, which means "vast west," has traditionally been one of the parts of China most neglected by missionaries. In the 1920s workers lamented that there were "areas inhabited by [minority] tribes where no Christian worker would be familiar with the languages spoken and where the country has not as yet been explored."[5] Today no more than 0.3% of Guangxi's 45 million inhabitants claim to be Christians. Protestants in Guangxi number between 50,000[6] and 90,000,[7] in addition to 30,000 Catholics.[8]

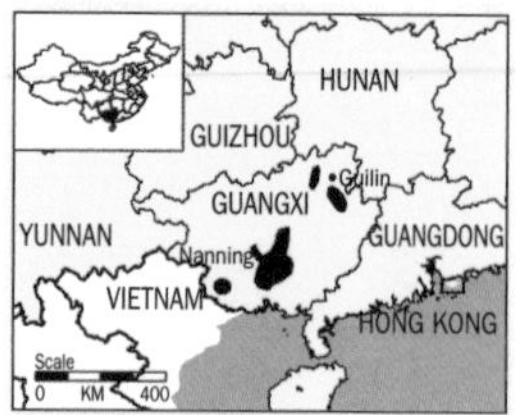

Population in China:
2,000,000 (1987)
2,338,000 (2000)
2,642,000 (2010)
Location: Guangxi
Religion: No Religion
Christians: 8,000

Overview of the Pinghua Chinese

Countries: China

Pronunciation: "Ping-hwa"

Other Names: Pinghua, Ping, Pinghwa, Penghua, Penhwa, Pengwa

Population Source: More than 2,000,000 (1987 *LAC*);
Out of a total Han population of 1,042,482,187 (1990 census)

Location: *Guangxi:* Between Lingchuan and Nanning

Status: Officially included under Han Chinese

Language: Chinese, Pinghua

Dialects (2): Guibei, Guinan

Religion: No Religion, Buddhism, Christianity, Daoism

Christians: 8,000

Scripture: None

***Jesus* film:** None

Gospel Recordings: None

Christian Broadcasting: None

ROPAL code: None

Status of Evangelization

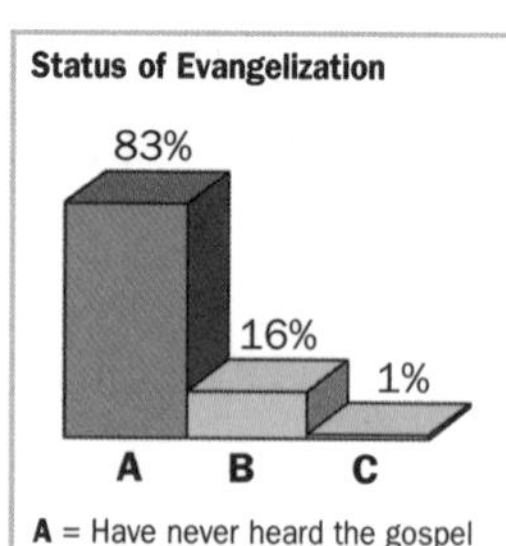

A = Have never heard the gospel
B = Were evangelized but did not become Christians
C = Are adherents to any form of Christianity

Han Chinese, Puxian 汉(莆田)

Location: Approximately two and a half million Puxian Chinese densely inhabit a relatively small area in eastern Fujian Province. The Puxian take their name from nicknames of the two counties they primarily inhabit: *Pu*tian and neighboring *Xian*you. Xianyou is also under the jurisdiction of Putian City. The Puxian language is spoken in an oval valley about 55 kilometers (34 mi.) wide and 100 kilometers (62 mi.) long.

Identity: Puxian people are often stereotyped by other Chinese as heroic and athletic people. Many of China's best track and field stars come from Putian.[1] In Southeast Asia the Puxian are known as the *Hinghua.*

Language: A Chinese proverb states for "every three *li* [about one mile], the dialect is different." The Puxian language is one such example of the linguistic diversity among the world's largest race. Puxian is lexically quite close to Min Nan, "but phonetically, it appears to be closer to Min Dong.... This group can be thus regarded as transitional between the Min Nan and Min Dong groups."[2]

History: *The Yuan (Mongol) Dynasty (1271–1368):* In 1213 the Mongols, led by Genghis Khan, broke through the Great Wall which had been designed to prevent them from entering China. The Mongols swept all opposition before them, winning more territory than any other kingdom in the history of world. Their realm stretched from Southeast Asia to Hungary in Europe. The Mongol armies were brutal, killing and plundering unmercifully wherever they went. One writer at the time recounted, "If anyone were to say that at no time since the creation of man by the great God had the world experienced anything like it, he would only be telling the truth.... The Mongols... spared none. They killed women, men and children, ripped open the bodies of the pregnant and slaughtered the unborn."[3]

Paul Hattaway

Customs: Chinese leaders have long been diligent in numbering and classifying the people of China. Although vital statistics of the population date back as far as the Xia Dynasty (2200–1700 BC), the first recorded nationwide census in China was conducted in 789 BC under the reign of Emperor Zhou Xuan.

Religion: The implementation of Communist policies resulted in a ban on all religious activity across China between 1966 and 1976. Thousands of temples, mosques, and churches were smashed to the ground, and believers were forced to practice their faith in secrecy.

Christianity: The Nestorian church disappeared from China in the fourteenth century, leaving almost no trace of its existence. The heads of 70,000 Christians were piled on a heap in Xian around 1300.[4] "This was the second disappearance of Christianity from China, and when it returned two hundred years later, the next wave of Christians seemed largely unaware that there had ever been Christians there before them."[5] Today approximately 100,000 (4%) of the Puxian Chinese are Christians — including more than 30,000 in Putian City alone,[6] and 90,000 in the whole of Putian County.[7]

JIANGXI ZHEJIANG HUNAN FUJIAN Fuzhou Putian GUANGDONG Xiamen TAIWAN HONG KONG Scale 0 KM 400

Population in China:
2,253,000 (1987)
2,633,700 (2000)
2,976,100 (2010)
Location: Fujian
Religion: No Religion
Christians: 100,000

Overview of the Puxian Chinese

Countries: China, Singapore, Malaysia

Pronunciation: "Pu-shee-un"

Other Names: Putian, Pu-Xian, Xinghua, Hinghua

Population Source:
2,253,000 (1987 *LAC*);
Out of a total Han population of 1,042,482,187 (1990 census);
6,000 in Singapore (1985);
Also in Malaysia

Location: *E Fujian:* Putian and Xianyou counties

Status: Officially included under Han Chinese

Language: Chinese, Puxian

Dialects (2): Putian, Xianyou

Religion: No Religion, Buddhism, Ancestor Worship, Christianity, Daoism

Christians: 100,000

Scripture: Bible 1912; New Testament 1900; Portions 1892

***Jesus* film:** None

Gospel Recordings: Hing Hwa #00421

Christian Broadcasting: None

ROPAL code: CPX00

Status of Evangelization

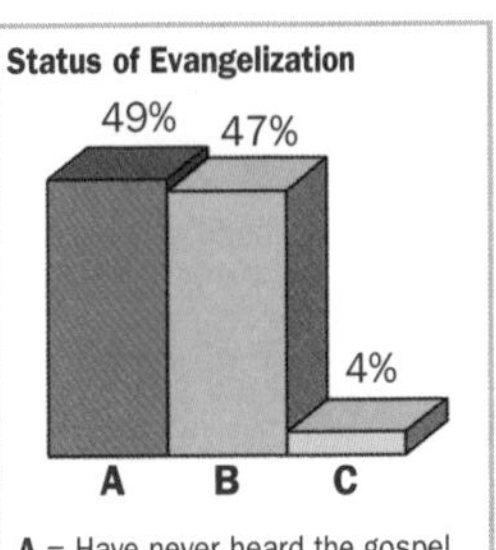

A = Have never heard the gospel
B = Were evangelized but did not become Christians
C = Are adherents to any form of Christianity

Han Chinese, Shaojiang 汉，邵江

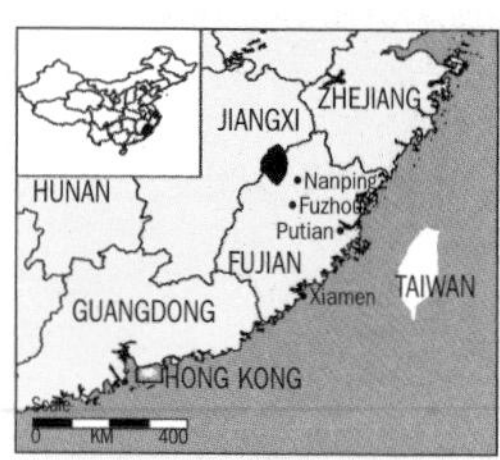

Population in China:
745,000 (1987)
870,900 (2000)
984,100 (2010)
Location: Fujian
Religion: No Religion
Christians: 30,000

Overview of the Shaojiang Chinese

Countries: China

Pronunciation: "Shaow-jung"

Other Names: Shaojiang

Population Source:
745,000 (1987 *LAC*);
Out of a total Han population of 1,042,482,187 (1990 census)

Location: *NW Fujian:* Shaowu, Guangze, Jiangle, and Shunchang

Status: Officially included under Han Chinese

Language: Chinese, Shaojiang

Dialects: 0

Religion: No Religion, Ancestor Worship, Buddhism, Daoism, Christianity

Christians: 30,000

Scripture: None

***Jesus* film:** None

Gospel Recordings: None

Christian Broadcasting: None

ROPAL code: None

Status of Evangelization

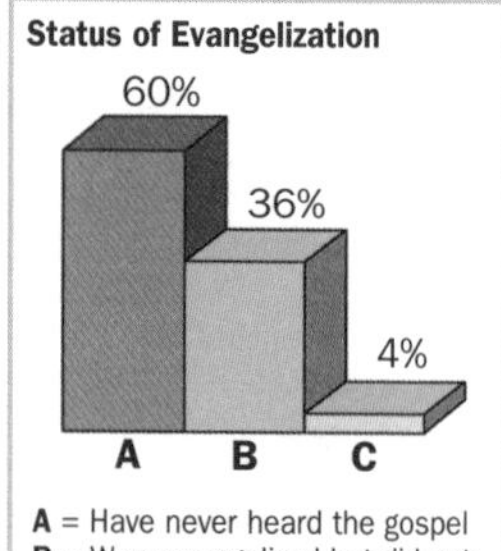

A = Have never heard the gospel
B = Were evangelized but did not become Christians
C = Are adherents to any form of Christianity

Location: A 1987 study listed 745,000 members of the Shaojiang Chinese language group.[1] Because of the careful implementation of China's one-child policy, the Shaojiang population growth has slowed in recent years. Their numbers are expected to be approximately 870,000 by the turn of the century and 984,000 by the year 2010. Compared to other Chinese language groups, the Shaojiang live in a relatively small geographical area. The majority are located in Shaowu, Guangze, Jiangle, and Shunchang counties. All four counties are situated west of the Futunxi River in northwest Fujian Province.

Identity: The members of the Shaojiang Chinese language group are considered part of the Han Chinese nationality, but they speak a language not understood by any other Chinese people.

Language: Shaojiang is part of the Min language group, which contains several distinct Chinese varieties. Most Shaojiang speakers are also able to speak Mandarin Chinese.

History: *The Ming Dynasty (1368–1644):* Until 1420 the Ming Dynasty rulers used Nanjing as its capital, until Yongle, the second Ming emperor, re-established the capital in Beijing, where it has remained until today. China slowly found its feet again after the violent reign of the Mongols. The first Ming emperor, Hongwu, is remembered for putting to death 10,000 scholars and their families in two purges. For the first time, China became a maritime nation. Zhang He "undertook seven great expeditions that took him and a huge fleet to Southeast Asia, Persia, Arabia and even eastern Africa."[2] Corruption, famine, and costly wars against the Japanese brought the country to bankruptcy and sparked an uprising that toppled the government.

Customs: The various peoples of Fujian were once considered extremely savage. Marco Polo, describing his travel through the interior of Fujian, wrote, "The people in this part of the country are addicted to eating human flesh, esteeming it more delicate than any other.... When they advance to combat they throw loose their hair about their ears, and they paint their faces a bright blue color.... They are a most savage race of men, inasmuch that when they slay their enemies in battle, they are anxious to drink their blood, and afterwards they devour their flesh."[3]

Religion: Many elderly Shaojiang follow Buddhist and Daoist teachings, while most Shaojiang youth are atheists.

Christianity: The first Catholic missionary in China was John of Montecorvino, who constructed a magnificent church in Beijing in 1299.[4] The jealous Nestorians called John a "spy, magician, and deceiver of men."[5] By 1305 he had won 6,000 converts. John claimed, "and if not for the above-named slanders I should have baptized more than 30,000."[6] One historian states, "Almost single-handedly [John] established the Roman Catholic faith in the capital of the mightiest empire of his time."[7] At the time of his death in 1328, there were 100,000 Catholic converts across China.[8]

Paul Hattaway

Han Chinese, Shaozhou 汉(韶州)

Paul Hattaway

Location: Approximately 930,000 speakers of Shaozhou Tuhua — or "Shaozhou native speech" — live in northern Guangdong Province, and possibly in the adjacent areas of Hunan and Jiangxi. The Shaozhou are spread across eight counties of northern Guangdong: Lianxian, Liannan, Lechang, Ruyuan, Qujiang, Shaoguan, Renhua, and Nanxiong.

Identity: The northern Guangdong area has been a crossroads for migrating peoples through the centuries. This has forced a wide range of influences upon the Shaozhou Chinese, resulting in their language being distinct from other Han groups.

Language: This century, Shaozhou speakers "have been swamped by Hakka speakers as the latter continue to migrate into the area."[1] There are many variants of Shaozhou, "each differing significantly from the others.... Other varieties of native dialects are also found in Jianghua, Jiangyong and Daoxian in the neighboring province of Hunan. Further studies are required to determine whether these dialects are related to Shaozhou Tuhua."[2]

History: *The Taiping Rebellion (1851–1864):* The Taiping Rebellion started in 1851 when the Manchu government tried to ban a movement in the south of China headed by Hong Xiuquan. Hong believed he was the brother of Jesus Christ and gathered a large number of followers with claims that he was on a mission from God to build a "Heavenly Kingdom of Great Peace." They smashed Buddhist and Daoist temples and abolished slavery and foot-binding. By 1853 they had captured the south of China and had grown to an army of 600,000 men and 500,000 women. The army were only allowed to adhere to the Taiping version of Christianity and were not allowed to smoke, drink, or gamble. In 1864 a multinational army attacked the Taiping base at Nanjing, completely slaughtering the rebels and abruptly ending the movement.

Customs: The Shaozhou Chinese are a part of the huge Han nationality. The Han generally consider themselves culturally superior to the minority groups of China. One government publication arrogantly points out, "The Han... are more developed than the minorities in the political, economic and cultural spheres."[3]

Religion: In 1900 many Chinese, outraged by foreign domination of its ports, caused the antiforeigner Boxer Rebellion to break out. Missionaries and their Chinese converts were especially targeted. In Shanxi alone, 159 missionaries were massacred.[4]

Christianity: In addition to the hundreds of foreign missionaries killed by the Boxers, some 32,000 Chinese Christians were butchered.[5] A *London Times* reporter in Beijing described the carnage: "As darkness came on, the most awful cries were heard in the city, most demonical and unforgettable, the cries of the Boxers — '*Sha kuei-tzu*' (kill the devils) — mingled with the shrieks of the victims and the groans of the dying. For Boxers were sweeping through the city, massacring the native Christians and burning them alive in their homes."[6]

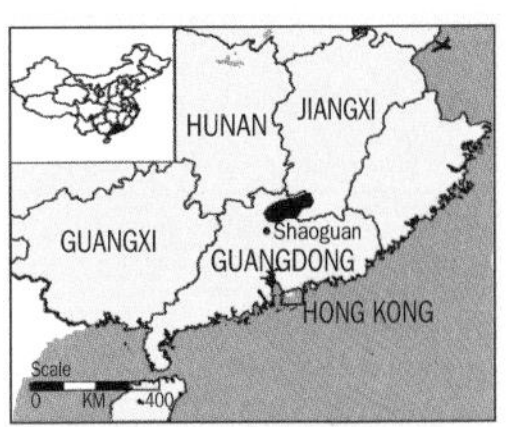

Population in China:
800,000 (1987)
935,200 (2000)
1,056,800 (2010)
Location: Guangdong
Religion: Daoism
Christians: 8,000

Overview of the Shaozhou Chinese

Countries: China

Pronunciation: "Shaow-joe"

Other Names: Shaozhou Tuhua, Shaozhou

Population Source: 800,000 (1987 *LAC*); Out of a total Han population of 1,042,482,187 (1990 census)

Location: *N Guangdong:* Lianxian, Liannan, Lechang, Ruyuan, Qujiang, Shaoguan, Renhua, and Nanxiong counties; Possibly also in *Jiangxi* and *Hunan* provinces

Status: Officially included under Han Chinese

Language: Chinese, Shaozhou Tuhua

Dialects: 0

Religion: Daoism, No Religion, Ancestor Worship, Buddhism

Christians: 8,000

Scripture: None

***Jesus* film:** None

Gospel Recordings: None

Christian Broadcasting: None

ROPAL code: None

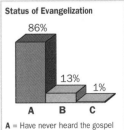

Status of Evangelization

	A	B	C
%	86%	13%	1%

A = Have never heard the gospel
B = Were evangelized but did not become Christians
C = Are adherents to any form of Christianity

Han Chinese, Waxiang 汉，瓦乡

Population in China:
300,000 (1995)
319,500 (2000)
361,000 (2010)
Location: Hunan
Religion: Animism
Christians: 500

Overview of the Waxiang Chinese

Countries: China

Pronunciation: "Wa-sheeung"

Other Names:
Waxianghua, Xianghua, Wogang

Population Source:
300,000 (1995 S. Milliken);
Out of a total Han population of 1,042,482,187 (1990 census)

Location: *W Hunan:* Yuanling, Chunxi, Jishou, Guzhang, and Dayong counties

Status: Officially included under Han Chinese

Language: Chinese, Xianghua

Dialects: 0

Religion:
Animism, No Religion, Daoism

Christians: 500

Scripture: None

***Jesus* film:** None

Gospel Recordings: None

Christian Broadcasting: None

ROPAL code: WXA00

Status of Evangelization

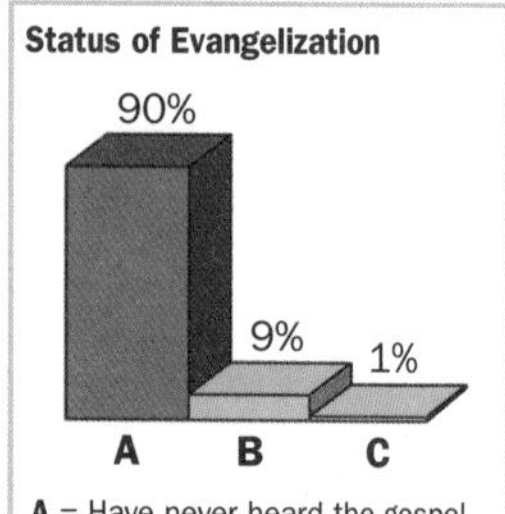

A = Have never heard the gospel
B = Were evangelized but did not become Christians
C = Are adherents to any form of Christianity

Paul Hattaway

Location: Approximately 320,000 speakers of the Waxiang language live scattered throughout an area of more than 6,000 square kilometers (2,340 sq. mi.) in western Hunan Province. The majority are located in the Wuling Mountains, including parts of Yuanling, Chunxi, Jishou, Guzhang, and Dayong counties.

Identity: Although officially considered part of the Han Chinese nationality, Waxiang may not even be a Chinese language. Little study has been conducted into Waxiang, but one scholar notes, "Some view it as a special variety of Chinese, others as a minority language, perhaps related to Miao."[1] It is possible that the Waxiang are a mixture of Miao and Chinese people who developed their own distinct characteristics after centuries of mutual contact.

Language: Waxiang differs greatly from both Mandarin and Hunanese (Xiang) Chinese. Neighboring Han, Miao, and Tujia do not understand Waxiang. In 1969 a Miao woman from the Waxiang region in Hunan tried to communicate with the Chinese authorities by using a unique script.[2]

History: *The Qing (Manchu) Dynasty (1644–1911):* The Manchus in the northeast took advantage of the peasant unrest throughout China and seized control of Beijing. Yet again, the Han Chinese majority were ruled by a neighboring minority tribe. It took a further four decades for the Manchu to take control of southern China. Today's Inner Mongolia, Tibet, and Xinjiang were all conquered and subdued, leading to ethnic unrest which persists to this day. The Manchu period witnessed the entrance of foreign powers into China and the seizing of key ports and regions. Hong Kong was taken by the British, Macau by the Portuguese, while the Dutch, Spanish, French, Japanese, and Russians all laid claim to parts of China. The Chinese consider the Manchu Dynasty one of the most humiliating of their long history.

Customs: Many of the customs of the more rural Waxiang are similar to those of the neighboring Ghao-Xong.

Religion: The majority of Waxiang practice animistic rituals. They appease spirits and ghosts who they believe dwell in their villages and influence their lives for good or for evil.

Christianity: There are few Christians among the Waxiang. The region has historically given a cold reception to those few missionaries who ventured into the Wuling Mountains. American Catholic priests, from the Blessed Gabriel Monastery in Massachusetts, USA, commenced work along the Hunan-Guizhou border in the 1920s. One early missionary reported, "The good work is moving but very slowly. The people are as hard as steel. They are eaten up both soul and body by the world, and do not seem to feel that there can be reality in anything beyond sense. To them our doctrine is foolishness, our talk jargon. We discuss and beat them in argument. We reason them into silence and shame; but the whole effort falls upon them like showers upon a sandy desert."[3]

Han Chinese, Wu 汉，吴

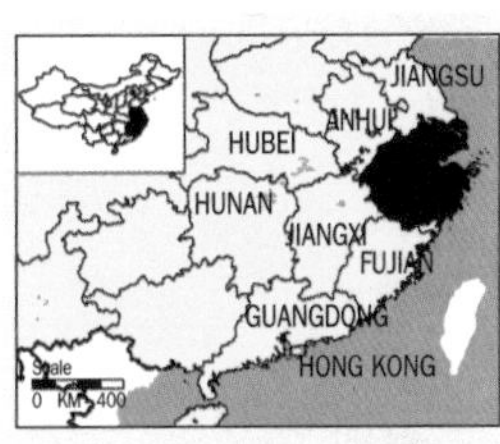

Population in China:
70,100,000 (1987)
81,947,000 (2000)
92,600,000 (2010)
Location: Zhejiang, Jiangsu, Shanghai, Jiangxi, Fujian, Anhui
Religion: No Religion
Christians: 4,000,000

Overview of the Wu Chinese

Countries: China

Pronunciation: "Woo"

Other Names: Wu, Shanghai, Shanghainese

Population Source: 70,100,000 (1987 *LAC*); Out of a total Han population of 1,042,482,187 (1990 census)

Location: *Zhejiang; S Jiangsu; Shanghai; Jiangxi; N Fujian; S Anhui*

Status: Officially included under Han Chinese

Language: Chinese, Wu

Dialects (14): Piling, Suhujia, Tiaoxi, Hangzhou, Linshao, Yongjiang, Taizhou, Oujiang, Wuzhou, Chuzhou, Longqu, Tongjing, Taiguo, Shiling

Religion: No Religion, Buddhism, Christianity

Christians: 4,000,000

Scripture: Bible 1908; New Testament 1868; Portions 1847

***Jesus* film:** Available

Gospel Recordings: Chinese: Wu #04694 Shanghai Chinese #00396

Christian Broadcasting: None

ROPAL code: WUU00

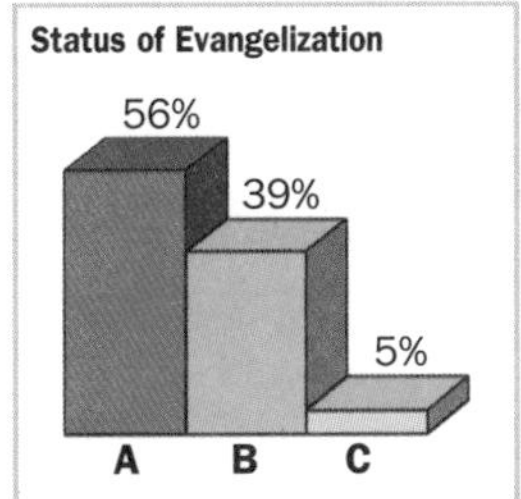

Location: The 1987 China Language Atlas listed 70.1 million speakers of the Wu Chinese language.[1] Wu is spoken over a widespread area of 137,500 square kilometers (53,600 sq. mi.) in six provinces of eastern China. The majority are located in Zhejiang Province (43 million by the year 2000), southern Jiangsu Province (19.3 million), and the city of Shanghai (13.9 million). Smaller numbers are also located in Jiangxi, northern Fujian, and southern Anhui provinces.

Identity: The Wu Chinese language is more commonly referred to as the Shanghai dialect, but in fact Wu is spoken in a far greater area than just Shanghai. The Wu are counted as part of the Han nationality.

Language: Wu consists of 14 dialects, all of which are very different from Mandarin Chinese. Most Wu, however, are bilingual in Mandarin because it has been used in all media and education for the past 40 years.

History: *The Republic of China (1911–1949):* Secret societies and triads were active throughout the Chinese countryside at the turn of the twentieth century. China was effectively run by local warlords. Discontent at foreign control over many parts of China led to the Boxer Rebellion in 1900, when more than 200 foreigners, mostly missionaries, were killed. The Boxers were themselves a secret society which originated in Shandong Province and stirred up anti-foreign sentiment throughout the land. In October 1911 Sun Yatsen set up the Republic of China and was promptly displaced as president by Yuan Shikai. Unrest in the countryside and economic chaos created a favorable environment for the Communist Party, headed by Mao Zedong. They won the hearts of China's oppressed peasants and waged a civil war against the Nationalists from 1927 to 1949. The Kuomintang army of the Nationalists were defeated and fled — along with the country's entire gold reserves — to Taiwan, from where they have claimed to be the rightful rulers of China until the present time.

Customs: In the 1990s the differences between China's poor and the wealthy reached epidemic proportions. In 1997 one magazine commented, "China has no shortage of workers who have reached the limit of their tolerance.... Widespread labour unrest doesn't just threaten economic reforms — it threatens the Party's hold on power."[2]

Religion: Most Wu Chinese do not practice any religion, although in recent years there has been widespread interest in the magical practice of Qi Gong.

Christianity: There were Nestorian churches in the region between Nanjing and Shanghai as early as AD 1279. At one time the Nestorians had seven monasteries in and around the city of Zhenjiang,[3] now in Jiangsu Province. In the 1800s almost all missionaries to China commenced their work in Shanghai, which was the first port of entry for foreigners. This has resulted in the region having the highest concentration of Christians in all of China today. The Wu number at least 4 million believers, including 2.5 million in Zhejiang[4] and 247,000 in Shanghai.[5]

Paul Hattaway

Han Chinese, Xiang 汉(湘)

Location: Approximately 35 million speakers of Xiang Chinese — or Hunanese — live in China.[1] The majority are located in Hunan Province. Others inhabit 20 counties of western Sichuan and parts of northern Guangxi and northern Guangdong provinces.

Identity: The Xiang are traditionally acknowledged as the most stubborn and proud of all Chinese peoples. "The people themselves... are the most clannish and conservative to be found in the whole empire, and have succeeded in keeping their province practically free from invasion by foreigners and even foreign ideas."[2]

Language: Xiang is a distinct Chinese language in transition. It is exposed to Mandarin from several directions. Hunanese women once possessed their own writing system. It was taught by women to women and could not be read by men.[3]

History: *The People's Republic of China (1949–):* The Communists seized control of China in 1949. Initial euphoria among the people soon vanished as famine, economic mismanagement, and the suppression of all opposition became the norm. The darkest period came between 1966 and 1976 when millions of innocent people were butchered in the name of progress. After Mao's death in 1976 a power struggle ensued. Deng Xiaoping, who stood alone with an agenda of economic reforms, took power and China gradually reopened to the outside world. A demonstration held in Tiananmen Square, Beijing, to demand political reform was forcefully broken up by the army on 4 June 1989. Fears that China would revert to the excesses of the 1960s and 1970s proved unfounded, however, and China continued to open up and become a thriving part of the world community throughout the 1990s.

Paul Hattaway

Customs: In 1911 the Xiang were described as "the best haters and best fighters in China. Long after the rest of the empire was open to missionary activity, Hunan kept its gates firmly closed against the foreigner."[4] The Xiang are renowned for their theaters and opera.

Religion: Recently there has been an upsurge in religious interest in Hunan, as people seek to fill the spiritual void in their hearts. "A monastery in Hunan... has witnessed tens of thousands of pilgrims arriving to worship the three 'gods' of Communist China — Chairman Mao, Zhou Enlai and Zhu De. This pilgrimage has set alarm bells ringing in the local government over the revival of superstition."[5]

Christianity: In 1861 Welsh missionary Griffith John met a Hunan military mandarin, who "boasted of the glory and martial courage of the Hunan men, and said there was no danger of their ever believing in Jesus or of His religion taking root there."[6] The pride of the Xiang has made them the most unreached of all Han Chinese peoples. Today only 80,000, or about 0.2%, of the Xiang are Christians. The entire Christian population of Hunan is numbered at no more than 120,000.[7] Because of internal strife, the Hunan church has been described as a "disaster area."[8]

HUBEI
ANHUI
HUNAN
FUJIAN
GUANGXI
GUANGDONG
HONG KONG
Scale
0 KM 400

Population in China:
30,850,000 (1987)
36,064,000 (2000)
40,752,000 (2010)
Location: Hunan, Sichuan, Guangxi, Guangdong
Religion: No Religion
Christians: 80,000

Overview of the Xiang Chinese

Countries: China

Pronunciation: "Sheeang"

Other Names: Hunanese, Hunan, Hsiang

Population Source: 30,850,000 (1987 *LAC*); Out of a total Han population of 1,042,482,187 (1990 census)

Location: *Hunan; Sichuan; Guangxi; Guangdong*

Status: Officially included under Han Chinese

Language: Chinese, Xiang

Dialects (9): Changsha, Changde, Xiangtan, Yiyang, Yueyang, Linxiang, Shaoyang, Yungshun, Shaungfeng

Religion: No Religion, Buddhism, Daoism, Ancestor Worship, Christianity

Christians: 80,000

Scripture: None

***Jesus* film:** Available

Gospel Recordings: None

Christian Broadcasting: None

ROPAL code: HSN00

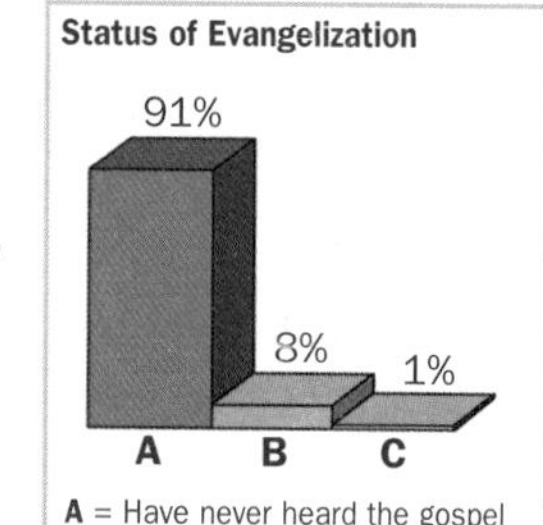

Han Chinese, Xunpu 汉(讯普)

Population in China:
1,000 (1997)
1,040 (2000)
1,170 (2010)
Location: Fujian
Religion: Daoism
Christians: 30

Overview of the Xunpu Chinese

Countries: China

Pronunciation: "Shun-poo"

Other Names: Xunpu, Xunbu

Population Source:
1,000 (1997 AMO);
Out of a total Han population of 1,042,482,187 (1990 census)

Location: *E Fujian:* Xunpu Village near Quanzhou City

Status: Officially included under Han Chinese

Language: Chinese, Min-Nan

Dialects: 0

Religion: Daoism, Ancestor Worship, No Religion, Christianity

Christians: 30

Scripture: None

***Jesus* film:** None

Gospel Recordings: None

Christian Broadcasting: None

ROPAL code: None

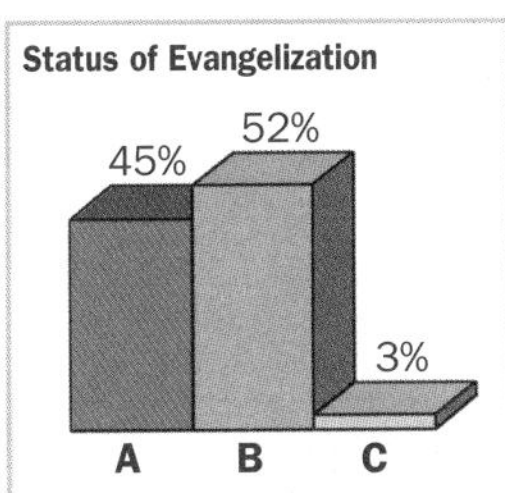

Location: Located just eight kilometers (five mi.) south of the large city of Quanzhou on the coast of Fujian Province, about 1,000 people live in the "tiny fishing village of Xunpu,"[1] situated near the Jinjiang River that runs through Quanzhou before emptying itself into the East China Sea.

Identity: Although officially considered part of the Han nationality, the inhabitants of Xunpu are the descendants of foreign immigrants. As one historian explains, "The nearby village of Yuanlu, which is a flower-growing center... was a private garden belonging to a superintendent of maritime trade at the time of the Yuan Dynasty (1271–1368). This person was an Arab by origin, whose name is rendered as Bu Shougeng. The interesting thing is that the surname of most of Yuanlu's residents is Bu, so there is a distinct possibility that they might be descended from this Yuan dynasty official."[2] Today the inhabitants of Xunpu consider themselves a distinct people. They wear spectacular, colorful costumes, keep their own traditions, and are called *Xunpu Ren* by other residents of the area.

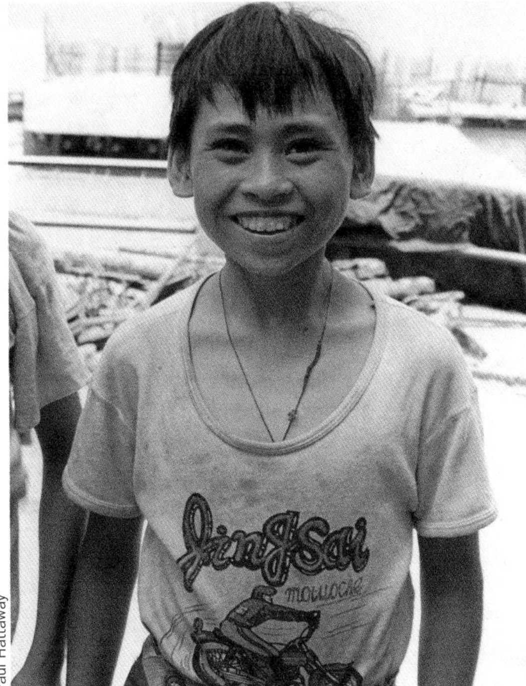

Paul Hattaway

Language: Today the people of Xunpu speak the standard Min Nan Chinese language of the surrounding communities.

History: In the past Quanzhou was known as *Zaitun*. Founded in 711, it grew to become the world's second largest port during the Song and Yuan dynasties (960–1368) and continued to be important until its harbor silted up during the Ming Dynasty (1368–1644). "Over the centuries, it attracted merchants, envoys and missionaries from faraway Persia, Arabia, India and Europe."[3] Another historian records, "A large number of Moslem, Nestorian, Catholic, Manichean and Hindu inscriptions are found in the area.... The inscriptions are in Arabic, Syriac and Tamil."[4]

Customs: The most eye-catching feature of the Xunpu women is the way they dress their hair. "It is twisted up into a bun or chignon, often fastened with strands of red wool, and set off by a garland or two of dozens of chrysanthemum, jasmine or magnolia buds."[5] Xunpu village is celebrated for its oysters. The outer walls of many of their homes are insulated with empty oyster shells collected from the nearby beach.

Religion: Today most Xunpu inhabitants adhere to traditional Chinese religions such as Daoism and ancestor worship. There are many strong Han Christian churches in nearby Quanzhou.

Christianity: Although there are now only a few believers among the Xunpu, the Quanzhou area has a long and rich Christian history. The first Christian community was started by Franciscan monks in the early 1300s.[6] In 1982 all the people of the nearby village of Shenghu, numbering 250, "were converted following an unusual case of exorcism."[7] Churches in Quanzhou City have experienced steady growth over a twenty-year period. One house church which numbered 100 to 200 people in 1975 had grown to 1,000 members by 1986.[8]

Hani 哈尼

Josie Plummer

Location: More than 600,000 Hani live across a wide stretch of land between the Ailao and Wuliang mountain ranges in southern Yunnan.[1] The Hani population is expected to surpass 750,000 by 2010.

Identity: The official Hani nationality numbered 1.25 million people in the 1990 census. This is the result of the inclusion of more than a dozen distinct people groups into the official classification. These groups have been separated and profiled individually in *Operation China*.[2] There are a multitude of self-appellations among the official Hani groups. They also "have over 100 ways of dressing themselves."[3] This Profile deals only with the speakers of "Hani proper."

Language: The Hani language consists of three tones and five dialects. More than 450,000 Hani can speak their language.[4] Differences with each of the major dialects "are relatively small, and speakers from the different sub-dialects can generally understand each other."[5] A Hani Roman alphabet was introduced in 1957 but was never widely embraced by the Hani who today have a literacy rate of just 29%.[6]

History: In Hani legend a Sky god named Abo-Momi sent a buffalo to the earth to teach man that grass and trees must be planted to enable crops to grow everywhere else. If man would do this they would be able to eat every second day. Unfortunately the buffalo had a poor memory and told them the *crops* must be planted. He also told them to let the grass and trees grow everywhere else. If they would do that, the buffalo said, they would be able to eat twice every day. Man obeyed the buffalo's message but found their lives did not improve at all. When the buffalo returned to the sky, Abo-Momi was displeased and sent the buffalo back to the earth to help the Hani cultivate the soil. The water buffalo is still revered today among the Hani. When a Hani man dies his buffalo is slaughtered and buried with him, so that the beast can guide him to the next world.

Customs: The Hani are a needy and poverty-stricken people. The central government ranked them the lowest of China's official minorities in a "quality of life index." The Hani scored 38.3%, compared to the national average of 62.7%.[7] They also ranked last for infant mortality, with 107 of every 1,000 Hani children dying during infancy. The Hani life expectancy is just 58 years.[8]

Religion: The Hani have three major religious clergymen. The *zuima* is a male from the oldest household who directs all religious activities. The *beima* perform magic rites and exorcisms. Male and female *nima* make predictions and administer medicinal herbs.[9]

Christianity: The Hani have traditionally been one of the most gospel-neglected of China's minorities. The few efforts to evangelize them have been met with resistance. One writer notes, "They have no Scriptures, no evangelists, no radio broadcasts and no *Jesus* film. In other words, even if a Hani wants to hear about Jesus Christ, he can't, no matter how hard he tries."[10]

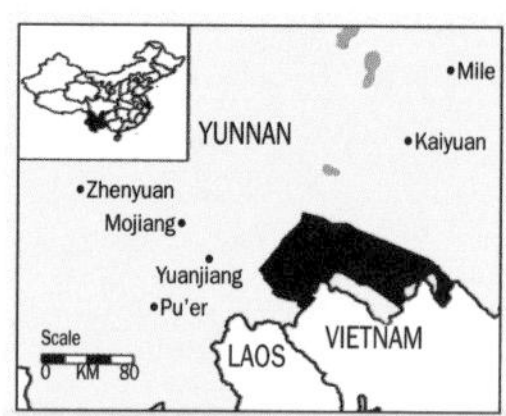

Population in China:
500,000 (1990)
614,500 (2000)
755,200 (2010)
Location: Yunnan
Religion: Polytheism
Christians: 200

Overview of the Hani

Countries: China, Vietnam, Laos

Pronunciation: "Ha-nee"

Other Names: Hanhi, Haw

Population Source: 500,000 (1990 J.-O. Svantesson); Out of a total Hani population of 1,253,952 (1990 census); 37,000 in Vietnam (1993 P. Johnstone); 1,122 in Laos (1995 census)

Location: *S Yunnan:* Yuanjiang and Mekong River basins; Mainly between the Ailao and Wuliang mountains

Status: An official minority of China

Language: Sino-Tibetan, Tibeto-Burman, Burmese-Lolo, Lolo, Southern Lolo, Akha, Hani, Ha-Ya

Literacy: 29%

Dialects: 5

Religion: Polytheism, Animism, Shamanism

Christians: 200

Scripture: Work in progress

***Jesus* film:** In progress

Gospel Recordings: Hani #04698

Christian Broadcasting: None

ROPAL code: HNI00

Status of Evangelization

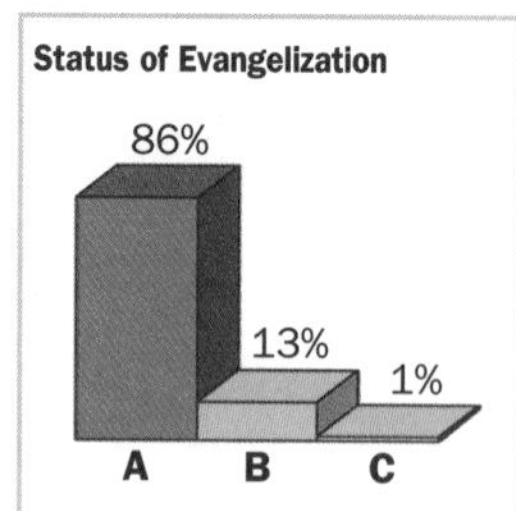

A = Have never heard the gospel
B = Were evangelized but did not become Christians
C = Are adherents to any form of Christianity

Han Tai 汉傣

Location: Approximately 55,000 Han Tai people inhabit the mountains of Mengyuan County in the Xishuangbanna Prefecture of China's Yunnan Province. "The area contains 539 species of wild animals and birds, including elephants, wild oxen, tigers, leopards, bears, wild boar, gibbons and monkeys."[1]

Identity: Although the Han Tai have never previously appeared in Christian research lists, they are a people group with their own customs, self-identity, and language. While Tai Lu (Shui Tai) women wear long, colorful sarongs, and put their hair up in a bun, "Han Tai women wear black, hand-woven sarongs with a bright blue fitted blouse and black turban."[2]

Language: The Han Tai speak their own distinct language. Most Han Tai (except those in more isolated villages) are also able to speak the regional Tai Lu language, which serves as the *lingua franca* throughout the region. The Han Tai speak Tai Lu to outsiders but continue to speak their own language in their villages. The Christian ministry *Gospel Recordings* recently produced three different cassettes in the Han Tai, Huayao Tai, and Shui Tai languages.

History: Over many generations, the Tai race slowly began to separate and form distinctive traditions and languages. They "eventually evolved into two groups: the lowland farmers or *Shui Tai* and the mountain nomads, or *Han Tai*."[3]

Customs: In contrast to the dominant Tai Lu, whose homes are built on stilts, the Han Tai build their homes flat on the ground, often in a long row of houses containing several families. The Han Tai celebrate the annual Songkran Festival. People splash water over each other, believing it cleanses the sins of the past year. A Tai legend tells about a powerful fire-breathing demon who was defeated by Yidanhan, a beautiful Tai maiden. "One night she made a special feast for the demon and got him drunk.... He told her that if someone was able to pull a hair from his head and wrap it around his neck, his head would fall off and he would die. Yidanhan did this, but the demon's head rolled away and set everything on fire. The Tai splashed water on the demon's head to quench the fire, and to wash the blood from Yidanhan's clothes."[4]

Dwayne Graybill

Religion: During the Cultural Revolution the Han Tai Buddhists suffered much persecution. Cadres even dug up the skeleton of a revered Buddhist abbot and used his bones as fertilizer, in a bizarre bid to provoke the people and destroy their religion.[5] Pa Ya Shanmudi, the legendary Tai folk hero, laid down several commandments to ensure the survival of his people. One of these instructs each village to build a shrine, called a *zaixin*, as the symbolic heart of the community. "It serves as a ritual center.... To destroy it or obstruct access to it would be the height of sacrilege."[6]

Christianity: A small number of Han Tai Christians who live in the Mengyuan area were won to Christ by an evangelist in recent years. In the 1960s many of the Tai church leaders in Xishuangbanna were killed by the fanatical Red Guards.

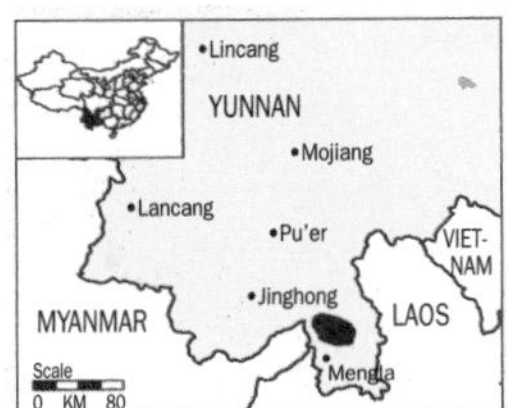

Population in China:
50,000 (1996)
55,500 (2000)
70,700 (2010)
Location: Yunnan
Religion: Buddhism
Christians: 200

Overview of the Han Tai

Countries: China

Pronunciation: "Hahn-Tie"

Other Names: Dai: Han, Dry Land Dai, Mountain Dai, Han Dai

Population Source: 50,000 (1996 AMO); Out of a total Dai population of 1,025,128 (1990 census)

Location: *SW Yunnan:* Xishuangbanna Prefecture: Mengyuan County and surrounding area

Status: Officially included under Dai

Language: Daic, Tai, Southwestern Tai, East Central, Northwest

Dialects: 0

Religion: Theravada Buddhism, Animism, Christianity

Christians: 200

Scripture: None

***Jesus* film** : None

Gospel Recordings: Han Dai #04794

Christian Broadcasting: None

ROPAL code: None

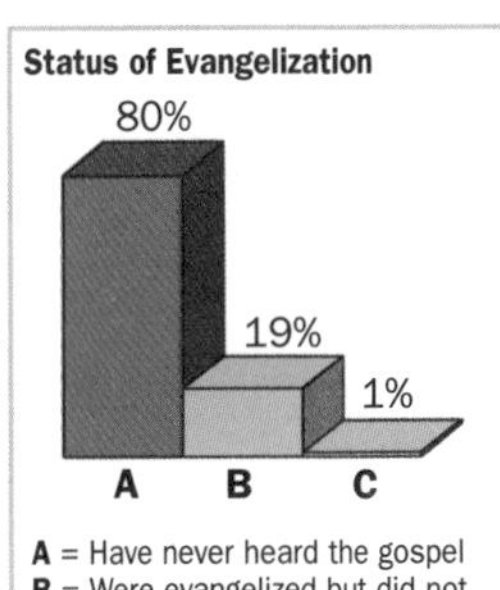

Haoni 豪尼

Population in China:
100,000 (1990)
122,900 (2000)
151,000 (2010)
Location: Yunnan
Religion: Polytheism
Christians: 5,000

Overview of the Haoni

Countries: China, possibly Vietnam

Pronunciation: "How-nee"

Other Names: Ouni, Uni, Ho, Honi

Population Source: 100,000 (1990 J.-O. Svantesson); Out of a total Hani population of 1,253,952 (1990 census); Possibly also in Vietnam

Location: *S Yunnan:* Mojiang, Yuanjiang, and Jiangcheng counties and surrounding areas; One village in Wuding county in northern Yunnan

Status: Officially included under Hani

Language: Sino-Tibetan, Tibeto-Burman, Burmese-Lolo, Lolo, Southern Lolo, Akha, Hao-Bai

Dialects: 0

Religion: Polytheism, No Religion, Animism, Christianity

Christians: 5,000

Scripture: None

***Jesus* film:** None

Gospel Recordings: None

Christian Broadcasting: None

ROPAL code: HOW00

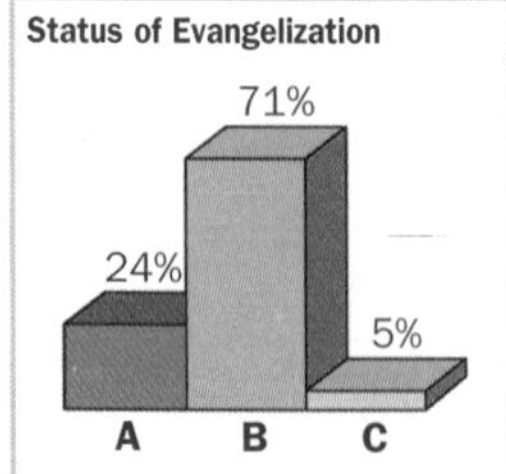

A = Have never heard the gospel
B = Were evangelized but did not become Christians
C = Are adherents to any form of Christianity

Location: In 1990 an estimated 100,000 Haoni were located in Mojiang County and surrounding areas of the Yuxi and Honghe prefectures. Honghe (Red River) Prefecture is located in the southern part of Yunnan Province. One village of Haoni people is located in Wuding County in northern Yunnan.[1]

Identity: The Haoni are counted as part of the Hani nationality in China, but they speak their own distinct language.

Language: In 1987 linguistic research listed 80,000 speakers of the Haoni language.[2] Haoni is close to Baihong. Speakers from the two groups who live near each other can communicate with relative ease. Those Haoni who live farther away from the Baihong struggle to understand them. Some consider Baihong to be a dialect of Haoni.

History: The Haoni people have a long history. They were originally part of a larger race known as *Heman* or *Heni* during the Tang Dynasty (AD 618–907). These names are still sometimes used today by the various Hani groups. In 1917 the Haoni joined forces with the local Miao and Tai in a five-year battle against oppressive landlords.[3]

Customs: The Haoni live in a harsh environment where it is difficult to grow the food they need. They have long been a poverty-stricken people. In 1955 when the Communist authorities in Mojiang sent cadres to investigate the Haoni, "the sight of abject poverty horrified the investigators. Most of the children were stark naked, and the rags they possessed were hardly enough to go around for adults. Eight villagers of the age of 20 had literally no clothes to wear and six of them were females. One family's belongings amounted to no more than a small iron pot and an earthenware bowl."[4] Today economic improvement has come to the Haoni in the valleys, but the plight of those dwelling on the mountaintops remains much the same.

Religion: The Haoni are rapidly becoming a secularized people. Few of the younger generation observe the intricate superstitions of their parents and grandparents. Traditionally the Haoni were slaves to a multitude of demons and ghosts. This has helped shape the worldview of the Haoni. Some believe "a man's body has nine souls located in the head, mouth, heart, eyes, chest, hands, ears, back, and feet; a woman's body, however, has one more soul located in her breasts."[5]

Christianity: Mojiang County was the center of activity for the German Pentecostal Vandsburger Mission and the Danish Assemblies of God. Between 1940 and 1947 a massive people movement to Christ flourished throughout the area, especially among the Biyo and Kado. Forty thousand tribesmen — 35% of the entire minority population at the time — started following Christ.[6] H. A. Baker, an independent Pentecostal missionary, also ministered widely in the area. Today an estimated 5,000 Haoni Christians meet in scattered churches throughout Mojiang County. Most Haoni use the Chinese language in their services because there has never been any translation work completed in the Haoni language of southern Yunnan.

Dwayne Graybill

Hdzanggur 藏股

Paul Hattaway

Location: Several thousand members of the Hdzanggur tribe inhabit a remote part of southeast Qinghai Province. They are primarily located in the Ger Zhung Valley around the Radja Monastery, northeast of Dawu on the banks of the Yellow River. Hdzanggur territory starts at the banks of the Yellow River and extends for several days' journey by foot or horse to the west. There are few roads in this hidden part of the world.

Identity: The Hdzanggur are one of the main tribes of Golog Tibetans. The name *Golog* means "those with heads on backwards," in reference to their rebellious nature. The Hdzanggur have a reputation for being robbers and murderers. They are heavily armed and practically independent from Chinese rule. One of the first outsiders to visit the Hdzanggur was the intrepid Joseph Rock in 1929. He wrote, "I crossed over... to see what these almost unknown and wild people were like. Though very suspicious of us, they showed the greatest curiosity about our appearance and clothing.... They formed a circle about me, feeling my clothes. My pockets in particular amused them.... They followed me about, shaking their heads in bewilderment."[1]

Language: The Hdzanggur speak a variety of Golog Tibetan, which is part of the larger Amdo Tibetan linguistic group. Few are able to read and write either Tibetan or Chinese.

History: For centuries the Hdzanggur have been cut off from contact with the rest of the world. To this day, they are without telephones, electricity, and a postal system. There are virtually no roads in their region. This primitive tribe practices crude forms of medicine, little changed for centuries. Rock reported, "I did manage to photograph one wild fellow.... His abdomen was covered with straight scars, made when he had held burning rags against his body to cure his stomach ache. These scars were so evenly placed that they looked like tattoo marks. Others had scars on wrists and hands, marks of fiery ordeals to cure rheumatism."[2]

Customs: Today there are boats available to ferry passengers across the Yellow River and, near the main towns, bridges now exist. But 70 years ago, the Hdzanggur were renowned for their unique method of crossing the river. "Here a ferry of inflated goatskins supporting a raft of poles was in operation. These skins soon went flat. After each trip the Tibetans had to blow up each skin — excellent exercise for the lungs. As many as 12 people would ride on one of these flimsy rafts."[3]

Religion: The Hdzanggur are fervent Tibetan Buddhists. They also worship a selection of fierce mountain deities. Several Western Buddhists are presently studying at Radja Monastery.

Christianity: The gospel of Jesus Christ has never penetrated this geographically, politically, and spiritually isolated part of the world. There has never been a known Hdzanggur believer. Unknown to Christendom, the Hdzanggur have perished in their sin for centuries without the slightest cry for help being heard from their midst.

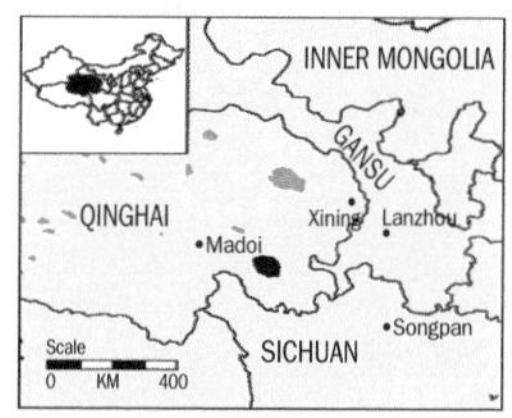

Population in China:
4,000 (1996)
4,370 (2000)
5,380 (2010)
Location: Qinghai
Religion: Tibetan Buddhism
Christians: None Known

Overview of the Hdzanggur

Countries: China

Pronunciation: "H-zung-gur"

Other Names:

Population Source:
4,000 (1996 AMO);
Out of a total Tibetan population of 4,593,330 (1990 census)

Location: *SE Qinghai:* West of the Yellow River in the Golog Tibetan Prefecture

Status:
Officially included under Tibetan

Language: Sino-Tibetan, Tibeto-Burman, Bodic, Bodish, Tibetan, Northern Tibetan

Dialects: 0

Religion:
Tibetan Buddhism, Polytheism

Christians: None known

Scripture: None

***Jesus* film:** None

Gospel Recordings: None

Christian Broadcasting: None

ROPAL code: None

Status of Evangelization

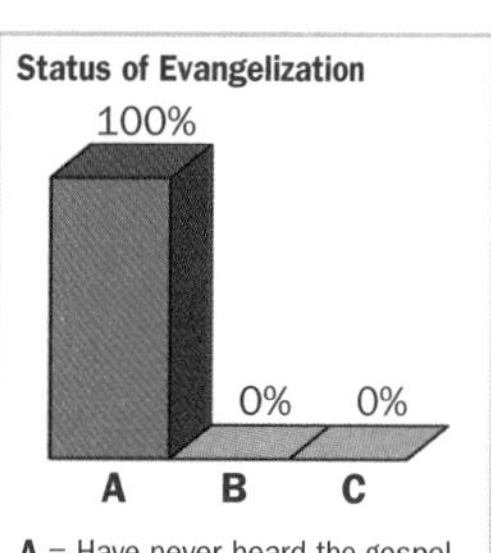

A = Have never heard the gospel
B = Were evangelized but did not become Christians
C = Are adherents to any form of Christianity

Hezhen 赫哲

Population in China:
4,245 (1990)
5,470 (2000)
7,060 (2010)
Location: Heilongjiang
Religion: Shamanism
Christians: 100

Overview of the Hezhen

Countries: Russia, China
Pronunciation: "Her-jen"
Other Names: Hezhe, Nanai, Ulcha, Olcha, Hoche, Olchis, Olca, Goldi, Gold, Hol-Chih, Heche, Sushen, Juchen, Ulchi, Olchi, Mangun, Mangoon, Naani, Nanay, Nani, Hedjen, Fish Skin Tatars, Ulych
Population Source:
4,245 (1990 census);
1,476 (1982 census);
718 (1964 census);
300 (1949);
12,000 in Russia (1993 United Bible Societies)
Location: *NE Heilongjiang:* Sanjiang River valley[1]
Status:
An official minority of China
Language: Altaic, Tungus, Southern Tungus, Southeast, Nanai
Literacy: 84%
Dialects (2): Hezhen, Qileng
Religion: Shamanism, Animism, No Religion, Ancestor Worship, Christianity
Christians: 100
Scripture: Portions 1884
***Jesus* film:** None
Gospel Recordings: None
Christian Broadcasting: None
ROPAL code: GLD00

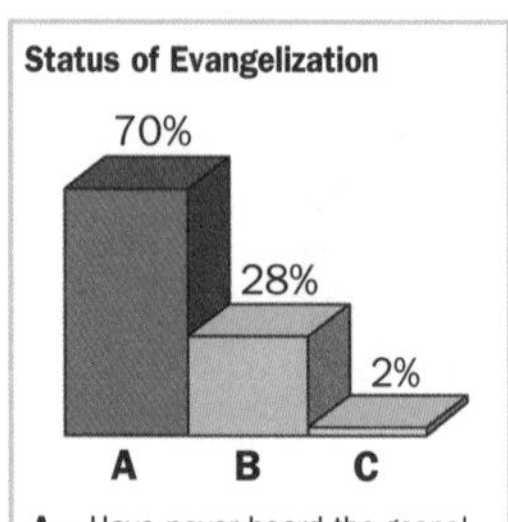

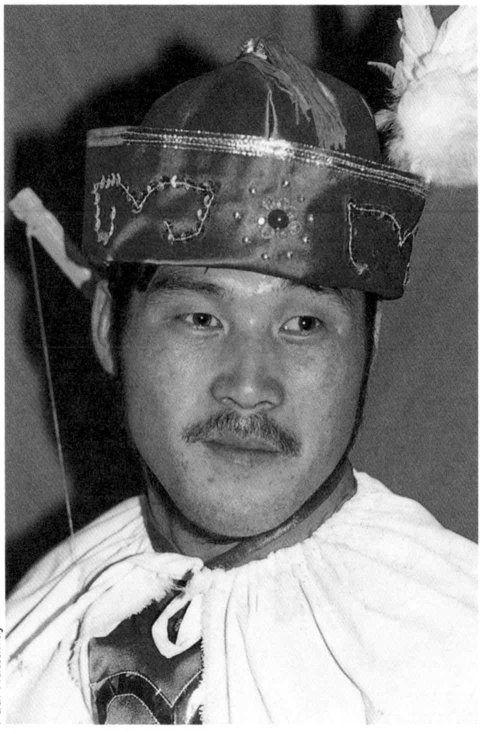
Paul Hattaway

Location: Approximately 5,500 Hezhen live in the extreme northeast of China. More than 12,000 are also located across the border in Siberia, where they are known as *Nanai.* The Hezhen in China live at the juncture of the Heilong, Wusali, and Songhua rivers in Heilongjiang Province. The Hezhen population has fluctuated numerically in recent centuries. There were more than 12,000 in the mid-1600s.[2] In the 1930s the Japanese invaders drove the Hezhen into the forests and banned them from fishing, hunting, and farming. Because of the resulting starvation and disease, by 1949 the Hezhen were close to extinction, numbering only 300 people.[3] They recovered to 700 by 1970 and numbered 1,476 in the 1982 census.

Identity: The Hezhen are the third smallest of China's 55 official minority groups. Only about 1,000 Hezhen are still ethnically distinct from the Han Chinese. The name *Hezhen* reportedly means "people living in the east or the lower reaches of rivers."[4]

Language: The Hezhen language is a part of the Tungus branch of Altaic languages making them distant relatives to the many small Siberian tribes and groups in China such as the Ewenki and Oroqen. The Hezhen teach their children history and culture by singing rhymed ballads and telling folk tales.[5] The Hezhen language is close to extinction. In 1987 it was reportedly spoken by only 40 elderly people.[6] All Hezhen youth now speak Chinese as their mother tongue. In Russia, however, the situation is better: 6,600 of the 12,000 Hezhen in that country — where the Hezhen language has an orthography — can still speak their mother tongue.[7]

History: Hezhen history dates back to the Sushen, a tribe who occupied the region as far back as 700 BC. In 1663 the Qing Dynasty rulers gave the Hezhen their current name.

Customs: During the summer months the Hezhen's beautiful homeland is flush with an abundance of deer, fish, bears, and pheasants. During the bleak winters, temperatures plummet to as low as minus 40 degrees. In the past the Hezhen were known as the *Fish Skin Tatars.* Their coats, trousers, and even shoes were made of fish skin. When a Hezhen child dies, the corpse is wrapped in a birch bark, placed in a tree, and is allowed to decompose naturally.[8]

Religion: For centuries the Hezhen worshiped the spirits of the sky, earth, sun, moon, stars, mountains, rivers, and trees. In the late 1960s shamans were still active among the Hezhen, but since that time the traditional beliefs of the Hezhen have been rapidly eroded by atheism and secularism.

Christianity: Scripture portions were translated into the Hezhen language in Russia in 1884, but these have long been unavailable and obsolete. Until recently, the Hezhen in China had never had a known church in their midst. In 1996 Chinese believers from Tongjiang conducted outreach to the Hezhen in Jiejinkou County. More than 60 Hezhen believed and were baptized. Today there are three house fellowships full of the new believers, but there are no organized Hezhen churches or trained church leaders available to pastor the flock.[9]

Hkauri 高日

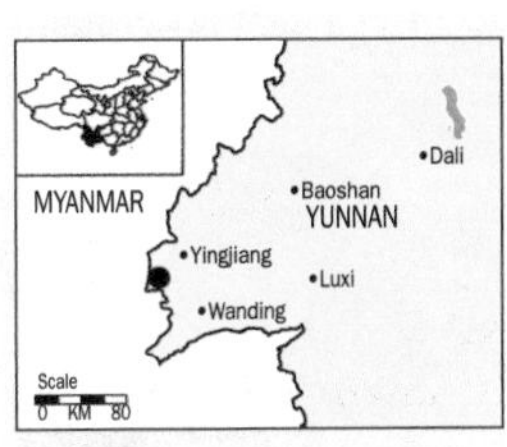

Population in China:
30 (1998)
31 (2000)
40 (2010)
Location: Yunnan
Religion: Christianity
Christians: 20

Overview of the Hkauri

Countries: Myanmar, China

Pronunciation: "Cow-ree"

Other Names: Gaori, Kao-jih, Khauri, Gauri, Kauri

Population Source:
30 (1998 AMO);
"A few dozen speakers" (1998 J. Matisoff);
Out of a total Jingpo population of 119,209 (1990 census);
Also in Myanmar

Location:
W Yunnan: Yingjiang County;
Also in Myanmar

Status:
Officially included under Jingpo

Language: Sino-Tibetan, Tibeto-Burman, Baric, Kachinic

Dialects: 0

Religion: Christianity, Animism

Christians: 20

Scripture: None

***Jesus* film:** None

Gospel Recordings: None

Christian Broadcasting: None

ROPAL code: CGP04

Status of Evangelization

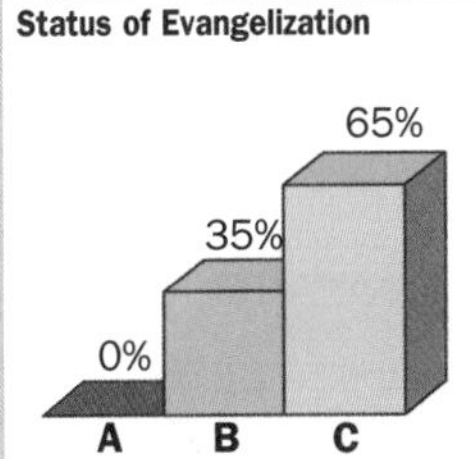

A = Have never heard the gospel
B = Were evangelized but did not become Christians
C = Are adherents to any form of Christianity

Location: Although the majority of people belonging to the Hkauri ethnic group live east and northeast of Bhamo in Myanmar's Shan State, a few also spill across the border into the western part of Yunnan Province, China. Only about 30 Hkauri people live within China's borders. One source states, "the speaking population in China numbers only a few dozen people."[1] The Hkauri live in one village within Yingjiang County in the Dehong Prefecture of Yunnan Province, immediately on the China-Myanmar border.

Identity: Although the Chinese authorities have placed the Hkauri under the official Jingpo nationality, they possess a different ethnicity and speak a distinct language from other Jingpo groups. In Myanmar, the Hkauri's claims as a separate tribe have recently been acknowledged. The various branches of the Kachin in Myanmar are encouraged to profess unity as one people. Different claims of ethnicity are seen as a sign of weakness, especially by the leaders of the Kachin Independence Army. The fact remains, however, that the Hkauri have their own name and language. Somewhat surprisingly, the present government of Myanmar acknowledges the Hkauri as one of that nation's 135 ethnic groups.

Language: Hkauri is related to Jingpo, yet mutual intelligibility between Hkauri and Jingpo is considered difficult. Early Baptist missionaries working among the Hkauri found their speech extremely divergent from other Jingpo varieties. One report stated, "The Gauris [Hkauri] in the hills east and northeast of Bhamo... speak a dialect so different from the other Jinghpaws [Jingpo] of that district that, in the early years, we favored making a separate dictionary for their language."[2]

History: According to Hkauri legends and folklore, their first ancestor was named Ning Gawn Wa. He was also involved with the creation of the earth. Later, he married an alligator. "Their great grandson, Wahkyet Wa, became the progenitor of the Jingpos. Of Wahkyet Wa's numerous sons (traditions as to the number of his wives vary from three to thirty), the five eldest sons of his first wife... became the founders of the five major Jingpo clans,"[3] including the Hkauri.

Customs: The Hkauri claim they migrated to their present location from a place far to the north known as Majoi Shingra Bum (Naturally Flat Mountain). A number of researchers have suggested all the Jingpo peoples once lived on the Tibetan or Qinghai Plateau in China. The Hkauri are a hardy, warrior type of people, yet are extremely friendly to outsiders.

Religion: The majority of Hkauri in both Myanmar and China today are Christians. Before their conversion they were animists, worshiping and appeasing a host of different deities and gods.

Christianity: Baptist missionary Josiah Cushing started work in the Hkauri area in 1876, although missionary Eugenio Kincaid had first passed through northern Burma in the 1830s. The Jingpo Bible is used by Hkauri Christians, but there may be a need for them to have the Scriptures in their own language. The *Jesus* film and gospel recordings are also unavailable in Hkauri.

Paul Hattaway

Hmong Be 赫蒙拔

Location: Approximately 1,000 members of the Hmong Be tribe live in a compact community in Luzhai Village near Babao Township. The area lies within Dafang County in the northwestern part of Guizhou Province. This part of southern China is a hilly region with lush forests watered by numerous rivers and streams.

Identity:[1] Chinese linguistic and anthropological literature in the past frequently mentioned the Hmong Be, despite their small population. The Chinese call them *Luzhai Miao* after the name of their village. They call themselves *Hmong Be* (Mountain Hmong).[2] The neighboring Hmong who live in Dananshan Village refer to them as *Hmong Nzhil* (Peppery Hmong), or *Hmong Drout Raol* (Six Village Hmong). They are one of several dozen ethnic groups combined to form the official Miao nationality in China. Although the Hmong Be speak the same language as the Hmong Dou, they claim a different ethnic identity. In addition, Hmong Be women wear their own unique style of dress.

Language: The Hmong Be speak a variety belonging to the Chuanqiandian (Western) Miao language group. Chuanqiandian is the most cohesive of the Miao language groups. Speakers from diverse places such as northwest Guizhou and southern Yunnan have little trouble communicating with each other. Farther east — in Guizhou, Guangxi, and Hunan — Miao languages show much greater variation.

History: In China many of the branches of the Miao do not accept each other as members of the ethnic group. This is because the Chinese have used the name *Miao* as a generic cover term to refer to the original inhabitants of Guizhou for more than 2,000 years. Today, centuries after they have splintered into numerous separate entities, they are still called *Miao* by the Chinese. In comparison, the former great Mon-Khmer race was never called by one generic name. They have splintered into today's groups such as the Lahu, Wa, De'ang, and Bulang, each acknowledged by the government as distinct nationalities. Today's Miao groups show just as much ethnolinguistic variety as the Mon-Khmer groups, but they are all officially included in the same nationality.

Customs: The Hmong Be celebrate several regional festivals, including an annual gathering when the youth come together to find partners.

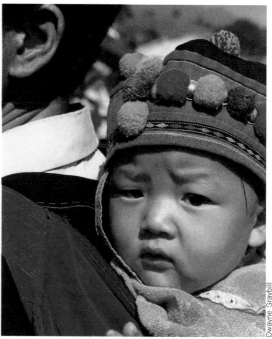

Dwayne Graybill

Religion: Animism is the primary religious belief system among the Hmong Be. Although animism is not technically an organized religion, the people's lives and communities reflect their bondage to the spirit world that surrounds them.

Christianity: Many Hmong Be have heard something of the gospel, mostly through the temporary witness of Christians passing through the area. As a result, few Hmong Be today have a full understanding of the concepts of grace and salvation. It is unknown whether there are presently any active believers among the Hmong Be.

Population in China:
1,000 (1998)
1,050 (2000)
1,360 (2010)
Location: Guizhou
Religion: Animism
Christians: None Known

Overview of the Hmong Be

Countries: China

Pronunciation: "Hmong-Beh"

Other Names: Hmong: Luzhai, Luzhai Miao, Mountain Hmong, Hmong Nzhil, Peppery Miao, Hmong Drout Raol, Six Village Miao

Population Source: 1,000 (1998 AMO); Out of a total Miao population of 7,398,035 (1990 census)

Location: *NW Guizhou:* Luzhai Village in Babao Township, Dafang County

Status: Officially included under Miao

Language: Hmong-Mien, Hmongic, Western Hmongic, Farwestern, Hua Miao, Northern Hua Miao

Dialects: 0

Religion: Animism, Ancestor Worship

Christians: None known

Scripture: None

***Jesus* film:** None

Gospel Recordings: None

Christian Broadcasting: None

ROPAL code: None

Status of Evangelization

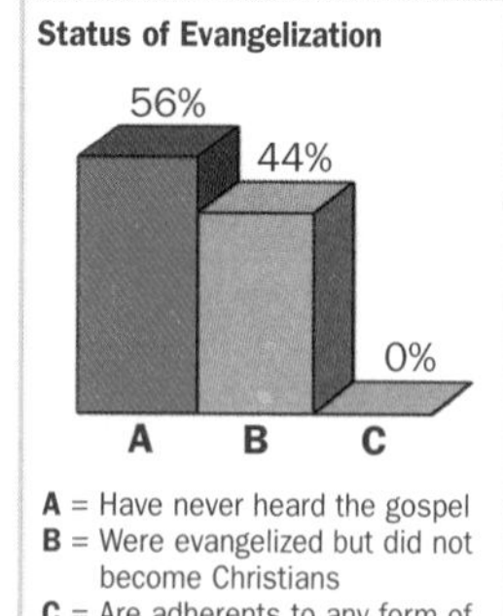

A = Have never heard the gospel
B = Were evangelized but did not become Christians
C = Are adherents to any form of Christianity

Hmong Bua 赫蒙部阿

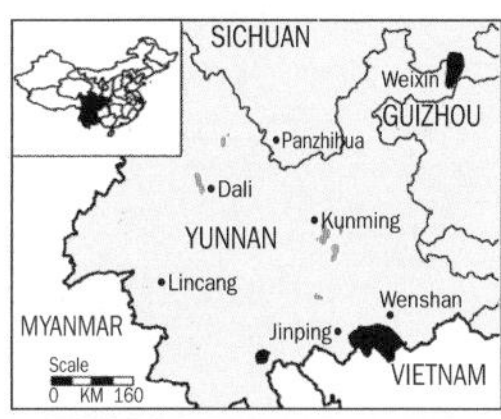

Population in China:
50,000 (1998)
52,900 (2000)
68,200 (2010)
Location: Yunnan, Sichuan
Religion: Polytheism
Christians: 600

Overview of the Hmong Bua

Countries: China, Vietnam

Pronunciation: "Hmong-Booah"

Other Names: Black Hmong, Black Miao, Hei Miao, Hmong Dlo, Hmong Si

Population Source:
50,000 (1998 M. Johnson);
Out of a total Miao population of 7,398,035 (1990 census);
20,000 in Vietnam (1998 M. Johnson)

Location: *SE Yunnan:* Jinping, Pingbian, and Hekou counties;
A few have recently migrated to Xishuangbanna Prefecture;
NE Yunnan: Weixin and Zhenxiong counties; *S Sichuan:* A few in Xuyong County;
Also in Vietnam

Status:
Officially included under Miao

Language: Hmong-Mien, Hmongic, Western Hmongic, Farwestern Hmong, Hua Miao, Black Miao

Dialects: 0

Religion:
Polytheism, Animism, Christianity

Christians: 600

Scripture: None

***Jesus* film:** None

Gospel Recordings: None

Christian Broadcasting: None

ROPAL code: None

Status of Evangelization

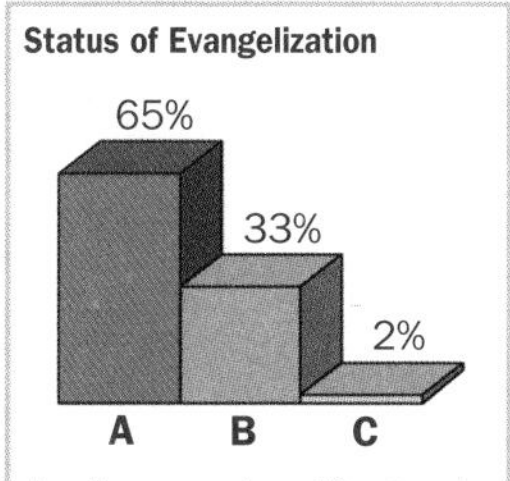

A = Have never heard the gospel
B = Were evangelized but did not become Christians
C = Are adherents to any form of Christianity

Dwayne Graybill

Location: A 1998 study listed a population of 50,000 Hmong Bua in China.[1] They live in two widely separated areas in Yunnan Province: Weixin and Zhenxiong counties in northeastern Yunnan (and Xuyong County in neighboring Sichuan Province); and Jinping County (especially Laomeng Township) in southeastern Yunnan. A few also live on the east bank of the Honghe River in Pingbian and Hekou counties. Some Hmong Bua recently migrated to Xishuangbanna Prefecture in southwest Yunnan. In addition, 20,000 speakers of the Hmong Bua language live in Lai Chau, Vietnam.

Identity: The Hmong Bua are a separate ethnic group, with a common identity, within the Miao nationality. The Hmong Bua in Jinping and Vietnam call themselves *Hmong Dlo* or *Hmong Bua*, meaning "black Hmong." In Weixin the autonym used is *Hmong Si*. It is important to note that this group is not related to the large Hmu group in Guizhou, who were also called *Black Miao* by missionaries in the past. Linguist Michael Johnson notes, "In the Weixin-Xuyong area the Hmong Si are ethnically closely tied with the Hmong Leng, another Northern Hua dialect."[2]

Language: Although the Hmong Bua language is mutually intelligible with other Hua Miao varieties in southern China, Johnson notes, "The varieties in this subgroup are phonologically the most conservative within the Hua Miao group in that they preserve a number of initial consonant contrasts that have been lost in all other Hua Miao dialects and yet are also amongst the most innovative in that they have developed a ninth tone."[3]

History: The Hmong Bua now living in southern Yunnan and Vietnam arrived in the region about 200 years ago. In contrast, the Hmong Bua in the northeastern Yunnan-Sichuan area first arrived there in 1573.[4] After several generations of separation from their homeland, the Hmong Bua developed their own identity. Today most of the various Miao subgroups in China do not acknowledge kinship with each other, even if they speak the same language.

Customs: Hmong Bua women's clothing features a black shirt, similar to the Hmong Leng, with embroidery on the cuffs. "The skirt is also dark... with oblique squares of cloth sewn to it. Women often use a small waist apron as a head covering."[5]

Religion: The majority of Hmong Bua are animists. In recent years the Hmong Bua in Jinping may have benefited from the Christian "radio revival" among the neighboring Hmong Daw, who speak a similar language.[6]

Christianity: As many as 20,000 of the neighboring Hmong Daw people have turned to Christ in southern Yunnan since 1994, due to gospel radio broadcasts produced by the Far East Broadcasting Company. The Hmong Bua are able to understand most of the Hmong Daw language and have probably been affected also. Many Hmong Bua could potentially use the Hmong Daw and Hmong Njua Scriptures, but very few are literate.

Hmong Daw 赫蒙兜

Miao Messenger

Location: Linguist Michael Johnson lists a figure of 220,000 speakers of Hmong Daw in China, of which more than 200,000 live in Wenshan Prefecture in Yunnan Province.[1] In addition, approximately 230,000 Hmong Daw live in Vietnam, 169,800 in Laos, 70,000 in the United States[2] (primarily in Minnesota and California), 60,000 in Thailand, and 10,000 in France. In China most Hmong Daw are located along the China-Vietnam border in Yunnan, in the western part of Guangxi, and in southwesten Guizhou.

Identity: The Hmong Daw (called "White Miao" by the Chinese) take their name from the traditional color of their women's skirts. However, "In many locations in China the Hmong Daw have adopted the dialect and clothing styles of other Hmong groups, most notably the Light Hmong [Hmong Leng] but in more remote areas... the dialect is still very strong and 'pure.'"[3]

Language: Hmong Daw is linguistically close to Hmong Njua. Speakers from the two groups are usually able to understand each other. Hmong Daw is relatively standard across a widespread area. Those in Thailand can communicate with those in China with few difficulties.[4]

History: The Hmong Daw are scattered throughout southern China and Southeast Asia as a result of Chinese military attacks. The conventional method of these wars was to besiege the Hmong [Miao] from three sides, leaving only mountains to the west open to escape. "The defeated Miao retreated through the hills... relying on their matchless climbing skills. This explains a Miao inclination to describe the west as a desirable destination."[5] A traditional Hmong rhyme says, "Over the western mountains of ten thousand cloud-capped crags and over the cliff, will be a paradise; over the peaks will be flourishing life."[6]

Customs: Hmong Daw women are skilled embroiderers. Mothers teach their daughters these skills at an early age.

Religion: For centuries the Hmong Daw were animists, living in fear of the spirits around them. Few Hmong Daw in China had heard the gospel, although many churches were established among their relatives in Thailand and Laos. In 1993 an old Hmong Daw man heard his language being spoken while tuning his radio. Soon thousands of Hmong Daw were listening to the gospel broadcasts daily, learning about Christ and the path of salvation. After a few months, 18 villages in southern China turned en masse to Christ.[7] Thousands of people reported receiving a "new heart."[8]

Christianity: In 1919 missionary Gladstone Porteous wrote, "Quite recently the White Miao [Hmong Daw] have shown interest in the Gospel.... [They asked] for an evangelist to go with them, and help them to burn up their objects of demon worship and teach them the Gospel."[9] Radio broadcasts have proven to be a highly effective tool for evangelizing the Hmong Daw. In the mid-1950s hundreds of Hmong Daw in Laos came to Christ as a result of radio broadcasts.[10] The recent "radio revival" has been fueled by the delivery of Bibles in their language.[11]

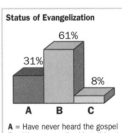

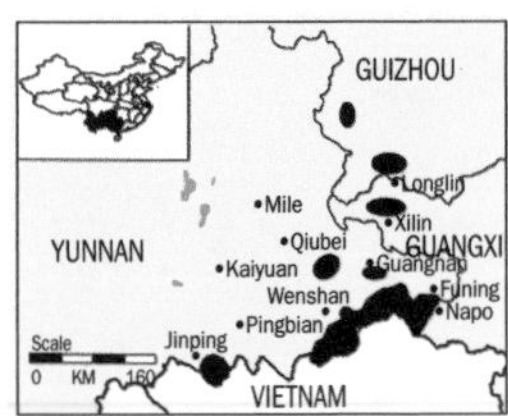

Population in China:
220,000 (1998)
232,700 (2000)
300,200 (2010)
Location:
Yunnan, Guangxi, Guizhou
Religion: Animism
Christians: 20,000

Overview of the Hmong Daw

Countries: Vietnam, China, Laos, Thailand, USA, France, Canada, French Guiana, Australia

Pronunciation: "Hmong-Doh"

Other Names: White Miao, Bai Miao, Bai Hmong, White Meo, Meo Kao, White Lum, Peh Miao, Pe Miao, White Hmong[12]

Population Source: 220,000 (1998 M. Johnson); Out of a total Miao population of 7,398,035 (1990 census); 230,000 in Vietnam (1998 M. Johnson); 169,800 in Laos (1995 AMO); 70,000 in USA (1987 UBS); 60,000 in Thailand (1998 M. Johnson); 10,000 in France; Also in Canada, French Guiana, Australia

Location: *SE Yunnan; NW Guangxi; SW Guizhou*[13]

Status: Officially included under Miao

Language: Hmong-Mien, Hmongic, Western Hmongic, Farwestern Hmong

Dialects: 0

Religion: Animism, Christianity

Christians: 20,000

Scripture: Bible 1997; New Testament 1975; Portions 1922

***Jesus* film:** Available

Gospel Recordings: White Hmong #00491

Christian Broadcasting: Available (FEBC)

ROPAL code: MWW00

Status of Evangelization

31% 61% 8%

A B C

A = Have never heard the gospel
B = Were evangelized but did not become Christians
C = Are adherents to any form of Christianity

Hmong Dlex Nchab 赫蒙乐插

Location: Linguist Michael Johnson listed a figure of 15,000 members of the Hmong Dlex Nchab ethnic group. They live in and around Tongchang Township in Jinping County[1] — the only place they are found in China. Jinping is located in the southern part of Yunnan Province close to China's border with Vietnam. There are a total of 80,000 Miao in Jinping County. The largest group is the Hmong Leng, followed by the Hmong Bua and the Hmong Daw. There are also a small number of Hmong Shuad in the area.

Identity: The Chinese call this group *Qingshui Miao*, meaning "clear water" Miao. This name corresponds to their autonym, *Hmong Dlex Nchab* (Clear Water Hmong). They also call themselves *Black Hmong*, but they are not the same group as the local Black Hmong (Hmong Bua) living in the same area.

Language: The Hmong Dlex Nchab are closely related to the Hmong Leng. The two groups can communicate without much difficulty. The major differences between the various Hmong groups in Jinping are ethnocultural, rather than linguistic. Johnson notes, "This dialect preserves the most number of features within the Southern Hua Miao group and both Hmong Leng and Hmong Njua could be synchronically derived from it."[2]

History: Historically, the Chinese have viewed the Hmong with contempt, believing them to be "uncivilized barbarians." Visitors to the minority peoples of China, however, have generally found them an extremely warm and hospitable people, often more than the Han Chinese themselves. Father De Mailla's comments on the tribes of Taiwan in the early 1700s still stand true for many of the minorities in China today. De Mailla wrote, "Savages though they may be according to the maxims of the Chinese world, I believe them to be nearer to the true philosophy than a great number of the most celebrated Chinese sages. One never sees among them, even upon Christian testimony, either cheating or quarreling, or robbery or litigation.... Their dealings are equitable, and they are attached to each other... they are circumspect in their words, and upright and pure in heart."[3]

Paul Hattaway

Customs: The Hmong Dlex Nchab join with other ethnic groups in the area to celebrate several major festivals each year, including the Chinese New Year and Spring festivals.

Religion: Most Hmong Dlex Nchab are polytheistic animists. Despite their fear of the spirit world, no Hmong in China are idolaters in the true sense of the word. They worship no idols or images in their rituals.

Christianity: Generations of Hmong Dlex Nchab have perished without receiving news of the sacrifice of Christ for their sins. The Jinping area is tightly controlled by the Chinese authorities. In 1994, in response to thousands of Hmong Daw coming to Christ through radio broadcasts, the local police arrested 18 church leaders, beat local Christians, and destroyed numerous Bibles and much Christian literature.[4]

Population in China:
15,000 (1998)
15,870 (2000)
20,400 (2010)
Location: Yunnan
Religion: Animism
Christians: None Known

Overview of the Hmong Dlex Nchab

Countries: China

Pronunciation: "Hmong-Dley-Ncha"

Other Names: Clear Water Hmong, Clear Water Miao, Qingshui Miao, Hmong Dlob, Black Hmong

Population Source: 15,000 (1998 M. Johnson); Out of a total Miao population of 7,398,035 (1990 census)

Location: *SE Yunnan:* Tongchang Township of Jinping County

Status: Officially included under Miao

Language: Hmong-Mien, Hmongic, Western Hmongic, Hua Miao, Southern Hua Miao, Qingshui Miao

Dialects: 0

Religion: Animism, Polytheism, Ancestor Worship

Christians: None known

Scripture: None

***Jesus* film:** None

Gospel Recordings: None

Christian Broadcasting: None

ROPAL code: None

Status of Evangelization

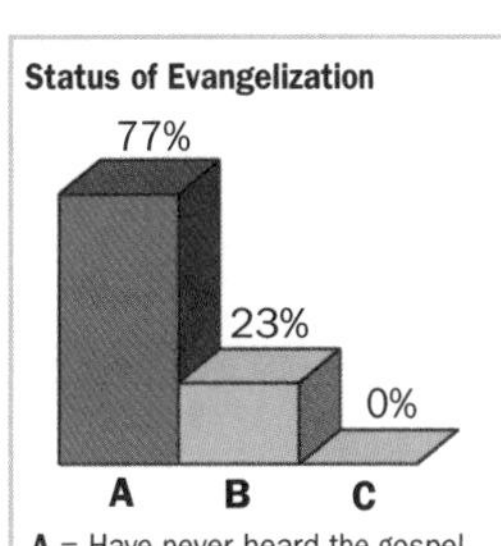

A = Have never heard the gospel
B = Were evangelized but did not become Christians
C = Are adherents to any form of Christianity

Hmong Dou 赫蒙抖

Population in China:
3,000 (1998)
3,170 (2000)
4,100 (2010)
Location: Guizhou
Religion: Animism
Christians: 300

Overview of the Hmong Dou

Countries: China

Pronunciation: "Hmong-Njah"

Other Names: Mo, Hongxian Miao, Downhill Hmong, Red Thread Miao, Red Top Miao

Population Source: 3,000 (1998 M. Johnson); Out of a total Miao population of 7,398,035 (1990 census)

Location: *W Guizhou:* Bijie County: Dananshan Village, and a few surrounding villages in Xiaoshao and Yanzikou townships. Some have moved to Daguan and Xiehe districts of Qianxi County.

Status: Officially included under Miao

Language: Hmong-Mien, Hmongic, Western Hmongic, Farwestern Hmong, Hua Miao, Northern Hua Miao

Dialects: 0

Religion: Animism, Christianity

Christians: 300

Scripture: None

***Jesus* film:** None

Gospel Recordings: None

Christian Broadcasting: None

ROPAL code: None

Status of Evangelization

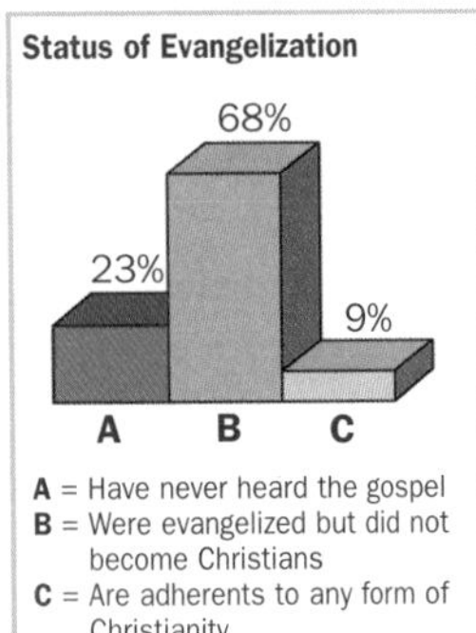

A = Have never heard the gospel
B = Were evangelized but did not become Christians
C = Are adherents to any form of Christianity

Location: Approximately 3,200 Hmong Dou live in the large Dananshan Village in Bijie County, located in the western part of Guizhou Province. Small numbers also live in a few surrounding villages in Xiaoshao and Yanzikou townships. In addition, some Hmong Dou have migrated to the Daguan and Xiehe districts of Qianxi County.[1]

Identity: Although they speak a language mutually intelligible with other Western Miao (Hmong) varieties, the Hmong Dou possess their own ethnic identity. They do not consider other Miao/Hmong groups to be of the same ethnic stock and do not usually intermarry outside of their communities. The Chinese call them *Hongxian Miao*, which means "red thread Miao." The Hmong Be (Mountain Hmong) in Luzhai Village of Dafang County call them *Hmong Dou* which means "downhill Hmong."

Language: The village of Dananshan was chosen by Chinese linguists as the standard location for the Chuanqiandian (Western) Miao language family. Scholars have conducted extensive research there since the 1950s, and based the Chuanqiandian orthography on the pronunciation of the occupants of this village. Linguist Michael Johnson recently researched the Hmong Dou, however, and found "a number of differences from the Chuanqiandian standard. It could be that I did not meet people whose speech matches the standard or else the standard is an artificially constructed dialect actually based on a number of close Northern Hua Miao varieties in the northwest Guizhou locality."[2] Some mission lists have mistaken Dananshan to be the name of a Miao ethnic group when it is only the name of a village.

History: Centuries of discrimination and military campaigns against them by the Chinese have splintered the Miao/Hmong into their numerous present-day ethnic groups and languages — including the Hmong Dou.

Customs: The Hmong Dou were given their Chinese name (*Hongxian* "red thread" *Miao*) because the women "often make their hair into a large bun that bulges on each side of the head. The bun is held in place by red thread wrapped around the forehead in a band about three inches in height."[3]

Religion: For centuries the Hmong Dou have been diligent to appease demons, offering annual sacrifices in a bid to keep peace with the spirit world. They believe spirits can be either good or bad and can locate themselves in a person, animal, or some other object of nature.

Christianity: Because they live alongside the Gha-Mu, who have thousands of Christians, most Hmong Dou have some awareness of the gospel, and a small number have placed their trust in Jesus Christ. Missionary J. R. Adam worked in the area in the early 1900s and included the Hmong Dou in one of his 1907 mission reports.[4]

Michael Johnson

Hmong Leng 赫蒙冷

Michael Johnson

Location: Approximately 250,000 Hmong Leng live in southern and southeastern Yunnan Province — including 30,000 in Jinping County alone.[1] Others are scattered in Pingbian County, parts of Wenshan Prefecture, and as far north as Kaiyuan County. In addition, large numbers of Hmong Leng live outside of China in Vietnam, Laos, Thailand, and as refugees in various Western nations, particularly the United States. The total world population for the Hmong Leng exceeds 500,000,[2] the majority found in Vietnam.

Identity: The Hmong Leng have been included under the official Miao nationality in China. Their self-name is *Hmong Len* or *Hmong Shib* which means "light Hmong." In Jinping County one subgroup is called *Hmong Liab* (Red Hmong) or *Hmong Liab Haut* (Red-Headed Hmong), but they speak the same language as the Hmong Leng.

Language: The Hmong Leng language, which has two dialects, is part of the Southern Hua Miao linguistic group.

History: The Hmong Leng are "a geographically widespread and populous group. There are a number of Hmong Leng ethnic and geographic subgroups speaking identical or extremely similar dialects. The differences amongst the subgroups are mostly obvious in clothing styles, geographical locations, and autonym but some socio-cultural differences may also exist. The closeness within the group indicates that they probably formed a single ethnolinguistic group, with no internal variation, in the southeast Yunnan area only a few hundred years ago."[3]

Customs: The Hmong Leng are among the most economically progressive minority groups in south China. Hmong Leng youth frequently travel to cities and towns in search of employment and have a reputation for being good businessmen. Hmong Leng women wear dresses made from hempcloth. A flat, round turban consisting of black and white cloth is also worn. In Jinping the clothing style includes a black or blue shirt and a flap of red cloth with sharply pointed corners at the back of the neck.

Religion: Hmong Leng homes customarily have a spirit and ancestral altar that is placed in a prominent location on a wall in the main room of the house. Offerings of fruit and incense are placed on the altar to honor and nourish the souls of their dead ancestors and to seek the spirits' blessings.

Christianity: There are few believers among the Hmong Leng in China, although in Southeast Asia and the United States, Hmong Leng Christians number in the thousands. Generally speaking, the Hmong Leng near the Vietnam border have a far greater chance of hearing the gospel than their counterparts farther north. Around Kaiyuan County there are few Christian communities and the Hmong Leng remain largely untouched. There may be a small number of Hmong Leng believers mixed in with the Hmong Daw churches in Jinping County and other parts of Wenshan Prefecture.

Population in China:
235,000 (1998)
248,600 (2000)
320,700 (2010)
Location: Yunnan
Religion: Animism
Christians: 200

Overview of the Hmong Leng

Countries: Vietnam, China, Laos, USA, Thailand

Pronunciation: "Hmong-Leng"

Other Names: Miao Leng, Hmong Sib, Light Hmong, Hmong Lens, Red Hmong, Hmong Bal Hout, Red-Headed Hmong, Hongtou Miao, Red-Headed Miao

Population Source: 235,000 (1998 M. Johnson); Out of a total Miao population of 7,398,035 (1990 census); 145,600 in Laos; Also in Vietnam, USA, Thailand

Location: *SE Yunnan:* Pingbian, Jinping, and Kaiyuan counties, and other parts of Wenshan Prefecture

Status: Officially included under Miao

Language: Hmong-Mien, Hmongic, Western Hmongic, Farwestern Hmong, Hua Miao, Southern Hua Miao

Dialects (2): Light Hmong, Hmong Leng (30,000)

Religion: Animism, Polytheism, Ancestor Worship

Christians: 200

Scripture: None

***Jesus* film:** None

Gospel Recordings: None

Christian Broadcasting: None

ROPAL code: MWW02

Status of Evangelization

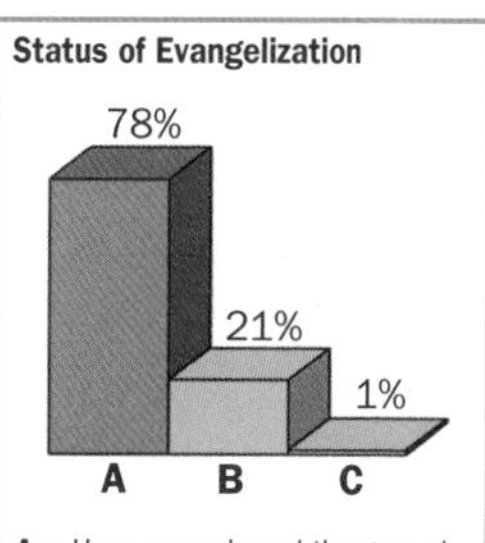

A = Have never heard the gospel
B = Were evangelized but did not become Christians
C = Are adherents to any form of Christianity

Hmong Njua 赫蒙巨额

Population in China:
40,000 (1998)
42,300 (2000)
54,500 (2010)
Location: Yunnan
Religion: Animism
Christians: 400

Overview of the Hmong Njua

Countries: China, Vietnam

Pronunciation: "Hmong-Juua"

Other Names: Blue Miao, Green Miao, Hmong: Njua, Qing Miao, Lu Miao, Miao Njua

Population Source: 40,000 (1998 M. Johnson); Out of a total Miao population of 7,398,035 (1990 census); Also in Vietnam

Location: *SE Yunnan:* Malipo and Maguan counties

Status: Officially included under Miao

Language: Hmong-Mien, Hmongic, Western Hmongic, Farwestern Hmong, Hua Miao, Southern Hua Miao, Green Miao

Dialects: 0

Religion: Animism, Polytheism, Christianity

Christians: 400

Scripture: New Testament 1975; Portions 1955

***Jesus* film:** Available

Gospel Recordings: Hmong: Blue #00492

Christian Broadcasting: Available (FEBC)

ROPAL code: BLU00

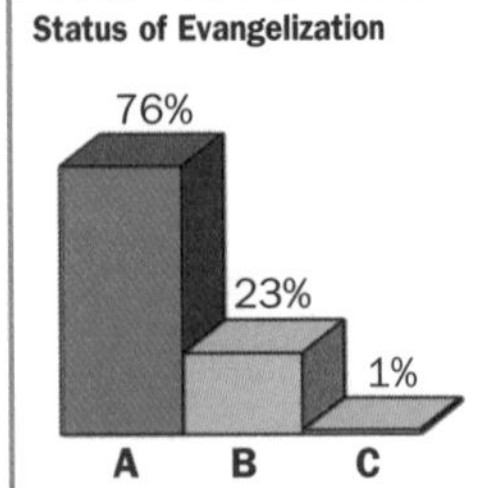

Paul Hattaway

Location: Approximately 40,000 Hmong Njua live in Malipo and Maguan counties in Wenshan Prefecture, in the southeastern part of Yunnan Province. Small numbers of Hmong Njua are also located near Sa Pa in northern Vietnam.

Identity: The Hmong Njua are not the same ethnic group, nor do they speak the same language as the identically named Hmong in Thailand, Vietnam, and Laos. In their language, the same word is used for both *green* and *blue*. For this reason, the Green Hmong have been listed as *Blue Hmong* in many publications. In an attempt to simplify the situation some scholars have listed them by their autonym, *Hmong Njua*. Chinese sources use the names *Qing Miao* or *Lu Miao* to describe this group. Hmong Njua women's clothing in China is very similar to the clothing of the Hmong Leng group. In Vietnam, however, the Hmong Njua clothing style is very different. "All the clothing is made from heavily indigo-dyed hemp cloth with no embroidery. Both women and men wear knee-length trousers and a long jacket… because of cold weather in Sa Pa."[1]

Language: The Hmong Njua language is closely related to, yet different from, the Hmong Daw and Hmong Leng. It is part of the Farwestern branch of the Hmongic language family.

History: As a result of the numerous wars waged against the Hmong during the Qing Dynasty, most of the survivors "dispersed in several directions."[2] The Hmong in Vietnam and Laos migrated from China at the end of the 1700s and the beginning of the 1800s. "Due to geographical separation… the two Hmong Njua groups [China and Vietnam] have no extensive socio-cultural contact and do not consider each other to belong to the same group."[3]

Customs: There are several ways for young Hmong Njua to show their admiration for each other. In some areas, lovers give each other fruit tree saplings which they plant together. For years to come they go into the woods together and tend to their growing trees.[4] Some crops harvested in southern Yunnan include sugarcane, tea, hemp, cotton, and maize.

Religion: Most Hmong Njua are animists. They are susceptible to being deceived by strong influential figures. One of their legends tells of a Hmong savior who will come and lead them into their own land where they will be left alone in peace.[5] In recent years thousands of Hmong in Vietnam have followed a miracle-working leader who claims to be the Hmong savior.[6]

Christianity: Although there are large Christian communities among the Hmong Njua in Vietnam, their counterparts in China are an unreached people group. More than half have yet to receive a clear presentation of the gospel. The *Jesus* film is available in "Blue Miao" — the only translation completed in any Miao/Hmong language. Most Hmong Njua in China are able to understand it, depending on the amount of contact they have had with their Hmong Daw neighbors.[7] Many Hmong Njua can also understand the Hmong Daw gospel radio programs.

Hmong Shuad 赫蒙数阿

Population in China:
250,000 (1998)
264,500 (2000)
341,200 (2010)
Location: Guizhou, Yunnan
Religion: Animism
Christians: 2,000

Overview of the Hmong Shuad

Countries: China, Vietnam

Pronunciation: "Hmong-Shoo-ah"

Other Names: Hmong Sua, Chinese Miao, Sinicized Miao, Hmong Sa, Hmong La, Paddy Field Miao, Waishu Miao, Biantou Miao, Mushu Miao, Shuixi Miao, Han Miao

Population Source:
250,000 (1998 M. Johnson);
Out of a total Miao population of 7,398,035 (1990 census);
2,000 in Vietnam
(1998 M. Johnson)

Location: *Guizhou:* Zhijin, Anshun, Shuicheng, Nayong, Dafang, Qinlong, Xingren, Pu'an, Anlong, Xingyi, Puding, Ziyun, Guanling, Qinglong, and Qianxi counties; *SE Yunnan:* Wenshan Prefecture and Jinping County

Status:
Officially included under Miao

Language: Hmong-Mien, Hmongic, Western Hmongic, Farwestern Hmong, Hmong Shuad

Religion: Animism, Polytheism, Ancestor Worship, Christianity

Christians: 2,000

Scripture: None

***Jesus* film:** None

Gospel Recordings:
Miao: Waishu #04948

Christian Broadcasting: None

ROPAL code: MSC00

Status of Evangelization

	A	B	C
%	68%	31%	1%

A = Have never heard the gospel
B = Were evangelized but did not become Christians
C = Are adherents to any form of Christianity

Location: More than 260,000 Hmong Shuad live in southern China.[1] They primarily occupy parts of Zhijin and Anshun counties in the western part of Guizhou Province. Small communities are also found in southeastern Yunnan,[2] and southward into Vietnam where about 2,000 Hmong Shuad live.

Identity: The Hmong Shuad are a distinct ethnolinguistic people group. Their language is very different from all other Miao languages. Most of this group use the autonym *Hmong Shuad* which means "Sinicized Miao." However, the Hmong Shuad still speak their own Miao language and wear traditional clothing. The Chinese call different Hmong Shuad subgroups by local names, such as *Waishu Miao* (Lopsided Comb Miao), *Biantou Miao* (Flat Head Miao), *Mushu Miao* (Wooden Comb Miao), and *Shuixi Miao* (West of the Water Miao).[3]

Language: Linguist Michael Johnson has researched the Hmong Shuad language. He says, "It is one of the most divergent Miao dialects.... There are many phonological features which are not shared with other dialects... that show a close relationship with Hmong Daw — especially as regards kinship terms in the lexicon — and also to some degree with A-Hmao."[4]

History: The Miao have a woeful history of warfare and genocide inflicted on them by the Chinese. One attack was launched in 1726. Qing Dynasty troops set more than 1,000 Miao villages on fire, butchered tens of thousands of people, and destroyed their farmland.[5] In response, in 1727 various Miao tribes unified against the Chinese, constructing stone signal towers at one-mile intervals along mountain ridges. The Miao took blood oaths to fight the Chinese to the death. They even killed their own wives and children, so they could face the advancing enemy as men with nothing to lose.[6] In 1795 the Miao took up knives and long poles in another revolt against Qing troops. The Miao occupied many townships for more than a decade. Another uprising occurred from 1851 to 1874. The Miao forces were victorious and gained control of almost the entire northwest area of Guizhou Province.[7]

Customs: Some Hmong Shuad claim their ancestors were soldiers sent to Guizhou from Jiangxi. The soldiers settled down and married Miao women. As a result, today many Hmong Shuad do not even claim Miao ethnicity. Other Miao groups call them "Chinese Hmong."

Religion: The majority of Hmong Shuad are animists. They also worship their ancestors, a practice that probably stems from their Chinese origins.

Christianity: Because they are such a widespread group, the influence of Christianity among the Hmong Shuad is difficult to gauge. However, there is a Christian presence in Anshun and Shuicheng, two of the areas where the Hmong Shuad live. Jinping County in Yunnan also contains many Hmong Daw believers. A number of Hmong Shuad attend Han Chinese churches in the region.

Paul Hattaway

Hmong Vron 赫蒙润

Location: More than 4,4000 members of the Hmong Vron people group inhabit 12 villages in the Suoga District, near Luzhi in western Guizhou Province. Luzhi is part of the Lupanshui (Six Plate Water) Municipality. The area has been described as a "sea of coal.... A wide range of coal types is extracted from tunnel mines and exports, including coke, are sent to Hong Kong, Japan, India, and the U.S.A."[1] The Hmong Vron live just south of the Gha-Mu area.

Identity: Hmong Vron women wear long wooden horns connected to their hair. Because of this they are called *Long Horn Miao* in English. *Hmong Vron* means "forest Hmong." The Chinese call them *Qing Miao*, which means "forest Miao." There is another group of Hmong near Bijie who also wear horns, but the two groups are only distantly related. In *Operation China* this latter group is called *Horned Miao.*

Language: The Hmong Vron speak a language belonging to the Farwestern Hmong language group. It is probably most closely related to Horned Miao. Hmong Vron is not understood by other Miao in the area.

History: The Hmong Vron, like many other Miao/Hmong groups in China, have been ensnared by dire poverty for centuries. When the Communists passed through Guizhou in 1934 on their Long March, they were horrified at the condition of the Miao. "They sat huddled in nakedness beside straw cooking fires.... Girls of seventeen and eighteen worked naked in the fields. Many families had only one pair of trousers to share among three or four adult males.... They owned no land. They were in debt to the landlord from birth to death. There was no escape. They sold their children if anyone would buy them. They smothered or drowned baby girls. That was routine. The boys were killed too, if there was no market for them."[2]

Robert Sussland

Customs: To produce their striking appearance, Hmong Vron women first tie a big wooden horn on their heads. "Then, cords of hair are bound around the wooden horn.... In fact, the cords are made from the hair of her deceased elder relatives handed down through the generations.... Tradition has it that long ago a villager caught an exceptionally beautiful pheasant. It caused a sensation among the villagers, who wished to dress themselves as beautifully as the golden pheasant."[3]

Religion: In the past, each Hmong Vron village had its own shaman. Today most are animists, living in constant fear of evil spirits.

Christianity: The Hmong Vron are an unreached people group with no known believers despite the fact that they are neighbors of the Gha-Mu (Small Flowery Miao) — the majority of whom are Christians. The gospel has not spread to the Hmong Vron because of linguistic and social barriers. This situation highlights the necessity for the Christian world to view the many Miao groups as separate entities. The Gha-Mu speak a completely different language from the Hmong Vron. Also, the two groups do not particularly like each other. As a result, there is little contact between them.

Population in China:
4,000 (1996)
4,460 (2000)
5,750 (2010)
Location: Guizhou
Religion: Animism
Christians: None Known

Overview of the Hmong Vron

Countries: China

Pronunciation: "Hmong-Vron"

Other Names: Qing Miao, Forest Miao, Long-Horn Miao

Population Source: 4,000 (1996 Ouyang Changpei); Out of a total Miao population of 7,398,035 (1990 census)

Location: *W Guizhou:* Suoga District of Luzhi County

Status: Officially included under Miao

Language: Hmong-Mien, Hmongic, Western Hmongic, Farwestern Hmong

Dialects: 0

Religion: Animism, Polytheism

Christians: None known

Scripture: None

***Jesus* film:** None

Gospel Recordings: Miao: Ching

Christian Broadcasting: None

ROPAL code: None

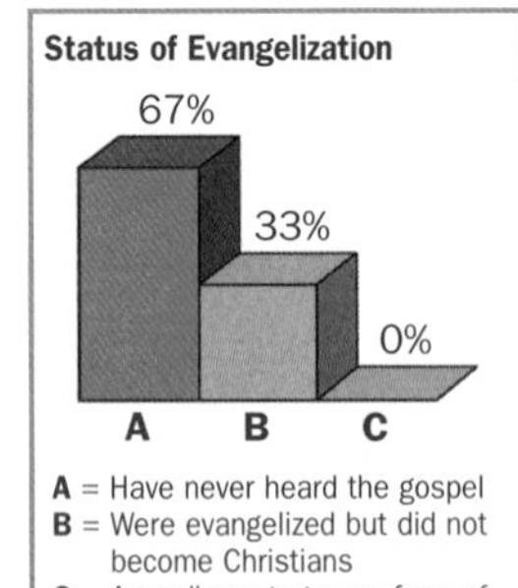

Hmu, Eastern 赫目(东)

Population in China:
350,000 (1990)
451,500 (2000)
582,400 (2010)
Location: Guizhou, Hunan
Religion: Animism
Christians: 1,000

Overview of the Eastern Hmu

Countries: China

Pronunciation: "H-moo"

Other Names: Hmong: Eastern Qiandong, Eastern East Guizhou Miao, Eastern Qiandong Miao, Hmu, Hei Miao, Black Miao

Population Source: 350,000 (1995 Wang Fushi – 1990 figure); 200,000 (1985 Wang Fushi – 1982 figure); Out of a total Miao population of 7,398,035 (1990 census)

Location: *E Guizhou:* Jinping, Jianhe, and Liping counties; *SW Hunan:* Huitong, Jingzhou, and Tongdao counties

Status: Officially included under Miao

Language: Hmong-Mien, Hmongic, Eastern Hmongic

Dialects: 0

Religion: Animism, Polytheism, Ancestor Worship, Christianity

Christians: 1,000

Scripture: Portions 1928

***Jesus* film:** None

Gospel Recordings: None

Christian Broadcasting: None

ROPAL code: HMQ00

Status of Evangelization

	A	B	C
%	86%	13%	1%

A = Have never heard the gospel
B = Were evangelized but did not become Christians
C = Are adherents to any form of Christianity

Location: Approximately 450,000 Eastern Hmu speakers inhabit Jinping, Jianhe, and Liping counties in the fareastern corner of Guizhou Province, as well as Jingxian, Tongdao, and Huitong counties of neighboring Hunan Province. The Qinghsui River, which flows through the region, contains a breed of giant salamanders, each weighing up to 39 kilograms (66 lb.).[1]

Paul Hattaway

Identity: The Eastern Hmu, who are one of the many components of the great Miao minority, call themselves *Hmu.* Missionaries in the past called them the *Black Miao*, but this name has never been used by the people themselves. Linguists label them the *Eastern Qiandong Miao.*

Language: The Eastern group of Miao languages is very different in structure, vocabulary, and phonology from other Miao language groups. There is "very low intelligibility" among the three Hmu languages.[2] A linguist "met one situation in which speakers in one village had a remarkably different pronunciation of certain vowels and tones from another village in the same valley within one hour's walking distance."[3]

History: After the many Miao rebellions and wars during the Ming Dynasty, the survivors scattered across the country. Around that time, the group known today as the Eastern Hmu arrived in their present location.[4]

Customs: Many Miao groups in Guizhou, including the Eastern Hmu, have a legend describing the creation of the human race. They say a long time ago a rat and a small animal called the *jiao-ao* chewed away the roots of a pine tree. Worms laid twelve eggs in the branches of the fallen tree, but none of the eggs would hatch. At last, a swan was able to hatch the eggs. From ten of them came Thunder and nine different types of animals. The swan thought the two other eggs had died, and began to peck the eggs open. The eggs cried out, "Don't peck us! Wait another two days!" Two days later a boy named Ang emerged from one shell and his sister from the other.[5]

Religion: The Eastern Hmu have a 1,000 line poem that tells how the heavens and the earth were created by a heavenly king named Vang-vai and his son Zie-ne.[6] Today the Eastern Hmu know little about any Creator. Most are trapped in slavery to evil spirits.

Christianity: Of the few Christians among the Eastern Hmu, most are members of Catholic churches. The vast majority of this group, however, have never heard the gospel. Protestant work began in Guizhou in 1877, but it was not until 1896 that an effort was made to target the Hmu. The three Hmu language groups have proven more resistant to Christianity than Miao in other parts of China.[7] Today, despite their considerable population, there are no more than a handful of ministries conducting any Christian work among the Eastern Hmu. No Scriptures or gospel recordings exist that the Eastern Hmu can readily comprehend.[8]

Hmu, Northern 赫目(北)

Miao Messenger

Location: Approximately 1.6 million Northern Hmu are concentrated in eastern Guizhou Province and areas of northern Guangxi. The main center for the Northern Hmu is the city of Kaili. Others are located in southeast Guizhou. Scattered pockets are also found in southwest Guizhou and in Longlin County in northwest Guangxi.

Identity: The Northern Hmu are a linguistic distinction within the large, official Miao nationality in China. Their autonym is *Hmu*. "Miao" is a Chinese name. There are three Hmu language groups, of which Northern Hmu is the largest.

Language: Northern Hmu is a part of the Eastern branch of the Hmongic linguistic family. It contains at least seven dialects, some of which may also qualify as distinct languages. An orthography was introduced by the government in the 1950s, but it has never gained widespread acceptance among the people.

History: The Chinese have despised the Hmu for centuries. The Chinese called the Hmu "men-dogs," believing they had tails. Stories were circulated that when the Hmu were born, their feet were cauterized to make it impossible for them to get tired.[1]

Customs: Perhaps the greatest Hmu festival is the annual Dragon Boat Festival. Legend has it that at one time an evil dragon lived in a palace in the depths of the Qingshui River. Occasionally he would rise up to cause destruction among Hmu communities. An old man swam to the bottom of the river and set fire to the dragon's palace.

Religion: When a Hmu dies, a shaman "opens the road" by giving directions to enable the soul of the deceased to reach heaven after a long journey. He says, "When you come to the snow mountain, don't fear the cold. When you come to the door of heaven, an old man guards it and will not let you in. Tell him who you are and all about yourself, and he will allow you to enter."[2]

Christianity: The gospel has never taken root among the Northern Hmu. F. B. Webb commenced Protestant mission work at Panghai in 1896.[3] In 1898, CIM missionary W. S. Fleming and the first Hmu convert, Pan Xiushan, were murdered. Thirty-two Hmu "Christian inquirers" were "seized and beheaded without trial or defense."[4] This caused great harm to the advance of Christianity. M. H. Hutton described the cool reception he received at a Hmu village 14 years later: "Some of the men began to curse my men for leading us to their village. They said they did not want the foreigner nor his Gospel, for some years ago, they said, all those who had anything to do with the Gospel Hall were killed."[5] Hutton later reported that "work is steady, with families coming to Christ several at a time."[6] By 1934 he had completed his translation of the Black Miao (Hmu) New Testament. Today only about 50 believers near Kaili "know Hutton's Black Miao writing.... Hymns are still sung from the 1928 hymn book."[7]

Population in China:
1,250,000 (1990)
1,612,500 (2000)
2,080,100 (2010)
Location: Guizhou, Guangxi
Religion: Animism
Christians: 2,000

Overview of the Northern Hmu

Countries: China

Pronunciation: "H-moo"

Other Names: Hmong: Northern Qiandong, Hei Miao, Black Miao, Chientung Miao, Hmu, Northern Qiandong Miao

Population Source: 1,250,000 (1995 Wang Fushi – 1990 figure); 900,000 (1985 Wang Fushi – 1982 figure); Out of a total Miao population of 7,398,035 (1990 census)

Location: *SE Guizhou:* Songtao, Kaili, Majiang, Danzhai, Leishan, Tajiang, Huangping, Jianhe, Zhenyuan, Sansui, Fuquan, Zhenning, Xingren, Zhenfeng, Guanling, and Ziyun counties; *NW Guangxi:* Longlin County

Status: Officially included under Miao

Language: Hmong-Mien, Hmongic, Eastern Hmongic

Dialects (7): Taikung, Kaili, Lushan,Taijiang, Chengfeng, Jungchiang, Yanghao

Religion: Animism, Polytheism, Christianity

Christians: 2,000

Scripture: New Testament 1934; Portions 1928

***Jesus* film:** None

Gospel Recordings: Black Miao #04664

Christian Broadcasting: None

ROPAL code: HEA00

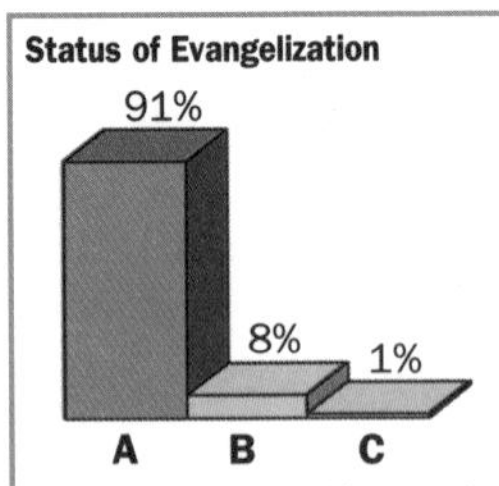

Hmu, Southern 赫目(南)

Location: The Southern Hmu — one of the groups labeled *Black Miao* by early missionaries — numbered 500,000 people in 1990. They inhabit parts of the Qiandongnan Prefecture in eastern Guizhou Province and adjacent parts of the Guangxi Autonomous Region. The Southern Hmu live in one of the poorest and most remote regions of China. Many villages are located more than a mile above sea level. Temperature variation over a vertical mile is equal to temperature variation over a land distance of up to 2,500 kilometers (1,560 mi.) horizontally. One Hmu woman commented, "We buy our land not with money like you, we buy it with our tears."[1]

Identity: The Hmu are part of the official Miao nationality. *Miao* is a Chinese term and is not used by the various groups that are termed "Miao." *Hmu* is the name this group calls itself. For countless centuries most Southern Hmu have lived alongside the Dong minority. In some places the distinction between the Hmu and Dong has become blurred. The two groups often wear identical ethnic dress and celebrate the same festivals.

Language: Southern Hmu is the second largest of the three Hmu languages in China. In northern Guangxi it has been heavily influenced by the Dong and Zhuang languages.

History: Records suggest the ancestors of the Hmu already had a well-developed culture in the Yellow River valley region of Central China more than 2,000 years ago. Chi You, their leader, founded their religion, invented a detailed code of criminal law, and initiated the use of arms.[2]

Customs: Many Southern Hmu are unable to attend school because their communities need every family member to work in the fields. In other areas the cost of schooling is beyond what most families can afford.

Paul Hattaway

Religion: During the annual Hmu Worship of the Door Festival the door is closed at sunset, and a young female pig is sacrificed. The pig's blood is drained into a hole under the door jamb. The family then observes a long period of silence. Eventually the family members retire for the night, except the father and oldest son. They stay up until just before daybreak, solemnly reciting the phrase, "We worship thee, O door. Keep away sickness, keep away disease, keep away slander and all that is injurious."[3]

Christianity: The Catholic church commenced work in Guizhou in the 1600s. In 1870, 300 Hmu from a diaspora group were baptized at Zhengfeng in Guizhou Province.[4] In 1927, Carlo — the first *Vicaire Apostolique* at Anlong — baptized 150 Hmu believers.[5] Protestant work among the Southern Hmu was slow to develop. In 1950 Ivan Allbut wrote, "In a tribe conservatively estimated to include 500,000 people, there are about 100 who have confessed the Lord in baptism.... They have the Black Miao [Hmu] New Testament in their language, but are still waiting for missionaries to teach them how to use it."[6]

Population in China:
500,000 (1990)
645,000 (2000)
832,000 (2010)
Location: Guizhou, Guangxi
Religion: Animism
Christians: 400

Overview of the Southern Hmu

Countries: China

Pronunciation: "H-moo"

Other Names: Hmong: Southern Qiandong, Southern East Guizhou Miao, Hmu, Black Miao, Hei Miao, Southern Qiandong Miao

Population Source: 500,000 (1995 Wang Fushi – 1990 figure); 300,000 (1985 Wang Fushi – 1982 figure);
Out of a total Miao population of 7,398,035 (1990 census)

Location: *S Guizhou:* Rongjiang, Congjiang, Danzhai, and Sandu counties;
N Guangxi: Rongshui and Sanjiang counties

Status:
Officially included under Miao

Language: Hmong-Mien, Hmongic, Eastern Hmongic

Dialects: 0

Religion: Animism, Polytheism, Ancestor Worship

Christians: 400

Scripture: None

***Jesus* film:** None

Gospel Recordings: None

Christian Broadcasting: None

ROPAL code: HMS00

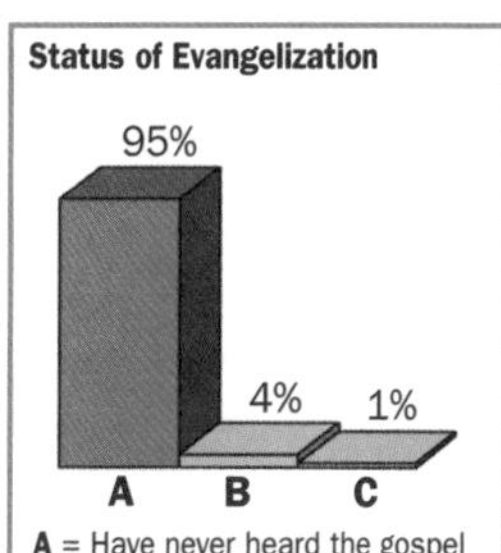

A = Have never heard the gospel
B = Were evangelized but did not become Christians
C = Are adherents to any form of Christianity

Hongjin Tai 宏金傣

Population in China:
150,000 (1995)
170,500 (2000)
217,300 (2010)
Location: Yunnan, Sichuan
Religion: Animism
Christians: 2,000

Overview of the Hongjin Tai

Countries: China

Pronunciation: "Hong-jin-Tie"

Other Names: Hongjin Dai, Tai Hongjin, Huagongji Dai, Flowery Rooster Dai, Yongren Tai

Population Source: 150,000 (1995 Luo Meizhen); Out of a total Dai population of 1,025,128 (1990 census)

Location: *N Yunnan:* Scattered communities in Honghe, Jinshajiang, Yuanjiang, Xinping, Maguan, and Wuding counties; *S Sichuan:* Huili and Dukou counties

Status: Officially included under Dai

Language: Daic, Tai, Southwestern Tai

Dialects: 0

Religion: Animism, Polytheism, Theravada Buddhism, No Religion, Christianity

Christians: 2,000

Scripture: None

***Jesus* film:** None

Gospel Recordings: Dai: Wuding #04854

Christian Broadcasting: None

ROPAL code: TIZ00

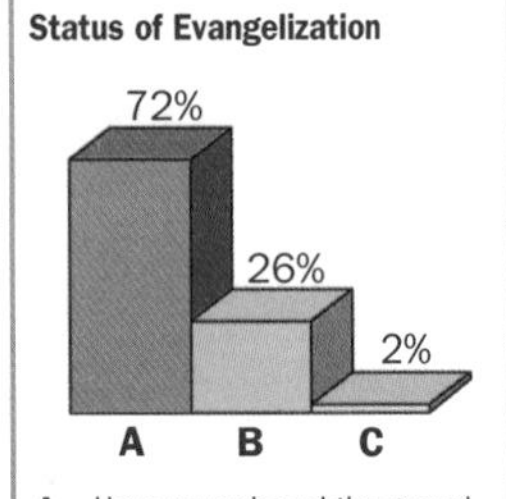

Location: In 1995 Chinese linguist Luo Meizhen described the Hongjin Tai language for the first time.[1] He numbered 150,000 speakers, scattered in small communities across southwest China, from the southern part of Sichuan Province down to the China-Vietnam border. The Hongjin Tai have migrated along the Honghe and Yangtze river systems. By 1952, the established households of Hongjin Tai in Wuding County of northern Yunnan Province numbered 2,706.[2]

Identity: The Hongjin Tai are also known in the Wuding area as the *Hua Gongji* (Flowery Rooster) Tai. The description of Hongjin Tai seems to be a broad one and may be a generic description of those Tai groups in China who do not fit into one of the recognized classifications.

Language: The farther north one goes, the less vigorous the Hongjin Tai language (which belongs to the Southwestern Tai language group) is used. Most Hongjin Tai are illiterate.

History: The golden era of the Tai (Dai) nationality in China began in 1340 when the Tai chief, Sifeka, established an independent kingdom in Luchuan (present-day Dehong).[3] The kingdom lasted for 100 years, until it was attacked by Ming Dynasty troops from 1441 to 1448. An army of 150,000 soldiers was mobilized from all over China to attack the Tai Kingdom and bring it to its knees.[4] To this day the Tai have never again had their own homeland in China. Numerous Tai fled the warfare and scattered throughout southern China — they are the ancestors of today's Hongjin Tai. Those living along the Yangtze River in northern Yunnan are described as "a hidden pocket of 10,000 Tais who long ago moved far away from their southwest homeland."[5]

Customs: Many of the Hongjin Tai have assimilated to Chinese culture. Few now wear any traditional clothing, and many of their children cannot speak the language.

Religion: Various Hongjin Tai groups practice different religions depending upon their location. These include animism, polytheism, and Theravada Buddhism.

Christianity: There are approximately 1,000 Hongjin Tai Christians in the Luquan area of northern Yunnan. The China Inland Mission commenced work among them in the early 1900s. In the 1980s "the Lipo used Mandarin Chinese to bring the Gospel to the Hua Gongji ('Flowery Rooster') tribe.... So many hundreds of Tais have come to the Lord... this year they have dedicated their first church."[6] The Hongjin Tai living in the southern part of Sichuan Province were visited in 1914 by William Dodd, a missionary working in northern Thailand. Seventeen Hongjin Tai families soon became Christians. Dodd taught them to read the Northern Thai script, enabling them to read the Bible.[7] It is not known if they still use this script — which is practically extinct in Thailand. Dodd reported, "Three families from the same village destroyed their idols and put away all traces of demon worship, accepted Christ and came for study faithfully. There are but thirty families in the village and twenty of them are now Christian."[8]

Paul Hattaway

68

69

70

71

68. A *Northern Hmu* woman's festival silver headdress, Shidong, Guizhou. [Paul Hattaway]
69. Some *Southern Hmu* girls from northern Guangxi. [*Miao Messenger*]
70. *Southern Hmu* from the mountains of Rongjiang County, Guangxi. [*Miao Messenger*]
71. A headdress of the *Northern Hmu* in Shidong, Guizhou. [Paul Hattaway]

72

73

74

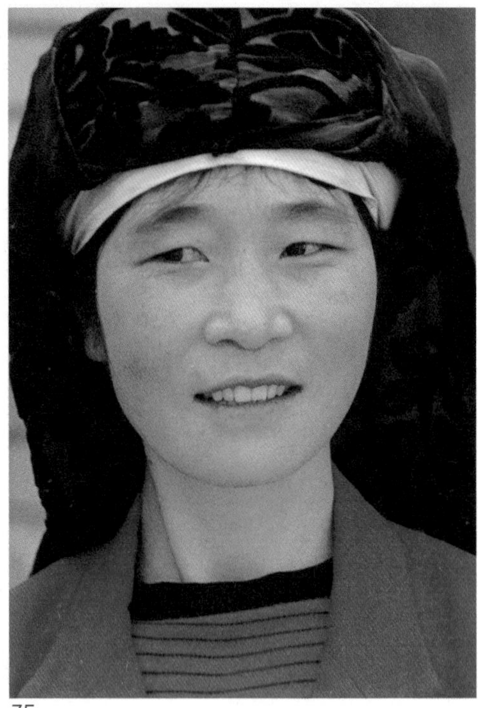

75

72–75. More than 10 million *Hui* Muslims — the descendants of Arab and Persian traders — live scattered throughout China. The Hui are probably the largest ethnic group in the world without a single known Christian fellowship or church. [all by Paul Hattaway]

76

77

78

76–77. The 70,000 *Huayao Tai* (Flowery Belt Tai) live scattered throughout southern Yunnan Province. [76 Paul Hattaway; 77 Midge Conner]

78. The Red Cone-Headed Yao, a subgroup of the *Iu Mien*, are located on both sides of the China-Vietnam border. Many have come to Christ in recent years as the result of gospel radio broadcasts in their language. [YWAM COM]

79 80 81 82

79–82. Four of the different branches of the unevangelized *Iu Mien* are pictured. More than one million Iu Mien live scattered across five provinces of southern China. In China the Iu Mien are known by a number of different local names given to them by the Chinese. Despite their wide dispersion, the Iu Mien language is reasonably uniform. Iu Mien from most areas have little problem communicating with each other.
[79 Midge Conner; 80 & 81 Paul Hattaway; 82 Dwayne Graybill]

Horned Miao 角苗

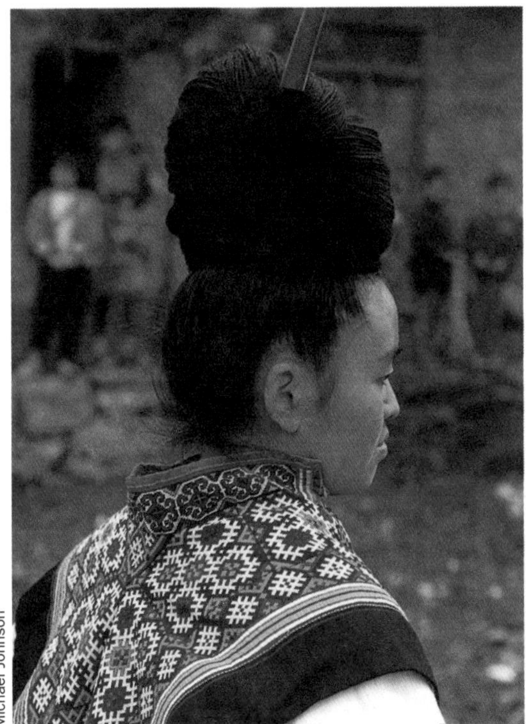
Michael Johnson

Location: Linguist Michael Johnson, an expert on the Miao languages, listed a 1998 population of 50,000 Horned Miao living in southern China.[1] They are located on a thin strip of land that stretches from Zhenxiong County in northeastern Yunnan Province all the way southeast to Guiyang Municipality, the capital of Guizhou Province. The main concentration of Horned Miao inhabit the Shuangshau, Xiangshui, and Pojiao districts of Dafang County in Guizhou.

Identity: The Horned Miao have been officially counted as part of the large Miao nationality in China, but they have a distinct ethnolinguistic identity. The Chinese call them *Jiaojiao Miao* in Mandarin, or *Koko Miao* in the local Chinese dialect. We have called them *Horned Miao* because of their women's practice of wearing large wooden horns on their head.[2] The Miao in Bijie call them *Hmong Soud* which means "lively" or "bustling." This name is a reflection of the energetic way the Horned Miao celebrate festivals.[3] The Horned Miao are not the same as the Hmong Vron (Long Horn Miao), who live in northwest Guizhou.

Language: The Horned Miao speak a language belonging to the Chuanqiandian (Western) Miao family. "Horned Miao shares a large number of phonological and phonetic features with Gha-Mu [Small Flowery Miao] including the loss of all syllable-final nasal consonants... and various phonetic (pronunciation) features... Horned Miao also shows a number of similarities with the Sinicized Hmong [Hmong Shuad] group.... The majority of Horned Miao now live on the borders of the Sinicized Hmong [Hmong Shuad] region."[4]

History: The Horned Miao call themselves Hmong Khuat Shuad Ndrang which means "guest of the Chinese plain Hmong." Johnson notes, "This autonym is somewhat ironic in that the local Hmong claim they lived in the small plain just north of Bijie before the Chinese did, and were the driven out to the surrounding hilly regions by Chinese settlers."[5]

Customs: The Horned Miao women have a striking appearance. "Their hair, along with false hair, is wrapped around a large horn-shaped wooden comb. In the past this comb was smaller and the tips only just protruded out from the hair. In more recent times, and especially amongst older people, the comb is extremely wide, almost the size of buffalo horns. During festival times the young women wear as many as thirty skirts and several long jackets."[6]

Religion: The majority of Horned Miao share the animistic and polytheistic practices of their Hmong neighbors. They are a superstitious people, believing a finely balanced harmony must be kept between them and the spirit world.

Christianity: Despite living near the heavily Christianized A-Hmao and Gha-Mu groups, linguistic and cultural barriers have prevented the Horned Miao from hearing the gospel. In the past there was no Christian work among them, resulting in few today having heard of Christ. There are no known Horned Miao believers or churches.

Population in China:
60,000 (1998)
63,480 (2000)
81,900 (2010)
Location: Guizhou, Yunnan
Religion: Animism
Christians: None Known

Overview of the Horned Miao

Countries: China

Pronunciation: "Jeeow-jeeow-Meow"

Other Names: Horn Miao, Jiaojiao Miao, Bai Miao, White Miao, Hmong Soud, Koko Miao

Population Source: 60,000 (1998 M. Johnson); Out of a total Miao population of 7,398,035 (1990 census)

Location: *Guizhou:* Dafang, Zhijin, Qingzhen, Bijie counties; Guiyang Municipality; *NE Yunnan:* Zhenxiong County

Status: Officially included under Miao

Language: Hmong-Mien, Hmongic, Western Hmongic, Farwestern Hmong, Horned Miao

Dialects: 2

Religion: Animism, Polytheism, Ancestor Worship

Christians: None known

Scripture: None

***Jesus* film:** None

Gospel Recordings: None

Christian Broadcasting: None

ROPAL code: HHO00

Status of Evangelization

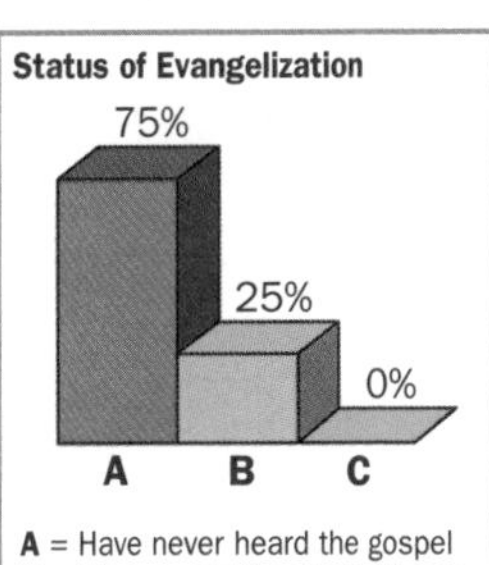

A = Have never heard the gospel
B = Were evangelized but did not become Christians
C = Are adherents to any form of Christianity

Hu 户

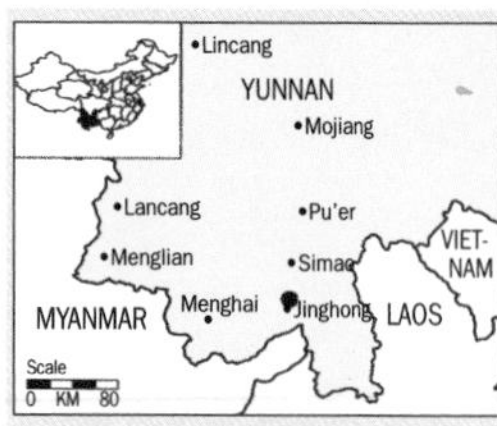

Population in China:
1,000 (1984)
1,460 (2000)
1,890 (2010)
Location: Yunnan
Religion: Buddhism
Christians: None Known

Overview of the Hu

Countries: China

Pronunciation: "Hoo"

Other Names:

Population Source:
1,000 (1984 J.-O. Svantesson)

Location: *SW Yunnan:* The Hu live in five communities in the Xiaomengyang District of Jinghong County in the Xishuangbanna Dai Prefecture.

Status: Counted in census as an *Undetermined Minority*

Language: Austro-Asiatic, Mon-Khmer, Northern Mon-Khmer, Palaungic, Western Palaungic, Angkuic

Dialects: 0

Religion:
Theravada Buddhism, Animism

Christians: None known

Scripture: None

***Jesus* film:** None

Gospel Recordings: None

Christian Broadcasting: None

ROPAL code: HUO00

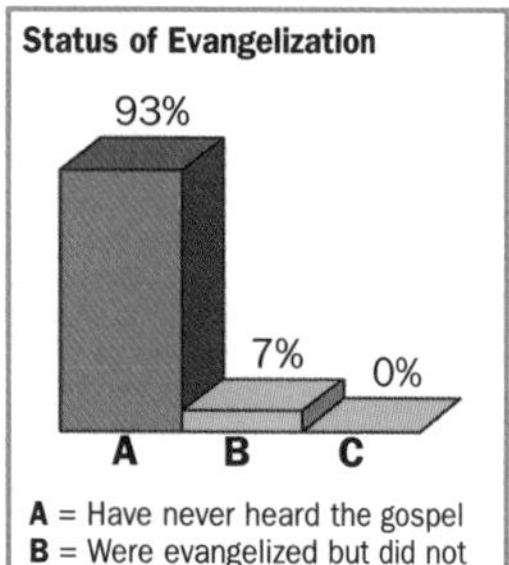

A = Have never heard the gospel
B = Were evangelized but did not become Christians
C = Are adherents to any form of Christianity

Dwayne Graybill

Location: Linguist J.-O. Svantesson listed a 1984 figure of 1,000 speakers of the Hu language.[1] They inhabit five villages in the Xiaomengyang District of Jinghong County in Xishuangbanna Prefecture.[2] The Hu live near the Manmet people and are also surrounded by Tai Lu and Bulang communities. The area inhabited by the Hu — the extreme southwest of China — is semi-tropical. It is warm and humid most of the year, while the rainy season inundates the crops between May and September every year.

Identity: The Hu are a distinct ethnolinguistic people group. Although their language is related to the Manmet and Angku who live in the same area, it does have significant differences. The Hu applied to be recognized as a separate minority in the 1950s, but their application was rejected. The authorities then offered the Hu a chance to be included as part of one of the several minority groups in the area, which they, in turn, refused to accept. In the 1982 Chinese census, the Hu were listed in a category of *Undetermined Minorities*.

Language: The tonal Hu language is part of the Angkuic branch of the Mon-Khmer language family. The Hu do not use a written script, but some of the Hu village leaders can read Chinese.

History: Although little is known about the origins of the Hu, they were probably part of a larger collection of Mon-Khmer peoples in the region who later came to form the official Bulang minority group. The Hu were formerly oppressed by Tai Lu and Chinese landowners until the Communist takeover of China in 1949. The land redistribution programs of the 1950s ended their oppression.

Customs: The Hu live simple lives, tending to their rice paddies that are skillfully built into the mountain slopes.

Religion: Although on the surface the Hu claim to be Buddhists, their daily lives are much more influenced by animistic beliefs. They fear demons and believe all sickness and bad luck comes upon them as a result of upsetting the delicate balance between the natural and spiritual worlds.

Christianity: The Hu are a people group untouched by the message of the gospel. Few have ever heard the name of Jesus Christ. In the past 200 years there have been numerous courageous missionaries in China, but none ever visited the Hu. Hudson Taylor, the most famous of all missionaries to China, once issued this challenge which can accurately be applied to the Hu today: "His Name, His attributes, they have never heard; His kingdom is not proclaimed among them. His will is not made known to them. Do you believe that each unit of these millions has a precious soul, and that there is no other Name under heaven given to men by which they must be saved except that of Jesus? Do you believe that He alone is the Way, the Truth and the Life?; that no man comes to the Father but through Him? If so, think of the state of these unsaved ones and solemnly examine yourself in the sight of God to see whether you are doing your utmost to make Him known to them."[3]

Hua Miao 花苗

Population in China:
564,000 (1998)
596,700 (2000)
769,700 (2010)
Location:
Guizhou, Yunnan, Sichuan
Religion: Animism
Christians: 1,000

Overview of the Hua Miao

Countries: China, Vietnam, Thailand, Laos, USA

Pronunciation: "Hwa-Meow"

Other Names: Hua Hmong, Hmong Sou, Hmong Dous, Downhill Hmong, Hmong Ghuad Dus, Shangfang Ren, Zhanjia Ren, Hmong Ndrou, Hmong Nraug, Hmong Bel

Population Source:
564,000 (1998 M. Johnson);
Out of a total Miao population of 7,398,035 (1990 census);
Also in Vietnam, Thailand, Laos, USA

Status:
Officially included under Miao

Location:
Guizhou: Weining, Dafang, Pan, and Hezhang counties;
S Sichuan; *Yunnan*

Language: Hmong-Mien, Hmongic, Western Hmongic, Farwestern Hmong, Hua Miao

Dialects: 0

Religion: Animism, Polytheism, Ancestor Worship, Christianity

Christians: 1,000

Scripture: None

***Jesus* film:** None

Gospel Recordings: None

Christian Broadcasting: None

ROPAL code: HHN00

Status of Evangelization

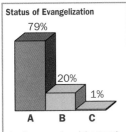

	A	B	C
	79%	20%	1%

A = Have never heard the gospel
B = Were evangelized but did not become Christians
C = Are adherents to any form of Christianity

Location: Approximately 600,000 Hua Miao are scattered over a wide area of Yunnan, Sichuan, and Guizhou provinces in southern China. One source lists a figure of 1.1 million Hua Miao speakers,[1] but this includes the Hua Miao outside of China and also groups such as the Chuan Miao, Hmong Njua, Hmong Bua, and Hmong Leng — all of which have been profiled separately in this book.

Identity: Although the Chinese call all members of this group *Hua Miao*, they are not the same as the Big Flowery (Hua) Miao or the Small Flowery (Hua) Miao. Among the Hua Miao there are numerous different self-names, ethnic groups, and dress styles, but all speak one common language. Linguist Michael Johnson has coined the term *Hua Miao* for this large group. They have been called by many other names in the past. Johnson explains, "I have labeled this linguistic grouping by the rather ambiguous term Hua Miao because there is no one 'Miao + modifier' autonym that is used throughout the group.... Many of the subgroups within Hua Miao are in fact called *Hua Miao* 'Flowery Miao' by the Chinese. The geographic extent of the group also makes it difficult to use a geographic based name."[2]

Language: Johnson further notes, "Within Hua Miao mutual intelligibility is generally extremely high, especially when two dialects are in local contact. Intelligibility is hindered between Hua Miao in China and those outside of China because of the past 150 years or more of lost contact and influence from surrounding minority languages."[3]

History: Despite their present ethnic divisions, the Hua Miao were once one group. "Given the comparatively minor extent of linguistic variation within Hua Miao it is feasible that the group formed a single ethnolinguistic group... perhaps only 600 years ago. The present geographical scattering is due mostly to migrations during the Qing Dynasty which were fueled by persecutions and other social unrest."[4]

Customs: Hua Miao probably contains several dozen self-appellations and varieties of dress. Among this collection of groups are the *Hmong Dous* (Downhill Hmong) in southern Sichuan, who are called *Hmong Ghuad Dus* (Buffalo Dung Hmong) by other Miao groups in the area in reference to their style of turban.[5]

Religion: The Hua Miao, being scattered over a large area, have several main religious beliefs, including animism, polytheism, and ancestor worship.

Christianity: There are as few as 1,000 scattered Hua Miao Christians in China — only one out of every 600 people. The Hua Miao are sparsely populated over a wide geographical area; therefore, their only chance of hearing the gospel comes if they happen to live near one of the few evangelized Miao groups — the A-Hmao and Gha-Mu in Guizhou or the Hmong Daw in Yunnan, for example. Significant ethnic and cultural barriers, and age-old prejudices combine to prohibit the gospel from spreading easily from one Miao group to another.

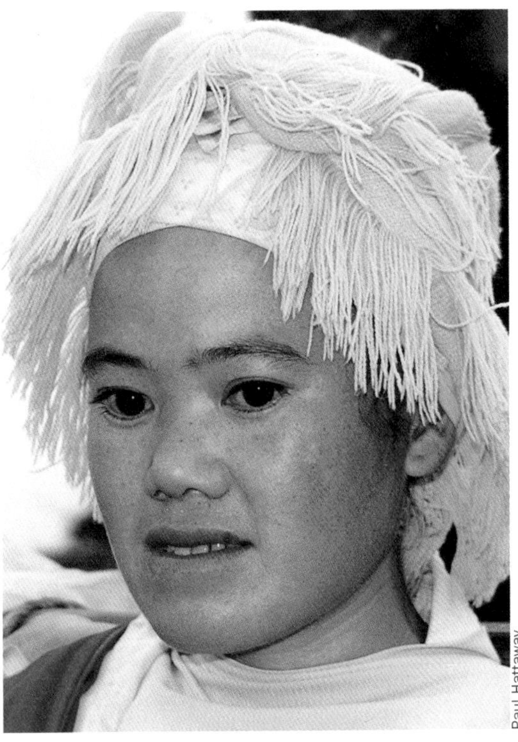
Paul Hattaway

Huayao Tai 花腰傣

Location: Fifty-five thousand Huayao Tai were reported in a 1990 official Chinese government survey. They live in stockaded villages in the foothills of the mountains in Xinping and Mengyang counties in the southern part of Yunnan Province. The Huayao Tai live in simple flat-roofed adobe homes that are built flat on the ground, as opposed to the neighboring Tai Lu who build their wooden homes on stilts. Small numbers of Huayao Tai also live along the banks of the Honghe River in Yuanjiang County.[1]

Identity: Although the Huayao (Flowery Belted) Tai are a part of the officially constructed Dai nationality in China, they desire to be recognized as a separate minority group. Their language shares some similarities to Tai Lu, but the two are reported to be mutually unintelligible.[2] It is possible that the Huayao Tai were a Tai group who originally lived in eastern Yunnan and migrated to their present location in the Xishuangbanna Prefecture. All Huayao Tai are also able to speak Tai Lu, which serves as the *lingua franca* of the region. The Huayao Tai observe different festivals from the other Tai groups. They do not celebrate *Songkran*, the annual Water Splashing Festival.

Language: Most people erroneously believe *Huayao Tai* is a term used merely for social distinction within the Tai Lu, but Huayao Tai language and self-identity are strongly separate. Where they live near Tai Lu, their language seems to have changed to accommodate communication with the Lu, but the speakers of more isolated Huayao Tai villages have great difficulty in communicating with other Tai speakers. Most Huayao Tai under the age of 40 are also able to speak and read Chinese.

History: The Huayao Tai are historically part of the great and ancient Tai race. One writer claimed that the Tai predate even the Chinese. "Gathered from Chinese and Burmese annals, as well as from their own, this history shows them to be older than the Hebrews or the Chinese themselves, to say nothing of such moderns as the Slavs, the Teutons or the Gauls."[3]

Paul Hattaway

Customs: Huayao Tai women are instantly recognizable by their huge circular hats. They also carry with them a small bamboo basket, containing needle and thread, cosmetics, or food. The distinctive dress of the Huayao Tai differs from one area to another, "by variations in their dress and the ornaments which they wear."[4] The Huayao Tai celebrate the annual Flower Street Festival.[5]

Religion: The Huayao Tai practice a mixture of Theravada Buddhism and animism. "Animism in its Tai form ranges from the worship of natural forces... to include the practice of shamanism, sorcery and black magic."[6]

Christianity: A small number of Huayao Tai believers live in Mengyang County. In recent years evangelists have been active among them, establishing several house churches. Few Huayao Tai outside of Mengyang have heard of Christ. The Huayao Tai believers use the Tai Lu and Chinese Scriptures. Gospel recordings have recently been produced in the Huayao Tai language.

Population in China:
55,000 (1990)
70,000 (2000)
89,200 (2010)
Location: Yunnan
Religion: Buddhism
Christians: 200

Overview of the Huayao Tai

Countries: China

Pronunciation: "Hwa-yaow-Tie"

Other Names: Hwayao Dai, Flowery Belt Dai, Flowery Waist Dai, Color Belt Dai

Population Source: 55,000 (1990 official figure); Out of a total Dai population of 1,025,128 (1990 census)

Location: *SW Yunnan:* Mengyang, Yuanjiang, and Xinping counties

Status: Officially included under Dai

Language: Daic, Tai, Southwestern Tai, East Central, Northwest

Dialects: 0

Religion: Theravada Buddhism, Animism, Christianity

Christians: 200

Scripture: None

***Jesus* film:** None

Gospel Recordings: Hua Yao Dai #04795 Hua Yao Gasa #04941

Christian Broadcasting: None

ROPAL code: None

Status of Evangelization

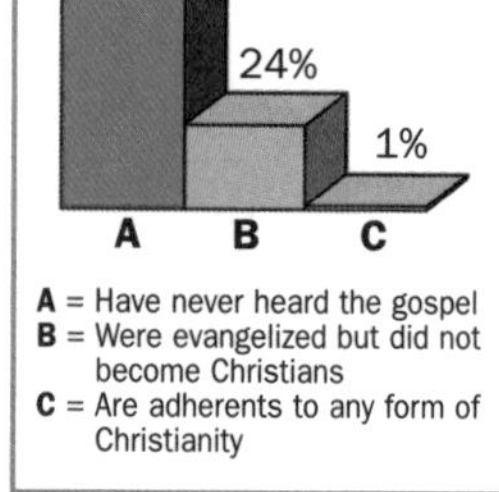

A = Have never heard the gospel
B = Were evangelized but did not become Christians
C = Are adherents to any form of Christianity

Hui 回

Population in China:
8,623,978 (1990)
10,676,500 (2000)
13,217,500 (2010)
Location: Ningxia, Gansu, Qinghai, Hebei, and most of China
Religion: Islam
Christians: 200

Overview of the Hui

Countries: China, Myanmar, Taiwan, Kyrgyzstan, Kazakstan, Thailand, Mongolia

Pronunciation: "Hway"

Other Names: Chinese Muslim, Dungan, Khotan, Panthay, Haw, Tungan

Population Source:
8,602,978 (1990 census);[1]
7,227,022 (1982 census);
4,473,147 (1964 census);
3,559,350 (1953 census);
100,000 in Myanmar;[2]
60,000 in Taiwan;
38,000 in Kyrgyzstan;
12,000 Kazakstan;[3]
2,000 in Mongolia[4]

Location: *Ningxia; Gansu; Qinghai; Hebei; Yunnan; Guizhou; Xinjiang; Henan; Anhui; Liaoning; Beijing* [5]

Status:
An official minority of China

Language: Chinese, Mandarin

Literacy: 58%

Dialects: 0

Religion: Islam

Christians: 200

Scripture: Chinese Bible

***Jesus* film:** Available in Mandarin

Gospel Recordings:
Chinese: Ningxia #4665
Chinese: Tongxin #4684

Christian Broadcasting:
Available (FEBC) – Mandarin but focused on the Hui

ROPAL code: None

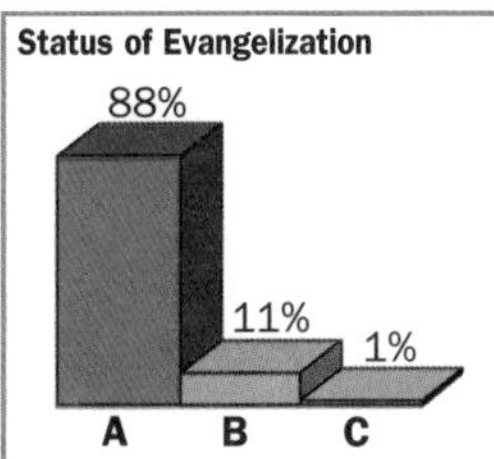

Paul Hattaway

Location: The Hui are the third largest minority group in China. Approximately 10.6 million Hui live scattered throughout almost every part of China. Remarkably, Hui reportedly live in 2,310 of the 2,369 counties and municipalities in China.[6] More than 200,000 Hui also live in the surrounding countries of Myanmar, Taiwan, Kyrgyzstan, Kazakstan, Mongolia, and Thailand. In these countries they are known by different names, including *Dungan*, *Panthay*, and *Khotan*. The majority of Hui in China inhabit the Ningxia Hui Autonomous Region, a barren wasteland established in 1958 in north central China.[7]

Identity: The Hui are an official minority of China. Their high cheekbones and round eyes give many Hui a very different appearance from the Han Chinese.

Language: The Hui speak standard Mandarin; although, in some locations, Persian and Arabic words have been added to their vocabulary.

History: By the middle of the seventh century, Arab and Persian traders and merchants traveled to China in search of riches. In addition, in the thirteenth century the Mongols turned people into mobile armies during their Central Asian conquests and sent them to China. These civilians were expected to settle down at various locations to farm while maintaining combat readiness. As artisans, scholars, officials, and religious leaders, they spread throughout China. These people are the ancestors of today's Hui. One of the worst cases of genocide in history took place against the Hui in Yunnan from 1855 to 1873. One million Hui people were massacred.[8]

Customs: The Hui are forbidden to eat pork, but that prohibition is often overlooked by calling the meat "mutton." A Chinese joke is that "One Muslim traveling will grow fat; two on a journey will grow thin."[9] The Hui are renowned as sharp businessmen. A Chinese proverb from the 1800s states, "A Chinese awake is not the equal of a Hui sleeping."[10]

Religion: Almost all Hui are Sunni Muslims. They worship in thousands of mosques throughout China. Islam first came to China via Abu Waggas, one of Mohammed's contemporaries. He preached in southern China and had the Beacon Tower built in memory of Mohammed in AD 627.[11] In recent years, an increasing number of Hui have traveled to Mecca for the annual Haj pilgrimage.

Christianity: Although there are a small number of scattered Hui believers in China,[12] the Hui are probably the largest people group in the world without a single known Christian fellowship group.[13] Mission work among the Hui in Ningxia commenced in 1885.[14] A few Hui converts were numbered among the Hui in Manchuria,[15] Gansu, and Qinghai[16] by the 1920s. In 1934 an American missionary known as Hai Chun Sheng baptized several Hui Muslim leaders in Qinghai.[17] Recently a mission team secretly distributed 35,000 gospel tracts and cassette tapes to the Hui.[18] A large church has emerged in northern Ningxia,[19] but almost all the believers are Han Chinese, and few of them have a desire to reach out to the Hui. Most Hui have yet to hear the gospel of Christ.

Indonesian 印度尼西亚人

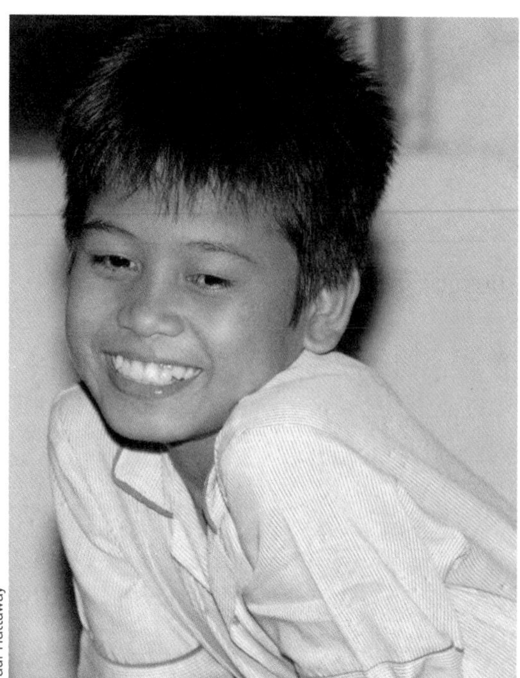

Paul Hattaway

Location: More than 8,500 Indonesians are located in four provinces of southern China. About 4,000 live on Hainan Island, with nearly the same number located in Fujian Province. A few hundred Indonesians live in southern Guangxi, and one small group has recently settled south of Kunming in Yunnan Province. The main body of Indonesians were placed in the Xinglong Overseas Chinese Farm on Hainan Island, an area good for coffee, pepper, coconut, and rubber production.

Identity: In 1952, 20,000 overseas Chinese refugees moved to Hainan Island after the Communist government issued an invitation for overseas Chinese to return to the "Motherland." The refugees from Malaysia were ethnic Han Chinese and have assimilated back to China easily. Today they are counted as part of the Han Chinese nationality by the government. Many of the Indonesians, however, were not of Chinese descent at all. Today they call themselves *Oran Toraja*, which means "people from Toraja." They have remained an ethnolinguistically distinct people group. One observer noted, "Not only do the villages speak Indonesian, but also their lifestyle remains Indonesian."[1]

Language: The majority of Indonesians in China came from the Toraja region in Sulawesi. Although Sulawesi is an ethnically diverse island — home to 114 distinct Malayo-Polynesian languages[2] — the Indonesians who migrated to China decided to speak standard Indonesian. Many are also proficient in English.

History: An additional 1,500 Indonesians came to China in the early 1960s after the failed Communist coup in Indonesia. The Chinese authorities resettled one group on Hainan Island and the other in Fujian Province. They encountered great hardship upon arrival in China. "Many of the new arrivals broke down in tears.... They were not farmers; they had to learn from the beginning how to plant crops and reap harvests."[3]

Customs: Ethnically, many of the Indonesians in China were from one of the tribal groups in the Toraja Mountains. They have largely forsaken their traditional clothing and customs, although some families remember their heritage on special occasions. During the Cultural Revolution, "although life was hard, they were still able to maintain a personal and ethnic identity."[4]

Religion: Although Islam is the state religion of Indonesia, the immigrants to China are not Muslims. Most came from the heavily Christianized Sulawesi Islands.

Christianity: Close to half of the Indonesians in China profess faith in Christ. The remainder are nonreligious. On Hainan Island the Indonesians meet in their own churches, both official and underground fellowships.[5] During the 1960s Christian worship was banned and many of the Indonesian believers were persecuted. The Indonesian church on Hainan Island is strong and meets nearly every day of the week. Since the mid-1980s Christian leaders from Sulawesi have come to Hainan to encourage and train the Indonesian believers.

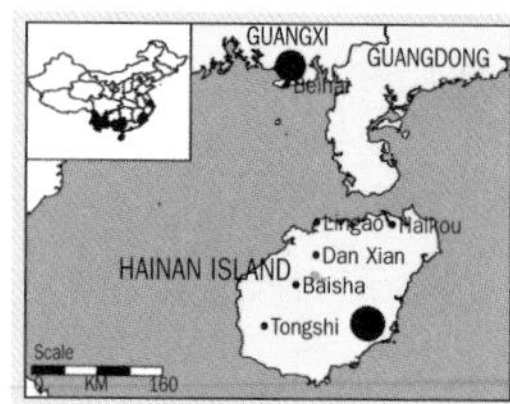

Population in China:
8,500 (1997)
8,830 (2000)
9,980 (2010)
Location: Hainan Island, Fujian, Guangxi, Yunnan
Religion: Christianity
Christians: 4,000

Overview of the Indonesians

Countries: Indonesia, Saudi Arabia, Singapore, Netherlands, China, USA

Pronunciation: "In-do-nee-seun"

Other Names: Oran Toraja, Indonesians: China

Population Source: 8,500 (1997 AMO); 140,000,000 in Indonesia (1993); 37,000 in Saudi Arabia (1993); 10,000 in Netherlands; 8,000 in Singapore (1993); 2,520 in USA (1975)

Location: *Hainan Island; Fujian; Guangxi; Yunnan*

Status: Officially included under Han Chinese

Language: Austronesian, Malayo-Polynesian, Western Malayo-Polynesian, Sundic, Malayic, Malayan

Dialects: 0

Religion: Christianity, No Religion

Christians: 4,000

Scripture: Bible 1974; New Testament 1968; Portions 1955

***Jesus* film:** Available

Gospel Recordings: Indonesian #00035

Christian Broadcasting: Not available in China

ROPAL code: INZ00

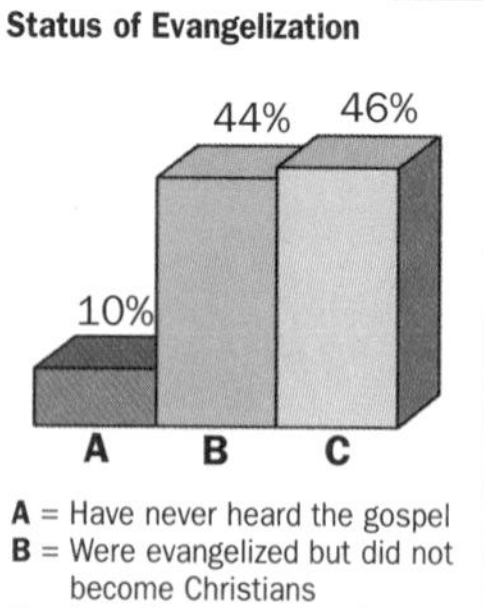

Iu Mien 与敏

Location: More than 980,000 Iu Mien live scattered across four provinces (and approximately 150 counties) of southern China. The majority are located in Guangxi, where the Iu Mien comprise 50% (615,000 people) of the total Yao population.[1] Others are scattered in parts of Yunnan, Guizhou and Jiangxi provinces. An additional 400,000 Iu Mien live in Southeast Asia, especially in Vietnam, Laos, and Thailand. Iu Mien refugee communities are also found in several Western nations.[2]

Identity: The Iu Mien are the largest of the groups who form the official Yao nationality in China. This group calls themselves *Iu Mien* or simply *Mien*, but in China they are widely known by their Chinese name *Pan Yao*. Little was known about this isolated group until recent years. In 1937 one traveler commented, "In these lofty areas are the aboriginal tribes called the *Iu people*, the 'Red Indians' of China. They are yet to be studied in detail."[3]

Language: The Iu Mien language is remarkably uniform considering the wide dispersion of its speakers. In 1987, Iu Mien able to speak their language numbered 692,000 (97%).[4] The remainder now speak Chinese.

History: The Iu Mien have a long history of fleeing oppression. This explains why the Chinese sometimes call them the *Guoshan* (Crossing the Mountains) Yao. Linguist Herbert Purnell explains, "The Iu Mien have been profoundly influenced by the Chinese over many centuries of contact. Perhaps the most significant development from these contacts has been the evolution and preservation of Taoist rituals written in Chinese characters.... The Iu Mien have therefore possessed for several centuries what many other Asian peoples only dream of — an extensive written literature."[5]

Customs: The Han Chinese call the Iu Mien *Pan Yao* after their legendary ancestor and pioneer of the Yao race, Pan Hu.[6] Pan can be traced in historical Chinese records as far back as the fifth century AD. The *Chronicles of the Later Han Dynasty ("Hou Han Shu")* "tells the story of Pan Hu, the pet dog of Emperor Gao Xin (2435–2365 BC) who killed his lord's arch-enemy, General Wu, the chief of the Quan Rong tribe. The dog was rewarded by marrying a young princess."[7] Their descendants, known as "the race of Pan Hu," became the forefathers of the Iu Mien. At some time the Imperial Court issued *The King Ping's Charter*. This proclamation was designed to reward the Yao by perpetually releasing them from paying taxes.[8]

Midge Conner

Religion: The Iu Mien are Daoists who also worship their ancestors. They believe Pan created the heavens and the earth. "After the death of King Pan... the feudal court allowed his descendants to worship and make a picture of him with human features."[9]

Christianity: Although one source estimates 10,000 Iu Mien/Yao Christians in China,[10] the true number is probably much lower. In recent years, at least 1,000 "Red Head" Yao (an Iu Mien group) living in Jinping County, Yunnan Province, have come to Christ because of FEBC gospel radio broadcasts in their language.[11]

Population in China:
712,000 (1987)
980,400 (2000)
1,264,700 (2010)
Location: Guangxi, Yunnan, Guizhou, Jiangxi
Religion: Daoism
Christians: 1,500

Overview of the Iu Mien

Countries: China, Vietnam, Thailand, USA, Laos, France, Canada, Myanmar, Denmark, New Zealand, Taiwan, Switzerland, and Australia

Pronunciation: "Yoo-Mee-en"

Other Names: Pan Yao, Youmian, Yumian, Yiu Mien, Mien, Mian, Myen, Highland Yao, Dao, Mien (Guangxi-Yunnan), Guoshan Yao, Man

Population Source: 712,000 (1987 *LAC*); 300,000 in Vietnam; 40,000 in Thailand; 23,000 in USA; 18,000 in Laos; 2,000 in France; 100 in Canada; 100 in Myanmar; 12 in Denmark; 7 in New Zealand; Also in Taiwan, Switzerland, Australia

Location: *Guangxi*; *Yunnan*; *Guizhou*; *Jiangxi*[12]

Status: Officially included under Yao

Language: Hmong-Mien, Mienic, Mian-Jin

Dialects: 0

Religion: Daoism, Ancestor Worship, Polytheism, Christianity

Christians: 1,500

Scripture: New Testament 1975; Portions 1932[13]

***Jesus* film:** In progress

Gospel Recordings: Yao #00417; Tuyao: Bama Dongshan #04975; Yao: Pang; Yao: Bangu

Christian Broadcasting: Available (FEBC)

ROPAL code: IUM00

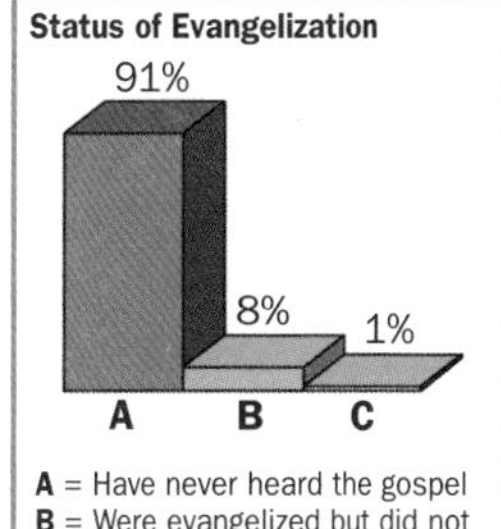

Iu Mien, Changping 与敏(常平)

Population in China:
20,000 (1990)
25,800 (2000)
33,200 (2010)
Location: Guangxi
Religion: Polytheism
Christians: None Known

Overview of the Changping Iu Mien

Countries: China

Pronunciation: "Chung-ping-Yoo-Mee-en"

Other Names: Pan Yao

Population Source: 20,000 (1995 Wang Fushi – 1990 figure); Out of a total Yao population of 2,134,013 (1990 census)

Location: *NE Guangxi:* Mengshan, Zhaoping, Pingle, and Lipu counties

Status: Officially included under Yao

Language: Hmong-Mien, Mienic, Mian-Jin

Dialects: 0

Religion: Polytheism, Animism, Ancestor Worship, Daoism

Christians: None known

Scripture: None

***Jesus* film:** None

Gospel Recordings: None

Christian Broadcasting: None

ROPAL code: IUM01

Status of Evangelization

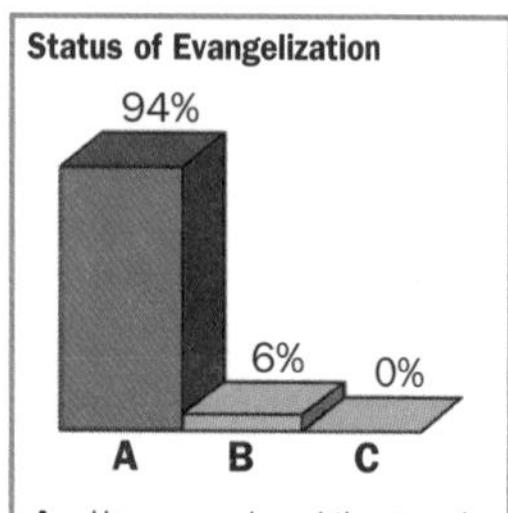

A = Have never heard the gospel
B = Were evangelized but did not become Christians
C = Are adherents to any form of Christianity

Location: More than 25,000 Changping Iu Mien live in northeast Guangxi, in Mengshan, Zhaoping, Pingle, and Lipu counties.

Identity: The Changping Iu Mien are one of four main Iu Mien language groups in China, all of which are included under the official Yao nationality.

Language: Chinese linguists have only recently determined that the Changping variety of Iu Mien is a distinct language, mutually unintelligible with other Iu Mien varieties.[1]

History: The Iu Mien have been harassed by the Han Chinese almost continually for a thousand years. The Han have traditionally viewed the Iu Mien with utter contempt, despising everything about them that is characteristic. One nineteenth-century Chinese historian was moved so far as to write, "The Yao [Iu Mien] are stupid and violent in nature and they do not have any intercourse with the Chinese. The Chinese take advantage of their stupidity by wresting things from them by force, by stealing from them, and by raiding and insulting them.... The Yao accumulate malice and hatred and then rebel, and events [tribal rebellions] have ever followed this course."[2]

Customs: The Pan Hu Festival is the greatest occasion among the Iu Mien. People gather from far away to celebrate and honor their mythical progenitor. There are several different stories explaining the origins of this festival. One legend states that "during a hunting trip in the mountains, Pan Hu was knocked off a cliff by a wild goat and died as a result of his injuries. Overwhelmed by grief at his death, his Yao followers chopped down a catalpa tree and vengefully killed the goat, using its hide and the wood from the tree to make a drum which they played while mourning their leader."[3] Another story relates that the descendants of Pan formed twelve tribes which were driven from their homeland by the Chinese. During the course of their escape they were trapped in a storm at sea. "For seven days and nights they burned joss sticks and prayed to Pan Hu to deliver them from danger until, finally, they managed to reach land. To express their gratitude to their ancestral hero for his intervention... they started to hold a commemorative festival on a certain date."[4]

Religion: Although the Iu Mien do not consider their worship and honor of Pan Hu a religion, there is no doubt that it constitutes the main spiritual aspect of their lives. Spirit priests are employed to offer sacrifices to Pan and to intercede on behalf of the people. At times during the Pan Hu Festival, people are known to enter into a demonic frenzy as the focus of their energies reach a climax.

Christianity: The Changping Iu Mien are a people in desperate need of the liberating gospel of Jesus Christ. There are no known believers among them. With few confirmed Christians among the entire 800,000 Iu Mien population in China, few workers are available to take the gospel to the Changping Iu Mien in their language.

Josie Plummer

Iu Mien, Hunan 与敏(湖南)

Paul Hattaway

Population in China:
130,000 (1990)
167,700 (2000)
216,300 (2010)
Location: Hunan
Religion: Polytheism
Christians: None Known

Location: An official government study in 1995 listed 130,000 speakers of the Iu Mien language living in southern Hunan Province.[1] They inhabit at least 17 different counties within Hunan, including Yongzhou, Shuangpai, Xintian, Changning, Daoxian, Lanshan, Lingxian, Ningyuan, Jianghua, Jiangyong, Dong'an, Linwu, Guiyang, Xinning, and Yizhang. In many locations the Iu Mien live alongside Ghao-Xong and Han Chinese. There are no speakers of the Hunan variety of Iu Mien reportedly living outside of China.

Identity: Although they are part of the great Yao nationality in China, the Iu Mien living in Hunan Province have been found to speak a dialect that differs and is considered mutually unintelligible with Iu Mien varieties elsewhere.

Language: The language of the Iu Mien in Hunan has probably changed because of influences from neighboring languages such as Ghao-Xong and Xiang Chinese. Today speakers of Hunan Iu Mien struggle greatly to understand the speech of their counterparts in Guangxi, Guizhou, and Yunnan provinces. Hunan Iu Mien is closer to the speech of the Iu Mien in northern Guangdong Province, but it is still different enough to be labeled a separate *fangyan* (language, in a Western sense) by contemporary Chinese scholars.[2]

History: There has been great conflict between the Iu Mien (Yao) and the Han for many centuries. Until this century the Chinese character for writing *Yao* used the radical for "insect" instead of the radical for . "people." A series of rebellions occurred among the Iu Mien in Hunan, starting in 1836. The fight was over the control of the opium trade. Most drugs going from southern China to the northern provinces passed through Xinning County, just to the west of the Xiang River valley. The Iu Mien in this region were involved with the trade as well as several Chinese triad societies, including the *Qinglian Jiao* (Black Lotus Society) and the *Bangbang Hui* (Cudgel Society). In 1847 another revolt occurred in Xinning, led by an Iu Mien, Li Caihao. The Iu Mien were savagely defeated after fighting lasted for several months. Thousands of Iu Mien were killed.[3]

Customs: Many of the Iu Mien in Hunan live in isolated villages at the summits of high mountains. Because of their location, the Iu Mien pipe fresh water to their villages through a skillfully constructed system of bamboo pipes.

Religion: The Hunan Iu Mien share three religious belief systems. They worship Pan Hu, the mythical progenitor of their race, they appease spirits and demons, and they also observe rituals borrowed from Daoism (which includes ancestor worship).

Christianity: The Iu Mien in Hunan are among China's most unreached people groups. There is very little Christian influence of any sort in Hunan, and few believers have ever dared to venture into the isolated mountains inhabited by the Iu Mien since time immemorial.

Overview of the Hunan Iu Mien

Countries: China

Pronunciation: "Hoo-nahn-Yoo-Mee-en"

Other Names: Hunan Yao, Mien, Pan Yao

Population Source: 130,000 (1995 Wang Fushi – 1990 figure); Out of a total Yao population of 2,134,013 (1990 census)

Location: *S Hunan:* Yongzhou, Shuangpai, Xintian, Changning, Daoxian, Lanshan, Lingxian, Ningyuan, Jianghua, Jiangyong, Dong'an, Linwu, Guiyang, Xinning, and Yizhang counties

Status: Officially included under Yao

Language: Hmong-Mien, Mienic, Mian-Jin

Dialects: 0

Religion: Polytheism, Animism, Ancestor Worship, Daoism

Christians: None known

Scripture: None

***Jesus* film:** None

Gospel Recordings: None

Christian Broadcasting: None

ROPAL code: IUM03

Status of Evangelization

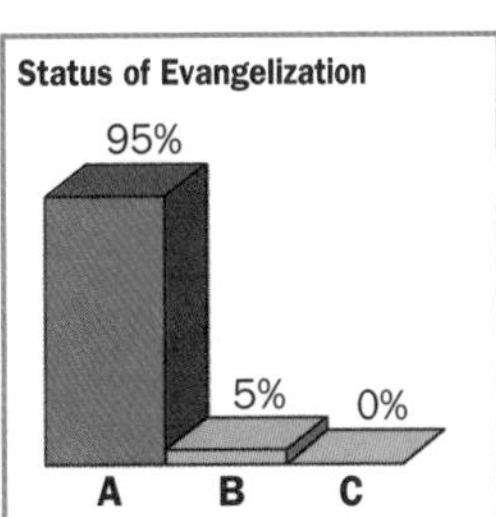

A = Have never heard the gospel
B = Were evangelized but did not become Christians
C = Are adherents to any form of Christianity

Iu Mien, Luoxiang 与敏(罗相)

Population in China:
3,000 (1990)
3,870 (2000)
4,990 (2010)
Location: Guangxi
Religion: Polytheism
Christians: 15

Overview of the Luoxiang Iu Mien

Countries: China

Pronunciation: "Luoh-sheung-Yoo-Mee-en"

Other Names: Pan Yao, Guoshan Yao

Population Source: 3,000 (1995 Wang Fushi – 1990 figure); Out of a total Yao population of 2,134,013 (1990 census)

Location: *Guangxi:* Jinxiu Yao Autonomous County

Status: Officially included under Yao

Language: Hmong-Mien, Mienic, Mian-Jin

Dialects: 0

Religion: Polytheism, Animism, Ancestor Worship, Daoism, Christianity

Christians: 15

Scripture: None

***Jesus* film:** None

Gospel Recordings: None

Christian Broadcasting: None

ROPAL code: None

Status of Evangelization

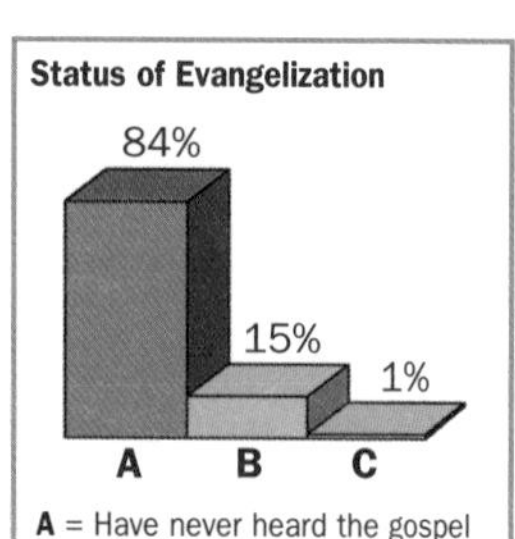

A = Have never heard the gospel
B = Were evangelized but did not become Christians
C = Are adherents to any form of Christianity

Location: Approximately 3,900 Luoxiang Iu Mien people live in the Dayaoshan (Big Yao Mountains) of the Jinxiu Yao Autonomous County within the Guangxi Zhuang Autonomous Region in southern China. Jinxiu is one of the most fascinating areas in all of China for anthropologists and linguists. Five distinct Yao subgroups, each speaking a different language, live in a small area.

Identity: The Luoxiang Iu Mien are part of the Yao nationality in China. The Chinese call them *Pan Yao*, meaning "Yao who worship Pan." The other Yao groups in Jinxiu County are the Kiong Nai, Lakkia, Ao Biao, and Kim Mun.

Paul Hattaway

Language: Chinese linguists have recently determined the Iu Mien language in Jinxiu to be a distinct language from all other Iu Mien varieties in China. They labeled it *Iu Mien, Luoxiang*.[1] There are at least four main Iu Mien languages in China. It is not surprising that Luoxiang Iu Mien language is different, as they have been influenced by centuries of contact with their neighbors who speak unique languages. The Iu Mien live very near the Lakkia village of Liuxiang and have probably absorbed parts of their language. The Lakkia speak a Tai language not even related to the Yao language family.

History: The Iu Mien and Kim Mun were the last two groups to migrate into the Dayao Mountains. They found the best land was already taken by the Ao Biao and the Lakkia. The Iu Mien struggled in extremely harsh conditions for many years, were forbidden to own land, and forced to live in bamboo sheds while rendering manual labor to the original inhabitants.[2] Another source states the Iu Mien "came to the Dayaoshan Mountains rather late and found no space for settlement in the wooded hills or river valleys suitable for farming. So they had to live in scattered mountain villages at a high altitude. Earlier, they did not even have a fixed place to live in and, like nomadic tribes, roamed from one mountain to another. They are, therefore, also known as the *Guoshan Yao* (the Yao who keep crossing mountains)."[3]

Customs: Despite their extreme poverty, the dress of the Luoxiang Iu Mien is elaborate. Both men and women wear large turbans. The greatest festival for the Iu Mien is the annual Pan Hu Festival, dedicated to the legendary ancestor of the Iu Mien. The Changgu (Long Drum) Dance is the most famous dance of the festival. "The drums used in this dance are shaped like an egg-timer, and their ends are covered with goat's hide. Before the performance, the drums are smeared with yellow mud, presumably to alter the pitch."[4]

Religion: Numerous stories abound regarding the heroic exploits of Pan Hu, who is worshiped by the Iu Mien as a spiritual savior.

Christianity: The first known penetration of the gospel among the Luoxiang Iu Mien occurred in 1996. A Hong Kong-based ministry won approximately 30 Ao Biao and Iu Mien in Jinxiu County to Christ.

Japanese 日本人

Location: According to a 1988 article in the *Christian Science Monitor*, some 5,000 Japanese people remain in China as a result of the Japanese occupation of Manchuria in the 1930s and 1940s.[1] The total of 5,000 does not include transient Japanese businessmen and officials who presently work in China but only those people who have been displaced in China for more than half a century. This figure is expected to lower, as many have taken advantage of the services of *Nii No Kai* (The Rainbow Group) — a Tokyo-based volunteer group who arrange for the war-displaced to be returned to Japan. Nii No Kai helped relocate 2,600 Japanese from China between 1972 and 1988. There is no single cohesive Japanese community or village in China. They are scattered throughout towns and villages in what was formerly called Manchuria, now the northeastern Chinese provinces of Heilongjiang, Jilin, and Liaoning.

Identity: Despite having adapted to Chinese language and culture, some Japanese in China have stubbornly retained their ethnic identity and have longed to return to their homeland. Yu Kita Otosaka, a mother of four who returned to Japan in 1974, said, "I must not forget how well the Chinese people treated me, though I had fleas and lice all over... but I always wanted to come back to this homeland."[2]

Language: All displaced Japanese were forced to learn Mandarin in order to survive in China. Consequently, many of their children are now unable to speak Japanese.

History: As a result of the *hakkio-ichiu* (the whole world under one roof) policy, 300,000 Japanese troops invaded northeast China in 1932.[3] Until 1945 they occupied a vast territory, which they renamed Manchkuo. Their rule was a reign of terror. "Undisciplined soldiers looted, raped and killed as they desired. Thousands of Chinese girls were gang raped, then killed for sport.... The only safe place was with foreigners. When soldiers were about, mission schools, hospitals and homes were jammed with Chinese women and girls."[4] Due to the sudden defeat and withdrawal of the Japanese forces, many orphans and women were left behind in China.

Customs: After the war ended, most of the Japanese women who were left behind married Chinese men and settled down to raise children, with many of their traditional Japanese customs being abandoned.

Religion: The belief of most Japanese in China is a mixture of Mahayana Buddhism and ancestor worship. Many others, because of the influence of Communism, are now atheists.

Christianity: There are no known Christians among the Japanese in China, although the recent revival among the Han Chinese in Heilongjiang Province may have touched the lives of some displaced Japanese. Living in Chinese communities for several decades, at least one-fourth of the Japanese in China are estimated to have heard the gospel. The Japanese Bible is unavailable in China, but most can no longer read the Japanese script anyway.

Paul Hattaway

Population in China:
5,000 (1988)
5,700 (2000)
6,580 (2010)
Location:
Heilongjiang, Jilin, Liaoning
Religion: Buddhism
Christians: None Known

Overview of the Japanese

Countries: Japan, Brazil, USA, Peru, Canada, Mexico, Argentina, Singapore, Germany, Paraguay, United Kingdom, Taiwan, Dominican Republic, United Arab Emirates, Panama, Mongolia, Philippines, and Thailand

Pronunciation: "Nee-hong-o"

Other Names: Nihongo

Population: 5,000 (1988 *Christian Science Monitor*); 125,182,000 in Japan (1993); 1,200,000 in Brazil (1993); 804,000 in USA (1993); 109,000 in Peru; 43,000 in Canada; 35,000 in Mexico[5]

Location: *Heilongjiang; Jilin; Liaoning*

Status: Unidentified; Probably included under Han Chinese

Language: Sino-Tibetan, Japanese

Dialects: 0

Religion: Mahayana Buddhism, No Religion, Ancestor Worship

Christians: None known

Scripture: Bible 1883; New Testament 1879; Portions 1837

***Jesus* film:** Available

Gospel Recordings: Japanese #00096

Christian Broadcasting: None in China

ROPAL code: JPN00

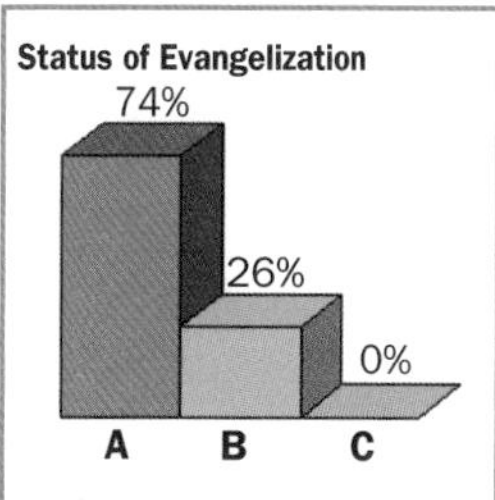

Jiarong, Chabao 嘉戎(查保)

Location: Approximately 14,000 speakers of the Chabao Jiarong language live in northwest Sichuan Province. They are primarily concentrated in the Longerjia, Dazang, and Shaerzong townships in Chabao District. Chabao lies within Barkam County in Aba Prefecture. Barkam is called *Ma'er-kang* by local Jiarong and Tibetans. The Chabao Jiarong live on grassland plateaus between several rivers that run through the region. The Chabao Jiarong dominate the total population of Chabao District.[1]

Identity: The Chabao Jiarong have been counted as part of the Tibetan nationality by the Chinese. "Barkam has a mixed population of Chinese, Jiarong, and Khampa Tibetans. The town was constructed in the 1950s on the site of a regionally important monastery after the Chinese built a road to open up this mountainous region."[2]

Language: Chabao Jiarong — which is not mutually intelligible with the other Jiarong languages — is part of the Qiangic branch of Tibeto-Burman. The Chabao Jiarong have been influenced by the Tibetans more than the four other Jiarong language groups have been. Most can also speak the local dialect of Khampa. Jiarong adults are reported to have a 27% literacy rate.[3] Most scholars in the West (and some in China) believe Jiarong is an independent language, while others think it is merely a dialect of Tibetan. "Political and sociological arguments brought into this discussion tend to cloud objectivity."[4]

History: The Jiarong population has been kept relatively low over the centuries because of wars and disease. In the 1930s it was reported: "Aborigines [minorities] seize and kill members of other nationalities.... Abandoned hovels and wasteland due to pillage by them are common sights. Violent attacks on communities... as well as government punitive actions against them, cost many tens of thousands of lives."[5]

Paul Hattaway

Customs: The Chabao Jiarong have survived the extreme Barkam winters for centuries. Little fruit or vegetables grow in the area. Their main crop is barley. The Jiarong diet mainly consists of fat, meat, and soured yogurt.

Religion: Approximately 20% of the Jiarong follow the Bon religion.[6] Bon, a mixture of black magic and demon worship, was the religion of all Tibetans before Buddhism arrived from India during the seventh century AD. Buddhism was incorporated into existing Bon rituals.

Christianity: The good news that Christ has defeated the devil has not yet reached the ears of the Chabao Jiarong. Isobel Kuhn once wrote, "The only person who does not believe that the devil is a person is someone who has never attempted to combat him or his ways.... The simple tribesman going through his animistic incantations is wiser than such a drugged intellectual. He, at least, knows there is a devil; and he has ways to appease him temporarily."[7]

Population in China:
12,197 (1993)
14,170 (2000)
17,450 (2010)
Location: Sichuan
Religion: Tibetan Buddhism
Christians: None Known

Overview of the Chabao Jiarong

Countries: China

Pronunciation: "Cha-baow-Gee-ah-rong"

Other Names: Gyarong, Gyarung, Rgyarong, Chiarong, Jarong, Chabao, Northeastern Jiarong, Northern Jiarong

Population Source: 12,197 (1993 Lin Xiangron); Out of a total Tibetan population of 4,593,330 (1990 census)

Location: *NW Sichuan:* Chabao District of Barkam County

Status: Officially included under Tibetan

Language: Sino-Tibetan, Tibeto-Burman, Qiangic, Jiarong

Dialects: 0

Religion: Tibetan Buddhism, Bon

Christians: None known

Scripture: None

***Jesus* film:** None

Gospel Recordings: None

Christian Broadcasting: None

ROPAL code: JYA00

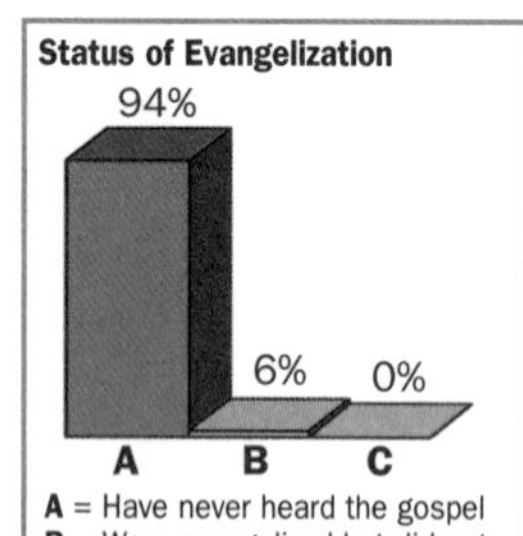

Jiarong, Guanyingqiao 嘉戎(观音桥)

Population in China:
5,000 (1999)
5,110 (2000)
6,300 (2010)
Location: Sichuan
Religion: Tibetan Buddhism
Christians: None Known

Overview of the Guanyingqiao Jiarong

Countries: China

Pronunciation: "Gwan-ying-cheeow-Gee-ah-rong"

Other Names: Gyarong, Gyarung, Rgyarong, Chiarong, Jarong, Chiajung, Guanyingqiao

Population Source: 5,000 (1999 AMO); Out of a total Tibetan population of 4,593,330 (1990 census)

Location: *NW Sichuan:* Jinchuan, Barkam, and Zamtang counties

Status: Officially included under Tibetan

Language: Sino-Tibetan, Tibeto-Burman, Qiangic, Jiarong

Dialects (8): Xiaoyili, Siyaowu, Muerzong, Guangyingqiao, Ergali, Taiyanghe, Ere, Yelong

Religion: Tibetan Buddhism, Polytheism

Christians: None known

Scripture: None

***Jesus* film:** None

Gospel Recordings: None

Christian Broadcasting: None

ROPAL code: JIQ00

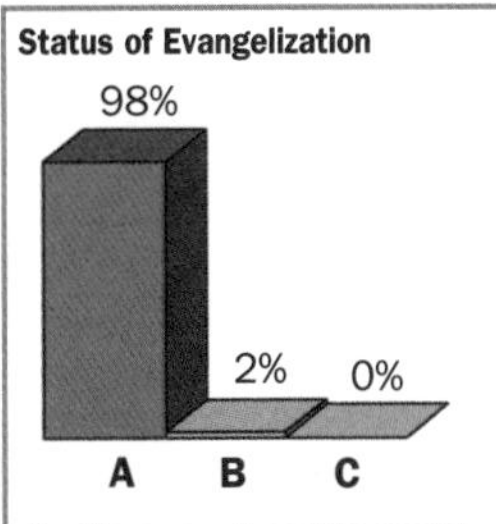

Location: Several thousand speakers of the Guanyingqiao Jiarong language live in the remote northwestern part of Sichuan Province. According to linguist Jonathon Evans, "The language is spoken along the tributaries of the Jinchuan River in the southwestern tip of Ma'erkang (Barkam) County, northwestern Jinchuan County, and southeastern Zamtang County. It has been named Guanyingqiao after the district in Jinchuan County which is the focal point of the Guanyingqiao-speaking area."[1] Although no specific figure for the Guanyingqiao Jiarong has been published, they are believed to number approximately 5,000 speakers. Their location is shared with Tibetans. Very few outsiders have ever ventured as far as the Guanyingqiao area.

Luke Kuepfer

Identity: Although the Guanyingqiao Jiarong have officially been classified as members of the Tibetan nationality, they do not even speak a language closely related to Tibetan and are known to have a different history, origin, and customs. Whereas certain Chinese experts were in favor of giving the Jiarong status as a distinct minority group, certain Tibetan leaders are believed to have campaigned for their inclusion in the Tibetan nationality, fearing that the exclusion of the Jiarong would weaken the Tibetan cause.

Language: Guanyingqiao Jiarong is a member of the Qiangic branch of the Tibeto-Burman language family. It is related to Ergong and Shangzhai Jiarong. Despite their small population, studies indicate the existence of eight dialects within Guanyingqiao Jiarong. "Representative local varieties of Guanyingqiao, some very different, include Xiaoyili and Siyaowu in Zamtang County, Muerzong in Barkam County, Guanyingqiao, Ergali, Taiyanghe, Ere and Yelong in Jinchuan County."[2]

History: Thousands of years ago the various branches of the Jiarong in Sichuan were more closely related to today's official Qiang nationality. The Jiarong, however, migrated into Tibetan areas and have been culturally assimilated to Tibetan ways.

Customs: Although the dress and most customs of the Jiarong are now identical to their neighboring Tibetans, they proudly retain their ancient stone defense towers, called *tianlu*, which show their historic relationship with the Qiang peoples.

Religion: Tibetan Buddhism is embraced by all Jiarong people. Polytheism and shamanism are also present. The deities most feared by the Jiarong are the Mountain gods, which they believe dwell inside large mountains and are responsible for most bad things that happen.

Christianity: The extreme geographic remoteness of the Guanyingqiao Jiarong has separated them from gospel witness throughout their history. There are few roads in this sparsely populated part of China, and most local people here have never seen a Westerner. Very few Han Chinese have settled in this part of Sichuan, except for government officials and some adventurous merchants. Few Guanyingqiao Jiarong have ever heard the name of Jesus Christ.

Jiarong, Shangzhai 嘉戎(上寨)

Paul Hattaway

Location: More than 4,000 speakers of the Shangzhai Jiarong language live in an isolated and sparsely populated part of northwest Sichuan Province. The area inhabited by the Shangzhai Jiarong was previously part of the Tibetan empire but was annexed by the Chinese and integrated into Sichuan Province. The Shangzhai Jiarong are located "near the confluence of the Doqu River and its tributary, the Zhongke River, in Shili, Zongke and Puxi townships of Shangzhai District, in southern Zamtang County."[1]

Identity: Shangzhai is one of five distinct languages of the Jiarong ethnic group in China (six if Ergong is included). The Jiarong, in turn, were officially placed under the Tibetan nationality by the Chinese authorities, even though their languages are far removed from Tibetan. There has been some talk in Chinese circles of further investigation being conducted to see if the Jiarong should be classified as a separate minority, but officials in Beijing believe the task of classifying minorities has been completed and will not consider any more applications.

Language: Shangzhai Jiarong, and the other Jiarong languages, are members of the Qiangic branch of Tibeto-Burman. Jonathon Evans notes, "This language remains almost totally unrepresented in the available literature except for isolated words and sample paradigms in one source."[2] Shangzhai seems closer to Ergong than to any other Jiarong languages. The internal diversity of Shangzhai is uncertain but its major local varieties, Dayili, Zongke and Puxi, appear to be quite distinct."[3] The Dayili dialect was included in a survey of Qiangic languages in 1993.[4]

History: The Shangzhai Jiarong are one of many people groups in the area who inhabit what has been labeled an "ethnic corridor." "This corridor, a borderland of Sino-Tibetan and Yi-Tibetan contact, has been an arena of political tug-of-war. This is also the area where the so-called Qiang, Di, and Rong ethnic groups lived and thrived and where many local governments of varying power and duration have appeared... this area should be fertile ground for exploration by historians as well as linguists."[5]

Customs: Visually and culturally the Jiarong are similar to the Tibetans who live in the area. Today, the Jiarong dress identically to the Tibetans, eat the same food, and celebrate the same festivals.

Religion: Tibetan Buddhism and spirit appeasement dominate every aspect of the daily lives of the Shangzhai Jiarong.

Christianity: The area inhabited by the Shangzhai Jiarong has been blocked off from Christian presence throughout its history. Lawless bandits, remote mountain ranges rising to 7,000 meters (23,000 ft.) above sea level, lack of roads, and the powerful influence of Tibetan Buddhism have prevented news of Jesus Christ from ever reaching the ears of the unreached Shangzhai Jiarong.

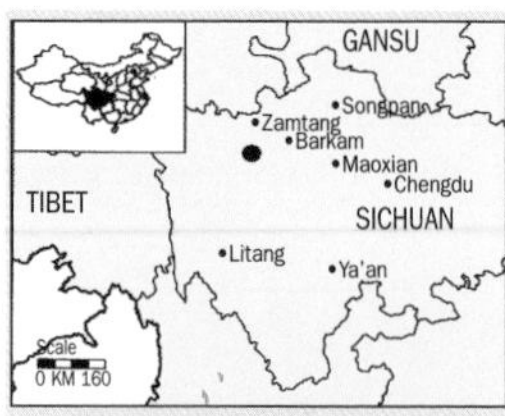

Population in China:
4,000 (1999)
4,090 (2000)
5,040 (2010)
Location: Sichuan
Religion: Tibetan Buddhism
Christians: None Known

Overview of the Shangzhai Jiarong

Countries: China

Pronunciation: "Shang-jai-Gee-ah-rong"

Other Names: Gyarong, Gyarung, Rgyarong, Chiarong, Jarong, Chiajung, Shangzhai

Population Source: 4,000 (1999 AMO); Out of a total Tibetan population of 4,593,330 (1990 census)

Location: *NW Sichuan:* Zamtang County

Status: Officially included under Tibetan

Language: Sino-Tibetan, Tibeto-Burman, Qiangic, Jiarong

Dialects (3): Dayili, Zongke, Puxi

Religion: Tibetan Buddhism, Polytheism

Christians: None known

Scripture: None

***Jesus* film:** None

Gospel Recordings: None

Christian Broadcasting: None

ROPAL code: JIH00

Status of Evangelization

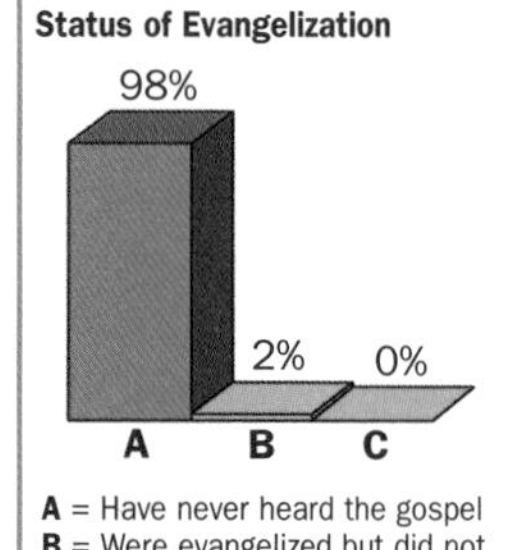

A = Have never heard the gospel
B = Were evangelized but did not become Christians
C = Are adherents to any form of Christianity

Jiarong, Sidabao 嘉戎(斯达宝)

Location: Approximately 5,500 Sidabao Jiarong live in an extremely remote and relatively widespread area of northwest Sichuan Province. "Most of its speakers live in the three townships of Caodeng, Kangshan and Ribu in the Sidabao District of Ma'erkang (Barkam) County, hence the language name Sidabao. Small outlying communities, however, exist both to the north in certain villages of Kehe and Rongan townships at the southwestern corner of Aba County, and, to the west, along the middle Doqu River between Wuyi and Shili townships in Zamtang County, spilling over even to a small area near the confluence of the Sertar and Doqu rivers in Sertar County. Exact population statistics of Sidabao are not available, but should run to several thousand."[1]

Identity: Although they have been officially included as part of the Tibetan nationality, Chinese scholars have considered the Jiarong distinct for several decades. In 1957 the Chinese Academy of Science listed a population of 70,000 Jiarong. One linguist notes, "The Jiarong... are within the cultural orbit of Tibetan Buddhism but speak distinct languages."[2]

Language: Sidabao Jiarong is part of the Qiangic branch of Tibeto-Burman. There are two main dialects of Sidabao: Ribu and Caodeng. Ribu further divides into "several quite different local varieties, such as Shili in Zamtang County, Rongan in Aba County, Ribu proper and Dawei in Barkam County."[3]

History: One Chinese source claims the Jiarong "are a branch of Tibetans who moved in remote antiquity from Qungbu in Tibet to live in the Songpan Plateau of northern Sichuan."[4] Buddhism arrived in Tibet during the reign of King Songsten Gampo (c. AD 605–650). It officially replaced the Bon religion and gradually worked its way to the extremities of the Tibetan world, including the area inhabited by the Jiarong today.

Paul Hattaway

Customs: The Jiarong are looked down upon by both the Chinese and the Tibetans. "Those Jiarong in the towns hold no more than low-level clerical jobs, as they are generally poorly educated."[5]

Religion: There is a revival of the ancient Bon religion in recent years among the Jiarong. For the past 13 centuries, Buddhism has been something of a veneer on ancient Bon rituals. The spiritism and black magic, still prevalent in Tibetan Buddhism, stem from Bon.

Christianity: The few attempts to evangelize the Jiarong in the past met with some success. In 1934 missionaries listed 34 Jiarong believers.[6] Another book from the 1930s lists a number of Jiarong Christians, but presently there is no indication of any believers among them. "Social ostracism of possible converts, and persecution to the extent of the placing of severe curses by the lamas, or poisoning through family members, are other hindrances to spreading the Gospel."[7] There are no Scriptures, gospel recordings or other ministry tools available to help evangelize the Jiarong.

Population in China:
5,000 (1995)
5,580 (2000)
6,850 (2010)
Location: Sichuan
Religion: Tibetan Buddhism
Christians: None Known

Overview of the Sidabao Jiarong

Countries: China

Pronunciation: "See-da-baow-Gee-ah-rong"

Other Names: Western Jyarung, Gyarong, Gyarung, Rgyarong, Chiarong, Jarong, Sidaboa, Western Jiarong

Population Source: 5,000 (1995 AMO); Out of a total Tibetan population of 4,593,330 (1990 census)

Location: *NW Sichuan:* Barkam, Aba, Zamtang, and Sertar counties

Status: Officially included under Tibetan

Language: Sino-Tibetan, Tibeto-Burman, Qiangic, Jiarong

Dialects (2): Caodeng, Ribu

Religion: Tibetan Buddhism, Bon, Polytheism

Christians: None known

Scripture: None

***Jesus* film:** None

Gospel Recordings: None

Christian Broadcasting: None

ROPAL code: JIW00

Status of Evangelization

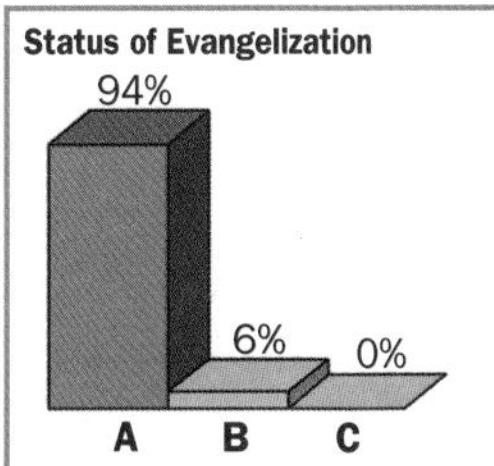

A = Have never heard the gospel
B = Were evangelized but did not become Christians
C = Are adherents to any form of Christianity

Jiarong, Situ 嘉戎(斯土)

Population in China:
139,000 (1993)
161,550 (2000)
199,050 (2010)
Location: Sichuan
Religion: Tibetan Buddhism
Christians: None Known

Overview of the Situ Jiarong

Countries: China

Pronunciation: "See-too-Gee-ah-rong"

Other Names: Eastern Jyarung, Gyarong, Gyarung, Rgyarong, Chiarong, Jarong, Chia-jung, Situ, Eastern Jiarong

Population Source: 139,000 (1993 Lin Xiangron); Out of a total Tibetan population of 4,593,330 (1990 census)

Location: *Sichuan:* Lixian, Wenchuan, Xiaojin, Barkam, and Jinchuan counties

Status: Officially included under Tibetan

Language: Sino-Tibetan, Tibeto-Burman, Qiangic, Jiarong

Dialects (4): Lixian, Jinchuan, Xiaojin, Barkam

Religion: Tibetan Buddhism, Polytheism

Christians: None known

Scripture: None

***Jesus* film:** None

Gospel Recordings: None

Christian Broadcasting: None

ROPAL code: JIR00

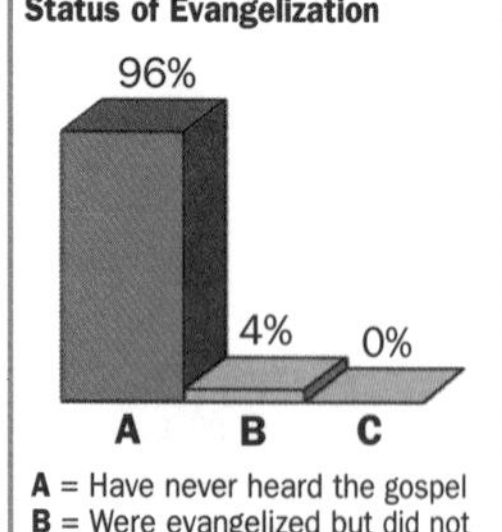

Location: A 1993 study listed a total of 139,000 Situ Jiarong people in Sichuan Province.[1] They are the dominant Jiarong group in China. The Situ, also known as the Eastern Jiarong, inhabit parts of Li, Wenchuan, and Xiaojin counties in central Sichuan, as well as sections of Barkam (Ma'erkang) and Jinchuan counties. Many Situ Jiarong live in a V-shaped valley between the Zagunao River — which originates in the Zhegu Mountains — and the upper section of the Min River.

Identity: The name *Situ* "refers to the traditional territory of the four chieftaincies of Zhuokeji, Suomo, Songgang and Dangba in the heartland of Jiarong country. The term is adopted since it is now a widely used local label for this language."[2] The several Jiarong groups in China have been officially counted under the Tibetan nationality by the Chinese authorities. The Jiarong, however, speak their own distinct languages and believe they are ethnically and historically different from the Tibetans. They have been listed as one of the people groups in China that "need further investigation."[3]

Language: The classification of Jiarong has baffled Chinese scholars. "The languages of the Jiarong who live in Aba and Garze areas of Sichuan are a puzzle. Their language is different from Tibetan in terms of grammar, and akin to the Qiang and Pumi languages. They are considered the 'language bridge' between Tibetan and Burmese."[4] Differences in the five Jiarong languages are great. Situ Jiarong has only 55% lexical similarity with Sidabao Jiarong and 75% with Chabao Jiarong.[5]

History: Until 1949 the Jiarong were divided into 18 small kingdoms. They kept the Chinese military at bay for ten years during the eighteenth century. The Jiarong languages suggest that they may have originally been part of the Qiang group who, after many generations of contact with Tibetans, became a distinct people.[6]

Customs: The majority of Situ Jiarong are farmers, herding livestock and growing crops along the river basins in central Sichuan. A number of urban Jiarong are merchants and shop owners.

Religion: Almost all Jiarong farther to the west are Tibetan Buddhists, but many of the Situ Jiarong have adopted the polytheistic practices of the Qiang.

Christianity: The Jiarong were first targeted in the early 1900s by the American Baptists — who had a mission base at Ya'an — and by the Border Mission of the Church of Christ in China in the 1910s. One writer summarized their efforts: "In the early half of this century some missionaries stationed in areas relatively close to the Jiarong took some trips into Jiarong territory. This led to the translation of some tracts. It was not until the 1930s that an effort to specifically learn and analyze the Jiarong language got underway. A draft translation of the book of Jonah was in progress when the invasion of the Red Army in 1936 made work impossible. All materials were lost in the war."[7]

Midge Conner

Jiasou 戛叟

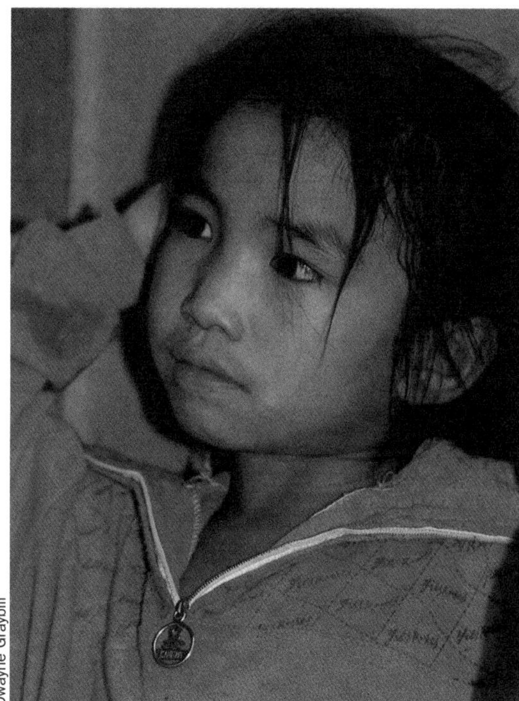
Dwayne Graybill

Location: According to a 1999 estimate, 30,000 ethnic Jiasou people live in Guangnan County within the Wenshan Prefecture of Yunnan Province.[1] There is some intermixing between the Jiasou and the Mengwu in Guangnan. It is possible that some of the people counted in this profile as Jiasou should belong to the Mengwu figures.

Identity: Despite the fact that they speak their own language and possess a unique ethnic name and set of customs, the Jiasou were officially included under the Yi nationality by the Chinese authorities in the 1950s. Sir Reginald F. Johnston explained that it was futile to call all Yi people by one cover term: "I venture to express a doubt whether we should gain much by classing under one such designation a number of peoples who, whatever their origin, have been so long separated from one another that they refuse to acknowledge any mutual connection, and to some extent have different customs and speak different languages."[2]

Language: According to Chinese sources, all Yi languages in Wenshan Prefecture belong to the Southeastern Yi branch of the Tibeto-Burman family. No specific study of Jiasou has ever been documented. It is believed to be partially related to Mengwu.

History: The Jiasou say they originated along the shores of Lake Dian in Kunming in ancient times. Many centuries ago they migrated southward to the southeastern corner of Yunnan Province, where they experienced numerous clashes and battles with other ethnic groups. It seems probable that the Jiasou were once part of the same group as the Mengwu, but after centuries of separation they have evolved into two distinct ethnicities. Only in Guangnan County do members of both the Jiasou and Mengwu ethnic groups still live together.

Customs: When a Jiasou person dies, a ceremony is held to send the soul back to the Jiasou's ancestral home. "The path of a Jiasou soul is thought to go first to Guangnan, then to Kaiyuan, and then to the Kunming lake-shores. This suggests the ancient path of migration taken by the Jiasou."[3]

Religion: In addition to ancestor worship, the Jiasou appease a number of protective spirits. Early on, they recognized their inability to withstand the Chinese who were continually encroaching on their land. They sought the blessing of warring spirits who would attack their enemies. Some Jiasou say they once worshiped an all-powerful God of Heaven who was above all spirits, but they lost contact with him and have been harassed by demons ever since.

Christianity: The Jiasou are a completely unreached and largely unevangelized people group. Few Christians reside in the Guangnan area, even among the Han Chinese majority. Catholic work in adjoining parts of Guangxi impacted the region in a general way prior to 1949, but little fruit from those endeavors remains today. There are no Scriptures or recordings available in the Jiasou language, and no ministries are known to be targeting them for church planting. Few outsiders have ever heard of the Jiasou.

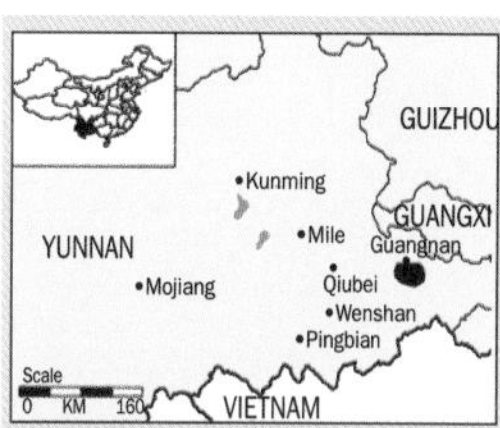

Population in China:
30,000 (1999)
30,750 (2000)
38,600 (2010)
Location: Yunnan
Religion: Ancestor Worship
Christians: None Known

Overview of the Jiasou

Countries: China

Pronunciation: "Jeeah-souh"

Other Names:

Population Source:
30,000 (1999 J. Pelkey);
Out of a total Yi population of 6,572,173 (1990 census)

Location:
SE Yunnan: Guangnan County

Status:
Officially included under Yi

Language: Sino-Tibetan, Tibeto-Burman, Burmese-Lolo, Lolo, Northern Lolo, Yi, Southeastern Yi

Dialects: 0

Religion:
Ancestor Worship, Animism

Christians: None known

Scripture: None

***Jesus* film:** None

Gospel Recordings: None

Christian Broadcasting: None

ROPAL code: None

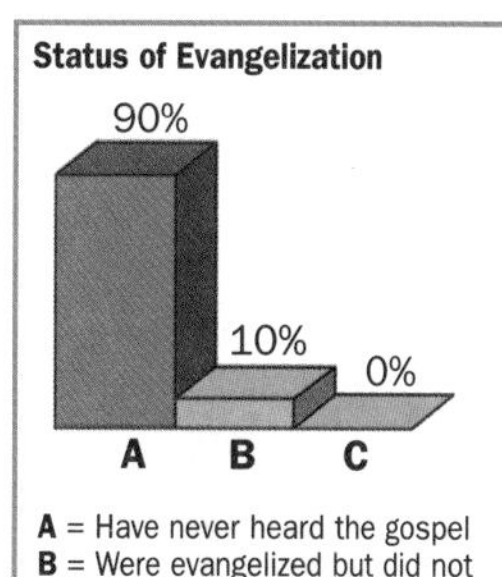

Jing 京

Population in China:
18,915 (1990)
24,400 (2000)
31,470 (2010)
Location: Guangxi, Guangdong
Religion: Daoism
Christians: 600

Overview of the Jing

Countries: China

Pronunciation: "Jing"

Other Names: Gin, Vietnamese in China, Kinh, Ching

Population Source:
18,915 (1990 census);
11,995 (1982 census);
4,293 (1964 census)

Location: *S Guangxi*: The Jing inhabit three islands, Wanwei, Wutou, and Shanxin, immediately off the southern coast of Guangxi, within Fangcheng County;
A few Jing live in *Guangdong*.

Status:
An official minority of China

Language: Austro-Asiatic, Mon-Khmer, Viet-Muong, Vietnamese

Literacy: 65%

Dialects: 0

Religion: Daoism, Buddhism, Animism, Christianity

Christians: 600

Scripture: Vietnamese Bible (not available in China)

***Jesus* film:**
Available (Vietnamese)

Gospel Recordings:
Vietnamese: North #00680

Christian Broadcasting:
Available (FEBC, TWR)

ROPAL code: VIE00

Status of Evangelization

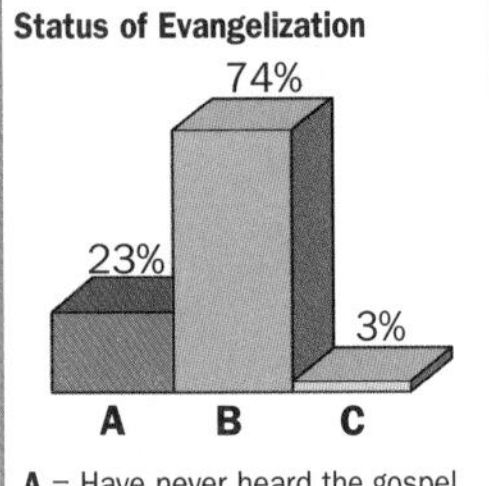

A = Have never heard the gospel
B = Were evangelized but did not become Christians
C = Are adherents to any form of Christianity

Location: More than 24,000 members of the Jing minority live in southern China, on the Shanxin, Wanwei, and Wutou islands. These three islands are within Fangcheng County in Guangxi.[1] Papaya, banana, and other varieties of tropical fruit grow abundantly. The Jing also eat horseshoe crabs and other delicacies which they gather from the sandy beaches. More than 700 species of fish live in the Beibu Gulf, "in addition to pearls, sea horses, and sea otters, which are prized for their medicinal value."[2] A small number of Jing live on the Chinese Mainland in Guangdong Province.

Midge Conner

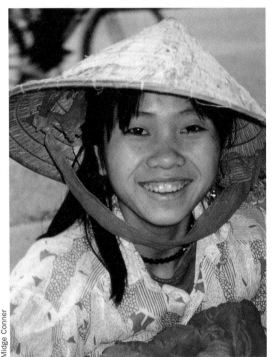

Identity: The Jing are one of the 55 official minorities of China. Some scholars classify them simply as "Vietnamese in China." The name *Jing* comes from the word *Kinh* which is the self-name of the Vietnamese people. After more than 500 years of separation, however, the Jing now possess their own customs and traditions.

Language: The Jing language is similar to varieties of Northern Vietnamese but has many influences from Cantonese and Mandarin. "The Vietnamese language is undoubtedly Mon-Khmer; though it has undergone millennia of Chinese influence."[3] Because they do not understand the Vietnamese script, the Jing use Chinese characters for reading and writing. In the past they claim to have had their own script, called *Zinan* or *Nanzi*, which was mainly used for religious purposes. The script was lost, possibly when they migrated to China.

History: The Jing are believed to have migrated to China from the city of Tushan and other places in northern Vietnam in the 1500s. When they arrived in southern China the mainland was already occupied by Chinese and Zhuang people, so they took possession of three unoccupied islands off the coast. Before 1958 the Jing were called *Yue*.

Customs: The Jing have developed many romantic traditions. "When a young man and girl are mutually attracted, they go the beach in the moonlight by tacit agreement. At a certain point, the man will cough loudly. This is the first signal of an intended proposal. On hearing it, the girl slows down her walking and waits for the man to catch her up. The man comes up and makes a small pile of sand with his feet which he then kicks in the direction of the girl who, if she is willing, stands her ground.... The girl, having no objection to the boy's proposal, gives him a smile and kicks back sand towards him."[4]

Religion: The main beliefs among the Jing are Daoism and animism. There are also many professing Catholics among them, but their worship is often mixed with Daoist and Buddhist idolatry.

Christianity: The first Protestant work among the Jing commenced in 1886 when E. G. Horder, an Anglican missionary, established the Pu Ren Hospital at Beihai in southern Guangxi. In 1991, 80 leper Christians still lived there, meeting in the *Simon Church*.[5] The great majority of Jing believers today are Catholic. They meet in both registered churches and independent house groups, and use Chinese Bibles, since they cannot read the Vietnamese script.

Jingpo 景颇

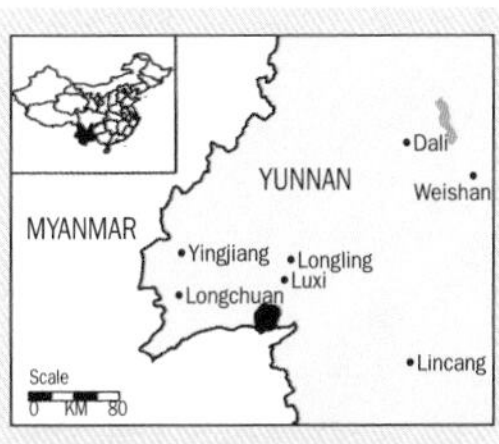

Population in China:
20,000 (1990)
25,800 (2000)
33,200 (2010)
Location: Yunnan
Religion: Christianity
Christians: 7,000

Overview of the Jingpo

Countries: Myanmar, China, India, Thailand

Pronunciation: "Jing-poh"

Other Names: Kachin, Keqin, Jingpaw, Chingpaw, Chingpo, Singpo, Marip, Singfo, Dashan, Dashanhua, Nhkum

Population Source:
20,000 (1990 J-O. Svantesson);
Out of a total Jingpo population of 119,209 (1990 census);
625,000 in Myanmar (1993 P. Johnstone);
7,200 in India (1983);
One village in Thailand

Location:
W Yunnan: Dehong Prefecture

Status:
Officially included under Jingpo

Language: Sino-Tibetan, Tibeto-Burman, Baric, Kachinic

Literacy: 38%

Dialects (2): Nhkum, Shidan

Religion: Christianity, Animism, Polytheism, Theravada Buddhism

Christians: 7,000

Scripture: Bible 1927; New Testament 1912; Portions 1895

***Jesus* film:** Available

Gospel Recordings:
Jingpaw #00175

Christian Broadcasting:
Available (FEBC)

ROPAL code: CGP00

Status of Evangelization

	A	B	C
	0%	72%	28%

A = Have never heard the gospel
B = Were evangelized but did not become Christians
C = Are adherents to any form of Christianity

Location: More than 25,000 Jingpo inhabit the western part of Yunnan Province along the China-Myanmar border. They are mainly concentrated in Yingjiang, Ruili, Lianghe, Longchuan, and Luxi counties of Dehong Prefecture.[1] In addition, 625,000 Kachin live in northern Myanmar.[2] The term *Kachin* refers to a collection of ethnic groups rather than a linguistic classification, but most of the Kachin in Myanmar are part of the group the Chinese call *Jingpo*. More than 7,000 Jingpo live in India. One village of Jingpo is also located in Chiang Mai, northern Thailand.

Identity: Although there were 119,209 people in China counted under the Jingpo nationality in the 1990 census, the official Chinese classification includes members of the Zaiwa, Maru, Lashi, and Bela people groups, in addition to Jingpo proper. In China the Jingpo are known locally as the *Dashan* (Big Mountain) people.

Language: The Jingpo language in China — where it has two dialects — is reported to differ phonologically in many ways from that spoken in Myanmar.[3] In recent years newspapers and books in the Jingpo Roman script have been published in China.

History: The Jingpo claim to have originated on the Tibetan Plateau. The fact that some scholars believe the present-day Deng language in southeast Tibet is related to Jingpo, adds credence to their claims. During the Yuan and Ming dynasties (1271–1644) the Jingpo were known as the Yeren. They had probably arrived at their present location in western Yunnan by the start of the sixteenth century.[4] From there they migrated south into northern Myanmar, where today they are the largest group in Kachin State.

Customs: Jingpo and Zaiwa are almost identical in every aspect of their historical and socioeconomic backgrounds, except for their political organization. The highest leader in Jingpo society is called *Pumtu* in Jingpo and *Pumtsau* in Zaiwa, meaning "master of the mountains." For centuries the Jingpo have practiced *lashi* or *naji*, meaning "snatching cows by military operation." This leads to on-going conflict with other nationalities. From 1980 to 1982 three Jingpo settlements reported 443 cases of *lashi*. The consequences were 7 deaths, 153 people wounded, and 338 cattle stolen.[5]

Religion: Many Jingpo today are Christians, having been converted through the ceaseless efforts of missionaries starting in the 1870s. Jingpo legends "tell a story of the passage over a bridge, to the after-life... these folk-myths came down from a long-gone past, like the far-carried boulders of the Glacial ages."[6]

Christianity: The first missionary working among the Jingpo in Myanmar (formerly Burma) was Josiah N. Cushing in 1876. By 1941, the baptized Jinpo in Burma numbered 47,526.[7] In the same year the Jingpo in China numbered 415 converts.[8] Today, estimates for the total number of Christians among the five Jingpo groups in China range from 7,000 to 8,000[9] and as many as 55,000.[10] Because the large Zaiwa group have proven highly resistant to the gospel, the higher figure is very unlikely. The Jingpo in Myanmar have evangelized many other people groups in their country.

Paul Hattaway

Jino 基诺

Location: Numbering about 22,000, the Jino have survived for countless centuries in the forests of southern Yunnan. They live in 46 villages — covering an area of 3,000 square kilometers (1,170 sq.mi.) — in the jungles and mountains of the Xishuangbanna Prefecture in southwest China.[1]

Identity: The Jino gained recognition as an official minority in 1979, becoming the 55th and most recent group to gain status in China. Previously, the Jino were considered part of the Dai nationality. The name *Jino* comes from the words *ji* "uncle" and *nuo* "descendants", therefore meaning "the descendants of the uncle."[2]

Language: The Jino language is part of the Tibeto-Burman stock and is similar to Sanda and Ake — two related groups also in Xishuangbanna. There are two mutually unintelligible Jino languages: Jino proper and Buyuan Jino — which is spoken by 1,000 people. The differences are mainly in vocabulary. All Jino are able to speak their language. Many can also speak Tai Lu, Chinese, or Akha, depending on their location. The Jino do not have a written script. In the past, they tied strings around their wrists or carved notches in wood or bamboo to help remind them of things they needed to do. In the event of an emergency, the Jino sent a feather or a piece of charcoal to their neighbors as a sign they needed help.

History: One link between the Jino and the Bible is the Great Flood. Every Lunar New Year in February, the Jino celebrate by dancing around a large ox-hide drum. For centuries the Jino have orally passed on from generation to generation a story about how the human race perished in a huge flood. Their ancestors were able to survive because they found shelter in a huge drum. Being directed by a god, they received ten calabash seeds that sprouted and produced all the races in the world.

Paul Hattaway

Customs: Jino women are easily identified by their large triangular hoods. When a Jino dies, they are buried in a hollowed-out tree and small huts are constructed over the graves.

Religion: The Jino have their own unique religion. Around AD 200, Kong Ming — also known as Chu-ko-Liang or Zhu Geliang — helped establish the Minor Han Dynasty. The Jino served in Kong Ming's military campaign into southwest China, but many were left behind.[3] Kong Ming remains a favorite war hero of the Chinese. In 1724 he was included in a kind of Chinese *Hall of Fame* when his tablet was admitted to the Confucian Temple.[4] Kong Ming is the main god among many worshiped by the polytheistic and superstitious Jino.

Christianity: Until recently there had never been a known Jino church or believer. In 1994 Tai Lu and Han Chinese believers from Jinghong and Mengla targeted the Jino. As a result, 31 Jino house churches have been established in a short period of time, containing more than 300 believers.[5] The young church has met with strong persecution. The local authorities handed out aid to all Jino except the Christians after a severe hailstorm destroyed their crops in 1997.[6] Churches have been ordered to close by village leaders who are afraid of the new religion.

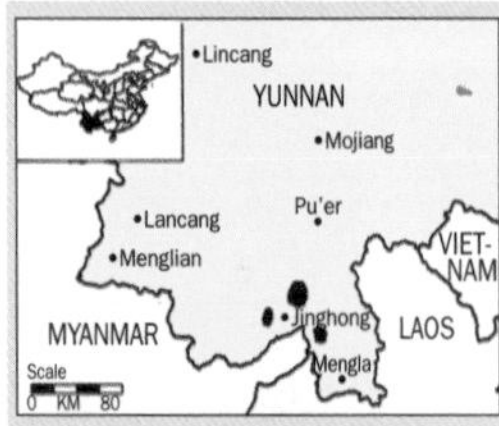

Population in China:
17,021 (1990)
21,950 (2000)
28,320 (2010)
Location: Yunnan
Religion: Polytheism
Christians: 300

Overview of the Jino

Countries: China

Pronunciation: "Jee-nor"

Other Names: Jinuo, Youle, Chi-no

Population Source: 18,021 (1990 census);[7] 11,974 (1982 census)

Location: *SW Yunnan:* 12,000 live in Jino Mountains of Jinghong County. The rest are scattered in Jinghong and Mengla counties in the Xishuangbanna Dai Prefecture.

Status: An official minority of China

Language: Sino-Tibetan, Tibeto-Burman, Burmese-Lolo, Lolo, Southern Lolo, Jino

Literacy: 49%

Dialects: 0

Religion: Polytheism, Animism, Christianity

Christians: 300

Scripture: None

***Jesus* film:** None

Gospel Recordings: Jino #04792

Christian Broadcasting: None

ROPAL code: JIU00

Status of Evangelization

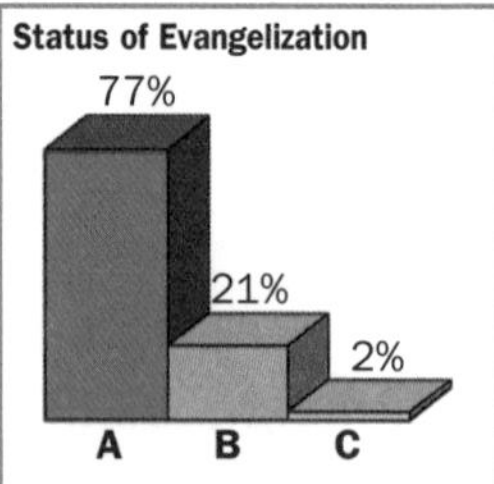

A = Have never heard the gospel
B = Were evangelized but did not become Christians
C = Are adherents to any form of Christianity

Jino, Buyuan 基诺(捕远)

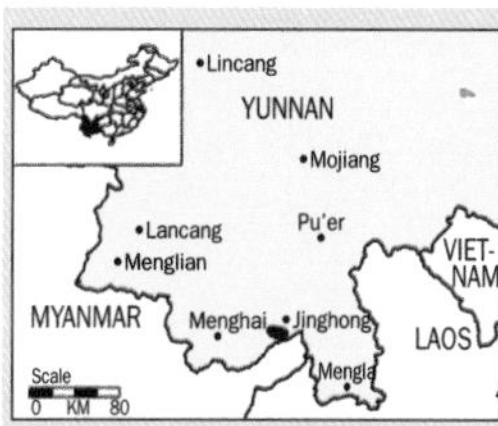

Population in China:
1,000 (1991)
1,260 (2000)
1,620 (2010)
Location: Yunnan
Religion: Polytheism
Christians: 20

Overview of the Buyuan Jino

Countries: China

Pronunciation: "Boo-yooahn-Jee-nor"

Other Names: Buyuan, Pu-yuan Chi-no

Population Source: 1,000 (1991 *EDCL*); Out of a total population of 18,021 Jino (1990 census)

Location: *SW Yunnan:* Buyuanshan District of Jinghong County

Status: Officially included under Jino

Language: Sino-Tibetan, Tibeto-Burman, Burmese-Lolo, Lolo, Southern Lolo, Jino

Dialects: 0

Religion: Polytheism, Animism, Christianity

Christians: 20

Scripture: None

***Jesus* film:** None

Gospel Recordings: None

Christian Broadcasting: None

ROPAL code: JIY00

Status of Evangelization

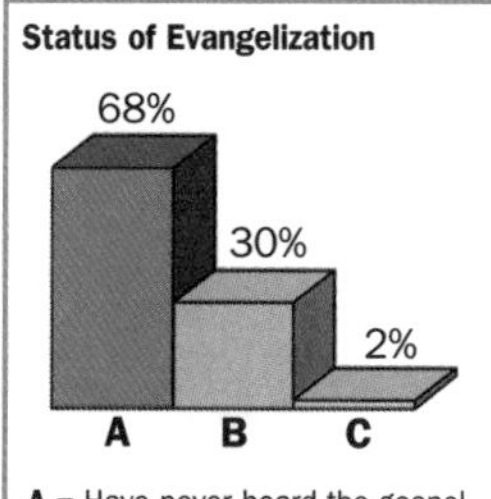

A = Have never heard the gospel
B = Were evangelized but did not become Christians
C = Are adherents to any form of Christianity

Paul Hattaway

Location: One thousand speakers of the Buyuan Jino language were listed in a 1991 study.[1] They live on the Buyuan Mountains in Jinghong County, Xishuangbanna Prefecture, located in the extreme southwest corner of China. Despite their close proximity to Laos and Myanmar, there is no evidence of Jino being found in either country. The Buyuan region is a thickly forested area. Over 200 wild elephants, as well as leopards, golden-haired monkeys, and wild oxen still roam the unspoilt forests. Small bears also inhabited the jungle, but their numbers have been reduced to near extinction by the expert Jino hunters.

Identity: Although the Buyuan Jino belong to the official Jino minority group, they speak their own distinct language.

Language: The exact genetic affiliation of the Jino languages is yet to be determined. It is known that they are members of the Tibeto-Burman language group. The speakers of Buyuan Jino must speak Chinese or Tai Lu in order to communicate with the Jino who live in the Youle Mountains.

History: In 1942 the Kuomintang authorities dispatched an officer to the Jino Mountains to collect a "tobacco tax." He died on the way back. The government used this incident to accuse the mountain people of poisoning the tax collector. The KMT "sent soldiers to loot, burn and kill. The Jino people rose up and notified the villages of the Tai Lu, Yao, Lahu, Akha and Han nationalities by urgent letter that their delegates should assemble on Jino Mountain. There they pledged in the blood of a slain ox to rally to the support of the Jino people. The armies attacked unmercifully and numerous Jino were slaughtered. Despite the failed uprising, the Tai Lu sing, 'The strongest animal in the forest is the rhinoceros, the bravest people on the mountain are the Jino!'"[2]

Customs: An aspect of Jino culture unique among China's peoples is the *longhouse*. Whole Jino extended families live together in the same home. In the early 1950s the largest home contained 127 people![3] In the past, the ears of newborn babies were pierced and inserted with decorated pieces of cork or bamboo.[4] The Jino's village boundaries are marked by wooden or stone tablets bearing an emblem of a sword or spear.[5]

Religion: The Buyuan Jino are polytheists, worshiping a multitude of demons and gods. They also worship Kong Ming. Jino homes are constructed in the shape of a cube with a pointed roof to resemble the hat Kong Ming reputedly wore into battle. Jino boys wear shirts with a circular pattern embroidered on the back, alleged to be the eight diagrams Kong Ming used in his divination.[6]

Christianity: A small number of Buyuan Jino have been won to Christ by evangelists from Jinghong in recent years. All the new Christians are teenagers. This has prevented the gospel from permeating the authority structures of the Jino and from winning favor with the leaders of their communities. Most older Buyuan Jino view Christianity with suspicion.

Kado 卡多

Dwayne Graybill

Location: More than 122,000 Kado live in communities scattered throughout the southern part of Yunnan Province. Although most are concentrated in Mojiang County in Honghe Prefecture, Kado can be found as far southwest as Jinghong County in Xishuangbanna Prefecture.[1] In 1983, 128,500 Kado were also reported living in Myanmar. An additional small group of 200 Kado lives in northern Laos.

Identity: The Kado are one of 18 groups combined by the Chinese authorities to form the official Hani nationality. The Kado possess their own language, although diminishing numbers of Kado children are now able to speak it. Many Kado have become culturally indistinguishable from the Han Chinese.

Language: The Kado language is part of the Bi-Ka branch of the Tibeto-Burman language family.[2] It is most similar to Biyo and Woni. In Myanmar — where there are six Kado dialects reported — many scholars believe Kado and Ganaan to be separate languages.[3] Kado is not the same as Katu, a Mon-Khmer language spoken in Vietnam and Laos, nor is it the same as Kaduo, the Tibeto-Burman language spoken by the Mongols in Yunnan.

History: Until recently the Kado lived under the yoke of powerful landlords who controlled their society. When the Communists attempted to condemn the oppressive landlords in the 1950s, the Kado Christians refused to be involved, saying it was better to forgive them.[4]

Customs: For the past 200 years the Kado have been gradually Sinicized. Today few wear their traditional costume — the mark of their ethnic identity.

Religion: There are many strong Christian churches among the Kado. It was not always the case, however. In the past the Kado lived in deep spiritual bondage. A survey of one Kado village found 93% of the adults were infected with a sexually transmitted disease.[5]

Christianity: H. A. Baker, an independent Pentecostal missionary, commenced work among the Kado in 1932,[6] sowing the seed for a great revival among them between 1940 and 1947. A 1941 report commented, "Several new stations have been added as the blessed message of Life spread from one village to another. Several thousands of these needy people have made a confession of Christ. Many of these are busy learning to read the newly translated Scripture portions in their own language."[7] By 1950, 33 Kado churches had been established, but all of them were forced to close between 1952 and 1953.[8] Both the Assembly of God and the Seventh Day Adventists had many Kado converts. During the Cultural Revolution, the Communists hoped to destroy the Kado church by dividing them over the issue of the Sabbath. Sensing the principle of unity was more important than the letter of the law, the Adventists agreed to meet with the Assembly of God believers on Sundays.[9] By 1986 the Kado numbered 40,000 believers[10] — most of whom used Chinese Scriptures — and 156 Kado were engaged in full-time Christian work.[11] A 1986 study of 5,201 believers in Mojiang County indicated that 31% were teenagers.[12]

Population in China:
100,000 (1990)
122,900 (2000)
151,000 (2010)
Location: Yunnan
Religion: Christianity
Christians: 40,000

Overview of the Kado

Countries: Myanmar, China, Laos

Pronunciation: "Kha-doe"

Other Names: Kadu, Katu, Kato, Kudo, Gado, Asak, Sak, Thet, That, Mawteik, Puteik, Ka Dwo

Population Source:
100,000 (1990 J.-O. Svantesson);
Out of a total Hani population of 1,253,952 (1990 census);
128,500 in Myanmar (1983), including 90,300 Kado and 38,200 Ganaan speakers;
200 in Laos (1996 D. Bradley)

Location: *S Yunnan:* Mojiang, Yuanjiang, and Jinghong counties

Status:
Officially included under Hani

Language: Sino-Tibetan, Tibeto-Burman, Burmese-Lolo, Lolo, Southern Lolo, Akha, Bi-Ka

Dialects (6): Kadu, Ganaan, Andro, Sengmai, Chakpa, Phayeng

Religion:
Christianity, Animism, Polytheism

Christians: 40,000

Scripture: Portions 1939

***Jesus* film:** None

Gospel Recordings:
Katu #01929

Christian Broadcasting: None

ROPAL code: KDV00

Status of Evangelization

0% 67% 33%

A B C

A = Have never heard the gospel
B = Were evangelized but did not become Christians
C = Are adherents to any form of Christianity

Kawa 阿佤

Location: A 1990 study listed 60,000 speakers of the Kawa language in China.[1] They live in remote villages high in the mountains of western Yunnan Province. Kawa communities are located in Ximeng and Menglian counties, in addition to a small number in neighboring Lancang County. Kawa villages are situated at least 1,500 meters (5,000 ft.) above sea level.

Identity: The Kawa, traditionally known as the *Wild Wa*, are one of three distinct language groups that were combined to form China's official Wa nationality. The Chinese divide the Wa into three sociolinguistic groups: the Kawa, or Wild Wa; the Lawa, or Tame Wa; and the Sinicized Wa.[2]

Language: The nontonal Kawa language, which is called *Vo* or *Awa*, is partially intelligible with Parauk Wa but very different from Lawa.

History: The Kawa are the most primitive and reclusive group of Wa in China. Because of their isolated settlements, they rarely come into contact with outsiders and have retained their customs and traditions more than the Lawa or Parauk Wa. Until the 1960s the Kawa practiced head-hunting. Members of other nationalities dared not venture into Kawa territory for fear of being decapitated. Between 1948 and 1950, a Kawa cut off five Han merchants' heads because of a business dispute. He then sold the heads for ¥300 for the beardless ones and ¥2000 for those with a full beard.[3] In 1946 the Kawa in Asai attacked the Wa in Gouhe, butchering 67 people and sparing only one life. "The booty of gory heads was carried back by eight cows."[4] Villagers immediately took revenge for such attacks, causing a cycle of mutual killings that continued for years.

Customs: The Kawa do not generally like outsiders and prefer to be left alone. They grow a variety of crops, including rice, corn, and maize.

Paul Hattaway

Religion: The cruelty of the Kawa is unquestionably without equal among all the peoples of China. "Their infamous head-hunting, intended to beg for a good harvest, displayed their inhuman cruelty, for example, by buying a child Wa slave girl at the age of ten to be customarily killed by the procedure of a slow death."[5] One writer summarized the spiritual condition of groups like the Kawa: "The ignorant minorities existed in constant fear: fear of demons, fear of the government officials, fear of landlords, fear of hostile tribes, and even fear of their own evil souls. The ghastly and bloodcurdling practices they developed to assuage their fears only resulted in further exacerbating them."[6]

Christianity: Although there are at least 75,000 Wa Christians in China,[7] almost all of them are among the Parauk Wa and Lawa. Most Kawa stubbornly resist change and remain an unreached people group. Chinese historian T'ien Ju-K'ang explains, "Enthusiastic response for Christianity came only from the Tame Wa in Cangyuan district. In 1954, 78 churches, 73 local pastors, 108 Christian villages and 25,076 believers were reported.... In 1957, there were 97 villages in the Ximeng Mountains with 59,493 Kawa inhabitants, but no Christians were recorded."[8]

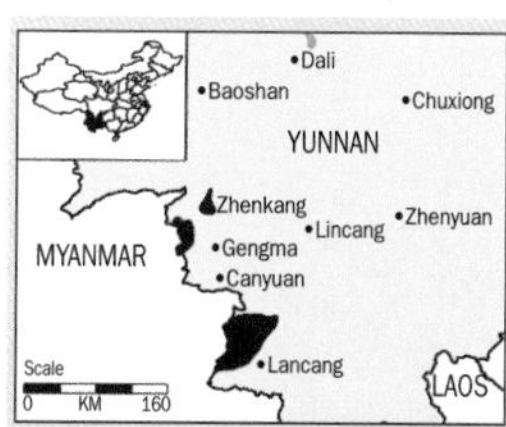

Population in China:
60,000 (1990)
73,300 (2000)
89,700 (2010)
Location: Yunnan
Religion: Animism
Christians: 100

Overview of the Kawa

Countries: Myanmar, China

Pronunciation: "Kah-wa"

Other Names:
Vo, Wa Pwi, Wakut, Wild Wa, Awa

Population Source:
60,000 (1990 J.-O. Svantesson);
Out of a total Wa population of 351,974 (1990 census)

Location: *W Yunnan:* Ximeng, and Menglian counties, and parts of Lancang County

Status:
Officially included under Wa

Language: Austro-Asiatic, Mon-Khmer, Northern Mon-Khmer, Palaungic, Western Palaungic, Waic, Wa

Dialects: 0

Religion: Animism, Polytheism, Shamanism, Christianity

Christians: 100

Scripture: None

***Jesus* film:** None

Gospel Recordings: None

Christian Broadcasting: None

ROPAL code: WBM00

Status of Evangelization

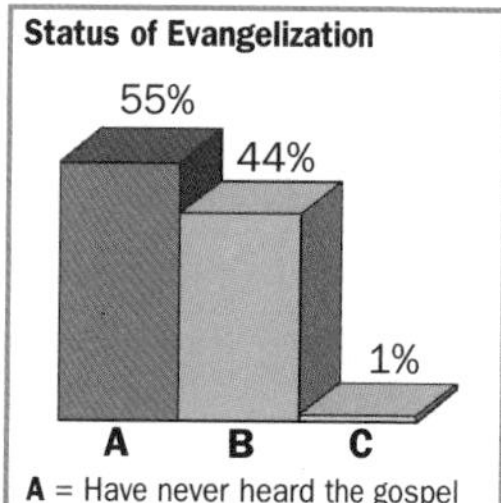

A = Have never heard the gospel
B = Were evangelized but did not become Christians
C = Are adherents to any form of Christianity

Kazak 哈萨克

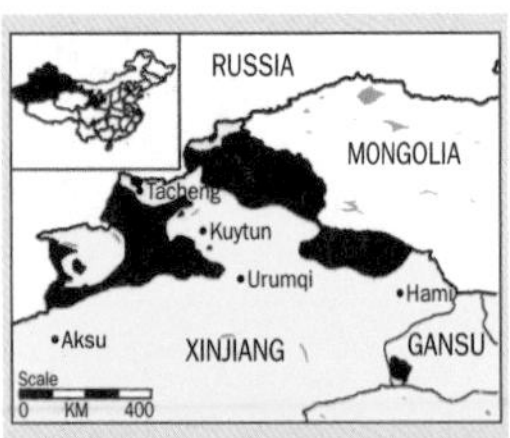

Population in China:
1,109,718 (1990)
1,419,300 (2000)
1,815,300 (2010)
Location: Xinjiang, Gansu
Religion: Islam
Christians: 30

Overview of the Kazaks

Countries: Kazakstan, China, Russia, Uzbekistan, Mongolia, Turkmenistan, Kyrgystan, Iran, Afghanistan, Turkey, Germany
Pronunciation: "Kar-zark"
Other Names: Kazakh, Kazax, Hazake
Population Source: 1,111,718 (1990 census);[1] 908,414 (1982 census);[2] 6,556,000 in Kazakstan (1979 census); 808,000 in Uzbekistan (1993 P. Johnstone); 636,000 in Russia[3]
Location: *N Xinjiang:* Ili Prefecture; Mori and Barkol counties; *NW Gansu:* Aksay County
Status: An official minority of China
Language: Altaic, Turkic, Western Turkic, Aralo-Caspian
Literacy: 72%
Dialects (2): Northeastern (830,000), Southwestern (70,000)
Religion: Islam, Shamanism, Animism, Ancestor Worship
Christians: 30
Scripture: New Testament 1820–1910; Portions 1818; Work in progress
***Jesus* film:** Available
Gospel Recordings: Kazak #03377
Christian Broadcasting: Available (FEBC, TWR)
ROPAL code: KAZ00

Status of Evangelization

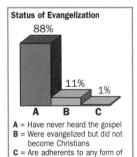

	A	B	C
%	88%	11%	1%

A = Have never heard the gospel
B = Were evangelized but did not become Christians
C = Are adherents to any form of Christianity

Location: Approximately 1.1 million Kazaks were counted in the 1990 Chinese census. They are centered primarily in the Ili Prefecture in northern Xinjiang.[4] After dark the streets of Yining are full of drunk Kazaks and Uzbeks who often use knives and other weapons to settle quarrels. A smaller number of Kazaks live in the northwest part of Gansu Province. In addition, about nine million Kazaks are scattered throughout Central Asia, Russia, and as far away as Turkey and Germany.

Identity: The Kazaks are one of China's official minority groups. The name *Kazak* means "the breakaways" or "secessionists".[5] Chinese publications, however, not wanting to flame the Kazaks desire for independence, claim their name means "white swan".[6]

Language: Since 1980 the Kazaks in China have used a modified Arabic script. There are two main Kazak dialects in China: Southwestern and Northeastern Kazak. The Southwestern variety includes the tribes of Alban and Suwen.[7] Kazak is a "relatively uniform language, without any major dialectal differences, so that Kazaks from different places have no difficulty in conversing with one another."[8]

History: Over the centuries the various Islamic groups in northwest China have attempted to establish their own homeland. Several brutal massacres have reinforced Chinese rule and the deep hatred the Kazaks have for the Han. At least 100,000 Kazaks migrated into China from Russia between 1916 and 1920, after the Tsarist government imposed conscription on them.[9] In the early 1950s the Kazaks in China were forced into a communal society and were forbidden to enjoy the nomadic lifestyle their ancestors had enjoyed for over a thousand years. In 1962, 60,000 Kazaks decided to cross back into the Soviet Union. The massive migration represented more than one-tenth of the entire Kazak population in China at the time.

Customs: Images of proud nomadic Kazak horsemen have long stirred the imagination of the world. Being the rulers of vast open grasslands, they lived as they pleased and moved their livestock wherever and whenever they desired: the Kazaks love their freedom. When a Kazak girl goes to the altar on her wedding day, "she is carried off after the ceremony, slung over a horse and delivered to the family of her husband-to-be."[10]

Religion: Although the Kazaks embraced Islam in the sixteenth century and consider themselves to be Muslims today, their practices and rituals are combined with elements of spiritism, black magic, animism, and shamanism.

Christianity: Few of the Kazaks in China — despite having the Scriptures, *Jesus* film, gospel recordings, and gospel radio broadcasts available in their own language — believe in Christ. In the 1930s the Swedish Missionary Society planted one small Kazak church in Xinjiang, but persecution wiped it out.[11] Presently there are only "a handful of Kazak Christians in China."[12] In neighboring Kazakstan, however, in recent years "approximately 3,500 Kazaks have come to faith in Christ."[13]

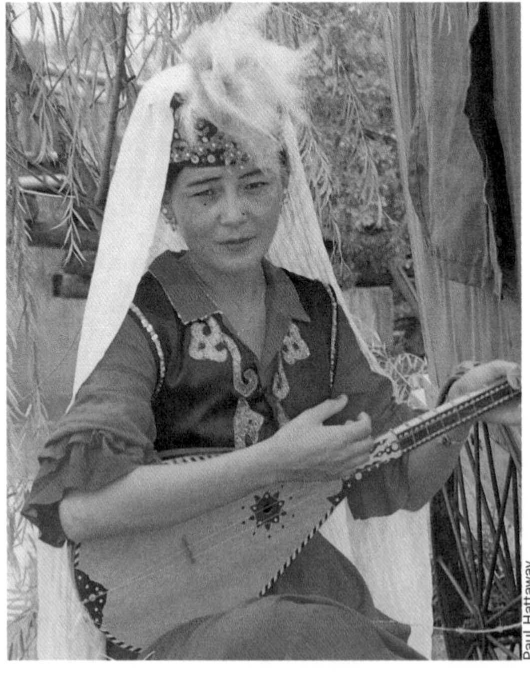
Paul Hattaway

Kazak, Qinghai 哈萨克(青海)

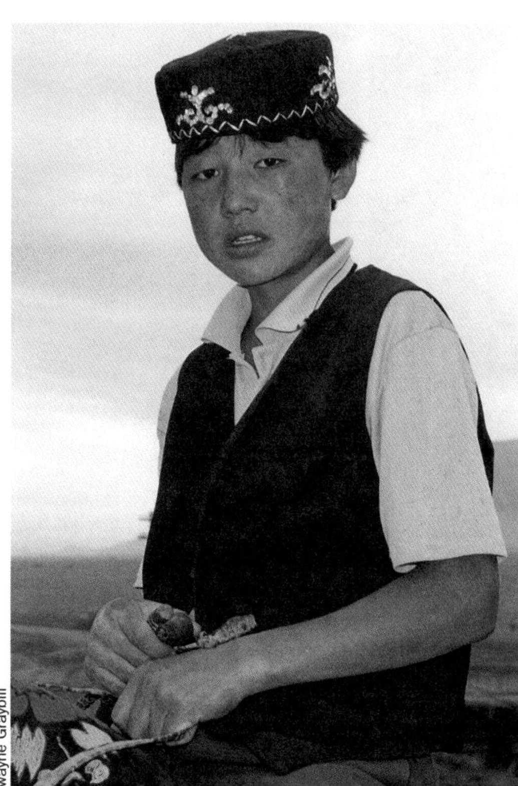
Dwayne Graybill

Location: Approximately 2,900 members of an isolated Kazak people group live in the northwest section of Qinghai Province.[1] Being seminomadic, they inhabit a wide stretch of land in the Haixi Autonomous Prefecture which is jointly administered by the Mongols, Tibetans, and Kazaks. They are the only group of Kazaks found in Qinghai (Blue Sea) Province.

Identity: Although the Qinghai Kazaks are part of the official Kazak nationality in China, they now consider themselves to be a distinct people group. Their language has also become different from other Kazaks in Xinjiang. The Qinghai Kazaks have a common affinity and kinship for each other because of the horrendous events of their history.

Language: The Qinghai Kazaks speak a variety of Kazak that has been heavily influenced by other peoples in the area because of trade, including the Oirat Mongols and Tibetans. The Qinghai Kazaks do not use their own written script, although some can read Chinese and Tibetan.

History: In 1936 a group of 10,000 Kazaks left northern Xinjiang and migrated south to Qinghai. "Beset there by Mongol nomads, the Kazaks moved further south in 1939, only to be caught and massacred by a local warlord. Of 10,000 Kazaks, they say all but 700 perished. Today they have recovered to become a commune of about 2,000 semi-nomads, who raise sheep, horses, cattle and camels and live in houses near Golmud in winter."[2] The Kazaks have long desired to have their own independent state. In the 1940s a man named Osman led his fellow Kazaks in a rebellion. This rebellion gave them control of a large area of southwest Xinjiang. Several years later in 1951, Osman was captured and executed. In 1953, the Communists slaughtered 12,600 of the 15,000 Kazaks who attempted to flee China.[3]

Customs: The Qinghai Kazaks are nomads who migrate seasonally in search of new pastures. Their yurts are designed to be quickly assembled and easily transported. Their livestock includes sheep, goats, and some cattle. One of their favorite drinks is called *kumyss*, a wine made from fermented mare's or horse's milk. When a young Kazak couple marries, the "bride-price" is often paid in horses.

Religion: Although they claim to be Muslims, the Qinghai Kazaks are essentially animists. They also engage in ancestor worship. They are surrounded by Tibetan Buddhists on every side but have stubbornly refused to embrace their religion. The Qinghai Kazaks still admit to being Muslims; but without the *Qur'an*, teachers, or a mosque to worship in, their devotion has gradually eroded.

Christianity: Famous Scottish missionary George Hunter translated the first Scriptures for the Kazak in China. Books of the Bible were printed by the British and Foreign Bible Society in 1922.[4] Today the Kazaks of Qinghai are a completely untouched group and have no knowledge whatsoever of Christ or the gospel.

Population in China:
2,000 (1984)
2,890 (2000)
3,700 (2010)
Location: Qinghai
Religion: Animism
Christians: None Known

Overview of the Qinghai Kazaks

Countries: China

Pronunciation: "Ching-hai-Kar-zark"

Other Name: Kazakhs, Haixi Kazaks

Population Source: 2,000 (1984 Wong How-Man); Out of a total Kazak population of 1,111,718 (1990 census)

Location: *NW Qinghai:* Haixi Mongol-Tibetan-Kazak Prefecture

Status: Officially included under Kazak

Language: Altaic, Turkic, Western Turkic

Dialects: 0

Religion: Animism, Shamanism, Ancestor Worship, Islam

Christians: None known

Scripture: None

***Jesus* film:** None

Gospel Recordings: None

Christian Broadcasting: None

ROPAL code: None

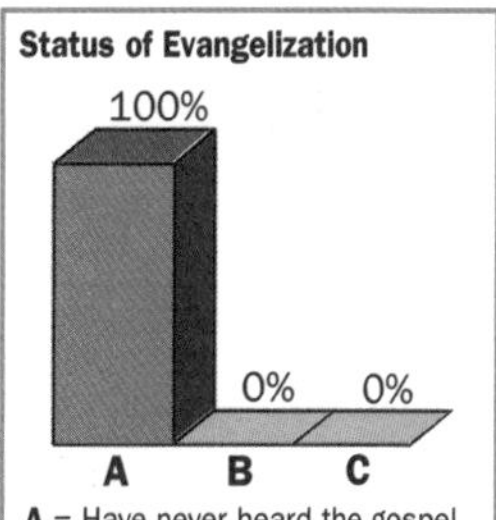

Keji 科计

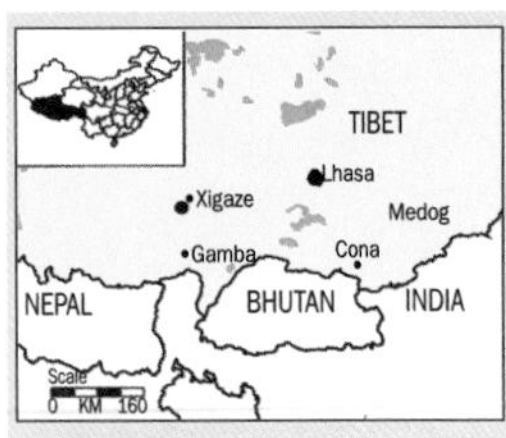

Population in China:
1,650 (1991)
2,000 (2000)
2,480 (2010)
Location: Tibet
Religion: Islam
Christians: None Known

Overview of the Keji

Countries: China

Pronunciation: "Kerr-jee"

Other Names: Tibetan Muslims, Kejis, Ka Che

Population Source: 1,650 (1991 *Global Prayer Digest*); 1,000 in Lhasa (1998 *ARAMCO World*) Out of a total Hui population of 8,602,978 (1990 census)

Location: *Tibet*: Lhasa, Xigaze, and other cities

Status: Officially included under Hui

Language: Sino-Tibetan, Tibeto-Burman, Bodic, Bodish, Tibetan, Central Tibetan

Dialects: 0

Religion: Islam

Christians: None known

Scripture: None

***Jesus* film:** None

Gospel Recordings: None

Christian Broadcasting: None

ROPAL code: None

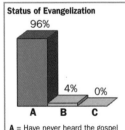

Status of Evangelization

	A	B	C
%	96%	4%	0%

A = Have never heard the gospel
B = Were evangelized but did not become Christians
C = Are adherents to any form of Christianity

Midge Conner

Location: Approximately 2,000 Keji, or Tibetan Muslims, live scattered throughout various cities in Tibet. One thousand of them live in the capital city of Lhasa,[1] where they worship in the small *Chota Masjid* mosque. Hundreds of tourists — both five-star and backpackers — can be found in Lhasa on any given day. Upon arrival in Lhasa, many people are disappointed in their high expectations of the "city of the gods," although it has improved a little since Lowell Thomas' unflattering 1949 report: "Nothing is known of modern plumbing. Refuse piles up on all corners... once a year these offal heaps are transferred to the fields to stimulate crops. The odors are not entirely pleasant. The nobles hold scented handkerchiefs to their noses as they ride along.... Dead animals are tossed in refuse piles to be fought over and devoured by the city's scavengers — thousands of mangy dogs and ravens."[2]

Identity: The Keji have been included in the Hui nationality in China simply because they are Muslims. The proud Keji, however, speak Tibetan and are ethnically distinct. Few people are aware of the existence of the Keji in Tibet. One writer notes, "Even the *Chinese Encyclopedia on Nationalities* makes no mention of their existence."[3]

Language: The Keji speak the Tibetan language of whatever community they live in. They had their own language from Kashmir in the past, but this has been lost.

History: There are two groups of Muslims in Tibet. The larger group are the Hui: Chinese-speaking Muslims who are descended from Arab and Persian traders. The Hui are believed to have migrated into Tibet some time before 1766.[4] The second group are the Keji. "The Kejis have their ancestral roots in Kashmir, India, from which their ancestors migrated in the 1600s. They came to Tibet as traders and still earn a comfortable living that way."[5] The Keji in Lhasa were noticed by the 5th Dalai Lama (1617–1682). "The Dalai Lama spotted a [Keji] man at prayer every day... worshipping according to the precepts of his religion... on the hill because no mosque existed in the area. Impressed with his faith, the Dalai Lama sent a bowman to a site near the hill and had him shoot arrows in each of the four cardinal directions. A house was built at the place from which the arrows were shot, and the land around it, extending as far in each direction as the arrows had flown, was deeded to the Muslim community. The place came to be called The House of Far-Reaching Arrows, and became the site of Lhasa's first mosque and cemetery."[6]

Customs: The Keji have their own Islamic restaurants, tea shops, and mosque in Lhasa. Keji women in some locations wear a distinctive blue dress.

Religion: All Keji are Sunni Muslims. Islam in Tibet dates back to when the ruler of Kabul, a vassal of the Tibetan king, converted from Buddhism to Islam between AD 812 and 814. "As a token of his sincerity, he presented... a gold statue of the Buddha, which was melted down to make coins."[7]

Christianity: There has never been a known Christian among the Keji in Tibet. Because all missionaries who go to Tibet focus on the needs of the Tibetans, the Keji have yet to hear the gospel for the first time in their long history there.

Kemei 克蔑

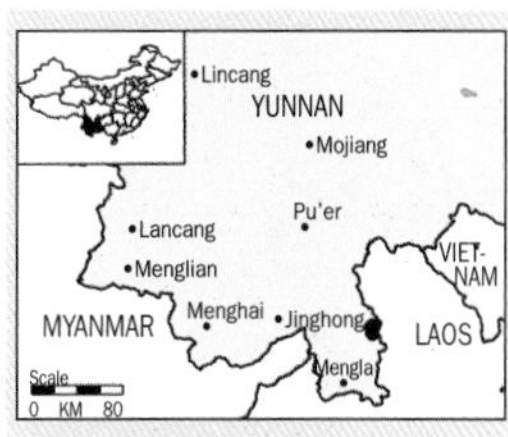

Population in China:
1,000 (1991)
1,260 (2000)
1,620 (2010)
Location: Yunnan
Religion: Animism
Christians: None Known

Overview of the Kemei

Countries: China, Laos

Pronunciation: "Keh-may"

Other Names: Kemeihua, Ka Mi, Kebi

Population Source: 1,000 (1991 *EDCL*); 450 (1996 D. Graybill); Also in Laos

Location: *SW Yunnan:* Jinghong and Mengla counties in Xishuangbanna Prefecture

Status: Unidentified

Language: Austro-Asiatic, Mon-Khmer, Northern Mon-Khmer, Khmuic, Unclassified

Dialects: 0

Religion: Animism, Ancestor Worship, Theravada Buddhism

Christians: None known

Scripture: None

***Jesus* film:** None

Gospel Recordings: None

Christian Broadcasting: None

ROPAL code: KFJ00

Status of Evangelization

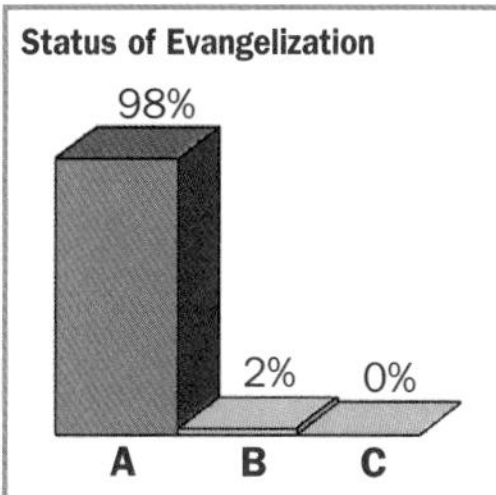

A = Have never heard the gospel
B = Were evangelized but did not become Christians
C = Are adherents to any form of Christianity

Location: The *Encyclopedic Dictionary of Chinese Linguistics* listed a 1991 population of 1,000 Kemei in southern China.[1] Researcher Dwayne Graybill who visited the area in 1996, however, listed a total of only 450 Kemei living in two villages. The largest village, Kami Zhai, contained 285 inhabitants in 47 households.[2] The Kemei villages are west of Meng Ban and south of Mengla, in the Xishuangbanna Prefecture. The Kemei also claim to have relatives living in Laos.

Identity: The Kemei are a little-known group. It is not known in what minority, if any, the Kemei are counted by the Chinese authorities, who officially spell their name *Ka Mi*. The Kemei are not the same as the Khmu people group, who live in the same county and whose language is also from the Mon-Khmer linguistic family. Although their name resembles *Khmer*, the usual Chinese transliteration of Khmer is *Gaomian*.[3]

Language: The Kemei language retains many linguistic similarities with Khmu. Both languages are part of the Northern Mon-Khmer linguistic branch of the Austro-Asiatic language family. Some Kemei are reportedly able to read the Tai Lu "temple script."[4]

History: The Kemei claim they were once part of the Khmu race of Laos. They migrated to China approximately 60 years ago to escape war in Laos. They tell a colorful story explaining why they split from the Khmu. Long ago the two groups went out into the mountains on a hunting expedition. The Khmu killed an elephant, but the Kemei did not believe in eating elephants and caught pigs instead. The Kemei complained, saying it was not fair because the Khmu got to eat much more meat than they did. The quarrel grew so fierce that they decided to separate and have remained apart to this day.[5]

Customs: Because of their small numbers, the Kemei intermarry outside their tribe. At the end of the year, the Kemei hold a festival to bring in the New Year. All Kemei wear red and yellow flowers during the celebration. They say this stems from a long time ago when a prince in Laos was murdered by a farmer. To mourn his death, all the people brought red and yellow flowers to his funeral. When a Kemei dies, they kill his pig and place it next to the corpse along with rice, vegetables, and his knife.

Religion: The Kemei practice animism, with a demonic element to their rituals. To determine where a burial site should be, they carry an egg to the mountains and, with the help of mediums, are led by the spirits. When they reach the appointed place, the egg supernaturally turns black. The Kemei say the spirit of a dead person often returns home, so they continue leaving out food on the table for it.[6]

Christianity: An impromptu survey of the members of a Kemei community in 1996 revealed none had ever before heard of Jesus Christ. Dwayne Graybill reported, "Puzzled looks came upon the faces of both old and young when asked if they had heard of Him. There has never been a church among the Kemei, nor has there ever been a single known believer among their entire tribe."[7]

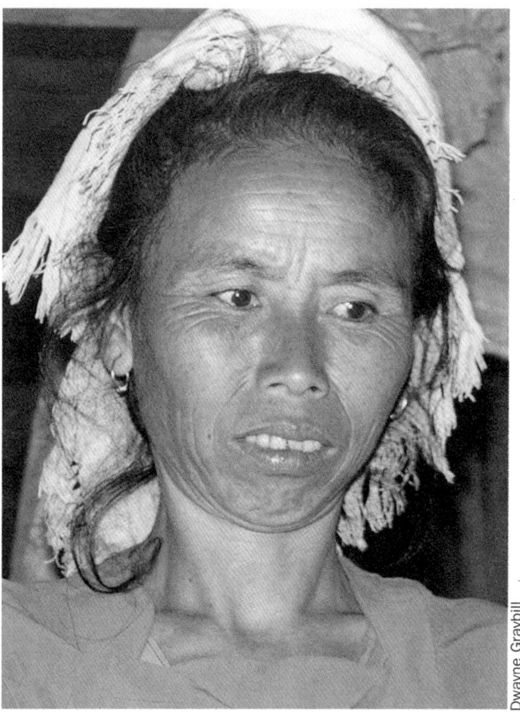

Dwayne Graybill

Keriya 克日亚

Location: Approximately 100 families of the Keriya tribe live "at the southeastern edge of the great Taklimakan Desert... in a green corridor that extends sporadically into the depths of the desert."[1] The largest Keriya community is Tangzubast Village, about 300 kilometers (185 mi.) north of the town of Yutian, in the Xinjiang Uygur Autonomous Region. Tangzubast has been placed under the jurisdiction of Liuabuyi Township in Yutian County. The only way for travelers to visit the area is to follow the dry Keriya River bed north, as there are no roads. *The Record of Buddhist Countries*, written by a fourth century pilgrim, described the Taklimakan Desert: "Monstrous heat-waves are frequent in the desert. Coming across such a phenomena means inevitable death. No birds can be seen in the sky nor animals on the ground. The only things to catch the eye are skeletons which mark the trail of travelers."

Identity: The Keriya have been officially counted as part of the Uygur nationality in China. Although they now speak Uygur as their own language, they claim to be descended from the Gug tribe who fled into the desert centuries ago to escape the attacking Ladakhis from Kashmir.

Language: The Keriya once had their own language, but today they speak only the Yutian Uygur language.

History: After they were attacked by the Ladakhis, "a small number of Gug people crossed the Kunlun Mountains and settled in the Keriya River valley, where they reclaimed land, hunted and herded animals and lived a self-sufficient life until today."[2] The Keriya live on the ruins of the ancient city of Keladun, which is now buried beneath the sand. Archaeologists have found items of pottery dated from the Han Dynasty (206 BC – AD 220). Ruins of twenty similar cities are found throughout the desert. The Keriya people were first "discovered" by Swedish explorer Svan Anders von Hedin in 1896 after he had traveled 12 days into the desert, following the Keriya River. It recently dried up after a sudden change in course and can no longer be followed.

Paul Hattaway

Customs: The Keriya live in widely scattered communities. When there is a wedding or other celebration, "the invitation is written on a slip of paper and passed from family to family, which usually takes a fortnight to do the rounds."[3] Most Keriya families herd goats and sheep. Many also raise camels, horses, and donkeys. Mutton pancakes, called *somitikubaxi*, are the main staple of the Keriya's diet.

Religion: The Keriya have embraced the Sunni Islamic beliefs of most of the people groups in Xinjiang. They do not have their own mosques but are careful to observe all Muslim rules and regulations.

Christianity: The hidden Keriya people have never heard the gospel. They present a significant physical challenge for any would-be evangelist who must venture deep into the awesome and hostile Taklimakan Desert to reach these precious souls. *Taklimakan* is a Turkic word which means "many go in, but few come out." Summer temperatures in the area frequently rise to over 50° Celsius (122°F).

XINJIANG
•Urumqi
•Aksu
•Korla
•Kashgar
Hotan
•Minfeng
•Yutian
Scale
0 KM 400

Population in China:
600 (1996)
660 (2000)
830 (2010)
Location: Xinjiang
Religion: Islam
Christians: None Known

Overview of the Keriya

Countries: China

Pronunciation: "Kerr-yah"

Other Names: Keriya Uygurs

Population Source:
600 (1996 AMO);
100 families
(1996 *China Tourism*);
Out of a total Uygur population of 7,214,431 (1990 census)

Location:
S Xinjiang: Yutian County

Status:
Officially included under Uygur

Language:
Altaic, Turkic, Eastern Turkic

Dialects: 0

Religion: Sunni Islam

Christians: None known

Scripture: None

***Jesus* film:** None

Gospel Recordings: None

Christian Broadcasting: None

ROPAL code: None

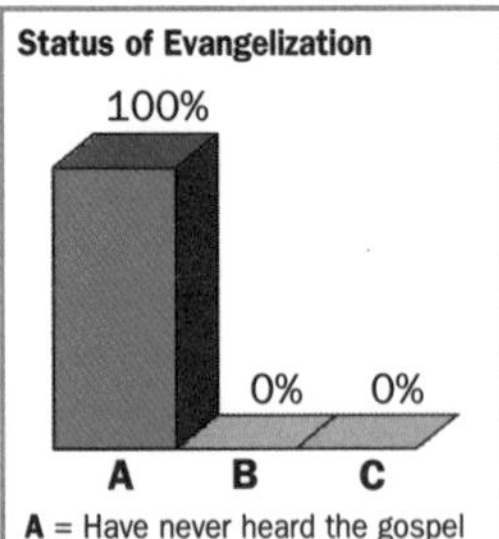

A = Have never heard the gospel
B = Were evangelized but did not become Christians
C = Are adherents to any form of Christianity

83

84

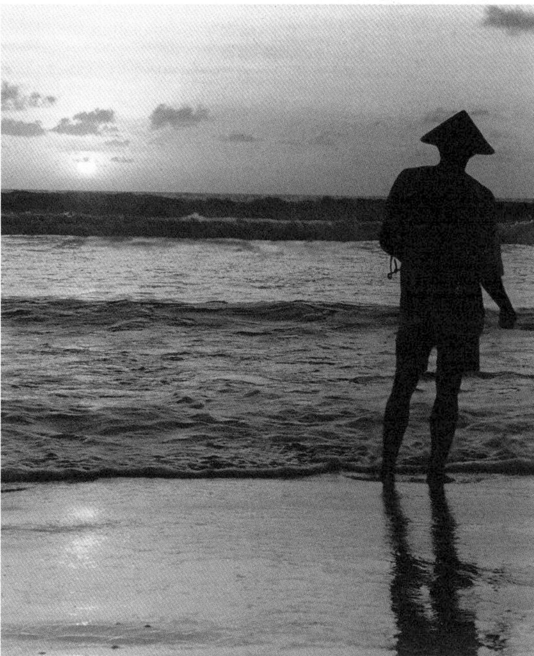

85

83. The 22,000 *Jino* of Xishuangbanna, Yunnan, worship Kong Ming. They consider this war hero to be their forefather. [Midge Conner]
84. For centuries, the *Jiarong* have lived in isolation among massive mountains in western Sichuan. [Midge Conner]
85. A *Jing* fisherman at sunset; Beibu Gulf, Guangxi. [Paul Hattaway]

86

87

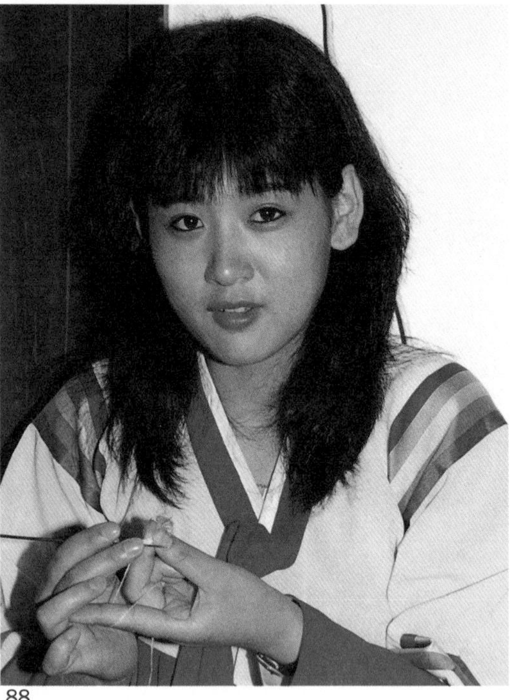
88

89

86. A woman from the 1.4 million-strong *Kazaks* in northwest China. [Midge Conner]
87. The *Kucong* are despised by other groups as cowards since they surrendered to the Qing Dynasty armies in the 1800s. [Paul Hattaway]
88. More than 2 million *Koreans* live in northeast China. Thousands of Korean families migrated to China in 1869 after a severe famine in North Korea. [Paul Hattaway]
89. The *Jingpo*, who live along the Yunnan-Myanmar border, are one of the strongest Christian minorities in China. [Paul Hattaway]

90

91

92

93

90. More than 178,000 *Kirgiz* live in China's extreme northwest border area. Although they profess to be Muslims, most Kirgiz follow a form of black magic. [Dwayne Graybill]
91. A *Khampa* Tibetan woman from western Sichuan. [Midge Conner]
92. The *Kim Mun* (called *Lanten* by the Chinese) are scattered across a wide area of southern China. [Dwayne Graybill]
93. A *Kazak* woman from Xinjiang adorned in her festive best. [Paul Hattaway]

94

95

96

97

94. A *Khampa* Tibetan woman from Kangding, Sichuan. [Paul Hattaway]
95. A *Keji* man keeping warm in his yak-skin coat. The 2,000 Keji are a Tibetan Muslim minority among millions of Tibetan Buddhists. [Revival Christian Church]
96. A *Kirgiz* girl from the China-Kyrgyzstan border. [Dwayne Graybill]
97. The *Khampa* have a reputation of being the most violent and warlike branch of the Tibetan race. [Paul Hattaway]

Khakas 哈卡斯

Population in China:
1,197 (1990)
1,540 (2000)
1,990 (2010)
Location: Heilongjiang
Religion: Tibetan Buddhism
Christians: None Known

Overview of the Khakas

Countries: Russia, China

Pronunciation: "Khar-kuss"

Other Names: Khakhas, Khakhass, Abakan Tatar, Yenisei Tatar, Heilongjiang Kirgiz, Fuyu Kirgiz, Fuyu Keerkezi, Xakas, Khakassian

Population Source:
1,197 (1990 census);
875 (1982 census);
Out of a total Kirgiz population of 141,549 (1990 census);
64,800 in Russia
(1993 United Bible Societies)

Location: *Heilongjiang:* Fuyu County, north of Qiqihar

Status:
Officially included under Kirgiz

Language:
Altaic, Turkic, Northern Turkic

Dialects: 0

Religion: Tibetan Buddhism, Animism, Shamanism, No Religion

Christians: None known

Scripture: None

***Jesus* film:** None

Gospel Recordings: None

Christian Broadcasting: None

ROPAL code: KJH00

Status of Evangelization

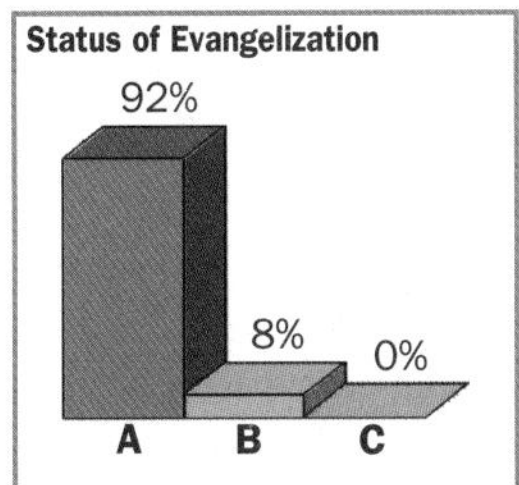

A = Have never heard the gospel
B = Were evangelized but did not become Christians
C = Are adherents to any form of Christianity

Location: The 1990 Chinese census listed 1,197 members of the Khakas people group before they were combined into the official Kirgiz nationality. In contrast to the Kirgiz who live in northwest China, the Khakas live in Fuyu County in Heilongjiang Province in China's northeast. The largest Khakas community in China is Qujiazi Village. In 1979 it contained 219 Khakas,

Dwayne Graybill

327 Han Chinese, 84 Mongols, 21 Daur, and 2 Manchus.[1] The Khakas live along the eastern bank of the Nonni River. Another group of Khakas used to live in the Imim region of Inner Mongolia, but they were ethnically assimilated by other nationalities during the early part of the twentieth century. The vast majority of Khakas today (about 65,000) live in the Altai region of Russia.

Identity: Although the Chinese officially consider the Khakas to be a part of the Kirgiz nationality, their languages and culture "differ considerably."[2] In Russia the Khakas are a collection of the five nomadic Turkic-speaking tribes of Kacha, Kyzyl, Sagai, Beltir, and Koibal.[3]

Language: The Khakas language in China is nearly extinct. In 1982 there were only ten fluent speakers of Khakas remaining.[4] The youngest speaker was 60 years old. The Khakas have been bilingual in Olot, Mongolian, or Chinese for several generations. Now all Khakas youth speak only Mandarin.[5] For the time being the Khakas is the easternmost Turkic-speaking group in the world. In Russia, where there is a Khakas script, the language is not under immediate threat.

History: During the Ming Dynasty (1368–1644) the Kirgiz fought with the Oirats. When the latter were defeated by the Eastern Mongols, most Kirgiz tribes moved to the Tianshan Range in Xinjiang where they still live today. A few Kirgiz remained in their homeland on the upper Yenisei River in today's Russia. Others lived just south of there, in the Altai Mountain range, as late as the eighteenth century. "When the Qing forces defeated the Jungars in the 1750s, they removed these Kirgiz [Khakas] to China's northeast. The first group moved there in 1758 and a second group followed them in 1761 from the Altai and Kang'ai mountain ranges. These two groups form the core of today's Kirgiz [Khakas] in Heilongjiang."[6]

Customs: Most Khakas no longer practise their own customs. They have adapted to Chinese culture and before long will probably cease to be a distinct people.

Religion: Unlike the Kirgiz, there are no Muslims among the Khakas. They were converted to Tibetan Buddhism by their Mongol neighbors. "Until the 1950s you could still find shamans, called *Gam* in the Khakas villages."[7] Today the Khakas are rapidly becoming a secularized group. Few of the present generation of Khakas youth have any interest in religion.

Christianity: There has never been a single known believer among the Khakas in China. Their relatives in Russia are also an unreached people who follow animistic practices. Although they have a written script, the Scriptures have never been translated into Khakas.

Khampa, Eastern 康巴(东)

Luke Kuepfer

Location: Approximately 1.2 million Khampa Tibetans speak the Eastern Khampa language. They inhabit a vast area but are primarily concentrated in western Sichuan Province as far east as Kangding, a large portion of eastern Tibet, and parts of southern Qinghai Province. The Eastern Khampa town of Litang lies 4,700 meters (15,400 ft.) above sea level. Chamdo is another important town — at an altitude of 3,200 meters (10,500 ft.). The Chamdo Monastery was built in 1473 and now houses 2,500 monks. Other main towns include Bayi, where a massive textile and carpet factory employs 1,300 workers, and Batang, which is 2,700 meters (8,856 ft.) above sea level.

Identity: The Khampa have a fearsome reputation as the most hostile and violent of Tibetans. "Tall and well-built men, fearless and open of countenance, they resemble Apache Indians, with plaited hair hanging from each side of well-modeled heads."[1]

Language: The Eastern Khampa language is by far the largest of the Khampa varieties. It is reported to have eight dialects[2] and 80% lexical similarity with Central Tibetan.[3]

History: The Khampa have a long history of conflict with the Chinese, who annexed most of Kham Province to Sichuan in 1720. "No Chinese dares to enter the territory for fear of being murdered."[4] Military clashes between the two groups occurred in 1918, 1928, and 1932. In 1950 the Chinese captured the town of Chamdo without firing a shot. The Khampa fled in terror when the Chinese set off a huge fireworks display on the outskirts of the town. In late 1955 the Chinese authorities ordered the monks of Litang Monastery to produce an inventory for tax assessment. The monks refused to oblige. In February 1956, the Chinese laid siege to the monastery which was defended by several thousand monks and farmers. Litang and surrounding areas were bombed by Chinese aircraft. In 1959 the Khampa in Lhasa organized a revolt against Chinese rule. "The fighting lasted three days with the Tibetans caught up in a religious fervor, not caring whether they lived or died."[5]

Customs: Sexual immorality among the Khampa is considered normal behavior. A 1950s survey "found the rate of venereal diseases was 40% in peasant areas and 50.7% in pasture areas."[6]

Religion: The Khampa, like all Tibetan groups, are devout followers of Buddhism.

Christianity: Catholic work among the Khampa commenced in the mid-1800s. The Catholic mission at Batang Township was demolished in 1873 and 1905 — after two priests had been killed and converts who would not deny their faith were shot.[7] By 1924 the mission numbered 2 bishops, 15 French missionaries, and 4,800 baptized converts of whom "about two-fifths were Tibetans."[8] Today there are 200 Khampa Catholics near Kangding and some near Batang and Yajiang.[9] Protestant work among the Khampa commenced in 1897. The missionaries ran hospitals, schools, and orphanages, but saw little fruit. By 1922 the Protestant station at Batang had won ten converts.[10]

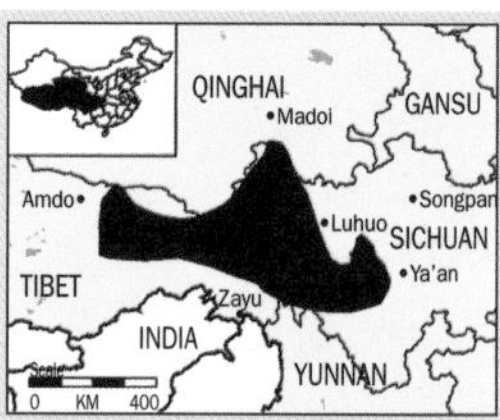

Population in China:
956,700 (1987)
1,245,200 (2000)
1,534,100 (2010)
Location:
Sichuan, Tibet, Qinghai
Religion: Tibetan Buddhism
Christians: 400

Overview of the Eastern Khampa

Countries: China, India, Nepal

Pronunciation: "Kum-ba"

Other Names: Kham, Khams, Khams-Yal, Khams-Bhotia, Kam, Khamba, Kang, Konka, Konkaling

Population Source: 956,700 (1987 *LAC*); Out of a total Tibetan population of 4,593,330 (1990 census); Also in India and Nepal

Location: *W Sichuan:* Garze Prefecture; *E Tibet; S Qinghai*

Status: Officially included under Tibetan

Language: Sino-Tibetan, Tibeto-Burman, Bodic, Bodish, Tibetan, Northern Tibetan

Dialects (8): Dege, Karmdzes, Chamdo, Braggyab, Nyingkhri, Batang, Nyagchu, and an unknown dialect

Religion: Tibetan Buddhism, Bon, Christianity

Christians: 400

Scripture: Tibetan Bible 1948; New Testament 1885; Portions 1862

***Jesus* film:** None

Gospel Recordings: Kham #02508; Khamba #00796

Christian Broadcasting: None

ROPAL code: KHG01

Status of Evangelization

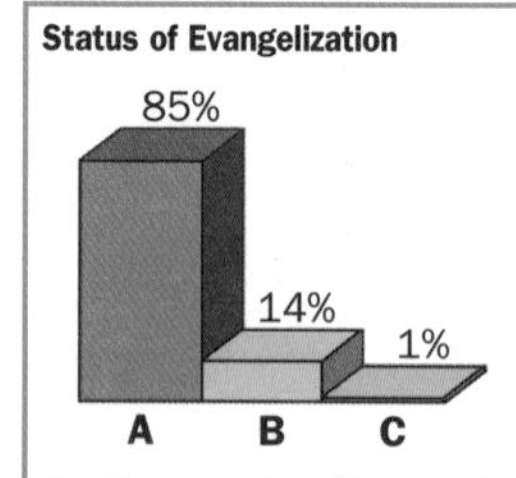

A = Have never heard the gospel
B = Were evangelized but did not become Christians
C = Are adherents to any form of Christianity

Khampa, Northern 康巴(北)

Location: A 1987 linguistic study listed 91,000 speakers of the Northern Khampa Tibetan language.[1] They occupy the large, sparsely populated Yushu Tibetan Autonomous Prefecture in southern Qinghai Province. Northern Khampa is spoken as far north as the 5,214-meter-high (17,100 ft.) Mount Yagradagze. In addition, a small number of Northern Khampa spill over the border into northeast Tibet. The nomadic Northern Khampa live on a high plateau where they herd sheep, goats, and yaks.[2]

Identity: The Northern Khampa are part of the Tibetan nationality in China. Anthropologist Michael Peissel described them in 1964: "The Khampas stood a good six feet in height ... wore great heavy boots and flowing khaki robes that flapped like whips as they walked, advancing with their feet slightly apart as if to trample the grass to extinction.... Unlike Tibetans of Lhasa, their features were not Mongoloid, but straight, with large fierce eyes set beside beak-like noses, and long hair braided and wound around their heads, giving them a primitive allure."[3]

Language: Northern Khampa is one of three Khampa groups, "each speaking its own language and living in different areas. Due to the migration of peoples and the many political developments, Tibet has become very ethnically complex."[4]

History: Heinrich Harrier, famous for his book *Seven Years in Tibet*, walked through Khampa areas in the 1940s. Harrier described the Khampa: "They live in groups in three or four tents which serve as headquarters for their campaigns.... Heavily armed with rifles and swords they force their way into a nomad's tent and insist on hospitable entertainment on the most lavish scale available. The nomad in terror brings out everything he has. The Khampas fill their bellies and their pockets and, taking a few cattle with them for good measure, disappear into the wide-open spaces. They repeat the performance at another tent every day till the whole region has been skinned.... Stories were told of the cruelty with which they sometimes put their victims to death. They go so far as to slaughter pilgrims and wandering monks and nuns."[5]

Luke Kuepfer

Customs: Khampa men are easily identifiable by the red and black tassels braided into their hair. They say that they wear this to protect their scalps during knife fights. Khampa superstition says a man without an earring will be reincarnated as a donkey. Turquoise, red coral, bone, and silver ornaments decorate nomad Khampa women's hair.

Religion: Although they profess to be Buddhists, the Khampa nomads' religion is little more than a crude imitation of the ideals of the pure form of Buddhism.

Christianity: Two thousand years since the birth of Christ, the Northern Khampa remain completely untouched by the gospel. They are separated by geographic, linguistic, cultural, and religious barriers. There has never been any kind of church or Christian witness in the extremely isolated and practically impenetrable Yushu Prefecture.

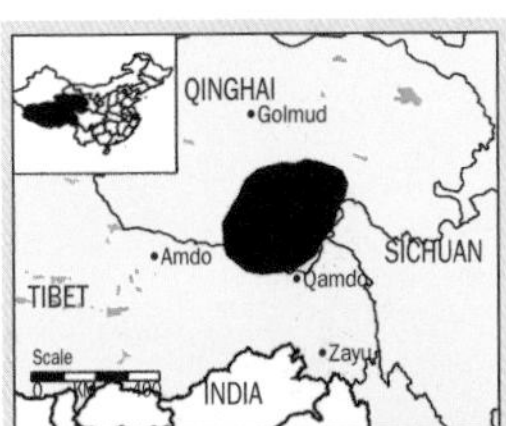

Population in China:
91,000 (1987)
118,400 (2000)
145,900 (2010)
Location: Qinghai, Tibet
Religion: Tibetan Buddhism
Christians: None Known

Overview of the Northern Khampa

Countries: China

Pronunciation: "Kum-ba"

Other Names: Kham, Khamba

Population Source:
91,000 (1987 *LAC*);
Out of a total Tibetan population of 4,593,330 (1990 census)

Location: *S Qinghai:* Yushu Prefecture; *NE Tibet*

Status:
Officially included under Tibetan

Language: Sino-Tibetan, Tibeto-Burman, Bodic, Bodish, Tibetan, Northern Tibetan

Dialects (4): Bristod, Khrihdu, Kuergu, Nagnchen

Religion: Tibetan Buddhism

Christians: None known

Scripture: Tibetan Bible 1948; New Testament 1885; Portions 1862

***Jesus* film:** None

Gospel Recordings: None

Christian Broadcasting: None

ROPAL code: KHG04

Status of Evangelization

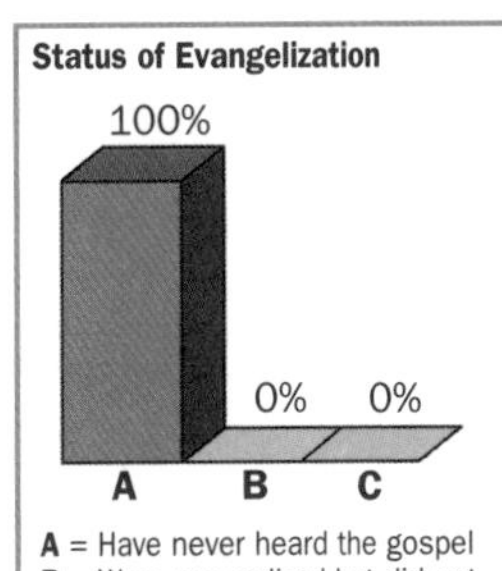

A = Have never heard the gospel
B = Were evangelized but did not become Christians
C = Are adherents to any form of Christianity

Khampa, Western 康巴(西)

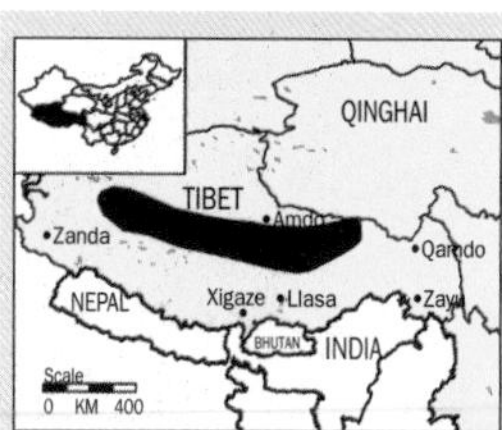

Population in China:
157,700 (1987)
205,200 (2000)
252,800 (2010)
Location: Tibet
Religion: Tibetan Buddhism
Christians: None Known

Overview of the Western Khampa

Countries: China

Pronunciation: "Kum-ba"

Other Names: Kham, Khamba

Population Source:
157,700 (1987 *LAC*);
Out of a total Tibetan population of 4,593,330 (1990 census)

Location:
N Tibet: Nghari Prefecture

Status:
Officially included under Tibetan

Language: Sino-Tibetan, Tibeto-Burman, Bodic, Bodish, Tibetan, Northern Tibetan

Dialects (2): Ger-rtse, Nagchu

Religion: Tibetan Buddhism

Christians: None known

Scripture: Tibetan Bible 1948; New Testament 1885; Portions 1862

***Jesus* film:** None

Gospel Recordings: None

Christian Broadcasting: None

ROPAL code: KHG03

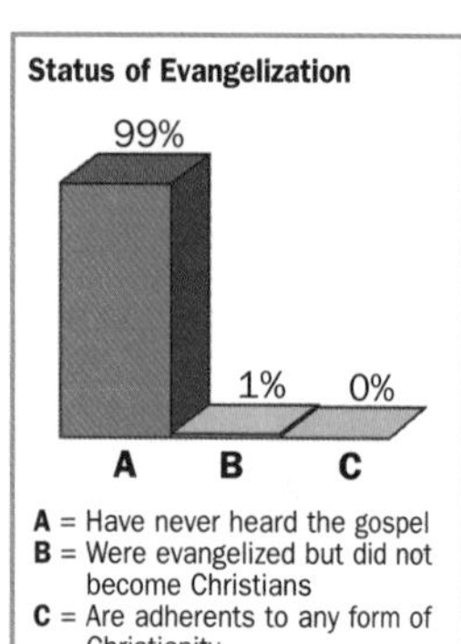

Location: Approximately 205,000 Tibetans living in the massive Nghari Prefecture in central and northern Tibet speak the Western Khampa language. They have "a very sparse population in a band to the northeast and extending to the north of almost the entire central Tibetan area."[1] The region is mostly a high, desolate plateau. "At 17,000 feet [5,180 meters], the rarefied atmosphere has only half as many oxygen particles as at sea level. As early as AD 100 a Chinese official described the Tibetan Plateau as 'Headache Mountains'."[2]

Identity: The suffix *pa* means "people" in Tibetan. *Kham-pa*, therefore means "people of Kham." Kham was a province of Tibet until it was annexed by the Chinese and incorporated into Qinghai and Sichuan provinces. The Western Khampa, however, live wholly within Tibet itself, which the Chinese call *Xizang* (Hidden West).

Language: Western Khampa is unintelligible with the Central Tibetan languages or Amdo Tibetan. Despite living in a huge area approximately the size of England, only two dialects are reported within the Western Khampa language.

History: For centuries the Khampa have terrorized other Tibetans. During the 1950s they formed guerrilla groups and took over considerable territory. "In 1958 they attacked a Chinese market town, killing several thousand of them."[3]

Customs: Living in some of the harshest conditions in the world, the traditional long-sleeved coats of the Khampa are tied up with a belt, which conceals a large knife or sword. Many wear lucky charms, magical strings, or amulet boxes around their neck. Khampa men, who often get around on horseback, are never without a weapon. *Polyandry* (the practice of brothers sharing the same wife) still occurs in some places. Life expectancy for Khampa living on the bitter plateau averages only about 45 years.

Religion: The Khampa rely on demons, ghosts, and the spirits of disembodied deities to guide their decisions. Many monks are able to call up fearsome demons, who sometimes visualize in front of them. The most devout monks are reported to be able to transport themselves spiritually from one place to another, and have been reputed to appear in different widespread locations on the same day. The Khampa also worship *Yama*, the god of Death. They believe he is the king of the underworld and that he controls all the events of their lives.

Christianity: The Western Khampa Tibetans are the epitome of an unreached people group. Missionaries in the past, frustrated at not being allowed into Tibet, loaded up dozens of yaks with Tibetan tracts and sent them randomly into the vast Tibetan frontiers.[4] In the 1920s one writer lamented, "This region is not only without a resident missionary, but even the scouts of Christianity have barely touched it except at one or two points.... All these are realms to conquer in West China. Large areas are unknown absolutely, and still larger ones remain relatively unknown."[5]

Luke Kuepfer

Khmu 克木

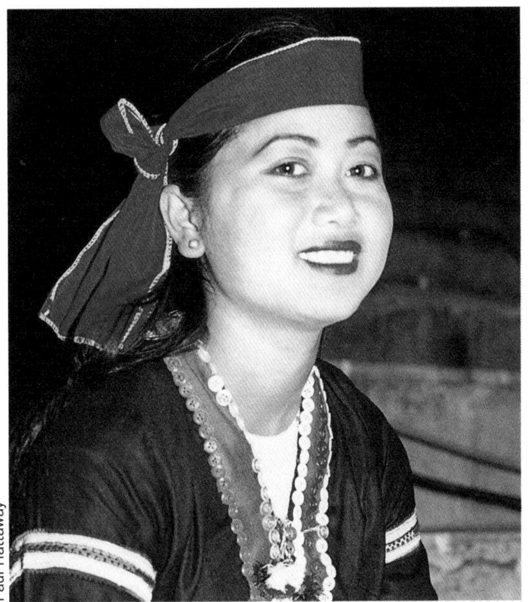

Location: The 1,400 Khmu in China are located in the extreme southwest corner of the country. More than 560,000 Khmu also live throughout Southeast Asia, particularly in Laos where 500,000 are found. The Khmu in China came from northern Laos into Xishuangbanna earlier this century. Twenty-five hundred Khmu have also settled in Western countries as refugees.[1] In Yunnan, "the area they inhabit is surrounded by mountains and situated in the Shanyong District adjacent to China's border with Laos and south of the Nanla River in Mengla County."[2]

Identity: There has been much talk of the Khmu in China being granted status as China's 56th official minority. Twenty Chinese experts "urged that the Khmu be classified as a separate nationality."[3] The government has so far resisted and has included the Khmu in a list of *Undetermined Minorities*. The Khmu have been described in such unflattering terms as "poverty stricken, dirty, and primitive."[4]

Language: Khmu is a Mon-Khmer language. The Khmu in Jinghong use a classical written script — called *Duota* — while those in Mengla have no orthography, which suggests linguistic differences between the two.[5]

History: Despite being recognized as the original inhabitants of Laos,[6] the Khmu have a long history of oppression and conflict with other peoples. They were driven from the most prosperous land on the plains by Lao invaders from southern China almost 1,000 years ago. Many Khmu became slaves of the Lao. Still today the Khmu are known as *Kha* — a derogatory name meaning "slaves." In the latter part of the 1800s the Khmu were attacked by the Hmong in northern Laos after the Khmu had unwisely demanded tribute from the newly arrived Hmong.[7]

Customs: In Khmu culture, sons take their father's family names, and daughters take their mother's. Surnames represent an animal or plant which those who bear that name are not allowed to touch.[8] The Khmu in China, who refuse to marry outside of their tribe, "have no special festivals but in their times of leisure, the villagers, men and women, like to sit in a ring with wine jars put in the middle from which the wine can be sucked up through long straws."[9]

Religion: Most Khmu believe their lives are controlled by the spirit world. This complex hierarchy of spirits includes the spirit of heaven, the spirit of thunder, the spirit of the water snake, etc. Every year the Khmu in Laos hold festivals to worship the spirits of the village and their ancestors, as well as to pray for a plentiful harvest and good fortune.

Christianity: There are only a handful of believers among the Khmu in China, but in Laos they are one of the strongest Christian groups. Various missions were prominent in the early 1900s, sowing seeds for the harvest of at least 50,000 Khmu believers in Laos today.[10] Many Khmu in Laos are coming to Christ through gospel radio broadcasts in the Khmu language. Some believe the Khmu in Laos are on the verge of mass conversion.[11] Bible portions were translated into the Khmu language almost 80 years ago, but new Bible translation projects are currently under way.

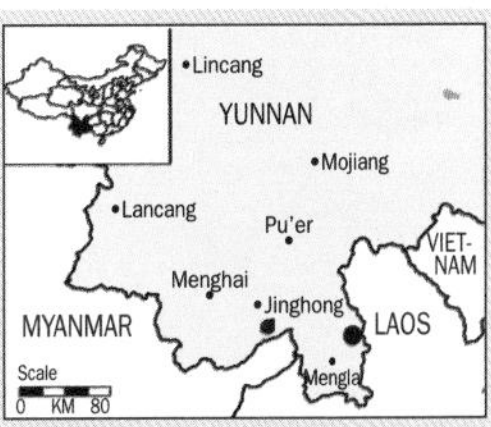

Population in China:
1,100 (1990)
1,420 (2000)
1,830 (2010)
Location: Yunnan
Religion: Animism
Christians: 10

Overview of the Khmu

Countries: Laos, Vietnam, Thailand, USA, China, Myanmar

Pronunciation: "Keh-Mu"

Other Names: Kemu, Khamu, Mou, Khamuk, Pouteng, Theng, Kha, Kamhmu, Kamu, Lao Terng, Kammu, Khomu, Samon

Population Source:
1,600 (1990 census);[12]
500,957 in Laos (1995 census);
42,853 in Vietnam (1989 F. Proschan);
15,000 to 40,000 in Thailand;
2,000 in USA; 500 in France;
Also in Myanmar

Location: *SW Yunnan:* Banhuiai Village, Mengla County, in Xishuangbanna Dai Prefecture; Also in Jinghong County

Status: Counted in census as an *Undetermined Minority*

Language: Austro-Asiatic, Mon-Khmer, Northern Mon-Khmer, Khmuic, Mal-Khmu, Khmu

Dialects: 0

Religion: Animism, Theravada Buddhism

Christians: 10

Scripture: Portions 1918; Work in progress

***Jesus* film:** In progress

Gospel Recordings: Khamu #01005

Christian Broadcasting: Available (FEBC)

ROPAL code: KJG00

Status of Evangelization

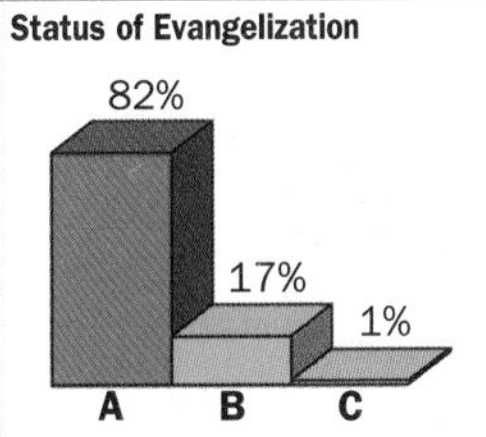

A = Have never heard the gospel
B = Were evangelized but did not become Christians
C = Are adherents to any form of Christianity

Kim Mun 金们

Population in China:
200,000 (1990)
258,000 (2000)
332,800 (2010)
Location: Yunnan, Guangxi, Hainan Island
Religion: Daoism
Christians: 300

Overview of the Kim Mun

Countries: China, Laos, Vietnam, Myanmar, Switzerland, USA

Pronunciation: "Gehm-Moon"

Other Names: Gem Mun, Juim Mun, Man, Lanten, Lowland Yao, Jim Mun, Shanzi Yao, Lantien, Kem Mun, Jinmen, Hainan Miao, Miao of Hainan Island, Landian

Population Source: 200,000 (1995 Wang Fushi – 1990 figure); Out of a total Yao population of 2,134,013 (1990 census); 8,500 in Laos (1999 AMO); Also in Vietnam, Myanmar, Switzerland, USA

Location: *SE Yunnan; Hainan Island; Guangxi*

Status: Officially included under Yao, except those on Hainan Island who are officially included under Miao

Language: Hmong-Mien, Mienic, Kim Mun

Dialects: 0

Religion: Daoism, Polytheism, Ancestor Worship, Christianity

Christians: 300

Scripture: None

***Jesus* film:** None

Gospel Recordings: Lanten #03122; Yao: Lantien; Miao: Tongjia

Christian Broadcasting: None

ROPAL code: MJI00

Status of Evangelization

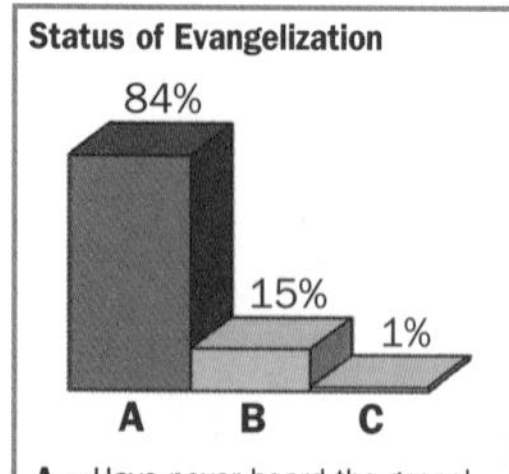

A = Have never heard the gospel
B = Were evangelized but did not become Christians
C = Are adherents to any form of Christianity

Dwayne Graybill

Location: More than 250,000 speakers of the Kim Mun language live in China.[1] The majority are located in the Jinping area of southeastern Yunnan Province, in addition to parts of Guangxi. Approximately 50,000 people living on Hainan Island are officially included as part of the Miao nationality, but they speak the same language as the Kim Mun on the Mainland who are included as part of the Yao nationality. More than 8,500 Kim Mun live in two subgroups within northern Laos, and an unspecified number live in Vietnam. In Laos the Kim Mun population is decreasing because of rampant drug addiction.

Identity: Most of the Kim Mun in China are also known as *Lantien* and are counted as part of the Yao nationality. Those on Hainan Island, however, have been included as part of the Miao (apparently at their own insistence), although linguists agree that they speak Kim Mun.[2] The name *Lantien* is a Chinese term meaning "those who make dye." *Kim Mun* means "the people in the forest." To complicate matters further, some Kim Mun are also referred to as the *Shanzi Yao* by the Chinese, meaning "mountaineer Yao."

Language: Despite the distances between some of their locations, the Kim Mun language is quite uniform. Speakers from widespread regions can understand each other without too much difficulty.[3]

History: For centuries the Kim Mun were oppressed by greedy landlords. They migrated in large numbers south and west in search of their own land. "Legend has it that the forefathers of these two branches of Yao [Kim Mun and Iu Mien] were brothers who separated during migration, thus forming two groups."[4]

Customs: The Kim Mun are famous for their many ingenious customs and inventions,[5] including the tradition of making paper from roots and leaves.[6] Until recently, a young Kim Mun man taking a wife had to pay a price. "Betrothal was actually a negotiation of the bride price, which was divided into five different grades, depending on such natural qualities as the girl's beauty and health. The girl's parents would not let the man take their daughter away until the price had been paid in full. The five different grades ranged from 72 to 12 ounces of silver."[7] During courtship, Kim Mun youth sing romantic songs to each other. "If a girl falls in love with a boy, she bites his arm as a token of her love for him."[8]

Religion: The Kim Mun believe that when bad people die they go to a terrible place, their perception of hell — a thick, dark forest with no villages or clearings. It is believed that good people will go to one of several levels of heaven, depending on how much care their eldest son gives the spirit of his dead parent. Men without sons, therefore, do whatever it takes to procure a son, since their soul will be lost without one. The Kim Mun worship their ancestors by sacrificing pigs three times each year to honor them.

Christianity: The Kim Mun are an unreached people, although there are tiny pockets of believers scattered throughout southern China, including several confirmed believers in Mengla. The Kim Mun have no Bible in their language, and few ministries are reaching out to them.

Kiong Nai 炯奈

Population in China:
1,500 (1991)
1,890 (2000)
2,400 (2010)
Location: Guangxi
Religion: Polytheism
Christians: None Known

Overview of the Kiong Nai

Countries: China

Pronunciation: "Chee-ong-Nai"

Other Names: Hwa Lan Yao, Hua Lan Yao, Jiongnai, Jiongnaihua, Kion Nai, Flowery Blue Yao, Qiungnai, Kiang Nai

Population Source:
1,500 (1991 *EDCL*);
822 (1982 census);
Out of a total Yao population of 2,134,013 (1990 census)

Location: *E Guangxi:* Jinxiu Yao Autonomous County

Status:
Officially included under Yao

Language:
Hmong-Mien, Hmongic, Kiang Nai

Dialects: 0

Religion: Polytheism, Animism

Christians: None known

Scripture: None

***Jesus* film:** None

Gospel Recordings: None

Christian Broadcasting: None

ROPAL code: PNU00

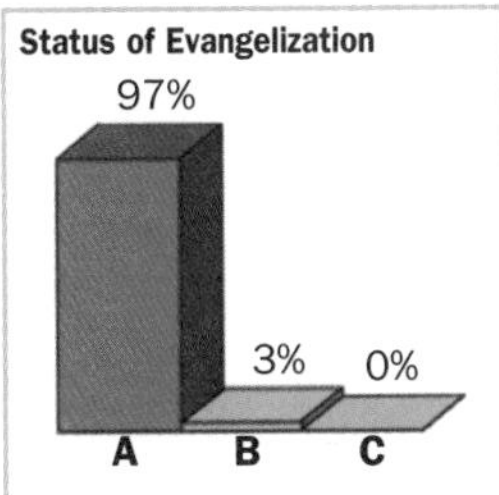

Location: The small Kiong Nai tribe, which numbered 1,500 people in a 1991 study,[1] are one of five distinct Yao groups living in the Dayaoshan (Big Yao Mountains) in eastern Guangxi's Jinxiu County. The 1982 Chinese census listed only 822 Kiong Nai, but later research placed the number higher. The Kiong Nai are the smallest and most different of the five Yao groups, who together total 36,000 people.[2] The various groups "speak different languages and each has its own peculiar customs and living habits."[3] The Kiong Nai inhabit the nine villages of Longhua, Nanzhou, Dajin, Liuxiang, Mentou, Gubu, Ludan, Liutian, and Chang'e.

Identity: Although they are officially (and ethnically) considered part of the Yao nationality, the Kiong Nai speak a language related to Miao. *Kiong Nai* is the self-name of this small tribe. The Chinese call them *Hualan Yao* which means "flowery blue Yao." It can also mean "Yao with baskets of flowers."

Language: Kiong Nai is totally unintelligible with the speech of the surrounding Yao communities. Although it is considered part of the Bunu linguistic group, Kiong Nai has only 52% lexical similarity with Bunuo, the main Bunu language.[4] Kiong Nai is considered one of the intermediary languages between Miao and Yao.[5]

History: The Kiong Nai live alongside the Iu Mien and Lakkia in the Dayaoshan Mountains. These groups migrated into the area at different times. The Kiong Nai's homes are "built with brick and wood.... The Pan [Iu Mien] and Shanzi Yao [Kim Mun], however, had no land in the Dayaoshan, suggesting that these two groups were later arrivals in the area. They had to ask to use land from the three established Yao groups, and had to pay rent and render manual labor to them. These two groups could not settle down, but lived in rustic bamboo sheds."[6]

Customs: Kiong Nai women wear beautiful dress, which is "embroidered with fine lace and consists of three wraps, one large, one smaller, and one a medium size.... A small bamboo basket is carried on the back and a long knife at the waist. A pair of short pants and a puttee completes the outfit."[7] The Kiong Nai are renowned throughout the area for their skill in making silver ornaments.

Religion: The Kiong Nai are polytheists. They worship a variety of gods and spirits. Their religion has made them indifferent to the sanctity of human life. "It is their custom... to control the size of their population. They plan their families according to their wealth and the size of the land they will till. Generally, there will be one or two children in a family. In order to maintain their living standard, they do not hesitate to resort to abortion if and when their planning goes wrong."[8]

Christianity: The Kiong Nai are completely untouched by the gospel. They have never had a known believer or Christian fellowship among them. There are geographic, cultural, and linguistic barriers that prevent the Kiong Nai from hearing the message of salvation from other people groups.

Paul Hattaway

Kirgiz 柯而克孜

Location: Approximately 140,000 Kirgiz were counted in the 1990 Chinese census. In addition, 2.23 million Kirgiz live in their new homeland, Kyrgyzstan. Others live in Uzbekistan, Tajikistan, Afghanistan, and in a small refugee community in Turkey. In China, 80% of the Kirgiz are located in more than 20 counties within the Kiziksu Prefecture in the Xinjiang Uygur Autonomous Region.[1]

Identity: In the 1950s the Kirgiz were granted status as one of China's official minority groups. The name *Kirgiz* means "44 lasses."[2] The Kirgiz believe they are descended from 44 maidens. The Kirgiz in China still retain their tribal identities. "To this day one can distinguish the following tribes: Kipchak, Naiman, Taiyit, Kaisaik, Chongbash, Qielik, Kuqu, Salu, Salbash, Mengduzi, Mengguldar, Ketay, Buwu, and Sayak."[3]

Language: Kirgiz is a Turkic language. They used to have their own script, called the *Yenisei* script, until it was lost in the eighth century.[4] No trace of it remains today. The Kirgiz language in China contains two dialects: Northern and Southern Kirgiz. Both dialects have the same vocabulary but employ different pronunciations.

History: In AD 751 the Chinese armies were defeated by the Arabs in a significant battle at Talas, in what is now Kyrgyzstan. One historian wrote, "This encounter... was one of the most fateful battles in history. It marked the end of Chinese control over Central Asia.... It also marked the beginning of Arab conquest of Central Asia. Soon the area was permanently converted to Islam."[5] By the early 830s the Kirgiz had clashed with the Uygurs for control of Central Asia and defeated them. In 1944 the Chinese Nationalist government ordered the closure of many Kirgiz pasture lands, under the pretext of "border security." The Kirgiz, outraged at losing their livelihood, formed a government that gave birth to the Puli Revolution.

Dwayne Graybill

Customs: The Kirgiz have a famous epic, the *Manas*, that describes their past. The *Manas* is a virtual encyclopedia describing the customs, habits, and philosophies of the Kirgiz, as well as recording their struggle for independence and freedom. Most Kirgiz in China are involved with the production of carpets, horse gear, cloth, and wool.

Religion: In reality — although they are outwardly Muslims — most Kirgiz follow a form of shamanism and black magic, where power through seductive signs and wonders is exerted. Demonstrations of this evil power are often aired on public television in Kyrgyzstan. The Snake god, in particular, is held in great fear.

Christianity: Swedish missionaries in Xinjiang listed 163 baptized believers by 1933, "mostly Uighers and Kirgiz, with some Chinese."[6] In 1933 the missionaries were arrested and brought before Abdullah Khan, who "personally kicked and beat them. He threatened to kill them, claiming that their religious teaching was destroying the faith of many of his people."[7] Most of the new Kirgiz believers were murdered. Those whose lives were spared were imprisoned for many years. There are just a few known believers among the Kirgiz in China today, although some ministries are targeting them.

Population in China:
138,600 (1990)
178,800 (2000)
230,600 (2010)
Location: Xinjiang
Religion: Islam
Christians: 10

Overview of the Kirgiz

Countries: Kyrgyzstan, Uzbekistan, China, Tajikistan, Afghanistan, Turkey

Pronunciation: "Kerr-geez"

Other Names: Kirghiz, Kara, Ke'erkezi

Population Source: 141,549 (1990 census);[8] 113,999 (1982 census);[9] 2,230,000 in Kyrgyzstan; 175,000 in Uzbekistan; 64,000 in Tajikistan; 25,000 in Afghanistan; 1,137 in Turkey

Location: *SW Xinjiang:* 80% live in Kiziksu Kirgiz Prefecture.[10]

Status: An official minority of China

Language: Altaic, Turkic, Western Turkic, Aralo-Caspian

Literacy: 59%

Dialects (2): Northern (50,000), Southern (50,000)

Religion: Islam, Polytheism, Ancestor Worship

Christians: 10

Scripture: New Testament 1988; Portions 1818

***Jesus* film:** Available

Gospel Recordings: Kirghiz #03374

Christian Broadcasting: Available (FEBC, TWR)

ROPAL code: KD000

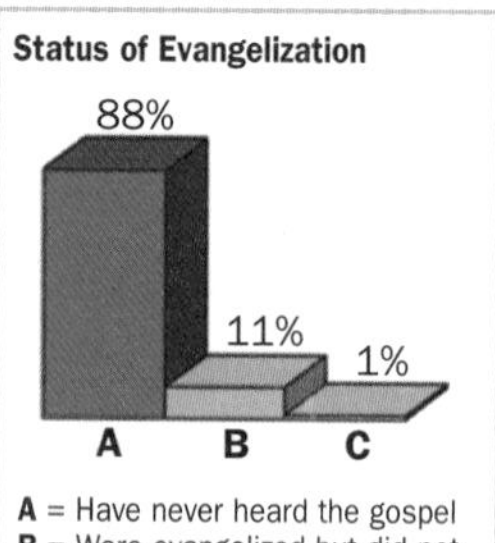

Kong Ge 控各

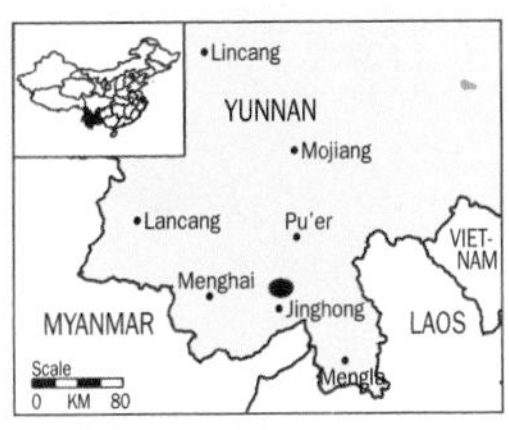

Population in China:
1,300 (1996)
1,450 (2000)
1,870 (2010)
Location: Yunnan
Religion: Ancestor Worship
Christians: None Known

Overview of the Kong Ge

Countries: China, possibly Myanmar

Pronunciation: "Kong-Ger"

Other Names: Kong Geh, Kon Keu, Kui Ge

Population Source: 1,300 (1996 Asia for Christ); 3,000 (1995 Luo Yunzhi); 400 (1991 R. Morse); Also possibly in Myanmar

Location: *SW Yunnan:* Jinghong County in Xishuangbanna Prefecture

Status: Officially included under Bulang

Language: Austro-Asiatic, Mon-Khmer, Northern Mon-Khmer

Dialects: 0

Religion: Ancestor Worship, Animism

Christians: None known

Scripture: None

***Jesus* film:** None

Gospel Recordings: None

Christian Broadcasting: None

ROPAL code: None

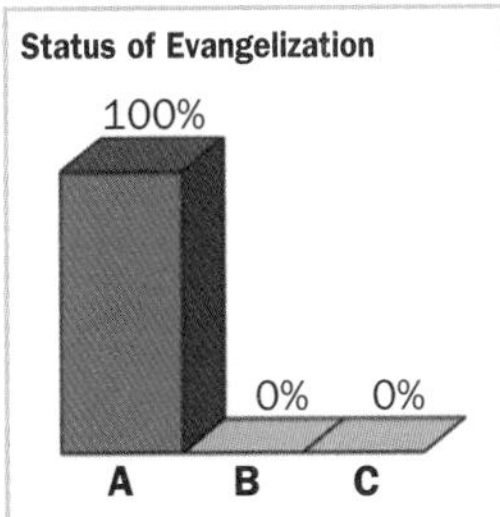

Dwayne Graybill

Location: The Kong Ge inhabit five remote villages north of Jinghong City in the southwestern part of Yunnan Province. Two different sources list populations for the Kong Ge of 400[1] and 3,000.[2] Dwayne Graybill, who visited the Kong Ge in 1996, says the Kong Ge themselves say they number 1,300 people, with 400 living in their largest village, Na Hui Pak.[3] The Kong Ge claim to also have relatives living in Myanmar.

Identity: The Chinese include the Kong Ge as part of the Bulang nationality, a point that does not sit well with the Kong Ge. The Kong Ge refuse to intermarry with the Bulang and separated from them many generations ago. "So far, scholars are divided about their identity.... Their dark complexion and thick lips gave me the impression that I was among a tribe in Africa."[4]

Language: The Kong Ge language is part of the Northern Mon-Khmer linguistic branch. It is related to, yet distinct from, Bulang. The Kong Ge people love to sing. "When they go to work they sing about work, and when they attend a wedding they sing about marriage."[5] Only Kong Ge children aged 15 or under — who have been educated in Mandarin — are able to speak the national language.

History: The ancestors of today's Kong Ge in Xishuangbanna claim to have migrated from an area near Simao 300 to 400 years ago. At that time they were part of the Bulang minority. Their legend tells how two Kong Ge families came to the area where they now live. One of the wives had a baby, so they decided to remain. The first Kong Ge village was called *Man Ba Boo.* The people were so successful at growing cotton that many outsiders joined their village.

Customs: The Kong Ge are hardworking agriculturists, harvesting rice, corn, rubber, and cotton. Although some youngsters have married Han in recent years, most Kong Ge prefer to marry only within their tribe. It is especially forbidden to intermarry with the Bulang whom they despise. After marriage the bride always goes to live in her husband's village. Every year the Kong Ge celebrate the Spring Festival. They build a huge bonfire and celebrate the start of the new year.

Religion: Before the Communist Revolution in China the Kong Ge believed in *Zao Zi,* a protective spirit. The Kong Ge sacrificed a cow before planting their rice to ensure that the spirits would allow the rice to grow. Every Kong Ge family worships their ancestors. Ancestral worship ceremonies are held after the planting season to ask for a good crop.

Christianity: The Kong Ge's small, isolated communities and their linguistic uniqueness have prevented them from hearing the gospel. In 1996 one researcher asked a 57-year-old Kong Ge man if he had heard of Jesus. The man thought for a while and looked puzzled. Finally, determined not to appear ignorant, he asked what nationality this Jesus was.[6] This man is indicative of all Kong Ge. They have absolutely no awareness of the existence of the gospel, and there has never been a single known Christian believer among their tribe.

Korean 朝鮮

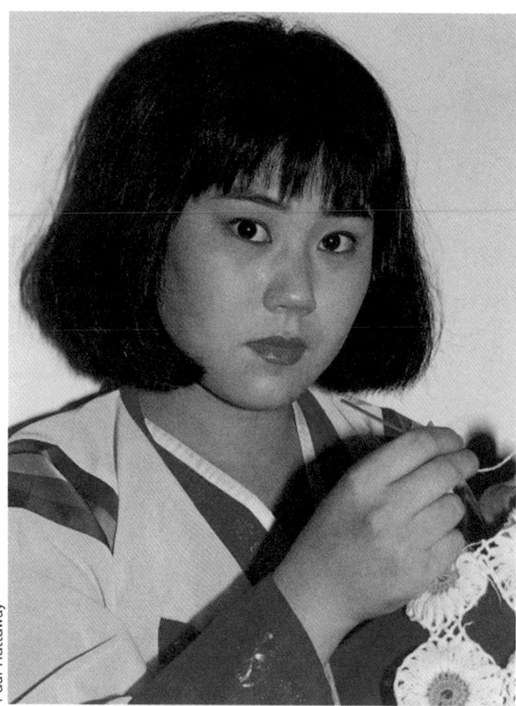

Paul Hattaway

Location: More than two million Koreans live in the northeastern part of China, especially in the provinces of Jilin, Heilongjiang, and Liaoning. Unofficial sources state there are at least three million Koreans in China.[1] More than 74 million Koreans are found worldwide.

Identity: The Koreans are an official minority nationality in China. They are "a completely unassimilated people who speak and write their own language, operate schools... and maintain the society and culture of their homeland."[2]

Language: Most linguists consider Korean to be a language isolate, while others place it as a member of the Altaic family. "Korean does not have tones like Chinese, but certain words have different meanings depending on whether they are pronounced high and short, or low and long."[3] The speech of the Koreans in China is more similar to the North Korean dialect than South Korean. In addition, their language contains some Chinese loanwords.

History: Koreans have long played an important role in Chinese history. A famous Korean general named Kao Hsien-chih was sent by the Imperial Court to fight the marauding Tibetan armies in AD 741.[4] The Sui Dynasty (AD 589–618) fell soon after three disastrous and costly military campaigns in North Korea.[5] The Ming Dynasty (1368–1644) also fell, partly because the country was bankrupt as a result of the massive cost of defending Korea from the Japanese.[6] The first wave of Korean migrants arrived in China in the late 1600s. Sizable numbers arrived later after a severe famine in North Korea in 1869.[7] "When Koreans first arrived in China, they worked for Chinese landlords who furnished them with seed and all supplies. As this tended to throw the Koreans into debt, many of them frequently moved."[8]

Customs: The Koreans — known as *Chaoxian* in China — boast the highest education rate of any of China's minorities: 43 out of 1,000 attend university.[9] Their rate was twice as high as the national average and close to the 1979 USA level (46 out of 1,000 people).

Religion: Most Koreans in China today are atheists. In addition, there are a sizable number of Mahayana Buddhists and Christians among them.

Christianity: It is not recorded if Nestorian missionaries penetrated as far as Korean territory during their time in China from the seventh to the fourteenth century, but in 1927 archaeologists excavated a tomb near the present Korea-China border. "They found the remains of seven bodies and at the head of each a clay cross... they were able to date the grave at between 998 and 1006 by Chinese coins of the Song Dynasty left with the bodies."[10] Today there are estimated to be 600,000 Korean Christians in China,[11] although a 1992 source listed only 122,000.[12] Many Korean Bibles have been smuggled into China from abroad in recent years, in addition to the 189,487 printed by the government-sanctioned Amity Press.[13] Many of these Bibles have been carried across the border into North Korea.

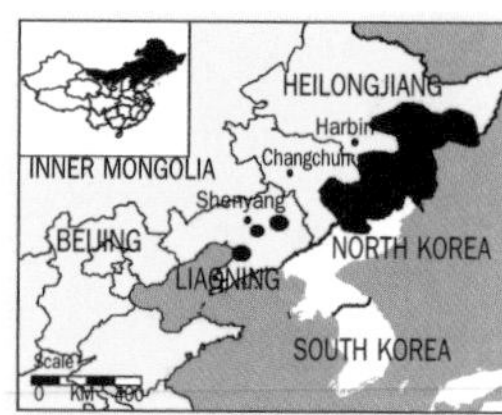

Population in China:
1,920,597 (1990)
2,130,000 (2000)
2,362,000 (2010)
Location: Jilin, Heilongjiang, Liaoning, Inner Mongolia, Beijing
Religion: No Religion
Christians: 600,000

Overview of the Koreans

Countries: South Korea, North Korea, China, USA, Japan[14]

Pronunciation: "Chao-shee-ahn"

Other Names: Chaoxian

Population Source:
1,920,597 (1990 census);
1,766,439 (1982 census);[15]
44.8 million in South Korea;
25.5 million in North Korea;
800,000 in USA; 720,000 in Japan; 183,000 in Uzbekistan; 107,000 in Russia[16];

Location: *Jilin;*[17] *Heilongjiang; Liaoning; Inner Mongolia; Beijing; Hebei; Tianjin; Shanghai*

Status:
An official minority of China

Language: Korean

Literacy: 89%

Dialects: 0

Religion: No Religion, Christianity, Buddhism

Christians: 600,000

Scripture: Bible 1911; New Testament 1887; Portions 1882

***Jesus* film:** Available

Gospel Recordings:
Korean #00103
Korean: Northern China #04856

Christian Broadcasting:
Available (TWR)

ROPAL code: KKN00

Status of Evangelization

18% A, 53% B, 29% C

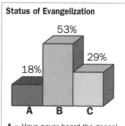

A = Have never heard the gospel
B = Were evangelized but did not become Christians
C = Are adherents to any form of Christianity

Kuan 宽

Location: More than 1,200 Kuan live in Jinghong County in Xishuangbanna Prefecture, located in the southwestern corner of Yunnan Province.[1] More than 8,000 live in nearby Laos. A number of Kuan families also live on the West Coast of the United States: in Richmond, California; and in Seattle, Washington. They were accepted into America as refugees from Laos following the 1975 Communist takeover of their country.

Identity: The Kuan have appeared in research under several different spellings. Their name has been listed as *Khuen*, *Kuanhua*, *Kween*, *Khween*, and *Khouen*. Some publications have listed *Kuan* and *Khuen* as two separate groups, but they are the same people. The Kuan are also different from the *Khun*, a Tai group found in eastern Myanmar. It is uncertain under which minority group, if any, the Chinese authorities have placed the Kuan.

Language: Kuan is a member of the Mon-Khmer language family and is related to Khmu. "The typological features of all Mon-Khmer languages include extensive morphology, including infixation.... In phonology, many Mon-Khmer languages of the core Southeast Asian area have developed a register (phonation-type) system."[2]

History: The Kuan live in Jinghong — the center of Tai Lu culture in southern China. The Tai Lu have the following tale of how Jinghong was discovered by accident several thousand years ago: A hunter named Bayalawu had led some youths into the forest to hunt, where they came upon a golden deer. "Bayalawu purposely shot an arrow into its leg to stop it so that they could take it home to raise. But the golden deer escaped with the arrow in its leg. He then led the young hunters in a chase after it, taking them over 77 peaks and 99 rivers before there suddenly appeared before their eyes a glittering golden lake into which the golden deer leapt and vanished from sight. In a twinkling the lake was filled with lotus flowers."[3]

Dwayne Graybill

Customs: The Kuan wear their own distinctive clothing. Many aspects of their culture are similar to the Khmu, including their family names — which are taken from the names of sacred animals or plants. For the duration of their lives, the Kuan are not allowed to touch the particular animal or plant that bears their name.

Religion: Some Kuan have been converted to Theravada Buddhism by the Tai Lu. They also worship a hierarchy of demons and ghosts. Every year the Kuan hold a festival to worship the spirits of the village and their ancestors.

Christianity: Although Xishuangbanna Prefecture in 1996 had "more than 10,000 Christian believers... from half a dozen different national minorities,"[4] the hidden Kuan remain an unreached and unevangelized people group. Few Kuan have any awareness of the gospel. Most of the believers in the area are among the Han Chinese, Tai Lu, Jino, and Akha minorities. As of yet, few have any vision to reach the numerous small, isolated groups such as the Kuan. There are no Scriptures or other evangelistic resources available in a language the Kuan easily understand.

Population in China:
1,000 (1991)
1,260 (2000)
1,620 (2010)
Location: Yunnan
Religion: Buddhism
Christians: None Known

Overview of the Kuan

Countries: Laos, China, USA

Pronunciation: "Khoo-ahn"

Other Names: Kuanhua, Khuen, Kween, Khween, Khouen

Population Source:
1,000 (1991 *EDCL*);
8,000 in Laos (1995 L. Chazee);
Also in USA

Location: *SW Yunnan:* Jinghong County in the Xishuangbanna Dai Prefecture

Status: Unidentified

Language: Austro-Asiatic, Mon-Khmer, Northern Mon-Khmer, Khmuic, Mal-Khmu, Khmu

Dialects: 0

Religion: Theravada Buddhism, Animism, Ancestor Worship

Christians: None known

Scripture: Work in progress

***Jesus* film:** None

Gospel Recordings: None

Christian Broadcasting: None

ROPAL code: QAK00; KHF00

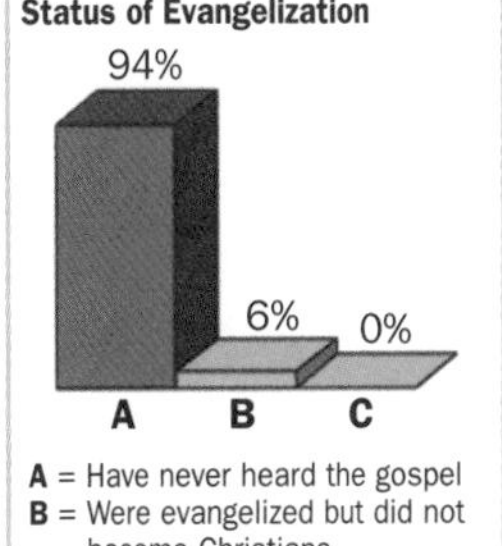

Kucong 苦聪

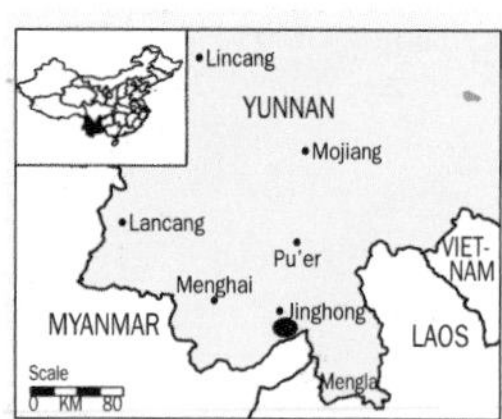

Population in China:
30,000 (1988)
40,400 (2000)
52,150 (2010)
Location: Yunnan
Religion: Buddhism
Christians: 500

Overview of the Kucong

Countries: China, Myanmar, Laos, Thailand, USA, possibly Vietnam

Pronunciation: "Koo-tsung"

Other Names: Kutsung, Kui, Shi, Yellow Lahu, Kwi, Lahu Shi, Lahu Xi

Population Source:
30,000 (1988 *Yunnan Nanjian*);
9,500 in Myanmar
(1992 B. Grimes – 1983 figure);
Out of a total Lahu population of 411,476 (1990 census);
6,268 in Laos (1995 census);
600 in USA;
Also in Thailand;
Possibly in Vietnam

Location: *SW Yunnan:* Mojiang, Xinping, and Mengla counties

Status: Officially included under Lahu since 1987

Language: Sino-Tibetan, Tibeto-Burman, Burmese-Lolo, Lolo, Southern Lolo, Akha, Lahu

Dialects: 0

Religion: Theravada Buddhism, Animism, Christianity

Christians: 500

Scripture: None

***Jesus* film:** None

Gospel Recordings:
Lahu: Yellow #00565

Christian Broadcasting: None

ROPAL code: KDS00

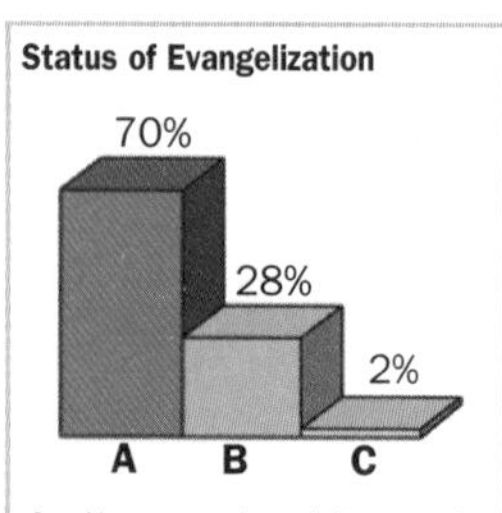

A = Have never heard the gospel
B = Were evangelized but did not become Christians
C = Are adherents to any form of Christianity

Location: The Kucong people of southwest China have had various figures reported for their population, including "5,000,"[1] "about 20,000,"[2] and "less than 30,000."[3] The 1988 *Yunnan Nanjian* lists a population of 30,000 Kucong.[4] In addition, 10,000 are located in northern Myanmar, 6,300 in Laos, a few in Thailand, and about 600 refugees in Visalia, California, USA.[5] In China the Kucong live in Mojiang, Xinping, and Mengla counties.[6]

Identity: The Kucong are also known as the Yellow Lahu, or Lahu Shi and have been officially included as part of the Lahu in China since 1987. Before that time they were included in a list of *Undetermined Minorities*. The Kucong have lived in dire poverty for generations. "Their lives were primitive, like wild animals, until they were discovered in the virgin jungles by their civilized compatriots about twenty years ago, when they were on the verge of extinction."[7]

Language: Kucong is very different from standard Lahu or Lahu Na.[8] The Kucong language has changed after many generations of isolation from other Lahu. "They had fled from the banks of the Honghe River to escape the centuries-long plunder of the ruling classes."[9]

History: Between the fourteenth and nineteenth centuries the Lahu had strong leadership in their wars of resistance against their Han and Tai rulers. Not until an irretrievable defeat in 1799 did they begin to collapse. This defeat caused the Lahu to flee into the mountains; from that point on they fragmented as a people. The Black Lahu claim to be pure Lahu and express contempt for the Kucong for having surrendered to the Qing army in the combat of the last century.[10] Since that time the Kucong have been hated and oppressed by all other Lahu. "Many of the Kucong died, not just from starvation, but attacked also by wild animals and disease. Between 1947 and 1949 alone, a third of the village population succumbed."[11]

Customs: The autumn harvest provides Kucong families with a small amount of grain for the year. Their meals are supplemented by wild berries and herbs and with any birds or animals that can be caught. All Kucong women have their heads shaven. "When they go into town they wear hats, embarrassed the people of other minorities will mock them for their baldness."[12]

Religion: The Kucong are primarily Theravada Buddhists, in comparison to the majority of Lahu who are either animists or Christians. In the past, Christianity was not able to spread from the Lahu to the Kucong because of the many prejudices between the two groups.

Christianity: Although there are fewer believers among the Kucong than among the Lahu, H. A. Baker — the great Pentecostal missionary — left a spiritual legacy at a Kucong village called *Stony Stockade* in an untraversed mountain ridge in Mojiang County. "The whole village of 29 households were converted after hearing Baker's fiery preaching, and they have earnestly adhered to the faith until this day. Right up to the present, the old inhabitants still enjoy very much recounting to visitors, vividly and nostalgically, anecdotes of 'Ben Mooshi' (Pastor Baker)."[13]

Dwayne Graybill

Kyakala 科压卡拉

Dwayne Graybill

Location: Approximately 2,000 members of the Kyakala were reported in 1996. None, however, are able to still speak the Kyakala language.[1] The majority are concentrated to the south of Heihe County in Heilongjiang Province. Heihe is located on the China-Russia border. Due to the recent thawing in relations between the two countries, Chinese tour groups are now able to cross the border from Heihe into the Russian town of Blagovenshcensk. "Chinese tourists don't find much to buy in Russia, but are impressed to see a city where nobody spits and people actually stand in line."[2] Smaller numbers of Kyakala live in various cities between the Ussuri and Sungari river basins.

Identity: The Kyakala are the remnant of a people whose assimilation into surrounding nationalities was hastened by the large populations of their neighbors. The Kyakala were initially consumed into the Manchu nationality, which in turn has largely been swallowed up by the Han Chinese. Assimilation occurs when "members of minority groups have absorbed the characteristics of the dominant group to the exclusion of their own and become indistinguishable from members of the majority."[3]

Language: Kyakala, once a vibrant Tungic language, has been extinct since the early 1900s[4]. "After an initial integration into Manchu, the language has been replaced by Mandarin Chinese."[5] Today knowledge of written Manchu is reportedly still encountered among some Kyakala scholars.[6] Little precise information is known about the Kyakala language. The language seems to have died before any linguistic research was done. Finnish Linguist Juha Janhunen suggests that Kyakala was "a Manchurian variety of Udehe, possibly transitional towards Manchu... historically the ethnonym Kyakala has also been applied to the speakers of Udege."[7] The Kyakala remain proud of their ethnic identity and historical roots.

History: The Kyakala area was controlled by the Japanese between 1932 and 1945. Horrific cruelty was inflicted on the inhabitants of Manchuria. "Over 4,000 were exterminated in bestial fashion; some were frozen or infected with bubonic plague, others were injected with syphilis, and many were roasted alive in furnaces."[8] Fu Yuguang of the Jilin Institute of Ethnic Studies in Changchun is presently the most competent scholar on the Kyakala.

Customs: Many Kyakala people today earn their living from their involvement in cross-border trade with the Russians, which has increased markedly since the collapse of the Soviet Union. The main items traded are food, clothing, and household goods.

Religion: Once a people dominated by shamanism, the Kyakala show few traces of their former religion today. Most of these people are nonreligious, although many elderly Kyakala retain ancestor worship practices in their homes.

Christianity: There are no known Kyakala Christians. A revival in the 1990s swept through many parts of Heilongjiang Province but did not encompass the Kyakala area in the northwest of the province. The Kyakala would now best be reached by using the Chinese Scriptures.

Population in China:
2,000 (1993)
2,230 (2000)
2,880 (2010)
Location: Heilongjiang
Religion: No Religion
Christians: None Known

Overview of the Kyakala

Countries: China

Pronunciation: "Key-ah-kah-lah"

Other Names: Udege Kyakala, Kiakala, Kiakla, Qiakala

Population Source:
2,000 (1993 J. Janhunen);
Out of a total Manchu population of 9,821,180 (1990 census)

Location: *N Heilongjiang:* South of Heihe; Also scattered in cities between the Ussuri and Sungari basins

Status:
Officially included under Manchu

Language: Chinese (traditonally Altaic, Tungic)

Dialects: 0

Religion:
No Religion, Ancestor Worship

Christians: None known

Scripture: None

***Jesus* film:** None

Gospel Recordings: None

Christian Broadcasting: None

ROPAL code: None

Status of Evangelization

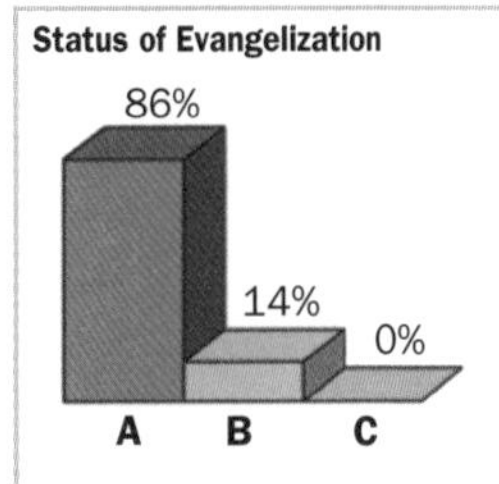

A = Have never heard the gospel
B = Were evangelized but did not become Christians
C = Are adherents to any form of Christianity

Kyerung 科容

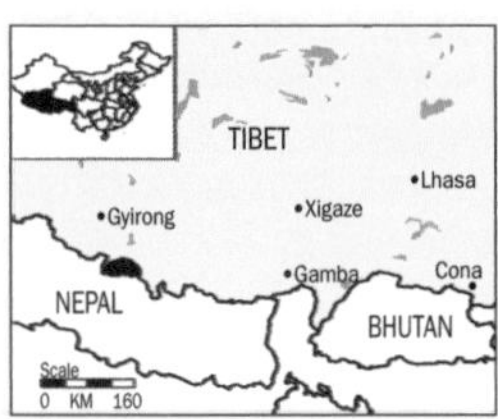

Population in China:
6,113 (1995)
6,820 (2000)
8,400 (2010)
Location: Tibet
Religion: Tibetan Buddhism
Christians: None Known

Overview of the Kyerung

Countries: Nepal, China

Pronunciation: "Geeh-rong"

Other Names: Kyirong, Gyirong

Population Source:
6,113 (1995 GEM);
Out of a total Tibetan population of 4,593,330 (1990 census);
Also in Nepal

Location: *S Tibet:* Along Nepal-China border near Mt. Everest

Status: Officially included under Tibetan

Language: Sino-Tibetan, Tibeto-Burman, Bodic, Bodish, Tibetan

Dialects: 0

Religion: Tibetan Buddhism

Christians: None known

Scripture: None

***Jesus* film:** None

Gospel Recordings: None

Christian Broadcasting: None

ROPAL code: KGY00

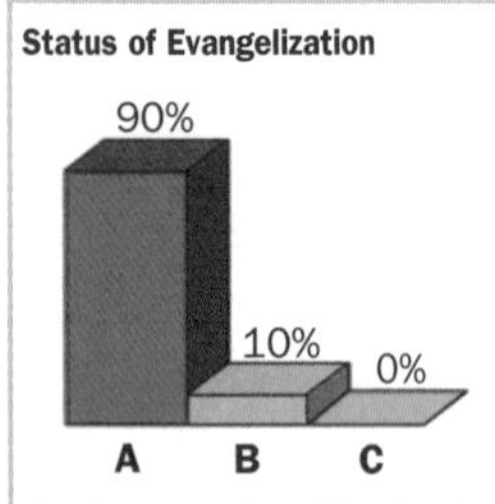

A = Have never heard the gospel
B = Were evangelized but did not become Christians
C = Are adherents to any form of Christianity

Paul Hattaway

Location: A 1995 figure placed 6,113 speakers of the Tibetan Kyerung language living in southern Tibet,[1] along Nepal's northern border with China. The majority of Kyerung live in Nepal, especially in the villages of Rasua Gari, Birdim, Thangjet, Syabru and Syabrubensi. These villages are located in the Rasuwa District of the Bagmati Zone in Nepal's Langtang region. There are also "large concentrations [of Kyerung] in Kathmandu,"[2] the capital city of Nepal.

Identity: The Kyerung are ethnic Tibetans and have been officially counted as part of the Tibetan nationality in China; however, they speak their own language, unintelligible with other Tibetan varieties. The Kyerung make up a significant portion of the 60,000 or more Tibetans in Nepal. The Kyerung are not the same as the Jiarong people of Sichuan Province, although when pronounced in Tibetan the two names sound similar.

Language: Kyerung is a part of the Bodic branch of the Tibeto-Burman linguistic family. It is reported to share 65% lexical similarity with Central Tibetan. Kyerung has 68% lexical similarity with Lhomi and 57% with Sherpa[3] — all spoken in southern Tibet.

History: The seventh and eighth centuries saw a rapid increase in the Tibetan empire. Tibet's rule extended into Kashmir, China, Turkestan, Sikkim, Bhutan, Nepal, and northern Burma. In 1788 the Tibetans turned to the Chinese for military assistance when they were being besieged by an invading Gurkha army from Nepal. After this, Chinese influence in Tibet increased greatly. The states of Sikkim, Bhutan, and Nepal splintered and became separate political units. By the mid-1800s Manchu power in China was waning; and when the Gurkhas again invaded Tibet in 1856 the Chinese did not help. The Nepalese extracted annual tribute from the Tibetans. By the end of 1959 an estimated 20,000 Tibetans had fled across the border into Nepal and India. Today the number of Tibetans in exile has grown to approximately 200,000. They are scattered in communities in India, Nepal, Bhutan, and Taiwan, in the mountains of Switzerland, in the United States, Norway, Australia, France, and England.

Customs: The Kyerung are willing to accept other people's beliefs. They have a greeting, *Tashiteleg*, which means "I recognize the divine qualities in you." Traditionally a man can marry two sisters, or several brothers may share the same wife (although this is now only practiced in remote communities).

Religion: The Kyerung, like all Tibetan ethnic groups, zealously follow Tibetan Buddhism.

Christianity: There are no known Christian believers among the Kyerung in either Tibet or Nepal. Faithful workers are needed like William E. Simpson, an American missionary to Tibet, who was martyred in 1932. Simpson summarized his life when he wrote, "Are not all the trials, the loneliness, the heartache, the weariness and pain, the cold and fatigue of the long road, the darkness and discouragements, and all the bereavements, temptations and testings, deemed not worthy to be compared with the joy of witnessing to this 'glad tidings of great joy'?"

Laba 喇叭

Population in China:
150,000 (1982)
228,300 (2000)
294,500 (2010)
Location: Guizhou, Jiangxi, Hunan, Sichuan
Religion: Ancestor Worship
Christians: 500

Overview of the Laba

Countries: China

Pronunciation: "Lah-ba"

Other Names: Huguang, Huguangren, Laobazi, Nabazi, Laba Miao

Population Source: 150,000 (1982 *Minzu Shibie Wenxian Ziliao Huibian*); Out of a total Miao population of 7,398,035 (1990 census)

Location: *SW Guizhou:* Qinglong, Shuicheng, Pu'an, and Panxian counties; Also in *Jiangxi*; *Hunan*; and *Sichuan*

Status: Officially included under Miao since 1985; Previously included in a list of *Undetermined Minorities*

Language: Chinese

Dialects: 0

Religion: Ancestor Worship, Animism, No Religion, Christianity

Christians: 500

Scripture: None

***Jesus* film:** None

Gospel Recordings: Miao: Laba

Christian Broadcasting: None

ROPAL code: None

Status of Evangelization

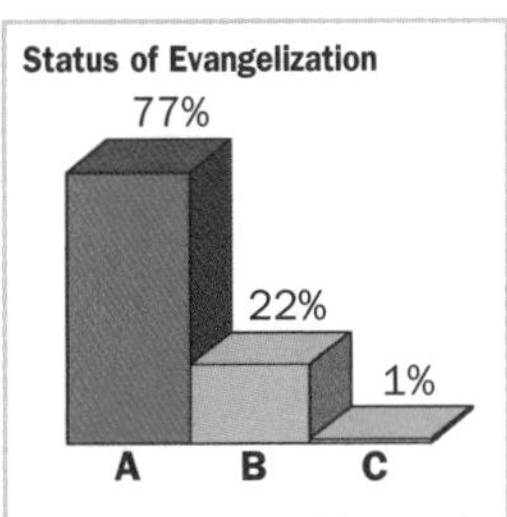

A = Have never heard the gospel
B = Were evangelized but did not become Christians
C = Are adherents to any form of Christianity

Location: More than 200,000 people belonging to the Laba ethnic group live in Guizhou Province in southern China. The population of the Laba in 1982 was given at 150,000 by a Chinese official publication.[1] The Laba predominantly live in Qinglong, Shuicheng, Pu'an, and Panxian counties in southwest Guizhou. There are also reports of Laba people in parts of Jiangxi, Hunan, and Sichuan provinces.[2]

Identity: When Chinese scholars first visited the Laba in the 1950s they were unable to determine what ethnolinguistic relationship the Laba had with other groups. The Laba shared many of the customs of their Gha-Mu (Small Flowery Miao) neighbors yet seemed to only speak a form of Chinese. In the 1982 census the Laba were included in an extensive list of *Undetermined Minorities*, which included more than 900,000 people in 80 groups, most of which were located in Guizhou Province.[3] In 1985 the government officially reclassified the Laba under the Miao nationality.[4] One source says that although the Laba are now considered Miao, "really they are Han."[5] The Laba are also widely known as the *Huguang*, or *Huguangren*. *Laba* is the name they call themselves.

Language: The history of the Laba language is fascinating. They originally spoke a form of Chinese, before they intermarried with the Miao and absorbed many influences from that language. In recent decades, however, the Laba language has started to show signs of losing its Miao traits. One report states that Laba "is slowly changing back to Chinese."[6]

History: One alternative name for the Laba is *Huguangren*. This is because they reportedly originated in Huguang County of Hunan Province, before migrating across Guizhou and settling in their present location. During the Qing Dynasty there were still 4,500 Laba in Hunan Province.[7] The Laba were probably a garrison of Han Chinese soldiers who were sent to Guizhou to fight the Miao. After hostilities ceased, the soldiers stayed behind, married local women, and gradually developed a separate ethnicity until they forgot their roots as Han people.

Customs: The customs and celebrations of the Laba also reflect both Miao and Han influences. For many years the main cultural connection between the Laba and Miao was the fact that they prepared and ate the same kind of food, which is significant in China.

Religion: Ancestor worship and animism are the primary religious systems practiced by the Laba. In the past, a cow was sacrificed to the spirits of the Laba's ancestors every three years. The Laba believed the meat was able to nourish the souls of their forefathers in the next life.

Christianity: Although approximately 500 Laba follow Christ, the gospel has never taken root among this group as it has among other peoples in the area. More than 70% of the Gha-Mu (Small Flowery Miao), for example, are Christians. The first Protestant missionary in the area was J. R. Adam, who commenced work near Anshun in 1899. In 1998 gospel recordings were produced in the Laba language.

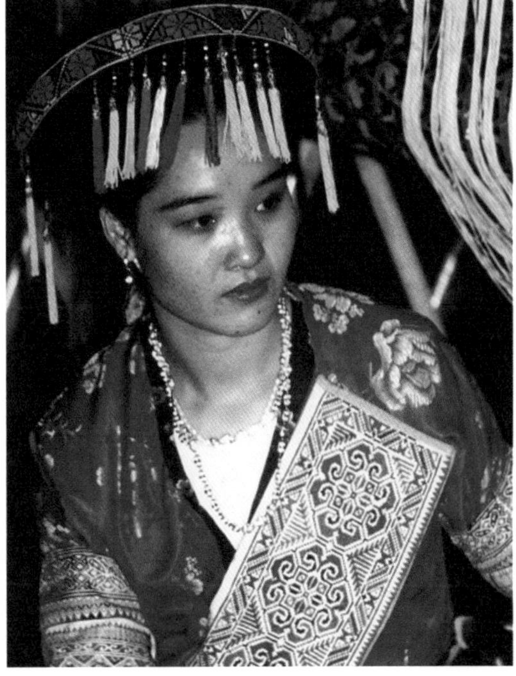

Miao Messenger

Labapo 腊拔泼

Location: Six thousand four hundred Labapo people were counted in a 1999 study of Honghe Prefecture.[1] They inhabit more than 20 villages in the Baige and Dazhuang districts of Kaiyuan County in southern Yunnan Province. The Labapo live in the same district as the 9,400 Daizhan, who are a related people group.

Identity: The Labapo have been combined with four other tribes in Kaiyuan County into a group called *Aza*.[2] None of the five groups calls itself by that name. The Aza, in turn, have been officially included by the Chinese authorities under the large Yi nationality which contains 120 distinct ethnolinguistic groups. The Labapo (Laba Tribe) are not the same as the Laba, a large group in Guizhou Province who have recently been classified as Miao.

Language: Labapo is a part of the Southeastern Yi language family. The use of their mother tongue has become seriously endangered under pressure from Yunnanese Chinese.

History: The Labapo know little of their history, except that they originated farther to the north of their present location and migrated across the mountains at least 300 years ago.

Customs: The Labapo still retain some of their customs and festivals. At various times of the lunar calendar, all Labapo gather for celebrations and festivities that last two and a half days; during this period they eat communal meals. Every family invites relatives from other villages to be their guests. The feasting is always accompanied by copious amounts of alcohol, singing, and revelry. It gives the Labapo a chance to unwind and also affords young people the opportunity to find a spouse.

Dwayne Graybill

Religion: The Labapo worship their ancestors. They also live in fear of the spirit world. Many Yi groups share a legend about a great flood that inundated the ancient world. Today, their ancestral tablets are still made of *pieris* wood (the same wood that the ark was constructed of, according to Yi legend). The Labapo believe in three main types of ghosts: spirits of accidental or unclean deaths, invisible demons, and *slota* (unusual phenomena which cause disasters). Twice a year a pig and a chicken are sacrificed at a worship stone near the sacred village tree which they believe houses a protective dragon.[3]

Christianity: There has never been a Christian church among the Labapo. They remain a completely unreached people. Whoever first takes the gospel to the Labapo will need to respect their customs and beliefs without compromising the essence of the gospel. Despite being almost 350 years old, the following Catholic declaration dating from 1659 contains sound advice for foreign missionaries that still applies today: "Do not regard it as your task, and do not bring any pressures to bear on the peoples, to change their manners, customs and uses, unless they are evidently contrary to religion and sound morals. What could be more absurd than to transport France, Spain or Italy, or some other European country to China? Do not introduce all that to them, but only the faith, which does not despise or destroy the manners and customs of any people, always supposing they are not evil, but rather wishes to see them preserved unharmed."[4]

Population in China:
6,400 (1999)
6,560 (2000)
8,200 (2010)
Location: Yunnan
Religion: Ancestor Worship
Christians: None Known

Overview of the Labapo

Countries: China

Pronunciation: "Lah-ba-po"

Other Names: Laba Aza, Azar, Laba, Pula

Population Source: 6,400 (1999 J. Pelkey); Out of a total Yi population of 6,572,173 (1990 census)

Location: *Yunnan:* Baige and Dazhuang districts of Kaiyuan County in Honghe Prefecture

Status: Officially included under Yi

Language: Sino-Tibetan, Tibeto-Burman, Burmese-Lolo, Lolo, Northern Lolo, Yi, Southeastern Yi

Dialects: 0

Religion: Ancestor Worship, Animism, Polytheism, No Religion

Christians: None known

Scripture: None

***Jesus* film:** None

Gospel Recordings: None

Christian Broadcasting: None

ROPAL code: None

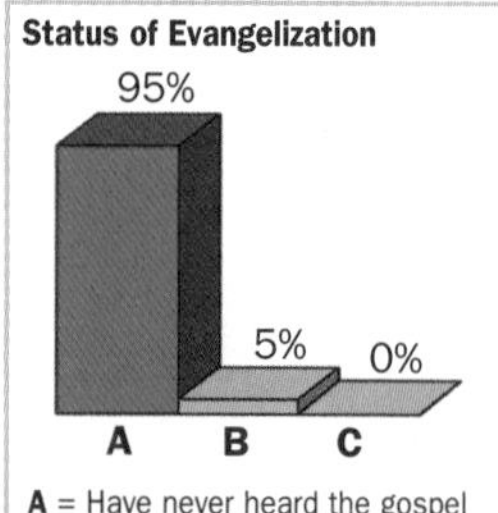

Ladakhi 腊大课

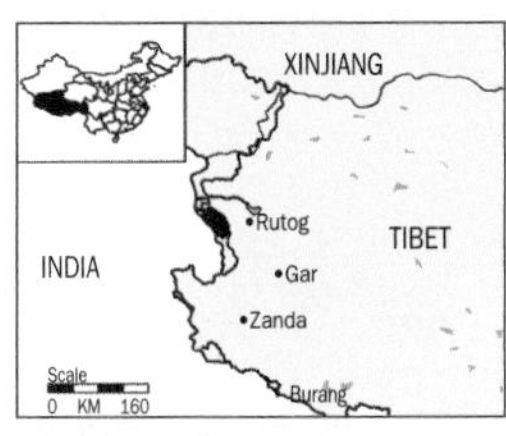

Population in China:
2,445 (1995)
2,720 (2000)
3,360 (2010)
Location: Tibet
Religion: Tibetan Buddhism
Christians: None Known

Overview of the Ladakhi

Countries: India, China

Pronunciation: "Lah-dah-kee"

Other Names: Lodokhi, Ladakh, Ladaphi, Ladhakhi, Lodak, Ladwags, Ladak

Population Source:
2,445 (1995 *GEM*);
Out of a total Tibetan population of 4,593,330 (1990 census);
97,000 in India (1994 India Missions Association)

Location:
W Tibet: Aksai Chin area

Status:
Officially included under Tibetan

Language: Sino-Tibetan, Tibeto-Burman, Bodic, Bodish, Tibetan, Western Tibetan, Ladakhi

Dialects: 0

Religion: Tibetan Buddhism

Christians: None known

Scripture: Portions 1904

***Jesus* film:** Available

Gospel Recordings:
Ladakhi #00902

Christian Broadcasting: None

ROPAL code: LBJ00

Status of Evangelization

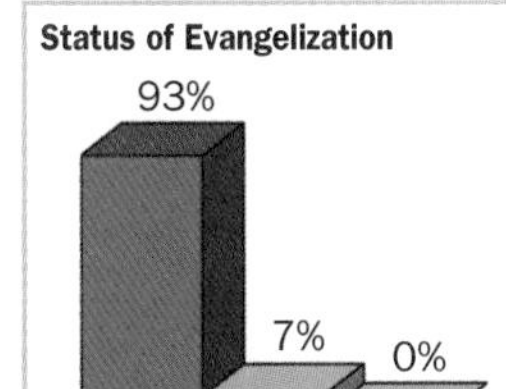

A = Have never heard the gospel
B = Were evangelized but did not become Christians
C = Are adherents to any form of Christianity

Paul Hattaway

Location: The Global Evangelization Movement lists a 1995 population of 2,445 Ladakhi in Tibet.[1] Their inclusion in China was unplanned and outside of their control. Before 1949 all Ladakhi lived in India. The Chinese invaded northern Ladakh in 1949, annexing 38,000 square kilometers (14,820 sq. mi.) of the Aksai Chin region in remote Himalayan territory.[2] Those mountain passes near the China-India border have claimed the lives of many men and beasts. Bleached human and animal bones mark the trail like signposts at regular intervals. Approximately 100,000 Ladakhi live on the Indian side of the border. The Aksai Chin area is so remote that the Indian government did not discover the Chinese had constructed a road there until two years after it was completed.

Identity: The Ladakhi are a Tibetan group, but they have major linguistic and historical differences from their counterparts in Tibet. The closely related *Nubra* people group are also found in China.

Language: Ladakhi serves as the *lingua franca* among most people on the southern slopes of the Himalayas. Ladakhi shares only 30% to 40% lexical similarity with Central Tibetan.[3]

History: Leh, the capital of Ladakh, was the home of an independent Ladakhi monarchy for a thousand years. Today a Ladakhi royal family still exists in Leh, but their influence has been merely symbolic since the independence of India in 1947.[4] The Ladakhi royal family trace their lineage back to the legendary King Nya Tri Tsanpo who ruled in the third century BC.

Customs: Life for the Ladakhi is hard. Hidden away in the highest mountains in the world, the region sees little rainfall — no more than three inches per year. Farmers rely on melted snow to water their crops. Winter temperatures remain constant at minus 30° Celsius (–22°F).

Religion: The Ladakhi share the beliefs of their Tibetan neighbors. Tibetan Buddhism, mixed with images of ferocious demons from the pre-Buddhist Bon religion, has been the stronghold in Ladakh for more than a thousand years. Traces of influence from the dark, distant past are found in the demonic masks and reenactments of human sacrifices that make up their festivals. The Ladakhi believe hell is a miserably cold place.

Christianity: The first Christians to the Ladakhi were probably Nestorian traders in the eighth century. Georgian crosses have been found inscribed on boulders in Ladakh.[5] In 1642 a Portuguese priest, Antonio de Andrade, established a base near present-day Zanda. The mission was torn down soon after by the king of Ladakh. The Moravians commenced work in Ladakh in 1856 and by 1922 numbered 158 converts.[6] They reported, "There is no very active opposition to Christian work.... The people are very willing to accept anything we can give them in the way of medicine, education, or even Scriptures and religious tracts."[7] Although the Moravians are still working among the Ladakhi in India, there are no known Christians among the small number of Ladakhi in Tibet.

Lagou 腊勾

Jamin Pelkey

Location: More than 6,000 people belonging to the Lagou ethnic group live in Weining County in northwestern Guizhou Province, and in Yiliang County in northeastern Yunnan Province. Two thousand Lagou live within Yunnan Province.[1] In Guizhou, the Lagou are concentrated near the town of Majie.[2]

Identity: The self-name of this people group is *Lagou*, although few people apart from the members of the group know it. The Han Chinese call them *Hong Yi* (Red Yi). The Lagou were former slaves of the Nasu. In the 1950s they were liberated by the Communist authorities.

Language: The speech of the Lagou may be exactly the same as the Nasu in Guizhou. They may have originally spoken their own dialect but adopted the language of their masters while under slavery. Lagou is part of the Eastern Yi branch of Tibeto-Burman.

History: Weining County in Guizhou has long been viewed as a strategic location by military leaders. To the dismay of the Chinese, however, Weining was inhabited by a large number of Yi people who steadfastly resisted Chinese rule, giving rise to many armed conflicts. In 1381 Weining was selected by Fu Youde, "the general who conquered the south," as a defense post. A garrison of 5,600 Imperial troops was stationed there. Later, when the Manchus assumed rule of China (1644), they launched a massive campaign against the Yi of Zhaotong and Weining. For the first time the area was fully brought under Chinese control.[3] It was at this time that many Yi people left the area, crossed the Yangtze River, and fled into the Daliangshan Mountains in southern Sichuan.

Customs: Despite their history of oppression, the Lagou today are a very colorful and fun-loving people. One visitor to Majie in Guizhou commented: "The Yi people of Majie are *Red Yi* [Lagou]; in the old days, they would have been slaves of the *Black Yi* [Nasu], in other words, at the very bottom rung of the social ladder. The Red Yi of today's world have gained a reputation for their expertise in basketry, as well as in the manufacture of other bamboo articles, so that they are now often referred to jokingly as 'that tribe of bamboo craftsmen'. I was much taken by the blue dress of their womenfolk with collar, shoulders, front opening and sleeves all trimmed with broad bands of embroidery and braiding. A villager told me that the clothing worn by Yi women around Majie is old-fashioned, reflecting the styles of the Ming and Qing dynasties, and is rarely seen elsewhere, even within the area of Weining."[4]

Religion: Ancestor worship and Christianity are the two main religious beliefs among the Lagou.

Christianity: Before 1949 the China Inland Mission planted 16 churches among the Yi in Weining County. The Methodists also joined in the work, so that by 1950 there were 25 private Christian schools in the county. Today there are an estimated 2,000 Lagou believers in China — or approximately one-third of the population. One official publication estimates that 50% of all Yi in Weining County are Christians.[5]

Population in China:
6,000 (1999)
6,150 (2000)
7,720 (2010)
Location: Guizhou, Yunnan
Religion: Ancestor Worship
Christians: 2,000

Overview of the Lagou

Countries: China

Pronunciation: "Lah-gaow"

Other Names: Lagoupu, Hong Yi, Red Yi

Population Source: 6,000 (1999 AMO); 2,000 in Yunnan (1999 J. Pelkey); Out of a total Yi population of 6,572,173 (1990 census)

Location: *NW Guizhou:* Weining County; *NE Yunnan:* Yiliang County

Status: Officially included under Yi

Language: Sino-Tibetan, Tibeto-Burman, Burmese-Lolo, Lolo, Northern Lolo, Yi, Eastern Yi

Dialects: 0

Religion: Ancestor Worship, Christianity, Animism

Christians: 2,000

Scripture: None

***Jesus* film:** None

Gospel Recordings: None

Christian Broadcasting: None

ROPAL code: None

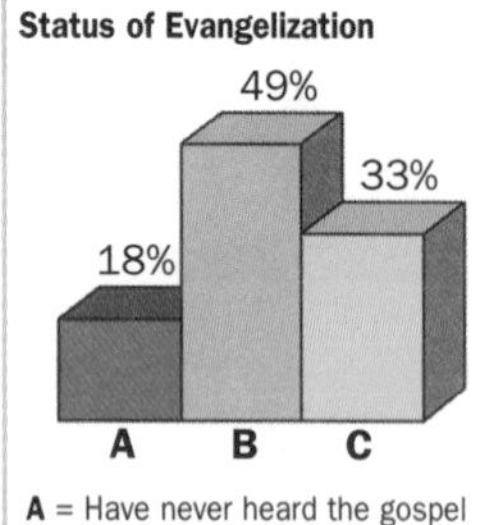

Lahu 拉怙

Location: More than 475,000 Lahu inhabit seven counties in the western part of Yunnan Province.[1] Their villages are often situated on mountains at least 1,500 meters (4,920 ft.) above sea level. In addition, significant numbers of Lahu are located in Myanmar, Thailand, Vietnam, and Laos.

Identity: The Lahu are one of China's 55 official minority groups. The name *Lahu* reportedly means "to roast tiger meat by fire," although others say the name has no particular meaning. Their skill as hunters has given them their nickname of *Musso*, which is used throughout Southeast Asia. Since 1890, when the Lahu surrendered their rebellion against their Yi and Tai landlords, they have been viewed as cowardly by other minority groups in Yunnan. An old Lahu man said, "Ever since the defeat, the Lahu lost heart and were despised by other groups."[2]

Language: Lahu — which has seven tones — has been vividly described as "perhaps the most exquisite form of speech ever devised by the mind of man."[3] Lahu from different locations often struggle to understand each other.[4]

History: The Lahu have a long history of war and armed conflict against their oppressors. They rebelled more than 20 times throughout the eighteenth and nineteenth centuries. The region they occupied west of the Lancang River was branded "a place of constant riot."[5]

Customs: Lahu women give birth in the privacy of their own rooms. Three days after the birth they invite old people to a small feast where a name is given to the child. However, if an unexpected visitor should come in the meantime, he or she is given the honor of naming the newborn. When a Lahu dies, three shots are fired into the air to scare away the spirits and to announce the news to the village.

Paul Hattaway

Lahu communities have long been plagued by stealing[6] and rampant alcoholism. "It is common to see a group of Lahu drunk and beating their fists on the roadside and shouting as they are led homeward."[7]

Religion: The Lahu believe in a supreme god named *G'ui Sha*. Many Lahu villages have a temple consecrated to this deity. This belief in One Supreme Being played a large part in their mass conversion to Christianity.

Christianity: When American Baptist missionary William Young first preached the gospel to the Lahu in northern Burma in 1901, they exclaimed, "We as a people have been waiting for you for centuries.... We even have meeting houses built in some of our villages in readiness of your coming."[8] Many of the Lahu men wore strings on their wrists. They explained, "We Lahu have worn [strings] like these since time immemorial. They symbolize our bondage to evil spirits. You alone, as the messenger of G'ui Sha, may cut these manacles from our wrists — but only after you have brought the lost book of G'ui Sha to our very hearths!"[9] Lahu tribesmen came all the way from China to hear Young preach. Six thousand Lahu were baptized in 1905 and 1906.[10] Today there are between 35,000[11] and 50,000[12] Lahu Christians in China, "mostly concentrated in Banli, Mujia, Gengma and Menglian."[13]

Population in China:
369,400 (1990)
476,500 (2000)
614,700 (2010)
Location: Yunnan
Religion: Animism
Christians: 50,000

Overview of the Lahu

Countries: China, Myanmar, Thailand, Laos, Vietnam
Pronunciation: "La-hoo"
Other Names: Lohei, Lahuna, Laku, Kaixien, Namen, Mussuh, Muhso, Musso, Moso, Mussar, Lohe, Laho
Population Source:
411,476 (1990 census);[14]
304,174 (1982 census);[15]
125,000 in Myanmar (1993);
28,000 in Thailand (1993);
8,702 in Laos (1995 census);
5,400 in Vietnam (1991)
Location: *SW Yunnan:* Lancang, Menglian, Gengma, Shuangjiang, Cangyuan, Menghai, and Ximeng counties

Status:
An official minority of China
Language: Sino-Tibetan, Tibeto-Burman, Burmese-Lolo, Loloo, Lolo, Southern Lolo, Akha, Lahu
Literacy: 17%
Dialects (2):
Black Lahu, Red/White Lahu
Religion:
Animism, Buddhism, Christianity
Christians: 50,000
Scripture: Bible 1987; New Testament 1932; Portions 1924
***Jesus* film:** Available
Gospel Recordings: Black Lahu #00085; Red Lahu #00566
Christian Broadcasting:
Available (FEBC)
ROPAL code: LAH00

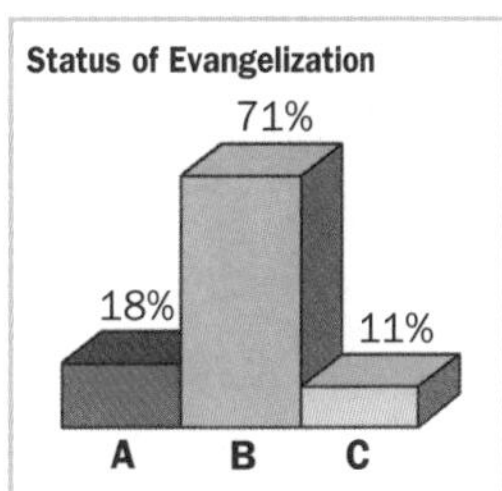

Lahuli, Tinan 腊户力提喃

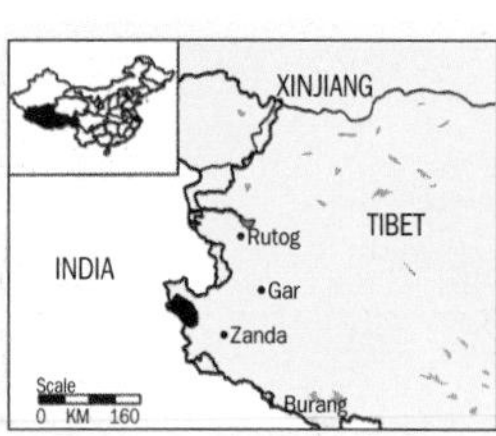

Population in China:
1,600 (1977)
2,450 (2000)
3,020 (2010)
Location: Tibet
Religion: Tibetan Buddhism
Christians: None Known

Overview of the Lahuli Tinan

Countries: India, China

Pronunciation: "La-hoo-lee-Tee-nun"

Other Names: Lahuli, Bhotia of Lahul, Lahauli, Lahouli, Rangloi, Gondla, Tinani

Population Source: 450 to 1600 (1977 Voegelin & Voegelin); Out of a total Tibetan population of 4,593,330 (1990 census); 24,534 in India (1994 India Missions Association)

Location: *W Tibet:* Border between Tibet and Himachal Pradesh, India

Status: Officially included under Tibetan

Language: Sino-Tibetan, Tibeto-Burman, Bodic, Bodish, Himalayish, Kanauri

Dialects: 0

Religion: Tibetan Buddhism

Christians: None known

Scripture: Portions 1908

***Jesus* film:** None

Gospel Recordings: Lahouli Tinan #02425

Christian Broadcasting: None

ROPAL code: LBE00

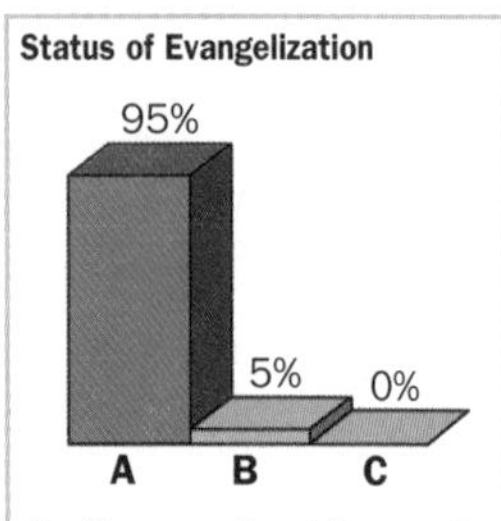

Location: Linguists C. F. and F. M. Voegelin listed a 1977 population of between 450 and 1,600 Lahuli Tinan living in western Tibet.[1] Geographic and political barriers keep this small group separated from contact with the outside world. The majority of Lahuli Tinan are located in India where more than 24,000 live in the Spiti and Lahul Subdivision, which is situated in the lower Chandra-Bhaga Valley in the northern part of the Indian state of Himachal Pradesh. The main Lahuli Tinan village in India is Gondla.

Identity: The Lahuli Tinan — who are counted under the Tibetan nationality in China — are also known as *Bhotia.* The term *Bhotia* refers to people of Tibetan stock in general. The name *Lahuli* is also a generic term used to describe the inhabitants of the Lahul District, which was formerly controlled by the British. A 1922 missionary survey explained, "The name Tibet is unknown in the country itself, having been given to it by the Turks and Persians. Its true name is Bod or Bodyu, ie. Bodland, the original name of the inhabitants being Bodpa.... Little Tibet, to the west of Tibet proper, consists of Lahoul and Spiti, which belong to England."[2]

Language: Lahuli Tinan is a distinct language from Lahuli Chamba. It is part of a group which includes "several West Himalayish/Kanauri languages."[3] Other Tibetans cannot understand Lahuli Tinan. It has 32% to 37% lexical similarity with Bunan, 21% with Spiti, and only 13% with Central Tibetan.[4]

History: The Lahuli region was part of the Ladakhi Kingdom in the tenth century. Border clashes in the area in the 1950s and 1960s resulted in the Chinese seizing a large tract of land from India. The region, which is home to the Lahuli people, is called *Aksai Chin.*

Customs: Lahuli men are skillful merchants and traders. Lahuli women are known for their independence. "Since their husbands are usually off on trading expeditions, the women feel free to take more than one husband. The men trade salt, grain and wool to other people in the Himalayan region and in the process sometimes become quite wealthy."[5]

Religion: The strength of Tibetan Buddhism in northern India depends to a great extent on the prosperity and generosity of the Lahuli Tinan. "They, in turn, feel spiritually secure because of the religious merit they gain by dispensing charity and generously supporting the temples."[6]

Christianity: There are a handful of Lahuli Tinan believers in India, but none are known on the Tibetan side of the border. Few have ever heard of Jesus Christ. Mission work in Lahul began after Karl Gutzlaff challenged the Moravians to begin a mission in Tibet. "The first missionaries, A. W. Heyde and E. Pagell, settled down in Kyelang, a Tibetan village in the province of Lahul."[7] Scripture portions were translated into Lahuli Tinan in 1908 but have been out of print since 1915. Gospel recordings are currently available in the Lahuli Tinan language.

Paul Hattaway

Laka 腊卡

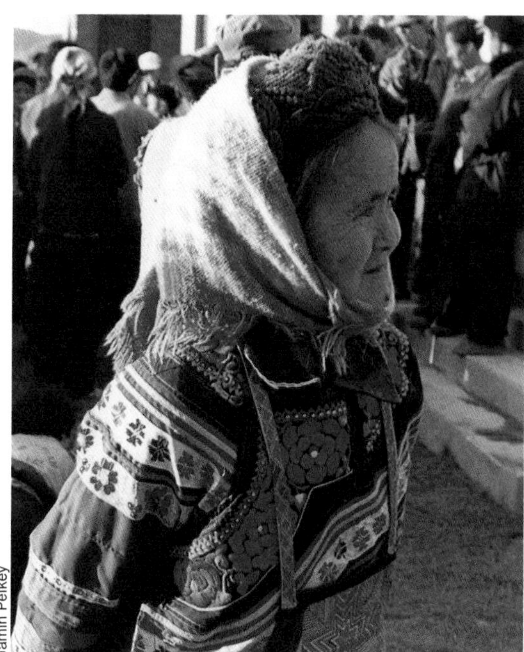
Jamin Pelkey

Location: More than 6,000 members of the Laka group live in the northernmost reaches of Yunnan Province, on the southern banks of the Yangtze River in Wuding County.[1] The Yangtze is the border between Yunnan and Sichuan. In 1911 missionary Samuel Clarke recounted the first visit to the Laka people by Australian missionary Arthur Nicholls: "The Laka are another branch of the Nosu [Yi] race. From the hill-tops, when Mr. Nicholls visited them, he saw the River of Golden Sand, as the Yangtze River is called in that part of its course. Across the river was the province of [Sichuan], which there, following the course of the river, projects like a promontory far away to the south."[2]

Identity: The Laka are a subgroup of the Naluo, who are officially considered a subgroup of the Yi.[3] The name "Laka" may originate from the Chinese term *laogan* "old workers"[4] or a Yi term meaning "artisan."[5] In the early 1900s the Laka may have been workers who helped construct the railroad in northern Yunnan. Samuel Clarke unflatteringly described them as "very drunken and immoral."[6] The Laka are often confused with the Lakkia people of the Guangxi Zhuang Autonomous Region, a Yao group who are also sometimes called *Laka*.

Language: Even though the Laka consider themselves a people group, they speak basically the same language as the Naluo in northern Yunnan. Early missionaries, however, "clearly differentiated [the two groups] to the point of having two different Bibles while being served by the same missionaries."[7]

History: The Laka are part of the splintering of people groups that has taken place in the mountains of southwest China over the past 2,000 years. One source states that the main difference between the Laka and the Naluo is that the Laka were slaves and serfs of the Nasu while the Naluo were not.[8] This historical and social separation has created a distinct self-identity among the two groups today.

Customs: The Laka earn their livelihood from the bounty of the Yangtze River. This part of the Yangtze contains a nearly extinct breed of albino dolphins found nowhere else in the world.

Religion: The Laka were traditionally animists and polytheists until they were converted by missionaries prior to 1949. Today many Laka are nonreligious and have adopted many of the customs of the Han Chinese people in the area.

Christianity: Mission outreach to the Laka commenced in the early 1900s. In 1908 it was reported that "the work among the Laka is now being consolidated by the appointment of Mr. Metcalf as their own missionary."[9] The Gospel of Mark was translated into the Laka language using the Pollard script and distributed between 1912 and 1936. Today most Laka are mixed in with Eastern Lipo communities and few outsiders know of their existence. Missiologist Ralph Covell has stated, "The name Laka people is repeatedly mentioned in missionary literature about Yunnan. Always it appears with the sorry refrain that although the Laka wanted to believe, no one was available to go to them, either to evangelize or disciple."[10]

Population in China:
6,000 (1999)
6,150 (2000)
7,700 (2010)
Location: Yunnan
Religion: Christianity
Christians: 2,000

Overview of the Laka

Countries: China
Pronunciation: "Lah-ka"
Other Names: Lagou, Laga
Population Source: 6,000 (1999 AMO); Out of a total Yi population of 6,572,173 (1990 census)
Location: *N Yunnan:* Wuding County
Status: Officially included under Yi
Language: Sino-Tibetan, Tibeto-Burman, Burmese-Lolo, Lolo, Northern Lolo, Yi, Eastern Yi
Dialects: 0
Religion: Christianity, No Religion, Animism
Christians: 2,000
Scripture: Portions 1912
***Jesus* film:** None
Gospel Recordings: None
Christian Broadcasting: None
ROPAL code: None

Status of Evangelization

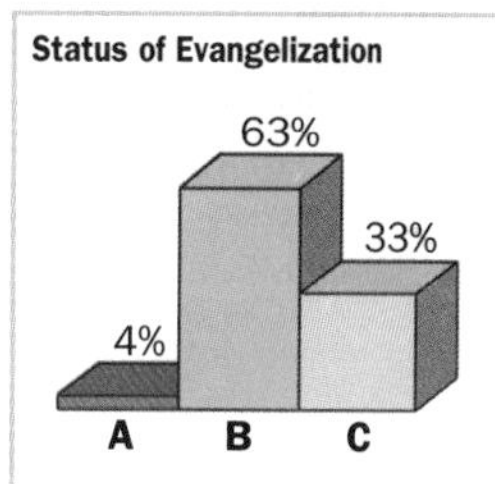

A = Have never heard the gospel
B = Were evangelized but did not become Christians
C = Are adherents to any form of Christianity

Lakkia 拉珈

Population in China:
11,068 (1987)
15,200 (2000)
19,600 (2010)
Location: Guangxi
Religion: Animism
Christians: None Known

Overview of the Lakkia

Countries: China

Pronunciation: "Lah-kee-uh"

Other Names: Lakkja, Lakja, Tai Laka, Lakia, Lajia, Chashan Yao, Tea Mountain Yao, Laka

Population Source:
11,068 (1987 D. Bradley);
Out of a total Yao population of 2,134,013 (1990 census)

Location: *Guangxi:* Jinxiu Yao Autonomous County

Status:
Officially included under Yao

Language: Daic, Kam-Sui

Dialects: 0

Religion: Animism, Polytheism, Ancestor Worship

Christians: None known

Scripture: None

***Jesus* film:** None

Gospel Recordings: None

Christian Broadcasting: None

ROPAL code: LBC00

Status of Evangelization

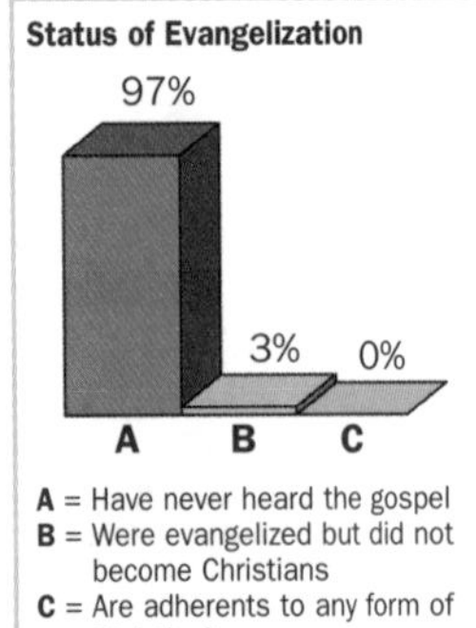

A = Have never heard the gospel
B = Were evangelized but did not become Christians
C = Are adherents to any form of Christianity

Location: A 1987 source lists a figure of 11,068 Lakkia people in China.[1] The number of speakers of the Lakkia language is less than the total population. Different linguists have listed figures of 8,000,[2] 8,900,[3] and 9,000[4] speakers. The Lakkia are located along both banks of the Jinxiu River, in the Dayaoshan (Big Yao Mountains) in Guangxi. They live in a concentrated area and are not found in any other part of China.[5]

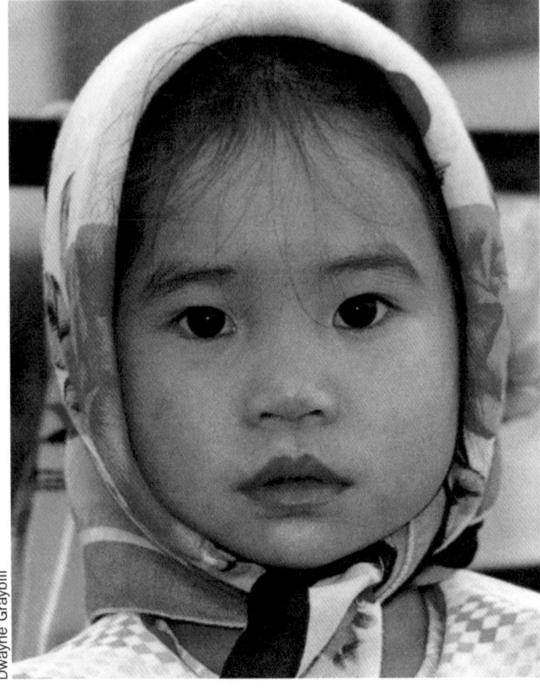
Dwayne Graybill

Identity: The Lakkia have been officially included as part of the Yao nationality in China. Although they are culturally similar to some Yao groups, the Lakkia speak a language from the Dong-Shui linguistic branch. *Lakkia* is the self-name of this people group. The Chinese call them *Chashan Yao*, meaning "Yao of the tea mountains." Formerly they were called *Changmao Yao* meaning "long-haired Yao" because they used to wear their long hair in buns. The Lakkia should not be confused with the Laka of northern Yunnan,[6] the identically named Lakkia of Vietnam, or the Laqua in Yunnan who have also been known to call themselves Lakkia.

Language: The Lakkia language is unique among the various Yao groups in China because it is not even a part of the Yao or Miao (Hmong-Mien) language family.[7] Lakkia has 45% lexical similarity with Dong and 44% with Northern Zhuang.[8]

History: Acknowledged to be the original inhabitants of the Dayaoshan Mountains, they are said to have arrived in the area from Guangdong, passing through Wuzhou in Guangxi before entering their present location via Teng and Pingnan counties.[9] It is possible the Lakkia were originally a Tai group who, after centuries of living alongside the Yao, became assimilated to the Yao culture but still retained their original language.

Customs: Lakkia houses are long and deep and are approached through three or four successive gates. Inside the front gate are cattle and pigs. The living quarters are located in the rear of the house. Lakkia courting customs are simple. "At a suspension tower... boys stand at one corner and girls at another, singing to each other.... Through singing one looks for one's dream girl or ideal man and love songs are sung by way of courtship. When a boy and a girl come to like each other in the course of singing, they exchange bracelets or waist belts as a token of their love. The boy's family will then send a match-maker to the girl's and the two will get married on an auspicious day."[10]

Religion: Most Lakkia could be considered animists, with fewer traces of Daoism in their beliefs than in those of the four other Yao groups in the Dayaoshan Mountains.

Christianity: There are no known believers among the Lakkia. The area was mentioned in a 1922 report: "Just north of Pingnamyun there is a large area known as the Yao Mountain district still uncharted, where a local dialect prevails of which little is known."[11] In 1998, Gospel recordings in the Xinping language were produced for the first time.

Lalu, Xinping 腊鲁(新平)

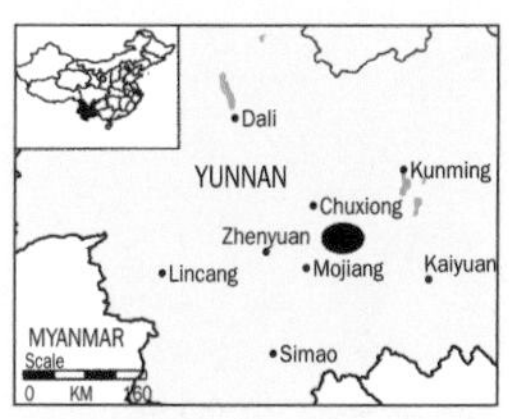

Population in China:
38,000 (1999)
38,950 (2000)
48,900 (2010)
Location: Yunnan
Religion: Polytheism
Christians: 150

Overview of the Xinping Lalu

Countries: China

Pronunciation: "Shin-ping-Lah-loo"

Other Names: Lalu

Population Source:
38,000 (1999 J. Pelkey);
Out of a total Yi population of 6,572,173 (1990 census)

Location: *S Yunnan:* Xinping (28,700), Zhenyuan (8,000), Mojiang (1,000), and Yuanjiang (400) counties

Status:
Officially included under Yi

Language: Sino-Tibetan, Tibeto-Burman, Burmese-Lolo, Lolo, Northern Lolo, Yi, Western Yi

Dialects: 0

Religion: Polytheism, Animism, Ancestor Worship, Christianity

Christians: 150

Scripture: None

***Jesus* film:** None

Gospel Recordings:
Yi: Lallu #04936

Christian Broadcasting: None

ROPAL code: None

Location: More than 38,000 Xinping Lalu are distributed throughout the soaring Ailao Mountain range in southern Yunnan Province. They are primarily found in the southwestern districts of Xinping County (28,700) and in the western districts of Zhenyuan County (8,000). A small number spill over into Mojiang (1,000) and Yuanjiang (400) counties.

Identity: The loconym *Xinping* has been added to this group to distinguish them from other Lalu and Laluo groups in southern China. The various Lalu peoples, although all officially counted as part of the Yi nationality, have little in common with each other except their names. Each group possesses distinct customs and languages. Jamin Pelkey has said about this group, "The Lalu have a strong sense of identity, and do not consider themselves to be part of the Yi nationality. For that matter, other peoples in Lalu regions do not consider the Lalu to be Yi either."[1]

Language: Although they were once part of the great Laluo group of Menghua, the Xinping Lalu are believed to have migrated away from the main body of that ethnic group long ago. For this reason, their language is today one of the most divergent of the Lalu or Laluo varieties in China. Xinping Laluo is part of the Western Yi language group. Xinping Lalu living in some villages near the Honghe River basin have begun to lose the use of their mother tongue, but all those living in the mountains retain vigorous use of their language.

History: The Xinping Lalu are recognized as among the earliest inhabitants of the Ailao Mountains. For centuries they have been influenced by Han, Hani, and Hongjin Tai cultures more than by the Yi.

Customs: The Xinping Lalu greatly enjoy music. They love to get together and sing old traditional songs and play folk instruments. During the second lunar month of each year, on the day of the ox, the Xinping Lalu hold a singing competition. The victorious young man and girl are considered the most eligible marriage partners by the community. They will be greatly sought after by prospective suitors from that time on.

Religion: For generations the Lalu have been polytheists who worship many gods, ghosts, demons and disembodied spirits. They believe that when people die they will become either good or bad spirits, depending on their character while living.

Christianity: There is a church among the Hongjin Tai people in the Mosha District of Xinping County. This church uses the Tai language to worship, and some of the believers who are bilingual in Chinese are known to have taken the gospel to their Xinping Lalu neighbors. As a result, there are about 150 Christians among the Lalu in Xinping today, meeting in two churches. Kado and Biyo believers in Mojiang and Yuanjiang may have impacted the small number of Lalu living there. In 1998 gospel recordings in Xiaping Lalu language were produced for the first time.

Jamin Pelkey

Lalu, Xuzhang 腊鲁(徐掌)

Location: The small Xuzhang Lalu group, who number 4,100 people, live in several villages within the Xuzhang Community in Wafang District of Baoshan County. Baoshan is located in the western part of Yunnan Province. The principal village of the Xuzhang Lalu is named Sikeshu.

Identity: Although they have been officially placed under the Yi nationality in China, the Xuzhang Lalu are different from all other ethnic groups. They possess their own identity, language, and customs. A local government source, the *Baoshan Xian Zhi*, states, "There are numerous divisions of the Yi in Baoshan County; based on a combination of autonyms [self-names], languages, and distribution, there are five kinds all together."[1] Three of the Yi groups in Baoshan, the book concludes, are legitimate, distinct people groups.

Language: The Xuzhang Lalu language is part of the Western Yi branch of languages, but is mutually unintelligible with other Yi varieties in the area. One Chinese source states, "They speak Yi, but language differences between this and other groups in the county are fairly sizable."[2]

History: It seems likely that the Xuzhang Lalu were once part of the large and influential Laluo people of Menghua who dominated the region from at least the eighth century AD. For an unknown reason, perhaps as they searched for more arable land, the ancestors of the Xuzhang Lalu migrated westward from the main body of Laluo. After centuries of separation they developed their own language, customs, and identity, although their name is only slightly different from the Laluo today.

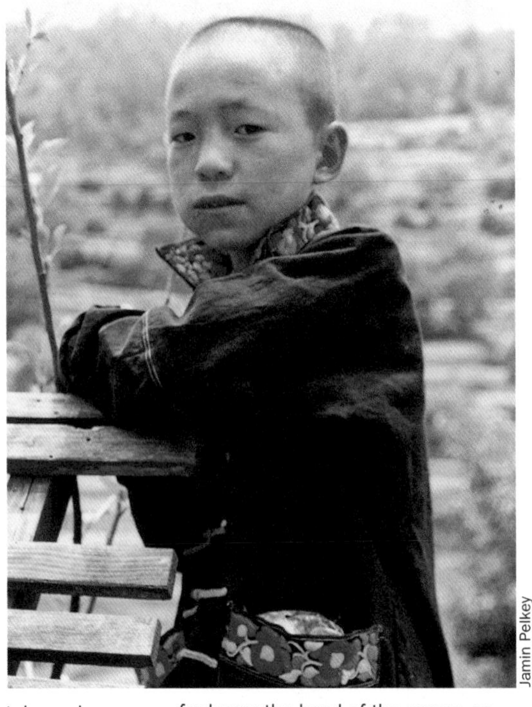

Jamin Pelkey

Customs: Every year during the sixth and seventh months of the lunar calendar, activities known as the Flower Street Festival are organized in some Lalu communities. "On these occasions, people from all over the district come to an open area on a mountain peak.... The young boys and girls participate in singing and dancing. Should a boy wish to pursue a certain girl, he will throw a white handkerchief at her. If the girl is willing to take him as a boyfriend, she will indicate this by picking the handkerchief up."[3]

Religion: When a Lalu man dies, his relatives hold a feast of mourning which they call *za*. "A pig or sheep is sacrificed in the doorway.... The nearer kindred, on hearing of the death of a relative, take a fowl and strangle it.... The mourner then proceeds to his house and sticks the fowl near the head of the corpse as an offering."[4] This ritual represents the beliefs of the Xuzhang Lalu, which are a combination of spirit worship and ancestor worship.

Christianity: Although Baoshan County contains a number of Lisu and Jingpo Christians, they have not been able to take the gospel to most Xuzhang Lalu because of communication barriers. As a result, there are still no known believers among this group, who have no access to God's Word in printed or audio form in a language they can easily understand.

Population in China:
4,000 (1999)
4,100 (2000)
5,150 (2010)
Location: Yunnan
Religion: Polytheism
Christians: None Known

Overview of the Xuzhang Lalu

Countries: China

Pronunciation: "Shoo-jung-Lah-loo"

Other Names: Lalu, Tujia

Population Source: 4,000 (1999 J. Pelkey); Out of a total Yi population of 6,572,173 (1990 census)

Location: *W Yunnan:* Xuzhang Community in Wafang District of Baoshan County

Status: Officially included under Yi

Language: Sino-Tibetan, Tibeto-Burman, Burmese-Lolo, Lolo, Northern Lolo, Yi, Western Yi

Dialects: 0

Religion: Polytheism, Animism, Ancestor Worship

Christians: None known

Scripture: None

***Jesus* film:** None

Gospel Recordings: None

Christian Broadcasting: None

ROPAL code: None

Lalu, Yangliu 腊鲁(杨柳)

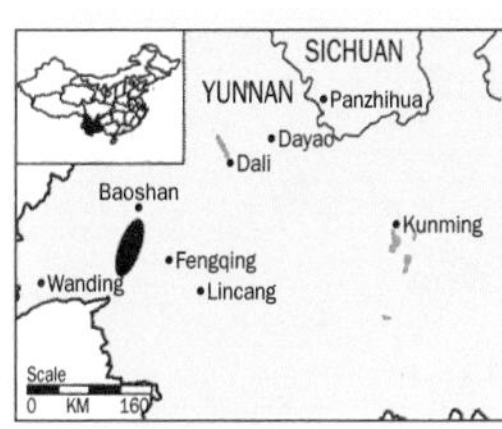

Population in China:
37,000 (1999)
37,900 (2000)
47,600 (2010)
Location: Yunnan
Religion: Polytheism
Christians: None Known

Overview of the Yangliu Lalu

Countries: China

Pronunciation:
"Yung-leeooh-Lah-loo"

Other Names:
Lalu, Tuli, Tujia, Xiangtang

Population Source:
37,000 (1999 J. Pelkey);
Out of a total Yi population of 6,572,173 (1990 census)

Location: *W Yunnan:* Baoshan (11,000), Shidian (11,000), Zhenkang (9,000), Longling (5,000), and Luxi (1,000) counties

Status:
Officially included under Yi

Language: Sino-Tibetan, Tibeto-Burman, Burmese-Lolo, Lolo, Northern Lolo, Yi, Western Yi

Dialects: 0

Religion: Polytheism, Animism, Ancestor Worship

Christians: None known

Scripture: None

***Jesus* film:** None

Gospel Recordings: None

Christian Broadcasting: None

ROPAL code: None

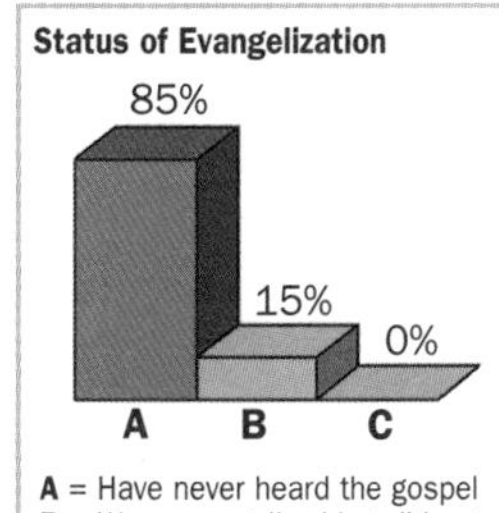

A = Have never heard the gospel
B = Were evangelized but did not become Christians
C = Are adherents to any form of Christianity

Location: With a population of more than 37,000, the Yangliu Lalu inhabit areas in the western part of Baoshan County (11,000), Shidian (11,000), Zhenkang (9,000), Longling (5,000), and Luxi (1,000) counties. All of these places are situated within the boundaries of the Dehong Dai Autonomous Prefecture in the western part of Yunnan Province. The Yangliu Lalu are the nearest Yi group to Myanmar in this part of Yunnan.

Jamin Pelkey

Identity: Today, the Yangliu Lalu are different from the Xuzhang Lalu. The two groups possess different customs and cannot easily understand each other's language.

Language: The Yangliu Lalu are on a rapid slide to assimilation. Many cannot speak their own language, especially those who have had prolonged contact with Chinese or who live in ethnically mixed communities. Yangliu Lalu is part of the Western Yi branch of Tibeto-Burman.

History: The Yangliu Lalu are believed to have migrated to their present location from Menghua (present-day Weishan and Nanjian counties) at different stages during the Ming and Qing dynasties (1368–1911). They fled Menghua to escape the wars between the Laluo and the Han Chinese immigrants who flooded into the area. The Chinese seized the best land and forced the Laluo into the mountains, from where they launched military attacks and wrought revenge for their losses. Many Yi groups in Yunnan have had a long history of violence against their oppressors. Pressured by unfair taxes, they killed many Han landowners between 1847 and 1872: "Though pacified and forced to return the land, the Yi had put an end to the feudal system. Eventually some even bought land. In the traditional serf system, the land was divided among 42 families, each paying dues in kind, plus 15 days' service a year and building materials. They were not free to leave the village without permission.... After the revolt, only rent was collected, not services. After revolt, the Chinese became absentee landlords and had difficulty in collecting rents, therefore they were eager to sell."[1]

Customs: Yangliu Lalu homes are constructed of wood and customarily consist of three rooms. The central room serves as a kitchen and as a place for receiving guests and relatives. At the same time that other Yi groups in Yunnan celebrate the Torch Festival, "the Yangliu Lalu celebrate Girl's Day. All females return to the home of their mother and father for a time of rest."[2]

Religion: Being animists and ancestor worshipers, the Yangliu Lalu believe that the soul of a dead person does not go to the next world but rather stays to roam the earth.

Christianity: There are many Tibeto-Burman-speaking Christians in Dehong Prefecture, especially among the Jingpo, Lashi, Maru, and Achang; however, these groups do not live in the vicinity of the Yangliu Lalu, most of whom have never heard the gospel. The Yangliu Lalu have never had a known church or fellowship in their midst.

Laluo, Jiantou 腊罗(尖头)

Dwayne Graybill

Location: A total of 30,000 Jiantou Laluo live in three counties within the Dali Bai Autonomous Prefecture in Yunnan Province. About half (15,000) live in Weishan County, 7,000 in Midu County, and 8,000 in Xiaguan County which encompasses the ancient town of Dali. The Jiantou Laluo mostly live in high mountains.

Identity: Although this group simply calls itself *Laluo* in their own language, the Chinese call them *Jiantou Yi* or *Jiantou Laluo* to distinguish them from the Mishaba Laluo who live in the same general area. *Jiantou* is a Chinese term meaning "cone head" and is applied to this group because of their custom of wearing large, cone-shaped turbans. Married Jiantou Laluo women also wear small, green ceramic cones on their foreheads. Although the government has included the Jiantou Laluo as part of the Yi nationality, neighboring people do not consider them Yi. They call them *Maganfang*, after a place name in the Jiantou Laluo region. The Jiantou Laluo are a different ethnic and language group from the Mishaba Laluo.

Language: The Jiantou Laluo speak a Western Yi language. Although the Jiantou Laluo and the Mishaba Laluo both live near each other in Weishan County, their languages are so different that they must use Chinese to communicate. A group of Mishaba Laluo in Miaogai District said they could only understand about 40% of Jiantou Laluo vocabulary, although the Jiantou Laluo in Dacang District believe they can understand 80% of the speech of their Mishaba Laluo neighbors.[1] The Jiantou Laluo language still enjoys vigorous use and is not immediately endangered.

History: Little is known about the history of the Jiantou Laluo. Because they have no written language, no records have been kept of their migrations and experiences.

Customs: Jiantou Laluo women retain their traditional dress, "which is predominantly green with intricate embroidery and silver-colored sequins plotted out pleasantly on their blouses — all complimented by a unique headdress."[2]

Religion: The Jiantou Laluo are animists. They seem to have something of a fixation on spiders and have several legends involving them. One states that long ago a group of Laluo girls hid in a cave to escape the evil advances of a group of soldiers. As soon as they entered the cave, a spider came down and spun a web over the cave entrance, prohibiting the soldiers from entering. In honor of the insects, many Jiantou Laluo women embroider patterns of spiders on their clothing and headdress.

Christianity: There are believed to be a few Jiantou Laluo Christians, meeting in the Three-Self church in Dali Township. The large majority of this group, however, are completely unaware of the existence of Christianity. Because of their Hui neighbors, they have had more exposure to Islam than to Christianity.

Population in China:
30,000 (1999)
30,750 (2000)
38,600 (2010)
Location: Yunnan
Religion: Animism
Christians: 20

Overview of the Jiantou Laluo

Countries: China

Pronunciation: "Jeeuhn-tow-Lah-luoh"

Other Names: Laluo, Lalu, Laloba, Jiantou Lolo, Dongshan Yizu, Maganfang

Population Source: 30,000 (1999 J. Pelkey); Out of a total Yi population of 6,572,173 (1990 census)

Location: *Yunnan:* Weishan (15,000), Xiaguan (8,000), and Midu (7,000) counties

Status: Officially included under Yi

Language: Sino-Tibetan, Tibeto-Burman, Burmese-Lolo, Lolo, Northern Lolo, Yi, Western Yi

Dialects: 0

Religion: Animism, Ancestor Worship, Daoism, Christianity

Christians: 20

Scripture: None

***Jesus* film:** None

Gospel Recordings: None

Christian Broadcasting: None

ROPAL code: None

Status of Evangelization

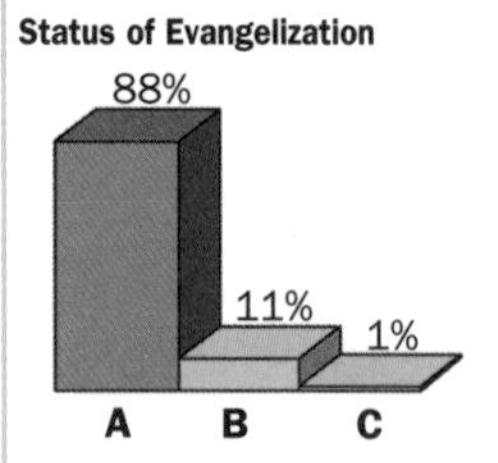

A = Have never heard the gospel
B = Were evangelized but did not become Christians
C = Are adherents to any form of Christianity

Laluo, Mishaba 腊罗，迷撒拔

Location: More than 575,000 Mishaba Laluo people are distributed throughout 16 counties of north central Yunnan Province. They are concentrated in the counties of southern Dali Prefecture, northern Lincang Prefecture, and eastern Baoshan Prefecture. Jingdong County in northern Simao Prefecture is also represented by a large number of Mishaba Laluo.[1]

Identity: The Mishaba Laluo are the largest Western Yi group in China. Until the 1950s, present-day Weishan and Nanjian counties were one administrative unit called Menghua. Since the beginning of the Tang Dynasty (AD 618) Menghua had been inhabited almost exclusively by the Laluo. As a result, the Mishaba Laluo are often called *Menghua* or *Menghuazu* by their neighbors. This group could be said to have two self-names in their language: *Laluo* and *Mishaba*. Laluo denotes their ethnic identity while Mishaba denotes their regional identity. "This people has, since ancient times, been 'the Laluo from the land of Misha', and, in their hearts, consider themselves as nothing else — certainly not 'Yi'."[2]

Language: Mishaba is a Western Yi language, although many have already lost the use of their mother tongue and have assimilated to Han culture and language. An estimated 400,000 Laluo (about 70%) still speak their language.[3]

History: Although they had exclusively inhabited the Menghua region since the eighth century, by the start of the Qing Dynasty (1644) the Laluo made up just 70% of the population. Large-scale Han migrations to the area during the eighteenth to the twentieth centuries made the Laluo a minority in their homeland and forced many to seek refuge in the mountains for the first time, in order to retain their culture and identity.

Jamin Pelkey

Customs: In Weishan County, the Laluo celebrate the Festival of the Tree King on the eighth day of the second lunar month. The entire community gathers around a large tree that stands outside the village. A black piglet is sacrificed and the pig's front teeth are offered to the spirit of the tree. The rest of the pig is cooked and eaten by the people, who sing a song in praise of the power of the Tree god.

Religion: Most of the Mishaba Laluo are animists. On the fifth day of the second lunar month they hold a ceremony called Calling Back the Spirit of the Rice. A young man dressed in a goatskin is responsible for making contact with the spirit. He cracks a whip and shouts toward the hills. If an echo is heard, the spirit is believed to have entered their presence. In one region around Weibao in Weishan County the Mishaba Laluo engage in Daoism, which they inherited from the Chinese centuries ago. Some Laluo have even become Daoist priests.

Christianity: The extent of Christianity among the Mishaba Laluo is uncertain, but there are believed to be a small number of Christians, mostly among assimilated Laluo. The majority of this people group, however, have no knowledge of the gospel and no contact with any Christian communities.

Population in China:
565,000 (1999)
579,400 (2000)
727,100 (2010)
Location: Yunnan
Religion: Animism
Christians: 500

Overview of the Mishaba Laluo

Countries: China
Pronunciation: "Mee-sha-bah-Lah-luoh"
Other Names: Mishaba, Misan, Misanxu, Menghua, Menghuazu, Turen, Misanru, Misapha, Laluopo, Lalu, Pingtou Lolo, Laloba, Misabo, Misapo, Misaru, Xishan Yi, Tutiaozi
Population Source: 565,000 (1999 J. Pelkey); Out of a total Yi population of 6,572,173 (1990 census)
Location: *Yunnan:* Fengqing, Yunxian, Nanjian, Weishan, Midu, Yangbi, Jingdong, Yongping, Baoshan, Changning, Shuangjiang, Lincang, Gengma, Yongde, Cangyuan, and Nanhua counties
Status: Officially included under Yi
Language: Sino-Tibetan, Tibeto-Burman, Burmese-Lolo, Lolo, Northern Lolo, Yi, Western Yi
Dialects (3+): Weishan,Fengqing, Jingdong
Religion: Animism, Ancestor Worship, Daoism, Christianity
Christians: 500
Scripture: None
***Jesus* film:** None
Gospel Recordings: None
Christian Broadcasting: None
ROPAL code: None

Status of Evangelization

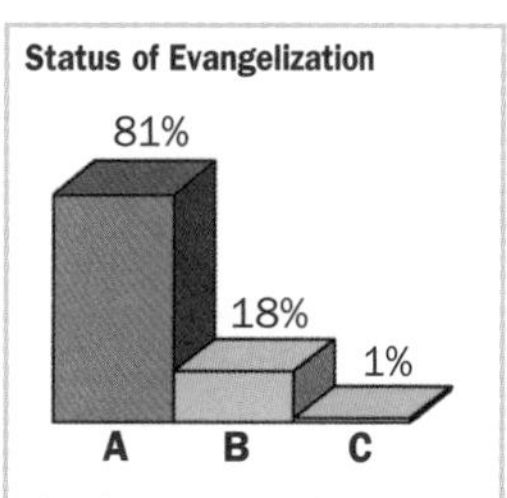

A = Have never heard the gospel
B = Were evangelized but did not become Christians
C = Are adherents to any form of Christianity

Lama 腊麻

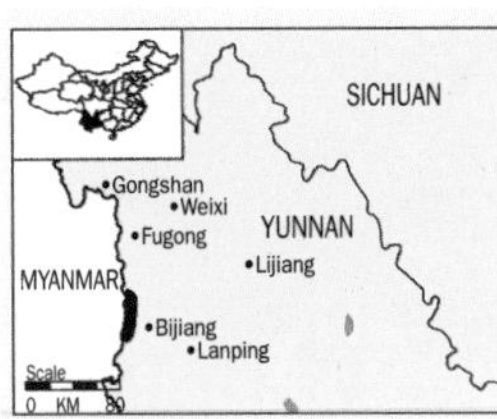

Population in China:
1,000 (1997)
1,060 (2000)
1,290 (2010)
Location: Yunnan
Religion: Polytheism
Christians: 100

Overview of the Lama

Countries: Myanmar, China

Pronunciation: "Lah-ma"

Other Names:

Population Source:
1,000 (1997 AMO);
Out of a total Nu population of 27,123 (1990 census);
3,000 in Myanmar and China (1977 Voegelin & Voegelin)

Location:
NW Yunnan: Bijiang County

Status:
Officially included under Nu

Language: Sino-Tibetan, Tibeto-Burman, Lolo, Northern Lolo, Unclassified

Dialects: 0

Religion:
Polytheism, Animism, Christianity

Christians: 100

Scripture: None

***Jesus* film:** None

Gospel Recordings: None

Christian Broadcasting: None

ROPAL code: LAY00

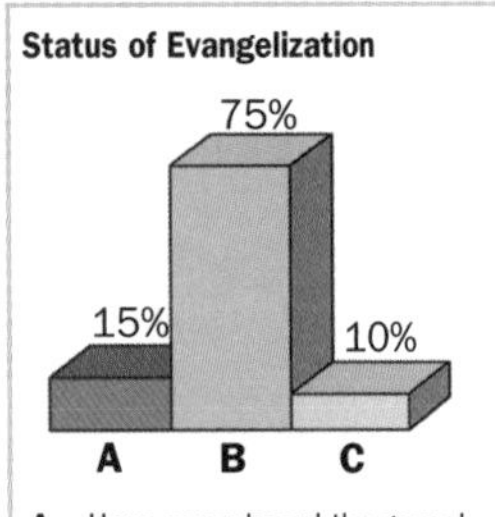

Location: More than 1,000 Lama are located within a thin strip of land along the China-Myanmar border, primarily in and around the town of Bijiang in Yunnan Province. A 1977 figure placed a total of 3,000 Lama in both China and Myanmar.[1] Their villages are constructed on steep 75-degree slopes. Yesterday's dangerous cane bridges across the turbulent river have given way to today's chain and rope bridges.[2] The region is extremely mountainous, with the highest peaks rising more than 3,000 meters (9,840 ft.) above sea level. "Dense virgin forests of pines and firs cover the mountain slopes and are the habitat of tigers, leopards, bears, deer, giant hawks and pheasants."[3]

Identity: The Lama are one of several distinct language groups combined to form the official Nu nationality in China.

Language: The Lama language — which has six tones — is part of the Lolo branch of the Tibeto-Burman language family. Lama is closely related to the Norra language spoken in northern Myanmar.

History: In 1896 the explorer Henri d'Orleans said the wild Lisu constantly raided the Lama and took them as slaves.[4] Today, Lama villages in Bijiang retain vestiges of a patriarchal clan system. Ten clans were located in ten different villages where each had communal land. According to a 1953 survey, "a landlord economy had emerged in Bijiang County, with an increasing number of land sales, mortgages, and leases. In some places, rich peasants exploited their poorer neighbors by a system called *washua*, under which peasants labored in semi-serf conditions. Slavery was practiced in a fraudulent form of son adoption."[5]

Customs: The Lama have a custom of naming a man three times during his lifetime. The first time occurs just after birth. A male elder, usually a grandfather, gives the baby a name which will be used all his life. At the age of 14 or 15 he is given another name which can only be used among his friends and people of his own generation. When a man gets married, he is named a third time. His name is connected to his father's by prefixing his name with the last sound of his father's name.[6]

Religion: In the past, clan leaders among the Lama also doubled as the village shamans. Their main job was to practice divination to ensure a bountiful harvest.

Christianity: Today there are believed to be a small number of Catholic believers among the Lama in China. The first Catholic missionaries in the Lama region were sent out by the Paris Foreign Missionary Society in the late 1800s. Father Jen Anshou established a work at Bai Halo. Most Catholic churches in China are not plagued by the idolatry that is often a feature of Catholicism in other countries. A Protestant mission book in the 1920s went as far as to state: "Go where you will in China, enter their churches when you will, and you will almost invariably find someone at prayer. Or again, if you are passing a little country church at the hour of its daily mass, you will find on any week day a goodly few from the village gathered there for worship."[7]

Dwayne Graybill

98

99

100

98. More than 350,000 *Central Luoluopo* inhabit the Chuxiong Prefecture in Yunnan. [Jamin Pelkey]
99. The *Lahu* first converted to Christianity in 1901. For centuries they had been waiting for a messenger to come with the lost Book of God. [Paul Hattaway]
100. The *Ladakhi*, who have their own monarchy in India, have been traders in the high Himalayan passes between India and Tibet for centuries. [Paul Hattaway]

101

102

103

101–102. The small *Lhoba* minority — who live in a virtually inaccessible part of southern Tibet — wear extensive jewelry, in addition to tiger, leopard, and bear fur. [101 Midge Conner; 102 Paul Hattaway]

103. Few people are aware of the *Lemo* people on the China-Myanmar border; Lushui, Yunnan. [Dwayne Graybill]

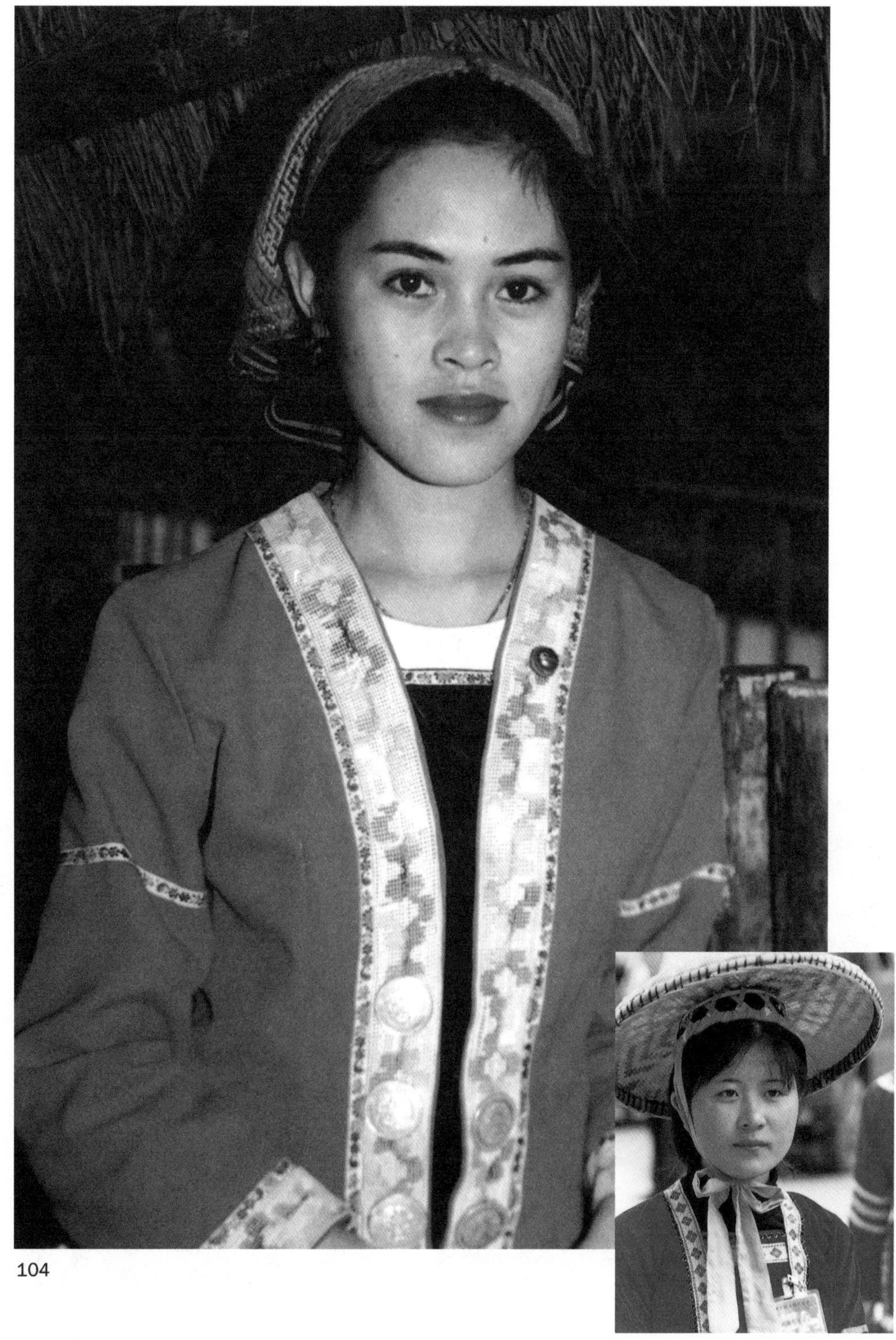

104

105

104–105. The *Li* nationality — a collection of five different tribes and languages — were the original inhabitants of Hainan Island. The Li language is distantly related to the Tai linguistic family. [both by Paul Hattaway]

106

107

108

106. The *Eastern Lipo* number at least 60,000 Christians. They have taken the gospel to many other tribes in Yunnan. [Jamin Pelkey]

107. The 146,000 *Western Lipo*, on the other hand, are an unreached people with few believers. They have a different language, customs, and ethnicity from the Eastern Lipo. Because of these differences, Eastern Lipo Christians have struggled to communicate the gospel to their Western Lipo neighbors. [Jamin Pelkey]

108. Of the 353,000 *Central Luoluopo* of Yunnan Province, there are only a handful of known Christians. [Jamin Pelkey]

Lami 腊米

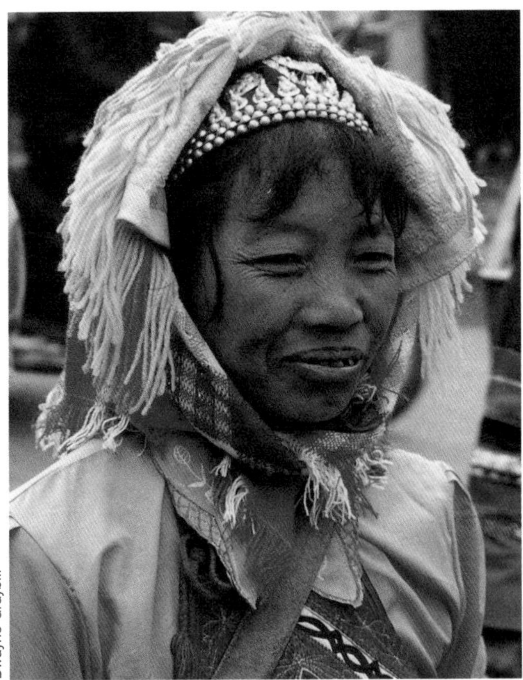

Dwayne Graybill

Location: Approximately 100,000 members of the Lami tribe inhabit seven different counties in Yunnan Province. One of the largest Lami villages is Habo in Yuanyang County which is described as "a small hamlet with about two hundred Lami households living in high and spacious houses. Built with solid mud bricks and straw on a stone foundation half-way up the mountain, the houses resemble each other in style. Their white-washed walls present a neat appearance."[1] The Lami are also located in northern Vietnam where they are one of the official subgroups of the Hani minority.

Identity: Approximately 13,000 Lami in Pu'er County have been officially classified under the Hani nationality.[2] The majority of Lami, however, have been officially included as part of the Yi nationality. The name Lami may mean "dirty" or "lowly." Some Hani may identify themselves as Lami so they can be treated as a separate group.

Language: The Lami language is part of the Western Yi branch of the Tibeto-Burman language family. Many Lami adults are also able to speak and write Chinese. Because the authorities do not encourage the use of Lami, all schooling is done in Mandarin.

History: In the distant past the Lami were a part of a large group of Tibeto-Burman peoples, including today's Akha, Hani, and Yi. Research indicates the formation of today's distinct Hani groups started in the thirteenth century, probably as a result of Genghis Khan's conquest of Yunnan.[3]

Customs: The Long Dragon Banquet is a Lami festival held on the third and fourth days of the 12th lunar month every year. Tables, dishes, trays, and wine cups are placed in a pattern to resemble the scales of a dragon. Each household is required to prepare "a table of fifteen to twenty dishes of delicacies comprising of food they grudge eating at ordinary times, that is, birds, beasts and aquatic produce. No ingredients such as carrots or cabbage are to be used."[4]

Religion: The Lami keep strictly to the customs handed down from their ancestors. Angmatu, their principal festival, is considered the best time for them to worship their deity and ask for blessings. "The god of Strength is the deity they worship, the god they believe can dispel disasters and sweep away all evils and monsters, and endow them with auspiciousness, fortune, longevity and bumper harvests."[5] Festival leaders among the Lami are selected after they have been approved by the deities. Chickens are slaughtered and their liver patterns studied to determine who should take up the sacred posts. During the festival, the leaders must sleep on one side of their body and abstain from sexual intercourse and from eating meat. For one month prior to the festival they must separate themselves from all people, including their own families.[6]

Christianity: There are a few thousand known Lami Christians, due to the witness of large Christian communities among the nearby Kado and Biyo. The Lami zealously guard their traditions and refuse to allow outside influences into their culture. The introverted nature of the Lami has kept most from seeing their need of God.

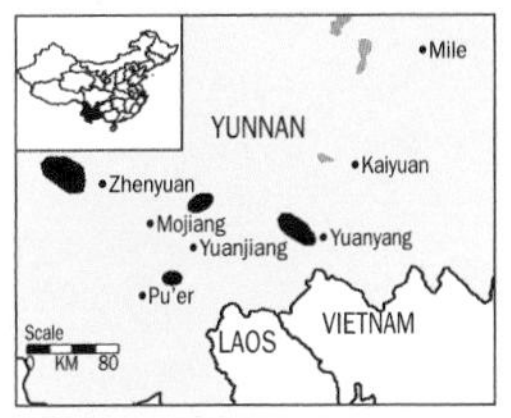

Population in China:
80,000 (1990)
100,400 (2000)
126,000 (2010)
Location: Yunnan
Religion: Polytheism
Christians: 2,000

Overview of the Lami

Countries: China, Vietnam

Pronunciation: "La-mee"

Other Names: Liumi, Ban

Population Source: 80,000 (1990 AMO); Also in Vietnam

Location: *Yunnan:* Yuanyang County in southern Honghe Prefecture; and Jingdong, Jinggu, Pu'er, Mojiang, Yunxiang, and Fengqing counties

Status: Officially included under both Hani and Yi

Language: Sino-Tibetan, Tibeto-Burman, Burmese-Lolo, Northern Lolo, Yi, Western Yi

Dialects: 0

Religion: Polytheism, Animism, Ancestor Worship, Christianity

Christians: 2,000

Scripture: None

***Jesus* film:** None

Gospel Recordings: None

Christian Broadcasting: None

ROPAL code: None

Status of Evangelization

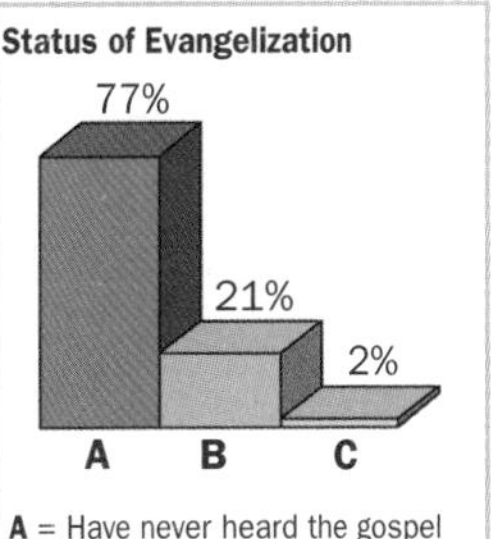

A = Have never heard the gospel
B = Were evangelized but did not become Christians
C = Are adherents to any form of Christianity

Laopang 劳旁

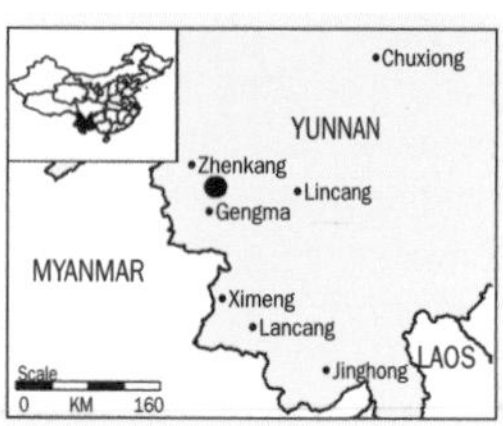

Population in China:
12,226 (1995)
14,000 (2000)
18,050 (2010)
Location: Yunnan
Religion: Animism
Christians: 400

Overview of the Laopang

Countries: Myanmar, China

Pronunciation: "Laow-pung"

Other Names: Laopa

Population Source: 12,226 (1995 GEM); Also in Myanmar

Location: *W Yunnan*

Status: Probably officially included under Lahu

Language: Sino-Tibetan, Tibeto-Burman, Burmese-Lolo, Lolo, Unclassified

Dialects: 0

Religion: Animism, Christianity

Christians: 400

Scripture: None

***Jesus* film:** None

Gospel Recordings: None

Christian Broadcasting: None

ROPAL code: LBG00

Status of Evangelization

	A	B	C
%	59%	38%	3%

A = Have never heard the gospel
B = Were evangelized but did not become Christians
C = Are adherents to any form of Christianity

Location: The population of the Laopang tribe in southern China numbered just over 12,000 in 1995.[1] Additional communities of Laopang live in northern Myanmar. The only location ever given for the Laopang in China was in 1945, after missionary John Kuhn conducted a detailed survey of the tribes in Yunnan. Kuhn listed the Laopang as living at "Yungpeh."[2] Yungpeh is the old spelling for what today would be Yongbei, but Yongbei has not been located on any map of Yunnan. Today the Laopang may be located at Yongde or Yongkang — two towns located near the Lahu areas in the western part of Yunnan Province.

Dwayne Graybill

Identity: Little is known about the Laopang people group or language. They may have been included under the Lahu nationality. The Laopang language has been described as "possibly the same as a group of Lahu near the Lao-Thai border."[3]

Language: The Laopang language belongs to the so-called Lolo (Yi-Hani) branch of the Tibeto-Burman language family. Foreigners — whether businessmen, missionaries, or diplomats — have long struggled to come to terms with learning Chinese languages. The famous British missionary C. T. Studd once jokingly stated that he believed the Chinese language was invented by the devil to prevent the Chinese from ever hearing the gospel properly.[4] In the early 1900s missionary Luella Miner expressed her frustrations with her lack of progress in the Chinese language: "I have been in China more than a year and a half and have labored under the delusion hitherto that I both understood and could speak a little of the vernacular. But the jargon which these country-women, speaking a slightly different dialect, poured into my ears fairly started the cold sweat, and it was equally appalling to see the vacant stare with which my supposedly choice Pekinese was received by many of the women.... My umbrella now and then proved more interesting than the difference between the true God and temple idols."[5]

History: The Laopang are probably considered a branch of the Lahu minority. A legend says that long ago, people from different nationalities shared a tiger they had hunted together. They ate the meat in different ways. "Because the way the Lahus ate their share was most characteristic... they were given the nickname, 'brave tiger-hunting people'."[6]

Customs: Today there are few tigers left in the western Yunnan area. The Laopang have turned to rice cultivation as their main source of food production. They also grow vegetables, corn, and maize.

Religion: The majority of Laopang people are animists who worship various spirits.

Christianity: The Laopang are part of the Lahu minority, which contains 50,000 Christians in China,[7] mostly concentrated in Banli, Mujia, Gengma, and Menglian.[8] At least several hundred of these are believed to be Laopang people. The gospel was excitedly accepted by the Lahu groups because of a legend of a foreigner who would come and bring them the true religion they had lost. By 1906 American missionary William Young had baptized 6,000 Lahu converts, including some Laopang.[9]

Laowu 老乌

Population in China:
6,300 (1999)
6,450 (2000)
8,100 (2010)
Location: Yunnan
Religion: Polytheism
Christians: None Known

Overview of the Laowu

Countries: China

Pronunciation: "Laow-woo"

Other Names: Lawu

Population Source:
6,300 (1999 J. Pelkey);
Out of a total Yi population of 6,572,173 (1990 census)

Location: *S Yunnan:* Western part of Jinping County in Honghe Prefecture

Status:
Officially included under Yi

Language: Sino-Tibetan, Tibeto-Burman, Burmese-Lolo, Lolo, Northern Lolo, Yi, Southern Yi

Dialects: 0

Religion: Polytheism, Animism, Ancestor Worship

Christians: None known

Scripture: None

***Jesus* film:** None

Gospel Recordings: None

Christian Broadcasting: None

ROPAL code: None

Status of Evangelization

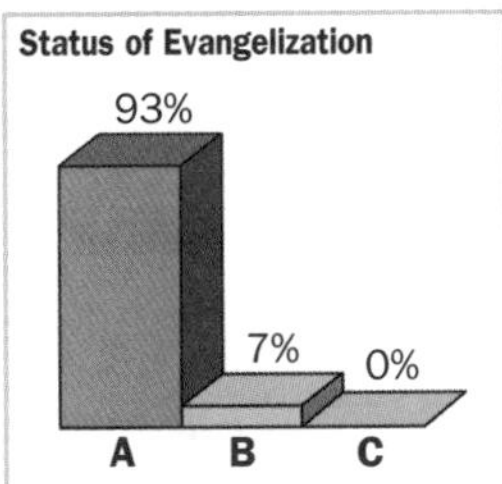

A = Have never heard the gospel
B = Were evangelized but did not become Christians
C = Are adherents to any form of Christianity

Location: Six thousand three hundred Laowu people were reported in a 1999 ethnographic study of Yi peoples in Yunnan Province.[1] They live in the western part of Jinping County within the Honghe Yi-Hani Autonomous Prefecture.[2] Although the Laowu live near China's border with Vietnam, there is no evidence of their existence within Vietnam.

Identity: The Laowu are part of the official Yi nationality in China. Unfortunately, most outsiders view the Yi as one people group. In reality they are a complex collection of ethnolinguistic peoples. Scholars have stated that the Yi consist of "several dozen branches,"[3] and that they are "made up of 93 tribes."[4] The Laowu are not the same ethnolinguistic group as the similarly named *Lawu* (who speak a Western Yi language) or *Luowu* (an Eastern Yi group), even though all three are part of the Yi nationality.

Language: Laowu is a distinct language within the Southern Yi linguistic group. It is partially related to other Southern Yi varieties such as Nisu, Pula, Boka, Xiuba, and Muji. The Laowu do not possess their own orthography. The Chinese script is used for reading and writing.

History: The Laowu in Jinping County seem to have once been distributed over a far wider area than they are today. Many non-Laowu villages in other parts of the county bear the name *Laowuzhai* (Laowu Village).

Customs: Laowu marriages are traditionally arranged through a matchmaker. A shaman is consulted. If the horoscopes of both parties are agreeable and if the parents on both sides give their consent, the two may become engaged. Before a Laowu wedding can be held, the family of the bride must donate articles such as clothes, blankets, a standing closet, and a trunk. When a Laowu bride leaves her home on the wedding day, she must be singing the "crying song" accompanied by her brothers, uncles, and maid-of-honor. Immediately before the bride and groom cross the threshold of their new home, the groom's sisters or mother takes a gourd filled with oats, wheat, corn, and beans and smashes it at their feet. This represents a wish for a lifetime of prosperity for the new couple.

Religion: After entering the house, the newly wed Laowu couple pay their respects first to heaven and earth, then to their ancestors, and finally to their parents. After a few more rituals, the couple is considered married. This ritual shows the polytheistic worldview of the Laowu. They believe a complex hierarchy of spirits guide and control their lives. They also consider it important to worship their ancestors.

Christianity: There is no Christian presence among the Laowu people in China. Little is known about the history of Christian missionary work in Jinping County prior to 1949. The area was a political hotbed, influenced by the restrictive French control of nearby Vietnam and Laos. In recent years thousands of Hmong and Iu Mien people in Jinping have come to Christ as a result of gospel radio broadcasts in their languages. These new believers, though they speak completely different languages from the Laowu, represent the best chance of the Laowu hearing the gospel.

Jamin Pelkey

Lashi 勒期

Location: Less than 2,000 Lashi live in the western part of Yunnan Province.[1] They are primarily located in Lushui County along the China-Myanmar border. In addition, more than 55,000 Lashi live in northern Myanmar. Many Lashi suddenly found themselves living in China after the redrawing of the China-Burma border in the 1950s and 1960s.

Identity: The Chinese call the Lashi *Chashan Ren*, meaning "tea mountain people." This name signifies the primary occupation of the Lashi: tea cultivation. The Lashi are one of six tribes who have been combined to form the official Jingpo nationality in China. In Myanmar, the Lashi are considered part of the generic Kachin group — a collection of loosely related tribes. They are pressured not to seek a separate ethnic identity from the Kachin. According to one source, the Lashi are "a group that arose largely by intermarriage between the Atsi and the Maran clan of the Jingpo."[2]

Language: The Lashi language — which has four tones — is closely related to Zaiwa. Some linguists have even described Zaiwa as a dialect of Lashi.

History: Many of the Lashi in China claim to be descended from a battalion of soldiers who were pushed across the border into China by advancing British troops in 1885.[3]

Customs: Most Lashi families own several copper guns. Living in dense forests, the Lashi use the weapons to defend themselves against wild animals and to hunt. They also fire shots into the air to announce a death or to celebrate a wedding. A man who is a skilled shooter is considered particularly attractive to a Lashi woman. Until recently the Lashi made their own gunpowder — a mix of fertilized soil, charcoal, sulphur, and plantain juice.

Paul Hattaway

Religion: In the past the Lashi relied on shamans to mediate between the material and the spiritual worlds. The shamans maintained a tight control over the people, reducing them to dire poverty while indulging in personal luxury. The Lashi still sometimes offer sacrifices to demons in a bid to heal a sickness. Some believe demons have the power to bite them, but if they bring appropriate offerings, this punishment can be forestalled. Often, to exorcize a case of disease, such as malaria, treacherous sorcerers demanded a family's livestock to be sacrificed one by one, effectively plunging the family into debt for generations.

Christianity: Although there are numerous churches among the Lashi, many of the professing believers have a superficial faith. A group of young Christians, in discussion with local officials, listed 15 causes why they believed they were poor. The list included: sickness, cruel and greedy sorcerers, vendettas, floods, wind and frost on crops, laziness, wife's pregnancy, marriage, death of the chief laborer, house building, fire, loss of cattle, being shorthanded, and causing another person's girlfriend to become pregnant.[4] Work is currently underway in Myanmar to translate the Scriptures into the Lashi language for the first time.

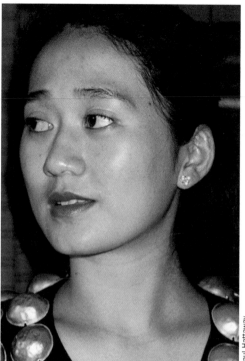

Lushui
Dali
MYANMAR
Tengchong
Baoshan
YUNNAN
Longling
Longchuan
Lincang
Scale 0 KM 80

Population in China:
1,800 (1997)
1,950 (2000)
2,520 (2010)
Location: Yunnan
Religion: Christianity
Christians: 640

Overview of the Lashi

Countries: Myanmar, China

Pronunciation: "Lah-shee"

Other Names: Lasi, Letsi, Lechi, Lashi-Maru, Lachikwaw, Chashan, Ac-ye, Leqi, Chashanhua

Population Source:
1,800 (1997 AMO);
Out of a total Jingpo population of 119,209 (1990 census);
55,500 in Myanmar (1983)

Location:
W Yunnan: Lushui County

Status:
Officially included under Jingpo

Language: Sino-Tibetan, Tibeto-Burman, Burmese-Lolo, Burmish, Northern Burmish

Dialects: 0

Religion:
Christianity, Animism, Polytheism

Christians: 640

Scripture: Work in progress

***Jesus* film:** None

Gospel Recordings:
Lashi #01044

Christian Broadcasting: None

ROPAL code: LSI00

Status of Evangelization

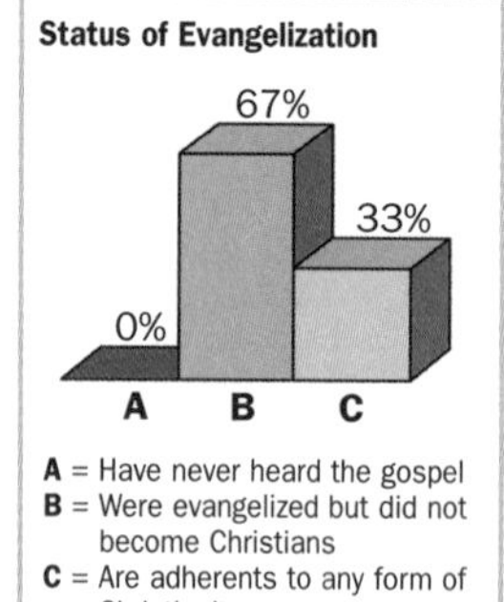

A = Have never heard the gospel
B = Were evangelized but did not become Christians
C = Are adherents to any form of Christianity

Lati 腊基

Population in China:
1,634 (1990)
2,050 (2000)
2,570 (2010)
Location: Yunnan
Religion: Animism
Christians: None Known

Overview of the Lati

Countries: Vietnam, China

Pronunciation: "Lah-tee"

Other Names: Akhu, Pula, Tai Lati, Lachi, Lipulio, Fula, Foula, Lipu, Lipute, Lipuchio, Lipuke, Liputio, Lipupi, Lipupo

Population Source:
1,634 (1990 Liang Min);
2,000 (1999 J. Pelkey);
Out of a total Yi population of 6,572,173 (1990 census);
7,863 in Vietnam (1991 census)

Location: *SE Yunnan:* Maguan County in the Wenshan Zhuang-Miao Prefecture; Possibly a few in Hekou County

Status:
Officially included under Yi

Language: Daic, Kadai, Lati-Kelao

Dialects (6): Lipute (Bag Lati), Liputcio (Han Lati), Lipuke (Red Lati), Lipuliongtco (Flowery Lati), Liputio (Black Lati), Lipupi (Long-Haired Lati)

Religion:
Animism, Ancestor Worship

Christians: None known

Scripture: None

***Jesus* film:** None

Gospel Recordings: None

Christian Broadcasting: None

ROPAL code: LBT00

Status of Evangelization

A: 83%
B: 17%
C: 0%

A = Have never heard the gospel
B = Were evangelized but did not become Christians
C = Are adherents to any form of Christianity

Dwayne Graybill

Location: The Lati — despite having a relatively small 1990 population of just 1,634 people living in 306 households — have several colorfully named subgroups, each speaking a separate dialect. Approximately half of the Lati call themselves *Han Lati.* Seventy-two households refer to themselves as *Flowery Lati*, 37 households as *Bag Lati* and 27 households as *Red Lati.* The Lati in China are located in Maguan County, Wenshan Prefecture in the southern part of Yunnan Province. There may also be a few in Hekou County. Across the border in Vietnam are the *Long Hair*, *White*, and *Black* Lati.[1]

Identity: The Lati in China are officially counted under the Yi nationality, yet they do not even speak a Sino-Tibetan language and have no kinship with the Yi. The incorrect categorization of the Lati is an example of the hurried approach that the Chinese authorities employed in their classification of China's ethnic peoples.

Language: The Lati language is part of the Tai family. Seventy percent of the Lati in China are able to speak their language. Most Lati are bilingual in Chinese and Nung. Some can also speak the languages of the neighboring Hmong and Tai. One linguist has described Lati as "a possibly extinct Kadai language in northern Vietnam."[2] The linguistic mix of Lati is reflected in a study which found it shares 36% lexical similarity with Gelao, 33% with Laqua, 34% with Buyang, 28% with Northern Zhuang, 25% with Li, 23% with Laka, and 22% with Dong.[3]

History: The Lati in Vietnam claim two historical founders of their race: Hoang Din Thung and Pu Lo To. They are reputed to have created many different species and to have educated the people how to live and farm.

Customs: Most Lati live simple lives. They cultivate rice. Lati women are renowned for their skill in weaving and indigo dyeing. Each family clan owns drums and gongs which are used in ritual ceremonies. At weddings the groom's family must provide a suitable amount of money to the bride's parents to repay the cost of the girl's upbringing. Lati homes are constructed on stilts and consist of three sections. The largest room contains the ancestral altar.

Religion: The Lati hold annual ceremonies determined by the lunar calendar. They pray for seeds before they plant them, believing each seed has a soul. They invoke the spirits to watch over the harvest, to ensure plenty of food for the entire village. The New Rice Festival along with the New Year and Seventh Month festivals are the largest, most colorful, and most important festivals of the year.

Christianity: The Lati are blocked off from Christian witness because the atheistic governments of both China and Vietnam forbid evangelism. There are no known Lati believers on either side of the border, and no missionaries are known to have ever targeted them. The nearest Christian communities to the Lati are among the Hmong Daw and Hmong Leng, but the Lati do not share a common language with the Hmong. The two groups rarely have contact with each other.

Lawa 腊佤

Paul Hattaway

Location: Approximately 55,000 Lawa live in Yongde and Zhenkang counties in southwest China's Yunnan Province. Their communities are located in thickly forested areas on the outskirts of the Ximeng Mountains. In addition, 30,000 members of the Bulang nationality also speak Lawa as their mother tongue.

Identity: The Lawa were also known historically as the *Tame Wa*. They assimilated more quickly to the cultures of surrounding peoples than did the Kawa, or Wild Wa, who live in isolated communities at least 1,500 meters (5,000 ft.) up in the mountains.

Language: The Lawa language in China is not intelligible with Lawa spoken in Thailand, which has "surprisingly great dialect differences."[1] Despite their relatively small population, the Christian ministry *Gospel Recordings* has produced cassettes in seven different Lawa dialects in Thailand alone.[2] The Lawa now use a Roman script, but in the past they communicated by engraving bamboo strips or sending objects to other villages. "Objects used implied specific meaning or feelings. For instance, sugarcane, banana or salt meant friendship, but pepper meant anger, feathers urgency, and gunpowder and bullets the intention of clan warfare."[3]

History: The Lawa are a part of the great Mon-Khmer race of Asia, which includes ethnolinguistic groups ranging from India to the Philippines.

Customs: Having adopted Theravada Buddhism under the influence of the Tais many centuries ago, the Lawa became a more gentle people than their head-hunting cousins in the mountains. The Lawa's Buddhism is cloaked with traditional animistic and polytheistic rituals, as well as with ancestor worship.

Religion: In addition to their adherence to Buddhism, the Lawa believe in "house spirits, local spirits, and the spirits of the iron mines. They also rely heavily on witchdoctors. Many deities are regarded as disembodied spirits of ancient heroes."[4] Christian churches are also found in many Lawa villages in China.

Christianity: The 10,000 Lawa Christians in China first received the gospel in the 1920s from William Young of the American Baptist Foreign Mission Society and later from his two sons: "Young succeeded against all odds to win the crude Wa tribe to Christianity."[5] The Lawa's conversion was attained not only by preaching and words, but by Young's self-sacrificial concern for the people. Historian T'ien Ju-K'ang recorded: "At the onset he was fiercely opposed by the Wa who threatened to cut off his head if he ever dared to approach their settlement again. Once in 1924, Young discovered the body of a dying woman lying in a ditch outside a village. She was apparently a victim of smallpox who had been left for dead. Young immediately erected a shed and brought in the woman for treatment, washing her sores continuously for three days. To draw out the puss, Young did not hesitate to use his own mouth. His devotion and compassion opened the hearts of countless Wa to receive his message."[6]

Population in China:
45,000 (1990)
55,000 (2000)
67,300 (2010)
Location: Yunnan
Religion: Buddhism
Christians: 10,000

Overview of the Lawa

Countries: China, Myanmar, Thailand

Pronunciation: "Lah-wa"

Other Names: Western Lawa, Mountain Lawa, Lava, Luwa, L'wa, Lavua, Tame Wa

Population Source: 45,000 (1990 J.-O. Svantesson); Out of a total Wa population of 351,974 (1990 census); 14,000 in Thailand (1993 P. Johnstone); Also in Myanmar, and Thailand

Location: *W Yunnan:* Yongde and Zhenkang counties

Status: Officially included under Wa

Language: Austro-Asiatic, Mon-Khmer, Northern Mon-Khmer, Palaungic, Western Palaungic, Waic, Lawa

Dialects: 0

Religion: Theravada Buddhism, Animism, Christianity

Christians: 10,000

Scripture: New Testament 1972; Portions 1961

***Jesus* film:** None

Gospel Recordings: Lawa: Chang Maw #02187 Lawa: La-oop #01154

Christian Broadcasting: None

ROPAL code: LCP00

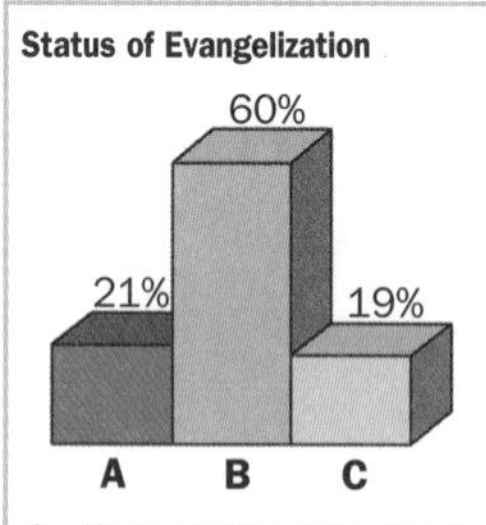

Lawu 拉乌

Location: Approximately 20,000 Lawu live in the soaring Ailao Mountains of Simao and Yuxi prefectures in southwest China's Yunnan Province. Besides the 12,500 living in the northwestern part of Xinping County, many more Lawu can be found in Zhenyuan and Jingdong counties of Simao Prefecture. The highest concentration of Lawu live on steep slopes in the Shuitang District of Xinping County. More than 60% of the district's total population are Lawu people.[1]

Jamin Pelkey

Identity: Although they have been officially classified as part of the generic Yi nationality in China, the Lawu are a distinct ethnolinguistic group. They have never before been listed in any ethnographic survey of China's people groups and, therefore, have never been on any mission lists of China's unreached peoples either.[2] The Lawu are culturally and linguistically different from three other similarly named Yi groups in Yunnan: the Awu, the Laluo, and the Lalu.

Language: Although they are located in southwestern Yunnan, the Lawu speak a language belonging to the Western Yi branch of the Tibeto-Burman language family.

History: Even though the Yi minority in China is comprised of more than 100 tribes and subgroups speaking numerous languages and dialects, some of these groups share common historical roots. Many Yi (and some Hani) believe a man named Zzemuvyvy (Zhongmuyu in Chinese) was their original ancestor.[3] Zzemuvyvy and his six descendants are referred to in Yi manuscripts from as far as Sichuan to southern Yunnan and Guizhou provinces.

Customs: Every five days (on days 5, 10, 15, 20, 25, and 30 of each month), the Lawu from Shuitang District in Xinping County come down from the mountains to trade with the Tai and Han living in the Gasa River valley.

Religion: For countless generations the Lawu have adhered to the superstitions of animism, polytheism, and ancestor worship. Their belief system reveals itself in a number of different ways. One example is *Mi Ga Ha*, which in the Lawu language is the "Dragon Worship Festival." During the second lunar month, a day is chosen for all villagers to gather around a large tree and hold a ceremony to worship the dragon. They believe the dragon is responsible for rainfall and many other natural phenomena. They hope to appease the dragon in order to quell floods and prevent drought. At the same time many other Yi people celebrate the Torch Festival, the Lawu observe a day of worshiping their ancestors.

Christianity: There are believed to be a handful of Christians among the isolated Lawu people. They are not considered resistant to the gospel but have simply never heard it. Paul Vial, a French Catholic missionary among the Sani in the late 1800s, held great hopes for all Yi groups becoming Christian, especially because of their belief in Creation and the Universal Flood. He wrote, "Christianity... will make them understand what is beautiful, good, and true, and the [Yi] will no longer think to search elsewhere for that which he will find henceforth in himself."[4]

Population in China:
19,500 (1999)
19,950 (2000)
25,100 (2010)
Location: Yunnan
Religion: Polytheism
Christians: 10

Overview of the Lawu

Countries: China

Pronunciation: "Lah-woo"

Other Names: Lao-wou, Lao-wu

Population Source:
19,500 (1999 J. Pelkey);
Out of a total Yi population of 6,572,173 (1990 census)

Location: *Yunnan:* Xinping County in Yuxi Prefecture (12,500); Zhenyuan County in Simao Prefecture (7,000)

Status:
Officially included under Yi

Language: Sino-Tibetan, Tibeto-Burman, Burmese-Lolo, Lolo, Northern Lolo, Yi, Western Yi

Dialects: 0

Religion: Polytheism, Animism, Ancestor Worship, Christianity

Christians: 10

Scripture: None

***Jesus* film:** None

Gospel Recordings: None

Christian Broadcasting: None

ROPAL code: None

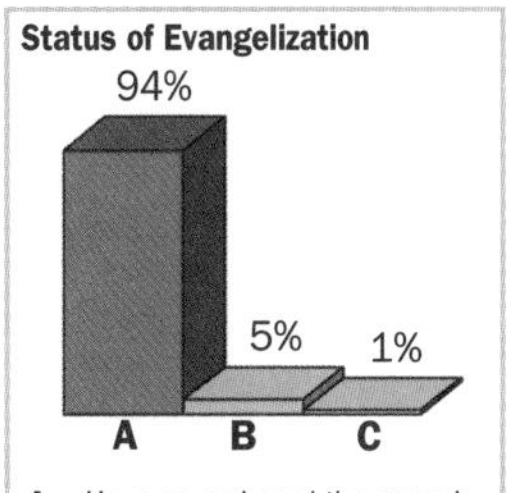

A = Have never heard the gospel
B = Were evangelized but did not become Christians
C = Are adherents to any form of Christianity

Lemo 勒墨

Population in China:
2,000 (1997)
2,140 (2000)
2,670 (2010)
Location: Yunnan
Religion: Buddhism
Christians: None Known

Overview of the Lemo

Countries: China

Pronunciation: "Lee-mo"

Other Names: Lu-k'ou, Laimo

Population Source:
2,000 (1997 D. Graybill);
Out of a total Lisu population of 574,856 (1990 census)

Location: *W Yunnan:* Lemo, 78 kilometers (48 mi.) north of Liuku Township in Lushui County

Status:
Officially included under Lisu

Language: Sino-Tibetan, Chinese

Dialects: 0

Religion: Theravada Buddhism, Animism, Ancestor Worship

Christians: None known

Scripture: None

***Jesus* film:** None

Gospel Recordings: None

Christian Broadcasting: None

ROPAL code: None

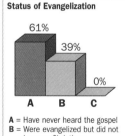

Status of Evangelization

	A	B	C
	61%	39%	0%

A = Have never heard the gospel
B = Were evangelized but did not become Christians
C = Are adherents to any form of Christianity

Location: More than 2,000 people who use the ethnic name Lemo live in the small town of Lemo, 78 kilometers (48 mi.) from Liuku Township in western Yunnan Province. The Lemo live along the Nujiang River, near the mountainous China-Myanmar border and close to communities of Lisu and Nu people.

Identity: The Lemo may be an ethnic group who developed as the result of intermarriage between the Tai Mao and Lisu. Francis Ward, writing in 1913, described them as racially mixed people who spoke and dressed like the Chinese.[1] Today, the Lemo still see themselves as different from surrounding communities, and they still wear their own spectacular ethnic dress. The Chinese authorities have included the Lemo as part of the Lisu nationality.

Language: Being a mix of Lisu and Tai Mao, which are two completely unrelated languages from two different linguistic families, the Lemo chose to speak Chinese among themselves at an early stage. Today some Lemo men speak Lisu, but it has been relearned to enable them to trade with the Lisu, who are the largest ethnic group in northwest Yunnan. There are few or no traces of the Tai Mao language remaining among the Lemo.

History: The Lemo say they were once great hunters who fed their families by killing wild game in the mountains. These days most Lemo are agriculturists, although the men still possess bows and arrows, and swords. Since the government's inclusion of the Lemo under the Lisu minority — a classification the Lemo strongly disagree with — their identity as a distinct people group has gradually eroded. Neighboring people, who are forced to believe China has only 55 minority nationalities, now call them *Lisu.* This has resulted in some comical situations. When several researchers visited the Lemo in 1997, they asked at the home of a Bai man, who said he had never heard of such a group. They then knocked on the door of another home about 20 feet away. The family who lived there excitedly said they were Lemo, and all the people in that particular village were Lemo except the Bai home they first visited![2]

Customs: In the 1950s the Lemo were the focus of a government crop project. Due to irrigation and the use of 72 tons of manure per hectare, grain output dramatically increased from 100 kilograms (220 lb.) to 1.25 tons (2,750 lb.) per capita.[3] In addition to agriculture, many Lemo are engaged in fishing and hunting.

Religion: Most Lemo people, especially the elderly, are Theravada Buddhists. They are superstitious people who believe in ghosts, deities, and the existence of good and evil spirits. If someone dies from an accident it is considered impure and a bad omen. Nine grains of rice (seven for women) are placed in the mouth of the deceased to appease the spirit of death.

Christianity: Although the Lemo live in a strong Christian area which contains thousands of Lisu, Nu, and Han Chinese believers, there are no known Christians among the Lemo. The Lemo's strong belief in Buddhism and their isolated cultural mind-set have prevented them from accepting the gospel from their neighbors.

Dwayne Graybill

Lesu 勒苏

Jamin Pelkey

Location: Approximately 15,000 Lesu people live in dense mountain forests at least 2,300 meters (7,546 ft.) above sea level, in Xinping, Jinping, Zhenyuan, and Eshan counties of Yuxi Prefecture in southern Yunnan Province. A mere 37 Lesu reportedly live in Shaungbai County,[1] and an additional 600 Lesu live in Shiping County of Honghe Prefecture.[2]

Identity: The government has included the Lesu as part of the Yi nationality in China, an artificially constructed classification that contains at least "several dozen branches" of different ethnic groups.[3] *Lesu* or *Leisu* is the self-name of this group. The Chinese call them *Shansu*, meaning "mountain people." The Lesu who live west of the Gasa River in the Ailao Mountains of Mosha District reportedly no longer speak their mother tongue, having reverted to Chinese. Because of this, the people in the area call them *Jia Shansu*, meaning "fake Shansu."

Language: The Lesu language is classified as a dialect of the Southern Yi branch of the Tibeto-Burman family, but their language is so different from the other Southern Yi speakers around them that they must use Chinese in order to communicate. Even Chinese sources, which tend to downplay differences between Yi subgroups, admit that the Lesu language is quite unique. "Given such a sporadic distribution with such distances between clusters of Lesu villages, there are probably a number of Lesu dialects. *Leisu* ('Laysoo') is reportedly a variant name for the Lesu and could be a separate group if dialect differences prove to be wide enough."[4]

History: The Lesu were once named the *Ma Long* people, who were part of the *Sou* tribe dating back to the Han and Western Jin dynasties (220 BC – AD 316). "The Lesu entered Yuanjiang County during the Yuan Dynasty (1271–1368) and by the Ming Dynasty (1368–1644) had spread to Xinping and Shiping counties."[5] There are two different sets of festivals celebrated by the Lesu of different areas. Those in Eshan, Xinping, and Shuangbai celebrate a festival called Traditional Flower Fair, while those in Yuanjiang celebrate a Mountain Sacrifice Festival. The Flower Fair of the first region is celebrated every 24th day of the sixth lunar month (the same day as the Torch Festival among the Nisu and Nasu), and repeated every 15th day of the seventh month of the Lunar calendar. The festival stems from an old legend in which a Han and a Lesu fell in love. Their parents strongly disagreed with the engagement, however. One night the couple went to the peak of Daxishan where they danced and sung. On that night the two committed suicide together. The festival is now held in their honor.[6]

Religion: The Lesu people greatly revere the Mountain god, but only those in Yuanjiang County hold a yearly day of sacrifice in order to appease him. On this day Lesu are forbidden to work in their fields for fear the Mountain god will be offended.

Christianity: The Lesu were a completely unevangelized and unreached people group until 1999, when a Lesu family — who helped record the first gospel recording in their language — gave their lives to Jesus Christ after considering the message.

Population in China:
14,800 (1999)
15,170 (2000)
19,040 (2010)
Location: Yunnan
Religion: Polytheism
Christians: 5

Overview of the Lesu

Countries: China

Pronunciation: "Leh-soo"

Other Names: Shansu, Shanshu, Leisu, Chesu

Population Source: 14,800 (1999 J. Pelkey); Out of a total Yi population of 6,572,173 (1990 census)

Location: *Yunnan:* Xinping (6,800), Yuanjiang (6,100), Eshan (1,000), Zhenyuan (200), and Shuangbai (100) counties of Yuxi Prefecture; Shiping County (600) of Honghe Prefecture

Status: Officially included under Yi

Language: Sino-Tibetan, Tibeto-Burman, Burmese-Lolo, Lolo, Northern Lolo, Yi, Southern Yi

Dialects: 2+

Religion: Polytheism, Animism, Shamanism, Christianity

Christians: 5

Scripture: None

***Jesus* film:** None

Gospel Recordings: Yi: Shansu #04940

Christian Broadcasting: None

ROPAL code: None

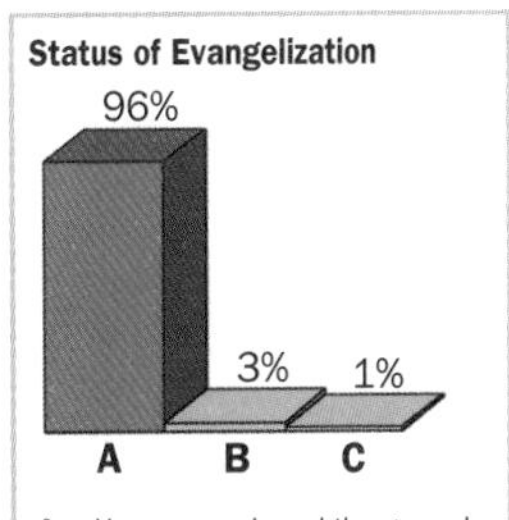

Lhoba, Bogar 珞巴，博嘎而

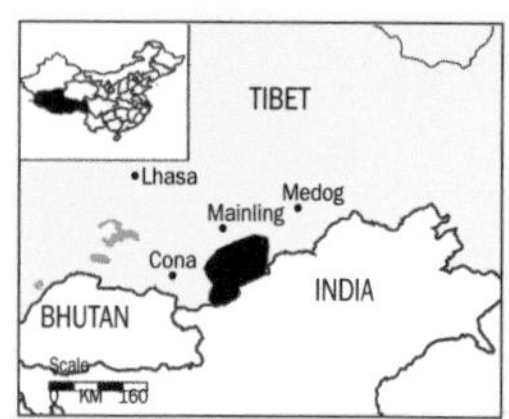

Population in China:
3,000 (1987)
3,580 (2000)
4,100 (2010)
Location: Tibet
Religion: Shamanism
Christians: None Known

Overview of the Bogar Lhoba

Countries: China, India

Pronunciation: "Low-bar-Bo-gah"

Other Names: Lhoba: Boga'er, Boga'er, Bengi-Boga'er, Bokar

Population Source:
3,000 (1987 *LAC*);
Only 2,312 Lhoba were counted in the 1990 census;
3,375 in India (1981 census)

Location: *SE Tibet:* Lhunze and Mainling counties, south of the Yaluzangjiang River

Status:
Officially included under Lhoba

Language: Sino-Tibetan, Tibeto-Burman, Baric, Mirish

Dialects (2):
Upper Bogar, Lower Bogar

Religion: Shamanism, Animism, Tibetan Buddhism

Christians: None known

Scripture: None

***Jesus* film:** None

Gospel Recordings: None

Christian Broadcasting: None

ROPAL code: LHO00

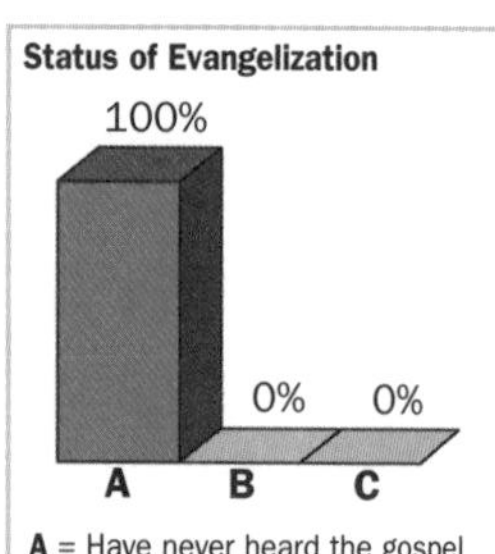

Dwayne Graybill

Location: Approximately 3,500 speakers of the Bogar language inhabit a sparsely populated area of southeast Tibet. They live south of the Yaluzang (Yarlung Zangbo) River in the two large counties of Lhunze and Mainling. Medog Prefecture is the size of Holland, yet contains just 9,000 people.[1] It is closed for most of the year due to snow and landslides. One study remarks that "an unknown number of Bogar can also be found on the south slope of the eastern section of the Himalayan ranges."[2] The 1981 census of India listed 3,375 *Bokar* living in the state of Arunachal Pradesh.

Identity: The Bogar form part of the official Lhoba nationality in China. In the 1990 census, only 2,312 Lhoba were counted. A 1987 study, however, reported 3,000 speakers of Bogar and 7,000 speakers of Yidu Lhoba. Some publications have incorrectly reported a population of 200,000 Lhoba in Tibet.[3] The name *Lhoba* means "southerners" in the Tibetan language. The Lhoba are not the same group as the *Lopa* (Mustang) Tibetans of Nepal.

Language: The Bogar language is distinct from Yidu Lhoba and Adi. Speakers of each language are unable to communicate with each other. Bogar Lhoba is a member of the Mirish branch of Tibeto-Burman.[4]

History: Until the 1950s the Bogar were frequently bullied and oppressed by the Tibetans. The Bogar were not allowed to intermarry with other nationalities and were not allowed to leave their area without the permission of the Tibetans.[5] In August 1965, the State Council of China officially recognized the Lhoba as a distinct minority group. The first satellite TV dish was installed in Medog Prefecture in 1989, linking this remote area with the rest of China.

Customs: Few peoples in the world are as isolated as the Bogar. The barefooted tribesmen are skilled hunters and fishermen. The forests they inhabit still contain many Bengali tigers and 40 species of other rare protected animals.[6] There are two classes among the Bogar: *maide* and *nieba*. The *maide* class are free to keep slaves and hold authority in the society. The word *nieba* means "those who are not allowed to lift their heads casually."[7] They are slaves who have no rights.

Religion: Most Bogar are worshipers of evil spirits. When they become sick, they believe they are being afflicted by demons. A shaman is summoned to heal the sick person by calling the soul back to the body. Every Bogar village has an altar where sacrifices and divination take place. The most common form of telling the future is to study the lines of a rooster's liver. Sometimes dozens or even hundreds of roosters will be killed in order to secure a favorable decision.[8]

Christianity: The Bogar of Tibet are a completely unevangelized people. They presently have no access to the gospel. Their area is effectively sealed off from the rest of the world by geographic, political, and religious barriers.

Lhoba, Yidu 珞巴，蒉都

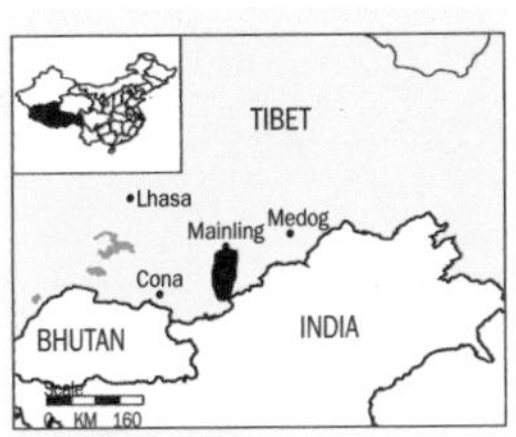

Population in China:
7,000 (1987)
8,350 (2000)
9,600 (2010)
Location: Tibet
Religion: Shamanism
Christians: None Known

Overview of the Yidu Lhoba

Countries:
China, India, possibly Bhutan

Pronunciation: "Low-bah-E-doo"

Other Names:
Lhoba: Yidu, Yidu, Idu

Population Source:
7,000 (1987 *LAC*);
Only 2,312 Lhoba were counted in the 1990 census;
8,569 in India (1981 census);
Possibly also in Bhutan

Location: *SE Tibet:* Lhunze and Mainling counties

Status:
Officially included under Lhoba

Language: Sino-Tibetan, Tibeto-Burman, Baric, Mirish

Literacy: 31%

Dialects: 0

Religion: Shamanism, Animism, Tibetan Buddhism

Christians: None known

Scripture: None

***Jesus* film:** None

Gospel Recordings: None

Christian Broadcasting: None

ROPAL code: LON00

Status of Evangelization

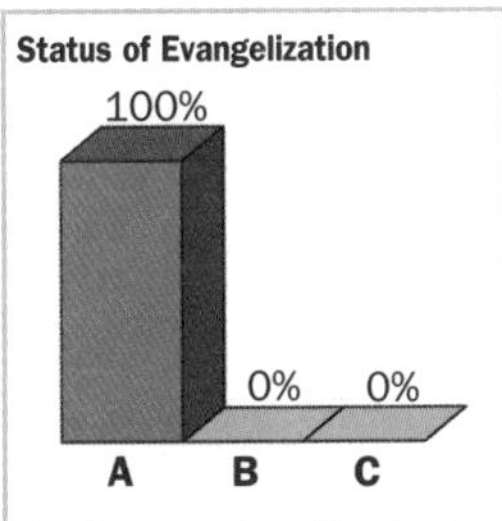

A = Have never heard the gospel
B = Were evangelized but did not become Christians
C = Are adherents to any form of Christianity

Location: The extremely isolated Danba River valley and the surrounding mountain slopes in southeast Tibet are home to more than 8,000 Yidu Lhoba. This sparsely populated region borders northern India. More than 8,500 *Idu* live in Arunachal Pradesh, India. Some reports have incorrectly stated that there are 200,000 Lhoba living in northern India.[1]

Identity: Yidu is a distinct language that differs from Bogar Lhoba, which is spoken by members of the same minority group farther to the east of the Yidu. The Yidu have been combined with the Bogar and Adi to form the official Lhoba nationality in Tibet. However, the Chinese government's 1990 census findings of only 2,312 Lhoba do not match the figures of independent linguists and researchers who report a minimum of 10,000 Lhoba in China.

Language: The exact classification of the Yidu language is uncertain. Linguist Ning Yu has placed it in the Tibeto-Burman family, but the Chinese have not yet assigned it an affiliation.[2] Some scholars believe the two Lhoba languages are related to Jingpo.[3]

History: Until recently the Lhoba were a virtually unknown and extremely primitive people. Because they have no written script, the Lhoba have no record of where they originated. In the past they tied strings around their wrists or notched marks in wood to remind them of important things they needed to do.

Customs: Most Lhoba marriages take place sometime within the full moon days of September to December. "On that day... the bride and groom take a sip from their own bowls first and then exchange the bowls and keep on drinking.... On the second day after the wedding, friends and relatives of the groom will present a gift which they consider the best of all gifts — rat meat. Rat meat is, for the Lhobas, the best dish a host can offer his guests."[4]

Religion: For thousands of years the Lhoba have handed down oral traditions about the genesis of the world. Their beliefs form the Lhoba worldview. They say in the beginning the sky was empty, and only the sun, moon, and stars could be seen. The earth was bare, and only the mountains, rivers, and rocks existed. "*Maidong* (the sky) and *Shijin* (the earth) sat together trying to break the absolute tranquillity that embodied the world. They decided to get married and soon after the earth was pregnant. Their first child, before birth, dissipated into a pool of blood. The blood then changed into rain and nourished the various forms of life on earth. Later on, the earth gave birth to another child who became the ancestor of the Lhoba nationality."[5] To please their Tibetan neighbors, many Yidu Lhoba outwardly adhere to Tibetan Buddhism, but in reality they practice shamanism and spirit appeasement.

Christianity: The Yidu Lhoba have no awareness of the name of Jesus Christ. There are a few churches in Assam, northern India, among the related Adi people, but no Christians are known to have crossed into the Yidu Lhoba part of Tibet with the gospel.

Dwayne Graybill

Lhomi 珞米

Location: More than 1,300 Lhomi inhabit the border area between southern Tibet and Nepal. Despite their relatively small population, the Lhomi are found in three countries. The majority (4,000) live in six villages in the eastern hills of the Sankhvwasawa District in the Koshi Zone of eastern Nepal. They live near the Arun River and are bilingual in the Nepali language. An additional 1,000 Lhomi speakers live in the famous tea-growing and tourist region of Darjeeling in India. The Lhomi live at the juncture of the former nations of Sikkim and Tibet, and the current nations of India and Nepal.

Identity: Although they are considered part of the Tibetan nationality, the Lhomi possess their own distinct language and culture. *Lhomi* means "southern people."[1]

Language: The Lhomi language was studied extensively in the 1970s by linguists Oliva and Marja Vesalanen.[2] Lhomi, which is a part of the Central Bodic branch of Tibeto-Burman, is reported to have 65% lexical similarity with Central Tibetan and Kyerung and 58% with Sherpa.[3] The dialect spoken by the Lhomi in Tibet may differ from those spoken in Nepal and India.

History: The Lhomi are a Tibetan people who have been influenced by non-Tibetans over the course of many centuries. This has led to the mixture of cultural, linguistic, and religious traits that today identify them as a distinct people group.

Customs: Over the past 20 years, some Lhomi in Nepal have moved and settled down in the nation's capital, Katmandu, where they work as laborers and builders. Most of the Lhomi men who work in Katmandu send money back to their families. They are only able to travel back to their home villages once or twice a year. "This independent tribe grows a few crops, in particular millet for making gruel and beer. They raise sheep for wool and meat, and weave cotton-like garments from wild sisal hemp."[4]

Paul Hattaway

Religion: The Lhomi believe in the existence of spirits and natural forces that control the affairs of their lives. Their religion has been described as "unrefined Buddhism.... Their shamans (animistic priests) are as active as the Buddhist lamas. Although animal sacrifice is abhorrent to orthodox Buddhists, the Lhomis make several ritual animal sacrifices during the year."[5] Before millet is planted in September, the Lhomi kill three sheep to placate the patron deity of their village.

Christianity: Due to the large foreign missionary contingent formerly based in Darjeeling, northeast India, many Lhomi there have some awareness of the gospel, and a few have believed in Christ. In recent years more than 100 Lhomi in Nepal have also put their faith in Christ. They are now sending evangelists to other people groups. Lhomi Scripture portions were first printed in 1976, and gospel recordings are also available. Further linguistic work is reportedly in progress to translate more of the Bible into Lhomi. Despite the existence of Lhomi Christians in Nepal and India, it has proven difficult for the gospel to spread to their counterparts in Tibet, due to the political situation there and the tightly controlled borders.

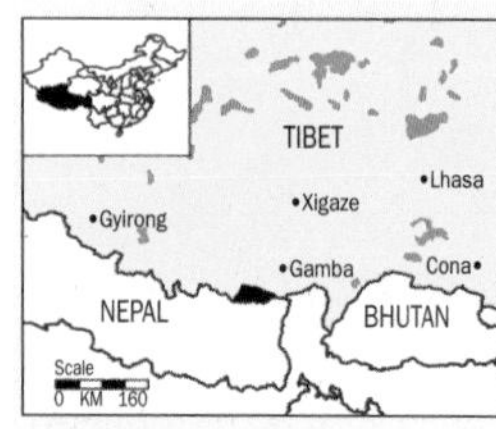

Population in China:
1,000 (1985)
1,350 (2000)
1,660 (2010)
Location: Tibet
Religion: Animism
Christians: None Known

Overview of the Lhomi

Countries: Nepal, China, India

Pronunciation: "Low-mee"

Other Names: Lhoket, Shing Saapa, Kathe Bhote, Kar Bhote, Shingsawa

Population Source: 1,000 (1992 B. Grimes – 1985 figure); Out of a total Tibetan population of 4,593,330 (1990 census); 4,000 in Nepal; 1,000 in India (1985)

Location: *S Tibet:* Along the Nepal border, east of Mt. Everest

Status: Officially included under Tibetan

Language: Sino-Tibetan, Tibeto-Burman, Bodic, Bodish, Tibetan, Central Tibetan

Dialects: 0

Religion: Animism, Tibetan Buddhism, Shamanism

Christians: None known

Scripture: Portions 1976; Work in progress

***Jesus* film:** None

Gospel Recordings: Lhomi #04092

Christian Broadcasting: None

ROPAL code: LHM00

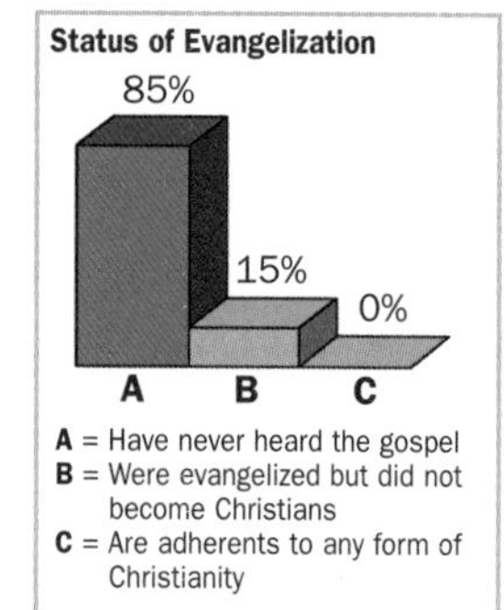

Li, Bendi 黎,本地

Population in China:
44,000 (1987)
60,600 (2000)
78,100 (2010)
Location: Hainan Island
Religion: Polytheism
Christians: None Known

Overview of the Bendi Li

Countries: China

Pronunciation: "Ben-dee-Lee"

Other Names: Bli, Bendi

Population Source:
44,000 (1987 *LAC*);
Out of a total Li population of 1,110,900 (1990 census)

Location: *Hainan Island:* The eastern half of Baisha County, and in areas north to Yinggeling

Status:
Officially included under Li

Language: Daic, Kadai, Li-Laqua

Dialects (2): Baisha (36,000), Yuanmen (8,000)

Religion:
Polytheism, Animism, Shamanism

Christians: None known

Scripture: None

***Jesus* film:** None

Gospel Recordings: None

Christian Broadcasting: None

ROPAL code: LIC04

Status of Evangelization

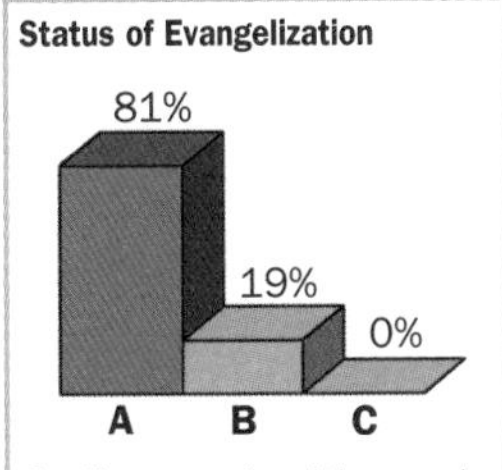

A = Have never heard the gospel
B = Were evangelized but did not become Christians
C = Are adherents to any form of Christianity

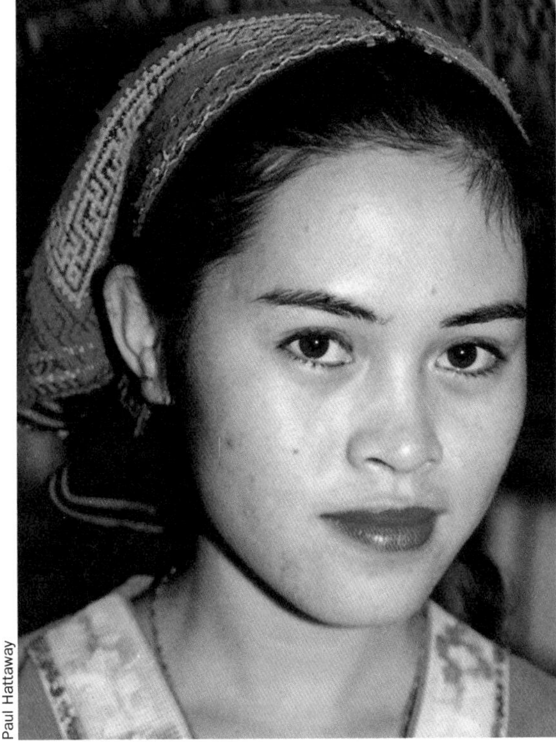

Paul Hattaway

Location: A 1987 linguistic survey listed 44,000 speakers of the Bendi Li language.[1] The Bendi language further divides into the Baisha dialect (36,000 speakers) and the Yuanmen dialect (8,000 speakers). The Bendi Li are one of five distinct Li tribes located on southern China's tropical Hainan Island. The Bendi inhabit the central part of the island, including the eastern half of Baisha County and northward to Yinggeling.

Identity: Although the various Li groups on Hainan Island acknowledge a common historical kinship, "they are divided into several groups, distinguishable by their different dialects [and costumes]."[2] The name *Li* means "black" or "dark brown"; it can also mean "numerous."[3]

Language: *Bendi* is the Chinese name for the speakers of this distinct language. Although there is a small measure of intelligibility between the various Li languages, "The Li language is really more like a collection of related languages."[4] Bendi Li contains five or six tones, compared to nine tones in some of the other Li languages. Bendi Li is part of the so-called *Kadai* language family. "The Kadai languages form one of two branches of Thai-Kadai.... The term Kadai was coined by Benedict from the human prefix 'ka' and the general term for the Tai group. Most of the Kadai languages are spoken by small populations in widely scattered areas, and some have extensive internal diversity."[5]

History: The ancestors of the Li are believed to have migrated to Hainan Island from the Mainland approximately 3,000 years ago. The state of Li is mentioned at the beginning of the tenth book of the Chinese *Book of History.* The state was conquered by the Chief of the West in AD 1123.[6] Historically the Chinese have viewed Hainan as a backward, undesirable place. When Li Deyu — a Chinese prime minister during the Tang Dynasty (618 – 907) — was exiled to Hainan, he described his new home as "the gate to hell."[7]

Customs: Until recently the Bendi Li relied on hunting and fishing for their survival. One visitor to Hainan Island noted, "The natives do not use fish hooks, but dam the numerous interior rivers and pour in root poison which stupefies the fish, making them easy to spear."[8]

Religion: The Bendi Li are mostly polytheists and animists, worshiping a multiplicity of gods and spirits. Before the antireligion purges of the Cultural Revolution, most Li villages had their own shaman who acted as a medium between the community and the spirit world.

Christianity: There is no known Christian presence among the Bendi Li. Of the more than one million Li on Hainan Island, only 1,000 believe in Jesus Christ.[9] The majority have never heard the gospel before. Tragically there are no Scriptures, gospel recordings, or *Jesus* film available in any of the Li languages. Historically, most evangelism conducted on Hainan Island has been aimed at the Hainanese Chinese.

Li, Ha 黎, 哈

Paul Hattaway

Location: Approximately 540,000 speakers of Ha Li are located in the western part of Hainan Island. The Ha Li live primarily in Ledong, Yaxian, and Dongfang counties, although they can also be found on the fringes of four other neighboring counties. Hainan was a hunter's paradise until recently, and even now a large number of wild animals can still be found in the more mountainous regions. In 1938 one visitor reported, "Hainan's wild-life includes two species of deer... porcupines, foxes, flying squirrels, monkeys, and pythons... there are also boars... leopards, black gibbons, and numerous birds such as parrots, pheasants, mynas, pigeons and doves."[1]

Identity: The Ha are the largest of the groups under the official Li nationality.

Language: The Ha language is the *lingua franca* used by most of the Li on Hainan Island. It has three main dialects. A Roman orthography for the Li was created in 1957. Ha Li shares 30% lexical similarity with Northern Zhuang, 27% with Gelao, and 26% with Dong.[2]

History: For centuries the Li rebelled against Chinese rule of Hainan. During World War II, the Li joined the Communists to fight the Japanese who had invaded the island in 1939. Hainan was considered a part of Guangdong until 1988, when it was granted status as a separate province.

Customs: Ha Li women in the past wore 56 huge earrings during festivals.[3] One visitor described their appearance: "The ears of the Ha women were weighted down with silver and brass, and their ankles were circled with silver and gold bands. The women I saw did not cover their breasts. They were very coy and shy.... The men were tall, many six feet, and wore their black or brown hair in big knots extending out about four inches from their foreheads.... Many wore turbans of red, white, and blue through which they extended a big knot. They dressed in G-strings, and carried great knives in baskets at their backs."[4]

Religion: The Ha Li god, Pa-Thung, "is a good god, and lives in some unknown place. But his agents, devils sent to watch the [Ha Li] villages, are ever present and always live in a nearby cave, in a river, in the jungle, or on a nearby mountain.... The villages have paid priests, or witchdoctors, who complain to Pa-Thung when local devils spitefully send thunder, lightning, and rain... or when they bring famine or sickness to the people."[5]

Christianity: Of the approximately 1,000 Li believers on Hainan Island, the majority are among the Ha Li. Because they have no Bible in their language to govern them, many Li churches are filled with rampant heresies and cultic activities. One Christian visitor described a bizarre Li church service. "The leader drinks a cup of tea which has been blessed by the Holy Spirit and sprays it over the believers. Then they close their eyes and dance until they become exhausted and fall to the ground.... The Li Christians lack familiarity with the Bible."[6]

Population in China:
390,000 (1987)
537,000 (2000)
692,800 (2010)
Location: Hainan Island
Religion: Animism
Christians: 600

Overview of the Ha Li

Countries: China

Pronunciation: "Ha-Lee"

Other Names: Lai, La, Loi, Le, Dli, Bli

Population Source: 450,000 (1987 *LAC*);[7] Out of a total Li population of 1,110,900 (1990 census)

Location: *Hainan Island:* Li-Miao Prefecture, especially in Ledong, Yaxian, and Dongfang counties; Some also in Baisha, Changjiang, Baoting, and Lingshui counties

Status: Officially included under Li

Language: Daic, Kadai, Li-Laqua

Dialects (3): Hayan (193,000), Luohuo (166,000), Baoxian (73,000)

Religion: Animism, Polytheism, Shamanism

Christians: 600

Scripture: None

***Jesus* film:** None

Gospel Recordings: Li: Hainan Ledung #04972
Li: Hainan Tongjia #04973

Christian Broadcasting: None

ROPAL code: LIC01

Status of Evangelization

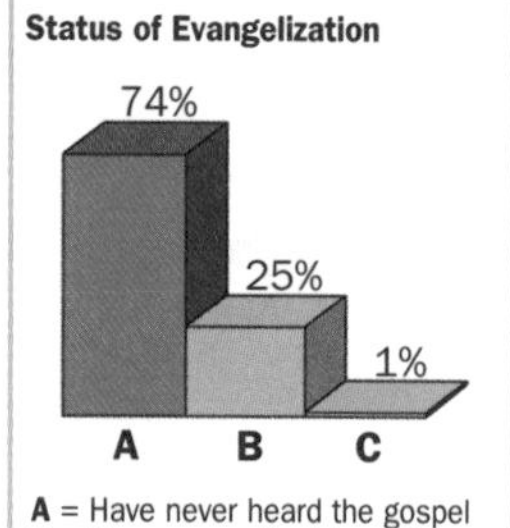

A = Have never heard the gospel
B = Were evangelized but did not become Christians
C = Are adherents to any form of Christianity

Li, Jiamao 黎,加茂

Location: Fifty-two thousand speakers of the Jiamao language were reported in a 1987 study.[1] They live in the southeastern part of Hainan Island, concentrated in the eastern and southern parts of Baoting County, as well as in parts of Lingshui and Qiongzhong counties. They live near Wuzhi (Five Finger) Mountain — the highest peak at 1,867 meters (6,124 ft.) on the island. The Lingshui River flows through Jiamao territory.

Identity: The Jiamao Li derive their name from the area they inhabit. Other Li groups call them *Kamau*. The Jiamao refer to themselves as *Tai*, which simply means "people."[2]

Language: The Jiamao language differs most from the other Li varieties and shares only about 40% of its lexicon with the other Li languages.[3] There are considerable differences between the Li languages, both phonetically and lexically. The Jiamao language consists of five tones, but "they do not correspond to those of the Ha, Qi, Bendi and Meifu dialects."[4] There are no dialect variations reported among the Jiamao.

History: The various Li groups, including the Jiamao Li, are proud of the fact that they are the original inhabitants of Hainan Island. During the Song and Yuan dynasties (960 – 1368), the Li staged 18 large-scale uprisings against oppressive Chinese rule on the island.[5] During the China-Vietnam War in the late 1970s, it was feared the Vietnamese would invade Hainan, but this fear proved unfounded. In recent years, territorial disputes over the Spratley Islands, which lie to the south of Hainan, have greatly increased tensions in the region. Virtually every country in Southeast Asia lays claim to the hundreds of tiny, oil-rich islands.

Paul Hattaway

Customs: For centuries Li women observed the custom of tattooing their bodies and faces at the onset of puberty. This was considered a mark of beauty. The Chinese have discouraged this practice. Today only old Li women can still be seen with tattoos.

Religion: The Jiamao Li are animists. They traditionally consulted shamans and witch doctors to deal with sickness. Today this practice has been replaced by Western and Chinese medicine. In the past, the Jiamao sacrificed animals to their gods and spirits. A chicken was killed for a minor sickness and a pig for a more serious illness. If someone was in danger of dying, the required sacrifice was to slaughter an ox in a vain bid to appease the offending spirits.

Christianity: The first recorded Christian presence on Hainan were the Jesuits, who came from Macau in 1630 and established a chapel at Fucheng.[6] The American Presbyterian Mission commenced work on Hainan Island in 1885 when Charles McCandliss was appointed as a missionary to the island. McCandliss and his wife lived on Hainan for 40 years. Their upright lives gave Christianity a good name among the people, and many came to Christ. Today there are a relative handful of Jiamao Christians. Most Jiamao have yet to hear the gospel, although gospel recordings are available in their language.

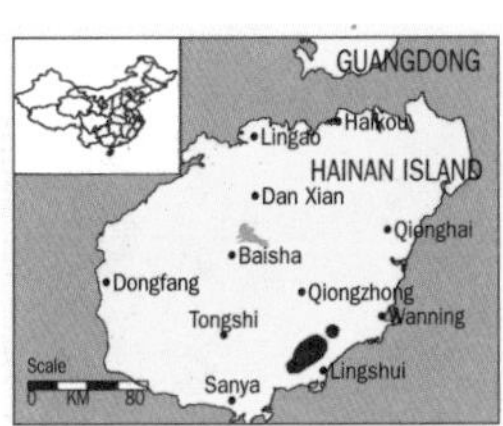

Population in China:
52,000 (1987)
71,600 (2000)
92,300 (2010)
Location: Hainan Island
Religion: Animism
Christians: 50

Overview of the Jiamao Li

Countries: China

Pronunciation: "Jeeah-maow-Lee"

Other Names: Kamau, Tai

Population Source:
52,000 (1987 *LAC*);
Out of a total Li population of 1,110,900 (1990 census)

Location: *SE Hainan Island:* Baoting, Lingshui, and Qiongzhong counties

Status:
Officially included under Li

Language: Daic, Kadai, Li-Laqua

Dialects: 0

Religion: Animism, Polytheism, Shamanism, Christianity

Christians: 50

Scripture: None

***Jesus* film:** None

Gospel Recordings:
Li: Baoting

Christian Broadcasting: None

ROPAL code: JIO00

Status of Evangelization

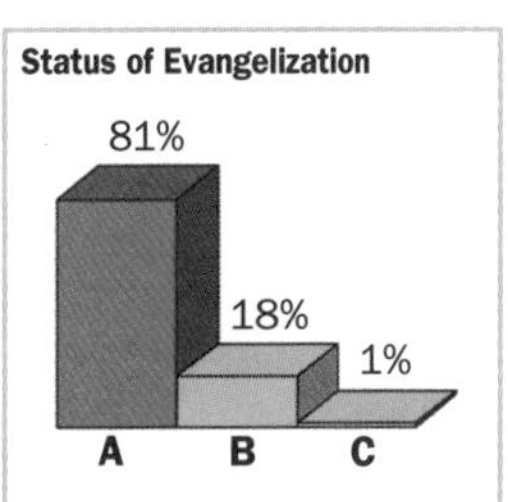

A = Have never heard the gospel
B = Were evangelized but did not become Christians
C = Are adherents to any form of Christianity

Li, Meifu 黎，美孚

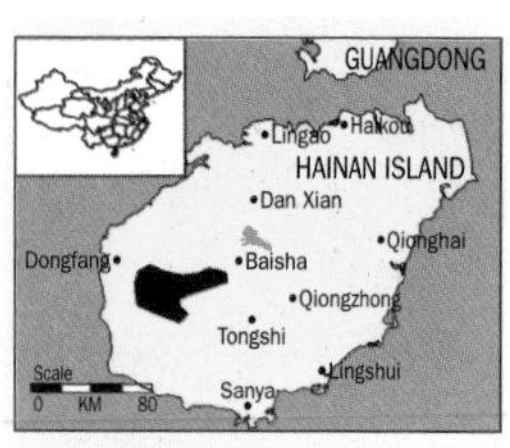

Population in China:
30,000 (1987)
41,300 (2000)
53,300 (2010)
Location: Hainan Island
Religion: Animism
Christians: None Known

Overview of the Meifu Li

Countries: China

Pronunciation: "May-foo Lee"

Other Names: Moifau

Population Source:
30,000 (1987 *LAC*);
Out of a total Li population of 1,110,900 (1990 census)

Location: *Hainan Island:* Cheyi and Dongfang counties

Status: Officially included under Li

Language: Daic, Kadai, Li-Laqua

Dialects: 0

Religion: Animism, Polytheism, No Religion

Christians: None known

Scripture: None

***Jesus* film:** None

Gospel Recordings: Li: Dongfang

Christian Broadcasting: None

ROPAL code: LIC03

Status of Evangelization

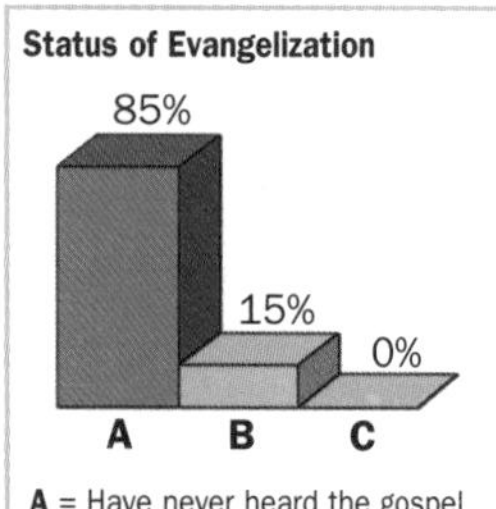

A = Have never heard the gospel
B = Were evangelized but did not become Christians
C = Are adherents to any form of Christianity

Location: The 1987 *Language Atlas of China* listed a population of 30,000 speakers of the Meifu Li language. The majority live along the western banks of the Changhua River in parts of the Cheyi and Dongfang counties. In the past the inhabitants of Hainan Island were decimated by disease, especially malignant malaria which wiped out whole villages. Minority populations grew little over the centuries and, in some areas, even declined. With the introduction of modern medicine, the Li people are experiencing rapid growth. The population of the Meifu Li is expected to rise to more than 41,000 by the year 2000, and 53,000 by 2010.

Identity: The Meifu are one of five different tribes that have been combined to form the official Li nationality in China.

Language: Meifu is a distinct language, not intelligible with other varieties of Li. Most Meifu Li are also able to speak the Ha Li language, which acts as the common language between members of the various Li groups. Speakers of Meifu Li refer to their language as *Moi Fau*, meaning "the Han people below."[1] Meifu has its own vocabulary, but it is phonetically similar to the Ha and Bendi Li languages.

History: The Li are believed to have once been part of the great Yue race which splintered to become today's Li, Zhuang, Bouyei, Shui, Dong, and Dai minority groups.[2] In the sixth century AD, Madame Xian, a political leader of the Yues in southern China, pledged allegiance to the Sui Dynasty.[3] This opened up Hainan Island to Chinese rule for the first time in history. The fact that the Meifu refer to themselves as "the Han people below" suggests that they may have been descended from Chinese migrants over the centuries, who intermingled with the Li and formed their own language.

Customs: In the past the Li lived in simple straw huts designed to withstand the many typhoons that strike the island every year. They dug a pit in the ground, placed bamboo or wood poles over it to form an oblong frame, and covered it with straw. The result was a low-lying structure that resembled an overturned boat.[4] As part of a Li wedding ceremony, the bride's family must kiss a pig and two fowls. The bride's eldest brother remains her legal guardian after the marriage.[5]

Religion: The Meifu Li traditionally believed in the existence of ghosts and devils, but now only the elderly practice spirit appeasement. The younger generation, having been educated in atheistic schools, rejects all such practices as foolish superstition.

Christianity: There are no known churches or Christians among the Meifu Li. Although many people on Hainan have come to Christ in recent years — the total number of believers has grown to approximately 70,000[6] — the majority of the converts are among the different Han Chinese language groups in the northern part of the island.

Paul Hattaway

Li, Qi 黎,杞

Location: The Qi Li are the second largest Li group on Hainan Island. Although numbering 178,000 speakers in 1987,[1] there are many more ethnic Qi Li who now can speak only Chinese. This people group is located in the central sections of Hainan Island, especially concentrated in Baoting and Qiongzhong counties.

Identity: The Qi Li are one of five distinct tribes of the official Li nationality. "The women of the Ki [Qi]... like those of all the Hainan tribes and sub-tribes, wore dress peculiar to their region. Their silver ornaments differed in design, and the headdress was a turban or sometimes a tasseled handkerchief."[2]

Language: The Qi Li are perhaps the most Sinicized of the various Li groups. Almost all Qi Li are bilingual in the Hainan dialect of Chinese. Qi consists of three dialects: Tongshi, Qiandui, and Baocheng. The Qiandui dialect group has been strongly influenced by the Chinese, both linguistically and culturally. In 1983, 78,000 members of the Li nationality were able to speak only Chinese.[3] The majority of these assimilated Li are from the Qi tribe. The Qi Li language has six tones.

History: The Qi Li have a long history of being bullied by Chinese landowners. Many chose to live back in the mountains beyond the reach of their oppressors, while those who remained in the valleys were gradually assimilated to Chinese culture and language.

Customs: Until recently divorce was not prohibited among the Li. "A [Li] widow cannot return to her parents; this is supposed to discourage prostitution, and promote marriage."[4]

Religion: The Qi Li living in more remote villages have many superstitions. They believe demons live in nature, especially in large mountains and waterfalls. In 1937 the Qi would not allow a Western traveler to visit a nearby waterfall, claiming it was the home of the devil.[5]

Christianity: The Qi Li are an unreached people group. Few have ever been approached with the gospel. The foundation of the American Presbyterian Mission on Hainan Island was laid by Carl C. Jeremiassen, a native of Denmark. He went to Hainan in 1881 as an independent, self-supporting missionary. "During that year he made a complete circuit of the island, treating the sick and distributing Chinese literature wherever he visited."[6] To the Qi Li, however, who had no prior knowledge of Christianity, this scattered seed fell on rocky soil. Decades later they told another foreigner about a man who had visited them long before and "who had stayed for only an hour. His name they did not know, but he distributed many papers showing a strange God with a beard!"[7] Today there are possibly several hundred believers among the Qi Li; however, without a Bible in their language, the few churches are weak and nominal.[8] There are no gospel recordings or other evangelistic tools available in the Qi Li language.

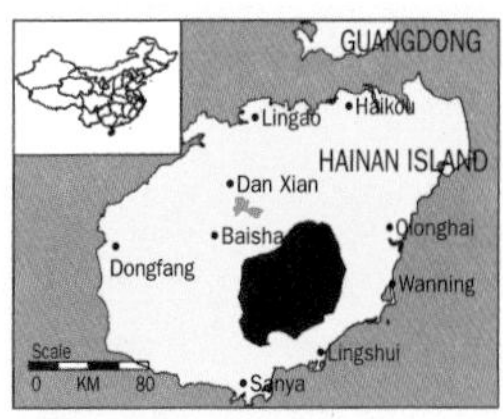

Population in China:
178,000 (1987)
245,100 (2000)
316,200 (2010)
Location: Hainan Island
Religion: Animism
Christians: 350

Overview of the Qi Li

Countries: China
Pronunciation: "Chee-Lee"
Other Names: Qi, Ki, Gei, Hei, Qiandui, Heitu
Population Source: 178,000 (1987 *LAC*); Out of a total Li population of 1,110,900 (1990 census)
Location: *Hainan Island:* Qiongzhong and Baoting counties
Status: Officially included under Li
Language: Daic, Kadai, Li-Laqua
Dialects (3): Tongshi (125,000), Qiandui (29,000), Baocheng (24,000)
Religion: Animism, Polytheism, No Religion, Christianity
Christians: 350
Scripture: None
***Jesus* film:** None
Gospel Recordings: None
Christian Broadcasting: None
ROPAL code: LIC02

Status of Evangelization

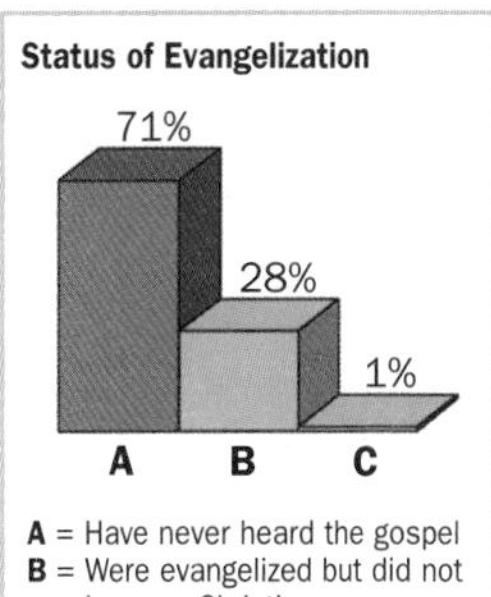

A = Have never heard the gospel
B = Were evangelized but did not become Christians
C = Are adherents to any form of Christianity

Limi 俐米

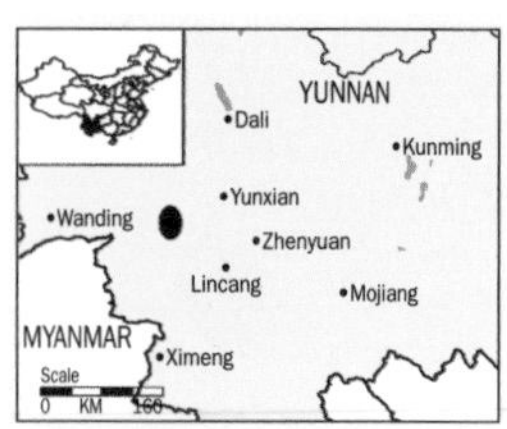

Population in China:
29,000 (1999)
29,700 (2000)
37,300 (2010)
Location: Yunnan
Religion: Polytheism
Christians: None Known

Overview of the Limi

Countries: China

Pronunciation: "Lee-mee"

Other Names:

Population Source:
29,000 (1999 J. Pelkey);
Out of a total Yi population of 6,572,173 (1990 census)

Location: *S Yunnan:* Yongde (24,000), Fengqing (4,000), and Yunxian (1,000) counties

Status:
Officially included under Yi

Language: Sino-Tibetan, Tibeto-Burman, Burmese-Lolo, Lolo, Northern Lolo, Yi, Western Yi

Dialects: 0

Religion: Polytheism, Animism, Ancestor Worship

Christians: None known

Scripture: None

***Jesus* film:** None

Gospel Recordings: None

Christian Broadcasting: None

ROPAL code: None

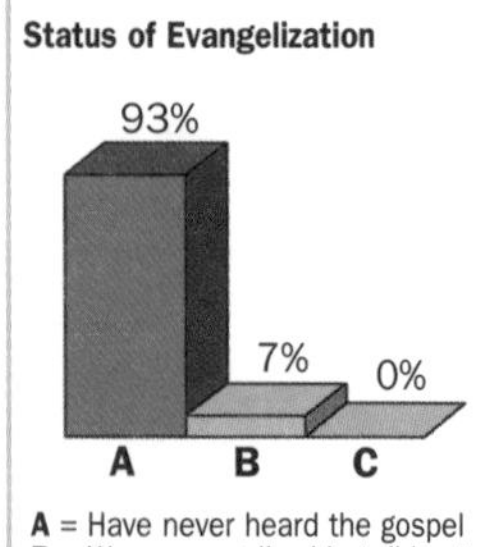

Location: Approximately 30,000 Limi live within southern Yunnan Province in southwest China. The majority inhabit areas within Yongde County. They are the majority group within the Wumulong District and make up a sizable portion of the population in Yalian District. Four thousand Limi live in Fengqing County where they are principally found in the southern part of Guodazhai District and in the southeastern part of Yingpan District. An additional 1,000 Limi live in Yunxian County.[1]

Jamin Pelkey

Identity: The Limi are one of more than 100 groups in Yunnan who have been combined into the official Yi nationality by the Chinese authorities. The Limi were first documented by China Inland Mission's John Kuhn in the 1940s. In his benchmark book, *We Found a Hundred Tribes*, Kuhn listed the Limi as a Lolo-speaking group located at "Qingku."[2] Qingku is the pre-1949 spelling of today's Jinggu County in Simao Prefecture.

Language: Limi is a part of the Western Yi linguistic branch of the Tibeto-Burman language family. Jamin Pelkey points out, "Most Limi villages are not mixed with Han Chinese or other minorities. The Limi language, as a result, has been very well preserved and is in active use. Judging from other unique aspects of Limi culture, their language is likely to be found widely different from other Western Yi varieties."[3]

History: The Limi claim that their ancestors came from a place called Dayuandi in Jingdong County long ago. They reportedly were slaves of a tyrannical master. One day the Limi escaped en masse and won their freedom. They moved to their present locations where they settled down and started new communities.

Customs: Compared to other Yi groups in the area, such as the Western Gaisu and some of the Laluo, the Limi culture has been well preserved. Until recently the Limi strictly refused to intermarry with the Han Chinese or even with other Yi groups. Because of this, they have gained a reputation for being something of an isolated, inward-looking group who have little contact with other people. The Limi joyously celebrate several festivals throughout the course of the year.

Religion: Polytheism, animism, and ancestor worship prevail among the Limi. Regular ceremonies are held to worship the spirits and honor their ancestors.[4]

Christianity: The independent mind-set of the Limi has contributed to them being unreached and largely unevangelized today. Few missionaries worked in the area prior to the expulsion of foreigners from China in the 1950s. If the Limi had been so fortunate to have workers like Gladys Aylward targeting them, they would have been greatly blessed. Aylward described the hardship she faced daily in China: "Life is pitiful, death so familiar, suffering and pain so common, yet I would not be anywhere else. Do not wish me out of this, or in any way seek to get me out, for I will not be got out while this trial is on. These are my people, God has given them to me, and I will live or die with them for Him and His glory."[5]

Limin 里民

Population in China:
50,000 (1982)
76,100 (2000)
98,100 (2010)
Location: Guizhou
Religion: Animism
Christians: 100

Overview of the Limin

Countries: China

Pronunciation: "Lee-min"

Other Names: Li Ren, Limingzi, Chiming, Turen, Jiuren, Tulao, Lijia

Population Source: 50,000 (1982 *Minzu Shibie Wenxian Ziliao Huibian*)

Location: *W Guizhou:* Luzhi, Guanling, Qinglong, Pu'an, Xingren, Zhenning, and Anlong counties; A few are in Guiyang, Qianxi, and Qingzhen counties.

Status: Officially included under Yi since 1985; Previously included in a list of *Undetermined Minorities*

Language: Sino-Tibetan, Tibeto-Burman, Unclassified

Dialects: 0

Religion: Animism, Ancestor Worship, No Religion, Christianity

Christians: 100

Scripture: None

***Jesus* film:** None

Gospel Recordings: None

Christian Broadcasting: None

ROPAL code: None

Status of Evangelization

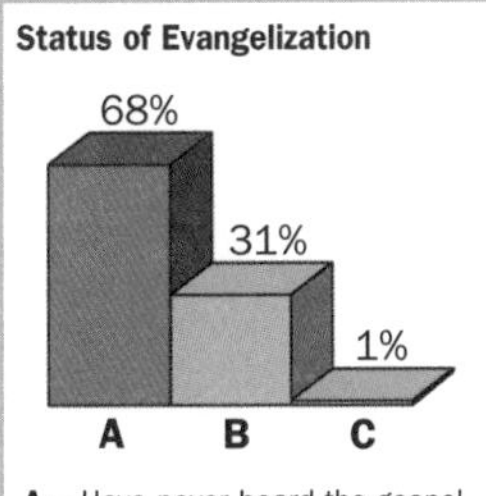

A = Have never heard the gospel
B = Were evangelized but did not become Christians
C = Are adherents to any form of Christianity

Location: In 1982 an official Chinese publication listed a population of 50,000 Limin people living in western Guizhou Province.[1] The Limin are primarily distributed throughout Luzhi, Guanling, Pu'an, Xingren, Zhenning, and Anlong counties. A small number of Limin are also found in Guiyang, Qianxi, and Qingzhen counties of Guizhou Province.

Identity: In the 1982 census the Limin were included in a list of *Undetermined Minorities*. When the Chinese authorities surveyed the groups on that list, however, the village leaders of the Limin told the government officials that they "wanted to be identified as Yi."[2] Their desire was granted in 1985, so that today they are officially considered part of the Yi nationality. Despite this event, most Limin still consider themselves to be a distinct people group. It is possible that they asked to be included in the Yi minority out of fear of being included in a group they did not like, rather than for any affinity they may feel for other Yi people. The Limin should not be mistaken for the Limi, a Yi group in Yunnan Province.

Language: Although all Limin people now adequately speak the Guizhou dialect of Mandarin Chinese, traces of the original Limin tongue remain in the more isolated villages. No thorough research has been conducted yet to determine how the Limin language relates to other members of the Tibeto-Burman family.

History: Before the reign of Emperor Dao Guan in the Qing Dynasty (1644–1911), there was no record of the Limin in Guizhou Province. It seems likely that they migrated into the area from another location at that time. During the latter half of the Qing Dynasty the Limin began to grow and become an influential group. Even today the Limin have a reputation for being good businessmen.

Customs: Most Limin have been assimilated by the Han Chinese who have migrated into the area in large numbers since the 1400s. In the last 200 years the Han population in western Guizhou has exploded. Although they are now officially Yi, most people in the area consider the Limin to be Han people. To complicate matters, Limin women's clothing resembles that of their Miao neighbors. The Limin, who celebrate Han festivals, are known as good poets. They love to write and recite romantic poetry.

Religion: The Limin do not consider themselves to be religious people. If an outsider asks them what religion they follow, their answer will invariably be "none." People in China do not consider animism to be a religion like Buddhism, Islam, or Christianity. In reality, the Limin practice spirit worship and also worship their ancestors.

Christianity: There are believed to be a few hundred scattered Limin Christians in Guizhou Province. In 1999 two Limin evangelists tried to reach out to their own people but, finding a cool reception, turned instead to the Bouyei living in the same area, resulting in 300 new converts.

Paul Hattaway

Lingao 临高

Location: More than 640,000 speakers of Lingao inhabit four counties in the northern part of Hainan Island, including the provincial capital Haikou, and as far west as Bolian Township. Visitors to Hainan are often surprised at the number of modern vehicles and electrical appliances used there. This is the result of government corruption during the 1980s. In 1983 the central government allocated massive amounts of valuable foreign exchange funds to Hainan, in an effort to improve the island's infrastructure and to make the province more attractive to foreign tourism and investment. Hainan officials saw it as an opportunity to indulge themselves. US$1.5 billion was used to purchase 90,000 new Japanese cars from Hong Kong. Most of these were then transported to the Mainland and sold at a massive profit. The shopping list also included 2.9 million color TVs, 252,000 video recorders, and 122,000 motorcycles.[1]

Identity: The Lingao, despite speaking their own Tai language, have been officially included as members of the Han Chinese nationality. "Although they regard themselves as Han people, they are regarded as Li people in historical records and by the Han people on Hainan Island."[2] The Lingao call their language the "village language" — the same name as the Cun people on the west coast of Hainan. To avoid confusion, the Chinese have labeled this group *Lingao*.

Language: Although the use of the Lingao language is widespread, "it has no orthography and is not taught in schools."[3] Scholars disagree regarding the linguistic affiliation of Lingao. Some consider it "closely related to Bouyei, Giay, and Northern Zhuang."[4] Many city-dwelling Lingao are bilingual in the local dialect of Chinese, and some speak Mandarin as a third language. Most rural Lingao, especially women and children, are unable to speak any language except their own.[5]

Paul Hattaway

Customs: Many Lingao fish in the Beibu Gulf between Hainan and the Chinese Mainland. Every year, between May and October, severe storms lash the area.

History: The Lingao language suggests they may have originally been Zhuang who migrated from the Mainland. Hainan has belonged to China for about 2,000 years. "Yet the Chinese have occupied little more than its fringe, and among them the legend still persists that the wild men of the interior have tails!"[6]

Religion: The majority of Lingao are animists. In some locations a multiplicity of spirit beings and ghosts are worshiped. Ancestor worship is also common.

Christianity: In 1630 Jesuit priests from Macau came and set up a chapel in Fucheng — then the capital of Qiongzhou.[7] More than 250 years later, in the 1880s, Danish missionary Carl Jeremiassen also "settled down in Fucheng, Qiongshan County, where he bought the Ancestral Hall... and turned it into a church."[8] Today, most of the Christians on Hainan are in the northern part of the island. Many Han and Lingao youth have found Christ in recent years, as both official and underground churches report overflowing crowds at their meetings.

Population in China:
520,000 (1982)
641,700 (2000)
725,100 (2010)
Location: Hainan Island
Religion: Animism
Christians: 5,000

Overview of the Lingao

Countries: China

Pronunciation: "Lin-gaw"

Other Names: Be, Ongbe, Vo Limkou, Limkou, Limkow

Population Source: 520,000 (1982 census); Out of a total Han population of 1,042,482,187 (1990 census)

Location: *North Central Hainan Island:* Lingao, Dengmai, Qiongshan, and Dan counties

Status: Officially included under Han Chinese

Language: Daic, Kadai

Dialects (3): Lincheng (350,000), Qiongshan (170,000), Lingao

Religion: Animism, Polytheism, No Religion, Ancestor Worship, Christianity

Christians: 5,000

Scripture: None

***Jesus* film:** None

Gospel Recordings: None

Christian Broadcasting: None

ROPAL code: ONB00

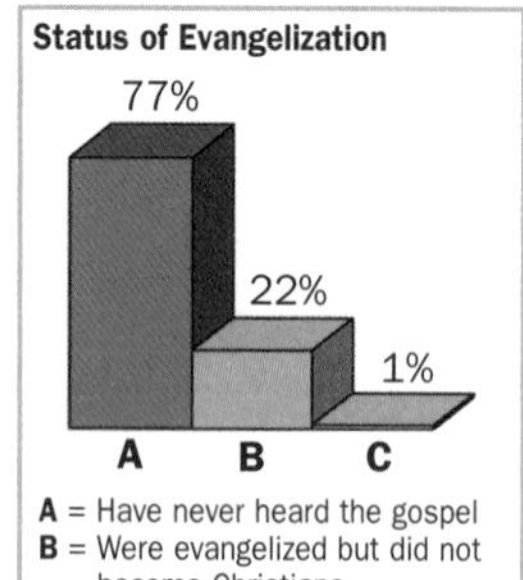

Linghua 伶话

Population in China:
20,000 (1991)
22,300 (2000)
25,200 (2010)
Location: Guangxi
Religion: Ancestor Worship
Christians: None Known

Overview of the Linghua

Countries: China

Pronunciation: "Ling-hwa"

Other Names:

Population Source:
20,000 (1991 *EDCL*);
Out of a total Han population of 1,042,482,187 (1990 census)

Location:
NE Guangxi: Longsheng County

Status: Probably officially included under Han Chinese

Language: Chinese, Linghua

Dialects: 0

Religion: Ancestor Worship, Polytheism, Animism

Christians: None known

Scripture: None

***Jesus* film:** None

Gospel Recordings: None

Christian Broadcasting: None

ROPAL code: None

Status of Evangelization

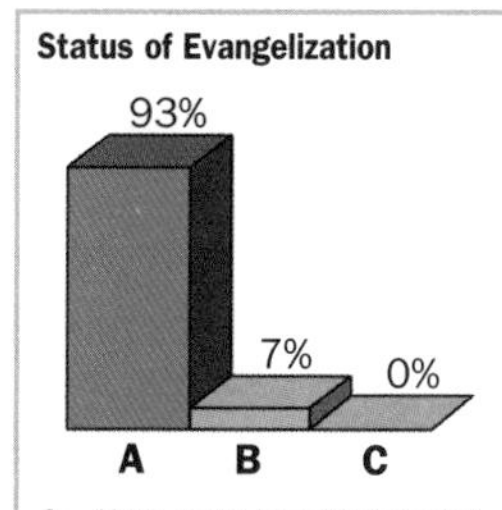

A = Have never heard the gospel
B = Were evangelized but did not become Christians
C = Are adherents to any form of Christianity

Paul Hattaway

Location: Linghua is a language reportedly spoken by 20,000 people in Longsheng County, in the northeast of the Guangxi Zhuang Autonomous Region.[1] Longsheng, a verdant mountainous area, is also home to the Younuo people group who are known locally as the *Red Yao*.

Identity: Linghua is an entirely linguistic classification. It is not known what ethnic name the speakers of this language call themselves. *Hua* means "speech" in China; *Linghua* is therefore a linguistic term. Linghua is not the same as Pinghua, a language spoken by approximately two million people in other parts of Guangxi, although the origins of the two languages may be similar. Even though their speech displays many influences from Miao, the Linghua have almost certainly been officially counted as members of the Han Chinese nationality.

Language: One scholar has stated that Linghua is "spoken by twenty thousand people in Longsheng, Guangxi,... and is possibly a Miao-Chinese mixture."[2] There are several languages of unusual interest in the Guangxi-Guizhou-Hunan border areas, including Mjuniang, Waxiang, and Aoka. These languages appear to be "hybrids of Chinese dialects and minority languages."[3]

History: The area now inhabited by the Linghua speakers was once solely the domain of tribal, non-Han Chinese people. As the Han expanded and multiplied, Han migrants started to enter the area several hundred years ago and found themselves a minority among a diverse collection of ethnic groups. Languages like Linghua are the result of fusion between the Han and minorities.

Customs: Living in mountains that contain a bulging population, there is little spare land available for the Linghua to cultivate rice and other crops. Many Linghua villages have water fed to them through bamboo pipes leading from the nearest river or stream.

Religion: The main religious adherence of the Linghua is ancestor worship. People in China who worship their ancestors do not consider it a religion, but it does dominate their spiritual thinking and requires a measure of devotion to the rituals and ceremonies associated with it.

Christianity: There are no known Christians among the 20,000 Linghua. Prior to 1949 Guangxi was one of the provinces in China most neglected by missionaries. Its lack of roads and infrastructure, and its diverse number of languages and tribal peoples made ministry and evangelistic progress in Guangxi difficult. A 1922 mission report stated, "In Guangxi 30 *hsiens* [counties] remain unclaimed by any Protestant mission society. Only eight *hsiens* report more than 100 communicants each.... There is an average of one Protestant church member to approximately 2,300 inhabitants in the province.... Over 33,000 sq. miles [85,470 sq. km.] of Guangxi remains unclaimed by any Protestant missionary society. Here and there occasional evangelistic work is done, but no Christian organization is seriously facing the need of these areas with a sense of sole responsibility."[4] The Linghua can be adequately reached through the use of Chinese materials.

Lipo, Eastern 理泼(东)

Jamin Pelkey

Location: Approximately 90,000 Eastern Lipo live in scattered communities across three counties in northern Yunnan and southern Sichuan provinces, primarily along the upper Yangtze River watershed.[1] The majority live in Wuding and Yuanmou counties. Eastern Lipo communities are located from Panzhihua in Sichuan all the way down to the outskirts of Kunming city in Yunnan.

Identity: Strangely, the Eastern Lipo have been included in the Lisu nationality at local administrative levels but are considered part of the Yi nationality at the national level — a classification that angers them.[2] They have more in common historically and linguistically with the Lisu than with the Yi. The Eastern Lipo have a different language, dress, and history from the Western Lipo.

Language: Although the Eastern Lipo language is closely related to Lisu on the China-Myanmar border,[3] the Chinese have classified Eastern Lipo as a Yi language.

History: The Eastern Lipo originally lived with the Lisu in the Salween Valley, but they migrated to the Wuding area after suffering a crushing military defeat at the Salween River in 1812.[4] In October 1995 a huge earthquake struck the Wuding District. One hundred and thirty thousand homes — many belonging to Eastern Lipo people — were destroyed. Fifty people were killed, 1,000 wounded, and 200,000 people were left homeless.

Customs: The Eastern Lipo occasionally intermarry with neighboring tribes. Most of their culture is now centered around the church and their strong Christian faith.

Religion: The majority of Eastern Lipo are professing Christians. They were first converted by Australian missionary-doctor Arthur Nicholls, who traveled to the area in 1906.[5] Conversions occurred almost immediately. In 1907, 60 Eastern Lipo believers traveled 97 kilometers (60 mi.) to Sapushan to participate in the Harvest Thanksgiving Service.[6] In 1913 the four Gospels were translated into Eastern Lipo, using the Pollard script.[7] By 1922 it was reported that the Lipo's "progress toward self-support is truly amazing and most gratifying. Already in many centers half of the working expenses are met by the native church."[8] The Eastern Lipo church experienced severe persecution during the 1960s and 1970s. In 1978 one pastor "had both his arms crippled from being hung up for 15 days with galvanized wire which was wrenched tighter with pliers after every refusal to give up his faith."[9]

Christianity: In 1986 the Eastern Lipo, Naluo, Gesu, Eastern Nasu, A-Hmao, and Han believers in Sayingpan built Yunnan's largest church (1,500 seats) with their own labor and money. Their dedication and sacrifice was a tremendous witness to the local authorities. By 1988, in Luquan County alone, 475 Communist cadres and 390 Communist Youth League members had accepted the gospel.[10] By 1990 there was estimated to be at least 60,000 Eastern Lipo believers.[11] In early 1998 Eastern Lipo churches sent evangelists to ten unreached minorities throughout southern China.

Population in China:
80,000 (1995)
90,200 (2000)
113,300 (2010)
Location: Yunnan, Sichuan
Religion: Christianity
Christians: 60,000

Overview of the Eastern Lipo

Countries: China

Pronunciation: "Lee-po"

Other Names: Eastern Lisu, Lipoo, Lipuo, Lisu Taku, He Lisu, Black Lisu, Taku, Machi, Machipuo, Lizu, Li-a, Heipo

Population Source: 80,000 (1995 J. Pelkey); Out of a total Yi population of 6,572,173 (1990 census)

Location: *N Yunnan:* Wuding (27,000), Yuanmou (17,000), and Luquan (10,000) counties; *S Sichuan:* Huili, Huidong, and Pingdi counties

Status: Officially included under Yi on a national level, and Lisu on a district, county, and prefecture level

Language: Sino-Tibetan, Tibeto-Burman, Burmic, Burmese-Lolo, Lolo, Northern Lolo, Lisu

Dialects: 0

Religion: Christianity, Animism

Christians: 60,000

Scripture: New Testament 1951; Portions 1913; Work in progress

***Jesus* film:** None

Gospel Recordings: Lipo #04669

Christian Broadcasting: None

ROPAL code: TKL00

Status of Evangelization

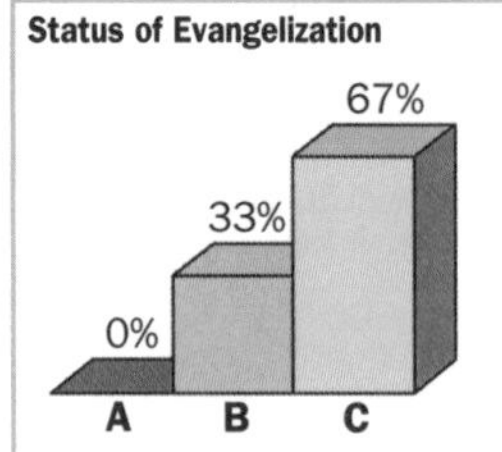

A = Have never heard the gospel
B = Were evangelized but did not become Christians
C = Are adherents to any form of Christianity

Lipo, Western 理泼(西)

Location: More than 146,000 Western Lipo live in an impoverished area of northern Yunnan Province. They inhabit six counties in Yunnan — Dayao, Yongren, Yuanmou, Binchuan, Yao'an, and Yongsheng. A small number of Western Lipo spill across the border into the Renhe District of Panzhihua County in Sichuan Province.

Identity: There is a great deal of confusion regarding the classification of the Lipo. The Lipo as a whole have been officially included as part of the Yi nationality in China, yet among the Lipo are two very distinct groups, which here are defined as Eastern and Western Lipo. The two do not consider themselves to be the same people. They have different histories, dress, customs, and languages. This century a further distinction has developed between the two groups: the Eastern Lipo are known as a Christian tribe while the Western Lipo have relatively few Christians. *Lipo* means "insiders." They refer to the Han Chinese as *Xipo*, or "outsiders."

Language: While Eastern Lipo is a language related to Lisu, Western Lipo is part of the Central Yi language group. One scholar believes that the two languages may share as little as 50% lexical similarity.[1] Western Lipo is quite closely related to Luoluopo. These two languages reportedly contain between 80% and 93% lexical similarity.[2]

History: One of the key elements in understanding the separation of the Lipo into two distinct groups is their past. While the Eastern Lipo are a Lisu-speaking group who migrated to their present location after a military defeat in 1812,[3] the Western Lipo claim to have originated in Nanjing or Jiangxi in eastern China. According to local accounts, "the ancestors of today's Lipuo [Western Lipo] came as soldiers at various times from the early Ming to the early Qing dynasties [late 14th century to late 17th century]. Historical records confirm that those dynasties did send military expeditions to the area that is now Yongren; we can speculate that today's Lipuo [Western Lipo] are descendants of intermarriage between Han troops... and local women."[4]

Jamin Pelkey

Customs: The headdresses of Western Lipo women "come in four or five motley varieties. Men and women alike wear long goat-skin cape-vests and sport magnificently hand-embroidered shoulder bags. Although the younger generations seem to be forgetting their folk-tales and legends, ethnic music, song, and dance are still flourishing."[5]

Religion: The majority of Western Lipo are polytheists. They worship many spirits and protective deities, including mountain deities. In most ways the Western Lipo mirror the religious beliefs of the Luoluopo.

Christianity: Although the Eastern Lipo are a thoroughly Christian group, few Western Lipo have been evangelized. Most of the 200 known Western Lipo Christians are Catholics. In northeastern Binchuan County and in the Yupaojiang and Tiesuo districts of Dayao County, Catholic churches were planted before 1949. These are believed to contain some Western Lipo members today.

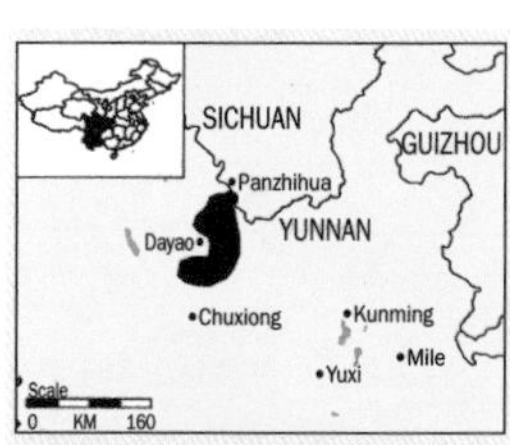

Population in China:
142,800 (1999)
146,400 (2000)
183,700 (2010)
Location: Yunnan, Sichuan
Religion: Polytheism
Christians: 200

Overview of the Western Lipo

Countries: China

Pronunciation: "Lee-po"

Other Names: Lipoo, Lipuo, Lipo: Dayao, Li, Lipa, Tujia, Lizu, Gaoshanzu

Population Source:
142,800 (1999 J. Pelkey);
Out of a total Yi population of 6,572,173 (1990 census)

Location: *N Yunnan:* Dayao (76,000), Yongren (44,600), Yuanmou (10,500), Binchuan (6,000), Yao'an (3,500), and Yongsheng (2,200) counties; *S Sichuan:* Renhe District in Panzhihua County

Status:
Officially included under Yi

Language: Sino-Tibetan, Tibeto-Burman, Burmic, Burmese-Lolo, Lolo, Northern Lolo, Yi, Central Yi

Dialects: 0

Religion: Polytheism, Animism, No Religion, Christianity

Christians: 200

Scripture: None

***Jesus* film:** None

Gospel Recordings: None

Christian Broadcasting: None

ROPAL code: None

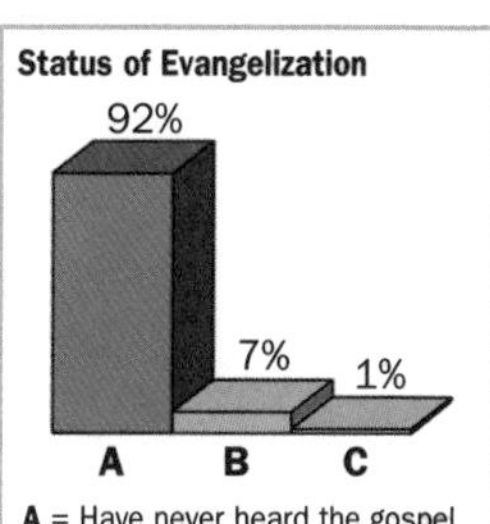

A = Have never heard the gospel
B = Were evangelized but did not become Christians
C = Are adherents to any form of Christianity

Lisu 傈僳

Population in China:
574,856 (1990)
715,100 (2000)
889,600 (2010)
Location:
Yunnan, Sichuan, Tibet
Religion: Christianity
Christians: 300,000

Overview of the Lisu

Countries:
China, Myanmar, Thailand, India

Pronunciation: "Lee-soo"

Other Names: Southern Lisu, Lissu, Lisaw, Lishaw, Lihsaw, Lu-tzu, Lesuo, Lishu, Leisu, Lusu, Khae, Leshuoopa, Loisu, Yaw Yen, Yawyin, Yeh Jen, Chung, Cheli, Chedi, Lipa, Lissoo

Population Source:
574,856 (1990 census);
480,960 (1982 census);[1]
126,000 in Myanmar;
16,000 in Thailand;
Also in India

Location:
W Yunnan;[2] *S Sichuan; SE Tibet*

Status:
An official minority of China

Language: Sino-Tibetan, Tibeto-Burman, Burmese-Lolo, Lolo, Northern Lolo, Lisu

Literacy: 28%

Dialects (6): Nujiang, Yongsheng, Luquan, Hua Lisu, White Lisu, Lushi Lisu

Religion: Christianity, Animism

Christians: 300,000

Scripture: Bible 1968; New Testament 1938; Portions 1921

***Jesus* film:** Available

Gospel Recordings:
Western Lisu #00108

Christian Broadcasting:
Available (FEBC)

ROPAL code: LISOO

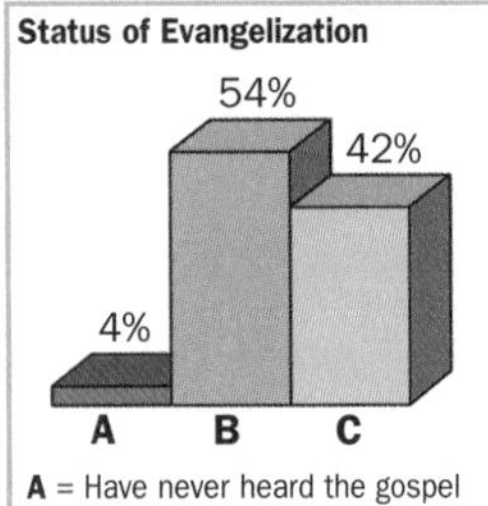

Location: More than 700,000 Lisu live among the massive mountains and deep valleys of the Nujiang, Salween, and Yangtze river basins in southwest China. The majority of Lisu live in Yunnan Province. An additional 15,000 live in Sichuan, and a small number can also be found in southern Tibet. Thousands of Lisu migrated from their original homeland during the last century. Many now live in faraway Myanmar, Thailand, and northeast India.

Identity: The Lisu are one of China's official minorities. The name *Lisu* means "come-down people." Their original home was in eastern Tibet, where they had a kingdom in the tenth century before they migrated to their present homes in China and Myanmar.[3]

Language: Lisu is part of the Yi branch of Tibeto-Burman. Although an early visitor stated that "nearly every village speaks a different dialect,"[4] the Lisu language today is reported to be fairly uniform.

History: The Lisu have a long history of being oppressed by greedy landlords and governments. The Lisu revolt of 1801–03 proved devastating. The Qing government mobilized a huge army of more than 10,000 soldiers from three provinces. Chinese writers criticized this campaign as "using a cattle knife to kill chickens."[5] During the 1940s the Lisu had to pay 65 different types of taxes and levies — including one of ¥3.5 for each airplane flying over their region![6] This provocation resulted in thousands of Lisu seeking life in a new country. Missionary Lilian Hamer described one scene as the Lisu she had sought to reach left en masse: "I saw little children clinging to their mother's skirts, older folk carrying iron cooking pots, blankets, oil lamps. I stood outside my door and watched this wholesale evacuation of the people I had served and loved, mourned and wept over."[7]

Customs: Before they embraced Christianity, the Lisu were described as "utter savages."[8] They were so given over to alcohol that when one newly converted village threw out all their liquor, all the pigs in the village got drunk![9] A passion for gambling often degraded the Lisu into an abyss of suffering. "When they have gambled away their money, they will often stake their children, their wives, and even themselves as slaves. As a result, in one night a whole family can be gambled away into life-long slavery."[10]

Religion: The conversion of the Lisu is one of the greatest stories in mission history. Their mass turning to Christ was due in part to their ancient belief in Wa Sa, a supreme god of Healing and a village guardian. During one interrogation by the Communists, a young Lisu man exclaimed, "Christianity has already penetrated into our flesh and blood and it will not be easy to tear it away from us."[11]

Christianity: A number of missionaries labored self-sacrificially among the Lisu prior to 1949, including James Fraser, A. B. Cooke, John and Isobel Kuhn, and the Morse family. In 1916 and 1917 alone, Fraser baptized 60,000 Lisu.[12] Today there are an estimated 300,000 Lisu believers in China.[13] The Lisu church has reached out to many other groups in the area, including the Deqen Tibetans.

Dwayne Graybill

Liude 六德

Target Ministries

Location: With a population of approximately 1,400 people, the Liude ethnic group inhabits a few villages within the Liude District of Yongsheng County in northern Yunnan Province.[1]

Identity: The Liude were one of 260 ethnic groups in Yunnan Province who applied for recognition as minority nationalities in the 1950s. The central authorities rejected the Liude, along with 90% of the other groups in Yunnan. Instead, the Liude were officially placed in the Yi nationality. The Liude are closely related to the 7,000 Talu people who live in the same area.

Language: The Liude language belongs to the Northern Yi branch of the Tibeto-Burman family. It has absorbed many features of Xiaoliangshan Nosu, who are the dominant Yi group in northern Yunnan.

History: For centuries the Liude, along with other Yi groups, have celebrated weddings with great excitement. Traditional customs are followed. According to one observer at a Yi wedding, "When we came to the bride's home, we saw many groups of girls busily filling jars, basins and even trays with water to be poured on the young fellows who came to take the bride to her new husband's home. At sunset, the escort team arrived at the bride's house with wine and meat as gifts. The moment they stepped into the house, the girls started splashing them with water. According to local custom, the young men could not counter-attack; all they could do was try and dodge. After the water-splashing, the girls began to smear the young men's faces with soot scraped from the bottom of a pan. This is actually a kind of social activity among the youth of the Yi nationality, giving them opportunity for furthering their acquaintance and possibly falling in love."[2]

Customs: According to Chinese writer Wu Si, the wedding rituals continue the following day, starting before sunrise. "The bride was carried pickaback out of her home by a male cousin. Local customs forbid a bride to start the journey after daybreak and, no matter how great the distance, she is not allowed to let her feet touch the ground.... But where was the groom? Well, he was not to be seen that day. On the following day the bride was escorted back to her own home by her cousin and stayed there for a night, and only then did the groom, accompanied by some of the young men of his village, appear. The party carried wine and meat and herded before them sheep and hogs, gifts for the bride's family. Even then it was a few more days before the groom could send people to his wife's home to bring her back. Then, and only then, were the couple considered man and wife."[3]

Religion: The Liude have many gods and spirits that must be appeased in order to maintain order in the community. Ancestors are also worshiped.

Christianity: There has never been a church or a known Christian among the Liude. They are one of many desperately needy unreached people groups living in the mountains of northern Yunnan Province. There are no Scriptures or recordings available in the Liude language.

Population in China:
1,400 (1999)
1,430 (2000)
1,800 (2010)
Location: Yunnan
Religion: Polytheism
Christians: None Known

Overview of the Liude

Countries: China
Pronunciation: "Lee-ou-deh"
Other Names: Liudepo
Population Source:
1,400 (1999 J. Pelkey);
Out of a total Yi population of 6,572,173 (1990 census)
Location:
N Yunnan: Yongsheng County
Status:
Officially included under Yi
Language: Sino-Tibetan, Tibeto-Burman, Burmese-Lolo, Lolo, Northern Lolo, Yi, Northern Yi
Dialects: 0
Religion: Polytheism, Animism, Ancestor Worship
Christians: None known
Scripture: None
***Jesus* film:** None
Gospel Recordings: None
Christian Broadcasting: None
ROPAL code: None

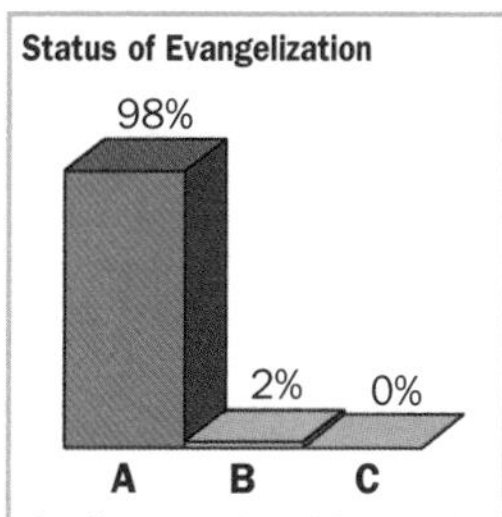

Liujia 六甲

Population in China:
4,000 (1999)
4,050 (2000)
4,570 (2010)
Location: Guizhou
Religion: Ancestor Worship
Christians: None Known

Overview of the Liujia

Countries: China

Pronunciation: "Lee-u-jeeah"

Other Names: Liu, Liujiaren

Population Source:
4,000 (1999 AMO);
Out of a total Han population of 1,042,482,187 (1990 census)

Location: *W Guizhou*

Status: Officially included under Han Chinese since 1985; Previously included in a list of *Undetermined Minorities*

Language:
Chinese, Guizhou dialect

Dialects: 0

Religion: Ancestor Worship, Animism, Daoism, No Religion

Christians: None known

Scripture: None

***Jesus* film:** None

Gospel Recordings: None

Christian Broadcasting: None

ROPAL code: None

Status of Evangelization

	A	B	C
%	90%	10%	0%

A = Have never heard the gospel
B = Were evangelized but did not become Christians
C = Are adherents to any form of Christianity

Location: More than 4,000 Liujia people inhabit villages in an unspecified part of western Guizhou Province in southern China.[1] Guizhou has a reputation in China as one of the poorest and most backward areas of the nation. The soil is generally rocky and yields poor harvests. Famine and starvation have been problems for the province's inhabitants throughout history.

Paul Hattaway

Identity: At the time of the 1982 census the Liujia, who are also known as the Liujiaren, had not been classified under any of China's 56 official nationalities. In 1985, after further investigation, the Liujia were placed in the Han Chinese nationality.[2] This decision was based on historical records which showed the Liujia were originally Han immigrants who moved to Guizhou. The Liujia, however, after living for centuries alongside minority peoples and absorbing many of their customs and identity, believe they are a minority group and are upset at being called Han.

Language: Although preliminary studies show that the Liujia have adopted a number of non-Chinese loanwords in their speech, the Liujia fundamentally speak the Guizhou dialect of Mandarin Chinese, known as *Guizhouhua*. The form of Mandarin spoken in this part of southern China is often looked down upon by Mandarin speakers from the north who consider the Guizhou accent uncouth.

History: One of the main reasons for the Liujia's opposition to being identified as Han Chinese results from the persecution and discrimination they have suffered from the Chinese over the centuries. The main bulk of Chinese settlers entered Guizhou between the fifteenth and eighteenth centuries. Before that time, with the exception of isolated cases such as the Liujia, Chuanlan, and Chuanqing peoples, Guizhou was inhabited entirely by tribal peoples. The later Han migrants also viewed the Liujia as a minority group, drove them off the best land into the remote mountains, and attempted to assimilate them by forbidding them to speak their own language or celebrate their festivals.

Customs: The Liujia possess their own traditional style of dress, similar to that of their minority neighbors. These days the dress is usually worn only for festivals and other special occasions, but it continues to make a statement that the Liujia do not consider themselves to be Han people. The Liujia have also absorbed other parts of minority culture, including food preparation and eating styles.

Religion: Liujia religious life consists of elements of ancestor worship, animism, and Daoism. Every home contains an ancestral altar on which incense and food is placed as an offering to the souls of their deceased relatives.

Christianity: The Liujia are believed to be an unreached people group with no known Christians in their midst. Catholic mission work dating back 300 years and Protestant mission work which commenced in 1877 have been carried out in various parts of Guizhou Province with mixed results, but the message of eternal life in Jesus Christ has yet to reach the ears of the Liujia people. Chinese Scriptures and gospel recordings in the Guizhou dialect are available.

Liwu 里乌

Population in China:
4,200 (1999)
4,300 (2000)
5,400 (2010)
Location: Yunnan
Religion: Polytheism
Christians: None Known

Overview of the Liwu

Countries: China

Pronunciation: "Lee-woo"

Other Names: Liang'e Ren

Population Source:
4,200 (1999 J. Pelkey);
Out of a total Yi population of 6,572,173 (1990 census)

Location:
N Yunnan: Yongsheng County

Status:
Officially included under Yi

Language: Sino-Tibetan, Tibeto-Burman, Burmese-Lolo, Lolo, Northern Lolo, Yi, Northern Yi

Dialects: 0

Religion: Polytheism, Animism, Ancestor Worship

Christians: None known

Scripture: None

***Jesus* film:** None

Gospel Recordings: None

Christian Broadcasting: None

ROPAL code: None

Status of Evangelization

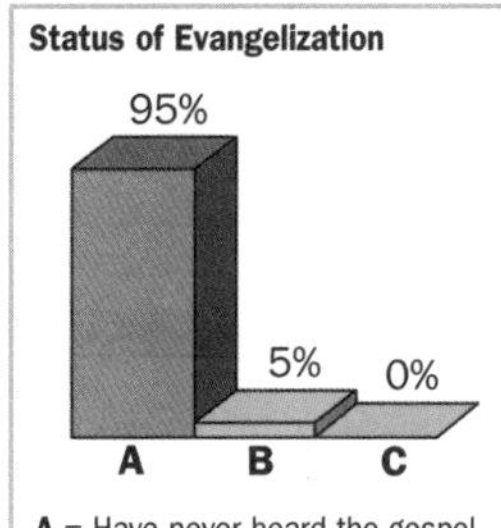

A = Have never heard the gospel
B = Were evangelized but did not become Christians
C = Are adherents to any form of Christianity

Location: Totaling 4,300 people, the only known members of the Liwu ethnic group live in the Liang'e and Jiehu communities of Xinghu District, in Yongsheng County of northern Yunnan Province.[1] The Liwu live in remote villages in high, isolated mountains.

Identity: Apart from their neighbors, few people have ever heard of the Liwu. They do not have much interaction with the other people groups in their area. In the 1950s the Chinese authorities turned down the claims of the Liwu, who asked to be recognized as a distinct ethnic group. Instead, they were placed in the official Yi nationality which contains approximately 120 different ethnolinguistic groups spread throughout southern China.

Language: Liwu belongs to the Northern Yi group of Tibeto-Burman languages. It has not been studied but is believed to be at least partially intelligible with other Northern Yi varieties in Yongsheng County: Northern Awu, Talu, Tagu, Naza, Xiaoliangshan Nosu, Naruo, Naru, Western Lipo, and Liude.

History: The last several hundred years of history for the inhabitants of Yongsheng County have been ones of terror and domination at the hands of the Xiaoliangshan Nosu, who took slaves at will and imposed their rulership on the other peoples.

Customs: In the past many men from different branches of the Yi nationality obtained their wives by force. When Samuel Clarke visited in the early 1900s, he reported, "The bridegroom gathers his friends and makes an attack on the maiden's home. Arming themselves with cudgels... they approach secretly and then rush towards the house. Strenuous efforts are made by the occupants to prevent their entering, and weighty blows are exchanged.... Occasionally during these fights the maiden's home is quite dismantled. The negotiations being concluded, preparations are made for escorting the bride to her new home. On arriving at the bridegroom's house there is a scuffle. The veil is snatched from the bride's face by her kinsmen, who do their utmost to throw it on the roof, to signify that she will rule over the occupants when she enters. The bridegroom's people, on the other hand, do all they can to trample it down on the doorstep as an indication of the rigor with which the newcomer will be subjected to the ruling of the head of the house. Much blood is sometimes shed, and people are often seriously injured in these skirmishes."[2]

Religion: The Liwu believe their souls live on after death, so great preparation is made to help the soul of a deceased Liwu find its way back to the ancestral home. For this reason, deceased Liwu are buried in their traditional clothing and with objects that help the spirits identify the person as a Liwu.

Christianity: The Liwu suffer the misfortune of living in one of the most unevangelized and neglected areas in all of China. As a result, there are no churches or known Christians in their midst. Most have never heard the name of Jesus Christ.

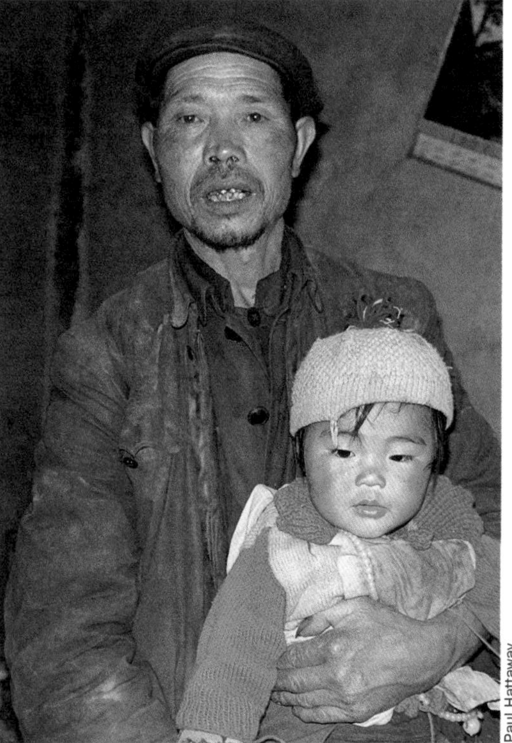

Paul Hattaway

Long 弄

Location: The Long are one of the smallest ethnolinguistic people groups in China. Approximately 1,300 of them inhabit five villages (Kazhai, Sheyin, Shemuduo, Suojugou, and Pusulu) in the Xincheng District of Huaning County.[1] Huaning is part of the Yuxi Prefecture in central Yunnan Province. Yunnan is easily the most ethnically diverse part of China.

Identity: Though small in number, the Long people are proud of their ethnicity and are considered a distinct group by other people in the area. The Chinese authorities have not been willing to recognize them separately, but included them as part of the large Yi nationality in the 1950s. The Yi classification was created probably to make administration of the numerous tribes in Yunnan an easier task. Instead of having to cater to so many groups and collective needs, the government now only has to deal with one group. The tragedy of such a policy is that groups like the Long now tend "not to exist." Only people living in the immediate area have any awareness of the Long's existence. As a further result, these people have never appeared on any Christian mission lists before.

Language: The Long speak a distinct language within the Southeastern Yi language group. The Long have only limited intelligibility with their Yi neighbors such as Ati and Xiqi, who also speak Southeastern Yi languages. The differences between classifications such as Southern Yi, Southeastern Yi, and Western Yi could be compared to the differences between European languages such as English, French, Spanish, and Italian.

Target Ministries

History: Centuries before the Han Chinese conquered Yunnan and migrated into China's southwest frontier, minority peoples had established independent kingdoms. The Ailao Kingdom, ruled by Tai princes, flourished in western Yunnan around the start of the Christian era. During the Tang Dynasty (618–907) the Long were part of the *Xie Me Tu* people. Along with the Xiqi and Ati, the Long were called *White Lolo* by the Han Chinese during the Yuan, Ming, and Qing dynasties (1271–1911).

Customs: The Long have struggled to retain their traditional customs this century as their culture and ethnicity have been gradually swallowed up and absorbed by the Chinese. The Long claim to have once held their own festivals, but today they have reverted to observing traditional Chinese holidays and celebrations.

Religion: Most elderly Long are polytheists. They believe a host of spirits control their lives and must be placated in order to have peace and prosperity. Most younger Long have been affected by atheism and no longer observe the rituals of their parents.

Christianity: Huaning County has largely been neglected by Christians throughout the centuries. A few Catholic and Three-Self churches exist in the townships, but very little vibrant witness has ever gone out to the inhabitants of the region. Although gospel recordings are available in their language, the numerically-small Long tribe remains a Christless people.

Population in China:
1,300 (1998)
1,360 (2000)
1,710 (2010)
Location: Yunnan
Religion: Polytheism
Christians: None Known

Overview of the Long

Countries: China

Pronunciation: "Long"

Other Names:

Population Source:
1,300 (1998 J. Pelkey);
Out of a total Yi population of 6,572,173 (1990 census)

Location: *Yunnan:* Xincheng District of Huaning County

Status:
Officially included under Yi

Language: Sino-Tibetan, Tibeto-Burman, Burmese-Lolo, Lolo, Northern Lolo, Yi, Southeastern Yi

Dialects: 0

Religion:
Polytheism, Animism, No Religion

Christians: None known

Scripture: None

***Jesus* film:** None

Gospel Recordings: Yi: Long

Christian Broadcasting: None

ROPAL code: None

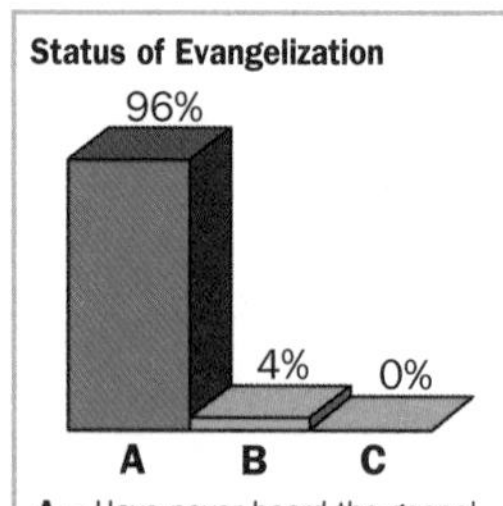

A = Have never heard the gospel
B = Were evangelized but did not become Christians
C = Are adherents to any form of Christianity

109

110

111

112

109–112. Approximately 300,000 of the 715,000 *Lisu* in Yunnan Province are Christians. They were won to Christ by missionaries (such as James Fraser, John and Isobel Kuhn, and the Morse family) in the first half of the twentieth century. Here are four varieties of dress worn by Lisu women, each featuring exquisite embroidery. [109 Midge Conner; 110 & 111 Paul Hattaway; 112 Dwayne Graybill]

113

114

115

116

113–114. The *Miao* are not one people group but a collection of more than 40 ethnic and dialect subgroups, each possessing its own customs and unique dress. A front and back portrait of a Miao lady from Huaxi, Guizhou. [both by *Miao Messenger*]

115. Two ladies from the *Pointed Hat Miao*, possibly a subgroup of the *Hua Miao*; Pingba, Guizhou. [*Miao Messenger*]

116. *Miao* sisters from Duyun, Guizhou. [*Miao Messenger*]

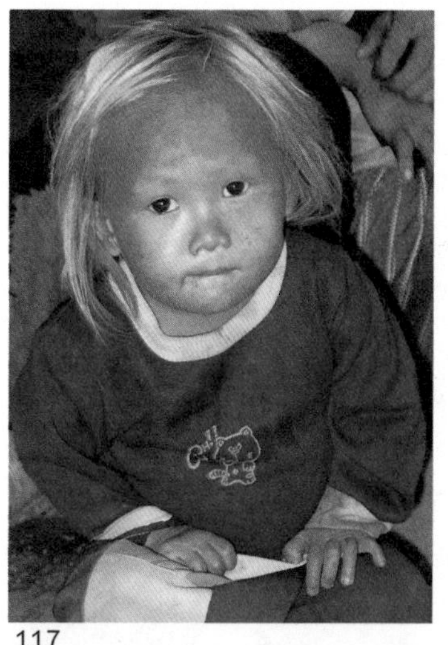
117

118

119

120

121

117–118. The Caucasian ancestry of the *Miao* can be clearly seen in these two girls. As recently as 100 years ago many Miao had blue or green eyes and blond hair. A Miao legend speaks of a homeland where "days and nights lasted six months, the water was frozen, and snow hid the ground.... The people, too, were short and squat, clothed in furs." [both by *Miao Messenger*]

119. This subgroup of the *Miao* were called *Cowrie Shell Miao* by early missionaries because they used shells as currency. [Paul Hattaway]

120–121. Festival time among this *Miao* group in Duyun, Guizhou. [both by *Miao Messenger*]

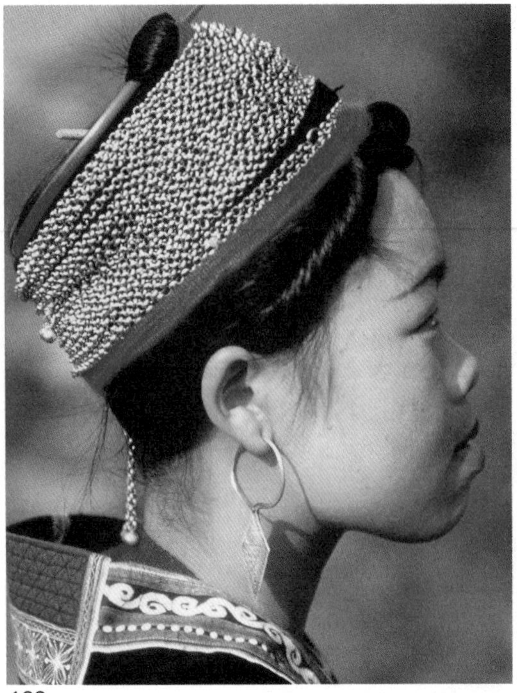
122

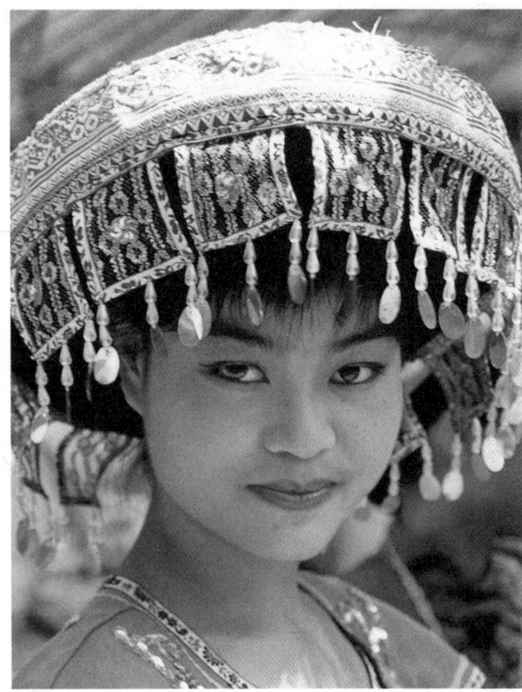
123

124

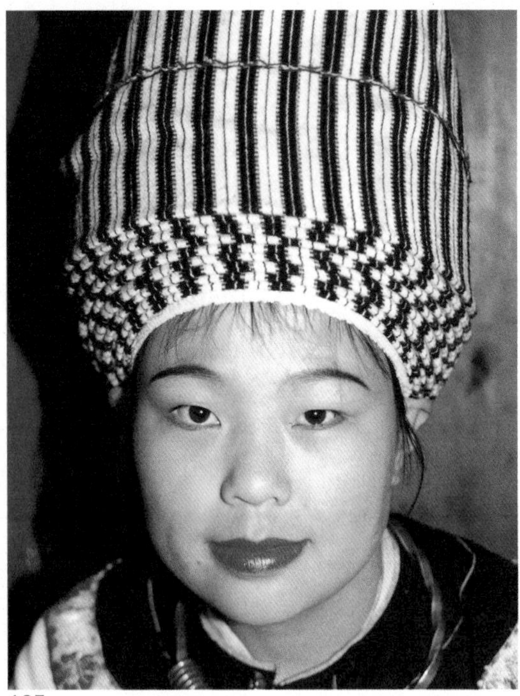
125

122. A *Miao* woman from Anshun, Guizhou. [*Miao Messenger*]
123. One of the numerous styles of dress worn by the *Hua Miao*. [Paul Hattaway]
124. A woman from the *Guiyang Miao* group, Guizhou. [Paul Hattaway]
125. Some *Miao* in northern Guangxi wear costumes very similar to the Dong people. They have lived alongside the Dong for centuries. [Paul Hattaway]

Longjia 龙家

Population in China:
2,000 (1982)
3,040 (2000)
3,920 (2010)
Location: Guizhou, Guangxi
Religion: Ancestor Worship
Christians: None Known

Overview of the Longjia

Countries: China

Pronunciation: "Long-jeeah"

Other Names: Long, Da Tou Long, Ma Mian Long, Gou Er Long, Bai Long

Population Source: 2,000 (1982 *Minzu Shibie Wenxian Ziliao Huibian*); Out of a total Bai population of 1,594,827 (1990 census)

Location: *Guizhou:* Pu'an, Pingba, and Qingzhen counties; *NW Guangxi:* Longlin County

Status: Officially included under Bai since 1987; Previously included in a list of *Undetermined Minorities*

Language: Chinese

Dialects: 0

Religion: Ancestor Worship, Animism, Daoism, No Religion

Christians: None known

Scripture: None

***Jesus* film:** None

Gospel Recordings: None

Christian Broadcasting: None

ROPAL code: None

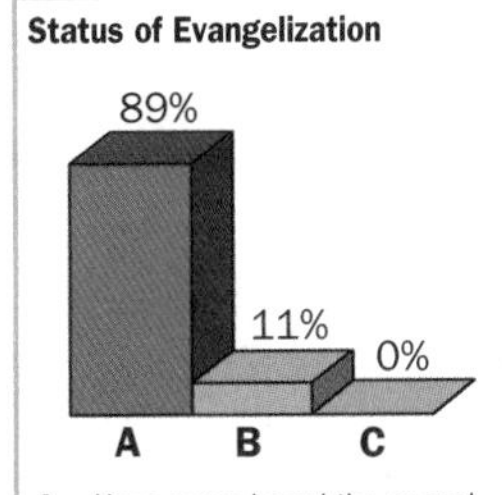

Paul Hattaway

Location: An official 1982 Chinese publication, the *Minzu Shibie Wenxian Ziliao Huibian*, listed a population of 2,000 Longjia people living in a widespread area of southern China.[1] The majority are located in Pu'an County in southwest Guizhou, and in Pingba and Qingzhen counties between Guiyang and Anshun cities in central Guizhou. Others live within Longlin County in the Guangxi Zhuang Autonomous Region. There are possibly also a few Longjia living in the Qingping District, just west of Kaili in central Guizhou.

Identity: The 1982 census listed the Longjia in a collection of *Undetermined Minorities*. In 1987 the Chinese authorities reclassified them as part of the Bai nationality. The suffix *jia* is a Chinese term meaning "household" or "family." The Longjia should not be confused with the 1,300 Long people who are a Yi group living in Huaning County of Yunnan Province. In reality, the Longjia share no historical or ethnic relationship with the Bai people of Yunnan. Their inclusion in the Bai minority was one of convenience for the government. Although they did not want to place the Longjia in a group which it would offend them to be part of, the authorities firmly oppose official recognition of small groups like the Longjia.

Language: The Longjia have lost the use of their mother tongue and now speak exclusively Chinese. There are several subgroups of the Longjia, including the colorfully named *Da Tou Long* (Big Head Dragon), *Ma Mian Long* (Horse Face Dragon), and *Gou Er Long* (Dog Ear Dragon).

History: The Longjia were once a large group in western Guizhou before they were assimilated into the Han Chinese culture and language. In the 27th year of the Yuan Dynasty (1298) the Longjia numbered 46,000 families.[2]

Customs: The Longjia ethnic group includes some members of the Nanjingren group. These two peoples have lived alongside each other for many centuries. They have become so intermixed that it is difficult for outsiders to distinguish one group from the other. Today, the Longjia wear Han clothing and speak Chinese. The Longjia have something of a bad reputation among their neighbors; they are known for their violence and drunkenness.

Religion: Ancestor worship mixed with animism are the main religious beliefs among the Longjia. Every year they hold a bullfighting ceremony which has many religious rituals attached to it. The people finally sacrifice the animal as an offering to the spirits of the harvest, the spirit of the water, village, etc., and they ask the guardian spirits to watch over their community in the coming year with blessing and protection. In Longjia culture, a family's wealth is measured by the number of water buffaloes and cows it owns.

Christianity: Despite being concentrated in Guizhou's Anshun Prefecture, which contains many Protestants and Catholics among the Han, Miao, and Bouyei, the Longjia remain an unreached people group with little access to the gospel. The Longjia would best be reached today by using Chinese-language Scriptures and other evangelistic tools.

Lopi 水田

Paul Hattaway

Location: More than 15,000 Lopi people live in small communities scattered throughout northern Yunnan and southern Sichuan. Anthropologist Stevan Harrell is the only scholar known to have researched the Lopi. He estimates between 2,000 and 3,000 Lopi live in Futian and Pingjiang districts, near Panzhihua in southern Sichuan Province.[1] The large and polluted town of Panzhihua is an "iron, steel, vanadium and titanium mining complex built since 1965."[2]

Identity: The Chinese authorities have counted the Lopi as part of the huge Yi nationality who, in 1945, were found to be a collection of 93 different tribes.[3] This classification, however, has angered the Lopi who "do not even agree that they are Yi; they think of the Yi as mountain barbarians and have no wish to be associated with them; they are both puzzled and bitter that they have not won recognition as a separate *minzu* [nationality]."[4] According to Harrell, the Han neighbors of the Lopi are aware of their claim of separate status, but "it is not much of an issue for them."[5] The future of the Lopi as a distinct people is endangered. Harrell notes, "Their system of kinship terminology like their dress, their religion, and their language, is now identical with that of the Han; only their sense of self-identity and their official classification as members of a minority distinguish them from their Han neighbors."[6] *Lopi* is the self-name of this group. The Chinese call them *Shuitian*, meaning "Watery fields people."

Language: It may already be too late to save the Lopi language from extinction. The Lopi used to speak a Yi language, but now "only a few older people still remember even basic vocabulary, and we could find no informants who knew kinship terms beyond those for primary relations."[7]

History: The Panzhihua area is a crossroads for many tribes and people groups. There are at least five kinds of Yi in the region, including the Eastern Lipo, Bai Yi, Nosu, and Michi who migrated from Guizhou. These groups are described as "all very different from each other."[8]

Customs: The Chinese name for the Lopi, (Watery Fields People) indicates their occupation. They are primarily engaged in cultivating rice which they grow in irrigated fields. There are few distinct customs left among the Lopi, who have been gradually assimilated by the Han Chinese in much the same way as "stomach juices will treat a steak."[9]

Religion: Most Lopi are nonreligious, although a few minor traces of animistic practices remain among the elderly Lopi in the mountains.

Christianity: Although there are few known Christians among the Lopi today, the area around Panzhihua has a rich missions history. The Catholic Paris Foreign Missionary Society commenced work in the region as early as 1790. In 1802 Monseigneur de Philomeile reported that "the Lolos [Yi] wish to become Christians in groups." In five or six days he counted as many as 500 potential converts.[10] In 1809 Monsieur Hamel baptized 74 adults in Huili, northeast of the Lopi area.[11] The neighboring Eastern Lipo group has many Christians.

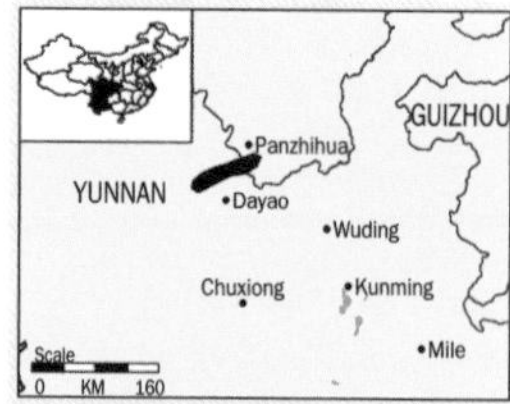

Population in China:
10,000 (1990)
15,060 (2000)
18,900 (2010)
Location: Yunnan, Sichuan
Religion: No Religion
Christians: 50

Overview of the Lopi

Countries: China
Pronunciation: "Lo-pee"
Other Names: Shuitian, Tu
Population Source:
10,000 (1990 AMO);
Out of a total Yi population of 6,572,173 (1990 census)
Location: *N Yunnan:* Huaping, Dayao, and Yongsheng counties; *S Sichuan:* Futian and Pingjiang districts
Status:
Officially included under Yi
Language: Sino-Tibetan, Tibeto-Burman, Burmese-Lolo, Lolo, Northern Lolo, Yi, Central Yi
Dialects: 0
Religion: No Religion, Animism, Ancestor Worship
Christians: 50
Scripture: None
***Jesus* film:** None
Gospel Recordings: None
Christian Broadcasting: None
ROPAL code: None

Status of Evangelization

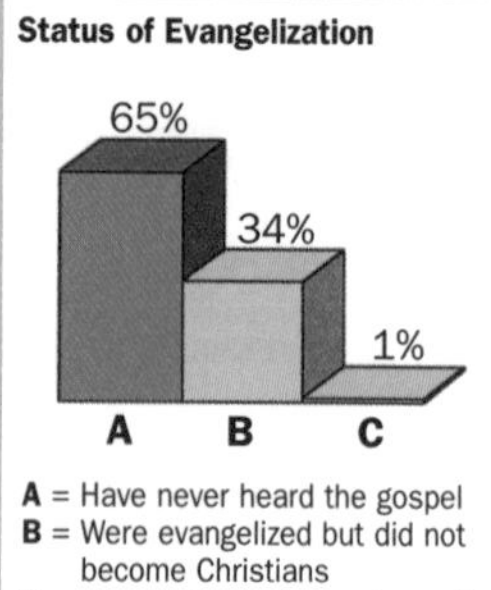

A = Have never heard the gospel
B = Were evangelized but did not become Christians
C = Are adherents to any form of Christianity

Lu 卢人

Location: The 1982 Chinese publication *Minzu Shibie Wenxian Ziliao Huibian* listed a population of 3,000 Lu people living in Dafang, Qianxi, and Bijie counties of Guizhou Province.[1]

Identity: Not to be confused with the Tai Lu people of southern Yunnan, who are also often referred to simply as *Lu*, the Lu of Guizhou are a small, ethnically distinct people group. The Lu registered their name with the government in the early 1950s for recognition as a minority group. Their application was rejected. Until the mid-1980s they remained a people without any official nationality. The 1982 census listed the Lu as one of 80 *Undetermined Minorities* in Guizhou Province alone. These 80 groups totaled more than 900,000 individuals.[2] In 1985, apparently after scholars had further investigated the claims of the Lu, they were placed under the Manchu nationality.[3] Most Manchu live in northeast Chinese, thousands of miles away from the Lu. There are scattered communities of Manchu people throughout all of China, however, resulting from the time when the Manchus founded the Qing Dynasty and ruled China from 1644 to 1911. As a result, Manchu people are found in no less than 2,092 of China's 2,369 counties and municipalities.[4] Despite this new classification, the Lu continue to view themselves as a distinct people group.

Language: The Lu have lost the use of their original language and now only speak the Guizhou dialect of Mandarin Chinese.

History: The first recorded mention of the Lu was during the Qing Dynasty (1644–1911), when they were known as the *Songjia*. Their sudden appearance on the scene in Guizhou indicates they may have been a group of troops and administrators who were sent to Guizhou by the Manchu rulers to represent their interests in the area.

Paul Hattaway

Customs: The Lu are also known by the nickname *Washing-Bone Miao* because of an old custom. The Lu traditionally dug up the bodies of people who had died, washed the bones, wrapped them in white cloth, and reburied them. This practice was repeated once or twice each year for seven years. When a Lu person was sick others would say, "It is because you haven't cleaned your ancestors bones."[5] This practice was forcibly stopped by the Communist authorities. Lu men wear green shirts and baggy trousers. They tie their hair. Lu women wear a one-piece dress.

Religion: The Lu live under the powerful controlling influence of ancestor worship. They fear that if they do not take care of and pray for the souls of their ancestors, their own souls will be lost in eternity. The Lu regularly offer food and drink to their forefathers and take great care to clean — and worship at — the ancestral altar.

Christianity: The influence of ancestor worship has prevented the Lu from accepting Christ, for to become Christians would be considered a grave offense to the spirits of their forefathers. There are a number of Miao, Han, and Yi believers in the area, but the Lu have little contact with them and prefer to be left alone.

SICHUAN, GUIZHOU, YUNNAN, GUANGXI, Guiyang, Zhenxiong, Weining, Bijie, Qianxi, Lupanshui, Guiyang, Anshun, Panxian — Scale 0 KM 160

Population in China:
3,000 (1982)
4,560 (2000)
5,890 (2010)
Location: Guizhou
Religion: Ancestor Worship
Christians: None Known

Overview of the Lu

Countries: China

Pronunciation: "Loo"

Other Names: Lu Ren, Lu Ge Zi, Songjia, Lugepo, Washing-Bone Miao

Population Source: 3,000 (1982 *Minzu Shibie Wenxian Ziliao Huibian*); Out of a total Manchu population of 9,821,180 (1990 census)

Location: *Guizhou:* Dafang, Qianxi, and Bijie counties

Status: Officially included under Manchu since 1985; Previously included in a list of *Undetermined Minorities*

Language: Chinese

Dialects: 0

Religion: Ancestor Worship, Animism, No Religion

Christians: None known

Scripture: None

***Jesus* film:** None

Gospel Recordings: None

Christian Broadcasting: None

ROPAL code: None

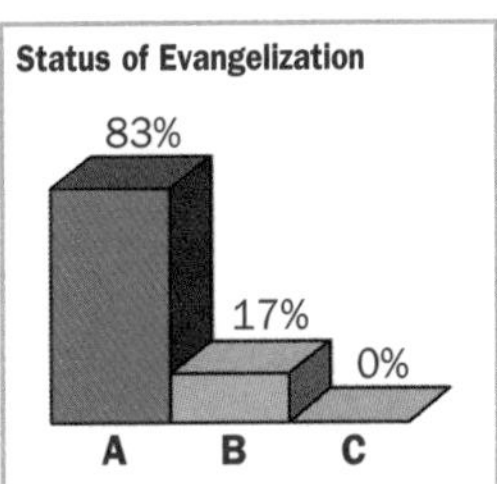

A = Have never heard the gospel
B = Were evangelized but did not become Christians
C = Are adherents to any form of Christianity

Luoluopo, Central 罗罗坡(中)

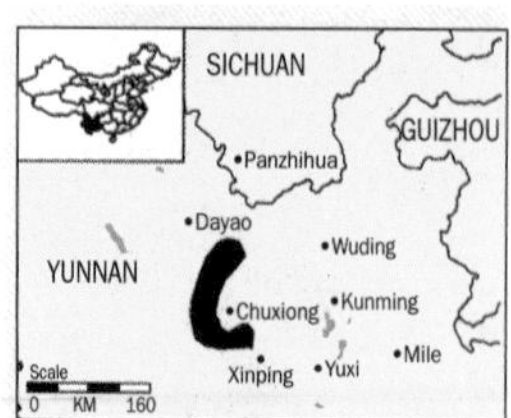

Population in China:
344,600 (1999)
353,400 (2000)
443,500 (2010)
Location: Yunnan
Religion: Polytheism
Christians: 200

Overview of the Central Luoluopo

Countries: China
Pronunciation: "Luoh-luoh-po"
Other Names: Luoluopuo, Lolo, Lolopo, Bai Yi, White Yi, Gaoshan, Tu, Alu, Lulupu, Luolu, Hei Yi, Black Yi, Gaoshanzu
Population Source:
344,600 (1999 J. Pelkey);
Out of a total Yi population of 6,572,173 (1990 census)
Location: *Yunnan:* Chuxiong (83,000), Nanhua (74,000), Yao'an (43,000), Jingdong (34,000), Shuangbai (33,600), Mouding (31,000), Lufeng (21,000), Xiangyun (8,000), Yuanmou (6,000), Wuding (3,400), Xinping (3,100), Nanjian (3,000), and Lijiang (1,500) counties
Status:
Officially included under Yi
Language: Sino-Tibetan, Tibeto-Burman, Burmese-Lolo, Lolo, Northern Lolo, Yi, Central Yi
Dialects (3):
Nanhua, Chuxiong, Yao'an
Religion:
Polytheism, Animism, Christianity
Christians: 200
Scripture: None
***Jesus* film:** None
Gospel Recordings:
Yi: Luoluopo #04937
Christian Broadcasting: None
ROPAL code: YICOO

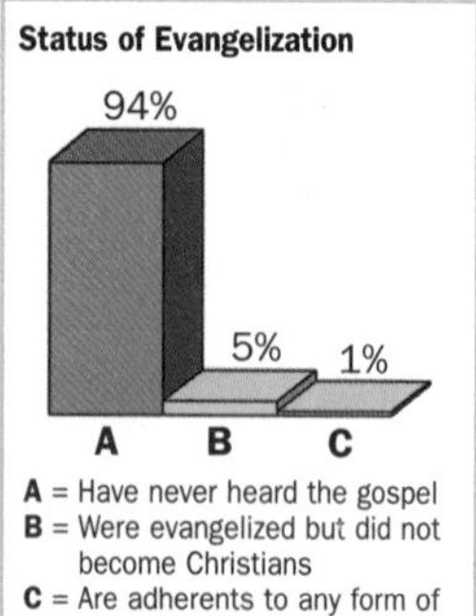

Location: More than 350,000 Central Luoluopo live in the central and north central parts of Yunnan Province. The great majority are located in Chuxiong Prefecture. In a 1957 study, Chuxiong reportedly contained 140,000 Luoluopo.[1]

Identity: The name *Luoluopo* means "tiger-dragon people" in the Luoluopo language. It is not the same name as *Lolo*, which was used by the Chinese in a derogatory manner to describe all Yi people until recently.[2] The Central Luoluopo are one of more than 100 subgroups of Yi in Yunnan.

Language: The Central Luoluopo speak a language belonging to the Central Yi language group, which in 1987 contained a total of 470,000 speakers.[3] The Yi script is not used by the Central Luoluopo.

History: The Central Luoluopo have been in their present location for many centuries. Over time the best land on the plains was taken by the Han. The Central Luoluopo were forced to migrate into the isolated mountains.[4]

Customs: The Central Luoluopo celebrate numerous festivals over the course of the year, most of which have religious significance. In January they observe the two-day Dragon Worship Festival. Sacrifices are made to the dragons of the water to ensure a good harvest and to prevent drought and famine. In Dayao County, the Central Luoluopo celebrate the Open Street Festival every February. It affords the chance for Luoluopo from different locations to meet and trade. Luoluopo youth dress in their finest clothes and take the opportunity to meet prospective partners. The social activities of the week include a unique traditional dance in which participants may only dance on their left foot. At all Central Luoluopo festivals a huge feast is prepared. Luoluopo men and women have the habit of smoking long pipes. Central Luoluopo youth are expected to be sexually active before marriage. All villages have a "flower house" where young people are allowed to come together after dark. Fidelity in marriage is stressed only after the first baby is born.

Religion: The Central Luoluopo celebrate the Tiger Festival between the eighth and the 15th days of the first lunar month. The Luoluopo believe they are descended from tigers. The hero of the festival is the tiger, a person in costume who, after dancing on the open ground, rides a Mountain god float to call on each home in the community and offer them a blessing.

Christianity: French Catholic missionary Alfred Liétard and his team worked among the Central Luoluopo in the early part of the twentieth century. They wrote a detailed account of the group in 1913.[5] The missionaries also translated the text of the "Prodigal Son" into Central Luoluopo,[6] although this is no longer available. Today there are a small number of Central Luoluopo Christians attending churches in the townships, but the majority of Luoluopo have never heard the gospel. Central Luoluopo gospel recordings were produced in 1998.

Jamin Pelkey

Luoluopo, Southeastern 罗罗坡(东南)

Paul Hattaway

Location: A total of more than 35,000 Southeastern Luoluopo live in southern Yunnan Province of China. The majority, more than 20,000, live in Maguan County. Some live in Funing and Xichou counties (5,000 each). An additional 4,000 live in Malipo County and 1,600 in Honghe County.[1] The Southeastern Luoluopo also spill across the border into northern Vietnam where approximately 3,200 are recognized as the official *Lolo* minority group.

Identity: Although they have received status as a separate ethnic group in Vietnam, the Southeastern Luoluopo have not been so fortunate in China where they are considered to be just one subgroup of the massive Yi nationality. The self-name of this group is *Luoluopo. Southeastern* has been added to distinguish this group from the other Luoluopo groups in China who speak completely different languages, even though they share the same autonym.

Language: As their name suggests, this group speaks a language belonging to the Southeastern group of Yi languages. Yi, in turn, is just one of the branches of the Tibeto-Burman language family.

History: According to Vietnamese sources, the Luoluopo migrated to Vietnam in two different waves: one in the fifteenth century and the other in the eighteenth century. This suggests that the Luoluopo have been living in southern China for more than 500 years. In recent years, many of the Southeastern Luoluopo in China who live near the townships or in the valleys have started mixed communities with the Han Chinese and are rapidly losing their language and culture.

Customs: When a Luoluopo dies, his or her relatives organize a "dance of the spirits." They believe this dance will help the soul find its way back to the resting place of its ancestors. At the dance the son-in-law of the deceased carries a bag on his shoulder. Inside the bag is a cloth ball which represents the head of the deceased person.

Religion: The Luoluopo are a very superstitious people. Even their homes are arranged to reflect this. The altar to the "spirit of the house"stands against the back wall. A room on the right side contains a bedroom with a fireplace and the room on the left side contains the kitchen and the ancestral altar. The oldest surviving member of each family is expected to maintain the altar and to faithfully execute all the ancestral ceremonies and rituals. In addition to their intricate system of ancestor worship, the Lolo believe in two gods who created the world, *Mit Do* and *Ket Do.* Ket Do created the entire universe and mankind, while Mit Do governs the earth and watches over the Luoluopo.

Christianity: The Southeastern Luoluopo are one of the most neglected and gospel-starved peoples in the region. There are no known believers in their midst in either China or Vietnam today. No Scriptures or evangelistic tools exist in their language and no ministries are known to be targeting them for salvation.

Population in China:
35,800 (1999)
36,700 (2000)
46,050 (2010)
Location: Yunnan
Religion: Polytheism
Christians: None Known

Overview of the Southeastern Luoluopo

Countries: China, Vietnam
Pronunciation: "Luoh-luoh-po"
Other Names: Lolo, Hanluo, Hualuo, Bailuo, Heiluo
Population Source: 35,800 (1999 J. Pelkey); Out of a total Yi population of 6,572,173 (1990 census); 3,134 in Vietnam (1989 census)
Location: *S Yunnan:* Maguan (20,000), Funing (5,200), Xichou (5,000), Malipo (4,000), and Honghe (1,600) counties
Status: Officially included under Yi
Language: Sino-Tibetan, Tibeto-Burman, Burmese-Lolo, Lolo, Northern Lolo, Yi, Southeastern Yi
Dialects (4): Han Lolo, Hua Lolo, Bai Lolo, Hei Lolo
Religion: Polytheism, Animism, Ancestor Worship
Christians: None known
Scripture: None
***Jesus* film:** None
Gospel Recordings: None
Christian Broadcasting: None
ROPAL code: None

Status of Evangelization

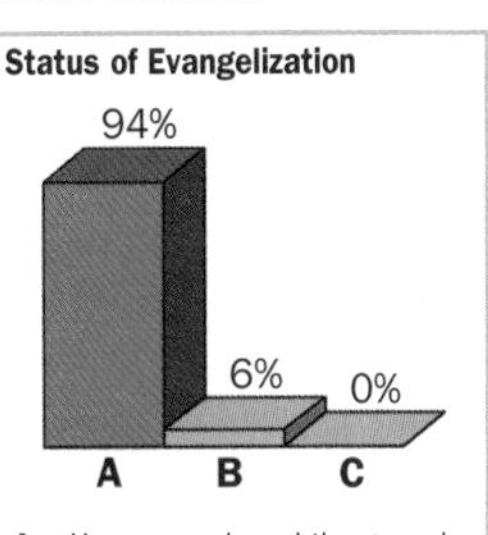

A = Have never heard the gospel
B = Were evangelized but did not become Christians
C = Are adherents to any form of Christianity

Luoluopo, Western 罗罗坡(西)

July 11

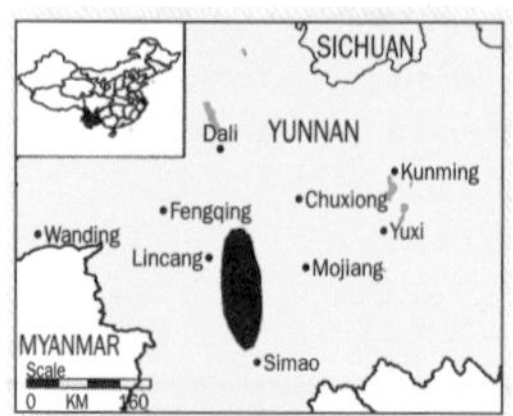

Population in China:
188,500 (1999)
193,300 (2000)
242,600 (2010)
Location: Yunnan
Religion: Polytheism
Christians: 100

Overview of the Western Luoluopo

Countries: China

Pronunciation: "Luoh-luoh-po"

Other Names: Lolo, Western Lolo, Lolopo

Population Source: 188,500 (1999 J. Pelkey); Out of a total Yi population of 6,572,173 (1990 census)

Location: *Yunnan:* Jingdong (57,000), Jinggu (47,000), Lancang (31,500), Zhenyuan (28,000), Simao (14,500), and Pu'er (10,000) counties

Status: Officially included under Yi

Language: Sino-Tibetan, Tibeto-Burman, Burmese-Lolo, Lolo, Northern Lolo, Yi, Western Yi

Dialects: 0

Religion: Polytheism, Animism, Ancestor Worship, Christianity

Christians: 100

Scripture: None

***Jesus* film:** None

Gospel Recordings: None

Christian Broadcasting: None

ROPAL code: None

Status of Evangelization

87% 12% 1%

A B C

A = Have never heard the gospel
B = Were evangelized but did not become Christians
C = Are adherents to any form of Christianity

Jamin Pelkey

Location: According to researcher Jamin Pelkey, 188,500 Western Luoluopo live in six counties of northern and central Simao Prefecture in Yunnan Province. In descending order, the Western Luoluopo are found in Jingdong County (57,000), followed by Jinggu (47,000), Lancang (31,500), Zhenyuan (28,000), Simao (14,500), and Pu'er (10,000).[1]

Identity: Although they share the same autonym with the Central Luoluopo and the Southeastern Luoluopo, the languages of these three groups differ widely. Each comes from a different branch of the Yi linguistic group. These names reflect each group's linguistic affiliation, rather than a geographic orientation: the Western Luoluopo speak a Western Yi language; the Central Luoluopo speak a Central Yi language, etc. *Luoluopo* is the self-name of these groups. In the past, Lolo came to be the derogatory term used freely by the Chinese to describe all Yi people. As a result, many Luoluopo today prefer to identify themselves as *Yi* to outsiders.

Language: Western Luoluopo is one of more than 20 distinct Western Yi varieties in China. In some locations, such as Jingdong County, the Western Luoluopo live near speakers of Central Luoluopo. Speakers from the two groups cannot understand each other without using Chinese.

History: The ancestors of the Western Luoluopo used to live farther to the north of their present location. In the past, war between different Yi tribes and clans was frequent, resulting in massive loss of life. Because of these conditions, many groups migrated out of the area. One historian described the hostilities: "War tactics were... mundane: ambushes and surprise attacks were favored; because of lack of ammunition, battles were often hand to hand; the goal was not so much to kill the enemy as to capture him. A Black Yi would be held for ransom or allowed to commit suicide; White Yi or slaves were held for ransom or enslaved. Witchcraft and amulets were used extensively."[2]

Customs: These battles were often ended "by the mediation of a third clan, or by a 'waiting-at-home' bride related to both parties (if her pleas were unsuccessful, she would commit suicide). Peace negotiations were long and required expert debaters: compensation had to be decided upon for each life lost."[3]

Religion: Polytheistic animism is the main religious adherence of the Western Luoluopo. Ancestor worship is also prevalent. Two or three ancestral rites are performed every year in honor of the Luoluopo forefathers.

Christianity: Although little is known about the extent of Christianity among the Western Luoluopo, there may be a small number of believers among them. Aa a result, The Luowu remain completely unreached today, although the first ever gospel recordings in the Luowu language were produced in 1999. With no Scriptures, recordings, or ministries targeting them, however, most Western Luoluopo have never heard of Christ.

Luowu 罗武

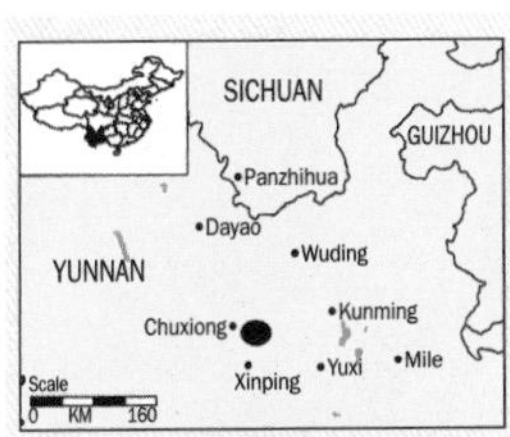

Population in China:
22,000 (1999)
22,550 (2000)
28,300 (2010)
Location: Yunnan
Religion: Polytheism
Christians: None Known

Overview of the Luowu

Countries: China

Pronunciation: "Luoh-woo"

Other Names: Lowu, Alu, Lou-wou, Nisu, Lao-wou

Population Source: 22,000 (1999 J. Pelkey); Out of a total Yi population of 6,572,173 (1990 census)

Location: *Yunnan:* Yimen (9,000), Lufeng (7,000), Shuangbai (4,000), and Chuxiong (2,000) counties

Status: Officially included under Yi

Language: Sino-Tibetan, Tibeto-Burman, Burmese-Lolo, Lolo, Northern Lolo, Yi, Eastern Yi

Dialects: 0

Religion: Polytheism, Animism, Ancestor Worship

Christians: None known

Scripture: None

***Jesus* film:** None

Gospel Recordings: Yi: Luowu

Christian Broadcasting: None

ROPAL code: None

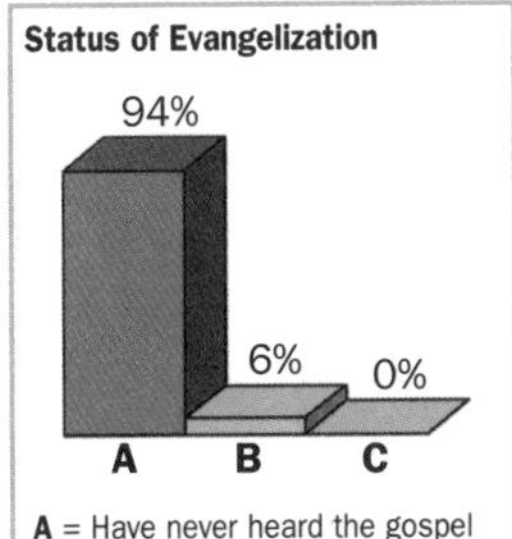

Location: More than 22,000 people belonging to the Luowu ethnic group live in the mountains of central Yunnan Province. They are distributed in Yimen (9,000), Lufeng (7,000), Shuangbai (4,000), and Chuxiong (2,000) counties.[1]

Identity: The Luowu, who were first referred to in a 1909 study,[2] are one of numerous subgroups of the official Yi nationality. The Luowu were described in 1913 as timid and peaceful. Ninety percent of the people suffered from goiter, while other prevalent diseases included malaria, smallpox, leprosy, typhoid fever, and tuberculosis.[3] The Luowu living in the Tongchang District of Yimen County call themselves *Alu*. These people reportedly speak a language so different from the Nisu (another Yi subgroup) in the southern part of their own district that they have to use Chinese to communicate with each other.[4]

Language: The Luowu language, which enjoys widespread usage among the people, is part of the Eastern Yi language affiliation.[5] Luowu is different from Laowu, which is reportedly a Western Yi variety, and from Lawu, said to be Southern Yi. The Luowu and Lawu, however, are said to be originally descended from the Laowu.

History: The Luowu are believed to have originated in Wuding County, northern Yunnan. Chinese records state that the Luowu lived there in the 1380s, in the early years of the Ming Dynasty (1368–1644). Because of their many expeditions the Luowu were allowed to serve in the local court of the area. They migrated to other parts of Chuxiong Prefecture and ended up where they live today.[6]

Customs: The 1995 *Chuxiong Xian Zhi* states, "The Luowu are monogamous and prefer to marry only other Luowu. A Luowu couple meets through a matchmaker and then becomes engaged. A Luowu wedding ceremony lasts for three days. On the first day the bridegroom gets up at daybreak and goes to the home of his bride where he meets with his matchmaker, bride, and all of her relatives to present wedding gifts to them. Many important rituals ensue. On the final day the *suona* (a long horn which emits a high-pitched sonorous wail) is blown. The bride and her entourage are forbidden to enter the house of the groom until the bride's family have blown the *suona* horn. The two are considered married when the bride has entered the home of her bridegroom."[7]

Jamin Pelkey

Religion: The Luowu are polytheists. They live in fear of and bondage to a number of deities and demons. They believe that, although some spirits are good, most are vengeful and bad, desiring to kill and destroy them. The Luowu also venerate their ancestors to the fourth or fifth generation.

Christianity: Many early missionaries were great ambassadors for Christ. Maria Dyer, who became Hudson Taylor's wife, revealed her deep commitment when she considered Taylor's marriage proposal. Dyer wrote, "If he loves me more than Jesus he is not worthy of me — if he were to leave the Lord's work for the world's honour, I would have nothing further to do with him." However, few missionaries working in China prior to their expulsion in 1949 targeted the groups in the mountains of central Yunnan. As a result, the Luowu remain unreached today, although gospel recordings in their language were produced in 1999.

Luzu 路组

Location: More than 1,000 ethnic Luzu people live in several villages within Muli County in the isolated southern part of Sichuan Province. The area was previously known as Xikang, before it was incorporated into Sichuan in the 1930s. Muli itself has been described as "a rich possession, and all the rivers, especially the Litang, carry gold and produce a considerable revenue."[1]

Identity: The Luzu have been officially classified as part of the Tibetan nationality, even though their language is not related to Tibetan and they have a distinct ethnicity. Several small ethnic groups in Muli were also classified as Tibetan, seemingly on the basis of their adherence to the Tibetan Buddhist religion rather than for ethnolinguistic reasons. One observer notes that "the Xifan [Chrame] of southwestern Sichuan [including the Luzu]... are a member of the Tibetan *minzu* [nationality], but feel that they have little in common with the Tibetans."[2]

Language: Although few people have ever heard of the Luzu, one linguist reports that it is similar to the Ersu language and is considered by some to be a dialect of Western Ersu, which belongs to the Qiangic language family.[3] Muli County contains several fascinating languages. One linguist says, "Muli... is an amazingly multi-lingual region, where at least the following Tibeto-Burman languages are spoken: Khams Tibetan, Namuyi, Luzu, Nosu, Naxi (both the Western and Eastern dialects), Shixing, and Pumi (Northern dialect)."[4]

History: The Luzu are one of numerous ethnic groups who speak a Qiangic language. In addition to the Qiang nationality presently recognized in China, smaller groups such as the Ersu, Ergong, Namuyi, Luzu, and Chrame have spread throughout southern Sichuan Province. Muli was a monastery town, presided over by a king until the 1950s. One foreign visitor to Muli commented, "The villagers occupy wooden shanties scattered over the hillsides below the town. They are very poor, and live in constant fear of the lama king and his parasitic satellites."[5]

Customs: Almost half of the families living in Muli practice either *polyandry* (brothers sharing a wife) or *polygamy* (sisters sharing a husband).[6] These practices probably started because of the large numbers of men who join the Buddhist monkhood, thus taking a vow of celibacy. To accommodate the needs of the women, nonconventional marriages were adopted.

Religion: All Luzu are followers of Tibetan Buddhism. Every aspect of their daily lives is influenced by their beliefs. Pilgrimages to important Buddhist sites are undertaken by all Luzu at some stage of their lives.

Paul Hattaway

Christianity: The Luzu as a people group in China is completely unreached by the gospel. Muli is a desperately needy and vitally strategic area for evangelists and church planters to target with the gospel, for there are several untouched people groups living there. The Luzu will need to be visited by evangelists in order for them to hear the gospel, as shortwave gospel radio broadcasts are unable to penetrate the high mountains.

Population in China:
1,000 (1998)
1,040 (2000)
1,280 (2010)
Location: Sichuan
Religion: Tibetan Buddhism
Christians: None Known

Overview of the Luzu

Countries: China
Pronunciation: "Loo-zoo"
Other Names: Lüzü
Population Source:
1,000 (1998 AMO);
Out of a total Tibetan population of 4,593,330 (1990 census)
Location: *S Sichuan:* Muli County
Status:
Officially included under Tibetan

Language: Sino-Tibetan, Tibeto-Burman, Qiangic, Ersu
Dialects: 0
Religion:
Tibetan Buddhism, Polytheism
Christians: None known
Scripture: None
***Jesus* film:** None
Gospel Recordings: None
Christian Broadcasting: None
ROPAL code: None

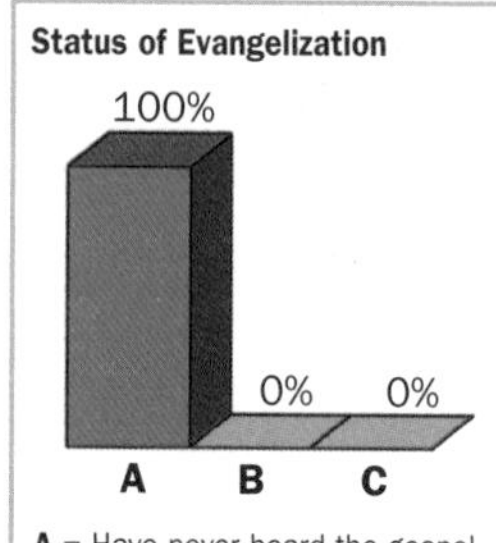

Malimasa 马理马撒

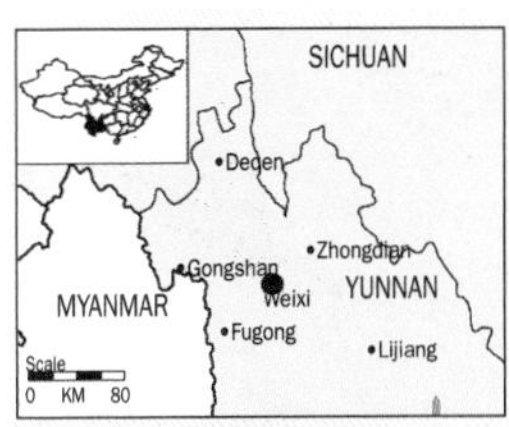

Population in China:
500 (1998)
515 (2000)
600 (2010)
Location: Yunnan
Religion: Tibetan Buddhism
Christians: None Known

Overview of the Malimasa

Countries: China

Pronunciation: "Ma-lee-ma-sa"

Other Names:

Population Source:
500 (1998 AMO);
100 families (1998 J. Matisoff);
Out of a total Naxi population of 278,009 (1990 census)

Location: *NW Yunnan:* Weixi County in the Deqen Tibetan Autonomous Prefecture

Status:
Officially included under Naxi

Language: Sino-Tibetan, Tibeto-Burman, Burmese-Lolo, Lolo, Northern Lolo, Naxi, Eastern Naxi

Dialects: 0

Religion:
Tibetan Buddhism, Polytheism

Christians: None known

Scripture: None

***Jesus* film:** None

Gospel Recordings: None

Christian Broadcasting: None

ROPAL code: None

Status of Evangelization

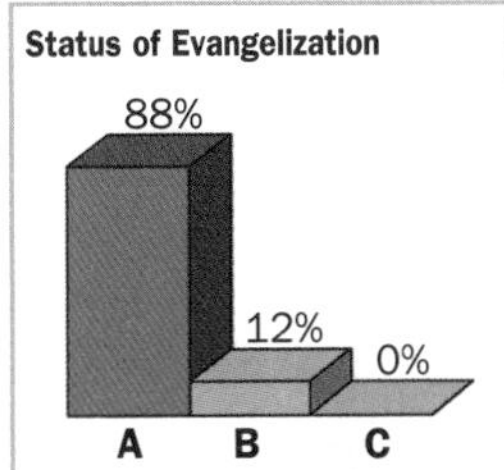

A = Have never heard the gospel
B = Were evangelized but did not become Christians
C = Are adherents to any form of Christianity

Dwayne Graybill

Location: Approximately 100 Malimasa families inhabit an area near the town of Weixi, in the northwest of Yunnan Province.[1] Weixi, five hours by road from the city of Zhongdian, is at the juncture where the Tibetan and Chinese worlds meet. Joseph Rock, an intrepid explorer and botanist, described Weixi in the 1920s as "a forlorn place of about 400 houses.... The town boasts a wall of mud with a few dilapidated gates."[2] The Malimasa people live in extremely remote communities. Severe snowfall often cuts their villages off from the outside world for weeks at a time during the winter months.

Identity: The other people in the Weixi region say they have viewed the Malimasa as a separate people group for at least one hundred years. The Chinese authorities, however, have included the Malimasa under the official Naxi nationality.

Language: The Malimasa language is part of the Eastern Naxi language branch, which is related to Mosuo. The people themselves say their vocabulary is comprised of 30% Tibetan words and 30% Bai words.[3] Despite their small number, the Malimasa have their own "syllabary script."[4]

History: The history of the Malimasa is shrouded in uncertainty, but their language suggests that they were once part of the Mosuo people who are today concentrated a considerable distance northeast of Weixi, on the Yunnan-Sichuan border. The Malimasa are still a purely matriarchal and matrilineal society, with women in complete control of all finances, possessions, and decision-making.

Customs: The Malimasa wear their own traditional dress, distinct from all other groups in the area. Women wear a large turban wrapped around their heads. Sickness and disease have long plagued people in this part of China. When Rock visited Weixi 70 years ago, he reported, "Nowhere have I seen goiter so prevalent as here. The people carried regular pouches in their throats, like certain monkeys when they fill up with peanuts."[5]

Religion: The Malimasa are 100% Tibetan Buddhist. There are a number of Tibetan, Lisu, and Naxi Christians in the Weixi area, but they have had little impact on the staunch belief system of the Malimasa.

Christianity: Catholic missionaries from the Grand St. Bernard Order commenced work at Latsa Pass near Weixi in 1931.[6] Several Protestant families also lived in Weixi prior to 1949. The great missionary statesman Hudson Taylor, writing of China's needs in general, stated, "The harvest here is indeed great, and the laborers are few and imperfectly fitted for such a work. And yet grace can make a few feeble instruments the means of accomplishing great things — things greater even than we can conceive."[7] Taylor's passionate desire was that national believers would be given the leadership of their own churches and have control over their own affairs. He wrote, "I look upon foreign missionaries as the scaffolding around a rising building. The sooner it can be dispensed with, the better; or rather, the sooner it can be transferred to other places, to serve the same temporary use, the better."[8]

Manchu 满

Paul Hattaway

Location: The majority of the more than 12 million Manchu are concentrated in China's northeastern provinces of Liaoning,[1] Jilin, and Heilongjiang — all of which were formerly part of Manchuria. For centuries the Manchu separated themselves from the Chinese and even erected a wooden stockade to keep them out.[2] In 1859 the Chinese were finally allowed to migrate into Manchuria. The Chinese entered in such massive numbers that today the Manchu are a minority in their homeland. Small numbers of Manchu may also live in Siberia and North Korea.[3] Manchu are found in no less than 2,092 of China's 2,369 counties and municipalities.[4]

Identity: Although they are considered China's second largest minority, most Manchu today are indistinguishable from the Han Chinese. As one historian notes, "The Manchus' political and military successes... were purchased at the expense of losing their ethnic identity. Long before the Qing Dynasty collapsed in 1911, most Manchus had ceased to be Manchus ethnically, linguistically, and culturally."[5]

Language: The Manchu language is practically extinct. Various studies have listed "less than 20,"[6] "70,"[7] and "1,000"[8] speakers of Manchu remaining among the entire ethnic group.[9] Manchu speakers are located in a few villages in Heilongjiang — Sanjiazi Village in Fuyu County and Dawujia Village in Aihui County. Most of the Manchu speakers use Mandarin as their first language and speak Manchu "with a pronounced Chinese accent."[10] Manchu was the only Tungus language to possess an orthography, but this too is now extinct.[11]

History: Although the name *Manchu* was first used in the early 1600s, their descendants date back 3,000 years to the Suzhen tribe.[12] In 1644 the Manchu broke through the Great Wall and, after several decades of conquest, established the Qing Dynasty which ruled China for 267 years.

Customs: All but about 200,000 Manchu have lost their cultural identity. Traditional Manchu dress is now reserved solely for tourist performances.

Religion: Before the Manchu were assimilated, they were known as shamanists who also worshiped their ancestors. Some aspects of these practices remain, but today most Manchu are considered nonreligious.

Christianity: The Catholics commenced work in Manchuria in 1620.[13] By 1922 they numbered 56,000 converts,[14] most of whom were Han Chinese. Protestant work among the Manchu began in 1869. A revival swept through Manchuria in the early 1900s. A blind evangelist, Chang Sen, traveled from village to village winning hundreds of converts to Christ. "Missionaries followed after him, baptizing converts and organizing churches."[15] In the first half of this century many Manchu Christians suffered severe persecution and torture, especially between 1931 and 1945 when northeast China was annexed by Japan and renamed *Manchukuo*. Today there are at least 10,000 scattered Manchu believers who meet in Chinese churches. Many have come to Christ as the result of the great Heilongjiang revival in the 1990s.[16]

Population in China:
9,819,180 (1990)
12,666,700 (2000)
16,340,100 (2010)
Location: Liaoning, Jilin, Heilongjiang, Hebei, and most of Eastern China
Religion: No Religion
Christians: 10,000

Overview of the Manchu

Countries: China, possibly in Russia and North Korea
Pronunciation: "Mahn-choo"
Other Names: Man, Manchou, Manju
Population Source: 9,821,180 (1990 census);[17] 4,304,160 (1982 census);[18] Possibly also in North Korea and Russia
Location: *Liaoning* (55% of all Manchu); *Heilongjiang; Jilin; Hebei; Inner Mongolia; Beijing; Henan; Tianjin; Shandong; Xinjiang; Shanxi; Gansu; Shaanxi; Ningxia; Guangdong; Qinghai; Jiangsu; Hunan*[19]
Status: An official minority of China
Language: Altaic, Tungus, Southern Tungus, Southwest
Literacy: 82%
Dialects: 0
Religion: No Religion, Ancestor Worship, Shamanism, Buddhism, Christianity
Christians: 10,000
Scripture: New Testament 1835; Portions 1822[20]
***Jesus* film:** None
Gospel Recordings: None
Christian Broadcasting: None
ROPAL code: MJF00

Status of Evangelization

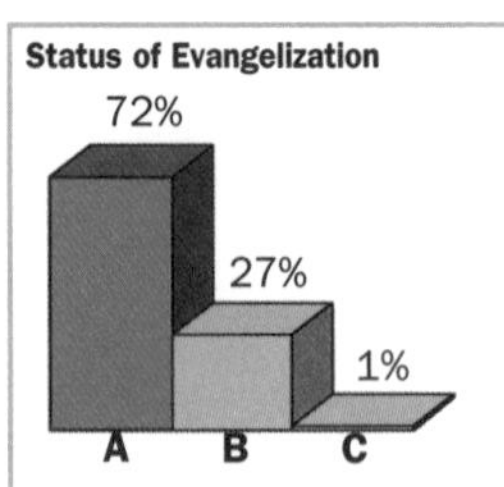

A = Have never heard the gospel
B = Were evangelized but did not become Christians
C = Are adherents to any form of Christianity

Mang 莽

Location: In 1997 a mere 408 Mang people lived in the remote and impoverished mountains of southern China.[1] The little-known Mang inhabit thick forests and mountain slopes in the Mengla District of Jinping County, near the Vietnam border. Their homes are a two-hour trek from the nearest road. The low population of the Mang is due to inbreeding, which has caused many Mang women to become sterile. Disease, malnutrition, and poor hygiene cause a high infant mortality rate. More than 2,000 Mang are located directly across the border in the Ha Giang area of Vietnam where they are one of that country's 54 official ethnic groups.

Identity: The Mang have been included in a list of *Undetermined Minorities* by the Chinese authorities. They are known by different names to different peoples in the area. The Dai call them *Chaman*; the Hani know them as *Manbu*; and the Kucong call them *Ba'e*. *Mang* is the self-name of this group.

Language: Mang is a Mon-Khmer language. "Mang is included in the Palaungic [language group] by some and is a separate group of Mon-Khmer for others."[2] Only a handful of Mang are able to understand Mandarin.

History: The Mang say they do not know where they come from. They have no special celebrations and do not even observe the popular Chinese Spring Festival. Despising themselves and feeling no self-worth, the Mang told one visitor, "We have no reason to live except to survive."[3]

YWAM COM

Customs: The Mang live in simple bamboo houses on stilts. They have no electricity and no schools. On the roofs of their houses are fixed two carvings of dragons — common among Mon-Khmer-speaking peoples. In the past, at the onset of puberty, young Mang girls were tattooed around their mouths for adornment and to show they had reached maturity. The Mang's diet consists primarily of rice and corn. They also raise pigs and hunt for rabbits, mice, and occasionally small deer. They hunt frequently because they have little food in their village. The local authorities sometimes give aid to Mang families to help them survive.

Religion: The Mang world is full of evil spirits who must be continually appeased to placate their anger. The Mang believe the universe and the human race were created by *Mon Ten*, the Creator god. They believe the universe is divided into four strata. The uppermost level is the *Mon phinh*. The realm of spirits on the earth is *Mon lom*; under the earth is *Mon lo* (the realm of demons); and in the water is *Mon chang* (the realm of dragons).[4]

Christianity: Due to the fact that they are a small and primitive people group who have virtually no contact with the outside world, the Mang in China are unaware of Christianity. They did not even know they had relatives across the mountains in Vietnam, no more than 50 kilometers (31 mi.) away. In addition to the gospel message, the Mang need practical help and assistance in community development to break them out of their dire physical poverty and economic struggle for survival. A handful of Mang families in Vietnam reportedly became Christians in 1999, but it appears these Mang have no contact with the Mang in China.

Population in China:
408 (1997)
440 (2000)
570 (2010)
Location: Yunnan
Religion: Animism
Christians: None Known

Overview of the Mang

Countries: Vietnam, China, Thailand

Pronunciation: "Mung"

Other Names: Mang Ren, Mang U, Xamang, Chaman, Manbu, Ba-e

Population Source: 408 (1997 YWAM COM); 500 (1991); 630 (1981); 2,250 in Vietnam (1991 census); 5 in Thailand (1992)

Location: *S Yunnan:* There are four villages of Mang in the Mengla District of Jinping County in the Honghe Hani-Yi Prefecture.

Status: Counted in census as an *Undetermined Minority*

Language: Austro-Asiatic, Mon-Khmer, Northern Mon-Khmer, Palaungic-Khmuic, Mang

Dialects: 0

Religion: Animism, Polytheism

Christians: None known

Scripture: None

***Jesus* film:** None

Gospel Recordings: None

Christian Broadcasting: None

ROPAL code: MGA00

Status of Evangelization

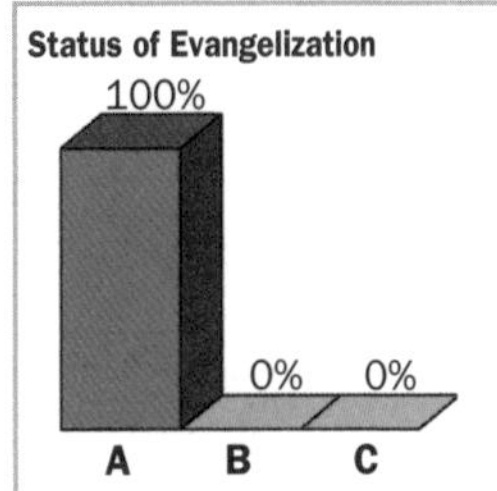

A = Have never heard the gospel
B = Were evangelized but did not become Christians
C = Are adherents to any form of Christianity

Manmet 曼米

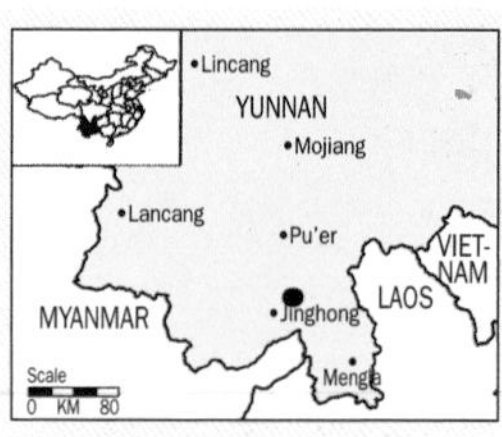

Population in China:
900 (1984)
1,310 (2000)
1,700 (2010)
Location: Yunnan
Religion: Buddhism
Christians: None Known

Overview of the Manmet

Countries: China

Pronunciation: "Mahn-met"

Other Names: Manmi, Manmit, Man Met

Population Source: 900 (1984 J.-O. Svantesson)

Location: *SW Yunnan:* The Manmet live in five communities in the mountainous areas near Jinghong County in Xishuangbanna Dai Prefecture.

Status: Counted in census as an *Undetermined Minority*

Language: Austro-Asiatic, Mon-Khmer, Northern Mon-Khmer, Palaungic, Western Palaungic, Angkuic

Dialects: 0

Religion: Theravada Buddhism, Animism

Christians: None known

Scripture: None

***Jesus* film:** None

Gospel Recordings: None

Christian Broadcasting: None

ROPAL code: MML00

Status of Evangelization

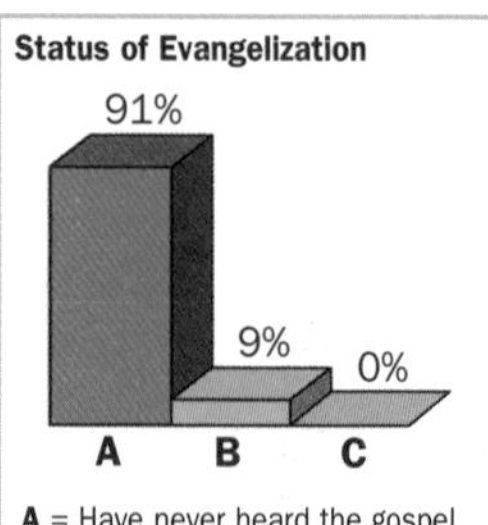

A = Have never heard the gospel
B = Were evangelized but did not become Christians
C = Are adherents to any form of Christianity

Location: More than 1,300 members of the Manmet people group live in five villages in the mountains northeast of Jinghong (City of Dawn) — the capital of Xishuangbanna Prefecture in southwest Yunnan Province. Although the Manmet are close to China's borders with the nations of Laos and Myanmar, no communities of Manmet are known to exist outside of China.

Identity: The Manmet were counted separately in the 1982 Chinese census and then combined into a large group of *Undetermined Minorities*. In the 1950s the Manmet applied to the central government in a bid to be recognized as a distinct minority group, but their application was rejected. Today the Manmet are looked down upon by both the neighboring Han Chinese and the Tai Lu people.

Language: The Manmet speak a distinct tonal language within the Angkuic branch of the Mon-Khmer linguistic family. Some Manmet men who have spent time as monks in a Buddhist temple are able to read the Tai Lu script.

History: In the twelfth century AD, a number of different tribes united with the Tai to establish the *Jinglong Golden Hall Kingdom*. The Nanzhao Kingdom, centered at Dali in central Yunnan, was overthrown by the advancing Mongol hordes of Kublai Khan in AD 1253. Thousands of minority people fled from the savage Mongols. Those who survived settled into the dozens of ethnic communities which sprang up in southern Yunnan. It was also at this time that the great Mon-Khmer race began to split into smaller, more distinct political units. The Manmet are one group today who owe their existence to this tumultuous period of history.

Customs: The Manmet are experts at tilling their sharply angled fields which seem to cling to the sides of the mountains. Every available patch of land near their villages is used for food production. They grow rice, corn, sugarcane, bananas, and various kinds of vegetables. They also raise chickens, water buffaloes, and pigs. Most Manmet women stay at home, but some earn income by selling produce at the Jinghong market. In recent years many Manmet youth have moved to the cities in search of education and work.

Religion: Most Manmet adhere to a mixture of animism and Theravada Buddhism, which is the prevalent religion in the Xishuangbanna region. Around Jinghong there are numerous temples, which serve as the focal point of each community's social life as well as a place for practising religious rituals.

Christianity: Christian churches, hospitals, and schools were established by Presbyterian missionaries in Jinghong during the 1930s and 1940s. "The people readily received the Gospel, but for many, it was very difficult to renounce sin; for them their faith was nominal.... During the Cultural Revolution [1966–1976]... many leaders of the church were killed."[1] Although missionaries were active in the Jinghong area, the shy Manmet escaped their attention. Few Manmet people today have any awareness of the gospel or the name of Jesus Christ.

Paul Hattaway

Manyak 曼牙科

Paul Hattaway

Location: Between 1,500 and 2,000 speakers of the Manyak language live in the isolated and thinly populated mountains of southern Sichuan Province. Their exact location is unknown, but they are part of the larger Ersu group which is dispersed throughout Shijin, Yanyuan, Ganluo, Yuexi, Mianning, Muli, and Jiulong counties in southern Sichuan.

Identity: Speakers of Manyak have been officially included under the Tibetan nationality in China. The Manyak are not the same as the Minyak, who are also sometimes called *Minya* or *Muya*. The Minyak live farther north than the Manyak. When Joseph Rock traveled to Muli in the 1920s, he stated, "One of the least known spots in the world is this independent lama kingdom of Muli.... Almost nothing has been written about the kingdom and its people, who are known to the Chinese as *Hsifan*, or Western Barbarians. The Europeans who have passed through during the last 100 years can be counted on the fingers of one hand."[1]

Language: Although few people have ever heard of this tribe, the Manyak language was first described by B. H. Hodgson in 1874.[2] Manyak is part of the Qiangic branch of Tibeto-Burman. Linguist Jackson Sun has identified Manyak as an Ersu language.

History: The history of the Manyak has been tied to the former Kingdom of Muli, which dominated the lives of its inhabitants until the Communists dethroned the king in the early 1950s. Manyak men were forcibly enlisted in the king's armies to ward off raids by the Nosu, who launched regular attacks from their home base in the Daliangshan mountains.

Customs: The Manyak lead incredibly difficult lives. Their attempts to cultivate crops often fail due to the steep slopes. Joseph Rock commented, "The kingdom is so mountainous that it is impossible to cultivate the soil except along the Litang River and in the narrow valleys of its tributaries descending from the mighty ranges."[3] Because of poor nutrition and hygiene, many Manyak die before their 40th birthday.

Religion: All Manyak belong to the Yellow Hat sect of Tibetan Buddhism. "Their cloaks are always red, but the distinguishing mark of the sect is the yellow ceremonial hat. It is usual for two or three out of every five male members of a family to become lamas. When there are three brothers in a family, two become lamas, and the third often marries several wives to carry on the family."[4] The Manyak also practice spirit worship and sacrifice. They live in constant fear of powerful demons and deities they believe have the power to cause affliction and bring epidemics if they are not appeased by the people.

Christianity: The Manyak are among the neediest unreached people groups in all of China. The great majority have never heard the name of Jesus Christ. They are without a witness and spiritually blinded by the powerful influence of Tibetan Buddhism. With no Bible, gospel radio, *Jesus* film, or audio recordings in a language they can understand, the Manyak have little chance of hearing the gospel.

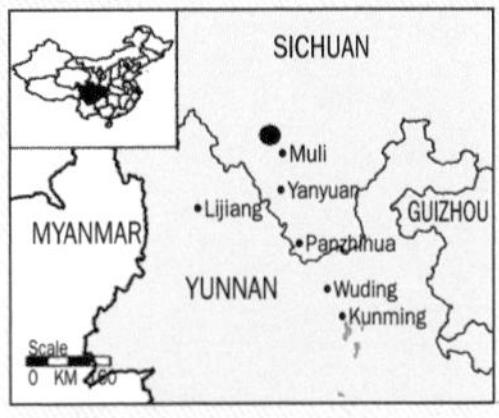

Population in China:
1,800 (1998)
1,880 (2000)
2,320 (2010)
Location: Sichuan
Religion: Tibetan Buddhism
Christians: None Known

Overview of the Manyak

Countries: China
Pronunciation: "Mahn-yahk"
Other Names:
Population Source: 1,800 (1998 AMO); Out of a total Tibetan population of 4,593,330 (1990 census)
Location: *S Sichuan:* Probably in Muli County
Status: Officially included under Tibetan
Language: Sino-Tibetan, Tibeto-Burman, Qiangic, Ersu
Dialects: 0
Religion: Tibetan Buddhism, Polytheism
Christians: None known
Scripture: None
***Jesus* film:** None
Gospel Recordings: None
Christian Broadcasting: None
ROPAL code: YMY00

Status of Evangelization

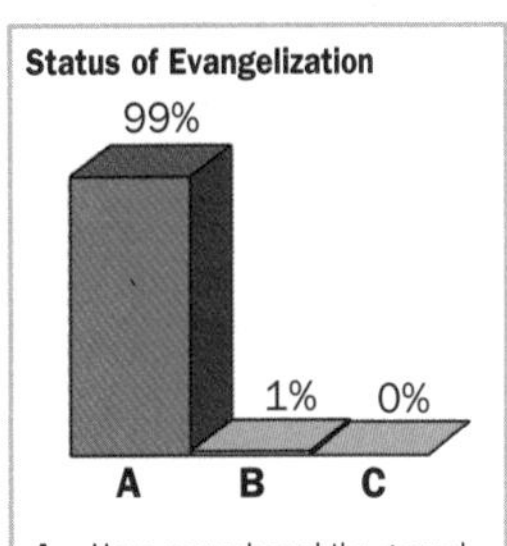

A = Have never heard the gospel
B = Were evangelized but did not become Christians
C = Are adherents to any form of Christianity

Maonan 毛南

Population in China:
40,000 (1990)
51,600 (2000)
66,500 (2010)
Location: Guangxi
Religion: Daoism
Christians: 3,000

Overview of the Maonan

Countries: China

Pronunciation: "Maow-nun"

Other Names: Ai Nan, Anan

Population Source:
71,968 (1990 census);[1]
38,135 (1982 census);
22,382 (1964 census)

Location: *N Guangxi:* Huanjiang Maonan Autonomous County

Status:
An official minority of China

Language: Daic, Kam-Sui

Literacy: 69%

Dialects: 0

Religion: Daoism, Ancestor Worship, No Religion, Christianity

Christians: 3,000

Scripture: None

***Jesus* film:** None

Gospel Recordings: None

Christian Broadcasting: None

ROPAL code: MMD00

Status of Evangelization

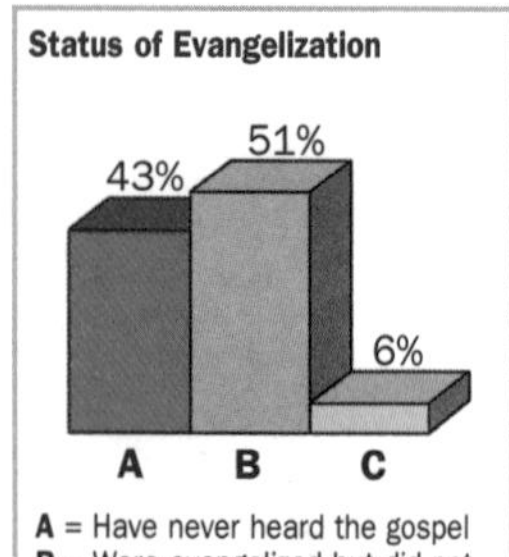

A = Have never heard the gospel
B = Were evangelized but did not become Christians
C = Are adherents to any form of Christianity

Paul Hattaway

Location: Approximately 70% of the 51,000 Maonan live in the Xianan District of Huanjiang Maonan Autonomous County in the northernmost part of Guangxi. Maonan communities are also located in nearby Hechi, Nandan, Yishan, and Du'an counties.[2] Picturesque karstic rock formations are found throughout the Huanjiang area. Many Maonan men are employed as stone masons.

Identity: The Maonan are one of China's 55 officially recognized minority groups. Their numbers grew from about 38,000 in 1982 to 72,000 in the 1990 census. Most of the population growth was not biological, but resulted from the government's inclusion of the Yanghuang people group into the Maonan nationality in 1990. The Maonan call themselves *Anan*, which means "local people" in their language.[3]

Language: The Maonan language is a part of the Dong-Shui branch of the Tai linguistic family and is similar to the Shui language spoken in Guizhou Province. Approximately half of the Maonan are able to speak their language, which has eight tones. The remainder speak either Chinese or Northern Zhuang, or both.

History: The Maonan did not appear in historical records as a separate people until the Ming Dynasty (1368–1644). They were ruled by cruel landlords, who often took away the daughters of Maonan families in payment for debts.

Customs: Up to 80% of the Maonan are surnamed Tan. They claim their ancestors lived in Hunan before migrating to their present location. Others are named Lu, Meng, Wei, and Yan, whose ancestral homes are said to have been in Shandong and Fujian provinces.[4] The Maonan live together in small villages according to their family names. The Maonan say they have three treasures — sweet yams, beef cattle, and bamboo hats. They have raised yams and cattle for at least 500 years. The northern Guangxi area is famous for its unique food. American missionary Eleanor Chestnut, who died in Guangxi in 1905, jokingly told her supporters back home this prescription she was given by her local doctor: "You must catch some little rats whose eyes are not yet open, pound them to a jelly, and add lime and peanut oil. Warranted to cure any kind of an ulcer."[5]

Religion: Most Maonan are Daoists. Each year the Maonan celebrate the Temple Festival. It is held to commemorate the Maonan patriarch, San Jie. He is believed to have taught the Maonan how to breed oxen for plowing, thereby enabling them to grow more food and to escape famine. A temple has been built to remember him, and each Maonan village annually slaughters a cow in his honor.

Christianity: The Maonan have been exposed to the gospel more than most of the other people groups in northern Guangxi. There are approximately 3,000 Maonan believers today.[6] Mission work was begun in Huanjiang in 1897. During the Cultural Revolution the Maonan church was destroyed, but in 1992 "a new church building was completed... with a big red cross on top that can be seen from far away."[7]

Maru 嫲鲁

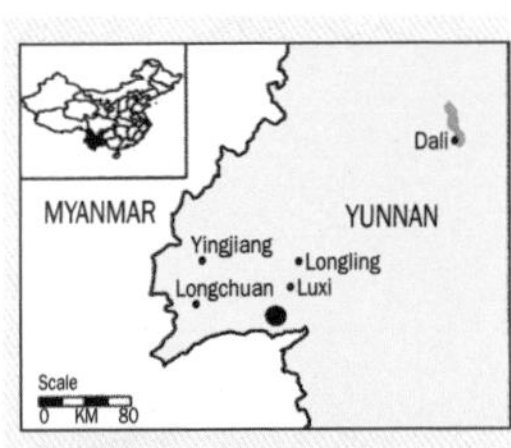

Population in China:
22,000 (1997)
23,900 (2000)
30,850 (2010)
Location: Yunnan
Religion: Christianity
Christians: 18,800

Overview of the Maru

Countries: Myanmar, China

Pronunciation: "Mah-roo"

Other Names: Malu, Matu, Lhao Vo, Lawng, Laungaw, Lansu, Lang, Mulu, Diso, Lang'e

Population Source:
22,000 (1997 AMO);
Out of a total Jingpo population of 119,209 (1990 census);
150,000 in Myanmar (1996 Tribes & Nations Outreach)

Location: *W Yunnan:* Luxi County in Dehong Prefecture

Status:
Officially included under Jingpo

Language: Sino-Tibetan, Tibeto-Burman, Burmese-Lolo, Burmish, Northern Burmish

Dialects: 0

Religion: Christianity, Animism

Christians: 18,800

Scripture: New Testament 1994, Portions 1940; Work in progress

***Jesus* film:** None

Gospel Recordings:
Maru #01159

Christian Broadcasting:
Available (FEBC)

ROPAL code: MHX00

Status of Evangelization

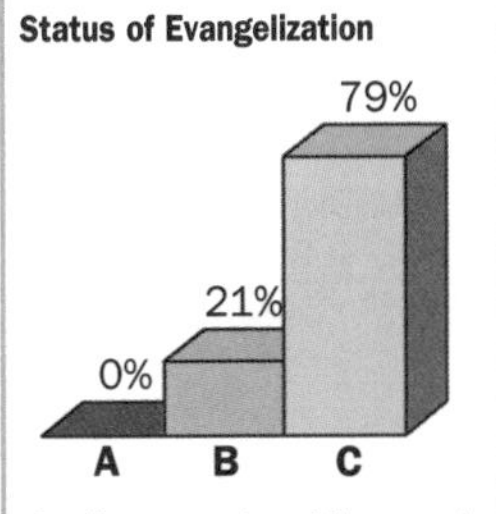

A = Have never heard the gospel
B = Were evangelized but did not become Christians
C = Are adherents to any form of Christianity

Location: Under the British Empire, all Maru lived within the borders of Burma. When the British left Burma in the 1940s and the borders were redrawn, approximately 10% of the Maru suddenly found themselves living in southern China. Today about 150,000 Maru live on the Burmese (now Myanmar) side of the border. An additional 23,900 live on Chinese soil.[1] It's believed that they live only in Luxi County, even though the *Encyclopedic Dictionary of Chinese Linguistics* states that the Maru live in parts of five counties: Luxi, Longchuan, Yingjiang, Ruili, and Lianghe.[2]

Identity: The name *Maru* is used by the Kachin and Jingpo to describe this group. The Maru call themselves *Lhao Vo*. In China the Maru have been classified as part of the Jingpo nationality, while in Myanmar they are viewed as part of the large Kachin ethnic group. The Maru earnestly oppose such classifications, insisting on a separate historical and cultural identity.

Language: The Maru language has three tones. It is related to the other Jingpo languages in China but contains loanwords from Chinese, Jingpo, Tai Mao, and Burmese. The Maru use a Roman script, devised in 1957.

History: The Maru claim to have migrated from the Tibetan Plateau thousands of years ago. They lived first in the Nujiang River valley in Yunnan before settling down in northern Myanmar. They claim to be the original inhabitants of Myanmar — an assertion that upsets the Burmans and Kachin.[3]

Customs: The Maru live in close-knit communities. When a house is being built, the whole village lends a hand in its construction. When a Maru family moves, they carry the fire from their old home along in a torch, believing the unbroken fire will ensure the continuing well-being of the family.

Religion: The majority of Maru in both Myanmar and China claim to be Christians, but in many cases their faith is nominal. One Maru church leader explains, "Many Maru animists decided to accept Christ for their convenience. They wanted to get rid of the burden of sacrificing offerings of chickens, buffaloes etc. to appease the spirits. They did not really know who Christ is. That's why when they received the copy of the Word of God in their own language, they learned that Jesus is the Redeemer; that they were redeemed from the hands of Satan to become the son of the Almighty Father; that they were a holy priesthood, a holy nation, not just plainly called Christians, but that they are an anointed people. They then understood the meaning of being a Christian for the first time."[4]

Christianity: Missionaries first targeted the Maru 100 years ago. As a result, most Maru in China and Myanmar are Christians — primarily Baptists and Catholics. However, despite the apparent success, Christianity never really took root in the people's hearts. This was primarily because the Bible was not translated in their own language. In 1994 the Maru New Testament was completed. Four thousand copies have been distributed in Myanmar.[5] At the present time three ministries are busy translating separate copies of the Maru Old Testament.[6]

Paul Hattaway

Meng 孟

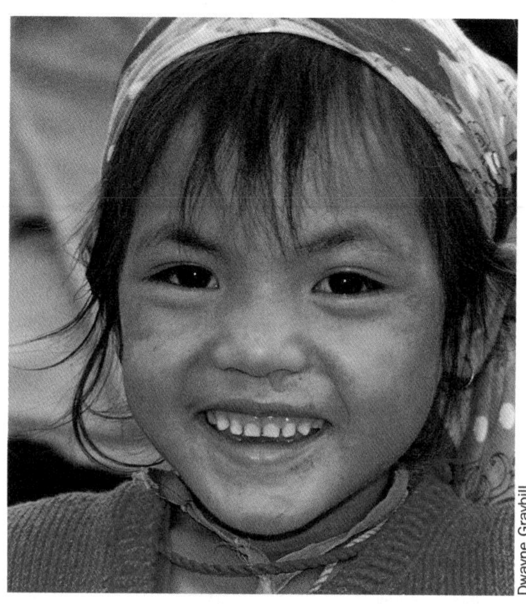
Dwayne Graybill

Location: Approximately 4,000 Meng are located in Shuangjiang County in Yunnan Province's Honghe Prefecture. The precise location of the Meng within the county is uncertain. One source simply locates the Meng as "south of Dali."[1] The Honghe (Red) River "meanders across the prefecture from northwest to southwest. Of the prefecture's 3.35 million inhabitants, 52.7% are minority people."[2] In addition to the different Hani groups, Honghe is also home to the Yi, Miao, Dai, Zhuang, Yao, Hui, Bouyei, and Lahu.

Identity: The Meng are one of many distinct Hani groups in the region. Little is known of them because Honghe is a tightly controlled area which foreigners have only recently been allowed to enter. In mission literature the Meng have usually been listed as *Menghua. Hua* means "speech" in Chinese and refers to the name of the language rather than to the people. Note that the Meng are not the same as the Mongolian nationality, who call themselves *Meng Zu* in Chinese.

Language: The Meng language is a member of the Akha branch of the Tibeto-Burman linguistic family. Tibeto-Burman contains more than 1,000 languages spoken across Asia.

History: The Meng were originally part of a large race who are the ancestors of today's Hani and Akha peoples. The various Hani groups place great importance on being able to recite their genealogies. Research into the historical relationship between the Hani tribes found that they share an identical genealogical record for the first 20 to 22 generations. After that time the groups broke off and became separate peoples. Significantly, the timing coincides with the Mongol invasion of Yunnan and the destruction of the Nanzhao Kingdom in AD 1252.[3]

Customs: Due to the horrific practice of female infanticide, the various Hani groups contained 126.5 men to every 100 women in 1987.[4] This imbalance is the worst of any minority in China. Among the Meng, the last syllable of the father's name is used to start the names of his children.[5] Many of the inhabitants of Honghe are employed in tin mines. "Both banks of the Honghe River abound luxuriantly in natural resources. This area is particularly important for the output of nonferrous metals.... The yield of tin ranks the first in the country. Because of this, Gejiu is known as the Capital of Tin."[6]

Religion: The majority of Meng are polytheists. For countless generations they have followed this primitive religion. In rice-growing areas the Thunder god and the wind ghost are the principal deities worshiped by the Meng.

Christianity: There is thought to be a small number of Christians among the Meng — the result of outreach by the neighboring Biyo and Kado. H. A. Baker, an independent Pentecostal evangelist, traveled extensively in the area throughout the 1930s and 1940s. "In spite of being short of funds,... Baker, with his traveling bag on his back and a long stick in his hand, continued his preaching as usual. He slept wherever he was able to find a place and ate whatever he could get hold of; both the [minorities] and he himself almost forgot his national identity."[7]

YUNNAN
•Zhenyuan
•Mojiang
Yuanjiang
•Yuanyang
LAOS
VIETNAM
Scale 0 KM 80

Population in China:
3,668 (1995)
4,090 (2000)
5,020 (2010)
Location: Yunnan
Religion: Polytheism
Christians: 200

Overview of the Meng

Countries: China

Pronunciation: "Mung"

Other Names: Menghua, Mehua, Menghwa, Mengwa

Population Source:
3,668 (1995 GEM);
Out of a total Hani population of 1,253,852 (1990 census)

Location: *S Yunnan:* Honghe Prefecture: Shuangjiang County

Status:
Officially included under Hani

Language: Sino-Tibetan, Tibeto-Burman, Burmese-Lolo, Lolo, Southern Lolo, Akha

Dialects: 0

Religion:
Polytheism, Animism, Christianity

Christians: 200

Scripture: None

***Jesus* film:** None

Gospel Recordings: None

Christian Broadcasting: None

ROPAL code: MJB00

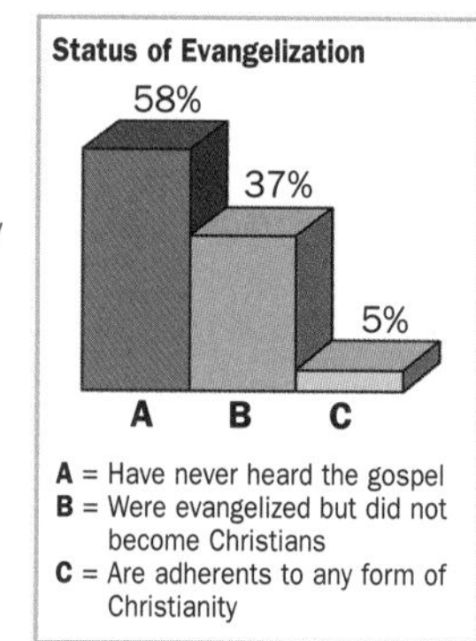

Mengwu 孟乌

Population in China:
18,200 (1999)
18,650 (2000)
23,400 (2010)
Location: Yunnan
Religion: Polytheism
Christians: None Known

Overview of the Mengwu

Countries: China

Pronunciation: "Mung-woo"

Other Names: Meng

Population Source:
18,200 (1999 J. Pelkey);
Out of a total Yi population of 6,572,173 (1990 census)

Location: *SE Yunnan:* Funing (8,000), Guangnan (7,000), Xichou (2,000), and Malipo (1,200) counties

Status:
Officially included under Yi

Language: Sino-Tibetan, Tibeto-Burman, Burmese-Lolo, Lolo, Northern Lolo, Yi, Southeastern Yi

Dialects: 0

Religion: Polytheism, Animism, Shamanism, Ancestor Worship

Christians: None known

Scripture: None

***Jesus* film:** None

Gospel Recordings: None

Christian Broadcasting: None

ROPAL code: None

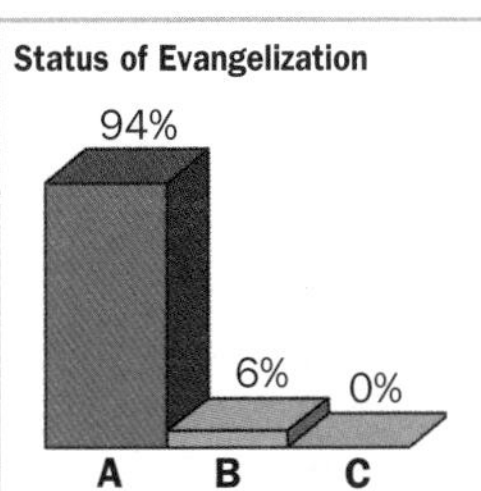

A = Have never heard the gospel
B = Were evangelized but did not become Christians
C = Are adherents to any form of Christianity

Location: A total of 18,650 Mengwu people live in the southeastern part of Yunnan Province in southern China. They are found living in valleys and on the mountainsides along the common borders of Xichou, Malipo, Guangnan, and Funing counties. Approximately 8,000 are in Funing, 7,000 in Guangnan, 2,000 in Xichou, and 1,200 in Malipo.

Identity: Although they possess their own ethnicity, customs, and language, the Mengwu have been officially included under the Yi nationality by the Chinese authorities. The Mengwu also simply call themselves *Meng*.

Jamin Pelkey

Language: The Mengwu language has never been studied in depth, but it is believed to be part of the Southeastern Yi branch of the Tibeto-Burman language family. Chinese sources state that all the Yi languages in Wenshan Prefecture are Southeastern Yi varieties.

History: The Mengwu claim that they originated near today's Kunming City. Many centuries ago they migrated south to their present location. Since then they have lived alongside the Han Chinese and other ethnic minorities.

Customs: The Mengwu observe many interesting ceremonies and festivals. Between the seventh and ninth days of the fourth lunar month they engage in a festival called *Dagongjie*, which celebrates their victory in an ancient battle. The Mengwu say their ancestors beat their adversaries by using golden bamboo in battle. Both Mengwu men and women wear white shirts. The women "have red and black bands around their wrist cuffs and circular black hats with white and black plaid material on top. In the back the women's headdress flow into long red and silver tassels accompanied by a braid of hair."[1]

Religion: The Mengwu are polytheists. They worship the creation rather than the Creator. Every year, on the 14th day of the eighth lunar month, the Mengwu get up in the small hours of the morning to worship the stars. The entire ceremony is presided over by a *bimo* (shaman) and the whole Mengwu population attends. "A white goat is prepared to be sacrificed by first sprinkling some clean water on its head to see whether or not the animal will shake off the water. If it does, this is regarded as a good omen. The sacrificial site is surrounded by *caoguo*, jingang pear, mulberry, and pine branches. It is said that the way an experienced bimo thrusts in these branches makes a sort of astrolabe, which denotes the relative positions of the stars being worshipped. The Mengwu burn sticks of incense and the goat is slaughtered. They hold a very similar ceremony to send off the soul of the deceased to be reunited with its ancestors in the afterlife."[2]

Christianity: There are no known Christians among the Mengwu, though it is possible that there are a handful who believe because of the influence of Han Chinese and Hmong Christians in the area. The Mengwu are unknown to the world of missions. They have never before appeared on any unreached peoples or ethnolinguistic lists of China. Consequently, they have never been targeted for Christian outreach.

Menia 么呢阿

Paul Hattaway

Location: Although it is difficult to estimate the population size of the Menia, there are believed to be more than 1,200 speakers of the Menia language living in southern Sichuan Province. Few outsiders have ever ventured into the area in and around Muli County. Still today, access is difficult and foreigners are not allowed to enter the region. When Joseph Rock launched an expedition from Lijiang in northern Yunnan Province in 1925, he offered a glimpse of the geographic wonders encountered along the way: "The mountains are pierced by the mighty Yangtze, which has cut a trench 13,000 feet deep through a wall of limestone rock covered with eternal snow.... The whole region is a vast conglomeration of peaks and mighty gorges, with very little level ground."[1]

Identity: Although they are now officially included under the Tibetan nationality, the Menia formerly belonged to the Chrame group who are commonly called *Xifan* (Western Barbarians) by the Chinese. Other tribes or subgroups of the Chrame include the Manyak and Hor.

Language: Menia is a member of the Qiangic branch of the Tibeto-Burman language family. Menia was first described by Edward Colborne Baber in 1881.[2] Based on the information Baber compiled and on later Chinese data, linguist Jackson Sun has identified Menia as belonging to the Ersu group of languages.[3]

History: From the Menia's language it appears that they can trace their ancestry to the Qiang race who roamed northwest China in former times. Over the course of many centuries the various tribes became dispersed across the vast geographical area of Sichuan and surrounding provinces. Some groups have been completely assimilated by the Tibetans or by the Chinese. Others, including the Menia, still retain their original language but have ceased to be culturally different from the surrounding peoples.

Customs: When, in the 1920s, a Western explorer visited the region inhabited by the Menia, he wrote, "We pitched camp on the banks of the Muli River, 8,000 feet above the sea, and here we made our first acquaintance with Muli villagers, especially the women, who barter grass and barley for the horses of caravans. Their dress consisted of dark-gray woolen skirts with fringes, and leather jackets. Their wealth of hair, a good deal of it false, was decorated with garlands of gilded Szechwan [Sichuan] rupees, a coin common in this region."[4]

Religion: The Menia were once controlled by the Chrame king, who was also the head lama of the Muli Monastery. Tibetan Buddhism still pervades every aspect of Menia society.

Christianity: There has never been a known Christian among the Menia. This is the tragic result of never having heard the gospel throughout their long history. Although they may show some interest in Christ, Buddhists do not believe in a God or a Creator and do not view sin as an act of the will, but rather an external influence. These beliefs have created additional barriers to the gospel's advance.

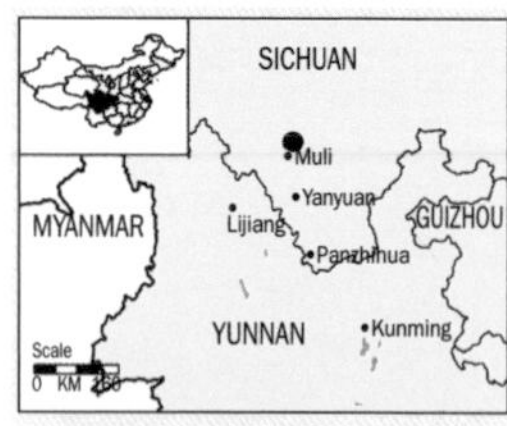

Population in China:
1,200 (1998)
1,250 (2000)
1,540 (2010)
Location: Sichuan
Religion: Tibetan Buddhism
Christians: None Known

Overview of the Menia

Countries: China
Pronunciation: "Mee-nya"
Other Names: Munia
Population Source: 1,200 (1998 AMO); Out of a total Tibetan population of 4,593,330 (1990 census)
Location: *S Sichuan:* Muli County and surrounding areas
Status: Officially included under Tibetan
Language: Sino-Tibetan, Tibeto-Burman, Qiangic, Ersu
Dialects: 0
Religion: Tibetan Buddhism, Polytheism
Christians: None known
Scripture: None
***Jesus* film:** None
Gospel Recordings: None
Christian Broadcasting: None
ROPAL code: None

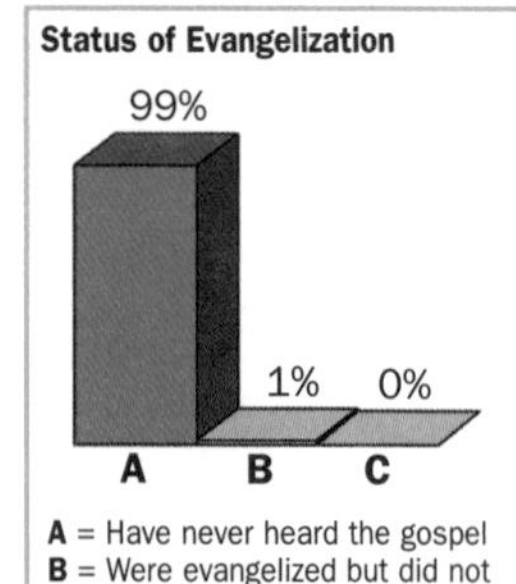

Miao, Baishi 苗 (拜师)

Location: Approximately 13,000 Miao people living in the Baishi District of Tianzhu County in the eastern part of Guizhou Province comprise their own ethnolinguistic group.[1] The area is mountainous, as is 97% of the total land in Guizhou Province. For centuries the Baishi Miao have grown crops in the poor, rocky soil. The Baishi Miao are only one branch of several distinct Miao ethnolinguistic groups who live in the region.

Identity: The Miao of Baishi have been counted as part of the Miao nationality in China, which contained approximately 7.4 million people in 1990. The Baishi Miao qualify as a distinct people group because of their language, which is not understood by any other Miao people.

Language: The Baishi Miao have lost the use of their original Miao language. They are recorded as speaking a variety of Chinese by linguists who have studied their speech, but it is not intelligible with any other Chinese varieties in China. This is probably due to a linguistic fusion of Chinese and the retention of Miao words from the past, which have survived intact in the Baishi Miao vocabulary. Most Baishi Miao cannot read Chinese well, although education is taking a more prominent role in their society; more youth are attending high school than in the past. Even though they now speak a Chinese language, the Baishi Miao believe they speak a unique Miao language. They are proud to be Miao people and have no desire to be recognized as Chinese speakers.

History: Although they are officially acknowledged as part of the Miao nationality, the Hmu and Ghao-Xong living in eastern Guizhou do not consider themselves to be related to the Baishi Miao. The Baishi Miao probably migrated into the area relatively recently (i.e. in the last 500 years) and brought with them different customs, traditional dress, and language.

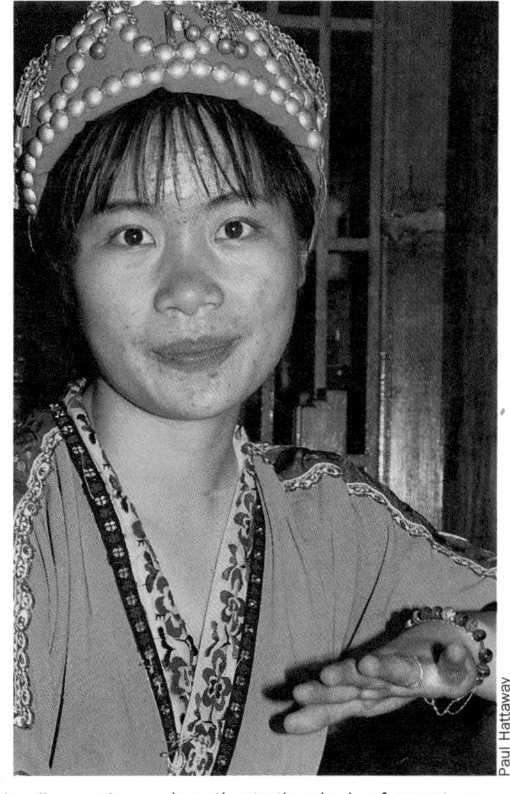
Paul Hattaway

Customs: The Baishi Miao faced opposition from other Miao groups in the past. When they migrated to Baishi they were forced to live on the worst land. In the last few decades they have been allowed to intermarry with other ethnic groups in the area. Weddings are elaborate affairs which often cost the groom's family the equivalent of two years' wages.

Religion: The Baishi Miao worship their ancestors. Elements of animism are also present in their religious rituals. The Baishi Miao believe that when a person dies, the soul remains in the village for a time before departing to the abode of ancestors. Offerings of paper money, food, and drink are made to the soul of the deceased, in a bid to provide for its needs in the next world.

Christianity: There is practically no Christian presence of any kind in the Baishi District of Guizhou Province. There are no known believers among the Baishi Miao and no ministries known to be targeting them for church planting. Few Baishi Miao have any awareness of Jesus Christ.

HUNAN
GUIZHOU
•Guiyang
•Kaili
•Hongjiang
•Chengbu
•Anshun
Rongjiang
Tongdao
•Sanjiang
GUANGXI
Scale
0 KM 100

Population in China:
10,000 (1990)
12,900 (2000)
16,600 (2010)
Location: Guizhou
Religion: Ancestor Worship
Christians: None Known

Overview of the Baishi Miao

Countries: China
Pronunciation: "Bai-shi-Meow"
Other Names:
Population Source:
10,000 (1990 AMO);
Out of a total Miao population of 7,398,035 (1990 census)
Location: *E Guizhou:* Baishi District in Tianzhu County
Status:
Officially included under Miao
Language: Chinese
Dialects: 0
Religion: Ancestor Worship, No Religion, Animism
Christians: None known
Scripture: None
***Jesus* film:** None
Gospel Recordings: None
Christian Broadcasting: None
ROPAL code: None

A = Have never heard the gospel
B = Were evangelized but did not become Christians
C = Are adherents to any form of Christianity

Miao, Chuan 苗，川

Population in China:
117,000 (1990)
150,900 (2000)
194,700 (2010)
Location: Sichuan
Religion: Animism
Christians: 2,000

Overview of the Chuan Miao

Countries: China, Myanmar

Pronunciation: "Chwun-Meow"

Other Names: Sichuan Miao, River Miao, Magpie Miao, Yaque Miao

Population Source: 117,000 (1995 Lang Weiwei – 1990 figure); Out of a total Miao population of 7,398,035 (1990 census); 10,000 in Myanmar (1992 Xiong Yuyou)

Location: *S Sichuan:* Xuyong, Gong, Gao, Junlian, and Gulin counties

Status: Officially included under Miao

Language: Hmong-Mien, Hmongic, Western Hmongic, Farwestern Hmongic, Hua Miao

Dialects: 0

Religion: Animism, Polytheism, No Religion, Christianity

Christians: 2,000

Scripture: Portions 1922

***Jesus* film:** None

Gospel Recordings: None

Christian Broadcasting: None

ROPAL code: None

Status of Evangelization

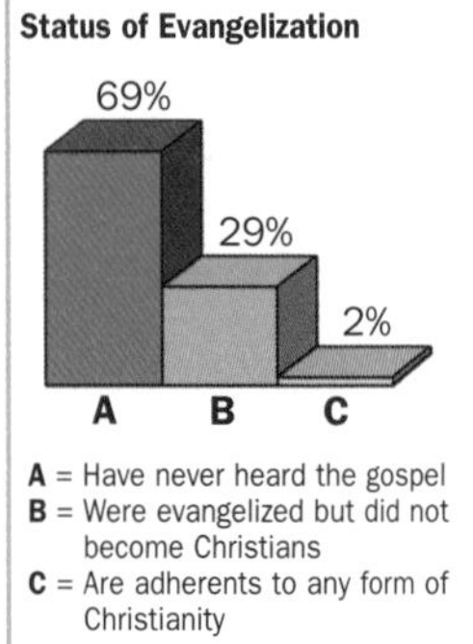

A = Have never heard the gospel
B = Were evangelized but did not become Christians
C = Are adherents to any form of Christianity

Location: The Chuan (River) Miao inhabit five counties in the southern part of Sichuan Province. They are located primarily in Xuyong, Gong, Gao, Junlian, and Gulin counties. In 1990 there were 117,000 Chuan Miao in China[1] — an increase from 1949 when they reportedly numbered between 60,000 and 70,000.[2] In addition, 10,000 Chuan Miao also live in Myanmar. They migrated there in the mid-1800s to avoid Chinese oppression.

Identity: Although the Chuan Miao speak a language similar to the Hmong Daw in southern Yunnan, they possess a distinct ethnicity and wear their own traditional dress.

Language: Chuan Miao — which has nine tones — is a part of the Chuanqiandian (Western) Miao language group. They do not have their own traditional script, but in 1912 the French explorer d'Ollone mentioned a kind of Miao writing used in southern Sichuan.[3] When missionaries first brought the gospel to the Chuan Miao, they thought the missionaries had been sent from Heaven to bring back their lost book.[4]

History: The Chuan Miao migrated north from southern Yunnan into Sichuan around 1806 to escape forced assimilation by the Han Chinese. Miao children were forced to attend Chinese schools, large tracts of Miao land were confiscated, and the Miao were banned from celebrating their traditional festivals.[5] During the Hui Rebellion in Yunnan (1855–1873), the Chuan Miao sided with the Hui against the Han Chinese. As a result, "Thousands of Miao were killed and many more migrated into Southeast Asia."[6]

Customs: The Chuan Miao love to sing. The early Christians among them "preached the Gospel by song... they will sing all night after a hard day's work, to be followed by another such day."[7]

Religion: The Chuan Miao's traditional animistic religion has gradually eroded under the influence of the Chinese.

Christianity: The China Inland Mission commenced work among the Chuan Miao in 1915 when Samuel Pollard opened a school for 40 Miao boys.[8] By 1922, 569 Chuan Miao had been baptized.[9] In 1923, 5,000 Chuan Miao were described as being interested in Christianity.[10] Thirty churches were planted by the CIM: 17 in Gulin County and 13 in Xuyong. Three thousand Chuan Miao were "under instruction from time to time."[11] The Gospel of Mark was translated into Chuan Miao in 1922, using the Pollard script. In 1937 the United Methodist missionary R. H. Goldsworthy also targeted the Chuan Miao. Within ten years, the Methodists numbered 113 baptized believers, in addition to 130 "on trial." They also had 406 students attending their schools.[12] In 1946 Ewart Wright wrote, "There is a great lack of Bibles and hymnals, both in Chinese and in River [Chuan] Miao. There is a felt desire to get the whole New Testament translated into River Miao."[13] Unfortunately, since the missionaries were deported in the 1940s, the Chuan Miao church has not significantly grown, and all the church buildings have been destroyed.

Paul Hattaway

Miao, Enshi 苗(恩施)

Paul Hattaway

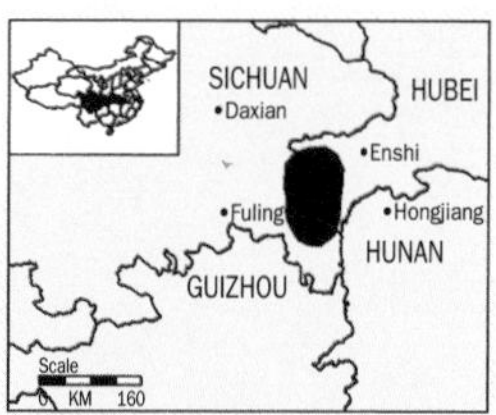

Population in China:
400,000 (1990)
516,000 (2000)
665,600 (2010)
Location: Sichuan, Hubei
Religion: Ancestor Worship
Christians: 300

Location: Approximately 500,000 Miao people — living in the southeastern part of Sichuan Province and in and around Enshi County in Hubei Province — speak Mandarin as their first language. More than 300,000 Chinese-speaking Miao live in eastern Sichuan Province alone.[1] Because they have lost the use of their original tongue, this group has not been included in linguistic studies of Miao language groups in China. The Enshi Miao are the northernmost Miao group in China. Many Tujia people also live in the Enshi area.

Identity: In *Operation China* this group is labeled *Miao, Enshi* even though far more of these people live in southeast Sichuan than in the Enshi County of Hubei. This is to avoid relating their name with Sichuan Province because of confusion with the *Chuan Miao* group who live farther to the west in Sichuan. The Enshi Miao and the Chuan Miao are two very different ethnolinguistic people groups.

Language: The Enshi Miao lost the use of their original Miao language at least 300 years ago. Today they speak the Sichuan dialect of Mandarin Chinese. Originally, the Enshi Miao are thought to have spoken the Ghao-Xong language, now primarily spoken in Hunan Province.

History: The Enshi Miao are a vivid example of what happens to a people group when assimilation takes place. Because they lived at the perimeter of Miao habitation, the Enshi Miao came into contact with the Han Chinese at a much earlier stage than other Miao groups. After centuries of contact, the Enshi Miao lost the use of their mother tongue and absorbed the Chinese language. Today there are no more than a few loanwords remaining from Miao. The Enshi Miao have also absorbed Chinese culture and customs. Few still wear a traditional style of dress, and few of their ways are different from the Chinese around them. The main distinguishing feature of the Enshi Miao is their official classification as part of the Miao nationality, which was based on their historical origins.

Customs: The Enshi Miao have lost all or most of their culture. They no longer celebrate Miao festivals, although in recent years a movement has commenced to rediscover their roots as Miao people. The Enshi Miao observe the major festivals of the Han Chinese, including the Spring Festival and the Chinese New Year.

Religion: Elderly Enshi Miao continue to worship their ancestors, especially during the annual ancestral rites when graves are cleaned and prayers are offered to the spirits of the dead. Most Enshi Miao under the age of 40 have no interest in religion.

Christianity: Very little mission work was ever undertaken in eastern Sichuan and western Hubei prior to 1949, except for work in the city of Chongqing. Today, there are thought to be only a few hundred Christians among the Enshi Miao, mostly Catholic believers living in the townships. Most Enshi Miao have never heard the gospel.

Overview of the Enshi Miao

Countries: China
Pronunciation: "En-shee-Meow"
Other Names:
Population Source:
400,000 (1990 AMO);
More than 300,000 in Sichuan (1998 M. Johnson);
Out of a total Miao population of 7,398,035 (1990 census)
Location: *SE Sichuan; SW Hubei:* Enshi County
Status:
Officially included under Miao
Language: Chinese, Mandarin
Dialects: 0
Religion: Ancestor Worship, No Religion, Animism
Christians: 300
Scripture: None
***Jesus* film:** None
Gospel Recordings: None
Christian Broadcasting: None
ROPAL code: None

Status of Evangelization

A = Have never heard the gospel
B = Were evangelized but did not become Christians
C = Are adherents to any form of Christianity

Miao, Guiyang (Northern) 苗(北贵阳)

Population in China:
84,000 (1990)
108,300 (2000)
139,800 (2010)
Location: Guizhou
Religion: Animism
Christians: 1,000

Overview of the Northern Guiyang Miao

Countries: China

Pronunciation: "Gway-yung-Meow"

Other Names: Hmong: Northern Guiyang, Kaisa

Population Source: 84,000 (1995 Wang Fushi – 1990 figure); 60,000 (1985 Wang Fushi – 1982 figure); Out of a total Miao population of 7,398,035 (1990 census)

Location: *Guizhou:* Guiyang Municipality; Pingba, Qianxi, Jinsha, Qingzhen, Xifeng, Xiumen, Guiding, and Kaiyang counties

Status: Officially included under Miao

Language: Hmong-Mien, Hmongic, Western Hmongic, Guiyang

Dialects: 0

Religion: Animism, Polytheism, Christianity

Christians: 1,000

Scripture: None

***Jesus* film:** None

Gospel Recordings: None

Christian Broadcasting: None

ROPAL code: HUJ00

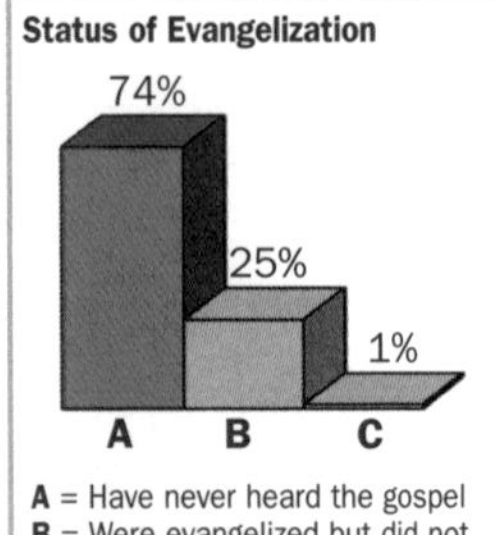

Dwayne Graybill

Location: Eighty-four thousand speakers of the Northern Guiyang Miao language were reported in 1990.[1] They occupy the western part of Guiyang Municipality and are also found in eight counties of Guizhou Province: Pingba, Qianxi, Jinsha, Qingzhen, Kaiyang, Xifeng, Xiumen, and Guiding.

Identity: A part of the official Miao nationality in China, Northern Guiyang Miao is one of four distinct Guiyang Miao languages. There are said to be more than 70 tribes of Miao in China, "each one with a distinctive costume."[2] The name *Miao* comes from the Chinese.[3] The character used in the Chinese *Book of History* means "tender blades of grass or sprouts."[4] One historian notes, "The various subgroups of Miao have no love for each other, and the Chinese have in the past been able to get some Miao groups to serve as mercenaries against other Miao groups."[5]

Language: The Guiyang Miao language group is divided into five distinct languages: Northern, Northwestern, South Central, Southern, and Southwestern.

History: In 1924 Father F. M. Savina of the Paris Foreign Missionary Society published his book *Histoire des Miao*, which caused a sensation in the Western world. Savina claimed the Miao were of Caucasian origin. He wrote, "In appearance [the Miao are] pale yellow in complexion, almost white, their hair is often light or dark brown, sometimes even red or 'corn-silk blond', and a few even have pale blue eyes."[6]

Customs: A Miao mother is not allowed to help her daughter during the delivery of a baby. The mother's sister-in-law is not even allowed to enter the delivery room, for if they do, Miao superstition dictates, the new mother will have no milk. When visitors come to see the new baby, often they will remark how ugly or dirty the baby is, so the demons will be tricked into thinking the baby is not worth their trouble and will leave the child alone.

Religion: The worldview of some Miao groups states that heaven is a flat land on top of the sky where the deceased souls of their ancestors live. It is a wonderful place, with no sickness or death, no mountains to climb, and no fields to plow. The sun always shines, and although it never rains, there is an abundance of water available.[7]

Christianity: The Northern Guiyang Miao were first visited by Protestant missionaries in the late 1800s. Several Protestant families lived in the Guiyang-Anshun region, but the Miao were described by the missionaries as "utterly indifferent to things spiritual."[8] The 1900 Boxer Rebellion broke out just as the work was seeing its first fruit, causing the mission to close and the missionaries to flee China. During the years the missionaries were gone, a military official and a noted village headman went throughout the entire district and threatened people with death if they joined the "foreign religion."[9] A small church remains today among the Northern Guiyang Miao.

Miao, Guiyang (Northwestern) 苗（西北贵阳）

Population in China:
5,000 (1982)
7,610 (2000)
9,810 (2010)
Location: Guizhou
Religion: Animism
Christians: None Known

Overview of the Northwestern Guiyang Miao

Countries: China

Pronunciation: "Gway-yung-Meow"

Other Names: Hmong: Northwest Guiyang

Population Source: 5,000 (1985 Wang Fushi – 1982 figure); Out of a total Miao population of 7,398,035 (1990 census)

Location: *Guizhou:* Qianxi, Pingba, Luzhi, and Qingzhen counties

Status: Officially included under Miao

Language: Hmong-Mien, Hmongic, Western Hmongic, Guiyang

Dialects: 0

Religion: Animism, Polytheism, Ancestor Worship

Christians: None known

Scripture: None

***Jesus* film:** None

Gospel Recordings: None

Christian Broadcasting: None

ROPAL code: None

Status of Evangelization

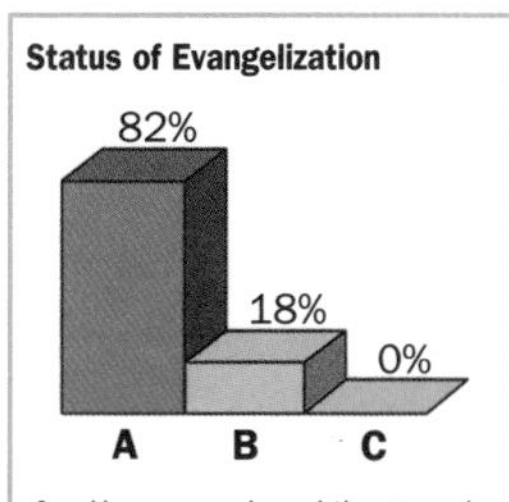

A = Have never heard the gospel
B = Were evangelized but did not become Christians
C = Are adherents to any form of Christianity

Location: In 1982, 5,000 speakers of the Northwestern Guiyang Miao language were reported in China. At that time, Chinese linguists began to investigate the numerous Miao languages and dialects, assigning them to their various classifications. The Northwestern Guiyang Miao live in Pingba, Qianxi, Luzhi, and Qingzhen counties, west of Guiyang City in Guizhou Province.

Identity: At the completion of studies based on the 1982 census findings, there were still eight unclassified Miao languages that did not fit into any of the government's recognized categories. One of these was a language labeled *Qianxi, Pingba, Qingzhen* after the names of three counties where it is spoken. In 1993 Chinese linguist Li Yunbing arrived at the conclusion that it was a part of the Guiyang Miao language cluster.[1] It has subsequently been called *Northwestern Guiyang Miao* by the Chinese authorities. None of the other seven Miao languages has yet been classified.

Language: Because of their relatively recent inclusion as a part of the Guiyang group, the Northwestern Guiyang Miao language has appeared in few linguistic studies.

History: The Northwestern Guiyang Miao have been forced from the best and most fertile land into the mountains by Han Chinese settlers. Organized and brutal attacks on the Miao were launched at regular intervals by the Chinese during the 1700s and 1800s when hatred for the Miao reached a fever pitch. Hundreds of thousands of troops were mobilized from all over China to attack the Miao. The official Chinese policy was one of genocide and complete extermination of the Miao race.

Customs: Linguists have ascertained that more than 5,000 people speak the Northwestern Guiyang Miao language. Within that number, however, there may be several ethno-socio subgroups, each wearing distinct dress and practising slightly different customs from the others.

Religion: The Miao believe that the gods are invisible unless they choose to reveal themselves. Among them, *Ntzi* is the highest god. He is kind, just, and powerful, controlling heaven and earth. Stories recount how he sent his daughter to earth to help the poor and unfortunate. Some Miao groups believe there was once a ladder that connected the earth with heaven, but the ladder was broken. Since that time no Miao have been able to visit heaven.

Christianity: Most of the Northwestern Guiyang Miao have never heard the gospel and live hidden away from any Christian influence. Those few who have heard the good news in Mandarin have found it interesting, but because it was not presented to them in their own language, it has proven to be something abstract or foreign. Specific cross-cultural evangelism will need to occur before the gospel takes hold in the hearts and minds of the Northwestern Guiyang Miao people.

Dwayne Graybill

Miao, Guiyang (South Central) 苗（中南贵阳）

Location: In 1985 Chinese linguist Wang Fushi listed a 1982 figure of 3,000 speakers of the South Central Guiyang Miao language in China. They are one of five Guiyang Miao languages spoken in China's Guizhou Province. The South Central Guiyang Miao live in parts of Ziyun and Zhenning counties.

Identity: The classification of the South Central Guiyang Miao was only made in 1995. Until that time scholars had not yet determined that it qualified as a distinct language. After the 1982 census the language was placed in a list of eight unclassified Miao languages and was named "Ziyun, Zhenning" after the counties where it was spoken. Finally it was agreed that South Central Guiyang Miao was unlike any of the other Miao languages and was set apart by itself. This group is one small part of the massive Miao nationality, whose ten million members are found throughout China and in the neighboring countries of Southeast Asia.

Language: South Central Guiyang Miao is part of the Western Miao language group, more closely related to the Hmong varieties in Yunnan than to the Hmu and Ghao-Xong languages in Guizhou and Hunan.

History: The areas now inhabited by the Guiyang Miao are believed to have once been home to many of today's Western and Farwestern Miao groups. The majority of these peoples fled Guizhou to Yunnan and beyond during times of persecution, while those that remained have, over the centuries, fragmented into small tribes and ethnic groups.

Dwayne Graybill

Customs: Miao families are renowned for being close-knit. Family and community relationships are prized above all among the Miao, who often frown upon individualism and decisions made without the input of others. The Guiyang Miao women are also known for their embroidery. In the past one of the subgroups of Miao in Guizhou was even known as *Mp'eo* or *De Mp'eo*, which means "embroidery."

Religion: The South Central Guiyang Miao are animists. Above all they revere the spirit of the dragon, and another spirit which they believe blesses their crops.

Christianity: While pre-1949 mission labors resulted in several wonderful people movements to Christ, there were quite simply not enough laborers to cover the numerous minority areas in southwest China. Most people groups missed out on the gospel. While people like Isobel Kuhn — who worked among the Lisu and once said, "When I get to heaven they aren't going to see much of me except my heels, for I will be hanging over the golden wall keeping an eye on the Lisu church!"[1] — were faithful to their call, other areas were completely neglected. As a result, the more than 3,000 hidden souls who speak the South Central Guiyang Miao language have never had any known Christians in their midst.

SICHUAN
GUIZHOU
•Lupanshui
•Guiyang
•Anshun
•Duyun
•Huishui
YUNNAN
•Xingren
GUANGXI
Scale
0 KM 160

Population in China:
3,000 (1982)
4,560 (2000)
5,890 (2010)
Location: Guizhou
Religion: Animism
Christians: None Known

Overview of the South Central Guiyang Miao

Countries: China

Pronunciation: "Gway-yung-Meow"

Other Names: Hmong: South Central Guiyang

Population Source: 3,000 (1985 Wang Fushi – 1982 figure); Out of a total Miao population of 7,398,035 (1990 census)

Location: *Guizhou:* Ziyun and Zhenning counties

Status: Officially included under Miao

Language: Hmong-Mien, Hmongic, Western Hmongic, Guiyang

Dialects: 0

Religion: Animism, Polytheism

Christians: None

Scripture: None

***Jesus* film:** None

Gospel Recordings: None

Christian Broadcasting: None

ROPAL code: None

Status of Evangelization

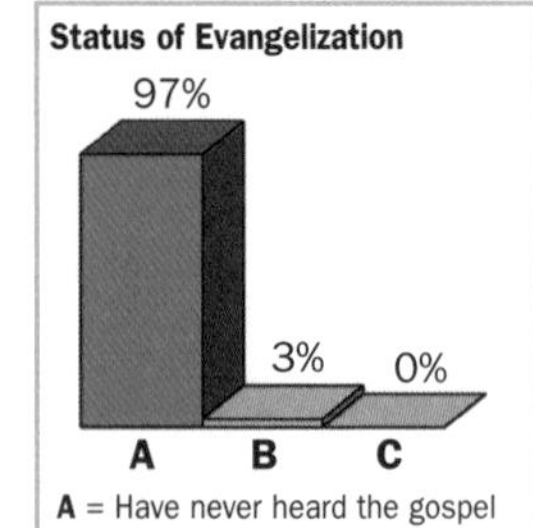

A = Have never heard the gospel
B = Were evangelized but did not become Christians
C = Are adherents to any form of Christianity

Miao, Guiyang (Southern) 苗(南贵阳)

Population in China:
28,000 (1990)
36,100 (2000)
46,600 (2010)
Location: Guizhou
Religion: Animism
Christians: 3,000

Overview of the Southern Guiyang Miao

Countries: China

Pronunciation: "Gway-Yung-Meow"

Other Names:
Hmong: Southern Guiyang

Population Source: 28,000 (1995 Wang Fushi – 1990 figure); 20,000 (1985 Wang Fushi – 1982 figure);
Out of a total Miao population of 7,398,035 (1990 census)

Location: *Guizhou*: Anshun, Changshun, Ziyun, and Zhenning counties

Status:
Officially included under Miao

Language: Hmong-Mien, Hmongic, Western Hmongic, Guiyang

Dialects: 0

Religion: Animism, Christianity, Ancestor Worship

Christians: 3,000

Scripture: None

***Jesus* film:** None

Gospel Recordings: None

Christian Broadcasting: None

ROPAL code: HMY00

Status of Evangelization

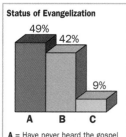

49% 42% 9%

A B C

A = Have never heard the gospel
B = Were evangelized but did not become Christians
C = Are adherents to any form of Christianity

Miao Messenger

Location: Approximately 36,000 Southern Guiyang Miao are located in the mountains of southern China, primarily in Anshun, Changshun, Ziyun, and Zhenning counties in Guizhou. Anshun was once an opium trading center and is now the commercial hub of western Guizhou.

Identity: Officially considered part of the Miao nationality, the Southern Guiyang Miao have lived in their current location for many centuries. They share the same part of China as the Bouyei minority.

Language: Southern Guiyang Miao is one of five Guiyang Miao languages that are mutually unintelligible. They form part of the Western Miao language family. People from one group are not able to communicate in their native tongues with people from the other four groups.

History: Miao legends from Laos depict the distant ancestors of the Miao as "white," with "pale skin and light hair."[1] During intense periods of Chinese persecution, the Miao were killed because they were easy to single out. An 80-year-old Miao man in Laos, Cher Sue Vue, remembers his childhood when the Chinese crossed into Laos looking for white babies. "At that time there was only one white baby in our village. The infant's parents were warned before the Chinese arrived, and they carried him into the forest where they hid."[2] The Miao have a legend of a homeland where "days and nights lasted six months, the water was frozen, and snow hid the ground. Only a few trees grew and they were small. The people, too, were short and squat, clothed in furs."[3]

Customs: Strict superstitions apply to the Miao when they are eating. If someone changes his chopsticks during a meal, he can expect either a divorce or a change of spouse. If he taps something with his chopsticks, he will become a beggar. If he finishes his meal by leaving the chopsticks standing straight up in his rice, someone will die. After a meal, if he turns his bowl upside down, he is cursing the host to be barren.[4]

Religion: The Southern Guiyang Miao believe all living things have a spirit. They seek to live in harmony with nature and are careful to avoid offending the spirits of the hills, river, crops, rain, etc. A number of Southern Guiyang Miao near Anshun have converted to Christianity.

Christianity: The first Protestant missionary in the region was J. R. Adam of the China Inland Mission, who commenced work near Anshun in 1899. A strong Miao church exists there today. One author who visited them comments, "They witness to God not by their appearance, but by their living. Their mouths are not filled with theological terms or biblical messages. Pastors do not wear ties, white shirts and dark blue pants.... What they wear are work clothes; what they carry are agricultural tools... the Miao Christians are a blessed community."[5]

Miao, Guiyang (Southwestern) 苗(西南贵阳)

Jamin Pelkey

Location: More than 90,000 speakers of the Southwestern Guiyang Miao language are located in Pingba, Qingzhen, and Changshun counties, as well as in the Guiyang and Anshun municipalities in Guizhou Province. China's largest waterfall and the province's chief tourist attraction, Huangguoshu Falls, is located about 40 kilometers (25 mi.) southwest of Anshun.

Identity: The Southwestern Guiyang Miao speak their own distinct language. One anthropologist has counted "72 different tribes of Miao in Guizhou alone."[1]

Language: There are no dialects reported within any of the four Guiyang Miao languages. Speakers of the various languages find it necessary to use Chinese to communicate with each other.

History: Speculation about the origin of the Miao race has led some to claim that they first lived in Persia or Babylon before migrating north into Siberia. After staying there for a time, the Miao moved again, passing through Mongolia and entering China. One writer has even asserted that there was a Miao princess named Mong Kao Lee who led the Miao in their great migration. "In her honor they called their former homeland by her name, Mongoli or Mongolia."[2] Chinese histories confirm the Miao used to be found in northern and central China before they were pushed south under Chinese pressure.

Customs: Southwestern Guiyang Miao women wear a style of clothing referred to as "flag clothing" by local people. Square and rectangular patterns on their jackets resemble the pattern of a flag. The Guiyang Miao live on the mountaintops where the land is poor. Often their homes are a long distance from streams and rivers. Water therefore carries a high price. Miao women are responsible for walking hours down the mountain and back again, to fetch drinking water in hollowed bamboo. In the most extreme cases, the women mix cow urine with the water, so that others they meet on the pathway will not be tempted to steal the water from them.[3] Young Miao women often base their answer to a marriage proposal on how far the would-be bridegroom's water supply is from his village.

Religion: Most Southwest Guiyang Miao are either animists or Christians. Some whole villages have converted to Christ, while others prefer to retain their ancient traditions and superstitions.

Christianity: Shortly after J. R. Adam commenced work in Anshun in 1899, he was forced to leave because of the Boxer Rebellion. When Adam returned to Anshun in 1902 he baptized 20 Miao at the first baptismal service. The work grew quickly, and by 1907 the number of baptized believers numbered 1,200. Adam started a Bible college where students came for four to eight weeks of study. Tragically, Adam's work was cut short when he was killed by a bolt of lightning while he stood in the doorway of his house in 1915.[4]

Population in China:
70,000 (1990)
90,300 (2000)
116,500 (2010)
Location: Guizhou
Religion: Animism
Christians: 2,000

Overview of the Southwestern Guiyang Miao

Countries: China

Pronunciation: "Gway-yung-Meow"

Other Names: Hmong: Southwestern Guiyang

Population Source: 70,000 (1995 Wang Fushi – 1990 figure); 50,000 (1985 Wang Fushi – 1982 figure); Out of a total Miao population of 7,398,035 (1990 census)

Location: *Guizhou:* Pingba, Qingzhen, and Changshun counties; Anshun and Guiyang municipalities

Status: Officially included under Miao

Language: Hmong-Mien, Hmongic, Western Hmongic, Guiyang

Dialects: 0

Religion: Animism, Polytheism, Christianity

Christians: 2,000

Scripture: None

***Jesus* film:** None

Gospel Recordings: None

Christian Broadcasting: None

ROPAL code: HMG00

Status of Evangelization

	A	B	C
%	79%	18%	3%

A = Have never heard the gospel
B = Were evangelized but did not become Christians
C = Are adherents to any form of Christianity

Miao, Huishui (Central) 苗(中惠水)

Location: Approximately 50,000 Miao speak the Central Huishui Miao language as their mother tongue. They are located in the suburbs of Guiyang City, in the Baijin area of Huishui County, and in parts of adjacent Changshun County.[1] These two counties are located south of Guiyang City in Guizhou Province.

Identity: Central Huishui is one of four Huishui Miao languages — totaling more than 140,000 speakers. They, in turn, are considered part of the official Miao nationality by the Chinese government.

Language: Central Huishui Miao is "inherently unintelligible" with all other Miao languages in China. The Miao have no written script today — except for orthographies devised by missionaries. In 1683, however, traveler Lu Ciyun's book *Dongqi-xianzhi* contained samples of Miao writing which he claims to have discovered on his travels through southern China. Lu wrote, "The Miao have writing, which is not like that on ancient bronze vessels, nor like the kedou script. One cannot find out who invented it."[2] His claims are strengthened by the *Annals of Baoqing Prefecture* in 1740, which mentions an edict from the Qing authorities banning the use of Miao writing.[3]

History: Because they do not have a written language, Miao history is handed down by word of mouth and through songs. Miao legend tells how human life originated when a maple tree metamorphosed into a butterfly. The butterfly then laid twelve eggs from which hatched Jiangyang, the ancestor of the Miao. The other eggs hatched, giving birth to Thunder, Centipede, Dragon, Elephant, Tiger, Snake, Rooster, Dog, Fish, and Water Buffalo.[4]

Miao Messenger

Customs: The lives of most Miao people in China have become more complicated in recent years as China's economic condition has improved. Today, a prospective partner for marriage is often required to own a television, radio, and motorbike before being considered marriageable.

Religion: Most Central Huishui Miao are animists, living in fear of a host of different demons and deities. Miao shamans and sorcerers possess great demonic power. An early missionary described his experiences: "As a rule I don't believe in devils but these wizards seem to have communications with a whole world of demons."[5] He went on to describe some of the supernatural things done by these men, such as putting white hot chains around their necks without being harmed.

Christianity: There are small numbers of indigenous Miao and ethnically mixed Christian fellowships in the Central Huishui Miao region. Approximately one percent of Central Huishui Miao are Christians, although most members of this group have yet to receive an adequate presentation of the gospel. There are no Scriptures in their language, and the Miao language used for the *Jesus* film is not understood by the Central Huishui Miao. They are relatively open to change, but few evangelists or missionaries have ever specifically targeted the Central Huishui Miao.

SICHUAN
GUIZHOU
•Guiyang
•Lupanshui
•Anshun
•Duyun
Huishui
•Pingtang
YUNNAN
•Xingren
•Wangmo
GUANGXI
Scale
0 KM 160

Population in China:
40,000 (1990)
51,600 (2000)
66,500 (2010)
Location: Guizhou
Religion: Animism
Christians: 300

Overview of the Central Huishui Miao

Countries: China

Pronunciation: "Hway-shway-Meow"

Other Names: Hmong: Central Huishui, Gaopo

Population Source: 40,000 (1995 Wang Fushi – 1990 figure); 30,000 (1985 Wang Fushi – 1982 figure); Out of a total Miao population of 7,398,035 (1990 census)

Location: *Guizhou:* Huishui and Changshun counties; Guiyang Municipality

Status: Officially included under Miao

Language: Hmong-Mien, Hmonic, Western Hmongic, Huishui

Dialects: 0

Religion: Animism, Shamanism, Polytheism, Christianity

Christians: 300

Scripture: None

***Jesus* film:** None

Gospel Recordings: None

Christian Broadcasting: None

ROPAL code: HMC00

Status of Evangelization

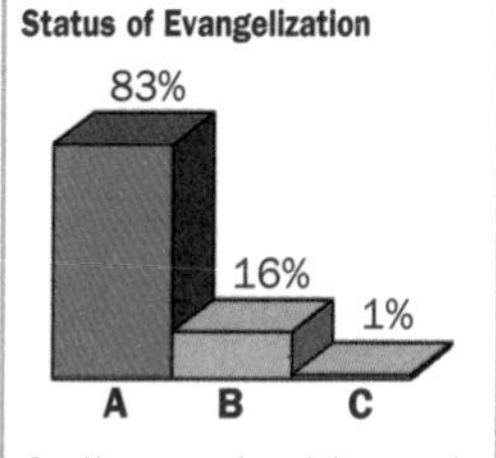

A = Have never heard the gospel
B = Were evangelized but did not become Christians
C = Are adherents to any form of Christianity

Miao, Huishui (Eastern) 苗(东惠水)

Population in China:
14,000 (1990)
18,050 (2000)
23,300 (2010)
Location: Guizhou
Religion: Animism
Christians: 50

Overview of the Eastern Huishui Miao

Countries: China

Pronunciation: "Hway-shway-Meow"

Other Names: Hmong: Eastern Huishui

Population Source: 14,000 (1995 Wang Fushi – 1990 figure); 10,000 (1985 Wang Fushi – 1982 figure);
Out of a total Miao population of 7,398,035 (1990 census)

Location: *S Guizhou:* Gaobaibang District of Huishui County; Luodian and Pingba counties

Status: Officially included under Miao

Language: Hmong-Mien, Hmongic, Western Hmongic, Huishui

Dialects: 0

Religion: Animism, Polytheism, Ancestor Worship

Christians: 50

Scripture: None

***Jesus* film:** None

Gospel Recordings: None

Christian Broadcasting: None

ROPAL code: HME00

Status of Evangelization

	A	B	C
	93%	6%	1%

A = Have never heard the gospel
B = Were evangelized but did not become Christians
C = Are adherents to any form of Christianity

Location: More than 18,000 Miao in southern Guizhou Province speak the Eastern Huishui language. They live in the Gaobaibang District of Huishui County, in the Xiguan District of Luodian County, and in Pingba County.

Identity: The Eastern Huishui Miao are one part of the Miao diaspora that has taken place at various stages over the last 1,000 years.

Language: Eastern Huishui Miao is distinct from all other Miao languages in China. It is unintelligible even with the other languages in the Huishui branch. In times of war the Miao developed what they called "feather letters" to communicate across the various linguistic barriers. The feather letters were "long wood sticks, about one inch thick, one end was split, and there were inserted two feathers, a piece of fuse... and two red peppers. This was said to be a Miao emergency message: the feather means emergency, the pepper means that the enemy is strong and the fuse means that the enemy has already opened fire. If somebody received such a 'feather letter' he would bring armed troops and come to their support."[1]

History: The Chinese hatred of the Miao reached a feverish climax during the Ming Dynasty (1368–1644) when the Imperial Court attempted to completely isolate the Miao territory from the rest of China. They set up stone guard posts and military stations, and in many places even erected walls to keep the Miao in the mountains. The remains of these stone towers can still be seen along ridges in Guizhou today. In 1650 the Miao rebelled, tore down the guard posts and walls, and "demolished the border between themselves and the Chinese."[2]

Customs: The Miao have many oral legends of great heroes. One heroine often portrayed on embroidery is Wu Yaoxi. Born in Shidong in Guizhou, she joined the Miao rebellion against the Qing Dynasty (1855–1872) and became a famous general. She was finally killed, but she is still proudly remembered by her descendants.[3]

Religion: A sinister part of the traditional Miao religion was the role of some women who produced an evil poison called *gu*. It was used in secret black magic rituals to put curses on their enemies, who often died because of it.[4] All Chinese people living near the Miao were afraid that these dark powers would be used against them and, therefore, lived in utter terror of the Miao.

Christianity: In the early years of Protestant missionary work, most workers focused on the needs of the A-Hmao and Gha-Mu in northwest Guizhou because of the readiness with which these peoples responded to the gospel. The Miao groups in southern Guizhou, such as the Eastern Huishui Miao, were comparatively neglected. There may be small numbers of believers among all of the Huishui Miao groups, but there are few vibrant fellowships meeting regularly. The handful of Christians live in small, scattered communities. Few Eastern Huishui Miao have been so fortunate as to receive the offer of salvation.

Miao Messenger

126

127

128

129

126–127. The *Manchu* ruled China for 250 years until 1911. Their domination was won, however, at the cost of their ethnic identity. Today only about 1,000 of the more than 12 million Manchu in China can still speak the Manchu language. [both by Paul Hattaway]

128–129. The *Monba* minority are one of the most unreached people groups in China. They live in a remote part of southern Tibet that is off-limits to foreign travelers. [both by Midge Conner]

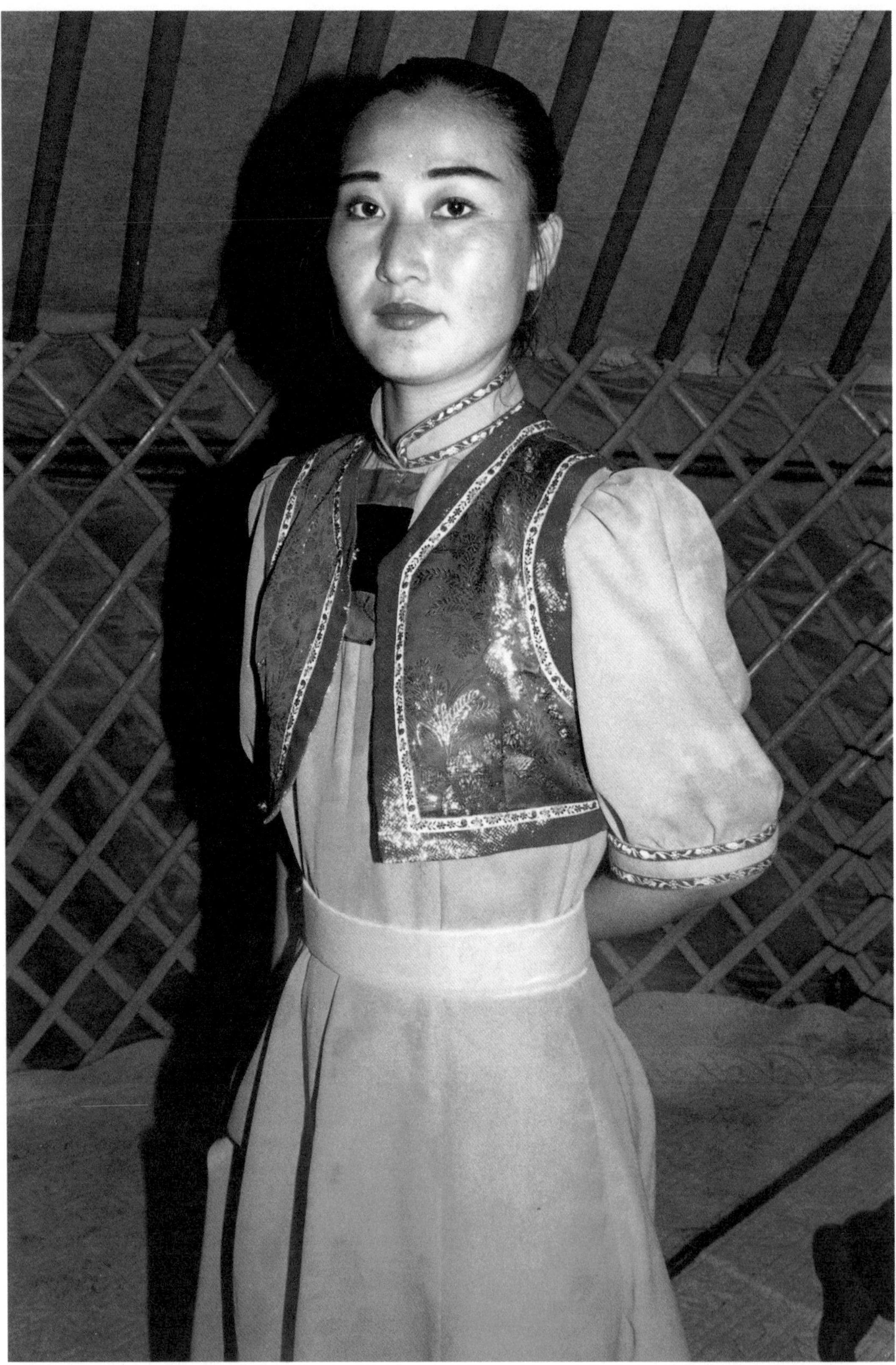

130. Approximately three times as many *Mongols* live within the borders of China than in the nation of Mongolia. [Paul Hattaway]

131

132

133

131. A *Mongol* lady inside her yurt. [Paul Hattaway]
132. An *Alxa Mongol* from the Alxa League in Inner Mongolia — also home to 200,000 double-hump Bactarian camels. Alxa contains the only Mongolian Muslim community in China. [Paul Hattaway]
133. Few people know about the 27,000 *Sichuan Mongols* who are descendants of Genghis Khan's thirteenth-century armies. A Mongolian prince still lives in the region, Muli, Sichuan. [China Passage]

134

135

136

137

134. *Mongol* horsemen once ruled over the largest empire the world has seen, stretching from Southeast Asia to Europe. [Paul Hattaway]
135. Most of the 46,000 *Mosuo* on the Yunnan-Sichuan border still live in a matriarchal society, where their communities are ruled by women. [Paul Hattaway]
136. A *Mosuo* woman rowing on beautiful Lugu Lake, Sichuan. [Midge Conner]
137. The 7,000 *Yunnan Mongols* are descended from seven administrators sent by the Mongols in 1252 to rule over the region. [Paul Hattaway]

Miao, Huishui (Northern) 苗(北惠水)

Miao Messenger

Location: The Northern Huishui Miao language is spoken by more than 90,000 people south of Guiyang Municipality — the capital of Guizhou Province. They live in the Gaopo District of Guiyang Municipality, and Huishui and Guiding counties.

Identity: The Northern Huishui Miao are defined as a group purely on the basis of a linguistic classification within the Miao nationality, which contains "30–40 languages in China."[1] The Northern Huishui Miao language group may consist of several ethnic subgroups.

Language: Northern Huishui Miao is inherently unintelligible with the Eastern, Central, or Southwestern Huishui Miao languages. Speakers from the different groups must use Mandarin to communicate.

History: According to legend, in about 2550 BC a Miao chief, Jiyou, was defeated by the Han race. The Miao were forcibly exiled to the inhospitable mountains in southern China. Military campaigns were launched against the Miao for centuries. Throughout the Ming Dynasty (1368–1644), more than 80 fierce attacks were made against the Miao — an average of one every three years.[2] In 1832 another Miao rebellion was directed by the self-appointed "Golden Dragon King," who dressed in yellow robes. He declared that the government of China had lost its "mandate from heaven" and, therefore, no longer had a right to rule over the Miao people.[3] He mobilized a large army with his promise to overthrow the Qing Dynasty, but without the arms or means to pose a threat, he was soon captured and executed, and the rebellion was crushed.

Customs: Music is always at the center of Miao celebrations and social gatherings, whether it involves singing, instrument playing, or leaf-blowing. Traditional love songs are handed down from generation to generation. Two young lovers may sing to each other in question-and-answer form to express their mutual feelings.[4] Many annual Miao festivals are held which offer a chance for young people from different villages to mix and for romance to blossom.

Religion: Most Northern Huishui Miao live in fear and bondage to evil spirits which harass them continually. Some Miao stories tell of a dark place inhabited by demons and ruled by a demon king. To the Miao, demons are the souls of humans, birds, or animals. If a deceased person had no descendants to continue his family line, or if his descendants do not make proper offerings, he becomes a demon and causes harm to people.[5]

Christianity: Few of the early missionaries targeted the Miao groups in southern Guizhou. As the great people movement to Christ unfolded in northwest Guizhou and in Yunnan among the A-Hmao and Gha-Mu, many of the missionaries placed among other Miao groups were summoned to lend a hand to disciple these new believers. This is one of the reasons why the gospel has never taken a firm foothold among most of the Miao groups in China. Most Northern Huishui Miao are completely unaware of Christ or the claims of the gospel.

Population in China:
70,000 (1990)
90,300 (2000)
116,500 (2010)
Location: Guizhou
Religion: Animism
Christians: 50

Overview of the Northern Huishui Miao

Countries: China
Pronunciation: "Hway-shway-Meow"
Other Names: Hmong: Northern Huishui
Population Source: 70,000 (1995 Wang Fushi – 1990 figure); 50,000 (1985 Wang Fushi – 1982 figure); Out of a total Miao population of 7,398,035 (1990 census)
Location: *Guizhou:* Gaopo District of Guiyang Municipality; Tangbao, Yangchang, and Pingfa districts of Huishui County; Guiding County
Status: Officially included under Miao
Language: Hmong-Mien, Hmongic, Western Hmongic, Huishui
Dialects: 0
Religion: Animism, Polytheism
Christians: 50
Scripture: None
***Jesus* film:** None
Gospel Recordings: None
Christian Broadcasting: None
ROPAL code: HMN00

Status of Evangelization

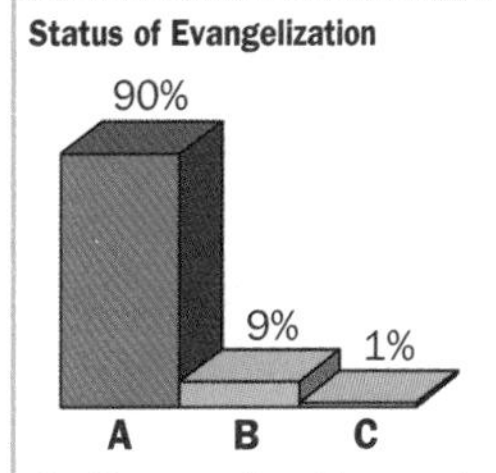

A = Have never heard the gospel
B = Were evangelized but did not become Christians
C = Are adherents to any form of Christianity

Miao, Huishui (Southwestern) 苗（西南惠水）

July 29

Population in China:
56,000 (1990)
72,200 (2000)
93,200 (2010)
Location: Guizhou
Religion: Animism
Christians: None Known

Overview of the Southwestern Huishui Miao

Countries: China

Pronunciation: "Hway-shway-Meow"

Other Names: Hmong: Southwestern Huishui

Population Source: 56,000 (1995 Wang Fushi – 1990 figure); 40,000 (1985 Wang Fushi – 1982 figure);
Out of a total Miao population of 7,398,035 (1990 census)

Location: *Guizhou:* Yashui, Sandu, Doudi, and Duansha districts in Huishui County; Baitang and Zhongguo in Changshun County

Status: Officially included under Miao

Language: Hmong-Mien, Hmongic, Western Hmongic, Huishui

Dialects: 0

Religion: Animism, Polytheism, Ancestor Worship, Shamanism

Christians: None known

Scripture: None

***Jesus* film:** None

Gospel Recordings: None

Christian Broadcasting: None

ROPAL code: HMH00

Status of Evangelization

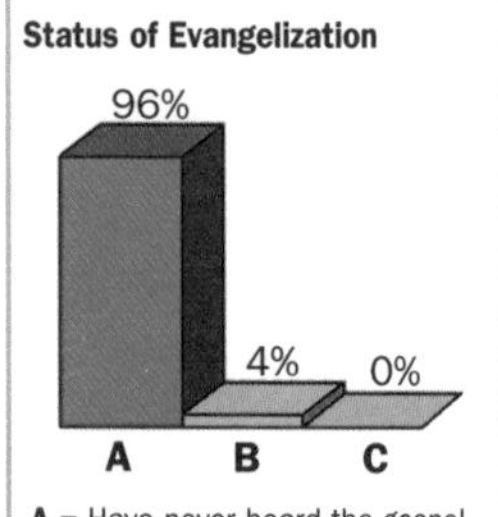

A = Have never heard the gospel
B = Were evangelized but did not become Christians
C = Are adherents to any form of Christianity

Miao Messenger

Location: More than 70,000 Southwestern Huishui Miao live quiet lives in the mountains of southern China. They are concentrated in four districts of Huishui County, and in the Baitang and Zhongguo districts of Changshun County. Both counties are located directly south of Guiyang City, the capital of Guizhou Province.

Identity: Although they were officially placed under the Miao nationality — which contained 7.4 million people in the 1990 census — the Southwestern Huishui Miao are a distinct ethnolinguistic people.

Language: The *Ethnologue* states that the Southwestern Huishui Miao language is "inherently unintelligible with other Hmong [Miao] varieties."[1] It is one of four Huishui Miao languages in Guizhou and one of more than 30 Miao languages in all of China.[2]

History: The Miao have a folk tale explaining why their language has never possessed a written form. They tell of a time long ago when they lived alongside the Chinese. The Chinese were too crafty for them, so they decided to move away and live by themselves. At that time the Miao knew only a few Chinese characters. When they came to a deep river they saw some water spiders walking about on the water. They asked, "If they can walk on water, why can't we?" So they tried to walk across the river but almost drowned, having swallowed much water. By the time they made it to the other side of the river they had swallowed all the characters they knew. That is why the Miao no longer have a written language.[3]

Customs: Sexual immorality is rampant among many of the Miao groups. Some practice what they call "free marriage." Young people are allowed to engage in sexual relationships with multiple partners before and after betrothal.[4] Families may build a separate room onto their homes so young men can visit their daughters at night, while many villages have "flower houses" set aside where young people can meet in sexual orgies that often last for several days.[5] Sexual diseases were so rampant that Samuel Pollard wrote, "When one mentions the *Miao disease* everyone knows what one means... it is so typical."[6]

Religion: The majority of Southwestern Huishui Miao villages are animists, with altars and incense boxes located inside their homes. They do not worship idols, however. Marriages, funerals, and major festivals are presided over by Miao men who fill the traditional role of spirit priest.

Christianity: Few Southwestern Huishui Miao have ever been exposed to the Christian message and no ministries are known to be targeting them. There are no known believers among this group, and no Scriptures or recordings are available in their mother tongue. At the present time, only four of the more than 30 to 40 Miao languages in China have ever had any portion of the Bible translated into them.

Miao, Luobohe 苗(罗泊河)

Population in China:
60,000 (1990)
77,400 (2000)
99,800 (2010)
Location: Guizhou
Religion: Animism
Christians: None Known

Overview of the Luobohe Miao

Countries: China

Pronunciation: "Luo-bo-her-Meow"

Other Names: Hmong: Luopohe, Xiamahe Miao, Luopohe

Population Source: 60,000 (1995 Wang Fushi – 1990 figure); 40,000 (1985 Wang Fushi – 1982 figure);
Out of a total Miao population of 7,398,035 (1990 census)

Location: *Guizhou:* Fuquan, Weng'an, Guiding, Longli, Kaiyang, and Kaili counties

Status:
Officially included under Miao

Language: Hmong-Mien, Hmongic, Western Hmongic, Luobohe

Dialects: 0

Religion:
Animism, Polytheism, Shamanism

Christians: None known

Scripture: None

***Jesus* film:** None

Gospel Recordings: None

Christian Broadcasting: None

ROPAL code: HML00

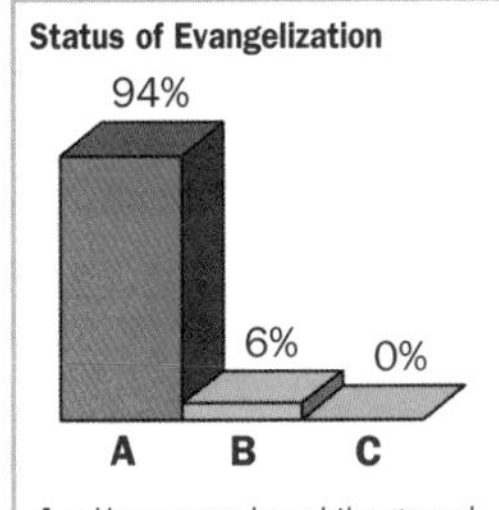

Location: Approximately 77,000 speakers of the Luobohe (Luobo River) Miao language live in southern China. They inhabit parts of Fuquan, Weng'an, Guiding, Longli, Kaiyang, and Kaili counties in central Guizhou Province. Visitors to the region are often overwhelmed at the enormous variety of different Miao subgroups. "Along the roads of central Guizhou, one cannot fail to notice a great variety of Miao. Every 50 kilometers or so we found that the women's dress and appearance varied. There were those with long skirts, those with short skirts, hair done in a knot, hair done in a more elaborate coiffure."[1]

Identity: Although considered part of the Miao minority, the Luobohe Miao speak their own language, making them a "mission-significant" people. The Chinese include the Xi people as part of the Luobohe Miao language group,[2] but the Xi have been profiled separately in *Operation China.*

Language: Luobohe Miao is part of the Chuanqiandian (Western) Miao language family and the Luobohe Miao is different from the large Hmu group they live among.

History: The long-standing enmity between the Chinese and the Miao continued during the reign of Emperor Qianlong (1736–1795). Chinese spies were sent to Miao territory pretending to be traders and merchants. There they led the Miao into evil activities and deliberately incited riots. As the Han Chinese population multiplied and land became a more valuable commodity, many Chinese peasants forcibly took land from the Miao along the Guizhou-Hunan border in the early 1790s. This led to yet another Miao uprising in 1795.[3]

Customs: Many Luobohe Miao homes are three stories high. Constructed of wood, they are often built on stilts against the hillside. The top room is used to store grain — keeping it as far away from rats and dampness as possible. The middle level of the house is reserved for the use of the family, while the bottom floor is reserved for the family's animals. Luobohe Miao women wear their own distinctive dress, which is noted for the intricate and skillfully embroidered patterns which decorate the hemline of the skirt.

Religion: Although the Luobohe Miao worship no gods and have no idols, in most of their villages shamans, or spirit priests, are summoned to mediate in all matters pertaining to the spiritual world. The Miao have great respect for the shamans who, in addition to warding off evil spirits, serve the people as doctors, counselors, and mediators of disputes between families.

Christianity: Few Luobohe Miao have any awareness of Christ at all. Most live their lives completely ignorant of the good news of the Christian faith. There are approximately 1,000 Miao believers in and around Kaili city, all from the Hmu and Ge groups. The majority of Luobohe Miao, however, live where there are no visible Christian communities. Most Luobohe Miao are illiterate, and there are currently no gospel recordings in a language they are able to understand easily. The Luobohe Miao are a desperately needy, unreached people with little access to the gospel.

Paul Hattaway

Miao, Lupanshui 苗(六盘水)

Midge Conner

Location: More than 50,000 Miao people living in the Lupanshui and Qinglong areas of western Guizhou Province form their own ethnolinguistic group, which we have labeled *Miao, Lupanshui*. Lupanshui (also spelled *Liupanshui*) is an amalgamation of several towns and districts, combined to form a municipality which contains 2.5 million people.[1] Qinglong County, farther to the south, contained a total of 51,555 Miao people in the 1990 census, of which about 30% are part of the Lupanshui Miao group.

Identity: The Lupanshui Miao are a peculiarity. Scholars have found that although they are ethnically members of the Miao nationality, they speak the Xiang (Hunanese) Chinese language. Their dialect is similar to the Xiang language spoken in Dongkou County in western Hunan Province, at least 400 kilometers (247 mi.) from their present location. Today the Lupanshui Miao are linguistically distinct from all of the other Miao groups in western Guizhou. Other Miao people view the Lupanshui as a different group and usually do not intermarry with them.

Language: Lupanshui Miao speak a dialect of Xiang Chinese that is only spoken in three counties of Hunan Province: Dongkou, Suining, and Longhui. The Lupanshui Miao probably lost the use of their original Miao speech at least 300 years ago. Their homeland in Hunan is near the home of today's Ghao-Xong ethnic group.

History: The precise reason why the Lupanshui Miao migrated away from their homeland in Hunan Province is uncertain. The 1990 Chinese census listed only 304 Miao people still living in Dongkou County in Hunan, suggesting that almost the entire people group were transplanted across the province to their present-day location in Guizhou. Chinese military campaigns against the Miao are a likely reason for their migration. On certain occasions, the authorities uprooted whole communities and forced them to move to sensitive areas as guards and soldiers, and to spy on other Miao groups.

Customs: Since the mid-1980s there has been a growing desire among young people to move to Lupanshui City or one of the other economically thriving towns in the area, to find work in a factory or on a construction site.

Religion: The Lupanshui Miao are not a particularly religious people. Most of them are hardworking agriculturists who do not center their lives around religion. Many older Lupanshui Miao practice animism and still worship spirits and the elements of nature, but many of the youth are atheists.

Christianity: There are no known churches or Christian believers among the Lupanshui Miao. Miao churches do exist among other subgroups in the vicinity, but they speak languages very different from the Lupanshui and have been unable, and perhaps unwilling, to communicate the gospel to them. Christians in the Lupanshui area have experienced severe persecution in the past.

SICHUAN
GUIZHOU
•Guiyang
•Lupanshui
•Anshun
•Duyun
Huishui
•Xingren
•Pingtang
•Wangmo
YUNNAN
GUANGXI
Scale
0 KM 160

Population in China:
40,000 (1990)
51,600 (2000)
66,500 (2010)
Location: Guizhou
Religion: Animism
Christians: None Known

Overview of the Lupanshui Miao

Countries: China

Pronunciation: "Loo-pahn-shway-Meow"

Other Names: Miao, Liupanshui

Population Source: 40,000 (1990 AMO); Out of a total Miao population of 7,398,035 (1990 census)

Location: *W Guizhou:* Lupanshui Municipality; Qinglong County

Status: Officially included under Miao

Language: Chinese, Xiang

Dialects: 0

Religion: Animism, Polytheism, Ancestor Worship, No Religion

Christians: None known

Scripture: None

***Jesus* film:** None

Gospel Recordings: None

Christian Broadcasting: None

ROPAL code: None

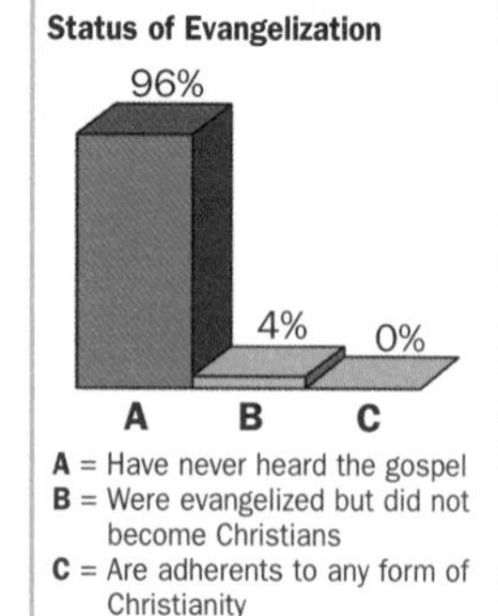

A = Have never heard the gospel
B = Were evangelized but did not become Christians
C = Are adherents to any form of Christianity

Miao, Mashan (Central) 苗(中麻山)

Population in China:
70,000 (1990)
90,300 (2000)
116,400 (2010)
Location: Guizhou
Religion: Animism
Christians: 200

Overview of the Central Mashan Miao

Countries: China

Pronunciation: "Ma-shahn-Meow"

Other Names: Hmong: Central Mashan, Bu Cao

Population Source: 70,000 (1995 Wang Fushi – 1990 figure); 50,000 (1985 Wang Fushi – 1982 figure); Out of a total Miao population of 7,398,035 (1990 census)

Location: *SW Guizhou:* Ziyun, Wangmo, and Luodian counties

Status: Officially included under Miao

Language: Hmong-Mien, Hmongic, Western Hmongic, Mashan

Dialects: 0

Religion: Animism, Polytheism, Christianity

Christians: 200

Scripture: None

***Jesus* film:** None

Gospel Recordings: None

Christian Broadcasting: None

ROPAL code: HMM00

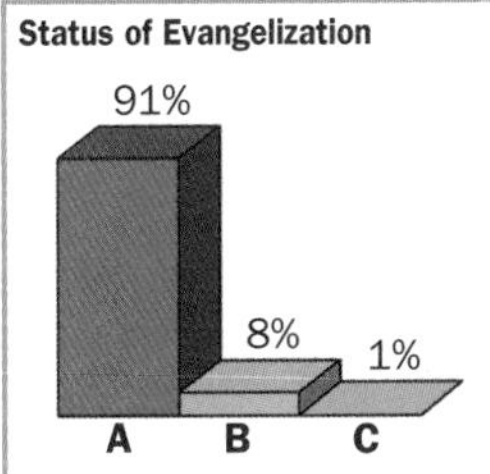

A = Have never heard the gospel
B = Were evangelized but did not become Christians
C = Are adherents to any form of Christianity

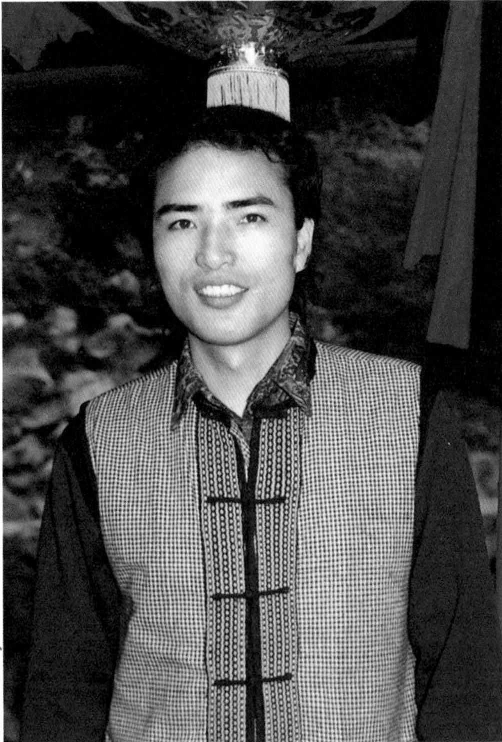

Paul Hattaway

Location: The 1995 *Miaoyu Jianzhi* lists a 1990 population of 70,000 Central Mashan speakers out of a total population of 92,000 for all four Mashan vernaculars. The Central Mashan Miao are found in the Zongdi District of Ziyun County, in the Dayi District of Wangmo County, and in the Banyuan District of Luodian County. The locals have a saying that the Chinese live at the base of the hills, the Bouyei halfway up, and the Miao at the very top.

Identity: There are four Mashan Miao language groups in Guizhou, designated Northern, Southern, Central, and Western Mashan. All four comprise part of the large Miao nationality — the fourth most populous of China's 55 official minorities. The Central Mashan Miao may call themselves *Bu Cao*.

Language: The Central Mashan Miao language — which contains an extraordinary 11 tones[1] — is not spoken in any other part of China.

History: Out of the extensive history of brutality waged by the Chinese against the Miao, what was probably the most vicious war commenced in 1800. A vast Chinese army was mobilized from provinces all over China in a bid to completely exterminate the Miao. Critics describing the war at the time stated that "elephant guns were used to hunt rabbits."[2] An estimated 500,000 Miao in Guizhou were butchered in the carnage, forcing the survivors to flee to more remote and mountainous regions. This and many similar historical influences have scattered the Miao, which resulted in them speaking such a wide variety of languages today.

Customs: According to legend, at one time there were two Miao sisters who were unhappy because they could not find suitable husbands. A special social gathering was arranged with a neighboring village, enabling them to meet two handsome young men, whom they married.[3] To this day the Central Mashan Miao — and most other Miao groups — prefer to marry outside of their village. Marriage outside of their tribe or clan is extremely rare, however, and is discouraged by community leaders.

Religion: The Central Mashan Miao believe that all sickness is caused by evil spirits. A farmer with a headache is often thought to have met the "Shrinking Head Spirit" on a mountain slope. The victim is required to throw a bowl of rice and water outside the village gate to appease the spirit.[4]

Christianity: Only a tiny fraction of the Central Mashan Miao profess to be Christians. A small number of them have believed the gospel, but they currently do not have the resources or initiative to spread the gospel throughout the remainder of their people, most of whom have yet to hear the gospel. There is a massive church among the A-Hmao and Gha-Mu about 200 kilometers (124 mi.) to the northwest. If the believers from these two "Miao" groups came to the Central Mashan Miao they would need to learn a new language and new customs, and they might not be socially accepted.

Miao, Mashan (Northern) 苗(北麻山)

Miao Messenger

Location: A 1990 linguistic survey reported 35,000 speakers of the Northern Mashan Miao language.[1] By the end of the twentieth century their population was expected to exceed 50,000. The Northern Mashan Miao live in one small location at the juncture of three counties: the Daihua District of Changshun County, the Bianyang District of Luodian County, and the Dongshan District of Huishui County. All are located in the southern part of Guizhou Province.

Identity: Officially included under the Miao nationality, the Northern Mashan Miao language is part of the so-called *Chuanqiandian* language group. This term was derived from the historical names of the three provinces of Sichuan (*Chuan*), Guizhou (*Qian*), and Yunnan (*Dian*). Although different sources have listed a variety of figures for the number of Miao groups in China — including "seventy,"[2] and "forty in Guizhou,"[3] all agree that the Miao are a collection of groups rather than one cohesive ethnolinguistic identity.

Language: Reported to have as many as 13 tones, the Northern Mashan Miao language is unintelligible with all other varieties of Miao.[4]

History: According to Miao tradition there were originally six suns, but their intense heat dried up everything on the earth. Then the people decided to shoot down all the suns, except one. But they discovered this was impossible to do and, instead, shot at the suns' reflections in the lake. The remaining sun became frightened and refused to come out, plunging the world into continual darkness. The Miao used various methods to coax the sun out, but nothing worked. Then a rooster crowed, and suddenly the sun appeared. The Miao conclude that this is why the sun rises every morning when the rooster crows.[5]

Customs: One of the numerous Miao festivals is *Sister's Day*. It is held every spring to enable young women to meet with young men from other villages. A series of games and dances is arranged, and glutinous rice dishes are prepared. Playing the *lusheng* (a bamboo instrument) is popular during these festivals. Young men who play skillfully are favored by the girls.

Religion: The Northern Mashan Miao offer sacrifices to a demon they believe dwells in the highest mountain. They also sacrifice to various other deities, believing their efforts can summon protective dragons to act on their behalf.

Christianity: The Northern Mashan Miao are an unreached people group who have never appeared on a list of unreached peoples. Most foreign agencies prefer to view all the Miao as one people, despite their multiplicity of languages and customs. There are no known churches or house fellowships among the Northern Mashan Miao, and no Scriptures or gospel audio recordings are available that they can comprehend. Their social and community structures are very exclusive, creating an additional barrier to the introduction of the gospel among them.

Population in China:
35,000 (1990)
45,150 (2000)
58,200 (2010)
Location: Guizhou
Religion: Animism
Christians: None Known

Overview of the Northern Mashan Miao

Countries: China

Pronunciation: "Ma-shahn-Meow"

Other Names: Hmong: Northern Mashan

Population Source: 35,000 (1995 Wang Fushi – 1990 figure); 25,000 (1985 Wang Fushi – 1982 figure); Out of a total Miao population of 7,398,035 (1990 census)

Location: *S Guizhou:* Daihua District of Changshun County; the Bianyang District of Luodian County; Dongshan District of Huishui County

Status: Officially included under Miao

Language: Hmong-Mien, Hmongic, Western Hmongic, Mashan

Dialects: 0

Religion: Animism, Polytheism

Christians: None known

Scripture: None

***Jesus* film:** None

Gospel Recordings: None

Christian Broadcasting: None

ROPAL code: HMO00

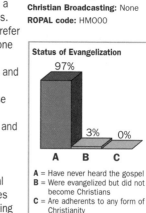

Status of Evangelization

	A	B	C
	97%	3%	0%

A = Have never heard the gospel
B = Were evangelized but did not become Christians
C = Are adherents to any form of Christianity

Miao, Mashan (Southern) 苗(南麻山)

Location: The Southern Mashan are one of the smallest of the distinct Miao language groups in China, with a 1990 population of 10,000 people.[1] Despite the one-child policy in China, many Southern Mashan Miao have several children. This has resulted in a rapid population increase: their number was expected to exceed 12,000 by the year 2000. The Southern Mashan Miao live in a small region in the Mashan and Lekuan districts of Wangmo County. Wangmo is located in the extreme southern part of Guizhou Province. Their villages are accessible only by a lengthy walk over treacherous trails. For much of the year the weather in the region is wet and miserably cold.

Identity: Although the government considers them a part of the Miao nationality, the Southern Mashan Miao are a distinct people group. They live in small and compact communities, speak their own language, and have little to do with the outside world.

Language: Southern Mashan Miao is one of the four Mashan Miao languages. It is part of the Chuanqiandian (Western) branch of the Miao language group.

History: The Southern Mashan Miao are a group who migrated south following persecution against them in the past. The Chinese *Canon of Shuen* records one Miao group, the "San Miao," being driven into the mountains of San Wei around 4,000 years ago.[2]

Customs: The Miao believe there was a time when dragons guarded their families, crops, animals, and trees against disease and pestilence. The people regularly sacrificed chickens to the dragons and burned paper money to procure their favor.

Miao Messenger

Religion: During funeral chants, which predate all Christian influence, many Miao groups refer to an outer place of darkness where the spirit of the deceased must travel. They believe it is a horrible place of demons, torments, and gnashing of teeth.[3] Legend claims there was once a time when the Miao were able to climb to heaven on a huge fir tree, but the gods struck it down. Left with no other way to communicate with heaven, the people in Yanpai village of Xijiang County in Guizhou climbed to the top of the highest mountain and thrust a bamboo branch into its crest, signaling to the gods, "All is not well."[4] The Southern Mashan Miao are animists, living in fear of evil spirits.

Christianity: Wangmo County, the sole area where the Southern Mashan Miao live, was largely neglected by mission organizations in the pre-Communist era. The Southern Mashan Miao remain an unreached people group with no Scriptures in their language and no known ministries targeting them. There are a few Catholic believers among the Bouyei minority to the north, but the Miao and Bouyei have little contact with each other and speak different languages. Most Southern Mashan Miao cannot speak more than basic Mandarin; fewer still are able to read or write Chinese.

Population in China:
10,000 (1990)
12,900 (2000)
16,600 (2010)
Location: Guizhou
Religion: Animism
Christians: None Known

Overview of the Southern Mashan Miao

Countries: China

Pronunciation: "Ma-shahn-Meow"

Other Names: Hmong: Southern Mashan

Population Source: 10,000 (1995 Wang Fushi – 1990 figure); 7,000 (1985 Wang Fushi – 1982 figure);
Out of a total Miao population of 7,398,035 (1990 census)

Location: *SW Guizhou:* Mashan and Lekuan districts in Wangmo County

Status: Officially included under Miao

Language: Hmong-Mien, Hmongic, Western Hmongic, Mashan

Dialects: 0

Religion: Animism, Polytheism

Christians: None known

Scripture: None

***Jesus* film:** None

Gospel Recordings: None

Christian Broadcasting: None

ROPAL code: HMA00

Status of Evangelization

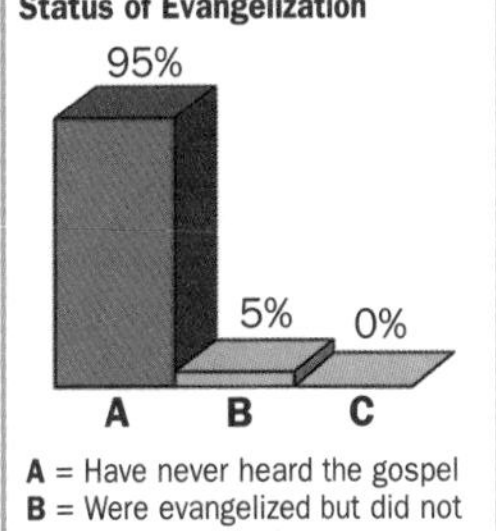

A = Have never heard the gospel
B = Were evangelized but did not become Christians
C = Are adherents to any form of Christianity

Miao, Mashan (Western) 苗(西麻山)

Population in China:
14,000 (1990)
18,050 (2000)
23,300 (2010)
Location: Guizhou
Religion: Animism
Christians: None Known

Overview of the Western Mashan Miao

Countries: China

Pronunciation: "Ma-shahn-Meow"

Other Names: Hmong: Northern Mashan

Population Source: 14,000 (1995 Wang Fushi – 1990 figure); 10,000 (1985 Wang Fushi – 1982 figure); Out of a total Miao population of 7,398,035 (1990 census)

Location: *S Guizhou:* Houchang and Sidazhai districts in Wangmo County

Status: Officially included under Miao

Language: Hmong-Mien, Hmongic, Western Hmongic, Mashan

Dialects: 0

Religion: Animism, Polytheism

Christians: None known

Scripture: None

***Jesus* film:** None

Gospel Recordings: None

Christian Broadcasting: None

ROPAL code: HMW00

Status of Evangelization

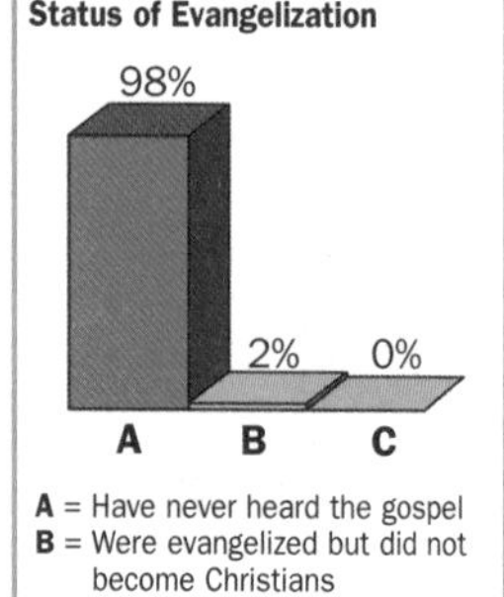

A = Have never heard the gospel
B = Were evangelized but did not become Christians
C = Are adherents to any form of Christianity

Location: More than 18,000 people in China speak the Western Mashan Miao language. Their villages are located in the small, remote area of Houchang and Sidazhai districts in Wangmo County. Wangmo, located in southern Guizhou Province, is a mountainous region rarely visited by outsiders. The total population of Guizhou fell from 14.7 million in 1928 to 9.2 million in 1935, mainly due to two civil wars.[1] Today the province's population has mushroomed to 35 million. Roads and facilities are poor or nonexistent in the region. The Western Mashan Miao live near the Bouyei, Yao, and Zhuang.

Identity: The minority peoples of southern Guizhou are among the poorest in Asia and face mounting health risks. According to United Nation's figures for the late 1980s, only 22% of Guizhou's rural villages had access to an improved water source (running water, pump, or well). "The main source is usually a river or pond which is affected by droughts and almost always polluted from factory waste, seepage of agricultural chemicals, and human and animal waste."[2]

Language: The Western Mashan Miao language — which has 13 recognizable tones[3] — does not have a written script.

History: A festival on the eighth day of the fourth lunar month commemorates the death of Ya Nu, who was killed in action as he led the Miao into battle against the Chinese 1,700 years ago.[4]

Customs: The majority of Western Mashan Miao are hardworking peasants. They are also talented musicians, composing songs for festivals and creating energetic and demonstrative dances. Because of the region's mountainous terrain, it often takes several hours to walk down into the valley and up again to reach a village on a nearby hill. Without the use of telephones, the Miao have learned to project their voices across the valleys and trees to reach a neighboring village.

Religion: The Western Mashan Miao put their trust in the spirit world. If a crop fails or a woman cannot produce children to help with work in the fields, the village could face starvation. As a result, an intricate system of spirit appeasement gradually developed. The Miao believe that if they make peace with the spirits, the survival and prosperity of their communities will be ensured.

Christianity: The Western Mashan Miao have no knowledge of the gospel. Little has changed since William Clifton Dodd traveled through southern China in the 1920s: "It was a Christless land that we passed through. A man can endure a few days of absolute heathenism if he has a few Christian companions. But to foot it for a thousand miles without any sight or sound giving any evidence of anything Christian, to march as boldly as may be for so long and so far against such a blank wall of heathenism; this is to enter the land of darkness that may be felt."[5]

Miao Messenger

Micha 密察

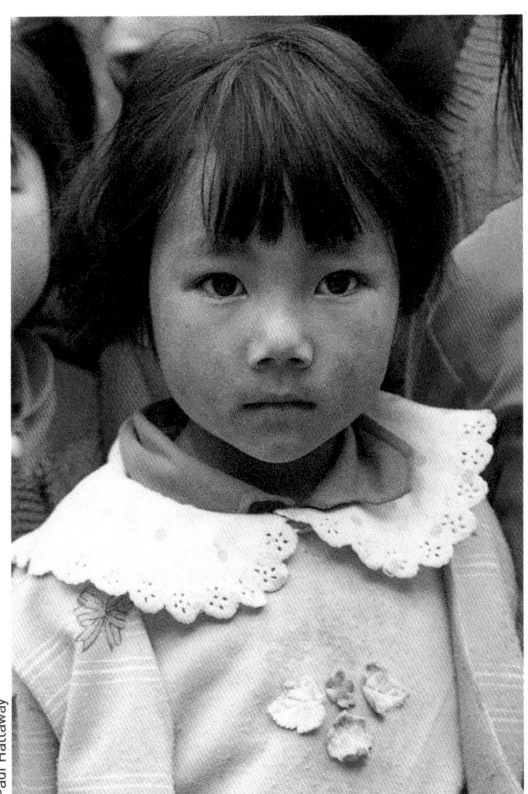

Paul Hattaway

Location: More than 1,000 people belonging to the Micha ethnic group live in areas in and around Aliwu and Santaishan in Nanjian County of Yunnan Province.[1] The Micha live at the northern end of the Ailao Mountains, southeast of the ancient town of Dali.

Identity: The Micha have been officially counted as part of the Yi nationality in China. It is uncertain how they relate to other Yi groups. Because of their similar names, it is possible the Micha were once related to the Michi people who live much farther east in Chuxiong Prefecture of Yunnan.

Language: Micha is an unclassified member of the Yi group of Tibeto-Burman languages. It is probably either a Western Yi or Central Yi variety.

History: At the time of the Ming Dynasty (1368–1644), eleven different Yi tribes were listed in the records of the region around Dali. Ralph Covell notes, "When the Mongols under Genghis Khan defeated the Dali kingdom... some of the Yi nationalities were dispersed throughout Yunnan. The area about the River of Golden Sand [Yangtze] to the north remained unconquered, and tribal kings remained in power there until as late as 1727. Even after the Manchus, with great savagery, suppressed the tribes and put their kings to death, thousands of [Yi] refused to acknowledge defeat and withdrew across the River of Golden Sand to the Daliangshan area. Here they remained in haughty arrogance, resisting Chinese control, at least in the high mountains, until the advent of the People's Republic of China. The Yi of Yunnan accepted Chinese rule and gradually, with periodic resistance, adopted Chinese culture and many features of Chinese religion."[2]

Customs: The *Mitcha* (Micha) were mentioned in an early book as one of only two people groups in Yunnan that the Yi were willing to marry, the other being the Bai. In turn, the Micha refused to intermarry with anyone except the Bai and the Lisu.[3] Today most Micha are hardworking agriculturists who prefer to be left alone in their mountain community. Many of their young people prefer to move to the cities and towns where they can earn more money — and to return home periodically for festivals and special occasions.

Religion: After living alongside the Han Chinese and Bai for many centuries, the Micha have absorbed many of the religious practices of their neighbors, including aspects of Daoism, Buddhism, and ancestor worship. Little remains of the traditional polytheistic beliefs of the Micha, although the elderly still worship various spirits including the spirit of the village which they believe resides in the largest tree near the community.

Christianity: The Micha are believed to be an unreached people group with no known Christians, although there is a small smattering of Three-Self (government-sanctioned) churches throughout the area, as well as some Catholic influence. The Micha, however, being a small and isolated group, are not exposed to Christian witness.

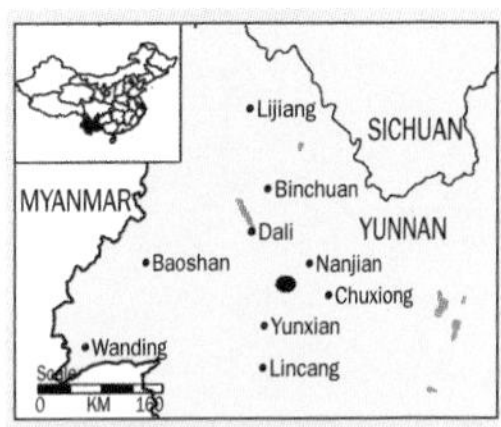

Population in China:
1,000 (1999)
1,020 (2000)
1,280 (2010)
Location: Yunnan
Religion: Animism
Christians: None Known

Overview of the Micha

Countries: China

Pronunciation: "Mee-cha"

Other Names: Micha: Nanjian, Mitcha

Population Source: 1,000 (1999 J. Pelkey); Out of a total Yi population of 6,572,173 (1990 census)

Location: *Yunnan:* Nanjian County

Status: Officially included under Yi

Language: Sino-Tibetan, Tibeto-Burman, Burmese-Lolo, Lolo, Northern Lolo, Yi, Unclassified

Dialects: 0

Religion: Animism, Ancestor Worship, Daoism, Mahayana Buddhism

Christians: None known

Scripture: None

***Jesus* film:** None

Gospel Recordings: None

Christian Broadcasting: None

ROPAL code: None

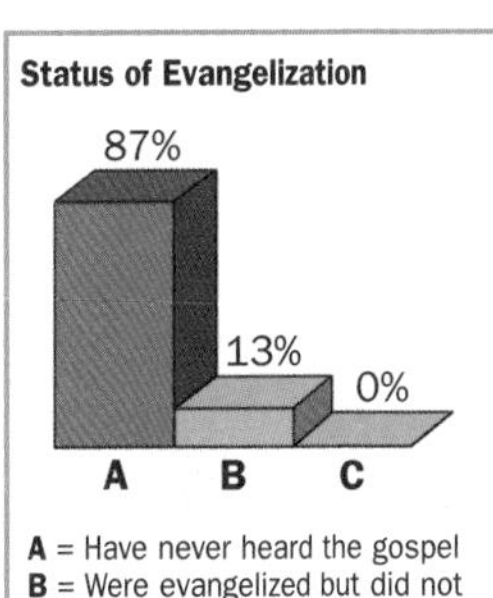

Michi 米切

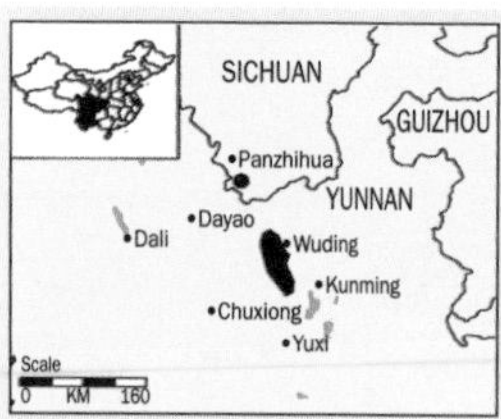

Population in China:
29,000 (1999)
29,700 (2000)
37,300 (2010)
Location: Yunnan, Sichuan
Religion: Ancestor Worship
Christians: 800

Overview of the Michi

Countries: China

Pronunciation: "Mee-chee"

Other Names: Red Yi, Hong Yi, Michia, Mijia, Minjia, Michipuo, Miqipuo, Sinicized Yi, Miqi, Miqipo, Micha, Hong Yi, Mi Qie Po, Min Chi, Minqi, Mizu

Population Source: 29,000 (1999 AMO); 24,500 in Yunnan (1999 J. Pelkey); Out of a total Yi population of 6,572,173 (1990 census)

Location: *N Yunnan:* Wuding (8,100), Fumin (7,000), Lufeng (4,500), Luquan (4,000), Yimen (800), and Anning (100) counties; *S Sichuan:* Panzhihua area of Miyi County

Status: Officially included under Yi

Language: Sino-Tibetan, Tibeto-Burman, Burmese-Lolo, Lolo, Northern Lolo, Yi, Unclassified

Dialects: 0

Religion: Ancestor Worship, Animism, Christianity

Christians: 800

Scripture: None

***Jesus* film:** None

Gospel Recordings: None

Christian Broadcasting: None

ROPAL code: None

Status of Evangelization

A = Have never heard the gospel
B = Were evangelized but did not become Christians
C = Are adherents to any form of Christianity

Jamin Pelkey

Location: Approximately 29,700 Michi live in communities on both sides of the Sichuan-Yunnan border. The majority are located in northern Yunnan Province, in addition to a small number living near the town of Panzhihua in southern Sichuan. A 1954 government study listed 2,854 Michi in Wuding.[1] A 1957 report listed 7,785 Michi living in Chuxiong Prefecture, which includes Wuding County.[2] The Michi are also found in Fumin, Lufeng, Luquan, Yimen, and Anning counties.

Identity: Although they have been counted as members of the Yi nationality by the Chinese authorities, the five "Yi" groups in the Panzhihua area "are all very different from each other... and have a strong sense of ethnic identity."[3] The Michi are also known as the *Red Yi* or *Michia*. The Michi are one of more than 100 branches of the Yi nationality living within the borders of Yunnan Province. The official Chinese *pinyin* spelling of their name is *Miqi*. The Michi have also been listed in literature as the *Sinicized Yi* due to their high level of assimilation into the Chinese culture.

Language: It is uncertain what Yi group the Michi language belongs to. Different Chinese sources list Michi as Central Yi, Eastern Yi, and Southeastern Yi. In many locations, however, the Michi language has already died out and is no longer being taught to children.

History: The Michi claim to have migrated to their present location from Guizhou. Chinese scholar T'ien Ju-K'ang explains the historical differences between the different groups in the area: "The divisional coverage and the farm land localities largely overlap. The number of high status Black Yi [Eastern Nasu] was high and proportional to the concentration of Gani [Naluo] as tenant serfs. The Han landlords parasitized on the Sinicized Micha [Michi]. The Miao, Lisu, and Gani [Naluo] who became Christians in groups had a common distinguishing feature: they were sparsely settled in the high mountains to avoid being assimilated."[4]

Customs: One of the few unique Michi customs remaining includes their ritual of constructing ancestral altars with pine branches. They also practice "double cross-cousin marriage."[5]

Religion: Unlike most Yi groups in China, who are polytheists, the Michi have little or no trace of spirit appeasement left in their religious practices. Elderly Michi worship their ancestors, while a growing number of youth are atheists.

Christianity: Australian missionary A. G. Nicholls first visited Sapushan in 1906. By 1952 there were 3,000 Nosu and 1,585 Naluo Christians, as well as small numbers of Michi and other believers in the area.[6] In the last ten years the Eastern Lipo have emerged as the strongest church in northern Yunnan and have thoroughly evangelized most Michi. The Michi believers do not have their own churches but are in mixed congregations with Chinese, Eastern Lipo, and Naluo believers. Despite their exposure to the gospel, relatively few Michi have followed Christ. Nominalism and the pressure of Communism have caused many Michi believers to fall away.

Miguba 米古巴

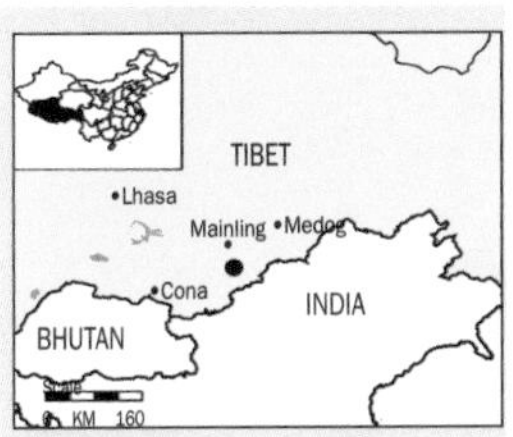

Population in China:
80 (1998)
82 (2000)
94 (2010)
Location: Tibet
Religion: Shamanism
Christians: None Known

Overview of the Miguba

Countries: China, probably India

Pronunciation: "Mih-goo-bah"

Other Names: Damu

Population Source: 80 speakers (1998 J. Matisoff); Probably also in India

Location: *SE Tibet:* Damu Village in Motuo County

Status: Possibly officially included under Lhoba

Language: Sino-Tibetan, Tibeto-Burman, Baric, Mirish

Dialects: 0

Religion: Shamanism, Animism, Tibetan Buddhism

Christians: None known

Scripture: None

***Jesus* film:** None

Gospel Recordings: None

Christian Broadcasting: None

ROPAL code: None

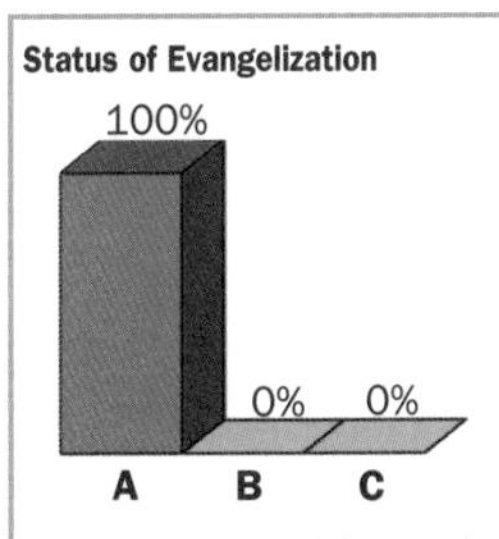

Location: According to linguist Jackson Sun, 80 speakers of the Miguba language live in just one village in southeastern Tibet: Damu Village is located in a densely forested area of Motuo County.[1] The region is one of the least populated places in China. The few other inhabitants in the vicinity, mostly Lhoba and Tibetans, call the members of this group *Damu* after the name of their village. The Miguba may be the same ethnic group as the Ashing Adi people in Arunachal Pradesh, India. The legends of the Miguba closely match those of the Ashing, who numbered 959 people in India according to the 1971 census.

Identity: The Miguba ethnic group was only recently discovered. They may have been officially counted as part of the small Lhoba nationality by the Chinese authorities. The Miguba share linguistic similarities with the Bogar and Yidu, two tribes combined by the Chinese to form the Lhoba minority.

Language: The Miguba speak a dialect from the Mirish branch of the Tibeto-Burman family. Most Miguba are illiterate.

History: According to Miguba mythology, Abo Tani was the first human. They say they migrated across the Himalayas to their present location from a place named Padong-Among, which means "land of rain." Child marriages were prevalent in the past, but today most Miguba marry when they are 15 to 17 years of age.

Customs: In the past, the Miguba wore hats made of cane. The men still wear a long coat and a *langoti* (loincloth). The Miguba love to eat meat, especially deer, tiger, pork, and chicken. Their diet is supplemented by vegetables and fruit such as jackfruit, bananas, pineapples, guavas, and oranges. Premarital sexual relations are not only allowed by the Miguba but are encouraged. A boy's hut called *bango* and a girl's hut called *rasheng* are located in their village. Girls are not allowed to enter the *bango*, but boys are permitted to spend a night with a girl of their choice in the *rasheng*.

Religion: The Miguba live in constant fear of demons and the spirit world. Numerous aspects of their lives reflect their bondage. Before a woman gives birth, "pre-delivery rituals are observed to avoid future complications, but in case of certain problems a ritual becomes a must to ward off evil spirits. The nature of animal sacrifice in the ritual depends upon the financial condition of the person concerned, as well as on the severity of the case. A name is given to the baby immediately after birth, either by the family or relatives, in order to save the baby from the clutches of evil spirits."[2] Some Miguba outwardly profess to be Buddhists, but this is done only to please the Tibetans.

Christianity: The whole region of southeast Tibet is somewhat of a mystery to outsiders. Few people have ever traveled to the area inhabited by the Miguba. The gospel has also failed to penetrate the thick forests and deep valleys of the northern Himalayas. There are no known Christians in the area to impact the Miguba, who have yet to be exposed to the gospel.

Paul Hattaway

Mili 咪哩

Location: Approximately 23,000 Mili people live in the mountains of central Yunnan Province. They inhabit a widespread area encompassing four counties. The majority live in the Anding and Wenlong districts of Jingdong County. About 9,000 inhabit Yunxian County while smaller numbers live in Zhenyuan and Xinping counties.

Identity: The Mili are one of approximately 120 tribes and people groups that the Chinese government combined into the official Yi nationality in China. The Mili are acknowledged by all other people who live near them as a distinct ethnic group with their own history, customs, dress, and language. The Mili first appeared in John Kuhn's 1945 tribal survey of Yunnan Province, located in "Qingku."[1] Qingku is the old spelling for today's Jinggu County in Simao Prefecture.

Language: Chinese scholars have classified Mili as a language belonging to the Western Yi linguistic classification. In Zhenyuan County, where all Yi languages are supposedly Western Yi, one official source states, "The language spoken by each individual Yi group in the county is rather complex, and when different groups are together they have much trouble communicating."[2]

History: The Mili have never before appeared on Chinese ethnolinguistic lists, simply because they have been lumped together with the many names and subgroups that make up the official Yi nationality in China. The Mili have a long history of being oppressed by the Chinese.

Customs: Mili culture, like their language, is well preserved. After the death of a Mili person, the sons and grandsons gather around the corpse and, "one-by-one, take turns blowing into the mouth of the deceased. They then each take a silver coin, a little rice, and some tea leaves and wrap them in a red cloth. Having done this, they then place their small, red parcels in the mouth of the deceased. The body stays this way, in the home, two or three days before the burial ceremony."[3] For the Mili, this act is a way of honoring their dead before the soul leaves for the next world. They believe the rice and tea will nourish the soul of the deceased, while the coins will provide for any needs that may arise on its journey. Mili weddings are very relaxed. Once a couple decides they are ready for marriage, they choose a day to go farther into the mountains and chop firewood together.

Jamin Pelkey

Religion: The Mili are polytheists and animists. They feel close to nature and are careful not to upset the spiritual balance they believe exists between themselves and their surroundings. Until the 1950s many Mili villages contained shamans.

Christianity: For hundreds of years the Mili have lived and died without the slightest knowledge of the gospel or the name of Jesus Christ. Without a church or any Christian witness, the Mili remain neglected and in spiritual darkness. No missionaries are known to have ever reached out to the Mili people. The areas inhabited by the Mili are practically devoid of any Christian presence, be it Han Chinese house churches or government-sanctioned believers. The Mili are isolated geographically, culturally, linguistically, and spiritually from outside influence.

Population in China:
23,200 (1999)
23,750 (2000)
29,850 (2010)
Location: Yunnan
Religion: Polytheism
Christians: None Known

Overview of the Mili

Countries: China

Pronunciation: "Mee-lee"

Other Names: Alie

Population Source: 23,200 (1999 J. Pelkey); Out of a total Yi population of 6,572,173 (1990 census)

Location: *Yunnan:* Jingdong (12,000), Yunxian (9,000), Zhenyuan (1,000), and Xinping (1,000) counties

Status: Officially included under Yi

Language: Sino-Tibetan, Tibeto-Burman, Burmese-Lolo, Lolo, Northern Lolo, Yi, Western Yi

Dialects: 0

Religion: Polytheism, Animism, Ancestor Worship

Christians: None known

Scripture: None

***Jesus* film:** None

Gospel Recordings: None

Christian Broadcasting: None

ROPAL code: None

Ming 命

Population in China:
10,000 (1994)
11,700 (2000)
15,100 (2010)
Location: Sichuan
Religion: No Religion
Christians: None Known

Overview of the Ming

Countries: China

Pronunciation: "Ming"

Other Names: Mingzu

Population: 10,000 (1994 AMO); Out of a total Qiang population of 198,252 (1990 census)

Location: *Sichuan:* Maoxian Qiang Autonomous County and Wenchuan County

Status: Probably officially included under Qiang

Language: Sino-Tibetan, Tibeto-Burman, Unclassified

Dialects: 0

Religion: No Religion, Animism, Polytheism

Christians: None known

Scripture: None

***Jesus* film:** None

Gospel Recordings: None

Christian Broadcasting: None

ROPAL code: None

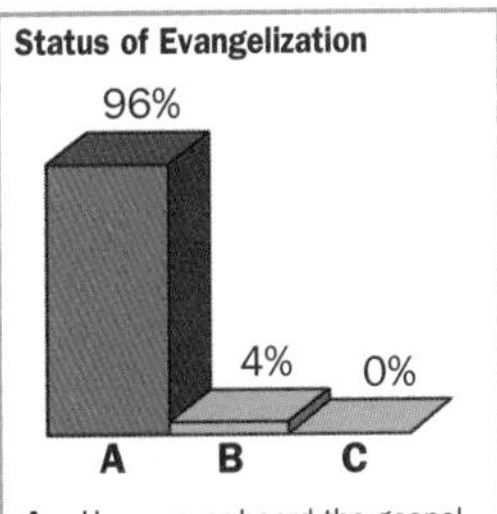

A = Have never heard the gospel
B = Were evangelized but did not become Christians
C = Are adherents to any form of Christianity

Paul Hattaway

Location: The 11,700 Ming people are a mixed race who live in and around the towns of Maoxian and Wenchuan counties in Sichuan Province. Maoxian County is the administrative seat of the Qiang Autonomous County — about eight hours by road from Chengdu, the capital city of Sichuan Province. Maoxian is one of the most beautiful locations in all of China, with the fast-flowing Min River cutting its way through massive cliffs that rise directly from the river banks.

Identity: The Ming people are an ethnic Han Chinese-Qiang mix. They formed their own communities after being ostracized by the other peoples in the region. The Ming wear distinct costumes marked by a white turban. They call themselves *Ming Zu*, meaning "Ming nationality." Scottish missionary Thomas F. Torrance notes, "In Weizhou [now called Wenchuan] most of the people are either Qiang or a mixed race, though there are some outsiders of Tibetan, Jiarong, Xifan, Nosu, Wazi, and Bolotsze... as well."[1]

Language: The Ming spoken language, like the race itself, is a mixture of Qiang and Chinese. All Ming are able to speak the local dialect of Mandarin and rely on Chinese for everyday communications. The Ming language has also been influenced by numerous Qiang and Tibetan loanwords.

History: A mixed race has existed in the Qiang region for at least a thousand years. During the zenith of the Tibetan empire (AD 600–900), many Qiang were assimilated by the Tibetans and by Han Chinese. According to one scholar, "Only a small number were not assimilated."[2] In the past there was prejudice against the members of this mixed race, who were not socially accepted by either the Qiang or the Han Chinese. They were forced to form their own communities and villages and to adopt a separate identity.

Customs: The Ming observe all traditional Chinese festivals, including the Chinese New Year and Spring Festival celebrations. Being the crossroads for several ethnic groups, Maoxian County hosts a large number of Tibetan and Qiang festivals and special occasions.

Religion: Although some Ming are animists, the majority can accurately be described as nonreligious. There are Daoist and Buddhist temples in Maoxian County, but many of the customs and beliefs that formed the identity of the people in the region have been set aside since the Communists took over China. The young generation of Qiang have been educated in atheistic schools and made to ridicule their parents' religious beliefs, which are mocked as "superstition."

Christianity: Catholic mission work in the late 1800s and Protestant work in the early 1900s established several churches among the Qiang in the geographically isolated Maoxian area, but no evidence of those labors remains today. There are currently no known churches or believers among the Ming. At least three teams of foreigners have been arrested in recent years for attempting to distribute gospel literature in Maoxian County. The local authorities strongly oppose such outreach.

Minglang 明廊

Jamin Pelkey

Location: More than 1,500 members of the Minglang tribe live in northern Yunnan Province. Their two main villages are Lower Lemei Village of Chadian District and Tianxin Village of Gaoqiao District within Wuding County. Others live in Maoshan District of Luquan County. The Minglang may also live in Fumin County. Accurate figures on the Minglang population are difficult to obtain because the government no longer considers them a specific people group. They have been combined with many other groups to form the huge Yi nationality. The most recent figure available which specifically mentions the Minglang tribe was a 1952 government study: it listed 103 Minglang households located in Wuding County.[1]

Identity: Wuding is home to numerous small people groups. Each group wears distinctive dress and is recognized as a separate entity by the local inhabitants. Although the Minglang speak a language related to Sani, they firmly consider themselves a unique tribe. In recent decades, under increasing pressure from large numbers of Han Chinese who have migrated into Wuding, the Minglang have commenced a gradual slide toward assimilation. Some Minglang children now exclusively speak Mandarin.

Language: The Minglang language is related to Sani, and many official publications list the Minglang as part of the Sani. Although they may have the same origins, today when a Minglang and Sani meet, they must speak Chinese in order to understand each other.

History: The Minglang have never possessed a written script of their own, although some of the Minglang Christians are able to read the Pollard script — devised by missionary Samuel Pollard in the early 1900s to help illiterate tribal people read the Bible.

Customs: The Minglang observe all the traditional Chinese festivals, in addition to several regional Yi celebrations.

Religion: In the past the Minglang were animists and polytheists, living in fear and bondage to a wide variety of spirits.

Christianity: The Minglang (and many other groups in the Wuding area) owe their salvation to the efforts of the Eastern Lipo Christians. "On the banks of the 'River of Golden Sand' in the upper Yangtze watershed between Sichuan and Yunnan provinces live the Yi people.... The Lipos, a Yi sub-group formerly called the Eastern Lisus, have had the Gospel for almost half a century.... These remarkable mountain people... have used their musical talent to share the Good News of salvation and freedom from all demonic control. Old hymns, packed with sound doctrine, were translated and memorized by the early Lipo Christians. Early on they became a singing church which not only preserved but also propagated its faith cross-culturally by singing hymns. Today, because of their witness, there are believers among many neighboring tribes in spite of the language barriers and lack of Christian literature. The Lipo have reached the Minglang, the Ming Cha, and the Samei peoples living among them."[2] Today as many as 400 of the 1,500 Minglang people in Wuding confess Christ.

Population in China:
1,500 (1999)
1,530 (2000)
1,930 (2010)
Location: Yunnan
Religion: Christianity
Christians: 400

Overview of the Minglang

Countries: China
Pronunciation: "Ming-lung"
Other Names: Sani, Sanipo
Population Source:
1,500 (1999 J. Pelkey);
Out of a total Yi population of 6,572,173 (1990 census)
Location: *N Yunnan:* Wuding and Luquan counties; Possibly also in Fumin County
Status:
Officially included under Yi
Language: Sino-Tibetan, Tibeto-Burman, Burmese-Lolo, Lolo, Northern Lolo, Yi, Southeastern Yi
Dialects: 0
Religion: Christianity, Animism
Christians: 400
Scripture: None
***Jesus* film:** None
Gospel Recordings: None
Christian Broadcasting: None
ROPAL code: None

Status of Evangelization

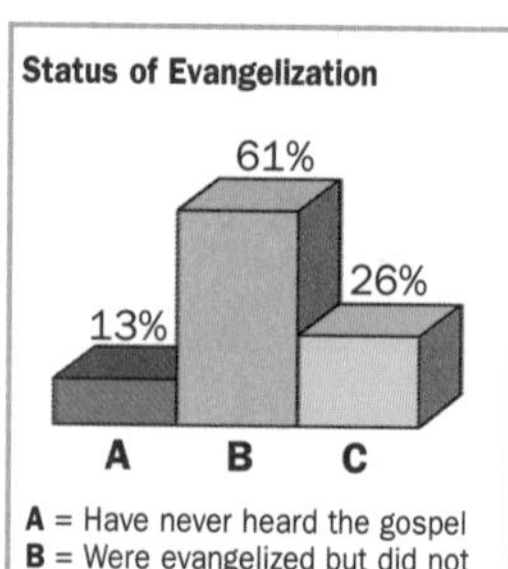

A = Have never heard the gospel
B = Were evangelized but did not become Christians
C = Are adherents to any form of Christianity

Minyak 木雅

Location: A 1983 study listed 15,000 Minyak living in extremely remote regions of central Sichuan Province.[1] The Minyak live in the shadow of the mighty 7,556-meter (24,783 ft.) Gongga Mountain (*Minya Konka* in Tibetan). The region was first described in 1930 by intrepid explorer Joseph Rock: "A scenic wonder of the world, this region is 45 days from the nearest railhead. For centuries it may remain a closed land, save to such privileged few as care to crawl like ants through its canyons of tropical heat and up its glaciers and passes in blinding snowstorms, carrying their food with them."[2]

Identity: The Minyak are part of the Tibetan nationality. They have been described as a "peaceful, sedentary Tibetan tribe, a most inoffensive, obliging, happy-go-lucky people."[3] Most of the members of this group call themselves *Minyak*, except for those living at Kangding and the Tanggu area of Jiulong County who call themselves *Buoba*.

Language: Minyak is part of the Qiangic linguistic branch.[4] It has two dialects, Eastern and Western Minyak, which reportedly have significant differences.[5] Many Eastern Minyak are bilingual in Chinese, while most Western Minyak also speak Khampa.[6]

History: The Minyak were once part of the now extinct Chiala Tibetan Kingdom in western Sichuan. Ancient *tianlu*, or stone defense towers, still stand in dilapidated condition at valley junctures.[7] For centuries the Minyak were bullied by the violent Khampa. Rock reported, "The Minya [Minyak] Tibetan's homes have been burned several times by [Khampa] outlaws. On previous raids the Minya people could only flee into the hills and leave their homes to the robbers."[8] The Minyak may be descended from survivors of the destruction of Minyak (in present-day Ningxia) by Genghis Khan in 1227.

Paul Hattaway

Customs: The Minyak live quiet lives in nearly complete isolation from the rest of the world. Most of their villages are accessible only by foot. The Minyak have many cultural links to the Qiang that show a common ancestry, including a reverence for white stones. In the past the Minyak lived in small isolated communities, but because of attacks by Khampa bandits they have constructed "large fortress-like community houses built of rock, looking like prisons of the Middle Ages."[9] Most Minyak spend their time raising livestock.

Religion: All Minyak adhere to Tibetan Buddhism. They observe Tibetan festivals and make pilgrimages to Tibetan holy sites.

Christianity: Although there are presently no known Christians among the Minyak, the China Inland Mission did have a station in Tatsienlu (now Kangding), on the edge of Minyak territory. The mission closed when the missionaries were forced to leave China in the early 1950s. When explorer Joseph Rock first entered the Minyak region he was besieged for medicine — a sure sign missionaries had been there before him. "Whenever we came to a village, the peasants would gather about us and with folded hands would beseech me to dispense medicine to sick relatives."[10] The Minyak today have no awareness of Jesus Christ or his grace. They are ignorant of Christianity, living and dying "without the slightest knowledge of the outside world."[11]

Population in China:
15,000 (1983)
20,900 (2000)
25,750 (2010)
Location: Sichuan
Religion: Tibetan Buddhism
Christians: None Known

Overview of the Minyak

Countries: China

Pronounciation: "Min-yahk"

Other Names: Munya, Miyao, Muyak, Muya, Minya, Minya Tibetans, Miyao, Buoba

Population: 15,000 (1983 Sun Hongkai); Out of a total Tibetan population of 4,593,330 (1990 census)

Location: *W Sichuan:* Garze Tibetan Prefecture: Kangding, Ya'an, Jiulong, and Shimian counties

Status: Officially included under Tibetan

Language: Sino-Tibetan, Tibeto-Burman, Qiangic, Minyak

Dialects (2): Eastern Minyak, Western Minyak

Religion: Tibetan Buddhism

Christians: None known

Scripture: None

***Jesus* film:** None

Gospel Recordings: None

Christian Broadcasting: None

ROPAL code: MVM00

Status of Evangelization

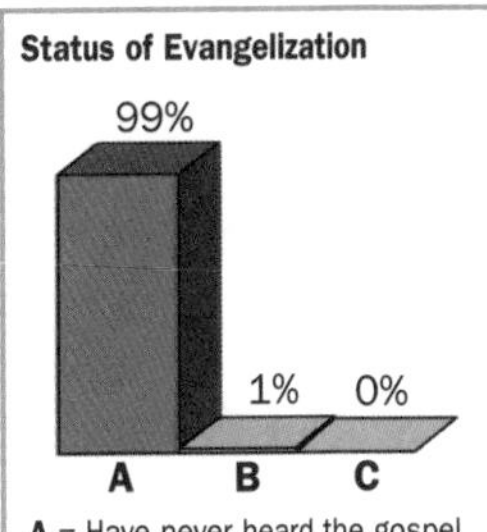

A = Have never heard the gospel
B = Were evangelized but did not become Christians
C = Are adherents to any form of Christianity

Mixisu 米习俗

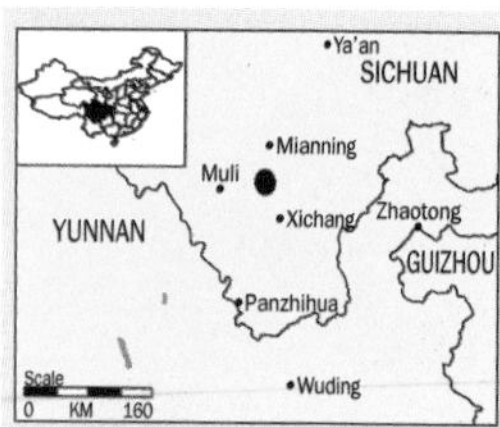

Population in China:
5,000 (1999)
5,120 (2000)
6,430 (2010)
Location: Sichuan
Religion: Animism
Christians: None Known

Overview of the Mixisu

Countries: China

Pronunciation: "Mee-shee-soo"

Other Names: Shuitian, Shuitian Ren, Shuitianzu

Population Source:
5,000 (1999 AMO);
Out of a total Yi population of 6,572,173 (1990 census)

Location: *S Sichuan:* Xichang and Mianning counties

Status:
Officially included under Yi

Language: Sino-Tibetan, Tibeto-Burman, Burmese-Lolo, Lolo, Northern Lolo, Yi, Northern Yi

Dialects: 0

Religion: Animism, Ancestor Worship, No Religion

Christians: None known

Scripture: None

***Jesus* film:** None

Gospel Recordings: None

Christian Broadcasting: None

ROPAL code: None known

Status of Evangelization

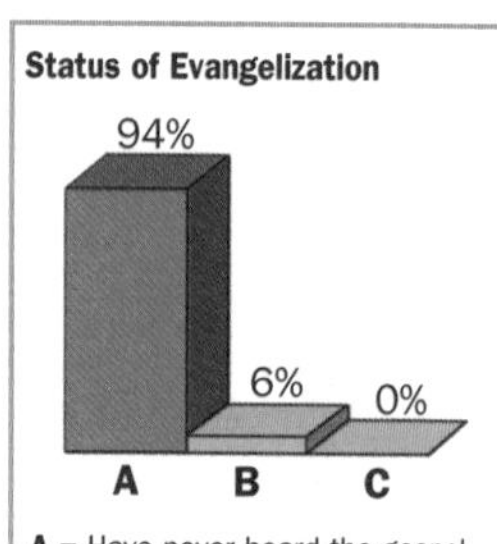

A = Have never heard the gospel
B = Were evangelized but did not become Christians
C = Are adherents to any form of Christianity

Location: Approximately 5,000 people belonging to the Mixisu ethnic group live in the mountainous southern part of Sichuan Province in southern China. The Mixisu inhabit villages within Xichang and Mianning counties in the Liangshan Yi Autonomous Prefecture.

Identity: The Mixisu have been officially included under the Yi nationality in China. The self-name of this group is *Mixisu*. Although they are surrounded on every side by the Shengzha Nosu people, the Mixisu continue to retain a separate ethnicity. The Han Chinese call the Mixisu *Shuitian Ren*, which means "water fields people." This generic Chinese name is used for several distinct groups throughout southern China.

Language: Because of their location in the heart of the Daliangshan (Big Cold Mountains) it can be assumed that the Mixisu speak a Northern Yi language. No specific research has yet been done to confirm this however. Many Mixisu may now have lost the use of their mother tongue and may exclusively speak either or both Chinese and Nosu.

History: In the distant past there were few Yi people living in southern Sichuan Province, but warfare between the Yi and Chinese in Guizhou and Yunnan forced many people to migrate into the lonely, wild mountains of southern Sichuan where they could retain their ethnicity without fear of invasion. According to French General Vicomte d'Ollone, "The first conquest [of the Yi in Guizhou] was effected by the Ming Dynasty about 1380, and another more serious one by the Manchu Emperor Yungcheng in 1727; and it was then that the irreducible populations sought an inaccessible refuge beyond the Blue River. We now saw the country-side which was once the home of the tribes we had already visited, the battle-fields where they often held their conquerors in check; we also found remnants of the same tribes which had preferred surrender, and which still preserve continuous relations with their fellow-clansmen across the river."[1]

Customs: The Mixisu were raided by the Nosu for generations and many were taken away as slaves and concubines. The Communist authorities "liberated" the area and abolished the slave system in the early 1950s. Today, the Mixisu lead quiet lives as farmers and herdsmen.

Religion: Although most Mixisu do not consider themselves to be religious, they still retain spirit worship and ancestor worship ceremonies which are held on several occasions throughout the lunar calendar.

Christianity: In many parts of southern China prior to 1949, the Nosu dominated the lives of their neighbors by using their authority as powerful landlords. "One Nosu landowner [in another area]... would not allow his Nosu tenants to become Christians as they were false and crafty, and if they entered the Church, it was from unworthy motives."[2] As a result, few Mixisu have ever been given the chance to hear the gospel. There are a few small Three-Self Chinese churches in Xichang City, but few have ever considered taking the gospel to the unreached Mixisu.

Midge Conner

Mjuniang 草苗

Paul Hattaway

Location: The *Encyclopedic Dictionary of Chinese Linguistics* listed a 1991 figure of 60,000 speakers of the Mjuniang language.[1] They live at the juncture of three southern provinces: Guangxi, Hunan, and Guizhou. In Guizhou they are located in Liping County; in Hunan they live in Tongdao County; and in Guangxi they are found in Sanjiang County. Liping County, which also contains many members of the Dong nationality, was captured by the Communists during the Long March in December 1934. Zhou En Lai chaired a meeting there at a shop belonging to a merchant named Xu. Today a small museum in Liping commemorates the Communist visit.

Identity: Although they have been officially included as members of the large Miao nationality in China, the Mjuniang speak a language closely related to Dong. The name *Mjuniang* is the autonym of this group. The Chinese invariably call them by the nickname *Cao Miao*, meaning "grass Miao." All the peoples in the area call the Mjuniang *Cao Miao*.

Language: Despite being ethnically and historically descended from the Miao ethnic group, the Mjuniang have been influenced by the Dong for centuries and have lost the use of their original language. Mjuniang may best be described as a dialect of Northern Dong. The Mjuniang language — which has six tones — is used in everyday communication. When the Mjuniang sing, however, they prefer to use Chinese.[2]

History: The Eurasian ancestry of the Miao (including the Mjuniang) was still apparent as recently as the nineteenth century. One visitor remarked, "They ate with spoons rather than chopsticks.... Even more odd were the many red or blond-haired Miao with light skin, and some with blue eyes."[3] For thousands of years the Han Chinese called themselves *Li-min*, which is generally translated "black-haired people." One writer asks, "Why, then, did they designate themselves the Black or Dark people? Did they at one time live in the neighbourhood of people who were fair-haired and of lighter complexion than themselves?"[4]

Customs: To accommodate their terrain, some Mjuniang villages consist of *hanging houses*. "These three-story wooden homes are built on stakes against the mountain slope. The top story is used to store the grain, the middle for bedrooms and living room, and the bottom for cattle, sheep and poultry."[5]

Religion: For centuries, Mjuniang shamans and sorcerers have possessed great demonic power. Since the advent of Communism in China, however, their influence has been diminished. In many locations shamans continue to operate in secret.

Christianity: The Lutherans worked in Liping until the 1930s, when they were forced to leave China. The church property was confiscated by the Communists. Today there are no known believers among the unreached Mjuniang. Most of the present generation have never heard of Christ, nor have they ever met a Christian.

Population in China:
60,000 (1991)
75,600 (2000)
97,600 (2010)
Location: Guizhou, Hunan, Guangxi
Religion: Animism
Christians: None Known

Overview of the Mjuniang

Countries: China

Pronunciation: "Jooh-nee-ah"

Other Names: Cao Miao, Grass Miao, Cao, Miao: Cao

Population Source:
60,000 (1991 *EDCL*);
Out of a total Miao population of 7,398,035 (1990 census)

Location:
SE Guizhou: Liping County;
SW Hunan: Tongdao County;
N Guangxi: Sanjiang County

Status:
Officially included under Miao

Language: Daic, Kam-Sui

Dialects: 0

Religion: Animism, Shamanism, Ancestor Worship

Christians: None known

Scripture: None

***Jesus* film:** None

Gospel Recordings: None

Christian Broadcasting: None

ROPAL code: COV00

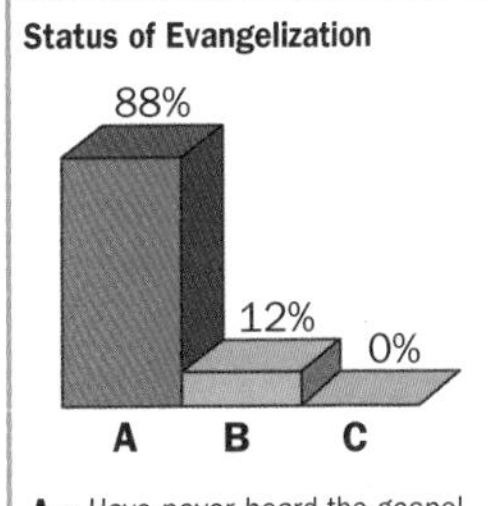

A = Have never heard the gospel
B = Were evangelized but did not become Christians
C = Are adherents to any form of Christianity

Mo 莫家

Population in China:
12,822 (1982)
18,550 (2000)
23,270 (2010)
Location: Guizhou
Religion: Daoism
Christians: 30

Overview of the Mo

Countries: China

Pronunciation: "Mo"

Other Names: Ching, Mak, Mo Jia, Mohua, Mochia, Mo Min, Sou Miao

Population Source:
12,822 (1982 *Minzu Shibie Wenxian Ziliao Huibian*);
4,400 (1976 J. Dreyer);
Out of a total Bouyei population of 2,545,059 (1990 census)

Location: S Guizhou: Jia Liang Township of Libo County; Dushan County

Status: Officially included under Bouyei since 1985; Previously included in a list of *Undetermined Minorities*

Language: Daic, Kam-Sui

Dialects (5):
Mak, Chi, Ching, Hwa, Lyo

Religion:
Daoism, Animism, Christianity

Christians: 30

Scripture: None

***Jesus* film:** None

Gospel Recordings: None

Christian Broadcasting: None

ROPAL code: MKGOO

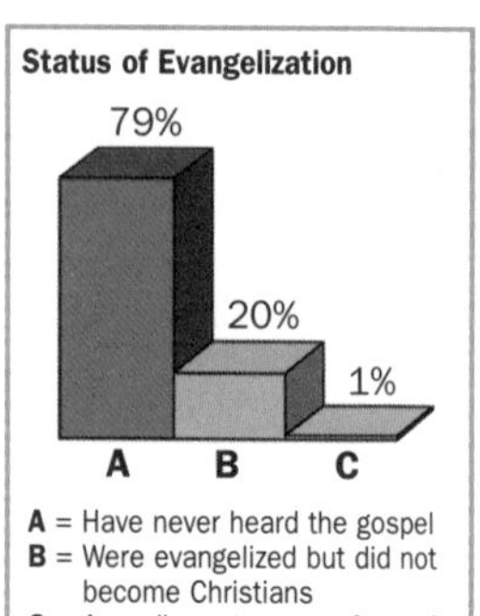

Paul Hattaway

Location: A total of 12,822 Mo people were listed in a 1982 Chinese official publication.[1] The majority are located in and around Jia Liang Township in the heart of Libo County in southern Guizhou Province, and in parts of Dushan County.[2] The Mo live near the Maolan Karst Forest, where "karst formations are cut by beautiful waterfalls. The natural vegetation remains and there are plants that have survived from very early periods, retaining characteristics of plants and trees that are now extinct.... This conservation area supports musk deer, rhesus monkey and, it is claimed, tiger, ox, bear and leopard."[3]

Identity: The Mo were included in a list of *Undetermined Minorities* in the 1982 census but were reclassified into the Bouyei nationality in 1985.[4] The Mo are also known as the *Mo Jia, Mak*, and *Ching*, which may be the names of Mo clans. Most of the inhabitants of Jia Liang are surnamed *Mo*.

Language: The Mo language — which has been described as "very close to Shui"[5] — is also related to Yanghuang and Rao. It is part of the Dong-Shui branch of the Tai linguistic family. It contains five dialects: Mak, Ching, Chi, Hwa, and Lyo. Most Mo men are able to speak Mandarin, with a heavy local accent. Many can also speak Bouyei as a trade language. Most Mo women, however, cannot speak any Mandarin at all.[6]

History: Because they do not possess a script, the exact history of the Mo is uncertain. From their language, it can be speculated that the Mo were originally part of the Shui, who migrated away from the main body of Shui several centuries ago.

Customs: Many of the Mo customs are the same as those of the Bouyei. When visiting a Mo home, "one may see cut-paper spells hanging in the doorway or in the windows. The door may have a mirror above it to reflect demons away or swords to pierce them if they try to enter."[7]

Religion: The Mo are a very superstitious people. Many adhere to the Chinese religion of Daoism. Although they do not have their own temples, most Mo homes contain pictures of fierce Daoist deities. Posters are plastered to the doors and gates of their houses in a bid to scare off afflicting demons.

Christianity: A Protestant mission station opened in Dushan County in 1895, but "the time of the missionaries was entirely given up to work among the Chinese."[8] In 1995 a Hong Kong-based mission presented the gospel to the Mo and succeeded in winning several of them to Christ. The new converts immediately started a house church. About 30 Mo have reportedly become Christians in the years since then.[9] These messengers of the gospel shared the great joy that many early pioneers found in presenting the message of eternal life to a people for the first time. One missionary wrote, "I know not whether anyone experiences emotion worthy to be compared with the thrill of joy which the missionary feels, when permitted for the first time to point out to a sin-enslaved people the Lamb of God which taketh away the sin of the world."[10]

Monba, Cona 门巴(措那)

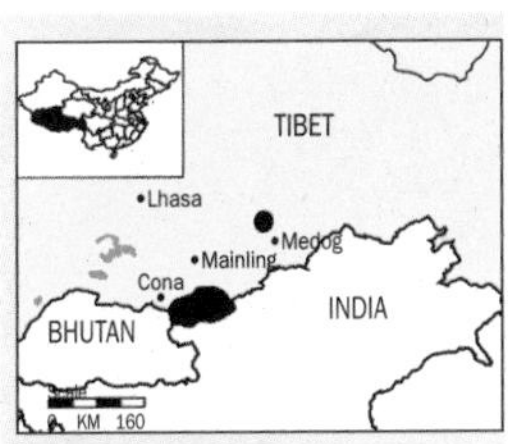

Population in China:
30,000 (1987)
34,850 (2000)
43,400 (2010)
Location: Tibet
Religion: Tibetan Buddhism
Christians: None Known

Overview of the Cona Monba

Countries: Bhutan, China, India

Pronunciation: "Co-nah-Mon-bah"

Other Names: Tsangla, Sangla, Tshangla, Cuona Monba, Motuo Monba, Central Monba, Moinba, Menba, Monpa, Mompa, Momba, Menpa, Memba, Southern Monba

Population Source:
30,000 (1987 *LAC*);
Only 7,475 Monba were counted in the 1990 census;
138,000 in Bhutan (1993);
43,649 in India (1994)

Location:
S Tibet: Cona and Medog counties

Status:
Officially included under Monba

Language: Sino-Tibetan, Tibeto-Burman, Bodic, Eastern Bodic Himalayan, Kiranti, Eastern

Dialects (2):
Northern Cona, Southern Cona

Religion: Tibetan Buddhism, Shamanism, Polytheism, Animism

Christians: None known

Scripture: None

***Jesus* film:** None

Gospel Recordings:
Bhutanese Tsangla #00595

Christian Broadcasting:
Available in Bhutan (FEBC)

ROPAL code: TSJ00 and MOB02

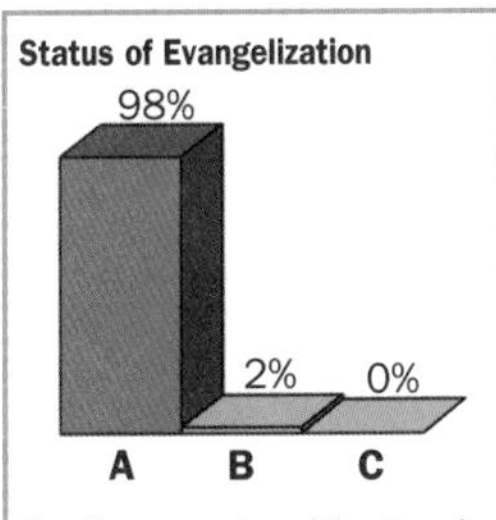

A = Have never heard the gospel
B = Were evangelized but did not become Christians
C = Are adherents to any form of Christianity

Location: More than 34,000 speakers of Cona Monba — which is known as *Tsangla* in Bhutan and India — live in the southern part of Tibet, particularly in Cona County.[1] Others are scattered far to the northeast in Medog County. The majority (138,000) of the speakers of this language live in eastern Bhutan. Approximately 44,000 also inhabit the Kameng District in Arunachal Pradesh, India.

Identity: Although the Monba are one of China's officially recognized nationalities, only 7,475 were listed in the 1990 census. Independent researchers agree there are more than 30,000 Cona Monba in China.

Language: Cona Monba is "quite distinct linguistically"[2] from Medog Monba. The speakers of the two Monba languages, which are part of the Eastern Himalayan branch of Tibeto-Burman, struggle to communicate with each other. The two groups must use Tibetan as a common language. Cona Monba has four tones, while Medog Monba does not contain any tones at all.[3]

History: Nearly three centuries ago the Monba people migrated across the Himalayas from the Moinyu area to southeast Tibet. Numerous Monba speakers today still live within the borders of India. Until 1959 the Monba were oppressed serfs of the Tibetans. They had to ask permission from the Tibetans even just to make a journey.

Customs: The Monba are the only minority group in China to practice "river burial," by which a corpse is cut into 108 pieces and hurled into a rushing river to be washed away. The Tibetans consider this to be the lowest form of burial and only use it for children and lepers. Some Monba practice Tibetan bird burials. The number 20 is the basic counting unit of the Monba. Thus, 67 becomes *three twenties plus seven*, and so on. Monba silversmiths are renowned for their skill in making intricate jewelry and ornaments.

Religion: Although most Monba are outwardly Tibetan Buddhists, the majority continue to practice numerous shamanistic and polytheistic rituals. The Monba believe all disease is caused by demons. They feel they are forced to sacrifice their valuable cattle and horses in order to pacify these angry demons and cause the affliction to cease. They also believe humans can be demons who cause sickness. A boy or girl who marries into a "demon family" too becomes a demon. Therefore "demon families" are allowed to intermarry only.[4]

Christianity: The Monba are one of the most unreached and inaccessible people groups in all of China. They have no knowledge of the gospel. Few Christians have ever prayed for them. Foreigners are not permitted to enter their region from either the Tibetan or the southern side of the border. There are currently shortwave gospel radio broadcasts in the Tsangla language of Bhutan which perhaps can be heard and understood by the Cona Monba. In 1996 several Bhutanese Christians crossed into Tibet for the purpose of evangelism.[5]

Midge Conner

Monba, Medog 门巴 (墨脱)

Location: A 1987 study reported 5,000 speakers of the Medog Monba living in China.[1] The majority are located in Medog County in southern Tibet. A few are also found in the Dongjiu area of Linzhi County. All Monba in Tibet are located in the vast Menyu Prefecture. One linguist states, "The Medog Monba live mainly in Medog County in Tibet as well as Siang District of Arunachal Pradesh. This is a very small group... with the majority in India, quite distinct linguistically from the [Cona] Monba."[2] Inaccessible for most of the year due to snow and landslides, Medog was the last county in China to become accessible to land vehicles. In 1994 a road was built there for the first time. Medog contains many Bengali tigers and 40 species of other rare, protected animals.[3]

Identity: Unlike some of the Cona Monba, who were counted in the Tibetan nationality, it appears that all of the Medog Monba have been counted as part of the Monba nationality.

Language: The Medog Monba language has been influenced by Tibetan more than the Cona Monba language. Medog Monba is not a tonal language, compared to Cona Monba which contains four tones. Many Medog Monba are bilingual in Tibetan and many can read the Tibetan script.[4]

History: The Medog Monba became poverty stricken following the implementation of a feudal system imposed on them by the Zhuba Geju faction in the fourteenth century. For centuries they were effectively slaves of the Tibetans.

Midge Conner

Customs: The Monba are known for their hospitality. They have a great love for music, singing, and dancing. "Most of them are able to play the traditional bamboo flute, a short thick instrument with four finger holes.... Their silversmiths are skillful in designing bracelets, earrings, necklaces, and other ornaments."[5] At Monba weddings, the bride's uncle is the most honored guest. According to tradition, he "finds fault in everything, complaining the meat slices are too thick and the drinks too cheap. He bangs on the table with his fists, glowering angrily at everyone who passes. He behaves in this way to test the groom's family and observe their reactions."[6]

Religion: The majority of Monba follow Tibetan Buddhism. Some, however, still maintain their traditional belief in unseen gods, demons, and ancestral spirits. Shamans and some Buddhist monks frequently use magic to cure the sick.

Christianity: The Medog Monba are completely unaware that Christ came two millennia ago and died for their sin. No missionaries were allowed to work in this area of Tibet in the past. There are no churches near Medog for more than a hundred miles in any direction. The Medog Monba have existed for generations without any flicker of spiritual light to brighten their lives. They have no Scriptures or recordings in their language. Few have ever interceded on their behalf for Christian workers to penetrate these lonely communities with the good news.

Population in China:
5,000 (1987)
6,590 (2000)
8,200 (2010)
Location: Tibet
Religion: Tibetan Buddhism
Christians: None Known

Overview of the Medog Monba

Countries: India, China

Pronunciation: "Meh-dog-Mon-bah"

Other Names: Cangluo Monba, Canglo Monba, Northern Monba, Motuo Monba, Eastern Monba

Population Source: 5,000 (1987 *LAC*); Out of a total population of 7,475 Monba (1990 census); Also in India

Location: *S Tibet:* Medog and Linzhi counties

Status: Officially included under Monba

Language: Sino-Tibetan, Tibeto-Burman, Bodic, Eastern Himalayan, Kiranti, Eastern Kiranti

Literacy: 57%

Dialects: 0

Religion: Tibetan Buddhism, Shamanism

Christians: None known

Scripture: None

***Jesus* film:** None

Gospel Recordings: None

Christian Broadcasting: None

ROPAL code: MOB01

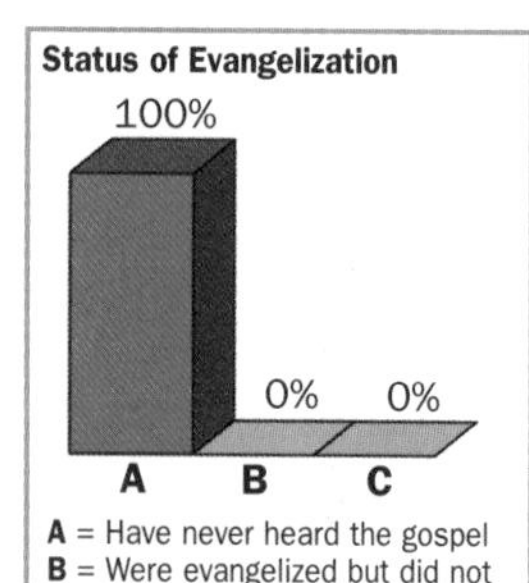

Mongol 蒙古

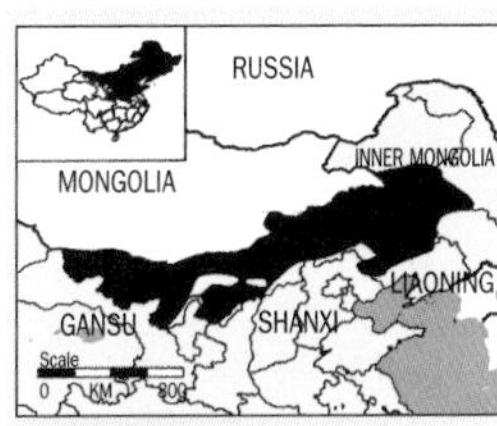

Population in China:
4,505,000 (1990)
5,811,400 (2000)
7,496,800 (2010)
Location: Inner Mongolia, Jilin, Liaoning, Hebei, Henan...
Religion: Shamanism
Christians: 12,000

Overview of the Mongols

Countries: China, Mongolia, Russia, Taiwan, USA
Pronunciation: "Mong-goll"
Other Names: Mongolian, Menggu, Meng Zu
Population Source: 4,806,849 (1990 census);[1] 3,416,881 (1982 census);[2] 1,614,000 in Mongolia (1993 P. Johnstone); 626,000 in Russia (1993); 6,000 in Taiwan (1993); Also in USA
Location: *Inner Mongolia Autonomous Region; Jilin; Liaoning; Hebei; Henan; Beijing; Jiangsu; Shaanxi; Shanxi; Tianjin; Shandong; Shanghai*
Status: An official minority of China
Language: Altaic, Mongolian, Eastern Mongolian, Oirat-Khalka, Khalka-Buriat
Literacy: 71%
Dialects (9): Chahar, Ordos, Tumet, Shilingol, Ulanchab, Jo-Uda, Jostu, Jirim, Ejine
Religion: Shamanism, Tibetan Buddhism, Animism, Christianity
Christians: 12,000
Scripture: New Testament 1952; Work in progress
***Jesus* film:** None
Gospel Recordings: Mongolian #00292
Inner Mongolian Chahar #04947
Sheeringgul: Hohhot
Christian Broadcasting: Available (FEBC)
ROPAL code: MVF00

Status of Evangelization

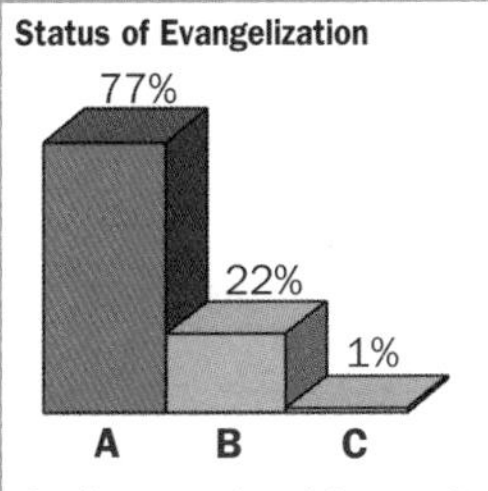

A = Have never heard the gospel
B = Were evangelized but did not become Christians
C = Are adherents to any form of Christianity

Paul Hattaway

Location: Almost six million Mongols are scattered across a wide area of northern China. Approximately three times as many Mongols live in China as in the nation of Mongolia. The population of Mongols living in Inner Mongolia fell from 450,000 to 300,000 in the 173 years between 1772 and 1945.[3] Although their numbers have since grown again, they are now swamped by the multitude of Han who have migrated into their homeland. In 1982, 1,863 of China's 2,369 counties and municipalities contained members of the Mongolian nationality.[4]

Identity: The Mongols — who consist of "as many as sixty separate Mongolian tribes"[5] — are one of China's official nationalities.

Language: The main Mongol language in China is similar to Hahl Mongol in Mongolia, "but there are phonological and important loan differences."[6]

History: In the thirteenth and fourteenth centuries the Mongols brutally established the largest empire the world has seen, stretching from Southeast Asia to Europe. They instituted the Yuan Dynasty and ruled China from 1271 to 1368. The terrified Europeans called the Mongols *Tatars*, meaning "people from hell" (Tartarus).

Customs: Through thousands of bitter winters the Mongols have lived in yurts, racing their horses, raising livestock, and worshiping the forces of nature.

Religion: At the mercy of their vast and windswept landscape, the ancient Mongols based their religion on the forces of nature. The moon, stars, and sun were all revered, as were rivers. In the past many Mongols were Christians, converted by Nestorian missionaries between the seventh and fourteenth centuries. Even a chapel outside the Great Khan's royal tent "resounded with the sound of public chants and the beating of tablets loudly announcing the appointed hours of Christian worship."[7] Hulagu Khan's wife was described as "the believing and true Christian queen."[8] The Keirats, a Mongol tribe, numbered 200,000 believers in AD 1007,[9] while there were about 30,000 Mongol Catholics recorded in China by 1368.[10]

Christianity: At times during the thirteenth and fourteenth centuries it seemed that the Mongols were on the verge of adopting Christianity as their religion. Kublai Khan issued this challenge to Marco Polo: "Go to your Pope and ask him to send me a hundred men learned in your religion, who in the face of these sorcerers... will show their mastery by making the sorcerers powerless to perform these marvels in their presence.... Then I will be baptized, and all my magnates and barons will do likewise, and their subjects in turn.... Then there will be more Christians here than there are in your part of the world."[11] In 1992 there were about 2,000 Mongol believers reported in China.[12] Today there are believed to be between 5,000 and 12,000.[13] In 1998 a German-based ministry claimed at least 200,000 Mongol Christians in China.[14] This has been strongly challenged by people close to the situation who say this source is unreliable and the claims are grossly exaggerated. The size of the Mongol church in China has long been a matter of dispute. Many have been unable to distinguish between Han believers living in Inner Mongolia, and ethnic Mongols.[15]

Mongol, Alxa 蒙古(阿拉善)

Paul Hattaway

Location: More than 21,000 Muslim Mongols live in the West Banner of the Alxa League, in the western part of Inner Mongolia. The Alxa League is surrounded on three sides by the Badain Jaran, Tengger, and Ulan Buh deserts.[1] The population of the entire Alxa League is only 150,000.[2] The League covers an area of 270,000 square kilometers (105,300 sq. mi.), 60% of which is desert. The main Alxa town is Bayan Hot, which means "city of wealth" in Mongolian.[3]

Identity: The Alxa Mongols are a distinct people group. They are the only group within the Mongolian nationality in China to profess Islam as their religion. As one mission agency notes, "They do indeed qualify as a people group, because, like caste, the difference is great enough to prevent intermarriage or even inter-friendship."[4] A Chinese writer adds, "The customs of the Mongolians in this area, like the terrain, are quite different from that of the eastern part of Inner Mongolia."[5] The Chinese call Alxa, "The Mongolia west of the Yellow River bend"[6] — a reference to both geographic and cultural differences.

Language: The Alxa Mongols use the *todo* "clear" script, also used by the Oirat and Torgut in Xinjiang. A Mongolian from farther east commented on the songs of the Alxa Mongols: "The melodies sounded booming and featured a broad range of notes."[7] The town of Bayan Hot is a linguistic mix, being home to members of 15 other nationalities.[8]

History: Alxa was the center of nomadic peoples such as the Hun, Wuhuan, and Qiang during the Qin and Han dynasties (221 BC – AD 220). One scholar states that the Alxa Mongols and the Dongxiang of Gansu were originally part of the Jagatai khanate, "who flourished during the Yuan period.... They were converted to Islam but were thereafter discriminated against by other Mongols who presumably resisted conversion.... They were compelled to move eastward.... When they reached Zhenfan they split into two routes. One group crossed the Helan mountains and went to Hetao where their descendants are today's Muslim Mongols of the Alashan [Alxa] West Banner."[9]

Customs: The Alxa Mongols rely on camels for survival. There are an estimated 200,000 camels in the region — one-sixth of the world's two-humped Bactarian camels.[10] Camel milk is not only used as drink but "is also fermented and made into an alcoholic beverage, cheese, butter and yogurt."[11] Due to a horrific infant mortality rate in the past, the Alxa Mongols do not celebrate a child's birth until it is three years old."[12]

Religion: The Alxa Mongols remain fervent followers of Islam to this day. Their faith constitutes their historical and ethnic identity as a people group.

Christianity: There are no known Christians among the Alxa Mongols. Few have ever heard the gospel. Because of their social and religious isolation, they will probably be one of the most difficult people groups to penetrate in all of China.

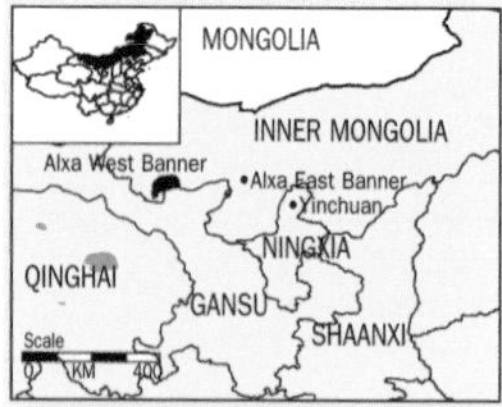

Population in China:
20,000 (1997)
21,700 (2000)
28,000 (2010)
Location: Inner Mongolia
Religion: Islam
Christians: None Known

Overview of the Alxa Mongols

Countries: China
Pronunciation: "Al-sha-Mon-gols"
Other Names: Muslim Mongols
Population Source:
20,000 (1997 AMO);
Out of a total Mongol population of 4,806,849 (1990 census)
Location: *W Inner Mongolia:* Alxa West Banner (County) of the Alxa League (Prefecture)
Status: Officially included under Mongolian
Language: Altaic, Mongolian, Eastern Mongolian
Dialects: 0
Religion: Islam
Christians: None known
Scripture: None
***Jesus* film:** None
Gospel Recordings: Alashanmeng
Christian Broadcasting: None
ROPAL code: None

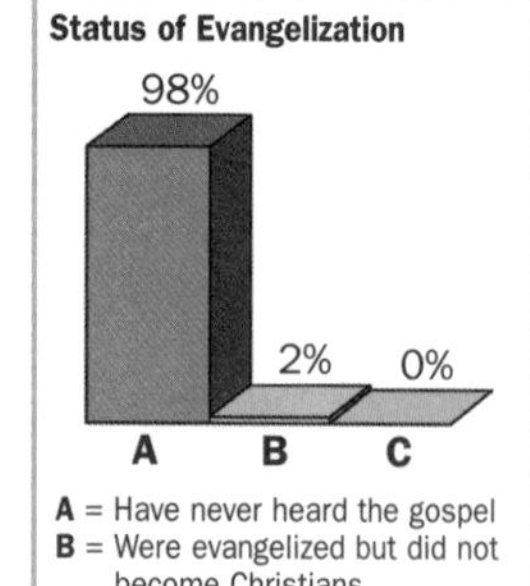

Mongol, Khalka 蒙古，卡拉卡

Location: The Khalka language, or *Hahl* for short, is the main language of the nation of Mongolia. In addition, approximately 50,000 speakers of Khalka are located along the China-Mongolia border.

Identity: The name *Khalka* means "shield."[1] The region of northern Mongolia has been called *the shield* since the sixteenth century. In the early 1900s one missionary described the Mongols as "well-built and sturdy. In appearance he is dirty and unkempt. His unwashed face and hands, tousled hair, and shaggy, greasy, sheep-skin garments create a prejudice against him.... On the other hand, he is simple-minded, fearless, and self-reliant; generous, and comparatively honest, kindly, hospitable, and easily approached and understood when treated with proper consideration."[2]

Language: The Khalka language is largely intelligible with the standard spoken by most Mongols in China. Speakers from the two countries have little trouble understanding each other; however, one linguist points out that the two languages "have important phonological and loan differences."[3]

History: The Khalka keep "carefully preserved genealogies to prove they are descendants of Genghis Khan."[4] For centuries they were ruled by a hereditary line of nobles and princes, until they were stripped of power by the Mongolian and Chinese Communist governments this century.

Customs: The greatest festival of the year for all Mongols is *nadam*, a word meaning "amusement." Mongols from far and wide gather for horse racing, wrestling, and other fun and games.

Midge Conner

Religion: The majority of Khalka Mongols in China follow Tibetan Buddhism, also known as Lamaism. "It has welded them together, has leavened their civilization with religious ideals, and has made them kind and hospitable.... But, on the other hand, it has robbed their manhood of its energy and natural ambition.... Until the power of Lamaism, with its overgrown, dissolute, and corrupting priesthood, is broken, there can be no hope of arresting the sure decay of the Mongols or of preventing their ultimate extinction."[5]

Christianity: There are a few known Christians among the Khalka in China. Prior to 1949 the Catholic Church claimed many converts (mostly Han Chinese) in Inner Mongolia, but one critic observed that "very often the incentive held out to the heathen is an economic one. The converts are invited to live on the land, each family is given an ox, a plow, a small field and sufficient seed."[6] Portions of the Bible were first translated into Khalka in the early twentieth century,[7] but the script used is now obsolete. Early missionary work was slow and difficult. "Looking back on our work in Mongolia it seems dark, having borne little fruit, but I lift my eyes upward to Him who can look deeper and farther than we can look and does not judge simply by the outward appearance as we do.... We believe there will be some saved souls from Mongolia in the great blood-washed multitude before the throne of the Redeemer."[8]

RUSSIA
MONGOLIA
INNER MONGOLIA
LIAONING
GANSU
SHAANXI
Scale
0 KM 300

Population in China:
49,000 (1995)
51,800 (2000)
66,800 (2010)
Location: Inner Mongolia
Religion: Tibetan Buddhism
Christians: 100

Overview of the Khalka Mongols

Countries: Mongolia, China, Taiwan, Russia, Kyrgyzstan

Pronunciation: "Hahl-ka"

Other Names: Khalka, Hahl

Population Source: 49,000 (1995 Joshua Project); Out of a total Mongol population of 4,806,849 (1990 census); 1,614,000 in Mongolia (1993 P. Johnstone); 6,000 in Taiwan; 1,774 in Russia (1959); Also in Kyrgyzstan

Location: *Inner Mongolia:* Along the China-Mongolia border

Status: Officially included under Mongolian

Language: Altaic, Mongolian, Eastern, Oirat-Khakla, Khalka-Buriat, Mongolian Proper

Dialects: 0

Religion: Tibetan Buddhism, Shamanism

Christians: 100

Scripture: New Testament 1990; Portions 1979

***Jesus* film:** Available

Gospel Recordings: Mongolian #00292

Christian Broadcasting: Available (FEBC)

ROPAL code: KHK00

Status of Evangelization

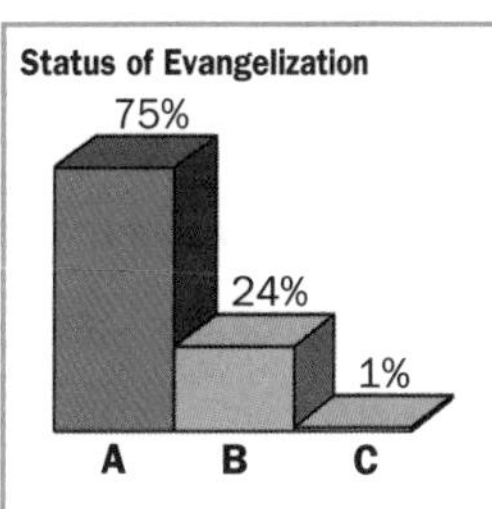

A = Have never heard the gospel
B = Were evangelized but did not become Christians
C = Are adherents to any form of Christianity

Mongol, Khamnigan 蒙古，康尼感

Population in China:
1,600 (1993)
1,920 (2000)
2,480 (2010)
Location: Inner Mongolia
Religion: Shamanism
Christians: None Known

Overview of the Khamnigan Mongols

Countries: China, Russia, Mongolia

Pronunciation: "Khahm-nee-gahn"

Other Names: Khamnigan, Kamnigan, Xamnigan, Hamunikan

Population Source: 1,600 (1993 J. Janhunen); Out of a total Mongol population of 4,806,849 (1990 census); Also in Russia, and Mongolia

Location: *NE Inner Mongolia:* Chen Baehru Banner of Hulunbuir League

Status: Officially included under Mongolian

Language: Altaic, Mongolian, Eastern Mongolian

Dialects: 2

Religion: Shamanism, Animism

Christians: None known

Scripture: None

***Jesus* film:** None

Gospel Recordings: None

Christian Broadcasting: None

ROPAL code: None

Status of Evangelization

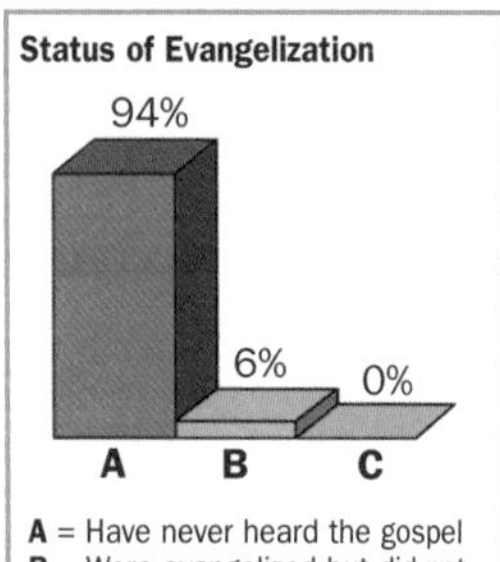

A = Have never heard the gospel
B = Were evangelized but did not become Christians
C = Are adherents to any form of Christianity

Location: The Khamnigan Mongols are scattered across Siberia, Mongolia, and the Chen Baehru Banner of the Hulunbuir League in China's Inner Mongolia. All of these locations are in the Onin-Argun region of the Trans Baikalia. A 1993 study listed 1,600 Khamnigan Mongols in China.

Identity: Although they are officially considered part of the Mongolian nationality, the small number of Khamnigan Mongols speak their own distinct language and have major cultural differences with other Mongolian groups. The Khamnigan Mongols have also never embraced Tibetan Buddhism.

Language: A 1993 study found 1,500 of the 1,600 Khamnigan Mongols were able to speak their language, described as "an archaic branch of northern Mongol."[1] Khamnigan children are still being taught to speak the language. Most Khamnigan Mongols are also able to speak the language of the neighboring Tungus Ewenki. Linguist Jahu Janhunen comments, "Although vigorous for the moment, the survival of Khamnigan Mongol in the long run is threatened by the increasing influx of Han Chinese settlers; both Chinese and Standard Mongolian are also present via the networks of radio and television as well as in the form of printed material."[2] Assimilation may have already occurred in Russia and Mongolia where the language is described as "possibly extinct."[3] In China the Khamnigan Mongol language consists of two dialects which show a mixture of influences from the Tungus Ewenki language.[4]

History: Little is known of the historical background of the Khamnigan Mongols. Their past has been intertwined with the Ewenki people for centuries. They have traded and intermarried with them for many generations. Today the two groups share many similar cultural traits.

Customs: *Khurund* is a milk curd thickened in the sun until it dries into a hard, gray cheese. In the days of Genghis Khan a warrior would mix a lump of khurund with water and put it into his saddlebag. "By their motion in riding," wrote Marco Polo, "the contents are violently shaken, and a thin porridge is produced upon which they make their dinner."[5]

Religion: Unlike most other Mongol groups, the Khamnigan Mongols have never adhered to Tibetan Buddhism. Their primary religion is shamanism. They worship the elements of nature, not unlike the Mongols at the time of Genghis Khan.

Christianity: One missionary visiting the Khamnigan Mongols in 1995 revealed that there are no known Christians or churches among them. Some may have heard the gospel through the witness of the Ewenki, who number more than 100 Eastern Orthodox believers in China. Most Khamnigan Mongols in China, however, remain completely ignorant of the person of Jesus Christ. No Scriptures or audio gospel recordings have been translated into the unique Khamnigan Mongol language.

Paul Hattaway

Mongol, Sichuan 蒙古(四川)

Paul Hattaway

Location: Approximately 27,000 Mongols live in the southern part of Sichuan Province. Although a few Mongol villages are within the borders of Yunnan Province — located on the shores of Lugu Lake among the Mosuo people — most are in Sichuan, spread out along two or three valleys in Yanyuan and Muli counties, northeast of Lugu Lake.

Identity: The Sichuan Mongols are officially counted as part of the Mongolian nationality in China. They are a distinct ethnolinguistic group, however, from all other Mongolian peoples.[1] They call themselves *Mongols* and possess their own clothing, history and language. All other peoples in the region recognize them as *Mengzu* (Mongols).

Language: Little research has been done regarding the language of the Sichuan Mongols. In the seven centuries since their arrival to the area, their speech has been heavily influenced by neighboring peoples. One visitor described their language as "Neither Mongolian, Mandarin, Yi, Mosuo nor Tibetan. I suspect it is a language taken from all or some of these languages."[2] The Mongol prince could "pick out a few words" of a Mongolian cassette played for him.[3]

History: Joseph Rock was the first recorded foreigner to visit the Sichuan Mongols in 1924. He described the town of Youngning as "the seat of three chiefs whose ancestors were Mongols, elevated to power by Kublai Khan in the 13th century."[4] Rock adds, "When the great Mongol Emperor marched through the territory about Youngning, 1253 AD, he left one of his relatives to rule the Hlihin tribesmen."[5] Before Communist rule, the Mongol king acted as a warlord over the whole region. "When the Communists took over, they deposed him, not killing him so as not to make him a martyr in the people's eyes."[6] The Mongol palace was destroyed and the prince was sent to a re-education camp for several years. The prince, La Ping Chu, is still alive today and respected by his people, although he is not allowed to rule. Many older Mongols still bow their heads in respect when they pass him on the street.

Customs: Most Sichuan Mongols are farmers or fishermen, leading quiet lives in their remote villages. They observe Buddhist festivals, "hoping some day their kingdom will be restored to them."[7]

Religion: Tibetan Buddhism — also known as Lamaism — is the stronghold of the Sichuan Mongols. There is a temple in active use just behind the prince's house. Most temples and altars were destroyed during the Cultural Revolution.

Christianity: Very few Sichuan Mongols have ever heard the name of Jesus Christ. One person who has heard the gospel is the prince himself, witnessed to by foreign visitors a few years ago. A prayer for healing was offered for the prince, who could not stand up straight because of a stomach ulcer. He was completely healed.[8] The Sichuan Mongols are surrounded by unreached people groups on every side; therefore, there are no Christian communities nearby who could reach them. Gospel radio broadcasts in Mandarin have had little effect because few understand Chinese.

Population in China:
21,033 (1990)
27,100 (2000)
35,000 (2010)
Location: Sichuan, Yunnan
Religion: Tibetan Buddhism
Christians: 5

Overview of the Sichuan Mongols

Countries: China
Pronunciation: "Mong-gawls"
Other Names: Lugu Lake Mongols, Mongolians: Sichuan, Hlihin, Hli-khin
Population Source: 21,033 (1990 census); Out of a total Mongol population of 4,806,849 (1990 census)
Location: *S Sichuan:* Yanyuan (13,619) and Muli (7,414) counties; A few live in adjacent areas across the Yunnan border.
Status: Officially included under Mongolian
Language: Sino-Tibetan, Tibeto-Burman, Unclassified
Dialects: 0
Religion: Tibetan Buddhism, Shamanism
Christians: 5
Scripture: None
***Jesus* film:** None
Gospel Recordings: None
Christian Broadcasting: None
ROPAL code: None

Status of Evangelization

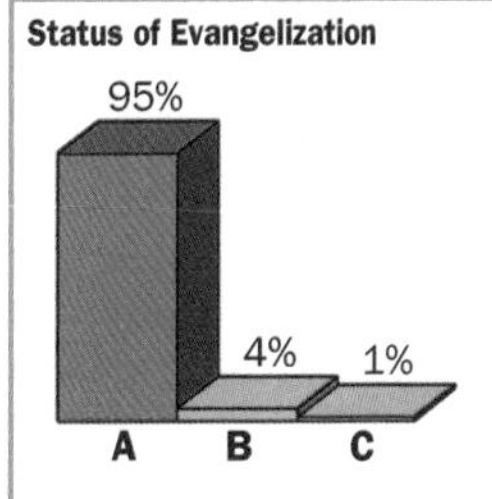

A = Have never heard the gospel
B = Were evangelized but did not become Christians
C = Are adherents to any form of Christianity

Mongol, Yunnan 蒙古(云南)

August 15

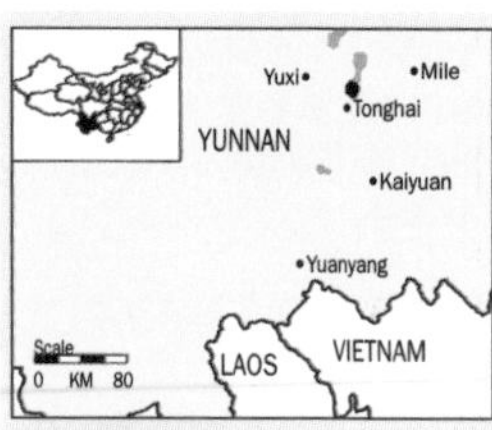

Population in China:
6,341 (1997)
6,890 (2000)
8,890 (2010)
Location: Yunnan
Religion: Daoism
Christians: None Known

Overview of the Yunnan Mongols

Countries: China, language in Laos

Pronunciation: "Mong-gawls-Yoo-nanh"

Other Names: Kaduo, Gazhuo, Yunnan Mongolians

Population Source: 6,341 (1997 *Yuxi Nianjian*); Out of a total Mongol population of 4,806,849 (1990 census); 5,000 speakers of Kaduo in Laos (1981 Wurm & Hattori)

Location: *Yunnan:* Near Jihulu Lake, Hexi District of Tonghai County, in Yuxi Prefecture

Status: Officially included under Mongolian

Language: Sino-Tibetan, Tibeto-Burman, Burmese-Lolo, Lolo, Northern Lolo, Unclassified

Dialects: 0

Religion: Daoism, Mahayana Buddhism, Polytheism, Islam

Christians: None known

Scripture: None

***Jesus* film:** None

Gospel Recordings: None

Christian Broadcasting: None

ROPAL code: KTPOO

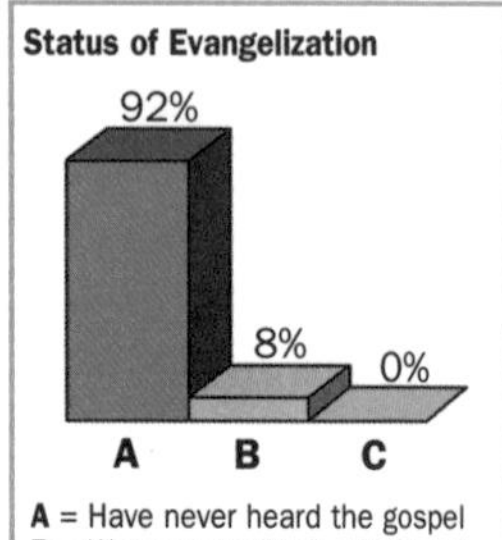

Location: Approximately 6,900 Mongolians inhabit a large village near Jihulu Lake in Tonghai County, Yunnan Province.[1] Intriguingly, an additional 5,000 people in northern Laos speak the same language, called *Kaduo*, although they do not identify themselves as Mongols.

Paul Hattaway

Identity: The Yunnan Mongols are a distinct people group. They deliberately separate themselves and refuse to intermarry with people from other nationalities.[2] Despite having been cut off from their homeland for seven centuries, the Yunnan Mongols proudly retain their ethnic identity as Mongols.

Language: Over the centuries the Yunnan Mongol's language has evolved to the point that it is unintelligible with other Mongolian languages. Having been influenced by neighboring peoples, the Yunnan Mongols today speak their own distinct Tibeto-Burman language, called *Kaduo* or *Gazhuo*. It is described as having eight tones[3] and as being similar to the Lisu and Sani languages.[4]

History: The Mongolian empire gained control over southwest China in 1252 when they overthrew the ancient Nanzhao Kingdom in Dali. They ruled Yunnan for 129 years, extracting annual taxes and tribute which were sent north to fill the coffers of the Yuan Dynasty rulers. In 1381, "Ming Dynasty troops routed the Yuan army by the shore of the Baishi River. The Mongol soldiers, their hopes to return to their homeland having been dashed, had no alternative but to settle down in the province."[5] Their ancestors have today grown to 7,000 people around Jihulu Lake.

Customs: The Yunnan Mongol women's dress is said to resemble the uniform of the original Mongol soldiers. In the milder climate they wore cloth instead of fur and cut off the sleeves. In the early 1980s village elders sent a delegation to Inner Mongolia to learn about Mongolian culture. They immediately adopted customs similar to Mongols in the north. Wrestling became their favorite sport when they saw how popular it was with other Mongols.[6]

Religion: The religion of the Yunnan Mongols is a mixture of Buddhism and Daoism. Posters of fierce Daoist deities hang on the doors and gates of their homes to ward off evil spirits. A few Mongol families are Muslims. They were converted to Islam by the neighboring Hui community, located near the entrance to the Mongolian village.

Christianity: There is no Christian church among the Yunnan Mongols. The few efforts to take the gospel to them have met with stubborn resistance and opposition from village leaders and local police. In the 1980s a Mongolian Christian was mobilized from northern China and visited this village, hoping he would be able to influence the Yunnan Mongols to become Christians.[7] He too was rejected by the locals, who are eager to preserve the Mongolian traditions they had neglected for centuries and who are careful to shun all change to their society.

Mongour 蒙古(土族)

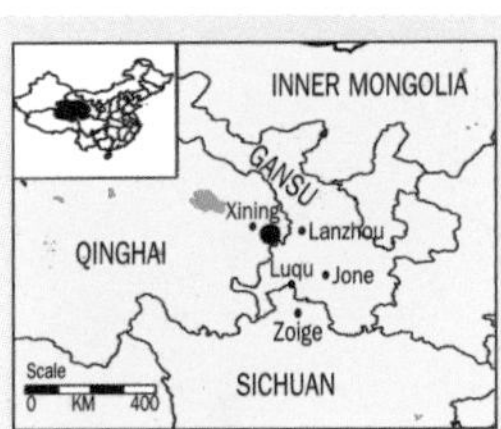

Population in China:
30,000 (1987)
39,800 (2000)
49,800 (2010)
Location: Qinghai
Religion: Tibetan Buddhism
Christians: None Known

Overview of the Mongour

Countries: China

Pronunciation: "Mong-gore"

Other Names: Mongour, Mongor, Monguor, Mongou, Minhe Tu

Population Source:
30,000 (1987 *LAC*);
Out of a total Tu population of 191,624 (1990 census)

Location: *E Qinghai:* Minhe County

Status:
Officially included under Tu

Language: Altaic, Mongolian, Eastern Mongolian, Mongour

Dialects: 0

Religion: Tibetan Buddhism, Shamanism, Daoism

Christians: None known

Scripture: None

***Jesus* film:** None

Gospel Recordings:
Tu, Minhe #04946

Christian Broadcasting: None

ROPAL code: MJG02

Status of Evangelization

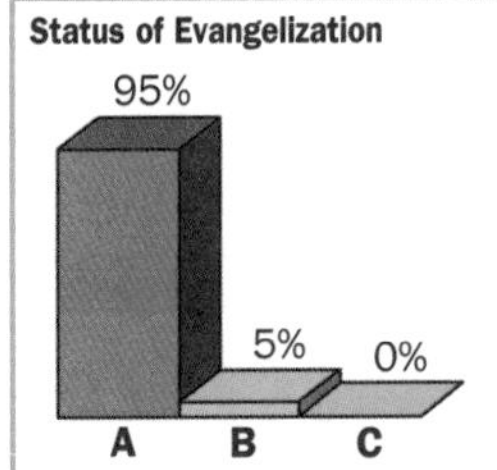

A = Have never heard the gospel
B = Were evangelized but did not become Christians
C = Are adherents to any form of Christianity

Location: Thirty thousand speakers of the Mongour language were reported in a 1987 study.[1] They primarily inhabit Minhe County in the eastern part of Qinghai Province. Minhe, formerly known as *Shangchuankou*, lies on the Huang Shui River. Minhe is situated east of the provincial capital Xining, a considerable distance from Huzhu County where the majority of the Tu people live.

Identity: Although the Mongour have been officially included as part of the Tu nationality, they speak a very different language and possess a separate identity from the Tu in other locations. As one researcher explains, "The Tu call themselves Mongol, except those living in Minhe, who form a minority, where the word is pronounced *Mongour*. This term has mistakenly been used by some Western scholars as the general name for all Tu."[2]

Language: The speakers of Mongour cannot communicate with other Tu in their own language and must revert to Chinese to be understood. "Differences [between Tu and Mongour] are mainly phonological, but there are also lexical and grammatical differences."[3] While Tu has many loanwords from Tibetan, Mongour contains numerous loanwords from Chinese. Mongour is considered "the most divergent Mongolian language of all."[4]

History: When the ancestors of today's Tu and Mongour people first came to Qinghai, the area was occupied by Tibetans, Uygurs, and a group called the Shato. By the late 1300s, the Tu had divided into 16 clans. Eight clans were called *Tu* (White Mongol), five *Shato*, one *Black Mongol*, one *Turkish* (Uygur), and one Chinese.[5]

Customs: The Mongour have several unique marriage customs. One is called "marriage to the pole" by which a girl stays with her family and takes in lovers. Any children born to her take her family's name. Another is the "marriage to the girdle" where a Mongour girl sleeps with a guest, who upon departure leaves his girdle behind. In case the girl becomes pregnant, she would be "married to the girdle."[6] During child delivery, the mother and baby stay confined to a room for one month. Men are barred from entry; only the closest female relatives are allowed to enter.

Religion: Two types of shamans are active among the Mongour. "White shamans" are used to heal sickness, while "black shamans" bring vengeance on enemies. Another highly regarded religious figure is the *kurtain*. This is a person who allows himself to be possessed by an evil Daoist spirit.

Christianity: By the 1920s Catholic missionaries were active in the Mongour region, but no church remains today. Although most Mongour can read, there are no Scriptures available in their language. Missionary Frank Laubach issued a warning to the Church in the 1930s: "Millions in China will soon be reading. Are we going to give them reading matter? Will they be flooded with the message of Christ or with atheism? Will they read love or hate? This is the most stupendous, most arresting, most ominous fact, perhaps on this planet."[7]

Revival Christian Church

Mosuo 摩梭

August 17

Location: A 1991 study numbered 40,000 Mosuo,[1] living on both sides of the Sichuan-Yunnan border. The Mosuo are primarily concentrated around the shores of beautiful Lugu Lake. Lugu is one of the highest inhabited lake areas in China, at an altitude of 2,685 meters (8,800 ft.) above sea level. Lion Mountain, home to the goddess Gammo, the chief Mosuo deity, rises majestically over the northern shore. No roads led to the lake until 1982. Before that time the Mosuo area was only accessible by foot or on horseback. Still today the whole area is snowbound and cut off from the rest of the world for months at a time during winter.

Identity: The Mosuo have been officially included as part of the Naxi nationality. The Mosuo deeply resent this and despise being called Naxi. The two groups have a different language, religion, and culture.

Language: Although distantly related to the Naxi, Mosuo speakers are not able to communicate with them and generally revert to Chinese. An earlier visitor found it "impossible to converse with these people, for their language is more than a mere dialect of the Lijiang Naxi."[2]

History: According to Mosuo legends, the ancestors of today's Naxi and Mosuo migrated down from the Tibetan Plateau about 1,000 years ago.[3] Part of the group stopped at Lugu Lake and became today's Mosuo people, while the remainder continued south until they reached Lijiang where today they are the Naxi. After many centuries of separation, the two groups have developed major ethnolinguistic differences.

Customs: The Mosuo have a matriarchal and matrilineal society. The *azhu* system means all property and assets are transferred to the female side of the family, from mother to youngest daughter. Even the family name is passed down from the mother. Instead of taking a husband, Mosuo women are able to have "walk-in" relationships. Men are only allowed to visit their lovers at night. They must leave the woman's house early the next morning and return to their mother's home. If a child is born, the responsibility to raise the child is borne by the mother and her brothers. Often the identity of the father is not known at all. Despite pressure from the government to discontinue the *azhu* system, a 1994 study revealed 60% of the Mosuo still conform to this way of life.[4]

Paul Hattaway

Religion: Tibetan Buddhism has a strong grip on the Mosuo. Altars of white stones are piled in pyramid formations on every corner and outside most homes. "Because the Mosuo have no written language, shamans had to memorize the equivalent of 71 volumes of text and recited them word for word during funerals, births and other events. From the first utterance to the last, a master's recitation took up to 60 hours."[5]

Christianity: There had never been a known Mosuo believer until recently, when a Mosuo family came to Christ under quite extraordinary, supernatural circumstances.[6] This family shared the gospel with their friends and neighbors, so that today there are about 20 Mosuo believers who meet together, of whom "five are strong Christians."[7]

Population in China:
40,000 (1991)
46,000 (2000)
53,700 (2010)
Location: Sichuan, Yunnan
Religion: Tibetan Buddhism
Christians: 20

Overview of the Mosuo

Countries: China

Pronunciation: "Mo-sor"

Other Names: Mosso, Moso, Lushi, Hli-khin, Musu, Moxie, Mo-hsieh, Jang

Population Source: 40,000 (1991 Shi Yuoyi); Out of a total Naxi population of 278,009 (1990 census)

Location: *Yunnan-Sichuan:* Lugu Lake, where Ninglang County, Yunnan, and Yanyuan County, Sichuan, meet

Status: Officially included under Naxi

Language: Sino-Tibetan, Tibeto-Burman, Burmese-Lolo, Lolo, Northern Lolo, Naxi, Eastern Naxi

Dialects: 0

Religion: Tibetan Buddhism, Polytheism, Shamnism, Christianity

Christians: 20

Scripture: None

***Jesus* film:** None

Gospel Recordings: Mosuo #04807

Christian Broadcasting: None

ROPAL code: None

Status of Evangelization

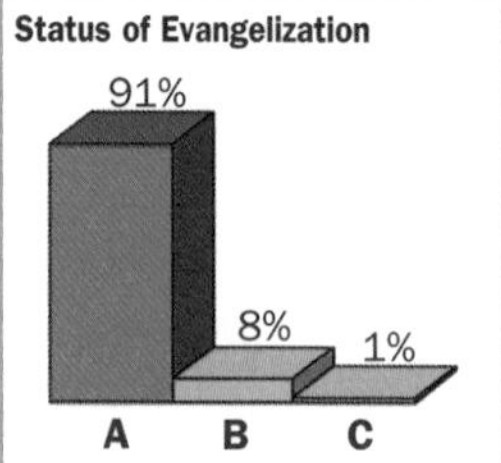

A = Have never heard the gospel
B = Were evangelized but did not become Christians
C = Are adherents to any form of Christianity

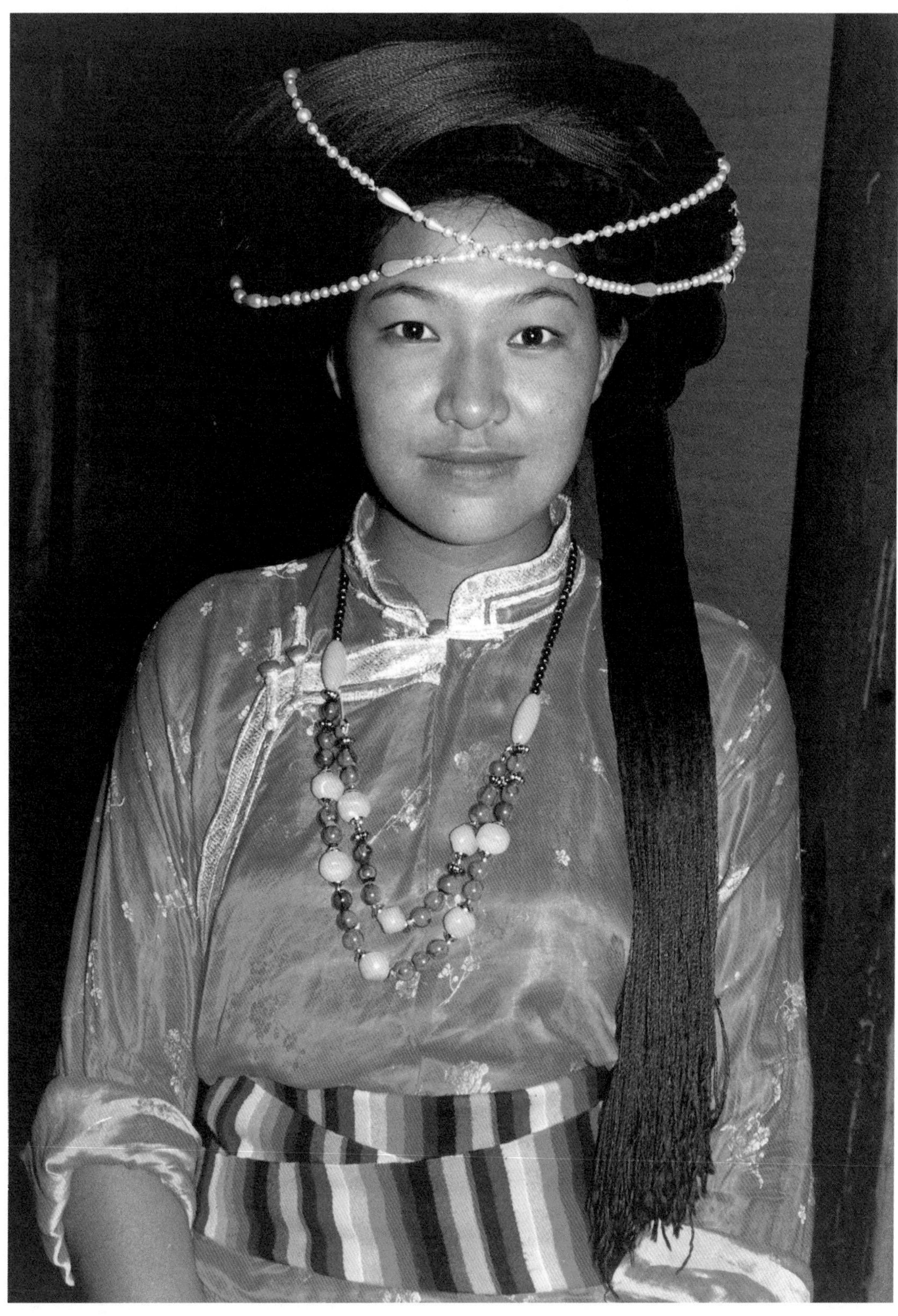

138. Most *Mosuo* women do not have husbands, but take “walk-in” lovers who must return to their mother’s house during the day. If a baby is born, the responsibility to raise the child is undertaken by the mother and her brothers. As a result, there is no word for “father” in the Mosuo language. [Paul Hattaway]

139

140

141

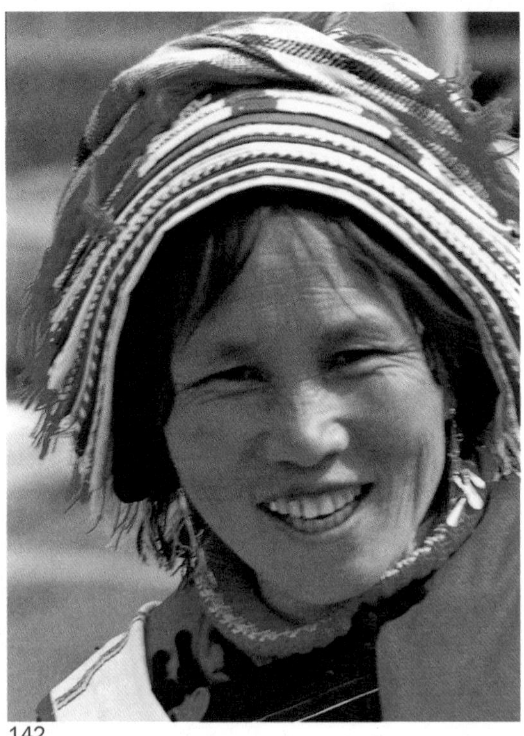
142

139. Three *Naxi* maidens, Lijiang; Yunnan. [Paul Hattaway]
140. A man from the *Nasu* people group, a branch of the Yi, out hunting in Yunnan Province. [Jamin Pelkey]
141. A *Naxi* farmer clothed in a goatskin vest, Lijiang, Yunnan. [Mary Adams]
142. Multilayered headdress of the *Naxi*; Qiaotou, Yunnan. [Paul Hattaway]

143

144

145

143. A *Nosu* bride on her wedding day. She must sit under this cloak for the entire wedding ritual, before her new husband uncovers her, and they commence a new life together; Daliangshan, Sichuan. [Target Ministries]
144. Until recently the *Nosu* kept slaves, Xichang, Sichuan. [Paul Hattaway]
145. A *Nosu* mother and her daughters, Panzhihua, Sichuan. [Target Ministries]

146 147 148 149

146. A lady from the *Jianshui Nisu* ethnic group; Honghe, Yunnan. [Jamin Pelkey]
147. The *Nung* live along the China-Vietnam border. [Midge Conner]
148–149. The *Xinping Nisu* are an ethnic group in central Yunnan with their own dress, language, and customs. [both by Paul Hattaway]

Mozhihei 莫治黑

Population in China:
4,000 (1991)
5,040 (2000)
6,500 (2010)
Location: Hunan
Religion: Animism
Christians: None Known

Overview of the Mozhihei

Countries: China

Pronunciation: "Moh-jerr-hay"

Other Names: Southern Tuchia, Southern Tujia

Population Source: 4,000 (1991 *EDCL*); Out of a total Tujia population of 5,704,223 (1990 census)

Location: *W Hunan:* Tanxi District of Luxi County

Status: Officially included under Tujia

Language: Sino-Tibetan, Tibeto-Burman, Burmese-Lolo, Lolo, Unclassified

Dialects: 0

Religion: Animism, No Religion, Ancestor Worship, Polytheism, Daoism, Shamanism

Christians: None known

Scripture: None

***Jesus* film:** None

Gospel Recordings: None

Christian Broadcasting: None

ROPAL code: TJS00

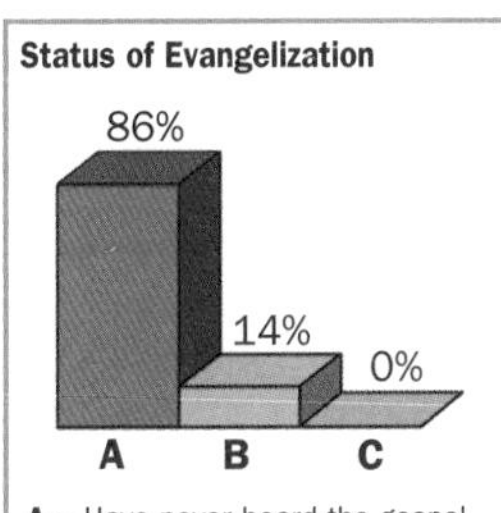

Location: More than 5,000 speakers of the Mozhihei language live in the Tanxi District of Luxi County, in the western part of Hunan Province.[1] The mountainous region — close to the juncture of Hunan, Sichuan, and Guizhou provinces — is largely inhabited by Miao people. Tanxi lies on the northern bank of the Wushui River, which serves as a tributary of the Yuanjiang River.

Identity: Although they are considered part of the Tujia nationality, the Mozhihei speak a very different language from other Tujia people. *Tujia* is the historical Chinese name for this group. The Southern Tujia call themselves *Mozhihei*, while the Northern Tujia speakers use the autonym *Bizika*. The two Tujia groups have separate customs, names, and languages.

Paul Hattaway

Language: According to Chinese linguist Chen Kang, out of a basic list of 600 words, the Northern and Southern Tujia languages shared only about 40% cognate vocabulary.[2] Mozhihei has four tones, structured similarly to the tones in Mandarin. It has many loanwords from Hunanese (Xiang) Chinese and Ghao-Xong. The Mozhihei have never possessed their own orthography. Today most use the Chinese script.

History: Han Chinese peasants migrated into western Hunan in the early twelfth century, bringing with them modern tools and farming expertise. Some Mozhihei youth joined the Communist Long March after it passed through their area in 1935. Some traveled all the way to northern China and fought against the Japanese.

Customs: The Mozhihei have a rich repertoire of traditional songs and dances. "The Hand Waving Dance, with its seventy ritual gestures that represent war, hunting, farming and other aspects of life, is popular at the New Year's festival."[3] The Mozhihei grow a variety of crops including wet rice, wheat, maize, and sweet potatoes. Cash crops include beets, cotton, and tea. Mozhihei men are proficient hunters, trappers, and fishermen.[4] From the time a Mozhihei girl is 10 or 11 years old, she begins practicing how to cry sufficiently for her future wedding, to show the wedding guests how much she will miss her parents. "How well she cries is considered a test of her abilities as well as her integrity. So, a girl who does not perform well enough in crying will probably be looked down upon."[5]

Religion: The beliefs of the Mozhihei are a mixture of shamanism, Daoism, ancestral worship, and ancient beliefs involving ghosts and evil spirits. Many of the Mozhihei who have moved to urban areas for work or education now consider themselves atheists.

Christianity: There are no known believers among the Mozhihei. For centuries they have lived and died without any knowledge of the Savior of the world. Few missionaries have ever braved the remote mountains of western Hunan, leaving it one of the most unevangelized areas in China today. The nearest Christian community is probably the 2,000 believers, mainly Han, in Danjiang County in neighboring eastern Sichuan Province.[6] The Mozhihei have no Scriptures in their mother tongue, and no Christian workers are specifically known to be targeting them for Christ.

Muda 母打

Josie Plummer

Location: More than 2,300 people belong to the Muda ethnic group in China. They inhabit the Nanliangshan (Nanliang Mountains) in the Gashai District of Jinghong County. Jinghong is the prefectural seat for the Xishuangbanna Dai Autonomous Prefecture in southern Yunnan Province.

Identity: The Muda are an ethnic subgroup of the Hani nationality in China. They call themselves *Muda* and speak a different language from other Hani groups in China. The Muda are possibly called *Sangkong* in Chinese.

Language: The Muda language was briefly studied and documented in 1993; this included lexical terms and a phonetic inventory.[1] It is part of the Phunoi branch of the Tibeto-Burman family, closely related to Bisu.

History: Because of ethnic and linguistic differences from the Akha who dominate the area, it is likely the Muda are a tribe or group of people who migrated into the area from a different location. The Akha have been scattered throughout many parts of Southeast Asia during the last 150 years. It is possible that ethnic Muda families have also participated in this diaspora, although no record exists of the Muda being in surrounding countries.

Customs: Muda villages are built, where possible, on ridges along the Nanliangshan Mountains. Their houses are stilted, with enveloping thatched roofs that often reach down to touch the ground on the high side of the hill. Muda houses have no windows. Inside their homes, there is a strict division between males and females: each gender has its own room. The family's ancestral altar stands in the center of the main room. It is considered sacred and must never be dishonored. When they move into a new house, the Muda must bring the household items into the home in a prescribed manner. First, the altar is carried in, followed by a tripod that is used to cook rice. After that, the other pieces of furniture and belongings may be brought in.

Religion: The ancestral altar is the focus for all ceremonies relating to the Muda's ancestors. The Muda share the Akha belief in a supreme being, Apoe Miyeh, who is also considered the link between their ancestors and the present-day generation. The Muda believe Apoe Miyeh to be their original male ancestor and the progenitor of their race. Great care is taken during ancestral rituals to feed and honor the spirits of the deceased. In this way the Muda also hope their children will take care of their souls after death. The Muda also worship "inside" and "outside" spirits.

Christianity: In recent years the church in Jinghong County has continued to grow, but so far almost all of the expansion has occurred among Han Chinese, Tai Lu, and Jino believers. Christianity has failed to make any impact among the Muda. Because of their small population, the Muda are likely to be passed over by mission agencies and evangelists, in favor of larger, more influential groups. It will require a specific, focused, cross-cultural church-planting effort to see the Muda won for Jesus Christ.

Population in China:
2,000 (1993)
2,320 (2000)
2,850 (2010)
Location: Yunnan
Religion: Ancestor Worship
Christians: None Known

Overview of the Muda

Countries: China

Pronunciation: "Moo-dah"

Other Names: Muta, Gashai, Sangkong

Population Source: 2,000 (1993 J. Matisoff); Out of a total Hani population of 1,253,952 (1990 census)

Location: *SW Yunnan:* Nanliang Mountains in Gashai District of Jinghong County in Xishuanbanna Prefecture

Status: Officially included under Hani

Language: Sino-Tibetan, Tibeto-Burman, Burmese-Lolo, Lolo, Southern Lolo, Phunoi

Dialects: 0

Religion: Ancestor Worship, Animism, Polytheism

Christians: None known

Scripture: None

***Jesus* film:** None

Gospel Recordings: None

Christian Broadcasting: None

ROPAL code: None

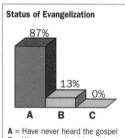

Status of Evangelization

A	B	C
87%	13%	0%

A = Have never heard the gospel
B = Were evangelized but did not become Christians
C = Are adherents to any form of Christianity

Muji 母基

Location: More than 53,000 Muji people live high in the mountains of several counties within southern Yunnan Province. The largest concentrations of Muji live in Gejiu and Mengzi counties, followed by Hekou, Pingbian, and Jinping counties. The Muji also used to live in the Xiaolila and Dalila villages of Tonghongdian District in Huaning County, but today the people in these villages have lost their original ethnicity and languages: they consider themselves Han Chinese.

Identity: The Muji were first listed in a 1903 survey of the tribes of western China.[1] Today, even though they consider themselves a distinct people group with their own traditional dress and language, the Chinese government includes the Muji as part of the large, diverse Yi nationality.

Language: In many locations the Muji who live near urban centers have lost the use of their language; only elderly people still speak it. In the mountains, however, even small children are able to speak Muji and cannot understand any Chinese. The Muji language is 70% similar to the Pula language and shares about 50% similarity with the Puwa language.[2] The Muji language is part of the Southern Yi language group.

History: Over the the last 200 years the Muji have been pushed deep into the mountains by Han Chinese and settlers from other minority groups. Those who chose to stay in the plains were soon assimilated. Because their villages are located high in the mountains, often on rocky soil, the staple food of the Muji is maize.

Jamin Pelkey

Customs: Although Muji women north of the Honghe River wear an intricately decorated headdress which covers their entire head, their counterparts south of the river prefer to wear theirs differently. The southern Muji women have a peculiar custom of braiding their long hair into one thick braid and wrapping the braid around their foreheads. A decorative headdress is then worked into the braid producing a lovely, natural crown.

Religion: When a baby is born to a Muji couple, the child is thought to need a godfather and godmother. When the child turns six or seven years old, a suitable relative or friend is chosen who will provide protection and safety through life and into the afterlife. "A ceremony is held for which the parents prepare chicken and whisky and take the child to the home of his or her selected godfather and godmother. The godparents bestow a surname on the child, and then give the child symbolic jewelry and clothing. The ceremony comes to an end when the 'spirit rope' is fastened around the child's wrist. The spirit rope is thought to ensure the safe passage of the child's soul through life and into death."[3]

Christianity: Although Miao churches exist in some of the areas inhabited by the Muji, there is very little contact and no linguistic similarity between the Miao and the Muji. There is at least one known Muji Christian, an elderly lady who said she believes in Christ because only he could heal her of her ailments.[4] There may be a small number of Muji attending the one church situated in Gejiu City; otherwise there are no other known Christians among the unreached Muji people group. Muji gospel recordings were first produced in 1999.

Population in China:
52,050 (1999)
53,300 (2000)
66,900 (2010)
Location: Yunnan
Religion: Polytheism
Christians: 20

Overview of the Muji

Countries: China

Pronunciation: "Moo-jee"

Other Names: M Ji, Mujipo, Puzu

Population Source:
52,050 (1999 J. Pelkey);
Out of a total Yi population of 6,572,173 (1990 census)

Location: *S Yunnan:* Gejiu (21,700), Mengzi (15,000), Jinping (12,700), Pingbian (2,150), and Hekou (500) counties; The Muji used to live in Huaning County but may have become extinct there.

Status:
Officially included under Yi

Language: Sino-Tibetan, Tibeto-Burman, Burmese-Lolo, Lolo, Northern Lolo, Yi, Southern Yi

Dialects: 0

Religion: Polytheism, Animism, Ancestor Worship, Christianity

Christians: 20

Scripture: None

***Jesus* film:** None

Gospel Recordings: Yi: Muji

Christian Broadcasting: None

ROPAL code: None

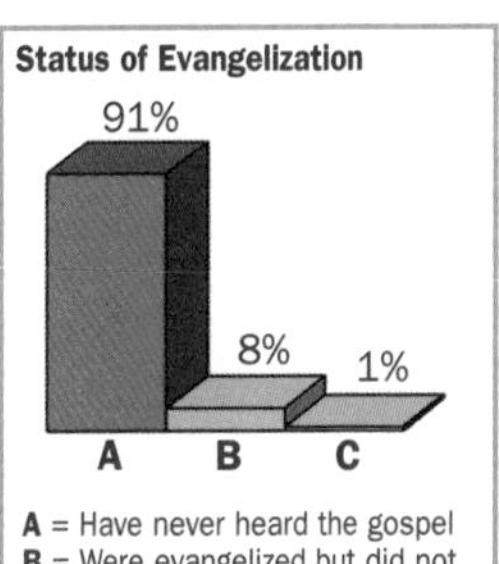

A = Have never heard the gospel
B = Were evangelized but did not become Christians
C = Are adherents to any form of Christianity

Mulao 仫老

Population in China:
159,328 (1990)
205,500 (2000)
265,100 (2010)
Location: Guangxi, Guizhou
Religion: Ancestor Worship
Christians: 1,600

Overview of the Mulao

Countries: China

Pronunciation: "Moo-laow"

Other Names: Mulam, Molao, Morlao, Mu, Abo, Muluo, Ayo, Mulao Miao

Population Source: 159,328 (1990 census); 90,426 (1982 census); 52,819 (1964 census)

Location: *N Guangxi:* Luocheng, Yishan, Liucheng, Xincheng, and Du'an counties; Liuzhou City; Guizhou: Kaili and Majiang counties

Status: An official minority of China

Language: Daic, Kam-Sui

Literacy: 65%

Dialects: 0

Religion: Ancestor Worship, Daoism, No Religion, Christianity

Christians: 1,600

Scripture: None

***Jesus* film:** None

Gospel Recordings: Mulao

Christian Broadcasting: None

ROPAL code: MLM00

A = Have never heard the gospel
B = Were evangelized but did not become Christians
C = Are adherents to any form of Christianity

Location: More than 159,000 Mulao were counted in the 1990 Chinese census. The majority live in the Luocheng Mulao Autonomous County in the northern part of the Guangxi Zhuang Autonomous Region.[1] A few villages of Mulao are located in central Guizhou Province. The people there refer to themselves as *Mu.* Guangxi contains some of the most spectacular scenery in the world. The landscape is dotted with many jagged limestone peaks that stretch hundreds of feet in the air, resembling sharp knives.

Identity: The Mulao are one of China's officially recognized minority groups. Some Mulao living in Luocheng refer to themselves as *Kyam.*[2] In 1945 the Mulao were described as being a part of the Lao race in China, which also included the Gelao and Tulao tribes.[3]

Language: Mulao is a part of the Dong-Shui branch of the Daic linguistic family. It has ten tones, and shares 65% lexical similarity with Southern Dong and 53% with Northern Zhuang.[4] Although Mulao is spoken by most members of the Mulao nationality, many are bilingual or multilingual in Chinese, Zhuang, and Dong. The Mulao have used the Chinese orthography for reading and writing since the Ming Dynasty (1368–1644).[5]

History: The Mulao, also known as *Mulam,* are the descendants of the ancient Liao and Ling tribes of the Jin Dynasty (AD 265–420). For centuries the Mulao have struggled to prevent their ethnic identity from being swallowed up by the dominant Han Chinese, Zhuang, Miao, and Dong groups. Today in the main center of Mulao civilization, Luocheng County, the Mulao no longer wear their traditional clothing. In addition, many Mulao youth now speak Mandarin as their mother tongue.

Customs: Guangxi is home to some of the most exotic food in China. In addition to the normal helpings of dog and cat that are available throughout Southern China, mouthwatering dishes that appear on local menus include snake-vile soup, bamboo rat, mutjac-horned pheasant, short-tailed monkey brain, gem-faced civet, ants, fruit-eating fox, and last but not least, armadillo face. Mulao who bear the surname of Luo or Wu, however, are not allowed to eat dog meat or the internal organs of animals.[6]

Religion: The Mulao used to be polytheists, but now religion does not play a large part in their everyday lives. In the past they observed the Yifan Festival. Pigs and sheep were sacrificed, lion and dragon dances were performed, and Mulao shamans chanted incantations.

Christianity: Several Christian research organizations list a figure of 1,600 Mulao believers in China,[7] but one recent visitor reported, "Nobody I spoke with had ever met a Christian before, and most did not even know what the word *Christian* meant."[8] There are no reports of missionaries prior to 1949 specifically targeting the Mulao. A 1997 article mentions a mud-brick and tile church building needing repair at Qiaoshan Village in Luocheng County, but it does not mention whether the members of this church are Han Chinese or Mulao.[9]

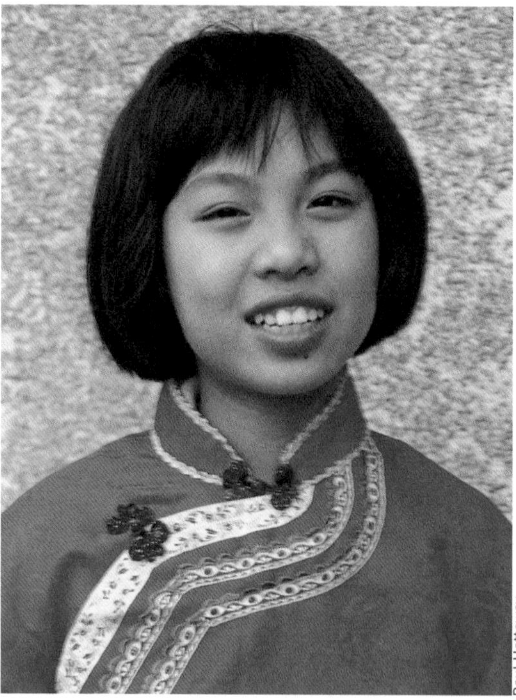
Paul Hattaway

Mulao Jia 木老家

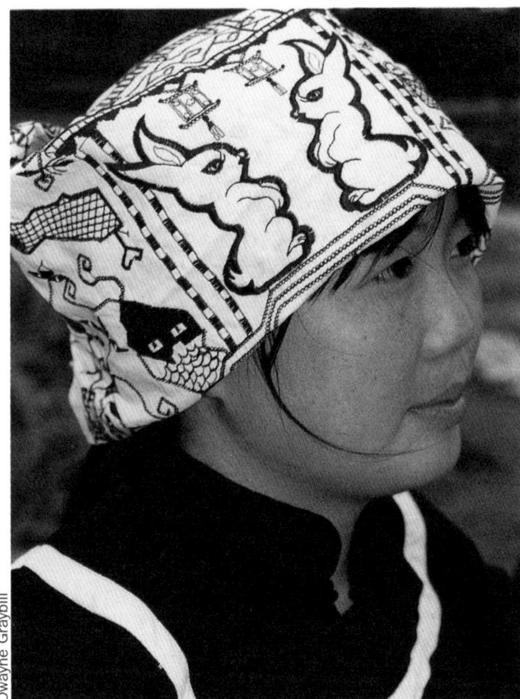

Dwayne Graybill

Location: In 1982 an official Chinese publication listed a population of "about 20,000" Mulao Jia people living in Kaili, Huangping, Duyun, Fuquan, Weng'an, and Majiang counties of Guizhou Province.[1] The main concentration of Mulao Jia live in the mountains of Majiang County. The Mulao Jia are not the same ethnic group — nor do they speak the same language — as the official Mulao nationality in northern Guangxi. There is a small group of people living in Xuanwei and Jidong villages of Majiang who refer to themselves as *Mu.* It is not known if these people are the same as the Mulao Jia, or if they should be considered a distinct people group.

Identity: The official classification of the Mulao Jia is extremely problematic. In the national census of both 1982 and 1990, the Mulao Jia were included in a list of *Undetermined Minorities.* In 1993, however, 2,800 Mulao Jia in Guizhou were placed in the official Mulao nationality of northern Guangxi, more than 200 miles away.[2] The reason why only a segment of the Mulao Jia were reclassified in such a way remains unclear. Most Mulao Jia consider themselves a distinct people and reject plans to include them as part of another nationality. Local people either consider the Mulao Jia a distinct people, or they consider them part of the Miao.

Language: Little information is available on the Mulao Jia, although it is known that many communities are now unable to speak their mother tongue and exclusively use the Chinese language and script.

History: The history of the Mulao Jia in central Guizhou dates back at least to the Ming Dynasty (1368–1644). At that time, they were known as a primitive people who made business contracts by carving notches on wood.[3]

Customs: Although many of their customs and festivals are now the same as those of the Han Chinese, the Mulao Jia are still known for their knife-making skills. They also beat drums to welcome friends and visitors, and drink wine from buffalo horns.

Religion: The Mulao Jia are animists. They worship a variety of ghosts and deities, including the spirit of the rice, water, trees, and forest. Many intricate animistic rituals are performed whenever there is an important community event such as a wedding or funeral. After a young Mulao Jia couple has agreed to marry, a bride-price is set by the parents of the bride and the parents of the groom. The price is always negotiated in a number of cows that the boy's family must pay the girl's. Cows are a sign of wealth and social standing among the Mulao Jia.

Christianity: Protestant missionaries commenced work in central Guizhou around the start of the twentieth century, but their work was primarily focused on reaching the Hmu and Ge peoples. After several frustrating decades, with little progress being made except for a small church in Panghai, west of Kaili, the missionaries were expelled from China. There is no record of work ever having been conducted among the Mulao Jia, who live in remote communities in the mountains. There are no known Christians among the Mulao Jia today. Few Christians have ever heard of this group's existence.

Population in China:
20,000 (1982)
30,400 (2000)
39,200 (2010)
Location: Guizhou
Religion: Animism
Christians: None Known

Overview of the Mulao Jia

Countries: China

Pronunciation: "Moo-laow-jeeah"

Other Names: Mulao, Mulaojia, Gwa-o, Qa-o, Lei-o

Population Source: 20,000 (1982 *Minzu Shibie Wenxian Ziliao Huibian*)

Location: *Guizhou:* Majiang, Kaili, Huangping, Duyun, Fuquan, and Weng'an counties

Status: Counted in census as an *Undetermined Minority*; In 1993, 2,800 Mulao Jia were placed in the official Mulao nationality.

Language: Daic, Tai, Unclassified

Dialects: 0

Religion: Animism, Ancestor Worship, Daoism, No Religion

Christians: None known

Scripture: None

***Jesus* film:** None

Gospel Recordings: None

Christian Broadcasting: None

ROPAL code: None

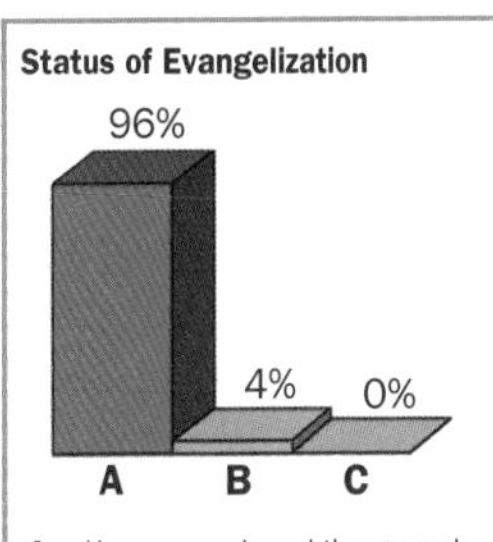

Muzi 母资

Population in China:
1,500 (1999)
1,530 (2000)
1,930 (2010)
Location: Yunnan
Religion: Polytheism
Christians: None Known

Overview of the Muzi

Countries: China

Pronunciation: "Moo-zi"

Other Names: Muji, Southern Muji, La'ou Yuxi Mujiren

Population Source: 1,500 (1999 J. Pelkey); Out of a total Yi population of 6,572,173 (1990 census)

Location: *S Yunnan:* Five villages (Gamadi, Adapo, Dimami, Liangshuigou and Bailedi) within Gamadi Community, Shuitian District in Mengzi County

Status: Officially included under Yi

Language: Sino-Tibetan, Tibeto-Burman, Burmese-Lolo, Lolo, Northern Lolo, Yi, Unclassified

Dialects: 0

Religion: Polytheism, Animism, Ancestor Worship

Christians: None known

Scripture: None

***Jesus* film:** None

Gospel Recordings: None

Christian Broadcasting: None

ROPAL code: None

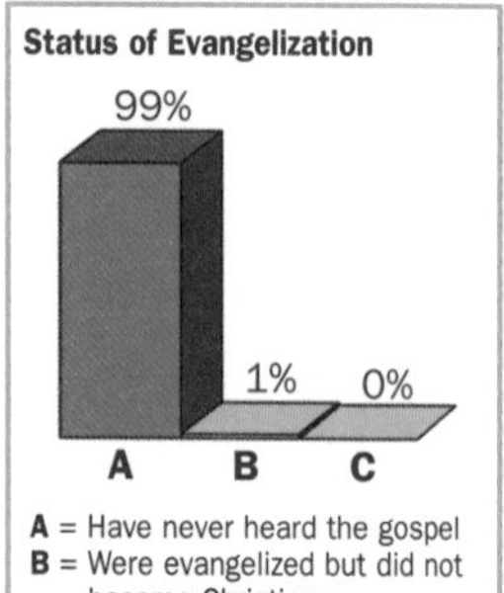

Location: A 1999 research paper listed a population of 1,500 Muzi people living in southern China's Honghe Prefecture in Yunnan Province.[1] The Muzi inhabit the five villages of Gamadi, Adapo, Dimami, Liangshuigou, and Bailedi — all within Gamadi Community of Shuitian District in Mengzi County. The Muzi are not reported to live in any other part of China.

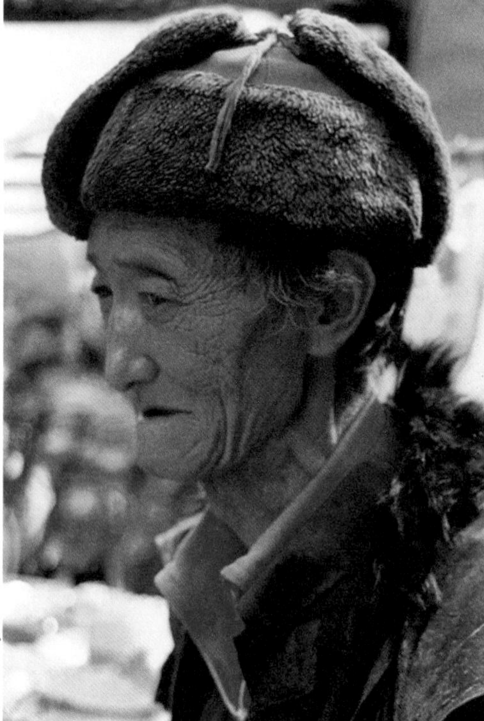
Jamin Pelkey

Identity: Despite their similar names and even though both have been included under the Yi nationality in China, the Muzi are not the same people group as the Muji. Jamin Pelkey explains, "The origin and development of the Muzi people are baffling. Not only are their customs and eating habits remarkably different from the Muji on all sides of them, but their language is divergent enough to be placed in a completely separate language family!"[2]

Language: Although Muzi remains an unclassified member of the Yi (Lolo) language family, it is known to be mutually unintelligible with Muji, Puwa, and other Southern Yi varieties in the area.

History: Despite the fact that the Muzi have a different language and customs today, historians speculate that at one time they were part of the Muji people. Historians say that the two groups "diverged late in the Yuan Dynasty (1279–1367) when the Muji went to war with the Puwa of present-day Xibeile District."[3]

Customs: Every Muzi home has a fire-pit dug into the middle of the floor of the main room. Beside this fire-pit is a rock on which to place the cooking pot. The Muzi believe "this rock and the area around it to be sacred — being the area where the guardian god of the home and the ancestors reside. No one is allowed to step on this rock."[4] Unmarried Muzi youth and widows usually live together in a *huafang* — a communal house where they can come together for sexual unions and courtship. "They may also spend the night with each other in rooms built above their homes adjoining goat stables."[5]

Religion: The Muzi set aside the first day of each third lunar month to worship the Dragon god. "On this day each Muzi village kills a pig, each family prepares fermented glutinous rice, and all gather around the altar at the sacred tree of the village to worship the dragon god. After the ceremonies the entire village feasts together on bean sprouts and pork. The dancing of the 'slap dance' and folk singing after the feast is reportedly lively, but the Muzi do not allow outsiders to participate.... In history past the Muzi were acclaimed hunters and felt a need to appease the god of the hunt. In order to show their reverence they would save the bones from every animal they killed and, after amassing a certain weight, would take them into the forest to dump the bones into a prepared hole. After burying the bones a Muzi hunter would pray to the god of the hunt for a rich supply of game."[6]

Christianity: The Muzi are completely unaffected by Christianity. Their isolated location and mind-set have separated them from the mainstream of Chinese society and, consequently, from any contact they might have with Christians.

Naheng 纳哼

Population in China:
1,200 (1998)
1,240 (2000)
1,440 (2010)
Location: Yunnan
Religion: Polytheism
Christians: None Known

Overview of the Naheng

Countries: China

Pronunciation: "Nah-heng"

Other Names: Beiquba Naxi, Pei-ch'u-paa Naxi

Population Source: 1,200 (1998 AMO); Out of a total Naxi population of 278,009 (1990 census)

Location: *N Yunnan:* Beiquba District of Ninglang County; Shaoping and Zhangzidan districts of Yongsheng County

Status: Officially included under Naxi

Language: Sino-Tibetan, Tibeto-Burman, Burmese-Lolo, Lolo, Northern Lolo, Naxi, Eastern Naxi

Dialects: 0

Religion: Polytheism, Animism, Ancestor Worship

Christians: None known

Scripture: None

***Jesus* film:** None

Gospel Recordings: None

Christian Broadcasting: None

ROPAL code: None

Status of Evangelization

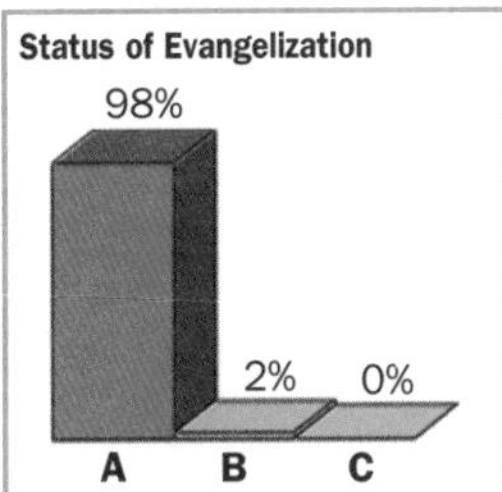

A = Have never heard the gospel
B = Were evangelized but did not become Christians
C = Are adherents to any form of Christianity

Location: The Naheng ethnic group, who number approximately 1,200 individuals, live primarily in the Beiquba District of Ninglang County, in northern Yunnan Province. Smaller numbers of Naheng also live in the adjoining Shaoping and Zhangzidan districts of Yongsheng County. The area is remote, poor, and rarely visited by outsiders. Few roads were constructed in the mountainous area until recently. Because of its geographic isolation, numerous ethnic groups inhabit this part of China, including the Eastern and Western Lipo, Naxi, Mosuo, Pumi, and the Xiaoliangshan Nosu. One study in 1922 found there to be "as many as 26 different tribes"[1] in the region surrounding Lijiang.

Identity: Although the Chinese authorities officially include the Naheng as part of the Naxi nationality, the Naheng have their own name, speak a distinct language, and view themselves differently from other communities. The Naheng may have originally been part of the Mosuo and Naru groups, but centuries of separation have caused them to possess a distinct ethnicity today.

Language: The Naheng speak a distinct language within the Eastern Naxi branch of the Tibeto-Burman language family. Other Eastern Naxi languages include Mosuo and Naru. The Naheng language is sometimes named *Beiquba Naxi*, after their principal location.[2]

History: The Naheng language suggests they were once part of the larger Mosuo group. For an unknown reason the Naheng separated from the main body of Mosuo at Lugu Lake and migrated southeast to their present location. Today the marked differences between the Mosuo and Naheng mean that the two groups no longer acknowledge historical kinship. The main difference, however, is that, whereas the Mosuo are zealous proponents of Tibetan Buddhism, the majority of Naheng are animists.

Customs: Naheng villages consist of closely clustered log homes that are surrounded by a courtyard and gate. The Naheng are hardworking agriculturists. Wheat, maize, and legumes are the primary crops grown. Some families also grow potatoes and turnips. Except for poultry and pigs, they do not herd livestock. The Naheng were once a matriarchal society. Today their families are monogamous.

Religion: The Naheng live just south of the influence of Tibetan Buddhism in China and just north of the influence of the traditional Naxi religion of Dongbaism. Dongbaism is a mixture of shamanism and the pre-Buddhist Tibetan religion of Bon. Most Naheng today are animists and ancestor worshipers, although they also have a legend of a god of Creation.

Christianity: Living in one of the most gospel-neglected parts of southern China, the Naheng are an unreached people group with practically no knowledge at all of Jesus Christ. The nearest believers to the Naheng are probably the Eastern Lipo farther east, but the Naheng have so far been outside the range of their evangelistic efforts.

Midge Conner

Naisu 乃苏

Location: Almost 50,000 Naisu live at the juncture of four counties — Lufeng, Yuanmou, Wuding, and Mouding — in northern Yunnan Province. The Naisu live in isolated mountain villages.

Identity: Naisu women wear distinctive red clothing and so are known locally as the *Hong Yi* (Red Yi). There are several different groups known as the Red Yi, so to avoid confusion, their self-name, *Naisu*, is used in *Operation China*.

Language: Naisu falls within the Eastern Yi language grouping and is apparently closely related to the Eastern Nasu language. One Chinese researcher has remarked that the two are as closely related as British and American English are.

History: During the past 2,000 years the various branches of the Yi have migrated far across southern China. At one time they were spread deep into Guizhou before most of them were driven back into Yunnan during the Ming Dynasty (1368–1644).[1] The Naisu and other tribes were practically independent until the nineteenth century. The Chinese brought the region back under their control after successful military campaigns were launched against the Yi in Zhaotong and Weining.

Customs: The Naisu have many folktales which they hand down from generation to generation. They say that in the past their community life revolved around a sacred azalea tree which was located in the center of their village. The tree was huge and had a very wide trunk. Before men went out to find a wife they would pray at the base of the tree in order to secure success. For many generations the Naisu numbered only 99 families and could not seem to grow any larger. The people went to a *bimo* (shaman) and sought his advice. He told them to cut the tree down. All the Naisu men gathered their axes and began to chop the tree. The trunk bled profusely. As it was about to fall, two white cranes flew out of the tree's branches and left the village. As soon as the sacred tree had fallen the Naisu started dying and the men had no more success at capturing brides. They went to another *bimo* who told them they were foolish to have chopped down the tree because the tree itself *was* the 100th family. The people were devastated at what they had done and migrated away from the area. Every year in the third lunar month the Naisu come together to celebrate the Flower Festival in remembrance of the tree, and to worship the Mountain gods.

Paul Hattaway

Religion: Most Naisu are animists. They have an ancient system of worshiping the spirits of the mountains, trees, and rivers.

Christianity: There are approximately 2,000 Naisu Christians in northern Yunnan. They were the first to hear the gospel from Lipo believers who had been converted by foreign missionaries in the early 1900s. The Eastern Lipo church was taught to take responsibility for winning other ethnic groups to Christ. They traveled extensively throughout the region sharing the gospel by song and dance. Many people came to Christ as a result of supernatural healing of the sick. Today Wuding has been saturated with the gospel. There are some believers in all the people groups. A-Hmao believers in Lufeng have reached out to the Naisu, resulting in a number of believers in Gaofeng District.

Population in China:
48,000 (1999)
49,200 (2000)
61,700 (2010)
Location: Yunnan
Religion: Polytheism
Christians: 2,000

Overview of the Naisu

Countries: China

Pronunciation: "Nai-soo"

Other Names: Nasu, Nisu, Hong Yi, Red Yi, Hongee, Luowu

Population Source: 48,000 (1999 J. Pelkey); Out of a total Yi population of 6,572,173 (1990 census)

Location: *N Yunnan:* Lufeng (17,000), Yuanmou (14,500), Wuding (10,500), and Mouding (6,000) counties

Status: Officially included under Yi

Language: Sino-Tibetan, Tibeto-Burman, Burmese-Lolo, Lolo, Northern Lolo, Yi, Eastern Yi

Dialects: 0

Religion: Polytheism, Animism, Christianity

Christians: 2,000

Scripture: None

***Jesus* film:** None

Gospel Recordings: Yi: Hong #04836

Christian Broadcasting: None

ROPAL code: None

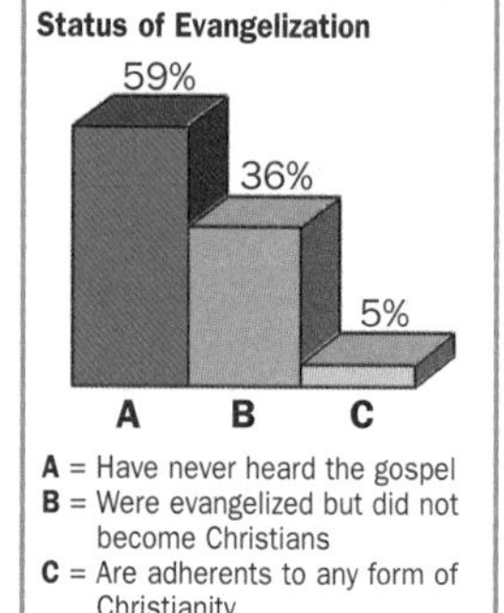

Naju 纳据

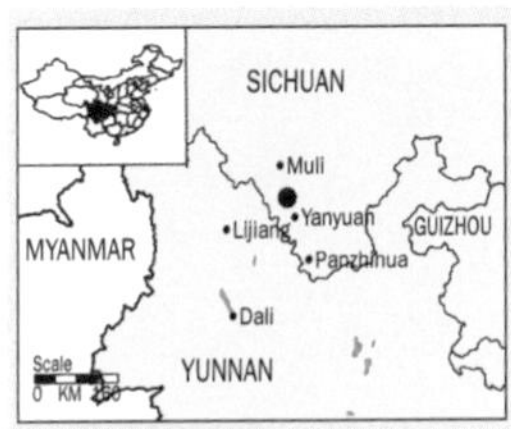

Population in China:
1,500 (1998)
1,550 (2000)
1,810 (2010)
Location: Sichuan
Religion: Tibetan Buddhism
Christians: None Known

Overview of the Naju

Countries: China

Pronunciation: "Nah-joo"

Other Names: Naru, Guabie Naxi, Kua-pie Naxi

Population Source: 1,500 (1998 AMO); Out of a total Naxi population of 278,009 (1990 census)

Location: *S Sichuan:* Guabie District in Yanyuan County; Bowa and Liewa districts in Muli County

Status: Officially included under Naxi

Language: Sino-Tibetan, Tibeto-Burman, Burmese-Lolo, Lolo, Northern Lolo, Naxi, Eastern Naxi

Dialects: 0

Religion: Tibetan Buddhism, Polytheism

Christians: None known

Scripture: None

***Jesus* film:** None

Gospel Recordings: None

Christian Broadcasting: None

ROPAL code: None

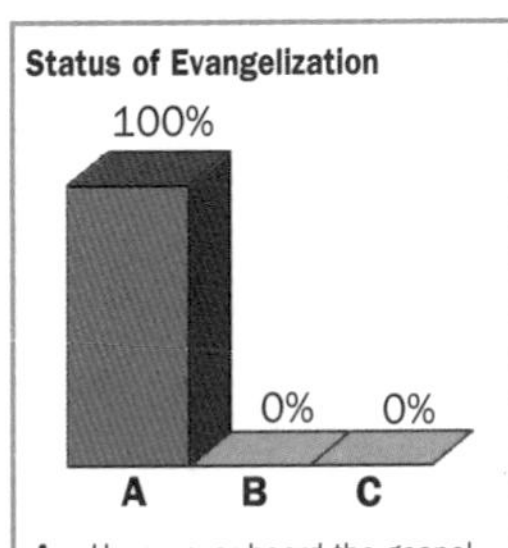

Midge Conner

History: The Naju claim to have originated on the Tibetan Plateau. Between 800 and 1,000 years ago they migrated down from the plateau. Some stayed behind at Lugu Lake on today's Sichuan-Yunnan border where they gradually developed into the group now known as *Mosuo*. The majority continued farther south to Lijiang and became today's *Naxi* people. Some time later, a group of the Mosuo left their homeland at Lugu Lake and they developed into the present-day *Naju* group. For several hundred years the Naxi and Mosuo had their own kings who dominated other ethnic groups and controlled commerce throughout the region.

Location: More than 1,500 people belonging to the Naju ethnic group live in a remote part of southern Sichuan Province. Their main community is located in the Guabie District of Yanyuan County. Others are found in the Bowa and Liewa districts of Muli County. The area is rarely visited by outsiders. Few roads connect the remote peoples of southern Sichuan who live in isolated mountain villages. The region is marked with great ethnic and linguistic diversity. Muli County contains people from the Chrame, Sichuan Mongol, Ersu, Nosu, and several other small ethnic groups.

Identity: Although they have been officially included under the Naxi nationality, the Naju have a different name, language, and history from the Naxi in Yunnan, and the Naheng and Mosuo in Sichuan. The Naju actually prefer to call themselves Naru, but their alternative name is used in *Operation China* to avoid confusion with the unrelated Naru of northern Yunnan.

Language: The Naju speak their own language, which has been named *Guabie Naxi* by some linguists because of their primary location in Guabie District in Yanyuan County.[1] The Naju language is part of Eastern Naxi, related to Mosuo and Naheng.

Customs: The whole western and southwestern part of Sichuan Province was formerly known as Xikang. It was a lawless and violent province where few outsiders dared to enter. Much of the murder and strife was the result of opium trade which flourished until Communist forces destroyed the poppy harvests in the early 1950s. Today most Naju live in poverty, growing vegetables and herding livestock.

Religion: Tibetan Buddhism is the predominant religious adherence among the Naju. They were originally polytheists but were converted to Buddhism by the Tibetans at least several centuries ago. Mixed in with their beliefs is a strong fear of powerful spiritual deities that they believe dwell inside mountains. As a result of these beliefs the Naju spend much of their time, energy, and money on appeasing and placating the spirit world.

Christianity: There is no record of missionary activity in Muli or Yanyuan counties prior to 1949. The geographic, linguistic, and cultural isolation of the Naju creates barriers to Christian outreach among them in the future. Perhaps a few believers live among the Lisu in southern Sichuan, but there is no record of any Christian activity among the needy Naju.

Naluo 纳罗

Target Ministries

Location: Approximately 37,000 Naluo inhabit the steep mountainsides along the rivers of northern Yunnan and southern Sichuan Provinces. The majority are located in Luquan, Wuding, Dongchuan, and Yuanmou counties.[1] Small numbers of Naluo reportedly live in Huize County of Zhaotong Prefecture and parts of Qujing Prefecture.

Identity: Despite insisting on their own distinct identity, the Naluo (also called *Alu* or *Gani* — Dry Yi) are considered part of the Yi nationality by the Chinese authorities. The *Laka* are a subgroup of the Naluo. The main difference between the two is sociohistorical.

Language: The Naluo speak a distinct Tibeto-Burman language. It cannot be understood by members of other Yi groups. Naluo is part of the Eastern Yi linguistic branch, distantly related to Michi, Gepo, Eastern Nasu, Naisu, and the Yi varieties spoken in Guizhou Province.

History: For centuries the Naluo were despised as slaves and serfs of the Nasu people. In the early 1950s the slave/serf system was abolished by the Communist authorities. The humble disposition of the Naluo helped many of them see their need for God. Many responded to the gospel when Protestant missionaries moved to their area in the early decades of the twentieth century.

Customs: In the same way that numerous languages and dialects are spoken among the many branches of Yi in China, they also have numerous distinct cultures. Catholic missionary Paul Vial explained, "The Lolo [Yi] do not have a single term that can be applied to an entire nation or a race of men, no more for others than for themselves.... With the Lolo [Yi], each tribe knows only the tribes around it; beyond this horizon, it knows nothing. In their books, the author uses the name of his tribe, sometimes in a limited sense, if it is a particular history; sometimes in a broad sense, if the history applies to the entire race."[2]

Religion: Most Naluo are worshipers of spirits. Others have embraced Christianity, though many who profess to be Christians have retained their former animistic rituals. In the past each Naluo village had a resident shaman.

Christianity: The first Protestant missionaries arrived in northern Yunnan in the early 1900s. Australian Arthur Nicholls was among the early pioneers of the gospel. Others joined him in a mission of love. Medical clinics were established, and large numbers of people were exposed to the gospel. Probably because of their history as a slave people, the Naluo were eager to accept the offer of freedom in Jesus Christ. They turned to Christianity, breaking themselves free from centuries of bondage to spirit worship. Thousands of Eastern Lipo and Eastern Nasu also came to Christ in the Wuding and Luquan areas. Today there are an estimated 11,000 Naluo believers. Many of them meet in ethnically mixed congregations. The Naluo living in Yuanmou County have had less exposure to the gospel. In the past many Naluo believers used the Pollard New Testament in the Eastern Nasu language, but today most prefer to use the Chinese Scriptures.

Population in China:
36,700 (1999)
37,600 (2000)
47,200 (2010)
Location: Yunnan, Sichuan
Religion: Animism
Christians: 11,000

Overview of the Naluo

Countries: China

Pronunciation: "Nah-luoh"

Other Names: Nalo, Gani, Alu, Dry Yi, Gan Yi, Nalu

Population Source: 36,700 (1999 J. Pelkey); Out of a total Yi population of 6,572,173 (1990 census)

Location: *N Yunnan:* Luquan (20,000), Wuding (10,300), Dongchuan (2,500), Yuanmou (1,500), Huize (1,400), and Qujing (1,000) counties; *S Sichuan:* Panzhihua area

Status: Officially included under Yi

Language: Sino-Tibetan, Tibeto-Burman, Burmic, Burmese-Lolo, Lolo, Northern Lolo, Yi, Eastern Yi

Dialects: 0

Religion: Animism, Christianity

Christians: 11,000

Scripture: None

***Jesus* film:** None

Gospel Recordings: None

Christian Broadcasting: None

ROPAL code: None

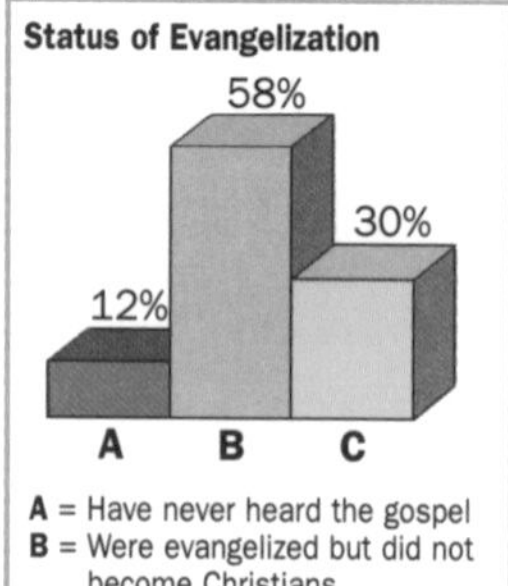

Namuyi 纳木义

Location: In 1983 Chinese linguist Sun Hongkai listed 5,000 speakers of the Namuyi language.[1] The majority are located in the western parts of the Liangshan (Cold Mountains) Prefecture in southern Sichuan Province. Although small in number, the Namuyi are geographically widespread, inhabiting parts of Mianning, Muli, Xichang, and Yanyuan counties in the Liangshan Prefecture, in addition to parts of Jiulong County in Garze Prefecture.

Identity: Although they officially belong to the Tibetan minority, the Namuyi — who call themselves *Namuzi* in Jiulong and Muli — speak a distinct language belonging to the Qiangic branch. The Namuyi, along with several similar groups such as the Jiarong, Ersu, Shixing, Ergong, and Minyak, have been combined into the Tibetan nationality solely on the basis of their religion.

Language: Little is known about the Namuyi language except that it is part of the Qiangic linguistic family. Most Namuyi are able to speak the languages of their neighbors, especially Khampa Tibetan. Those living in Muli County are bilingual in Chrame, while some of the easternmost Namuyi, who live in parts of Xichang County, can speak the Nosu Yi language. Namuyi does not possess a written script. Chinese is the most commonly used orthography.

History: Areas of the western Liangshan Prefecture used to be in a province called Xikang, which was grafted into Sichuan Province in 1939. Xikang was a violent region; murder and banditry were commonplace. "Much of the banditry and lawlessness in Sikang [Xikang] can be traced to the opium trade. Confusion and violent civil strife often break out in opium-growing districts after the harvest.... The prevalence of such lawlessness makes firearms almost a necessity, even for law-abiding citizens."[2] For more than 200 years, up until the 1950s, the Namuyi were subject to the powerful Chrame Kingdom that was based in Muli. The king ruled with "absolute spiritual and temporal sway"[3] over his subjects.

Paul Hattaway

Customs: The Namuyi practice traditional Tibetan wind burial. Corpses are cut up with an axe into small pieces and placed on a mountaintop. Ravens and other birds of prey descend and devour the flesh and organs. The Namuyi believe this enables the soul of the dead person to be scattered to the four winds.

Religion: Most Namuyi are Tibetan Buddhists, but those who live near the large and influential Nosu group have adopted their polytheistic practices.

Christianity: The Namuyi have yet to hear the gospel for the first time because of their geographic, social, and religious isolation. There are few Christians among any of the ethnic groups in the region. Of the hundreds of self-sacrificing missionaries who gave their lives for China, none is known to have worked in the Namuyi area. C. T. Studd, a well-known sportsman in England, gave up his fame and career to serve Christ in Africa and China. For Studd, the decision was not a difficult one to make. He simply explained, "If Jesus Christ be God and died for me, then no sacrifice can be too great for me to make for Him."[4]

Population in China:
5,000 (1983)
6,950 (2000)
8,570 (2010)
Location: Sichuan
Religion: Tibetan Buddhism
Christians: None Known

Overview of the Namuyi

Countries: China

Pronunciation: "Nah-moo-yee"

Other Names: Namuzi, Nameji

Population Source: 5,000 (1983 Sun Hongkai); Out of a total Tibetan population of 4,593,330 (1990 census)

Location: *S Sichuan:* Liangshan Yi Prefecture: Mianning, Muli, Xichang, and Yanyuan counties; Jiulong County in Garze Prefecture

Status: Officially included under Tibetan

Language: Sino-Tibetan, Tibeto-Burman, Qiangic, Namuyi

Dialects: 0

Religion: Tibetan Buddhism, Polytheism

Christians: None known

Scripture: None

***Jesus* film:** None

Gospel Recordings: None

Christian Broadcasting: None

ROPAL code: NMY00

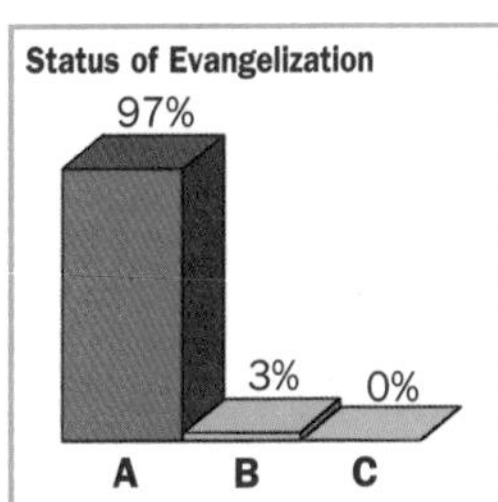

Nanjingren 南京人

Population in China:
80,000 (1982)
121,700 (2000)
157,000 (2010)
Location: Guizhou
Religion: Ancestor Worship
Christians: 1,000

Overview of the Nanjingren

Countries: China

Pronunciation: "Nahn-jing-ren"

Other Names: Nankingren, Nankingese, Nang Jing, Xienan, Xiejing, Awutu, Shiye, Gejiaoren, Nongjiazi, Longjiazi

Population Source: 80,000 (1982 *Minzu Shibie Wenxian Ziliao Huibian*)

Location: *W Guizhou:* Bijie, Dafang, Lupanshui, Qianxi, Weining, Jinsha, Nayong, Anshun, Qingzhen, and Zhijin counties

Status: Most have been officially included under Bai since 1987, but some have been counted under the Gelao, Yi, or Han Chinese;
Previously they were in a list of *Undetermined Minorities.*

Language: Sino-Tibetan, Tibeto-Burman, Unclassified

Dialects: 0

Religion: Ancestor Worship, Daoism, Animism, No Religion, Christianity

Christians: 1,000

Scripture: None

***Jesus* film:** None

Gospel Recordings: None

Christian Broadcasting: None

ROPAL code: None

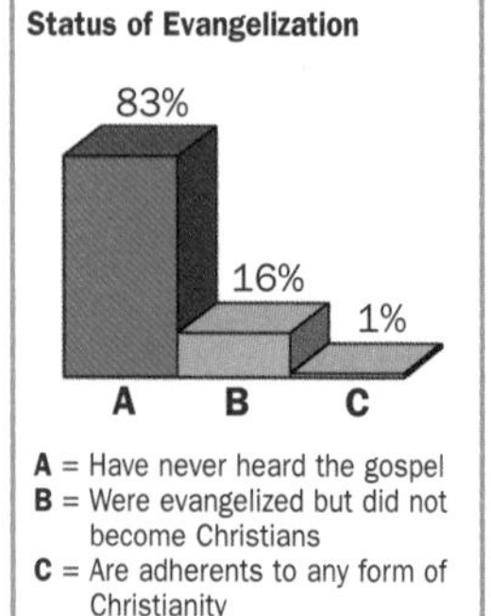

Location: More than 120,000 people who call themselves *Nanjingren* (Nanjing People) live in Bijie, Dafang, Lupanshui, Qianxi, Weining, Jinsha, Nayong, Anshun, Qingzhen, and Zhijin counties in western Guizhou Province.[1]

Identity: The official classification of the Nanjingren by the Chinese authorities has been extremely problematic. In the 1982 census they were placed in a list of *Undetermined Minorities*. In 1987 the authorities decided that most Nanjingren were assimilated, and that the remaining 2,000 people who retain their ethnicity had become members of the Longjia minority group. The Longjia themselves, however, were not granted status as a minority group. In the late 1980s they were "discovered" to be a branch of the Bai nationality, the majority of whom live around Dali in western Yunnan Province. To complicate an already confused situation, the Nanjingren were told they could choose which nationality they wanted to be under. As a result, today there are Nanjingren who are classified as Gelao, Yi, or Han Chinese. In Qianxi County the Nanjingren call themselves *Xienan*, and in Dafang they use the name *Xiejing*. The Yi call them *Awutu*; the Miao know them as *Shiye*; and the Han call them *Gejiaoren*.

Language: The Nanjingren speak the Guizhou dialect of Chinese. However, in some locations where they have retained their ethnicity better, they speak the Longjia language. This language has not been studied, but it is believed to be a variety of Tibeto-Burman.

History: The Nanjingren in Guizhou are historically similar to the Chuanqing and Chuanlan groups. Nanjing is the large, former capital city of China located on the east coast. The Nanjingren claim their ancestors were soldiers sent from Nanjing during the eighth and ninth centuries to fight against Miao insurgents in the mountains.

Customs: When a number of generations had passed after their arrival in the area, the Nanjingren adopted many minority customs, especially from the Miao, and no longer viewed themselves as Han Chinese. Later, Han settlers entered the region in the fourteenth century. Not only did they not consider the Nanjingren as Han people, but in many instances they persecuted and despised them. When the Nanjingren marry, the bride-price is customarily paid with cows. The traditional dress of the Nanjingren women consists of short-sleeved shirts, long skirts, and a headdress.

Religion: Most Nanjingren worship their ancestors. Each home has an ancestral altar on the wall of the main room. Offerings of incense and food are regularly made to the dead, in the belief that it will procure their souls a better existence in the afterlife. When a Nanjingren dies, Daoist priests are called in to conduct the funeral according to Daoist rites.

Christianity: Although most Nanjingren have never heard the gospel in such a manner as to intelligently accept or reject Christ, there are about 1,000 Catholic Christians and a few Protestants among them. These believers are the fruit of pre-1949 mission work in the region.

Paul Hattaway

Naru 纳儒

Paul Hattaway

Location: More than 11,500 Naru people live in northern Yunnan Province in southwest China. Seven thousand inhabit areas in the southern and central parts of Yongsheng County, while 4,500 live in southern Huaping County.[1]

Identity: The Naru have been officially included under the Yi nationality in China, even though they retain a separate ethnicity and history from other Yi groups. The Naru are called *Shuitian* (Watery Fields People) by the Chinese. This name, used by the Chinese for several small Yi groups, is not used by any of the groups to describe themselves.

Language: Naru is part of the Northern Yi branch of Tibeto-Burman. Jamin Pelkey has written, "The Naru language is very similar to the Naruo language. In Huaping County the Naru language is on the edge of extinction, but may enjoy more frequent use in Yongsheng County."[2]

History: The Naru claim they originated in Hunan and Jiangxi provinces in eastern China in ancient times. They were probably Chinese soldiers who were sent to patrol northern Yunnan Province. Over the centuries the descendants of the original soldiers intermarried with local Yi tribeswomen and gradually developed into a distinct ethnic group. One source claims, "The Naru are certain to have once been the same people as the Naruo with whom they now have only mild cultural and linguistic differences."[3]

Customs: When a Naru couple decides to get married, they tell their parents who then arrange for a meeting. Both sets of families come together and "engage in a whiskey drinking ceremony after which they playfully argue about the amount of gifts to be given and received until a compromise is reached. Rice whiskey also plays an important role in the actual wedding. If all the guests don't drink in agreement, then the couple cannot be considered married. Naru weddings are usually very festive and expensive occasions participated in by some 200 guests."[4]

Religion: The center of a Naru home is the kitchen fire-pit. "A day of grazing goats, cows and mules and working the corn, rice or tobacco fields climaxes around the lapping flames of the family fire-pit as the smoke wends its way through the open rafters. While gazing into the flames, all smoke their tobacco bongs or long-pipes and engage in story-telling and laughter."[5] The Naru worship a spirit that they believe actually resides in the fire-pit. They also worship their ancestors and experience more Daoist and Buddhist influence than most other Yi groups. This is possibly due to their origins as Chinese soldiers.

Christianity: The remote mountains of Yongsheng and Huaping counties have been formidable barriers to the introduction of the gospel into the area. Before the 1960s there were few roads in the region. As a result, no long-term missionary work was ever undertaken in this part of China. Today the Naru are an unreached people group with no church or believers.

Population in China:
11,500 (1999)
11,790 (2000)
14,800 (2010)
Location: Yunnan
Religion: Polytheism
Christians: None Known

Overview of the Naru

Countries: China

Pronunciation: "Nah-roo"

Other Names: Shuitian

Population Source: 11,500 (1999 J. Pelkey); Out of a total Yi population of 6,572,173 (1990 census)

Location: *N Yunnan:* Yongsheng (7,000) and Huaping (4,500) counties

Status: Officially included under Yi

Language: Sino-Tibetan, Tibeto-Burman, Burmese-Lolo, Lolo, Northern Lolo, Yi, Northern Yi

Dialects: 0

Religion: Polytheism, Ancestor Worship

Christians: None known

Scripture: None

***Jesus* film:** None

Gospel Recordings: None

Christian Broadcasting: None

ROPAL code: None

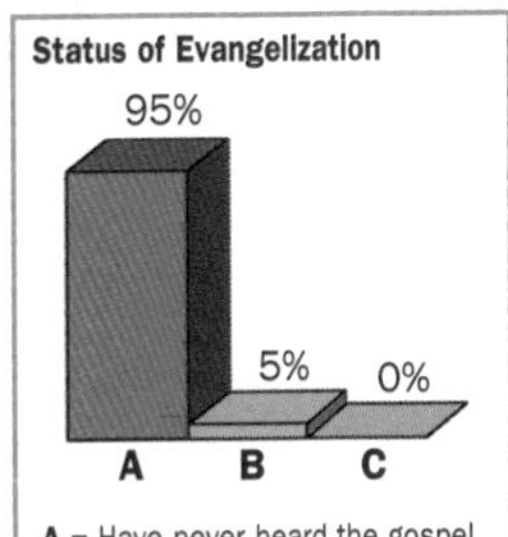

Naruo 纳若

Population in China:
11,900 (1999)
12,200 (2000)
15,300 (2010)
Location: Yunnan
Religion: Polytheism
Christians: None Known

Overview of the Naruo

Countries: China

Pronunciation: "Nah-roo-oh"

Other Names: Narou, Zhili, Naluo, Shui Yi

Population Source: 11,900 (1999 J. Pelkey); Out of a total Yi population of 6,572,173 (1990 census)

Location: *N Yunnan:* Yongsheng (7,400) and Huaping (4,500) counties; Possibly in *S Sichuan*

Status: Officially included under Yi

Language: Sino-Tibetan, Tibeto-Burman, Burmese-Lolo, Lolo, Northern Lolo, Yi, Northern Yi

Dialects: 0

Religion: Polytheism, Animism

Christians: None known

Scripture: None

***Jesus* film:** None

Gospel Recordings: None

Christian Broadcasting: None

ROPAL code: None

Status of Evangelization

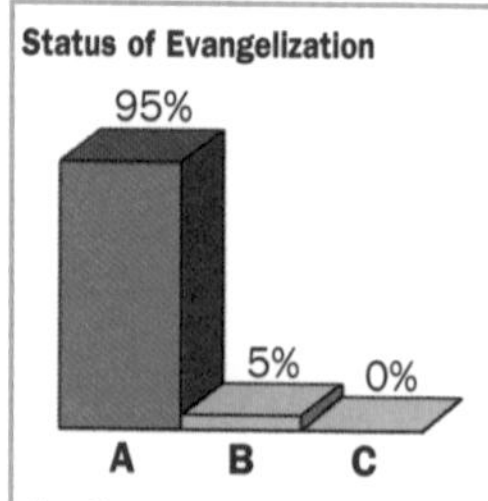

A = Have never heard the gospel
B = Were evangelized but did not become Christians
C = Are adherents to any form of Christianity

Location: The small Naruo tribe lives in the mountains of northern Yunnan Province. Numbering approximately 12,000 people, they inhabit parts of Yongsheng and Huaping counties. Most Naruo villages are only accessible by foot. Few roads have been constructed through the mountainous area. The Naruo are so remote that one anthropologist who visited the area was unable to locate them.[1] There may also be Naruo communities living across the border in neighboring Sichuan Province.

History: The slave system in use among the Nosu Yi in the Daliangshan (Big Cold Mountains) of southern Sichuan was officially abolished in the 1950s. For centuries slaves had been taken by the Nosu ruling class, who believed they were a superior race. They had no respect for any other tribes or for the Han Chinese. This brutal system contributed to the scattering of many smaller clans and tribes who felt it wiser to migrate away from the Nosu than to face the constant threat of being taken captive in slavery. Originally, the Naruo say they came from Hunan and Jiangxi provinces in eastern China. After a time the ancestors of the Naruo married local women and gradually formed their own distinct ethnic group.

Paul Hattaway

Customs: The Naruo believe it is far better to have a baby boy and do not rejoice at the birth of a girl. In some locations, exacerbated by China's one-child policy, the Naruo abort female foetuses or kill baby girls at birth. The Naruo have an annual ritual of offering sacrifices and burning incense to both good and evil spirits, asking them to allow boys to be born in their communities.

Identity: The Naruo are a little-known tribe. They have never before appeared in any Western ethnolinguistic research. They are one of the more than 100 Yi subgroups in Yunnan Province alone. *Naruo* is this group's self-name. Neighboring tribes call them *Zhili* or *Gan Yi*, while the Chinese often call them *Shuiyi* (Water Yi). The Naruo are closely related to the Naru who live in the same counties.

Language: Little research has been done into the Naruo language, but it is believed to be part of the Northern Yi group, related to Xiaoliangshan Nosu. In fact, it may turn out to be the same as Xiaoliangshan Nosu. Many elderly Naruo are unable to speak any other language than their own. The Naruo language does not have a written form.

Religion: The primary religious adherence among the Naruo is polytheism. They worship a wide range of demons and fearsome disembodied spirits.

Christianity: Because they were never targeted by missionaries in the past, there are no known Christians among the Naruo today. In the 1800s Griffith John challenged the Christian Church concerning China's lost millions. He wrote, "Shall not China remain in its state of darkness and death because of the worldliness and deadness of the people of God? Shall not the cry which now goes forth from this land penetrate our universities, colleges, and churches, and elicit a response in many a heart devoted to Christ, worthy of the urgency and solemnity of the occasion?"[2]

Nasu, Eastern 纳苏(东)

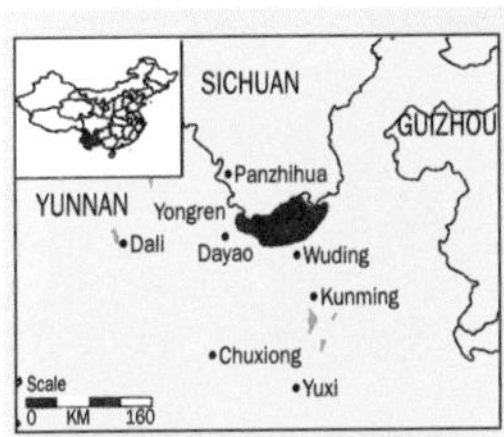

Population in China:
366,769 (1995)
413,500 (2000)
519,000 (2010)
Location: Yunnan, Sichuan
Religion: Animism
Christians: 120,000

Overview of the Eastern Nasu

Countries: China

Pronunciation: "Nah-soo"

Other Names: Gopu, Kopu, Gani, Nasu Puo, Gan Yi, Ganyi, Kang-i, Black Yi, Hei Yi

Population Source:
366,769 (1995 GEM);
141,600 (1999 J. Pelkey);
Out of a total Yi population of 6,572,173 (1990 census)

Location: *N Yunnan:* Wuding, Luquan, Xundian, Dongchuan, Yuanmou, Huize, and Qujing counties;
S Sichuan: Huili and Huidong counties

Status: Officially included under Yi

Language: Sino-Tibetan, Tibeto-Burman, Burmese-Lolo, Lolo, Northern Lolo, Yi, Eastern Yi

Dialects: 0

Religion: Animism, Christianity, Polytheism, Shamanism

Christians: 120,000

Scripture: Portions 1913

***Jesus* film:** None

Gospel Recordings:
Yi: Yunnan #04670
Yi: Gan #04775
Yi: Nasu #04938

Christian Broadcasting: None

ROPAL code: None

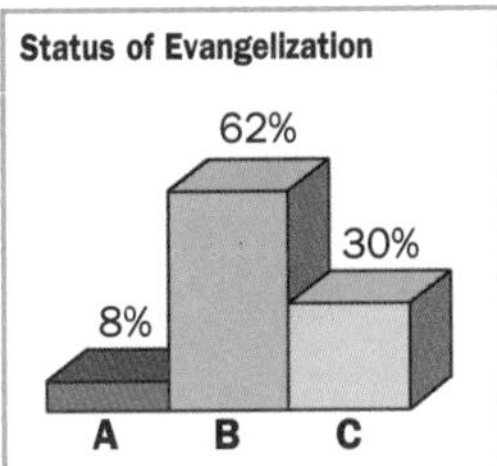

Location: More than 400,000 Eastern Nasu live in northern Yunnan Province, especially in Wuding, Luquan, Xundian, and Dongchuan counties.[1] They also spill across into Huili and Huidong counties in the southern part of Sichuan Province.

Identity: The Nasu call themselves *Nasu Puo*. (*Puo* is an Yi word meaning "tribe" or "nationality.") Their name means "black people." In the past the Chinese called the Nasu *Gani*, which means "dry Yi." Early missionaries called this group *Gani* or *Kopu*.

Language: Eastern Nasu — which has 24 vowels — is part of the Eastern Yi group of Tibeto-Burman. Nasu has an ancient script which can only be read by *bimos* (shamans).

History: For centuries — until the advent of Communism in 1949 — the Eastern Nasu captured slaves from among the Eastern Lipo and other ethnic groups in the region.

Customs: Prior to their conversion to Christianity, the Eastern Nasu carried around small baskets which they believed contained the souls of their ancestors. In 1909 Australian missionary Arthur G. Nicholls first contacted the Eastern Nasu. He reported, "These people... are very drunken and immoral.... We asked them if they were willing to throw away the baskets in which they profess to keep the spirits of their ancestors, and six families thereupon burnt their spirit baskets and other articles used in their dealings with demons."[2]

Religion: The Eastern Nasu were trapped in a never-ending cycle of spirit appeasement until they turned to Christ. At the beginning, comprehension of their new religion was slow. It was reported: "They understand very little of Christian doctrine. But they understand that Christianity means no whisky and clean living.... But when men and women are willing to take the spirit baskets their tribe has venerated for ages, and utensils used in demonolatry, and make a bonfire for them, it may be inferred that interest has deepened into conviction and conversion. Over all this region the Sun of Righteousness is rising, and the people are turning to the light."[3]

Christianity: By 1914 a few Eastern Nasu churches had been established in Salowu,[4] but the missionaries were stretched to the limit. "We are at our wits' end for workers. The work... is pitifully undermanned."[5] In response, the Lisu and A-Hmao churches sent evangelists to the Eastern Nasu.[6] The four Gospels were translated into Eastern Nasu in 1913, using the script invented by missionary Samuel Pollard.[7] By the 1940s the Eastern Nasu church was being "used of God not only in evangelizing their own districts but also in sending missionaries to seek out and find untouched sections of their tribe in dangerous and far-distant territories. Magnanimously they have given out of overwhelming poverty so that many evangelistic journeys could be taken, and the number of families won to the Lord are counted in the hundreds."[8] Today there are about 120,000 believers and hundreds of churches among the Eastern Nasu.[9]

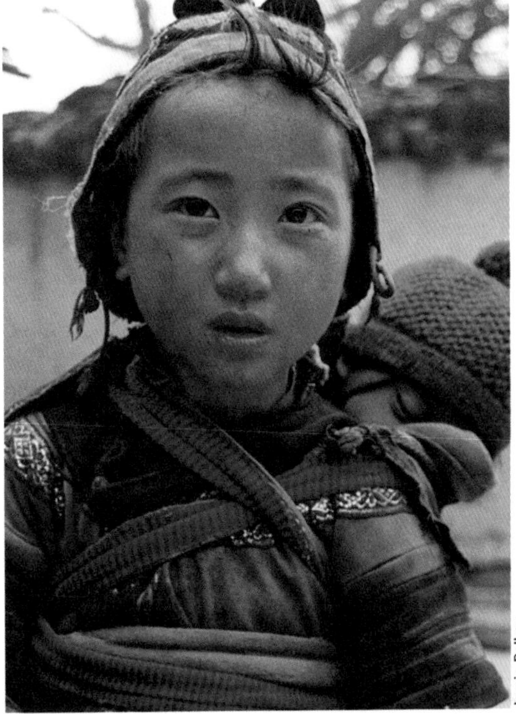
Jamin Pelkey

Nasu, Jinghong 纳苏(景洪)

Location: An estimated 18,450 Nasu people live in the southwestern corner of China. The majority, about 12,000, live in parts of western and northwestern Jinghong County, and 6,000 inhabit areas of northeastern Menghai County in Xishuangbanna Prefecture of Yunnan Province.[1] The area is better known as the home of the Tai Lu people, although numerous other small tribes and people groups also live in the mountains. The Lancang River, better known outside of China as the Mekong, flows through Jinghong before entering Southeast Asia.

Identity: The Jinghong Nasu have been officially counted as part of the Yi nationality in China. While the self-name of this group is simply *Nasu*, the loconym *Jinghong* has been added to distinguish this particular Nasu group from the several others in China who use the same autonym — but who speak widely varying languages.

Language: It is uncertain which linguistic affiliation the Jinghong Nasu language belongs to. Chinese sources do not comment on the Yi of Xishuangbanna who are comprised of only two groups: the Jinghong Nasu and the Xiangtang.

History: The Nasu in southwest Yunnan may have once been connected to one of the other Nasu or Nosu groups living farther north, before migrating to their present location at least 300 years ago. Some Jinghong Nasu are losing their culture.

Customs: Eagles are held in great honor by many Yi groups in southern China. One of their legends states, "In the mountains there lived a girl of sixteen whose beauty was so enchanting that the threshold of her home was soon worn out by the number of people coming to court her. But no one was sufficiently eligible for her. One day... as the girl was weaving cloth under a huge fir-tree, she was suddenly struck by the beauty of an eagle hovering overhead. She told herself it would be wonderful if only she could find herself a lover as brave as that noble bird! At this very moment, the eagle swooped down and shed three drops of blood on her: one drop fell on her head, snapping off nine of her hairs; another on her waist, penetrating the seven layers of clothes she was wearing; the third drop fell into her lap, seeping through her three-layered pleated skirt. Soon it became clear that she was pregnant and she gave birth to a boy with a square jaw and big eyes. This was the very hero in Yi mythology who shot arrows at the sun and the moon and who overpowered the god of Thunder."[2]

Paul Hattaway

Religion: Spirit worship is practiced by the Jinghong Nasu at certain times throughout the year. Despite living alongside the Theravada Buddhist Tai Lu for generations, no Nasu are known to have converted to Buddhism.

Christianity: A small number of Jinghong Nasu have become Christians in recent years in both Jinghong and Menghai counties. Some Yi are members of the large Three-Self congregation in Jinghong City, which has grown from 200 to around 1,000 people in the past ten years. Some Jinghong Nasu may also be members.

Population in China:
18,000 (1999)
18,450 (2000)
23,150 (2010)
Location: Yunnan
Religion: Animism
Christians: 100

Overview of the Jinping Nasu

Countries: China

Pronunciation: "Jin-ping-Nah-soo"

Other Names: Nasupo

Population Source: 18,000 (1999 J. Pelkey); Out of a total Yi population of 6,572,173 (1990 census)

Location: *SW Yunnan:* Jinghong (12,000) and Menghai (6,000) counties

Status: Officially included under Yi

Language: Sino-Tibetan, Tibeto-Burman, Burmese-Lolo, Lolo, Northern Lolo, Yi, Unclassified

Dialects: 0

Religion: Animism, Ancestor Worship, Christianity

Christians: 100

Scripture: None

***Jesus* film:** None

Gospel Recordings: None

Christian Broadcasting: None

ROPAL code: None

Status of Evangelization

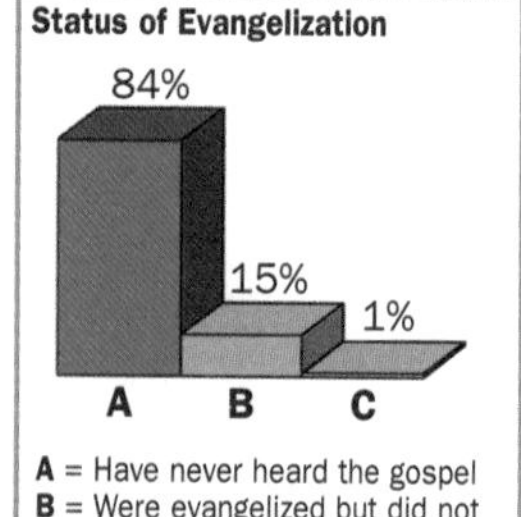

A = Have never heard the gospel
B = Were evangelized but did not become Christians
C = Are adherents to any form of Christianity

Nasu, Panxian 纳苏(盘县)

Population in China:
282,900 (1999)
290,100 (2000)
364,100 (2010)
Location:
Guizhou, Yunnan, Guangxi
Religion: Ancestor Worship
Christians: 5,000

Overview of the Panxian Nasu

Countries: China

Pronunciation: "Nah-soo-Pan-sheeun"

Other Names: Nasu, Nasupo, Xiaohei Yi, Panxian Yi, P'an-hsien Yi, Panlong Yi, Panbei Yi, Pannan Yi

Population Source: 282,900 (1999 AMO); Out of a total Yi population of 6,572,173 (1990 census)

Location: *W Guizhou:* Panxian, Shuicheng, Xingren, Xingyi, Pu'an, and Qinglong counties; *E Yunnan:* Fuyuan (44,000), Luoping (25,000), and Qujing (17,000) counties; *NW Guangxi:* Longlin County (3,422)

Status: Officially included under Yi

Language: Sino-Tibetan, Tibeto-Burman, Burmese-Lolo, Lolo, Northern Lolo, Yi, Eastern Yi

Dialects (2): Panbei, Pannan

Religion: Ancestor Worship, Animism, Christianity

Christians: 5,000

Scripture: None

***Jesus* film:** None

Gospel Recordings: None

Christian Broadcasting: None

ROPAL code: None

Status of Evangelization

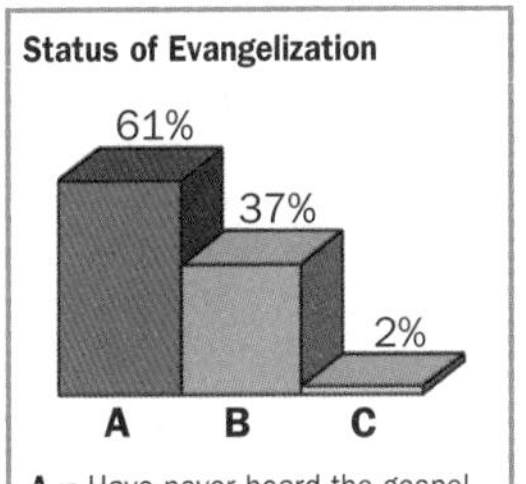

A = Have never heard the gospel
B = Were evangelized but did not become Christians
C = Are adherents to any form of Christianity

Paul Hattaway

Location: Approximately 290,000 Nasu people speaking a distinct language live in western Guizhou Province and in adjoining parts of eastern Yunnan Province. In Yunnan, where 86,000 are located, the Panxian Nasu live in Fuyuan, Luoping, and Qujing counties.[1] In Guizhou their villages are distributed in Panxian, Shuicheng, Xingren, Xingyi, Pu'an, and Qinglong counties. The Panxian Nasu are also found in Longlin County of the Guangxi Zhuang Autonomous Region. They are the largest group of the 6,000 Yi people in Guangxi.

Identity: The Panxian Nasu are officially considered part of the Yi nationality in China. Their culture, ethnicity, and language are different from other Yi groups however. *Panxian* is the name of a county in Guizhou Province. The county includes the large Lupanshui Municipality. This loconym has been added to the name of this group to distinguish it from the several other Nasu groups in southern China.

Language: Panxian Nasu is part of the Eastern Yi branch of Tibeto-Burman. Panxian Nasu contains two dialects: *Panbei* (Northern Panxian) and *Pannan* (Southern Panxian). In areas where the two dialects overlap, speakers can understand each other because they have had prolonged contact with each other. In other areas, however, speakers of Pannan and Panbei cannot understand each other until they have had a few weeks exposure to each other's vocabulary and accent. Panbei Nasu is primarily spoken in the northern part of Panxian County and in parts of Qinglong and Shuicheng counties in Guizhou, and in Yunnan Province. Pannan Nasu is primarily spoken in the southern part of Panxian County and in parts of Xingren and Pu'an counties in Guizhou.

History: The Panxian Nasu have lived in their present location for numerous centuries. Over the past three hundred years, under pressure from an influx of Han Chinese into their areas, many Panxian Nasu living near the townships have lost the use of their language, traditional dress, and culture.

Customs: The traditional dress of Panxian Nasu women consists of "a long gown in black or blue with buttons on the right side.... The headscarves are usually white in color. The waist is girded with a black apron with two floral streamers hanging down on the front.... Women of Longlin [County in Guangxi] look more plain and graceful.... They wear black headscarves, earrings, bracelets and embroidered shoes with a hawk head on the top."[2]

Religion: Ancestor worship is the main religion of the Panxian Nasu today. Only in mountainous areas do they still practice spirit worship.

Christianity: There are at least 5,000 Panxian Nasu believers. In Longyin Township of Pu'an County, where the Nasu have met in three large house churches since 1980, "the Christians are held in high esteem by their neighbors because of their constant display of public spirit."[3] The Panxian Nasu of southern Guizhou, Yunnan, and Guangxi have had less exposure to the gospel.

Nasu, Southern 纳苏(南)

Jamin Pelkey

Location: More than 100,000 Southern Nasu live in five counties of central and southern Yunnan Province. The majority (42,900) live in Eshan County, followed by Xinping County (33,300), while Yimen County contains 17,000 Southern Nasu. In addition, about 9,000 Southern Nasu live in the southern part of Anning County and the southwestern part of Jinning County in the Kunming Municipality.[1]

Identity: Although this people group calls itself merely *Nasu*, an added description is needed in order to separate them from other groups who refer to themselves as Nasu but who speak different languages and dialects.[2] The Southern Nasu are also different from the Nisu in Xinping and Yuanyang counties who have been profiled separately.

Language: The Southern Nasu speak a northwestern dialect within the Southern Yi branch of the Tibeto-Burman language family. Southern Nasu is reportedly very similar to the Xinping Nisu language. The two groups have little trouble communicating with each other in their own languages. The two groups, however, do have different customs, style of dress, and insist that they are distinct groups.

History: The Southern Nasu probably originated in southern Sichuan and northern Yunnan many centuries ago. The name *Nasu* means "black people." The color black is revered by the Nasu.

Customs: The Southern Nasu retain many aspects of their traditional culture, including the four-stringed guitar and a host of folk dances and songs. They also participate in the annual Torch Festival which takes place on the 24th day of the sixth lunar month.

Religion: The Southern Nasu are polytheists who attempt to placate a wide array of spirits and deities. Some spirits are considered helpful while others are evil and cause death, sickness, and destruction. One source says, "Animistic spirituality and ancestor worship is alive and well among this people. The Southern Nasu of Eshan County still have living *bimos* or sorcerers who perform rites and incantations from the ancient script to appease demons and ward off evil from sick persons, households, and at funerals. Besides the *bimo* there is a significant number of ordinary people who have linked themselves with the spirit world, and are able, through such channels, to heal sicknesses."[3]

Christianity: There are presently only about 100 known Christians among the Southern Nasu. These believers meet in Han Chinese churches in the townships of Yuxi Prefecture. There is no Nasu-language congregation in existence. Today most Southern Nasu have no knowledge of Christianity. Mission work among them prior to 1949 was nonexistent. In 1998 the Christian ministry Gospel Recordings produced audio tapes of the gospel message in Southern Nasu, resulting in a few people making decisions to follow Christ.

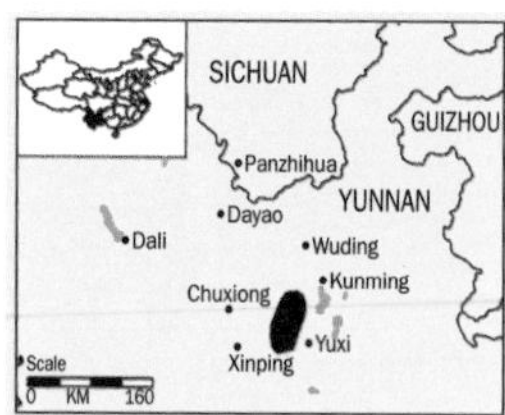

Population in China:
102,200 (1999)
104,800 (2000)
131,500 (2010)
Location: Yunnan
Religion: Polytheism
Christians: 100

Overview of the Southern Nasu

Countries: China

Pronunciation: "Nah-soo"

Other Names: Southern Yi

Population Source: 102,200 (1999 J. Pelkey); Out of a total Yi population of 6,572,173 (1990 census)

Location: *Yunnan:* Eshan (42,900), Xinping (33,300), and Yimen (17,000) counties of Yuxi Prefecture; Jinning and Anning (together 9,000) counties of Kunming Municipality

Status: Officially included under Yi

Language: Sino-Tibetan, Tibeto-Burman, Burmese-Lolo, Lolo, Northern Lolo, Yi, Southern Yi

Dialects: 0

Religion: Polytheism, Animism, Ancestor Worship, Shamanism, Christianity

Christians: 100

Scripture: None

***Jesus* film:** None

Gospel Recordings: Southern Nasu #04670

Christian Broadcasting: None

ROPAL code: None

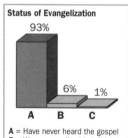

Status of Evangelization

	A	B	C
%	93%	6%	1%

A = Have never heard the gospel
B = Were evangelized but did not become Christians
C = Are adherents to any form of Christianity

Nasu, Western 纳苏(西)

Location: The 215,000 Western Nasu are a comparatively large ethnic group who spill across into parts of three large prefectures in a widespread geographical area of western Yunnan Province. The Western Nasu are concentrated in the western part of Dali Prefecture, the northern part of Lincang Prefecture, and in Baoshan Prefecture.

Identity: The Western Nasu are part of the official Yi nationality in China. Although many people use the autonym *Nasu*, they speak widely differing languages. Many Western Nasu are in the process of assimilation to Han Chinese culture and language.

Language: Western Nasu is a part of the Western Yi group of languages, as opposed to other speakers in Yunnan who call themselves *Nasu* and whose languages are from the Southern, Eastern, and Central Yi groups.

History: Ethnographic studies over the past few years have attributed the Nasu's leopard dancing to the reign of the fabled Yellow Emperor in the prehistoric period. Dancers at the time disguised themselves as animals during the Banishment of Evil Spirits Festival. "By the Zhou Dynasty (c.11th century – 212 BC) the ritual had evolved as part of the state ceremonial system and was presided over by priest-exorcists who were dressed up as beasts in much the same way as shamans among the Nasu today."[1]

Customs: The Western Nasu in some areas practice a ritualistic dance known as *Yugmo-Lhage-She* which means "dancing like a leopard." A team of young girls opens the ritual by beating drums, gongs, and cymbals. "In the cacophony the leopard dancers emerge... stamping the plank roof with their feet all the time, changing tempo and action in syncopated rhythm with the percussion."[2] When the musicians stop playing, the nearly naked leopard dancers "gnaw and prance at each other in mock fights.... This is a ritual to banish evil spirits out of the door."[3]

Dwayne Graybill

Religion: The polytheistic Western Nasu believe "everything in this world has a soul and that all ghosts are incarnations of human souls. They respect the good and hate the evil. Whenever someone dies a natural death they invite a shaman to pacify the soul of the deceased and send it to the midst of their ancestors, and whenever someone dies in an accident, they invite the shaman to drive his soul out of their way."[4] The Western Nasu also worship the spirits of certain animals, especially the tiger, bear, and ox. They believe spirits are more powerful than men. No effort is spared to placate the deities and ghosts that they believe control their lives.

Christianity: Although some publications report "approximately 200,000 Yi Christians in China,"[5] most outsiders are unaware that these believers are found mainly among the Eastern Lipo and Eastern Nasu subgroups in northern Yunnan. They speak distinct languages and have acute cultural differences with the Western Nasu. Few Western Nasu have ever heard the name of Jesus Christ.

Population in China:
200,000 (1997)
215,300 (2000)
270,200 (2010)
Location: Yunnan
Religion: Polytheism
Christians: None Known

Overview of the Western Nasu

Countries: China

Pronunciation: "Nah-soo"

Other Names: Yunnan Yi, Yi: Yunnan, Shui Nosu, Naso, Nyi, Nasu Puo, Nasu Yi, Yisupuo

Population Source: 200,000 (1997 J. Pelkey); Out of a total Yi population of 6,572,173 (1990 census)

Location: *W Yunnan:* Baoshan, Dali, and Lincang prefectures

Status: Officially included under Yi

Language: Sino-Tibetan, Tibeto-Burman, Burmese-Lolo, Lolo, Northern Lolo, Yi, Western Yi

Dialects: 0

Religion: Polytheism, Shamanism, Animism, Ancestor Worship

Christians: None

Scripture: None

***Jesus* film:** None

Gospel Recordings: None

Christian Broadcasting: None

ROPAL code: None

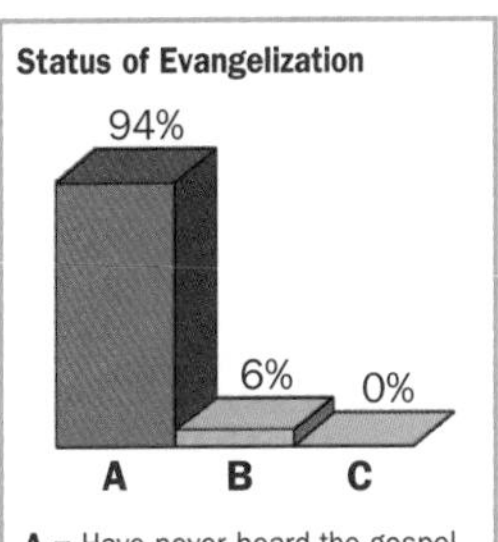

A = Have never heard the gospel
B = Were evangelized but did not become Christians
C = Are adherents to any form of Christianity

Nasu, Wusa 纳苏，乌撒

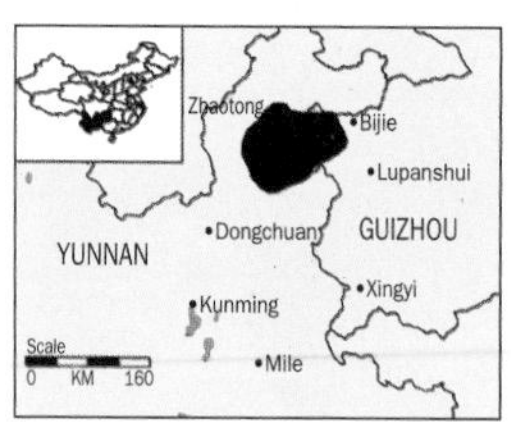

Population in China:
242,400 (1999)
248,500 (2000)
312,000 (2010)
Location: Guizhou, Yunnan
Religion: Polytheism
Christians: 60,000

Overview of the Wusa Nasu

Countries: China

Pronunciation: "Nah-soo-Woo-sa"

Other Names: Wusa, Nasu, Nasupo, Lousu, Henke Yi, Hezhang Yi

Population Source: 242,400(1999 AMO); 85,000 in Yunnan (1999 J. Pelkey); Out of a total Yi population of 6,572,173 (1990 census)

Location: *W Guizhou:* Weining, Shuicheng, Hezhang, Nayong, Dafang, Bijie, and Qianxi counties; *NE Yunnan:* Xuanwei (58,000), Yiliang (15,000), and Huize (12,000) counties

Status: Officially included under Yi

Language: Sino-Tibetan, Tibeto-Burman, Burmese-Lolo, Lolo, Northern Lolo, Yi, Eastern Yi

Dialects (3): Weining, Hezhang, Henke

Religion: Polytheism, Ancestor Worship, Christianity

Christians: 60,000

Scripture: None

***Jesus* film:** None

Gospel Recordings: None

Christian Broadcasting: None

ROPAL code: None

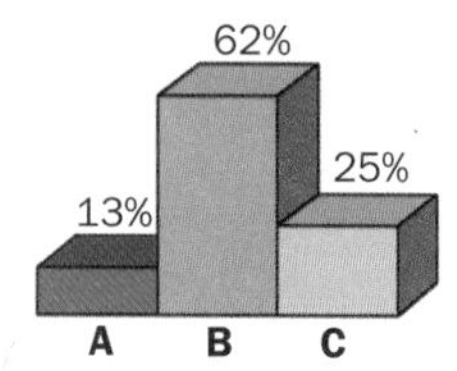

A = Have never heard the gospel
B = Were evangelized but did not become Christians
C = Are adherents to any form of Christianity

Location: Approximately 250,000 Wusa Nasu people live in seven counties of northwest Guizhou Province and in three counties of northeast Yunnan Province in southern China. The Wusa Nasu are the dominant Yi group in this region of China. The highest concentrations are found in Weining, Shuicheng, Hezhang, and Nayong counties of Guizhou; and in Xuanwei County of Yunnan where 58,000 reportedly live.[1]

Identity: The Wusa Nasu speak a different language from the several other Yi groups in southern China who use the autonym *Nasu*. The name *Wusa* is an ancient tribal name which formerly designated this people group.

Language: Wusa Nasu is part of the Eastern Yi group of Tibeto-Burman languages. In areas where their population is thin, the Wusa Nasu language is being lost to Chinese, but in densely concentrated areas the language is still used vigorously. In Weining County, for example, 85% of the Yi in the county still speak their native tongue and use it daily.[2]

History: The Wusa Nasu claim they are descended from their esteemed ancestor Dumu, "who had six sons after moving into the region of present-day Zhaotong. These six sons became separate tribes — one of the tribes being the *Wusa*. Among the other tribes were the *Wumeng* and *Mangbu Nosu*. These six tribes have developed quite separately in terms of language."[3]

Customs: Most Wusa Nasu are herders of goats, sheep, cattle, and pigs. Since the Ming Dynasty (1368–1644) the Wusa Nasu have used Chinese names, although many still also have Wusa names which consist of two characters. Folk dancing is an important part of Wusa Nasu culture. They dance at weddings, festivals, and at family get-togethers. Children often wear hats decorated with pictures of the sun, moon, and stars.

Religion: The Wusa Nasu used to bury their dead but now they cremate them. The people worry that their relatives' souls will not reach their ancestors' homeland, so shamans are called on to perform rituals over the dead body. Shamans still operate in Weining County, but most of them are over 60 years old. Nature worship is embedded in Wusa Nasu customs. They particularly revere the sun and the moon. In totem worship they idolize woodcarvings of bamboo, cranes, tigers, and dragons.

Christianity: At least 25% of Wusa Nasu are Christians today. Missionaries commenced work among them in the early 1900s. In 1907 the Wusa Nasu tried to murder Samuel Pollard because many of their A-Hmao tenants were being converted. The Wusa Nasu feared the missionaries were giving poison to the A-Hmao to put in their wells.[4] By 1911 the work was advancing slowly. It was reported: "Some of them [Wusa Nasu] gather a little consolation from the coming of Christianity, and hope that it means an arrest of their decline."[5] Large numbers of Wusa Nasu have followed Christ, including about 50% of the population in Weining County;[6] in other areas they have firmly resisted the advance of Christianity.

Paul Hattaway

Naxi 纳西

Paul Hattaway

Location: More than 270,000 Naxi are located in northern Yunnan Province, especially in Lijiang County, at the foot of the sacred and majestic Jade Dragon Mountain. The perennially snowcapped mountain towers 5,596 meters (18,350 ft.) above the Lijiang plain. Small numbers of Naxi live in Sichuan Province[1] and possibly in Myanmar.[2]

Identity: The Naxi have been combined with several smaller groups to form one of China's official minorities. The Naxi trace their origins to an elephant-headed god named Tabu, who helped them hatch from magic eggs. The name *Naxi* means "respectable people."[3]

Language: One of the most distinctive aspects of Naxi culture is their ancient pictographic script. The Naxi developed the system of 1,500 pictographs more than 1,000 years ago, perhaps so they could record their religious laws before setting out to their new lands. Today some 20,000 Naxi manuscripts appear in museums and private collections in China and around the world.[4] The pictographs were only read by the *Dongbas* — priests of the Dongba religion. In 1995 only three old men, aged 71, 76, and 86, could read the Naxi script. Naxi consists of three main dialects.[5] A Naxi-English dictionary exists.[6]

History: Since migrating from Tibet, the Naxi have lived in Lijiang approximately 1,000 years. References in Naxi literature to Lake Manasarovar and Mt. Kailas, both in farwestern Tibet, confirm the Naxi's origins. By the time the Mongol hordes swept through Lijiang in 1253, it was already populated by 1,000 families. On 3 February 1996, a huge earthquake shook Lijiang and surrounding districts. Three hundred people died, 40,000 were injured, and 300,000 were made homeless.[7]

Customs: Naxi society is traditionally known for its matriarchal practices. For centuries, all property and assets were passed down through the woman's side of the family. Naxi men were only entitled to visit their *azhu* (walk-in friend) at night for sexual purposes, and to return at dawn to their mother's house. Matriarchal society started to subside in 1723 when Lijiang came under Chinese control. Naxi women protested their falling status by killing themselves. The annual "Sacrifice to Heaven" was last practiced in Lijiang in 1949.[8] The favored way of dying was by taking poison. Today, matriarchal customs are seen more among the Mosuo farther to the north.

Religion: Although today many Naxi are nonreligious, in the 1940s there were more than 4,000 Naxi Dongba priests. Their religion was "characterized by a fascination with power and wonder-working, and belief in a multitude of gods and demons who are manipulated with magic."[9]

Christianity: The first missionaries to the Naxi arrived in 1912. By 1930 there were eight or nine baptized Naxi believers.[10] In 1932 the Dutch Pentecostal Mission Society translated Scripture portions into Naxi, but these are now obsolete. In the early 1950s the Naxi church was destroyed by the Communists. Today there are a small number of Naxi believers in Lijiang, and there are Naxi Catholics mixed in with Lisu and Tibetan congregations farther north. More than 1,000 Naxi are members of the Mentu Hui cult,[11] founded by Ji Sanbao, who claims to be a Second Christ.

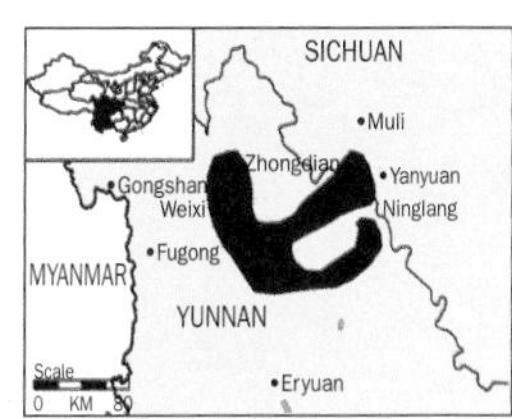

Population in China:
232,500 (1990)
271,300 (2000)
316,600 (2010)
Location: Yunnan, Sichuan
Religion: Animism
Christians: 200

Overview of the Naxi

Countries: China, possibly Myanmar

Pronunciation: "Na-shee"

Other Names: Nahsi, Nasi, Nakhi, Lomi, Mu, Nachi

Population Source: 278,009 (1990 census);[12] 245,154 (1982 census); 156,796 (1964 census); 143,453 (1953 census); Possibly also in Myanmar

Location: *NW Yunnan:* Lijiang, Weixi, Gongshan, Yongsheng, Zhongdian, and Ninglang counties; *S Sichuan:* Muli (3,618) and Yanbian (2,051) counties

Status: An official minority of China

Language: Sino-Tibetan, Tibeto-Burman, Burmese-Lolo, Lolo, Northern Lolo, Naxi

Literacy: 62%

Dialects (3): Lijiang (140,000), Dayazhen (30,000), Baoshanzhou (10,000)

Religion: Animism, No Religion, Dongbaism, Daoism, Christianity

Christians: 200

Scripture: Portions 1932; Work in progress

***Jesus* film:** None

Gospel Recordings: Naxi #04700

Christian Broadcasting: None

ROPAL code: NBF00

Status of Evangelization

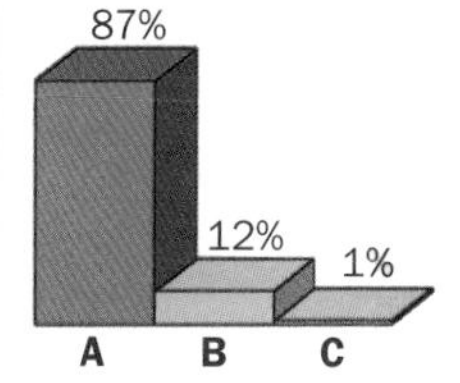

A = Have never heard the gospel
B = Were evangelized but did not become Christians
C = Are adherents to any form of Christianity

Naxi, Northern 纳西(北)

Population in China:
2,309 (1990)
2,690 (2000)
3,140 (2010)
Location: Tibet, Yunnan
Religion: Tibetan Buddhism
Christians: 100

Overview of the Northern Naxi

Countries: China

Pronunciation: "Na-shee"

Other Names: Deqen Naxi

Population Source:
2,309 (1990 census);
Out of a total Naxi population of 278,009 (1990 census)

Location:
SE Tibet: Markam County (1,236); *NW Yunnan:* Deqen County (1,073)

Status:
Officially included under Naxi

Language: Sino-Tibetan, Tibeto-Burman, Burmese-Lolo, Lolo, Northern Lolo, Naxi, Northern Naxi

Dialects: 0

Religion: Tibetan Buddhism, Polytheism, Ancestor Worship, Christianity

Christians: 50 to 100

Scripture: None

***Jesus* film:** None

Gospel Recordings: None

Christian Broadcasting: None

ROPAL code: None

Status of Evangelization

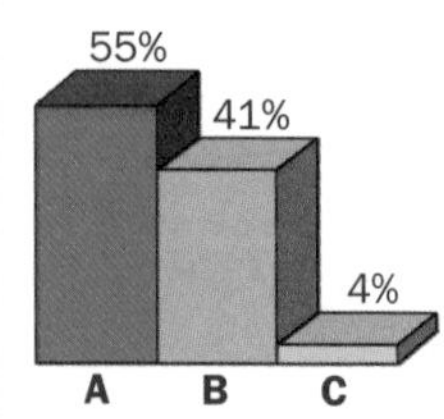

A = Have never heard the gospel
B = Were evangelized but did not become Christians
C = Are adherents to any form of Christianity

Paul Hattaway

Location: According to the 1990 census, 2,309 Northern Naxi live in the highlands between Yunnan and the Tibet Autonomous Region in southwest China. They inhabit villages on both banks of the Lancang (Mekong) River. Near the source of its origin, the river is crystal clear and narrow. By the time it spills into the ocean in Vietnam it is a vast, dirty waterway that measures 11 kilometers (6.8 mi.) wide at its broadest point. The majority of Northern Naxi (1,236) live in Markam County just inside the Tibet Autonomous Region. An additional 1,073 live in Deqen County in northern Yunnan Province.

Identity: The Northern Naxi are linguistically distinct from other groups of Naxi in China, including those who live in Zhongdian County. The Northern Naxi also possess a different style of dress and customs from their counterparts in Lijiang. The Northern Naxi, including those inside Tibet, still proudly identify themselves as members of the Naxi nationality.

Language: Although no detailed linguistic studies have been done to determine the difference between Northern and Lijiang Naxi, one missionary who visited the area played the new Naxi gospel recording and found the Northern Naxi could only understand about 60% of the vocabulary.[1] Because of several centuries of geographic separation, Northern Naxi today displays many influences from Deqen Tibetan, while Lijiang Naxi has been greatly influenced by Chinese.

History: Today's various branches of the Naxi nationality in China, including the Mosuo, Naru, and Naheng, all share the same migration stories. They claim they originated on the Tibetan Plateau and migrated en masse approximately 1,000 years ago in search of better pasturelands. The Northern Naxi claim they came to live in their present location by two means. Firstly, during the original migration certain families who had fallen sick or weak were left behind while the main body continued their journey south. They settled down along the banks of the Lancang River and gradually formed into communities. Secondly, the Northern Naxi say Naxi soldiers from Lijiang were sent north in the past to guard the fertile valleys from invaders and bandits. Many of these soldiers stayed behind in the area.

Customs: To an outsider, there is little to visually distinguish the Northern Naxi from neighboring Tibetans today. The Northern Naxi wear Tibetan clothing.

Religion: The Northern Naxi are comprised of several interesting religious elements. Most follow Tibetan Buddhism. Ancestors are also worshiped and revered. In addition, a small number of Northern Naxi have converted to Catholicism.

Christianity: Between 50 and 100 Catholic believers are found among the Northern Naxi. Most of them meet in Deqen Tibetan churches, including one church at Yanjing, just inside Tibet, which contains more than 700 ethnic Tibetan believers and a small number of Northern Naxi.

Naza 纳咱

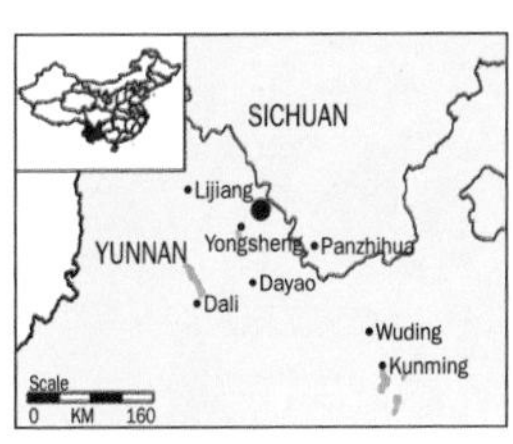

Population in China:
1,300 (1999)
1,330 (2000)
1,670 (2010)
Location: Yunnan
Religion: Polytheism
Christians: None Known

Overview of the Naza

Countries: China

Pronunciation: "Nah-za"

Other Names: Nazaren, Nazasu

Population Source:
1,300 (1999 J. Pelkey);
Out of a total Yi population of 6,572,173 (1990 census)

Location:
N Yunnan: Yongsheng County

Status: Officially included under Yi

Language: Sino-Tibetan, Tibeto-Burman, Burmese-Lolo, Lolo, Northern Lolo, Yi, Northern Yi

Dialects: 0

Religion: Polytheism, Animism, Ancestor Worship

Christians: None known

Scripture: None

***Jesus* film:** None

Gospel Recordings: None

Christian Broadcasting: None

ROPAL code: None

Status of Evangelization

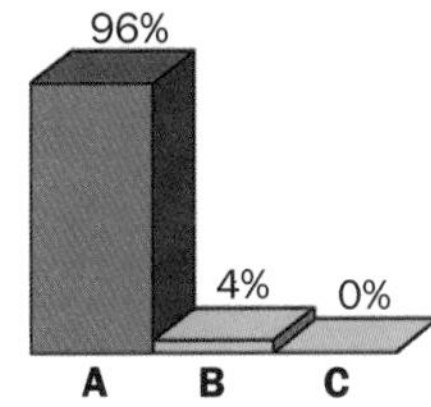

A = Have never heard the gospel
B = Were evangelized but did not become Christians
C = Are adherents to any form of Christianity

Location: More than 1,300 people of the Naza ethnic group inhabits just one village in the northern part of Yunnan Province in southern China. They live in the Nazi Village within the Liude Community, in the Liude District of Yongsheng County.[1] Yongsheng is a mountainous region bordered to the north by Sichuan Province.

Identity: The Naza have been officially counted in China as part of the Yi nationality. They live in the same district as the Liude people yet retain a separate ethnicity from the Liude and all other Yi groups in China. The Naza are also known as the *Nazaren* and *Nazasu.*

Language: Although the Naza language has not specifically been classified as a Northern Yi variety, Chinese linguists have designated the whole of Yongsheng County a Northern Yi area. The traditional Nosu script is not used by the Naza.

History: The Naza were formerly involved in the slave system that dominated people's lives in the northern Yunnan-southern Sichuan area. The history of the tribes in this region also featured regular warfare and conflict. Larger groups, such as the Xiaoliangshan Nosu, have used their population size to oppress and enslave smaller tribes, often raiding their villages and carrying away men, beasts, and goods.

Customs: The Naza today lead relatively quiet lives in the mountains. They raise pigs, goats, and poultry as well as grow rice and vegetables. Until the 1970s few people knew of the Naza. Their village is still accessible by foot only.

Religion: Polytheism, mixed with ancestor worship, is the main religious belief of the Naza. They worship the sun, moon, and stars, as well as a host of local spirits and deities. One missionary in the early 1900s, commenting on the spiritual beliefs of the Yi in a different area, wrote, "After the ingathering of buckwheat, when the crop is stacked on the threshing floor and the work of threshing is about to begin, the simple formula 'Thank you Je-so-mo' is pronounced. *Je-so-mo* seems to be a spirit who controls the crops; whether good or evil is not easy to determine. *Mo* is the generic name for 'sage' or 'spirit'. *Je-so* is so like the name *Je-su*, which the Chinese and Miao use for Jesus, that some of the Yi wished to use Je-so for the name of our Savior; but to this the missionaries very wisely did not consent, as they did not know who, or what sort of a person, Je-so-mo was. Je-so-mo is not God, for when the Nosu wish to speak of God they use the word Se, which means 'Master' or 'Lord'."[2]

Christianity: The Naza are an unreached and largely unevangelized people group. No more than a few of their population have ever received an intelligible gospel witness. Yongsheng County is almost completely devoid of Christian presence, except for a few Han Chinese and possibly Lisu believers. Because they do not have an orthography, there are no Scriptures available in the Naza language, and no gospel recordings or other evangelistic tools.

Jamin Pelkey

Neisu 聂素

Location: The Neisu tribe, who number more than 16,500 members, inhabit parts of the Honghe Hani and Yi Autonomous Prefecture, in the south central part of Yunnan Province. Honghe Prefecture shares its southern border with Vietnam.

Identity: Although officially counted as a Hani subgroup, the Neisu have possessed their own customs and national dress for centuries, as well as their own distinct language. One writer explains, "The term *Hani* can be a little misleading. In the 1950s, Communist government officials... found a host of various minority groups and began to combine those that had some sort of affinity into larger groups for administrative purposes."[1] Neisu women are easily identified by their distinctive rooster-shaped hat and the colorful decorations of silver and embroidery on their aprons.

Language: Neisu is a distinct language. Although it is partially related to other languages in the area such as Kado and Biyo, most speakers from the different groups use Chinese in order to communicate with each other. The Chinese list "five different subgroups and dialects in Mojiang County alone,"[2] but other sources indicate the situation is much more complex. One visitor reported "14 different Hani dialect groups in just one area."[3] Note the Neisu language of the Hani subgroup is not the same as the Nisu varieties in southern China.

History: The oral stories and poems of the Neisu are rich with images of high mountains and rice-terracing systems. The Neisu have been cultivating rice on the steep mountain slopes of southern China for many centuries.

Customs: Neisu villages are constructed, where possible, along mountain ridges. Their homes are built with thatched roofs. Inside there is a strict division between the men's part of the house and the women's. Males are not allowed in the women's section. Every year the Neisu traditionally carve a pair of male and female wooden figures. These are placed on paths leading to the village entrance. At the end of the year the figures are not removed but are simply left to rot. After a number of years the village entrance seems to be guarded by many of these distinctive carvings.

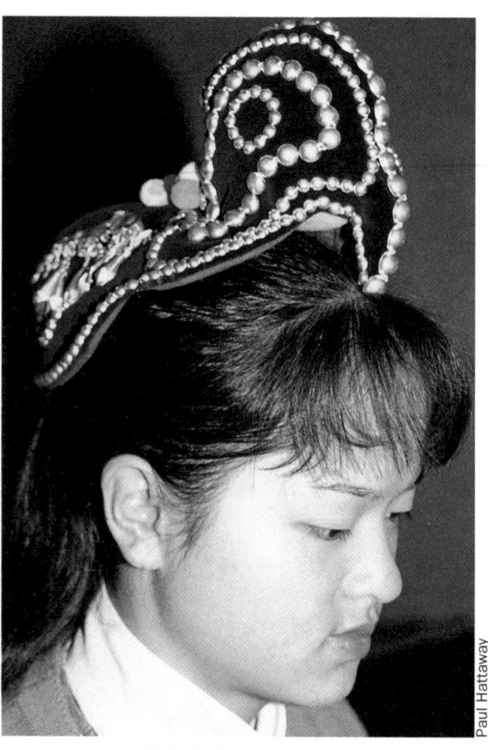

Paul Hattaway

Religion: The primary religion among the Neisu is polytheism. The term *polytheism* literally means "many gods." Indeed the Neisu worship a multiplicity of deities, from Chinese Daoist gods to ones portrayed as fearsome figures brandishing swords and clutching the severed heads of their human victims.

Christianity: There are believed to be several hundred Neisu Christians meeting in mixed churches with believers of other nationalities. In the 1950s and 1960s the Communist authorities launched a systematic plan to destroy the church in Honghe. Believers were forced to work on Sundays to prevent them from meeting together. Many worked twice as hard on Saturday to meet the quota for Sunday, so they could take the day off. Others continued to meet secretly on Sunday or stopped work to worship God in the fields.[4] Believers still suffer discrimination today.

Population in China:
15,000 (1995)
16,700 (2000)
20,500 (2010)
Location: Yunnan
Religion: Polytheism
Christians: 400

Overview of the Neisu

Countries: China

Pronunciation: "Nay-soo"

Other Names: Nisu

Population Source:
15,000 (1995 AMO);
Out of a total Hani population of 198,252 (1990 census)

Location:
S Yunnan: Honghe Prefecture

Status:
Officially included under Hani

Language: Sino-Tibetan, Tibeto-Burman, Burmese-Lolo, Lolo, Southern Lolo, Akha, Unclassified

Dialects: 0

Religion: Polytheism, Animism, Christianity, Daoism

Christians: 400

Scripture: None

***Jesus* film:** None

Gospel Recordings: None

Christian Broadcasting: None

ROPAL code: None

Status of Evangelization

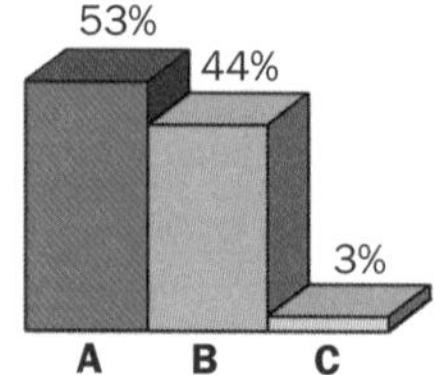

A = Have never heard the gospel
B = Were evangelized but did not become Christians
C = Are adherents to any form of Christianity

Neisu, Da Hei 聂素，大黑

Population in China:
6,300 (1999)
6,450 (2000)
8,100 (2010)
Location: Yunnan
Religion: Polytheism
Christians: None Known

Overview of the Da Hei Neisu

Countries: China

Pronunciation: "Da-Hay-Nay-soo"

Other Names: Da Hei Yi, Black Yi, Big Black Yi, Wopu, Nasu, Greater Neisu, Neisupo, Nisu, Xiqi

Population Source:
6,300 (1999 J. Pelkey);
Out of a total Yi population of 6,572,173 (1990 census)

Location: *Yunnan:* Mile (2,200), Luxi (1,500), Luliang (1,300), Lunan (800), and Shizong (500) counties

Status:
Officially included under Yi

Language: Sino-Tibetan, Tibeto-Burman, Burmese-Lolo, Lolo, Northern Lolo, Yi, Eastern Yi

Dialects: 0

Religion:
Polytheism, Animism, Shamanism

Christians: None known

Scripture: None

***Jesus* film:** None

Gospel Recordings: None

Christian Broadcasting: None

ROPAL code: None

Status of Evangelization

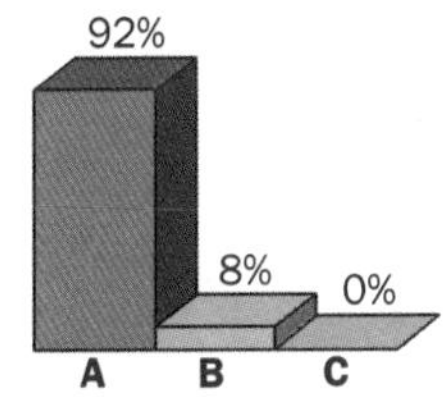

A = Have never heard the gospel
B = Were evangelized but did not become Christians
C = Are adherents to any form of Christianity

Paul Hattaway

Location: More than 6,300 Da Hei (Greater Black) Neisu live in Yunnan Province.[1] They inhabit widespread communities in four different prefectures. They live within Mile[2] and Luxi counties of Honghe Prefecture; Shilin (Lunan) County in Kunming Municipality; Shizong and Luoping counties of Qujing Prefecture; and Qiubei County in Wenshan Prefecture.[3]

Identity: Commonly called *Da Hei Yi* (Big Black Yi) by the Chinese, this people group refers to itself as *Neisu* or *Nasu* meaning "black people."[4] Linguist Jamin Pelkey has stated that "when widely different cultures and languages are encountered among one of these 'Black People' groups a clarifying title must be given to distinguish dissimilarities."[5]

Language: The language of the Da Hei Neisu is mutually intelligible with the Xiao Hei Neisu. In the past, the ruling castes felt that it was important to distinguish themselves by using a different dialect from the slave class. Today, "only in larger population pockets is the Da Hei Neisu language still spoken by young and old."[6]

History: Like the Nosu of Sichuan, the Da Hei Neisu have come from a society in which they were the traditional landlords and slave-owners. "Although their counterparts in Sichuan emerged from the slave system as late as the 1950s, this people seem to have begun slowly adopting new ways hundreds of years ago.... The Da Hei Neisu entered Honghe Prefecture from Luoping and Qiubei counties and from as far away as Zhaotong. That this people migrated from Zhaotong Prefecture lends credence to a possible connection between this and the Liangshan Nosu system of slavery."[7]

Customs: Although it is possible that dialects and cultures have diverged between the communities living so far apart, the Da Hei Neisu continue to see themselves as a homogeneous people group. A Da Hei Neisu wedding usually lasts from four to seven days. After marriage it is customary for the new husband and wife to sleep in separate beds. Da Hei Neisu traditional dress has disappeared in most regions, and many customs are also on the decline.

Religion: The Da Hei Neisu are polytheistic animists who believe a person's soul leaves the body at death or when the person is sick. To prevent this from happening, they tie string around the wrists of an ill person and fasten it to a bedpost or piece of furniture. Shamans are summoned to call the spirit back into the body.

Christianity: Although Catholic missionaries from the Paris Foreign Missionary Society worked among the Sani and Axi people in the 1880s, experiencing much success, no record exists of outreach to the Da Hei Neisu people farther south of the French mission stations. Today, there are no known believers among the Da Hei Neisu. Few have any awareness of the name of Jesus Christ. Much prayer is needed to break down the powerful influence of the occult among the Da Hei Neisu. There are presently no Scriptures or evangelistic materials available in the Da Hei Neisu language.

Neisu, Xiao Hei 聂素，小黑

Jamin Pelkey

Location: Approximately 7,500 Xiao Hei Neisu people live in the mountains of central Yunnan Province.[1] They are closely related to, yet distinct from, the Wopu ethnic group. The Xiao Hei Neisu are distributed throughout Malong (2,600), Mile (2,500), Shizong (2,000), and Luliang (300) counties in eastern Yunnan Province.

Identity: The Chinese call this group *Xiao Hei Yi,* meaning "small black Yi." They call themselves *Neisu.* The Chinese include the Xiao Hei Neisu as part of the official Yi nationality, a collection of 120 distinct ethnolinguistic groups. One scholar notes that there is "nothing in common between different Yi groups."[2]

Language: Xiao Hei Neisu is a dialect distinct from Da Hei Neisu and Gepo. It is a member of the Eastern Yi linguistic group. Their native tongue is presently in danger in the more urban locations, under pressure from Mandarin. In the mountains, however, Xiao Hei Neisu is still spoken by all community members, including children.

History: The Xiao Hei Neisu "were on the second tier of an ancient social stratum which evidently spanned the breadth of east-central Yunnan. Above them were the Greater [Da Hei] Neisu and below them were two slave classes of Gepo. Although the actual practice of slavery was lost long before Liberation, the Lesser [Xiao Hei] Neisu still retain a sense of distinct identity from the Greater Neisu and the Gepo, including a different dialect and different costume. In certain regions such as the common borders of Xiyi, Xinshao, and Wushan districts of Mile County, the Greater and Lesser Neisu, along with the Gepo can still be found living in very close proximity, suggesting the former nature of their distribution."[3]

Customs: Many Yi groups believe the progenitor of their race was Ou-lang and that he invented hunting and agriculture. Today, many villages hold an annual ceremony to worship Ou-lang. It affords the people a chance to socialize, trade, and catch up with relatives who live in different areas.

Religion: The Xiao Hei Neisu are polytheists. In their worldview, the earth is controlled by good and bad spirits. They offer regular sacrifices of sheep to ensure that they do not cause offense to the spirits. French missionary Crabouillet in 1873 found the Yi often hired shamans to chase evil spirits away from their villages by chanting and banging drums. The shamans determined the future by studying the organs of sacrificed sheep.[4]

Christianity: A few Xiao Hei Neisu became Christians in 1998 after Chinese Christians were mobilized to take the gospel to them. Most of the members of this group, however, have never heard the name of Jesus Christ. The Christian ministry Gospel Recordings produced a tape in the Xiao Hei Neisu language in 1998. This audio recording will prove greatly beneficial in reaching the Xiao Hei Neisu since most of them are illiterate.

Population in China:
7,400 (1999)
7,580 (2000)
9,520 (2010)
Location: Yunnan
Religion: Polytheism
Christians: 10

Overview of the Xiao Hei Neisu

Countries: China
Pronunciation: "Shaow-Hay-Nay-soo"
Other Names: Xiao Hei Yi, Black Yi, Small Black Yi, Wopu, Nasu, Niesupo, Lesser Neisu, Nisu, Er Yi
Population Source: 7,400 (1999 J. Pelkey); Out of a total Yi population of 6,572,173 (1990 census)
Location: *E Yunnan:* Mile (2,500), Malong (2,600), Shizong (2,000), and Luliang (300) counties; Possibly also in *Guizhou*
Status: Officially included under Yi
Language: Sino-Tibetan, Tibeto-Burman, Burmese-Lolo, Lolo, Northern Lolo, Yi, Eastern Yi
Dialects: 0
Religion: Polytheism, Animism, Christianity
Christians: 10
Scripture: None
***Jesus* film:** None
Gospel Recordings: Yi: Xiao Hei #04830
Christian Broadcasting: None
ROPAL code: None

Status of Evangelization

	A	B	C
%	88%	11%	1%

A = Have never heard the gospel
B = Were evangelized but did not become Christians
C = Are adherents to any form of Christianity

Niesu, Central 聂苏(中)

Location: According to Jamin Pelkey, 28,000 Central Niesu live along the common borders of Yangbi, Yunlong, and Yongping counties in the western part of Dali Prefecture in Yunnan Province. In Yangbi County, where 15,000 are found, the Central Niesu live in all the communities of Fuheng District; in the Goupi Community of Taiping District; in the Baizhang Community of Shangjie District; and in parts of Wanpo Community in Shuangjian District. In Yongping County, which contains 7,000 Central Niesu, they inhabit the Lishuping, Shuanghe, Heidouchang, and Liumi communities of Beidou District. In Yunlong County, the 6,000 Central Niesu live in all of the communities within Tuanjie District.[1]

Identity: The Central Niesu have been officially included as part of the Yi nationality in China. They are not the same as the similarly named Nisu, Neisu, Nasu, or Nosu groups in southern China who, even though they are all viewed as Yi groups, possess widely differing customs and languages. They are also not the same as a group in Weining County of Guizhou Province, also called Niesu.

Language: The Central Niesu language has been placed in the Central Yi group by Chinese linguists apparently on the basis that it displays similarities with the Western Lipo language, which has been classified a Central Yi variety.

History: According to past records, the Central Niesu were once part of the Lowu nationality, as were the present-day Luowu people group. Many centuries ago the ancestors of the Central Niesu migrated to their present location and settled down in the mountains.

Customs: A Niesu couple usually gets married by one of two ways. First, the couple needs the consent of both sets of parents. The couple then customarily lives in the home of the bride's family until the first child is born. Only after the birth is the couple officially considered married. They are free to move into their own home. Alternatively, when a girl "reaches the age of 16 she is given her own room above the goat shed or cattle stall. Her boyfriend then comes and spends the nights with her. When a child is born, the father of the child is her husband for life. Before a child is born... the 'marriage' may be broken off by a simple ceremony of splitting a stick, but after the first child, divorce is very uncommon."[2]

Paul Hattaway

Religion: The Central Niesu worship many gods and spirits. Some they see as helpful spirits that can bless and protect them, but most they see as vengeful and dangerous spirits that must be continually appeased and feared.

Christianity: The gospel has yet to reach the ears of at least 90% of Central Niesu people in China. Dali Prefecture contains one of the lowest percentage Christians of any area in Yunnan Province. Not only are the Central Niesu unreached, but they are surrounded by numerous other people groups in a similar unfortunate position.

Population in China:
28,000 (1999)
28,700 (2000)
36,050 (2010)
Location: Yunnan
Religion: Polytheism
Christians: None Known

Overview of the Central Niesu

Countries: China

Pronunciation: "Nay-soo"

Other Names: Niesupo, Neisu, Luowu

Population Source: 28,000 (1999 J. Pelkey); Out of a total Yi population of 6,572,173 (1990 census)

Location: *W Yunnan:* Yangbi (15,000), Yongping (7,000), and Yunlong (6,000) counties

Status: Officially included under Yi

Language: Sino-Tibetan, Tibeto-Burman, Burmese-Lolo, Lolo, Northern Lolo, Yi, Central Yi

Dialects: 0

Religion: Polytheism, Animism, Ancestor Worship

Christians: None known

Scripture: None

***Jesus* film:** None

Gospel Recordings: None

Christian Broadcasting: None

ROPAL code: None

Status of Evangelization

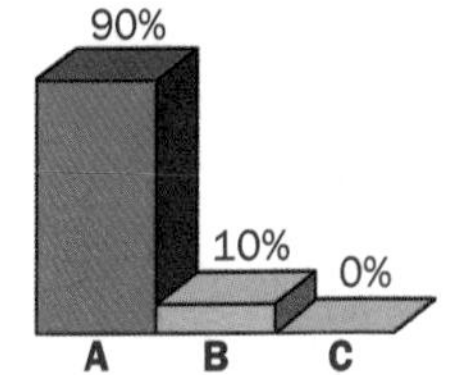

A = Have never heard the gospel
B = Were evangelized but did not become Christians
C = Are adherents to any form of Christianity

Nisu, Jianshui 尼苏(建水)

Population in China:
361,000 (1999)
370,200 (2000)
464,600 (2010)
Location: Yunnan
Religion: Polytheism
Christians: 400

Overview of the Jianshui Nisu

Countries: China

Pronunciation: "Nee-soo-Jee-uhn-shway"

Other Names: San Dao Hong, Neisu, Niesu, Nisu, Nisupo, Lolo, Luo, Luoluo, Luozu, Yizu

Population Source: 361,000 (1999 J. Pelkey); Out of a total Yi population of 6,572,173 (1990 census)

Location: *S Yunnan:* Jianshui (130,000), Shiping (110,500), Gejiu (54,700), and Mengzi (53,000) counties of Honghe Prefecture; Tonghai and Eshan counties in Yuxi Prefecture (13,000)

Status: Officially included under Yi

Language: Sino-Tibetan, Tibeto-Burman, Burmese-Lolo, Lolo, Northern Lolo, Yi, Southern Yi

Dialects: 0

Religion: Polytheism, Animism, Ancestor Worship, Shamanism, Christianity

Christians: 400

Scripture: None

***Jesus* film:** None

Gospel Recordings: None

Christian Broadcasting: None

ROPAL code: None

Status of Evangelization

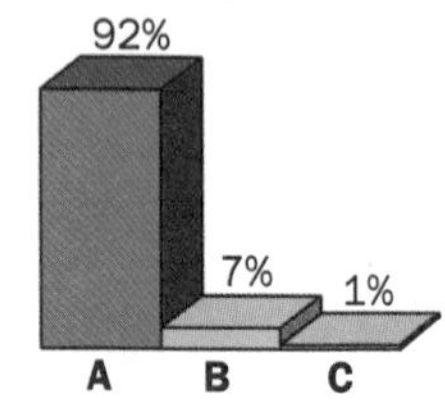

A = Have never heard the gospel
B = Were evangelized but did not become Christians
C = Are adherents to any form of Christianity

Location: Approximately 370,000 Jianshui Nisu people are located in southern Yunnan Province, primarily in Shiping, Jianshui, Gejiu, and Mengzi counties in Honghe Prefecture. About 13,000 live in Tonghai and Eshan counties of Yuxi Prefecture.

Identity: The Jianshui Nisu are part of the Yi nationality in China. Chinese records invariably mention two designations of Nisu in this part of the country: *Hua Yao* (Flowery Belt) and *San Dao Hong* (Three Stripes of Red). As one scholar found: "The Han titles are used in reference to costume differences; nevertheless, in this case, clothing styles correspond directly with the linguistic and cultural differences of two people groups — both of whom call themselves *Nisu*.... Garment differences vary among some of the Jianshui Nisu in Gejiu and Mengzi counties, however, and the title *San Dao Hong* is not always used to refer to this people."[1]

Language: The Jianshui Nisu language — which has about 20 vowels and 30 consonants — belongs to the Southern Yi linguistic branch. Jianshui Nisu is perhaps the oldest Southern Yi language. An ancient pictographic script of about 20,000 characters survives, 3,600 of which were commonly used. Today only a few *bimos*, or shamans, are still able to use the script for rituals. A 30-minute Jianshui Nisu radio broadcast is aired three times daily by the government station in Gejiu.

History: The Jianshui Nisu have been a dominant group in southern Yunnan for many centuries. Only during the past century have a small number of Jianshui Nisu been assimilated by Han Chinese who have settled in the area.[2]

Customs: Women of this group living in Jianshui and Shiping counties wear three tightly wound stripes of red yarn in their hair, often partially covered by a red or white headdress. In Shiping County, "the family of the bride is to make a new costume to present to the bride on her wedding day. She is to keep this set of garments until the day she dies. The bride, in turn, makes a pair of pants from coarse cloth, with the leg holes sewn closed, and presents them to her groom on the wedding day. The groom, much to his chagrin, must put the pants on in front of all his guests during the wedding ceremony. The party judges the groom's intelligence based on how soon he is able to break his feet through the cuffs and put the pants on."[3]

Religion: The Jianshui Nisu worship numerous spirits, some of whom are considered benevolent and others evil.

Christianity: The first missionaries in Jianshui arrived in 1933 and stayed for two years. In 1945 a Presbyterian work began in Jianshui and was joined by two Italian missionaries. By 1950 there were a reported 200 Christians in Jianshui — all of them Han Chinese.[4] In Shiping, a female missionary from the Seventh Day Adventists arrived in 1932. After a number of years she had gained about 30 disciples. All missionaries were expelled in 1949, but by 1958 there were still 50 believers in Shiping.[5] Today there are a small number of Nisu Christians in the Gaoda District of Tonghai County.[6]

Jamin Pelkey

Nisu, Xinping 尼苏(新平)

Jamin Pelkey

Location: More than 190,000 speakers of Xinping Nisu live in Xinping, Yuxi, Eshan, Yuanjiang, Jiangchuan, and Yimen counties of Yuxi Prefecture (143,400); Anning and Jinning Counties of Kunming Municipality (18,000); and Shiping County in Honghe Prefecture (31,000).[1] These locations are all within China's Yunnan Province.

Identity: Although the Xinping Nisu are officially included as part of the Yi nationality, they wear different dress, speak a distinct dialect from all other Yi groups, and possess their own self-identity. The Chinese call this group *Huayao Yi* (Flower Belt Yi) in reference to the clothing worn by the women. The Xinping Nisu in some areas call themselves *Tuli*, but they speak the same dialect as other Xinping Nisu.

Language: Xinping Nisu, which is mutually unintelligible with the other Nisu languages in southern China, is part of the Southern Yi language family. It has no written script.

History: Different Yi groups, including the Xinping Nisu, have developed their own identity and customs after centuries of isolation from each other.

Customs: Unmarried Xinping Nisu women wear gorgeous cockscomb hats made of wool tassels and silver bubbles. A legend states that there were once two Nisu villages in the Honghe area that were constantly harassed by an evil spirit. The demon was defeated by magic when a rooster crowed.[2] Of the many festivals observed by the Nisu in Yunnan, the one that takes place on the slopes of the Mopan Mountain in Xinping County is considered the greatest. When a Nisu girl turns 15 or 16 she is said to have entered the "spring time" of her life. When this time has come, her family sends her into the mountains with a selected boy from her village. The two pick a selection of beautiful flowers and grass and return home. The girl arranges a large structure of flowers on the roof of her house. When she has finished, her mother places a special headdress on her head and jewelry on her wrists. She also adorns herself with necklaces and earrings, and wears a special belt around her waist. Then her family and friends hold a ceremony where they drink wine and sing the following song: "Springtime has come to the mountains, The flowers are opening and the birds are beautiful on the hills; The young birds are flying away from their nests.... Springtime has come to this young maiden, She has blossomed and is beautiful; She too must leave her old home."[3]

Religion: Roosters are held in great reverence and are even worshiped by the Xinping Nisu. They also believe the spirits of dragons and the ox can protect them.

Christianity: Although an attempt by the China Inland Mission to reach the Tuli (a subgroup of the Xinping Nisu) apparently ended in failure,[4] there are a few known Xinping Nisu Christians in Yuanjiang County today. A 1989 study listed 528 Yi Christians in Yuxi Prefecture, of which 55% were in Yuanjiang County.[5] Most of these are probably Xinping Nisu.

Population in China:
192,400 (1999)
197,300 (2000)
247,600 (2010)
Location: Yunnan
Religion: Polytheism
Christians: 1,000

Overview of the Xinping Nisu

Countries: China
Pronunciation: "Shin-ping-Nee-soo"
Other Names: Huayao Yi, Flowery Belt Yi, Flowery Waist Yi, Hua Yao Yi, Nisu, Nisupuo, Tuli, Tuli Yi, Tuly, Niesu, Neisu
Population Source: 192,400 (1999 J. Pelkey); Out of a total Yi population of 6,572,173 (1990 census)
Location: *Yunnan:* Xinping (37,800), Yuxi (31,500), Eshan (28,900), Yuanjiang (28,000), Jiangchuan (12,700), and Yimen (4,500) counties of Yuxi Prefecture (143,400); Anning and Jinning (18,000) counties of Kunming Municipality; Shiping County (31,000) of Honghe Prefecture
Status: Officially included under Yi
Language: Sino-Tibetan, Tibeto-Burman, Burmese-Lolo, Lolo, Northern Lolo, Yi, Southern Yi
Dialects: 0
Religion: Polytheism, Animism, Christianity
Christians: 1,000
Scripture: None
***Jesus* film:** None
Gospel Recordings: Yi: Nisu #04976
Christian Broadcasting: None
ROPAL code: None

Status of Evangelization

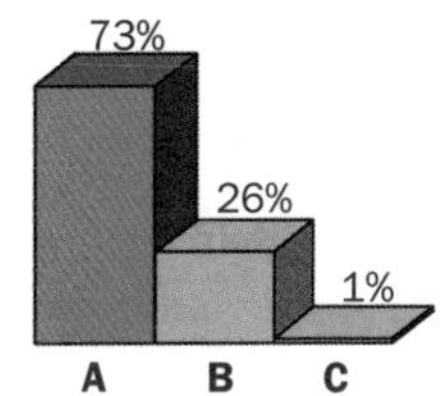

A = Have never heard the gospel
B = Were evangelized but did not become Christians
C = Are adherents to any form of Christianity

Nisu, Yuanyang 尼苏(元阳)

Population in China:
199,200 (1999)
204,200 (2000)
256,300 (2010)
Location: Yunnan
Religion: Polytheism
Christians: 2,000

Overview of the Yuanyang Nisu

Countries: China
Pronunciation: "Nee-soo-Yoo-ahn-yung"
Other Names: Neisu, Niesu, Nosu, Nisu, Nisupo, Hei Yi, Luoluo, Lolo, Nuosu
Population Source: 199,200 (1999 J. Pelkey); Out of a total Yi population of 6,572,173 (1990 census)
Location: *S Yunnan:* Yuanyang (83,300), Honghe (29,100), Jinping (11,600), Luchun (10,200), and Yuanjiang (2,000) counties of Honghe Prefecture; Mojiang (37,000), Jiangcheng (8,000), Pu'er (8,000), and Simao (10,000) counties of Simao Prefecture
Status: Officially included under Yi
Language: Sino-Tibetan, Tibeto-Burman, Burmese-Lolo, Lolo, Northern Lolo, Yi, Southern Yi
Dialects: 0
Religion: Polytheism, Animism, Shamanism, Christianity
Christians: 2,000
Scripture: New Testament 1948; Portions 1913
***Jesus* film:** None
Gospel Recordings: None
Christian Broadcasting: None
ROPAL code: None

Status of Evangelization

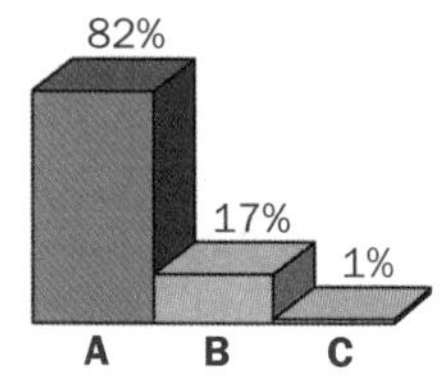

A = Have never heard the gospel
B = Were evangelized but did not become Christians
C = Are adherents to any form of Christianity

Paul Hattaway

Location: More than 200,000 Yuanyang Nisu live in southern Yunnan. Some 135,000 inhabit areas south of the Honghe River in Yuanyang, Honghe, Jinping, Yuanjiang, and Luchun counties.[1] Others live in Mojiang, Jiangcheng, Pu'er, and Simao counties.

Identity: The Yuanyang Nisu are different from the other Nisu groups in southern China because of dialect differences and cultural variation. They have been included in the official Yi nationality by the Chinese authorities.

Language: Yuanyang Nisu is part of the Southern Yi branch of the Tibeto-Burman language family. The linguistic complexity of Yi groups in southern Yunnan has created obstacles to the Chinese government's attempts to introduce a Roman script. An orthography has been created, but speakers from groups like the Yuanyang Nisu use different vocabulary from the standard that was selected. The result is that the script has gained acceptance only in the area where it was produced.

History: The Yuanyang Nisu are believed to have migrated into their present areas from locations to the north, such as Yuanjiang, Shiping, and Jianshui, during the Ming and Qing dynasties (1368–1911). Because of their geographic dispersion, their dialect and customs gradually evolved so that today this group should be considered distinct from other Nisu groups in China.

Customs: Unmarried Yuanyang Nisu girls wear cockscomb headdresses. Each hat contains as many as 1,200 silver beads. Even after marriage, Yuanyang Nisu women take pride in their clothing. Their headdresses are richly embroidered with laces that encircle the neck and flow down onto the back.

Religion: The Yuanyang Nisu are polytheistic animists. "They feel the need to appease many gods and ward off many forms of evil. On the first 'rat day' of the year, Yuanyang Nisu in some areas appoint one family from each village to appease the 'god of the path'. Two chickens are sacrificed at every path of entrance into the village. They construct crosses made of bamboo strips and fasten the chickens' heads, wings and feet to the crosses with rope. Having done so, the bloody crosses are erected at the gate of each village to ward off evil. Finally, the family in charge of the ritual chant the following spell: 'One mountain, one village, one village guardian, one village leader and all of the families under him — one path and all the doors along it — may the god of the path protect the paths to all the doors, may all the demons be frightened away. If we have succeeded, then come to our aid. We have worshipped you with a meat sacrifice; if you are satisfied then be our guardian from this day forward.'"[2]

Christianity: There are about 2,000 Catholic and Protestant believers among the Yuanyang Nisu in Yuanyang County and surrounding areas.[3] Missionaries translated Scripture portions into Yanyuang Nisu in 1913 and the entire New Testament in 1948, but the script used is now obsolete.

150

151

152

153

150–151. The small *Oroqen* minority, who live in China's far northeast, worship the bear and the tiger. The Oroqen are also renowned as great hunters and fishermen. [both by Midge Conner]

152. The Buddhist *Oirat* are ethnic Mongolians living in the Muslim-dominated northwest China. [Midge Conner]

153. Even though the *Nu* live in one of the most remote parts of China, missionaries reached out to them prior to 1949. Today, about 4,000 *Nu* are Christians. [Midge Conner]

154

155

156

157

154. A *Nu* woman, Nujiang River valley, Yunnan. [Paul Hattaway]
155. Despite numbering close to 30,000, the unreached *Puwa* of southern Yunnan Province are not known by many people outside of their area. [Jamin Pelkey]
156. This woman is from one of several small *Miao* ethnic groups in Duyun, Guizhou, who have yet to be officially classified. [Paul Hattaway]
157. A *Central Luoluopo* mother and child, Chuxiong, Yunnan. [Jamin Pelkey]

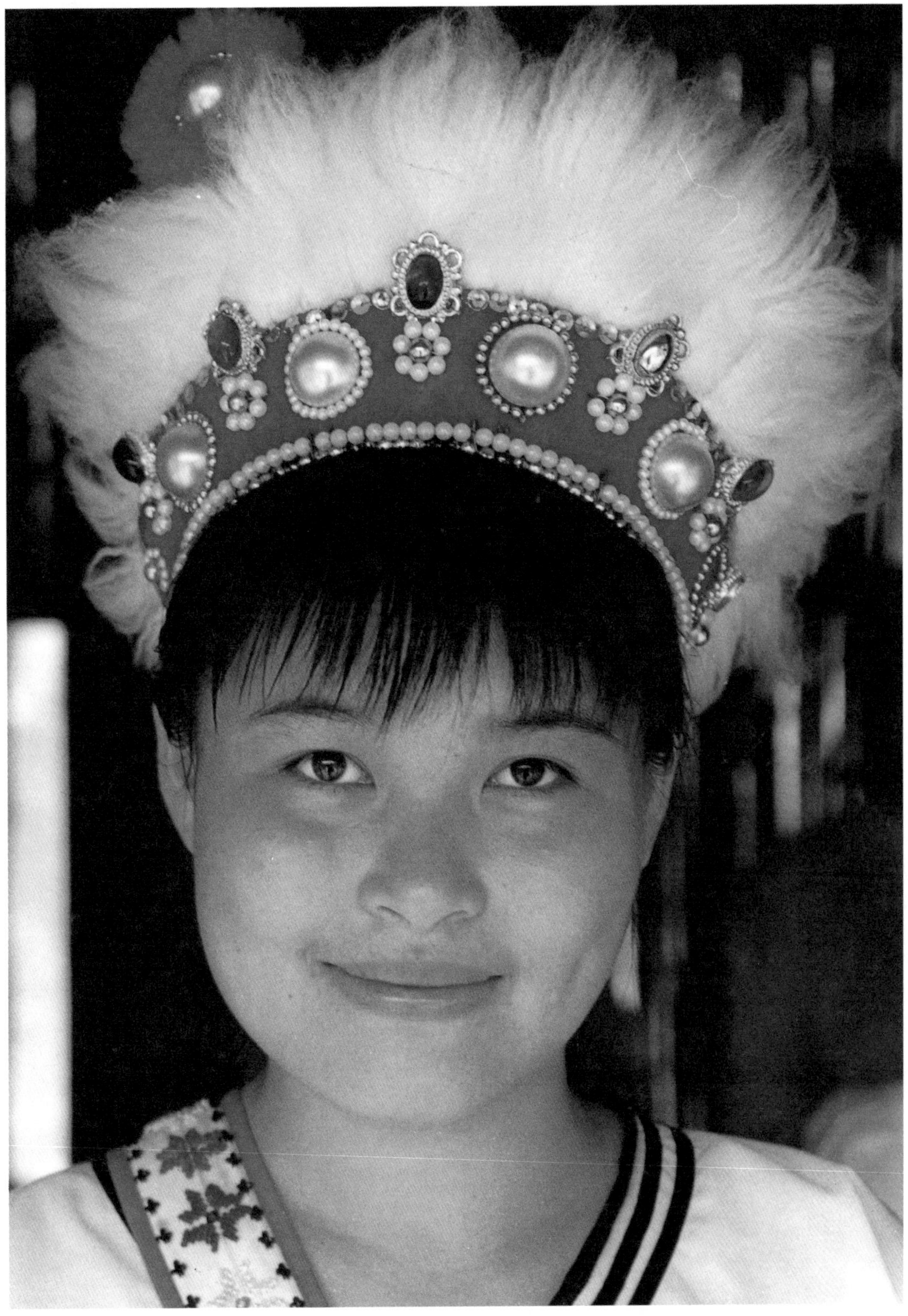

158. The *Paiwan* are one of three tribes in Fujian combined to form the official Gaoshan nationality in China. Others live in major Chinese cities such as Shanghai, Beijing, and Tianjian. Although numbering only several hundred people in mainland China, more than 80,000 Paiwan live in Taiwan. [Paul Hattaway]

159

160

161

162

159–160. The 37,000 *Pumi* live on the mountaintops of northern Yunnan. [159 Paul Hattaway; 160 Luke Kuepfer]
161–162. The beautiful costumes of the small *Paiwan* tribe, near Zhangzhou, Fujian. [both by Paul Hattaway]

Nosu, Butuo 诺苏(布拖)

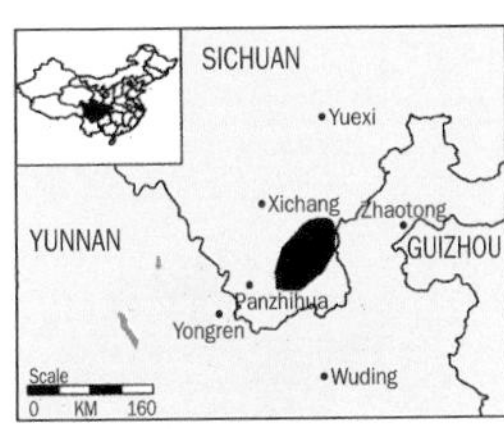

Population in China:
200,000 (1998)
210,200 (2000)
263,800 (2010)
Location: Sichuan
Religion: Polytheism
Christians: 200

Overview of the Butuo Nosu

Countries: China

Pronunciation: "Boo-twoh-Nor-soo"

Other Names: Pu-t'o Yi, Butuo Yi, East-Lower-Northern Yi, Boo Yi

Population Source: 200,000 (1998 J. Matisoff); Out of a total Yi population of 6,572,173 (1990 census)

Location: *S Sichuan:* Butuo, Puge, Ningnan, Huidong, and Huili counties

Status: Officially included under Yi

Language: Sino-Tibetan, Tibeto-Burman, Burmese-Lolo, Lolo, Northern Lolo, Yi, Northern Yi

Dialects: 0

Religion: Polytheism, Animism, Ancestor Worship, Christianity

Christians: 200

Scripture: None

***Jesus* film:** None

Gospel Recordings: None

Christian Broadcasting: None

ROPAL code: None

Status of Evangelization

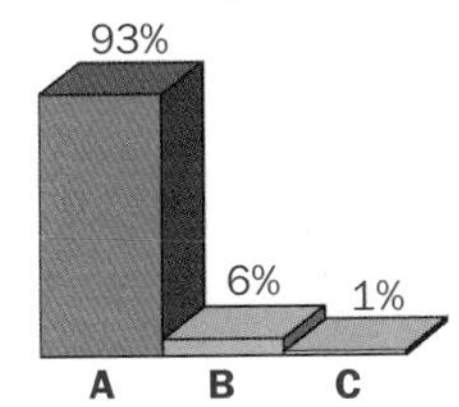

A = Have never heard the gospel
B = Were evangelized but did not become Christians
C = Are adherents to any form of Christianity

Location: According to Professor James Matisoff, who heads up the Department of Tibeto-Burman Linguistic Studies at the University of California at Berkeley, there are "about 200,000 speakers"[1] of the Butuo Nosu language in southern Sichuan Province. Their name comes from their primary location, Butuo County. Others are found across parts of Puge, Ningnan, Huidong, and Huili counties. The Butuo Nosu live at the southern end of the Daliangshan (Big Cold Mountains).

Identity: The Butuo Nosu are a distinct language group within the larger Nosu ethnicity. The Nosu, in turn, have been officially counted as part of the Yi nationality by Chinese authorities. The Butuo Nosu share very little in common with other Yi groups in Yunnan, Guizhou, and Guangxi, except for some legends and general cultural traits. In many locations the Butuo Nosu live alongside the Suodi.

Language: Butuo Nosu is considered a variety of Northern Yi, most closely related to Suodi, Shengzha Nosu, and Xiaoliangshan Nosu. Speakers of Butuo Nosu have only limited mutual intelligibility with these other languages. After being in contact with other Nosu speakers for a few weeks they pick up more vocabulary, but at the start communication is very difficult and speakers from different Nosu groups often have to revert to Chinese in order to understand each other.

History: The Butuo Nosu originally lived farther north of their present location. Speaking of a neighboring area in northern Yunnan Province, one historian notes, "Between 1796 and 1821, the Chinese extended their influence.... At times when the Chinese were weak, the [Nosu] expanded out of Daliangshan: for example in 1802, 1814, 1838–39, and from 1875 to 1892. By 1907, the Nosu controlled most areas, with the Chinese fortified in the towns. During the troubled times of the early Republic, the number of Chinese troops was reduced in the area, and the Nosu consequently became more troublesome: in 1919, they invaded Zhaojue, in 1920 they burned Xining, and in 1937 they killed the magistrate of Leibo."[2]

Customs: The Butuo Nosu pride themselves on being tough, residual, and aggressive people. Their homes and villages are constructed with high fences, a sign of their violent and murderous past.

Religion: The Butuo Nosu practice a complex form of polytheism. They fear and appease numerous mountain deities and spirits of war, harvests, and rivers, among others. They tie these beliefs in with deep reverence for their ancestors.

Christianity: The Butuo Nosu are a large, unreached people group. There are a few hundred Catholics among them, mostly elderly people who meet in Chinese-language churches. It is not known if the recent turning to Christ by 12,000 Nosu farther north has impacted the Butuo Nosu. Nosu audio tapes and the *Jesus* film are not understood by most Butuo Nosu.

Paul Hattaway

Nosu, Mangbu 诺苏(芒部)

Location: More than 65,000 Mangbu Nosu live in the northeastern part of Yunnan Province and in the adjoining areas of Hezhang County in Guizhou Province. The majority of Mangbu Nosu (48,800) live in the southern and central areas of Zhenxiong County in the Zhaotong Prefecture of Yunnan Province. More than 2,000 also live in the mountains of Weixin County.[1]

Identity: Although they have been officially included under the Yi nationality by the Chinese authorities, the Mangbu Nosu possess their own ethnicity, history, and language. This group calls itself *Nosu* (Black People). Mangbu is the name of a town in Zhenxiong County which is the geographic center of the Mangbu Nosu. One source states that "Mangbu is an ancient tribal name."[2]

Language: Mangbu Nosu is part of the Eastern Yi group of Tibeto-Burman languages. It is reportedly most closely related to the Shuixi Nosu, Wusa Nasu, and Wumeng languages. Mangbu Nosu is still used vigorously and is spoken in the home.

History: In the past, the Mangbu Nosu were one of six powerful tribes who ruled over the region. This alliance rejected Chinese rule of the area, which resulted in centuries of conflict and war between the Nosu and the various Chinese armies that were sent to subdue them. Today, the Mangbu Nosu long for their former glory, but they realize they have no chance of overpowering the Chinese. They view themselves as a defeated people.

Customs: Hatred between the Nosu and the Chinese fighters reached such a fever pitch that both sides resorted to cannibalism. Missionary Samuel Pollard, writing in the early 1900s, stated, "A sort of cannibalism is practiced in this area by both Chinese and Nosu. After a fight the warriors who are killed on either side are opened and their hearts removed, perhaps also their tongues, and these are cooked and eaten. It is supposed to be a way of inheriting the courage and valor of the deceased."[3]

Jamin Pelkey

Religion: Polytheism is the stronghold of the Mangbu Nosu. As a result, fewer Mangbu Nosu have believed in Christ than among other Yi groups in the area. Pollard recorded a sample of the resistance he experienced in 1905: "We crossed the sides of a big mountain... and finally arrived at the fort of a Nosu landlord called Loh-chig. He received us kindly and we stayed there the night, but he is a very unusual local baron. He told us straight he would rather lose his head than become a Christian. He refused all gifts of books, disputed all we said and denied all our attempts to win him over. He stuck up strongly for his religion and defended the worship of idols with great zest."[4]

Christianity: Although most Mangbu Nosu have refused to consider the gospel, there are about 1,000 believers among them, especially in Hezhang County of Guizhou. Villages there are often divided along religious lines, with Christians forced to live in separate communities.

Population in China:
65,200 (1999)
66,800 (2000)
83,900 (2010)
Location: Yunnan, Guizhou
Religion: Polytheism
Christians: 1,000

Overview of the Mangbu Nosu

Countries: China

Pronunciation: "Mung-boo-Nor-soo"

Other Names: Nosu, Mang-pu Yi, Mangbu Yi, Nuosu, Hei Yi, Black Yi, Bai Yi, White Yi

Population Source: 65,200 (1999 AMO); 50,900 in Yunnan (1999 J. Pelkey); Out of a total Yi population of 6,572,173 (1990 census)

Location: *NE Yunnan:* Zhenxiong (48,800) and Weixin (2,100) counties; *NW Guizhou:* Hezhang County (14,300)

Status: Officially included under Yi

Language: Sino-Tibetan, Tibeto-Burman, Burmese-Lolo, Lolo, Northern Lolo, Yi, Eastern Yi

Dialects: 0

Religion: Polytheism, Animism, Ancestor Worship, Christianity

Christians: 1,000

Scripture: None

***Jesus* film:** None

Gospel Recordings: None

Christian Broadcasting: None

ROPAL code: None

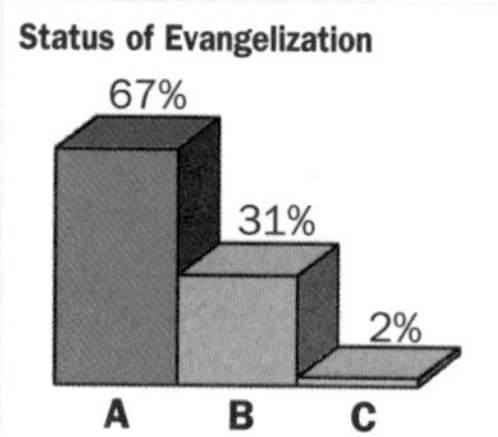

A = Have never heard the gospel
B = Were evangelized but did not become Christians
C = Are adherents to any form of Christianity

Nosu, Shengzha 诺苏(大凉山)

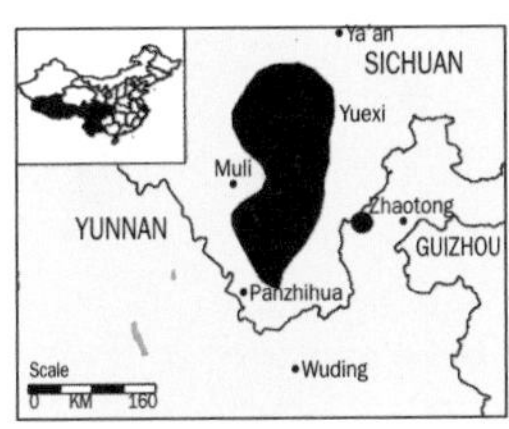

Population in China:
800,000 (1989)
1,024,400 (2000)
1,285,600 (2010)
Location:
Sichuan, Yunnan, Tibet
Religion: Polytheism
Christians: 12,000

Overview of the Shengzha Nosu

Countries: China, USA
Pronunciation:
"Shung-jah-Nor-soo"
Other Names: Northern Yi, Sichuan Yi, Lolo, North Lolo, Black Yi, Manchia, Mantzu, Naso, Nuosu, Daliangshan Nosu, Shengcha Yi, Shengzha Yi
Population Source:
800,000 (1989 Shi Songshan);
Out of a total Yi population of 6,572,173 (1990 census);
45 in USA[1]
Location: *S Sichuan:* Daliangshan Yi Autonomous Prefecture; *NE Yunnan:* Lushui and Zhaotong counties; *SE Tibet*
Status:
Officially included under Yi
Language: Sino-Tibetan, Tibeto-Burman, Burmese-Lolo, Lolo, Northern Lolo, Yi, Northern Yi
Dialects (1): Xide
Religion: Polytheism, Shamanism, Animism, Ancestor Worship, Daoism, Christianity
Christians: 12,000
Scripture: Portions 1913; Gospel tracts 1996
***Jesus* film:** Available
Gospel Recordings:
Yi: Sichuan #04671
Christian Broadcasting: None
ROPAL code: III00

Status of Evangelization

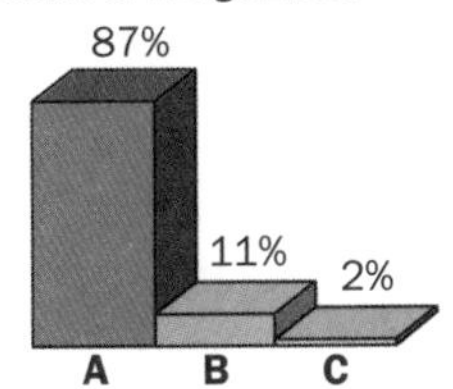

A = Have never heard the gospel
B = Were evangelized but did not become Christians
C = Are adherents to any form of Christianity

Paul Hattaway

Location: More than one million speakers of Shengzha Nosu live in southern Sichuan Province.[2] Their primary locations are in Xide, Yuexi, Zhaojue, Ganluo, and Jinyang counties. Other significant communities are in Puge, Leibo, Xichang, Dechang, Mianning, Yanyuan, and Yanbian counties; while small numbers can be found in Muli, Shimian, Jiulong, and Luding counties.[3] A few Shengzha Nosu spill over into northeast Yunnan and into southeastern areas of Tibet.

Identity: The name *Nosu* means "black people." Many early travelers who came into contact with the Nosu remarked on the beauty and Caucasian features of the Nosu women. One described them as "a black branch of the Caucasian race."[4] The Daliangshan area has a great level of ethnic complexity. A 1983 official government report seems to lament "44 Nosu subgroups with different self-designations and obscure dialects."[5] Another publication written by Chinese scholars mentions "more than 100 patriarchal clans in the Daliangshan alone,... independent of each other and with their own area of jurisdiction."[6]

Language: The Nosu possess an ancient pictographic syllabic script. It was mainly used by religious leaders prior to 1950,[7] but in recent years it has been taught to whole villages of Nosu.

History: Nosu history is one of violence and interclan warfare. For centuries the Nosu raided villages and took slaves, forcing them to do manual labor. One missionary noted, "In retaliation for the taking of slaves, it was not uncommon in the 1940s to see Chinese soldiers walking through city streets carrying on their backs large baskets filled with Nosu heads, still dripping with blood."[8] The Nosu region, in 1956, was the last part of China to come under Communist rule. In the violent clashes ten Chinese troops were killed for every Nosu, earning the Nosu the nickname, "Iron Peas."[9] Since the collapse of the slave system, the class structure among the Nosu has weakened. Today even the former Bai Yi slaves "tease and mock [the Nosu]... who are mockingly called princes and princesses."[10]

Customs: Early literature on the Nosu called them *Lolo*, in reference to the small basket they carried around with them which supposedly contained the souls of their dead ancestors.[11]

Religion: The Shengzha Nosu believe in Mo'm Apu, a supreme creator spirit who controls the universe. His son, Gee Nyo, gives rain, prosperity, and happiness.[12]

Christianity: Mission work among the Shengzha Nosu began in the late 1800s, but resulted in few conversions.[13] In the mid-1940s China Inland Mission worker James Broomhall tried to mobilize Yi Christians from Yunnan to evangelize the Nosu, but they could not adjust to the differences in language and culture.[14] After more than a century of labor and prayer, a breakthrough occurred in 1996 when 18 Nosu leaders of the Mentu Hui cult heard and believed the gospel. They publicly renounced the cult and by mid-1997 had led 12,000 Shengzha Nosu to faith in Christ.[15]

Nosu, Shuixi 诺苏(水西)

Jamin Pelkey

Location: Approximately 230,000 Shuixi Nosu live in the mountains of southern China. The majority are found in northern Guizhou Province, especially Bijie, Qianxi, Jinsha, Dafang, Zhijin, Nayong, and Qingzhen counties. An additional 20,900 Shuixi Nosu live in Zhenxiong County of Yunnan Province,[1] while a small number spill across the border into Gulin County of Sichuan Province.

Identity: This group calls itself *Nosu*. The loconym *Shuixi* has been added to distinguish them from the several other groups in southern China who call themselves Nosu, but who speak different languages from the Shuixi Nosu.

Language: Shuixi Nosu is part of the Eastern Yi group of languages. It is mutually unintelligible with other Nosu varieties in China, most of which are Northern Yi languages. Some old Shuixi Nosu men, former or present shamans, are able to read the traditional Yi orthography.

History: The Shuixi Nosu have migrated farther northeast than any other Yi group in southern China. Their migrations occurred as they fled Chinese military aggression.

Customs: Until 1949 many of the Shuixi Nosu owned large estates. In the early 1900s, Samuel Clarke reported they were "as big as an English county, and all the people on the estate are their tenants. The lairds are all of them Black Nosu, and the White Nosu are their slaves or serfs. These lairds are nearly all related to one another, as they constantly intermarry for the sake of joining and enlarging their estates. A Nosu heiress is always pestered and sometimes actually besieged by suitors. A laird always marries the daughter of some other laird, as there is but a limited number of them, this constant intermarriage has doubtless contributed to the decadence of the race and to the frequency of lunacy among them. They may, and often do, have Chinese and Miao women as concubines.... The lairds are glad to have the Miao as tenants; the rent they pay is mostly in kind, and not by any means high. As a matter of fact, the tenants, for the sake of mutual protection, group themselves in hamlets and villages. Besides the nominal rent they pay, the laird has the right to make levies on them on special occasions, such as funerals, weddings, and when he has litigation in the Chinese courts."[2]

Religion: The Shuixi Nosu have many gods and deities who, they feel, need to be frequently appeased in order to bring peace and prosperity to their communities.

Christianity: Today there are about 5,000 Shuixi Nosu Christians in China, mostly in the Dafang and Nayong counties of Guizhou Province. Many Shuixi Nosu have heard the gospel from the A-Hmao and Gha-Mu — two Miao groups who live intermingled with the Shuixi Nosu. On 2 July 1910, the famous missionary Samuel Pollard recorded in his diary: "Today I saw a miracle. At this lonely place of Ssu-fang-ching the Church was full of Nosu, and at their request Chang-yo-han was preaching to them. The proud Nosu listening to one of their Miao serfs."[3]

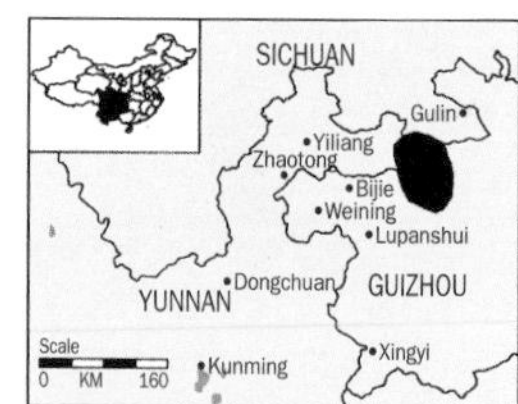

Population in China:
229,000 (1999)
234,800 (2000)
294,700 (2010)
Location:
Guizhou, Yunnan, Sichuan
Religion: Polytheism
Christians: 5,000

Overview of the Shuixi Nosu

Countries: China

Pronunciation: "Shway-shee-Nor-soo"

Other Names: Shuixi, Shuixi Yi, Shui-hsi Nosu, Bijie Yi, Dafang Yi, Qianxi Yi, Black Nosu

Population Source: 229,000 (1999 AMO); 20,900 in Yunnan (1999 J. Pelkey); Out of a total Yi population of 6,572,173 (1990 census)

Location: *NW Guizhou:* Bijie, Qianxi, Jinsha, Dafang, Zhijin, Nayong, and Qingzhen counties; *NE Yunnan:* Zhenxiong County; *SE Sichuan:* Gulin County

Status: Officially included under Yi

Language: Sino-Tibetan, Tibeto-Burman, Burmese-Lolo, Lolo, Northern Lolo, Yi, Eastern Yi

Dialects (3): Bijie, Dafang, Qianxi

Religion: Polytheism, Shamanism, Animism, Christianity

Christians: 5,000

Scripture: None

***Jesus* film:** None

Gospel Recordings: None

Christian Broadcasting: None

ROPAL code: None

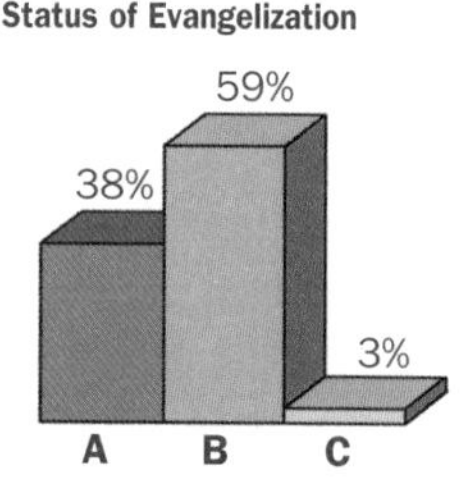

A = Have never heard the gospel
B = Were evangelized but did not become Christians
C = Are adherents to any form of Christianity

Nosu, Tianba 诺苏(天巴)

Location: More than 80,000 speakers of the Tianba Nosu language live in southern Sichuan Province.[1] The Tianba Nosu are the northernmost Yi group in China. They live at the northern end of the Daliangshan Mountains, primarily in Ganluo, Yuexi, and Ebian counties. Smaller numbers of Tianba Nosu live in Hanyuan County. Their territory stops at the central Sichuan plain where the population is completely Han Chinese.

Identity: The clothing and ethnic identity of the Tianba Nosu is similar to the Yinuo Nosu, but the two groups speak different languages and mutual communication is difficult. The Tianba Nosu are part of the Yi nationality.

Language: Tianba Nosu is part of the Northern Yi branch of the Tibeto-Burman family. It has also been heavily influenced by Chinese.

History: Violent conflict, intertribal and interclan warfare, and the taking of slaves were commonplace among the various branches of the Nosu until recently. When preparing for war, clear rules were followed by the Tianba Nosu. These included "sending out a wooden tablet calling on all members of the clan, its tenants, serfs, and slaves to assemble; each family would assent by making a mark on the tablet; tallying the marks would indicate how large a fighting force might be expected. War costumes were extremely colorful: some wore hats of woven bamboo covered with white cloth, thin woolen felts and yellow satin, with animal hair that would wave in the wind; they would carefully prepare their hair, interweaving it with a strip of cloth and tying it into a horn just above the forehead; some would cap this with a sheep horn wrapped in colorful silk and red pompons.... The Yi [Nosu] would run forward, shout out their names, and challenge their enemies to fight. The War songs were equally awe-inspiring: 'We are the famous Black Nosu! We are the tigers who eat up human flesh! We are the butchers who skin people alive! We are the supermen!'"[2]

Midge Conner

Customs: The Tianba Nosu have been influenced by Chinese culture more than the other Nosu groups in Sichuan, although they still retain their traditional dress and most of their ceremonies and customs.

Religion: The religious world of the Tianba Nosu is a complicated mixture of polytheism, animism, and ancestor worship. Because of Chinese influence, elements of Buddhism and Daoism are also present.

Christianity: There are no known Christian believers among the Tianba Nosu today. Catholic Father Baptistin Biron worked at Mabian, on the edge of the Tianba Nosu, in the early 1930s. "All seemed to be in place and orderly, with every necessary precaution taken. But then a few Lolos [Nosu], controlled by another chief, possibly irked that Biron had not come to live in his territory, argued with the priest and killed him... a victim of the savage Lolos."[3]

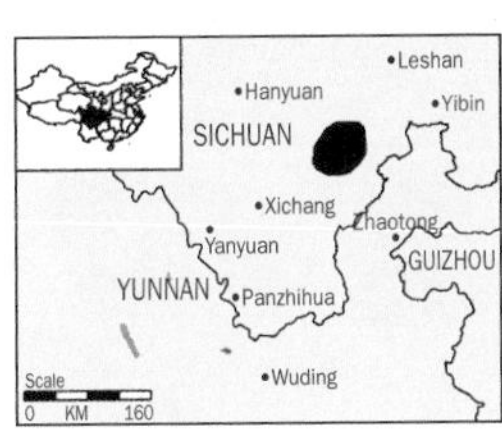

Population in China:
80,000 (1998)
84,080 (2000)
105,520 (2010)
Location: Sichuan
Religion: Polytheism
Christians: None Known

Overview of the Tianba Nosu

Countries: China

Pronunciation: "Tee-en-bah-Nor-soo"

Other Names: Tianba Yi, Tianba, T'ien-pa Yi

Population Source: 80,000 (1998 J. Matisoff); Out of a total Yi population of 6,572,173 (1990 census)

Location: *S Sichuan:* Ganluo, Yuexi, Hanyuan, and Ebian counties

Status: Officially included under Yi

Language: Sino-Tibetan, Tibeto-Burman, Burmese-Lolo, Lolo, Northern Lolo, Yi, Northern Yi

Dialects: 0

Religion: Polytheism, Animism, Ancestor Worship, Buddhism, Daoism

Christians: None known

Scripture: None

***Jesus* film:** None

Gospel Recordings: None

Christian Broadcasting: None

ROPAL code: None

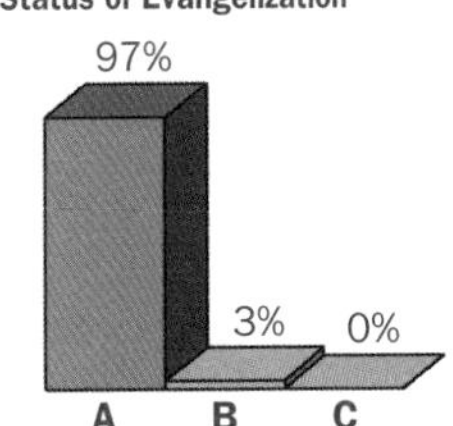

Nosu, Xiaoliangshan 诺苏(小凉山)

September 13

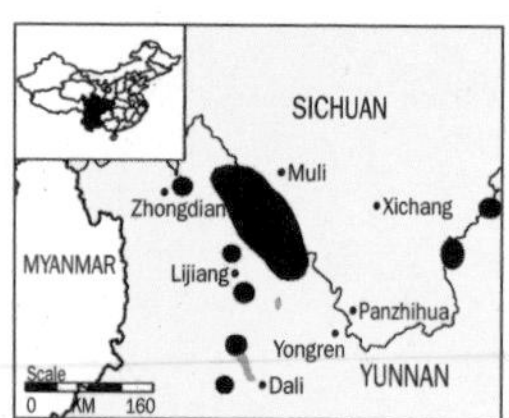

Population in China:
330,000 (1987)
439,400 (2000)
511,400 (2010)
Location: Yunnan, Sichuan
Religion: Polytheism
Christians: 100

Overview of the Xiaoliangshan Nosu

Countries: China

Pronunciation: "Shaow-leung-shan-Nor-soo"

Other Names: Lalaw, Green Yi, Xiaoliangshan Yi, Nuosu, Nosupo, Nisupo, Hei Yi, Black Yi

Population Source: 330,000 (1987 D. Bradley); 220,000 in Yunnan (1999 J. Pelkey); Out of a total Yi population of 6,572,173 (1990 census)

Location: *N Yunnan:* Ninglang (129,000), Yongsheng (16,000), Qiaojia (13,000), Eryuan (10,000), Zhongdian (8,900), Heqing (8,000), Yongshan (8,000), Lanping (5,500), Yangbi, Yunlong, Lijiang, and Weixi counties; *S Sichuan*

Status: Officially included under Yi

Language: Sino-Tibetan, Tibeto-Burman, Burmese-Lolo, Lolo, Northern Lolo, Yi, Northern Yi

Dialects: 0

Religion: Polytheism, Animism, Ancestor Worship, Christianity

Christians: 100

Scripture: None

***Jesus* film:** None

Gospel Recordings: None

Christian Broadcasting: None

ROPAL code: None

Status of Evangelization

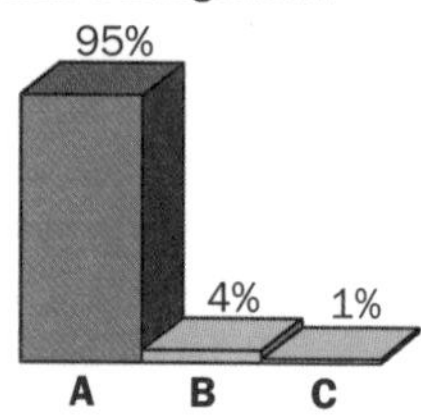

A = Have never heard the gospel
B = Were evangelized but did not become Christians
C = Are adherents to any form of Christianity

Location: More than 439,000 people belonging to the Xiaoliangshan Nosu group inhabit twelve widespread counties in the northwest and northeastern parts of Yunnan Province,[1] including Lijiang,[2] Dali, Zhongdian, Deqen, Weixi, Huaping, Yongsheng, Ninglang, and Yuanmou. In some locations the Xiaoliangshan Nosu live alongside the Bai, Naxi, Pumi, and Tibetans. The Xiaoliangshan Nosu also spill across into areas of southern Sichuan Province.

Identity: The Xiaoliangshan Nosu are ethnolinguistically related to the Shengzha Nosu in southern Sichuan. Most still call themselves *Nosu*, and their women's dress and large headdress are similar to what Shengzha Nosu women wear. *Xiaoliangshan* means "smaller cold mountains" — the primary habitation of this group. The Nosu in Sichuan live in the *Daliangshan* (Greater Cold Mountains). There may be several subgroups among the Xiaoliangshan Nosu.

Language: Xiaoliangshan Nosu, which is part of the Northern Yi language group, is only partially intelligible with the other Nosu languages in southern China.

History: The Xiaoliangshan Nosu came from the Daliangshan in Sichuan at various stages of their history. The first migration began in the sixth century. Large numbers migrated after the defeat of Yang in 1730. Others followed after Chinese raids in 1802, 1814 and 1839.[3] The Xiaoliangshan Nosu continued the practice of slavery that was the hallmark of their lives in the Daliangshan. After Communism, 10,000 slaves were liberated from Xiaoliangshan Nosu villages in Ninglang between October 1956 and March 1958.[4]

Customs: Prior to 1949 the Xiaoliangshan Nosu practiced a system of slavery. "Even today, Xiaoliangshan Nosu society is a very complex system of castes, tribes and clans. In northwest Yunnan there were four classes of Nosu... Nuo, Tunuo, Gajia, and Gaxi.... The Nuo were the highest caste of landlord and slaveowner. The second tier of the caste system, the Tunuo, made up 54.5% of the Nosu population. The final two classes, Gajia and Gaxi, were 43% of the total Nosu population. The Nuo held sway in the daily affairs of the Tunuo and had absolute power over the lives of the Gajia and Gaxi — frequently taking them as slaves. In 1957 80% of the Nuo were slave owners. The remnants of these class tensions are still an undercurrent in Nosu society today."[5]

Religion: A combination of polytheism, animism, and ancestor worship dominates the religious life of the Xiaoliangshan Nosu.

Christianity: There are only a few Xiaoliangshan Nosu believers scattered over a widespread area. They are often in mixed congregations with Han Chinese or Bai believers. Few Xiaoliangshan Nosu have ever heard the gospel. Samuel Zwemer once asked, "Does it really matter how many die or how much money we spend on opening closed doors, and in occupying different fields, if we really believe that missions is warfare and that the King's glory is at stake?"[6] The widespread geographic area of the Xiaoliangshan Nosu has hindered efforts to see a strong church planted in their midst.

Paul Hattaway

Nosu, Yinuo 诺苏，以诺

Midge Conner

Location: Chinese scholar Shi Songshan listed a 1989 population of 400,000 Yinuo Nosu people, living in remote northern areas of the Daliangshan (Big Cold Mountains) in southern Sichuan Province.[1] The main concentration of Yinuo Nosu live in Meigu, Mabian, Leibo, and Ebian counties, and in parts of Ganluo County. Smaller numbers of Yinuo Nosu live in Yuexi, Zhaojue, and Jinyang counties of Sichuan; and in Yongshan and Qiaojia counties of northeast Yunnan.[2]

Identity: Yinuo Nosu is a distinct language within the larger Nosu group in southern China. The Nosu are officially considered part of the Yi nationality. There are numerous subgroups and clans among the Nosu. One study reports "24 nationalities of Black Nosu Yi in the Liang Shan."[3] The Yinuo Nosu should not be confused with the Jino ethnic group of southern Yunnan Province whose name is also sometimes spelled *Yinuo.*

Language: Yinuo Nosu is part of the Northern Yi branch of Tibeto-Burman. It is related to Shengzha and Tianba Nosu, yet speakers from the respective groups who have not had regular exposure to the other dialects cannot understand them.

History: The Yinuo Nosu took slaves and fought against the Chinese authorities and other Nosu groups for centuries, until they were disarmed and the slave system was abolished by the Communists in the early 1950s. Still today, the Yinuo Nosu remain an aggressive and fierce people.

Customs: Because of the distinctive style of dress worn by the Yinuo Nosu, the region they inhabit is generally known as the "broad-legged trousers region." "The striking characteristic of men's garments is the broad bottoms of the trouser legs. Women also like to wear wide pleated skirts. The number of pleats sometimes comes to more than one hundred. Girls wear multi-colored headscarfs made of black cloth. Married women increase the layers of their headscarfs. After having a baby, they wear leaf-shaped bonnets."[4]

Religion: The various branches of the Nosu have a detailed legend of a great flood. They say there were once three brothers. "Because the eldest was undisciplined, God sent a messenger to the sons to warn them of the flood. The oldest wanted to kill the messenger. The second son bound the messenger and asked him questions. The third politely asked him why the flood was coming.... The youngest son, named Dum, built a boat out of wood in 20 days. Twenty days later the rains came. It rained seven days and nights and flooded the whole earth. The two older sons died. The boat landed in the snowy mountains of Tibet. Dum had three sons who populated the whole earth."[5]

Christianity: Despite this and other similarities with biblical stories, few Yinuo Nosu have ever heard the gospel. Intimidating mountains, rugged terrain, and cultural and linguistic barriers have prevented the gospel from spreading to the Yinuo Nosu. Today there are only a few hundred known Catholics among them.

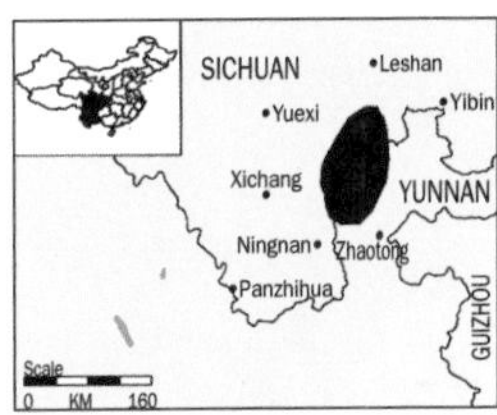

Population in China:
400,000 (1989)
512,200 (2000)
642,800 (2010)
Location: Sichuan, Yunnan
Religion: Polytheism
Christians: 200

Overview of the Yinuo Nosu

Countries: China
Pronunciation: "Yee-nuoh-Nor-soo"
Other Names: Yinuo, I-no, Yinuo Yi
Population Source: 400,000 (1989 Shi Songshan); Out of a total Yi population of 6,572,173 (1990 census)
Location: *S Sichuan:* Meigu, Mabian, Leibo, Ebian, Ganluo, Yuexi, Zhaojue, and Jinyang counties; *NE Yunnan:* Yongshan and Qiaojia counties
Status: Officially included under Yi
Language: Sino-Tibetan, Tibeto-Burman, Burmese-Lolo, Lolo, Northern Lolo, Yi, Northern Yi
Dialects: 0
Religion: Polytheism, Animism, Ancestor Worship, Christianity
Christians: 200
Scripture: None
***Jesus* film:** None
Gospel Recordings: None
Christian Broadcasting: None
ROPAL code: None

Status of Evangelization

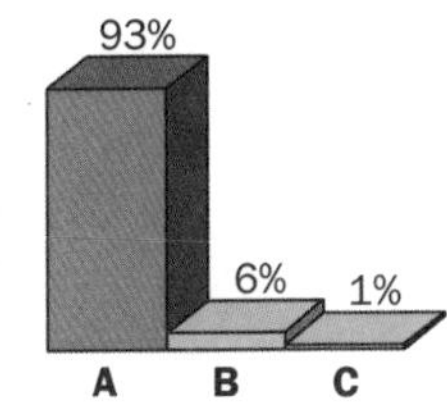

A = Have never heard the gospel
B = Were evangelized but did not become Christians
C = Are adherents to any form of Christianity

Nu 怒

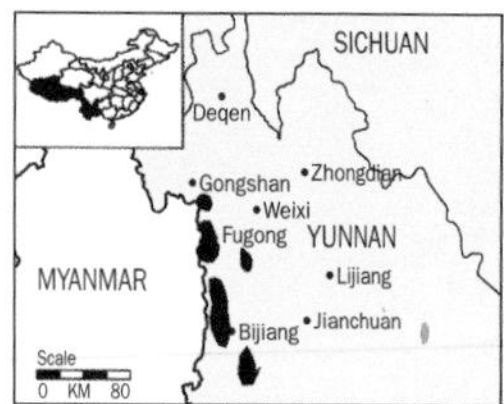

Population in China:
21,600 (1990)
26,200 (2000)
31,700 (2010)
Location: Yunnan, Tibet
Religion: Polytheism
Christians: 4,000

Overview of the Nu

Countries: China, Myanmar

Pronunciation: "Noo"

Other Names: Nusu, Nutzu, Nung, Anoong, Anu, Noutzu, Lutzu, Lu, Lutze, Kwinpang, Khupang, Kwingsang, Fuchye, Anong, A-nung, Nuzu, Nu-tsu, Luzi, Nuzi

Population Source:
27,123 (1990 census);[1]
23,166 (1982 census);
15,047 (1964 census);
Also in Myanmar

Location: *NW Yunnan:* Fugong, Gongshan, Lanping, Lushui, and Weixi counties;
SE Tibet: Changdu District in Zayu County (349)

Status:
An official minority of China

Language: Sino-Tibetan, Tibeto-Burman, Burmese-Lolo, Lolo

Literacy: 35%

Dialects (3): Northern Nu (2,000), Southern Nu (3,000), Central Nu (4,000)

Religion: Polytheism, Christianity, Tibetan Buddhism

Christians: 4,000

Scripture: New Testament 1991

***Jesus* film:** None

Gospel Recordings:
Kwinpang #00972

Christian Broadcasting: None

ROPAL code: NUF00 and NUN00

Status of Evangelization

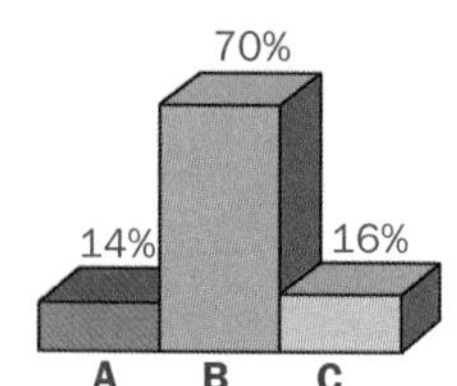

A = Have never heard the gospel
B = Were evangelized but did not become Christians
C = Are adherents to any form of Christianity

Midge Conner

Location: The majority of the 26,000 Nu live primarily in Gongshan, Fugong, and Lushui counties in northwest Yunnan. Small numbers are also found in Weixi and Lanping counties.[2] The Nu live high in mountainous jungle-like areas. In addition, Nu communities are also found in the southeastern corner of Tibet, although the Nu people there speak only Derung, and many are an ethnic mixture of Nu and Tibetan. Nu speakers are also located in northern Myanmar where they are called *Kwinpang*.

Identity: Those Nu living in the upper reaches of the Nujiang River call themselves either *Nu* or *Anu*. Those living in the lower reaches call themselves *Nusu*. Together, they have been combined with several smaller tribes to form the official Nu nationality.

Language: Approximately 8,000 people, (35%) of the Nu nationality, can speak the Nu language.[3] More than 5,500 ethnic Nu speak Derung as their first language.[4] Others speak Chinese, Lisu, or Tibetan. The Nu language has no traditional written form, although in recent years a Roman script has been introduced. In the past the Nu kept records by carving notches on wood.

History: Before their conversion to Christianity, the Lisu often bullied the Nu in the Salween Valley. The Lisu would frequently place a corpse on Nu land and claim the Nu had committed murder. "The demand for compensation, called *oupuguya* ('the ransom for a corpse') was imposed. This tyrannous annual exaction would be paid continuously for several generations. Each Nu village usually would have to pay six to eight such iniquitous taxes each year."[5]

Customs: Nu men are dangerous in the use of the crossbow and are skillful hunters. "Every little boy carries his bow and arrow and every living creature, from the smallest bird to the bear or traveler, serves as target. Their arrows are very strong and the points are poisoned with the root of aconite."[6] In the past the Nu made all their clothing from hemp; Nu in more remote areas continue this practice. "Almost all women adorn themselves with strings of coral, agate, shells, glass beads, and silver coins on their heads and chests.... In some areas, women adorn themselves in a unique way by winding a type of local vine around their heads, waists and ankles."[7]

Religion: Most Nu are polytheists. There are also significant numbers of Christians among the Nu, although they have never embraced the gospel en masse as the neighboring Derung and Lisu minorities have. A small number of Nu, mostly those living in mixed marriages with Tibetans, follow Tibetan Buddhism.

Christianity: Estimates of the current number of Nu believers range from 1,000[8] to 4,000.[9] J. Russell Morse and his family worked in the Upper Salween area for 25 years prior to 1949. Their mission base was described as "one of the most isolated stations in the world."[10] The family's zealous evangelism converted 6,900 Lisu and Nu and established 74 churches.[11] Today the Morse family continues to reach out from their base in Thailand.[12] Father André escaped the 1905 massacre of French Catholic missionaries in Deqen[13] to work single-handedly among the Nu for many years.

Nubra 努把

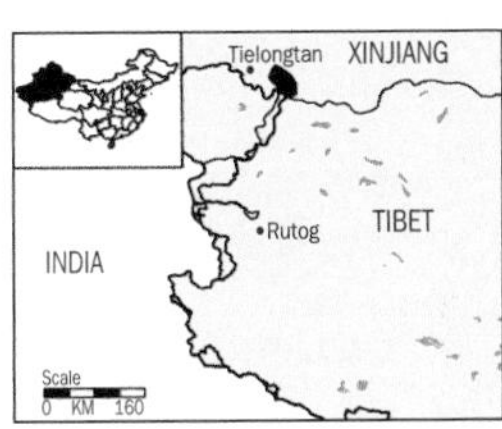

Population in China:
500 (1998)
520 (2000)
670 (2010)
Location: Xinjiang
Religion: Islam
Christians: None Known

Overview of the Nubra

Countries: India, China

Pronunciation: "Noo-bra"

Other Names: Nubran

Population Source:
500 (1998 AMO);
Also in India

Location: *SW Xinjiang:* Near the town of Tielongtan

Status: Unidentified; Possibly included under Uygur or Kirgiz

Language: Sino-Tibetan, Tibeto-Burman, Bodic, Bodish, Tibetan, Western Tibetan, Ladakhi

Dialects: 0

Religion: Sunni Islam

Christians: None known

Scripture:
Portions 1904 (Ladakhi)

***Jesus* film:** Available

Gospel Recordings:
Ladakhi #00902

Christian Broadcasting: None

ROPAL code: None

Status of Evangelization

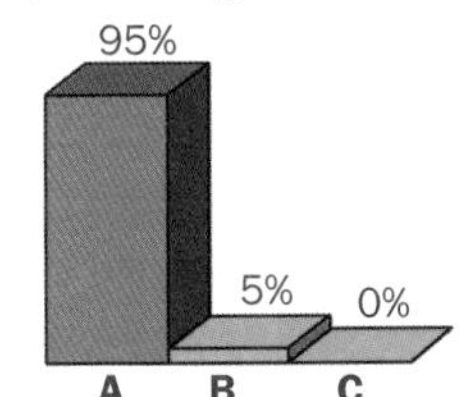

A = Have never heard the gospel
B = Were evangelized but did not become Christians
C = Are adherents to any form of Christianity

Location: Several hundred Nubra people live in the southwest corner of the Xinjiang Uygur Autonomous Region, near the juncture of Xinjiang, Tibet, Pakistan, and the Indian state of Jammu and Kashmir. The majority of Nubra live in India where they are considered a dialect group of the Ladakhi. The Nubra in India live in the Nubra Valley north of the town of Leh.

Identity: Historically, the Nubra were part of the Ladahki race. Although the Ladahki are primarily Tibetan Buddhist, most Nubra have converted to the Sunni sect of Islam. The Nubra do not appear in Chinese literature, so it is uncertain how they have been officially classified by the authorities. Local researchers in Xinjiang, however, are aware of the presence of this unique tribe who identify themselves as *Nubra* or *Nubran* to outsiders.

Language: Linguists consider the Nubra language a dialect of Ladahki. Traders from the two groups have little trouble communicating with each other. Most literate Nubra in India use the Urdu script, and many are bilingual in Kashmiri, the *lingua franca* of the area. The Nubra language is Tibetan related, although it now contains many Arabic loanwords due to the influence of Islam.

History: For centuries Nubra merchants have lived along the trade routes of the Old Silk Roads, which ran east into Tibet and north to Xinjiang and Central Asia. Tribes and bandits from the Ladakh region frequently raided areas inside today's China, including the Gug tribe who drove the Keriya people deep into the Taklimakan Desert before retreating back to their mountain hideouts.[1]

Customs: The Nubra experienced a complete cultural transformation when they converted from Tibetan Buddhism (with all its idols, demons, ghosts, and spirit appeasement) to Islam — which abhors idolatry and strictly opposes the worship of any deity other than Allah. The customs of the Nubra reflect their Islamic beliefs. Many Nubra also herd yaks, goats, and sheep.

Religion: The Nubra live near their fellow Muslims: the Uygur, Kazak, Tajik, and Kirgiz. Although they speak the Ladakhi language, the major religious differences between the Muslim Nubra and the Buddhist Ladakhis have caused the Nubra to develop a separate ethnicity.

Christianity: There are no known Christians among the Nubra either in China or India. Although there are about 120 Moravian believers among the Ladakhis in India, the church has not grown at all since 1922 when they numbered 158 believers.[2] In recent years an Indian mission, the Cooperative Outreach of India, has commenced medical and evangelistic work among the Nubra in India. After one of their trips they reported, "After having crossed the highest motorable road in the world one reaches the Nubra Valley.... We had 20 cataract surgeries and over 750 patients who came from far flung areas near the borders."[3] Because of the tense political situation, little has been done to help the Nubra living within China's borders. The Nubra remain unreached and unevangelized.

Dwayne Graybill

Numao 努毛

Location: The 1982 Chinese census listed a population of 1,147 Numao people living in the mountains of southern China. They are located in Libo County in southern Guizhou Province.[1] The Chinese authorities later amended their Numao population to 1,391 after they included the 244 Beidongnuo people with the Numao.

Yao Update

Identity: The Numao, despite their small size, are known by a variety of different names. Local Han Chinese people call them *Heiku Yao*, which means "black trouser Yao," after the Numao men's custom of wearing black trousers. One subgroup of the Numao are called the *Beidongnuo*. The Chinese have found that this small group speak the same language as the Numao. But the Beidongnuo are profiled separately in *Operation China* because they insist they are a different ethnic group. The Numao are one of eleven distinct tribes of the Bunu people, all of which have been officially included under the Yao nationality by the Chinese authorities.

Language: The Numao speak a language that is different from all others in China. It is most closely related to the Baonuo language spoken by about 15,000 people in southern Guizhou and northern Guangxi. Numao is part of the Bunuic branch of the Hmong (Miao) language family. Although the Numao and other Bunu groups speak a language related to Miao, they have been officially included under Yao because of cultural similarities.

History: Long before the start of the Christian era, it is generally believed, the numerous groups belonging to today's Miao, Yao, and She nationalities were part of the same great race. Chinese accounts place the ancestors of these people in northern China around 500 BC. Persecution forced them to migrate into southern China, especially into the regions that are today's Jiangxi and Hunan provinces. Further conflict forced these groups to splinter into dozens of smaller units who, after centuries of separation from other members of their original race, evolved into distinct ethnolinguistic groups.

Customs: Numao culture is similar to that of the Yao who live in the same part of China. They consider Pan Hu to be their progenitor and worship him at certain festivals throughout the year. All Numao are agriculturists, struggling to produce good crops from the poor soil where they live.

Religion: In addition to their worship of Pan Hu, the Numao revere and appease a hierarchy of spirits and deities — including the spirit of the soil — and demons, which they believe live inside the highest mountains in their region.

Christianity: Because of their small size, groups like the Numao tend to be overlooked by the Christian world. There has never been a known follower of Christ from among their tribe. God's Word has promised there will be redeemed representatives from all tribes, including the Numao, around his throne in heaven. Church planters need to view the Numao as an untouched group desperately in need of God, rather than ignore them because of their small numbers.

Population in China:
1,147 (1982)
1,745 (2000)
2,250 (2010)
Location: Guizhou
Religion: Polytheism
Christians: None Known

Overview of the Numao

Countries: China

Pronunciation: "Noo-maow"

Other Names: Nu-Mhou, Heiku Yao, Black Trouser Yao

Population Source:
1,147 (1982 census);
Out of a total Yao population of 2,134,013 (1990 census)

Location: *S Guizhou:* Libo County

Status:
Officially included under Yao

Language: Hmong-Mien, Hmongic, Bunuic, Naogelao

Dialects: 0

Religion: Polytheism, Animism, Ancestor Worship

Christians: None known

Scripture: None

***Jesus* film:** None

Gospel Recordings: None

Christian Broadcasting: None

ROPAL code: BWX05

Status of Evangelization

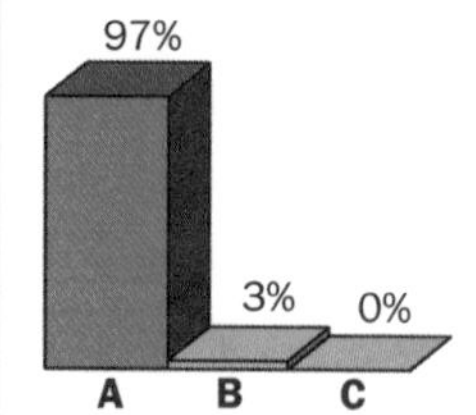

A = Have never heard the gospel
B = Were evangelized but did not become Christians
C = Are adherents to any form of Christianity

Nung 农

Population in China:
100,000 (1981)
137,200 (2000)
164,100 (2010)
Location: Guangxi, Yunnan
Religion: Shamanism
Christians: 1,000

Overview of the Nung

Countries: Vietnam, China, Laos, USA, Canada, Australia, England

Pronunciation: "Noong"

Other Names: Tai Nung, Thai Nung, Nong, Nawng, Lawng

Population Source:
100,000 (1981 Wurm & Hattori);
Out of a total Zhuang population of 15,489,630 (1990 census);
706,000 in Vietnam (1991);
A few in Laos;
7 in USA (1981 SIL);
Also in Canada, Australia, England

Location: *SW Guangxi; SE Yunnan:* Wenshan Prefecture

Status: Officially included under Zhuang

Language: Daic, Tai, Central Tai

Dialects (1): Longzhou

Religion: Shamanism, Ancestor Worship, Animism, No Religion, Christianity

Christians: 1,000

Scripture:
Portions 1971; Work in progress

***Jesus* film:** None

Gospel Recordings:
Thai Nung #3327

Christian Broadcasting:
Available (FEBC)

ROPAL code: NUT00

Status of Evangelization

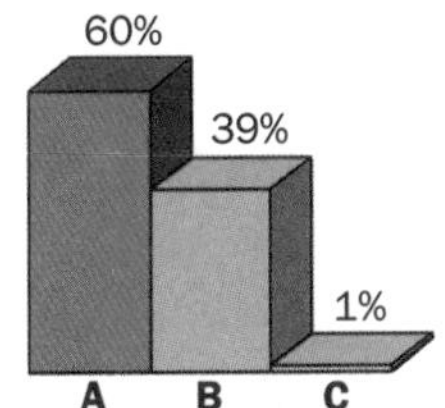

A = Have never heard the gospel
B = Were evangelized but did not become Christians
C = Are adherents to any form of Christianity

YWAM COM

Location: More than 137,000 Nung are located in southern China, along the China-Vietnam border in both Guangxi and Yunnan provinces. Most Nung (706,000) live in northern Vietnam where they are one of the largest of that nation's 54 official ethnic groups. Small communities of Nung are also found in Laos, the United States, Canada, Australia, and England.[1]

Identity: The Nung are closely related to the Tho. The Nung were listed as a distinct people group in a tribal survey of the early 1900s,[2] but since the 1950s they have been combined with other groups to form the official Zhuang nationality.

Language: The term *Nung* can refer to any of several different varieties of the Southern Zhuang language.[3] Nung is closely related to Tho and Southern Zhuang in China. Speakers of the Yaguang and Dejing varieties of Southern Zhuang, which are intelligible with Nung in Vietnam, refer to their languages as *Nong*. Rev. J. H. Freeman, a Presbyterian missionary, found the Nung tone and pronunciation were "quite close to [Tai] Lu [although] a large admixture of Cantonese and Mandarin caused difficulty in making them understand me."[4]

History: The Nung tribe suffered a massive military defeat in 1053. The Nung general, Nung Chih Cao, and his descendants fled to Guangning.[5] Later, during the Mongol reign of the thirteenth century, "a number of tribes pushed into Vietnam and Laos, such as the Tho and later the Nung."[6] In the 1860s the Nung in Vietnam sided with Sioung, a self-proclaimed Hmong king. Sioung's armies raided gold from Buddhist temples and seized large tracts of land from other peoples.[7]

Customs: Every Nung household has a plot of land to grow cotton and indigo. The cloth is dyed several times, then beaten until its surface becomes shiny.

Religion: The Nung have a deep-rooted sense of their ethnic identity and a great loyalty to each other. While many of the current generation of Nung youth are nonreligious, shamanism has traditionally been the religion of this group. More than 30 shaman priests still serve Nung communities in northern Vietnam.[8]

Christianity: Several books of the Bible were translated into Nung by missionaries Janice Saul and Nancy Freiberger between 1963 and 1966. The translators used the Vietnamese script which is not understood by the Nung in China. After 17 years of silence, the translators were encouraged when they received letters from the Nung in Vietnam, "telling of answers to prayer, of recent Nung converts and of the growth of the church."[9] The Nung in China's southwest Guangxi Zhuang Autonomous Region lived in the vicinity of the large and effective Lungchow (now Longzhou) and Ningming mission stations before 1949. Most of the Nung believers in China today are still located in that area. Gospel recordings are available in the Nung language. The Far East Broadcasting Company's gospel radio programs have allowed many Nung to hear the gospel, but the tightly controlled social structure of the Nung makes it difficult for them to change.

Nunu 努努

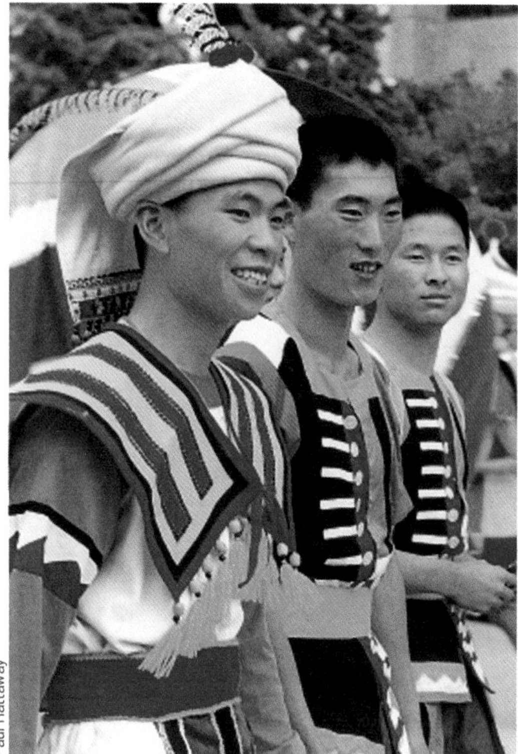
Paul Hattaway

Location: Numbering 31,928 speakers at the time of the 1982 Chinese language census, the Nunu people of Guangxi increased to more than 48,000 by the end of the twentieth century. They are one of 11 distinct Bunu subgroups, each speaking a different language. The Bunu totaled 439,000 people in 1982. Nunu communites are located in the northwestern part of the Guangxi Zhuang Autonomous Region: in Lingyun, Tianlin, Fengshan, and Donglan counties.

Identity: In most other countries, the Nunu would be classified as a distinct minority group in their own right. In China, however, they have been tucked away as part of the Bunu who, in turn, have been included under the official Yao nationality. Because of this classification, few people have ever heard of the Nunu even though they possess their own culture, history, language, and ethnicity.

Language: The Nunu speak their own language. They cannot communicate with the speakers of any other Bunu language, although Nunu is distantly related to the Dongnu and Bunuo languages. The Nunu have never possessed an orthography of their own. This has caused them to feel inferior to the Chinese and those other ethnic groups who possess a script.

History: Nunu history is shrouded in stories of past migrations and armed conflict with other people groups. Because of pressure from the Han and the Zhuang, the Nunu were driven from their land and forced into the remote mountains where the soil is poor and living conditions extremely harsh. In some places the Nunu must walk long distances to collect water from the nearest source.

Customs: Because of the poor soil and rocky ground, the Nunu have become accustomed to survive however they are able. Nunu men have traditionally been great hunters, but today their yields are limited to wild pigs and small game. In the past the region was home to many tigers, deer, and bears. Nunu women are experts at foraging in the forests for food supplements such as edible mushrooms and vegetables. In times of great hunger the Nunu have eaten roots and the bark from trees which they boil into a sticky substance.

Religion: Pan Hu is worshiped by the Nunu. At the great Pan Hu Festival, held on the 16th day of every tenth lunar month, thousands of people come together in a demonstration of devotion to Pan Hu that borders on demonic possession. The Nunu also worship their ancestors.

Christianity: The Nunu are trapped in complete spiritual darkness. They have no known believers or Christian witness. The Nunu are a childlike people. Early missionaries commented on the meekness of character possessed by China's minorities. Paul Vial, who worked among a group in Yunnan, wrote, "The [minority person] is born timid but not fearful; he shuns strangers as if they were bringing the plague.... He is not afraid, but he is not daring. In front of a Chinese, he is as a dog before a tiger.... He is like a large child who follows you, but who never precedes you."[1]

Population in China:
31,928 (1982)
48,600 (2000)
62,700 (2010)
Location: Guangxi
Religion: Polytheism
Christians: None Known

Overview of the Nunu

Countries: China
Pronunciation: "Noo-noo"
Other Names: Beilong Yao
Population Source:
31,928 (1982 census);
Out of a total Yao population of 2,134,013 (1990 census)
Location: *NW Guangxi:* Lingyun, Tianlin, Fengshan, and Donglan counties
Status:
Officially included under Yao
Language: Hmong-Mien, Hmongic, Bunuic, Bunu
Dialects: 0
Religion: Polytheism, Animism, Ancestor Worship
Christians: None known
Scripture: None
***Jesus* film:** None
Gospel Recordings: None
Christian Broadcasting: None
ROPAL code: BWX02

Status of Evangelization

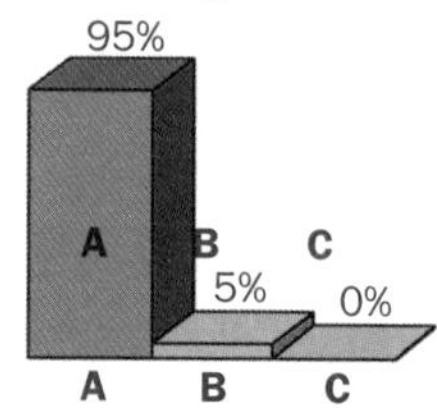

A = Have never heard the gospel
B = Were evangelized but did not become Christians
C = Are adherents to any form of Christianity

Oirat 伪拉特

Location: The 1982 China census numbered 166,000 Oirat in Qinghai, Xinjiang, and Gansu provinces. Of this number, 106,000 belong to the Torgut ethnic group, which have been profiled separately in this book. Although the Torgut and Oirat are closely related and speak the same language, they view themselves as distinct tribes. Most Oirat live in the remote mountains and verdant grasslands of northern Qinghai Province. Others live in Subei and Aksay counties in southwest Gansu Province.

Identity: The Oirat were acknowledged separately in the 1982 Chinese census, before being officially included under the Mongolian nationality. One expert described the Oirat as "physically smaller, more garrulous, friendlier and more inquisitive than [other Mongols]."[1] In Xinjiang the Torgut, Olot, Korbet, and Hoshut peoples are known as the "Four Tribes of Oirat."[2]

Language: Oirat has its own script — called *Tod* — which is different from the traditional Mongolian downward script. Although Oirat and Torgut can communicate easily, linguists have labeled the Oirat spoken in Qinghai and Gansu the *Kok Nur* vernacular of the Oirat language group.[3]

History: The Oirat have had a terrible history.[4] From 1755–57 the Qing armies crushed the Oirat, forcing the survivors to flee to the northern Caucasus Mountains in present-day Russia. There, oppression forced most of them to flee back into China in 1771. Only a few Oirat survived the long journey back to Xinjiang. "The rest died from famine or fell victim to the hostile raids of neighboring tribes."[5] Those who stayed behind on the Russian side of the border are called *Kalmyk* which means "to remain or stay behind."[6]

Paul Hattaway

Customs: The Oirat "burial in the fields" is unique in all of China. The corpse is placed on a wooden cart which is pulled furiously by a horse until the body falls from the back of the cart. Wherever it falls it is left to be devoured by beasts and birds of prey.[7] The Oirat have been described as "a squalid race, reputed never to change their clothes or wash. When one coat wears out, a new one is put over it and not until it rots off do they discard a garment."[8]

Religion: The majority of Oirat are followers of Tibetan Buddhism. Shamans are still used to perform many rituals and ceremonies. Some Oirat practice a crude form of black magic under the veneer of Buddhism. Every New Year the Oirat devote their prayers to Okeen Tenger, their female protector. She is believed to have saved the world from evil by bearing and later killing the offspring of the Lord of Evil, Erlik Khan.

Christianity: Few Christians have ever reached out to the Oirat with the gospel. Today there are no known believers, nor has there ever been a Christian fellowship among the Oirat in China. Percy Mather in 1914 was the first missionary to specifically target the Oirat. Mather, who was "widely regarded"[9] by the Oirat, compiled an Oirat dictionary. In 1922 the China Consultation Committee lamented, "There are no definite plans for reaching the [Oirat].... No missionaries as yet are planning to learn the dialect of the aborigines."[10] The Scriptures are presently being translated into Oirat.

GANSU
Zhangye
XINJIANG
Xining
QINGHAI
Madoi
Scale
KM 400

Population in China:
60,000 (1982)
91,300 (2000)
117,800 (2010)
Location:
Xinjiang, Qinghai, Gansu
Religion: Tibetan Buddhism
Christians: None Known

Overview of the Oirat

Countries: Mongolia, Russia, China, Germany, Taiwan, USA

Pronunciation: "Ooi-rut"

Other Names: Kalmyk-Oirat, Xinjiang Mongol, Western Mongol, Weilate

Population Source:
166,000 (1982 census) including 106,000 Torgut;[11]
Out of a total Mongol population of 4,806,849 (1990 census);
205,000 in Mongolia;
174,000 Kalmyk in Russia (1993 UBS);
Also in Germany, Taiwan, USA

Location:
Qinghai: Haixi Prefecture;
SW Gansu: Aksay and Subei counties; Parts of *SE Xinjiang*

Status: Officially included under Mongolian

Language: Altaic, Mongolian, Eastern Mongolian, Oirat-Khalkha, Oirat-Kalmyk-Darkhat

Dialects (4): Jakhachin, Bayit, Mingat, Khoshut

Religion: Tibetan Buddhism, Shamanism, Islam

Christians: None known

Scripture: New Testament 1827 (out of print); Work in progress

***Jesus* film:** None[12]

Gospel Recordings: Kalmyk #03205 (possibly in Russian dialect)

Christian Broadcasting: None

ROPAL code: KGZ00

Status of Evangelization

95%
5%
0%
A B C

A = Have never heard the gospel
B = Were evangelized but did not become Christians
C = Are adherents to any form of Christianity

Olot 鄂和他

Population in China:
2,000 (1993)
2,400 (2000)
3,100 (2010)
Location:
Heilongjiang, Inner Mongolia
Religion: Shamanism
Christians: None Known

Overview of the Olot

Countries: China

Pronunciation: "Ooh-lut"

Other Names: Manchurian Ölöt, Heilongjiang Ölöt, Mannai Ölöt, Ölët, Oold, Oleut, Elyut, Eleuth

Population Source: Less than 2,000 (1993 J. Janhunen); Out of a total Mongol population of 4,806,849 (1990 census)

Location: *Heilongjiang:* On the eastern bank of the lower Nonni River within Fuyu County; *Inner Mongolia:* Another group lives in the Imin region of Hulunbuir.

Status: Officially included under Mongolian

Language: Altaic, Mongolian, Eastern Mongolian

Dialects: 0

Religion: Shamanism

Christians: None known

Scripture: None

***Jesus* film:** None

Gospel Recordings: None

Christian Broadcasting: None

ROPAL code: KGZ04

Status of Evangelization

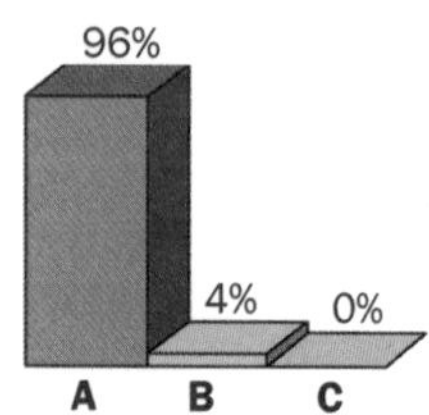

A = Have never heard the gospel
B = Were evangelized but did not become Christians
C = Are adherents to any form of Christianity

Location: "Less than 2,000" Olot were counted in a 1993 study.[1] The Olot inhabit the eastern bank of the Nonni River within Fuyu County in northeast China's Heilongjiang Province. Another group of Olot live in the Imin region of Hulunbuir, Inner Mongolia, but they have been unable to speak their language since the early 1900s.[2]

Identity: Although officially included as part of the Mongol nationality by the Chinese authorities, the Olot consider themselves to be a separate ethnic group. They speak a tribal dialect of Oirat that is unintelligible with the languages of all other surrounding communities. Oirat is the language spoken by most Mongols in northwest China on the opposite side of the country. In Xinjiang the Torgut, Olot, Korbet, and Hoshut peoples are known as the "Four Tribes of Oirat."[3]

Language: The Olot language is rapidly dying out. One linguist reported that the use of the Olot language has been extinct in Inner Mongolia since the start of the twentieth century, and that it is also headed toward extinction in Heilongjiang "due to assimilation by Chinese."[4] Athough it is still spoken by about 1,000 people, the youngest speakers of Olot today are in their 20s, and the language is no longer being taught to children. Many Olot can also speak the neighboring Daur language. The Olot language itself at one time served as a second language for the Khakas people in Heilongjiang.[5]

History: In 1758 the Qing Dynasty rulers of China conquered Jungaria in today's Xinjiang Uygur Autonomous Region. Jungaria was an area controlled by Oirat tribal chiefs who proved to be a thorn in the side of the Manchu emperors.[6] The Manchu government transferred a group of Olot to Manchuria, where they were split up and sent to the two locations they still inhabit today. One group was placed in Nonni and the other in Imin in Inner Mongolia. The Imin group gradually lost the use of their mother tongue, having been "influenced by the local Mongolic languages and dialects."[7]

Customs: The national drink of Mongolians across China is a fermented mare's milk called *airag* or *kumiss.* Made the same way today as it has been, for centuries, the milk is hung in a goatskin bag and stirred with a wooden stick until it sours. The Olot have been isolated from other Mongolian groups for such a long period that their culture today appears more similar to the cultures of the Daur and Han Chinese than to that of the Mongolians.

Religion: The majority of Olot are shamanists. Tibetan Buddhism has not gained a foothold among them as it has among most other Mongol groups. Each Olot village has a shaman who mediates between the spirit world and the community. The shamans were persecuted during the 1960s but have reappeared in the 1980s and 1990s.

Christianity: No Olot are known to have ever believed in Christ, although a strong Daur church has emerged in recent years and may be able to take the gospel to the neighboring Olot. For the time being the Olot remains an untouched people group.

Paul Hattaway

Ongkor 恩可

Dwayne Graybill

Location: The Ongkor are the smallest group profiled in this book, with just 20 people reported in a 1993 study.[1] Yet those 20 individuals view themselves as a separate ethnic community, speak (or spoke until recently) their own unique language, and hold to a rich history. As recently as the 1945 Xinjiang census, the Ongkor numbered 2,506 people.[2] Since that time they have intermarried with other groups, especially with the Western Daur and Western Xibe. They have rapidly lost their language and identity, so that today a mere 20 individuals could still be considered ethnically distinct. While many would discount the Ongkor as not worthy of mention, it should be remembered that in Vietnam the government has given official minority status to the 32 members of the O-Du tribe. The Ongkor inhabit one village near Yining in Xinjiang's Ili Prefecture.

Identity: The few remaining Ongkor have been included as part of the Ewenki nationality in China.[3] The Ongkor do not use the name *Ewenki* but sometimes refer to themselves as the *Xinjiang Solon.*

Language: In 1990 the Ongkor language was on the verge of extinction. Just one 79-year-old man could still speak the language fluently. "In addition to the last fluent speaker, a few individuals know some isolated phrases or words. There is widespread multi-lingualism in Daur, Kazak, Uygur, Chinese and other languages."[4] No Ongkor children are being taught the language, so it will soon become extinct.[5]

History: The Ongkor are the remnant from a tumultuous time in history. Their ancestors were a diaspora group of Solon Ewenki who were sent to Xinjiang from Manchuria in 1763. Other troops who made the year-long march across China included the ancestors of today's Western Xibe and Western Daur minorities. The reigning Manchu Dynasty ordered them to bring the hostile western front of China under control. After the collapse of Manchu rule, the soldiers and their families decided to stay in Xinjiang.

Customs: The Ongkor have few distinct customs left. They have adopted the lifestyles of their Western Daur and Han Chinese neighbors. The Ongkor emphasize courtesy in accordance with seniority. "When someone meets an older person, he offers tobacco to him, bends his knees, stands aside and bows to show his greeting. Even when he is on a horse, he should dismount to greet first."[6]

Religion: Although the other Ewenki groups in China have shamans and worship a wide range of gods and idols, the Ongkor have lost these practices. They could best be described as animists, believing all natural forces have a soul. Most Ongkor under the age of 40 are atheists who have no religious beliefs.

Christianity: Throughout their history, from the time they were a numerous people to their current state on the verge of extinction, the Ongkor people have never been touched by Christianity. There has never been a known Ongkor church. The western Xinjiang region — a stronghold of Islam — is one of the least evangelized places in the world.

Population in China:
20 (1993)
24 (2000)
31 (2010)
Location: Xinjiang
Religion: Animism
Christians: None Known

Overview of the Ongkor

Countries: China

Pronunciation: "Ong-kohr"

Other Names: Xinjiang Ewenki, Ongkor Solon, Onkor Solon, Sinkiang Solon, Turkestan Solon

Population Source: Less than 20 (1993 J. Jahunen); 2,506 (1945 Xinjiang census); Out of a total Ewenki population of 26,315 (1990 census)

Location: *NW Xinjiang:* Yining County in the Ili Kazak Prefecture

Status: Officially included under Ewenki

Language: Altaic, Tungus, Northern Tungus, Ewenki

Dialects: 0

Religion: Animism, Polytheism, No Religion

Christians: None known

Scripture: None

***Jesus* film:** None

Gospel Recordings: None

Christian Broadcasting: None

ROPAL code: None

Status of Evangelization

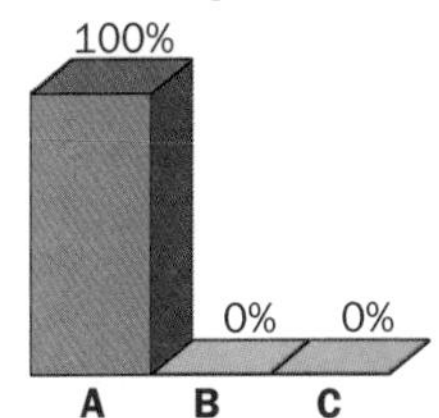

A = Have never heard the gospel
B = Were evangelized but did not become Christians
C = Are adherents to any form of Christianity

Oroqen 鄂伦春

Population in China:
6,965 (1990)
8,980 (2000)
11,590 (2010)
Location:
Inner Mongolia, Heilongjiang
Religion: Shamanism
Christians: 30

Overview of the Oroqen

Countries: China, Russia

Pronunciation: "Oro-chen"

Other Names: Orochen, Oronchon, Olunchun, Elunchun, Ulunchun

Population Source:
6,965 (1990 census);
4,132 (1982 census);
2,709 (1964 census);
2,262 (1953 census);
Also in Russia

Location: *E Inner Mongolia:* Hulunbuir Oroqen Prefecture; Butha Morindawa Daur Prefecture; *W Heilongjiang:* Huma, Aihui, Sunko, Qike, and Jiayin counties

Status:
An official minority of China

Language: Altaic, Tungus, Northern Tungus, Ewenki

Literacy: 84%

Dialects (4): Gankui, Biarchen, Kamarchen, Manyagir

Religion: Shamanism, Ancestor Worship, Polytheism, Christianity

Christians: 30

Scripture: None

***Jesus* film:** None

Gospel Recordings: Elenchun #04774

Christian Broadcasting: None

ROPAL code: ORH00

Status of Evangelization

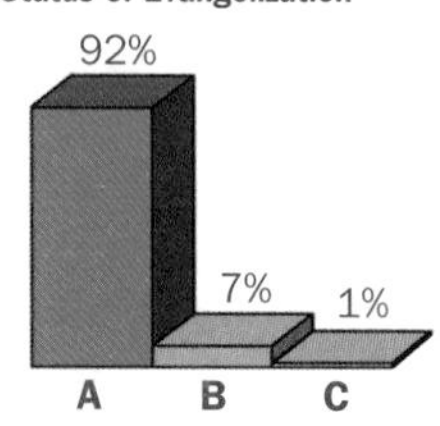

A = Have never heard the gospel
B = Were evangelized but did not become Christians
C = Are adherents to any form of Christianity

Paul Hattaway

Location: Approximately 9,000 Oroqen are spread over a vast area of the Outer Xingan Mountain range in northeast Inner Mongolia and in neighboring Heilongjiang Province. The Oroqen population has been affected by rampant disease and violence during the twentieth century. By 1953 their numbers had fallen to just 2,200. Despite their small population, the Oroqen live in a vast area measuring 58,000 square kilometers (22,970 sq. mi.), "slightly smaller than West Virginia (which has similar terrain) or Belgium and Holland combined."[1] When the Hulunbuir Prefecture was established in 1951, 774 of the 778 residents were Oroqen. By 1980 the population of 410,000 contained just 1,315 Oroqens.[2] A small number of Oroqen live across the border in eastern Siberia.[3]

Identity: In the 1950s the Oroqen were granted status as an official minority group in China. The name *Oroqen* means "people of the mountain range."[4]

Language: Oroqen is a member of the Northern Tungus language family. The Oroqen and Ewenki are said to be able to understand 70% of each other's language.[5] Some linguists consider the several dialects of Oroqen to be separate languages.[6]

History: The Oroqen were originally part of the Bei Shiwei people. It is believed that they broke away and formed their own identity sometime between AD 420 and 589. A Russian invasion of the area in the mid-1600s, followed by the Japanese occupation in the 1930s and 1940s, drove the Oroqen deep into the mountains and forests of China's northern border regions.

Customs: For generations the Oroqen lived in traditional tents called *xianrenzhu*, which they cover with birch bark in the summer and deerskin during the bleak winters, when the temperature can fall below minus 50° Celsius (–58°F). After a death occurs, the Oroqen wrap the corpse in birch bark and hang it at the top of a tree to decompose naturally. The Oroqen are great hunters and fishermen. Oroqen in some areas also raise reindeer. Today, due to the massive migration of Chinese to the northeast hinterlands, the Oroqen culture is being quickly assimilated.

Religion: Shamanism is the dominant religion among the Oroqen. They believe in an intricate system of demons and spirits. The Oroqen word for *shaman* means "agitated" or "frenzied" person. This name originated from the appearance of the shaman when he goes into a demonic trance to contact the spirit world. The Oroqen worship certain animals, especially the bear and the tiger, which they believe are blood relatives. They call the bear *amaha*, meaning "uncle" and the tiger *wutaqi*, meaning "old man."[7]

Christianity: Because of their reputation for violence and drunkenness, the few efforts to evangelize the Oroqen have met with resistance. In 1994 a Hong Kong-based ministry invited several Oroqen to work for them in southern China. Only one came; the rest chose to steal the train fare. The one who came was soon sent home after he threatened the other workers with a knife.[8] In 1995 the first ever breakthrough among the Oroqen occurred when 30 accepted Christ after hearing the gospel from the newly converted Daur believers in Heilongjiang Province. Recently gospel recordings were produced in the Oroqen language for the first time.

Paiwan 排湾

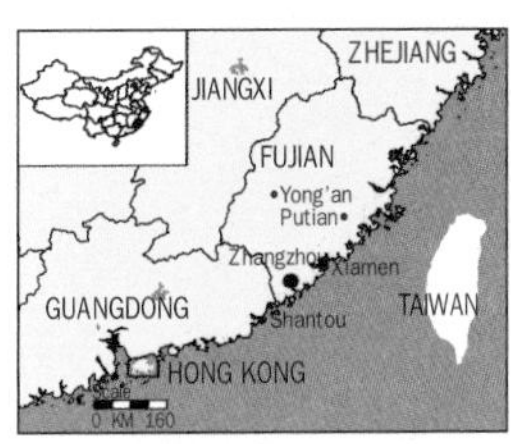

Population in China:
400 (1990)
510 (2000)
660 (2010)
Location:
Fujian, Beijing, Shanghai
Religion: Polytheism
Christians: None Known

Overview of the Paiwan

Countries: Taiwan, China

Pronunciation: "Pie-wohn"

Other Names: Paiuan, Payowan, Li-li-sha, Samobi, Samohai, Saprek, Tamari, Kadas, Kale-whan, Kapiangan, Katausan, Butanglu, Stimul

Population Source:
400 (1990 AMO);
Out of a total Gaoshan population of 2,909 (1990 census);
81,000 in Taiwan
(1993 P. Johnstone)

Location: *S Fujian:* In and around Zhangzhou City;
Some Paiwan live in *Beijing* and *Shanghai* municipalities.

Status:
Officially included under Gaoshan

Language:
Austronesian, Formosan, Paiwanic

Dialects: 0

Religion:
Polytheism, Ancestor Worship

Christians: None known

Scripture: New Testament 1973; Portions 1959; Not available in China

***Jesus* film:** None

Gospel Recordings:
Paiwan #01993

Christian Broadcasting: None

ROPAL code: PWN00

Status of Evangelization

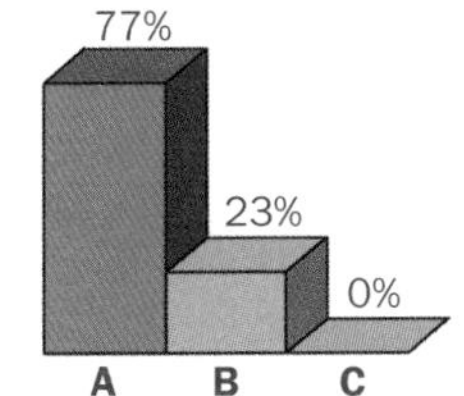

A = Have never heard the gospel
B = Were evangelized but did not become Christians
C = Are adherents to any form of Christianity

Location: Several hundred members of the Paiwan tribe live in and around the city of Zhangzhou in the southern part of Fujian Province. The great majority of Paiwan, 81,000, are located in southern Taiwan.

Identity: The Paiwan are one of three tribes, along with the Ami and Bunun, who were combined to form the official Gaoshan nationality in China. The name *Gaoshan* means "high mountain" in Chinese and is not the name of a specific ethnic group or language. The Paiwan believe they originated from an egg. Their legends say the sun laid two eggs that were hatched by a green snake.

Language: The Paiwan language is a member of the Formosan branch of the Austronesian language family. Although it is related to Ami and Bunun, speakers of the different languages usually have difficulty understanding each other and must revert to Chinese to communicate.

History: In the past the Paiwan had a fearsome reputation as head-hunters. When Paiwan warriors returned home from a head-hunting foray, "the women would gather together in front of the courtyard to welcome their heroes and would sing songs of triumph. The heads of their enemies were then hung on stone pillars in front of which were displayed wine and offerings. The sacrificial rite started, and the soul of the dead was duly consoled by the sorcerer. A tuft of hair was removed from the skull and solemnly put in a basket which was used for divination."[1] During the civil war, between 1946 and 1949, many Paiwan men were forcibly enlisted in the Kuomintang forces. When the war ended, some of the Paiwan remained behind in China and formed their own communities.[2]

Customs: Unlike other tribes in Taiwan, Paiwan society is divided into classes with a hereditary aristocracy. The Paiwan are not allowed to marry outside their tribe. On the day of their "five-yearly rite," "all marriage-seeking Paiwan men try to cut down as many trees as possible and offer the firewood thus procured to the family of the girl they want to woo."[3]

Religion: Traditionally the Paiwan have been polytheists. Their wooden carvings included images of human heads, snakes, deer, and geometric designs. In Taiwan, the Bataul branch of the Paiwan tribe holds a major sacrifice — called *maleveq* — every five years to invite the spirits of their ancestors to come and bless them.

Christianity: Christianity first came to the Paiwan people in the seventeenth century, when Taiwan was occupied by the Dutch. More than 5,000 tribesmen became Christians after only ten years, but all of them were massacred in 1661 when Cheng Gong Zheng liberated Taiwan. The missionaries were either killed or driven away, and the churches were destroyed.[4] Thousands of Paiwan people in Taiwan came to Christ in the late 1940s and 1950s. Whole villages embraced the good news and appropriated Christ's pardon and offer of salvation. Today the Presbyterian church in Taiwan claims 14,900 Paiwan members, meeting in 96 congregations.[5] The New Testament has been translated into Paiwan but is not available in Mainland China.

Paul Hattaway

Palyu 啪与

Location: More than 12,000 members of the Palyu tribe inhabit the farwestern part of the Guangxi Zhuang Autonomous Region — that section of Guangxi which juts out into Yunnan Province. The Palyu have been reported with vastly differing population figures. This is the result of linguists and anthropologists reporting according to their specific fields of interests. Most Palyu can no longer speak their language; they use the Chinese, Miao, or Yi languages spoken in the area. Linguists have reported figures of only 150, 500, and 800 speakers of Palyu.[1] Foreign travelers are presently not permitted to visit western Guangxi.

Identity: The Palyu have not been included under any nationality in China. They were included in a generic list of *Undetermined Minorities* in the Chinese census. *Palyu* is this group's self-name. The Chinese and neighboring peoples call them *Lai*.

Language: Most scholars describe Palyu as a Mon-Khmer language. One linguist states, "Palyu is clearly Mon-Khmer; many of this group now speak other languages but only 500 speakers remain."[2] Some older sources, however, classify Palyu as Sino-Tibetan and "similar to Zhuang-Dong."[3] There are 11 tones in the Palyu language — which also has two dialects: Xilin and Longlin. Linguists Jerold Edmonson and Kenneth Gregerson have written a recent report on the Palyu language.[4]

History: Although the Palyu are proud of their ethnic identity and are eager to preserve their customs, their language is gradually fading out and the people are fast being assimilated into the Han Chinese culture. According to Paul Benedict, the traditional homeland of the Palyu was in southwest Guizhou and southern Yunnan provinces, where the Palyu have assimilated to the cultures and languages of Yi groups.[5]

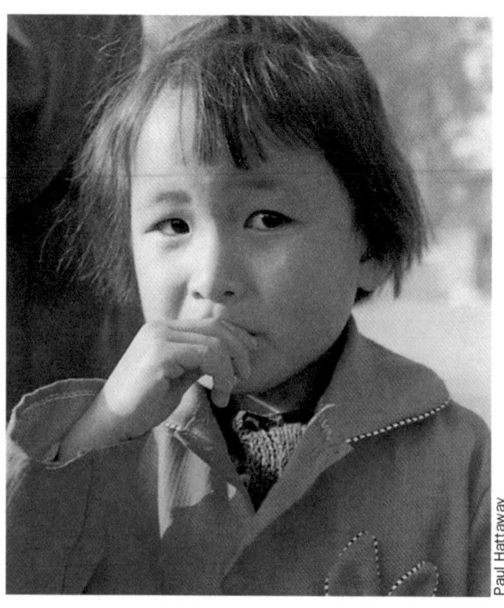

Paul Hattaway

Customs: The Palyu home is made of wood and consists of two stories. The lower area is for animals, while the upper level is where the family sleeps.

Religion: The Palyu have never been exposed to Buddhism, which many of the Mon-Khmer groups in western Yunnan have embraced. Instead, they practice animism and ancestor worship, and are careful not to offend the spirits they believe protect their communities.

Christianity: Western Guangxi is one of the most gospel-neglected areas in all of China. There are a few believers in the region but none known among the Palyu. Rev. W. H. Oldfield, writing in 1922, said, "From Liuchowfu [Liuzhou] one may travel for twelve days either northward or westward without seeing a Gospel chapel or entering a district in which a witness is being given to the Gospel... the districts surrounding these busy centers contain a large number of mixed tribesmen. These people are shut away from the rest of the province by huge mountain ranges. The greater part of this territory has not even been entered by a Gospel worker. No missionary in our province as yet speaks their language. To reach these people with the Gospel has for years been our hope and aim."[6]

Population in China:
10,000 (1993)
12,030 (2000)
15,510 (2010)
Location: Guangxi
Religion: Animism
Christians: None Known

Overview of the Palyu

Countries: China

Pronunciation: "Pal-yoo"

Other Names: Lai, Palju, Bolyu

Population Source: 10,000 (1996 B. Grimes – 1993 figure); 500 speakers of Palyu (1991)

Location: *W Guangxi:* Longlin and Xilin counties in the far-western corner of Guangxi; Possibly some in *Yunnan*

Status: Counted in the census as an *Undetermined Minority*

Language: Austro-Asiatic, Mon-Khmer, Palyu

Dialects (2): Longlin, Xilin

Religion: Animism, Ancestor Worship

Christians: None known

Scripture: None

***Jesus* film:** None

Gospel Recordings: None

Christian Broadcasting: None

ROPAL code: PLY00

Status of Evangelization

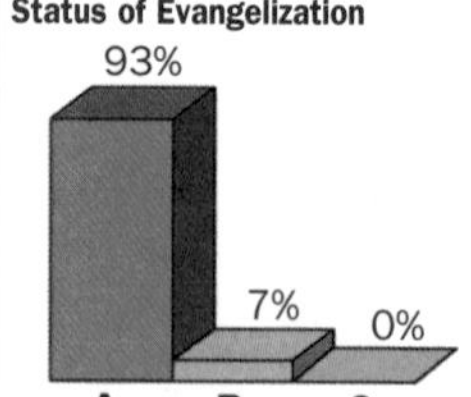

A = Have never heard the gospel
B = Were evangelized but did not become Christians
C = Are adherents to any form of Christianity

Pana 啪纳

Population in China:
4,000 (1999)
4,090 (2000)
5,020 (2010)
Location: Yunnan
Religion: Animism
Christians: None Known

Overview of the Pana

Countries: China, Laos

Pronunciation: "Pa-nah"

Other Names: Bana, Phana, Kai Pai

Population Source: 4,000 (1999 AMO); Out of a total Hani population of 1,253,952 (1990 census); 350 in Laos (1995 L. Chazee)

Location: *SW Yunnan:* Mengla County in Xishuangbanna Prefecture

Status: Officially included under Hani

Language: Sino-Tibetan, Tibeto-Burman, Burmese-Lolo, Lolo, Southern Lolo, Akha

Dialects: 0

Religion: Animism, Ancestor Worship

Christians: None known

Scripture: None

***Jesus* film:** None

Gospel Recordings: Bana #03121

Christian Broadcasting: None

ROPAL code: PHN00

Status of Evangelization

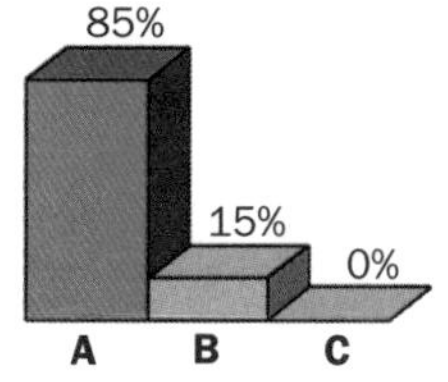

A = Have never heard the gospel
B = Were evangelized but did not become Christians
C = Are adherents to any form of Christianity

Paul Hattaway

Location: Several thousand ethnic Pana, or Bana, live in the extreme southern part of China along the border with Laos. The Pana live in Mengla County within the Xishuangbanna Prefecture in southwest Yunnan Province. An additional 350 Pana inhabit three villages in northern Laos. Two villages, Bopiet and Namtoung, are located in the Luang Namtha District of Luang Namtha Province, while one Pana village is in the Houaxay District of Bokeo Province near the Golden Triangle.[1]

Identity: The Pana are an ethnic subgroup of the Akha who, in turn, have been officially placed under the Hani nationality in China. Because of this classification, few people know about the Pana, who view themselves as a distinct people group. In many areas today it has become difficult to tell the Pana apart from the Tai Lu.

Language: The Pana language is part of the Akha branch of the Tibeto-Burman family and is believed to be most closely related to the Sila language of Laos and Vietnam. In China the Pana have learned how to speak Akha, but their original tongue is quite different from standard Akha. Some Pana in Laos are also able to speak Tai Lu, Lao, and Khmu.

History: The Pana now living in Laos say they migrated from China eight generations ago, under the authority of a Chinese leader named Lateu Kouang. They first arrived in the Viangphoukha District of Laos before settling down in their present locations. In China the Pana came under the control of the Xishuangbanna Tai Lu rulers in the past, who extracted tax and tribute from them.

Customs: Traditionally the Pana settled in the remote mountains, where they lived peacefully without trouble from other ethnic groups. The past 35 years in Laos have seen a number of Pana migrate down to the plains and valleys, where they have learned to grow irrigated crops. Despite their small population, at least three separate clan divisions exist among the Pana — each named after a sacred kind of bird, which the members of that clan are not allowed to kill. Most Pana no longer wear their traditional style of dress, except during festivals and other important occasions such as weddings and funerals.

Religion: Spirit worship and ancestor worship are practised by the Pana. In many respects the Pana rituals mirror those of their Akha neighbors and relatives, although it appears they do not follow the *Akhazang* system that is a dominant feature of the Akha throughout Southeast Asia.

Christianity: Although few outsiders have ever heard of the Pana ethnic group of southern China and northern Laos, the Christian ministry Gospel Recordings in 1967 produced a cassette tape message of the good news in the Pana language. Unfortunately, because of the relative obscurity of the Pana, few mission organizations have ever made use of this resource to take the gospel to the Pana in their own language. Today, there are no known Christians among the Pana in either China or Laos. There are very few believers among any of the ethnic groups in Mengla County.

Paxi 啪系

Paul Hattaway

Location: A 1996 Chinese television documentary put the population of the Paxi at "more than 1,000." The Paxi are located in two main villages, eight kilometers (five mi.) from Menghai Township, at the foot of Jingwang Mountain in Xishuangbanna Prefecture. Xishuangbanna is the most ethnically diverse area in China. It is home to more than 40 distinct ethnolinguistic people groups.

Identity: Linguistically, the Paxi are members of the Tai Lu language group. While almost all Tai Lu are Theravada Buddhists, the Paxi are Muslims. Today, the Paxi have been ostracized by the Tai Lu Buddhist community and have been forced to live in their own villages. They have a new name for themselves, *Paxi*, and have become socially distinct. Patrick Thornbury has described "fusion" between two cultures as "the process whereby two or more cultures combine to produce another, that is significantly different from the parent cultures."[1] The Paxi are a fusion of the Tai Lu and the Hui, who converted them to Islam. It is uncertain whether the Paxi have been officially counted as Hui or as part of the Dai nationality in China.[2]

Language: The Paxi speak standard Tai Lu, although a growing number of Arabic loanwords have been introduced in recent years. Arabic is learned by some Paxi youth to enable them to read the Qur'an and become Muslim clerics. All Paxi except the elderly are bilingual in Chinese.

History: The Paxi were converted to Islam approximately 200 years ago when the religion was introduced to them by Hui Muslim traders from Dali in central Yunnan Province. The Hui disguised themselves as raisin-sellers, but their real target was to convert people to their religion. Since their conversion the Paxi have struggled against continual persecution and prejudice from the Buddhist community. They were forced to leave their families and friends and had to build their own villages. Over the years some Hui from Dali have traveled to Menghai and married Paxi women.

Customs: The Paxi have abandoned the Tai Lu culture. They do not observe any of the Theravada Buddhist festivals and refuse to intermarry with non-Muslims.

Religion: The entire Paxi population are Sunni Muslims. Strictly adhering to the Muslim way of life, the Paxi follow Islamic teachings, do not eat pork, and worship in a small mosque. They receive frequent visits from Hui scholars and teachers who help them in their faith and understanding of the Qur'an.

Christianity: There are no Christians among the Paxi. They have a complete lack of knowledge and understanding of the gospel of Jesus Christ. It is a tragedy that Muslim missionaries won this people group to Islam approximately 100 years before the first appearance of Christianity in the region. There are a small number of Tai Lu who have converted to Christianity. Interestingly, the small Tai Lu Christian community was, like the Paxi, persecuted and forced to live in their own villages, but they retained more of the Tai Lu culture than the fanatical Paxi did.

Population in China:
1,000 (1996)
1,110 (2000)
1,400 (2010)
Location: Yunnan
Religion: Islam
Christians: None Known

Overview of the Paxi

Countries: China

Pronunciation: "Pah-shee"

Other Names: Dai Muslims, Tai Muslims

Population Source: More than 1,000 (1996 Chinese Televison)

Location: *SW Yunnan:* Two villages in Menghai County of Xishuangbanna Prefecture

Status: Probably officially included under Dai

Language: Daic, Tai, Southwestern Tai, East Central, Northwest

Dialects: 0

Religion: Sunni Islam

Christians: None known

Scripture: None

***Jesus* film:** None

Gospel Recordings: None

Christian Broadcasting: None

ROPAL code: None

Status of Evangelization

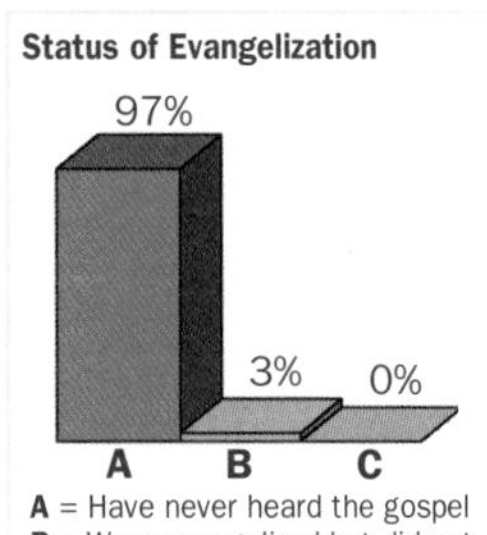

A = Have never heard the gospel
B = Were evangelized but did not become Christians
C = Are adherents to any form of Christianity

Pengzi 棚子

Location: The Pengzi, who number approximately 250 people, are one of the smallest ethnic groups in China. They live in the western part of Yunnan Province in southwest China, not far from the Myanmar border. The Pengzi are believed to live in the Wumulong District of Yongde County and possibly in the Mengban District as well.[1] The area, which lies within Lincang Prefecture, is mountainous and well forested.

Identity: Although small in number, the Pengzi view themselves as a distinct people group. They have also been mentioned in Chinese official sources from the area. The central government, however, has included the Pengzi as part of the official Yi nationality, which is a collection of about 120 different tribes and ethnic groups.

Language: Little is known about the Pengzi language, but it has been assumed that they speak a Western Yi variety because Chinese sources state that all Yi languages in Yongde County belong to the Western Yi branch of Tibeto-Burman. Other Yi languages in Yongde include Limi, Mishaba Laluo, Western Samadu, Suan, and Western Gaisu.

History: Without a written record of their origins, little is known about where the Pengzi came from and why. Over the past century, despite their dwindling population, the Pengzi have managed to cling to their ethnic identity.

Customs: The Pengzi live in a remote mountainous area. In China, rural areas have a particular charm about them. Vicomte d'Ollone, a French general who traveled through China between 1906 and 1909, wrote, "What a singular feeling obsesses one in the mountainous China, once the high-road has been left behind! The traveler feels himself a thousand leagues from all that pertains to civilization, organization, and society. There is no road communicating with the rest of the world; every one remains in his own home; there is neither post nor telegraph to bring news; men lead a tranquil existence, without troubling about matters of which they know nothing; there are no visits from officials from the outer world, no policemen, customs officers, highway inspectors, foresters, schoolmasters, or tax-collectors; there is no one but the village headman, appointed by the inhabitants.... All powers are concentrated in his person, yet he exercises none, for nothing is performed except by a common agreement, which is easily obtained."[2]

Jamin Pelkey

Religion: In the past the Pengzi practiced animal sacrifice to appease the spirits that governed their lives. In recent decades, however, and especially since the Cultural Revolution (1966–1976) when people were pressured to stop their animistic rituals, the Pengzi have become a more secularized people. The ancestors of the Pengzi are still worshiped at ceremonies held two or three times each year.

Christianity: The majority of the Pengzi live apart from all Christian influence. Few are aware of the gospel. Because of their small numbers, few outsiders, including both Chinese believers and foreign missionary organizations, have ever heard of the Pengzi.

Population in China:
250 (1999)
255 (2000)
320 (2010)
Location: Yunnan
Religion: Ancestor Worship
Christians: None Known

Overview of the Pengzi

Countries: China

Pronunciation: "Pung-zi"

Other Names:

Population Source:
250 (1999 J. Pelkey);
Out of a total Yi population of 6,572,173 (1990 census)

Location: *W Yunnan:* Wumulong and Mengban districts of Yongde County

Status:
Officially included under Yi

Language: Sino-Tibetan, Tibeto-Burman, Burmese-Lolo, Lolo, Northern Lolo, Yi, Western Yi

Dialects: 0

Religion: Ancestor Worship, Animism, No Religion

Christians: None known

Scripture: None

***Jesus* film:** None

Gospel Recordings: None

Christian Broadcasting: None

ROPAL code: None

Status of Evangelization

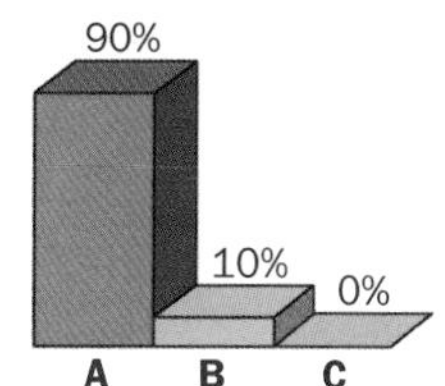

A = Have never heard the gospel
B = Were evangelized but did not become Christians
C = Are adherents to any form of Christianity

Pingdi 平地

Population in China:
1,000,000 (1996)
1,116,000 (2000)
1,439,600 (2010)
Location:
Guangxi, Hunan, Guangdong
Religion: Daoism
Christians: 400

Overview of the Pingdi

Countries: China

Pronunciation: "Ping-dee"

Other Names: Pingdi Yao, Pingding, Piongtuojo, Piongtoajeu

Population Source: 1,000,000 (1996 B. Grimes)

Location: *Guangxi:* Lipu Town; *Hunan*; *Guangdong*

Status: About half are officially included under Yao and half under Han Chinese.

Language: Chinese, Pingdi

Dialects: 0

Religion: Daoism, Animism, Ancestor Worship, Christianity

Christians: 400

Scripture: None

***Jesus* film:** None

Gospel Recordings: None

Christian Broadcasting: None

ROPAL code: None

Status of Evangelization

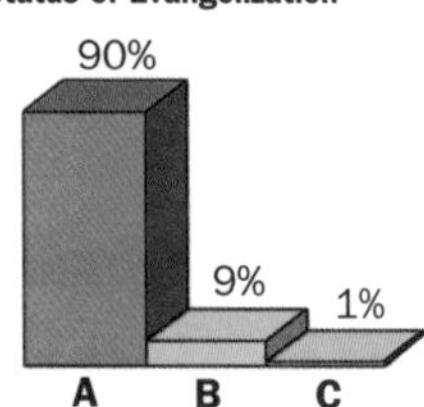

A = Have never heard the gospel
B = Were evangelized but did not become Christians
C = Are adherents to any form of Christianity

Location: More than one million speakers of the Pingdi language live in the mountainous area where Hunan, Guangxi, and Guangdong provinces meet.[1] The geographical center of the Pingdi is Lipu Township in northern Guangxi. The Pingdi live at the summits of high, remote mountains, which are divided by numerous streams and river valleys. "It is recorded in history that this distressful people, subject to endless bullying and humiliation, unable to settle down on the plains, had to bury themselves in the remotest mountains."[2]

Identity: In the 1990 national census, about half of the Pingdi were included under the Yao nationality, while the other half were included under Han Chinese. It appears the Pingdi speakers are a complicated mixture of Yao people who became Sinicized and, on the other hand, Han Chinese people who became "minoritized."[3] Although those Pingdi who have been counted as Yao speak a Chinese language, one study of the Yao states that even though "they have many branches, with different names, languages, customs, and economy, they preserve their common psychological quality which holds their ethnic group together."[4]

Language: The Pingdi, after centuries of intermingling between local Yao and Chinese people, produced their own language which is considered a form of Chinese. It still retains many words and features that reveal the genesis of a Yao language. Pingdi — which has seven tones — is also said to exhibit phonological characteristics of Daic (Tai) languages.[5]

History: The numerous Yao groups in China have splintered into their present divisions after centuries of forced migration. One historian notes, "The Yao were a very large component in the *Man* or Southern Barbarian tribes, pushed southwestwards over millennia by the Chinese. In fact the term *Man* is sometimes still used to refer to the Yao."[6]

Customs: The Pingdi area is rarely visited by outsiders. As a result, they have minimal interaction with other people groups. The majority of Pingdi are simple farmers engaged in rice cultivation.

Religion: Many Yao groups have a legend of a great flood. "Because the flood overflowed up to the sky for seven days and seven nights, on earth there were no people left except for Fuxi and his younger sister. Begging a Chinese tree to be their go-between, they became husband and wife. They gave birth to a lump of flesh, which they cut into 360 pieces and scattered around. Those pieces scattered in the green mountains changed into the Yao, the others became the Chinese people."[7]

Christianity: In the ancient past the Yao had a legend of a Creator god. The Yao claim, "Ages ago... before we crossed the sea, we worshipped someone called Tin Zay, who lives in heaven and is a holy god."[8] For centuries the Pingdi have lived and died without any knowledge of Christ and without a strong church in their midst. Although there is a Yao New Testament available in the Iu Mien language, the Pingdi speak a different language from Iu Mien. There are no Scriptures, recordings, or *Jesus* film available in the Pingdi language.

Paul Hattaway

Poluo 颇罗

Jamin Pelkey

Location: With a relatively large population of 230,000, the Poluo inhabit a widespread area in southeastern Yunnan Province. The highest concentration are found in Yanshan, Wenshan, and Qiubei counties of Wenshan Prefecture. Smaller numbers live in Maguan, Pingbian, Guangnan, Xichou, and Hekou counties. Yanshan County was only opened to foreign travelers in mid–1997. The Poluo are the dominant Yi group in southeastern Yunnan Province.

Identity: Despite their large population, very little is known about the Poluo, who are officially counted as part of the Yi nationality. The Poluo have never before been listed in ethnographic or linguistic lists from China. One researcher has stated, "The Poluo never refer to themselves as 'Yi' in their own language; instead, *Poluo* is used. The Han Chinese in their areas are also apt to call this people *Pu* instead of *Yi*. The title *Yi* is virtually meaningless in reference to this people."[1]

Language: The Poluo speak their own language which is part of the Southeastern Yi branch of Tibeto-Burman. Almost all Poluo retain the use of their native tongue. In many of the more isolated communities most of the people know only their own language and are not familiar with Chinese. Poluo is also mutually unintelligible with the other Southeastern Yi languages spoken in their area.

History: The Poluo are one of the most far-flung Yi groups in China today. They are believed to be the descendants of a large tribe that splintered into numerous ethnic groups during migrations many centuries ago.

Customs: Poluo houses are customarily built near streams or rivers to allow easy access to water. Bamboo pipes are arranged to carry the water into the village. Many Poluo live in extremely remote locations at the top of isolated mountains.

Religion: The vast majority of Poluo still adhere to the superstitions of animism, polytheism, and ancestor worship. In some locations a festival is observed on a dragon or ox day of the second lunar month. Each village chooses a day, and all the people gather around a large tree to hold a ceremony in worship of the dragon. The Poluo, along with many other peoples classified as Yi, believe the dragon is responsible for rainfall and other natural phenomena. They hope to appease the dragon in order to quell floods and prevent drought.

Christianity: The Poluo are unreached and largely unevangelized, without any Scriptures or recordings in their language. The first modern-day missionary in China, Robert Morrison, knew people must have the Word of God in their own language. He wrote, "I am still engaged in translation. My courage and perseverance almost fail me. This is a very lonely situation. I am under continual dread of the arm of the oppressor, and the natives who assist me are hunted from place to place and sometimes seized.... What a blessing it is to have the hope of eternal life rising brighter and brighter as we enter the valley."[2]

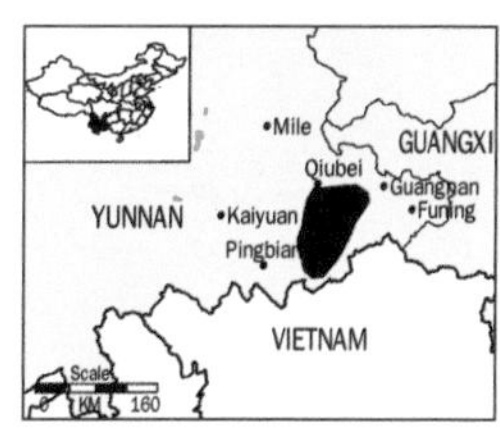

Population in China:
227,000 (1999)
232,700 (2000)
292,100 (2010)
Location: Yunnan
Religion: Polytheism
Christians: 100

Overview of the Poluo

Countries: China

Pronunciation: "Poh-luoh"

Other Names: Pu, Pola, Pula, Polo, Puzu, Aza

Population Source: 227,000 (1999 J. Pelkey); Out of a total Yi population of 6,572,173 (1990 census)

Location: *SE Yunnan:* Yanshan (74,000), Wenshan (67,000), Qiubei (63,000), Maguan (10,000), Pingbian (6,900), Guangnan (3,000), Xichou (2,200), and Hekou (1,000) counties in Wenshan Prefecture

Status: Officially included under Yi

Language: Sino-Tibetan, Tibeto-Burman, Burmese-Lolo, Lolo, Northern Lolo, Yi, Southeastern Yi

Dialects: 0

Religion: Polytheism, Animism, Ancestor Worship, Christianity

Christians: 100

Scripture: None

***Jesus* film:** None

Gospel Recordings: None

Christian Broadcasting: None

ROPAL code: None

Status of Evangelization

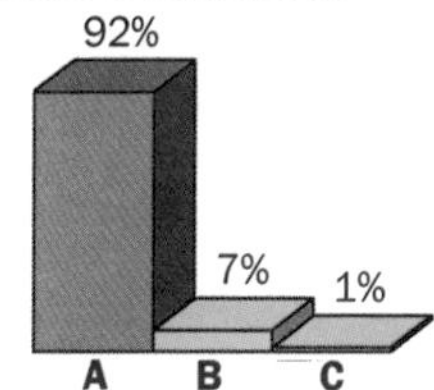

A = Have never heard the gospel
B = Were evangelized but did not become Christians
C = Are adherents to any form of Christianity

Popei 泼胚

Population in China:
5,000 (1999)
5,120 (2000)
6,430 (2010)
Location: Yunnan
Religion: Animism
Christians: None Known

Overview of the Popei

Countries: China

Pronunciation: "Poh-pay"

Other Names: Shuiyi, Shuiyipuo, Water Yi, Shui Yi, Shuitian, Shuiyizu, Shuitianyizi

Population Source:
3,000 to 5,000 (1999 J. Pelkey); Out of a total Yi population of 6,572,173 (1990 census)

Location:
N Yunnan: Chuxiong Prefecture: Dayao and Yongren counties; Lijiang Prefecture: Huaping County

Status:
Officially included under Yi

Language: Sino-Tibetan, Tibeto-Burman, Burmese-Lolo, Lolo, Northern Lolo, Yi, Central Yi

Dialects: 0

Religion: Animism, Daoism, Ancestor Worship

Christians: None known

Scripture: None

***Jesus* film:** None

Gospel Recordings: None

Christian Broadcasting: None

ROPAL code: None

Status of Evangelization

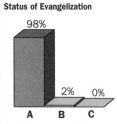

98%
2%
0%
A B C

A = Have never heard the gospel
B = Were evangelized but did not become Christians
C = Are adherents to any form of Christianity

Target Ministries

Location: Between 3,000 and 5,000 Popei people live in the northern part of Yunnan Province close to the border with Sichuan Province. About 1,000 Popei live in several villages in Huaping County which is part of Lijiang Prefecture. In addition, the Popei live in Dayao and Yongren counties of Chuxiong Prefecture. Other small pockets of Popei live scattered throughout the area. The Popei live in mountainous areas, alongside members of many other Yi subgroups such as the Eastern Nasu, Western Lipo, and Lopi.

Identity: The Popei have been officially combined with dozens of other distinct ethnolinguistic peoples to form the Yi nationality in China. The Popei are widely known by their Chinese name, *Shui Yi*, meaning "water Yi." The *Popei* (Shui Yi) are often mistaken for the *Shuitian* (Watery Fields) group, but the two groups are distinct and speak separate languages. *Popei* is this group's autonym.

Language: An official publication of the Lijiang Naxi Autonomous Prefecture states that the Popei are a distinct people group with their own language.[1] The Popei used to be more populous, but due to intermarriage with other tribes they have largely been assimilated. Jamin Pelkey states, "The Popei language reportedly shares 86% lexical similarity with the Central Luoluopo language but this comparison is based on a scant 29 word vocabulary list."[2]

History: Today's various branches of the Yi people, including the Popei, are believed to have come from common stock. Legends and records written in the ancient Yi script show that the Yi society was once matriarchal. The *Annals of the Yis in the Southwest* records that in ancient times the Yi people "only knew mothers and not fathers... and women ruled for six generations in a row."[3] As the Yi splintered into numerous divisions and migrated throughout southern China, each group gradually developed its own language and culture.

Customs: Although small in number, the Popei celebrate many traditional Yi festivals. Some of these include the Garment Contest Festival which takes place in Zhijie Township of Yongren County every February; and the Get-Together of Princes Festival which is held in Longjie Township of Dayao County on the eighth day of the fourth lunar month. The people throw water over each other, sing, dance, and create an edible "prince" which they bake and eat.

Religion: As the Popei were gradually absorbed by the Han Chinese, they adopted many of the Han's Daoist and ancestor worship rituals.

Christianity: The region inhabited by the Popei is one of the least evangelized in all of Yunnan Province. Various hidden tribes and groups in the area are locked away by remote mountains and rushing streams. Roads into the area were only constructed in the 1950s. Before then access was only possible by foot or on horseback from the nearest town. The result is that today there are no known believers among the unevangelized Popei. The nearest churches are among the Nasu and Lipo in Wuding.

Pubiao 普标

Population in China:
307 (1990)
385 (2000)
480 (2010)
Location: Yunnan
Religion: Animism
Christians: None Known

Overview of the Pubiao

Countries: Vietnam, China

Pronunciation: "Piu-bee-ow"

Other Names: Laqua, Pupeo, Ka Beo, Ka Bao, Ka Biao, Bendi Lolo, Man Laqua, Kubiao

Population Source:
307 (1990 Zhang Junru);
Out of a total Yi population of 6,572,173 (1990 census);
382 in Vietnam (1994 Hoang Luong)

Location: *SE Yunnan:* Malipo County in Wenshan Prefecture: Tiechang, Matong, Punong, Pucha, Pufeng, and Pialong villages

Status:
Officially included under Yi

Language: Daic, Kadai, Li-Laqua

Dialects: 0

Religion: Animism, Polytheism, Ancestor Worship

Christians: None known

Scripture: None

***Jesus* film:** None

Gospel Recordings: None

Christian Broadcasting: None

ROPAL code: LAQ00

Status of Evangelization

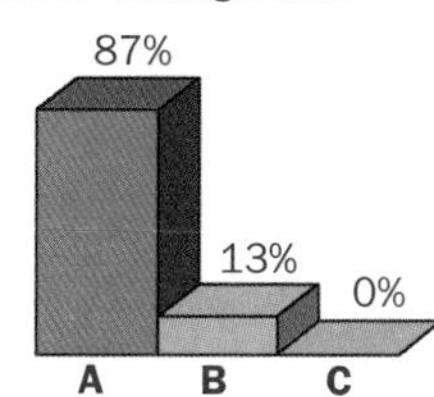

A = Have never heard the gospel
B = Were evangelized but did not become Christians
C = Are adherents to any form of Christianity

Location: The Pubiao people are evenly distributed on both sides of the China-Vietnam border. In 1990 the Pubiao numbered 307 people in southern China, while 382 were located in northern Vietnam where they are an official minority.[1] The Pubiao in China live near the Vietnam border in the Tiechang, Matong, Punong, Pucha, and Pufeng villages of Malipo County in the Wenshan Zhuang-Miao Prefecture of Yunnan Province. The Vietnam Pubiao are located in seven communes of Dong Van District in Ha Giang Province.

Identity: The Pubiao call themselves *Ka Biao*. In China the Pubiao have been officially included under the Yi nationality. The Chinese commonly call the Pubiao *Bendi Lolo*, which means "indigenous Lolo."[2]

Language: The language of the Pubiao, called *Laqua*, is nearing extinction. Only 50 elderly speakers were reported in 1991.[3] A Chinese linguist notes that although all Pubiao in China can speak Mandarin, "those who can still speak their own language are not numerous."[4] Laqua is "very similar to Laha in north-western Vietnam."[5] Every linguist who has studied Pubiao seems to have come to a different conclusion regarding which linguistic subgroup of Tai it belongs to. It has been variously described as "Zhuang-Dong,"[6] "Kadai,"[7] and "Daic."[8] The Pubiao living at Pialong can also speak Nung, while those at Matong are bilingual in Miao.[9]

History: For centuries Pubiao society has been monogamous. Today it is strictly forbidden for people of different generations to marry.

Customs: Until recently, Pubiao women wore two vests, in addition to ankle-length skirts. Lately they have abandoned wearing the outer vest and have only retained the inner one. This vest, called *bok tam*, has five panels and buttons under the right armpit. At the hems and around the neck and sleeves, bands of colored cloth are sewn which are similar to those adorning the costumes of the Giay. Pubiao women commonly draw their hair forward and hold it in place with a comb.

Religion: The Pubiao are animists. They believe a person has eight souls and nine spirits. These souls and spirits govern their existence and guide their activities. These beliefs shape the entire life and worldview of the Pubiao. The most revered place in a Pubiao home is the altar, reserved for three generations of ancestors. Each generation is symbolized by a small sandstone jar. A dried pumpkin and a bundle of ox-tail hair attached to a stick are believed to enable the ancestors to recognize their descendants.

Christianity: Many Pubiao customs are directed at preserving their unique culture, which makes it difficult for the gospel to penetrate their minds with the message of the Savior. At funerals the Pubiao offer prayers to the soul of the dead person. Texts are read reflecting the Pubiao concept of the universe, of mankind, and of their community. Some legends include a great flood in the past; the only survivors were a few who hid in a giant hollowed-out pumpkin.[10] This may be one key to introducing the gospel message to the unreached Pubiao.

Paul Hattaway

Pula 仆拉

Location: Approximately 20,000 Pula people live in China's southern Yunnan Province.[1] They live in Honghe, Yuanyang, Gejiu, Shiping, and Jianshui counties in the Honghe Yi-Hani Autonomous Prefecture; and in Yuanjiang County of Yuxi Prefecture.[2] In northwest Vietnam the Pula are better known as the *Phula* minority group. They numbered 6,424 people in the 1989 Vietnam census.

Identity: The Pula have been largely ignored in the complex ethnic patchwork of southern China.[3] The Chinese authorities have included them as part of the Yi nationality. In 1903 the Pula were described as being only about 4½ feet tall.[4]

Language: Little research has been conducted into the Pula language, but it is known to be part of the Southern Yi linguistic branch. The Pula were a tribal group on whom the Yi imposed their language.[5]

History: In China, the Pula are believed to have been among the first inhabitants of the areas where they now live. The Pula are believed to have migrated to Vietnam very long ago. Vietnamese writer Le Quy Don, famous for his book written in the mid–1700s, *Kien Van Tieu Luc* (Things Seen and Heard), described the Pula who at that time were already settled in northern Vietnam.

Customs: Traditional dress varies significantly among Pula in different areas along the Honghe River, a fact reflected in the headdress of different regions: "Pula women of southern Gejiu County wear multi-colored embroidered headpieces which stand up straight from their foreheads; Pula women in Yuanjiang County of Yuxi Prefecture often wear elaborate 'yarn bundle' headdresses, and married women of Honghe County plait their hair on the tops of their heads and wrap their heads with green turbans."[6] There are numerous social rules and superstitions among the Pula in Yuanjiang County. For example, if a child's upper tooth falls out the parents take the tooth and put it under the bed. On the other hand, if a lower tooth falls out, the tooth is placed on the roof. Only in this way, it is thought, can one be sure a new tooth will grow in its place. The Pula consider it impolite to ride a horse into another village. No one is allowed to sit in the doorway of a home for fear that the god of Wealth will be blocked from taking up residence there. Inside a Pula home, people are forbidden to sit on the rice-husking mortar, which they believe can bring a curse of famine on the family.

Paul Hattaway

Religion: The Pula believe that a god named Mumi created the heavens and earth, humans, and all spirits. "On the first 'rabbit' day after the Chinese New Year, the Pula worship the sky; on the first 'ox' day they worship the earth and the village god; and on the first 'tiger' day they call all the spirits to their aid in the new year. The Pula hold many ceremonies which... sacrifice a pig. After the sacrifice a feast is held beneath the sacred tree of the village."[7] In every Pula home the most sacred room is a central bay which contains the ancestral altar. Next to the altar is a tiny "spirit door" about 10 inches wide.

Christianity: There are just a few known Christians among the Pula in China, while only one or two families are known to have found Christ among this unreached group in northern Vietnam. Pula gospel recordings were first produced in 1999.

Population in China:
19,800 (1999)
20,300 (2000)
25,450 (2010)
Location: Yunnan
Religion: Ancestor Worship
Christians: 20

Overview of the Pula

Countries: China, Vietnam

Pronunciation: "Poo-lah"

Other Names: Phula, Bo Kho Pa, Mu Di Pa, Pulapo, Puwa, Pu, Puzu

Population Source:
19,800 (1999 J. Pelkey);
Out of a total Yi population of 6,572,173 (1990 census);
6,424 in Vietnam (1989 census)

Location: *S Yunnan:* Honghe (7,000), Yuanyang (3,800), Gejiu (2,200), Shiping (1,200), and Jianshui (500) counties in Honghe Prefecture; Yuanjiang (5,300) County in Yuxi Prefecture; Also in Vietnam

Status:
Officially included under Yi

Language: Sino-Tibetan, Tibeto-Burman, Burmese-Lolo, Lolo, Northern Lolo, Yi, Southern Yi

Dialects: 0

Religion: Ancestor Worship, Animism, Polytheism, Christianity

Christians: 20

Scripture: None

***Jesus* film:** None

Gospel Recordings:
Yi: Pula Yuanyang

Christian Broadcasting: None

ROPAL code: None

Status of Evangelization

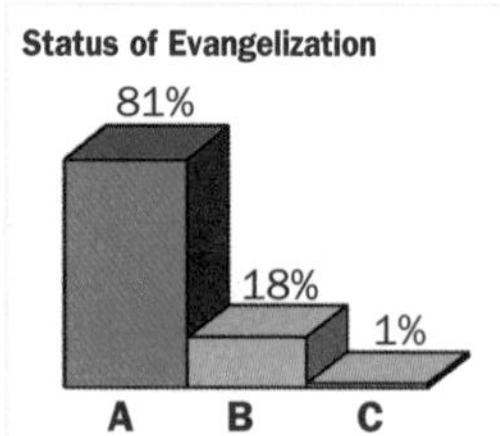

A = Have never heard the gospel
B = Were evangelized but did not become Christians
C = Are adherents to any form of Christianity

Puman 朴满

Population in China:
12,000 (1987)
16,520 (2000)
21,300 (2010)
Location: Yunnan
Religion: Buddhism
Christians: None Known

Overview of the Puman

Countries: China

Pronunciation: "Poo-mun"

Other Names: U, P'uman, Wa-la, Phuman

Population Source: 12,000 (1987 D. Bradley); 3,000 (1988 J.-O. Svantesson); Out of a total Bulang population of 82,280 (1990 census)

Location: *S Yunnan:* Shuangjiang and Mengla counties, and in several scattered communities throughout southern Yunnan

Status: Officially included under Bulang

Language: Austro-Asiatic, Mon-Khmer, Northern Mon-Khmer, Palaungic, Western Palaungic, Angkuic

Dialects: 0

Religion: Theravada Buddhism, Animism

Christians: None known

Scripture: None

***Jesus* film:** None

Gospel Recordings: None

Christian Broadcasting: None

ROPAL code: UUU00

Status of Evangelization

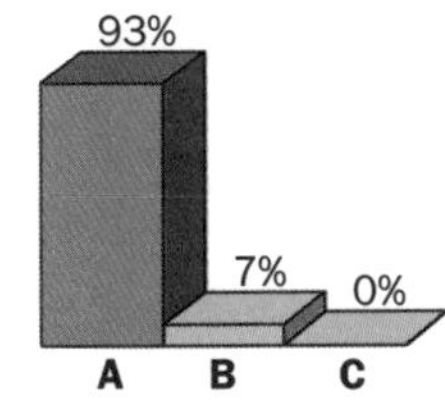

A = Have never heard the gospel
B = Were evangelized but did not become Christians
C = Are adherents to any form of Christianity

Paul Hattaway

Location: A 1988 source lists 3,000 speakers of the Puman language,[1] which is also called *U*. Another source lists a much higher population of 12,000 Puman.[2] The majority live west of the Lancang (Turbulent) River in Shuangjiang County in southern Yunnan Province. Several small Puman communities are scattered throughout other parts of southern Yunnan. Outside China, the Lancang River is known as the *Mekong*. The Mekong is the life-source for millions of people in Laos, Myanmar, Thailand, Cambodia, and Vietnam.

Identity: The Puman have been included as part of the Bulang nationality in China, although one linguist notes that they are "not very closely related."[3] The Puman are not the same as the Hu, who live in the same general vicinity and speak a similar language.

Language: The Puman speak a language belonging to Palaungic branch of the Mon-Khmer linguistic family. It is related to Wa and De'ang.

History: The Puman are part of the great Mon-Khmer race of Asia. Over the centuries, the Mon-Khmer splintered into numerous groups and today are spread as far as India's Nicobar Islands and Indonesia.

Customs: Traditionally the Puman cast lots every year before a statue of Buddha to determine where they should farm. Puman women adorn themselves with colorful head scarfs, often decorated with pieces of silver in the shape of shells or fish. This has baffled experts since their region is located far from the coast.[4]

Religion: The Puman are devoted members of the Theravada sect of Buddhism. In southwest China the Buddhists have many stories regarding the coming of a Savior, a blessed one who fits the description of Jesus Christ in many respects. Missionary William Clifton Dodd, who traveled extensively throughout the region in the 1930s, was intrigued to learn of some of the characteristics of this Theravada Buddhist messiah: "His coming is to be preceded by a falling away from the practice of religion, morality, and righteousness. His forerunner shall level every mountain, exalt every valley, make crooked places straight, and rough places smooth.... Only the pure in heart and life shall be able to see him. But those who see are to be delivered from the thralldom of rebirth. He is to be recognized by his pierced hand. And his religion shall be introduced from the south [Christianity came into southern Yunnan from Thailand], by a man with a white face and a long beard [a description that fits both Donald McGilvary and Dr. Wilson — the first missionaries to bring the gospel to Xishuangbanna]."[5]

Christianity: Despite their belief in a Savior, most Puman have yet to hear about Jesus Christ. Locked away in remote mountains and deep forests, few Christians have ever endeavored to take the gospel to them. There are no Scriptures available in a script the Puman can easily comprehend. Robert Morrison, the first Protestant missionary to China, stated, "This Bible is the one thing that can burn gates of brass and penetrate walls of rock.... I can secretly translate and circulate this Book, with the confidence that its divine message will operate with divine power."[6]

Pumi 普米

Luke Kuepfer

Location: More than 37,000 members of the Pumi minority inhabit the mountains of northern Yunnan Province. They live in approximately 500 villages, some of which are located 3,200 meters (10,500 ft.) above sea level.[1] In many locations the Pumi live beside members of the Naxi nationality. Despite 2,000 years of history, the Pumi population has remained relatively small because of disease, plague, famine, and assimilation to other tribes.[2]

Identity: The Pumi are one of China's officially recognized minority groups. In 1960 the government combined various tribes and labeled them *Pumi*. Prior to that, each tribe called themselves by a different name, including *Boukhai*.[3] The Pumi today call themselves a name which means "white men." The 30,000 Chrame people in Sichuan speak a language related to Pumi, but they have been counted in the Tibetan nationality.

Language: Pumi — which has five dialects — is a member of the Tibeto-Burman language family. Some scholars believe it was originally a Qiangic language.[4] Today after centuries of interaction, 15% of Pumi vocabulary consists of Chinese loanwords.

History: According to Pumi legends and historical records, the ancestors of the Pumi were a nomadic tribe who roamed areas hundreds of miles farther north of their present location. They were forcibly moved to Yunnan by the Mongolians in the 1300s.[5]

Customs: On the 15th day of the first month of the Pumi calendar, all Pumi, "clad in their holiday best, go camping on mountain slopes and celebrate around bonfires. The holidays are devoted to sacrifices to the 'god of the kitchen'. They celebrate with wild feasting, horse racing, shooting contests and wrestling."[6] At the age of 13, Pumi youth are considered adults. When a Pumi dies, a conch is blown three times to beckon villagers. A shaman then holds a *Gei Yangzi Yishi* (Sheep Guide) rite. The Pumi believe a sheep will lead the spirit of the deceased into the land of their ancestors.[7]

Religion: The Pumi live in fear of the spirit world. If offended, the deities can release a deluge of fierce, predatory beasts against their livestock. All Pumi worship Suoguonaba, the god of the Mountains. Worship of this powerful spirit is observed on the 5th, 15th, and 25th day of each lunar month. Ancestor worship is also practiced. Food is not eaten until it has been placed on the *guozhuang*, or tripod, to signify an invitation to the ancestors to eat first. Spirits are also believed to dwell in the wooden center post of their homes.

Christianity: Because of their linguistic variety and isolated communities, the Pumi have been largely neglected with the gospel. Prior to 1949, German missionaries reportedly witnessed to the Pumi, but little fruit remains. Although there is no organized church among the Pumi today, visitors report that they are a people "ripe unto harvest." In the early 1990s several Pumi were baptized by a Mosuo believer near Lugu Lake.[8] A potential breakthrough occurred in 1997 when 30 Pumi people prayed to receive Christ after viewing the *Jesus* film in Mandarin.[9]

Population in China:
29,657 (1990)
37,900 (2000)
48,500 (2010)
Location: Yunnan
Religion: Polytheism
Christians: 30

Overview of the Pumi

Countries: China

Pronunciation: "Poo-mee"

Other Names: Primi, Primmi, Baju, P'um, Pimi, Prummi, P'rome

Population Source:
29,657 (1990 census);
24,237 (1982 census);
14,298 (1964 census)

Location: *N Yunnan:* Lanping, Weixi, Yongsheng, Ninglang, and Lijiang counties; As far north as Lugu Lake

Status:
An official minority of China

Language: Sino-Tibetan, Tibeto-Burman, Qiangic, Pumi, Southern Pumi

Literacy: 39%

Dialects: 5

Religion: Polytheism, Animism, Shamanism, Ancestor Worship, Christianity

Christians: 30

Scripture: None

***Jesus* film:** None

Gospel Recordings: None

Christian Broadcasting: None

ROPAL code: PUS00

Status of Evangelization

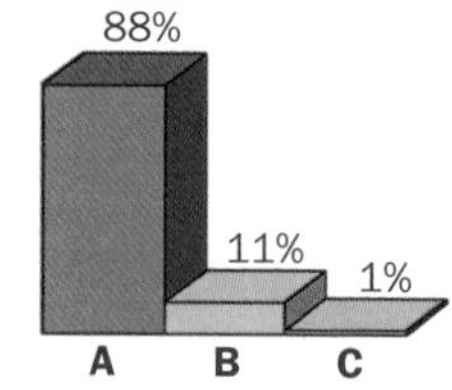

A = Have never heard the gospel
B = Were evangelized but did not become Christians
C = Are adherents to any form of Christianity

Purik 普日

Location: A small number of people belonging to the Purik people group live in Gar County on the Tibet-India border.[1] The vast majority of Purik inhabit the Suru Valley in the Kargil District of the Indian state of Jammu and Kashmir. The area is surrounded by Ladakh on the east and Baltistan (now controlled by Pakistan) to the north and northwest. The Purik's homeland is one of extremes. They live on the westernmost flange of the Himalayas — with peaks as high as 7,088 meters (23,250 ft.) and valleys as low as 265 meters (870 ft.) above sea level. Six months of the year Kargil is cut off from the rest of India; winter snows can accumulate up to 12.2 meters (40 ft.). Temperature between November and February often plummet to minus 45° Celsius (–49°F). The few Purik in Tibet live near the Bunan and Lahuli Tinan.

Identity: Few sources list the existence of the small Purik people group in China. It is not known what nationality, if any, they have been classified under by the government. "The name *Purig-Pa* [Purik] is given by the people of Ladakh and Baltistan to the inhabitants of the Kargil area in Jammu and Kashmir. *Purig-Pa* means 'Of Tibetan Origin'."[2]

Language: The Purik language, called *Purig-Skad*, is a hybrid of Ladakh Tibetan and the Balti language. "Since their conversion to Islam, their language has been influenced by Balti. All the religious sermons, hymns (*Qasidas*), and cultic mourning (*Natam*) are sung in Balti or Persian."[3] In its original form, Purik was a Western Tibetan language related to Ladakhi and the Lahuli varieties.

History: The Purik are one of the ancient peoples of northern India. They are a rare example of Tibetan Buddhists who recanted from their faith and embraced another religion — in this case, Islam.

Dwayne Graybill

Customs: Before their conversion to Islam, the Purik people held Tibetan Buddhism as their main religion. "Food and fodder were plentiful because a check on population was kept through such practices as polyandry, primogeniture and sending boys and girls to the monastery. With the introduction of Islam, the people started practicing polygamy, *Muta* (temporary concubinage) and division of the land among the children. As a result there has been a big increase in the population."[4]

Religion: With the exception of half a dozen villages, all the Purik population in India are Muslims of the fanatical Shi'a sect. It is uncertain if the small number of Purik in Tibet have re-converted to Tibetan Buddhism, or if they are practicing Muslims.

Christianity: The only outreach to target the Purik in India was undertaken by the Central Asian Mission, which worked in Kargil from the early 1900s until 1956. In addition to operating an orphanage and a medical clinic, missionary Daniel Berger translated the New Testament into Purik in 1950. Other laborers included the Mazzoni family, Nina Drew, and Betty Hall. Presently there are only three known Purik Christians in India; all live outside Kargil. There are no known Purik believers in Tibet. The Purik are considered extremely resistant to the gospel.

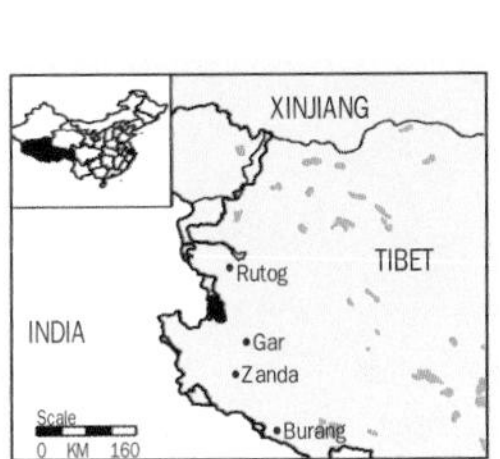

Population in China:
600 (1997)
650 (2000)
840 (2010)
Location: Tibet
Religion: Islam
Christians: None Known

Overview of the Purik

Countries: India, China, Pakistan

Pronunciation: "Boo-rig"

Other Names: Burig, Purigskad, Purik Bhotia, Purig, Purik-pa

Population Source:
600 (1997 AMO);
148,000 in India
(1977 Voegelin & Voegelin)

Location: *W Tibet:* Gar County

Status: Unidentified; Probably officially included under Tibetan

Language: Sino-Tibetan, Tibeto-Burman, Bodic, Bodish, Tibetan, Western Tibetan

Dialects: 0

Religion: Shi'a Islam, possibly Tibetan Buddhism

Christians: None known

Scripture: New Testament 1950; Portions 1938; Work in progress

***Jesus* film:** None

Gospel Recordings: Purig #01432

Christian Broadcasting: None

ROPAL code: BXR00

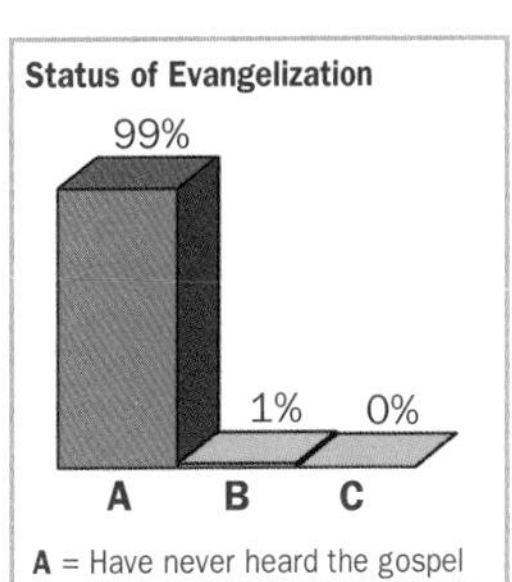

A = Have never heard the gospel
B = Were evangelized but did not become Christians
C = Are adherents to any form of Christianity

Puroik 巴绕克

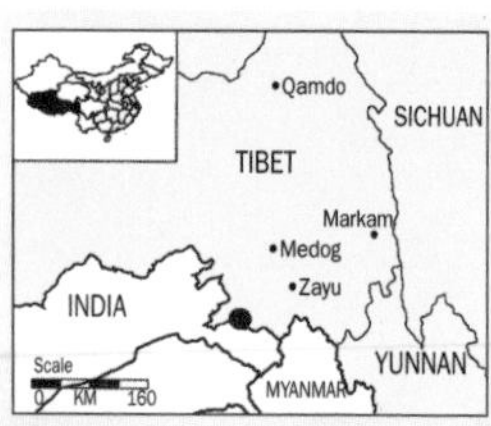

Population in China:
300 (1995)
340 (2000)
440 (2010)
Location: Tibet
Religion: Polytheism
Christians: None Known

Overview of the Puroik

Countries: India, China

Pronunciation: "Pooh-royk"

Other Names: Suling, Pariok, Sulung, Sulong

Population Source: 300 (1995 AMO); Out of a total Lhoba population of 2,312 (1990 census); 4,227 in India (1981 census)

Location: *SE Tibet:* Longzi County, near the Tibetan border with the East Kameng District in Arunachal Pradesh, India

Status: Officially included under Lhoba

Language: Sino-Tibetan, Tibeto-Burman, Unclassified

Dialects: 0

Religion: Polytheism, Animism

Christians: None known

Scripture: None

***Jesus* film:** None

Gospel Recordings: None

Christian Broadcasting: None

ROPAL code: SUV00

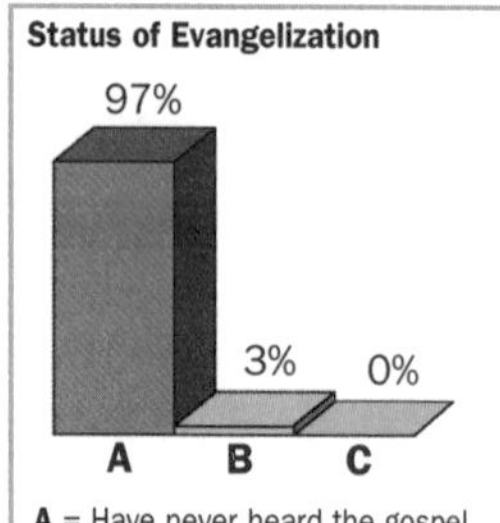

Location: Approximately 4,500 members of the small Puroik tribe inhabit mountainous jungle terrain in the East Kameng District in the northeast Indian state of Arunachal Pradesh. The region has a "drastic terrain thrown up by the sharp twisting of the Himalayan ranges as they turn suddenly from a southeasterly to a southerly direction and drop precipitously to the tropical forests of southern China and northern Burma."[1] A few hundred Puroik are also located in Longzi County on the Tibetan side of the border.[2] Traditionally the border region was controlled by India, but the Chinese took considerable territory from India after armed border clashes in 1959 and 1962.

Identity: The Puroik are officially counted as part of the Lhoba nationality in China. All people in Arunachal Pradesh in India know the Puroik as the *Sulung*, a Bangni term meaning "slaves."[3] Arunachal Pradesh is one of the most ethnically diverse regions in the world. "With a total population of less than one million, 70% is tribal, containing 21 major tribal groupings with over 100 ethnically distinct subgroupings."[4]

Language: Puroik is an unclassified member of the Tibeto-Burman family. It is very different from other varieties in the area, including Lhoba and Adi.

History: Although the Puroik claim to be the original inhabitants of the area, for centuries they have been virtual slaves of the larger Nishi tribe.[5] The Nishi formerly had intermediaries called *gingdungs* who arranged for the ransom of Puroik people, and in that way kept them trapped in dire poverty.[6] Puroik legends "tell of the great journeys they made over the wild and lonely hills and of the heroic pioneers who made the first clearings in the forest. It is part of their reverence for the dead, whose spirits they believe still haunt the countryside."[7]

Customs: The Puroik live in very small groups comprised of just a few families living together. They are a secretive and furtive people who prefer to be left alone. The Puroik are renowned as mighty hunters. The primitive mountains contain ten species of pheasants, as well as tigers, leopards, snow leopards, and goat antelope.

Religion: The primary religion among the Puroik is called *Donyi-Polo* (The Sun and the Moon). They also worship a complex hierarchy of spirits, gods, and ghosts. "Not only do particular parts of nature (plants, animals, celestial bodies, etc.) carry a divine presence, but there is a notion that spiritual energy can be exchanged between humans and these spiritually charged natural phenomena."[8]

Christianity: There are a handful of known Puroik believers on the Indian side of the border, but none in Chinese territory. Unlike other tribal areas in northeast India which have been heavily Christianized, Arunachal Pradesh remains largely animist.[9] One secular anthropologist reported, "The handful of Christians I met in Arunachal Pradesh all spoke of the importance of maintaining traditional rituals as a way of preserving their ethnic identity, despite the strong pressure against this on the part of fundamentalist Christian missionaries."[10]

Paul Hattaway

163

164

165

163–165. The *Qiang* minority in western Sichuan are a collection of 11 ethnolinguistic groups, each possessing its own language and distinctive dress. Qiang women are renowned for their skillfully embroidered hats, clothes, and even shoes (165). [all by Paul Hattaway]

166

167

168

166–168. Scottish missionary Thomas Torrance lived among the *Qiang* from 1895 to the 1930s. Torrance created a sensation by claiming the Qiang were a lost tribe of Israel. He documented numerous cultural and religious similarities between the Qiang and the Old Testament accounts. Although later scholars have dismissed Torrance's claims, the similarities between Old Testament teaching and existing Qiang customs and rituals present missionaries with a powerful starting point for explaining the gospel. [all by Paul Hattaway]

169

170

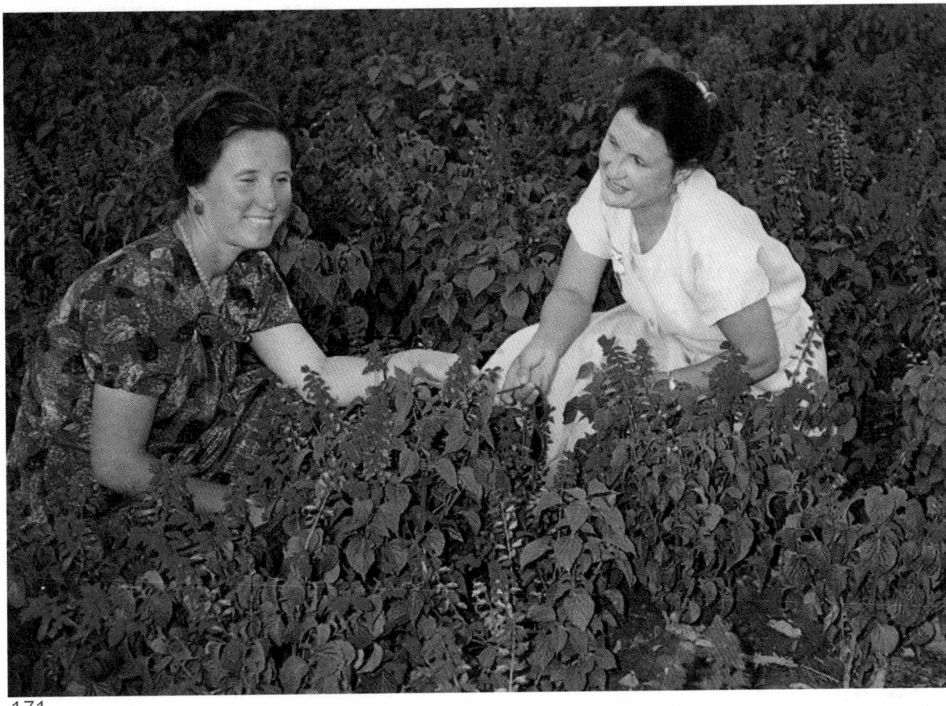

171

169. The small *Riang* tribe on the Yunnan-Myanmar border are the only group among the De'ang minority not to have embraced Buddhism. [Cooperative Baptist Fellowship]

170–171. The *Russians* are one of China's 55 official minority groups. Thousands of Russians migrated into China during the 1917 civil war. [170 Dwayne Graybill; 171 Midge Conner]

172

173

174

175

172–173. The Muslim *Salar* people speak a Turkic language. They claim to have migrated to China from Samarkand in present-day Uzbekistan. Today most Salar live in Xunhua, Qinghai. [both by Paul Hattaway]

174–175. Although more than 800,000 *She* people live in southeast China, all but a few have assimilated to Chinese culture and language. [both by Paul Hattaway]

Pusha 普沙

Dwayne Graybill

Location: Approximately 5,500 members of the Pusha tribe live in an unspecified location in southern China's Guangxi Zhuang Autonomous Region. In research literature the Pusha are often mentioned along with the Buyang, a group of similar size who inhabit three counties in the extreme southeastern arm of Yunnan Province.

Identity: One scholar explained how the Pusha came to be considered part of the official Zhuang minority in China: "Due to historical reasons, some ethnic minorities (the Bunong [Buyang] and the Busha [Pusha] who were later classified as Zhuang) have moved to different places and had different titles but still kept the same characteristics; the same language, customs and traditions."[1] Part of the confusion surrounding the Pusha is the result of their various names and identities in the past.

Language: The Pusha language has not been studied in any depth, but it is probably a part of the Kadai linguistic affiliation. The Pusha differ from other Zhuang groups who speak Northern or Central Tai languages. Most Pusha are adequately bilingual in the national language, Mandarin, since it is the common language for trade and commerce throughout the region.

History: Until recently the Pusha practiced slash-and-burn agriculture. They moved every time their farmland was exhausted. In 1953 the Pusha, along with the Buyang, were officially included as part of the huge Zhuang nationality.[2] It seems that they may have voluntarily accepted their inclusion into the Zhuang, even though they speak their own language and possess their own set of customs and traditions. One writer explains, "After the establishment of the People's Republic of China, during the stage of the 'recognition of nationalities', the Zhuangs from different districts agreed, through democratic consultation, that they be regarded as the Zhuang nationality as a whole."[3] They probably had the option to either accept inclusion as part of China's largest artificially constructed minority group or remain isolated and without the benefits of belonging to one of China's 56 politically recognized nationalities.

Customs: The Pusha live in makeshift homes because, until recently, they had to be ever ready to move to a new location.

Religion: Animism and ancestor worship are the predominant religious beliefs among the Pusha. Each home has an ancestral altar where frequent offerings are made to local deities.

Christianity: The Pusha are an unevangelized people group, living in complete ignorance, without a gospel witness. James Fraser, a missionary to the Lisu in the early part of the twentieth century, pleaded with believers around the world to intercede for the unreached: "I am not asking you to just 'help' in prayer as a sort of sideline, but I am trying to roll the main responsibility of prayer warfare on you. I want you to take the burden of these people on your shoulders. I want you to wrestle with God for them."[4] The Pusha need similar fervent prayer on their behalf.

Population in China:
5,000 (1995)
5,490 (2000)
6,560 (2010)
Location: Guangxi
Religion: Animism
Christians: None Known

Overview of the Pusha

Countries: China

Pronunciation: "Poo-sha"

Other Names: Busha

Population Source:
5,000 (1995 AMO);
Out of a total Zhuang population of 15,489,630 (1990 census)

Location: *SW Guangxi*

Status:
Officially included under Zhuang

Language: Daic, Kadai

Dialects: 0

Religion: Animism, Polytheism, Ancestor Worship

Christians: None known

Scripture: None

***Jesus* film:** None

Gospel Recordings: None

Christian Broadcasting: None

ROPAL code: None

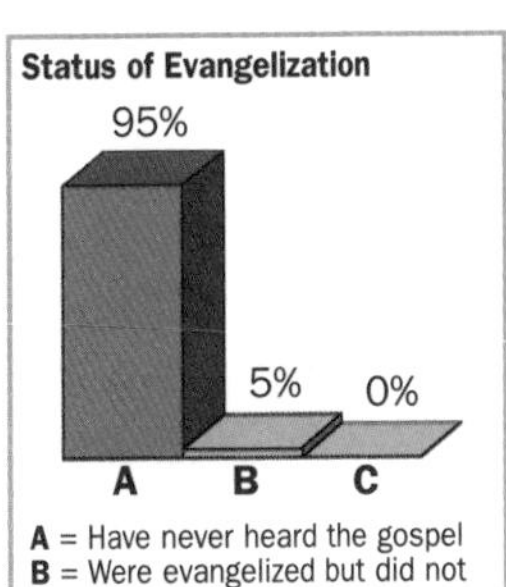

Puwa 仆瓦

Population in China:
29,000 (1999)
29,700 (2000)
37,300 (2010)
Location: Yunnan
Religion: Polytheism
Christians: 100

Overview of the Puwa

Countries: China

Pronunciation: "Poo-wah"

Other Names: Wapuo, Lapeitula, Lepeitulapuo, Pula, Pupula, Green Pu, Pu, Pupo, Puzu, Puren, Aza, Azar, Azarpuo

Population Source:
29,000 (1999 J. Pelkey);
Out of a total Yi population of 6,572,173 (1990 census)

Location: *SE Yunnan:* Mengzi (23,000), Yanshan (4,000), and Kaiyuan (2,000) counties

Status:
Officially included under Yi

Language: Sino-Tibetan, Tibeto-Burman, Burmese-Lolo, Lolo, Northern Lolo, Yi, Southeastern Yi

Dialects: 0

Religion: Polytheism, Animism, Ancestor Worship, Christianity

Christians: 100

Scripture: None

***Jesus* film:** None

Gospel Recordings:
Yi: Puwa Kaiyuan
Yi: Pula Mengzi

Christian Broadcasting: None

ROPAL code: None

Status of Evangelization

A = Have never heard the gospel
B = Were evangelized but did not become Christians
C = Are adherents to any form of Christianity

Location: More than 29,000 members of the Puwa tribe live in thatched-roof huts throughout the southern and southeastern parts of Yunnan Province. The majority (23,000) live in Mengzi County, while 4,000 live in Yanshan County, and 2,000 in Kaiyuan. The Puwa are one the largest of the Yi groups in the China-Vietnam border region, but they do not spill across into northern Vietnam.

YWAM COM

Identity: The name *Puwa* is both the autonym and the name used by all other people in the area to describe this group. There may be several distinct tribes or clans among the Puwa. The Puwa are not related to the ancient Pu tribe who founded the Ailao Kingdom in Yunnan between the first and fifth centuries AD. Today's Mon-Khmer peoples in Yunnan, such as the De'ang, Wa, and Bulang, are thought to be descended from the former Pu Kingdom. The Puwa are related to the larger Poluo group who inhabit areas in southeast Yunnan.

Language: The Puwa language is part of the Southeastern Yi group. It is still spoken by all members of this ethnic group, including children.

History: These people have a reputation for being very independent and hostile to outsiders. They rarely venture into the townships and marketplaces and, therefore, have little contact with members of other nationalities. The Puwa prefer to stay in their mountain villages where they retain their customs, language, and lifestyle without interruption.

Customs: The Puwa celebrate many festivals throughout the year. One of the largest is the Cattle Festival that takes place during the second month of the lunar calendar. The people pick flowers and place them in the horns of their cows and water buffalo. They also place flowers above the doors of their homes and stables. The primary reason for the festival is the worship of the Mountain god. The Puwa believe large and powerful demons live inside the highest mountains. They offer sacrifices in honor of these spirits, which — they believe — if not kept happy, can cause disaster to fall on their communities.

Religion: The Puwa are a superstitious people who worship numerous spirits. The most revered is the Dragon god. The first "dragon day" of every third lunar month is set aside to appease the dragon. Every village stops work and sacrifices a pig under the village dragon's tree.[1]

Christianity: There is at least one Puwa Catholic village in Mengzi County. Mengzi has the longest history of Christianity in all of Yunnan. Catholic missionaries first entered the county in 1716 from Sichuan. Beginning in 1894, much work was done in Laozhai and Mingjiu districts, mostly impacting the Hmong but also reaching at least one Puwa village for Christ.[2] Work was also started among the Puwa of Dayakou Village in Mengzi County in 1896. Through the years nine families believed, and a church was formed. After almost 50 years of persecution, however, none of the converts there still cling to Christ. Their church building still stands but has not been used since 1951.[3]

Qanu 喀努

Population in China:
10,000 (1995)
11,450 (2000)
14,700 (2010)
Location: Guizhou
Religion: Animism
Christians: None Known

Overview of the Qanu

Countries: China

Pronunciation: "Ga-Noo"

Other Names: Kanao, Gha-Nu, Qanu Miao

Population Source: 10,000 (1995 M. Johnson); Out of a total Miao population of 7,398,035 (1990 census)

Location: *Guizhou:* South of Kaili

Status: Officially included under Miao

Language: Hmong-Mien, Hmongic, Eastern Hmongic

Dialects: 0

Religion: Animism, Polytheism, Ancestor Worship

Christians: None known

Scripture: None

***Jesus* film:** None

Gospel Recordings: None

Christian Broadcasting: None

ROPAL code: None

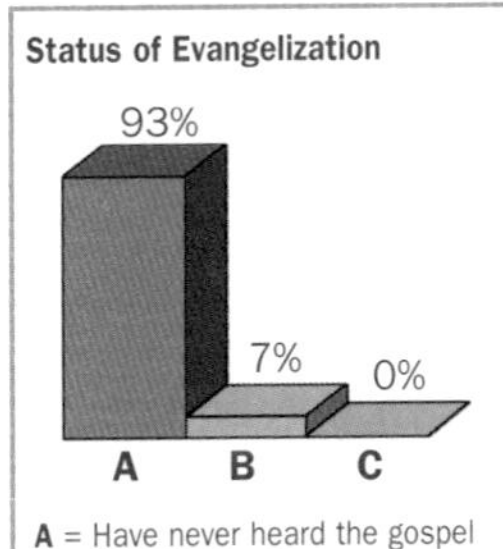

Location: Approximately 11,500 members of a Miao subgroup who call themselves *Qanu* are primarily located in villages to the south of the city of Kaili, in Guizhou Province's Qiandongnan Prefecture.[1] Kaili is the main center of the Northern Hmu language group.

Identity: Although they have been officially included as part of the Miao nationality in China, the Qanu possess their own distinct ethnic identity.[2] The Qanu may also be known as the "Miao with Combs in Their Hair" to local people. There are many smaller Miao groups in China, such as the Qanu, who have not yet been thoroughly researched by Chinese linguists. In southern Guizhou, six different Miao "dialects" remain unclassified. One linguist states they are "presumably mutually unintelligible languages."[3] These six unclassified groups amount to about 30,000 people.[4]

Language: Michael Johnson notes, "The speakers of another intelligible dialect group to the south of Kaili City call themselves *Qanu.*"[5] Although they possess a different ethnocultural identity, the Qanu speak the same language as the Northern Hmu. Remarkably — despite their small numbers and the fact that few people today are aware of their existence — a French-Qanu dictionary was complied by Joseph Esquirol in the 1930s.[6] Esquirol transcribed Qanu as *Kanao.*

History: The lack of a written script has caused great anguish among the Miao for centuries. A Miao pastor, Wang Mingji, declared his feelings: "We Miao do not have writing. For thousands of years we have been like the blind, it has been very bitter. Everybody knows that there is nothing worse in the world than to be blind, however shimmering is the sun in the sky, however shining is the moon in the sky, however clear are the rivers and mountains on the earth, however beautiful are the flowers in the wilderness, the blind cannot see them anyway."[7]

Customs: Most Qanu are agriculturists. Many families also raise livestock to supplement their meager incomes.

Religion: The majority of Qanu are animists. The spirit of the water is particularly held in great fear.

Christianity: There are no known believers among the Qanu. Many Protestant missionaries targeted the Gha-Mu and A-Hmao in northwest Guizhou and northern Yunnan prior to the advent of Communism, but few worked in the region of southeast Guizhou where the Qanu are located. Former missionaries in China are generally remembered as self-sacrificing servants who labored with the love of God for the people they lived among. The Communist authorities, however, have a very different view of history: "From the nineteenth century onwards the imperialists propagated Christianity in northwest Guizhou and in other Miao areas. They... printed the 'Bible' in order to poison and deceive the masses in the area of question. Furthermore, they sowed dissension and discord, spied, exploited, pillaged etc."[8]

Paul Hattaway

Qiang, Cimulin 羌(知木林)

Location: A Chinese source lists a 1990 figure of 9,800 speakers of Cimulin Qiang living in five districts within Heishui (Black Water) County in northwest Sichuan Province.[1] The total Qiang population in the 1990 census was 198,252 — a four-fold increase from the 1964 figure of only 49,105. Most of the increase can be attributed to the reclassification of additional peoples under the Qiang, rather than to biological growth.

Identity: The Cimulin Qiang language is very different from other varieties of Qiang. "The Chinese character for *Qiang* is a combination of *yang* (sheep) and *ren* (people), with the composite meaning of 'people tending sheep'."[2]

Language: Cimulin Qiang, which is a Northern Qiang language, is not tonal, whereas Southern Qiang varieties consist of between two to six tones.[3] Many of the Cimulin Qiang are bilingual in Tibetan, while others living near the towns are able to speak Chinese. In addition, more than 50,000 speakers of Northern Qiang dialects have been placed under the Tibetan nationality.[4]

History: Qiang history dates back as far as the Western Zhou Dynasty (1100–771 BC), when considerable numbers of Han people migrated west and formed mixed communities with the Di and Qiang.[5]

Customs: One of the Qiang festivals is called *Jishanhui*, which women are not allowed to attend. A cow or sheep is sacrificed on an altar to the god of the Mountains. They ask for a good harvest and peace for the village.

Paul Hattaway

Religion: The Northern Qiang language groups have embraced Tibetan Buddhism more zealously than the Southern Qiang, because of centuries of influence from neighboring Tibetans. The Northern Qiang also worship a multitude of Chinese and Tibetan deities, of which the Sky god is considered the greatest. In addition, shamans, witches, and mediums are located throughout the countryside. In 1994 one Christian interviewed a Qiang sorceress at a temple reputed to be 1,000 years old. The woman told the visitor, "'I have the power to put people into a trance, and make their spirits leave their bodies and travel to hell. Usually, we can then call their spirits back, but sometimes it doesn't work, and the person dies and is trapped in hell forever.' When we told her about a God who has the power to take her spirit to heaven, she was delighted and wanted to know more."[6] Most Qiang people, like this sorceress, have absolutely no awareness of the gospel.

Christianity: One Christian ministry has incorrectly reported there to be "no Qiang Christians remaining,"[7] but a small Qiang church does exist in China. There are a very small number of Northern Qiang Christians, including some families living in Songpan. "There are no church buildings any more, but still Christian believers."[8] It is not known, however, if there are any Christians specifically among the Cimulin Qiang. Several short-term missions teams in the early 1990s were arrested and expelled from China for distributing literature in the Qiang region.[9]

Population in China:
9,800 (1990)
12,600 (2000)
16,300 (2010)
Location: Sichuan
Religion: Tibetan Buddhism
Christians: None Known

Overview of the Cimulin Qiang

Countries: China

Pronunciation: "Chee-ung"

Other Names: Chiang: Cimulin, Chi'ang, Cimulin, Tz'u-mu-lin Ch'iang

Population Source: 9,800 (1998 Liu Guangkun – 1990 figure); Out of a total Qiang population of 198,252 (1990 census)

Location: *NW Sichuan:* Heishui County: Cimulin, Gewo, Wumushu, Rewo, and Qinglanggou districts

Status: Officially included under Qiang

Language: Sino-Tibetan, Tibeto-Burman, Qiangic, Qiang, Northern Qiang

Dialects: 0

Religion: Tibetan Buddhism, Polytheism, Animism, Shamanism

Christians: None

Scripture: None

***Jesus* film:** None

Gospel Recordings: None

Christian Broadcasting: None

ROPAL code: None

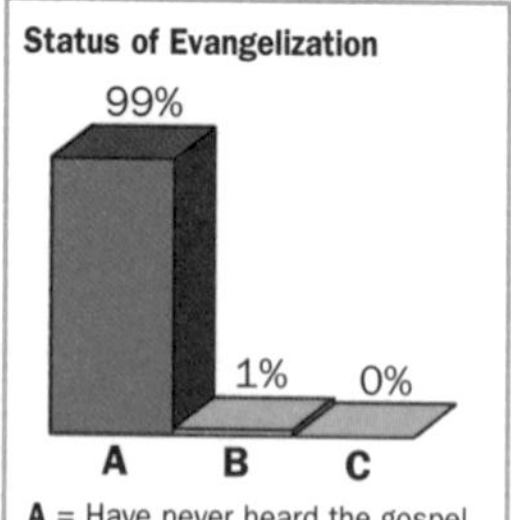

A = Have never heard the gospel
B = Were evangelized but did not become Christians
C = Are adherents to any form of Christianity

Qiang, Dajishan 羌(大吉山)

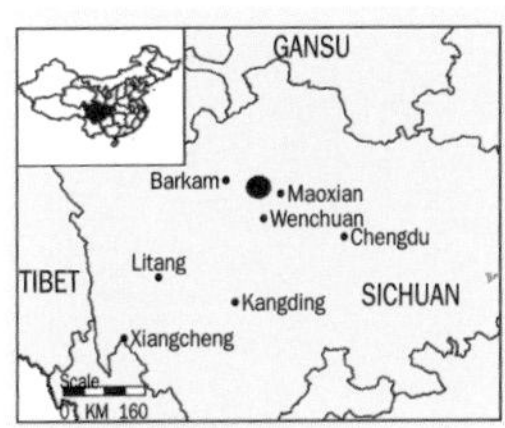

Population in China:
7,400 (1990)
9,540 (2000)
12,300 (2010)
Location: Sichuan
Religion: Polytheism
Christians: None Known

Overview of the Dajishan Qiang

Countries: China

Pronunciation: "Chee-ung-Dah-jee-shahn"

Other Names: Chiang: Dajishan, Dajishan, Daqishan Qiang, Ta-ch'i-shan Ch'iang

Population Source: 7,400 (1998 Liu Guangkun – 1990 figure); Out of a total Qiang population of 198,252 (1990 census)

Location: *W Sichuan:* Lixian County: Xuecheng, Shangmeng, Xiameng, Xinglong, Ganbao, Lielie, Jiuzi, Muka, Piaotou, and Puxi districts

Status: Officially included under Qiang

Language: Sino-Tibetan, Tibeto-Burman, Qiangic, Qiang, Southern Qiang

Dialects: 0

Religion: Polytheism, Animism, Ancestor Worship

Christians: None known

Scripture: None

***Jesus* film:** None

Gospel Recordings: None

Christian Broadcasting: None

ROPAL code: None

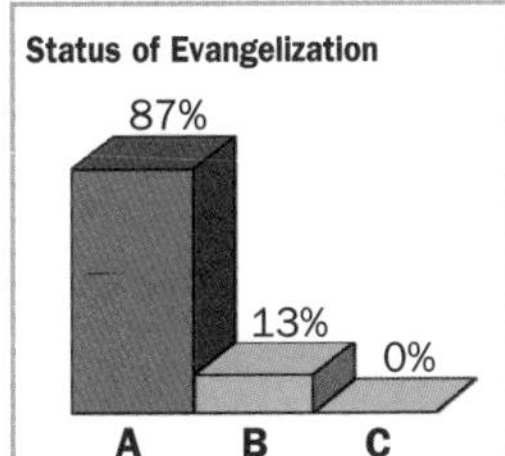

Location: A Chinese linguist in 1990 listed 7,400 speakers of the Dajishan Qiang language, living in ten districts within Lixian County in the Aba Prefecture of western Sichuan.[1] The Qiang, who total approximately 200,000 people, inhabit an extremely rugged region, with gushing emerald-colored rivers cutting their way past 18,000-foot (5,480 m) snowcapped mountains.

Paul Hattaway

Identity: The Qiang are one of the oldest and most famous of China's peoples. In ancient times they numbered 62 different tribes.[2] Today's official Qiang nationality is a collection of 11 different tribes and languages, including the Dajishan Qiang.[3]

Language: Linguist James Matisoff in 1991 discovered there to be "9 or 10 Qiangic languages."[4] The Qiang have a legend of once possessing a script and "lost book" of their own.[5] Dajishan Qiang is part of the Southern Qiang linguistic group. One linguist says, "Southern Qiang has been divided by researchers into five sub-dialects [including Dajishan] which are considered to be too divergent from each other to permit communication between people from different villages."[6]

History: Numerous references to the Qiang tribes, dating back 4,000 years, are found in Chinese history. Sandwiched between the wild, warlike Tibetans to the west and the expanding Chinese to the east, these various nomadic tribes came to be known as the *Qiang*, a name that one source says means "herdsmen."[7]

Customs: Almost all Qiang weddings and festivals are scheduled during the tenth month of the year. On the eve of the wedding day the bridegroom's family will send a "gift-bearer" to the bride's home with presents. After the wedding feast, which may last up to ten hours, the custom of "singing in the hall" commences. "The bride, whose face is veiled by a handkerchief, will first sing a song to bid farewell to her parents and thank them for her upbringing. She is then followed by the bridesmaids who will sing a song persuading her to go to the groom and live with him as man and wife."[8]

Religion: Most Qiang are polytheists. "They believe that everything on earth — the earth itself, the sky, the sun, trees, fire, saplings, doors, even cauldron supports, pillars, white stones etc. — has a soul and they are all to be worshipped. They have no idols of any deity but choose a kind of milk-white stone as the symbol of all deities.... Usually on the back wall on the top floor of every house there are five white stones representing deities of Heaven, Earth and Mountains."[9]

Christianity: Thomas F. Torrance, from Scotland, was the first Protestant missionary among the Qiang. He served with the China Inland Mission from 1895 to 1909 and then with the American Bible Society until the 1930s. Torrance reported, "scores and scores of Christian converts among these tribesmen, especially in the Wenchuan and Weizhou [Maoxian] areas, and seven meeting places established around Tongmenwai."[10] There are several hundred Qiang believers today, but it is unclear if any are from the Dajishan Qiang language group who live in Lixian County.

Qiang, Heihu 羌(黑虎)

Paul Hattaway

Location: More than 20,000 speakers of the Heihu Qiang language inhabit nine districts in the central and southern parts of Maoxian County in western Sichuan Province.[1] The various Qiang groups, including the Heihu, live in small, scattered communities, resulting in "large dialect differences."[2]

Identity: The Heihu Qiang have been combined with other related groups in Sichuan to form the official Qiang nationality.

Language: Linguist Robert Ramsey, in his overview of the Qiang, states, "The Qiang are bound together only loosely. Groups have diverged linguistically, and the Qiang in one area are frequently unable to understand the speech of those in another area.... No question of mutual intelligibility could possibly arise here; if groups from two areas were to come together, it is quite likely they would have to communicate with each other in Chinese."[3]

History: The Qiang have migrated a vast distance across China during their history. During the Qin and Han dynasties (221 BC – AD 220) they lived in the present-day Alxa Prefecture in Inner Mongolia. There they joined forces with the Hun and Wuhuan peoples to fight the Chinese. Because of numerous conflicts with other nationalities in the past, the Qiang built imposing stone fortresses, many of which still stand in the remote mountain passes of western Sichuan.[4]

Customs: The Qiang have a fond love for music. They are talented singers and dancers, and love to "dance to the accompaniment of gongs, tambourines, sonas and bamboos."[5]

Religion: Missionary Thomas Torrance amazed the world in the early 1900s with his claims that the Qiang people may be one of the lost tribes of Israel.[6] He found numerous practices in Qiang culture and religion that he believed could only have come from a knowledge of the Old Testament. On a visit to Oir in 1925, Torrance met a Qiang priest who "explained their ancient sacrificial rites, and told us of their two-fold sacrifice on their annual day of atonement: one goat was slaughtered at an altar in a sacred grove at a 'high place', and one goat was released into the wilds beyond. When my father read to the priest and his family the sixteenth chapter of the book of Leviticus, in which details of this same rite are found in the ancient Hebrew liturgy, the old priest leaped up from his stool in excitement, saying that these were the lost Qiang Scriptures!"[7]

Christianity: Mao's Communist forces destroyed several Qiang churches when the Long March passed through the region in the summer of 1935. "All Qiang pastors and most of their families were executed by Mao's men. The Communists tried to burn all Bibles and New Testaments, even tried to destroy the Christian's grain, so as to eliminate the Christian communities established in Wenchuan and Lifan counties. But in Tongmenwai the Christians saved some of their Bibles by burying them in caves. They resurrected them after Mao's forces had passed on."[8]

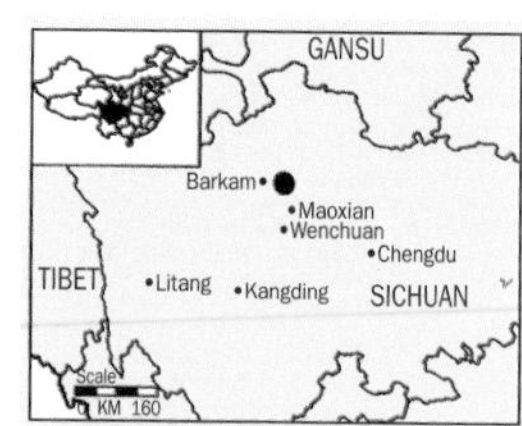

Population in China:
16,000 (1990)
20,640 (2000)
26,600 (2010)
Location: Sichuan
Religion: Polytheism
Christians: 150

Overview of the Heihu Qiang

Countries: China

Pronunciation: "Chee-ung-Hay-hoo"

Other Names: Chiang: Heihu, Heihu, Hei-hu Ch'iang

Population Source: 16,000 (1998 Liu Guangkun – 1990 figure); 30,000 (1998 J. Matisoff); Out of a total Qiang population of 198,252 (1990 census)

Location: *W Sichuan:* Maoxian County: Heihu, Sujiaping, Feihong, Goukou, Weimen, and Jiaoyuanping districts

Status: Officially included under Qiang

Language: Sino-Tibetan, Tibeto-Burman, Qiangic, Qiang, Southern Qiang

Dialects: 0

Religion: Polytheism, Animism, Ancestor Worship, Christianity

Christians: 150

Scripture: None

***Jesus* film:** None

Gospel Recordings: None

Christian Broadcasting: None

ROPAL code: None

Status of Evangelization

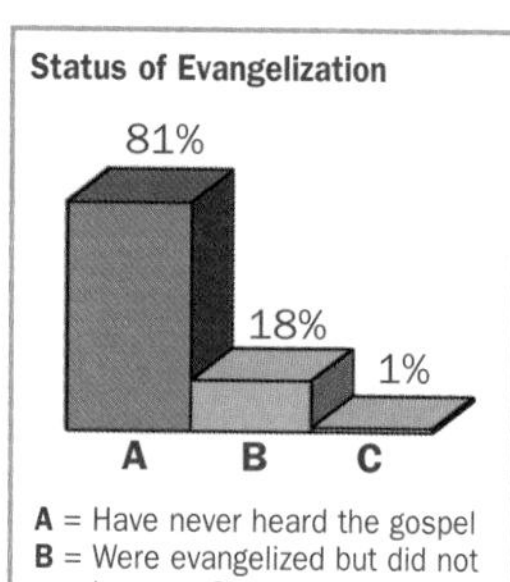

A = Have never heard the gospel
B = Were evangelized but did not become Christians
C = Are adherents to any form of Christianity

Qiang, Jiaochang 羌(较场)

Location: More than 24,000 speakers of the Jiaochang Qiang language live in the western part of Sichuan Province among rugged mountains near the Min River. The great majority live in Maoxian County, in the districts of Jiaochang (which lends its name to the dialect), Shidaguan, Taiping, and Songpinggou; others live in the Xice area of Zhenjiangguan District in Songpan County (which is the northernmost Qiang community in China). A small number of Jiaochang Qiang also live in parts of Beichuan County.[1]

Identity: The name Qiang is a Chinese term. The Qiang refer to themselves as *Rimai* in Maoxian County; *Rima* in Mao Township and Chibusu District; and *Ma* in Lixian County. "The meaning of these words is 'the righteousness of people'."[2]

Language: Jiaochang is spoken by more people than any other dialect of Southern Qiang in China. The linguistic diversity among the various Qiang groups scattered throughout Sichuan is bewildering. Captain William Gill was one of the first Westerners ever to pass through Qiang territory in the 1870s. Gill compiled a brief wordlist from a Qiangic language, but stated, "This orthography can convey but a feeble idea of the astounding noises the people make in their throats to produce these words."[3]

History: Between AD 600 and 900 many Qiang were assimilated by the Han and Tibetan cultures, leaving only a small group intact. This group is now known as the Qiang nationality.

Customs: Although they may struggle to understand each other's language, there are strong cultural ties between the various Qiang groups, including the mutual possession of stone towers. The Qiang believe their common ancestors constructed them.

Religion: The majority of Qiang people are polytheists and animists, deifying mountains, sheep, trees, storms, fire, etc. Others are followers of Tibetan Buddhism (especially those living close to Tibetan communities) and Daoism.

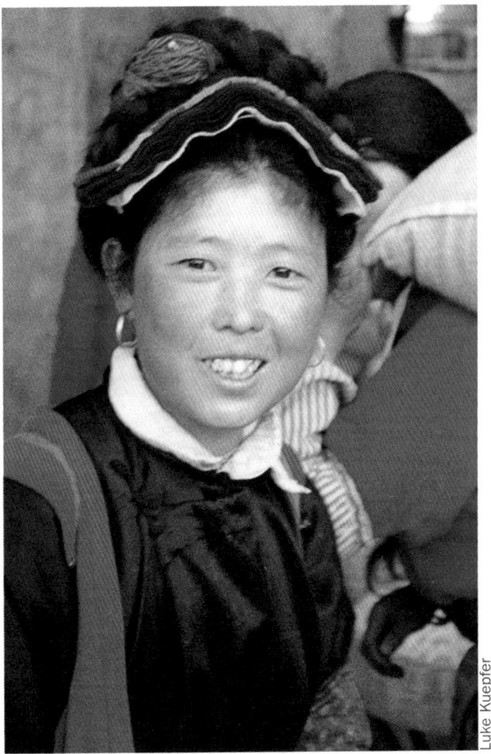
Luke Kuepfer

Christianity: There are approximately 100 Christians among the Jiaochang Qiang dialect group. They are the result of pre-1949 work by both Protestant and Catholic missionaries. In 1998 the Christian mission Gospel Recordings produced the first Christian audio recording in a Qiang language. It was recorded in Songpinggou District of Maoxian County, within the territory of the Jiaochang Qiang language. There are still no Scripture portions available in any of the 11 Qiang languages. Apart from the labors of Thomas Torrance, mission work among the Qiang includes a Catholic church that was established in Maoxian in 1898 by French missionaries. In 1906 a British missionary, whose Chinese name was Feigesheng, preached in Maoxian. In 1906 and 1909, the Catholic Church of England established a church, hospital, and school in the Qiang area. In 1918 an Englishman named Maosenwei also founded a school, medical clinic, and churches.[4]

Population in China:
19,000 (1990)
24,500 (2000)
31,600 (2010)
Location: Sichuan
Religion: Polytheism
Christians: 100

Overview of the Jiaochang Qiang

Countries: China

Pronunciation: "Chee-Ung-Jeeow-chung"

Other Names: Chiang: Jiaochang, Chi'ang: Jiaochang

Population Source: 19,000 (1998 Liu Guangkun – 1990 figure); Out of a total Qiang population of 198,252 (1990 census)

Location: *W Sichuan:* Maoxian County: Jiaochang, Shidaguan, Taiping, and Songpinggou districts; Songpan County: Xice area of Zhenjiangguan District; Some speakers of Jiaochang Qiang also live in areas within Beichuan County.

Status: Officially included under Qiang

Language: Sino-Tibetan, Tibeto-Burman, Qiangic, Qiang, Southern Qiang

Dialects: 0

Religion: Polytheism, Animism, Ancestor Worship, Daoism, Christianity

Christians: 100

Scripture: None

***Jesus* film:** None

Gospel Recordings: Qiang: Song Ping Gou #04835

Christian Broadcasting: None

ROPAL code: None

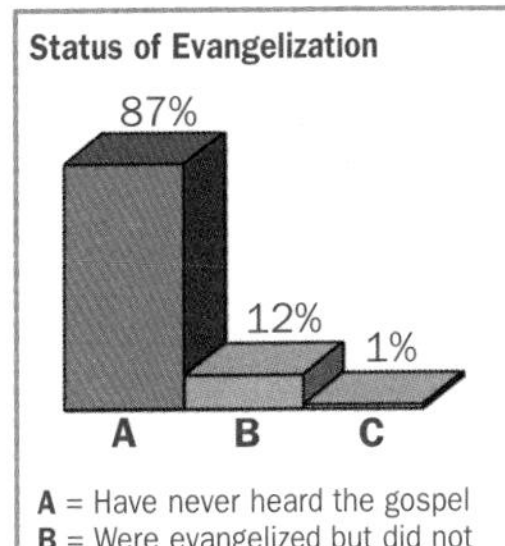

Qiang, Longxi 羌(弄西)

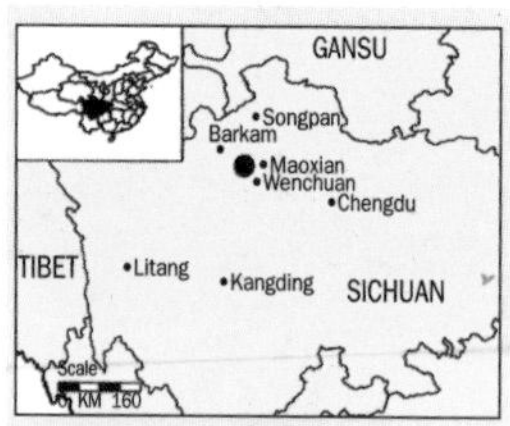

Population in China:
3,300 (1990)
4,250 (2000)
5,490 (2010)
Location: Sichuan
Religion: Polytheism
Christians: None Known

Overview of the Longxi Qiang

Countries: China

Pronunciation: "Chee-ung-Long-shee"

Other Names: Chiang: Longxi, Longxi, Lung-hsi Ch'iang

Population Source: 3,300 (1998 Liu Guangkun – 1990 figure); Out of a total Qiang population of 198,252 (1990 census)

Location: *W Sichuan:* Northern Wenchuan County: Longxi, Bulan, Baduo, Xiazhuang, and Mushang districts

Status: Officially included under Qiang

Language: Sino-Tibetan, Tibeto-Burman, Qiangic, Qiang, Southern Qiang

Dialects: 0

Religion: Polytheism, Shamanism, Animism, Ancestor Worship

Christians: None known

Scripture: None

***Jesus* film:** None

Gospel Recordings: None

Christian Broadcasting: None

ROPAL code: None

Status of Evangelization

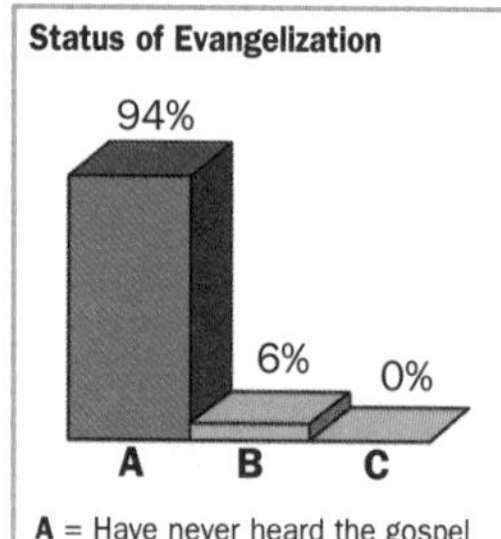

A = Have never heard the gospel
B = Were evangelized but did not become Christians
C = Are adherents to any form of Christianity

Location: More than 4,000 Longxi Qiang are one of at least ten Qiang language groups living in the Aba Prefecture in western Sichuan Province.[1] The Longxi Qiang live in the northern part of Wenchuan County. The 1,155-kilometer-long (712 mi.) Dadu River flows through the region. "It is sandwiched between sky-high cliffs on both banks and follows a course replete with rocks, precarious shoals and submerged reefs."[2]

Identity: Longxi Qiang is a distinct language spoken by members of the official Qiang nationality in China.

Language: Chinese scholars describe the various Qiang languages, including Longxi, as mere "dialects" of Qiang, but they are clearly distinct languages. The Southern Qiang languages have as many as six tones, while Northern Qiang is nontonal.[3]

History: The Qiang honor white stones, a tradition reportedly started after a conflict many centuries ago. The hostile Geji tribe ambushed the Qiang, who being caught unprepared, picked up sticks and white stones and fought with them. Despite their marked disadvantage, they defeated their enemies and won the right to live in the fertile valley that remains their home today.[4]

Customs: Qiang families spend much of their time around the fireplace and cauldron, which is located in the middle of their homes. The cauldron "is an iron or steel tripod over which hangs a hook known commonly as a 'rat's tail', which can be raised or lowered at will... to regulate the heat of the fire."[5]

Religion: During their annual sacrifice, the Qiang carry a sacred roll of white paper which represents the Word of God — even though it has nothing written on it. Torrance explains how "each year a fresh piece of white paper is rolled around the scroll to indicate the purity of the Word or Heaven-sent sin bearer which they termed variously *Je-Dzu*, *Nee-Dzu* or *Rin-Dzu*, meaning 'Saviour'. On hearing this my father then read the first chapter of St. John's Gospel which tells of the Word of God made flesh in Jesus Christ.... He told the Qiang that they had been tucked away in such a remote part of the world that they had never heard that the Word of God had come in Jesus Christ.... As he announced the Good News... the priest and all his household believed and were duly baptized."[6]

Christianity: After all of the Qiang church leaders had been martyred in 1935, missionary Thomas Torrance returned to Scotland. A Qiang Christian, Huang Taiqing, wrote to him: "Because of the Communist persecution, this book was hidden in a cave during the year of the Chinese Republic. Thus the book was saved from destruction. In memory of the Gospel Chapel of Tongmenwai, Lifan County."[7] The New Testament was sent to Torrance as a pledge that the church among the Qiang would rise again. Today there are Qiang believers living in Kegu, Kampo, Lixian, Songpan, and Maoxian counties, but it is not known if there are any Christians among the Longxi Qiang dialect group.[8]

Paul Hattaway

Qiang, Luhua 羌(龙溪)

Midge Conner

Location: The Chinese linguist Liu Guangkun lists a 1990 figure of 14,000 speakers of the Luhua Qiang language living in northwest Sichuan Province in western China.[1] The Luhua Qiang language is spoken in the Luhua, Shashiduo, Yangrong, Zegai, Ergulu, and Zhuogedu districts of Heishui (Black Water) County in the Aba Prefecture. Heishui County had a total population of 58,000 in the 1990 census, of which 49,600 (85.5%) speak Qiang languages.

Identity: Although they belong to the Qiang nationality and speak Qiang, many of the Qiang in Heishui County call themselves *Zangzu* (Tibetan) in Chinese but *R'ma* in their own language. Having been acculturated to Tibetan centuries ago, these Qiang no longer view themselves as a distinct people.

Language: Luhua Qiang is one of four distinct varieties of Northern Qiang in China. One researcher has noted, "Although Qiang does not have a large population, their language is divided into many dialects, and they are not intelligible from one to another. Even worse, each village uses a different dialect. It is therefore very difficult to research."[2]

History: For a long period of time before 1949, the Qiang lived in primitive conditions. A feudal landlord economy dominated production. Many of these poor peasants eventually lost their land due to excessive and unfair taxation. They became hired laborers and wandered from place to place to make a living.

Customs: In their small fields the Luhua Qiang grow corn, red peppers, potatoes, cabbages, beans, and wheat. They also grow a fruit called *whadjou*. In their mud-brick homes they keep pigs, sheep, goats, chickens, and some cattle.

Religion: White stones are not only representative of Qiang gods but are also a symbol of good fortune. Some Qiang believe that "bringing a white stone into a house on New Year's Day will bring more property. So, when they visit a neighbor or relative... they present a white rock and shout 'Property comes!' The host receives it carefully and then welcomes their blessing wholeheartedly by carefully placing it next to the ancestral tablets or the image of a deity."[3]

Christianity: Foreign missionaries who worked in the Qiang region in the late 1800s recounted this fascinating story of a brief encounter with an unknown tribe: "Years ago a deputation from Ngapa came to Kwanhsien [today's Guanxian County] with a request for pith helmets, guns, and Bibles. Their interest in the Gospel, like the order, seemed mixed, but... eleven years later, the writer met a Prince from Ngapa who greedily bought up 500 [Scripture] portionettes. 'No,' [the Prince] said, 'they are not for sale. My people are interested in this Gospel.'"[4] This interesting story reflects the interest in the gospel the Qiang people still have today. They are unreached not because they are resistant to the claims of Christ, but rather because few have ever been presented with the gospel in a way they could comprehend it and make an intelligent decision to accept or reject the Savior.

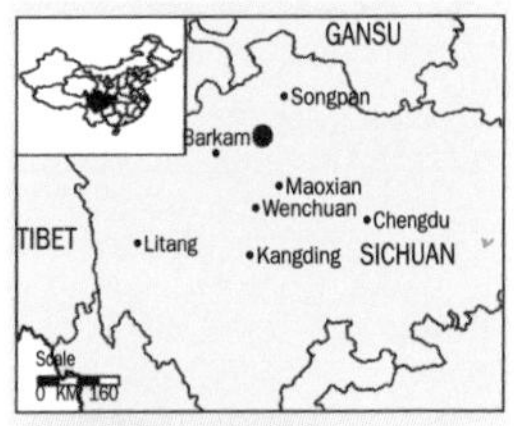

Population in China:
14,000 (1990)
18,060 (2000)
23,300 (2010)
Location: Sichuan
Religion: Tibetan Buddhism
Christians: None Known

Overview of the Luhua Qiang

Countries: China
Pronunciation: "Chee-Ung-Loo-hwa"
Other Names: Chiang: Luhua, Ch'iang, Luhua
Population Source: 14,000 (1998 Liu Guangkun – 1990 figure); 12,000 (1998 J. Matisoff); Out of a total Qiang population of 198,252 (1990 census)
Location: *W Sichuan:* Heishui County: Luhua, Shashiduo, Yangrong, Zegai, Ergulu, and Zhuogedu districts
Status: Officially included under Qiang
Language: Sino-Tibetan, Tibeto-Burman, Qiangic, Qiang, Northern Qiang
Dialects: 0
Religion: Tibetan Buddhism, Polytheism, Animism
Christians: None known
Scripture: None
***Jesus* film:** None
Gospel Recordings: None
Christian Broadcasting: None
ROPAL code: None

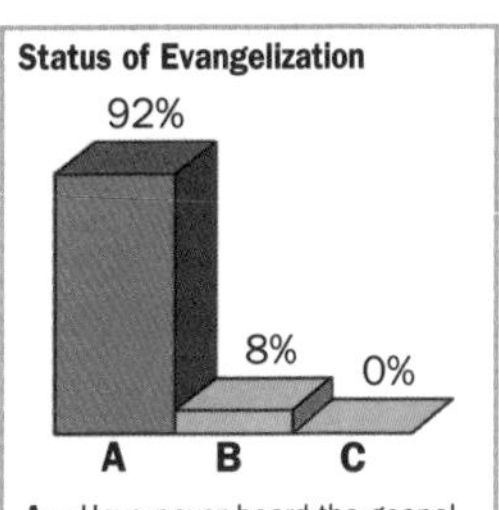

A = Have never heard the gospel
B = Were evangelized but did not become Christians
C = Are adherents to any form of Christianity

Qiang, Mawo 羌(麻窝)

Population in China:
12,000 (1990)
15,480 (2000)
19,950 (2010)
Location: Sichuan
Religion: Tibetan Buddhism
Christians: None Known

Overview of the Mawo Qiang

Countries: China

Pronunciation: "Chee-Ung-Mah-wo"

Other Names: Chiang: Mawo, Mawo

Population Source: 12,000 (1998 Liu Guangkun – 1990 figure); 15,000 (1998 J. Matisoff); Out of a total Qiang population of 198,252 (1990 census)

Location: *W Sichuan:* Heishui County: Mawo, Zhawo, Shuangliusuo, Xi'er, Hongyan, and E'en districts

Status: Officially included under Qiang

Language: Sino-Tibetan, Tibeto-Burman, Qiangic, Qiang, Northern Qiang

Dialects: 0

Religion: Tibetan Buddhism, Animism, Polytheism

Christians: None known

Scripture: None

***Jesus* film:** None

Gospel Recordings: None

Christian Broadcasting: None

ROPAL code: None

Status of Evangelization

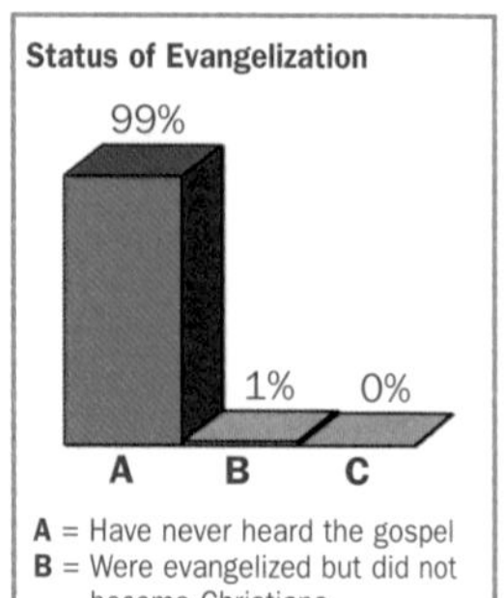

A = Have never heard the gospel
B = Were evangelized but did not become Christians
C = Are adherents to any form of Christianity

Paul Hattaway

Location: In 1990 there were 12,000 speakers of the Mawo Qiang language reported in China. They live wholly within the borders of Heishui County (in the districts of Mawo, Zhawo, Shuangliusuo, Xi'er, Hongyan, and E'en) in northwestern Sichuan Province.[1]

Identity: The Mawo Qiang are one subgroup of the official Qiang nationality in China. Interestingly enough, some Qiang claim to be descended from sheep, hence the character for their name. (The upper radical of the Chinese character for *Qiang* defines "sheep," the lower one "son.")

Language: Mawo Qiang is one of four varieties of Northern Qiang spoken in Sichuan Province. It takes its name from Mawo District which was the location chosen by scholars to study this language. Many Mawo Qiang are bilingual in Tibetan or multilingual in both Tibetan and the Sichuan dialect of Mandarin Chinese.

History: During certain occasions in the past, whole Qiang communities were wiped out because of plagues and disease. In recent years the government has given mass treatment of black fever and hookworm to the Qiang, which has greatly reduced the danger of these epidemic diseases.

Customs: Qiang men and women typically wear homespun linen gowns with sheep-skin vests called *guagua*. They wear their vests with the fur turned inward for cool weather and turned outward during rainy weather. Both men and women wear variously colored scarfs on their heads. Qiang women wear embroidered shoes called *Yun Yun* shoes. An old legend says that long ago a Han girl named Yun Yun enjoyed close friendship with her Qiang sisters and taught them spinning, weaving, and embroidery. One day Yun Yun and her Qiang sisters went up a mountain to cut firewood and got caught in a storm; Yun Yun slipped and fell into a deep valley, leaving behind only her embroidered shoes. In memory of Yun Yun the Qiang girls wear shoes patterned after hers and call them *Yun Yun* shoes. Unmarried girls often send their painstakingly embroidered Yun Yun shoes as gifts to the man they love. When they marry, they place several pairs in their dowry.[2]

Religion: One of the festivals celebrated by the Qiang is called *Zhuanshan* (Mountain Circling). In the past, villagers led an ox and carried food and wine up a mountain to sacrifice to the Mountain gods. Monkeys, wild boars, and rats, all made of paper, were set on fire to symbolize the destruction of the pests that devoured the Qiang's grain.

Christianity: The Mawo Qiang are possibly the most unevangelized of the Qiang groups in China. Their language is very different from the Southern Qiang language groups, which contain most of the known Qiang believers. If evangelists were to visit the Mawo Qiang they would need to communicate in Chinese which, although it is understood by some of the people, is not their "heart language." Mission history shows that the gospel must be presented in the native language of a people group for Christianity to penetrate to the core of a community and change it.

Qiang, Mianchi 羌(面斥)

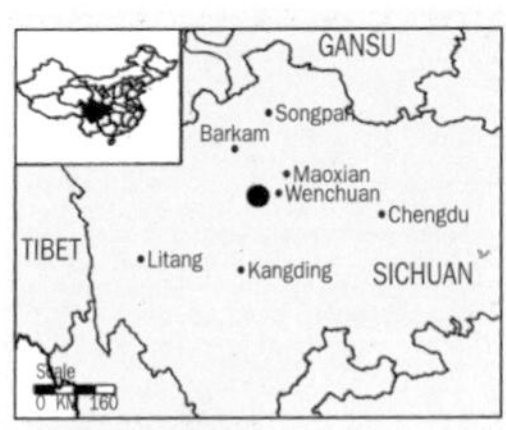

Population in China:
15,700 (1990)
20,250 (2000)
26,100 (2010)
Location: Sichuan
Religion: Polytheism
Christians: 150

Overview of the Mianchi Qiang

Countries: China

Pronunciation: "Chee-ung-Mee-an-chee"

Other Names: Chiang: Mianchi, Mianchi, Mien-ch'ih Ch'iang

Population Source: 15,700 (1998 Liu Guangkun – 1990 figure); Out of a total Qiang population of 198,252 (1990 census)

Location: *W Sichuan:* All of Wenchuan County except Longxi District.

Status: Officially included under Qiang

Language: Sino-Tibetan, Tibeto-Burman, Qiangic, Qiang, Southern Qiang

Dialects: 0

Religion: Polytheism, Animism, Ancestor Worship, Christianity

Christians: 150

Scripture: None

***Jesus* film:** None

Gospel Recordings: None

Christian Broadcasting: None

ROPAL code: None

Status of Evangelization

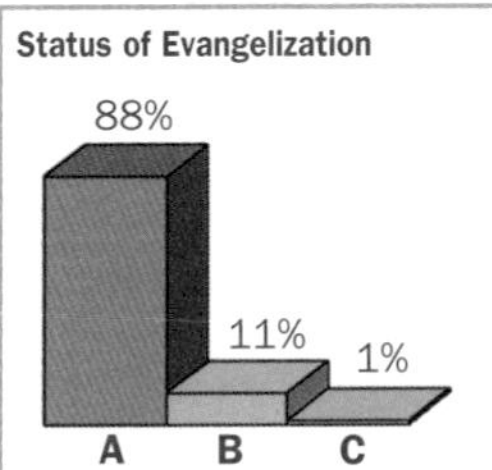

A = Have never heard the gospel
B = Were evangelized but did not become Christians
C = Are adherents to any form of Christianity

Location: Approximately 20,000 speakers of the Mianchi Qiang language live in every part of Wenchuan County (except Longxi District) in Sichuan Province. The region is criss-crossed by the mighty Min River. One visitor described the terror of crossing a 300-year-old chain bridge: "We saw the river underneath dashing out of a gorge, like a reinless horse to make a thunderous noise, and lashing at the rocks and reefs in its middle, to send up a white spray."[1]

Identity: The name *Qiang*, which means "herdsmen,"[2] has for centuries been a generic description for a large number of nomadic tribes along China's western border with Tibet. Mianchi is a distinct language that cannot be understood by the members of any other Qiang group in Sichuan.

Language: Mianchi Qiang is one of the "9 or 10 Qiangic languages"[3] spoken in Sichuan Province. At one time in history there were 62 Qiang tribes,[4] but many of these have since assimilated into larger peoples or have simply vanished because of disease, warfare, and famine.[5]

History: Records inscribed on bones and tortoise shells dating from the Shang Dynasty (1700–1100 BC) indicate that the ancestors of the Qiang were one of the first people recorded in Chinese history. "One branch of these peoples gradually moved to the upper reaches of the Min River and subsequently became today's Qiang."[6]

Customs: Because of invading armies and bandits in the past, many Qiang villages built stone watchtowers and forts — often 13 or 14 stories high — which are still seen on the mountain passes today. The two-story stone houses of the Qiang, called *qionglong*, are flat-roofed and resemble a watchtower. Builders construct them without the use of plans or measuring tools, depending entirely on their memory.[7]

Religion: In addition to worshiping a multitude of deities, the ancestors of the Mianchi Qiang are highly honored. Strict protocol is observed in the home so that the spirits of the ancestors are not offended. "Placed on the upper part of the support are memorial tablets of their ancestors. The cauldron support is under a taboo and the place near it is where the whole family eat their meals, get together, sing and dance on festive occasions and offer sacrifices to their ancestors."[8]

Christianity: There are about 150 Christians among the Mianchi Qiang, some of whom belong to the Quakers (Society of Friends).[9] Thomas Torrance Jr. met with the Qiang believers in 1994. He reported, "There is a whole cluster of Qiang Christians here in Wenchuan."[10] Many Qiang believers have moved to Wenchuan because of persecution and discrimination in their home areas. Torrance provided more than ¥200,000 (about US$28,500) to the Amity Foundation for the purpose of rebuilding the church, but it is uncertain if anything has been done to help the Qiang believers.[11] The believers in Wenchuan intend their church "to be the center for the spread of the Gospel and the Christian church throughout the whole Aba region."[12]

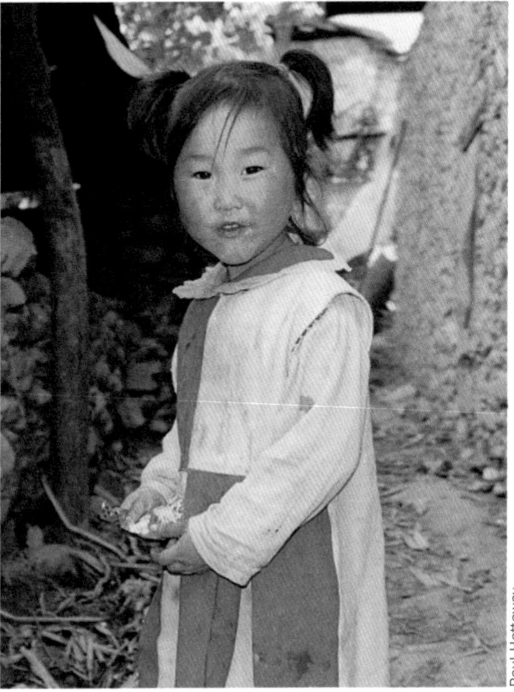
Paul Hattaway

Qiang, Sanlong 羌(三龙)

Location: More than 19,000 speakers of the Sanlong Qiang language live in the Fengyi, Sanlong, Shaba, Huilong, Baixi, Wadi, and Yazhuzhai districts of Maoxian County in western Sichuan Province. Maoxian, which is also known as Maowen, contained a total population of 89,000 people in the 1990 census, of which 72,000 (80.9%) were people who spoke Qiang languages.[1] Other inhabitants include Han Chinese, Tibetans, and a few families of minority groups such as Hui and Yi. Maoxian is part of the massive Aba Prefecture. The prefectural seat in the township of Aba is about two days' drive northwest of Maoxian.

Identity: The Sanlong Qiang are part of China's official Qiang nationality. Overall, the Qiang have one of the lowest education levels of any minority group. Only 34% of Qiang children attend primary school. From there the number declines to the 0.1% who attend university.

Language: The overall rate of literacy among the Qiang is 51%. Since the 1950s, the government has put in place an experimental program for primary school-age children (grades 1–3), to learn the Qiang language, with a standardized *pinyin* script. The writing system uses the Roman alphabet to convey about fifty different plain initial consonants. There is only about 55% shared vocabulary between the Northern and Southern Qiang varieties.

History: Today's Maoxian County was historically near the edge of Tibetan territory until the Chinese took control of western Sichuan in the 1700s.

Luke Kuepfer

Customs: Qiang women's clothing differs from men's in that the collar, cuffs, sash, and shoes are often cross-stitched with circles, triangles, and other designs. They are also decorated with a row of small silver plum-flower designs. The embroidered designs are mostly drawn from nature, depicting flowers and grass, deer, lions, rabbits, and human figures. Women like to wear especially large silver earrings, hairpins and finger rings, and silver and jade pins, among other decorations. At their waists women wear a silver sewing box, while men wear a silver tobacco box.

Religion: During the Qiang's *Zhuanshan* Festival, pieces of dough in the shape of the sun and half-moon are hung from an ox's horns. Sorcerers then proceed to call on the gods through a ceremonial drum dance. After the religious ceremony, people dance gaily to the sound of flutes, drums, and bells. Qiang folk dances today have evolved from this festival. The male dancers carry sheepskin drums with small handles and keep time with short curved drumsticks. The women dancers carry bells that are sounded in time with the drums.

Christianity: The Sanlong Qiang are an unreached people group. Few have ever heard the gospel, although some living in Maoxian may have heard of the existence of Qiang Christians in Wenchuan County. There are no Scriptures or resources available in the Sanlong Qiang language.

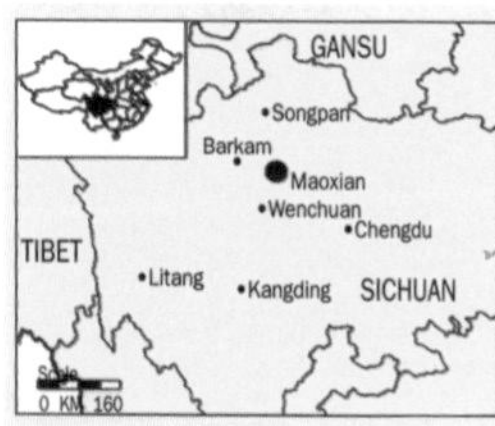

Population in China:
15,000 (1990)
19,350 (2000)
24,950 (2010)
Location: Sichuan
Religion: Polytheism
Christians: None Known

Overview of the Sanlong Qiang

Countries: China

Pronunciation: "Chee-Ung-Sahn-long"

Other Names: Chiang: Sanlong, Chi'ang: Sanlong

Population Source: 15,000 (1998 Liu Guangkun – 1990 figure); Out of a total Qiang population of 198,252 (1990 census)

Location: *W Sichuan:* Maoxian County: Fengyi, Sanlong, Shaba, Huilong, Baixi, Wadi, and Yazhuzhai districts

Status: Officially included under Qiang

Language: Sino-Tibetan, Tibeto-Burman, Qiangic, Qiang, Southern Qiang

Dialects: 0

Religion: Polytheism, Animism, Ancestor Worship, Shamanism

Christians: None known

Scripture: None

***Jesus* film:** None

Gospel Recordings: None

Christian Broadcasting: None

ROPAL code: None

Status of Evangelization

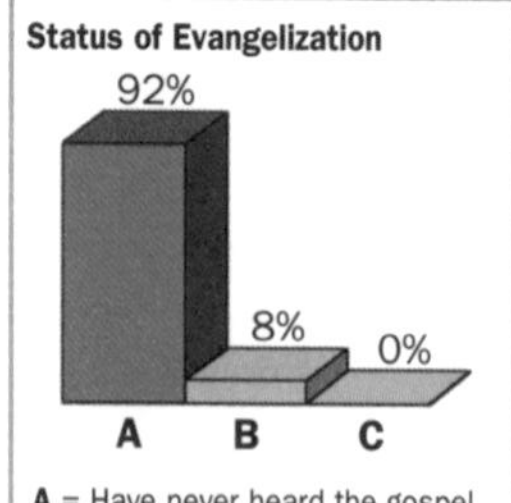

A = Have never heard the gospel
B = Were evangelized but did not become Christians
C = Are adherents to any form of Christianity

Qiang, Taoping 羌(桃坪)

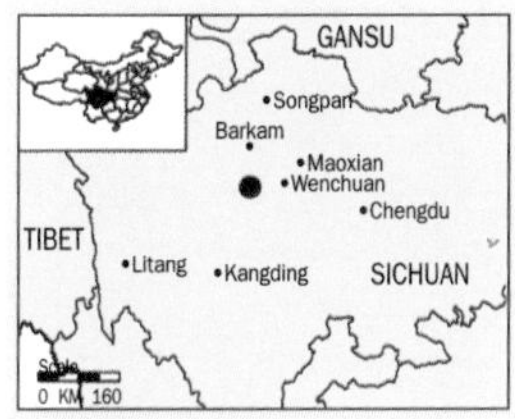

Population in China:
4,900 (1990)
6,320 (2000)
8,150 (2010)
Location: Sichuan
Religion: Polytheism
Christians: None Known

Overview of the Taoping Qiang

Countries: China

Pronunciation: "Chee-Ung-Taow-ping"

Other Names: Chiang: Taoping, Chi'ang, Jiang, T'ao-p'ing Ch'iang

Population Source: 4,900 (1998 Liu Guangkun – 1990 figure); Out of a total Qiang population of 198,252 (1990 census)

Location: *W Sichuan:* Lixian County: Taoping, Jiashan, Ganxi, Sancha, Cengtou, Niushan, Xishang, Tonghua, and Gucheng districts

Status: Officially included under Qiang

Language: Sino-Tibetan, Tibeto-Burman, Qiangic, Qiang, Southern Qiang

Dialects: 0

Religion: Polytheism, Animism, Ancestor Worship

Christians: None known

Scripture: None

***Jesus* film:** None

Gospel Recordings: None

Christian Broadcasting: None

ROPAL code: None

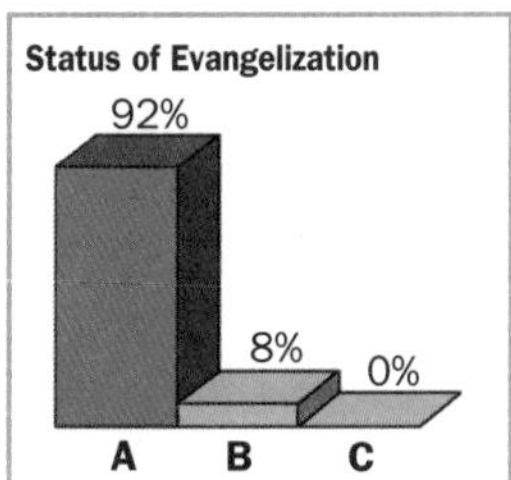

A = Have never heard the gospel
B = Were evangelized but did not become Christians
C = Are adherents to any form of Christianity

Paul Hattaway

Location: Approximately 6,300 speakers of the Taoping Qiang language live in Lixian County in western Sichuan Province.[1] Before 1949 landlords controlled the distribution of land among the Qiang. Eight percent of the population controlled 43% of the land.[2] Consequently, many Qiang lived in chronic poverty and bondage.

Identity: The Taoping Qiang are one of 11 Qiang language groups that make up the official Qiang nationality in China.

Language: The Southern Qiang languages, including Taoping Qiang, contain between two and six tones, depending on the location.[3] The Southern Qiang — located on the edge of Han Chinese civilization — are being assimilated. The farther north one travels the more culturally Tibetan the Qiang become.

History: For many centuries the Qiang have been sandwiched between the great Tibetan and Chinese empires. Numerous raiding armies and bandits have passed through the Qiang region, many leaving a violent mark on the pages of Qiang history.

Customs: The Qiang enjoy a tortilla-like bread called *sanchuisanda.* The term literally means "three blows, three hits." The bread is made of wheat flour and is "baked in hot ashes at the side of a fire.... But since the loaf is covered with ashes, one needs to blow on it two or three times and pat it as well."[4]

Religion: Most Qiang homes are two-story stone constructions. The ground floor is reserved for animals, while the family sleeps on the second floor. One room in every house is set aside by the Qiang to worship their ancestors. A shrine covered with red paper contains the family idols and ancestral tablets.

Christianity: There are no known Christians among the Taoping Qiang today. It is hoped the Mianchi Qiang believers will share Christ with all Qiang groups in China. Protestant and Catholic missionaries had been active among other Qiang groups before the end of the nineteenth century. Several churches were established but were destroyed, and most of the church leaders were martyred by the Communists in 1935. Today, the main church building at Tongwenmai — at the entrance of Longqi Township — still lies in ruins. The Wenchuan government offices now stand on the site of the former CIM premises.[5] In 1986 Thomas Torrance Jr. visited the Qiang for the first time since his family left China in the 1930s. Despite his long absence, he soon found his heart pounding for the people he had come to love more than 50 years before. Torrance wrote, "It was, I think, one of the most memorable days of my life. Apart from being in close contact with very lovely people I felt that I had been sent back by the Lord to help rekindle the flame of their Christian faith and start rebuilding the Church in their midst. I was deeply moved by the love and regard the Qiang people still retained for my father after more than half a century, and by the way they came to show their appreciation for what he was and had done for them in greeting and welcoming his son."[6]

Qiang, Yadu 羌(雅都)

Location: Yadu Qiang is spoken by more people than any other Qiang language in China. The majority of the approximately 30,000 Yadu Qiang live in the Chibusu, Yadu, Qugu, and Weicheng districts of Maoxian County; and in the Waboliangzi and Se'ergu districts of Heishui County farther to the north.[1]

Identity: Yadu Qiang is one of 11 groups that make up the official Qiang nationality in China.

Language: Yadu Qiang is a part of the Northern Qiang language group. Although varieties of the Northern Qiang appear to be more homogeneous than the Southern Qiang languages, which are very distinct from each other, Yadu Qiang speakers must still use Chinese or Tibetan to communicate with other Northern Qiang speakers.

Paul Hattaway

History: Although the Qiang are no longer considered a matriarchal society, women still play a leading role in agriculture and usually have the final say in the family. Young couples often live with the wife's family after the wedding.

Customs: Until recently, early marriages were common among the Qiang. It was not unusual for a boy to marry between the ages of seven and ten; and women between 12 and 18. Qiang women sing a sarcastic song to their guests. "It is the sixth moon, and the wheat flowers are blooming in the field. My husband is still an infant drinking milk. How long will it be before he grows up?" One of the games the Qiang play at festivals is called egg snatching. They place a number of rocks on the ground and while one person guards them, others try to snatch them. Whoever gets the most wins the contest. Another Qiang favorite is the log-pushing contest. Two people grab the log and try to push each other out of a circle. Whoever succeeds wins. The Qiang have their own unique cultural arts and crafts. Embroidery is a favorite pastime of the women. The Qiang enjoy singing and dancing as well. "Wine Song," "Plate Song," "Mountain Song," "Guozhuang," and the "Leather Drum" dances are very popular. These are played in accompaniment of gongs, tambourines, *sonas*, and bamboo flutes.

Religion: Most of the Yadu Qiang living in Heishui County have been thoroughly assimilated to Tibetan culture and religion. They follow Tibetan Buddhism, mixed with polytheism and animism. A belief in the power of the spirit world pervades all Qiang groups. Prayer flags and prayer beads are two of the common Buddhist symbols they have borrowed from the Tibetans.

Christianity: Despite having the largest population of the Qiang groups in Sichuan, there are no known Christians among the Yadu Qiang. Those in Maoxian County live nearer the Qiang believers, but there are major linguistic differences that create an obstacle to the Yadu Qiang's understanding of the gospel from Southern Qiang speakers. The Yadu Qiang living in Heishui County have even less chance of hearing the gospel. They live alongside Tibetan nomads who too are completely untouched by Christianity.

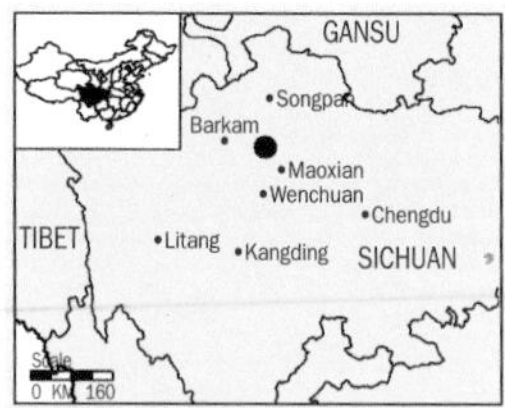

Population in China:
23,000 (1990)
29,650 (2000)
38,200 (2010)
Location: Sichuan
Religion: Tibetan Buddhism
Christians: None Known

Overview of the Yadu Qiang

Countries: China

Pronunciation: "Chee-Ung-Yah-doo"

Other Names: Chiang: Yadu, Yadu, Ya-tu Ch'iang

Population Source: 23,000 (1998 Liu Guangkun – 1990 figure); Out of a total Qiang population of 198,252 (1990 census)

Location: *W Sichuan:* Maoxian County: Chibusu, Yadu, Qugu, and Weicheng districts; Heishui County: Waboliangzi and Se'ergu districts

Status: Officially included under Qiang

Language: Sino-Tibetan, Tibeto-Burman, Qiangic, Qiang, Northern Qiang

Dialects: 0

Religion: Tibetan Buddhism, Polytheism, Animism

Christians: None known

Scripture: None

***Jesus* film:** None

Gospel Recordings: None

Christian Broadcasting: None

ROPAL code: None

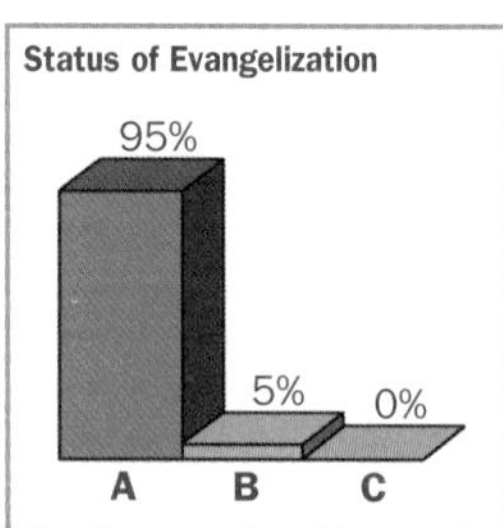

Qiangyi 羌夷

October 12

Location: Nine thousand Qiangyi people reside in the Xiangme, Ziqianglang, Huangcaoshao, Chuchang, and Chalangshao communities within the Midian District; and in the Daying and Xinxingzuo communities of Hedian District. These places are all within Xiangyun County in China's Yunnan Province. An additional 1,000 Qiangyi are believed to live in parts of southern Binchuan County as well.

Identity: The Qiangyi, who are officially classified as part of the Yi nationality, are one of the most interesting people groups in southern China. As Jamin Pelkey points out, "Many Tibeto-Burman peoples are said to have descended from the ancient Qiang tribes, but this is the only known case in Yunnan in which one of the people groups actually retains the name *Qiang* as part of their autonym. The suffix *yi* in the autonym is... probably a traditional Han name for the people meaning 'the Qiang foreigners' and may have been picked up by this people after having had centuries of contact with the Han Chinese."[1]

Language: Although the Qiangyi language is classified as a Western Yi variety, "at least one Chinese anthropologist says they may just as well be classified as Southern Qiang."[2] Most or all of the Qiangyi are adequately bilingual in Mandarin Chinese.

History: The history of the Qiangyi is fascinating in that they provide a living link between today's Tibeto-Burman-speaking tribes in southern China and the Qiang tribes who roamed China's northwest up to 4,000 years ago. One researcher has stated, "The Qiangyi are confirmed descendants of the ancient Qiang nation which migrated during the 'stone-ages' from Gansu to Sichuan — some of them moving into Yunnan. After crossing the Yangtze River into Yunnan, the Qiang separated into three distinct tribes, and slowly bifurcated into 11 other tribes which, in turn, became over 150 tribes. It seems that, finally, distinctions between tribes became so great and the multiplication and racial mixing so complex that historians lost count and the 'tribes' became known as separate 'peoples'."[3]

Customs: Little is known about the culture of the Qiangyi today and, outside the area where they live, few people have heard of them. Although the Qiangyi used to wear their own traditional dress, it is believed they now wear standard Han clothing except during festivals and special occasions.

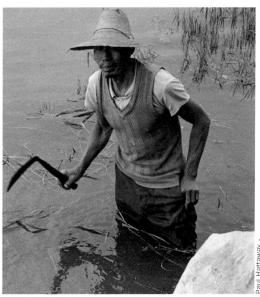

Paul Hattaway •

Religion: Polytheism (the worship of many gods) could accurately be described as the main religion among the Qiangyi. There are also elements of ancestor worship and Daoism present, which were probably adopted from their Bai and Chinese neighbors.

Christianity: Despite their long history, the Qiangyi are not known to have been impacted by Christianity. Today, there are no known Christians among them. Xiangyun and Binchuan counties, where the Qiangyi are found, have very little Christian presence except for a few small government-sanctioned churches affiliated with the TSPM. These churches are mostly comprised of elderly Han and Bai believers.

Population in China:
10,000 (1999)
10,250 (2000)
12,850 (2010)
Location: Yunnan
Religion: Polytheism
Christians: None Known

Overview of the Qiangyi

Countries: China

Pronunciation: "Chee-ung-Yee"

Other Names: Qiang Yi

Population Source: 10,000 (1999 J. Pelkey); Out of a total Yi population of 6,572,173 (1990 census)

Location: *Yunnan:* Xiangyun (9,000) and Binchuan (1,000) counties

Status: Officially included under Yi

Language: Sino-Tibetan, Tibeto-Burman, Burmese-Lolo, Lolo, Northern Lolo, Yi, Western Yi

Dialects: 0

Religion: Polytheism, Animism, Ancestor Worship, Daoism

Christians: None known

Scripture: None

***Jesus* film:** None

Gospel Recordings: None

Christian Broadcasting: None

ROPAL code: None

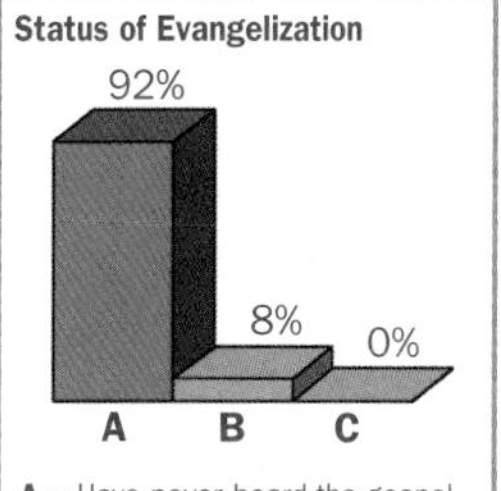

Qixingmin 七姓民

Population in China:
3,000 (1982)
4,560 (2000)
5,890 (2010)
Location: Guizhou, Yunnan
Religion: Buddhism
Christians: None Known

Overview of the Qixingmin

Countries: China

Pronunciation: "Chee-shing-min"

Other Names: Jing Ren, Bai Erzi, Bo, Boren

Population Source: 3,000 (1982 *Minzu Shibie Wenxian Ziliao Huibian*); Out of a total Bai population of 1,594,827 (1990 census)

Location: *NW Guizhou:* Shuicheng and Weining counties; *NE Yunnan:* Qiubei County

Status: Officially included under Bai since 1985; Previously included in a list of *Undetermined Minorities*

Language: Sino-Tibetan, Tibeto-Burman, Unclassified

Dialects: 0

Religion: Mahayana Buddhism, Animism, Ancestor Worship, Daoism

Christians: None known

Scripture: None

***Jesus* film:** None

Gospel Recordings: None

Christian Broadcasting: None

ROPAL code: None

Status of Evangelization

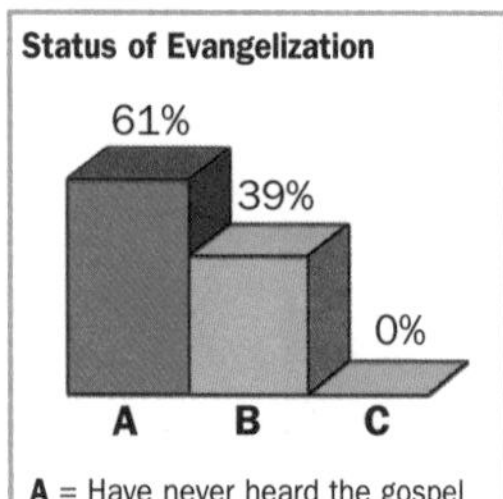

A = Have never heard the gospel
B = Were evangelized but did not become Christians
C = Are adherents to any form of Christianity

Location: According to a 1982 Chinese ethnographic survey, 3,000 Qixingmin people live in Shuicheng and Weining counties in western Guizhou Province, and in Qiubei County in Yunnan Province (where they may be better known as *Boren*).[1] This ethnically diverse area contains many Yi and Miao subgroups in addition to the majority Han Chinese population.

Identity: In the 1982 census the Qixingmin were not placed under any of the recognized nationalities but were instead placed in a list of *Undetermined Minorities* by the Chinese authorities. In 1985 they were reclassified under the Bai nationality who live more than 300 miles away in the Dali Prefecture of west central Yunnan.[2] Similarly, the Longjia and Nanjingren peoples of Guizhou were included under the Bai minority. One source states the identification of the Qixingmin ethnicity is a problematic one, primarily because they are known by three different ethnic names: *Qixingmin*, *Jing Ren*, and *Bai Erzi*.[3]

Language: Although the Qixingmin language, which may be called *Bo*, has never been studied in depth, it was mentioned in passing as a newly discovered language in a Chinese linguistic journal.[4] Today most Qixingmin are adequately bilingual in Mandarin Chinese, and the use of their mother tongue is in an endangered state.

History: The Qixingmin have lived in their present location and have been recognized as a distinct ethnic group for at least 400 years. During the Ming (1368–1644) and Qing (1644–1911) dynasties the Qixingmin were better known as *Bai Erzi*. During the Qing Dynasty they lived in mixed communities with the Yizi, Bouyei, Miao, and a group called the *Baolu*.

Customs: Despite their small numbers, the Qixingmin have a fierce reputation among their neighbors, who claim that the Qixingmin have hot tempers, that they are stubborn, and that they fight all the time. Visitors to a Qixingmin home are required to leave the house through a different door than the one by which they entered. The door is of great importance to the Qixingmin. Both the doors and the entrances to their villages are protected by regular cleansing ceremonies.

Religion: One of the main factors that make the Qixingmin a unique people in their area is their strong adherence to Buddhism. They are a Buddhist enclave surrounded by numerous animistic and Christian communities. Most Qixingmin use prayer beads to help them meditate, while some men become monks and join a monastery for extended periods of time, which is considered a great honor to their families.

Christianity: The Qixingmin are an unreached people group with no known believers, despite the fact that many have been exposed to the gospel from Han, Miao, and Yi believers living in the Weining and Shuicheng areas. The ethnic identity of the Qixingmin is integrally linked with Buddhism: to be a Qixingmin is to be Buddhist. The cost of going against their culture and the threat of probable expulsion from their community if they should become a Christian has proven too great an obstacle for the Qixingmin to overcome. Most churches in the area no longer attempt to evangelize them.

Paul Hattaway

Queyu 却育

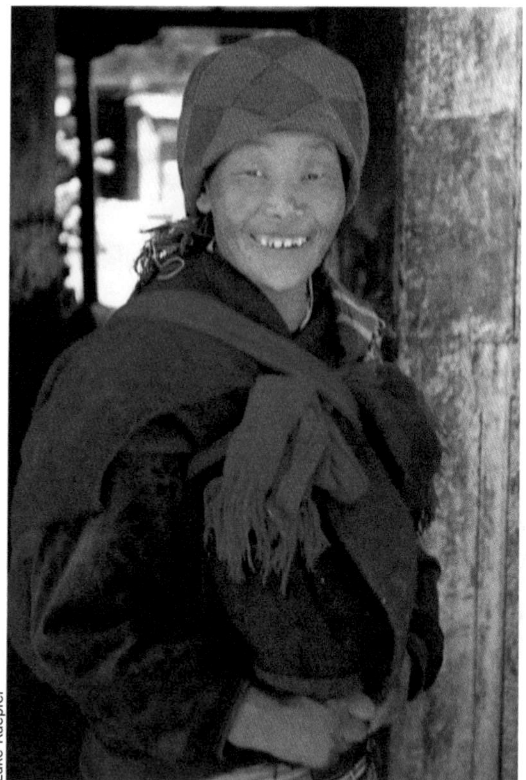
Luke Kuepfer

Location: Seven thousand speakers of the Queyu language were reported in a 1991 study.[1] Many Queyu men are applying to enter Tibetan Buddhist monasteries. Consequently, the population growth of the Queyu is expected to slow. The Queyu inhabit the three counties of Xinlong, Yajiang, and Litang in the large Garze Prefecture which covers a vast area of western Sichuan Province. Litang Township lies at an altitude of 4,700 meters (15,400 ft.) above sea level. The Queyu area was formerly part of the Kham Province of Tibet, until it was annexed and incorporated into China in the 1950s.

Identity: The Queyu have been officially counted as part of the Tibetan nationality, primarily because they follow the Tibetan Buddhist religion. Linguistically, however, the Queyu are closer to the Qiang minority.

Language: Throughout all the places where the Queyu are located, their language is reported to be inherently intelligible. There are no major dialect differences between the different regions. In the Tuanjie Township of Yajiang County the people call themselves *Zhaba*, although the same language as Queyu is spoken there. They should not be confused with another Qiangic language group called *Zhaba* who live in the Zhamai District, also within the Garze Prefecture. The Queyu language has four tones.

History: In late 1955 Chinese authorities ordered the monks of the large Litang Monastery to make an inventory of the monastery's possessions for tax assessment. The monks refused to oblige. In February 1956, the People's Liberation Army responded by laying siege to Litang Monastery, which was defended by several thousand monks and farmers, of whom many were armed with farm implements. Litang was bombed by Chinese aircraft, destroying the monastery and killing hundreds of people. The Tibetans, outraged by the attack, spread the conflict to the surrounding towns of Dege, Batang, and Chamdo.[2]

Customs: Although today the Queyu wear clothing similar to the Tibetans, there are a number of ancient *tianlu*, or stone watchtowers, scattered throughout the region inhabited by the Queyu, revealing this group's historic relationship to the Qiang.

Religion: All Queyu are Tibetan Buddhists, although there are also many aspects of shamanism and black magic within their religious practices.

Christianity: Protestant and Catholic missionaries worked in the Litang area until the early 1950s. Today there is a small Protestant church among the Khampa Tibetans in Litang County,[3] and there are some Catholics in Yajiang.[4] Most people in the area, however, have never heard the name of Christ, and there are no known Queyu believers. The situation has changed little since this report in 1922: "This region is not only without a resident missionary, but even the scouts of Christianity have barely touched it except at one or two points.... What is more serious is the fact that many border mission centers are undermanned or not manned at all."[5]

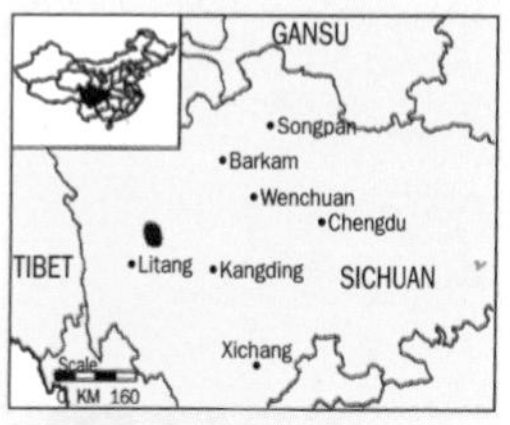

Population in China:
7,000 (1991)
8,460 (2000)
10,420 (2010)
Location: Sichuan
Religion: Tibetan Buddhism
Christians: None Known

Overview of the Queyu

Countries: China

Pronunciation: "Cue-yoo"

Other Names: Zhaba, Hokow

Population Source: 7,000 (1991 *EDCL*); Out of a total Tibetan population of 4,593,330 (1990 census)

Location: *W Sichuan:* Xinlong, Yajiang, and Litang counties in Garze Prefecture

Status: Officially included under Tibetan

Language: Sino-Tibetan, Tibeto-Burman, Qiangic

Dialects: 0

Religion: Tibetan Buddhism, Shamanism

Christians: None known

Scripture: None

***Jesus* film:** None

Gospel Recordings: None

Christian Broadcasting: None

ROPAL code: QEY00

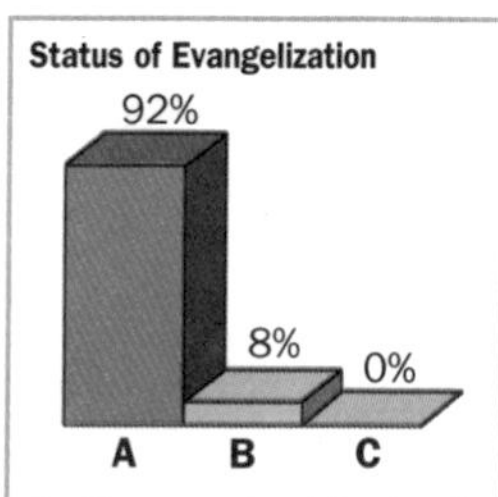

Rao 绕家

Population in China:
6,500 (1982)
9,890 (2000)
12,750 (2010)
Location: Guizhou
Religion: Animism
Christians: None Known

Overview of the Rao

Countries: China

Pronunciation: "Raow"

Other Names: Raojia, Yao Miao, Yao Bei Miao, Yaojia, Shui Gelao

Population Source: 6,500 (1982 *Minzu Shibie Wenxian Ziliao Huibian*); 7,000 (1997 D. Graybill)

Location: *SE Guizhou:* Duyun and Majiang counties

Status: The Rao in Duyun have been officially included under Bouyei, while the Rao in Majiang have been officially included under Yao since 1991. The Rao were included in a group of *Undetermined Minorities* in the 1982 census.

Language: Hmong-Mien, Hmongic, Eastern Hmongic

Dialects: 0

Religion: Animism, Polytheism, Ancestor Worship, No Religion

Christians: None known

Scripture: None

***Jesus* film:** None

Gospel Recordings: None

Christian Broadcasting: None

ROPAL code: None

Status of Evangelization

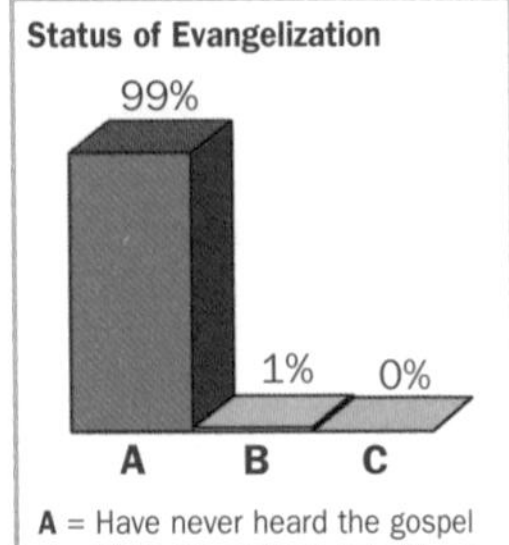

A = Have never heard the gospel
B = Were evangelized but did not become Christians
C = Are adherents to any form of Christianity

Dwayne Graybill

Location: Approximately 10,000 members of the Rao tribe are located in Guizhou Province. More than 4,000 live in six large villages in the Long Shan (Dragon Mountains) in Majiang County, west of Kaili City.[1] A further 2,454 Rao live in 21 villages in Duyun County to the south of Majiang.[2] The largest Rao villages in Duyun are Yako (356 Rao people), Ping (311), Xiao (215), Wan (181), and Zhahe (172).[3] Most Rao communities are isolated, set back into the mountains a few hours' walk from the nearest road. The Chinese characters for Guizhou mean "precious state." However, the original name for the region was *Kingdom of Demons*.[4]

Identity: The official classification of the Rao is a confusing matter. They are not recognized as a distinct group by the Chinese authorities, who have placed them as part of two other minority groups. The Rao in Majiang County have been officially included as part of the Yao nationality since 1991,[5] while those in Duyun, about 100 kilometers (62 mi.) to the south of Majiang, have been counted as part of the Bouyei nationality. Before 1949 the Rao in Majiang used another name, which meant "sudden death."[6]

Language: The Rao language is a part of the Miao linguistic family. Sixty percent of Rao vocabulary reportedly consists of Miao words.[7] The Rao speak a language distinct from any others in the area. One study has discovered that Rao is close to the Hmu language in Guizhou.[8]

History: The Rao claim to have migrated from Yunnan long ago. They say they were a Yao group who separated and gradually formed their own ethnic identity.[9] During the Ming Dynasty (1368–1644) the Rao were repeatedly attacked by the Chinese.[10]

Customs: The Rao are hardworking peasants. The medical care in rural Guizhou is the worst in China. United Nations figures show the ratio of health workers to rural population is 1:1263. The next worst area in China is Xinjiang with a ratio of 1:752.[11] Every November the Rao hold a winter festival where they remember their customs and acknowledge their uniqueness as a people. Each Rao village consists of members of the same family name. Rao are only permitted to marry within their own clan. Single women wear an embroidered headdress; but once they are married they wear black or dark blue headdresses.

Religion: In the past the Rao were animists, but they were forced to discontinue all spiritual practices during the antireligious campaigns of the Cultural Revolution in the 1960s.

Christianity: The Rao are a relatively untouched people group. They have never had a single known Christian believer, and no more than a relative handful are aware of the existence of Jesus Christ. There are no Scriptures or gospel recordings available in their language. The person privileged to take the gospel to the Rao will need the tenacity of Samuel Zwemer, who stated, "Frequent set-backs and apparent failure never disheartened the real pioneer. Occasional martyrdoms are only a fresh incentive. Opposition is a stimulus to greater activity."[12]

Rawang 热网

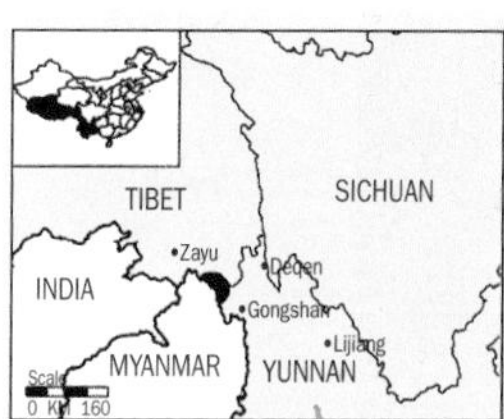

Population in China:
500 (1997)
540 (2000)
700 (2010)
Location: Yunnan, Tibet
Religion: Animism
Christians: 300

Overview of the Rawang

Countries: Myanmar, India, China, Thailand
Pronunciation: "Ra-wong"
Other Names: Qiuce, Kiutze, Chiutse, Chiutzu, Kiutzu, Khanung, Chopa, Zerwang, Nung Rawang, Ganung, Hkanung, Krangku, Taron, Serwang
Population Source:
500 (1997 AMO);
Out of a total Derung population of 5,816 (1990 census);
57,000 in India
(1995 Joshua Project);
80,000 in Myanmar
(1992 R. Morse);
A few in Thailand
Location:
NW Yunnan – SE Tibet border
Status:
Officially included under Derung
Language: Sino-Tibetan, Tibeto-Burman, Nungish
Dialects: 0
Religion: Christianity, Animism
Christians: 300
Scripture: Bible 1986; New Testament 1974; Portions 1952
***Jesus* film:** None
Gospel Recordings: Rawang #00285
Christian Broadcasting: Available (FEBC)
ROPAL code: RAW00

Status of Evangelization

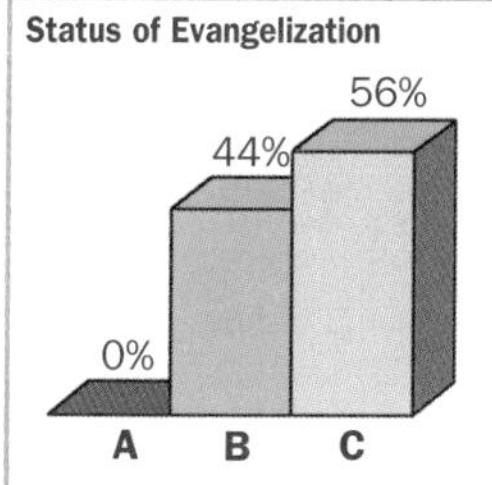

A = Have never heard the gospel
B = Were evangelized but did not become Christians
C = Are adherents to any form of Christianity

Location: Several villages of Rawang are located in an extremely remote area on the Yunnan-Tibet border in China. The Rawang, who are a collection of related dialect groups and clans, number more than 80,000 in northern Myanmar and 50,000 in northeastern India. The Rawang in China often visit their relatives in Myanmar by walking across the mountains, but "the way is difficult. They must follow trails through the mountains all night."[1] The Rawang area in China can only be accessed by hiking three days from the nearest village. They are isolated most of the year because of snow.

Identity: The Rawang have been officially included as part of the Derung nationality in China. Although the Rawang and Derung are related, their languages are inherently unintelligible. The Rawang consist of between 75 and 100 dialect groups in Myanmar, each with a different name. The Derung are the largest subgroup found in China, and so they were granted status by that name. The particular Rawang group referred to in this profile call themselves *Zerwang*.[2] The Zerwang in Myanmar are located in the Mondam area.

Language: The Rawang "language" is more a collection of languages, containing between 75 and 100 dialects.[3] Most of the dialects have some mutual intelligibility, although the closer a group is located to Tibet the more difficult it is for other Rawang to understand them. "When speakers of different Rawang varieties meet, they can often understand each other's speech, but cannot speak each other's language."[4] The Bible was translated into the Matwang dialect. This has made Matwang the *lingua franca* among the Rawang. The Kunglang dialect of Rawang is spoken in India, but they have been cut off from the Rawang in Myanmar since the 1950s.

History: When Rawang and Nu people greet each other they say, "In the remote past, we were brothers." They believe that they were separated by the river and then evolved into different groups. In the past, each Rawang clan had a shaman who directed warfare and settled disputes. The clans were "politically separate entities, which formed political alliances in times of danger from other communities."[5]

Customs: Many of the Rawang in China have intermarried with Tibetans and formed mixed communities. Rawang men are renowned for their hunting skills.

Religion: The mass movement of the Rawang in Myanmar to Christ is one of the great mission stories of the twentieth century. It is said that when the Morse family started ministering to them there were no Rawang Christians, but by the time they were forced to leave Burma in the 1960s there were just a few old men who were not believers.[6]

Christianity: Today 98% of the Rawang in Myanmar, and at least 50% in China, are Christians.[7] They have proven faithful to Christ and have taken the responsibility to send evangelistic teams to other groups in the Tibet-Yunnan-Myanmar border region. Largely because of the Morse family's labors, the Rawang have the full Bible in their language and their own gospel radio broadcasts.[8]

Midge Conner

Riang 日昂

Location: The Riang tribe, also known as the *Riang Liang*, inhabit parts of Zhenkang and Baoshan counties in the Dehong Prefecture, in China's Yunnan Province. One source listed a 1990 population of 1,200 Riang in China,[1] but a 1995 figure indicated a Riang population of 3,000.[2] In addition, as many as 50,000 Riang live in northern Myanmar. The most recent population estimate was done by a missionary in 1955. He estimated there were 25,000 Riang in Myanmar at that time. All population statistics from Myanmar are highly unreliable. The last census was conducted by the British in the 1930s. The present Myanmar regime is unwilling to conduct a new census, probably because the results could inflame the many ethnic tensions that exist in that troubled nation.

Paul Hattaway

Identity: The Riang, who have been officially counted as part of the De'ang nationality in China, have been known by several names in the past. The British mistakenly called them the *Black Karen* because of their appearance, but the Riang have no ethnolinguistic relationship with the Karen. The Riang are not related to the identically named Riang group in India and Bangladesh.

Language: Riang is the most divergent of the four De'ang languages in China. They cannot communicate with any of the other three De'ang language groups. This is mainly because they are animists, while the other three groups are Buddhists and their languages have therefore been influenced by Buddhist terms. All Riang are bilingual in Shan or Tai Mao. In Myanmar the Riang use a Roman script.

History: The Riang in Zhenkang County are the only De'ang group that retains features of the ancient clan and village commune system that used to prevail. In the past, Tai landlords controlled all the land in the area. Strict demarcation lines were clearly signposted between different villages and plots of land. Stone posts can still be seen today in the fields of Zhengkang.[3] Traditionally the Riang and other De'ang groups believe their first ancestor, Phu Sawti, was hatched from a serpent's egg — the result of a union between a Naga (female serpent-god) and a spirit.[4]

Customs: The Riang's belief in the above legend can be observed today in the dress of their women. "From their early teens, the women wear 40 or 50 cane hoops apiece, one resting upon another to a depth of a foot around their hips. The undulating movement when they walk resembles a snake's motion."[5]

Religion: The Riang are the only De'ang group who have never embraced Theravada Buddhism. The majority of Riang today are animists. They believe spirits live in objects of nature and must be placated before peace can be experienced in their communities.

Christianity: Missionaries worked among the Riang in Myanmar until they were expelled from the country in 1962. The Gospel of Mark was translated into Riang in 1950. Few members of this tribe have responded to the offer of salvation, however, and today there are no known churches among the Riang in either Myanmar or China.

Population in China:
1,200 (1990)
1,540 (2000)
1,990 (2010)
Location: Yunnan
Religion: Animism
Christians: None Known

Overview of the Riang

Countries: Myanmar, China

Pronunciation: "Ree-ung"

Other Names: Riang Liang, Yang Sek, Yang Wan Kun, Yin, Yanglam, Black Karen, Black Yang

Population Source: 1,200 (1990 J.-O. Svantesson); Out of a total De'ang population of 15,462 (1990 census); 20,000 in Myanmar (1955)

Location: *W Yunnan:* Zhenkang and Baoshan counties

Status: Officially included under De'ang

Language: Austro-Asiatic, Mon-Khmer, Northern Mon-Khmer, Palaungic, Eastern Palaungic, Riang

Dialects: 0

Religion: Animism, Shamanism

Christians: None known

Scripture: Portions 1950

***Jesus* film:** None

Gospel Recordings: None

Christian Broadcasting: None

ROPAL code: RIL00

Status of Evangelization

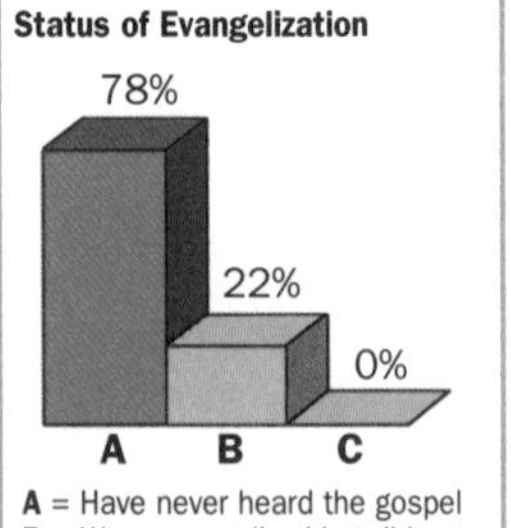

A = Have never heard the gospel
B = Were evangelized but did not become Christians
C = Are adherents to any form of Christianity

Russian 俄罗斯

RUSSIA
MONGOLIA
Altay
Tacheng
KAZAKSTAN
Yining
Urumqi
XINJIANG
Scale
0 KM 400

Population in China:
13,504 (1990)
17,400 (2000)
22,470 (2010)
Location: Xinjiang, Heilongjiang, Inner Mongolia
Religion: Christianity
Christians: 7,000

Overview of the Russians

Countries: Russia, all former USSR nations, Poland, USA, China
Pronunciation: "Rush-en"
Other Names: Russ, Eluosi, Olossu, Russki
Population Source: 13,504 (1990 census); 2,935 (1982 census); 1,326 (1964 census); 22,656 (1953 census); 120,000,000 in Russia (1993); 11,350,000 in Ukraine; 6,227,000 in Kazakstan; 1,650,000 in Uzbekistan[1]
Location: *N Xinjiang:* Majority of Russians live in Ili, Tacheng, and Altay; *Heilongjiang:* Xunke and Huma counties; *Inner Mongolia:* A few in the Hulunbuir League
Status: An official minority of China
Language: Indo-European, Slavic, Eastern Slavic
Literacy: 81%
Dialects: 0
Religion: Christianity, No Religion
Christians: 7,000
Scripture: Bible 1868; New Testament 1821; Portions 1815; Not available in China
***Jesus* film:** Available
Gospel Recordings: Russian #00049
Christian Broadcasting: Available (FEBC, TWR)
ROPAL code: RUS00

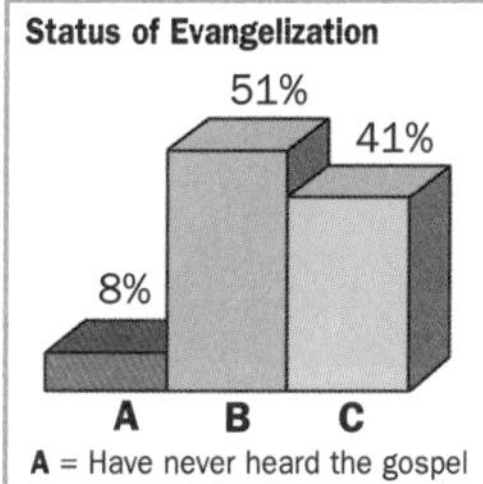

A = Have never heard the gospel
B = Were evangelized but did not become Christians
C = Are adherents to any form of Christianity

Midge Conner

Location: In 1953 Russians living in China numbered 22,656. This tally dropped when most decided to leave China because of the fanatical implementation of Communist policies. By the 1964 census, the Russian population in China had fallen to a mere 1,326. Today their numbers are on the increase again, with 13,504 occupying communities in three provinces along the China-Russia border. Most live in northern Xinjiang, while smaller numbers of Russians are located in Inner Mongolia and Heilongjiang.[2] This figure does not include the hundreds of young women from Russia reportedly working as prostitutes in cities like Beijing and Guangzhou. In addition, approximately 150 million Russians are located throughout the world, including all of the Republics of the former Soviet Union.

Identity: Most Russians in China are the descendants of troops who fled Russia in 1917 after their defeat in the civil war. They have been granted status as an official minority group in China. Today the majority of Russians are a mixed Russian-Chinese race. The few purebred white Russians remaining in China are members of a religious cult who instruct their members not to intermarry with other races.

Language: Over the decades there has been little opportunity for the Russians in China to read their own script. Today young Russians use written Chinese exclusively. One source indicates the Russian spoken in China differs in pronunciation and vocabulary from that spoken in Russia, due to influence from Chinese and Tungus languages.[3]

History: The city of Harbin in Heilongjiang Province was home to 200,000 Russians after the 1917 Russian Revolution. It was known as the "Moscow of Manchuria."[4] Most of these Russians either migrated back to the Soviet Union or became refugees to Western nations. In the 1950s Russia and China enjoyed good relations. Russian became the favored foreign language in Chinese schools. Border disputes and ideological differences in the 1960s, however, made the Chinese think less highly of the Russians.

Customs: Today many Russians living in the border regions are engaged in trade. Their ability to speak both Russian and Chinese is a marked advantage for them. Their products primarily include clothing, vodka, and cigarettes.

Religion: The Russians in China either adhere to Christianity or are atheists. Writers seem to differ regarding the extent of Christianity among the Russians in China. One source states, "The overwhelming majority belong to the Eastern Orthodox Church. In the absence of a church in the locality, they usually hold religious services at home. Thus in the... corner of every house there is inevitably an icon of the Virgin Mary or of Jesus Christ."[5]

Christianity: In addition to the Eastern Orthodox believers, there are also Baptist and Mennonite Russians in China.[6] Although most sources say the majority of Russians in China are Christians, another source lists only 300 Russian believers, fellowshiping in two official churches.[7] The Russian Bible is not available in China.

Salar 撒拉

Paul Hattaway

Location: Approximately 113,000 Salar live in north central China. More than 70% are located in Xunhua County in southeast Qinghai Province. Other Salar live in towns spread 50 kilometers (31 mi.) east to west and 40 kilometers (25 mi.) north to south. Additional communities are located in neighboring Gansu Province, while 1,447 Salar live in Yining County of Xinjiang — a vast distance from the main body of Salar.[1] Most Salar live in poor, mud-baked shacks.

Identity: Although the Salar hold the distinction of being one of China's official nationalities, they are very similar to the Uygurs of Xinjiang. Their language is virtually the same as Uygur. One expert lists Salar as a Uygur dialect, and notes that "The main difference between the Salar and the Uygurs of Xinjiang is geographical."[2]

Language: Approximately 80% of the Salar can speak their language, which is part of the Turkic family. Because the Salar live at the crossroads of several great civilizations, many are bilingual or multilingual in Chinese, Uygur, and Amdo Tibetan. A 1960 study found 7% of the Salar vocabulary was Persian-Arabic, in addition to a few Mongolian and Tibetan loanwords.[3]

History: The Salar have a colorful tale of their history. They say they originated in the famous city of Sarmarkand, located in today's Uzbekistan. In the eleventh century a tribe known as the *Salor* fled persecution in their homeland.[4] They were forced to migrate across the mountains of Central Asia. Not knowing where they were going, the Salar strapped a Qur'an to a camel's head and asked Allah to guide them to wherever he wanted them to settle. After many months of travel, a Salar *Imam* had a vivid dream of a beautiful waterfall. The next day the travelers came to the same waterfall. The camel stopped to drink and turned into a large white stone. Taking it as a divine sign, the tribe stopped there and began to build a community.[5] In 1781 the Qing armies crushed a Salar uprising.[6] The Salar suffered massive losses. As many as 40% of their entire population were obliterated in the battle.[7]

Customs: Divorce is a simple procedure for the Salar. The husband merely announces, "I don't want you any longer," and the woman leaves the home. She is free to marry again.

Religion: The Salar were reportedly converted to Islam as recently as 1750 by Muhammed Amin.[8] By the early 1980s, the Salar worshiped in 73 mosques throughout Xunhua County.[9] Many more mosques have been opened in recent years. Although they have lived beside Tibetans for centuries, the Salar have resisted all pressure to convert to Tibetan Buddhism.

Christianity: Before 1949 few missionaries reached out to the Salar. In the 1920s an appeal was made for "workers to give their whole time to the Salar."[10] Ralph Covell laments, "Missionaries talked about the Salar... but the rigors of a harsh climate, and a demanding geographical environment [meant] only a few were prepared for the necessary long-term commitment and sacrifices."[11] No church has ever been established among the Salar, although today there are a small number of Salar attending a Han Chinese church in Xining City.

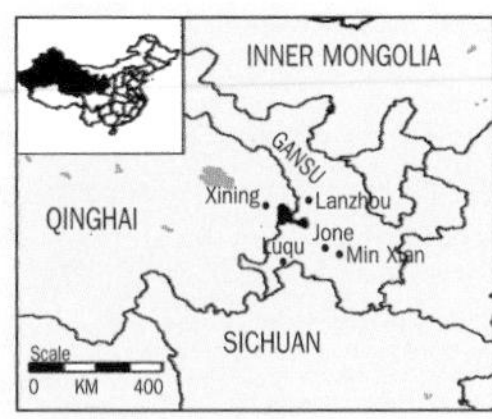

Population in China:
87,697 (1990)
113,100 (2000)
145,900 (2010)
Location:
Qinghai, Gansu, Xinjiang
Religion: Islam
Christians: 20

Overview of the Salar

Countries: China

Pronunciation: "Sar-lar"

Other Names: Sala, Turki Huihui, Turki Hwei Hwei

Population Source:
87,697 (1990 census);
69,102 (1982 census);
34,644 (1964 census);
30,658 (1953 census)

Location: *E Qinghai:* Xunhua and Hualong counties, and in eight other townships; A few also live in Xining City and in Gonghe, Guide, and Qilian counties.
Gansu: Jishishan County; Dahejia Township;
Xinjiang: Yining County

Status:
An official minority of China

Language:
Altaic, Turkic, Eastern Turkic

Literacy: 27%

Dialects (2): Jiezi, Mengda

Religion: Sunni Islam

Christians: 20

Scripture: None

***Jesus* film:** None

Gospel Recordings: None

Christian Broadcasting: None

ROPAL code: SLR00

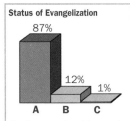

Status of Evangelization

87%

12%

1%

A B C

A = Have never heard the gospel
B = Were evangelized but did not become Christians
C = Are adherents to any form of Christianity

Samadu, Eastern 撒马多(东)

Location: Six hundred Eastern Samadu people live in just one village in southern China. They inhabit Zijun Village of Yiliiu District in Guandu County.[1] Guandu is part of the Kunming Municipality.

Identity: The Eastern Samadu are part of the massive Yi nationality in China. They speak a very different language from the Western Samadu, a group of 7,500 people who live across the province in the Lincang Prefecture near the China-Myanmar border. The Western Samadu claim to have migrated long ago from the Kunming area, so there would seem little doubt that these groups were once one people. Centuries of separation have caused them to become distinct, even though they still retain the same name. The Eastern Samadu, in fact, now pronounce their name slightly differently, as *Samaduo.*

Language: The Eastern Samadu language is part of the Eastern Yi branch of Tibeto-Burman, although some Chinese sources state that it is part of the Southeastern Yi branch. Eastern Samadu is believed to be nearing linguistic extinction and may now be spoken only by a few older people.

History: The Eastern Samadu were once a much larger group than they are today, but epidemics, assimilation, and migration caused them to reduce in size. Many Yi groups, including the Samadu, have legends about a great flood and about the origins of the human race: "A certain man had three sons. He received warning that a flood was about to come upon the earth, and the family discussed how they should save themselves when this calamity came upon them. One suggested an iron cupboard, another a stone one, but the suggestion of the third that they should make a cupboard of wood and store it with food was acted upon."[2]

Paul Hattaway

Customs: Although they no longer participate in many of their traditional festivals, the Eastern Samadu still celebrate the Torch Festival, as do many other ethnic groups in Yunnan Province. A large torch is lit to frighten away the evil spirits before the festival can proceed. In some locations the people drink chicken blood mixed with rice.

Religion: The homes of the Eastern Samadu are customarily built at the foot of a hill, and sacrifices are regularly offered on the hillside in the fourth month of each year. In the past the local shaman determined the most propitious day. An altar was erected, and a sheep and pig were sacrificed. Since the antireligion drives of the Cultural Revolution in the 1960s shamans have become scarce, although in recent years some have re-emerged.

Christianity: Although little is known about the status of Christianity among the Eastern Samadu, there may be a small number of believers among them. A number of churches, both from the Three-Self Patriotic Movement and unregistered house churches, are present in Guandu County. Most Eastern Samadu, however, have no knowledge of the gospel and have never been targeted for evangelism.

Population in China:
600 (1999)
615 (2000)
770 (2010)
Location: Yunnan
Religion: Polytheism
Christians: 10

Overview of the Eastern Samadu

Countries: China

Pronunciation: "Sah-mah-doo"

Other Names: Samaduo, Eastern Samaduo

Population Source: 600 (1999 J. Pelkey); Out of a total Yi population of 6,572,173 (1990 census)

Location: *Yunnan:* Zijun Village of Yiliiu District in Guandu County

Status: Officially included under Yi

Language: Sino-Tibetan, Tibeto-Burman, Burmese-Lolo, Lolo, Northern Lolo, Yi, Eastern Yi

Dialects: 0

Religion: Polytheism, Animism, Ancestor Worship, Christianity

Christians: 10

Scripture: None

***Jesus* film:** None

Gospel Recordings: None

Christian Broadcasting: None

ROPAL code: None

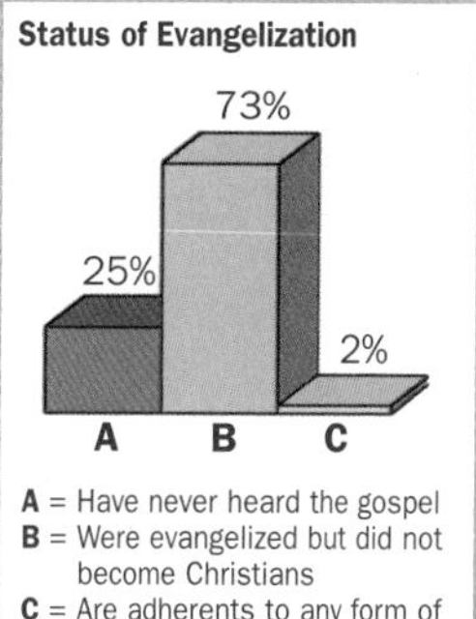

Samadu, Western 撒马堵(西)

Population in China:
7,500 (1999)
7,650 (2000)
9,650 (2010)
Location: Yunnan
Religion: Animism
Christians: None Known

Overview of the Western Samadu

Countries: China

Pronunciation: "Sah-mah-doo"

Other Names: Samou, Samaduo

Population Source:
7,500 (1999 J. Pelkey);
Out of a total Yi population of 6,572,173 (1990 census)

Location: *W Yunnan:* Zhenkang (6,000) and Yongde (1,500) counties

Status:
Officially included under Yi

Language: Sino-Tibetan, Tibeto-Burman, Burmese-Lolo, Lolo, Northern Lolo, Yi, Western Yi

Dialects: 0

Religion: Animism, Ancestor Worship, No Religion

Christians: None known

Scripture: None

***Jesus* film:** None

Gospel Recordings: None

Christian Broadcasting: None

ROPAL code: None

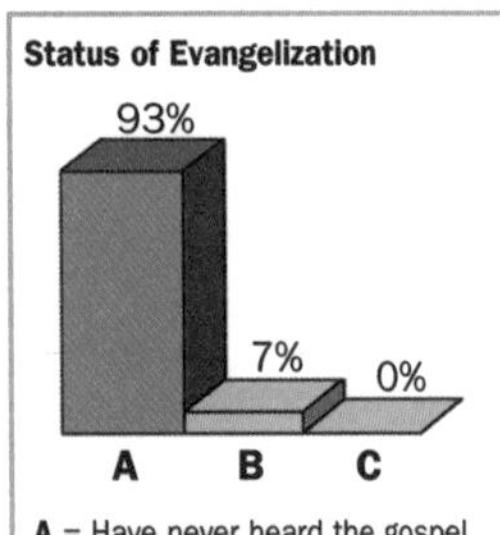

Location: According to a 1999 source, 7,500 Western Samadu people live in the western part of Yunnan Province in southwest China. The majority (6,000) live in Zhenkang County, while an additional 1,500 inhabit areas within neighboring Yongde County.[1]

Identity: The Western Samadu were originally Han Chinese soldiers who were sent from eastern China to Yunnan many centuries ago. They stayed in Yunnan, married local Yi women, and gradually evolved into a distinct ethnic group called the Samadu. Based on cultural and linguistic factors, the Western Samadu were officially included under the Yi nationality in China.

Language: There are two ethnic groups in Yunnan Province who use the autonym *Samadu*. One small group live southeast of Kunming City and are classified as speakers of an Eastern Yi language, while this Samadu group reportedly speak a Western Yi variety, at least among those few elderly people who still retain their language. Jamin Pelkey notes, "The Western Samadu language has reportedly been almost completely lost to Chinese. A few elderly speakers survive."[2]

History: The Samadu claim they originated in Jiangxi and Hunan provinces in eastern China. From there, they say they were sent to Kunming as soldiers in the Ming Dynasty armies, and from there some of them were dispatched to western Yunnan to patrol rebellious areas. In this regard they are similar to the Western Gaisu people, who also live in Yongde County.

Customs: Western Samadu culture is now virtually indistinguishable from the Han Chinese around them. The only factors that make them different today are their ethnic name, their history, and their language, which is fast becoming extinct.

Religion: Older Western Samadu practice animism and ancestor worship. The younger generation, having been educated in atheistic schools, are mostly non religious and view the superstitions of their forefathers with contempt. David Adeney, a former CIM missionary to China, found that Communism was not merely a political system but a religion set on conquering the hearts and minds of its subjects. "The Communist gospel says that God is not love, God is not personal; rather God is an inevitable necessity which moves in history to redeem men's bodies and minds from the slavery of hunger and injustice...Thus, while Communism has no concept of God, it supplies a substitute. Man in society becomes the God of Communism."[3]

Christianity: The Western Samadu are not known to contain any Christians. There are some Wa and Lahu believers in the general area they inhabit, but few believers have ever made a specific effort to reach out to the Western Samadu. There are several other Yi groups in Zhenkang and Yongde counties, including the Limi, Mishaba Laluo, Pengzi, Suan, Western Gaisu, and Yangliu Lalu, but all are unreached people groups in desperate need of the gospel. Because their language is on the verge of extinction, the Western Samadu could now best be reached by Chinese-language media.

Dwayne Graybill

Saman 撒满

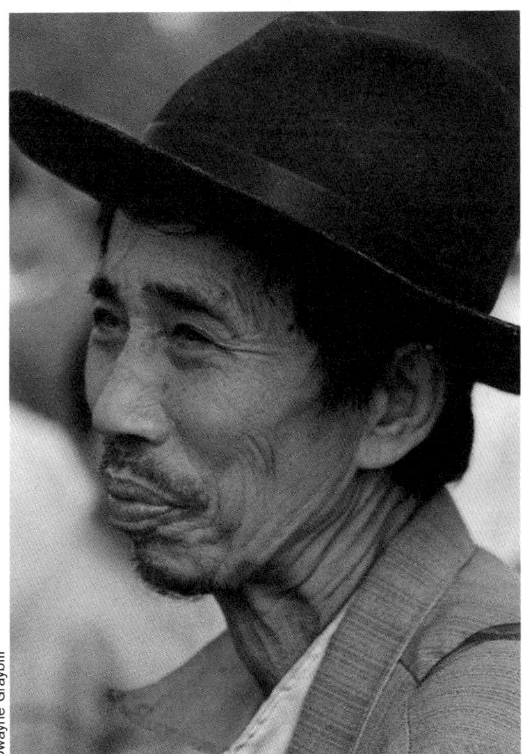

Dwayne Graybill

Location: The small and little-known Saman tribe live just to the north of the city of Qiqihar, in Fuyu County in northwestern China's Heilongjiang Province. Although the Saman today have been largely assimilated into the Han Chinese culture and language, they still proudly hold to their own ethnic and historic identity.

Identity: The exact classification of the Saman is uncertain. They may have been officially included under the Manchu nationality in China, although they claim to be a distinct people group. Traditionally, the Manchu were not one cohesive people, but rather a collection of smaller, related, Tungus-speaking tribes and clans.

Language: In 1987 there were a reported 40 speakers of Manchu remaining in Fuyu County — all elderly people over the age of 60.[1] If the Saman are indeed a Manchu group, then this figure refers to them. There are also Khakas, Daur, and Ewenki people living in Fuyu County.

History: The ancestors of the Saman may date back at least 3,000 years to the Suzhen tribe.[2] One publication goes much further, claiming the Saman have been "in existence since the Stone Age 40,000 years ago."[3] By the sixth century BC the Suzhen, together with the Yan and Hao tribes, occupied the vast territory of modern-day Heilongjiang Province. More specifically, the Saman may have been formerly related to the Wuji tribe, "descendants of the Suzhen and Yilou who in 493 AD overwhelmed the Fuyu and moved into the latter's territory on the Sungari. Soon thereafter, having acquired considerable power and a wide territory, the Wuji group came to be articulated into seven tribes: Sumuo, Boduo, Anchegu, Funie, Haoshi, Heishui, and Baishan."[4]

Customs: As part of their cultural resurgence, a Saman tribal village for tourists was opened in the city of Qiqihar in 1993 "to teach people about a little-known local tribe called the Saman.... The Saman still live relatively primitive lives. Visitors to this tribal recreation center can experience first-hand life with the Samans, and can even participate in religious rituals, horse racing, spear fishing, dancing, and other traditional activities of this group."[5]

Religion: Although the younger generation of this tribe have been heavily influenced by Chinese atheistic beliefs, the Saman were traditionally shamanists. "Each village had a shaman whose sole duty it was to be in touch with the spirits. The other kind of common shaman was in charge of managing rites within each clan. This task was part-time, with the shaman spending most of his time in the field.... Ancestor worship was also practiced, with virtually every home having an ancestor tablet... hanging on the west wall of the main room."[6]

Christianity: Despite their long history as a distinct tribe, there has never been a known Christian church among the Saman. Today few have ever heard the name of Jesus Christ. As they open up to the outside world, the present time affords the best opportunity to reach the primitive Saman with the gospel.

Population in China:
2,000 (1993)
2,580 (2000)
3,320 (2010)
Location: Heilongjiang
Religion: Shamanism
Christians: None Known

Overview of the Saman

Countries: China
Pronunciation: "Sah-mahn"
Other Names: Sa Man
Population Source:
2,000 (1993 AMO);
Out of a total Manchu population of 9,821,180 (1990 census)
Location: *W Heilongjiang:* Fuyu County, north of Qiqihar
Status: Probably officially included under Manchu
Language: Altaic, Tungus, Southern Tungus, Southwest
Dialects: 0
Religion: Shamanism, No Religion
Christians: None known
Scripture: None
***Jesus* film:** None
Gospel Recordings: None
Christian Broadcasting: None
ROPAL code: None

Status of Evangelization

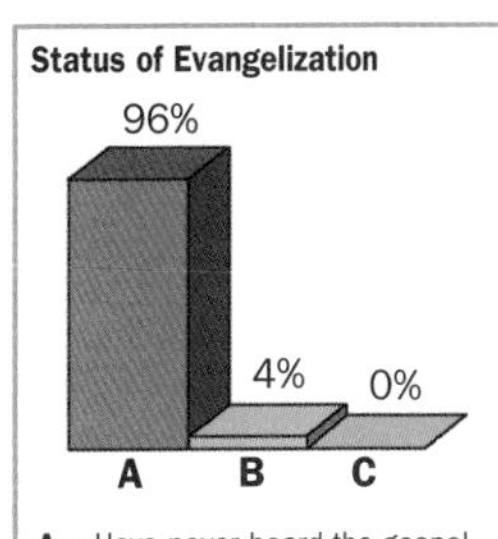

A = Have never heard the gospel
B = Were evangelized but did not become Christians
C = Are adherents to any form of Christianity

Samei 撒梅

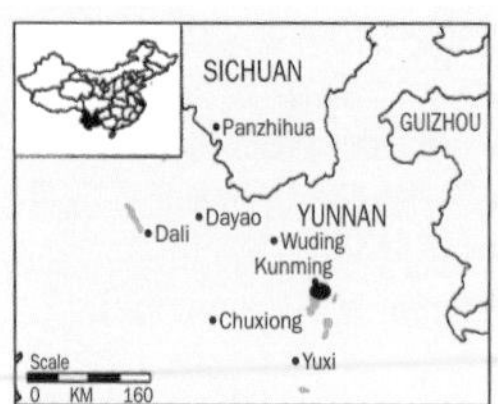

Population in China:
27,500 (1999)
28,200 (2000)
35,400 (2010)
Location: Yunnan
Religion: Animism
Christians: 300

Overview of the Samei

Countries: China

Pronunciation: "Sah-may"

Other Names: Soumi, Sani, Sanipo, Sameizu, Samin

Population Source: 27,500 (1999 J. Pelkey); Out of a total Yi population of 6,572,173 (1990 census)

Location: *Yunnan:* Guandu (26,000) and Yiliang (1,500) counties

Status: Officially included under Yi

Language: Sino-Tibetan, Tibeto-Burman, Burmese-Lolo, Lolo, Northern Lolo, Yi, Eastern Yi

Dialects: 0

Religion: Animism, Polytheism, Ancestor Worship, Christianity, No Religion

Christians: 300

Scripture: None

***Jesus* film:** None

Gospel Recordings: Yi: Sami

Christian Broadcasting: None

ROPAL code: SMH00

Status of Evangelization

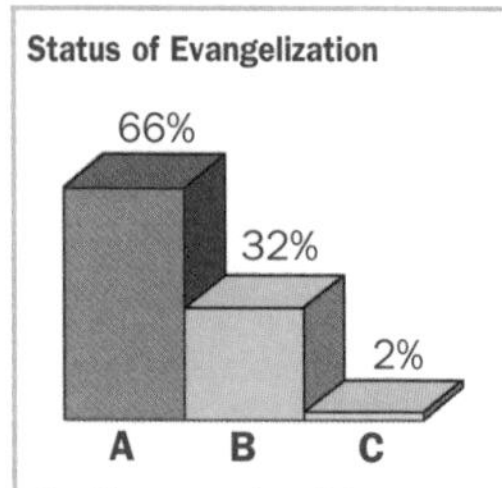

A = Have never heard the gospel
B = Were evangelized but did not become Christians
C = Are adherents to any form of Christianity

Paul Hattaway

Location: Approximately 28,000 members of the Samei tribe live just southeast of Kunming City in Yunnan Province, especially in the Ala and Dabanqiao districts of Guandu County. There are 13 Samei villages in the Dabanqiao District.[1] Most publications do not list a specific population for the Samei, simply mentioning they are "small,"[2] and there are "not many people."[3]

Identity: The Samei, who are part of the official Yi nationality in China, actually call themselves *Sani*. This, however, "does not mean they are the same people group as the famous Sani of the Stone Forest. The two should not be confused.... The Han Chinese have referred to this people as Samei for so long that the name has become fixed — even among anthropologists and linguists — to the point that their designation as anything else would probably be more confusing than helpful."[4]

Language: Jamin Pelkey explains how the Sani of the Stone Forest and the Samei "insist that they are different peoples. For one thing, the former has been classified as a 'Southeastern Yi' variety and the latter has been classified as an 'Eastern Yi' variety."[5] While many Samei adults know Chinese, most Samei children do not know Mandarin and can only speak their own language.[6]

History: For centuries the Samei have celebrated the annual Torch Festival. The Samei say that "long ago there was a brave Samei warrior king whose head, if cut off in battle, would grow back beneath the starlit sky at night. His wife leaked out the secret of his immortality, however, and he was finally killed in a battle.... The Samei went out to look for his soul with lit torches, and carry on the tradition every 24th day of the sixth lunar month."[7]

Customs: The Samei possess their own colorful dress. "A hat worn by young women of the Samei tribe on the outskirts of Kunming resembles the comb of a cock.... There are not many people in this tribe, but these hats are still worn by young women and are unique."[8]

Religion: Most Samei are animists. They believe their lives are controlled by the spirit world around them. Ancestor worship is also practiced, especially by older Samei. Many of the younger generation consider themselves nonreligious.

Christianity: The Samei have a long Christian history. Australian missionary Arthur Nicholls first pioneered work in the area in 1906. Nicholls received this glowing tribute from fellow missionary Samuel Clarke: "He may be reckoned among the heroes who are establishing the kingdom of heaven upon earth.... Loved and trusted by multitudes, despised and hated by many... like a man who has been touching the very bedrock of humanity, Arthur Nicholls goes on his way little thinking what a hero he is, and counting himself repaid over and over again because the people love him."[9] The Eastern Lipo of Wuding and Luquan counties have taken the gospel to the Samei in recent decades. "Because of their witness, there are believers among the neighboring tribes... including the Samei."[10]

Samtao 散套

Population in China:
100 (1993)
120 (2000)
155 (2010)
Location: Yunnan
Religion: Buddhism
Christians: None Known

Overview of the Samtao

Countries: Myanmar, Laos, China

Pronunciation: "Sahm-taow"

Other Names: Samtau, Samtuan, Sam Tao, Sen Chun, Kiorr, Saamtaav, Con, Col

Population Source: 100 (1996 B. Grimes – 1993 figure); Out of a total Bulang population of 82,280 (1990 census); 2,213 in Laos (1995 census); Also in Myanmar

Location: *SW Yunnan:* Xishuangbanna Prefecture

Status: Officially included under Bulang

Language: Austro-Asiatic, Mon-Khmer, Northern Mon-Khmer, Palaungic, Western Palaungic, Angkuic

Dialects: 0

Religion: Theravada Buddhism, Animism

Christians: None known

Scripture: None

***Jesus* film:** None

Gospel Recordings: None

Christian Broadcasting: None

ROPAL code: STU00

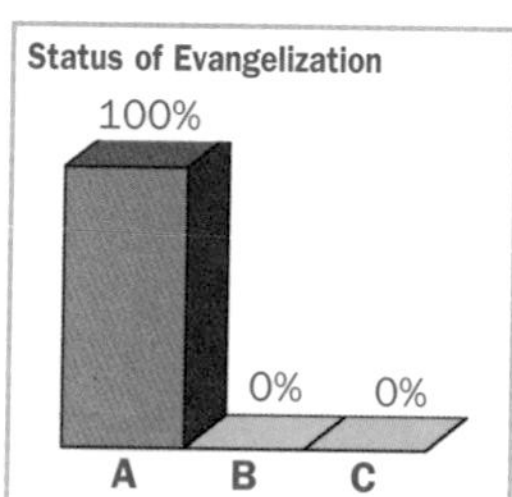

A = Have never heard the gospel
B = Were evangelized but did not become Christians
C = Are adherents to any form of Christianity

Location: The small Samtao tribe lives in the Bulang Mountains, in southwest China's Xishuangbanna Prefecture. Little information is available about the Samtao. A 1993 figure placed only 100 speakers of the Samtao language remaining in China,[1] but the number of people who belong to the Samtao ethnic group may be significantly higher. The vast majority of Samtao live in the eastern part of Myanmar's Shan State. They are primarily located in mountain villages northeast of the city of Kengtung. More than 2,000 Samtao also live in Laos.

Identity: The Samtao have been officially counted as part of the Bulang nationality in China. Although they share many cultural similarities with the Bulang, the Samtao speak their own separate language. The Samtao in Myanmar are part of what used to be a collection of three distinct tribes: Samtao, Samtuan, and Sen Chun.

Language: The Samtao language is part of the Western Palaungic language family. It is related to, yet distinct from, all other Mon-Khmer languages in the region such as De'ang, Wa, and Bulang. A visitor in the early 1920s noted, "They are mostly illiterate... but there are some members of the Wa-Palaung group who are literate, such as the Sen Chun, Sam Tao and Sam Tuan."[2]

History: The Samtao, although small in number, have a long and rich history. It is believed that they were originally Wa people who converted to Theravada Buddhism at least nine centuries ago.[3] The great majority of Wa have resisted Buddhism and remain animists or polytheists to this day. After many generations of separation, the Samtao emerged as a distinct people group with their own customs and language.

Customs: The primary occupation of the Samtao is tea cultivation. The Bulang Mountains are famous for the Pu'er variety of tea. Other crops include maize, rice, cotton, and sugarcane. Many Samtao men tattoo their limbs and torsos—often with passages of Buddhist scriptures. When a Samtao dies, his family kills a chicken to call back the soul of the deceased. The corpse is then bathed and dressed in new clothes; a turban is placed on the head and the body is positioned between white cloth sheets.

Religion: The Samtao are zealous followers of Theravada Buddhism. Their whole ethnic identity is wrapped up in their adherence to Buddhism. Missionary William Clifton Dodd wrote this about the Samtao in the 1920s: "These Sam Tao are one branch of the aboriginal stock found all over Indo-China, including the Khmu of French Laos State, the Lawa of North Siam [Thailand] and the Wild Wa of northern Burma and southern China. These three branches are not Buddhists, but the Sam Tao have been Buddhists for 900 years, and are the best Buddhists we have met."[4]

Christianity: There is not a single trace of Christianity among the Samtao today. They have never been targeted with the gospel throughout their long history and remain a completely unevangelized people group on both sides of the China-Myanmar border.

Dwayne Graybill

anda 散达

Location: Researcher Dwayne Graybill visited the little-known Sanda people in 1996. He reported a total of 1,000 people inhabiting six villages in the Sanda Mountains between Jinghong and Menglian in Xishuangbanna Prefecture.[1] They are the only people group living on the mountain that bears their name; therefore, they have managed to retain most of their traditional customs and identity. The region is in the southwest corner of China close to Laos and Myanmar. The late Robert Morse, a linguist who spoke more than 16 languages, listed a population of 700 Sanda in 1991.

Identity: The Chinese authorities surprisingly acknowledge the Sanda as a separate people, giving them the suffix *zu* (nationality), but consider them too small to be afforded status as one of China's official minorities. The Sanda were not counted under any nationality in the 1990 census but were combined into a list of *Undetermined Minorities*.[2]

Language: Sanda is a distinct Tibeto-Burman language, although the Sanda themselves say it is partially related to Jino and Ake — two other minority groups in Xishuangbanna.

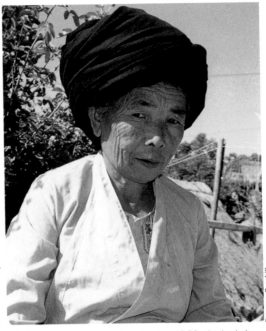

History: The Sanda believe that they have been living in the Sanda Mountains of southern Yunnan "since the beginning of the earth."[3] They claim to have been in Xishuangbanna long before their relatives — the Jino and Ake — migrated there. In the past, Sanda men and women were renowned for their excessively long hair, but this practice is no longer observed. Today the Sanda are widely known as expert hunters and gatherers who take much pride in their weapon-handling skills.

Customs: Rubber, bananas, and soybean are the main crops harvested by the Sanda. In addition to the government quota, they are allowed to sell their excess produce in the marketplaces of Jinghong and Menglian. In recent years many Sanda youth have moved to the towns to find work. Intermarriage with other tribes is common among the Sanda, especially with the Jino, Ake, and Tai Lu.

Dwayne Graybill

Religion: The inhabitants of the six Sanda villages are animists. All Sanda homes possess spirit altars, which are hung in a prominent position in the main room of their homes. The Sanda say that in the past they were a spiritual people, but during the Cultural Revolution they lost their soul.[4] The Sanda place great importance in burial practices. The corpse is placed in the ground for burial if the person was more than 60 years old. If someone dies by accident or before the age of 60, the body is cremated.

Christianity: Most Sanda have no awareness of the gospel. Few Sanda living in their mountain communities have ever heard the name of Christ, but there are a small number of believers among the Sanda migrant workers living in Jinghong. Richard F. Lovelace, an American theologian, said, "Let us remember that Jesus Christ is not to return again physically until the Gospel has first been preached to all nations.... It seems the millions of Muslims and Chinese should gain something more than a brief glimpse of a flare shot over another country."[5]

Population in China:
1,000 (1996)
1,110 (2000)
1,430 (2010)
Location: Yunnan
Religion: Animism
Christians: 15

Overview of the Sanda

Countries: China
Pronunciation: "Sahn-da"
Other Names: San Da
Population Source: 1,000 (1996 D. Graybill); 700 (1991 R. Morse)
Location: *SW Yunnan:* Xishuangbanna Dai Autonomous Prefecture: Between Jinghong and Menglian in the Sanda Mountains
Status: Counted in census as an *Undetermined Minority*
Language: Sino-Tibetan, Tibeto-Burman, Unclassified
Dialects: 0
Religion: Animism, Polytheism, Christianity
Christians: 15
Scripture: None
***Jesus* film:** None
Gospel Recordings: None
Christian Broadcasting: None
ROPAL code: None

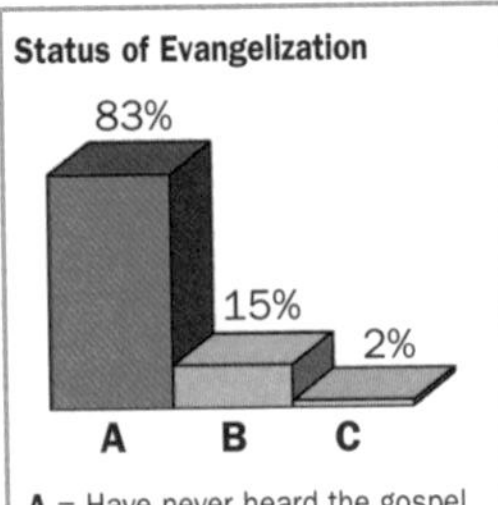

Sani 撒尼

Population in China:
103,000 (1999)
105,600 (2000)
132,500 (2010)
Location: Yunnan
Religion: Polytheism
Christians: 3,100

Overview of the Sani

Countries: China

Pronunciation: "Sah-nee"

Other Names: San Yi, San Yi Puo, Ming, Shani, Gni-p'a, Gni, Ni, Nipo

Population Source: 103,000 (1999 J. Pelkey); Out of a total Yi population of 6,572,173 (1990 census)

Location: *Yunnan:* Shilin (68,000), Yiliang (21,000), Luxi (2,000), Qiubei (10,000), and Mile (2,100) counties

Status: Officially included under Yi

Language: Sino-Tibetan, Tibeto-Burman, Burmese-Lolo, Lolo, Northern Lolo, Yi, Southeastern Yi

Dialects: 0

Religion: Polytheism, Animism, No Religion, Christianity

Christians: 3,100

Scripture: None

***Jesus* film:** None

Gospel Recordings: Yi: Sani #04939

Christian Broadcasting: None

ROPAL code: YIE01

Status of Evangelization

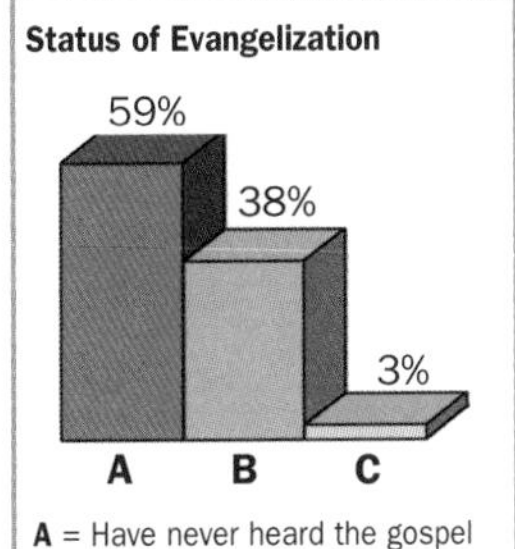

A = Have never heard the gospel
B = Were evangelized but did not become Christians
C = Are adherents to any form of Christianity

Paul Hattaway

Location: More than 105,000 Sani live in the central and eastern parts of Yunnan Province. The majority live in Shilin (formerly Lunan) County, especially around the famous Stone Forest. The Stone Forest, about 120 kilometers (75 mi.) southeast of Kunming, is a massive collection of limestone forms that stand up to 30 meters (98 ft.) high. Sani legend says the gods created the Stone Forest in order to help young lovers, who can find privacy among the towering pillars — which cover an area of 400 hectares (990 acres). In addition to 54,134 living in Shilin County,[1] the Sani are located in nearby Mile, Yiliang, Qiubei, and Luxi counties.[2]

Identity: Although they have been combined with numerous other people groups to form the large Yi nationality in China, the Sani possess their own unique language, customs, and ethnic identity.

Language: The Sani language is part of the Tibeto-Burman language family. It consists of 40 consonants, 24 vowels, and 5 tones. A Sani-Chinese dictionary was completed in 1986, using the traditional Nosu orthography.[3] The first two years of primary school education for Sani children are conducted in the Sani language, but all schooling after that point is conducted in Chinese.

History: The Sani are thought to have originated near Dali. Shortly after the Tang Dynasty (618–907) they left the region, traveled through Chuxiong, and settled among the rock formations of Shilin.

Customs:[4] A single Sani girl's turban contains all the colors of the rainbow. This results from a Sani legend. A long time ago a beautiful Sani girl named Musidama was rescued from a tiger by a handsome hunter named Stiasai, and the two fell in love. The local chief lusted after her, however, and desired to marry her first. One day Stiasai was attacked by a wild boar and died. Musidama's heart was broken. At his funeral, she leaped into the flames before the chief's men could stop her. Only two small pieces of her clothing were torn off. "Soon two colorful clouds rose from the flames and then converged together. The sky cleared and a beautiful rainbow appeared. The Sani call it *Saimusi-mudama* to remember the lovers."[5]

Religion: The Sani are polytheists. They believe the earth, sky, water, fire, mountains, stones, etc., have their own spirits. They also worship their ancestors.

Christianity: Père Paul Vial of the Paris Foreign Missionary Society commenced work among the Sani in 1887. In the early 1900s he reported the Sani to be a haven of Catholicism with 7,360 converts[6] and Sani priests ministering in 30 villages.[7] Vial was a colorful figure, whose battles with Chinese officials led to attempted murder in 1894.[8] Today there are Catholic believers in 22 of the 124 Sani villages in Shilin County. The 3,000 Sani Catholics in Shilin worship in seven main churches.[9] In addition, a small number of Catholics are found among the Sani in Honghe Prefecture. Although there are only a relative handful of Protestants among the Sani, the Sani Catholics represent a great resource and hope for the salvation of many other Yi peoples in the area. Their persistence and faithfulness in the face of opposition have been a powerful witness.

Sanie 撒聂

Paul Hattaway

Location: A total of 25,300 Sanie people lived within Kunming Municipality in Yunnan Province in 1999. The Sanie inhabit most of Gufeng and Tuanjie districts in Xishan (West Mountains) County; parts of Fumin County; and parts of Qinglong District in northern Anning County.[1]

Identity: The Sanie are one of 120 distinct ethnolinguistic people groups who have been combined by the Chinese authorities to form the Yi nationality. Although the Han Chinese refer to this people as *White Yi* or *White Lolo*, in their own language they refer to themselves only as Sanie.

Language: Linguists David Bradley, Maya Bradley, and Li Longxiang of the Yunnan Academy of Social Sciences have conducted extensive linguistic surveys among the Sanie. In 1997, at the 30th International Conference on Sino-Tibetan Languages and Linguistics, they published a paper entitled, *The Sanyie of Kunming: a Case of Yi Language Death*. They found that there are fewer and fewer speakers of Sanie in villages the farther one travels from Kunming. Nevertheless, the language is still being spoken by young and old in parts of Gufeng, Tuanjie, and Qinglong districts. Despite their small numbers, Bradley reports that "the degree of dialectical differentiation within Sanie is very great despite the small distances involved."[2]

History: Despite their similar names, the Sanie are not the same ethnic group, nor do they speak the same language, as the Sani or Samei. Long ago they may have been related.

Customs: Sanie customs are in the process of assimilation to the pervasive Han Chinese culture. In Xishan County, the Sanie, along with the Bai and Han, celebrate the *Taiyinhui* or "Moon Fair" on two occasions each year. The first celebration takes place on the sixth day of first lunar month. According to Jamin Pelkey, "Most of the participants in the festival are elderly women. Burning sticks of incense, they present various food offerings to the moon, and, after having arranged nine pieces of yellow paper in three small piles they get down on their knees and bow three times."[3]

Religion: The Taiyinhui Festival reflects the main religious beliefs of the Sanie, which are a mixture of polytheism and ancestor worship. Pelkey continues: "Following this, passages of the *Taiyangjing* (the Moon's Scripture) are chanted in unison. In the passages, the moon is praised for all of its qualities and personified as a tender, nocturnal messenger blessing the earth with refreshing dew. The second celebration takes place in conjunction with the mid-Autumn Festival, on the 15th day of the eighth lunar month."[4]

Christianity: There are believed to be a small number of Sanie Christians near Kunming. Before 1949 many Protestant and Catholic missionary organizations worked in Kunming City and surrounding areas. The majority of Sanie, however, have no awareness of the gospel or its life-giving message.

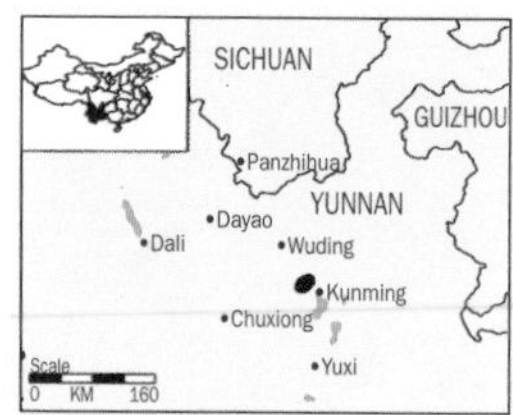

Population in China:
25,300 (1999)
25,900 (2000)
32,550 (2010)
Location: Yunnan
Religion: Polytheism
Christians: 100

Overview of the Sanie

Countries: China

Pronunciation: "Sah-nieh"

Other Names: Shanie, Shaniepu, Sanyie, Bai Yi, White Yi, Bai Lolo, Shansu

Population Source: 25,300 (1999 J. Pelkey); Out of a total Yi population of 6,572,173 (1990 census)

Location: *Yunnan:* Xishan (22,500), Fumin (2,500), and Anning (300) counties

Status: Officially included under Yi

Language: Sino-Tibetan, Tibeto-Burman, Burmese-Lolo, Lolo, Northern Lolo, Yi, Eastern Yi

Dialects: 0

Religion: Polytheism, Animism, Ancestor Worship, Christianity

Christians: 100

Scripture: None

***Jesus* film:** None

Gospel Recordings: None

Christian Broadcasting: None

ROPAL code: None

Status of Evangelization

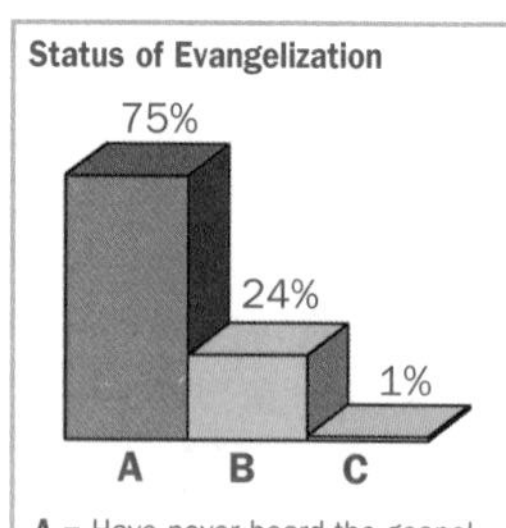

A = Have never heard the gospel
B = Were evangelized but did not become Christians
C = Are adherents to any form of Christianity

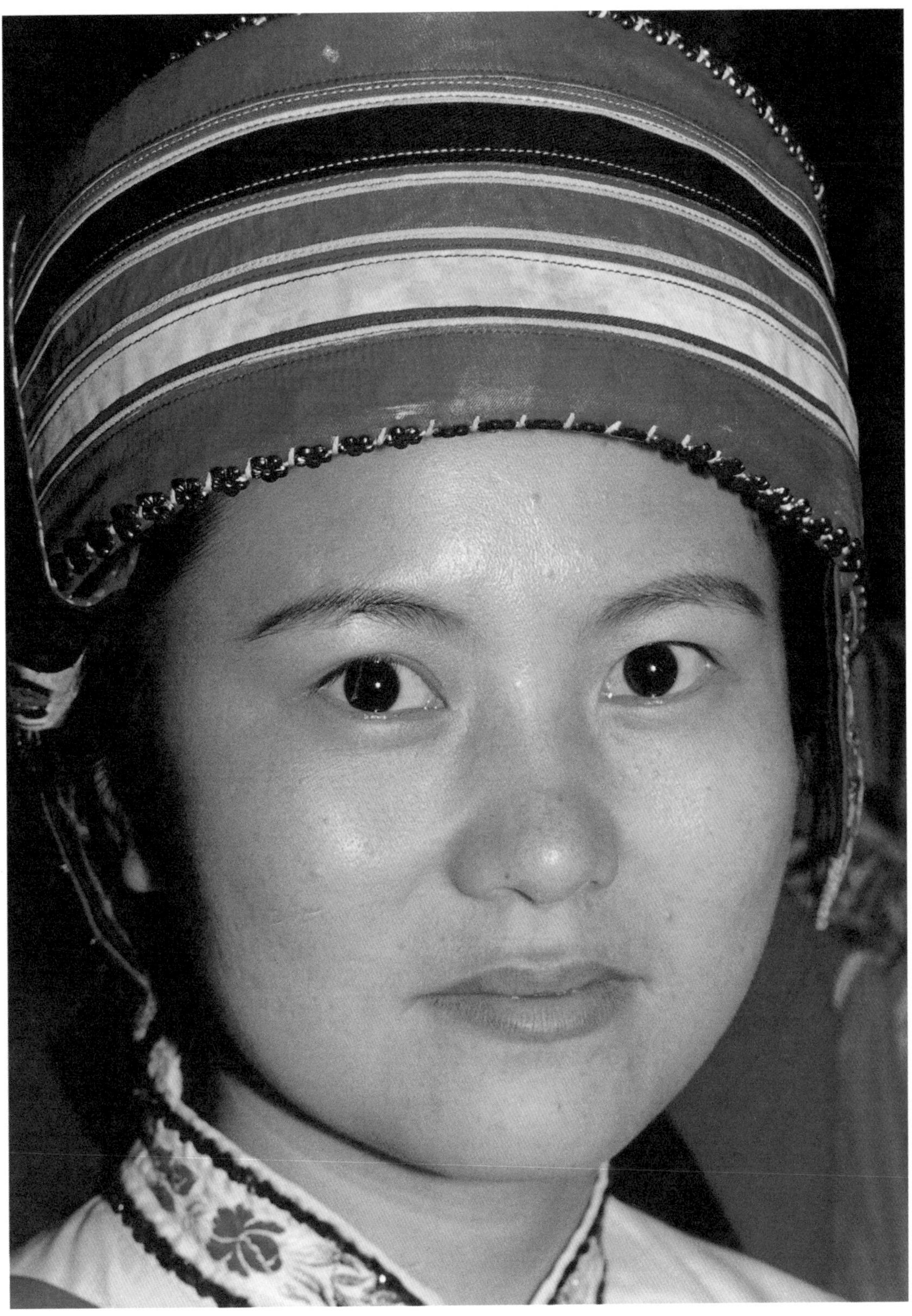

176. An unmarried *Sani* girl's headdress contains all the colors of the rainbow. More than 105,000 Sani live in and around the Stone Forest — a collection of limestone forms covering an area of 990 acres in Shilin County, Yunnan. [Paul Hattaway]

177

178

179

180

177. *Shui* women wear a white headdress for three years after the death of a relative, Duyun, Guizhou. [Paul Hattaway]

178–180. The 40,000 *Tajik* in China speak two distinct Persian (Iranian) languages: Sarikoli and Wakhi. The Tajiks are Muslims of the Shi'ite sect who live in the southwest part of Xinjiang. [all by Dwayne Graybill]

181

182

183

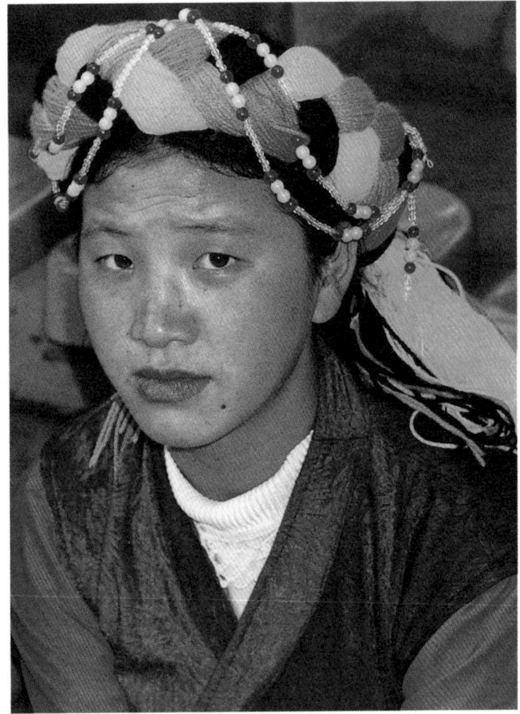
184

181. Although they number more than 7 million people worldwide, only about 6,000 Muslim *Tatar* people live in northwest China. [Paul Hattaway]
182. Most *Tai Dam* people live in Vietnam and Laos, with 34,000 also found in southern China. [Paul Hattaway]
183. A *Tibetan* Buddhist lama. [Revival Christian Church]
184. A *Tibetan* woman with traditional headdress, Sichuan. [Paul Hattaway]

185

186

187

188

185–186. Faces of *Tibetans* — a people without their own country. [both by Paul Hattaway]

187. The distinctive dress of the *Zhongdian Tibetans* from northern Yunnan. The Zhongdian Tibetans have their own culture and language. [Midge Conner]

188. A *Tibetan* nomad with a prayer wheel. Tibetans believe that every time they spin the wheel a prayer is released into the heavens. [Paul Hattaway]

Sanqiao 三锹

Location: It is estimated that more than 5,000 Sanqiao people live in the southeastern part of Guizhou Province, possibly in Liping County. The Sanqiao area is near the juncture of Guizhou and Hunan provinces, and the Guangxi Zhuang Autonomous Region.

Identity: The official classification of the Sanqiao people is extremely confusing. In the 1950s they applied for recognition as a distinct minority group, but their application was rejected. It appears that because some Sanqiao wear Dong clothing and have Dong customs, while others have been assimilated to the Miao culture, the authorities did not know how to classify the Sanqiao. In the 1982 census they were included in a list of *Undetermined Minorities.*[1] In 1985 those Sanqiao people who lived near the Dong and who had adopted Dong customs were officially included in the Dong nationality, while those who lived near the Miao and showed characteristics of the Miao people were included under the Miao nationality.[2] This division is not accepted by the Sanqiao who view themselves as a distinct group, different from both Miao and Dong. More research needs to be done to determine if the Sanqiao are related to the Mjuniang, who live in the same part of China and appear also to be partly absorbed into Miao and Dong culture. It may turn out that the Sanqiao are a subgroup of the Mjuniang, who have been profiled separately in *Operation China.*

Language: The Sanqiao are just as mixed linguistically as they are ethnically. While all except the most remote Sanqiao are able to speak Chinese, they also speak their own language, which appears to be related to Dong, in their homes. It is uncertain if this group was originally a Han Chinese group who absorbed Dong language and culture, or if they have always spoken the Dong language, which is part of the Kam-Sui branch of the Tai linguistic family.

Yao Update

History: The valleys of southeast Guizhou Province have seen numerous wars and interracial conflict over the centuries. Millions of Han Chinese have used this area to migrate from northern to southern China. As a result, there are numerous ethnic groups living among the mountains in this region.

Customs: As previously mentioned, the Sanqiao have lost their own identity and now practice the customs of the people who live nearest to them. Some Sanqiao practise Dong customs while others have taken up the Miao way of life.

Religion: Although the Sanqiao do not consider themselves to be a particularly religious people, they do worship their ancestors and hold ceremonies to appease local spirits on a few occasions throughout the year. Many Sanqiao youth are nonreligious.

Christianity: Little is known about the status of Christianity among the Sanqiao, but their location is one of the more gospel-neglected parts of southern China. Few missionaries ever ventured into the mountains of southeast Guizhou prior to 1949, and few believers exist among the local Dong or Miao.

Population in China:
5,000 (1999)
5,140 (2000)
6,630 (2010)
Location: Guizhou
Religion: Ancestor Worship
Christians: None Known

Overview of the Sanqiao

Countries: China
Pronunciation: "Sahn-cheeow"
Other Names: San Qiao
Population Source: 5,000 (1999 AMO)
Location: *SE Guizhou:* Possibly Liping County
Status: Officially included under both Miao and Dong since 1985; Previously included in a list of *Undetermined Minorities*
Language: Daic, Kam-Sui
Dialects: 0
Religion: Ancestor Worship, Animism, No Religion
Christians: None known
Scripture: None
***Jesus* film:** None
Gospel Recordings: None
Christian Broadcasting: None
ROPAL code: None

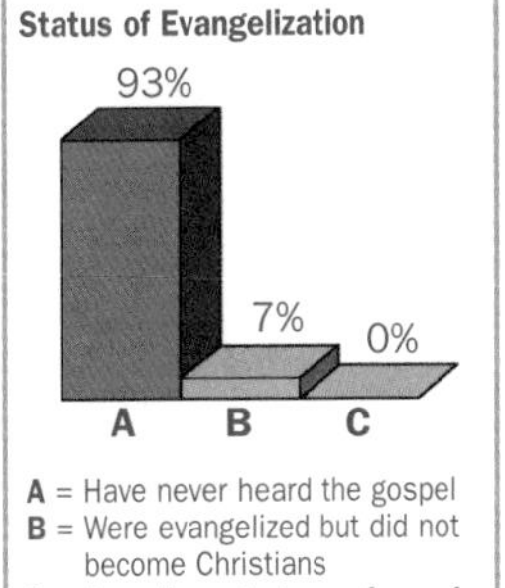

Sansu 散苏

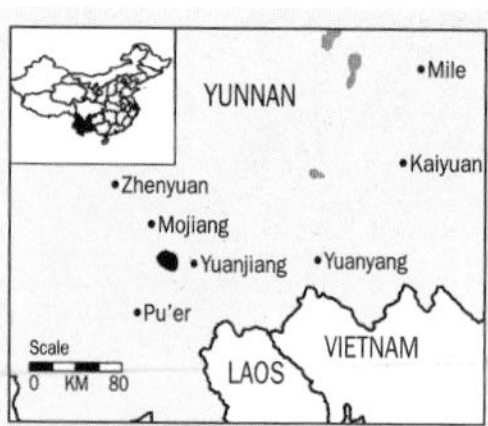

Population in China:
12,000 (1995)
13,370 (2000)
16,440 (2010)
Location: Yunnan
Religion: Polytheism
Christians: 300

Overview of the Sansu

Countries: China

Pronunciation: "Sahn-soo"

Other Names:

Population Source:
12,000 (1995 Joshua Project); Out of a total Hani population of 1,253,952 (1990 census)

Location: *S Yunnan:* Yuanjiang County in Yuxi Prefecture

Status:
Officially included under Hani

Language: Sino-Tibetan, Tibeto-Burman, Burmese-Lolo, Lolo, Southern Lolo, Akha

Dialects: 0

Religion: Polytheism, Animism, Christianity, Ancestor Worship

Christians: 300

Scripture: None

***Jesus* film:** None

Gospel Recordings: None

Christian Broadcasting: None

ROPAL code: SCA00

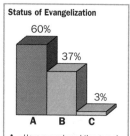

Status of Evangelization

60% (A) — 37% (B) — 3% (C)

A = Have never heard the gospel
B = Were evangelized but did not become Christians
C = Are adherents to any form of Christianity

Location: The Joshua Project listed a 1995 population of 12,000 Sansu — a poverty-stricken and destitute tribe located in the highest mountains of Yuanjiang County in southern Yunnan Province's Yuxi Prefecture. Yuanjiang, located on the banks of the Honghe (Red) River, is predominantly inhabited by members of the Han, Yi, and Hani nationalities.

Identity: For reasons of perceived historical kinship, the Sansu — along with more than a dozen other tribes — have been included in the Hani nationality by the Chinese authorities, who are not apt to grant official status to minorities with relatively small populations.

Language: Although the Sansu speak their own distinct Tibeto-Burman language, they do not possess an orthography. In 1957 the government tried to introduce a Roman script for the various Hani peoples in Honghe. The authorities' unwillingness to recognize the true linguistic diversity among the different groups caused the project to fail. Groups like the Sansu did not use words found in the "Hani language" literature. The Sansu were originally a non-Tibeto-Burman-speaking tribe who were taken as slaves and had another language imposed on them.[1]

History: For generations the Sansu were slaves of the ruling Yi people. "They are considered very low on the scale of tribal society, actually being servants to the Lolo [Yi] tribe and given so little recognition by the government that they are even exempt from taxation and military service. Tattered, torn, scanty togs; coarse mountain food; dark smoky hovels — these are their daily lot. The Sansu are some of the earth's poorest."[2]

Customs: The various Hani-related peoples, including the Sansu, have developed a long list of "at least 500 known medicinal plants as well as medicinal practices such as bone-setting, massage, and blood circulation techniques."[3]

Religion: The Sansu are zealous polytheists. They worship a multitude of evil spirits who rule over them. The Sansu also venerate their ancestors, especially the spirits of their in-laws.

Christianity: Of the more than 1,000 Hani Christians reportedly living in Yuanjiang County,[4] approximately 200 to 300 are believed to be members of the Sansu tribe. China Inland Mission's John Kuhn — who conducted an intensive ethnic survey of Yunnan Province in 1945 — joyfully recounted his meeting with the first Sansu believer. "At Yuanchiang [Yuanjiang] on the Red River, my cup ran over! I saw my first Sansu. I had never heard of that tribe before.... And there, my first Sansu sat before me, little of stature, shy, quiet, with a soft voice and distant look. His awkwardness bespoke his inner thought, 'Why should the White Man wish to talk to me?' Simply because the White Man wished to size up a Sansu, lowest in the scale of humanity of those parts, yet an object of the grace of God, for he had been brought to Christ by a Lolo. Wonderful! Are there any more Sansu? Yes, many more. Then we can expect a grand harvest, for the saving of the first is proof that He can save all."[5]

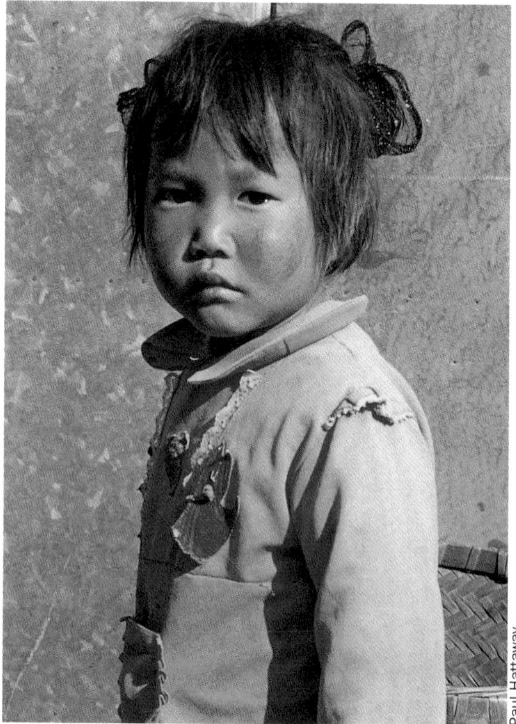
Paul Hattaway

Shan 山

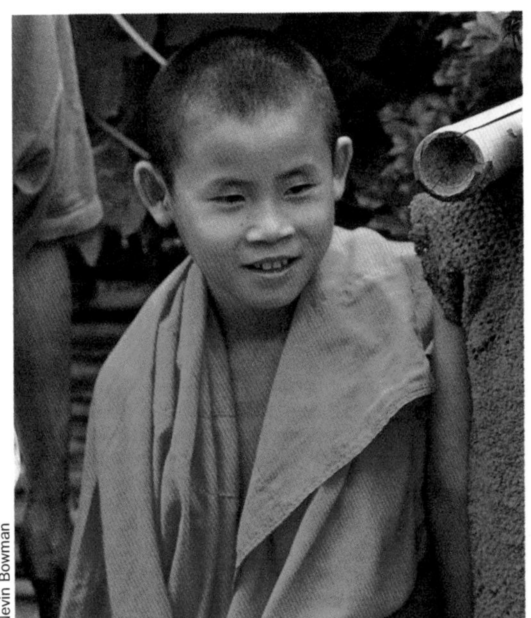
Nevin Bowman

Location: Although almost three million Shan inhabit the northern section of Myanmar, the members of only one village in China speak the same language as the Shan of Myanmar. This village is located in a remote area that juts into Myanmar, in a densely forested and mountainous region. The Shan live in the Dehong Prefecture of western Yunnan Province, an area open to foreigners. In addition, 56,000 Shan live in northwest Thailand. Small Shan communities also exist in the United States.[1]

Identity: The inhabitants of the one Shan village in China have been included under the Dai nationality. The name *Shan* is used by different Tai groups in various ways throughout China. The predominant Tai group in the Dehong Prefecture are the Tai Mao, who sometimes call themselves *Shan*. Furthermore, the Tai Nua are often called *Yunnanese Shan*. The Shan are very proud of their racial identity. They call themselves *Tai Yay*, meaning "greater Tai." Although the different Tai peoples view themselves as from the same ethnic stock, for reasons of determining Christian strategy it is important to classify them according to their various ethnic and linguistic affiliations.

Language: Linguists note that the Shan in one location of Dehong are "sometimes called Tai Nua, but the same Shan as Burma is spoken there,"[2] and "the dialect seems close to — but not identical with — the Tai-Mao dialect of Northern Shan (i.e. that spoken on the Burmese side of the border). The two groups used to share the same writing system."[3] The Shan of Myanmar and the Tai groups of China use several different scripts.

History: The Shan are one of the great peoples of Southeast Asia. They dominate the state in northern Myanmar that bears their name. Desiring their own independent homeland, rebel Shan armies have been fighting the Burmese since the end of World War II.

Customs: Traditionally all Shan boys are sent to a temple at the age of seven or eight, where they receive their education from Buddhist monks. In recent decades the region has seen rampant drug trafficking between China and Myanmar.

Religion: The Shan have been ardent followers of Theravada Buddhism for many centuries. Gold-colored temples are scattered throughout the jungles and mountains of Shan State. All Shan community life is centered around their religion. Unlike most Buddhists who believe in karma, the Shan believe they are protected from evil by the spiritual power of Buddha idols and spirits.[4]

Christianity: Mission research ministries have designated the Shan of Myanmar the ninth largest unreached people in the world. Missionaries first started reaching out to the Shan in 1860, and the Shan New Testament was completed in 1882. Historically, few Shan have responded to the gospel, largely because of their ethnic pride and identity as Buddhists. In recent years some breakthroughs have occurred in Myanmar. There are no Christians reported among the Shan in China, even though the Bible, the *Jesus* film, and gospel radio broadcasts are all available in the Shan language.

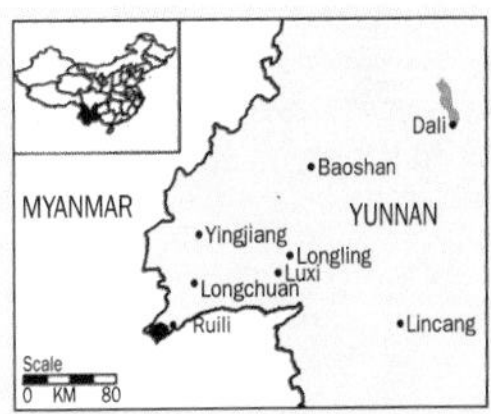

Population in China:
400 (1990)
500 (2000)
640 (2010)
Location: Yunnan
Religion: Buddhism
Christians: None Known

Overview of the Shan

Countries: Myanmar, Thailand, China, USA

Pronunciation: "Shahn"

Other Names: Sha, Tai Yay, Tai Shan, Great Thai

Population Source: 400 (1990 AMO); Out of a total Dai population of 1,025,128 (1990 census); 2,920,000 in Myanmar (1993 P. Johnstone); 56,000 in Thailand (1993 P. Johnstone); Also in USA

Location: *SW Yunnan:* One village in Dehong Prefecture

Status: Officially included under Dai

Language: Daic, Tai, Southwestern Tai, East Central, Northwest

Dialects: 0

Religion: Theravada Buddhism, Animism

Christians: None known

Scripture: Bible 1892; New Testament 1882; Portions 1871

***Jesus* film:** Available

Gospel Recordings: Shan #00083

Christian Broadcasting: Available (FEBC)

ROPAL code: SJN00

Status of Evangelization

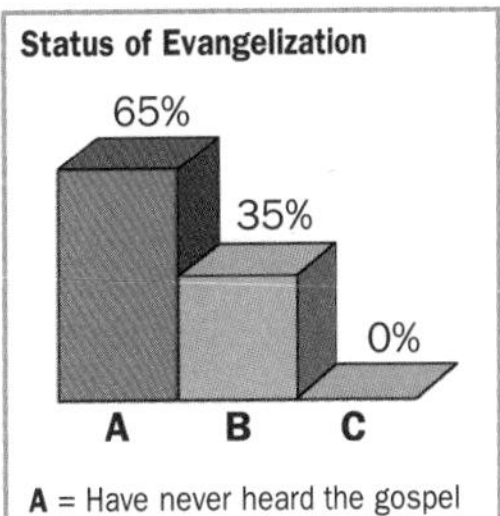

A = Have never heard the gospel
B = Were evangelized but did not become Christians
C = Are adherents to any form of Christianity

She 舍

Population in China:
630,378 (1990)
813,200 (2000)
1,049,000 (2010)
Location: Fujian, Guangdong, Zhejiang, Jiangxi, Anhui
Religion: Daoism
Christians: 1,000

Overview of the She

Countries: China

Pronunciation: "Sher"

Other Names:
Shanha, Huo Nte, Ho Nte

Population Source:
630,378 (1990 census);
368,832 (1982 census);
234,167 (1964 census)

Location: *Fujian* (461,000): Fu'an (58,002), Xiapu (37,892), Shanghang (30,699), Fuding (28,170), Ningdeshi (19,609), Zhangpu (18,690), and many other counties; *Guangdong*; *Zhejiang*; *Jiangxi*; and *Anhui*

Status:
An official minority of China

Language: Hmong-Mien, Ho Nte

Literacy: 51%

Dialects (2): Luofu, Lianhua

Religion: Daoism, Ancestor Worship, Shamanism, Animism, Christianity

Christians: 1,000

Scripture: None

***Jesus* film:** None

Gospel Recordings: None

Christian Broadcasting: None

ROPAL code: SHX00

Status of Evangelization

61%
38%
1%
A B C

A = Have never heard the gospel
B = Were evangelized but did not become Christians
C = Are adherents to any form of Christianity

Location: The 1990 China census listed 630,378 members of the She nationality. The majority (461,000) live in the mountainous areas of Fujian Province. She communities are located throughout more than 120 counties and townships in eastern China, including Guangdong and Zhejiang provinces, while "a few tiny communities" are also found in Jiangxi and Anhui provinces.[1]

Midge Conner

Identity: The She are one of the 55 official minorities of China. The vast majority of She have been assimilated to the Han Chinese or Hakka culture and language.

Language: Less than 1,000 She are still able to speak their language, primarily those living in Buluo, Zengcheng, Huidong, and Haifeng counties in Guangdong Province. The rest mostly speak Hakka as their first language.[2] The She are reported in some sources to speak two distinct languages,[3] which have between six and eight tones. She is described as an intermediary language between Miao and Yao.[4] In addition to Hakka, many She speak Cantonese, Min, or Mandarin Chinese, depending on the locality.

History: The She were known as the *Hsia-min* in historical records. The linguistic affiliation of the She suggests they were once part of the ancient Yue race, from which today's Yao and Miao peoples are also descended. Much of the She's past has been one of harassment and struggle against the exploitation of greedy Chinese landlords. The She have been pushed from the fertile land into the mountains.

Customs: Music is important to the She: "They sing in the fields, as well as on special festival occasions."[5] When a guest comes to their village they are asked to sing songs. Most She spend their days tending to rice fields on their hilly land which also yields cotton, tea, and grain. When visiting a She home, visitors must place their umbrella outside the door: placing the umbrella inside is a way of announcing a death.

Religion: The main religious adherence among the She is Daoism, mixed with ancestor worship. The She share the Yao belief in Pan Hu, the dog-king they believe was the forefather of their race. She folk songs, handed down orally from one generation to another, tell of the life of Pan Hu, who had a dragon's head, a dog's body, and was seven meters (22 ft.) in length.[6] The She formerly worshiped the totem of this legendary animal and held a large festival in its honor every three years. Today every She clan has a scepter on which is sculpted a dragon's head — a symbol of their former worship of the totem.

Christianity: Although Roman Catholic missionaries were active among the She in the late 1800s, one recent report indicates little or no fruit of their labor remains.[7] Although there are scattered Christian communities among the Chinese who live near them, the gospel has never taken root among the She. They are an unreached people group, living their lives with little knowledge of the claims of God or his offer of salvation through Christ's sacrifice. Most She could be effectively evangelized through the medium of the Hakka language.

Shenzhou 神州人

Population in China:
4,000 (1999)
4,050 (2000)
4,570 (2010)
Location: Guizhou
Religion: Ancestor Worship
Christians: None Known

Overview of the Shenzhou

Countries: China

Pronunciation: "Shen-joe"

Other Names: Shenzhouren

Population Source:
4,000 (1999 AMO);
Out of a total Han population of 1,042,482,187 (1990 census)

Location: *W Guizhou*

Status: Officially included under Han Chinese since 1985; Previously included in a list of *Undetermined Minorities*

Language:
Chinese, Guizhou dialect

Dialects: 0

Religion: Ancestor Worship, Animism, Daoism, No Religion

Christians: None known

Scripture: None

***Jesus* film:** None

Gospel Recordings: None

Christian Broadcasting: None

ROPAL code: None

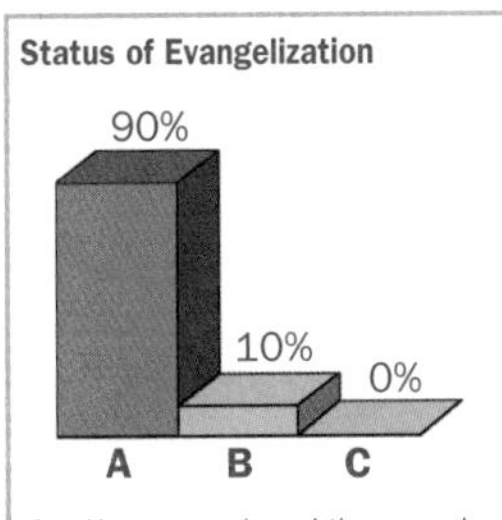

Location: With an estimated population of more than 4,000 people, the little-known Shenzhou people group inhabit areas of western Guizhou Province in southern China.[1] The precise location of the Shenzhou is uncertain, but it is likely that they live in Anshun Prefecture.

Identity: The Shenzhou, who are also known in China as the *Shenzhouren*, are one of several groups in Guizhou Province who possess a Chinese ancestry. Due to living alongside minority peoples (such as the Miao, Yi, and Bouyei) for many centuries they have lost their original ethnicity and now see themselves as a minority group. Other groups in Guizhou who fit this description are the Chuanlan, Chuanqing, Liujia, and Nanjingren. In the 1982 census the Shenzhou were not granted status as a nationality but were instead included in a list of *Undetermined Minorities*. In 1985, when researchers proved the Shenzhou were historically Han people, they were placed under the Han Chinese nationality.[2] This was not accepted by the Shenzhou who insist that they are a minority group. Although the Shenzhou do speak Chinese, the fact that they view themselves so differently from other Chinese justifies their inclusion as a separate ethnocultural group.

Language: The Shenzhou speak *Guizhouhua* (Guizhou Speech) which is a variety of Mandarin Chinese. Most Shenzhou can also read and write Chinese. The language of the Shenzhou also contains some loanwords from neighboring minority languages.

History: The ancestors of the Shenzhou were Chinese soldiers sent to Guizhou Province to quell uprisings by the Yi and Miao more than 800 years ago. After the fighting subsided, many soldiers stayed behind in Guizhou, took wives from among the local minorities — there were no other Han Chinese to speak of in the province at that time — and settled down. After generations passed, a new mixed people group evolved with aspects of minority culture and dress yet who still retained their Chinese language.

Customs: The overwhelming trend in China today is for the Han Chinese to assimilate non-Han minorities, which causes them to lose their identity. Therefore, it is ironic that there are pockets of people who fiercely insist on being called minority people even though the government has classified them as Han. The Shenzhou practise many customs, ceremonies, and festivals borrowed from minorities.

Religion: Although the Shenzhou do not think of themselves as religious people, ancestor worship still has a firm hold on the lives of most Shenzhou, especially the elderly. Some spirit worship, such as worship of the spirit of the house and village, are also practiced.

Christianity: Because their exact location has yet to be ascertained, nothing is known about the status of Christianity among the Shenzhou people. If they happen to live near some of the Miao communities in Anshun Prefecture, then there is a good chance that some of the Shenzhou have been exposed to the gospel; otherwise, most areas of southern Guizhou are unreached and unevangelized.

Paul Hattaway

Sherpa 西而巴

Location: The Sherpa, despite being a relatively small group, are one of the most well-known peoples of Asia. Approximately 50,000 Sherpa live on both sides of the Himalayan Range. In Tibet, the exact Sherpa population is uncertain. Various publications have listed "a mere 400 in China's territory,"[1] "800 speakers in China,"[2] and "no more than 1,000."[3] The Sherpa in Tibet inhabit parts of Dinggye, Tingri, and Zhangmu counties. Tingri County is directly on the road from Katmandu to Lhasa, a route frequented by many tour groups during the summer months.

Identity: The Sherpa in Tibet have been officially included as part of the Tibetan nationality. The Chinese are conducting an investigation to see if they should be classified as a distinct group. The name *Sherpa* means "eastern people." "They are distinguishable from Tibetans in part because their faces are smaller and they wear a colorful apron on their backside rather than the front."[4]

Language: Because the Sherpa language is related to Tibetan, most can communicate in a simple form of Tibetan.[5] Few of the 20,000 Sherpa in the Darjeeling area of India are still able to speak the Sherpa language.[6]

History: It is believed that all Sherpa once lived in Tibet before their descendants migrated west in the fifteenth century. "At that time, a Mongol King attempted to force them to convert to his sect of Buddhism. The people fled to the Khumbu region."[7] A Chinese account states, "They believe themselves to be descendants of Tibetans from the Kangba region in Sichuan Province. Many, many years ago, their ancestors, returning from a pilgrimage to Buddhist temples in India and Nepal, settled down here."[8]

Paul Hattaway

Customs: To many, the name Sherpa is irretrievably linked to the mystique of Mount Everest, the highest mountain on earth. The first men to climb Mount Everest were New Zealander Sir Edmund Hillary and Sherpa Tenzing Norgay. Numerous Sherpa guides have since led foreign climbing teams up the world's highest peak. The Sherpa charge around US$2,000 per expedition, making them one of the wealthiest groups in Nepal.[9] The Sherpa in China cremate their dead, as opposed to the Tibetans who practice wind burial. The *Gyawa* Festival takes place 49 days after the death of a loved one. The Sherpa eat as much food as they can during the festival, believing the food will nourish the loved one who has died.

Religion: The Sherpa are Tibetan Buddhists, although "with far less piety than the Tibetans. To have... a Buddhist statue and to recite or chant scriptures is all they do by way of religious practice."[10]

Christianity: In 1985 a Sherpa boy in Nepal had a vision where he was visited by Jesus. The boy's conversion was followed by the gradual conversion of his extended family and several families in his village. The boy later went to Bible school and returned to pastor the local church in his village.[11] There are reported to be a few dozen Christian Sherpas around the Mt. Everest region in Nepal.[12] Despite this wonderful breakthrough, there are no known Sherpa Christians in China. They are politically and geographically isolated from contact with their counterparts in Nepal.[13]

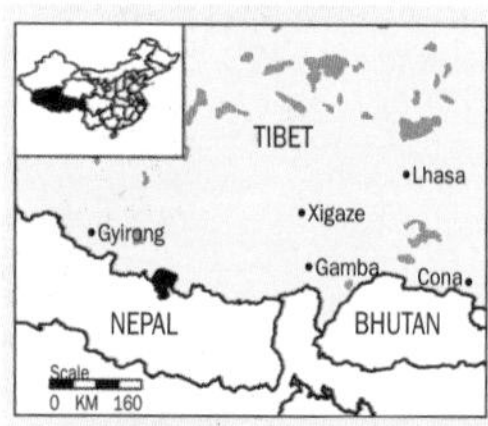

Population in China:
800 (1994)
910 (2000)
1,120 (2010)
Location: Tibet
Religion: Tibetan Buddhism
Christians: None Known

Overview of the Sherpa

Countries: Nepal, India, China

Pronunciation: "Sher-pah"

Other Names: Sharpa, Sharpa Bhotia, Xiaerba, Xiarba, Serwa

Population Source: 800 (1996 B. Grimes – 1994 figure); Out of a total Tibetan population of 4,593,330 (1990 census); 29,000 in Nepal (1993 P. Johnstone); 21,000 in India (1995)

Location: *S Tibet:* Dinggye, Tingri, and Zhangmu counties in Xigaze Prefecture

Status: Officially included under Tibetan

Language: Sino-Tibetan, Tibeto-Burman, Bodic, Bodish, Tibetan, Southern Tibetan

Dialects: 0

Religion: Tibetan Buddhism, Shamanism

Christians: None known

Scripture: Portions 1977; Work in progress

***Jesus* film:** None

Gospel Recordings: Twerpa #04242 Sherpa: Solukhumbu #00673 Sherpa Helumbu #02708

Christian Broadcasting: None

ROPAL code: SCR00

Status of Evangelization

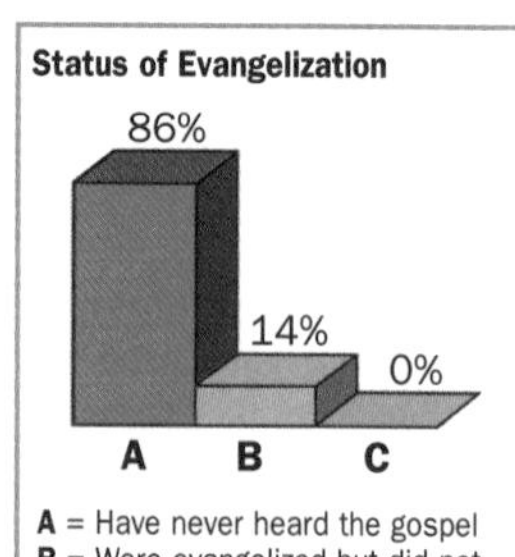

A = Have never heard the gospel
B = Were evangelized but did not become Christians
C = Are adherents to any form of Christianity

Shixing 是兴

Population in China:
2,000 (1983)
2,780 (2000)
3,430 (2010)
Location: Sichuan
Religion: Tibetan Buddhism
Christians: None Known

Overview of the Shixing

Countries: China

Pronunciation: "Sher-Shing"

Other Names: Shihing, Shuhin, Xumi

Population Source: 2,000 (1983 Sun Hongkai); Out of a total Tibetan population of 4,593,330 (1990 census)

Location: *SW Sichuan:* Muli County in the Liangshan Yi Prefecture

Status: Officially included under Tibetan

Language: Sino-Tibetan, Tibeto-Burman, Qiangic, Shixing

Dialects: 0

Religion: Tibetan Buddhism

Christians: None known

Scripture: None

***Jesus* film:** None

Gospel Recordings: None

Christian Broadcasting: None

ROPAL code: SXG00

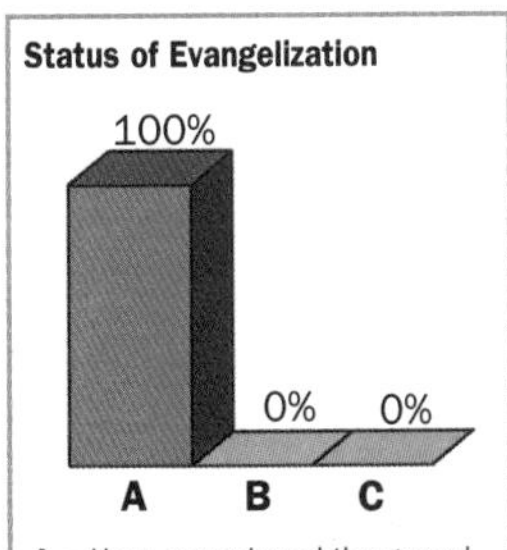

Paul Hattaway

Location: A 1983 report listed 2,000 speakers of the Shixing language "living along the fast-flowing Shuilo River and its downstream tributary, the Chongtian River,"[1] in the First District of Muli County in southern Sichuan Province. Mountain trails leading to the Shixing villages rise to an altitude of 4,680 meters (15,000 ft.). One visitor to the Shixing described the remarkable variation in terrain: "We found the stifling heat in the gorges of the Shou Chu next to unbearable, especially as we passed from cool forest regions to a temperature of over 100° Fahrenheit within a couple of hours."[2] The region is a botanist's paradise. "We found wild flowers, anemones, blue poppies, and many primroses of all colors, forming a veritable carpet of exquisite designs."[3]

Identity: The Shixing are one of many small groups in southern and central Sichuan who have been officially counted as part of the Tibetan nationality. The name *Shixing* means "iron people." The Chrame call their Shixing neighbors *Xumi.*

Language: Recently the Shixing language has been found to belong to the Qiangic linguistic branch, "hitherto virtually unknown to Western scholars.... Extensive lexical and grammatical material has been collected on the Shixing."[4] When explorer Joseph Rock visited the Shixing in 1930, he remarked that their language "seems to be a mixture of Nashi [Naxi], Tibetan and Hsifan [Chrame]; yet it is not understood by any of the three."[5]

History: The area inhabited by the Shixing has a long and rich history. Their villages are "guarded by watchtowers erected by powerful Naxi kings several hundred years ago."[6] The Naxi's interest in the region may have been due to the abundance of gold once found in the Shou Chu River. The river was extensively mined by the great Naxi king, Mutien Wang.[7]

Customs: The Shixing live isolated lives farming rice and maize on thin strips of land leading down to the river. The Shixing villages are "peculiar conglomerations of huts built one against the other, with flat roofs, permitting one to step from house to house over the entire village."[8]

Religion: All Shixing are Tibetan Buddhists; they were converted centuries ago. Outside many of their homes one will find *mani* piles (pyramids of white stones) which are engraved with the sacred Tibetan prayer, *Om mani padme hum* — "Hail the Jewel of the Lotus." In the past the Shixing lived under the rule of the Chrame king in Muli, along with his powerful religious rulers.

Christianity: The Muli region in southwest Sichuan Province is one of the most gospel-neglected places on earth. No missionaries are known to have worked there in the past. There has never been a known believer or Christian fellowship among the Shixing people. The nearest believers to the Shixing are the Lisu in northwest Yunnan, but they are still a considerable distance away over some of the most remote terrain in the world.

Shui 水

Paul Hattaway

Location: Approximately 430,000 members of the Shui minority live in southern Guizhou Province, primarily in Duyun, Sandu, and Libo counties. In addition, small numbers of Shui are located in northern Guangxi.[1] The descendants of eight Shui families who migrated out of China about 50 years ago live in northern Vietnam.

Identity: The Shui are one of China's 55 official minorities. Their name, which means "water" in Chinese, reflects their history. They were originally part of the Luo-yue tribe who lived along China's southeastern coast. Centuries later they were forced to migrate inland to their present mountainous location. Today the Shui still have more than ten different words for "fish."

Language: Shui is a member of the Daic (Tai) linguistic family. The Shui language of Yunnan and the Shui of Sandu in Guizhou are mutually unintelligible. There is a simple script in use among the Shui, but it is only known by village leaders and is not used by the common people. "The Shui have a system of symbols that is used for divination and geomancy. It is far too simple to have much of a linguistic function and seems to be little more than a set of magic symbols. A few of the 150 or so graphs are real drawings (such as a bird or a fish).... Most of the rest are borrowings from Chinese and are often written upside down or backwards, apparently to give the symbol more magical power."[2]

History: The Shui are proud of their history, which dates back as far as 200 BC in Chinese records. The Shui have traditionally enjoyed good relationships with the Chinese. A Shui man, Teng Enming, was a founding member of the Chinese Communist Party.

Customs: Shui women wear a white headdress for three years after the death of a relative. After the three-year period they can wear black again. Most Shui village leaders are able to read the 500 to 600-year-old ancient Shui script. The book contains a Shui code of ethics and behavior. Some leaders are teaching the script to young Shui boys. The Shui live in villages that are arranged according to family clans.

Religion: All Shui worship their ancestors. This is considered their main religion. It keeps them in bondage to the past and prevents them from receiving Christ, because to do so would be considered an insult to their ancestors.

Christianity: Several French Catholic missionaries first went to the Shui in 1884. By the early 1900s some 30 Catholic churches and 5,000 Shui Christians existed. However, all the believers were put to death or fell away during the anti-Christian movement of 1906. In recent years, missionaries have traveled to the villages that formerly contained Catholic churches and have not found a trace of Christianity remaining — neither old buildings nor any knowledge of the gospel among the people. Today there are reported to be only "a small number of Christians"[3] among the Shui. Another source adds, "a handful of Catholic believers remain."[4] A breakthrough came in late 1997 and 1998 when approximately 100 Shui people came to Christ and were being discipled by Chinese believers.[5]

Population in China:
341,600 (1990)
430,000 (2000)
541,400 (2010)
Location: Guizhou, Guangxi
Religion: Ancestor Worship
Christians: 200

Overview of the Shui

Countries: China, Vietnam
Pronunciation: "Shway"
Other Names: Sui, Ai Sui, Sui Li, Suipo, Shuijia, Suijia
Population Source:
345,993 (1990 census);[6]
286,487 (1982 census);
156,099 (1964 census);
133,566 (1953 census);
55 speakers of Shui live in Vietnam (1978).
Location: *S Guizhou:* Sandu, Duyun, Rongjiang, Duyun City, Dushan, Danzhai, and Libo counties;
N Guangxi: Nandan, Yishan, and Rongshui counties
Status:
An official minority of China
Language: Daic, Kam-Sui
Literacy: 37%
Dialects (3):
Sandong, Yang'an, Pandong
Religion: Ancestor Worship, Animism, Daoism, No Religion, Christianity
Christians: 200
Scripture: None
***Jesus* film:** None
Gospel Recordings: Shui #04855
Christian Broadcasting: None
ROPAL code: SWI00

Status of Evangelization

89%
10%
1%
A B C

A = Have never heard the gospel
B = Were evangelized but did not become Christians
C = Are adherents to any form of Christianity

Shui, Yunnan 水(云南)

Location: The 1990 national census listed a total of 7,314 Shui people living in Yunnan Province.[1] More than 6,800 live in the Huangnihe District of Fuyuan County, while 490 inhabit the Dahe and Long'an districts of Yiliang County.

Identity: The Yunnan Shui have been officially included as part of the Shui nationality — which numbered approximately 350,000 people in the 1990 census — by the Chinese authorities. However, Chinese linguists Wei Ch'ing-wen and Li Fang-Gui both state that the Shui in Yunnan speak a language mutually unintelligible with the Shui in Guizhou Province.[2] For this reason the Yunnan Shui are profiled separately and are considered a "mission-significant" people group. It is possible that this group has not always identified themselves as *Shui*. The government has included several small language groups who are more closely related to the Shui, such as the Mo and Rao, in the official Bouyei nationality in Guizhou. The government's classifications are often based on cultural similarities and not on any proven historical, linguistic, or ethnic kinship.

Language: The Shui in Yunnan speak a language from the Kam-Sui (Dong-Shui) branch of the Daic linguistic family. Most Yunnan Shui are adequately bilingual in Chinese. The Shui in Yunnan do not use the rudimentary Shui script known to many Shui village leaders in Guizhou. The Yunnan Shui pass down stories and fables which "praise the diligence, bravery, wisdom and love of the Shui ethnic group and satirize the stupidity of the feudal rulers."[3]

History: The Shui in Yunnan are a diaspora group who migrated to their present location at least 250 years ago. Today they live several hundred kilometers (200–250 mi.) west of the main body of Shui in central Guizhou. During their lengthy separation the Yunnan Shui have developed their own customs.

Paul Hattaway

Customs: The Yunnan Shui have a festive dance called the Copper Drum Dance, which is greatly enjoyed by all. It is performed during special occasions such as the Duan Festival, celebrated each September after the harvest has been gathered. Traditional musical instruments include gongs, lusheng, huqin, and suona horns.

Religion: Most Shui in Yunnan are animists. Ancestor worship does not appear to take such a prominent place among the Yunnan Shui as it does among the Guizhou Shui.

Christianity: The Shui in Yunnan are an unreached people group without a single known Christian among them. Few have ever been exposed to the gospel message since they live in one of the most spiritually neglected areas of Yunnan Province. Because they speak their own language, the Yunnan Shui will not be able to understand the Shui gospel recordings or *Jesus* film presently being considered for translation. The Chinese language may be the best medium for evangelizing the Yunnan Shui. Most now read and write Chinese, and all but the elderly can speak the Southwestern dialect of Mandarin.

Population in China:
7,314 (1990)
9,200 (2000)
11,550 (2010)
Location: Yunnan
Religion: Animism
Christians: None Known

Overview of the Yunnan Shui

Countries: China

Pronunciation: "Yoo-nahn-Shway"

Other Names:

Population Source:
7,314 (1990 census);
Out of a total Shui population of 345,993 (1990 census)

Location: *E Yunnan:* Huangnihe District of Fuyuan County (6,824), and the Dahe and Long'an districts of Yiliang County (490)

Status:
Officially included under Shui

Language: Daic, Kam-Sui

Dialects: 0

Religion: Animism, Polytheism, Ancestor Worship

Christians: None known

Scripture: None

***Jesus* film:** None

Gospel Recordings: None

Christian Broadcasting: None

ROPAL code: None

Status of Evangelization

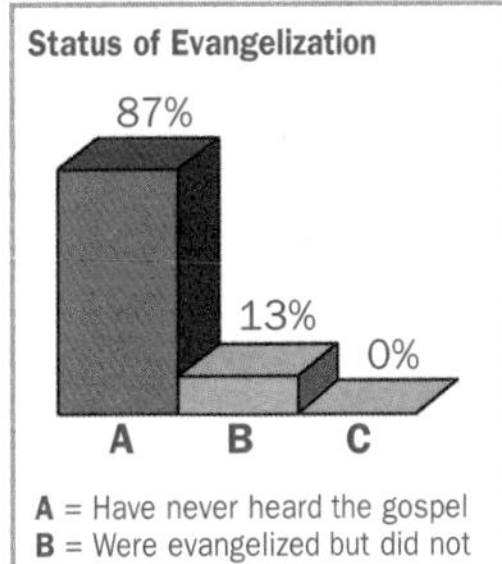

A = Have never heard the gospel
B = Were evangelized but did not become Christians
C = Are adherents to any form of Christianity

Sogwo Arig 阿日刊

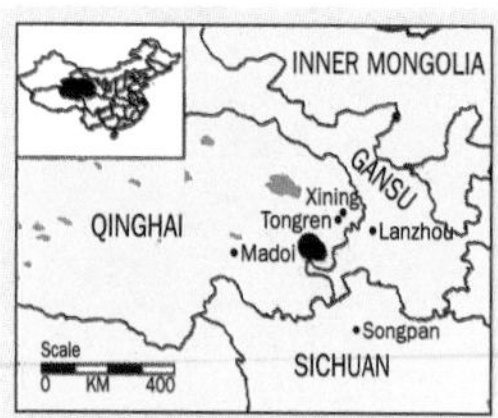

Population in China:
35,000 (1998)
37,000 (2000)
47,700 (2010)
Location: Qinghai
Religion: Tibetan Buddhism
Christians: None Known

Overview of the Sogwo Arig

Countries: China

Pronunciation: "Sog-wo-Ah-rig"

Other Names: Sogwo Arik, Arig Tibetan, Alike, A-li-k'oa, Tatze

Population Source: 35,000 (1998 AMO); Out of a total Mongol population of 4,806,849 (1990 census)

Location: *SE Qinghai:* Tongde and He'nan counties in Hainan Prefecture

Status: Officially included under Mongolian

Language: Sino-Tibetan, Tibeto-Burman, Bodic, Bodish, Tibetan, Northern Tibetan

Dialects: 0

Religion: Tibetan Buddhism, Shamanism, Bon

Christians: None known

Scripture: None

***Jesus* film:** None

Gospel Recordings: None

Christian Broadcasting: None

ROPAL code: None

Status of Evangelization

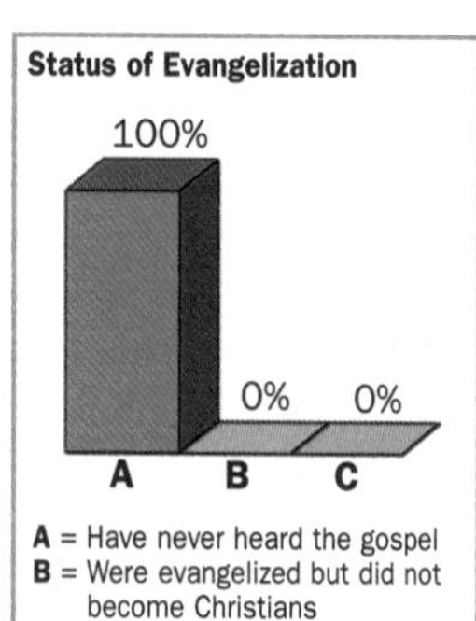

A = Have never heard the gospel
B = Were evangelized but did not become Christians
C = Are adherents to any form of Christianity

Location: Approximately 37,000 members of the Sogwo Arig tribe live in Tsanggar Gonpa, a district within Tongde County in the Hainan Golog Prefecture; and in parts of neighboring He'nan County.[1] Tongde lies to the east of the Yellow River in Qinghai Province. The Qinghai Plateau — at a minimum elevation of 3,500 meters (11,500 ft.) above sea level — is snowbound nine months of the year, and turns into a muddy bog the other three months. The area is home to the *Darakar Tredzong* (White Monkey Fortress), considered one of the three most sacred sites in all of the Amdo Tibetan areas.

Identity: The Sogwo Arig are a Mongolian tribe living in the midst of countless small Tibetan clans in one of the most remote locations in the world. Over the course of many centuries, the Sogwo Arig language and culture have gradually assimilated to the Tibetan. Still today, however, Tibetans in the area know the Sogwo Arig are of Mongol ancestry and view them as a separate people.[2]

Language: The Sogwo Arig language has become practically extinct during the course of the twentieth century. Today the Sogwo Arig speak the Amdo Hbrogpa Tibetan language, but they still retain various words in their vocabulary that show their Mongolian ancestry.

History: The Sogwo Arig claim to have been the Mongol rulers of Hunan Province. This fact was discovered by a surprised French explorer in 1906, when the Sogwo Arig prince signed a letter with the title of "King of Hunan." Vicomte d'Ollone explains, "When the Mongols were expelled from China, the dynasty of the kings of Ho-Nan [Hunan] — kings without a kingdom — retired to their steppes; and when in their turn the Manchus seized the empire [1644] they utilized the Mongols for the purpose of holding the Tibetans in check, for which reason a horde was sent to establish itself in this region."[3] The Sogwo Arig continued to have a succession of kings until the 1950s, when the Communist authorities stripped the Sogwo Arig royal family of its authority, at least as far as appearances are concerned.

Customs: Today one of the few remaining Sogwo Arig cultural features is their Mongolian style of *yurt.* Sogwo Arig men will not leave their homes without being armed with their rifle. When they go on hunting expeditions, they take wooden tripods for resting their weapons on when firing.

Religion: All Sogwo Arig are followers of either Tibetan Buddhism or Bon. They worship at crude sacrificial altars, constructed of yak dung piled about three feet high, upon which they regularly offer animal sacrifices to various gods and demons.

Christianity: Hidden away in communities virtually inaccessible to the outside world, the Sogwo Arig are untouched by Christianity. Intrepid evangelists will need to overcome severe weather, rugged terrain, linguistic and cultural barriers, and fierce packs of dogs which the Sogwo Arig have trained to attack strangers.

Paul Hattaway

Suan 蒜

Jamin Pelkey

Location: According to researcher Jamin Pelkey, 250 people belonging to the Suan ethnic group live in the Wumulong District and/or in the Mengban District of Yongde County. Yongde is situated within the Lincang Prefecture in western Yunnan Province.[1]

Identity: The Suan have been mentioned in a few local Chinese publications. Outside of their immediate area, however, the Suan are completely unknown. The government has officially counted them as part of the Yi nationality. The Suan are usually mentioned along with the Pengzi, who reportedly live in the same area and have the same population as the Suan, yet appear to be two different ethnic groups.

Language: Chinese sources state that all Yi languages in Yongde County are part of the Western Yi group, but no specific research has been conducted into Suan to see how vigorous its use is or to determine its relationship to other Yi varieties.

History: Nothing is known about the history of the Suan — where they originated or how they came to evolve into a distinct ethnic group.

Customs: Today, most Suan customs have been swallowed up by the pervasive Han culture. In the past, however, the Suan had a proud culture. They shared many of the traits that other Yi groups possess, including funeral rites. Visiting one Yi group in the early 1900s, famous missionary Samuel Pollard wrote, "The custom is that at death an imposing ceremony is held in the home. Then the tablets of wood are placed in the bags or baskets and left there for three years. In this time the ancestors are supposedly being worshipped in the home. After that time, a goat is killed in sacrifice, the tablets are escorted out. A short log is selected, split in two, the interior scooped out, and the ancestral baskets with tablets placed inside and the halves roped together again. The bound log is left on a hillside or cliff.... The old and new spirits are thought to reside in this trough of wood."[2]

Religion: When the three-year period after the death of a person has expired, the Suan believe bad people will go to hell to be tormented by demons. "The [Devil] has under his orders evil spirits who play all sorts of objectionable tricks; the most notable are those that cause illness in men and animals. The [Suan] therefore use no remedies; the *pimo* [shaman], by various procedures, consults destiny, discovers what evil spirit is incarnated, and chases it out of the body of the sufferer by ritual formula, accompanied by the sacrifice of an animal."[3]

Christianity: Groups that are small in size tend to be lost in the thicket of human souls in China. Although the Suan are a small, precious ethnic group, they have never appeared on any mission list of peoples in China and have never been targeted for church planting. They are an unreached and unevangelized people. Perhaps the best chance for them to hear the gospel has been through Chinese-language gospel radio broadcasts. There are few Christians in Yongde County who could potentially reach out to them. Until someone does, the Suan will remain untold.

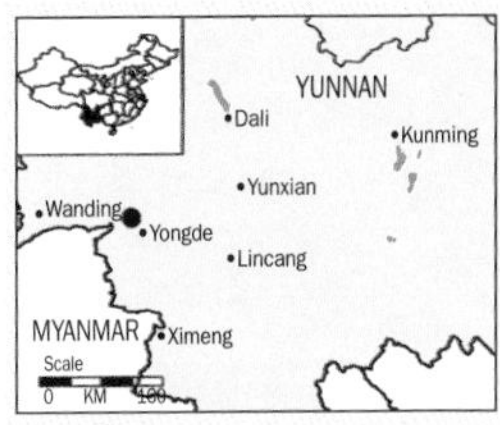

Population in China:
250 (1999)
255 (2000)
320 (2010)
Location: Yunnan
Religion: Ancestor Worship
Christians: None Known

Overview of the Suan

Countries: China

Pronunciation: "Soo-ahn"

Other Names:

Population Source: 250 (1999 J. Pelkey); Out of a total Yi population of 6,572,173 (1990 census)

Location: *W Yunnan:* Wumulong and/or Mengban districts of Yongde County in Lincang Prefecture

Status: Officially included under Yi

Language: Sino-Tibetan, Tibeto-Burman, Burmese-Lolo, Lolo, Northern Lolo, Yi, Western Yi

Dialects: 0

Religion: Ancestor Worship, Animism, Shamanism

Christians: None known

Scripture: None

***Jesus* film:** None

Gospel Recordings: None

Christian Broadcasting: None

ROPAL code: None

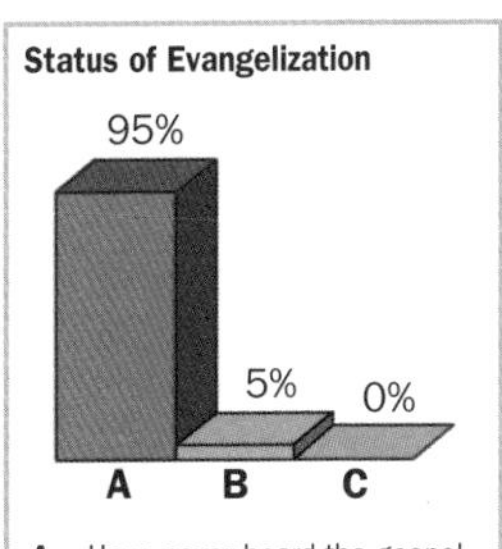

A = Have never heard the gospel
B = Were evangelized but did not become Christians
C = Are adherents to any form of Christianity

Subei 苏北

November 2

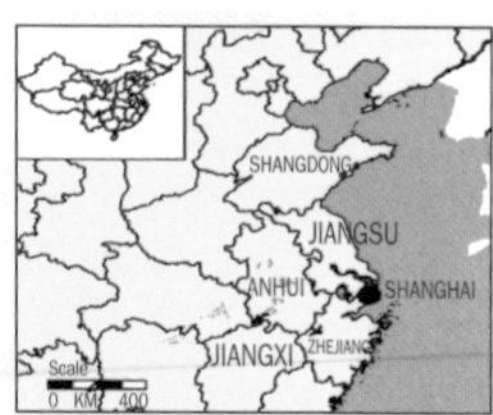

Population in China:
1,500,000 (1949)
2,494,500 (2000)
2,818,800 (2010)
Location: Shanghai
Religion: No Religion
Christians: 40,000

Overview of the Subei

Countries: China

Pronunciation: "Soo-bay"

Other Names: Jiangbei

Population Source: 1,500,000 (1949 Xie Junmei); Out of a total Han population of 1,042,482,187 (1990 census)

Location: *Shanghai Municipality*

Status: Officially included under Han Chinese

Language: Chinese, Mandarin

Dialects: 0

Religion: No Religion, Ancestor Worship, Christianity

Christians: 40,000

Scripture: Chinese Bible

***Jesus* film:** Available (Mandarin)

Gospel Recordings: Mandarin #00037

Christian Broadcasting: Available (FEBC, TWR)

ROPAL code: None

Status of Evangelization

A	B	C
65%	33%	2%

A = Have never heard the gospel
B = Were evangelized but did not become Christians
C = Are adherents to any form of Christianity

Location: The present population of the Subei people in Shanghai is almost impossible to measure, as the Chinese authorities do not count them as a separate people. The most recent population for the Subei was by Chinese scholar Xie Junmei who estimated 1,500,000 — or about one-fifth of Shanghai's population in 1949 — were Subei people.[1] They were originally located in the central areas of the city, but were pushed out by the Wu-speaking Chinese during the Qing Dynasty (1644–1911).

Paul Hattaway

Identity: Although they are part of the Han Chinese nationality, the Subei — who are also called *Jiangbei* — have a distinct identity. The Subei are immigrants who came from northern (*bei*) Jiangsu (*su*). The Subei "are socially looked down upon and economically and educationally disadvantaged.... The term 'Subei swine' is an extreme insult in the Shanghai dialect. The government recognizes them as Han, but they claim separate ethnicity and exhibit group solidarity.... If you ask any one from Shanghai who they are, they'll probably know exactly who you're talking about and be willing to spread a whole lot of slander about how dirty and stupid these people are. The only reason they're dirty is because they're poor, and they're poor because they are uneducated and they are uneducated because they are discriminated against."[2] Zhou Enlai, the Communist leader, was a Subei from Huai'an County.

Language: The Subei speak a dialect of Mandarin from northern Jiangsu Province. Their different speech makes them stand out from other Shanghai residents.

History: Refugees from northern Jiangsu migrated into Shanghai in large numbers after floods in 1911 and 1921. The worst flood took place in 1931, resulting in 78,045 Subei people coming to Shanghai.[3] Their numbers continued to grow. In 1946, nearly 59,000 Subei natives registered with the Committee for the Salvation of Subei Refugees.[4]

Customs: To outsiders today, the Subei are largely indistinguishable from the other Chinese around them. Until recently Subei women wore "red and green silk clothes, embroidered shoes, pink or red stockings, and other brightly colored clothes."[5] Even today, Shanghai women shun red cloth and often say to women wearing red, "You Subei person — that's ugly!"[6] A 1986 study showed that 80% of Subei marry spouses of Subei origins.[7] The Subei have a reputation for working in Shanghai's lowest and filthiest jobs, such as bathhouse attendants, barbers, and pig farmers. A 1958 study found 77% of the pedi-cab drivers in Shanghai were Subei people.[8]

Religion: There are a few traces of Chinese traditional religious beliefs remaining among elderly Subei people, but most Subei under the age of 50 are atheists.

Christianity: There are a significant number of Subei Christians in Shanghai. This city, which was the traditional port of arrival for missionaries, has received more gospel witness than most other parts of China. In 1996 Shanghai's more than 14 million inhabitants included 127,000 Protestants[9] and 120,000 Catholics.[10] These 247,000 believers, however, amount to only 2% of Shanghai's population.

Suodi 所地

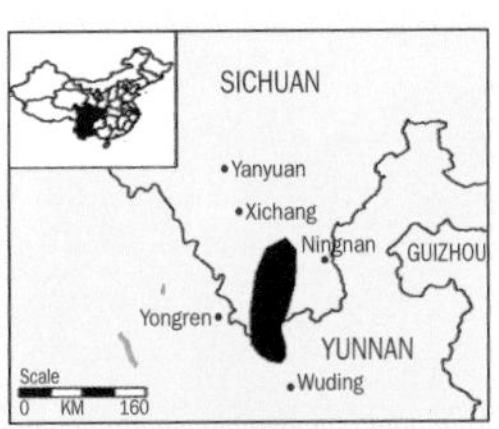

Population in China:
184,500 (1999)
189,200 (2000)
237,400 (2010)
Location: Sichuan, Yunnan
Religion: Polytheism
Christians: 200

Overview of the Suodi

Countries: China

Pronunciation: "Swohr-dee"

Other Names: Suod, So-ti, Huili Yi, Suodi Nosu, Nuosu, Black Yi

Population Source: 184,500 (1999 AMO); 170,000 in Sichuan (1998 J. Matisoff); 14,500 in Yunnan (1999 J. Pelkey); Out of a total Yi population of 6,572,173 (1990 census)

Location: *S Sichuan:* Huili, Dechang, Miyi, and Puge counties; *N Yunnan:* Yuanmou (6,000), Luquan (6,000), and Yongren (2,500) counties

Status: Officially included under Yi

Language: Sino-Tibetan, Tibeto-Burman, Burmic, Burmese-Lolo, Lolo, Northern Lolo, Yi, Northern Yi

Dialects: 0

Religion: Polytheism, Animism, Ancestor Worship, Christianity

Christians: 200

Scripture: None

***Jesus* film:** None

Gospel Recordings: None

Christian Broadcasting: None

ROPAL code: None

Status of Evangelization

	A	B	C
	93%	6%	1%

A = Have never heard the gospel
B = Were evangelized but did not become Christians
C = Are adherents to any form of Christianity

Location: Approximately 190,000 ethnic Suodi people live in the high mountains of southern China, including some 170,000 in Huili, Dechang, Miyi, and Puge counties of southern Sichuan Province,[1] and 14,500 in Yuanmou, Luquan, and Yongren counties of northern Yunnan Province.[2]

Identity: Few people have ever heard of the Suodi. Most publications have failed to distinguish the Suodi from the Nosu, who are the largest Yi group inhabiting the Daliangshan in southern Sichuan. Although the Suodi and Nosu languages are related, they are different enough that speakers have difficulty in communicating and often must revert to Chinese in order to be understood. Just as important, *Suodi* is the autonym of this group. They do not call themselves Nosu or Yi. The Suodi have been included under the official Yi nationality by the Chinese authorities.

Language: The Suodi language is part of the Northern Yi branch of Tibeto-Burman. The Nosu pictographic script is used in some Suodi villages. Prior to 1949 it was only used by shamans, so the script never gained widespread use among the common people.

History: For centuries the Suodi have been caught up in violence, slavery, and warfare with their Nosu neighbors and between respective clans of Suodi. As Chinese influence expanded into the Suodi area, frequent clashes between the Suodi and Chinese soldiers erupted. In 1911 the Suodi took several hundred people into slavery to avenge a surprise Chinese attack near Huili a few weeks earlier. "Jubilant in victory, the Chinese loaded four ponies with Lolo [Suodi] heads to bring them to Ningyuanfu. Since this load was too heavy, the Chinese cut off the ears and brought them into the city to be presented to their commander."[3]

Customs: The Suodi are engaged in a wide variety of occupations, including traders, farmers, and herders. In the past many Suodi were opium addicts — a vice that is slowly resurfacing among Suodi youth.

Religion: A complex form of polytheism is practiced by the Suodi. They worship a host of deities and spirits, hoping their devotion will prevent disaster coming upon their families and villages. They also believe in *Yasomu*, an all-powerful deity, and they keep ancestral tablets.

Christianity: Catholic missionaries first reached out to the Suodi in Huili in 1802. In 1809, "Monsieur Hamel sent Thomas Tsin into this area, and he founded five stations, baptized seventy-four adults, and registered the names of thirty-six catechumens."[4] American and Australian Baptist missionaries were also stationed at Huili before 1949. Little long-term work actually survived in the area. Numerous obstacles were placed before the missionaries by Chinese officials. "The desire of the missionaries was to plant a strong church among the savages in the mountains, but the opposition from both the [Suodi] and the Han Chinese was too great. They had to settle for spreading the faith among the Chinese."[5] Today there are no more than a few hundred Catholic believers among the Suodi. Most members of this group have yet to hear the gospel for the first time.

Target Ministries

Ta'er 塔尔

Location: Approximately 1,000 ethnic Ta'er people live in an unspecified location within Ninglang County in northern Yunnan Province.[1] Ninglang borders Sichuan Province and is home to several ethnic groups.

Identity: The Ta'er are one of the smallest and least-known branches of the official Yi nationality in China. Other small Yi groups in Ninglang County include the Tagu and Talu peoples. Although linguistically and culturally related, each of these three groups views itself as being distinct from the others.

Language: No specific research has been done on the Ta'er language, but Chinese linguists have designated Ninglang County as a "Northern Yi" area. The Yi group of languages is part of the Tibeto-Burman language family. Usually, when the Xiaoliangshan Nosu took slaves, they would forbid the slaves to speak their own language and would force them to speak the dialect of their captors. Because of this, many smaller groups have lost their original tongue.

History: In the past the Ta'er were oppressed by the Xiaoliangshan Nosu who number more than 130,000 just in Ninglang County alone. The Xiaoliangshan Nosu took the Ta'er as slaves and continually raided their villages. False charges were often laid against the Ta'er, such as a corpse being placed on their land and charges of murder being made. Full retribution would be demanded. As a result, the Ta'er are an impoverished people, with few possessions and a low self-esteem. Even though the slavery system was officially abolished by the Communist government in the late 1950s, the social stigma and class prejudice still exists today between the different Yi peoples.

Paul Hattaway

Customs: Because of their small numbers, the Ta'er have been forced to intermarry with the Han Chinese and other people groups in recent decades. Prior to liberation, the Xiaoliangshan Nosu were strictly forbidden to marry their slaves, under pain of death. Most Ta'er families are hardworking agriculturists. When a Ta'er girl becomes engaged to be married, she is allowed to "wander the hills" and sleep with her former boyfriends. After this time of immorality she is expected to settle down and be faithful to her husband.

Religion: The Ta'er believe that after death the soul of the deceased flies to heaven and becomes a star. The Ta'er have a centuries-old system of spirit worship which carefully appeases a host of vengeful demons. The Ta'er also worship their ancestors, especially those who have died within the past three generations.

Christianity: Although missionary work was conducted extensively among Yi groups in the Wuding and Luquan areas of northern Yunnan and in parts of central and northeast Yunnan, few or no foreign missionaries have ever worked in Ninglang County. As a result, the Ta'er have no knowledge of the gospel today, and no access to a Christian witness. The Ta'er do not easily understand gospel radio broadcasts in Chinese and have no Scriptures, gospel recordings or any other ministry tools available in their own language.

Population in China:
1,000 (1999)
1,025 (2000)
1,280 (2010)
Location: Yunnan
Religion: Polytheism
Christians: None Known

Overview of the Ta'er

Countries: China

Pronunciation: "Tah-ehr"

Other Names:

Population Source:
1,000 (1999 J. Pelkey);
Out of a total Yi population of 6,572,173 (1990 census)

Location:
N Yunnan: Ninglang County

Status:
Officially included under Yi

Language: Sino-Tibetan, Tibeto-Burman, Burmese-Lolo, Lolo, Northern Lolo, Yi, Northern Yi

Dialects: 0

Religion: Polytheism, Animism, Ancestor Worship

Christians: None known

Scripture: None

***Jesus* film:** None

Gospel Recordings: None

Christian Broadcasting: None

ROPAL code: None

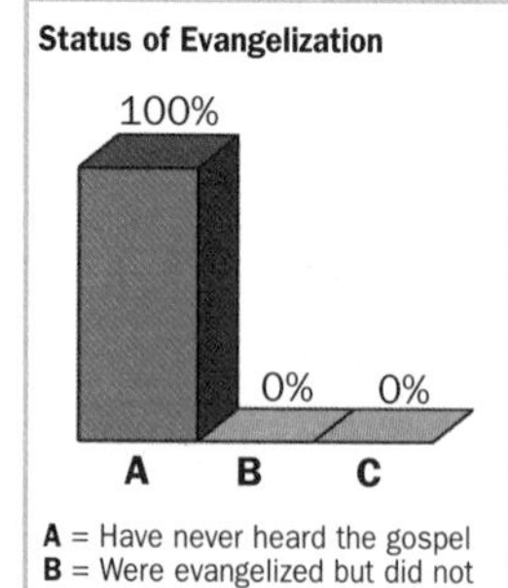

Tagu 塔谷

Population in China:
3,500 (1999)
3,590 (2000)
4,500 (2010)
Location: Yunnan
Religion: Polytheism
Christians: None Known

Overview of the Tagu

Countries: China

Pronunciation: "Tah-goo"

Other Names: Taguren, Tagupo

Population Source:
3,500 (1999 J. Pelkey);
Out of a total Yi population of 6,572,173 (1990 census)

Location: *N Yunnan:* Ninglang (2,000) and Yongsheng (1,500) counties

Status:
Officially included under Yi

Language: Sino-Tibetan, Tibeto-Burman, Burmese-Lolo, Lolo, Northern Lolo, Yi, Northern Yi

Dialects: 0

Religion: Polytheism, Animism, Ancestor Worship

Christians: None known

Scripture: None

***Jesus* film:** None

Gospel Recordings: None

Christian Broadcasting: None

ROPAL code: None

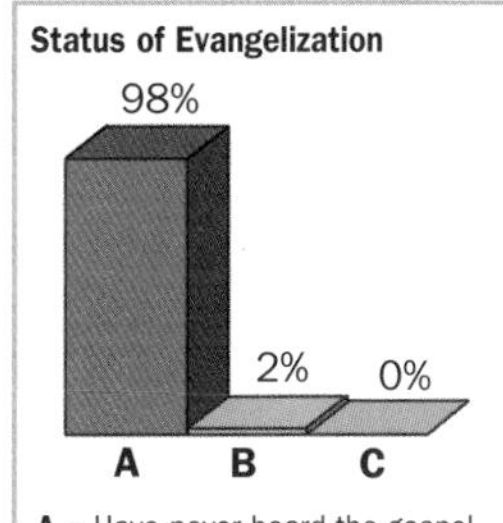

A = Have never heard the gospel
B = Were evangelized but did not become Christians
C = Are adherents to any form of Christianity

Target Ministries

Location: More than 3,500 people belong to the Tagu ethnic group in northern Yunnan Province of southern China. The Tagu mainly inhabit villages in the Dongshan and Gai communities of Dongshan District in Yongsheng County. The principal village of the Tagu is Taguping.[1] The Tagu are also known to live in Ninglang County, but their specific location is unknown.

Identity: The Tagu are part of the official Yi nationality in China, although they view themselves as distinct from all other ethnic groups. The Tagu are not the same as the Talu — a different Yi group also found in Yongsheng and Ninglang counties.

Language: Tagu has been classified as part of the Northern Yi branch of the Tibeto-Burman language family.

History: The Tagu may have been a tribe who came out of southern Sichuan Province centuries ago to escape the slave system practiced by the Nosu people there. After several generations, the ancestors of the Tagu forgot their origins and developed their own ethnicity, language, and culture.

Customs: When a missionary visited a Yi village in the early 1900s, he was given a never-to-be-forgotten meal: "As we sat on bear rugs on the ground a goat was brought in and presented to us, and there and then they set to slaughter and prepare it for the meal. This is considered very respectful to the guest and assures him that the meat is fresh and that the animal has been killed especially for his benefit. When the carcass was ready, the heart and liver were thrown into the ashes of the wood fire and after a few minutes they were taken out, placed on wooden plates and handed to the visitors. I ate mine with as much delight as I could.... Staying among these wild people convinces me that in their homes and among their own people they are worthy of our best efforts to evangelize among them. I found a warm welcome wherever I went and nowhere met with the ill-treatment predicted for me by the Chinese."[2]

Religion: One of the main deities feared by Yi people everywhere, including the Tagu, are the powerful Mountain gods they believe dwell inside the largest mountains in each area. Offerings and sacrifices are made to placate these demons. It is possible that the legends related to the power of the Mountain gods started as a result of volcanic activity long ago: this convinced the people a powerful being was responsible for displaying his wrath and venting his anger through the mountain. The Tagu also worship many local spirits, such as the spirit of the soil, the spirit of the rice harvest, and the spirit of the forest.

Christianity: Ninglang and Yongsheng, for all practical purposes, have only been connected to the rest of China for the last few decades. Before the 1950s there were few or no roads in the area and, therefore, they experienced little Chinese influence. For the same reason, no missionaries are known to have lived in the Ninglang or Yongsheng areas before 1949. Today there are no known believers or churches among the Tagu. They have little access to the gospel, and most Tagu have never yet met a Christian.

Tai Dam 黑傣

Nevin Bowman

Location: More than 34,000 Tai Dam live in Jinping County in southern China's Yunnan Province. The majority of Tai Dam are found in northern Vietnam where approximately half a million live around the city of Dien Bien Phu. They also extend into nearby areas of Laos and "to the south-west into central Thailand due to conquest and deportation by the (Bangkok) Thai in the early nineteenth century."[1] Most of the 50,000 Tai Dam now living in Laos fled there in the 1950s after the Communist terror in north Vietnam.[2] Refugee communities of Tai Dam are also located in such diverse places as Iowa, USA;[3] Sydney, Australia; and Paris, France.

Identity: The Tai Dam (Black Tai) are so named because of the predominant color of their traditional clothing, and also because they live along the banks of the Black River. In China, where they have been included in the official Dai nationality, the Tai Dam are also known as the *Jinping Tai* after the county they inhabit.

Language: The Tai Dam use an ancient Indic script, which seems to have been the forerunner of the current script used by the Thai people in Thailand. Tai Dam has some intelligibility with Tai Kao.[4]

History: The Tai Dam people are believed to have originated in southern China but gradually migrated into Southeast Asia due to oppression by the Chinese. The Tai Dam even had their own government in north Vietnam for a short time in the 1950s. The spread of smallpox, cholera, tuberculosis, and malaria was rampant among the Tai Dam in the past, decimating entire communities.

Customs: It is common for all the elders of a Tai Dam family to be equally responsible for raising children. Each village is under the control of a *Chao Muong*, or prince.[5]

Religion: The Tai Dam are one of the few members of the great Tai race never to have embraced Buddhism. They are animists. They believe that "non-human objects have spirits, and that people have multiple souls.... These spirits must be appeased so that they might avoid curses and receive blessings."[6] The Tai Dam in Vietnam believe in the *King of Heaven* who founded the city of Dien Bien Phu, formerly called "Heavenly City" by the Tai Dam. They believe there used to be a vine which reached from the earth to heaven. One mother was upset because her son kept climbing the vine to fellowship with God. She cut the vine and ever since then the Tai Dam have been unable to communicate with God.[7]

Christianity: Several years ago a young Tai Dam man was imprisoned in southern Vietnam. He found Christ through the witness of a Vietnamese pastor, who was incarcerated at the same time for his faith. After his release, the young man returned to his village and shared his new faith. Impressed by the dramatic change in the ex-criminal's life, 753 Tai Dam turned to Christ and were baptized.[8] In contrast to the Tai Dam church in Vietnam, which now numbers several thousand,[9] few of their counterparts in China have ever heard the gospel. Translation work is currently under way to bring more of God's Word to the Tai Dam people.[10]

Population in China:
30,500 (1995)
34,700 (2000)
44.200 (2010)
Location: Yunnan
Religion: Animism
Christians: 50

Overview of the Tai Dam

Countries: Vietnam, Laos, Thailand, China, USA, France, Australia
Pronunciation: "Tai-Dahm"
Other Names: Jinping Dai, Black Tai, Black Dai, Tai Noir, Thai Den, Do, Tai Do, Ty Dam
Population Source:
30,500 (1995 GEM);
Out of a total Dai population of 1,025,128 (1990 census);
500,000 in Vietnam (1993);
50,000 in Laos (1995 L. Chazee);
20,000 in Thailand;
4,000 in USA;
1,500 in France;
Also in Australia
Location:
S Yunnan: Jinping County
Status:
Officially included under Dai
Language: Daic, Tai, Southwestern Tai, East Central
Dialects: 0
Religion:
Animism, Polytheism, Christianity
Christians: 50
Scripture: Portions 1982; Available in the Tai Dam, Vietnamese, and Lao scripts; Work in progress
***Jesus* film:** In progress
Gospel Recordings:
Tai: Black #00794
Christian Broadcasting:
Available (FEBC)
ROPAL code: BLT00

Status of Evangelization

A = Have never heard the gospel
B = Were evangelized but did not become Christians
C = Are adherents to any form of Christianity

Tai Kao 白傣

Location: Approximately 11,000 Tai Kao live on the banks of the Honghe River in Jinping County in the southern part of Yunnan Province. Jinping borders Vietnam where approximately 200,000 Tai Kao live — a similar number to the Tai Kao population in northern Laos. Small Tai Kao refugee communities are also found in France and the United States.[1]

Identity: Although the Tai Kao are part of the official Dai nationality in China, they possess their own spoken and written language and are fiercely proud of their distinct ethnic identity. Their name *Tai Kao* means "white Tai."

Language: Tai Kao is part of the Southwestern Tai language family, which also includes Tai Lu and Tai Dam. One linguist notes that there are 190,000 speakers of Tai Kao in Vietnam, and that the language is also spoken in southern China. "Speakers who have had prolonged contact with Tai Dam [Black Dai] have become bilingual in it."[2] A Tai Kao dictionary has been complied by J. Donaldson.

History: The majority of the Tai race in north China lived farther to the north prior to the thirteenth century, when invading Mongol armies pushed the Tai into southern China. Some groups — such as the Tai Kao, Tai Dam, and Red Tai — moved from Guangxi into Yunnan Province and farther south into Vietnam and Laos.[3]

Customs: The Tai Kao live in compact communities along the Honghe River. Most are engaged in agriculture and fishing.

Religion: The animistic Tai Kao have never converted to Buddhism. They "have a number of statues and altars... to the spirit of the soil, to the tiger god, and to Tan Sin and Kouan-Yin, local heroes now deified by the White Tai."[4] Unlike most people in this region, the Tai Kao believe in a sovereign, supreme god who is active in their lives. "One of their legends states that their ancestors emerged from a pumpkin in which they had taken refuge during a divinely decreed flood that drowned all the other inhabitants of the earth because of their wickedness."[5]

Paul Hattaway

Christianity: Despite the availability of weekly gospel radio broadcasts and Scripture portions in the Tai Kao language since 1969, few have shown any interest in Christianity. They have been described as "the most unreached of all the Tai groups."[6] Little has changed since the 1920s, when missionaries in the region outlined their strategy for reaching the branches of the Tai in southern China: "We are not deaf to the call to plant and preach over the whole world; not among certain promising races only, nor alone in coastwise provinces. Neither do we put much reliance in the project to have the Chinese Christian assume entire responsibility for the evangelization of this disgracefully big unoccupied territory in Southwest China. There is too much racial antipathy. Chinese, unless under foreign guidance, will ever patronize the Tai... and the Tai are as proud as the Chinese and resent being either abused or patronized."[7]

Population in China:
10,000 (1995)
11,350 (2000)
14,500 (2010)
Location: Yunnan
Religion: Animism
Christians: None Known

Overview of the Tai Kao

Countries: Laos, Vietnam, China, France, USA

Pronunciation: "Tie-Kaow"

Other Names: White Tai, Dai Kao, Thai Trang, Tai Don, Tai Kaw, Tai Blanc, Tai Lai, Tai Khao, Tai D

Population Source: 10,000 (1996 B. Grimes – 1995 figure); Out of a total Dai population of 1,025,128 (1990 census); 200,000 in Laos (1995 AMO); 190,000 in Vietnam (1984); Also in France, USA

Location: *S Yunnan:* Jinping County

Status: Officially included under Dai

Language: Daic, Tai, Southwestern Tai

Dialects: 0

Religion: Animism, Polytheism

Christians: None known

Scripture: Portions 1969; Work in progress

***Jesus* film:** None

Gospel Recordings: White Tai #04322

Christian Broadcasting: Available (FEBC)

ROPAL code: TWH00

A = Have never heard the gospel
B = Were evangelized but did not become Christians
C = Are adherents to any form of Christianity

Tai Lu 傣历

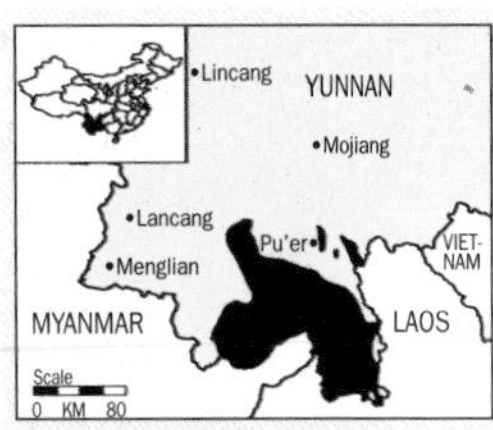

Population in China:
444,000 (1986)
614,300 (2000)
782,600 (2010)
Location: Yunnan
Religion: Buddhism
Christians: 2,000

Overview of the Tai Lu

Countries: China, Myanmar, Laos, Thailand, USA, Vietnam

Pronunciation: "Tie-Leuu"

Other Names: Pai-i, Shui Pai-i, Lue, Lu, Dai Lu, Ly, Xishuangbanna Dai, Sipsongpanna Dai, Shui Dai

Population Source: 550,000 (1986 T'ien Ju-K'ang);[1] Out of a total Dai population of 1,025,128 (1990 census); 200,000 in Myanmar (1981 SIL); 119,100 in Laos (1995 census); 78,000 in Thailand (1993); 4,000 in USA (1998); 3,684 in Vietnam (1989 census)

Location: *SW Yunnan:* Xishuangbanna Dai Prefecture

Status: Officially included under Dai

Language: Daic, Tai, Southwestern Tai, East Central, Northwest

Dialects: 0

Religion: Theravada Buddhism, Animism, Christianity

Christians: 2,000

Scripture: New Testament 1933 (Reprinted 1996); Portions 1921

***Jesus* film:** None

Gospel Recordings: Lu #01147

Christian Broadcasting: None

ROPAL code: KHB00

Status of Evangelization

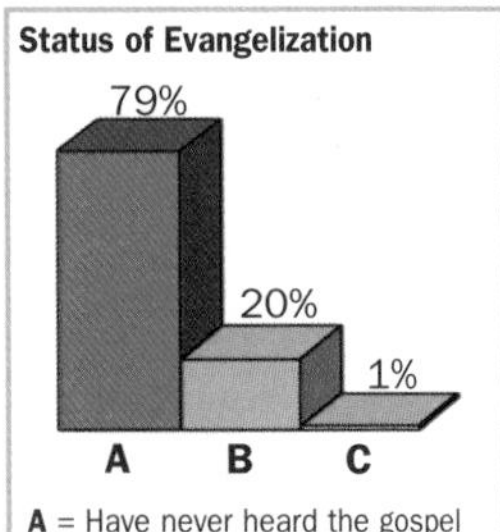

A = Have never heard the gospel
B = Were evangelized but did not become Christians
C = Are adherents to any form of Christianity

Location: More than 600,000 Tai Lu live in Xishuangbanna Prefecture in the extreme southwestern corner of China. Researchers vary on the population of the Tai Lu, with estimates ranging from 250,000[2] to 770,000.[3] Because Tai Lu varieties are spoken in a diverse area, population estimates are "especially precarious."[4] Xishuangbanna is a transliteration of the Tai name, *Sip-Song-Pan-Na*, which means "twelve thousand rice fields." The Tai Lu are also located throughout Laos, Vietnam, Thailand, and Myanmar. Massive deforestation and a rapid population growth have virtually destroyed the ecology of Xishuangbanna.[5]

Identity: The Tai Lu are part of the official Dai nationality in China. Although the name "Tai" is said with a "t" sound, the Chinese pronounce it as "Dai." One early missionary described them in unflattering terms: "The Lu impressed me as less civilized as any Tai people I had ever met. They are less polite and deferential, more talkative, even rude in their manners. But they are less timid, more sturdy, more hospitable, more receptive."[6]

Language: The Tai Lu possess an ancient script, still used by Buddhists in the region. This profile refers to the Shui (Water) Dai in China who speak a different language from the Han Tai and Huayao Tai.

History: By the ninth century AD, the Tai Lu had a well-developed agricultural system. They used oxen and elephants to till the land and constructed extensive irrigation systems.[7]

Customs: Each year the Tai Lu celebrate the Songkran Festival, when people splash water over each other, symbolizing the cleansing of sin from the previous year and a fresh start for the new year.

Religion: The Tai Lu are Theravada Buddhists. They believe that if they live good lives they will be reborn into a higher social position, but if they are wicked they will come back as degraded animals.[8] At certain times the Tai Lu pay homage to the spirits of those who have contributed greatly to the well-being of their descendants. "Sacrifices are offered to the spirits [and] the village is shut in on itself; all roads and tracks giving access to the community are blocked with barricades of trees and branches... the whole village is encircled with ropes made of straw or a line of white cotton thread, to represent symbolically an encircling wall preventing entry or exit. No outsiders of any description, not even monks or members of the elite ruling class, are permitted to attend these rites."[9]

Christianity: Not just physical barriers but also spiritual blockages exist among the Tai Lu. They have proven to be relatively resistant to the gospel. Presbyterian missionary Daniel McGilvary and his coworkers first ventured into Tai Lu territory in 1893 — riding elephants north from their base in Chiang Mai, northern Thailand — and shared the Gospel wherever they went.[10] The first Tai Lu church was formed in the early 1920s. Persecution against the new believers forced them to construct their own village, Bannalee, which remains Christian today. The Tai Lu New Testament was first translated in 1933 and reprinted in 1992 and 1996 for Tai Lu believers in China and Myanmar.[11]

Aisan Studies Institute

Tai Mao 傣毛

Paul Hattaway

Location: The Tai Mao — sometimes called *Mao Shan*, or in Burmese *Shan Tayok* meaning "Chinese Shan" — are a group living in the Dehong Prefecture of western Yunnan Province.[1] There are approximately 320,000 Tai Mao speakers in China, in addition to sizable communities in Myanmar, Laos, and possibly Vietnam.

Identity: The Tai Mao are known by a variety of names, including Dehong Dai, Shan, Chinese Shan, Kang, and Dai Nua. They are part of the official Dai nationality in China, which includes more than ten Tai language groups scattered throughout Yunnan and Sichuan provinces.

Language: The Tai spoken in Dehong is closely related to varieties of Shan spoken in adjacent areas of northern Myanmar; however, linguists say it is similar but not identical to Shan in Myanmar. The same Shan language of Myanmar is spoken in only one village in China.[2] The Tai Mao and Shan also use different scripts. The Tai Mao use a "square" orthography. "This has been revised and improved, and is still in use in China."[3]

History: The Tai Mao have long possessed an advanced culture. By the thirteenth century they had created a Tai calendar, written books explaining the eclipses of the sun and moon, and composed a number of poems, legends, and fairy tales. A Tai tale tells of a cataclysmic flood that long ago destroyed most of the people and animals of the world. Through intermarriage among the survivors, the people began to multiply so much that soon the land could not support the needs of so many people.

Customs: "Door Festivals" are held every half-year to help the people focus on agricultural production. Between 15 July and 15 October, the Tai do not hold any social or religious activities, nor do they visit their relatives or arrange marriages. "When the busy season is over, they hold the Door Opening Festival, during which time people beat gongs and drums, and dance... to announce the end of the farming season."[4]

Religion: The Tai Mao are Theravada Buddhists, although aspects of animism and shamanism influence their belief system. The Tai Mao also revere family ancestral spirits, called *diulahagun*.

Christianity: The Tai Mao are an unevangelized people group, despite living in a region with many Christian churches among the neighboring peoples. Scripture portions were translated into Tai Mao in 1931. Some Tai Mao are also able to read the Bible in the Shan script of Myanmar. John Kuhn conducted meetings among the Tai Mao in Longling in the 1940s. He reported that there were "some fifty thousand people right on that spot and without a single witness to the Gospel.... We preached to a group in a home... a young lad in his late teens raised his hand to say 'I will let the Saviour in.' He belonged to the Kang clan of the [Tai Mao] race. I sat and gazed at the young Kang as the first convert in all that area!"[5] In 1993, 34 Tai Mao received Christ after a short-term missions team from Taiwan traveled to Dehong.[6] For several years now, FEBC has broadcasted gospel radio programs in the Tai Mao language.

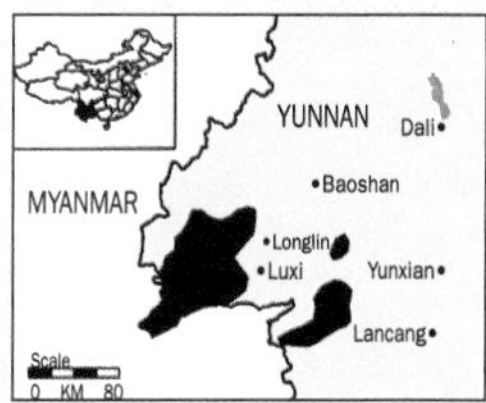

Population in China:
250,000 (1990)
318,500 (2000)
405,800 (2010)
Location: Yunnan
Religion: Buddhism
Christians: 200

Overview of the Tai Mao

Countries: China, Myanmar, Laos, possibly Vietnam

Pronunciation: "Tie-Maow"

Other Names: Kang, Kong, Chinese Shan, Maw, Mao, Dai Mao, Tai Long, Tai Nuea, Dehong Dai, Dehong, Tai Dehong, Tai Le, Dai Le, Tai Loe, Dai Loe, Tai Mo, Dai Mo

Population Source:
250,000 (1990 J.-O. Svantesson); Out of a total Dai population of 1,025,128 (1990 census); 72,400 in Myanmar (1983); 35,000 in Laos (1995 L. Chazee); Possibly in Vietnam

Location:
W Yunnan: Dehong Prefecture

Status:
Officially included under Dai

Language: Daic, Tai, Southwestern Tai, East Central, Northwest

Dialects (3): Southwestern Tai, East Central, Northwest

Religion:
Theravada Buddhism, Animism, Christianity

Christians: 200

Scripture: Portions 1931

***Jesus* film:** None

Gospel Recordings: None

Christian Broadcasting:
Available in "Chinese Shan" (FEBC)

ROPAL code: TDD01

Status of Evangelization

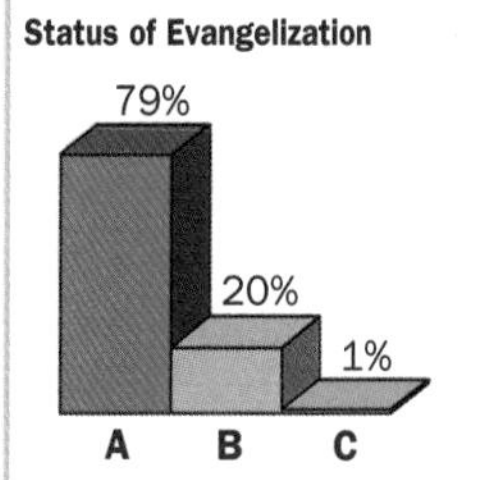

A = Have never heard the gospel
B = Were evangelized but did not become Christians
C = Are adherents to any form of Christianity

Tai Nua 傣努阿

Population in China:
100,000 (1987)
135,600 (2000)
172,800 (2010)
Location: Yunnan
Religion: Animism
Christians: None Known

Overview of the Tai Nua

Countries: China

Pronunciation: "Tie-Nooua"

Other Names: Dai Nuea, Tai Nuea, Dai Kong, Chinese Shan, Tai Le, Dai Le, Tai Loe, Dai Loe, Paiyi, Loe, Han-Paiyi, Dai Lu

Population Source: 100,000 (1987 D. Bradley); Out of a total Dai population of 1,025,128 (1990 census)

Location: *Yunnan:* Along rivers in south central Yunnan, south of Dali Prefecture

Status: Officially included under Dai

Language: Daic, Tai, Southwestern Tai

Dialects: 0

Religion: Animism, Theravada Buddhism, Polytheism, Ancestor Worship

Christians: None known

Scripture: None

***Jesus* film:** None

Gospel Recordings: None

Christian Broadcasting: None

ROPAL code: TDD00

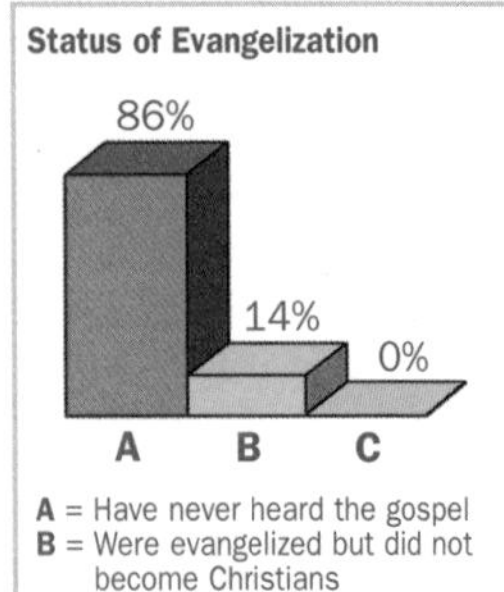

Location: There is a great deal of confusion regarding the names used to classify the various Dai/Tai groups in China. Many publications call the Tai in the Dehong Prefecture *Tai Nua*, a name meaning "northern Tai." The Tai in Dehong are profiled in *Operation China* under the name *Tai Mao*, according to the classification of linguist David Bradley. "The Tai Nua or 'Northern Tai' live in southwestern Yunnan along river valleys; they number about 100,000."[1]

Midge Conner

Identity: Although the Tai Nua are part of the official Dai nationality in China, they speak their own distinct language. They should not be confused with the identically named but different Tai Nua of Laos.

Language: Linguists have pointed out that Tai Nua is "a name given to at least two quite different southwestern branch groups."[2] The Tai Nua profiled here are members of the Southwestern branch of the Tai language family, while the Tai Mao language spoken throughout Dehong Prefecture is similar to the Shan language of Myanmar. The confusion of names is caused partly by "the Chinese tendency to group languages together into nationalities, exemplified by the Dai nationality, which includes all the Southwestern Tai languages of China."[3]

History: The Tai Nua are historically part of the great Tai race of Asia, which dispersed during the past millennia to now inhabit parts of China, Laos, Vietnam, Myanmar, India, and, of course, Thailand. "Based on evidence from Neolithic finds unearthed by archeologists... during recent decades... it is now believed that before migrating southwards, the forefathers of the present day Thais lived in most parts of Guangxi and Sichuan, plus parts of Guizhou and Yunnan."[4]

Customs: After a Tai Nua wedding ceremony the bridegroom goes to live with his bride's family. Traditionally he must take with him gifts of tea, rice, meat, bananas, four eggs, and two salted fish for his new in-laws. Upon arrival, the village elder takes the packets of tea and rice out to the road and calls on the spirits of heaven and earth to witness the marriage. He then ties a white thread seven times around the wrist of the bride and once around the wrist of the groom to indicate their unbreakable commitment to each other.[5]

Religion: Although they are nominally Theravada Buddhists, the Tai Nua have many aspects of animism and polytheism mixed into their beliefs. The very first Tai god was Shalou, the god of Hunting. "Before a hunt, sacrifices were... offered to Shalou to avert danger and to ensure success in the hunt."[6]

Christianity: There are no known Christians among the Tai Nua and very little outreach is presently focused on bringing the gospel to them. Little improvement in their spiritual condition has taken place since the 1920s when one missionary lamented, "There is not a missionary working south of [Kunming] to Mohei.... I am here alone and my little candle is the only light. Yet in these mountains are thousands of tribesmen who have never heard of the Gospel."[7]

Tai Pong 傣棚

Population in China:
66,000 (1987)
89,500 (2000)
114,000 (2010)
Location: Yunnan
Religion: Animism
Christians: 200

Overview of the Tai Pong

Countries: China

Pronunciation: "Tie-Pong"

Other Names: Pong, Dai Pong, La, You

Population Source: 100,000 (1987 D. Bradley);[1] Out of a total Dai population of 1,025,128 (1990 census)

Location: *S Yunnan:* Along the Honghe River valleys, including Jinping County

Status: Most are officially included under Dai, while some have been included under Zhuang.

Language: Daic, Tai, Southwestern Tai

Dialects (2): La, You

Religion: Animism, Polytheism, Ancestor Worship, No Religion, Christianity

Christians: 200

Scripture: None

***Jesus* film:** None

Gospel Recordings: None

Christian Broadcasting: None

ROPAL code: TDD02

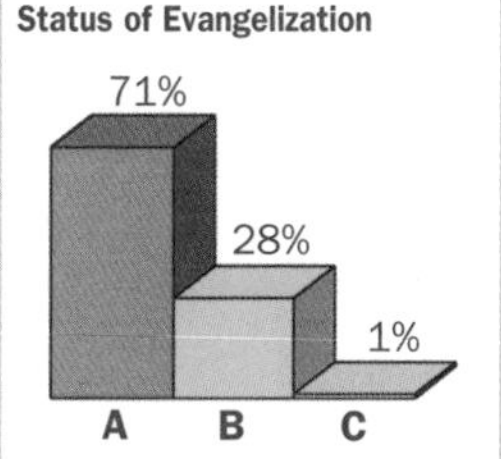

A = Have never heard the gospel
B = Were evangelized but did not become Christians
C = Are adherents to any form of Christianity

Location: Various subgroups comprising the Tai Pong language group live in a widely scattered area along the banks of the Honghe River in the southern extremity of Yunnan Province. The Honghe River changes its name to the Red River once it crosses into Vietnam. No speakers of Tai Pong are reported there. Linguists say Tai Pong is spoken "by as many as 100,000 speakers."[2] This figure includes the 34,000 members of the Ya ethnic group who have been profiled separately in *Operation China.*

Identity: The official classification of the Tai Pong is confusing. Most Tai Pong have been included in the Dai nationality by the Chinese government, but others have been included under the Zhuang.[3] In addition, there are various subgroups among the Tai Pong — such as the La and the You — which may qualify as distinct ethnolinguistic groups. Little research has been conducted into the relatively obscure Tai Pong.

Language: Linguist David Bradley states that the Tai Pong use "an Indic orthography, the furthest northeast example, and is composed of a variety of named subgroups along the rivers of south-eastern Yunnan. From north to south, these include Tai La, Tai You and Tai Ya (with further subgroups Tai Ka and Tai Sai). A few of the Zhuang nationality in Yunnan form part of Tai Pong, but most are [members of the] Dai nationality."[4]

History: Records of contact between the Tai and the Chinese date back to 109 BC when Emperor Wu Di of the Han Dynasty established the Yizhou Prefecture in present-day southern China. The Tai sent tribute to the Han Court at Luoyang and also sent musicians and acrobats to entertain the emperors. The Han Court gave the title "Great Captain" to the Tai chief.[5] The Tai Pong have lived along the Red River for centuries. They use the same script as the Tai Dam and Tai Kao, which suggests historical kinship between these different groups.

Midge Conner

Customs: Many of the Tai Pong are indistinguishable from the local Chinese and Hani, alongside whom they have lived for many generations. Most Tai Pong no longer wear traditional clothing, nor do they celebrate any of their own historical festivals.

Religion: Because the Tai Pong live at the eastern extremity of the Tai groups in China, they did not come under the influence of Theravada Buddhism when it first arrived from India. They have retained their polytheistic and shamanistic practices, although many of the younger generation of Tai Pong are nonreligious and consider themselves atheists.

Christianity: There are a small number of Christians today among the Tai Pong. Mission activity among them was already underway in 1919. In 1945 missionary John Kuhn joyously reported his visit to a mission station among the Tai Pong: "I shall never forget the Red River Valley. At Mosha I attended the twenty-fifth anniversary of the formation of the Shan [Tai] church and school there."[6] Presently, however, the majority of Tai Pong have yet to receive a clear gospel witness. The small number of known Tai Pong believers are concentrated in one or two areas.

Tajik, Sarikoli 塔吉克，撒里库而

Dwayne Graybill

Location: An estimated 33,000 speakers of the Sarikoli Tajik language live in China's far northwest corner, near the border with Afghanistan, Kyrgyzstan, and Pakistan. The majority live in and around the town of Taxkorgan, which means "stone fortress."[1] Although there are more than eight million Tajiks scattered throughout Central Asia — the majority being in Afghanistan, Tajikistan and Uzbekistan — the Sarikoli Tajik in China are a separate ethnolinguistic group from the Central Asian Tajik.

Identity: The Tajik nationality in China speaks two distinct languages: Sarikoli and Wakhi. The Tajik are probably the one group in China most unlike the Han Chinese. They are a Caucasian people with light skin. Many have green or blue eyes and fair hair. They speak a Persian (Iranian) language which is part of the Indo-European language group. The term *Tajik* is applied to various Iranian-speaking groups of Central Asia in differing ways.

Language: Three-quarters of China's Tajiks speak Sarikoli. It is described as "a language entirely different from the majority language spoken in Tajikistan."[2] The Tajik in China do not have their own written script, but some use the Uygur orthography. The two Tajik languages in China are reportedly different enough that speakers from each group must use Uygur to communicate.

History: The history of the Tajik dates back to the biblical time of Abraham. Around 1000 BC the first Persians started to forge a prominent place in history for themselves. The Old Testament records the Persians some 43 times, showing them to have a key role in God's redemptive plan. The Persian King Darius, mentioned in the sixth chapter of Daniel, today lends his name to the Tajik language called *Dari* in Tajikistan and *Farsi* in Afghanistan.

Customs: The Sarikoli Tajiks have lived in tribal and clan structures for centuries. Their homes are built with stone for protection against the extreme cold.

Religion: The Tajiks are one of the few groups in China who adhere to the Shi'a sect of Islam. They do not have mosques. Instead, they meet in their homes once a week for prayer and worship. Before the arrival of Islam in the tenth century, most Tajiks were Christians, having been converted by Nestorian missionaries starting in the seventh century. The Apostolic Church of the East — which had eight million Christians throughout Asia — was destroyed, and all trace of Christianity disappeared.

Christianity: The Tajik are one of the most unreached groups in China. In the 1920s a lone worker stated, "I am sorry to say that in accordance with my knowledge of conditions I cannot pretend this field to be ready for harvest, however, the need of sowing is utterly pressing. Workers intending to scatter the gospel seed in this country ought to know beforehand that their task is not to gather harvest in joy but to sow in tears."[3] Although today there are more than 400 believers in Tajikistan,[4] the Tajik Scriptures and *Jesus* film are not understood by the Sarikoli Tajik in China, although gospel recordings are available in their language.

Population in China:
25,800 (1990)
33,300 (2000)
42,900 (2010)
Location: Xinjiang
Religion: Islam
Christians: None Known

Overview of the Sarikoli Tajik

Countries: China

Pronunciation: "Sar-ree-kor-lee-Tah-jick"

Other Names: Sarikoli, Sarakoly, Sarykoly, Shughni, Tajike, Tajiki, Tadzik, Persian

Population Source: 25,800 (1990 AMO); Out of a total Tajik population of 33,538 (1990 census)

Location: *SW Xinjiang:* In and around Taxkorgan, near the Afghanistan border; Smaller groups of Tajik live in the Yarkant, Poskam, Kargalik, and Gumad districts.

Status: Officially included under Tajik

Language: Indo-European, Indo-Iranian, Iranian, Eastern Iranian, Northeastern, East Scythian, Pamir, Shugni-Yazgulami

Dialects: 0

Literacy: 52%

Religion: Ismaili Shi'a Islam, Animism

Christians: None known

Scripture: None

***Jesus* film:** None

Gospel Recordings: Shughni #03370

Christian Broadcasting: None

ROPAL code: SRH00

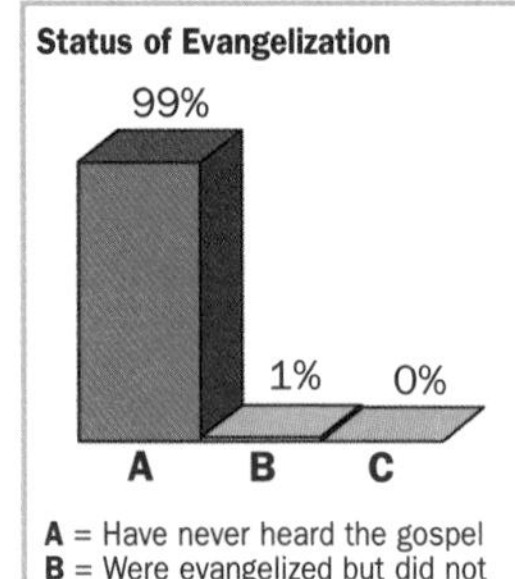

Tajik, Wakhi 塔吉克, 瓦罕

Population in China:
7,700 (1990)
9,930 (2000)
12,800 (2010)
Location: Xinjiang
Religion: Islam
Christians: None Known

Overview of the Wakhi Tajik

Countries: Pakistan, China, Tajikistan, Afghanistan

Pronunciation: "Wa-kee-Tah-jick"

Other Names: Vakhan, Wakhani, Wakhigi, Khik

Population Source: 7,700 (1990 AMO); Out of a total Tajik population of 33,538 (1990 census); 9,100 in Pakistan (1992); 7,000 in Tajikistan (1993); Also in Afghanistan

Location: *SW Xinjiang:* Taxkorgan Tajik County: Pishan and Taxkorgan townships

Status: Officially included under Tajik

Language: Indo-European, Indo-Iranian, Iranian, Eastern Iranian, Southeastern, Pamir

Dialects: 0

Religion: Ismaili Shi'a Islam, Animism

Christians: None known

Scripture: In progress

***Jesus* film:** None

Gospel Recordings: Wakhi #03380

Christian Broadcasting: None

ROPAL code: WBL00

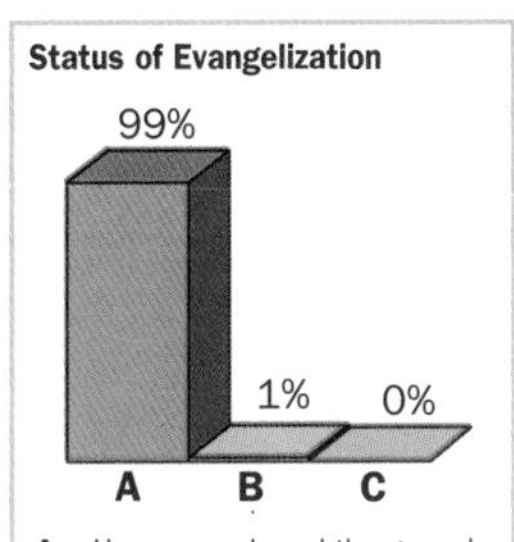

A = Have never heard the gospel
B = Were evangelized but did not become Christians
C = Are adherents to any form of Christianity

Dwayne Graybill

Location: The Wakhi live on both sides of China's remote border with Pakistan. Other Wakhi are located in Afghanistan and Tajikistan. In the Xinjiang Uygur Autonomous Region, the 9,900 Wakhi comprise about one-fourth of the total Tajik population. They are concentrated around the town of Daftar and also in the mountains south of Pishan. In northern Pakistan the Wakhi inhabit the Khunjerab Valley. *Khunjerab* means "valley of blood," a reference to the gangs of local bandits who for centuries plundered caravans and traders passing through the area.

Identity: The Wakhi have been combined with the Sarikoli to form the official Tajik nationality in China, but the languages of the two groups are very different.

Language: Wakhi is a language distinct from Sarikoli Tajik.[1] One linguist notes that "useful intelligibility between the two languages seems unlikely."[2] Many Wakhi in China can also speak Uygur and Kirgiz.

History: The Wakhi region in China was once the seat of the State of Hepant, which reached its peak of power between AD 420–589. A town in the southern part of Taxkorgan, called *Kezikurgan* (Princess Town), contained more than ten Buddhist temples — with a total of about 500 monks — centuries before the Wakhi were converted to Islam.[3] In 1986, after 20 years of construction, the Karakoram Highway was opened, linking China with Pakistan and making contact between the Wakhi in the two countries possible after centuries of isolation.[4] Marco Polo described the area when he passed through more than 700 years ago: "When the traveler leaves this place [Wakhan] he goes... through mountains all the time, climbing so high that it is said to be the highest place in the world.... No birds fly here because of the height and the cold.... The inhabitants live very high up in the mountains. They are idolaters and utter savages, living entirely by the chase and dressed in the skins of beasts."[5]

Customs: The Wakhi have a fond respect for eagles, who live in isolated and lonely mountains, much like themselves.[6] The Wakhi live in extended-family households, with the oldest male serving as the head. With few exceptions, the Wakhi do not marry outside of their group. Before a wedding a price must be paid to the bride's family. The payment often includes livestock, clothing, and silver.

Religion: Although the Wakhi have been Shi'a Muslims for centuries, they have retained many animistic rituals. They rely heavily on amulets to ward off evil spirits. The amulets are small boxes worn around the neck, containing bits of paper that have been written on by a *Pir* (Muslim cleric).[7]

Christianity: Swedish missionaries were active in the southern Xinjiang region during the 1920s and 1930s. Although they won more than 200 Muslim converts, no Wakhi or Sarikoli Tajiks were included in that number. There are no known Wakhi Christians in China or in any of the other countries they inhabit today. Work has recently begun in Moscow to translate the Gospel of Luke into the Wakhi language.

Talu 塔录

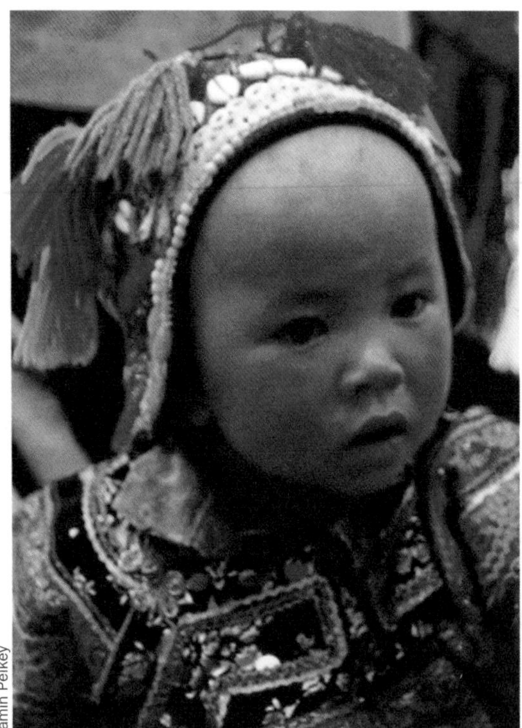
Jamin Pelkey

Location: More than 7,000 people belong to the Talu ethnic group in southern China. About 4,000 are concentrated in the Shuanghe, Yushui, Yunshan, and Liude villages in the Liude District of Yongsheng County in northern Yunnan Province. An additional 1,800 Talu live in the Yongningping District of northern Ninglang County, while others inhabit Weixing and Tongda areas of northwest Huaping County.[1] All areas inhabited by the Talu are located in the mountains of northern Yunnan Province.

Identity: Little is known about the Talu, except that they have been officially included under the Yi nationality in China. The Talu, who are also known as the *Talusu*, have never before appeared in any mission lists of people groups in China.

Language: Although the Talu language has never been specifically studied, it is believed to be part of the Northern Yi branch of Tibeto-Burman. Chinese linguists have formally classified Yongsheng, Ninglang, and Huaping counties as "Northern Yi" areas.

History: Despite the existence of a number of smaller Northern Yi-speaking groups in China, most sources, when speaking of the Northern Yi, do not mention any groups other than the dominant Nosu people. Jamin Pelkey explains, "The great, proud Nosu of Sichuan clasp the imagination with their history of slavery and savagery. As a result, much attention has been paid to the details and nuances of their culture while the linguistic and ethnic diversity of the tribes and peoples included in their numbers have gone unheeded.... The Nosu population also spills over into Yunnan, and by paying closer attention to detail in Yongsheng and Ninglang counties, what was previously thought to be *Nosu* has exploded into nine other small, and previously unknown tribes and peoples whose autonyms and dialects are distinct from the Nosu around them."[2]

Customs: The Talu believe that when people are sick it is the result of a demonic curse. Often the sick are abandoned to a room where they stay until they show signs of improvement.

Religion: The Talu, and some of the neighboring Yi peoples, observe funeral customs that are designed to help the soul of the deceased find rest: "the horse which the deceased used to ride is brought to the door and saddled by the exorcist. The command is then given to lead the horse to the grave. All the mourners follow, and, marching or dancing in intertwining circles, cross and re-cross the path of the horse until the poor creature, bewildered and frantic with fear, rushes and kicks in a wild confusion. The whole company thereupon raise a great shout, and say, 'The soul has come to ride the horse! The soul has come to ride the horse!'"[3]

Christianity: Few parts of China have been so thoroughly neglected by the ambassadors of Christianity than the areas inhabited by the Talu. Yongsheng, Ninglang, and Huaping counties are practically entirely devoid of any Christian presence. As a result, the Talu are a completely unreached and unevangelized people group with no knowledge of Jesus Christ.

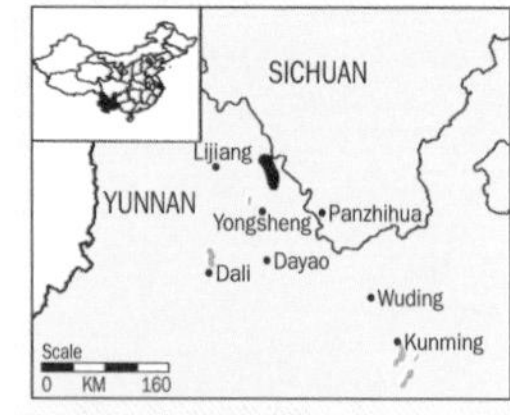

Population in China:
7,000 (1999)
7,150 (2000)
9,000 (2010)
Location: Yunnan
Religion: Polytheism
Christians: None Known

Overview of the Talu

Countries: China

Pronunciation: "Tah-loo"

Other Names: Talusu

Population Source: 7,000 (1999 J. Pelkey); Out of a total Yi population of 6,572,173 (1990 census)

Location: *N Yunnan:* Yongsheng (4,000), Ninglang (1,800), and Huaping (1,200) counties

Status: Officially included under Yi

Language: Sino-Tibetan, Tibeto-Burman, Burmese-Lolo, Lolo, Northern Lolo, Yi, Northern Yi

Dialects: 0

Religion: Polytheism, Animism, Ancestor Worship

Christians: None known

Scripture: None

***Jesus* film:** None

Gospel Recordings: Yi: Talu

Christian Broadcasting: None

ROPAL code: None

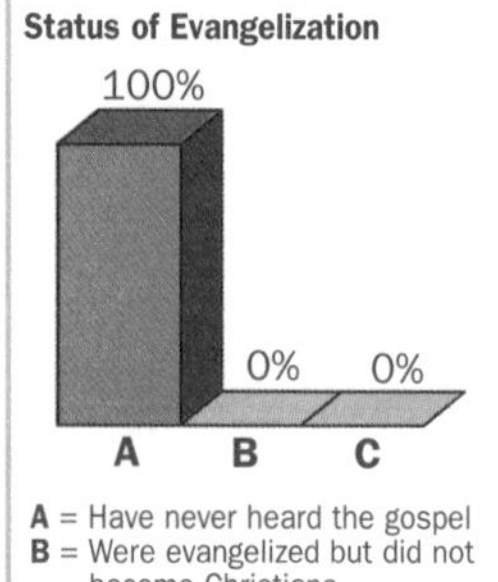

Tanglang 堂郎

Location: The small Tanglang people group — who numbered 947 people within 185 families in a 1996 study — inhabit eight villages in the isolated Tanglang Basin in the southern part of Lijiang County.[1] The locals call the basin *Tanglangba*. Administratively the Tanglang live in the Hongmai Community of Tai'an District. The Tanglang Basin is watered by the Tanglang River and is surrounded by a rim of mountains. During the rainy season, roads to the Basin are impassable; visitors are required to hike three hours from the nearest road in order to reach them.

Identity: The Tanglang tribe has been officially included as part of the Yi nationality in China. In the 1920s one study in Lijiang County alone listed 26 different minority groups.[2] The Tanglang believe they are a unique people group, with their own set of customs and their own language. The name *Tanglang* may mean "praying mantis" in Chinese.

Language: The language of the Tanglang appears to be a mixture of Lisu and Bai and is not even a Yi variety. It suggests the Tanglang may have been completely misclassified as a Yi group. Tanglang children are still taught their language, which is used extensively despite their small population. Most Tanglang are adequately bilingual in Chinese.

History: Some Tanglang claim that they migrated to their present location about 200 years ago.[3] They traveled on horseback from an unspecified location in the north and settled in the verdant basin, unoccupied at the time. Other Tanglang say that they have always lived in their present location. Despite living in the vicinity of minority groups such as the Naxi, Pumi, and Bai, the Tanglang have managed to preserve their own distinct culture and customs.

Jamin Pelkey

Customs: A massive earthquake rocked Lijiang County on 3 February 1996, killing 300 people, injuring 40,000, and leaving 300,000 homeless. The epicenter of the earthquake was near the Tanglang area. Many of their homes were destroyed, and because they are desperately poor, they have expended much energy since that time repairing their homes and trying to get their lives back to normal.

Religion: Every year the whole Tanglang community gathers to offer sacrifices to a sacred Mountain god. They believe a demon lives inside the largest mountains in the region. The demon must be placated for their lives to prosper and for no ill fortune to come their way. The Tanglang had a sacred pagoda, but it was destroyed in the 1996 earthquake. They make a pilgrimage to their sacred mountain every 13th day of the fifth lunar month. They offer sacrifices to the Mountain god.

Christianity: The Tanglang have never appeared in any previous ethnolinguistic people group lists of China. They are a completely unevangelized and unknown group. The Tanglang's remote location has prevented outside Christians from having any contact with them. The nearest significant Christian community to them are the Lisu believers farther to the west.

SICHUAN
Lijiang
Dali
Chuxiong
Wuding
Kunming
MYANMAR
YUNNAN
Xinping
Scale
0 KM 160

Population in China:
947 (1996)
1,040 (2000)
1,300 (2010)
Location: Yunnan
Religion: Polytheism
Christians: None Known

Overview of the Tanglang

Countries: China

Pronunciation: "Tung-lung"

Other Names: Tanglang Jiang

Population Source:
947 (1996 J. Pelkey);
Out of a total Yi population of 6,572,173 (1990 census)

Location: *NW Yunnan:* Tanglang Basin in Lijiang County

Status:
Officially included under Yi

Language: Sino-Tibetan, Tibeto-Burman, Burmese-Lolo, Lolo, Northern Lolo, Unclassified

Dialects: 0

Religion: Polytheism, Animism, Ancestor Worship

Christians: None known

Scripture: None

***Jesus* film:** None

Gospel Recordings: None

Christian Broadcasting: None

ROPAL code: None

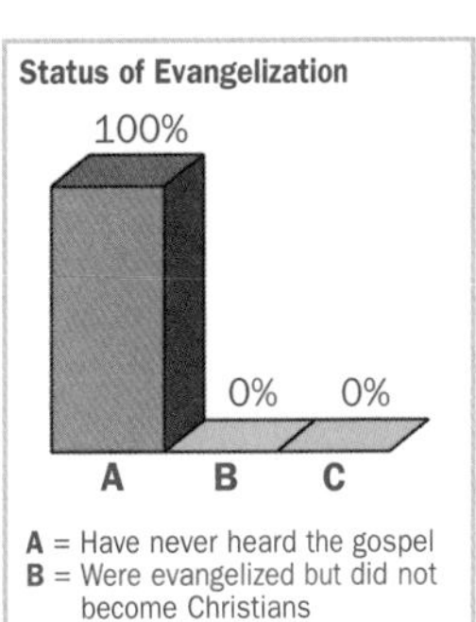

Tatar 塔塔而

Population in China:
4,873 (1990)
5,970 (2000)
7,320 (2010)
Location: Xinjiang
Religion: Islam
Christians: None Known

Overview of the Tatar

Countries: Russia and all former Soviet republics, Turkey, Romania, USA, Bulgaria, China, Afghanistan

Pronunciation: "Tah-tar"

Other Names: Tartar, Tata'er, Dada, Dadan

Population Source: 4,873 (1990 census); 4,127 (1982 census);[1] 5,522,000 in Russia (1993); 468,000 in Uzbekistan (1993); 328,000 in Kazakstan (1993); 87,000 in Ukraine (1993); 72,000 in Tajikistan (1993); 70,000 in Kyrgyzstan (1993)[2]

Location: *N Xinjiang:* Tacheng, Urumqi, and Yining cities

Status: An official minority of China

Language: Altaic, Turkic, Western Turkic, Uralian

Literacy: 86%

Dialects (1): Nogai

Religion: Sunni Islam

Christians: None known

Scripture: New Testament 1989; Portions 1864; Not available in China

***Jesus* film:** Available in Kazan Tatar

Gospel Recordings: None

Christian Broadcasting: Available in Kazan Tatar

ROPAL code: TTR00

Status of Evangelization

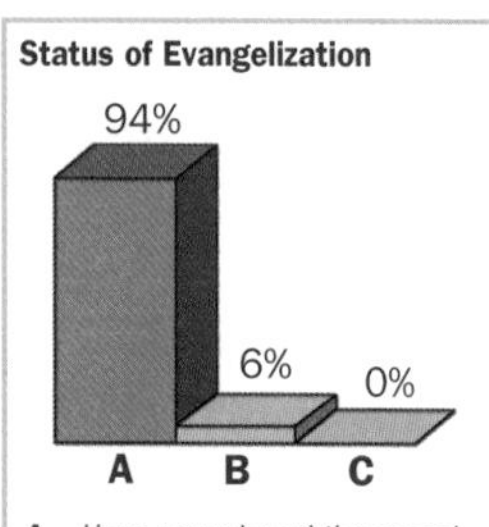

A = Have never heard the gospel
B = Were evangelized but did not become Christians
C = Are adherents to any form of Christianity

Location: Less than 6,000 members of the Tatar nationality live hidden away in tiny communities in the far northwestern corner of China. The majority live in the cities of Tacheng, Urumqi, and Yining in the Xinjiang Uygur Autonomous Region. The term *Tatar* is widely used throughout the nations of the former Soviet Union and Central Asia. More than seven million Tatar live in 20 different countries: the majority are spread throughout Russia, from Moscow to Eastern Siberia. Others are located in nations as diverse as Turkey, Afghanistan, Romania, and Finland. Approximately 10,000 Tatar also live in New York and San Francisco in the United States.

Identity: The Tatar are the fourth smallest of China's 55 officially recognized minorities. The name *Tatar* appears to have originated during the Mongol Empire of the thirteenth century. As the Mongol hordes pillaged their way across Asia, the terrified Europeans called them "The People from Hell." The Latin word for hell is *Tatarus*.

Language: Only about 1,000 of the Tatar in China are able to speak their language,[3] which is a member of the Turkic family. It is now mainly spoken by middle-aged and elderly people and is only taught to children in "pure" Tatar households.[4] It may be the same as Kazan Tatar in Russia. Although they possess no written language of their own, most Tatars in China use the Uygur or Kazak scripts.

History: The Tatar were known in China in the eighth century as *Dadan*. In the ensuing centuries after the collapse of the Mongol Empire, it seems to have been a favorable practice for various tribes to call themselves *Tatar*. Because of this, there are many Tatar throughout Russia and Central Asia who should be viewed as separate ethnolinguistic groups.

Customs: When a Tatar dies, relatives wrap the body in a white cloth and place a knife or rock on it. The corpse is then placed on a platform and removed from the house, head first.[5] Tatar wedding ceremonies are usually held at the bride's home. The newly married couple drink sweet water from the same cup, to show they will remain a devoted couple to the end of their lives.[6] The bridegroom often lives in his father's home for a time after the marriage, and some do not live with their wife until their first baby is born. Forty days after the birth of a child, the baby is bathed. The water for the bath is fetched from 40 places, representing as many good wishes for the baby's growth.[7]

Religion: The Tatars in China are Muslims of the Sunni sect. They worship in mosques along with Uygur and Kazak people.

Christianity: Percy Mather was the first missionary to reach out to the Tatar in China in 1914. "He sang at their festivals, and lived a similar life to them, and helped their sick.... He spent much time in the city of Chuguchak ('the land of flies') and his name was widely regarded among Russian, Tatar, Chinese and Mongolian sections of the city."[8] Although the Tatar in other lands have the New Testament and evangelistic material available in their language, they are not understood by the Tatar in China. There are no known believers among them.

Midge Conner

Teleut 贴邻股特

Location: Although their numbers in China are reported to be a mere 13 families or approximately 50 individuals,[1] the Teleut speak their own language and have their own historical and cultural identity. They are located in the Altai District in the extreme northernmost point of China's Xinjiang Uygur Autonomous Region. The area, which suffers from extremely cold winters, is situated at the juncture of China, Russia, and Mongolia. The vast majority of Teleut live in Russia, especially in the Kemerovo and Novosibirsk Oblasts in the Northern Altai region. There are 71,600 speakers of both Northern and Southern Altai on the Russian side of the border.[2]

Identity: The tiny Teleut group in Xinjiang view themselves as a separate people group and have officially registered their existence with the Chinese authorities. Historically, the Teleut were also known as the *White Kalmuck* and are called *Tielingute* by the Chinese. The authorities in China have probably counted the Teleut as part of the Kazak nationality.

Language: Teleut is a Turkic language from the Altaic family. Teleut is described as "endangered" in Russia, even though it is still being taught to children, and it is still spoken in many homes.[3] Recently there has been a revival of Teleut culture among the Teleut in Russia, which has also caused the use of their language to be invigorated. The Teleut in Russia have a written script using the Cyrillic alphabet. There is little information about the use of the Teleut language in China; it may have been linguistically consumed by the Oirat and Kazak languages long ago.[4]

History: The Teleut were dispersed throughout Russia by political developments in the seventeenth and eighteenth centuries. The tiny Teleut group in China are thought to be the descendants of a diaspora group who migrated south into China, probably in the early 1800s.[5]

Customs: The Altai region is one of the most inhospitable and harsh in all of China. Temperatures regularly plummet to minus 40° Celsius (–40°F) during the long winter months. Rich, virgin forests cover the slopes of steep mountains that rise over 4,000 meters (13,120 ft.) above sea level. Teleut men spend the summer months hunting and fishing to store up supplies for the winter.

Religion: The Teleut have long been under pressure from the Mongols, Tuva, and Kazaks who inhabit the Altai area, to convert to Tibetan Buddhism or Islam. The Teleut in Russia practice traditional animism and shamanism. Many have become atheists in recent decades.

Christianity: There are no known believers among the Teleut in China. Indeed, except possibly among the Russians, there is not a single known church fellowship in the entire Altai region of northern Xinjiang. Missionaries in Russia translated portions of the Bible into the Teleut language in 1910, but these are now out of print. Work has commenced in recent years to translate the Teleut Bible. While it will greatly benefit the small number of Teleut believers living on the Russian side of the border, the unevangelized Teleut in China are not able to read the Cyrillic script.

Population in China:
50 (1993)
59 (2000)
76 (2010)
Location: Xinjiang
Religion: Animism
Christians: None Known

Overview of the Teleut

Countries: Russia, China
Pronunciation: "Tel-oot"
Other Names: Telengut, Tielingute, White Kalmuck, Altai, Southern Altai
Population Source: 50 in 13 families (1993 J. Janhunen); 71,600 in Russia, including Northern Altai
Location: *N Xinjiang:* Altai District
Status: Probably officially included under Kazak
Language: Altaic, Turkic, Northern Turkic
Dialects: 0
Religion: Animism, Shamanism, No Religion
Christians: None known
Scripture: Portions 1910
***Jesus* film:** None
Gospel Recordings: None
Christian Broadcasting: None
ROPAL code: ALTOO

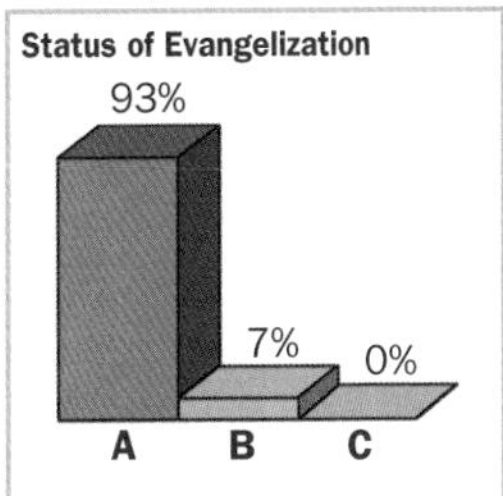

Thami 塔米

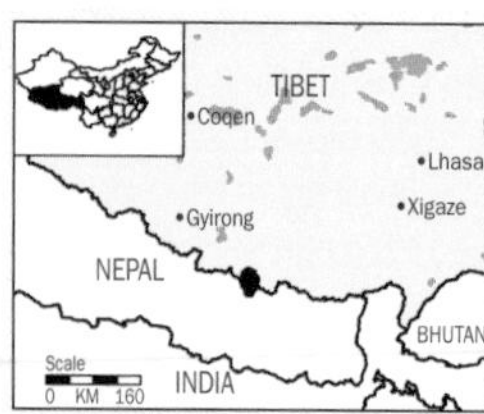

Population in China:
400 (1995)
460 (2000)
590 (2010)
Location: Tibet
Religion: Animism
Christians: None Known

Overview of the Thami

Countries: Nepal, China, India

Pronunciation: "Tah-mee"

Other Names:

Population Source:
400 (1995 AMO);
20,000 in Nepal (1985);
Also in India

Location: *S Tibet:*
Eastern Nepal-Tibet border:
In and around the town of Zhangmu

Status: Unidentified

Language: Sino-Tibetan, Tibeto-Burman, Bodic, Bodish, Himalayish, Eastern Himalayish

Dialects: 0

Religion: Animism, Hinduism, Tibetan Buddhism

Christians: None known

Scripture: None

***Jesus* film:** None

Gospel Recordings:
Thami #04174

Christian Broadcasting: None

ROPAL code: THF00

Status of Evangelization

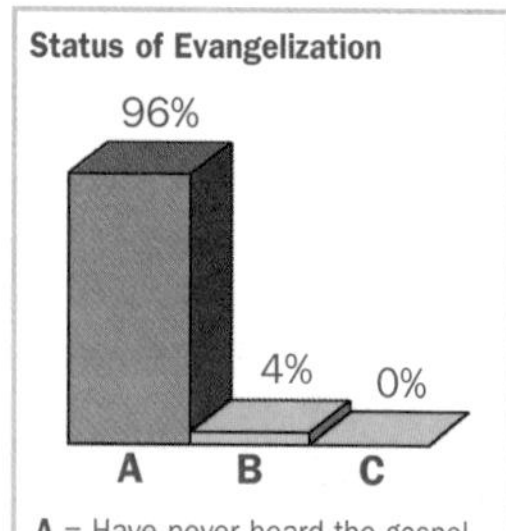

A = Have never heard the gospel
B = Were evangelized but did not become Christians
C = Are adherents to any form of Christianity

Paul Hattaway

History: Legend states that the first Thami couple had seven sons and seven daughters. In order to find suitable marriage partners for all of them, they were allowed to intermarry with other tribes.[3]

Customs: Most Thami men are employed as stonecutters. Many Thami women wear large gold earrings and nose rings. Some still wear traditional *labaedas*, clothing made from plants that are beaten and woven together.[4] The main diet of the Thami is fish and a porridge made with maize flour. Despite their poverty, the Thami willingly go into debt in order to host an elaborate feast or celebration. These festivals add color and variety to their otherwise mundane existence.

Location: More than 20,000 Thami live in and around the town of Dolakha in eastern Nepal. Several hundred Thami also live in Zhangmu County, on the Tibetan side of the border. The Thami were originally a nomadic tribe who settled just east of Katmandu, Nepal. In recent years many Thami men have migrated to India to seek employment.

Identity: It is not known how the Thami in Tibet were classified in the Chinese census. The physical appearance of the Thami suggest they are of Mongoloid descent. In Tibet it is possible the Thami are known by a different name.[1] It may be the Thami in Tibet are simply known as "Nepalese" to the local people. One publication comments on Zhangmu Township: "Crossing a bridge over the boundary river, you set foot [in Tibet].... Some, such as the Nepalese, have settled down here."[2]

Language: The Thami language is one of the few from the so-called Eastern Himalayish linguistic family. It is related to the Baraamu language of Nepal. Thami, which is not a written language, is still spoken in all Thami homes in Nepal, while the national Nepalese language is used for communication with other people groups.

Religion: Most Thami are animists, but many Hindu influences are intermingled with their beliefs. Three days after the birth of a child, the house is cleaned with cow dung and water. The people are sprinkled with cow urine to purify them. The baby is then named in accordance with the day of birth.[5] Those Thami in Tibet who are Hindus are possibly the only practicing Hindus in all of China apart from Indians in Hong Kong.

Christianity: Twenty to thirty Thami in Nepal received Christ in 1993 after listening to gospel recordings in their language.[6] Christian workers reported an "open heaven" as the Thami in Nepal eagerly received the message of salvation. The Thami believers meet in a small church. In 1997 an elderly Thami Buddhist monk in Nepal was visited by a missionary, whose arrival was expected. He explained, "I had a vision two years ago that a foreigner would come and give me a little golden book about the truth. I have been praying and watching each day. I know you are that man."[7] While the Thami in Nepal are a group ripe for harvest, there are no known believers among the Thami in China. Those inside Tibet have so far been cut off from receiving evangelists. Few have ever heard of Jesus Christ.

189

190

191

192

189–191. The *Tu* minority believe they are descended from white feathers that were left behind by a flock of cranes. Today all but a handful of the 200,000 Tu are zealous followers of Tibetan Buddhism. [189 & 191 Dwayne Graybill; 190 Revival Christian Church]

192. Few people have heard of the *Tujia*, even though they number 7 million people. [Paul Hattaway]

193

194

195

196

197

193–197. Approximately 9 million *Uygur* live in Xinjiang, northwest China. The Uygur are a Turkic-speaking people who dream of establishing their own Islamic state. The Uygur's desire is strongly opposed by the Chinese government, who have resettled millions of Han Chinese in Xinjiang since the 1950s — making the Uygur a minority in their own homeland.

[193 Dwayne Graybill; 195 Midge Conner; 194, 196, 197 Revival Christian Church]

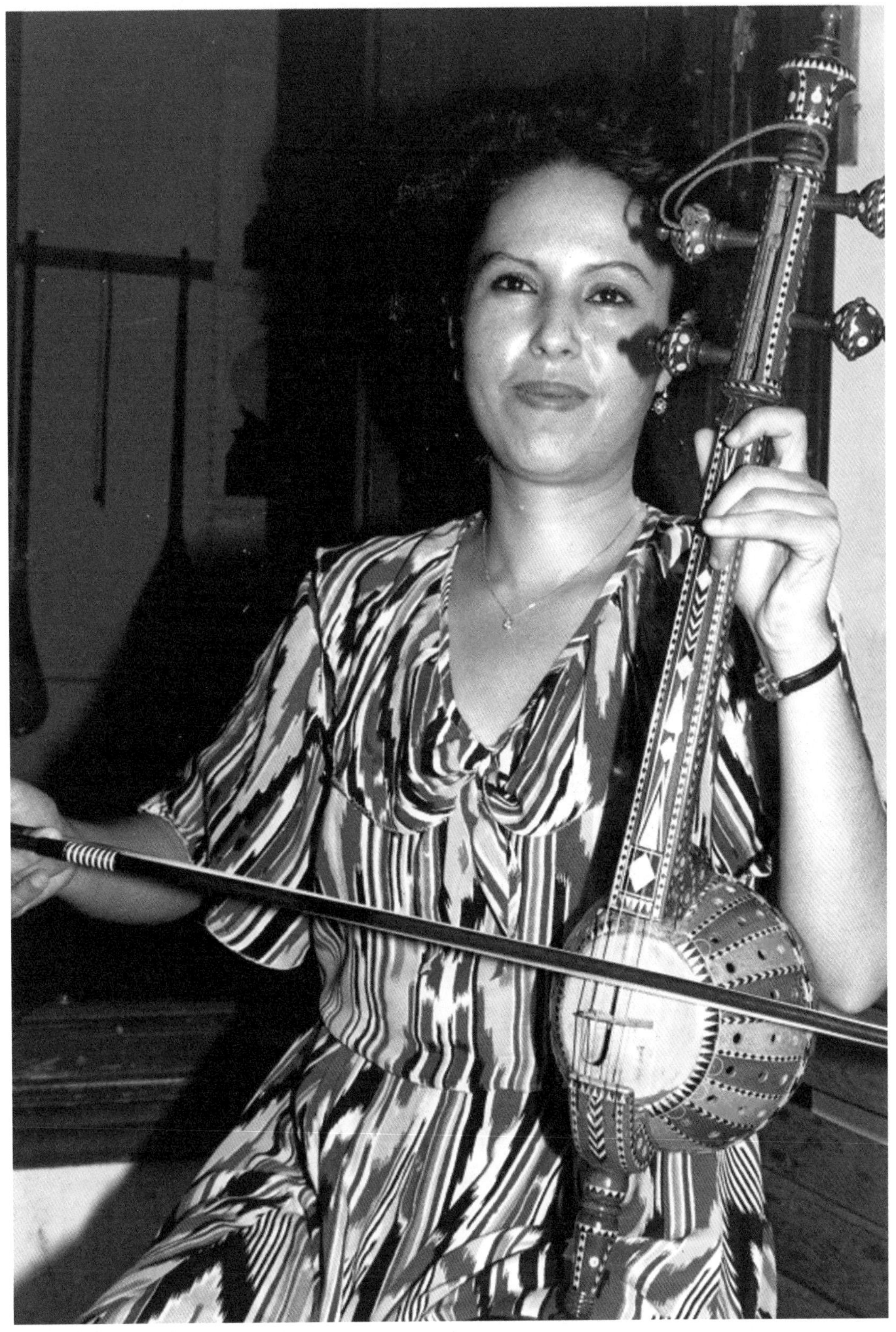

198. A *Uygur* woman's dress is designed to reflect their pre-Islamic religion of fire worship. When the women dance and twirl around, their appearance resembles a flame. [Paul Hattaway]

199

200

201

202

199–200. Although they number almost 20 million people in Central Asia, only about 17,000 *Uzbek* live in cities throughout the Xinjiang Uygur Autonomous Region in northwest China. [both by Paul Hattaway]

201–202. Until recently all people along the China-Myanmar border region lived in terror of the *Wa*, who cut off their neighbors' heads every year to ensure a good harvest. [201 Paul Hattaway; 202 Midge Conner]

Tho 妥

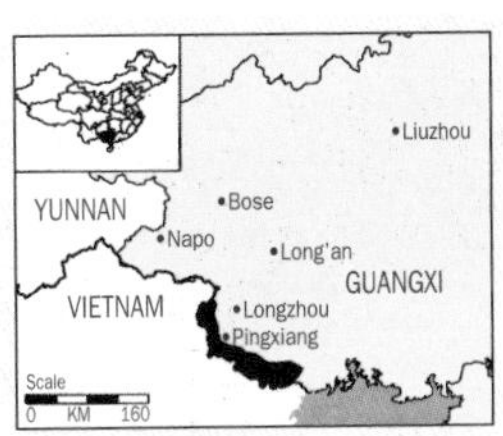

Population in China:
122,000 (1995)
134,000 (2000)
160,200 (2010)
Location: Guangxi
Religion: Ancestor Worship
Christians: 8,000

Overview of the Tho

Countries: Vietnam, China, USA, France, possibly Laos

Pronunciation: "Toh"

Other Names: Thu, To, Tai Tho, Tay, Tai-lo

Population Source: 122,000 (1995 GEM); Out of a total Zhuang population of 15,489,630 (1990 census); 1,190,000 in Vietnam (1989 census); Also in USA, France, possibly Laos

Location: *SE Guangxi:* Pingxiang County near the Vietnam border

Status: Officially included under Zhuang

Language: Daic, Tai, Central Tai

Dialects: 0

Religion: Ancestor Worship, Animism, Christianity

Christians: 8,000

Scripture: Portions 1938

***Jesus* film:** None

Gospel Recordings: Tho #00792

Christian Broadcasting: Available (FEBC)

ROPAL code: TOU00

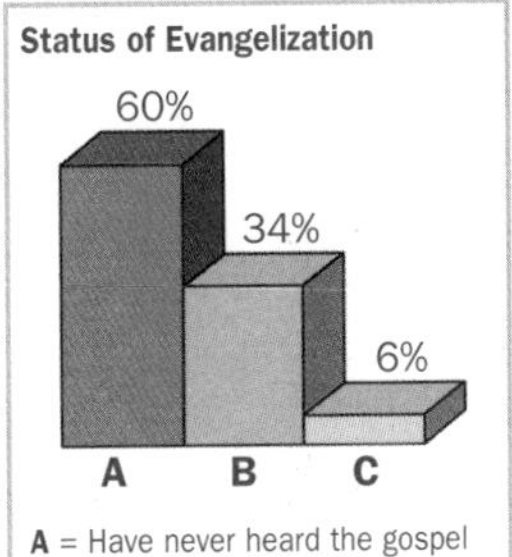

A = Have never heard the gospel
B = Were evangelized but did not become Christians
C = Are adherents to any form of Christianity

Location: Approximately 134,000 Tho are located in the Guangxi Zhuang Autonomous Region in, southern China. Most live in and around the town of Longzhou. In addition, more than one million Tho are located in northern Vietnam.[1] In Guangxi, "the Zhuang predominate in the eastern end of the province and the Tho in the western. They are so closely related it is difficult to distinguish between them."[2]

Identity: In China the Tho have been included as part of the large Zhuang nationality. In Vietnam the Tho are known as *Tay*. They are different from another group in Vietnam also named *Tho*.

Language: In the early 1900s Presbyterian missionary J. H. Freeman surveyed the Tho language. He reported, "Tone and pronunciation are quite close to [Tai] Lu. I made a vocabulary of 400 common words, and found only 67, or one in six, which cannot readily be identified with anything in the [northern Thai] dialect. There is, however, a large admixture of Cantonese and Mandarin in their words."[3] One recent study remarks that "speakers of southern Zhuang varieties, such as Debao... call themselves Tho, but for speakers in Vietnam the term appears to be considered pejorative."[4]

History: The ancestors of the Tho migrated south into Guangxi under pressure from the advancing Mongol armies in the thirteenth century. "From Guangxi a number of tribes pushed into Vietnam and Laos, such as the Tho."[5] The Tho in northern Vietnam were the only tribe who would not submit to the rule of the Hmong king, Sioung, in the late 1800s. Sioung was outraged and led a military campaign against the Tho for 12 years. Countless villages were burned and thousands of Tho were murdered. Most Tho fled the mountains to the lowlands to get beyond the reach of the Hmong.[6]

Customs: The Tho choose to live at the foot of a mountain or near a stream. Their homes consist of two main rooms, the front one for men and the rear one for women. The Tho possess a rich traditional folklore of poems, songs, and dances. One form of song is the *luon*, a duet where lovers sing romantic verses to each other.

Religion: Ancestor worship is the primary religion among the Tho in China today. An early missionary describes the external differences he saw between the Tho and Nung: "There are several factors which seemed to designate the Tho as the more strategic tribe of the two: The Tho are much finer looking; in fact they are the finest looking people we have seen among the natives of Indo-China; They cultivate their fields and gardens better, live in cleaner houses, and seem generally thriftier and more intelligent than the Nung."[7]

Christianity: There are a small number of Christians among the Tho in both China and Vietnam. Many have been exposed to the gospel through the FEBC radio broadcasts. As early as 1913 there were a reported 4,000 to 5,000 Tho Catholics in China.[8] Missionaries translated several books of the Bible into Tho in 1938, but these have been out of print since 1963. The script used was an ancient form of sixteenth-century Chinese characters; few, if any, would be able to read it today. Two Tho dictionaries exist to aid those who wish to learn their language.

Midge Conner

Tibetan, Boyu 藏(钵盂)

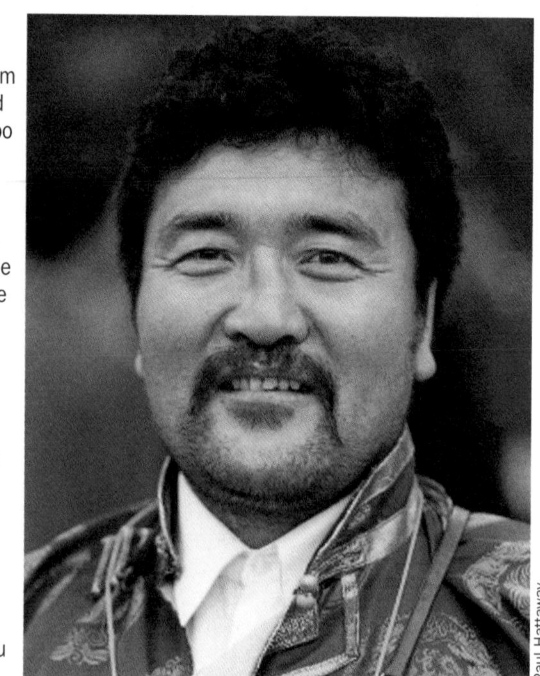

Paul Hattaway

Location: The Boyu Tibetans live in the large Boyu Village in Zhugqu County. Zhugqu is within the Gaanan Prefecture in poverty-stricken Gansu Province. They live atop a 3,000-meter-high (9,840 ft.) mountain. "Boyu is located at the heart of a complex of high peaks and deep ravines, and the paths along which they climb lead through magnificent scenery... dotted with all kinds of flowers: azaleas, camellias, peonies, wolf-berries."[1]

Identity: The Boyu Tibetans are a distinct ethnolinguistic people group. As one visitor remarked, "their language and costume is now very different from Tibetans elsewhere."[2] During festivals, Boyu women wear special dress, unique among all Tibetan peoples. "A breastplate is made of around five to six thousand coral beads, and an enormous silver medallion at waist level — known as *meilong*.... The body of the medallion is scattered with motifs executed in colored enamels, including Tibetan Buddhist symbols and talismans to ward off evil spirits."[3] The Boyu are ethnolinguistically distinct from other Tibetans in the area.

Language: The Boyu tribe arrived in Gaanan at a different time from other Tibetan groups presently in the prefecture, bringing with them their own distinct language. The Boyu language may be from the Qiangic branch of Tibeto-Burman.

History: The Boyu women's special costume "is thought to be associated in some way with the army of Tubo, the Tibetan kingdom which was founded by Songtsen Gampo in 629 and lasted for around two hundred years.... Legend has it that the forebears of the Boyu Tibetans were soldiers from the hinterland of Tibet who were sent to guard the border areas. However, they began to farm the land and eventually decided to settle there."[4]

Customs: The Flower-Gathering Festival of the Boyu is unique to this one small area. It takes place annually on the fifth day of the fifth month of the lunar calendar. "They believe if they drink the spring water on the mountain before the sun touches it... it will keep them free from disease. And if they bathe in the water, all evil will be kept from them."[5]

Religion: During the Flower-Gathering Festival the Boyu worship *Lianzhi*, the goddess of flowers. One of their legends relates that the Boyu lived in abject poverty in ancient times. Touched by their misery, "the gods eventually took pity and sent a young girl, Lianzhi, from heaven to teach them how to reclaim land and grow crops, how to spin and weave cloth.... This went on until one year... she went into the mountains to gather flowers... and never came back.... The people made offerings to her and named her the *Goddess of Flowers*."[6]

Christianity: There are no known Christians among the Boyu Tibetans today, although the Christian & Missionary Alliance worked in nearby Min Xian prior to 1949. The missionaries, who first arrived in 1889, included William Christie, W. W. Simpson, Robert Ekvall, Calvin Snyder, and William Ruhl.[7]

Population in China:
3,000 (1997)
3,260 (2000)
4,200 (2010)
Location: Gansu
Religion: Polytheism
Christians: None Known

Overview of the Boyu Tibetans

Countries: China

Pronunciation: "Bo-yuu"

Other Names: Boyu

Population Source:
3,000 (1997 AMO);
Out of a total Tibetan population of 4,593,330 (1990 census)

Location: *SE Gansu:* In and around Boyu Village in Zhugqu County of Gaanan Tibetan Prefecture

Status:
Officially included under Tibetan

Language: Sino-Tibetan, Tibeto-Burman, Unclassified

Dialects: 0

Religion: Polytheism, Tibetan Buddhism, Animism

Christians: None known

Scripture: None

***Jesus* film:** None

Gospel Recordings: None

Christian Broadcasting: None

ROPAL code: None

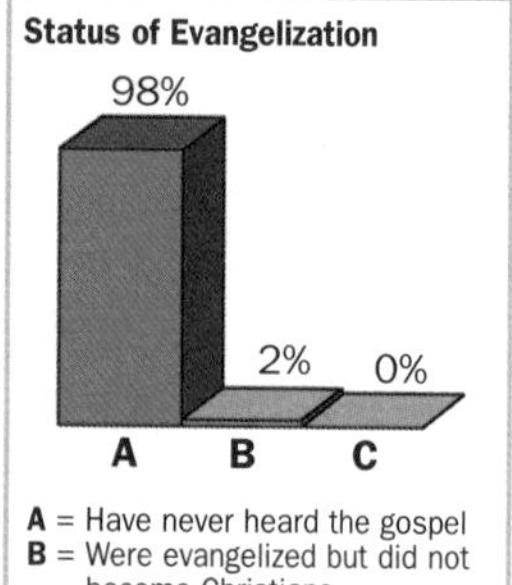

A = Have never heard the gospel
B = Were evangelized but did not become Christians
C = Are adherents to any form of Christianity

Tibetan, Central 藏(拉萨)

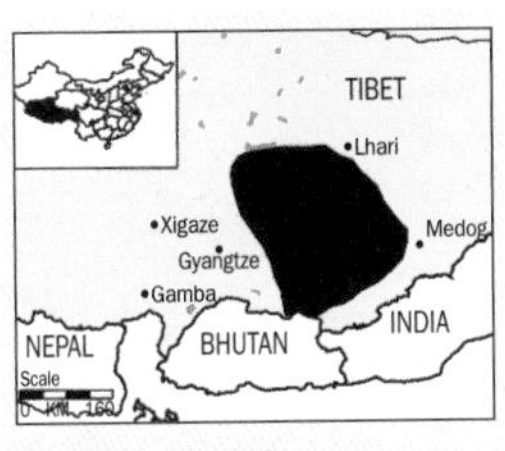

Population in China:
569,300 (1987)
741,000 (2000)
912,900 (2010)
Location: Tibet
Religion: Tibetan Buddhism
Christians: 50

Overview of the Central Tibetans

Countries: China, India, Bhutan, Nepal, Taiwan, Switzerland, USA, Norway, France, Australia, United Kingdom

Pronunciation: "Zung"

Other Names: Zang, Wei, Weizang, Bhotia, Phoke, Dbus, Dbustsang, Lhasa, Lhasa Tibetan, U

Population Source:
569,300 (1987 *LAC*);
Out of a total Tibetan population of 4,593,330 (1990 census)
120,000 in India (1995);
50,000 in Bhutan
(1987 D. Bradley);
2,000 in Nepal (1973)[1]

Location:
Tibet Autonomous Region

Status:
Officially included under Tibetan

Language: Sino-Tibetan, Tibeto-Burman, Bodic, Bodish, Tibetan, Central Tibetan

Dialects (5): Lhasa, Chushur, Phanpo, Testhang, Lunrtse

Religion: Tibetan Buddhism, Bon

Christians: 50

Scripture: Bible 1948; New Testament 1885; Portions 1862

***Jesus* film:** Available

Gospel Recordings:
Lhasa #00690
Tibetan, Colloquial #04380

Christian Broadcasting:
Available (FEBC)

ROPAL code: TIC02

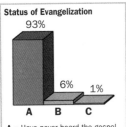

Status of Evangelization

	A	B	C
%	93%	6%	1%

A = Have never heard the gospel
B = Were evangelized but did not become Christians
C = Are adherents to any form of Christianity

Paul Hattaway

Location: Approximately 740,000 speakers of Central Tibetan live in the city of Lhasa and surrounding counties in the Tibet Autonomous Region.[2] Tourists to Lhasa often find the city falls short of the mystique they desire, although it has certainly improved since Thomas Manning's description in the early 1800s: "There is nothing striking, nothing pleasing in its appearance. The habitations are begrimed with smut and dirt. The avenues are full of dogs, some growling and gnawing bits of hide which lie about in profusion, and emit a charnel-house smell; others limping and looking livid; others ulcerated; others starving and dying, and pecked at by the ravens; some dead and preyed upon. In short, everything seems mean and gloomy."[3]

Identity: Although the Tibetans strongly maintain they are one people and are opposed to any attempts to classify them as separate groups, the Tibetan nationality clearly divides into numerous linguistic components.[4]

Language: Central Tibetan — which contains five dialects — "is more commonly known as central *Bus* (transliterated from *U*, the spoken version of the same word).... Educated people from other areas of Tibet traditionally retained their local variety and learned the literary variety of Central Tibetan."[5]

History: Written records of Tibetan history have survived from the seventh century AD, but it is known that nomadic tribes roamed Tibet as early as the second century BC. The cradle of Tibetan civilization is the Yarlung Valley area, about 80 kilometers (49 mi.) southeast of Lhasa. There, according to tradition, the union of a monkey and a she-devil created the Tibetan race. Around AD 600 the warrior-king of Yarlung, Namri Gampo, unified the clans of Tibet. He acquired a princess from Nepal and another one from China to be his wives. Under the persuasion of these two women, he combined the ancient Tibetan religion of Bon with Buddhist teachings.

Customs: For centuries the Chinese have claimed Tibet as an "unalienable part of China," despite Tibetans being culturally, historically, linguistically, and religiously distinct from Chinese. In the 1950s the Chinese took full control of Tibet.

Religion: The Tibetan Buddhist religion is the life-blood of the Tibetan people. It was placed over the powerful Tibetan religion of Bon, which is a mixture of magic, divination, demon worship, and sacrifices. The patron saint of Tibet is Chenrezig, whose image has up to 11 heads and from 2 to 1,000 arms.

Christianity: Tibet has long been one of the greatest challenges for Christianity. In 1892 Hudson Taylor said, "To make converts in Tibet is similar to going into a cave and trying to rob a lioness of her cubs."[6] Timothy, the Nestorian patriarch in Baghdad (778–820), referred to Christians in Tibet and indicated he was willing to assign a missionary to them.[7] Today there are just one or two small Tibetan fellowships in Lhasa.[8] Would-be missionaries face opposition from Buddhist monks, the Chinese authorities, and pro-Tibet foreigners living in Tibet.

Tibetan, Deqen 藏(德钦)

Paul Hattaway

Population in China:
73,560 (1987)
95,750 (2000)
117,900 (2010)
Location:
Yunnan, Tibet, Sichuan
Religion: Tibetan Buddhism
Christians: 7,500

Location: Much confusion surrounds the classification and population of the Deqen Tibetans, whom some researchers refer to as *Atuence*. Atuence is the old name for the Tibetan town of Deqen in northern Yunnan Province. Some sources list more than 500,000 *Atuence* speakers, but our research indicates there are only around 95,000.[1] In addition, there are nine villages of Deqen Tibetans in the northernmost tip of Myanmar.[2]

Identity: The language and many customs of the Deqen Tibetans are distinct from other Tibetan peoples. One Chinese scholar was "surprised to find that the life and customs of the people of the Deqen Prefecture differ from those of the Qinghai-Tibet Plateau. Besides traditional Tibetan customs, they have developed quite a few of their own."[3]

Language: Different linguists over a 60-year period have classified the Deqen, or Atuence, language in different ways. It has been described as "an ancient nomad dialect of Tibetan," "Central Bodish," and "Central Tibetan."[4] The authoritative *Language Atlas of China* lists it as the Southern Kham variety of Tibetan.[5]

History: Formerly located in Tibet, Deqen was annexed by the Chinese in 1703 and has since been a part of Yunnan Province. Tibetans had migrated south into the region many centuries earlier.

Customs: The extreme north of Yunnan is an isolated, mountainous region with abundant rain and snowfall. Hot springs located throughout the region help the people alleviate their winter struggles.[6]

Religion: Although most Deqen Tibetans are Buddhists, this group also has the largest number of professing Christians among any Tibetan group in the world.

Christianity: Three Deqen Tibetan villages numbering 600 people, located on the Tibetan side of the border, are Catholic.[7] Another 700 Tibetans meet in a large Catholic church in Yanjing.[8] The area was first converted by workers with the Paris Foreign Missionary Society in the late 1800s.[9] The mission reached out in love to people all over the Tibetan world. In 1905 Tibetan lamas killed all of the French missionaries and the head of Father Dubernard was hung on the monastery gate.[10] The Chinese authorities responded by demolishing several Tibetan temples in the region.[11] Around the same time, emissaries of the Dalai Lama were dispatched to a Christian village near Yanjing to order the people to renounce Christianity. They shot several Christian families in a field that is called the "Field of Blood" to this day. Instead of intimidating the believers, this cruel act solidified their faith and helped them to renounce Buddhism. It has remained Christian ever since. By 1922 there were a reported 1,610 Tibetan Catholic converts in the area.[12] The Pentecostal Missionary Union commenced work in Deqen in 1912 but gained few converts. In recent years Lisu evangelists have been sent to the Deqen Tibetans and have discipled hundreds of Tibetans in the ways of Christ. According to a Tibetan priest, Lu Rendi, there are 6,500 Tibetan Catholics in Southeast Tibet and at least a further 3,000 in neighboring areas of Yunnan Province.[13]

Overview of the Deqen Tibetans

Countries: China, Myanmar
Pronunciation: "Der-chen"
Other Names: Atuentse, Atuence, Anshuenkun Nyarong, Mekong Tibetan, Nganshuenkuan, Deqin Tibetan, Te-ch'in Tibetan
Population Source:
73,560 (1987 AMO);
Out of a total Tibetan population of 4,593,330 (1990 census);
1,000 in Myanmar (nine villages)
Location: *Yunnan-Tibet* border, especially in Deqen Tibetan Prefecture; Also in a large area of *SW Sichuan*
Status:
Officially included under Tibetan
Language: Sino-Tibetan, Tibeto-Burman, Bodic, Bodish, Tibetan, Northern Tibetan
Dialects (4): Derong, Deqen, Gyalthang, Phyagphreng
Religion:
Tibetan Buddhism, Christianity
Christians: 7,500
Scripture: Tibetan Bible 1948; New Testament 1885; Portions 1862
***Jesus* film:** None
Gospel Recordings:
Zang: Deging
Christian Broadcasting: None
ROPAL code: ATF00 (Atuence); KHG02 (Southern Kham)

Status of Evangelization

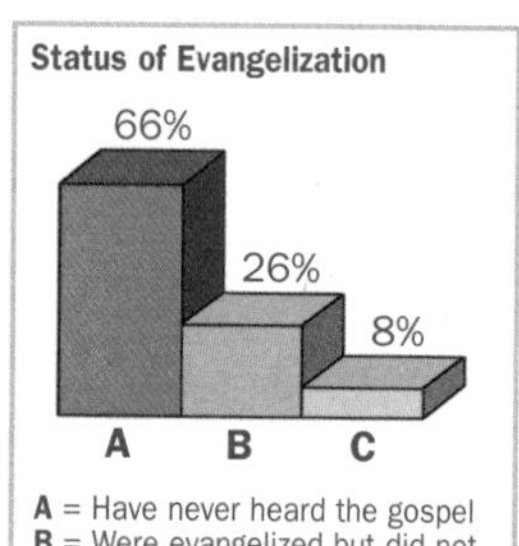

A = Have never heard the gospel
B = Were evangelized but did not become Christians
C = Are adherents to any form of Christianity

Tibetan, Gtsang 藏(格桑)

Paul Hattaway

Location: Almost 600,000 Tibetans belong to the Gtsang Tibetan dialect group. They are located in a wide geographical area, stretching east to west over roughly the entire length of the Tibet-Nepal border. Gtsang is spoken in the cities of Xigaze and Gyantse, the second and fourth largest cities in Tibet. The main attraction of Gyantse is the immense pagoda, or *Kumbun*, built by Rapten Kunsang Phapa (1389–1442).

Identity: The Gtsang Tibetans are part of the Tibetan nationality, but they speak a language only partly intelligible with other Tibetan varieties. Captain O'Conner, the British trade agent at Gyantse in the early 1900s, described the Gtsang Tibetans as "superstitious indeed to the last degree, but devoid of any deep-rooted religious convictions or heart-searchings, oppressed by the most monstrous growth of monasticism and priest-craft which the world has ever seen."[1]

Language: Gtsang Tibetan — which has 19 dialects[2] — is a variety of Central Tibetan. It is largely intelligible with Lhasa and Ngahri Tibetan. Despite their differences in speech, all Tibetans use the same Sanskrit-based orthography. In the seventh century, King Songtsen Gampo sent his minister, Thonmi Sambhota, with a delegation to India where he produced the script.

History: Xigaze, the capital of Tibet from 1618 to 1642, is the traditional seat of the Panchen Lama, Tibet's second most powerful ruler after the Dalai Lama. In 1954 the city was nearly destroyed by floods. After putting down a revolt in 1959, the Chinese imprisoned 400 monks in the Tashilhunpo Monastery.

Customs: The Xigaze New Year Festival is held in the first week of the 12th lunar month. Thousands of visitors have flocked to Gyantse since 1408 for the annual Horse Racing and Archery Show.

Religion: The Gtsang region is home to several Buddhist sects, including the *Nyingmapa* (Ancient), *Kagyupa* (Oral Transmission), and *Sakya* (Gray Earth) schools. After the death of the Panchen Lama in 1989, the Chinese filled his position with their own choice of successor. In May 1995 the exiled Dalai Lama announced a new Panchen Lama who was immediately rejected by the Chinese. Monks at the Tashilhunpo Monastery, and a number of lay Tibetans, rioted in protest. Eighty monks were interrogated by the police, and the city of Xigatse was sealed off for several days. Tensions have remained high since then.

Christianity: Jesuit missionary Antonio de Andrade arrived in Tibet from India in 1624 by disguising himself as a Hindu pilgrim. "Andrade outwitted hostile local officials, made his way north to the Himalayas, endured altitude sickness and snow blindness, fought his way over a 17,900-foot pass into Tibet, and finally reached Tsaparang.... There he impressed the king and queen with his piety, and they gave him permission to return, establish a mission, and preach the Gospel."[3] A revolution in Tsaparang in 1635 abruptly ended the Jesuit mission. Today there are just a handful of Gtsang Tibetan Christians.

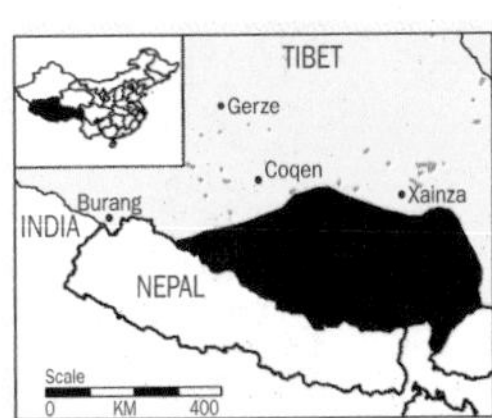

Population in China:
457,700 (1987)
595,700 (2000)
733,900 (2010)
Location: Tibet
Religion: Tibetan Buddhism
Christians: 20

Overview of the Gtsang Tibetans

Countries: China, Nepal, India

Pronunciation: "Git-zung"

Other Names: Xigatse Tibetan, Xigatze, Gyantse, Sagya, Tsang

Population Source: 457,700 (1987 *LAC*); Out of a total Tibetan population of 4,593,330 (1990 census); 50,000 in Nepal (1987 D. Bradley); Also in India

Location: *S Tibet:* A large area roughly north of the entire length of Nepal, including Xigaze and Gyantse counties

Status: Officially included under Tibetan

Language: Sino-Tibetan, Tibeto-Burman, Bodic, Bodish, Tibetan, Central Tibetan

Dialects (19): Dolpo, Reng Pungmo, Tichurong, Kag, Lo, Nar, Gyasumdo, Nubri, Tsum, Kachad, Langtang, Kagate, Jirel, Halung, Kyidgrong, Dingri, Zhiskartse, Gyalrtse, Nadkarrtse

Religion: Tibetan Buddhism, Bon

Christians: 20

Scripture: Tibetan Bible 1948; New Testament 1885

***Jesus* film:** None

Gospel Recordings: None

Christian Broadcasting: None

ROPAL code: TIC01

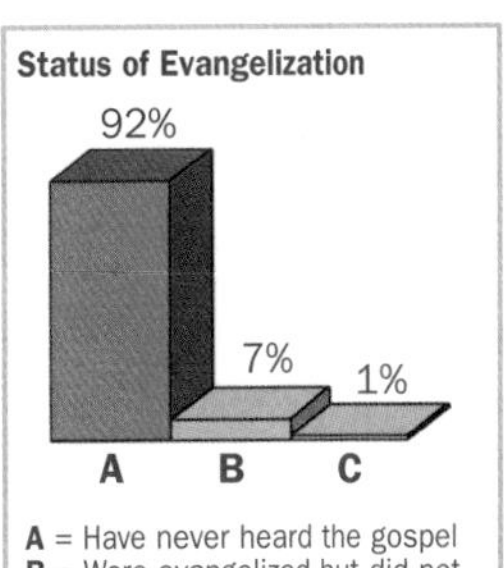

A = Have never heard the gospel
B = Were evangelized but did not become Christians
C = Are adherents to any form of Christianity

Tibetan, Jone 藏(遮呢)

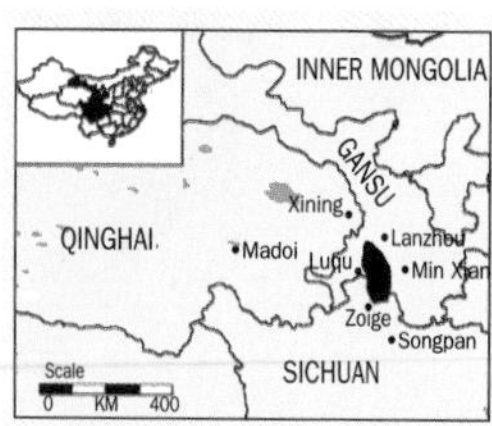

Population in China:
77,000 (1987)
100,200 (2000)
123,400 (2010)
Location: Gansu, Sichuan
Religion: Tibetan Buddhism
Christians: 200

Overview of the Jone Tibetans

Countries: China

Pronunciation: "Joe-nee"

Other Names: Choni, Chona, Chone, Jone, Cone, Zhuoni Tibetan

Population Source:
77,000 (1987 *LAC*);
Out of a total Tibetan population of 4,593,330 (1990 census)

Location: *S Gansu:* In and around Jone and Lintan counties; Also in *N Sichuan*

Status:
Officially included under Tibetan

Language: Sino-Tibetan, Tibeto-Burman, Bodic, Bodish, Tibetan, Northern Tibetan

Dialects: 0

Religion:
Tibetan Buddhism, Christianity

Christians: 200

Scripture: None

***Jesus* film:** None

Gospel Recordings: None

Christian Broadcasting: None

ROPAL code:
CDA00; TIC01; KHG06

Status of Evangelization

A = Have never heard the gospel
B = Were evangelized but did not become Christians
C = Are adherents to any form of Christianity

Location: Approximately 100,000 speakers of the Jone Tibetan language inhabit Jone County in the southwestern part of Gansu Province. A small number live in the adjacent parts of northern Sichuan. Some publications have incorrectly given their location as the "Yunnan-Tibet border."[1] Their name was previously spelled *Choni*, and they still appear in many publications by that name. The To River flows through Jone County. One traveler described the location: "Nowhere else [in Gansu] are there such forests, and the scenery is unsurpassed."[2]

Identity: Few have heard of the existence of the Jone Tibetans. In 1928 Joseph Rock wrote, "I — in common with some 300 million Chinese and perhaps as many foreigners — was totally unaware of the existence of the Choni [Jone]."[3] Little has changed in the 70 years since then. Although they are now officially considered part of the Tibetan nationality, the Jone Tibetans speak their own language and possess their own ethnic and historical identity. The name *Jone* may be of Tibetan origin, meaning *Jo* "pine trees" and *nyi* "two."

Language: The Jone language is related to Khampa Tibetan. Possible dialects or related languages in the area include Dpari, Rebkong, Wayen, and Horke.[4]

History: Jone was the site of an independent kingdom until 1928, when Chinese General Fengyu Shang stripped the prince of his title and confiscated his land.[5] A detailed history of the Jone appeared in a 1928 *National Geographic* article: "The prince represents the twenty-second generation, but is not of direct descent. His ancestors, a Tibetan official family, left their own country and made their way across [Sichuan] and the Min Shan Range... to the Tao River in 1404, conquering and pacifying the tribes and villages on the way. Upon informing the Imperial Court in Peking [Beijing] of their conquest of the territory for the Chinese Empire, they were made hereditary chiefs of Choni and the subjugated tribal lands. At the same time the Emperor, Yung Lo, gave them a seal and the Chinese name Yang."[6] Today many of Jone's inhabitants are still surnamed Yang.[7]

Customs: In the past the Jone prince was selected by rules of succession. If a prince had two sons, the elder succeeded him, and the second became the lama of the monastery. If there was only one son, he took both positions concurrently.[8]

Religion: Most Jone Tibetans are Tibetan Buddhists. Jone formerly contained a huge monastery, "containing 172 buildings and 3,800 monks at its zenith."[9]

Christianity: A 1922 mission report stated, "The prince of Choni alone governs 48 clans and we can easily travel among these clans, as the prince is friendly and would protect us.... If we had the workers to employ we would press toward the west from the line we are now occupying."[10] Today there are about 200 Jone Tibetan believers in Lintan County, to the northwest of Jone County. A church was constructed in 1997 — the first ethnic Tibetan fellowship in Gansu Province. "One woman sold her hair, and another family sold their TV to help build the new church."[11]

Paul Hattaway

Tibetan, Nghari 藏(纳日)

Paul Hattaway

Location: Despite having an approximate population of only 50,000, the Nghari Tibetan language is spoken over a vast area of western Tibet. Nghari Prefecture, which has an area of 306,000 square kilometers (119,340 sq. mi.), lies north of the Himalayas at an average altitude of 4,500 meters (14,760 ft.) above sea level. The Himalayas contain more than 17,000 glaciers. Almost all Nghari Tibetans are nomads, struggling to survive in the bleak conditions.[1]

Identity: The inhabitants of the Nghari region are also known as the *Chang Tang* (Northern Plain) Tibetans. Although they are ethnically Tibetan, they speak a language far removed from other Tibetan varieties. Their lifestyles have changed little over the last thousand years and are still devoid of any technology or machinery.

Language: The Nghari Tibetan language group extends into northwestern Nepal. It has seven dialects, named after their principal towns of habitation.[2] The Tibetan alphabet consists of 30 consonants and four vowels, plus six symbols used for Sanskrit words.

History: Western Tibet is a holy site for the followers of the four religions of Buddhism, Hinduism, Jainism, and Bon. Every year, thousands of pilgrims flock to the sacred Mount Kailas, a 6,714-meter (22,021 ft.) peak near Tibet's border with India and Nepal. During the Cultural Revolution (1966–1976) ten of the 13 monasteries in the region were demolished.

Customs: The favored kind of burial for Tibetans is "wind burial." The corpse is cut into small pieces and laid out on an exposed rock for vultures and ravens to eat. In the 1980s tourists in Lhasa secretly tried to take photographs of the ritual, an act considered a major offense by Tibetans. "An Australian tried to hide up the mountain and take telephoto pics. Whilst hopping around on the skyline, he scared the birds away — an exceptionally evil omen. The irate burial squad gave chase brandishing knives and showered him with rocks." Another group of tourists were "bombarded with rocks, chased with knives or threatened with meaty leg-bones ripped straight off the corpse."[3]

Religion: Immersion in one of two holy lakes south of Mount Kailas is thought to release people from their sins for a lifetime. Pilgrims who trek to the top of the 5,640-meter-high (18,500 ft.) Dolma Pass are believed to be born again in the process. Folk Tibetans believe in a hell divided into eight hot and eight cold levels. Sinners are made to suffer until they have worked off their demerits.

Christianity: The first recorded Tibetan church was built by Jesuit missionaries in Lhasa in 1726. Twenty-seven baptized converts and 60 inquirers attended the church. "At the end of April, 1742, a new convert named Pu Tsering publicly refused to bow before the Dalai Lama.... This threw the town into an uproar.... Twelve of the Christians were flogged with 20 lashes each. The missionaries fled to Nepal, but their church was attacked by a mob who destroyed everything except the church bell."[4] Today there are no known Christians among the Nghari Tibetans.

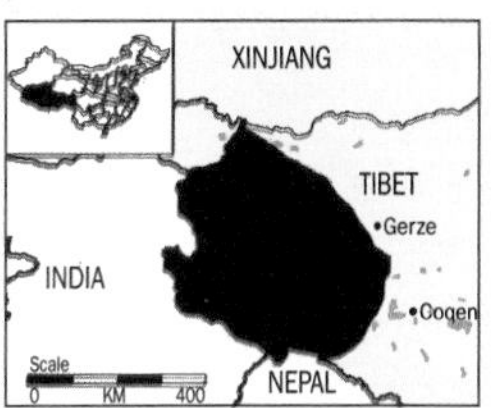

Population in China:
38,400 (1987)
49,900 (2000)
61,500 (2010)
Location: Tibet
Religion: Tibetan Buddhism
Christians: None Known

Overview of the Nghari Tibetans

Countries: China, Nepal

Pronunciation: "Nah-ree-Zung"

Other Names: Nghari, Ngharis, Mngahris, Drokpa, Drokwa

Population Source: 38,400 (1987 *LAC*); Out of a total Tibetan population of 4,593,330 (1990 census); Also in Nepal

Location: *W Tibet:* Nghari Prefecture: Rutog, Gartok, Zamda, Burang, Coqen, and Gerze; A few speakers also in Xigaze Prefecture

Status: Officially included under Tibetan

Language: Sino-Tibetan, Tibeto-Burman, Bodic, Bodish, Tibetan, Central Tibetan

Dialects (7): Rutog, Gartok, Zamda, Burang, Coqen, Gerze, Xigaze

Religion: Tibetan Buddhism, Shamanism

Christians: None known

Scripture: Tibetan Bible 1948; New Testament 1885; Portions 1862

***Jesus* film:** None

Gospel Recordings: None

Christian Broadcasting: None

ROPAL code: TIC03

Status of Evangelization

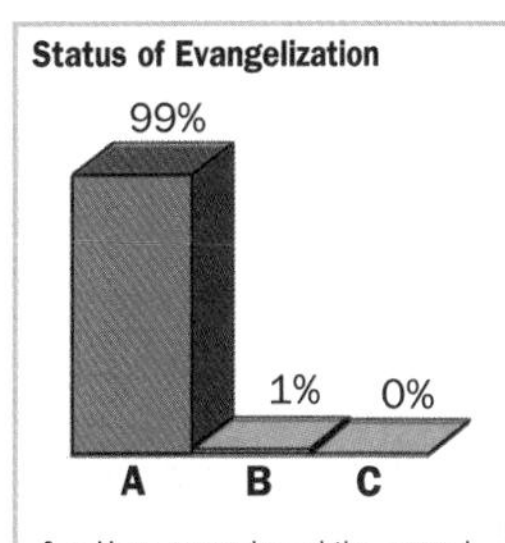

A = Have never heard the gospel
B = Were evangelized but did not become Christians
C = Are adherents to any form of Christianity

Tibetan, Zhongdian 藏(中甸)

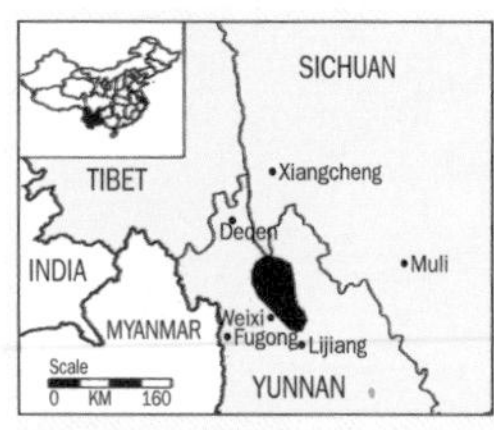

Population in China:
60,740 (1990)
74,800 (2000)
92,100 (2010)
Location: Yunnan
Religion: Tibetan Buddhism
Christians: 2,000

Overview of the Zhongdian Tibetans

Countries: China, Switzerland

Pronunciation: "Jong-dee-an"

Other Names: Zang, Khampa, Chung-tien Tibetan, Chongtien, Rgyalathang

Population Source:
60,740 (1990 AMO);
Out of a total Tibetan population of 4,593,330 (1990 census);
A few families in Switzerland

Location: *N Yunnan:* Zhongdian (50,302), Weixi (8,581), and Lijiang (1,849) counties; Possibly also located in counties in NW Yunnan

Status:
Officially included under Tibetan

Language: Sino-Tibetan, Tibeto-Burman, Bodic, Bodish, Tibetan, Northern Tibetan

Dialects: 0

Religion:
Tibetan Buddhism, Christianity

Christians: 2,000

Scripture: Tibetan Bible 1948; New Testament 1885; Portions 1862

***Jesus* film:** None

Gospel Recordings:
Zang: Xiaozhongdian; Zang: Weixi

Christian Broadcasting: None

ROPAL code: ATF00

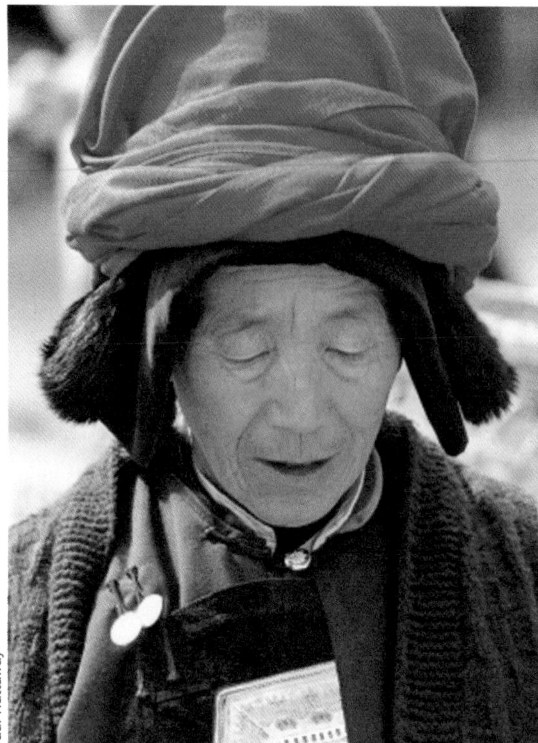

Paul Hattaway

Location: Approximately 75,000 linguistically distinct Tibetans inhabit villages in Zhongdian, Weixi, and Lijiang counties in the northern part of Yunnan Province. According to the 1990 national census, 50,302 live in Zhongdian County, 8,581 in Weixi, and 1,849 in Lijiang. The extent of their territory seems to extend to the Hengduan Pass between the towns of Zhongdian and Deqen, located farther to the north. Beyond the pass the dialect changes markedly. Hengduan literally means "cut off vertically."[1] In autumn, the Zhongdian Plateau abounds with colorful flowers. "Azaleas in full bloom on the sheep pastures provide a cheering contrast while, higher up, maple saplings signal in a blaze of reds and oranges."[2] A few Zhongdian Tibetan families have reportedly migrated to Switzerland.[3]

Identity: The Zhongdian Tibetans wear a different traditional dress from the Deqen Tibetans and all other Tibetans. Zhongdian women prefer to wear a cone-shaped headdress which they wrap inside a scarf.

Language: Researchers who have traveled into Tibetan areas of northern Yunnan Province report that the dialect variation between Zhongdian and Deqen is different enough to seriously affect mutual intelligibility between Tibetans from the two areas. Zhongdian Tibetan, which is related to the Khampa Tibetan group, has experienced much greater exposure to Chinese than the Deqen Tibetan language.[4]

History: Local legends say the ancestors of the Zhongdian Tibetans were Qiang people who came to Zhongdian, fought and overcame the locals in battle, and eventually became assimilated to Tibetan ways. This would explain the linguistic, clothing, and cultural differences they have today with other Tibetan groups.[5]

Customs: The inhabitants of the Zhongdian area live in two-story wooden houses. Except for a few new roads and electricity lines, life has not changed much in this remote part of China.

Religion: The great majority of Zhongdian Tibetans adhere to Tibetan Buddhism. The large Jietang Songlin Monastery, which houses several hundred monks, is located just to the north of Zhongdian Township.

Christianity: French Catholic missionaries commenced work among the Zhongdian Tibetans in the late 1800s. Today, a large French-style cathedral still stands at Tchronteu, near Weixi.[6] "The purpose of the monks of Saint Bernard was to minister to all in need who traveled over the high mountain trails in trade and commerce. Their most valuable helpers were huge Saint Bernard dogs — half Swiss and half Tibetan. In the city of Weixi, the monks, helped by the Cluny Sisters of Saint Joseph and two Tibetan nuns, ran a mission school attended by children from Sikkim, Nepal, Bhutan and Tibet."[7] A Catholic priest is responsible for 9,500 Tibetan believers in his area. Of these, about 7,500 belong to the Deqen Tibetan group and 2,000 to the Zhongdian Tibetans.

Tibetan, Zhugqu 藏(竹曲)

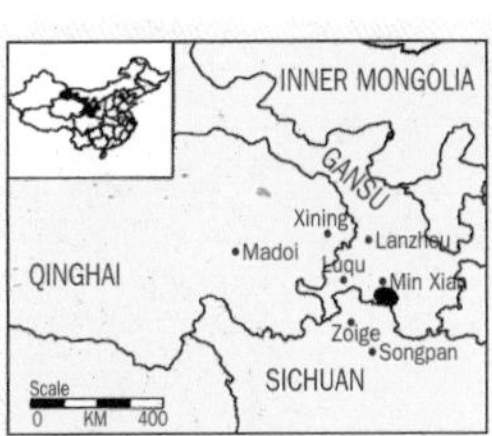

Population in China:
29,500 (1987)
38,300 (2000)
47,300 (2010)
Location: Gansu
Religion: Polytheism
Christians: None Known

Overview of the Zhugqu Tibetans

Countries: China

Pronunciation: "Zhoog-choo"

Other Names: Zhugqu, Hbrugchu, Zhouqu Tibetan, Chou-ch'ua Tibetan, Brugchu

Population Source: 29,500 (1987 *LAC*); Out of a total Tibetan population of 4,593,330 (1990 census)

Location: *SE Gansu:* Zhugqu County in Gaanan Prefecture

Status: Officially included under Tibetan

Language: Sino-Tibetan, Tibeto-Burman, Bodic, Bodish, Tibetan, Northern Tibetan

Dialects: 0

Religion: Polytheism, Tibetan Buddhism, Animism, Bon

Christians: None known

Scripture: None

***Jesus* film:** None

Gospel Recordings: None

Christian Broadcasting: None

ROPAL code: CDA01; KHG05

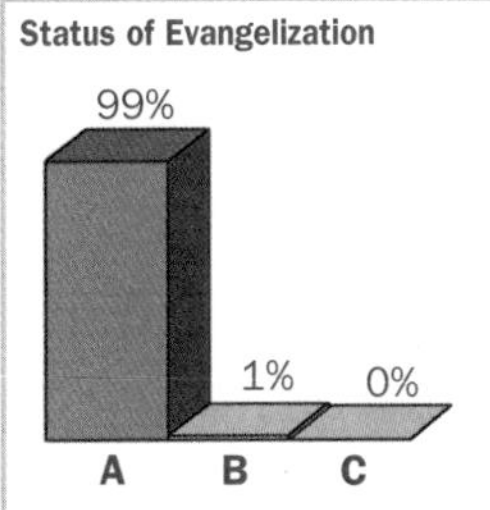

Location: More than 38,000 Zhugqu Tibetans live in Zhugqu County, in the Gaanan Prefecture of Gansu Province.[1] They are the most easterly of all Tibetan peoples in China. The Bai Long (White Dragon) River flows through mountainous Zhugqu County.

Identity: The Tibetans of Zhugqu are counted as part of the Tibetan nationality, but along with several other groups in southern Gansu — such as the Baima and the Boyu Tibetans — they are a specific ethnolinguistic group with their own language and customs.

Language: The Zhugqu language is a form of Khampa Tibetan, although it has great differences with other Khampa varieties farther to the south. The Zhugqu Tibetans cannot understand the speech of their neighbors, the Jone Tibetans, even though both are reported to be Khampa languages.

History: The Zhugqu Tibetans have a long history. A Chinese writer remarked, "Their forebears fled from the horrors of war (during the Southern Song Dynasty, 1127–1279) and eventually settled here and in surrounding areas, where they have multiplied over the generations."[2]

Customs: The homes of the Zhugqu Tibetans are one-story, built of mud, stone, and wood. Due to the lack of level ground, "nearly every household has a flat platform which serves many purposes.... Some people, when they walk out their own door, are in fact standing on the neighbor's roof."[3] Every year, usually in the fifth lunar month, the Zhugqu Tibetan men celebrate the Arrow-Planting Ceremony. Women are not allowed to participate. The men ride horses up to the mountaintop and plant prayer flags on the summit. "A respected elder of the tribe directs the sacrificial rites. Each in turn lays roasted flour, butter, barley and tea on to a pile of heaped-up cypress branches, which are then set alight and burned. These are offerings to the mountain god."[4]

Religion: The Zhugqu Tibetans are polytheists. Their pre-Buddhist belief of Bon includes the belief that mountains are holy. They believe powerful demons live inside the highest mountains. "They pray to the mountain god to make their hopes and wishes come true: peace, security, thriving livestock and abundant harvests."[5] There are different legends explaining the origin of the Arrow-Planting Festival. One states that there was a "certain man of dignity and fame who, after he died, was found by the gods to be too bad for heaven but too good for hell. Accordingly, he stayed on the earth, creating a great deal of mischief and disturbing the peoples' peace. Eventually a Living Buddha took pity on him and settled him on the mountain, directing him to give up evil and devote himself to good."[6]

Christianity: The Zhugqu Tibetans have never been reached with the gospel. Few members of this group have any awareness of the existence of Christianity. There are no Christian communities in the region, and no record exists of any missionary activity among them at any stage throughout their long history.

Paul Hattaway

Torgut 特股

Location: More than 146,000 Torgut Mongolians live alongside Kazak and Uygur communities in Xinjiang. Many live in the Junggar Basin which is more verdant than the vast Tarim Basin to the south. The Junggar landscape consists primarily of grasslands which are amply watered by the region's abundant rainfall.

Identity: The Torgut are an ethnic subgroup of the Oirat. The Oirat were acknowledged separately in the Chinese census, then officially included in the Mongolian nationality. The Torguts speak basically the same language as the Oirat, but they view themselves as ethnically separate. They have been described as "a law unto themselves, with their Tibetan religion, Mongolian language, and unspeakable customs."[1]

Language: The Torgut language is a variant of Oirat, but speakers of the two groups can converse with relative ease.

History: Torgut history closely mirrors that of the Oirat. They migrated from Xinjiang to Russia, where they lived until 1771 when Russian pressure forced most Torgut to flee back to China. Thousands died of starvation or were killed and plundered by bandits on the return journey to Xinjiang.[2]

Customs: Folk dancing is a favorite pastime of the Torgut. The *bielgee*, or "dance of the body," originated during the Qing (Manchu) Dynasty. Large public gatherings were outlawed because the Manchus feared a Mongol uprising. Traditional dances had to be performed privately inside the yurt where there was little leg room. The dancers expressed themselves by using their arms, legs, and other parts of their bodies in rhythmic movements.[3]

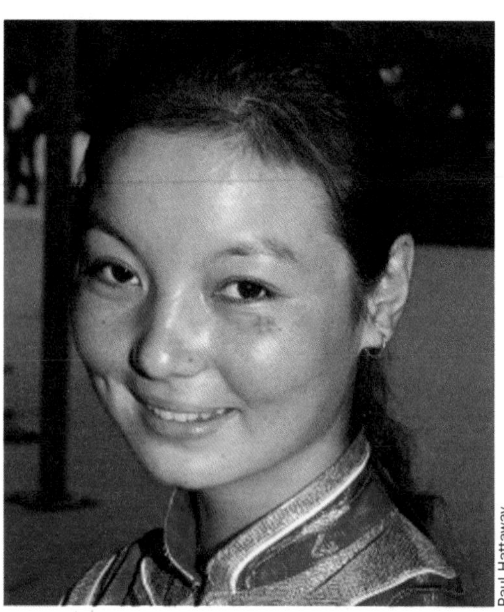
Paul Hattaway

Religion: Although all Torgut claim to be Tibetan Buddhists, many practice shamanism. The black magic and secret arts of the Mongol shamans were vividly described 700 years ago, when Marco Polo challenged the Great Khan to become a Christian. He replied, "On what grounds do you desire me to become a Christian?... You see that these sorcerers do what they will. When I sit at the table the cups in the middle of the hall come to me full of wine or other beverages without anyone touching them, and I drink from them. They banish bad weather in any direction they choose and perform many marvels. And, as you know, their idols speak and give them predictions as they ask.... If I am converted to the faith of Christ and become a Christian... these sorcerers, who with their arts and sciences achieve such great results, could easily compass my death."[4]

Christianity: There is no church today among the Torgut of China, despite the past efforts of self-sacrificing missionaries. During the Boxer Rebellion of 1900, "seven Alliance missionaries and seven children tried to flee on camels into Mongolia. Robbers intercepted them and took everything, even their clothes. In the trauma two of the missionaries gave birth. French missionary priests found the fourteen and the two infants naked in the desert and subsisting on roots. The priests gave them covering and took them back to the Catholic mission station.... The Boxers killed them with guns and swords, then set fire to the church."[5] The Scriptures have never been translated into Torgut.

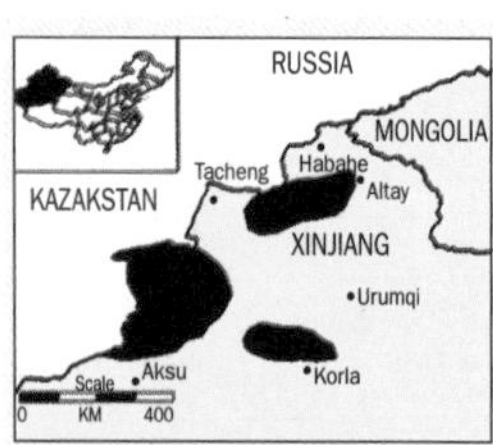

Population in China:
106,000 (1987)
146,000 (2000)
188,300 (2010)
Location: Xinjiang
Religion: Tibetan Buddhism
Christians: None Known

Overview of the Torgut

Countries: China

Pronunciation: "Tour-goot"

Other Names: Torgot

Population Source:
106,000 (1987 *LAC*);
Out of a total Mongol population of 4,806,849 (1990 census)

Location: *Xinjiang:* The Torgut primarily live in the Junggar Basin of northern Xinjiang, the Ili Kazak Prefecture, and the area northwest of Korla in central Xinjiang.

Status: Officially included under Mongolian

Language: Altaic, Mongolian, Eastern Mongolian, Oirat-Khalkha, Oirat-Kalmyk-Darkhat

Dialects: 0

Religion:
Tibetan Buddhism, Shamanism

Christians: None known

Scripture: None

***Jesus* film:** None[6]

Gospel Recordings: None

Christian Broadcasting: None

ROPAL code: None

Status of Evangelization

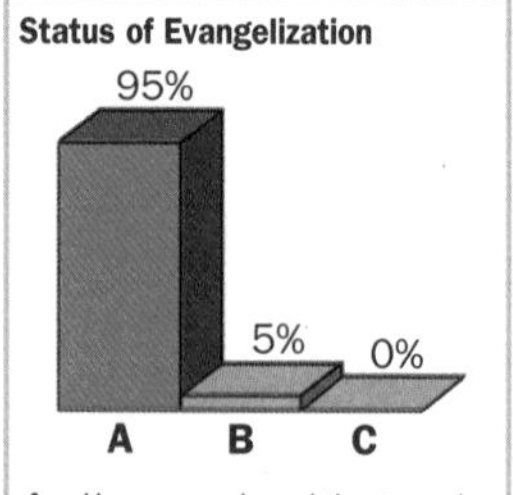

A = Have never heard the gospel
B = Were evangelized but did not become Christians
C = Are adherents to any form of Christianity

Tu 土

Population in China:
159,624 (1990)
199,800 (2000)
250,200 (2010)
Location: Qinghai, Gansu
Religion: Tibetan Buddhism
Christians: None Known

Overview of the Tu

Countries: China

Pronunciation: "Too"

Other Names: Huzhu, White Mongols

Population Source: 191,624 (1990 census);[1] 159,426 (1982 census); 77,349 (1964 census); 53,277 (1954 census)

Location: *E Qinghai:* Huzhu and Datong counties; A few in Ledu, Menyuan, and Tianzhu counties; *Gansu:* Yongdeng and Linxia districts

Status: An official minority of China

Language: Altaic, Mongolian, Eastern Mongolian, Mongour

Literacy: 42%

Dialects (11): Aragwa, Fulannara, Khalchiguor, Linxia, Mingho, Naringuor, Sanchuan, Datong, Tienyu, Wuyangpu, Yongjing

Religion: Tibetan Buddhism, Shamanism

Christians: None known

Scripture: None

***Jesus* film:** None

Gospel Recordings: None

Christian Broadcasting: None

ROPAL code: MJG00

Status of Evangelization

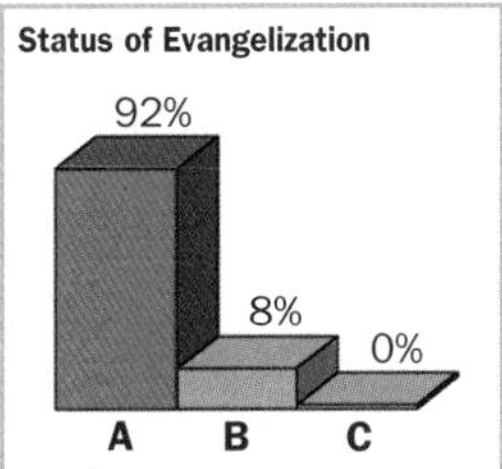

A = Have never heard the gospel
B = Were evangelized but did not become Christians
C = Are adherents to any form of Christianity

Dwayne Graybill

Location: Approximately 200,000 Tu live in north central China, especially in the Huzhu Tu Autonomous County in Qinghai Province. Others are scattered throughout other parts of Qinghai, as well as in neighboring areas of Gansu Province.[2]

Identity: The Tu — who are one of China's official minorities — believe they are descended from white feathers that were left behind by a flock of cranes.[3] The Tibetans consider the Tu to be a part of the Tibetan nationality and accuse the Chinese of trying to weaken the unity of the Tibetan world by granting the Tu a separate identity. However, there is no doubt that the Tu are distinct from the Tibetans historically, culturally, and linguistically. There are two distinct languages spoken among the Tu: Huzhu, which is profiled here, and Mongour, which is covered separately.

Language: Sixty percent of Tu vocabulary is still Mongolian in nature after 800 years of isolation. In 1979 a Tu script based on the Roman alphabet was created. It soon became popular among the Tu. The script is taught in local Tu schools today. A massive 70,000-entry Tu-Chinese dictionary was published in 1988. There are 11 different dialects within the Tu language. The Tu living in Datong County can now only speak Chinese. In addition, more than 4,000 ethnic Tu people speak Bonan as their mother tongue.[4]

History: The Tu were first recorded in AD 1227, when a Mongol garrison was dispatched to control the area that the Tu still inhabit today. The troops remained there and later married women from local tribes. A bronze statue of the first Mongol general still stands in the Youning Monastery. Another historian states, "Their ancestors are believed to be the Tuguhuns who moved in the third and fourth centuries to Gansu and Qinghai provinces and mingled with local people of different nationalities. Places where the Tu people live in compact communities are still called Tuhun in the Tu language."[5]

Customs: Until recently Tu girls were expected to be married by the age of 15. After that age, the girl was considered "married to heaven." If a Tu woman is still single by her mid-20s, she is allowed to sleep around, thus saving herself from disgrace in the eyes of the community. Any resulting children are raised by the entire Tu village. Unmarried Tu women wear a single ponytail to advertise their status to prospective partners.

Religion: The Tu are ardent followers of Tibetan Buddhism. Their main religious center is the Youning Monastery, founded in 1604. Shamans and mediums are also active among the Tu. The annual Nadun Festival focuses around the *fala*, a Tu medium who "impales himself with as many as 12 iron nails and is possessed by the spirit of the Erlang god."[6]

Christianity: Prior to the forced deportation of missionaries from China in the early 1950s, a handful of Tu Christians attended Han Chinese churches in the area.[7] Although there are no known Christians among the Tu today, there are about 400 Han Chinese believers living in the mountains 25 kilometers from Huzhu. They interact with the Tu and even speak the Tu language.

Tuerke 土而克

Dwayne Graybill

Location: In 1980 R. F. Hahn reported the existence of at least 30 Tuerke households, numbering approximately 120 people.[1] Another source lists a 1991 population of 200 Tuerke.[2] There are probably also some Tuerke living in Kazakstan. The Tuerke in China live near the city of Yining (formerly called Kuldja) within the Ili Valley in the northwest Xinjiang Uygur Autonomous Region. Located 700 kilometers (432 mi.) west of the provincial capital, Yining is predominantly a Kazak and Uzbek town. Ethnic unrest between Xinjiang's Muslim population and the Han Chinese creates a tension in this part of the country. "Chinese appear uneasy here and warn against staying out after dark, when knives are fast and streets unsafe.... The local Kazaks and Uzbeks can be a rough bunch (regularly drunk in the evenings and occasionally involved in street fights) but very friendly towards foreigners, whom they put in a different category from those in authority."[3]

Identity: The Tuerke, who are ethnically and linguistically distinct from all other peoples in the region, were only "discovered" by the Chinese in 1956. Their name is a generic term for all Turkic peoples. They are also known as the *Ili Turki*, named after their location.

Language: Despite the small population of the Tuerke, their language has been extensively researched.[4] Tuerke is now only spoken by middle-aged and older people.[5] Because younger Tuerke intermarry with the Uygur and Kazak, the use of the Tuerke language is rapidly declining. Some linguists believe Tuerke is a link between the Chagtai and Kypchak dialects of Uzbek.[6] Tuerke has also been greatly influenced by Kazak and Uygur and has borrowed words from the Arabic, Persian, Chinese, and Russian languages.

History: The oral history of the Tuerke states that they migrated from the Ferghana Valley — in today's Uzbekistan or Kyrgyzstan — about 200 years ago. The Ili Valley has long been a focal point for bandits. The Russians, angered at China's inability to control the border area, invaded Ili in 1871. They returned the region to China in March 1882. In 1962 there were several major China-Soviet military clashes along the Ili River.

Customs: Although the Tuerke possess their own set of customs, they are gradually replacing them with those of the Kazaks and Uzbeks. The Tuerke are fond of dancing and telling folk tales. In keeping with Islamic regulations, Tuerke women are required to wear veils; these are not the full face veils worn in the Middle East.

Religion: All Tuerke are Sunni Muslims. Although they do not have their own mosques, the Tuerke are faithful in observing Islamic law and prayer times.

Christianity: The far northwestern part of Xinjiang — which was formerly part of the Eastern Turkestan alliance — was one of the most missionary-neglected regions in China prior to 1949. There are few Christian communities in the area today, and there are no believers among the Tuerke. Gospel radio programs, aired in the Uzbek, Kazak, and Uygur languages, are the best opportunity the Tuerke have of hearing the gospel in a language they understand.

Population in China:
120 (1980)
189 (2000)
244 (2010)
Location: Xinjiang
Religion: Islam
Christians: None Known

Overview of the Tuerke

Countries: China, Kazakstan

Pronunciation: "Too-er-ke"

Other Names: Ili Tuerke, Ili Turki, T'urk, Ili Turk

Population Source: 120 (1980 R. F. Hahn); Probably also in Kazakstan

Location: *NW Xinjiang:* Approximately 30 households in the Ili Valley near Yining in the Ili Kazak County

Status: Unidentified; Possibly not included under any official minority

Language: Altaic, Turkic, Eastern Turkic

Dialects: 0

Religion: Sunni Islam

Christians: None known

Scripture: None

***Jesus* film:** None

Gospel Recordings: None

Christian Broadcasting: None

ROPAL code: ILI00

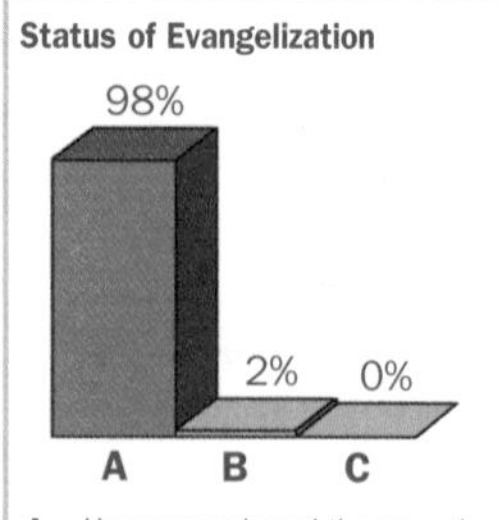

Tujia 土家

Location: More than 5.7 million members of the Tujia nationality were reported in the 1990 census. They live at the juncture of Guizhou, Hunan, Hubei, and Sichuan provinces.[1] The population given for the Tujia doubled between 1982 — when they numbered 2.8 million — and 1990. This was due more to the redefinition of minority status by the Chinese authorities than to biological growth.

Identity: The Tujia, whose name means "natives" or "original inhabitants," are one of China's officially recognized nationalities. Most Tujia today are ethnically indistinguishable from the Han Chinese. The vast majority have been assimilated since the Ming Dynasty (1368–1644) when they were sent as soldiers to fight Japanese pirates on the east coast of China.[2]

Language: Only 170,000 Tujia (approximately 3%) are able to speak their language. The rest speak Chinese or the local dialect of Ghao-Xong. Speakers of Tujia are concentrated mainly in the Youshuihe, Mengdonghe, and Xichehe river areas of the Xiangxi Prefecture in Hunan Province. In these areas education is conducted in the Tujia language until the third grade; after that, Mandarin is used. It is possible the Tujia once possessed a script which may have been lost as they assimilated to Chinese culture. In 1890 the British Consul Borne discovered a document in an unknown script. Borne was located at Tchong-Kiu — present day Zhong County in eastern Sichuan — north of the Tujia area.[3] The speakers of Northern Tujia call themselves *Bizika*,[4] while Southern Tujia speakers call themselves *Mozhihei*.

History: There are several theories about the origin of the Tujia. Some say they are the descendants of the ancient Ba tribe. Many Tujia still call themselves *Ba*. By the early 900s the Tujia were already recognized as a distinct people group in western Hunan.[5]

Paul Hattaway

Customs: One of the common motifs on Tujia embroidery is the bull's eye. This refers to a Tujia legend, which relates how one autumn day a herd of bulls was attacked by a tiger while grazing on a mountain slope. "At first sight of the tiger, the bulls were startled, even frightened, but they soon regained their composure. The bulls then charged at the tiger, which fled in panic. To this day the Tujia regard the bull's eye as a symbol of the victory of good over evil. Other common motifs include the snake and the white tiger since these were the totems of the Ba tribe."[6]

Religion: The Tujia of Guizhou practice *nuo* (exorcism) ceremonies. The Tujia evoke the spirits of Fuxi and Nuwa — the first human beings according to Chinese legend. The ceremony includes supernatural feats such as climbing ladders of sharp knives and walking on hot coals or glass.[7]

Christianity: Roman Catholic and Protestant missionaries first penetrated Tujia areas with the gospel near the end of the nineteenth century and established a small number of churches, schools, and medical clinics among the Tujia. Today it is estimated that there are between 13,000[8] and 30,000[9] Tujia Christians, a tiny proportion (0.22 - 0.41%) for such a large group. There are no Scriptures, gospel recordings, or *Jesus* film available in the Tujia language.[10]

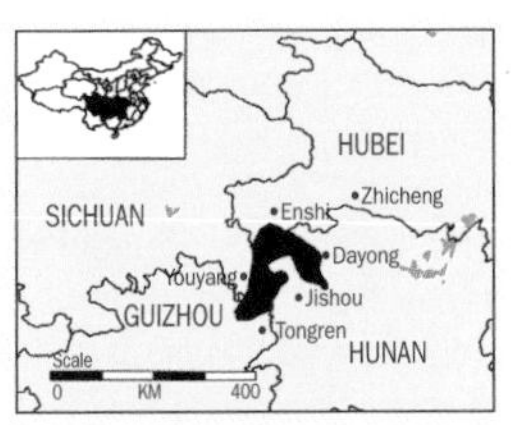

Population in China:
5,700,223 (1990)
7,353,300 (2000)
9,485,700 (2010)
Location: Hunan, Hubei, Sichuan, Guizhou
Religion: Animism
Christians: 30,000

Overview of the Tujia

Countries: China

Pronunciation: "Too-jeeah"

Other Names: Tuchia, Ba, Northern Tujia, Bizika, Tudja, Biseka, Pi-tse-k'a, Bizeka

Population Source: 5,704,223 (1990 census);[11] 2,834,732 (1982 census); 524,755 (1964 census)

Location: *NW Hunan; S Hubei; SE Sichuan; NE Guizhou*

Status: An official minority of China

Language: Sino-Tibetan, Tibeto-Burman, Burmese-Lolo, Lolo, Tujia

Dialects (2): Longshan, Baojing

Literacy: 67%

Religion: Animism, No Religion, Ancestor Worship, Polytheism, Christianity

Christians: 30,000

Scripture: None

***Jesus* film:** None

Gospel Recordings: None

Christian Broadcasting: None

ROPAL code: TJI00

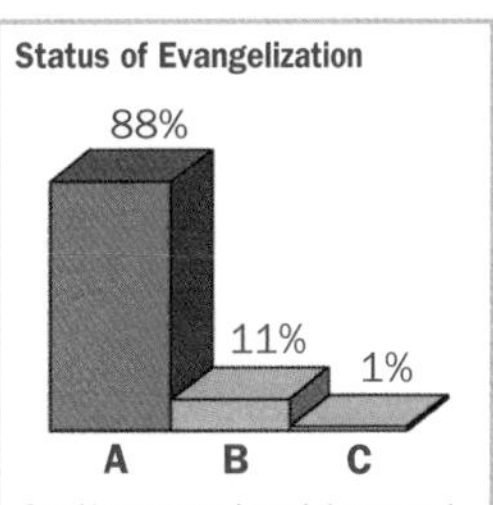

A = Have never heard the gospel
B = Were evangelized but did not become Christians
C = Are adherents to any form of Christianity

Tulao 土老

Population in China:
4,000 (1997)
4,140 (2000)
4,750 (2010)
Location: Yunnan
Religion: Animism
Christians: None Known

Overview of the Tulao

Countries: China, Vietnam

Pronunciation: "Too-laow"

Other Names:
Thu Lao, Budai, Bu Dai

Population Source:
4,000 (1997 AMO);
Out of a total Zhuang population of 15,489,630 (1990 census);
500 in Vietnam (1997)

Location: *SE Yunnan:* Maguan, Wenshan, Malipo, and Kaiyuan counties

Status:
Officially included under Zhuang

Language: Daic, Tai, Central Tai

Dialects: 0

Religion: Animism, Ancestor Worship, Daoism

Christians: None known

Scripture: None

***Jesus* film:** None

Gospel Recordings: None

Christian Broadcasting: None

ROPAL code: None

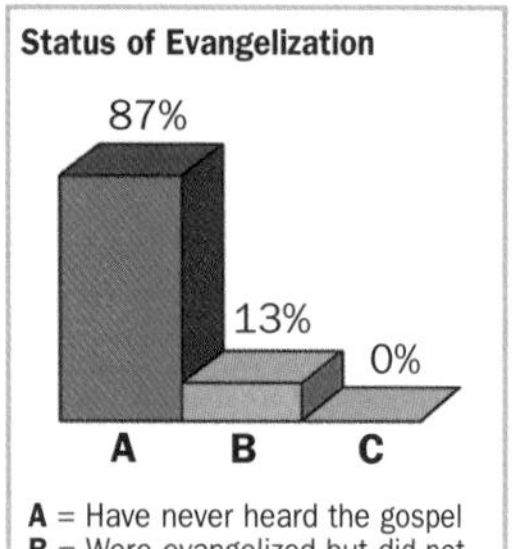

A = Have never heard the gospel
B = Were evangelized but did not become Christians
C = Are adherents to any form of Christianity

Location: Approximately 4,000 Tulao people live in southeastern Yunnan Province. They inhabit the villages of Xinhuilong and Luchaichong in Maguan County. Others are reported to live in Wenshan, Malipo, and Kaiyuan counties. In northern Vietnam the Tulao live in communities immediately facing their counterparts on the Chinese side of the border. They live in two villages in two different districts of Vietnam's Lao Cai Province: Thai Giang Sau Village in Ta Gia Khau Township of Muong Khuong district; and Doil Village in Xa Nam San Township of Bac Ha District. Their homeland is north of the Red River in an area that juts northward into China.

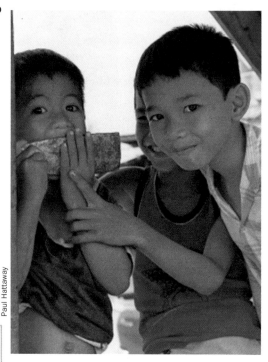

Paul Hattaway

Identity: Although they are a group with their own language, customs, and ethnicity, the Tulao in China have been placed under the massive Zhuang nationality. Because of this, they have become largely forgotten amid the numerous ethnic groups. Recent studies in China have brought them into the limelight after decades of obscurity.[1] In Vietnam they have been included under the generic *Tay* minority group. The Tulao do not refer to themselves by that name but use the autonym *Bu Dai*.

Language: Tulao is a member of the Central Tai linguistic family, related to Nung. Anthony Diller described Tulao as "a Southern Zhuang or Nung-type variety."[2] There are numerous Central Tai varieties in China who have been officially included in the Zhuang nationality. In some cases these do not constitute distinct languages or ethnic groups. In the case of the Tulao, however, they have their own ethnicity, history, and customs.

History: The Tulao were probably part of the large migration of Tai-speaking peoples who moved into southern Yunnan and Southeast Asia at various stages over the past 1,000 years. The Taiping Rebellion of 1851–1864 caused tens of thousands of people to flee the carnage that was taking place as the Taiping troops marched throughout southern China. The leader of the Taiping armies, Hong Xiuquan, believed he was the brother of Jesus Christ and that he was called by God to set up an earthly kingdom in China. The Tulao may well have migrated to their present location at that time, but this cannot be proven as the Tulao have no written account of their past.

Customs: In the past, the Tulao in Vietnam say, they crossed the border into China for weddings, funerals, and other festival occasions. The Sino-Vietnam war in 1979 brought great tension between the two Communist governments which caused interaction between the Tulao to cease. The Tulao have their own festivals, customs, and marriage and funeral practices.

Religion: The Tulao are animists. Buddhism has not reached their part of the world. There are also elements of Daoism and ancestor worship among the Tulao, probably as a result of Han Chinese influence.

Christianity: There are no known Christians among the Tulao on either side of the China-Vietnam border. Few have been exposed to the gospel.

Tushu 土数

Jamin Pelkey

Location: More than 5,000 Tushu people live in Weining County of northwest Guizhou Province and in adjoining areas of Yiliang County in northeast Yunnan Province. One researcher estimates 2,000 Tushu people live on the Yunnan side of the border.[1]

Identity: The Tushu are not the same ethnic group as the Tusu, even though both are officially included under the Yi nationality in China. The Tushu, who speak an Eastern Yi language, live a considerable distance apart from the Western Yi-speaking Tusu.

Language: The Tushu language is part of the Eastern Yi branch of Tibeto-Burman. Some publications have overstated the level of cultural and linguistic assimilation among the Yi groups in Guizhou Province. In one book it was stated, "Today in Guizhou only approximately 30 per cent of the Yi people speak their own language, the rest use Chinese."[2] An official Chinese publication, the *Weining Yizu Huizu Miaozu Zizhixian Minzuzhi* (The Annals of the Minority Nationalities of the Weining Yi, Hui, and Miao Autonomous County), however, states that 85% of the Yi in Weining County still speak their native tongue and use it daily. Only in those districts where there is a smaller concentration of Yi (i.e., districts with less than 1,000 Yi) has the language been lost.[3]

History: Although many people presume the various Yi groups were the original inhabitants of the Weining area, the Yi themselves claim that when they first entered the region "they found a people already in possession of the land, whom they call the *P'u*, and whom the Chinese today speak of as the *Yao-ren*.... The Nosu [Yi] say the Yao-ren moved to Szechuan [Sichuan]."[4]

Customs: Because of the poor quality of the soil, the Tushu cannot grow rice or most vegetables. Instead, the main crops in the area are corn and potatoes. In many places they also brew their own liquor, which is central to their culture.

Religion: Polytheism is the main religion of the Tushu. Spirit priests, or shamans, were once prevalent in their villages but are now rarely seen. Missionary Samuel Pollard, who worked in the area extensively in the early 1900s, noted in his diary: "Had a visit from a Nosu Wizard. He believes that chanting sacred books is expiation for the sins of dead people. In olden times, he told me, they had a book of chanting by which Wind and Rain could be called. But during the Mohammedan Rebellion the book was lost and has never been found again. They believe that all people go to Hades and that there is no Heaven. People saved by chanting come back again."[5]

Christianity: There are at least 400 Tushu Christians today, especially in the Weining area. In 1907 Pollard started to see the firstfruits of large-scale turning to Christ among the Yi of Guizhou. Not only the slaves but the landowners themselves were being saved. He wrote,"A blind Nosu [Yi] here who has become a Christian has released all his slaves and burnt the papers that bound them to him. He told them that they could remain as tenants. He has persuaded his nephew to do the same and other families have followed suit. Some he has persuaded to destroy their idols."[6]

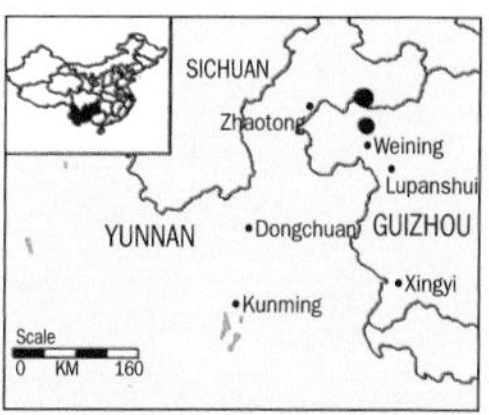

Population in China:
5,000 (1999)
5,120 (2000)
6,430 (2010)
Location: Guizhou, Yunnan
Religion: Polytheism
Christians: 400

Overview of the Tushu

Countries: China
Pronunciation: "Too-shoo"
Other Names: Tushupo, Tusu, Bai Yi, White Yi
Population Source: 5,000 (1999 AMO); 2,000 in Yunnan (1999 J. Pelkey); Out of a total Yi population of 6,572,173 (1990 census)
Location: *NW Guizhou:* Weining County; *NE Yunnan:* Yiliang County
Status: Officially included under Yi
Language: Sino-Tibetan, Tibeto-Burman, Burmese-Lolo, Lolo, Northern Lolo, Yi, Eastern Yi
Dialects: 0
Religion: Polytheism, Animism, Ancestor Worship, Shamanism, Christianity
Christians: 400
Scripture: None
***Jesus* film:** None
Gospel Recordings: None
Christian Broadcasting: None
ROPAL code: None

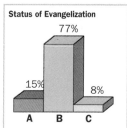

Status of Evangelization

	A	B	C
%	15%	77%	8%

A = Have never heard the gospel
B = Were evangelized but did not become Christians
C = Are adherents to any form of Christianity

Tusu 土族

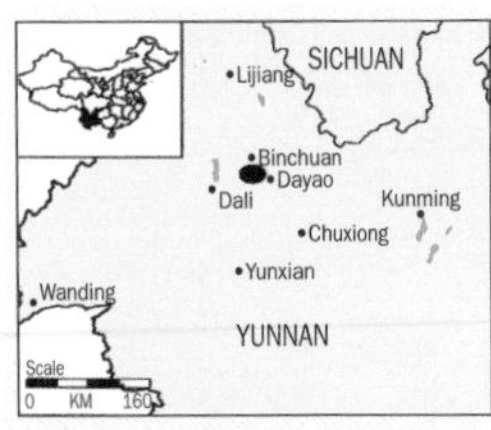

Population in China:
31,000 (1999)
31,750 (2000)
39,900 (2010)
Location: Yunnan
Religion: Polytheism
Christians: 20

Overview of the Tusu

Countries: China

Pronunciation: "Too-soo"

Other Names: Tusupo, Tu, Turen, Tuzu

Population Source: 31,000 (1999 J. Pelkey); Out of a total Yi population of 6,572,173 (1990 census)

Location: *N Yunnan:* Xiangyun (15,000), Binchuan (13,000), and Dayao (3,000) counties

Status: Officially included under Yi

Language: Sino-Tibetan, Tibeto-Burman, Burmese-Lolo, Lolo, Northern Lolo, Yi, Western Yi

Dialects: 0

Religion: Polytheism, Animism, Ancestor Worship, Christianity

Christians: 20

Scripture: None

***Jesus* film:** None

Gospel Recordings: None

Christian Broadcasting: None

ROPAL code: None

Jamin Pelkey

Location: Approximately 31,000 Tusu people live in the western central part of Yunnan Province in southwest China. In Xiangyun County the Tusu inhabit the Da'aonai Community of Luwu District; the Jindan, Zhifang, and Dacang communities of Xiazhuang District; the Jiangwei Community of Pupeng District; and all the communities within Dongshan District. In Dayao County the Tusu mainly inhabit villages within the Beiyangdi Community in the Sanchahe District, but are also thought to live in some villages of Tiesuo District. The Tusu also live in Binchuan County, but their exact distribution in Binchuan has yet to be determined.

Identity: The Tusu actually call themselves *Tu*, but in *Operation China* their alternate name is used to avoid confusion with the official Tu nationality of Qinghai Province. The Chinese refer to many tribal peoples as *Tu* or *Tuzu*. As Jamin Pelkey explains, "In Chinese *tu* means 'dirt' or 'native' and *turen* means 'natives' or 'aborigines'. Nevertheless, this people actually refer to themselves as *Tusu* (Tu people) in their own language — that is to say, Tu is their autonym. This people began to call itself *Tu* in the seventh century AD."[1]

Language: The language of the Tusu has been classified by the Chinese as a variety of Western Yi. Tusu speakers, however, cannot understand the speech of other Western Yi groups in their region and must revert to Chinese in order to communicate.

History: For more than 1,300 years the Tusu have appeared in Chinese records of Yunnan Province. The Tusu "are said to be descendants of the ancient Muocha tribe which moved from Baoshan to Weishan in ancient times. In the seventh century AD they moved to present-day Xiangyun County and later spread into southeastern Dayao and parts of Binchuan County."[2]

Customs: In some areas the Tusu love to come together and participate in local festivals, since it gives them a chance to relax and forget about their hardships and struggles. The festivals also serve as a reunion for relatives and friends. The Tiger Dance Festival is held for one week during the first lunar month each year. Large feasts are held, and tribesmen take the opportunity to trade with each other.

Religion: At another time of the year the Tusu indulge in ceremonial washing and bathing, which represents a cleansing from sin for the past year's transgressions. Houses are also thoroughly cleaned out as the people bid to start the upcoming year afresh. They also eat glutinous rice, dance, sing, and get drunk. Polytheism (the worship of many gods), animism (spirit appeasement), and ancestor worship are the three main religions among the Tusu people.

Christianity: The status of Christianity among the Tusu is uncertain, but there are believed to be about 20 Catholic believers in Binchuan County. There are a number of Han Chinese and Bai churches in the area, but most of the people do not really understand the gospel. Many others have no awareness of the existence of Christianity at all. There are at present no Scriptures or recordings available in the Tusu language.

Tuva 图瓦

Population in China:
3,000 (1993)
3,260 (2000)
4,200 (2010)
Location: Xinjiang
Religion: Tibetan Buddhism
Christians: None Known

Overview of the Tuva

Countries:
Russia, Mongolia, China

Pronunciation: "Too-va"

Other Names: Tuvin, Uryangkhai, Altai Uryangkhai, Altai Uriangkhai, Altai Tuva, Tuwa, Monchak, Monjak, Soyon, Shor, Urinkhai

Population Source:
3,000 (1993 J. Janhunen);
2,600 (1982 census);
Out of a total Mongol population of 4,806,849 (1990 census);
206,000 in Russia (1993 P. Johnstone);
27,000 in Mongolia (1993 P. Johnstone)

Location: *N Xinjiang*, near Russia-Mongolia-China border: Ili Kazak Prefecture: Altay and Burqin towns, Kanas Village; And in Fuyun and Habahe counties.

Status: Officially included under Mongolian

Language:
Altaic, Turkic, Northern Turkic

Dialects: 0

Religion: Tibetan Buddhism, Shamanism, No Religion

Christians: None known

Scripture: Portions 1996. Work in progress

***Jesus* film:** Available (but not understood by Tuva in China)

Gospel Recordings: None

Christian Broadcasting: None

ROPAL code: TUN00

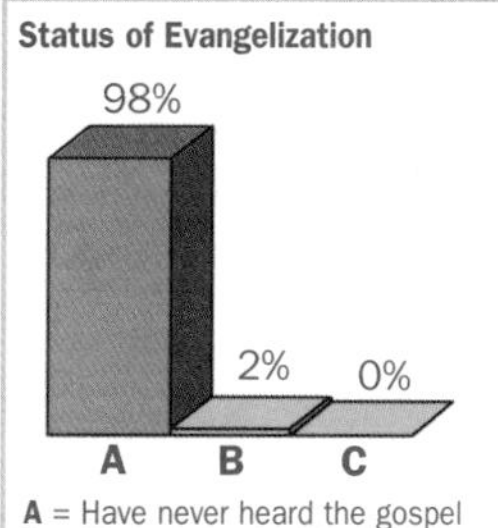

Location: More than 3,000 Tuva are located in the extreme north of China's Xinjiang Uygur Autonomous Region near the juncture of China, Mongolia, and Russia. The vast majority (87%) of Tuva are located in the Tuva Republic in Russia, where they were originally known as the *Soyon* and *Urinkhai* and sometimes as *Shor*. Approximately 27,000 Tuva live in western Mongolia.

Identity: The Tuva in China are a diaspora group who migrated to their present location in the early 1800s. Although the Tuva were "discovered" as a distinct people by the Chinese authorities in 1986, they are still officially classified as part of the Mongolian nationality.

Language: Tuva is a Turkic language. Because of contact with other peoples, 90% of the Tuva in China can speak Kazak and 30% can speak Oirat.[1] Most can also speak Mandarin. "The use of the [Tuva] language is rapidly declining on both sides of the China-Mongolia border,"[2] although it is reportedly still spoken by most Tuva children.[3] About half of the Tuva in China are able to speak their language,[4] which they call *Diba* or *Kok Mungak*.[5] The Tuva in Russia use a Cyrillic script.

History: The Tuva in China separated from the main Tuva population in the early 1800s, when a group migrated to the Altai region of Xinjiang. Today their language is different from Tuva in Russia and Mongolia, and they have become their own distinct people group. In the late 1800s the Tuva in China started to call themselves Mongolians "to avoid oppression by the then ruling Qing Dynasty, and to enjoy the favored status of the Mongolians, who were allies of the Manchurian court."[6] Tuva was declared an independent state by the Tzarist government in Russia in 1912; at the same time Mongolia gained independence from China. Freedom was short-lived however. Tuva became a Russian protectorate in 1914.

Customs: The Tuva do not live in yurts as do the Mongolians, "but in square houses built of logs with a roof plastered with thick mud."[7] Chinese scholars note that the Tuva "speak Mongolian with outsiders and have adopted many of the manners and customs of the surrounding Mongolian tribes, but they speak their own Turkic language among themselves."[8]

Religion: The Tuva in all three of the countries they inhabit adhere to Tibetan Buddhism. They were converted by Tibetan missionaries in the 1700s,[9] although shamans and mediums are still active among the Tuva communities in China. Most Tuva youth in China now consider themselves atheists.

Christianity: Very few Tuva in China have ever heard the name of Christ, and there are no known believers among them. The situation among the Tuva in Russia is better, with a reported "17 registered evangelical churches."[10] One Tuva believer in Russia was recently martyred. His death was reported on television, causing a growth of interest in the gospel among many people.[11] One Christian handed a Mongolian New Testament to a Tuva girl in China. "She started reading and wouldn't let up, walking away towards the hills with her treasure."[12]

Midge Conner

Tuwo 土窝

Location: Approximately 1,000 people belonging to the Tuwo tribe live along the border of western Yunnan Province and the nation of Myanmar. The largest concentration of Tuwo is found in Shui Li Village in Lushui County where 170 Tuwo live in relative isolation.

Identity: The Tuwo are one of several distinct tribes who were combined by the Chinese authorities to form the Nu nationality. The Tuwo live alongside other Nu communities and some small groups such as the Lemo. Today the Tuwo still call themselves *Tuwo* to outsiders and do not readily accept the government's classification of them as part of the Nu.

Language: Little conclusive research has been conducted into the Tuwo language. The Tuwo themselves believe their language is unique. They cannot communicate with any of the other people groups in the area unless they use Chinese.

History: Living near some of the deepest gorges and river valleys in the world, the various branches of the Tibeto-Burman race became separate entities soon after they split from a main body of people and migrated to their own areas. The Tuwo are one such group who have developed their own language and customs.

Customs: The Tuwo's single-story homes are simple structures made of bamboo and baked mud. Until recently Tuwo women wore their own distinct dress, but their ethnic costumes are now reserved for festivals and other special occasions.

Religion: Elderly Tuwo are more religious than the younger generation, who are mostly atheists. In the past, the Tuwo were polytheists, especially worshiping the spirit of the tiger and the god of the Mountains. There is also a Christian presence among the Tuwo, although their faith does not seem to be particularly lively. Researcher Dwayne Graybill was told by one group of Christians: "We go to church every now and then when we feel like it."[1]

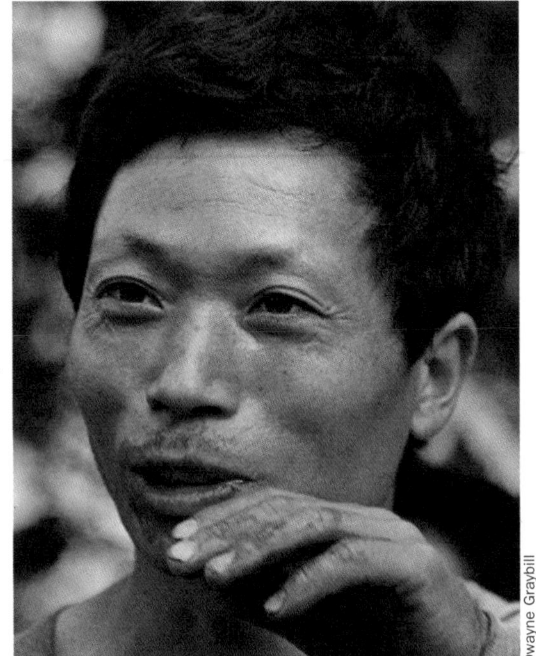

Dwayne Graybill

Christianity: Although there are some believers among the Tuwo — mostly meeting in Lisu and Nu churches — the gospel has never made an inward impact on them. Thousands of faith-filled missionaries have served in China over the decades. Some, such as Lizzie Atwater, who was martyred during the Boxer Rebellion in 1900, paid for their call with their lives. In her last letter home to her family, Atwater wrote, "Dear ones, I long for a sight of your dear faces, but I fear we shall not meet on earth.... I am preparing for the end very quietly and calmly. The Lord is wonderfully near, and He will not fail me. I was very restless and excited while there seemed a chance of life, but God has taken away that feeling, and now I just pray for grace to meet the terrible end bravely. The pain will soon be over, and oh the sweetness of the welcome above! My little baby will go with me. I think God will give it to me in heaven... I cannot imagine the Savior's welcome. Dear ones, live near to God and cling less closely to earth. There is no other way by which we can receive that peace from God which passeth understanding.... I do not regret coming to China."[2]

Population in China:
1,000 (1997)
1,060 (2000)
1,290 (2010)
Location: Yunnan
Religion: Animism
Christians: 100

Overview of the Tuwo

Countries: China

Pronunciation: "Too-woe"

Other Names:

Population Source:
1,000 (1997 D. Graybill);
Out of a total Nu population of 27,123 (1990 census)

Location:
W Yunnan: Lushui County

Status:
Officially included under Nu

Language: Sino-Tibetan, Tibeto-Burman, Burmese-Lolo, Lolo, Unclassified

Dialects: 0

Religion:
Animism, Christianity, No Religion

Christians: 100

Scripture: None

***Jesus* film:** None

Gospel Recordings: None

Christian Broadcasting: None

ROPAL code: None

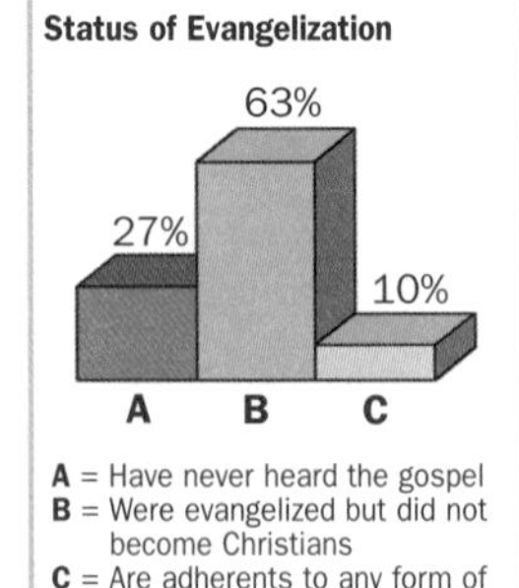

Utsat 回辉

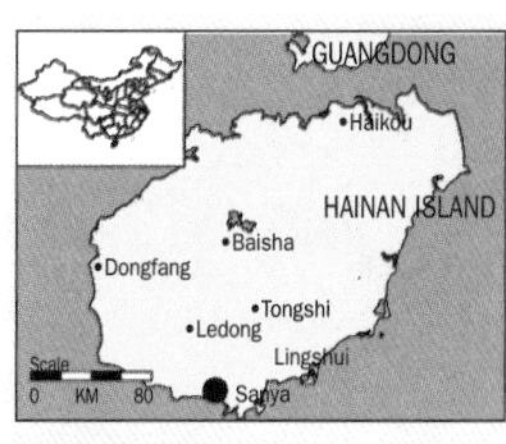

Population in China:
6,000 (1996)
6,570 (2000)
8,130 (2010)
Location: Hainan Island
Religion: Islam
Christians: None Known

Overview of the Utsat

Countries: China

Pronunciation: "Oot-sat"

Other Names: Huihui, Hainan Cham, Utset, Tsat, Sanya

Population Source:
6,000 (1996 AMO);
4,500 (1991 I. Maddieson);
Out of a total Hui population of 8,602,978 (1990 census)

Location: *S Hainan Island:* Huihui and Huixin villages in the Yanglan District, Yaxian County, near Sanya

Status:
Officially included under Hui

Language: Austronesian, Malayo-Polynesian, Western Malayo-Polynesian, Sundic, Malayic, Achinese-Chamic, Chamic, Northern Chamic

Dialects: 0

Religion: Islam

Christians: None known

Scripture: None

***Jesus* film:** None

Gospel Recordings: None

Christian Broadcasting: None

ROPAL code: HUQ00

Status of Evangelization

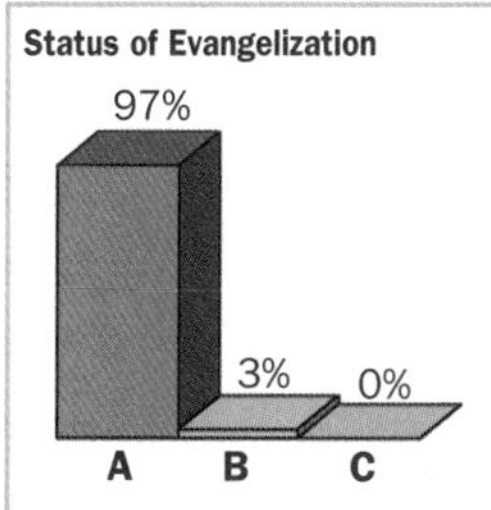

A = Have never heard the gospel
B = Were evangelized but did not become Christians
C = Are adherents to any form of Christianity

Paul Hattaway

Location: More than 6,500 Utsat live on the southern tip of China's tropical Hainan Island. The majority live in the two large villages of Huihui and Huixin in the Yanglan District of Yaxian County, on the outskirts of Sanya City.[1]

Identity: The Utsat are known by a variety of names. The Chinese call them *Huihui*, a repetition of Hui — the generic term for Muslims in China. They call themselves *Utsat* or *Tsat*. Linguists in the past have called them *Hainan Cham*, in reference to their linguistic affiliation to the Cham people of Southeast Asia. The Utsat have been officially included as part of the Hui nationality in China, based solely on their adherence to Islam. The Utsat share no ethnic, historical, or linguistic relationship with the Hui. One writer comments, "It is unfortunate the [Utsat] have been assigned to this larger 'nationality', since the association is likely to discourage research directed specifically at this tiny group of Muslims."[2]

Language: Utsat is unique among the languages of China because it is a member of the Chamic branch of the Malayo-Polynesian language family.[3] All Utsat are able to speak their mother tongue which, due to a long history of isolation, has diverged substantially from other Chamic languages.[4] The Utsat are a multilingual race. In addition to their own tongue, many can also speak Li, Mandarin, Cantonese, and Maihua — a local dialect of Cantonese.[5] An increasing number of Utsat men are also learning Arabic to enable them to read the Qur'an.

History: German ethnographer Hans Stubel first "discovered" the Utsat people in 1930, but their history on Hainan Island is believed to date back to the eighteenth or nineteenth centuries, when they claim to have migrated by sea from present-day Vietnam or Cambodia. The Utsat still derive most of their income from fishing.

Customs: Utsat women wear traditional Muslim head coverings, except on special occasions when they wear a multicolored, flamboyant ethnic dress indicative of their unique origins. The southern part of Hainan Island is frequently lashed by severe typhoons. Much of the Utsat's time is spent recovering from the damage these storms cause. Fishing nets, boats, and homes are destroyed every year.

Religion: The Utsat were already Muslim by the time they arrived in China, and they have never wavered in their beliefs. They are the only Muslim community on Hainan Island. Muslim teachers from Malaysia have traveled to Hainan Island and taught the Qur'an to the Utsat since the mid-1980s. The Utsat do not eat pork, and they live in tightly structured communities.

Christianity: Few Utsat have ever heard the gospel, and there has never been a single known Christian from among their group. They are considered resistant to change, since much of their identity as a people is strongly linked with their religion. The nearest vibrant Christian community to the Utsat are the Indonesians on Hainan Island. It is possible that audio gospel materials in the Cham language of Southeast Asia may be usable among the Utsat.

Uygur 维吾尔

Paul Hattaway

Location: More than nine million Uygurs live in the Xinjiang Uygur Autonomous Region in northwest China. In 1876 Eastern Turkestan was invaded by the ruling Manchu army, and its name changed to Xinjiang, which means "new dominion." Since the 1950s millions of Chinese have migrated into Xinjiang and, by their sheer numbers, have put an end to the Uygur's hope for an independent homeland.[1] Two thousand Uygur live in Hunan Province.[2] In addition, approximately 20,000 Uygur have recently migrated to Guangzhou in southern China.[3]

Identity: Before 1921 the various Turkic groups in Xinjiang called themselves by the name of the oasis near which they lived. When Turkic leaders met in Tashkent in 1921, they chose the name *Uygur* as the mark of their identity.[4] *Uygur* means "unity" or "alliance."

Language: Uygur is a Turkic language, related to Uzbek, Kazak, and Kirgiz. It also contains loanwords from Chinese, Arabic, Persian, Russian, and Mongolian.[5]

History: In the mid-eighth century the Uygur inhabited part of present-day Mongolia. Around AD 840 they were attacked from the north by the Kirgiz and fled southwest to their current homeland.[6]

Customs: Many Uygur cultivate cotton, grapes, melons, and fruit trees through an ingenious irrigation system which pipes mountain water into the desert oases.

Religion: Most Uygur follow a folk Islam mixed with superstition. Islam is stronger in southern Xinjiang than in the north. Today, although almost all Uygur confess to be Muslims, few are aware of the time in history when the majority of Uygur were Christians.

Christianity: When Nestorian missionaries first appeared in China in 635 AD, after they had already been working in Central Asia for a century.[7] One of the forerunners of today's Uygur were the Turkic Keirat tribe. By 1009, 200,000 Keirat had been baptized.[8] During the twelfth and thirteenth centuries "the whole tribe were considered Christian."[9] It has recently been estimated there were as many as eight million Christians in Central Asia.[10] In the fourteenth century Christianity disappeared from among the Uygur for 500 years, and they converted to Islam. The Swedish Missionary Society recommenced work among the Uygur in 1892. By the 1930s more than 300 Uygurs had been converted, primarily in Kashgar. When Abdullah Khan came to Yarkant in 1933 he expelled the missionaries and eliminated the Uygur believers in a mass execution.[11] Abdullah claimed, "It is my duty, according to our law, to put you to death, because by your preaching you destroyed the faith of some of us."[12] Despite the presence of many Han Christians in Xinjiang, few have a vision to reach the Uygurs. One visitor reported, "Many [church] leaders openly acknowledge, without guilt or shame, that they do not have such a burden for these people."[13] One church elder, when asked about evangelizing Uygurs, "responded by shouting, 'You're crazy!'"[14] Today about 50 known Uygur Christians meet in two small fellowships in China,[15] although 400 Uygur believers have recently emerged in neighboring Kazakstan.[16] Recent reports indicate that many Uygur in China may be on the verge of accepting Christ.[17]

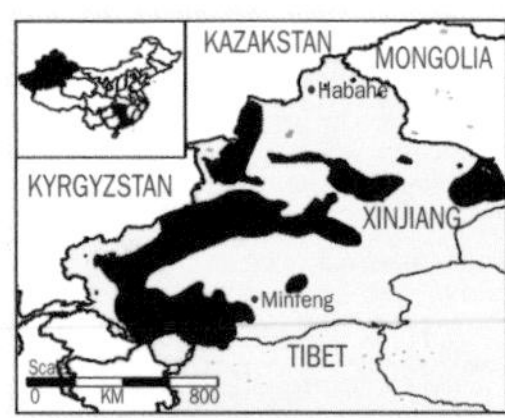

Population in China:
7,164,231 (1990)
9,041,200 (2000)
11,410,000 (2010)
Location: Xinjiang, Hunan, Guangdong, Beijing
Religion: Islam
Christians: 50

Overview of the Uygur

Countries: China, Kazakhstan, Kyrgyzstan, Uzbekistan, Afghanistan, Mongolia, Pakistan[18]

Pronunciation: "Wee-gur"

Other Names: Uighur, Uigur, Uighuir, Uiguir, Weiwuer, Yuanhe, Huihe

Population Source:
7,214,431 (1990 census);[19]
5,962,814 (1982 census);[20]
300,000 in Kazakstan (1993);
37,000 in Kyrgyzstan;
36,000 in Uzbekistan (1993);
3,000 in Afghanistan;
1,000 in Mongolia;
1,000 in Pakistan[21]

Location: *Xinjiang;*[22] *Hunan; Guangdong; Beijing*

Status:
An official minority of China

Language: Altaic, Turkic, Eastern Turkic, Southeast

Literacy: 56%

Dialects (2): Central Uygur, Hotan

Religion: Islam, Animism

Christians: 50

Scripture: Bible 1950; New Testament 1914; (Obsolete script); Portions 1898

***Jesus* film:** Available

Gospel Recordings:
Uygur #03371; Qashqari #03376

Christian Broadcasting:
Available in three dialects (FEBC)

ROPAL code: UIGOO

Status of Evangelization

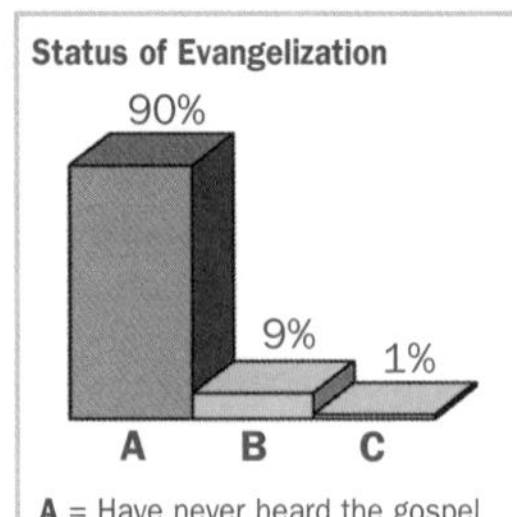

A = Have never heard the gospel
B = Were evangelized but did not become Christians
C = Are adherents to any form of Christianity

Uygur, Lop Nur 维吾尔(罗布泊)

Location: A 1987 study listed 25,000 speakers of the Lop Nur Uygur language in the eastern part of the Xinjiang Uygur Autonomous Region.[1] They live near Lop Nur Lake, in a widespread area which includes Yuli County and Miran Township of Ruoqiang County. The area is also near the site of China's nuclear bomb tests. Marco Polo described his travels through the Lop region more than 700 years ago: "At the point where the traveler enters the Great Desert, is a big city called Lop... I can tell you that travelers who intend to cross the desert rest in this town for a week to refresh themselves and their beasts. At the end of the week they stock up with a month's provisions for themselves and their beasts. Then they leave the town and enter the desert."[2]

Identity: Although the Lop Nur people have been officially included as part of the Uygur nationality, "they differ from the Uygur people in both language and appearance — looking more like Mongolians."[3]

Language: Most Chinese sources list Lop Nur as a dialect of Uygur, but it is not intelligible with any other Turkic varieties within China.

History: The Lop Nur Uygurs are "believed to be descended from the ancient Loulan people.... Their ancestors all lived at Lop Nur and were engaged in fishing and hunting.... When Lop Nur dried up several decades ago, they were forced to move and settle down in Miran."[4] When Marco Polo visited the ancient city of Lop, now buried deep beneath the sand, he noted, "There are many springs of bad and bitter water, though in some places the water is good and sweet. When it happens that an army passes through the country, if it is a hostile one, the people take flight with their wives and children and their beasts two or three days' journey into the sandy wastes to places where they know there is water and they can live with their beasts."[5]

Dwayne Graybill

Customs: Seven centuries ago, Marco Polo described the effect the Taklimakan Desert had on stray travelers. "When a man is riding by night through the desert and something happens to make him loiter and lose touch with his companions... he hears spirits talking in such a way that they seem to be his companions. Sometimes, indeed, they even hail him by name. Often these voices make him stray from the path, so that he never finds it again. And in this way many travelers have been lost and have perished."[6]

Religion: The Lop Nur Uygurs converted to Islam several centuries ago. They retain many features of their pre-Islamic spirit-appeasement rituals, including the worship of the sun, moon, stars, and wind.

Christianity: There is no apparent Christian presence among the people living in the desolate wastes of the Lop Nur region. Nestorian missionaries from the eighth to thirteenth centuries established churches along the Silk Road townships, but all memory of them and their message has long since been obliterated by the all-encompassing sands of the Taklimakan Desert.

MONGOLIA
XINJIANG
•Urumqi
•Korla
•Ruoqiang
•Qiemo
QINGHAI
Scale 0 KM 400

Population in China:
25,000 (1987)
33,500 (2000)
42,200 (2010)
Location: Xinjiang
Religion: Islam
Christians: None Known

Overview of the Lop Nur Uygur

Countries: China

Pronunciation: "Lop-noor-Wee-gur"

Other Names: Lop Nor Turks, Lop Nur

Population Source: 25,000 (1987 *LAC*); Out of a total Uygur population of 7,214,431 (1990 census)

Location: *E Xinjiang:* Lop Nur Region: Yuli County, and Miran Township of Ruoqiang County

Status: Officially included under Uygur

Language: Altaic, Turkic, Eastern Turkic

Dialects: 0

Religion: Sunni Islam, Polytheism

Christians: None known

Scripture: None

***Jesus* film:** None

Gospel Recordings: None

Christian Broadcasting: None

ROPAL code: UIG03

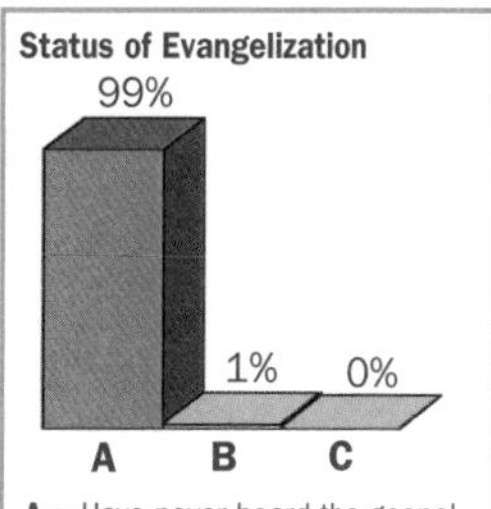

A = Have never heard the gospel
B = Were evangelized but did not become Christians
C = Are adherents to any form of Christianity

Uygur, Taklimakan 维吾尔(塔克拉玛干)

Population in China:
200 (1990)
250 (2000)
310 (2010)
Location: Xinjiang
Religion: Islam
Christians: None Known

Overview of the Taklimakan Uygur

Countries: China

Pronunciation: "Tahk-lee-mar-khan"

Other Names: Uygur: Taklamakan, Taklamakan, Taklemakan

Population Source: "More than 200" (1990 *China Daily*)

Location: *Xinjiang:* In the heart of the Tarim Basin in the Taklimakan Desert

Status: Officially included under Uygur (since discovered)

Language: Altaic, Turkic

Dialects: 0

Religion: Islam

Christians: None known

Scripture: None

***Jesus* film:** None

Gospel Recordings: None

Christian Broadcasting: None

ROPAL code: None

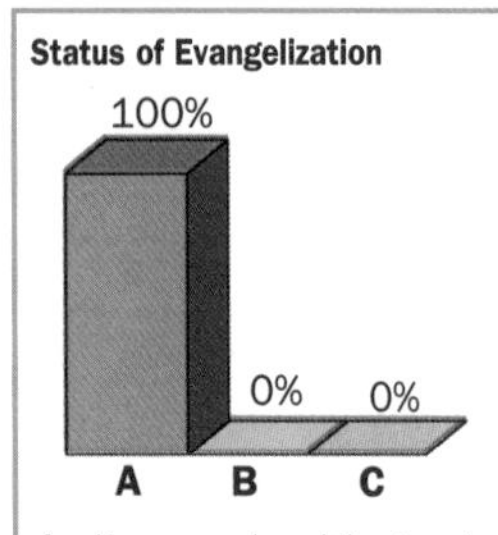

Location: Deep in the heart of what many consider one of the most inhospitable places on earth lies one of the most fascinating stories found among China's peoples. A tribe of "more than 200"[1] Uygurs live in the heart of the Tarim Basin in the desert of *Taklimakan*, a Uygur word which means "those who go in never come out." A vast expanse of shifting sand and wasteland in China's northwest, it covers an area of 337,000 square kilometers (131,400 sq. mi.) — about equal in size to the combined area of the eleven other deserts in China.[2] Surface and subterranean streams, "fed by water from the melted snow on the Tianshan and Kunlun Mountains, flow quietly on or beneath the desert, forming here and there ponds and small lakes. Oases big and small crisscross the desert."[3]

Identity: In early 1990 a Chinese oil exploration team[4] came across a village of people living around an extremely remote oasis in the heart of the desert. They were described as having a "gentle culture, living primitive lives in extreme isolation."[5] Experts discovered this tribe had been out of touch with the world for 350 years. "As a result, they... knew nothing of the historical fact of the Qing Dynasty (China's last dynasty) or about anything else up to the present time."[6]

Language: They were unable to communicate in standard Uygur, so scholars were called in to attempt to speak with the tribe. They found the tribe speaks a variety of ancient Uygur.

History: It is not known why the ancestors of the Taklimakan Uygur fled deep into the desert three and a half centuries ago. It may have been to escape the marauding bandits who infested the area at the time. The Xinjiang authorities — never slow to spot a money-making opportunity — sold the rights to film the tribe to the London-based Third Eye Television for US$2.8 million.[7] This will no doubt have a massive impact on this tribe which had never seen a machine or electric appliance before. They will probably be consumed into mainstream Uygur culture before too long.

Customs: At the time of their discovery, the Taklimakan Uygurs "told the time by the sun, had no form of government or authority structure, and no schools or writing system. They lived around an oasis, farming animals and growing crops for their existence."[8] Temperatures in the desert are as harsh as anywhere in the world. Andir, in the western part of the desert, once registered a temperature of 67.2° Celsius (153°F).[9]

Religion: Despite their isolation, reports indicate that the Taklimakan Uygur were still Muslims when they were discovered.

Christianity: The Taklimakan Desert is surrounded by the ancient Silk Road, which witnessed the arrival of Buddhism, Islam, and Christianity in China. At the Dunhuang oasis which skirts the desert, startled archaeologists in the early 1900s began to unearth hundreds of Nestorian Christian documents.[10] Accessible by helicopter only, the Taklimakan Uygur are the epitome of an unevangelized people group.

Dwayne Graybill

Uygur, Yutian 维吾尔(于田)

Midge Conner

Location: More than 50,000 Yutian Uygurs live in Yutian and Qira counties, about 160 kilometers (99 mi.) east of the city of Hotan in China's Xinjiang Uygur Autonomous Region.[1] Between Qira and Yutian the desert landscape is broken by occasional green fields and reedy marshes.

Identity: The Yutian Uygurs are visibly, culturally, and historically a distinct group. As one Chinese writer notes, "The Uygurs of Yutian differ from the Uygurs of other parts."[2] Married Yutian women are easily identified by their tiny black lambskin cap called *tailebaike* which "looks like an inverted teapot on the head."[3] This kind of cap, which used to be given to the host on the occasion of a wedding or funeral, has now become the accepted headgear for married Yutian women.

Language: The Yutian Uygur may have once possessed their own distinct language, but today they are considered to be speakers of the Hotan dialect of Turkic Uygur. Hotan and Lop Nur are the two dialects different from standard Uygur. "All other forms of speech are more vernaculars of a common dialect spoken everywhere in Xinjiang."[4]

History: Yutian used to be an independent kingdom called *Jumi*. After the Jagatai state broke up in 1370, it was succeeded by several local states, including Jumi. One historian notes that "the ancestors of the Yutian people are said to have moved here from Kashgar."[5] This fact is reflected in the style of the Yutian Uygur's homes which are similar to those of the Uygurs in the Kashgar area.

Customs: Elderly Yutian Uygur women wear a long gauze when going out, covering all but their eyes. The hairstyle of unmarried women is very unusual: "A fringe covers their forehead and hair from the temples reaches the neck in front. In addition, the top of the head is shaven and pigtails fall from the back.... On approaching marriage, a young girl may let the hair grow on the top of her head. At the age of twenty-eight she may wear a long gown and comb back her hair."[6] Former generations of Yutian Uygur women wore huge earrings, but today it is rare to see these. The Yutian men's hat is also unique among the Uygur. Made of lambskin, its color inside contrasts with the color of the outside of the hat.

Religion: As with almost all the Turkic-speaking peoples of China, the Yutian Uygur are Sunni Muslims. Seven centuries ago many of the Turkic peoples in China and Central Asia were Christian. The last Christian group of Uygurs were forcibly converted to Islam around 1390.[7]

Christianity: There are no known Christians or church fellowships among the Yutian Uygur. In 1947 God gave a specific vision to the Han Chinese *Bian Chuan Tuan* Church of Shaanxi Province: to preach the gospel along the Old Silk Road from Xian all the way to Jerusalem. "When they arrived in southern Xinjiang several months later, they led some Uygurs to Christ and established a fellowship. There were scores of Uygur believers... but no sooner had it begun when persecution from the local Muslim authorities scattered them completely."[8]

Population in China:
50,000 (1997)
53,900 (2000)
68,000 (2010)
Location: Xinjiang
Religion: Islam
Christians: None Known

Overview of the Yutian Uygur

Countries: China

Pronunciation: "Yuu-tee-en-Wee-Gur"

Other Names: Yutian

Population Source: 50,000 (1997 AMO); Out of a total Uygur population of 7,214,431 (1990 census)

Location: *S Xinjiang:* Yutian and Qira counties

Status: Officially included under Uygur

Language: Altaic, Turkic, Eastern Turkic, Southeast

Dialects: 0

Religion: Sunni Islam

Christians: None known

Scripture: None

***Jesus* film:** None

Gospel Recordings: None

Christian Broadcasting: None

ROPAL code: None

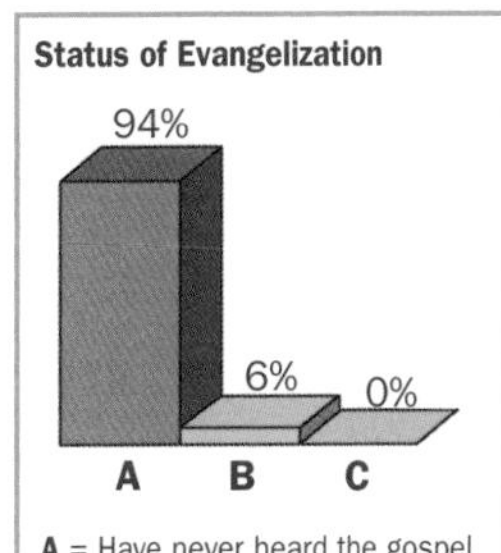

A = Have never heard the gospel
B = Were evangelized but did not become Christians
C = Are adherents to any form of Christianity

Uzbek 乌兹别克

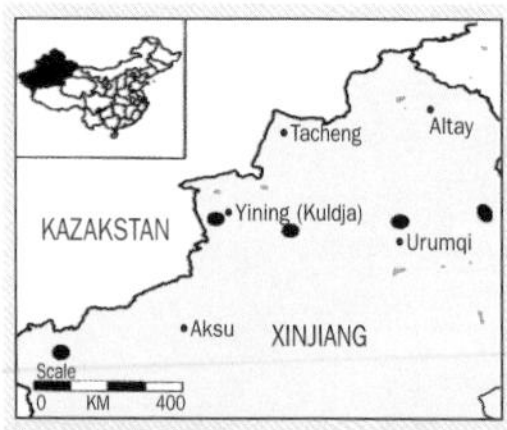

Population in China:
14,502 (1990)
17,470 (2000)
21,050 (2010)
Location: Xinjiang
Religion: Islam
Christians: 50

Overview of the Uzbek

Countries: Uzbekistan, Afghanistan, Tajikistan, Kyrgyzstan, Kazakstan, Turkmenistan, Pakistan, China

Pronunciation: "Wooz-beck"

Other Names: Wuzibieke, Ozbek, Ouzbek, Usbeki, Usbaki

Population Source:
14,502 (1990 census);
12,453 (1982 census);[1]
14,200,000 in Uzbekistan;
1,500,000 in Afghanistan (1993);
1,198,000 in Tajikistan (1993);
550,000 in Kygyzstan (1993);
332,000 in Kazakstan[2]

Location:
N & W Xinjiang: Ili Prefecture; Others live in Qoqek, Kashgar, Urumqi, Yarkant, and Kargilik.

Status:
An official minority of China

Language:
Altaic, Turkic, Eastern Turkic

Literacy: 79%

Dialects: 0

Religion: Sunni Islam

Christians: 50

Scripture: New Testament 1989; Portions 1891

***Jesus* film:** Available

Gospel Recordings:
Uzbek: Northern #04510

Christian Broadcasting:
Available (FEBC, TWR)

ROPAL code: UZB00

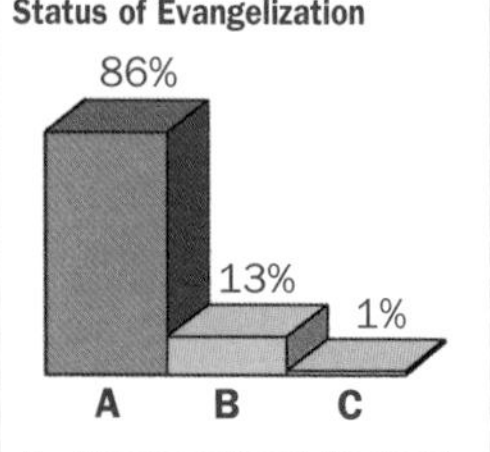

A = Have never heard the gospel
B = Were evangelized but did not become Christians
C = Are adherents to any form of Christianity

Dwayne Graybill

Location: The 18 million Uzbeks are one of the great peoples of Central Asia. Of this number, 14 million proudly live in their own homeland, Uzbekistan. China has a relatively small number of Uzbeks. Only 14,500 were counted in the 1990 census. Most live in the city of Yining in the Xinjiang Uygur Autonomous Region. Small numbers are also found in the large cities of Qoqek, Kashgar, Urumqi, Yarkant, and Kargilik.[3]

Identity: The Uzbek are one of China's 55 official minority groups. Their numbers have varied greatly over the course of recent decades. In 1953 there were more than 13,600 Uzbeks in China. By the 1964 census, however, their numbers had dwindled to only 7,700: many Uzbeks chose to flee to the Soviet Union to escape from Mao Zedong's extreme policies.

Language: All Uzbeks in China are bilingual in Uygur. Their speech includes loanwords from Uygur, Arabic, Persian, Russian, and Chinese, [4] which is similar to the standard spoken in Uzbekistan, though the Uzbek language in Afghanistan and Turkey is different.[5]

History: Uzbek history in China dates back to the time of the Mongol hordes who dominated Central Asia and China in the thirteenth century. The Uzbek in China are descended from traders who traveled along the Silk Road. Others arrived in the 1750s after the Chinese armies defeated the Jungars. The name *Uzbek* probably came from Ozbeg Khan, a Mongol ruler of the Golden Horde who spread Islam throughout many parts of the Empire in the fourteenth century. Those who remained in the area under Ozbeg Khan's rule became known as *Uzbeks*. Previously, they were called *Kazaks*.[6]

Customs: The Uzbek's Islamic faith permeates every area of their daily lives. Funerals are major events in Uzbek society. The dead person's children stay in mourning for a full seven days. Forty, 70, and 100 days after a death, Muslim priests are called to chant portions of the Qur'an inside the home of the grieving family.

Religion: For centuries the Muslim clergy have been responsible for the religious and secular education of Uzbek children. When the Chinese announced that all children in China were required to attend a state school, the Uzbek were outraged and refused to send their children to be educated by an atheistic regime. The Uzbek are committed Muslims, perhaps more so than any of the other Muslim peoples in Xinjiang.

Christianity: There are an estimated 50 Uzbek Christians in China today — significant considering the strength of Islam among the Uzbek.[7] Most Uzbek, however, are completely unaware of the gospel. The Uzbek in China are a difficult group to penetrate for Christ because of their small numbers and close-knit communities. A breakthrough has started to occur in Uzbekistan, however. More than 46 churches have been planted in recent years.[8] In 1996, 40 Uzbek believers volunteered to become church planters in the countries of Central Asia.[9]

Vietnamese 越南人

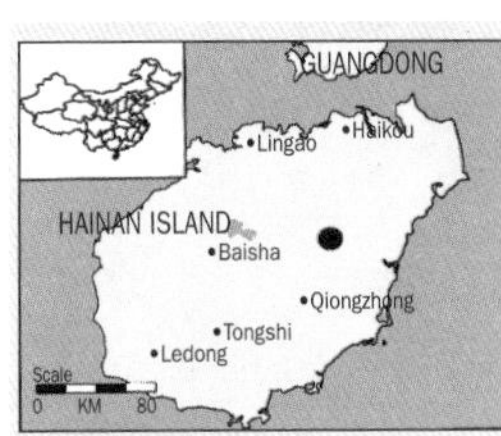

Population in China:
2,000 (1998)
2,110 (2000)
2,720 (2010)
Location: Hainan Island
Religion: No Religion
Christians: 40

Overview of the Vietnamese

Countries: Vietnam, USA, Cambodia, Norway, Laos, Germany, Canada, Australia[1]

Pronunciation: "Vee-et-nahm-ees"

Other Names: Viet, Annamese, Kinh

Population Source: 2,000 (1998 Christian Far East Ministry); 65,051,000 in Vietnam (1993); 859,000 in USA (1993); 600,000 in Cambodia; 99,000 in Norway; 76,000 in Laos (1993); 60,000 in Germany; 60,000 in Canada; 35,000 in Australia; 22,000 in United Kingdom[2]

Location: *Hainan Island:* Pyng Chu San

Status: Unidentified; Possibly included under Han Chinese

Language: Austro-Asiatic, Mon-Khmer, Viet-Muong, Vietnamese

Dialects: 0

Religion: No Religion, Daoism, Buddhism, Christianity

Christians: 40

Scripture: Bible 1916; New Testament 1914; Portions 1890 (Not available in China)

***Jesus* film:** Available

Gospel Recordings: Vietnamese: North #00680

Christian Broadcasting: Available (FEBC, TWR)

ROPAL code: VIE00

Status of Evangelization

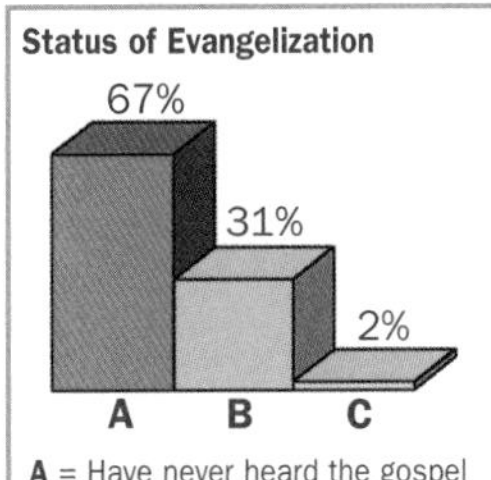

A = Have never heard the gospel
B = Were evangelized but did not become Christians
C = Are adherents to any form of Christianity

Location: More than 2,000 Vietnamese people live in Pyng Chu San Village in the central part of Hainan Island. More than 70 million Vietnamese are scattered throughout numerous nations of the world.

Identity: The official classification of the Vietnamese people on Hainan is a problematic one. They have not been included under the Jing nationality, although the Jing are fellow Vietnamese who have earned official status as one of China's 55 minority groups. This profile refers only to ethnic Vietnamese in China and not to the hundreds of thousands of ethnic Chinese who have fled from Vietnam to China since the late 1970s. As one commentator explains, "During outbreaks of racial hostility in Vietnam in 1978, thousands of Vietnamese of Chinese descent fled in confusion to their home country which they had left many years, sometimes generations, earlier.... About 100,000 went to Guangxi, and another 110,000 settled elsewhere in China."[3] Because those refugees are ethnic Han Chinese, they have easily assimilated back into China. "Since these refugees can no longer return to Vietnam, the aim of the Chinese government is to repatriate them as Chinese citizens. The teaching medium in schools is therefore Chinese. After several years of hard work, the residents are now no different from other Chinese."[4] The Vietnamese profiled here, however, are ethnic Vietnamese who speak the Vietnamese language. Their official classification is uncertain.

Language: Although many of the Vietnamese on Hainan have now learned Chinese, Vietnamese remains their mother tongue and is used in their homes.

History: The Vietnamese came to Hainan in 1986 by accident. They had set out as refugees onboard fishing vessels bound for Hong Kong, but only managed to reach Hainan Island. Hong Kong — which at one point housed almost 100,000 Vietnamese refugees — offered escapees the chance for repatriation to Western nations. Not all of the refugees who made it to safety in Hong Kong, however, came by sea from Vietnam. Many crossed the border into China, traveled by train to Guangdong Province, changed their appearance to look as if they had endured great hardship at sea, and then boarded vessels to take them the few miles into Hong Kong waters.[5]

Customs: Because of the exorbitant amount of money charged by the owners of the fishing vessels, most of the refugees came from wealthy families in northern Vietnam. They were willing to give up all they had in the hope of gaining entry to the United States or another Western nation.

Religion: Most Vietnamese on Hainan Island are nonreligious, although there are some who follow Daoism, Buddhism, or Catholicism.

Christianity: Only about 2% of the Vietnamese refugees on Hainan claim to be Christians. Because they originated in northern Vietnam where there are few churches, most have little awareness of the gospel. One missionary dropped off a few hundred Vietnamese gospel tracts and a *Jesus* film in 1997, but no organizations are known to be specifically targeting this group.

Paul Hattaway

Wa 佤

Location: Approximately 300,000 Wa live in the mountains of Yunnan Province. The majority are located in Cangyuan, Ximeng, Lancang, Gengma, Menglian, Yongde, Shuangjiang, and Zhenkang counties. An additional 558,000 Wa live in Myanmar.[1]

Identity: The Wa are one of the most prominent groups in southern China. They have been granted official status by the Chinese, although the Kawa, Lawa, and Ben are also included as part of the nationality. The name *Wa* means "mountaineer."[2]

Language: The speakers of the main Wa group call their language *Parauk*. The Chinese transliteration of this word is *Baraoke*. There are as many as 45 Wa dialects in Myanmar alone.[3] In 1957 a Wa orthography was introduced using Roman characters. Despite that effort, few Wa have ever learned to read or write.

History: For centuries the Wa engaged in head-hunting for the purpose of ensuring a good harvest. The practice is still rumored to continue in remote parts of Myanmar's Shan State. The evil spirits that control the Wa demanded human sacrifice to guarantee a good crop. In 1962 a Wa man from Daigela Village cut off a person's head by mistake while working in the fields. The victim's village retaliated by cutting off the heads of more than 60 people from Daigela.[4] In the past, incidents like this often sparked a sequence of killings that would continue for generations. In 1936 more than 100 households in the Ximeng Mountains of China were butchered by the Wa of Zhongke. Only three people were able to escape. "The booty of severed heads was transported back in the loaded saddle-bags of eight cows."[5] There are hundreds of stories of similar diabolical actions. The Wa have an expression, "There is no sight so beautiful as the three-pronged fork" — referring to the poles in their villages that they used to hang the heads of their victims on.

Paul Hattaway

Customs: Even in the 1950s, after the Communists came to power in China, no effective measures could be found to stop the Wa's head-hunting. There were 110 reported cases in 1956 and 34 in 1957.[6]

Religion: Before 1956 the Ximeng Wa settlement sacrificed 3,000 cows a year to appease spirits and to obey the orders of the local shamans. Yuesong Village was particularly notorious. This village of 407 households with 1,487 people slaughtered 874 cows for religious purposes between 1955 and 1957 — an average of two cows per household.[7] This kept the people trapped in dire poverty. All the Wa children were stark naked in this village; their parents could not afford to buy clothes.

Christianity: American Baptist missionary William Young was used by God to first bring the gospel to the Burmese Wa in the early 1900s. In a remarkable testimony of God's love and power, thousands of heathen Wa were swept into God's kingdom.[8] Young moved to China in the 1920s. By 1948, 22,369 Wa in China had been baptized.[9] Vincent Young translated the New Testament into Wa in 1938. Although one recent report lists a figure of 75,000 Wa Christians in China,[10] few of these "believers" have even a basic understanding of salvation.[11]

Baoshan
Dali
Chuxiong
YUNNAN
Zhenkang
Gengma
Lincang
Zhenyuan
MYANMAR
Ximeng
Lancang
LAOS
Scale
0 KM 160

Population in China:
245,000 (1990)
299,600 (2000)
366,400 (2010)
Location: Yunnan
Religion: Animism
Christians: 75,000

Overview of the Wa

Countries: Myanmar, China

Pronunciation: "Wa"

Other Names: Va, Praok, Parauk, Baraoke, Baraog

Population Source:
351,974 (1990 census);[12]
298,591 (1982 census);
200,272 (1964 census);
286,158 (1953 census);
558,000 in Myanmar (1993)

Location: *W Yunnan:* Cangyuan, Ximeng, Lancang, Gengma, Menglian, Yongde, Shuangjiang, and Zhenkang counties

Status:
An official minority of China

Language: Austro-Asiatic, Mon-Khmer, Northern Mon-Khmer, Palaungic, Western Palaungic, Waic, Wa

Literacy: 31%

Dialects: 0

Religion:
Animism, Polytheism, Christianity

Christians: 75,000

Scripture: New Testament 1938; Portions 1934

***Jesus* film:** Available

Gospel Recordings: Wa #00086

Christian Broadcasting:
Available (FEBC)

ROPAL code: PRK00

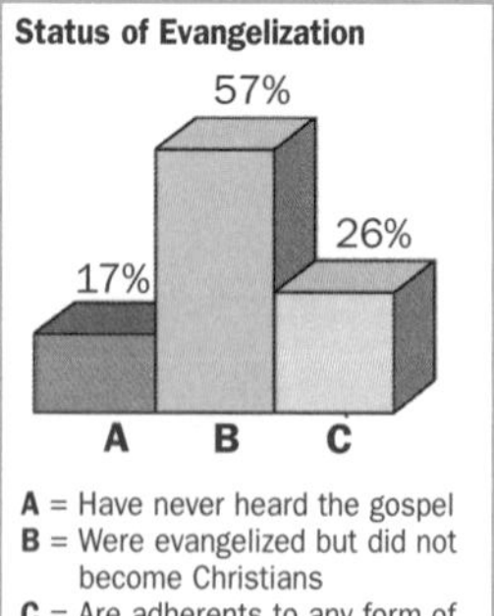

A = Have never heard the gospel
B = Were evangelized but did not become Christians
C = Are adherents to any form of Christianity

Woni 窝尼

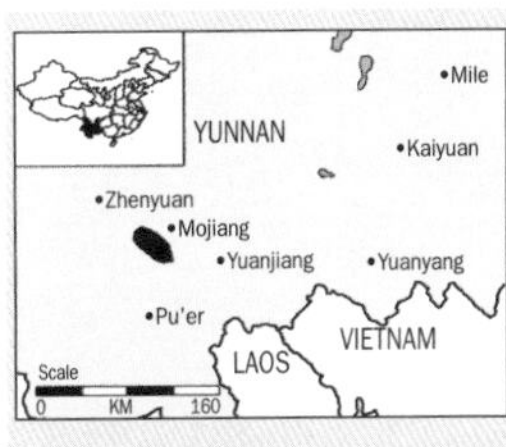

Population in China:
85,000 (1987)
110,300 (2000)
135,600 (2010)
Location: Yunnan
Religion: Animism
Christians: 4,000

Overview of the Woni

Countries: China

Pronunciation: "Woe-nee"

Other Names: Woniu

Population Source:
85,000 (1987 AMO);
Out of a total Hani population of 1,253,952 (1990 census)

Location: *S Yunnan:* Mojiang, Pu'er, and Simao counties

Status:
Officially included under Hani

Language: Sino-Tibetan, Tibeto-Burman, Burmese-Lolo, Lolo, Southern Lolo, Akha, Bi-Ka

Dialects: 0

Religion: Animism, No Religion, Ancestor Worship, Christianity

Christians: 4,000

Scripture: None

***Jesus* film:** None

Gospel Recordings: None

Christian Broadcasting: None

ROPAL code: None

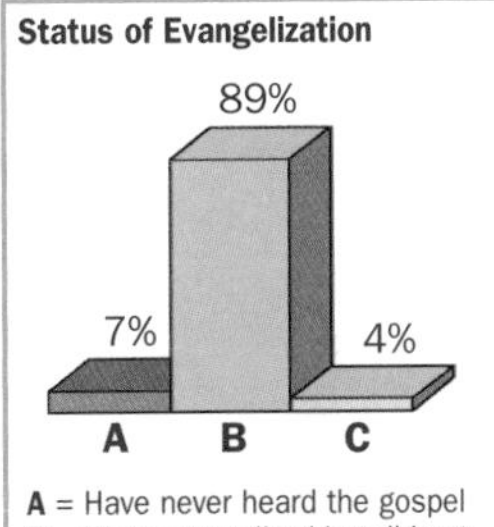

A = Have never heard the gospel
B = Were evangelized but did not become Christians
C = Are adherents to any form of Christianity

Paul Hattaway

Location: Approximately 110,000 Woni live in Mojiang, Pu'er, and Simao counties in the southern part of Yunnan Province. The Woni plant crops and have rice paddies in places that others would consider an impossibility. Many Woni villages are situated at an altitude of more than 1,500 meters (4,800 ft.) above sea level.

Identity: The Woni are part of the Hani nationality in China. The Hani are a collection of at least "17 subgroups who speak at least six (and probably closer to 12) mutually unintelligible dialects.... Each group is characterized by its own identity and tribal costume."[1] An early ethnographer Henry Davies said the Yi mixed with the Mon-Khmer peoples to form the Woni.[2] There is some confusion because the name *Woni* was also formerly used to describe all Hani in China. The Woni profiled here, however, are a distinct ethnolinguistic group.

Language: The Woni language was spoken by "60,000 or more" people in a 1987 study.[3] It is a part of the Bi-Ka branch of Hani, similar to Kado and Biyo. Woni is not the same as Haoni, a different group which is often referred to by their alternative name of *Woni*.

History: Most Woni are impoverished peasants. Their average life expectancy is just 58 years, compared to the high national average of 72 years for members of the Manchu nationality.[4]

Customs: The Woni are perceived as shy and distrustful of outsiders. "Despite this, they are noted for their warm, genuine hospitality once one gets to know them. When a guest enters their home, he is offered wine and strong tea. If he declines, the family will be highly offended."[5] The Woni celebrate the New Year Festival: "At noon on New Year's Day, an announcer throws three balls of blackened rice behind him to bid farewell to the old year. He then greets the new year by tossing three balls of white rice in front of him. Next, he pushes the ropes of a special swing and all of the people, regardless of sex or age, begin swinging."[6] The most interesting part of a Woni woman's dress is the long piece of square cloth attached to the turban. "One wonders how comfortable it is... this woman's annex to the turban."[7]

Religion: The Woni venerate the spirits of their parents-in-law. Each year in the second lunar month they hold a grand offering service. The whole village participates in praying to the spirit world for health, prosperity, and an abundant harvest. There is also a strong Christian presence among the Woni.

Christianity: There are at least 48,000 Christians among the various Hani subgroups in China[8] — the majority of whom are located in the Honghe Prefecture. Several thousand of these believers are members of the Woni ethnic group. In Mojiang County approximately 8,000 of the Hani believers are members of the government-sanctioned Three-Self Church.[9] The Three-Self Movement has only one ordained pastor, Li Suyi, who was sent from Kunming to shepherd them. The remainder of the Christians belong to unregistered house churches.

Wopu 窝普

Midge Conner

Location: More than 3,000 members of the Wopu ethnic group live in Xingyi County of Guizhou Province and in adjacent areas of Luoping County of Yunnan Province. Although the specific location of the Wopu in Guizhou is uncertain, in Yunnan they are known to inhabit the Dayiben, Jiudaogou, and Jigu villages within the Magai District; and Satuge Village of Agang District in Luoping County.[1] According to the 1990 census, there were a total of 7,337 Yi people in Xingyi County of Guizhou Province. This figure includes the Wopu. There may also be a small number of Wopu living in the western extremity of the Guangxi Zhuang Autonomous Region.

Identity: Being one of numerous subgroups of the official Yi nationality in China, the Wopu are commonly called *Da Hei Yi* (Big Black Yi) by their Chinese neighbors. In this regard they are similar to the *Da Hei Neisu*, although the two groups speak different languages.

Language: Wopu is classified by Chinese sources as part of the Eastern Yi group of the Tibeto-Burman language family.

History: The Wopu were formerly slave-owners and landlords. Considered the highest class of Yi people, they inherited the privilege to keep slaves and could demand free labor on their lands by force.

Customs: Like other Yi groups in Yunnan, Guizhou, and Sichuan provinces, the Wopu have "emerged from a slavery society in which they were the infamous landlords and slave-owners; and just as the Liangshan Nosu [in Sichuan], this society of 'Black People' evidently had structured a multi-tiered class system — four castes to be exact. The top ruling classes were both termed 'Black' while the bottom two were referred to as 'White'. Although their counterparts in Sichuan emerged from the slave system as late as the 1950s, this people seem to have begun slowly adopting new ways hundreds of years ago.... Although the slaves of this system — the Gepo — seem to have spoken the same language, the ruling castes felt it important to distinguish themselves by using two different dialects."[2]

Religion: The religious beliefs of the Wopu appear to be a combination of spirit worship, black magic, and ancestor worship. The center of a Wopu home is the kitchen fire-pit. They believe a "spirit of the kitchen" resides there. They also appease the spirit of the village, house, mountains, rivers, and forest. Some elements of Daoism, which have been absorbed from the Chinese, are also present.

Christianity: Unlike many of their Yi counterparts in northwest Guizhou, most of the Wopu have never received a witness of the gospel. They remain an unreached people group. Having been forced to give up their former identity as slaveholders, the Wopu are facing something of an identity crisis and may be open to the claims of Christ at the present time. Their remote location, distinct language, and small numbers have contributed to a lack of interest in their evangelization. No Scriptures or gospel audio tools are available in any language easily understood by the Wopu.

Population in China:
3,000 (1999)
3,070 (2000)
3,860 (2010)
Location: Guizhou, Yunnan
Religion: Polytheism
Christians: None Known

Overview of the Wopu

Countries: China

Pronunciation: "Woh-poo"

Other Names: Da Hei Yi, Big Black Yi

Population Source: 3,000 (1999 AMO); 600 in Yunnan (1999 J. Pelkey); Out of a total Yi population of 6,572,173 (1990 census)

Location: *W Guizhou:* Xingyi County; *E Yunnan:* Luoping County (600)

Status: Officially included under Yi

Language: Sino-Tibetan, Tibeto-Burman, Burmese-Lolo, Lolo, Northern Lolo, Yi, Eastern Yi

Dialects: 0

Religion: Polytheism, Ancestor Worship, Animism, Daoism

Christians: None known

Scripture: None

***Jesus* film:** None

Gospel Recordings: None

Christian Broadcasting: None

ROPAL code: None

Status of Evangelization

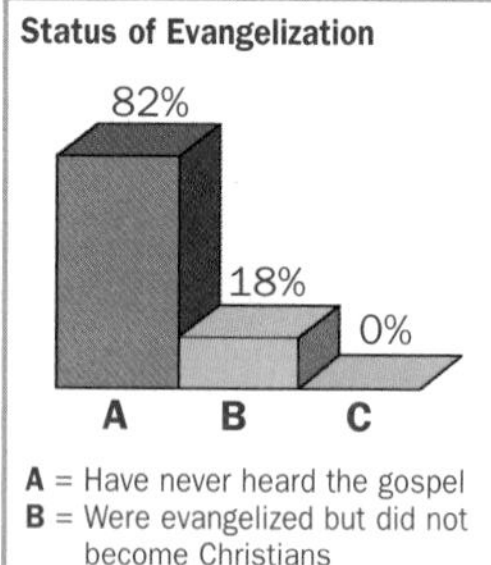

A = Have never heard the gospel
B = Were evangelized but did not become Christians
C = Are adherents to any form of Christianity

Wumeng 乌蒙

Location: In 1999 ethnographer Jamin Pelkey listed a population of 38,300 Wumeng people in China. They live in four counties of Zhaotong Prefecture in northeast Yunnan Province. "In Zhaotong County the Wumeng live mainly in the Buga, Siwang, Xiaolongtong, Beizha, Qinggangling, Panhe and Sayu districts, as well as Dashanbao and Tianba districts in the western arm of the county. In Yongshan County, Wujia District contains the highest concentration of Wumeng. The Wumeng also inhabit parts of northern and northeastern Ludian County and much of Shanggaoqiao District of Daguan County."[1] Although the Wumeng live close to the provincial border with Guizhou, they are believed to live exclusively within Yunnan Province.[2]

Identity: *Wumeng* is an ancient tribal name that has been used for centuries to describe this people. It is probably just a loconym invented by the Chinese because this group lives in the Wumeng Mountain range. It is uncertain what name the Wumeng use for themselves, or whether they have adopted the use of *Wumeng* as their name.

Language: Wumeng is part of the Eastern Yi group of Tibeto-Burman languages. It is related to Shuixi Nosu, Mangbu Nosu, and Wusa Nasu, although speakers of these languages have only limited mutual intelligibility and usually revert to Chinese in order to communicate with each other.

History: The Wumeng are relatively recent arrivals in the region, having migrated there within the last 300 to 400 years. Their situation was described by Samuel Clarke, who wrote that "two days to the north of Anshun begin the estates and residences of the large Nosu [Yi] landholders, which stretch away as far as Zhaotong, Yunnan, one hundred and fifty miles away as the crow flies."[3]

Midge Conner

Customs: In the past the Wumeng were relatively wealthy slaveholders and landlords. Today they are still a proud people who discourage intermarriage with other ethnic groups, including other peoples classified as "Yi." In recent years a few Wumeng have married partners from other ethnic groups, only to have their families disown them and cut them off.

Religion: Polytheism, ancestor worship, and, in the past century, Christianity are the main religions among the Wumeng.

Christianity: The Paris Foreign Missionary Society commenced work in Zhaotong in 1780. The China Inland Mission and the Methodists arrived in the area at the start of the twentieth century. On Christmas Day, 1905, Samuel Pollard recorded in his diary: "This Christmas for the first time we have had [Yi] visitors. More than thirty came as a result of the preaching of Mr. Wang. They are a strange-looking lot, much wilder than the Miao, and fiercer-looking. One of them was a Yi wizard who taught me some characters. They say there are about eight or nine hundred families who wish to come. Does this mean that salvation for them has come at last?"[4] Today, there are believed to be approximately 5,000 Wumeng Christians in northeastern Yunnan, meeting in small house fellowships throughout the mountains.

Population in China:
38,300 (1999)
39,250 (2000)
49,300 (2010)
Location: Yunnan
Religion: Polytheism
Christians: 5,000

Overview of the Wumeng

Countries: China

Pronunciation: "Woo-meng"

Other Names: Wumeng Yi

Population Source:
38,300 (1999 J. Pelkey);
Out of a total Yi population of 6,572,173 (1990 census)

Location: *NE Yunnan:* Zhaotong (16,000), Yongshan (9,000), Ludian (8,400), and Daguan (4,900) counties

Status:
Officially included under Yi

Language: Sino-Tibetan, Tibeto-Burman, Burmese-Lolo, Lolo, Northern Lolo, Yi, Eastern Yi

Dialects: 0

Religion: Polytheism, Animism, Christianity, Ancestor Worship

Christians: 5,000

Scripture: None

***Jesus* film:** None

Gospel Recordings: None

Christian Broadcasting: None

ROPAL code: None

Status of Evangelization

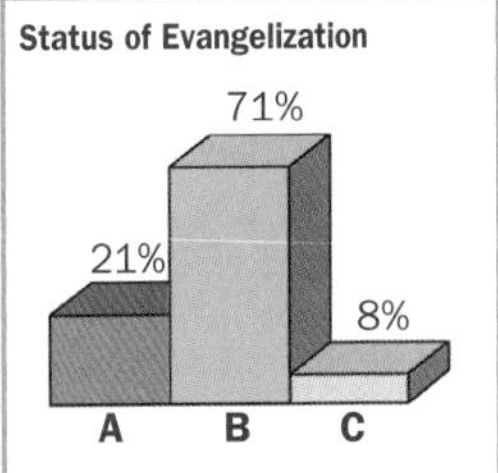

A = Have never heard the gospel
B = Were evangelized but did not become Christians
C = Are adherents to any form of Christianity

Wunai 晤奈

Population in China:
7,000 (1987)
9,630 (2000)
12,400 (2010)
Location: Hunan
Religion: Polytheism
Christians: None Known

Overview of the Wunai

Countries: China

Pronunciation: "Woo-nai"

Other Names: Ngnai, Bunu: Wunai, Hmnai, Hm Nai, Huayi Yao, Flowery Shirt Yao

Population Source:
7,000 (1987 D. Bradley);
3,980 (1982 census);
Out of a total Yao population of 2,134,013 (1990 census)

Location: *W Hunan:* Chengbu, Xinning, Tongdao, Longhui, Dongkou, and Chenxi counties

Status:
Officially included under Yao

Language: Hmong-Mien, Hmongic, Bunuic, Bahengic

Dialects: 0

Religion: Polytheism, Animism, Ancestor Worship, Shamanism

Christians: None known

Scripture: None

***Jesus* film:** None

Gospel Recordings: None

Christian Broadcasting: None

ROPAL code: BWN00

Status of Evangelization

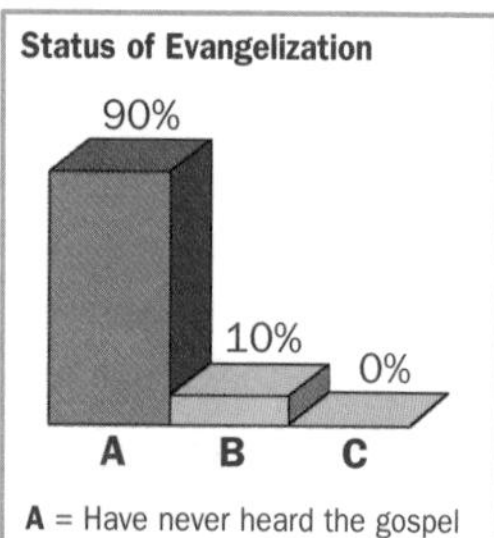

A = Have never heard the gospel
B = Were evangelized but did not become Christians
C = Are adherents to any form of Christianity

Location: A 1987 report listed 7,000 speakers of the Wunai language.[1] The Wunai are widely distributed in Chengbu, Xinning, Tongdao, Chenxi, Longhui, and Dongkou counties in the mountainous western part of Hunan Province. The 1982 census listed a figure of only 3,980 Wunai people.

Identity: The Wunai are officially considered part of the Bunu branch of the Yao nationality in China. The term *Bunu* is a generic name and does not refer to a specific people group or language; it simply means "us people." The Wunai do not refer to themselves as *Bunu* but use the self-name *Hm Nai*, which has been transcribed *Wunai* by the Chinese. The Han also call them by the nickname *Huayi* (Flowery Shirt) Yao.

Language: Although they have absorbed aspects of Yao culture, the Wunai speak a language related to Miao. It is unintelligible with any of the other Bunu languages in China. The differences between the Bunu languages "are mainly lexical. There is a large number of non-cognate words and a number of discrepancies of usage which impede intelligibility among dialects."[2] Wunai is not a written language. They use the Chinese script for everyday purposes.

History: The various "Bunu" groups are believed to be the descendants of the "savage Wuling tribes" who lived about 2,000 years ago. During the Song Dynasty (960–1279), agricultural skills developed among the ancestors of today's Wunai. They made "forged knives, indigo-dyed cloth and crossbow weaving machines."[3]

Customs: The Zhuzhu Festival is a grand occasion among the Wunai. *Zhuzhu* means "to remember forever." The people remember and make offerings to Miluotuo who is considered the mother of their race. The Wunai are hard workers. In the evenings, after dinner, it is customary for the males of the house to gather around the fireplace to drink and discuss the day's activities.

Religion: The Wunai are worshipers of Pan Hu, who they believe to be the progenitor of their race. When a person dies, a shaman is quickly summoned to chant the "opening of the way" over the corpse. The chant helps the soul of the deceased find its way back through many obstacles and paths to the village where their ancestors have gone. The Wunai believe after dwelling there for a time the dead will be reincarnated and come back to the earth. In the past, Wunai communities were controlled by shamans, but this practice has been driven underground since the Cultural Revolution. One of the spirits Wunai shamans call up is the god of Archery. At the beginning of time, the Wunai believed there were nine suns encircling the earth that inflicted great discomfort on the people and caused the waters to evaporate. The god of Archery came and shot eight of the suns out of the sky with his bow.

Christianity: The founder of Wycliffe Bible Translators, Cameron Townsend, once stated, "The greatest missionary is the Bible in the mother tongue. It never needs a furlough, is never considered a foreigner."[4] The Wunai do not have the Word of God in their language. They are an unreached people group with no known Christians in their midst.

Paul Hattaway

203

204

205

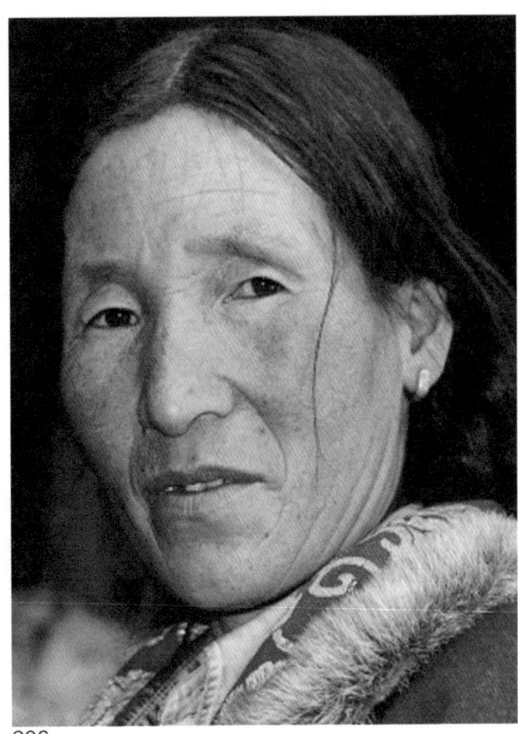
206

203. The little-known *Xi* people in Guizhou worship trees, rocks, and wood; Kaili, Guizhou. [Paul Hattaway]

204. The *Xibe* people are divided into two groups — on opposite sides of China — after a Xibe garrison was sent to Xinjiang in 1763. [Paul Hattaway]

205–206. Although they number only 2,000 people, the *Wutun* have their own culture and language; Tongren, Qinghai. [both by Dwayne Graybill]

207

208

209

207. The small *Yakut* tribe in China herd reindeer in a remote region where temperatures often plummet to minus 40° [Midge Conner]

208. A lady from the *Younuo* ethnic group; Longsheng, Guangxi. [*Yao Update*]

209. The *You Tai*, or Chinese Jews, are the remnant of a once-thriving Jewish community in central China. Their street sign is written in Chinese, Hebrew, and English; Kaifeng, Henan. [Midge Conner]

210

211

212

210–212. The *Yi* nationality in southern China is a government-constructed classification that includes 120 distinct tribes and subgroups who speak numerous languages and dialects. To say the Yi are one people is similar to calling all the Native Americans in the United States one people group, even though they speak numerous languages and practice different customs. Here are just three of the dozens of regional costumes worn by Yi women. [210 & 212 Terry Alber; 211 Paul Hattaway]

213

214

215

213. The *Zhuang* are China's largest official minority group. Their total population of 17 million is approximately the same as the population of Australia. The Zhuang consist of many smaller ethnic groups and clans. [Paul Hattaway]

214. A *Yi* girl from Chuxiong, Yunnan. [Paul Hattaway]

215. Two *Yi* sisters; Dayao, Yunnan. [Terry Alber]

Wutun 五屯

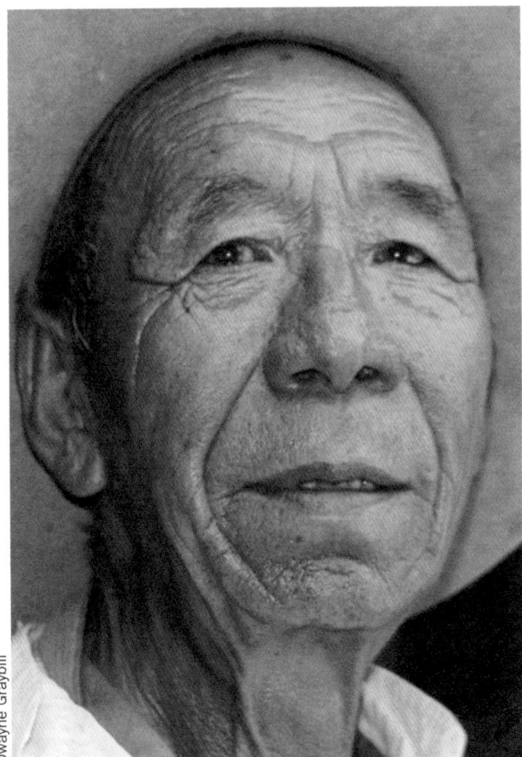
Dwayne Graybill

Location: The 1991 *Encyclopedic Dictionary of Chinese Linguistics* lists a population of 2,000 Wutun people.[1] They live in three main villages: Wutun Xiazhuang, Wutun Shangzhuang, and Jiangchama, located in the Longwu District of Tongren County in the eastern part of Qinghai Province.

Identity: The Chinese government does not recognize the Wutun as a separate people group but includes them under the Tu nationality. The 2,000 Wutun resist this classification and insist on their own status. There are also ethnic Tu people in the same area, but the two groups cannot understand each other's language. Neighboring Tibetan peoples refer to the Wutun as *Sanggaixiong,* meaning "the center of the lion."

Language: The Wutun language is a mixture of Chinese and Tibetan. Their vocabulary contains just under 60% Chinese and 20% Tibetan words. Most linguists believe Wutun is either "a variety of Chinese heavily influenced by Tibetan or perhaps a Tibetan language undergoing relexification with Chinese forms."[2] Wutun is not a written language. Most Wutun men are able to read Chinese, while the Tibetan script is used for religious purposes.

History: According to Wutun oral history, a long time ago a Tibetan king sent soldiers to where the Wutun now live to drive off other groups in the area. The soldiers stayed and married women from other tribes. Together they eventually became the Wutun people. It is claimed that the soldiers came from Lhasa. The Wutun children began to speak their mother's language and could not speak Tibetan — the language of their fathers — so they lost their original language.[3] Today all Wutun family names are Tibetan-language names and not Tu names.

Customs: The Wutun are skilled artists. Buddhist scenes and the Buddha himself are the most common subjects of their paintings. They claim their artistic skills came about because the original soldiers studied art in Nepal.[4]

Religion: Tibetan Buddhism is the only religion among the Wutun. They are fanatical believers. Their whole ethnic identity is bound up in their religion. Although they do not have their own temples, the Wutun frequent Tibetan temples in the Tongren area. Like all Buddhists, the Wutun believe they will end up in a state of bliss after death. But, being better and more privileged, they believe they will go there directly, while other Buddhists achieve enlightenment only after going through many trials and testings.[5]

Christianity: The Wutun have an almost complete lack of knowledge about the existence of Christianity. In the 1920s and 1930s there were Christian & Missionary Alliance workers nearby. In 1996 a 74-year-old Wutun man told a visitor, "When I was a small boy I heard something about this Jesus religion, but I did not understand. There are no believers in any other religions among us Wutun except for Buddhism. We are not interested in any new religions because we know that we have the best and only true religion in the world."[6]

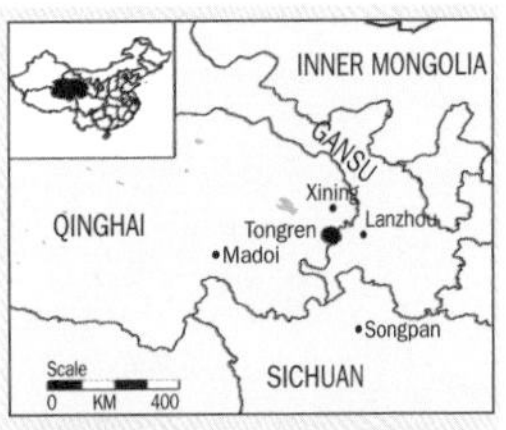

Population in China:
2,000 (1991)
2,450 (2000)
3,070 (2010)
Location: Qinghai
Religion: Tibetan Buddhism
Christians: None Known

Overview of the Wutun

Countries: China
Pronunciation: "Woo-toon"
Other Names: Wutunhua, Wutu, Sanggaixiong
Population Source: 2,000 (1991 *EDCL*); Out of a total Tu population of 191,624 (1990 census)
Location: *E Qinghai:* The Wutun inhabit the villages of Wutun Xiazhuang, Wutun Shangzhuang, and Jiangchama in the Longwu District of Tongren County.
Status: Officially included under Tu
Language: Sino-Tibetan, Tibeto-Burman, Unclassified
Dialects: 0
Religion: Tibetan Buddhism
Christians: None known
Scripture: None
***Jesus* film:** None
Gospel Recordings: None
Christian Broadcasting: None
ROPAL code: WUH00

Status of Evangelization

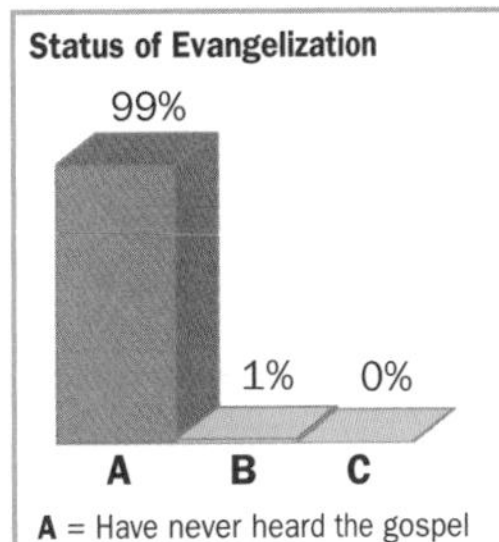

A = Have never heard the gospel
B = Were evangelized but did not become Christians
C = Are adherents to any form of Christianity

Xi 西家

Population in China:
1,200 (1997)
1,300 (2000)
1,680 (2010)
Location: Guizhou
Religion: Animism
Christians: None Known

Overview of the Xi

Countries: China

Pronunciation: "Shee"

Other Names: Xi Jia, Si Jia, Ximahe Miao, Xijia Miao, Gu Miao

Population Source:
1,200 (1997 AMO);
1,000 (1995 Wang Fushi – 1990 figure)

Location: *Guizhou:* 21 villages in Majiatun and Dapaomu districts near Kaili City; Others in Huangping, Majiang, and Guiding counties

Status: Officially included under She since 1997; Counted under Miao between 1985–1997; Previously included in a list of *Undetermined Minorities*

Language: Hmong-Mien, Hmongic, Western Hmongic, Luobohe

Dialects: 0

Religion: Animism, No Religion, Ancestor Worship

Christians: None known

Scripture: None

***Jesus* film:** None

Gospel Recordings: None

Christian Broadcasting: None

ROPAL code: None

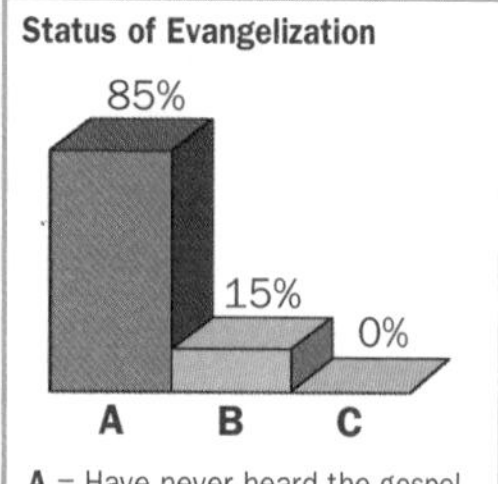

Location: Approximately 1,300 members of the Xi tribe are located in central Guizhou Province, including approximately 1,000 Xi who live in 21 villages surrounding Kaili City.[1] Other Xi settlements in the area include Pingzhai Village of Longchang Township; and Xiangma, Loumiao, and Fuzhuang villages of Lushan Township. In addition, the Xi live in mixed communities with the Miao and Ge in Kaili, Huangping, Guiding, and Majiang counties. The Xi are related to the Luobohe Miao who are scattered throughout parts of Fuquan, Guiding, Longli, and Kaiyang counties.

Paul Hattaway

Identity: The Xi applied for official recognition as a minority in the 1950s, but were rejected.[2] In 1982 they were included in a list of *Undetermined Minorities*; in 1985 they were incorporated into the Miao nationality. The Xi history, language, and customs are completely different from that of surrounding Miao groups. The most closely related people to the Xi are the Ga Mong, a group living in the area who were also included as part of the Miao until 1997. At that time the government reclassified both groups under the She nationality. This new status was done for political reasons and is not ethnohistorically accurate.[3]

Language: The use of the Xi language is extensive, and all Xi children are still being taught to speak it. Older Xi women are unable to speak Mandarin, but most are able to speak the local Chinese dialect. The Chinese classify Xi as part of the Luobohe Miao language, which "includes the so-called Xijia language."[4] A 1982 study claimed there were 40,000 Luobohe speakers.[5] Xi has four tones and has been described as "very different from all Miao languages."[6] The Xi of the large Shiban Village cannot communicate with the neighboring Ge village, even though they have lived a short walk from them for generations. The Xi do not have their own orthography.

History: The Xi claim to have originated in Gansu or Shaanxi many centuries ago. They fought with the Miao and Ge against the Qing Dynasty armies in the seventeenth and eighteenth centuries.

Customs: Xi women regularly wore their beautiful traditional dress, until a few years ago. Now they wear it only on special occasions. All Xi people come together to celebrate festivals. Xi are allowed to take Ge, Miao, or Han spouses, but if they marry another Xi it must be someone from a different village than their own.

Religion: The Xi are animists. They particularly worship the spirits of trees and the forest — and even worship a spirit they believe inhabits the wood used in the construction of their homes.

Christianity: The Xi have never had a church in their midst. Chinese Christians visited the Xi in early 1998, and while the Xi did politely listen to the evangelists, they were unwilling to accept Christ. They complained that they had been previously abused by members of the indigenous Chinese *Er Liang Mifan* (200 Grams of Rice) cult. The people in this group eat only 200 grams of rice per day. The Xi could not discern the difference between their Christian visitors and the cult, which has created a significant obstacle to future advancement of the gospel among the Xi.

Xialusi 下路司

Population in China:
3,000 (1999)
3,080 (2000)
3,980 (2010)
Location: Guizhou
Religion: Ancestor Worship
Christians: None Known

Overview of the Xialusi

Countries: China

Pronunciation: "Sheeah-loo-si"

Other Names:

Population Source:
3,000 (1999 AMO);
Out of a total Dong population of 2,514,014 (1990 census)

Location: *SE Guizhou*

Status: Officially included under Dong since 1985; Previously included in a list of *Undetermined Minorities*

Language: Unidentified; Possibly Chinese

Dialects: 0

Religion: Ancestor Worship, Animism, No Religion

Christians: None known

Scripture: None

***Jesus* film:** None

Gospel Recordings: None

Christian Broadcasting: None

ROPAL code: None

Status of Evangelization

	A	B	C
%	93%	7%	0%

A = Have never heard the gospel
B = Were evangelized but did not become Christians
C = Are adherents to any form of Christianity

Location: A 1982 Chinese report listed an ethnic group called the Xialusi living in an unspecified part of southeast Guizhou Province in southern China.[1] The Xialusi are believed to be a relatively small group numbering about 3,000 people.

Identity: The Xialusi are one of more than 400 ethnic groups who applied to the Chinese authorities in the early 1950s to be recognized as an official minority group. The Xialusi, and approximately 350 other groups, were disappointed when the government rejected their claims. In 1982 the Xialusi were counted in the census as an *Undetermined Minority*. In the mid-1980s research teams totaling more than 280 linguists, historians, and ethnographers were sent throughout Guizhou to investigate the claims of the unclassified groups. In 1985 it was determined the Xialusi should be part of the Dong nationality.[2] They were incorporated into the Dong who number more than 2.5 million people. Despite the official maneuvering, the Xialusi continue to view themselves as a distinct people, as do their neighbors.

Language: Nothing is known about the Xialusi language. The fact they have been officially viewed as Dong suggests they speak a Kam-Sui language, but many Dong people in southern China have lost the use of their mother tongue and now exclusively speak Chinese. The Xialusi may also have lost their original language.

History: Despite their strong struggle to retain their ethnic identity and customs, the Xialusi are at present in the process of assimilation to Han Chinese language and culture. Xialusi women are believed to have once worn their own unique style of dress, but now they choose to wear the same clothing as the Han Chinese and Dong around them.

Customs: The Xialusi hold several ceremonies throughout the year which are marked by their paying of respect to the progenitors of their ethnic group and the spirits which the people believe protect and bless their communities. The Xialusi cultivate rice and tend water buffaloes, goats, chickens, and pigs.

Religion: Ancestor worship is the main religion practiced by the Xialusi. Older people are eager to continue the rituals of their ancestors, but many younger Xialusi find the lure of jobs and wealth more attractive than continuing the superstitions of their forefathers.

Christianity: Although nothing is known about the status of Christianity among the Xialusi, it can be assumed that they are an unreached people since the entire region of southeast Guizhou is unreached, with little gospel witness. Although foreign Protestant missionaries have worked in the province since 1877, the work gravitated toward the receptive A-Hmao and Gha-Mu ethnic groups in western Guizhou, with almost no focus on the remote, mountainous part of the province where the Xialusi live. In the last 15 years several Chinese indigenous house-church movements have started outreach in Guizhou, but none are known to have targeted the Xialusi.

Paul Hattaway

Xiandao 仙岛

Location: The tiny Xiandao tribe — who numbered only 136 people in 1997[1] — inhabit Munmian Village in western Yunnan Province. Of the 137 Xiandao people, only 47 still live in their village; the rest have traveled to cities to find employment. Even though the Xiandao live directly next to the Myanmar border, there is no evidence of any living outside of China. The Xiandao village is near Pingwyan Township in Yingjiang County in the Dehong Dai Autonomous Prefecture. More than a dozen colorful groups share the multiethnic Dehong Prefecture.

Identity: The Xiandao are counted as part of the Achang nationality, but they claim they are not related. The Xiandao language is distinct from the three Achang dialects. The Xiandao may be the group described by one writer as a "Burmese tribe living in the Chinese Shan States... spoken of as *Lao-Mien*, Old Burmese."[2]

Language: The Xiandao language, called *Zhangta*, consists of four tones. It is part of the Burmish branch of Tibeto-Burman, related to Achang and Jingpo. Some linguists consider Xiandao to be a dialect of Achang, while other researchers have found it to be a distinct language.[3]

History: A recent interview with the Xiandao village leader recounts a bizarre history — no doubt a mixture of truth and legend: "A thousand years ago we numbered 400 people and were the richest tribe in the region. Then we had a fierce war with the De'ang. We lost and fled to the Huoyan Mountains on the Myanmar-China border. Slowly we filtered back into China. Because of the defeat we lost our wealth and have been poor to this day."[4] They claim that after the war many died of disease. They "grew red lumps on their faces and died." It is uncertain what disease this is, but the Chinese authorities give regular vaccinations against it.[5] More likely, the Xiandao are the descendants of one of the tribes who fled into China from Myanmar in 1885 to escape assaults by the British military.[6]

Dwayne Graybill

Customs: The Xiandao live quiet lives cultivating the *haoangong* rice that grows in the area. In recent years almost all Xiandao youth have left their village to find work in the region's towns and cities. Many have gained employment in the logging industry. Because of their small numbers, the Xiandao have been forced to intermarry with Achang, Dai, Jingpo, and the Han Chinese. The Xiandao share their village with Han Chinese families. All Xiandao can also speak Mandarin.

Religion: Almost the entire Xiandao population are Christians. They were first evangelized by Jingpo believers from a nearby village in the mid-1970s, and embraced the gospel en masse.

Christianity: The Xiandao have their own church in their village. The pastor is a Xiandao, even though they use the Jingpo Bible in their services. Of the 47 Xiandao left in Munmian Village, 46 are members of the church. The only one who is not is the village leader, who says that if he were a believer he would not be allowed to represent his people to the Communist government.[7] In 1976 the leader's wife was one of the first Xiandao to be converted.

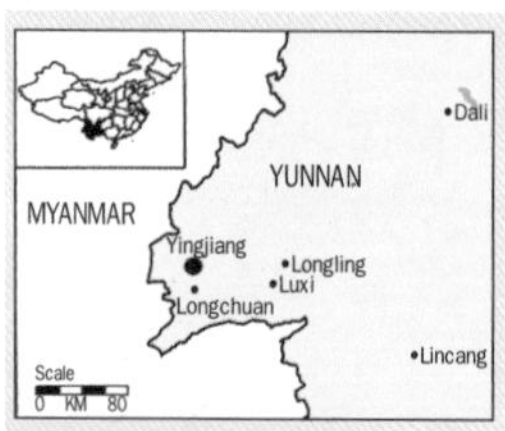

Population in China:
136 (1997)
148 (2000)
190 (2010)
Location: Yunnan
Religion: Christianity
Christians: 130

Overview of the Xiandao

Countries: China

Pronunciation: "Shee-ahn-Dow"

Other Names: Zhangta

Population Source:
136 (1997 D. Graybill);
Out of a total Achang population of 27,708 (1990 census)

Location: *W Yunnan:* Munmian Village in Yingjiang County, within Dehong Prefecture

Status:
Officially included under Achang

Language: Sino-Tibetan, Tibeto-Burman, Burmese-Lolo, Burmish

Dialects: 0

Religion: Christianity

Christians: 130

Scripture: None

***Jesus* film:** None

Gospel Recordings: None

Christian Broadcasting: None

ROPAL code: XIA00

Status of Evangelization

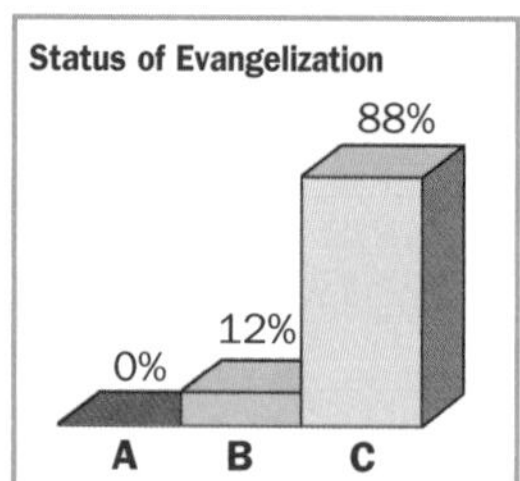

A = Have never heard the gospel
B = Were evangelized but did not become Christians
C = Are adherents to any form of Christianity

Xiangcheng 乡城

Population in China:
10,000 (1995)
11,160 (2000)
13,700 (2010)
Location: Sichuan
Religion: Tibetan Buddhism
Christians: None Known

Overview of the Xiangcheng

Countries: China

Pronunciation: "Shee-ung-cheng"

Other Names: Hsiangcheng, Qagcheng Tibetan, Phyagphreng

Population Source:
10,000 (1995 AMO);
Out of a total Tibetan population of 4,593,330 (1990 census)

Location: *SW Sichuan:* In and around Xiangcheng Township, Garze Prefecture

Status:
Officially included under Tibetan

Language: Sino-Tibetan, Tibeto-Burman, Unclassified; Possibly Qiangic

Dialects: 0

Religion: Tibetan Buddhism

Christians: None known

Scripture: None

***Jesus* film:** None

Gospel Recordings: None

Christian Broadcasting: None

ROPAL code: None

Status of Evangelization

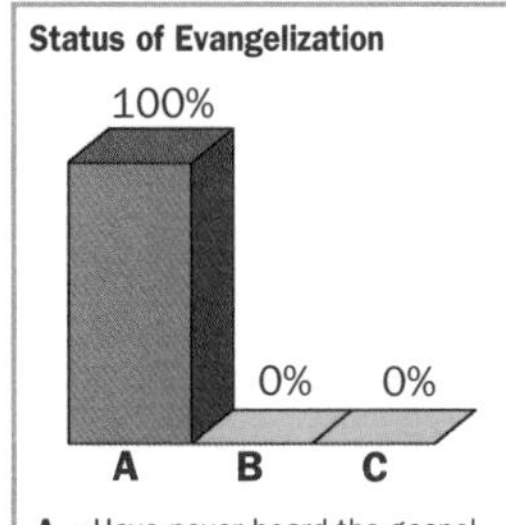

A = Have never heard the gospel
B = Were evangelized but did not become Christians
C = Are adherents to any form of Christianity

Paul Hattaway

Location: More than 11,000 people who inhabit a valley in and around the township of Xiangcheng in southwest Sichuan Province speak a distinct language and possess their own unique historical heritage.[1] The region is extremely remote. One visitor described Xiangcheng: "The town looked magnificent. The solid residential houses were all built with big blocks of stone, but their windows tended to be very small, probably for the purpose of defense, in addition to keeping warm. We were told that in the old days, horse drivers were afraid of bandits here."[2]

Identity: The government has not recognized the Xiangcheng as an independent minority but has included them as part of the Tibetan nationality. "The Xiangcheng people identify themselves as the descendants of Tibetan, Naxi, and Subi people.... In his southern expedition, Kublai Khan of the Yuan Dynasty (1271–1368) brought a great number of Subi people of Mongolian origin here to settle down in Xiangcheng. Ruins of ancient castles can still be found here."[3]

Language: It appears the Xiangcheng language is a mixture of several elements. They speak their own language within their families, but most use Khampa Tibetan when speaking to outsiders. Xiangcheng may be a Qiangic language.

History: For centuries the Xiangcheng area has remained virtually untouched — a remote outpost along the ancient caravan route that linked Yunnan with Tibet and Sichuan. One writer has noted, "Xiangcheng's geographic location provides a unique strategic location, which perhaps has also nurtured the firm character of the Xiangcheng people. Xiangcheng controls Zhongdian to the south, defends the ancient Yunnan-Tibet route in the west, and blocks the Sichuan-Tibet route from Batang to Dajianlu [now Kangding]. Since ancient times Xiangcheng has been contested by all strategists."[4] When Joseph Rock visited in 1930, he found the Xiangcheng territory was ruled by Sashatimba, a bandit chief based at the Sangpiliang Monastery. "Other bandit chiefs assist Sashatimba to rule the land. Together they loot and rob and murder. They even go on journeys of many weeks to hold up caravans or loot peaceful settlements. No Chinese dares to enter the Hsiangcheng [Xiangcheng] territories."[5]

Customs: The Xiangcheng build beautiful houses, which have white rocks on the roofs like those of the Qiang people. Xiangcheng homes are square-shaped, two stories, with colorful decorations around the window frames. They are very different from the houses of their neighbors, the Khampa.

Religion: The Xiangcheng are zealous believers in Tibetan Buddhism. Their beliefs form a large part of their identity as a people. There are numerous Buddhist temples and pagodas throughout the region.

Christianity: The Xiangcheng are one of the most untouched people groups in China. Few — perhaps none — have ever heard of Jesus Christ. There are no Christian communities in the region and no gospel literature or recordings in their language. There has been no history of missionary work in the vicinity of this hidden location.

Xiangtang 香堂

Jamin Pelkey

Location: Approximately 80,000 Xiangtang people live in nine widely scattered counties in southwestern Yunnan Province.[1] About 1,400 Xiangtang also live in the farwestern part of Luchun County in Honghe Prefecture.[2] Missionary John Kuhn documented the existence of the Xiangtang in 1945. He called them *Hsiangtan*, which is the old way of spelling Xiangtang. Kuhn described them as living in "Mengka and Malipa."[3] The first Western reference to the Xiangtang was by French ethnographer L. Gaide in 1903. Gaide called them the *Siang-Tan He-lou-jen*.[4]

Identity: The Chinese authorities have placed the Xiangtang under the official Yi nationality. Many Xiangtang in Simao have been thoroughly assimilated to Han Chinese culture and language. Only pockets of Xiangtang people living in more remote locations still retain their traditional way of life.

Language: Xiangtang is a part of the Western Yi linguistic branch of the Tibeto-Burman language family. Although many Xiangtang have lost the use of their mother tongue, there may still be large tracts of speakers left in Mengla, Jinghong, and other areas.

History: The Xiangtang are one of the southernmost Yi groups in China; this suggests that they may have been one of the earliest groups to migrate from the Yi homeland in today's Guizhou Province.

Customs: Since many Xiangtang have been gradually assimilated during the course of the twentieth century, most of their original customs have been lost. In the past, Xiangtang men had to pay a bride-price of five taels of silver to procure a wife. Alternatively, they could agree to work three years for the bride's family. In a Xiangtang home, guests of high status are seated behind the hearth, the host is seated on the right, and lower status people sit nearest the door. The main diet of the Xiangtang is maize, buckwheat, bean curd, pancakes, and sour and dried vegetables.

Religion: The Xiangtang in rural areas are a superstitious people. Ancestor worship, mixed with animism, remains the dominant religion among the Xiangtang, although many who live in urban areas have forsaken all religious practices. The Xiangtang living in Honghe are the only speakers of a Western Yi language in that prefecture. "While their language is widely different from the Yuanyang Nisu they live beside, the Xiangtang of Luchun County have been influenced by the Nisu culturally. Both groups worship and revere the dragon, but the Xiangtang also have reverence for the 'spirit of the ravine' whom they call to their aid every eighth day of the second lunar month."[5]

Christianity: The Xiangtang are one of many people groups in Yunnan Province with few or no known believers or Christian churches. It is possible that there are a few assimilated Xiangtang individuals attending Han Chinese churches. There are several thousand believers in the Jinghong and Mengla areas of Xishuangbanna Prefecture, but they are not known to be specifically targeting unreached people groups for evangelism. The Xiangtang have been without a resident missionary or church-planting effort throughout their entire history.

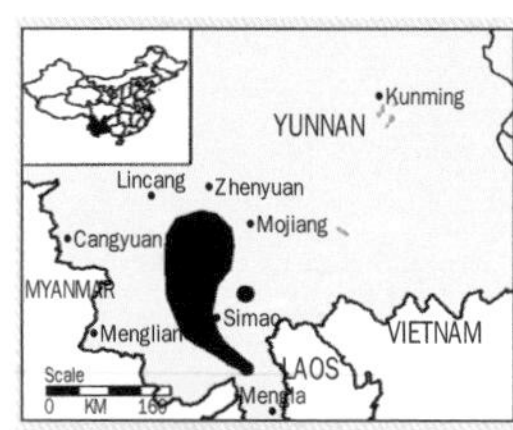

Population in China:
80,000 (1999)
82,400 (2000)
103,400 (2010)
Location: Yunnan
Religion: Ancestor Worship
Christians: 100

Overview of the Xiangtang

Countries: China
Pronunciation: "Shee-ung-tahn"
Other Names: Hsiangtan, Xiangtan, Siang-Tan He-lou-jen, Xiangtangpo
Population Source: 80,000 (1999 J. Pelkey); Out of a total Yi population of 6,572,173 (1990 census)
Location: *SW Yunnan:* Jinggu (20,000), Mengla (19,400), Zhenyuan (13,000), Lincang (7,000), Pu'er (7,000), Jinghong (5,300), Jiangcheng (5,000), Mojiang (2,000), Luchun (1,400)
Status: Officially included under Yi
Language: Sino-Tibetan, Tibeto-Burman, Burmese-Lolo, Lolo, Northern Lolo, Yi, Western Yi
Dialects: 0
Religion: Ancestor Worship, Animism, Christianity
Christians: 100
Scripture: None
***Jesus* film:** None
Gospel Recordings: None
Christian Broadcasting: None
ROPAL code: None

Status of Evangelization

A = Have never heard the gospel
B = Were evangelized but did not become Christians
C = Are adherents to any form of Christianity

Xibe 锡箔

Location: Approximately 180,000 members of the Xibe nationality inhabit more than 25 counties within Liaoning Province in northeast China.[1] This figure does not include the 32,900 Western Xibe who live in Xinjiang on the opposite side of the country. They have been profiled separately.

Identity: The Xibe are one of China's official minority groups. Today, the Xibe are actually two distinct people groups living on opposite sides of China. Each group has formed its own language, culture, and customs. For mission purposes, there is no doubt that the two Xibe groups should be viewed as separate ethnolinguistic peoples. The name *Xibe* refers to the people's former custom of wearing an animal-shaped leather hook.[2]

Language: Spoken Xibe is considered to be colloquial Manchu and is a part of the so-called Tungus branch of the Altaic language family. Today most Xibe in northeast China speak Mandarin Chinese as their mother tongue. According to Xibe folklore, they once had their own written script, but no record of its existence has ever been found. Today the Xibe use a borrowed script — a reformed Manchu orthography.

History: Xibe history dates back to at least AD 400. Some historians believe they are descended from the ancient Xianbei tribe. Indeed, most Xibe today regard the Xianbei as their ancestors. Historical accounts often mention features of blond hair and blue-green eyes among the Xibe.[3] One visitor said, "One can still find some Xibe with these features in... Fuyu County in the northeast."[4] Between 1690 and 1701, the Qing government moved large numbers of Xibe soldiers and civilians to Beijing, Shengjing, Kaiyuan, Jinzhou, and twenty other cities in Liaoning Province.[5]

Customs: Today most of the Xibe are culturally and linguistically indistinguishable from the Han Chinese. In the past the Xibe were divided into *hala* and *mokon*, common to all nationalities in the northeast. "A *hala* is a clan whose members all have the same surname. A *hala* consists of several *mokon*, localized kin groups... claiming common descent from a progenitor."[6] Until recently Xibe homes consisted of at least three generations of family members living under the same roof.

Religion: Most Xibe are nonreligious in everyday matters, although elements of ancestor worship and polytheism remain evident. Every March the Xibe offer fish to their ancestors. In July they offer melons. Some of their gods include the Insect king, the Dragon king, the earth spirit, and the smallpox spirit. They pay special homage to *Xilimama*, the god who provides domestic tranquility, and *Haierkan*, the god who protects livestock.

Dwayne Graybill

Christianity: Although overall they remain an unreached people group, in recent years a few Xibe churches have been established north of Shenyang. This is largely through the witness of neighboring Korean believers. There are at least 300,000 Protestants[7] and 60,000 Catholics[8] in Liaoning Province today. No Scriptures have ever been translated into the Xibe language, although in recent years Xibe gospel recordings were produced for the first time. Many Xibe now speak Mandarin as their first language and can be adequately evangelized in that language.

Population in China:
139,950 (1990)
180,500 (2000)
232,900 (2010)
Location: Liaoning
Religion: No Religion
Christians: 400

Overview of the Xibe

Countries: China

Pronunciation: "Shee-ba"

Other Names: Xibo, Sibo, Shibe, Sibin

Population Source: 172,847 (1990 census);[9] 83,629 (1982 census); 33,438 (1964 census); 19,022 (1953 census)

Location: *Liaoning:* Shenyang, Kaiyuan, Yixian, Wafangdian City, Fengcheng, and Fuyu counties

Status: An official minority of China

Language: Altaic, Tungus, Southern Tungus, Southwest

Literacy: 88%

Dialects: 0

Religion: No Religion, Ancestor Worship, Shamanism, Polytheism

Christians: 400

Scripture: None

***Jesus* film:** None

Gospel Recordings: Xibe #04943

Christian Broadcasting: None

ROPAL code: SJO00

Status of Evangelization

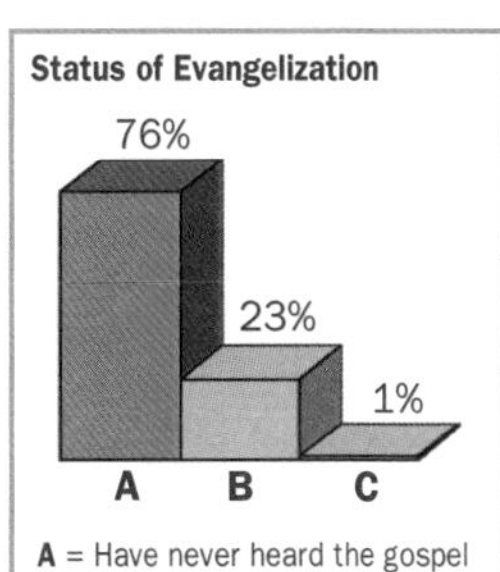

A = Have never heard the gospel
B = Were evangelized but did not become Christians
C = Are adherents to any form of Christianity

Xibe, Western 锡箔(西)

Population in China:
27,364 (1983)
42,400 (2000)
54,800 (2010)
Location: Xinjiang
Religion: Shamanism
Christians: 200

Overview of the Western Xibe

Countries: China

Pronunciation: "Shee-ba"

Other Names:
Xinjiang Xibe, Xibo, Sibo

Population Source:
27,364 (1983 *Minzu Tuanjie*); 10,626 (1945 Xinjiang Census); Out of a total Xibe population of 172,847 (1990 census)

Location: *W Xinjiang:* Qapqal (19,365), Urumqi City (2,675), Huocheng (2,658), Yining City (2,497), Gongliu (1,430), Tacheng City (1,111), and Nileke (607)

Status:
Officially included under Xibe

Language: Altaic, Tungus, Southern Tungus, Southwest

Dialects: 0

Religion: Shamanism, Tibetan Buddhism, Polytheism, Christianity

Christians: 200

Scripture: None

***Jesus* film:** None

Gospel Recordings: None

Christian Broadcasting: None

ROPAL code: SJO00

Status of Evangelization

A = Have never heard the gospel
B = Were evangelized but did not become Christians
C = Are adherents to any form of Christianity

Location: According to a 1983 study, 27,364 Western Xibe were living in the Xinjiang Uygur Autonomous Region.[1] This figure was expected to rise to approximately 42,000 by the start of the year 2000. The majority are located in the Qapqal Xibe Autonomous County, southwest of Yining City. Other Xibe communities are found in Huocheng, Gongliu (Tokkuztara), and Qoqek counties in the Ili Kazak Prefecture.[2] The Western Xibe region is close to the Kazakstan border.

Identity: There are major cultural and linguistic differences between Western Xibe and the Xibe in northeastern China. The Western Xibe have "preserved their own speech, clothing, and housing much better."[3]

Language: More than two centuries of separation from the Xibe in Liaoning has resulted in "a fair number of words"[4] that are different. Many Western Xibe are bilingual or multilingual in Chinese, Kazak, Uygur, Russian, and Mongolian. Xibe is a written language which uses a reformed Manchu script. About half of the Xibe in Xinjiang can speak their language.

History: The Western Xibe are the descendants of a Manchu garrison, 3,000-strong, sent to Xinjiang in the spring of 1763 to rule the territory of the recently defeated Jungars. "The officer in charge of the migration, lining his pockets with the money earmarked for the migration, cut down the time for the journey from two years to one. Many died on the way from exhaustion and practically all the infants had to be abandoned in the wilderness as they moved on."[5] Three hundred and fifty babies were born during the arduous year-long trek to Xinjiang.[6]

Customs: The Western Xibe "excel at archery and are known for their remarkable horsemanship. Their enemies know well how lethal their iron arrow-heads really are. Even Nu'erhachi, a leader of the Manchurian aristocrats, was wounded in the skull in a battle against the Xibes when an arrow-head actually pierced his iron helmet."[7] When a Western Xibe girl is born, the family hangs a red banner at the door as an announcement to their neighbors. When a boy is born, an archer's bow is displayed.

Religion: The primary religion among the Western Xibe is shamanism. Others follow Tibetan Buddhism, while still others are classified as polytheists who worship the traditional Xibe deities of *Xilimama* and *Haierkan*. Despite being surrounded by Muslims, the Western Xibe have resisted all pressure to convert to Islam.

Christianity: A visitor to Xinjiang recently commented, "Many Xibe have adopted the religion of their Han neighbors which means that some have even become Christians!"[8] They are the first known believers among the Western Xibe. They are being formed into indigenous Xibe churches. Hudson Taylor once stated, "Why should a foreign aspect be given to Christianity? We wish to see churches of such believers presided over by pastors of their own countrymen, worshipping God in their own tongue, in edifices of a thoroughly native style."[9]

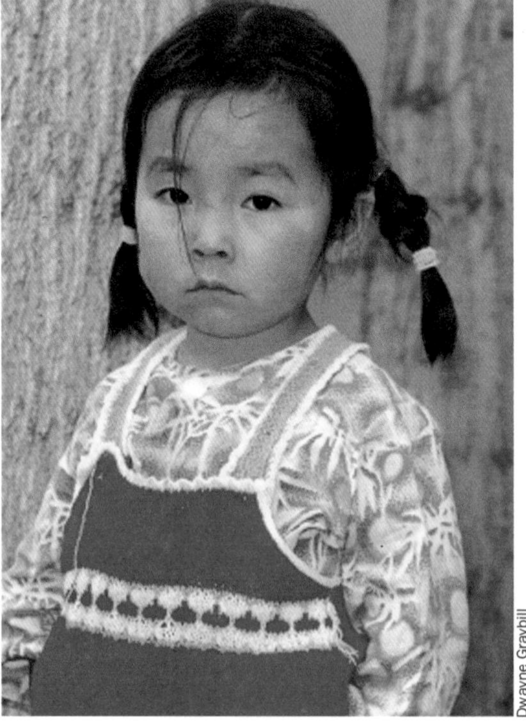

Dwayne Graybill

Xijima 洗期麻

Jamin Pelkey

Location: Thirty thousand people belonging to the Xijima ethnic group live in the central part of Yunxian County in the Lincang Prefecture of Yunnan Province. Yunxian is a hilly area inhabited by a number of distinct ethnic groups as well as the dominant Han Chinese.

Identity: The Xijima are one of 120 subgroups of the Yi nationality in China. They are also perhaps the most assimilated of all the Yi groups. After living alongside the Han Chinese for centuries, most of the Xijima's customs, language, and identity have been absorbed by the Han. Despite their similar names, the Xijima are not related to the Xiqi ethnic group farther east in Yuxi Prefecture. The Xiqi speak a Southeastern Yi language.

Language: The Xijima language, which is officially recorded as part of the Western Yi group of Tibeto-Burman languages, "is very close to extinction and only spoken by a handful of elderly individuals."[1] The rest of the group has reverted to using Mandarin Chinese.

History: Little is known about the history or migrations of the Xijima. Han Chinese settlers migrated into Yunxian County in large numbers during the eighteenth and nineteenth centuries. The Xijima, unable to retain their identity against the forceful influence of the Han, gradually lost the use of their language and most of their culture.

Customs: One observer of the Xijima has found that they "retain their folk-dances, certain festivals, and religious beliefs. These, however, along with their bloodline, are the only factors separating them from the pervasive Han culture."[2]

Religion: The Xijima have also been influenced by Chinese religious practices. Their ancestor worship closely mirrors that of their Han neighbors, while Daoist principles have been adopted by many. Posters of fierce Daoist deities clutching the severed heads of their victims are glued to the doors of many homes. Most of the younger generation of Xijima, however, are nonreligious. They have been influenced in their thinking by their atheistic education and have been taught to view their parents' religious beliefs as backward and foolish superstition.

Christianity: One factor of Xijima life that has remained constant is their ignorance of the gospel. There has never been a single known Xijima church, and there are no known believers in their midst today. Communism has placed additional barriers in the way of would-be evangelists and church planters among this group. David Adeney explains, "Communism attempts to provide a substitute not only for Christian doctrine and experience, but also for many of the methods and activities used in the church. Indeed, Communists have often adapted Christian methods and have proved themselves to be more thorough and efficient in using them than the Christians from whom they were borrowed."[3] Although the Xijima can best be reached by Chinese-language literature, recordings, and media, the gospel has yet to make an impact in this remote part of China.

Population in China:
30,000 (1999)
30,700 (2000)
38,600 (2010)
Location: Yunnan
Religion: Ancestor Worship
Christians: None Known

Overview of the Xijima

Countries: China
Pronunciation: "Shee-jee-ma"
Other Names: Xiqima
Population Source: 30,000 (1999 J. Pelkey); Out of a total Yi population of 6,572,173 (1990 census)
Location: *Yunnan:* Yunxian County
Status: Officially included under Yi
Language: Sino-Tibetan, Tibeto-Burman, Burmese-Lolo, Lolo, Northern Lolo, Yi, Western Yi
Dialects: 0
Religion: Ancestor Worship, Animism, Daoism, No Religion
Christians: None known
Scripture: None
***Jesus* film:** None
Gospel Recordings: None
Christian Broadcasting: None
ROPAL code: None

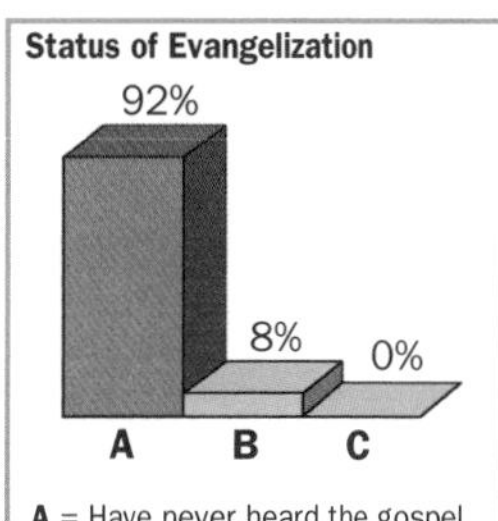

Xiqi 西期

Population in China:
13,300 (1999)
13,630 (2000)
17,100 (2010)
Location: Yunnan
Religion: Polytheism
Christians: 10

Overview of the Xiqi

Countries: China

Pronunciation: "Shee-chee"

Other Names: Siqi

Population Source:
13,300 (1999 J. Pelkey);
Out of a total Yi population of 6,572,173 (1990 census)

Location: *Yunnan:* Huaning County of Yuxi Prefecture: Tonghongdian, Panxi, Chengjiao, Huaxi and Qinglong districts; Some "Siqi" live in northern Panjiang District of Jianshui County in Honghe Prefecture.

Status:
Officially included under Yi

Language: Sino-Tibetan, Tibeto-Burman, Burmese-Lolo, Lolo, Northern Lolo, Yi, Southeastern Yi

Dialects: 0

Religion: Polytheism, Animism, Ancestor Worship

Christians: 10

Scripture: None

***Jesus* film:** None

Gospel Recordings: None

Christian Broadcasting: None

ROPAL code: None

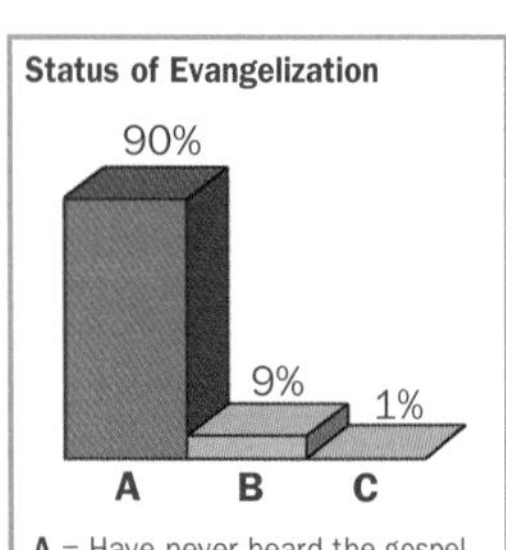

Jamin Pelkey

Location: More than 13,000 Xiqi (pronounced "Shee-chee") people live in the Zhuoqi Mountains of Huaning County in central Yunnan Province. In Tonghongdian District, the Xiqi live mainly in the villages of Suomeizao and Dapozuo. In Panxi District the Xiqi inhabit the area in and around Yide, Fagao, Dayaxi, and Longtanying villages. In Huaxi District the Xiqi can be found in and around Xishajing and Dujiacun villages. Some Xiqi also live in Shanzhi and Qize villages in south central Qinglong District. Others live on Denglou Mountain in Chengjiao District. All of these places are in Yuxi Prefecture. In addition, "the only hint of Xiqi living in Honghe Prefecture is a people referred to as 'Siqi' living in northern Panjiang District [Jianshui County], neighboring a Xiqi area of Huaning County."[1]

Identity: The Xiqi are one of more than 100 distinct tribes or people groups among the official Yi nationality in China. The name *Yi* was created by the government in the 1950s as a generic term that covers many Tibeto-Burman speaking groups in China.

Language: Little is known about the Xiqi language except that it is part of the Southeastern Yi group of languages.

History: Although now hidden in obscurity, the Xiqi were some of the earliest people to arrive in the region during the Yuan Dynasty (twelfth century AD). Before the seventeenth century Yunnan was largely controlled by non-Han peoples. As early as the Han Dynasty (206 BC – AD 220) the Chinese rulers tried to gain control of Yunnan in order to have unrestricted land access to India and Southeast Asia. Around 100 BC armed conflict erupted between China and the Ailao Kingdom when the latter refused to allow an emissary of Emperor Wu Di to enter its territory.

Customs: A small number of Xiqi women have gained employment in recent years making embroidered hats, clothing, and bags for the Huaning Trading Corporation, which sells the items all around the world. The extra income is a welcome relief for the Xiqi who are mostly impoverished farmers living very hard lives. For centuries the ability to sew and embroider has been important in Xiqi communities. Young men were attracted to a woman depending on her ability with the needle. Many Xiqi families keep pigs, poultry, and water buffaloes.

Religion: The majority of Xiqi are polytheists. They believe protective spirits live inside sacred trees. No one is allowed to harm or cut these trees, as that would bring disaster on the community. Offerings of food and sacrifices of animals are made at the foot of the tree trunk to ensure peace and prosperity for the entire village. The Xiqi also worship their ancestors, believing this will ensure a better existence for the dead person's soul.

Christianity: Despite their long history, a mere handful of Xiqi people are known to believe in Jesus Christ. They meet in one small church along with some Han Chinese believers. There are a small number of Christians among the Ati people in Huaning, but their presence has had minimal influence on the linguistically similar Xiqi. Because this group has never been documented before, no evangelistic tools have been produced in their language.

Xiuba 羞拔

Population in China:
950 (1999)
970 (2000)
1,220 (2010)
Location: Yunnan
Religion: Polytheism
Christians: None Known

Overview of the Xiuba

Countries: China

Pronunciation: "Shoo-ba"

Other Names: Xiuba Yi, Xiupo

Population Source:
950 (1999 J. Pelkey);
Out of a total Yi population of 6,572,173 (1990 census)

Location: *S Yunnan:* Three villages (Upper Feizuke, Lower Feizuke, and Poutai) in Xinhua District of Pingbian County in the Honghe Prefecture

Status:
Officially included under Yi

Language: Sino-Tibetan, Tibeto-Burman, Burmic, Burmese-Lolo, Lolo, Northern Lolo, Yi, Southern Yi

Dialects: 0

Religion:
Polytheism, Animism, Shamanism

Christians: None known

Scripture: None

***Jesus* film:** None

Gospel Recordings: None

Christian Broadcasting: None

ROPAL code: None

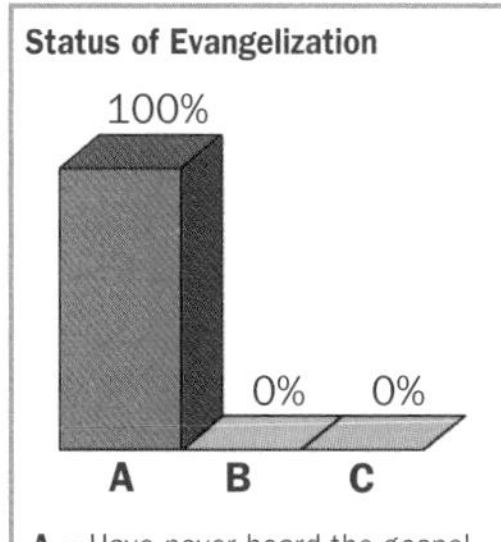

Location: The Xiuba are a small group of about 950 people[1] living in three remote mountain villages in the northern part of Xinhua District in Pingbian County, in southern Yunnan Province. Feizuke Village contains 300 people in 67 households.[2] There are no Xiuba communities in any other part of China.

Identity: Although they are one of many subgroups of the large Yi nationality, the Xiuba have their own unique customs, language, and traditional dress. The Xiuba have little contact with the outside world; they have separated themselves from all other nationalities by dwelling in these remote mountains. Pingbian is an autonomous county of the Miao minority, who live in villages surrounding the Xiuba.

Language: Little is known about the Xiuba language except that it is a member of the Southern Yi linguistic group.[3] All Xiuba children speak their language at home.

History: The origins of the small Xiuba tribe are uncertain, but it seems that they have been living in the same region of China for many generations. They claim to have first moved to Pingbian from Jianshui, farther to the northwest of their present location.[4] Xiuba history has been one of isolation and hardship, struggling to survive from one harvest to the next.

Customs: Bad soil and lack of access to the outside world have resulted in the Xiuba continuing their traditional slash-and-burn agricultural practices. The Xiuba are described as "an honest and warm hearted people."[5] When eating a meal, the Xiuba always honor the eldest guest by giving him the chicken's head. Xiuba women wear boots, colored belts and bow-shaped hats with two strings of chained tassels dangling from the ends. One researcher notes, "Xiuba women's headdresses are the most visible distinction of this resilient people: from a decorated cap, the headdresses rise into a magnificent arching display of silver-colored beads and balls of red yarn."[6] The Xiuba love to sing and especially love to perform the *Sanbuxian*, a traditional Xiuba dance.

Religion: A mix of polytheism and spirit appeasement forms the religious worldview of the Xiuba. They believe large mountains, trees, rivers, and even rocks have a spirit living in them. The Xiuba seek to live in harmony with nature and are trapped in a cycle of fear to evil spirits. Atheistic education has somewhat eroded the superstitions of the current generation of Xiuba, but many continue to conduct their lives with an acute realization of the spiritual realm that surrounds them. Much of the Xiuba's material poverty is caused by their practice of sacrificing valuable cows and poultry in obedience to the demands of the village shamans.

Christianity: The Xiuba are completely untouched by Christianity. There are small pockets of Miao Christians near the Xiuba in Pingbian County, but the various ethnic groups there have almost no contact with each other. The Xiuba were a completely undocumented people group prior to 1991 and have never appeared on Christian mission research lists.

Terry Alber

Ya 雅

Location: The 1982 China language census listed 34,000 speakers of the Ya language. Ya villages are located in the Ya and Chung districts of Yuanjiang County and also in the Mosha District of the neighboring Xinping County.[1] Both counties, which have only recently been opened to foreign visitors, are located in the southern part of Yunnan Province. The Ya language is also spoken in a few villages in Chiang Rai Province in northern Thailand.

Identity: Despite being acknowledged as a separate language by the Chinese, the Ya were combined with other related groups to form the official Dai nationality. The Ya are also known locally as the *Cung* and *Tai Ya*.[2] Subgroups of the Ya include the Tai Sai and Tai Ka.[3]

Language: Ya is a member of the Tai linguistic family. It is related to other Tai languages in China, such as the Tai Dam and Tai Kao, but contains many Chinese and Hani loanwords. Linguists list Ya as being "different from all other varieties of Tai,"[4] and "an identifiable Southwestern Tai variety originally associated with Mu'ang Ya in Yunnan... transported into Thailand and spoken in a few villages in Chiang Rai."[5]

History: The Ya were originally part of the great Tai group. Today, after centuries of migration, as many as 20 million people scattered across southern China still belong to Tai-related groups — including members of the Zhuang, Bouyei, Shui, and Dai nationalities. Other Tai groups have migrated as far west as northeast India, and as far east as China's Hainan Island and Vietnam.

Customs: The practice of tattooing has long held a prominent place in Ya culture. Legend has it that a long time ago there was no sun in the sky. Instead, a big pearl on a *pipal* tree gave light to the people. One day a demon stole the pearl. Wannapa, a Tai hero, started a long expedition to the edge of hell to recover it. On his way he recorded line maps on his body using sap, to enable him to find his way back. However, he found that after a few days the lines faded from the rain and sweat so he courageously bore the pain of pricking thorns into his skin to make the maps sustainable. Chinese records from the Tang Dynasty (AD 618–907) nickname the Tai "those with embroidered feet" in reference to their custom of tattooing.

Dwayne Graybill

Religion: The Ya are polytheists and animists. "The Buddhist Tai call all these illiterate Tai, *Tai Ya*. They say that the Lord Buddha once tried to teach these Tai, but found them so 'thick' that he desisted," recorded a researcher in the 1920s.[6] Each year before the Ya plant their seeds, offerings are made to the spirit of the field and the goddess of rice.

Christianity: Although Scripture portions may have been translated into Ya in 1922, few Ya today have ever heard of Christ. There are no known believers among them.[7] Little has advanced in regard to Christianity among the Ya since one missionary who worked in southern China in the 1920s wrote, "Most of the tribes people are very ignorant and many have no written language of their own. Throughout that part of the province which is inhabited by tribal people, little Christian work has yet been done. Many areas have never even been explored."[8]

Population in China:
34,000 (1982)
50,700 (2000)
64,600 (2010)
Location: Yunnan
Religion: Polytheism
Christians: None Known

Overview of the Ya

Countries: China, Thailand

Pronunciation: "Yah"

Other Names: Tai Ya, Tai Chung, Cung, Chung, Tai Cung, Dai Ya

Population Source: 34,000 (1982 census); Out of a total Dai population of 1,025,128 (1990 census); Also in a few villages in Thailand

Location: *S Yunnan:* Ya and Chung districts of Yuanjiang County; And Mosha District of Xinping County

Status: Officially included under Dai

Language: Daic, Tai, Southwestern Tai, East Central, Northwestern

Dialects (2): Tai La, Tai Sai

Religion: Polytheism, Animism

Christians: None known

Scripture: Portions 1922

***Jesus* film:** None

Gospel Recordings: Tai Ya #00508

Christian Broadcasting: None

ROPAL code: YYA00; CUU00

A = Have never heard the gospel
B = Were evangelized but did not become Christians
C = Are adherents to any form of Christianity

Yakut 压库

Population in China:
1,700 (1990)
2,190 (2000)
2,820 (2010)
Location: Inner Mongolia
Religion: Shamanism
Christians: None Known

Overview of the Yakut

Countries: Russia, China

Pronunciation: "Yah-kut"

Other Names: Sakha, Ewenki: Yakut, Ewenki: Aoluguya

Population Source:
1,700 (1990 AMO);
Out of a total Ewenki population of 26,315 (1990 census);
328,000 in Russia (1979 census)

Location:
NE Inner Mongolia: Ergun Banner

Status:
Officially included under Ewenki

Language: Altaic, Tungus, Northern Tungus, Ewenki

Dialects: 0

Religion: Shamanism

Christians: None known

Scripture: Portions 1858

***Jesus* film:** Available

Gospel Recordings:
Yakut #04451

Christian Broadcasting: None

ROPAL code: UKT00

Status of Evangelization

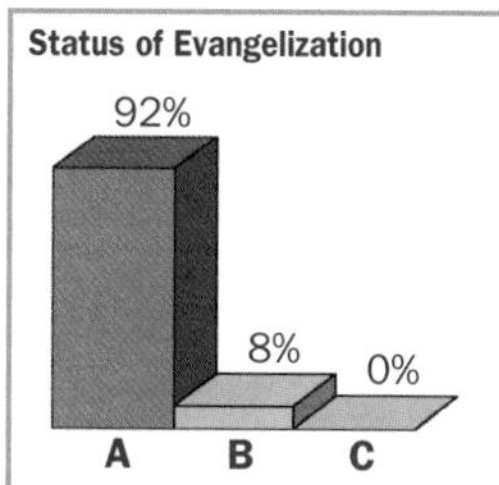

A = Have never heard the gospel
B = Were evangelized but did not become Christians
C = Are adherents to any form of Christianity

Midge Conner

History: In the late 1800s a small Yakut group migrated from far inside the Yakutia region of Siberia, stopping first in the Buriat region before finally proceeding into China. They are the ancestors of today's Yakut in China.

Customs: The Yakut live uncomplicated, seminomadic lives, tending reindeer and dwelling in simple tents. Alcohol abuse is rampant among the Yakut of China. In fact, it is so prevalent that the number of murders, early deaths, and suicides attributable to alcohol abuse may seriously jeopardize the future of this small group. Around the world the Yakut are renowned for their strong, hardy, massive Yakut draft horses from Siberia.

Location: A 1990 report listed more than 1,700 Yakut living in China.[1] They were originally part of the large group of more than 400,000 Yakut living in the Yakutia region near the Arctic Ocean in Russia. In China the Yakut are the most northern Ewenki group. They inhabit dense forests in the Ergun Banner of Inner Mongolia.

Identity: Although the Yakut have officially been included as part of the Ewenki nationality in China, they have their own language and customs. They identify themselves as "Yakut" to outsiders.

Language: Because they arrived in China only about 100 years ago, the Yakut language has not varied greatly from the Yakut spoken in Siberia. The elderly Yakut in China still speak a little Russian. Today most members of this tribe under the age of 40 can speak and read Chinese. Although their language has been officially labeled the *Aologuya* dialect of Ewenki in China, the Yakut cannot understand any of the other Ewenki languages. In fact, their language is more intelligible with Oroqen.[2] In Russia where they have their own newspapers, books, television, radio programs, and universities, the Yakut use the Cyrillic script.

Religion: The Yakut are shamanists. In the late 1800s anthropologist Waldemar Jochelson vividly described a Yakut religious ceremony: "A shaman has come to heal a sick woman, whose soul has been captured by evil spirits. He has put himself into a trance by inhaling tobacco, dancing, and beating his drum. Now his soul will travel to the spirit world and do battle in order to retrieve the woman's soul and thus restore her. His assistant holds the shaman by a chain so that if he gets lost or trapped in the spirit world he can be pulled back. Some of the flat iron pendants on the shaman's robe represent bird feathers, which allow the shaman's soul to fly.... As the shaman dances, the noise made by these pieces and by the copper bells and rattles on the robe, as well as the sound of his drum and singing, help summon the spirits."[3]

Christianity: Although the Yakut in Russia were evangelized by Russian Orthodox missionaries in the eighteenth and nineteenth centuries, few experienced a living faith in Christ. There are no known believers among the Yakut in China. In 1996 four evangelists traveled to the Yakut in China, taking with them a gospel recording of Bible stories in the Yakut language from Russia. The recipients were overjoyed to hear their own language.[4]

Yanghuang 扬黄

Dwayne Graybill

Location: A 1982 study numbered 32,000 Yanghuang in China.[1] Linguist David Bradley in 1987 listed a lower figure of 24,000 Yanghuang.[2] They are located in parts of three counties in China's southern Guizhou Province: Pingtang, Huishui, and Dushan.

Identity: The official classification of the Yanghuang is a complicated matter. In the 1982 census they were included in a list of *Undetermined Minorities*. By the time of the 1990 census, however, they had been reclassified as part of the Maonan nationality. The Yanghuang are a combination of two distinct ethnic groups, although they speak the same language. Consequently, the Yanghuang have two different ethnic names for themselves: *Ten* and *Rao*. It may be that the Ten have been counted as Maonan and the Rao as Shui. *Yanghuang* is the Chinese name for them and is the name all people in the region identify this group by.

Language: The Yanghuang language is "very closely related to Shui."[3] It may be the same language as Mo, although the speakers of Mo have a different ethnic identity.[4] Most Yanghuang are bilingual in the local dialect of Chinese, and some can also speak Bouyei as a third language.[5] The Yanghuang language does not have an orthography.

History: The origins of the Yanghuang are uncertain. Their language suggests a close historic affiliation with the Shui. They appear to have been two clans of Shui who migrated to the Bouyei areas in the past. After many generations of separation from the main bulk of Shui farther to the north and northeast, the Yanghuang gradually developed their own language and customs. Little was known of the southern part of Guizhou until the Japanese invaded China in the 1930s and the Kuomintang armies were forced to the south and southwestern parts of the country. There they constructed roads and railway lines through remote regions, which for centuries had been the unexplored domain of dozens of non-Han minority groups.

Customs: The Yanghuang lead peaceful lives among the verdant hills of southern Guizhou. The region was one of the most poverty-stricken in the country, but China's recent economic boom has helped the Yanghuang.

Religion: The Yanghuang are polytheists and animists. They believe their lives are controlled by a complex hierarchy of demons and gods who must be continually placated to ensure success and peace for the community.

Christianity: The majority of Yanghuang people are without any knowledge of the name of Jesus Christ. The few Christian missionaries who have visited them in recent years have reported a complete lack of any presence of Christianity among the Yanghuang. There has recently been a small breakthrough among the related Mo people in Libo County, who now have the first Christian church ever established among their people. It is hoped that the new Mo believers will be motivated and equipped to take the gospel to the linguistically related Yanghuang.

Population in China:
32,000 (1982)
48,700 (2000)
62,800 (2010)
Location: Guizhou
Religion: Polytheism
Christians: None Known

Overview of the Yanghuang

Countries: China
Pronunciation: "Yahng-hooung"
Other Names: Ten, T'en, Then, Yanghwang, Buong Yao
Population Source:
32,000 (1982 *Minzu Shibie Wenxian Ziliao Huibian*);
24,000 (1987 D. Bradley);
Out of a total Maonan population of 71,968 (1990 census)
Location: *S Guizhou:* Pingtang, Huishui, and Dushan counties
Status: Officially included under Maonan since 1990; Previously included in a list of *Undetermined Minorities*
Language: Daic, Kam-Sui
Dialects: 0
Religion: Polytheism, Animism, No Religion
Christians: None known
Scripture: None
***Jesus* film:** None
Gospel Recordings: None
Christian Broadcasting: None
ROPAL code: TCT00

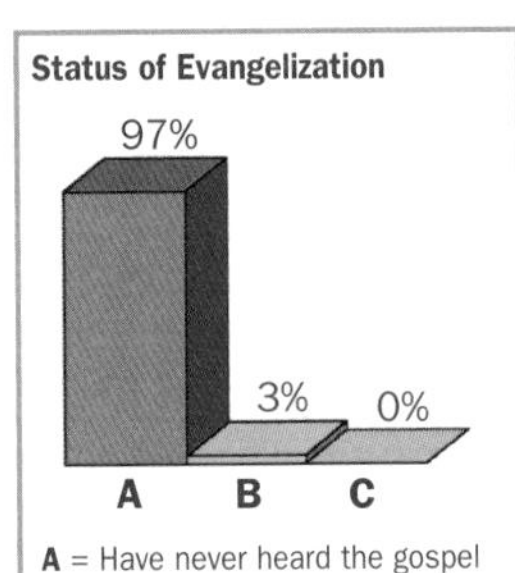

Yerong 耶容

Location: Chinese scholar Liang Min listed a 1990 population of only 300 to 400 Yerong in China.[1] In addition, about half of the members of the Buyang tribe (1,000 to 1,500 people) can also speak the Yerong language.[2] The Yerong are located in the Longhe and Pohe townships of Napo County in the southwest corner of Guangxi, just north of the juncture where Yunnan, Guangxi and Vietnam intersect.

Identity: The Yerong are also known to locals as the *Daban Yao*, or simply as *Daban*. Although there is a community of *Daban Yao* in Yunnan's Xishuangbanna Prefecture, the two groups are unrelated. The Yunnan Daban Yao speak the Iu Mien language. The Yerong are included as part of the Yao nationality in China, even though they speak their own, very different language. In 1945 the Yao were described as being made up of 39 different tribes.[3] Among these tribes, however, are a staggering number and variety of subgroups. "There are thought to be as many as 300 such different appellations among the Yao in China, making research and classification ethnically an impossible task. Because many Yao groups "have different self-denominations... they are probably not of the same ethnic stock."[4]

Language: The Yerong language is a part of the so-called *Kadai* language group. Kadai is a generic name invented by linguists to group together languages that do not comfortably fit into the Tai language family or any other linguistic affiliation.

History: In the past the numerous Yao groups in China were governed by a "tablet" system. The inhabitants of several villages banded together and erected a stone tablet, engraved in Chinese characters, containing the rules and regulations to be observed by members of the group. "Apparently a sort of social pact, this set of rules defined rights and prerogatives within the group; the social order, customs and practices to be maintained; and the sanctions imposed for infringement or violation of these rules."[5]

Dwayne Graybill

Customs: The Yerong, who wear their own distinctive dress, are renowned as an honest and hardworking people. The small population of the Yerong is the result of much intermarriage with other races and tribes. As more Yerong youth leave their home communities to marry and live with other people groups, the very existence of the Yerong is becoming increasingly endangered.

Religion: The Yerong are animists. They do not observe the custom of worshiping Pan Hu, as do most of the other Yao groups in Guangxi.

Christianity: There are no known believers or churches among the Yerong. They are still waiting to hear the gospel for the first time in their history. Foreign missionaries will struggle to effectively penetrate the isolated Yerong by themselves. Believers from related minority groups or from Han Chinese churches are best suited for effective evangelism. Because of the strong ethnic unity of the clan system, one observer points out, "Cross-cultural missionaries would have a very marginal part in such a thrust, but would be needed for encouragement and counseling."[6]

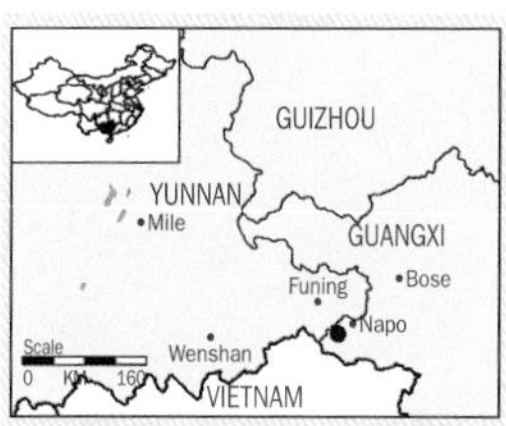

Population in China:
400 (1990)
510 (2000)
660 (2010)
Location: Guangxi
Religion: Animism
Christians: None Known

Overview of the Yerong

Countries: China

Pronunciation: "Yer-rong"

Other Names: Daban, Daban Yao, Yeyong

Population Source: 300 to 400 (1990 Liang Min); Out of a total Yao population of 2,134,013 (1990 census)

Location: *SW Guangxi:* Longhe and Pohe townships in Napo County

Status: Officially included under Yao

Language: Daic, Kadai, Bu Rong

Dialects: 0

Religion: Animism, Ancestor Worship

Christians: None known

Scripture: None

***Jesus* film:** None

Gospel Recordings: None

Christian Broadcasting: None

ROPAL code: YRN00

Status of Evangelization

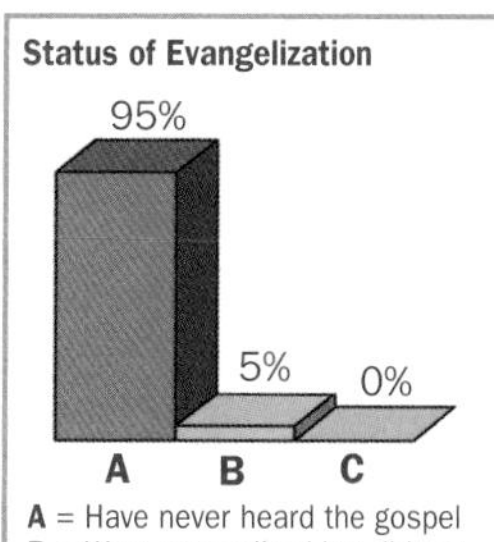

A = Have never heard the gospel
B = Were evangelized but did not become Christians
C = Are adherents to any form of Christianity

Yiche 以车

Population in China:
15,000 (1987)
19,460 (2000)
23,900 (2010)
Location: Yunnan
Religion: Polytheism
Christians: 100

Overview of the Yiche

Countries: China

Pronunciation: "Yee-cher"

Other Names: Yeche

Population Source:
15,000 (1987 Xie Shixun);
Out of a total Hani population of 1,253,952 (1990 census)

Location: *S Yunnan:* Honghe Prefecture: Chegu, Landi, and Dayangjie townships

Status:
Officially included under Hani

Language: Sino-Tibetan, Tibeto-Burman, Burmic, Burmese-Lolo, Lolo, Southern Lolo, Akha

Dialects: 0

Religion: Polytheism, Animism, Ancestor Worship, Christianity

Christians: 100

Scripture: None

***Jesus* film:** None

Gospel Recordings: None

Christian Broadcasting: None

ROPAL code: None

Status of Evangelization

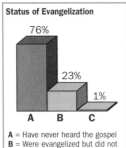

	A	B	C
%	76%	23%	1%

A = Have never heard the gospel
B = Were evangelized but did not become Christians
C = Are adherents to any form of Christianity

Location: Approximately 19,000 members of the Yiche tribe inhabit isolated villages in the Ailao Mountains. They are located in parts of Chegu, Landi, and Dayangjie townships. Honghe Prefecture is divided by two large rivers: the Honghe (Red) River which flows south into Vietnam and the Nanpanjiang River which is the upper section of the Pearl River. Banana, pineapple, and pomegranate are grown, while sugarcane, peanuts, and tobacco are important cash crops.

Identity: The Yiche are part of the Hani nationality in China. Yiche women are unique among all the peoples of China because they wear shorts. They also wear conical hats, similar to the Jino people, and short-sleeved blue blouses held together by five-colored girdles. "The clothes are layered one on top of each other, numbering from six to more than a dozen.... The layers indicate a family's financial standing. Women wear black shorts with pleats at the legs."[1]

Language: Yiche is similar to other Hani languages in the area. The Yiche's knowledge of Mandarin is poor, especially among women and children.

History: Little is known about the origins of the Yiche people, because they have never possessed a written script. Legends are handed down orally from generation to generation. The Yiche say they were once part of a tribe of 7,000 families, living "on a vast fertile plain away in the east where the sun rises."[2]

Customs: Yiche houses are two stories high and have tiled roofs. The upper floor serves as a storehouse and the lower floor as the living quarters. Every year in the fifth lunar month the Yiche celebrate the Kuzhazha Festival. "According to traditional custom, every family must light pine torches after sunset. Burning torches in hand, they walk around the house to perform a 'mopping up' and then follow a forked chestnut rod to the top of the road outside the hamlet and place the torches beside the chestnut rod. This drives evil away from the house ensuring the coming year is filled with peace and happiness."[3]

Religion: The Yiche are polytheists. "Most of their villages have temples where a multitude of gods are worshipped. These gods are associated with the earth, water, and fire, as well as famous ancestors. It is common for brothers of the same family to worship their dead parents at the eldest brother's house."[4] On the lunar New Year's Eve, Yiche children hear stories about their ancestors and learn their family genealogies.

Christianity: Some parts of Honghe Prefecture experienced a mass people movement to Christ in the 1940s as a result of the labors of missionaries. During the Cultural Revolution great persecution broke out against the church. Many fledgling believers fell away, but others "conducted Sunday services in cattle stables or on mountain peaks."[5] Today most believers in the area are Kado or Biyo, but there may be a few Yiche Christians.

Paul Hattaway

Yizi 羿子

Paul Hattaway

Location: The 1982 Chinese publication *Minzu Shibie Wenxian Ziliao Huibian* listed a population of 1,500 Yizi people living in southern China.[1] Despite their tiny population, the Yizi are distributed in three different provinces. The majority are located in Bijie County of northern Guizhou Province. Smaller numbers live in nearby Zhenxiong County in Yunnan Province and in Gulin County in Sichuan Province.

Identity: Despite their similar names, the Yizi are not related to any of the Yi groups in China who are speakers of Tibeto-Burman languages. The Yizi are also known as *Yiren* or "Yi people," which further confuses the matter. In the 1950s the Yizi applied for recognition as one of China's official minority groups. They were rejected. At the time of the 1982 national census they still had not been classified and were included in a list of *Undetermined Minorities*. After some debate, the Yizi were placed under the Gelao nationality in 1985.[2] The Yizi, who have a separate ethnicity from the Gelao, are not entirely happy with this decision. They view themselves as different from all other groups in China. The Yizi may call themselves *Wo*. The Miao call them *Ke*; the Han call them *Yizi*; and the Gelao know this group as *Yipu*.

Language: The Yizi have lost the use of their mother tongue and now speak exclusively the Southwest dialect of Mandarin Chinese. A few can also speak some Yi which they have learned from their Yi neighbors. Most Yizi also read and write Chinese.

History: Although today there are less than 2,000 ethnically distinct Yizi remaining, during the Ming Dynasty (1368–1644) they were recorded to have a population of more than 20,000.[3] During the Qing Dynasty (1644–1911) the Yizi were considered a Yi group, even though they have never claimed to be Yi themselves. Today, most Yizi have been assimilated to Han and Yi culture.

Customs: Most Yizi are now sedentary agriculturists, but before the advent of Communism in 1949 they were renowned and feared throughout the region as a fierce people. Still today, neighboring peoples despise the Yizi and claim they are all thieves.

Religion: Some of the more remote communities of Yizi are animists, although in most places now only the elderly continue to observe animistic rituals and appease spirits. Ancestor worship is a common thread that ties the Yizi together. The Yizi in different locations have the same ancestors. At least three times each year a ceremony is held to honor the spirits of those family members who have gone before.

Christianity: Because of a lack of specific information about the Yizi, it is not known if there are any Christians among them. It is possible they do include believers, however, because of the high density of Christians in the Bijie area of Guizhou Province especially among the A-Hmao, Gha-Mu, and the various branches of the Yi nationality. Samuel Pollard is credited for being used by God to bring the gospel to the people in the northeast Yunnan and northwest Guizhou areas. Pollard labored sacrificially among several people groups, seeing thousands come to Christ.

Population in China:
1,500 (1982)
2,280 (2000)
2,940 (2010)
Location:
Guizhou, Yunnan, Sichuan
Religion: Ancestor Worship
Christians: None Known

Overview of the Yizi

Countries: China

Pronunciation: "Yee-zee"

Other Names: Yiren, Wo, Ke, Yipu

Population Source:
1,500 (1982 *Minzu Shibie Wenxian Ziliao Huibian*);
Out of a total Gelao population of 437,997 (1990 census)

Location:
NW Guizhou: Bijie County;
NE Yunnan: Zhenxiong County;
S Sichuan: Gulin County

Status: Officially included under Gelao since 1985; Previously included in a list of *Undetermined Minorities*

Language: Chinese

Dialects: 0

Religion: Ancestor Worship, Animism, No Religion

Christians: None known

Scripture: None

***Jesus* film:** None

Gospel Recordings: None

Christian Broadcasting: None

ROPAL code: None

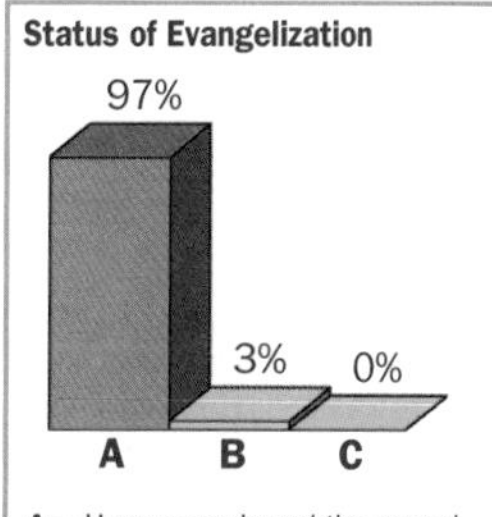

Yongchun 用春

Population in China:
12,226 (1995)
13,400 (2000)
16,050 (2010)
Location: Yunnan
Religion: Polytheism
Christians: None Known

Overview of the Yongchun

Countries: China

Pronunciation: "Yong-choon"

Other Names: Yungchun, Yungshun

Population Source: 12,226 (1995 GEM); Out of a total Zhuang population of 15,489,630 (1990 census)

Location: *SE Yunnan*

Status: Officially included under Zhuang

Language: Daic, Tai, Central Tai

Dialects: 0

Religion: Polytheism, Animism, Ancestor Worship

Christians: None known

Scripture: None

***Jesus* film:** None

Gospel Recordings: None

Christian Broadcasting: None

ROPAL code: YUG00

Status of Evangelization

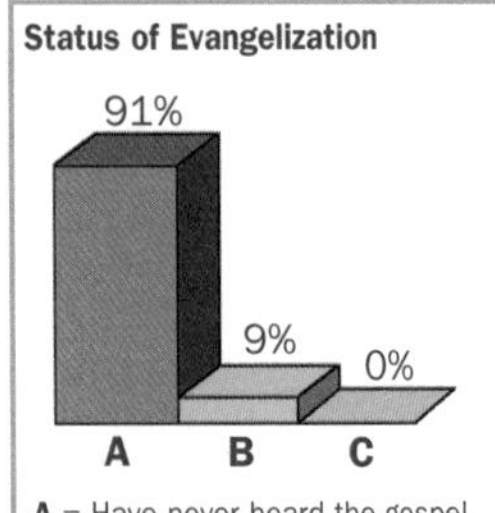

A = Have never heard the gospel
B = Were evangelized but did not become Christians
C = Are adherents to any form of Christianity

Location: The Global Evangelization Movement listed a 1995 population of 12,226 members of the Yongchun tribe in southern China. The Yongchun live in the southeastern part of Yunnan Province, but their exact location is uncertain. It is known that they live close to where Yunnan borders the Guangxi Zhuang Autonomous Region. The Han Chinese, Miao, Yi, Buyang, Lati, Giay, Nung, Cao Lan, Tho, and Southern Zhuang are also located in the region.

Dwayne Graybill

Identity: The Yongchun applied for status as a separate nationality in the 1950s. When their application was rejected — along with more than 350 other groups in China — the Yongchun leaders met and agreed to be combined into the official Zhuang nationality.

Language: The Yongchun language has simply been described as "a variety of Zhuang spoken in Yunnan Province."[1] The 1992 *Ethnologue* listed Yongchun as a separate language, but the 1996 edition did not mention them at all. Yongchun is a member of the Central Tai linguistic affiliation and is related to Southern Zhuang. There are more than 50 dialects of Zhuang in China,[2] many of which are mutually unintelligible. Speakers from different Zhuang groups often greet each other in their respective Zhuang dialects before conducting business in Mandarin or Cantonese.

History: After centuries of isolation, the various Tai peoples of southern China, including the Yongchun, gradually splintered and became distinct ethnolinguistic people groups.

Customs: During holidays and festival times the Yongchun like to make multi-colored eggs, which they use to find partners. "Chicken, duck, or goose eggs are boiled and then dyed red, yellow, orange, blue and purple.... When a young man spots a woman he likes, he takes an egg and smashes it on the egg she is carrying in her hand. If the woman is interested, she allows her egg to be smashed and then the two of them wander away from the crowd to talk in private."[3]

Religion: The Yongchun are polytheists. They are enslaved and tormented by the demands of evil spirits, to whom they offer regular sacrifices.

Christianity: There are no known Christians among the Yongchun people. In the 1800s, famous missionary statesman Hudson Taylor motivated thousands to prayer and action for China's lost by his heartfelt challenges. Taylor once asked: "Shall not the low wail of helpless misery arising from one-half of the heathen world pierce our sluggish ear and rouse us, spirit, soul and body, to one mighty, continued, unconquerable effort for China's salvation?... that strong in God's strength and in the power of His might, we may snatch the prey from the hand of the mighty; that we may pluck these brands from the everlasting burning, and rescue these captives from the thralldom of sin and Satan; to grace the triumph of our Sovereign King, and to shine forth forever as stars in His diadem."[4]

Yonzhi 用之

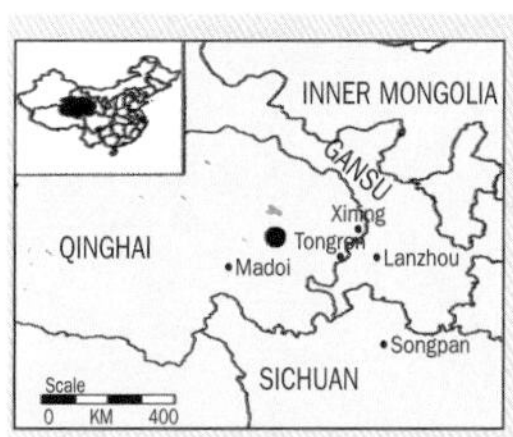

Population in China:
3,000 (1996)
3,270 (2000)
4,030 (2010)
Location: Qinghai
Religion: Tibetan Buddhism
Christians: None Known

Overview of the Yonzhi

Countries: China

Pronunciation: "Yon-jee"

Other Names:

Population Source:
3,000 (1996 AMO);
Out of a total Tibetan population of 4,593,330 (1990 census)

Location: *E Qinghai:* Near the Anye Machen Mountains in Gonghe County

Status:
Officially included under Tibetan

Language: Sino-Tibetan, Tibeto-Burman, Bodic, Bodish, Tibetan, Northern Tibetan

Dialects: 0

Religion:
Tibetan Buddhism, Polytheism

Christians: None known

Scripture: None

***Jesus* film:** None

Gospel Recordings: None

Christian Broadcasting: None

ROPAL code: None

Status of Evangelization

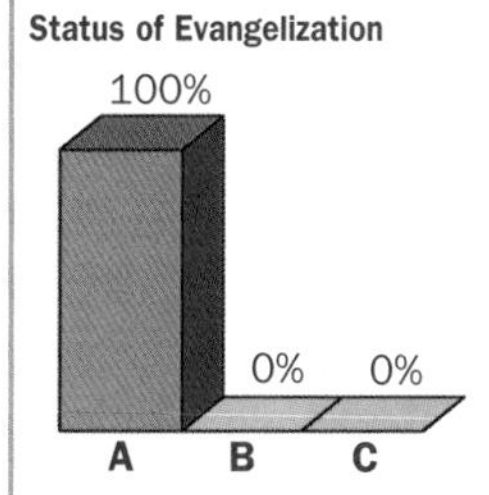

A = Have never heard the gospel
B = Were evangelized but did not become Christians
C = Are adherents to any form of Christianity

Location: More than 3,000 members of the Yonzhi tribe, a nomadic Tibetan people group, live in a virtually inaccessible area of eastern Qinghai Province. They primarily inhabit the Heha Chen Valley, near the town Tibetans call *Cheb Chu.* The Yonzhi area lies within Gonghe County, east of the Yellow River. The imposing Anye Machen Mountain range, considered sacred by all Tibetans, lies to the east of the Yonzhi tribe. The highest peak is the 6,282-meter (20,604 ft.) Machen Gangri. In the short summer months the area comes alive with flowers. "Red and blue poppies, bright, fresh, and unharmed, looked happily out of their bed of snow.... The scenery became more and more beautiful as we descended. The little meadows, clearings in the juniper forest, were full of flowers... out in all their glory."[1] The Yonzhi share their homelands with many blue sheep, gazelles, and wolves.

Identity: The Yonzhi are a distinct ethnic group who live in a remote area that has changed little for hundreds of years. They are considered by some to be a part of the Golog, who in turn are officially counted as part of the Tibetan nationality in China.

Language: The Yonzhi speak a variety of Golog Tibetan, the regional language. Few Yonzhi have a knowledge of Chinese.

History: For countless generations the Yonzhi have lived simple lives, unaffected by events in the rest of the world. Joseph Rock, the famous botanist and explorer, stumbled across the Yonzhi in 1929. He recalls, "The people were astonished at sight of our party. One asked, 'Why this array of arms and force when visiting our territory?' We continued up the valley to the very foot of Amnyi Druggu, the mountain god of the Yonzhi tribe. The last few tents we passed were cursed by some plague, the nomads said. The inmates lay dying outside, covered with yak-hair rugs."[2]

Customs: The Yonzhi are nomadic, living in yak-hair tents and moving every few weeks to find new pastures for their yaks, sheep, and goats.

Religion: In addition to worshiping Amnyi Druggu, the Yonzhi's Mountain deity, the Yonzhi live in the vicinity of Anye Machen Mountain. They believe it contains a powerful god of the same name. He is often represented in pictures riding a white horse, with the sun and a rainbow to his right and the moon to his left. "All Tibetans worship Anye Machen; every monastery has either a picture or image of him. *Anye* means 'old man' and corresponds to our 'saint'. *Ma* means 'peacock' and *chen* 'great'."[3]

Christianity: The Yonzhi are one of the most unreachable people groups in China — if not all the world. Their region is snowbound for most of the year with temperatures plummeting to minus 40° Celsius (–40°F). The Yonzhi move around frequently, relocating their homes and herds to new pastures. Their communities are only accessible by foot or horseback. To the Yonzhi, the gospel remains untold. It is possible no Yonzhi has ever heard the name of Jesus Christ.

Paul Hattaway

Youmai 油迈

Location: About 2,000 people belonging to the little-known Youmai ethnic group live in an unspecified part of southern Guizhou Province in southern China.[1] Although no location for the Youmai has ever been given, the few members of the Yao nationality — under which the Youmai were included — in Guizhou Province live in a few pockets along the southeast and southern parts of the province.

Identity: When the Chinese authorities first surveyed the ethnolinguistic composition of Guizhou Province in the 1950s, they found the Youmai people group so distinct that they were unable to place them under any of the officially recognized nationalities that had been created. By the time of the 1982 census, the Youmai were still unclassified and were placed in a generic list of *Undetermined Minorities.* The status for this small group changed in 1985 when the Youmai were included as part of the Yao nationality.[2] This classification has not been appreciated by the Youmai, who see themselves as a completely distinct group with no relationship to other minorities in southern China. Living in a nation where governmental decisions are not open to debate, the Youmai have little choice but to accept their bureaucratic identity. The people living near them, however, recognize them as a distinct ethnic group.

Language: The Youmai language has never been studied before. Because of their inclusion in the Yao minority group, the Youmai probably speak a Mienic language, although there are other Yao groups in China who speak languages belonging to the Tai and Hmongic language groups. More research needs to be conducted to find the linguistic relationship the Youmai share with other groups.

History: The Youmai may be related to the various Bunu people groups in Guizhou, who are culturally Yao but linguistically Hmong people. After more than a thousand years of living near the Yao, these groups have absorbed many of their customs and habits.

Paul Hattaway

Customs: The Youmai observe several key festivals throughout the year, including the Zhuzhu Festival. The date set for the festival is believed to be the birthday of their foremother, Miluotuo, in the fifth month of the lunar calendar. The Huiqi Festival is held at the same time as the Autumn Festival in other parts of China. Traditional singing contests are held, and people from the countryside crowd into the village which has been chosen as the sponsor for that year. Hosts entertain guests with sumptuous food. No festival or celebration is conducted by the Youmai without copious amounts of rice wine and whiskey being served.

Religion: Spirit worship, ancestor worship, and Daoism are the three most prevalent religious beliefs among the Youmai.

Christianity: Because researchers have yet to find the exact location of the Youmai in Guizhou Province, nothing is known of the status of Christianity among them. Few people groups in this part of China, however, have ever heard the gospel.

Population in China:
2,000 (1999)
2,055 (2000)
2,650 (2010)
Location: Guizhou
Religion: Animism
Christians: None Known

Overview of the Youmai

Countries: China

Pronunciation: "You-my"

Other Names: Youmairen

Population Source:
2,000 (1999 AMO);
Out of a total Yao population of 2,134,013 (1990 census)

Location: *S Guizhou*

Status: Officially included under Yao since 1985; Previously included in a list of *Undetermined Minorities*

Language: Hmong-Mien, Mienic

Dialects: 0

Religion: Animism, Ancestor Worship, Daoism

Christians: None known

Scripture: None

***Jesus* film:** None

Gospel Recordings: None

Christian Broadcasting: None

ROPAL code: None

Status of Evangelization

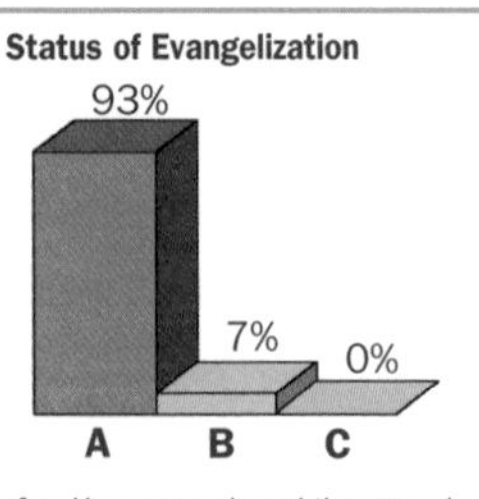

A = Have never heard the gospel
B = Were evangelized but did not become Christians
C = Are adherents to any form of Christianity

Younuo 有诺

Population in China:
13,000 (1987)
17,900 (2000)
23,000 (2010)
Location: Guangxi
Religion: Polytheism
Christians: None Known

Overview of the Younuo

Countries: China

Pronunciation: "Yoou-noou"

Other Names: Bunu: Younuo, Yunuo, Yuno, Red Yao, Hong Yao, Ju-Nuo, Shanhua Hong Yao, Mountain Speech Red Yao

Population Source:
13,000 (1987 D. Bradley);
2,920 (1982 census);
Out of a total Yao population of 2,134,013 (1990 census)

Location: *NE Guangxi:* Longsheng and Xing'an counties

Status:
Officially included under Yao

Language: Hmong-Mien, Hmongic, Bunuic, Bahengic

Dialects: 0

Religion: Polytheism, Animism, Ancestor Worship

Christians: None known

Scripture: None

***Jesus* film:** None

Gospel Recordings: None

Christian Broadcasting: None

ROPAL code: BUH00

Status of Evangelization

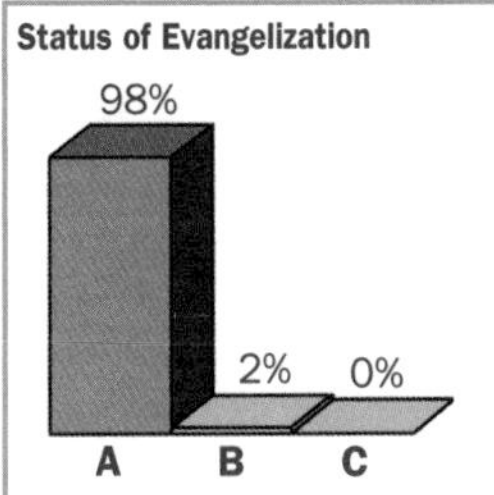

A = Have never heard the gospel
B = Were evangelized but did not become Christians
C = Are adherents to any form of Christianity

Yao Update

Location: Approximately 18,000 members of the Younuo tribe[1] — known locally as the *Hong Yao* (Red Yao) — live in concentrated communities within Longsheng and Xing'an counties in the northeastern part of the Guangxi Zhuang Autonomous Region. They share the region with members of the Dong and Miao minorities. The 1982 Chinese census listed only 2,920 Younuo. Subsequent research found their numbers to be higher.

Identity: The Younuo people have been officially classified as part of the Bunu in China, who in turn are considered part of the Yao nationality. The term *Bunu* does not necessarily refer to a specific people group; it simply means "us people."[2]

Language: The Younuo language — which has six tones — contains many Chinese loanwords in its vocabulary. Younuo is most closely related to Wunai, spoken in the mountains across the border in Hunan.

History: Traditionally, Younuo men were hunters, although the practice has diminished in the last generation. The Younuo's favorite weapons are the crossbow and the muzzle-loading musket. Wild pigs and deer become more scarce every year.

Customs: The Younuo rarely marry outside their ethnic group, although there is no rule prohibiting this. Often, Younuo women consider the location of their suitor's village — to determine how far she will have to walk to fetch water — before deciding if she will accept his proposal. Sexual immorality is rampant among the Younuo. Premarital sex is openly permitted. A young man may secretly come to his girlfriend's house after dark — knowing exactly where in the house she sleeps — and will call out to her between the cracks in the wall. If the girl accepts the boy's advances, she will leave the house and spend the night with him.

Religion: The Younuo have a flood legend. They claim the waters once rose up so high on the earth that they reached into heaven. Man then sounded a gong at the rooftop of the earth which woke the Thunder god. The Thunder god saw man's distress and came down to rescue them, causing the flood to end. They also worship a powerful dragon spirit, Zaj Laung, who they believe controls the waters and lives at the bottom the sea. He also controls the weather and must be placated to ensure enough rain for a bountiful harvest. The Younuo believe the dragon can take the form of a rainbow. They also worship the sun and moon.

Christianity: The Younuo, and all the Bunu groups in southern China, are unreached with the gospel. Rev. W. H. Oldfield longed to reach the people groups in Guangxi in the early part of the twentieth century. "How we wished we could speak their dialect and tell them plainly the Gospel message.... To this people, as yet, the Gospel has not been given. No missionary in [Guangxi] speaks their dialect; no Chinese worker is laboring among them; no Christian chapel has been opened in their territories. They live, they die, unreached, unhelped, and unheeded. For decades they have been groping in darkness, for decades more they will have to grope, unless someone comes to give them the message."[3]

You Tai 犹太人

Midge Conner

Location: Approximately 750 You Tai — or Chinese Jews — live scattered throughout several cities of eastern China. The majority, "200 to 300,"[1] are located in Kaifeng City in Henan Province.[2]

Identity: In the 1990 census the government officially noted the You Tai, before classifying them as part of the Han Chinese nationality. The You Tai are already extinct as an ethnolinguistic people, but they do retain a common pride in their lost heritage. One visitor reported, "They were very curious about their origins, though physically and culturally they seemed indistinguishable from other Chinese."[3] Most of the inhabitants of Kaifeng are aware of the existence of the You Tai and can direct visitors to the location where their synagogue used to stand.

Language: There are no traces of a Hebrew or Aramaic language still in use among the You Tai. All now speak and read Chinese.

History: Although now more of a historic novelty than a distinct people group, the You Tai have a rich and fascinating past. Jews have been in China since at least the ninth century AD. One scholar claims the You Tai migrated to China from Persia and Yemen 1,000 to 1,500 years ago.[4] In the thirteenth century Marco Polo described Jews living in mixed communities with Nestorian Christians at various places along the Old Silk Road.[5] When the Jesuits reached China in the sixteenth century they "found a colony of Jews in Kaifeng, but no Christians."[6] Matteo Ricci established that there were 10 or 12 families of Israelites in Kaifeng — "all expert in the Hebrew language"[7] — but discovered a much larger Jewish community in a place he refers to as *Cequian* at the capital of *Hamcheu*. Scholars have not been able to identify these places. The Jews in Kaifeng constructed a synagogue in 1163 which was destroyed by a flood in 1461.[8] Kaifeng grew to a thriving population of 20,000 Jews and was known as the "Jerusalem of China."[9] Another flood of the Yellow River in 1642 again destroyed the synagogue.[10] In the seventeenth century there were a dozen Jewish communities throughout China and Tibet.[11] They retained their religious practices as Jews right up to about 1850, when, "poverty stricken and isolated for centuries from any contact with other Jews, they demolished their own synagogue and sold the bricks."[12]

Customs: The You Tai today have completely assimilated to the Han Chinese culture and have no distinct customs left.

Religion: After the final destruction of the synagogue in 1850, all practice of Judaism among the You Tai ceased. Scrolls of the Pentateuch (five Books of Moses), which had been carefully preserved for centuries, were sold to Christian missionaries in the late 1800s.[13] Most You Tai are nonreligious, while a few families in Kaifeng have been converted to Islam by neighboring Hui communities.

Christianity: There are no known Christians today among the You Tai. A letter from the You Tai leaders in 1870 said in part, "Morning and night with tears in our eyes and with offerings of incense, we implore God that our religion may flourish again."[14]

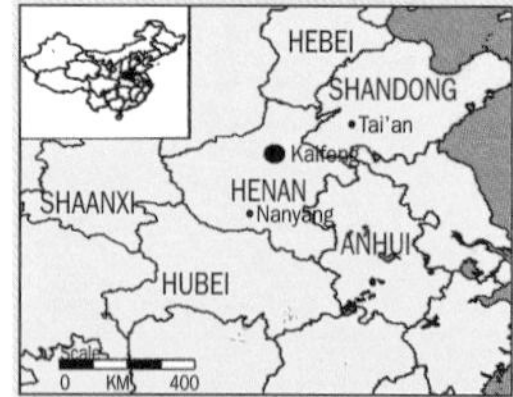

Population in China:
700 (1995)
750 (2000)
840 (2010)
Location: Henan
Religion: No Religion
Christians: None Known

Overview of the You Tai

Countries: China

Pronunciation: "Yo-Tai"

Other Names: Chinese Jews, Jews

Population Source:
700 (1995 AMO);
Out of a total Han population of 1,042,482,187 (1990 census)

Location: *Henan:* Kaifeng City, and several other locations throughout eastern China

Status: Officially counted separately, then included under Han Chinese

Language: Chinese, Mandarin

Dialects: 0

Religion: No Religion, Islam

Christians: None known

Scripture: None

***Jesus* film:** None

Gospel Recordings: None

Christian Broadcasting: None

ROPAL code: None

Status of Evangelization

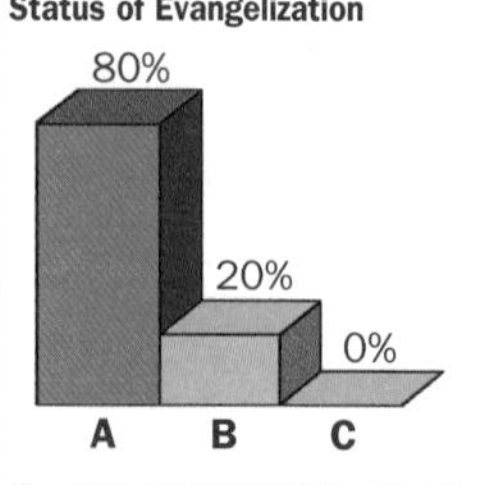

A = Have never heard the gospel
B = Were evangelized but did not become Christians
C = Are adherents to any form of Christianity

Yugur, Enger 裕固，恩格而

Location: The small Yugur (not to be mistaken for the *Uygur*) minority live in the Gansu corridor. They are one of the most unique people groups in China, speaking two completely unrelated languages. The Enger (Eastern) Yugur live in the eastern part of the Sunan Yugur Autonomous County in northern Gansu Province.[1] A 1987 study listed 4,000 speakers of Enger Yugur, representing about a third of all Yugur.

Identity: The Enger Yugur, who speak a Mongolian language, have been combined with the Turkic-speaking Saragh Yugur to form the official Yugur minority in China.

Language: Enger Yugur is a Mongolian language. Only a handful of people, living in the Dahe District of Sunan Yugur County, can speak both Yugur languages. Enger Yugur is closely related to Bonan, Tu, Dongxiang, and Mongolian. "Its phonology is closer to the first three languages, whereas in vocabulary and grammar it is somewhat more akin to Mongolian."[2] A significant number of Yugur, living in Jiuquan, Huangnibao, and parts of Sunan County, can now speak only Chinese. In addition, some Yugur are bilingual in the Tibetan language.

History: Most scholars believe the Yugur are descended from a nomadic tribe known as the Huiqu. The Huiqu were first recorded during the Tang Dynasty (AD 618–907). In the mid-800s, "heavy snowfall, combined with an attack from the forest-dwelling Kirgiz from the north, forced the Yugurs to flee their Mongolian homeland."[3] They moved to Gansu where they came under the control of the Tibetans. The Yugur region was largely unknown and cut off from the world for centuries until the completion of the Lanzhou-Urumqi railway line in 1963 which passes through the Yugur area.

Tallis Chang

Customs: The Yugur practice bird burials, similar to the Tibetans. Dead corpses are cut up into pieces and taken to a mountaintop where ravens and other birds of prey come and devour the flesh. Historically the Yugur were divided into nine separate clans. Each clan controlled its own herding area.

Religion: When the Yugur first arrived in the area in the ninth century, they believed in Manichaeanism. They were soon converted to Buddhism by the Tibetans. Today most Yugur remain followers of Tibetan Buddhism. In recent years there has been a revival of the ancient shamanistic religion and the cult of the "Emperor of Heaven," *Han Tengri*.

Christianity: Although few Enger Yugur today have ever heard the name of Jesus Christ, the region had many Christians in the past. The Ongkuts developed a widespread Christian culture, witnessed to by the many Christian crosses found by archaeologists.[4] The Yugur are thought to be the descendants of this tribe. When Marco Polo visited Dunhuang, near the Yugur's homeland, he reported, "It is true there are some Turks who hold to the religion of the Nestorian Christians."[5] In 1992 the first Enger Yugur people believed in Christ. Today there are approximately 50 Christians.

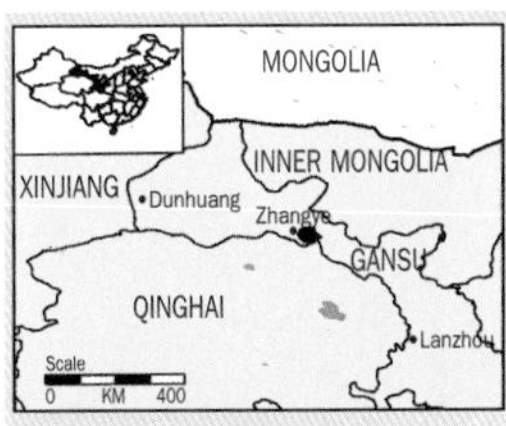

Population in China:
4,000 (1987)
4,810 (2000)
5,800 (2010)
Location: Gansu
Religion: Tibetan Buddhism
Christians: 50

Overview of the Enger Yugur

Countries: China

Pronunciation: "Eng-gur-Yoo-gur"

Other Names: East Yugur, Enger, Mongolian Yugur, Shira Yugur, Shera Yugur, Eastern Yogor, Yugar, Yugu, Yogur

Population Source: 4,000 (1987 *LAC*); Out of a total Yugur population of 12,297 (1990 census)

Location: *NW Gansu:* Sunan Yugur County: Kangle, Hongshiwo, and Qinglong townships of Kangle District, and Dongtan and Beitan townships of Huangcheng District

Status: Officially included under Yugur

Language: Altaic, Mongolian, Eastern Mongolian, Mongour

Literacy: 59%

Dialects: 0

Religion: Tibetan Buddhism, Shamanism, Christianity

Christians: 50

Scripture: None

***Jesus* film:** None

Gospel Recordings: Yugur, East #04864

Christian Broadcasting: None

ROPAL code: YUY00

Status of Evangelization

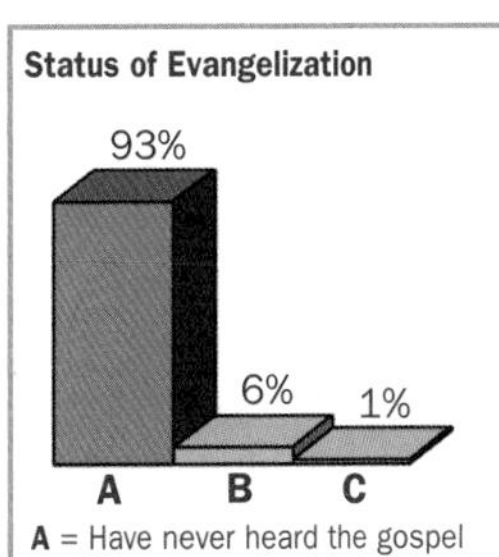

A = Have never heard the gospel
B = Were evangelized but did not become Christians
C = Are adherents to any form of Christianity

Yugur, Saragh 裕固, 撒里

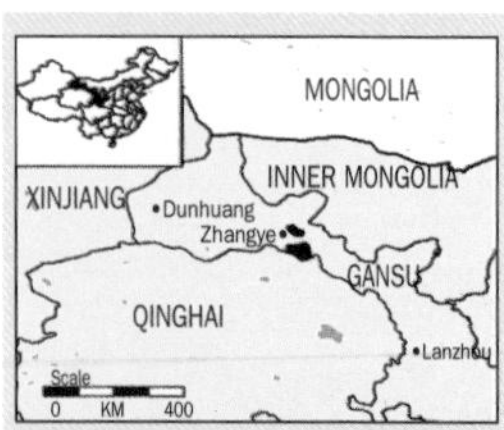

Population in China:
8,197 (1990)
9,870 (2000)
11,880 (2010)
Location: Gansu
Religion: Tibetan Buddhism
Christians: 50

Overview of the Saragh Yugur

Countries: China

Pronunciation: "Sah-rahg-Yoo-gur"

Other Names: West Yugur, Saragh, Saraygh, Sarig, Ya Lu, Yellow Uighur, Sari Yogur, Yuku, Yugu, Yohur, Yaofuer

Population Source:
8,197 (1990 AMO);
Out of a total Yugur population of 12,297 (1990 census)

Location: *NW Gansu:* Sunan Yugur County: Dahe and Minghua districts; Also some Yugur inhabit the Huangnibao area near Jiuquan City in western Gansu.

Status:
Officially included under Yugur

Language:
Altaic, Turkic, Eastern Turkic

Dialects: 0

Religion: Tibetan Buddhism, Shamanism, Christianity

Christians: 50

Scripture: None

***Jesus* film:** None

Gospel Recordings:
Yugur, West #04865

Christian Broadcasting: None

ROPAL code: YBE00

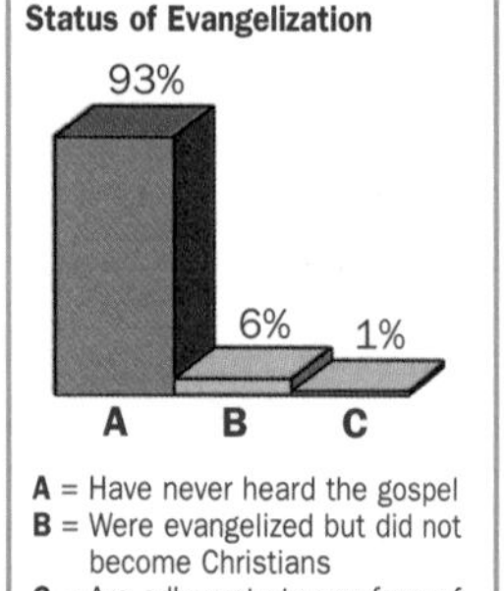

A = Have never heard the gospel
B = Were evangelized but did not become Christians
C = Are adherents to any form of Christianity

Location: Approximately 10,000 Saragh (Western) Yugur live in the western part of the Sunan Yugur Autonomous County, in the narrow northern corridor of Gansu Province. The nearest town to the Saragh Yugur is Zhangye. Other Saragh Yugur communities are located in the Dahe and Minghua districts, and in the Huangnibao area near Jiuquan City in western Gansu.

Identity: The Saragh Yugur, also known as *Yaofuer*, are the Turkic half of the official Yugur nationality. They live in a separate area from the Enger Yugur.

Language: Whereas Enger Yugur is a Mongolian language, Saragh Yugur is a completely different language — a member of the Turkic language family. The two Yugur groups have little contact with each other, but when they do meet they must use Chinese to communicate. One expert notes that Saragh Yugur "still preserves many features of the language of medieval Turkic literature."[1] Because they do not have their own script, written Chinese is in common use among the Yugur.

History: The Yugur region was controlled by the Tibetans until the Tangut state of Xixia conquered them in 1028.[2] The Tanguts, in turn, were annihilated by the Mongols in the early 1200s. The Chinese finally assumed control of the area during the Ming Dynasty (1368–1644). There were 300,000 Yugurs at that time, most of whom were living outside the Great Wall at Jiayuguan,[3] farther to the west of their present location. Today, their descendants are no longer called Yugur and probably have become part of the Uygurs in Xinjiang, who also speak a Turkic language. A small number of people migrated back inside the wall to avoid the conflict between the Turfan and Hami rulers. They are believed to be the Yugur's ancestors.

Customs: Most Saragh Yugur live in yak-hair *yurts*. A visitor who comes by horseback should leave his whip, rifle, ammunition, and all meat outside the yurt. The Yugur believe the god of Hair dresses in red and rides a reddish horse, so visitors dressed in red are not allowed inside a Yugur home.[4] The Yugurs are heavy drinkers. Each evening meal is followed by strong alcohol. Revelry often goes far into the next morning. They do not consider themselves to be good hosts unless their guests get drunk.

Religion: The Saragh Yugur adhere to a mixture of Tibetan Buddhism and shamanism. Each family clan has a shaman who consults the spirit world for them.

Christianity: This group had no knowledge whatsoever of Christianity until 1997, when about 15 Saragh Yugur believed in Christ after watching the *Jesus* film in Mandarin.[5] This number grew to around 50 believers by May 2000. The authorities in Sunan are strongly opposed to the introduction of Christianity. During the 1980s and early 1990s one mission agency sent workers several times to distribute gospel literature among the Yugur, but on every occasion the workers were arrested before they could complete their task.[6]

Tallis Chang

Za 杂

Paul Hattaway

Location: Approximately 2,500 people belonging to an ethnic group called the Za live in a remote area of southeastern Tibet. The Za, who were originally a collection of tribal peoples including relatives of today's Geman Deng people, live between Xiachayu and the Wanong Valley in Zayu County. Very few foreigners have ever ventured into this extremely remote part of China.

Identity: The Za ethnic group is one of the most fascinating examples of fusion in China today. About 200 years ago the Za were believed to be the same as today's Geman Deng people, but at that time Tibetan political and religious leaders entered the area and exerted their influence over the people there. The result is a new ethnic group called *Za* by the Tibetans, who speak a distinct language from the Deng and who practice different customs. The Za were not counted under any official nationality in the 1990 China census but instead were included in a list of *Undetermined Minorities.*

Language: Chinese linguist Sun Hongkai, who visited the Za in 1976, wrote, "Today the Za people only use their own language at home; outside the home they use Tibetan. The language that they use at home is about 60% Tibetan loanwords, and the grammar is also basically Tibetan. Recent Geman Deng immigrants into this area can only understand about 30% of the speech of the Za people.... Two hundred years of language contact, because of political, economic, cultural and religious dominance, caused one language to be heavily influenced by another and gradually lose its unique characteristics. In the recognition and comparison of this type of language we see how social factors play a crucial role in the process of language change in contact situations. Za is an unclassified part of the Tibeto-Burman language family."[1]

History: Two hundred years ago, the Tibetans entered this area and set up a combined rule of government and religion, and subsequently the original inhabitants of the area slowly became Tibetanized. The Tibetans ruled the Za with an iron fist. The Za were not even allowed to travel outside the area without prior permission of the monk or administrator. Today, the Za have changed from the Geman Deng so much that they deserve to be viewed as a distinct ethnolinguistic group.

Customs: The Za have lost the use of all of their original customs and festivals; these are still practiced by Geman Deng people who lived outside the influence of Tibetan rule. Culturally the Za have become identical to the Tibetans.

Religion: The forefathers of the Za people were polytheists, worshiping nature and a host of spirits. However, the Tibetans took over the area long ago, and today the Za have been thoroughly converted to the Tibetan Buddhist religion.

Christianity: Christianity has yet to make its presence felt in the isolated part of Tibet inhabited by the Za. Few roads led into the area until recently. Contact between the Za and the outside world is now possible. Today, the Za remain unaware of the existence of Christianity and are a completely unreached people group.

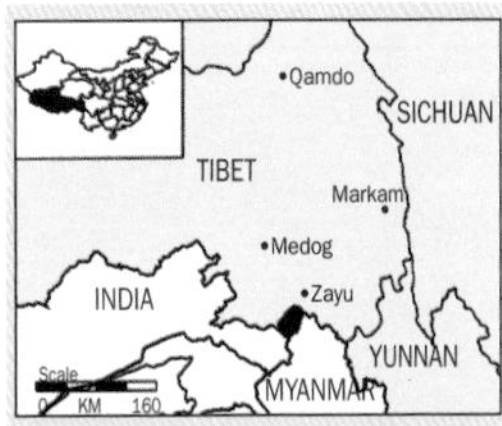

Population in China:
2,500 (1998)
2,640 (2000)
3,410 (2010)
Location: Tibet
Religion: Tibetan Buddhism
Christians: None Known

Overview of the Za

Countries: China
Pronunciation: "Za"
Other Names: Deng Za
Population Source:
2,500 (1998 AMO)
Location: *SE Tibet:* Between Xiachayu and the Wanong Valley in Zayu County
Status: Counted in the census as an *Undetermined Minority*
Language: Sino-Tibetan, Tibeto-Burman, Unclassified
Dialects: 0
Religion:
Tibetan Buddhism, Polytheism
Christians: None known
Scripture: None
***Jesus* film:** None
Gospel Recordings: None
Christian Broadcasting: None
ROPAL code: None

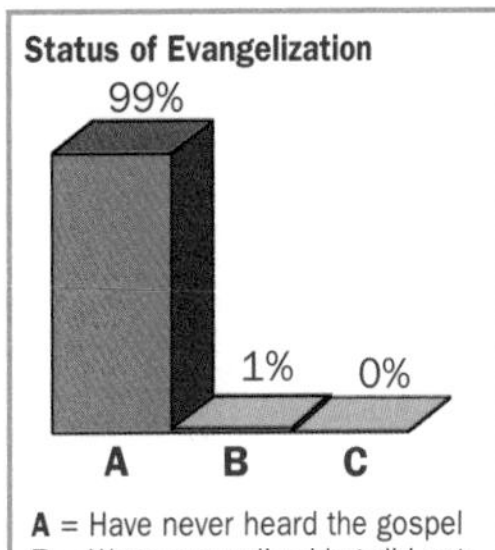

Zaiwa 载瓦

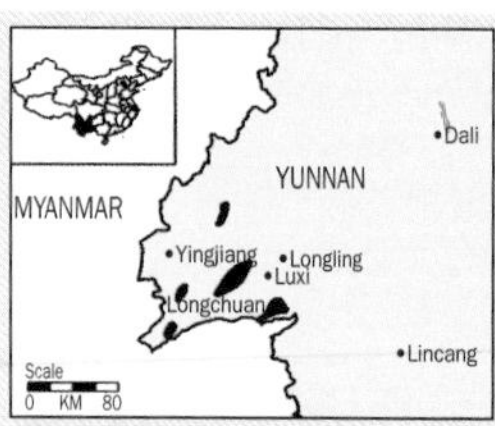

Population in China:
70,000 (1990)
90,300 (2000)
116,400 (2010)
Location: Yunnan
Religion: Polytheism
Christians: 200

Overview of the Zaiwa

Countries: China, Myanmar

Pronunciation: "Zay-wah"

Other Names: Atsi, Tsaiwa, Atzi, Szi, Atshi, Aci, Azi, Atsi-Maru, Xiaoshanhua, Xiaoshan, Aji

Population Source: 70,000 (1990 J.-O. Svantesson); Out of a total Jingpo population of 119,209 (1990 census); 13,200 in Myanmar (1983)

Location: *W Yunnan:* Luxi, Ruili, Longchuan, and Yingjiang counties

Status: Officially included under Jingpo

Language: Sino-Tibetan, Tibeto-Burman, Burmese-Lolo, Burmish, Northern Burmish

Dialects (3): Zaiwa, Langwa, Polo

Religion: Polytheism, Animism, Shamanism, Christianity

Christians: 200

Scripture: Portions 1939; Work in progress

***Jesus* film:** None

Gospel Recordings: Atsi #01176

Christian Broadcasting: Available (FEBC)

ROPAL code: ATB00

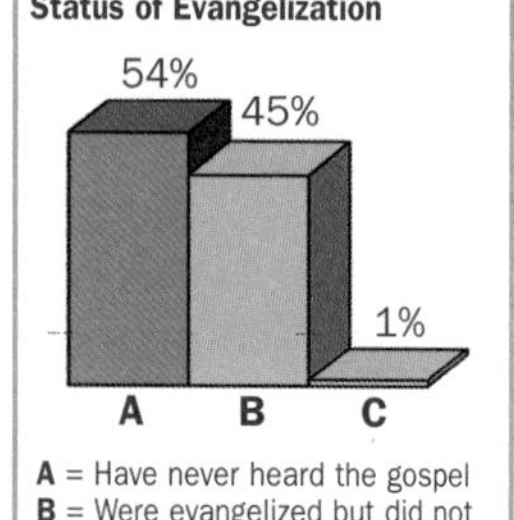

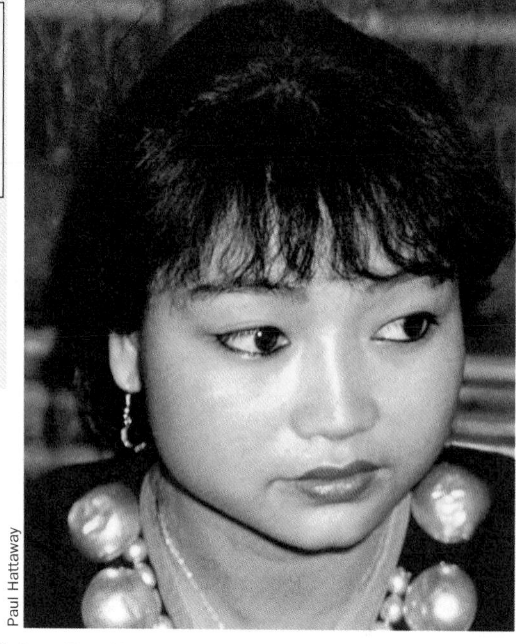
Paul Hattaway

Location: Linguist Jan-Olof Svantesson listed a 1990 population of 70,000 Zaiwa in China.[1] The Zaiwa comprise 73% of the total Jingpo population in Yunnan Province's Dehong Prefecture.[2] They are concentrated in the east and west mountains of Luxi County.

Identity: The Zaiwa are the largest subgroup of the official Jingpo nationality in China. The Zaiwa, who are called *Xiaoshan*, meaning "small mountain" by the Chinese, have a fearsome reputation. In 1911 James Fraser described the Zaiwa as "the wildest people around here by a long way. Inveterate robbers, their hand is against every man and every man's hand is against them. Dirty, unkempt, ignorant, everybody despises them. They are savages only and not cannibals."[3]

Language: In 1957 an orthography based on the Roman alphabet was devised for the Zaiwa.[4] Previously the Zaiwa kept records by notching wood or tying knots. Calculations were done by counting beans.

History: The Zaiwa have forged a reputation for themselves as a local version of the Mafia. Their *gumsa* system encourages a "belligerent, competitive, authoritarian society whose chiefs are chosen by public consent."[5] The large Zaiwa village of Banwa forced 44 neighboring villages, amounting to 1,020 households, to pay them "protection" money.[6]

Customs: The Zaiwa are enslaved by almost every kind of vice imaginable. Zaiwa young men "do not sleep at home. They usually spend the night flirting with young women at the youth club. Sexual relations are so disorderly as to have rendered them unfit for physical labor. A girl who gets pregnant without a proposal will not easily find another boy to marry her and will be considered a widow because of the heavy bride-price."[7] In Banwa Village alone, there were 55 such "widows" from a total of 134 households.[8]

Religion: The Zaiwa are enslaved by evil spirits. In the past they even bullied Lisu households into paying a tax of three squirrels per year, to be used as an offering to the spirits.[9] One tragic example of the Zaiwa's bondage is retold here: "Elder Dai's daughter-in-law died of fever after having a difficult labor. Before her death, several head of cattle were sacrificed to the demons. During the cremation, the firewood did not burn steadily due to its dampness. The sorcerer thereby proclaimed that the deceased's personal effects be thrown into the fire to annul her parsimony. As the fire still did not burst into a blaze, the sorcerer then attributed the cause to the deceased's reluctance to leave her newborn baby behind, thus resulting in the baby being thrown into the fire."[10]

Christianity: Despite living alongside strong Jingpo Christian communities, "the demon-worshipping Zaiwa never showed the slightest inclination to turn to Christianity."[11] Moreover, Zaiwa who became Christians in some of the mixed villages were ostracized by their own tribe, "who would expel them from the village and confiscate their land and livestock, compelling them eventually to abandon their alien belief."[12] There are a reported 4,000 Zaiwa Christians, mostly in Myanmar, with few in China.[13] Gospel radio broadcasts in Zaiwa started in 1996, while work is in progress to translate the Scriptures into Zaiwa.

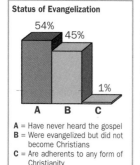

Zaomin 造敏

Population in China:
29,737 (1993)
35,700 (2000)
46,100 (2010)
Location: Guangdong, Hunan
Religion: Animism
Christians: 200

Overview of the Zaomin

Countries: China

Pronunciation: "Zaow-min"

Other Names: Yao Min, Bapai, Dzao Min, Yau Min, Pai Yao

Population Source: 29,737 (1996 B. Grimes – 1993 figure); Out of a total Yao population of 2,134,013 (1990 census)

Location: *N Guangdong:* Liannan and Yangshan counties; *S Hunan:* Yizhang County

Status: Officially included under Yao

Language: Hmong-Mien, Mienic, Zaomin

Dialects: 0

Religion: Animism, Daoism, Buddhism, Christianity

Christians: 200

Scripture: None

***Jesus* film:** None

Gospel Recordings: None

Christian Broadcasting: None

ROPAL code: BPN00

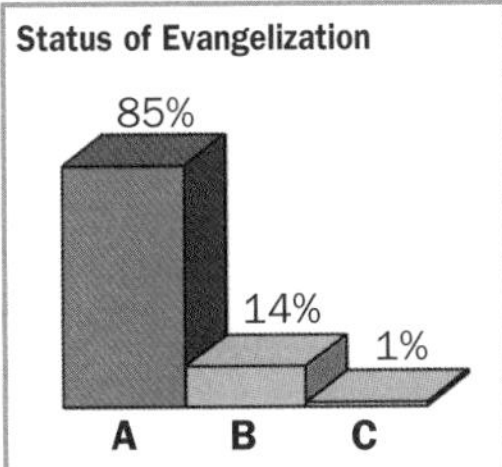

A = Have never heard the gospel
B = Were evangelized but did not become Christians
C = Are adherents to any form of Christianity

Location: Approximately 30,000 Zaomin were counted in a 1993 government study.[1] Living among rugged mountain terrain, the Zaomin are located in Liannan and Yangshan counties of northern Guangdong Province, and in the neighboring Yizhang County of Hunan Province.

Identity: The Zaomin are part of the large Yao nationality. The Chinese call them Bapai Yao, meaning "eight row Yao."[2] Their self-name is *Yaomin* or *Zaomin*.[3] The Zaomin "do not consider themselves to be originally of Yao stock, but rather immigrants from the north who became assimilated to the Yao through isolation and the development of common regional interests with the Iu Mien against the Han or Hakka Chinese."[4]

Language: Zaomin is "related to, although unintelligible with, other Yao dialects."[5] The Zaomin live near the Biao Mien; however, there are only 18 consonants in the Zaomin language compared to 36 in Biao Mien.[6] Zaomin contains nine tones[7] and is a member of the Hmong-Mien language family.

History: There were already large numbers of Yao living in Guangdong before the start of the Ming Dynasty (1368). Between 1368 and 1566 many Yao were attacked during large-scale military campaigns launched by the Chinese.[8] After 52 separate wars,[9] thousands of Yao fled Guangdong to the west, resulting in the fragmenting of today's Yao subgroups throughout 140 counties of China and into Southeast Asia.

Customs: It is the Zaomin women's job to collect firewood. Men say a quick way to find out whether a woman is industrious is to check the fuel piles outside her home. In the event of a divorce, couples share possession of the children. If there is only one child, the person who initiated the divorce loses custody.[10]

Religion: The Zaomin have a flood legend common among many Yao groups of how the Thunder god opened the "River of Heaven," causing a flood that drowned all of mankind except two people. With the help of the gods, from these two came all the peoples of the world.[11] One story, the *Narcissus Girl*, tells of a time long ago when there was no separation between the gods and humans. Both could go up and down to visit each other.[12] Today most Zaomin adhere to a religious mixture that includes Daoist, animist, and Buddhist elements. The Zaomin believe that when they die their moral conduct will have to be accounted for. Numerous songs and chants record what they will be asked. Their answers determine whether their soul will be able to enter into rest or not.[13]

Christianity: The American Presbyterian missionary H. V. Noyes commenced work in Lianxian in 1872. His church and medical clinic were burned down and five people murdered during a riot in September 1905, caused by missionary interference at a local ghost festival.[14] Some Zaomin in Lianxian have assumed leading positions in the local administration "because of education given to them by the church in the past."[15] In recent years several Zaomin became Christians in Guangzhou. They returned to their village and led 60 teenagers to Christ.[16]

Midge Conner

Zauzou 柔若

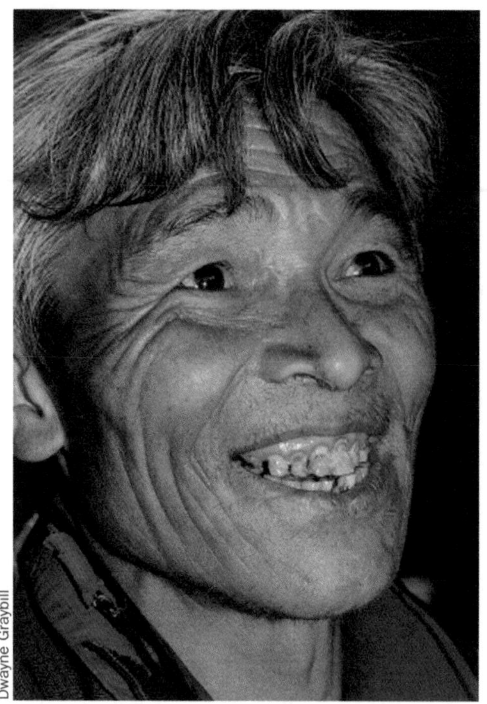

Dwayne Graybill

Location: More than 2,500 Zauzou live in the mountainous Lanping and Lushui counties in northwestern Yunnan Province.[1] The Zauzou are the most southern of the several Nu groups in China. The mighty Nujiang and Lancang rivers roar through the region, forming two sizable obstacles to travel in the area. The Nujiang rages up to 180,000 cubic feet per second during the rainy season, causing massive landslides.

Identity: The Zauzou have been officially included in the Nu minority in China, but they speak a different dialect from other Nu communities. A visitor in the 1920s commented on the dire state of the Zauzou, "They live solely on corn, their staple food, which they use for making a liquor of which they drink a great deal."[2]

Language: The Zauzou language has not been extensively studied, although it is known to contain six tones. One source states that 1,500 Zauzou people are able to speak their language.[3] Zauzou is part of the Lolo branch of Tibeto-Burman, but its specific affiliation has yet to be determined.

History: In the eighth century the whole of western Yunnan Province came under the control of the Nanzhao Kingdom. During the Yuan and Ming dynasties (1271–1644), Nanzhao came under the control of a Naxi headman in Lijiang. The Zauzou in Lanping County are the most Sinicized of the Nu groups in China. Prior to 1949 "their methods of production and standard of living were similar to those of the Hans, Bais, and Naxis."[4]

Customs: The various Nu groups bury a man on his back with straightened limbs, while a woman is laid on her side with bent limbs. If both the husband and wife are buried together, the wife's body is bent toward her husband, symbolizing her submission.[5] Deaths are announced with the loud blowing of bamboo trumpets. The number of trumpet blasts is determined by the age and status of the deceased — one for an unmarried man, two for a married man, three for a married man with children, five or six for a village elder or clan leader. All the villagers go to the house of the deceased and mourn with the grieving family.

Religion: For centuries the Zauzou have been animists. They slavishly worshiped the sun, moon, stars, mountains, rivers, trees, and rocks. In recent decades the practice of animism has subsided due to pressure from the Communist authorities who brand it "superstition." There are also believed to be a small number of Christians among the Zauzou.

Christianity: During the Korean War the Communists showed films of the war in one village, hoping to create anti-American fervor. However, the people responded, "American missionaries created written characters for us, enabling our adults and children to read and write. They told us about the benefits of believing in Jesus and abolishing superstition. They educated us to work hard and live thriftily.... They have done so much good for us, we have been constantly concerned about them after they left. How could we say anything against them?"[6]

Population in China:
2,500 (1991)
2,970 (2000)
3,600 (2010)
Location: Yunnan
Religion: Animism
Christians: 100

Overview of the Zauzou

Countries: China

Pronunciation: "Zaaw-zo"

Other Names: Rouruo, Raoruo, Jao-jo

Population Source: 2,500 (1991 *EDCL*); Out of a total Nu population of 27,123 (1990 census)

Location: *NW Yunnan:* Lanping and Lushui counties

Status: Officially included under Nu

Language: Sino-Tibetan, Tibeto-Burman, Burmese-Lolo, Lolo, Unclassified

Dialects: 0

Religion: Animism, Christianity

Christians: 100

Scripture: None

***Jesus* film:** None

Gospel Recordings: None

Christian Broadcasting: None

ROPAL code: ZAL00

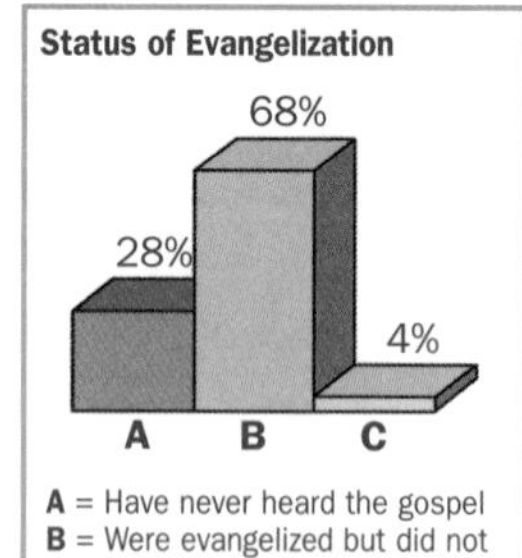

Zhaba 扎巴

Population in China:
15,000 (1983)
20,900 (2000)
25,750 (2010)
Location: Sichuan
Religion: Tibetan Buddhism
Christians: None Known

Overview of the Zhaba

Countries: China

Pronunciation: "Zhar-ba"

Other Names: Zaba, Zhaboa, Buozi

Population Source: 15,000 (1983 Sun Hongkai); 7,700 (1991 *EDCL*); Out of a total Tibetan population of 4,593,330 (1990 census)

Location: *W Sichuan:* Zhamai District of Yajiang County and Zhaba District of Daofu County; Possibly also in Litang and Xinlong counties

Status: Officially included under Tibetan

Language: Sino-Tibetan, Tibeto-Burman, Qiangic, Zhaba

Dialects (2): Western Zhaba, Eastern Zhaba

Religion: Tibetan Buddhism, Shamanism

Christians: None known

Scripture: None

***Jesus* film:** None

Gospel Recordings: None

Christian Broadcasting: None

ROPAL code: ZHA00

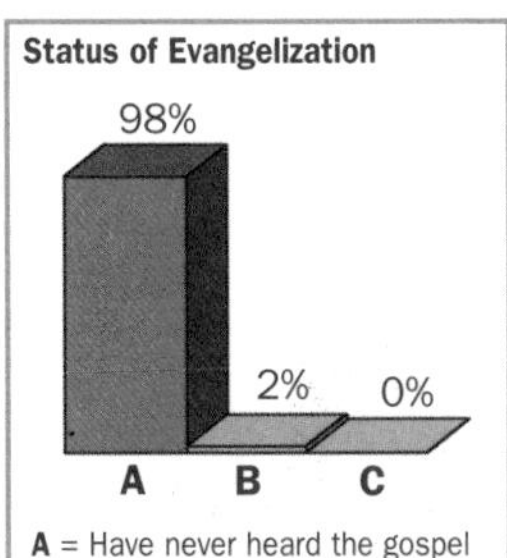

Paul Hattaway

Population: A 1983 source listed 15,000 people belonging to the Zhaba ethnolinguistic group.[1] They live in parts of Yajiang and Daofu counties within the massive Garze Tibetan Autonomous Prefecture in western Sichuan Province. The area was originally part of Kham Province in Tibet until it was annexed by the Chinese in the 1950s. The Sichuan-Tibet highway, begun in 1950 and completed in 1954, "is one of the world's highest, roughest, most dangerous and most beautiful roads.... Towns experience cold temperatures, with up to 200 freezing days per year; summers are blistering by day and the high altitude invites particularly bad sunburn."[2]

Identity: The Zhaba are counted as part of the Tibetan nationality, although they speak a Qiangic language. The Zhaba may call themselves *Buozi*. *Zhaba* appears to be the name used to describe them by their Khampa Tibetan neighbors.

Language: The Zhaba language belongs to a recently discovered branch of the Tibeto-Burman language family, which has amazed linguists and anthropologists. One scholar explains, "The most exciting recent development in Tibeto-Burman studies is the discovery of a new branch of the family, hitherto virtually unknown to Western scholars. These are the Qiangic languages of Sichuan. Extensive lexical and grammatical material has been collected on a dozen languages of the Qiangic group. Besides Qiang, other languages in the group include Baima, Ergong, Ersu, Jiarong, Guiqiong, Minyak, Namuyi, Pumi, Shixing, and Zhaba."[3]

History: When Marco Polo passed through rural Tibetan areas in the thirteenth century he found unique local customs. Polo wrote, "No man of that country would on any consideration take to wife a girl who was a maid; for they say a wife is worth nothing unless she has been used to consort with men.... When travelers come that way, the old women of the place get ready, and take their unmarried daughters... to whomsoever will accept them.... In this manner people traveling in that way... shall find perhaps 20 or 30 girls at their disposal."[4]

Customs: Promiscuity continues to be rife among the Zhaba. A 1950s survey of the Garze area found the rate of venereal diseases was 40% among people in peasant areas and 50.7% among people living in the pasture areas.[5]

Religion: The Zhaba worship a wide variety of demons and ghosts. These influences date back to the pre-Buddhist Tibetan religion of Bon. They believe large demons live inside mountains, and so they offer frequent sacrifices to appease them.

Christianity: There are no known Christians among the Zhaba, although there are a few Tibetan Catholics farther west near Litang. The Zhaba lead hard lives. Workers seeking to reach them will need to help them physically and not just spiritually. Isobel Kuhn, a missionary to the Lisu, said, "I have been a missionary for 27 years, but have never met a heathen tribesman who was looking for salvation.... They don't know enough to reach out a hand for heavenly aid. Their eyes look not up but down — down on the earth and upon their bodily appetites."[6]

Zhuang, Northern 壮(北)

Paul Hattaway

Location: The Zhuang are the largest minority group in China. With more than 17 million people, their population is approximately the same as the population of Australia. More than 11 million people speak Northern Zhuang. The majority are located in the central and western parts of Guangxi in southern China. Others are scattered throughout 15 of the other 29 provinces in China, including one small Zhuang enclave in distant Shaanxi Province.[1]

Identity: The name *Zhuang* "seems to be a cover term, officially including any and all Tai speakers who live in Guangxi and eastern Yunnan."[2] Most Zhuang are assimilated to Chinese language and culture and consider themselves to be Han people. "Of 152 clans examined in one district of Guangxi Province, not one claimed to be non-Han. Many are reported to be so anxious to be Chinese they have falsified genealogical records in order to find a suitable Han ancestor."[3]

Language: Zhuang has two orthographies: a Roman script introduced in 1986 and a script which uses Chinese characters to mirror the sound of Zhuang words.[4] Northern Zhuang is basically the same language as Bouyei.[5] Although the Chinese list only seven Northern Zhuang dialects, other sources state that there are more than fifty.[6] One worker in the area says, "Almost every Zhuang village has its own little village language.... Zhuang from one village may not understand Zhuangs who live 25 miles from them.... After greeting each other in their respective dialects of Zhuang, they do their business in Cantonese or Mandarin."[7]

History: During the Ming Dynasty (1388–1644) the Zhuang revolted 218 times against Chinese rule.[8] In the middle of the sixteenth century the Zhuang formed an army and beat back the invading Japanese pirates who had landed along the Guangxi coastline.

Customs: Today most Zhuang are culturally indistinguishable from the local Han Chinese. The Zhuang were not even considered a separate nationality in the past; they were counted as Han Chinese in the 1938 census.[9] Very few Zhuang wear their traditional clothing on a daily basis, although many do still wear it during festivals.

Religion: Most Northern Zhuang in the countryside worship their ancestors, while the majority of those who live in urban areas are atheists.

Christianity: In 1991 there were a reported 30,000 Zhuang Christians meeting in more than 250 house fellowships in the Guangxi Zhuang Autonomous Region.[10] Gospel radio broadcasts, gospel audio recordings, and the *Jesus* film are available in the Northern Zhuang language. These tools are allowing large numbers of Zhuang to be exposed to the gospel for the first time in their history. More Zhuang have believed in Christ since 1990 than in the previous 130 years of mission outreach.[11] Han Chinese house-church movements from several provinces have sent evangelists to work among the Zhuang. There is a great need for the Bible to be translated into Northern Zhuang.

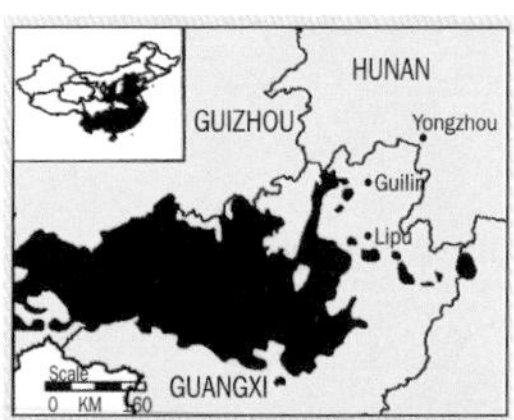

Population in China:
10,000,000 (1992)
11,568,000 (2000)
13,835,000 (2010)
Location: Guangxi, Yunnan, Guizhou, Hunan, Guangdong, Hebei
Religion: Ancestor Worship
Christians: 40,000

Overview of the Northern Zhuang

Countries: China
Pronunciation: "Zhoo-ung"
Other Names: Chwang, Chuang, Tai Chuang, Wuming, T'u, Cangva, Vah Cuengh, Bou-Tsuung, Bou-Shuung
Population Source: 10,000,000 (1992 J. Edmonson); Out of a total Zhuang population of 15,489,630 (1990 census)[12]
Location: *Guangxi; Yunnan; Guizhou; Guangdong; Hunan; Hebei; Fujian; Jiangxi; Beijing; Henan; Tianjin; Shandong; Shaanxi; Zhejiang; Anhui; Shanghai*
Status: Officially included under Zhuang
Language: Daic, Tai, Northern Tai
Dialects (7+): Hongshuihe (2,738,000), Yongbei (1,562,000), Guibe (1,299,000), Liujiang (1,271,000), Guibian (828,000), Youjiang (732,000), Quibe
Religion: Ancestor Worship, No Religion, Christianity
Christians: 40,000
Scripture: None
***Jesus* film:** Available
Gospel Recordings: Zhuang: Northern #04978 Zhuang: Luocheng #04980
Christian Broadcasting: Available (FEBC)
ROPAL code: CCX00

A = Have never heard the gospel
B = Were evangelized but did not become Christians
C = Are adherents to any form of Christianity

Zhuang, Southern 壮(南)

Location: Approximately four million speakers of Southern Zhuang live in the southwestern part of Guangxi and the adjoining areas of southeastern Yunnan Province, of which 770,000 live in Wenshan Prefecture.[1] Technically, there are also speakers of Southern Zhuang varieties in Vietnam and Laos, but they are known by different names in different places. The Chinese officially classify several groups as Southern Zhuang, which include the Giay, Tho, Nung, Cao Lan, and Buyang. In *Operation China* they are profiled separately.

Identity: The Southern Zhuang are a collection of related Central Tai language groups which have been combined with the Northern Zhuang — a collection of Northern Tai language groups — to form China's official Zhuang nationality. There are many tribes, clans, and self-designations among the Southern Zhuang. Names such as *Debao* and *Heiyi* frequently appear in Chinese linguistic research.

Language: There are numerous dialects spoken among the Southern Zhuang, many of which may be distinct languages. Many Southern Zhuang can speak Northern Zhuang as a second language.[2]

History: During the Qin Dynasty (221–207 BC), half a million Han convicts were exiled by Emperor Qin Shihuang to the Lingnan region in southern China (now Guangxi and Guangdong). There they intermingled with the various branches of the Bai Yue nationality.[3] The Zhuang today, especially the Southern Zhuang, are thought to be the descendants of the Bai Yue. Historically, the Zhuang were called *Tuliao* or *Sharen*.

Paul Hattaway

Customs: Because they are primarily engaged in agriculture, the Zhuang are also locally known as the *T'u* or "People of the Soil." Their homes are usually built on stilts. A newly married woman stays with her parents until after the birth of the first child. Only then does she go to live with her husband in his village.

Religion: The Southern Zhuang are a superstitious people. They are careful not to offend the spirit world that surrounds them. They believe in the spirits of the water, forest, mountain, village, etc.

Christianity: The first Protestant missionary to the Zhuang was R. H. Graves, a Southern Baptist, who arrived in Guangxi in 1862. In 1895 the Christian & Missionary Alliance commenced work in Guangxi. They established 65 churches over a 50-year period. Most of these churches were attended by Han Chinese, but small numbers of Southern Zhuang also attended. Today there are far fewer Southern Zhuang Christians than there are Northern Zhuang believers. The Southern Zhuang, because of their linguistic diversity, have no Scriptures, recordings, or *Jesus* film. Little has changed since this 1922 report describing Guangxi: "There are 58 cities, 700 market towns, and over 17,000 villages, all teeming with human lives for whom no effort whatever is being put forth."[4]

Population in China:
3,515,000 (1990)
4,203,900 (2000)
5,027,900 (2010)
Location: Guangxi, Yunnan
Religion: Animism
Christians: 6,000

Overview of the Southern Zhuang

Countries: China, Vietnam

Pronunciation: "Zhoo-ung"

Other Names: Pu Nong, Pu To, Kun To, Longming, Lungming, Bou Rau, Bou Lau, Bou Baan, Bu Maan

Population Source: 4,000,000 (1990 J.-O. Svantesson)[5]; Out of a total Zhuang population of 15,489,630 (1990 census); Southern Zhuang varieties are also spoken in Vietnam.

Location: *SW Guangxi; SE Yunnan*

Status: Officially included under Zhuang

Language: Daic, Tai, Central Tai

Dialects (10+): Zuojiang (1,384,000), Yongnan (1,360,000), Dejing (1,025,898), Wenma (100,000), Yanguang, Wenshan, Maguan, Debao, Yongning, Daxin

Religion: Animism, Ancestor Worship, Daoism, Christianity

Christians: 6,000

Scripture: None

***Jesus* film:** None

Gospel Recordings: Zhuang: Southern #04979 Zhuang: Jingxi #04981

Christian Broadcasting: None

ROPAL code: CCY00

A = Have never heard the gospel
B = Were evangelized but did not become Christians
C = Are adherents to any form of Christianity

Zuoke 作科

Population in China:
6,300 (1999)
6,450 (2000)
8,100 (2010)
Location: Yunnan
Religion: Polytheism
Christians: None Known

Overview of the Zuoke

Countries: China

Pronunciation: "Zuoh-keh"

Other Names: Niuweiba, Changpu, Baipu

Population Source: 6,300 (1999 J. Pelkey); Out of a total Yi population of 6,572,173 (1990 census)

Location: *SE Yunnan:* Wenshan County: Dongshan, Guanlijie, and Panzhihua districts

Status: Officially included under Yi

Language: Sino-Tibetan, Tibeto-Burman, Burmese-Lolo, Lolo, Northern Lolo, Yi, Southeastern Yi

Dialects: 0

Religion: Polytheism, Animism, Ancestor Worship

Christians: None known

Scripture: None

***Jesus* film:** None

Gospel Recordings: None

Christian Broadcasting: None

ROPAL code: None

Status of Evangelization

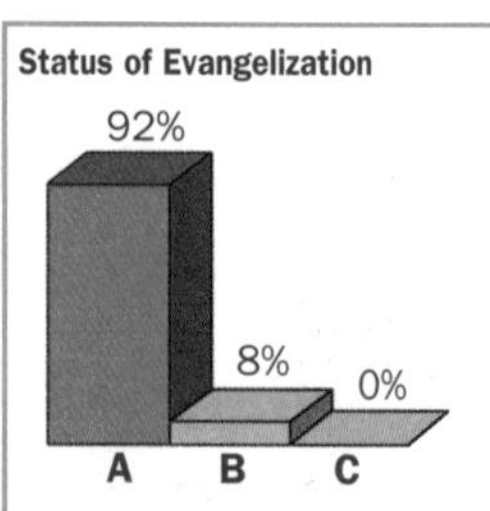

A = Have never heard the gospel
B = Were evangelized but did not become Christians
C = Are adherents to any form of Christianity

Location: More than 6,300 people belonging to the Zuoke ethnic group live in Wenshan County of Wenshan Prefecture, in the southeastern part of China's Yunnan Province. They live in a number of unmixed villages (i.e., communities inhabited solely by Zuoke people): Daxing, Wujia, Nanlinke, Kemali, Yahu, Shangziongdong, Shazipo, Jiahu, Yujiake, Bairenjiao, Shujingwan, and Liujia. Only in four villages do the Zuoke live in mixed communities with other nationalities: Xiaxiongdong, Banzhai, Youshidongzhong, and Guniang.[1] In total, there are 16 Zuoke villages, all situated in the southeastern part of Wenshan County. All of the Zuoke villages are under the jurisdiction of either Dongshan or Guanlijie districts, except for Guniang Village which lies within Panzhihua District.

Identity: The Zuoke are a distinct ethnic group. They are proud of their unique ethnicity and history as a people and do not see themselves to be the same as any other people group. Despite these facts, the Chinese authorities have placed the Zuoke under the large and all-embracing Yi nationality which contains 120 different groups. Jamin Pelkey notes, "The Zuoke consider themselves different from the Poluo around them, and certainly do not consider themselves to be Yi."[2] Some of the alternate names for the Zuoke include *Niuweiba* (Cowtail), *Changpu* (Long Pu) and *Baipu* (White Pu). These are probably names given to them by other ethnic groups and are not used by the Zuoke themselves.

Language: Although little is known about the Zuoke language, it is part of the Southeastern Yi branch of the Tibeto-Burman family. Zuoke is still spoken by all members of the ethnic group and is not in immediate danger.

History: According to Zuoke oral history, they originally lived in the Dali area of west central Yunnan and migrated to Wenshan around the time of the Nanzhao Kingdom (possibly about AD 900).

Customs: Chinese anthropologist Lu Jinyu visited the Zuoke extensively in the early 1990s. He studied Zuoke culture in all 16 of their villages and published a 30-page paper in Chinese.[3] Lu found that the Zuoke culture and language are thriving. The Zuoke practice a number of special customs and festivals throughout the year, when they dress up in their traditional attire.

Religion: The Zuoke are polytheistic animists. Their worldview is shaped by their belief in the spirit world. The Zuoke live in simple houses near streams or some other water source. Traditionally, they do not dig wells, for fear of "striking the veins of the dragon" that they believe lives in the water underneath the earth.

Christianity: The Zuoke have no known Christians in their midst. Their close-knit communities and strong desire to maintain their culture possibly mean they will view Christianity as a threat to their way of life. To date, few Zuoke have ever heard of Jesus Christ. They are a unique unreached people group with no Scriptures, recordings, or ministries known to be targeting them with the gospel.

Jamin Pelkey

APPENDIX 1:
Other Possible Groups

In addition to the 490 groups profiled in *Operation China*, we are aware of numerous other names of tribes and people groups that have appeared in books, manuscripts, and magazines over the years. In most cases, we have been unable to find any other source of information to justify including these groups, even though we believe many of the names below represent genuine ethno-linguistic identities. In some instances the names listed below may be alternate names for groups we have already profiled. It is hoped that future research will determine which of these should be considered as distinct people groups.

Amdo tribes

Early sources frequently mentioned a number of tribes and people groups living in the Amdo Tibetan territory in Gansu and Qinghai provinces. These include the Ngolo, Ngapa, Paotso, Samsa, Tatze, Pan-Yul, Lai-wa, Lhardi (who inhabited four villages near Labrang in Gansu), and Mbulu.[1] Although a century ago these groups appeared to be distinct and frequently at war with each other, today they have largely lost their tribal identity. All of these groups are included in the Amdo profiles in *Operation China*.

Amu

The Amu are possibly a subgroup of the Hani nationality, living in one valley within Mojiang County in southern Yunnan Province.

Arakanese

(ROPAL code MHV00) Approximately two million speakers of the Arakanese language live in Myanmar, particularly in Arakan State. Other significant Arakanese communities are found in Bangladesh and India. The *Ethnologue* states that Arakanese may also be spoken in China.[2] No other sources list this group or language in China.

Bajia

The Bajia appear in a list of "small groups... which need further investigation."[3] We have not seen this name in any other sources.

Bapu

The Bapu are a Yi tribe in Yunnan Province, mentioned in a 1917 publication. No other source mentions this group.[4]

Bargut

The Buriat language in the Xin Baerhu Banner of the Hulunbuir region in eastern Inner Mongolia is divided into the New Bargut (47,000) and Old Bargut (14,000) vernaculars.[5] It is unclear whether these "vernaculars" are dialects of Buriat or mutually unintelligible languages. One linguist describes Bargut as a "Manchurian branch of Eastern Buryat that has developed under the increasing influence of the northern dialects of Mongolia proper."[6] Research needs to be done to determine the degree of intelligibility between New Bargut, Old Bargut and Buriat proper.

Bawang Rong Ke

A language called Bawang Rong Ke was first described by missionary J. H. Edgar in 1934. Based on his information, linguist Jackson Sun "identified it as a Ergong language."[7] The Ergong are a small Qiangic-speaking ethnic group in a remote part of Sichuan Province.

Behee

This group was listed in John Kuhn's 1945 tribal survey of Yunnan Province to be located in "Wuding, Lufeng, and Fumin" in northern Yunnan.[8] They have probably been officially included as part of the Yi nationality.

Behma

This group was listed in John Kuhn's 1945 tribal survey of Yunnan Province to be located in the southern Yunnan border area.[9] It is not certain how this group relates to today's recognized nationalities.

Ben

There are a small number of Christians reported among the "Ben" in Mengla County of Xiahuangbanna Prefecture, Yunnan.[10] They are almost certainly not the same as the Ben group profiled in *Operation China* as a Wa group in western Yunnan.

Buguo

The Buguo were included on a list of small groups in China... "which need further investigation."[11]

Bukong

This Hani group lives in Mojiang County, in the Honghe Prefecture of Yunnan Province.[12]

Buli

This Akha tribe was briefly mentioned in a 1945 study as living at "Fuhai" in Yunnan Province.[13] They were also mentioned in a 1943 study.[14]

Bupeng

This group was listed in John Kuhn's 1945 tribal survey of Yunnan Province, located in the southern Yunnan border area.[15] It is not certain how this group relates to today's recognized nationalities.

Burmese

There are no recognized Burmese (Myen) communities in China today, although a few traders pass through. In 1974 one anthropologist stated, "A few Burmese tribes living in the Chinese Shan States are spoken of as Lao-mien, Old Burmese."[16]

Busa

This group was listed in John Kuhn's 1945 tribal survey of Yunnan Province, located in the southern Yunnan border area.[17] It is not certain how this group relates to today's recognized nationalities.

Chama

The Chama were listed in John Kuhn's 1945 tribal survey of Yunnan Province, located in the southern Yunnan border area.[18] It is not certain how this group relates to today's recognized nationalities.

Chang Teo Fah

This small group in the Jinghong area of Xishuangbanna Prefecture, Yunnan Province, is viewed as distinct by surrounding communities. They may have been officially included under the Yao nationality.

Chaodo

The Chaodo were included on a list of small groups in China... "which need further investigation."[19]

Chidi

This group was listed in John Kuhn's 1945 tribal survey of Yunnan Province, located in the southern Yunnan border area.[20] It is not certain how this group relates to today's recognized nationalities.

Choutien

The Choutien are an unidentified group in Yunnan, possibly a subgroup of the Yi, who were listed in a 1912 study.[21]

Danau

(ROPAL code DNU00) Approximately 10,000 ethnic Danau live in Myanmar. The *Ethnologue* states that the Danau may also be found in China.[22] No other sources list this group or language in China.

Dongchuan

This group was listed in John Kuhn's 1945 tribal survey of Yunnan Province, located in "Yuanjiang and Dongchuan" in southern Yunnan.[23]

Draba

This group of 15,000 Tibetans lives in the Garze Prefecture of western Sichuan Province. It is possible *Draba* may be an alternate spelling for *Zhaba*.

Duchi

The Duchi were listed in John Kuhn's 1945 tribal survey of Yunnan Province to be located in the southern Yunnan border area.[24] It is not certain how this group relates to today's recognized nationalities.

Eechi

This group was listed in John Kuhn's 1945 tribal survey of Yunnan Province, located in the southern Yunnan border area.[25] It is not certain how this group relates to today's recognized nationalities.

Eren

This group was listed in John Kuhn's 1945 tribal survey of Yunnan Province, located in "Ning Erh and Qingku [Jinggu]" in Simao Prefecture of Yunnan Province.[26] They have probably been officially included as part of either the Yi or Hani nationality. The Eren are not the same as the E people of Guangxi. *E-ren* may simply mean "Yi people."

Gaoshan

This is the name of a group living in the mountains near the Yunnan border with Tibet.... "They are possibly a subgroup of Lisu, but speak their own language."[27] The name *Gaoshan* means "high mountain." It is therefore uncertain if this refers to a specific tribe or group, or is a generic description of a group of people in that area, who we may have already profiled under another name. This group is not the same as the Gaoshan in Fujian Province, who are one of China's 55 officially recognized minorities.

Guzong

The Guzong are possibly a subgroup of the Yi, mentioned in a 1931 Chinese publication.[28]

Han Chinese Groups

In the past there were many social distinctions among the Han Chinese. Groups such as the Duomin, or "fallen people," in Zhejiang and the "musician households" of Shanxi and Shaanxi were discriminated against. They were regarded as entirely different from and socially beneath the rest of the Han population. Since the advent of Communism most of these class distinctions have been eradicated and these groups no longer represent true ethno-linguistic identities. Some groups have retained their identity, such as the Subei people of Shanghai and the Dan people of southern China, both of which are profiled in *Operation China*.

Hknong

This group was listed in John Kuhn's 1945 tribal survey of Yunnan Province, located in the "NW Burma-Yunnan border" area.[29] Kuhn listed the Hknong as part of his *Lolo* section, which means they are probably officially included today as part of either the Yi or Hani nationality.

Howan

This group was listed in John Kuhn's 1945 tribal survey of Yunnan Province, located in "Baoshan" in western Yunnan.[30] Kuhn listed the Howan as part of his *Lolo* section, which means they are probably officially included today as part of either the Yi or Hani nationality.

Huang Lolo

The Huang Lolo were listed in John Kuhn's 1945 tribal survey of Yunnan Province, located in "Yuanjiang-Mehjiang" in the Honghe and Yuxi Prefectures in southern Yunnan.[31] Kuhn notes they were also known as the *Long and Short-tailed Lolo*. They have probably been included as part of the present-day Hani nationality.

Jieduo

The Jieduo were included on a list of small groups in China... "which need further investigation."[32]

Kabie

The Kabie are possibly a subgroup of the Hani nationality, living in one valley within Mojiang County in southern Yunnan Province.

Kantsa

This Tibetan tribe lives near Kokonor in Qinghai Province. The Assemblies of God missionary Victor Plymire was visited by Ga

Lo, head of the Kantsa tribe, who requested the two of them make a blood covenant.[33]

Kentse

This group was listed in John Kuhn's 1945 tribal survey of Yunnan Province, located along the southern Yunnan border area.[34] They have probably been officially included as part of either the Yi or Hani nationality.

Khamti

The Khamtis, or Khamti Shan, are a Tai group. 12,000 live in northeast India[35] and approximately 60,000 speakers live in northern Myanmar. There is no confirmation of their presence in China, although some publications mention the possibility of Khamtis living in China.[36] If so, it is probable they have been assimilated to the related Dai groups in Yunnan Provinvce. In India most Khamtis are Hindus. They live near the Tibetan border, in northernmost Myanmar.

Khao

Also called *Khang*, this language is spoken by about 10,000 people, mostly in Vietnam. One source states, "There may be some speakers in China as well."[37]

Khla

Also known as *Tai-Khla*, this Tai language is reportedly spoken in the Honghe Prefecture in southern Yunnan Province.[38]

Khmer

The 1996 *Ethnologue* lists a 1993 figure of 1,000 speakers of Khmer (Cambodian) living in China.[39] This listing appears in the sections for Vietnam and Cambodia, but not in the China section. No other source lists the Khmer in China.

Kongsat

Numbering only 94 people in 16 families within northern Laos, the small Kongsat group lives on the border between Laos and Mengla County in Yunnan Province. The Kongsat say they came from nearby China, but there is no evidence of a similarly named group in this part of Yunnan. The Kongsat almost certainly have ethnolinguistic relatives in China, probably known by a different name.

La

The La are recorded as an Austro-Asiatic group of 40,000 living in western Yunnan Province.[40] This may be an alternate name for the *Lawa*.

Lahuli, Chamba

Listed by the Global Evangelization Movement, this group of 1,223 people live "along the border of western Tibet with Kashmir, India."[41] Alternate names are Patni, Manchad, Pattaini, and Chamba. They are related, yet distinct from the Lahuli Tinan group profiled in *Operation China*. No other sources list Chamba Lahuli in China.

Lam

"A Yunnanese Tai variety spoken in the Honghe Hani-Yi-Dai autonomous County in Yunnan Province."[42]

Lama-jen

A branch of the Bai people living north of the city of Dali were called *Lama-jen* in old sources.[43] It is not clear whether this name is still used, or whether they retain any ethnolinguistic distinction from other Bai people.

Lohei

A 1899 source mentions the Lohei people, who lived in "Chen Pien" in Yunnan Province.[44] This group may have been a Yi subgroup which has since been assimilated or who are now known by a different name.

Lomi

This Yi group was reported to be living in the Wuding area of northern Yunnan, near the Samei, Gani, and Michi.[45] Possibly another group called Lomi (alternative name, Black Hani) was mentioned in a 1903 article.[46]

Longan

This group is described as "A Southern Zhuang variety in the Yunnan-Guangxi border area (Funing)."[47]

Lopa

Also called *Loba, Loyu* and *Mustang Tibetans*, 2,445 Lopa are listed by the Global Evangelization Movement as living on the Tibetan side of the China-Nepal border.[48] No other sources mention the Lopa in China.

Lulu

This group has a small number of Christians in Mengla County of Xiahuangbanna Prefecture, Yunnan.[49] Possibly the same as *Lolo*, or *Dai Lu*.

Luso

This group was listed in John Kuhn's 1945 tribal survey of Yunnan Province, located in "Simao and Qingku [Jinggu]" in Simao Prefecture of southern Yunnan Province.[50] They have probably been officially included as part of either the Hani or Yi nationality.

Maliu

A group of people living in the town of Maliu in northern Sichuan are mentioned in one magazine article.[51] The article does not mention what ethnic group they belong to, but their embroidery and costumes are not similar to any other groups in the area. Maliu is near the juncture of Sichuan, Gansu, and Shaanxi Provinces. They may be a separate people group, but lack of further information prevents us from including them at this time.

Mengka

There may be a small tribe called the Mengka, who speak a Kam-Tai language and live in Southwest Yunnan. No sources mention this name, which may be the same as *Menghua*, or *Meng*.

Miao, Dananshan

The 1992 *Ethnologue* lists "Hmong, Dananshan" as a language (ROPAL code: HMOOO) spoken in Northwest Guizhou.[52] However, Dananshan is not the name of a Miao language, but rather the name of a village in Xianjin, Bijie County, Guizhou, that was chosen by the Chinese authorities as the standard for the Chuanqiandian Miao language group.[53]

Miehlantse

This group was listed in John Kuhn's 1945 tribal survey of Yunnan Province, located in the Wuding area in northern Yunnan.[54] They have probably been officially included as part of the Yi nationality.

Mizo

A small number of speakers of Mizo, also known as Lushai, or "men of the hills," were reported in China by the 1992 *Ethnologue*.[55] However, no location, sources, or other information were given. The Mizo are primarily located in India, Myanmar, and Bangladesh. No other sources mention the Mizo in China. The 1996 *Ethnologue* did not list the Mizo in China. In 1999 a Mizo informant from India told the author he knew of three or four village names in Yunnan Province that were Mizo names, although he had not personally visited them.

Mon

Also known as *Mok*, or *Amok*, this language "is found in China but there included in the Bulang nationality; and probably also in Burma."[56] There is a total of only 500 Mon speakers in all countries. This group is not the same as the large and well-known Mon ethnic group of Myanmar and Thailand.

Mu

A small number of people living in the Xuan Wei and Ji Dong villages of Majiang County in Guizhou Province call themselves *Mu*. It is not known if they are the same as the Mulao Jia or Mulao people groups, or if they should be considered a distinct group.

Nee

The Nee, an unidentified group in Yunnan, and possibly a subgroup of the Yi, were listed in a 1912 study.[57]

Nepalese

Chinese sources frequently mention the "Nepalese" living in Tibet. "Contacts between people of the two countries living on either side of the border are frequent and easy. Crossing a bridge over the boundary river, you set foot on foreign soil. Actually some of these foreign 'visitors', such as the Nepalese, have settled down here."[58] We believe this refers to the members of the Thami ethnic group, who live in and around Zhangmu Town near the Nepal border. There may also be a small number of traders from other Nepalese ethnic groups in Tibet.

Nobee

This group was listed in John Kuhn's 1945 tribal survey of Yunnan Province, located in Mojiang in southern Yunnan.[59] They have probably been officially included as part of the Hani nationality.

Norra

The Norra (Nora, Nurra, Noza: ROPAL code NOROO) are a group related to the Nu in northwest Yunnan Province. They are described as having a total population of 10,000, and living in northern Myanmar and in China.[60] Other sources do not mention this group, and subsequent editions of the *Ethnologue* do not list them in China.

Nuomei

This Hani group lives in the Yangjie area of Honghe Prefecture, Yunnan Province.[61]

Pala

A total of 4,000 Pala people inhabit 26 vilages in northern Laos, near the Yunnan border. The Pala are related to the Akha, but appear to have a separate ethnicity and language. One source says the Pala may have spilled over into China.[62]

Panang

The 1996 *Ethnologue* lists a language called Panang (ROPAL code: PCROO) in Tibet. Alternate names for Panang are Panags, Panakha, Pananag, Banag, Banang, Sbanag, and Sbranag. However, no sources, population figures, or location are given. The *Ethnologue* also notes that Panang "may not be a separate language."[63] No other sources list this language.

Peren

This group was listed in John Kuhn's 1945 tribal survey of Yunnan Province, located in "Mengting" in Yunnan Province. Kuhn notes, "Within... the China Inland Mission... we have not a little completely virgin soil among the tribal populations... including the Peren of Mengting."[64]

Peunn-jen

This group was mentioned in a 1903 study of Yi groups in Yunnan Province.[65] It is uncertain how this name relates to today's Yi groups in China.

Phunoi

According to the 1995 census in Laos, 35,635 Phunoi people inhabit 70 villages in northern Laos, near the Chinese border. One source states the Phunoi are "probably in China as well"[66] although no other source lists them in China. The Phunoi language may be spoken in China but the speakers may be known by a different ethnic name.

Phu Tai

"A somewhat problematic term, literally meaning 'Tai Person(s)'. In a restricted sense, it refers to identifiable subgroup of Southwestern Tai varieties spoken by 150,000-300,000 speakers in scattered locales in southern Laos, especially in Hua Phan Province, Vietnam and northeastern Thailand.... These varieties show strong affinity to White and Black Tai.... A dialect with the same name has been reported for the Wenshan prefecture of Yunnan."[67] If the Phu Tai reported in China are the same as the Phu Tai in Southeast Asia, they almost certainly qualify as a distinct group. The Phu Tai in Southeast Asia strongly consider themselves a distinct people.

Piza

The Piza were described by Augustine Henry in 1903.[68] They were a Hani group living south of the Red River in southern Yunnan Province. No other source mentions this group and it is uncertain how they relate to known Hani groups today.

Poo Maw

A tribe called the Poo Maw have been mentioned by H. A. Baker as a group living near other Hani tribes in southern Yunnan Province. Baker sent evangelists to the Poo Maw, "where an additional forty families yielded to their persuassions and threw away their idolatrous possessions."[69] This group has not been listed in any other literature from the area, but is probably related to one of the Hani or Yi tribes near Mojiang.

Poussang

A total of 1,850 Poussang people inhabit eight vilages in northern Laos, near the Yunnan border. The Poussang are related to the Akha but appear to have a separate ethnicity and language. One source says the Poussang may have spilled over into China.[70]

Pu Te

There may be a small Yi group in Jiangchuan and Tonghai counties in Yuxi Prefecture, Yunnan Province, called the Pu Te, but evidence is inconclusive. They may have been culturally and linguistically assimilated to the Nisu, who live in the same area.

Qiang groups

In addition to the 12 Qiang groups profiled in *Operation China*, a 1959 book mentions the names of five more Qiang tribes living along the Dadu River: *Tampa, Badi, Bawang, Yuetung* and *Lifan*.[72] It is uncertain how these names relate to the groups we have profiled, or whether they constitute distinct ethnolinguistic identities today. Another source from 1958 mentions the Wassu and Chiajung people also living in the Qiang areas.[73]

Romani Gypsies

The Joshua Project 2000, in compiling profiles of the world's least evangelized peoples, surprisingly included "Romani Gypsies" as one of their groups in China. They stated, "The Balkan Gypsies are also known as the Balkan 'Rom' Gypsies. They are located in parts of Eastern Europe and Southwestern Asia, including Yugoslavia. Moldova, Turkey, Iran, and Ukraine. There is even a significant community in China, however little else is known about them."[71] The author has never before heard mention of Gypsies living within China's borders, nor has he sighted any other source that mentions their existence. There are a number of people in Xinjiang, in China's northwest, who could be considered physically similar in appearance to Romani Gypsies, but these have been included under the Uygur nationality and speak the Uygur language.

Sai

This is a "Yunnanese Tai variety spoken in Wenshan Prefecture," in the southeastern part of Yunnan Province.[74] It is also known as *Tai-Sai*, or *Saaj*. Sai may be the same language as Dai, Pong.

Sharen

The Sharen were considered a separate nationality in China in the 1953 census (112,433 people). In 1974 an anthropologist stated, "There are 128,000 Sha-jen, a Tai group in the Southeast of Yunnan."[75] We are not sure what the Sharen people were reclassified as, but by their location it is likely they are now included as part of either the Zhuang or Dai nationality.

Sobi

This group was listed in John Kuhn's 1945 tribal survey of Yunnan Province, located in Yuanjiang and Mojiang in southern Yunnan.[76] They have probably been officially included as part of the Hani nationality.

Sotatipo

The 1992 *Ethnologue* lists a language called *Sotatipo* (ROPAL code: SCS00) in Tibet.[77] However, no sources, population, or location are given. No other known sources list this language.

Spiti

Some sources suggest there may be small numbers of speakers of the Spiti Tibetan language on the Tibetan side of the China-India border... "Known to its over 10,000 speakers as Piti, this variety is spoken in the Spiti Valley."[78]

Stau

A language or dialect of Ergong called *Stau* was identified by linguist Jackson Sun in 1992.[79] No other sources mention this name.

Straight Lolo

This group was listed in John Kuhn's 1945 tribal survey of Yunnan Province, located in Simao in south-west Yunnan.[80] They are probably officially included today as part of either the Yi or Hani nationality.

Tai Loi

About 2,000 Tai Loi, possibly also known as *Tai Doi*, live on both sides of the Mekong River between Myanmar and Laos. They are mentioned in one source as possibly also being in China.[81]

Taofu

Taofu is the name of a language or dialect similar to Ergong, in southern Sichuan Province. It was first studied by Andre Migot in 1957.[82] Little other information is available that mentions the Taofu.

Ta T'ou

A publication from the end of the the nineteenth century lists a group called the Ta T'ou, possibly a Yi subgroup, living in "Sumao" in Yunnan Province.[83]

Tebbus

The Tebbus are a Tibetan tribe mentioned in literature from the 1930s. They lived on the southern slopes of the Min Shan Range, which today forms the border between Gansu and Sichuan Provinces. The Tebbus were under the dominion of the Choni Tibetan Kingdom.[84]

Thongho

A 1955 linguistic survey of Yi groups in Yunnan Province included the Thongho.[85] No other sources mention this group.

Tseku

This is a Central Tibetan language (ROPAL code: TSK00) aparently spoken in Tibet, Bhutan, and possibly Nepal. The 1988 *Ethnologue* listed the Tseku in China,[86] but later editions did not. No population or location details were given, and no other sources cite this language.

Tula

The Tula were listed in John Kuhn's 1945 tribal survey of Yunnan Province, located in Shiping County in central Yunnan.[87] They have probably been officially included as part of either the Yi or Hani nationality. An earlier source in 1899 mentioned the Tula as living in "Kai Hua."[88]

Tudza

This group used to be one of the ruling classes of Nosu Yi in the Liangshan mountains of Sichuan Province, but today the Tudza (and Wazi) cannot be considered ethnolinguistically distinct, or socially distinct.

Waxiang

The "Waxiangren" were briefly mentioned as one of the ethnic groups in China who do not yet have official status.[89]

Wazi

The Wazi were formerly Han Chinese people who had been captured as slaves by the Nosu in the Daliangshan in Sichuan Province. Other spellings of their name include *Wa Tse*, *Han Wa Tse*, and *Wa Dz*. The Wazi lived separately from their masters and were allowed to possess their own slaves. Since the abolishment of the slaveholding system in the 1950s, the Wazi no longer can be construed as a viable ethnolinguistic identity.[90] In some literature the lower class of Nosu (80% of all Nosu) was also sometimes called Wazi, which has created confusion.

Weits'un

Chinese scholars in 1943 described the Weits'un people, a Han Chinese-Yi mixed group in Yunnan Province.[91] It is uncertain who these people are today.

Woma

This group was listed in John Kuhn's 1945 survey of Yunnan, located in "Longren, Pingpien, and Mengtse" in the Yunnan border area.[92]

Yassi

The Yassi appeared in a 1953 study by Roy Claude.[93] They are possibly a subgroup of the Yi, and may be an alternate name for Axi.

Yi groups

A 1932 study by Hsu Itang listed several subgroups of Yi that do not match any of today's known groups. They include the *Hai* (Sea) Yi, the *Kan* (Land) Yi, the *Sa-mi* (possibly the Sani), the *A-tcho* (possibly Azhe), *Sa-wan*, and *A-hie* (possibly A Che).[94] Similarly, Alfred Liétard in 1904 listed the following names of unrecognized Lolo (Yi) groups in China: *A-li*, *Tsi-cho*, *P'u-p'a*, and *Co-ko*.[95] Some of the additional tribes, clans, and various subgroups of Yi may include the following names the author has come across in research for this book: Ako, Daignet, Duampu, Huithom, Kangxiangying, Khaskhong, Kiaokio, Laichau, Lasu, Misa, Nameji, Nipu, Nuoku, Pakishan, Phupha, Pyen, Ulu, Won, Zijun, Zogo.

Yolo

A Hani group, called the Yolo (mentioned separately from the Lolo), were listed in a 1943 German study of southern Yunnan.[96]

Yueh

The Yueh are an extinct Han Chinese group. They "derive their name from the vassal state of Yueh in Chou [Zhou] times [1100-221 BC], centered around present-day Hangzhou in Zhejiang. Yueh peoples were mentioned from the 6th century BC until the end of the Han Dynasty [AD 220]. They were distributed along the coasts of Shandong, Jiangsu, Zhejiang, Fujian, Guangdong, Guangxi, Anhui, Jiangxi and Hunan. They had also spread as far as Vietnam. The Yueh were China's sea-faring people of old, and are believed to have sailed to the islands and across the Pacific, reaching the South American coast."[97] The Yueh have been assimilated into the Han Chinese.[98]

Ywe

This is possibly a subgroup of the Hani in Yunnan Province. The Ywe were mentioned in a 1962 Chinese article.[99]

Zangsari

The Global Evangelization Movement listed a 1995 population of 1,223 Zangsaris in Tibet. The majority of Zangsaris live in Kashmir, India.[100] No other sources list the Zangsari in China.

Zechian

This group was listed in John Kuhn's 1945 tribal survey of Yunnan Province, located in the Kunming area, capital city of Yunnan Province.[101] They have probably been officially included as part of the Yi nationality. The name of this group was formerly spelt *Tsechian*.

Zhuang, Guangdong

There is a small pocket of people in western Guangdong Province, officially counted as part of the Zhuang nationality, who appear to consider themselves a separate ethnolinguistic people group... "Those belonging to a branch of the Zhuang who to this day are still leading their age-old, traditional way of life, unaffected by the province's wide contacts with the outside world."[102]

Zoko

This Yi language was listed in southeastern Yunnan Province.[103] No other information refers to this name or language.

APPENDIX 2: Index of Alternate Names

In China, often the names of people groups have been spelled a host of different ways. In addition to different spelling, many tribes and people groups are known by different names according to their location. For example, the small Mang tribe are known as the *Chaman* by the local Dai people, *Manbu* by the Hani people, and *Ba'e* by the Kucong. The names of certain groups who appeared in pre-1949 missions literature have now changed. This index of 2,800 alternate names will hopefully assist the reader in avoiding confusion. This index lists all known names and the spelling of names for each group. The names in bold are the names used in the profiles.

Name:	See:
Arjie	Azhe
Asahei	
Asahei Aza	Asahei
Asaheipo	Asahei
Asak	Kado
Asci	Axi
Ashi	Axi
Ashu	Chin, Asho
Ati	
Atsam	Ai-Cham
Atsang	Achang
Atshi	Zaiwa
Atsi	Zaiwa
Atsi-Maru	Zaiwa
Atuence	Tibetan, Deqen
Atuense	Tibetan, Deqen
Atuentse	Tibetan, Deqen
Atzi	Zaiwa
Au	Ao Biao
Au Byau	Ao Biao
Awa	Kawa
A-wou	Awu, Southeastern
Awu, Northern	
Awu, Southeastern	
Awupu	Awu, Northern
Awupuo	Awu, Southeastern
Awutu	Nanjingren
Awuzhe	Awu, Northern
Awuzi	Cai
Axhebo	Axi
Axi	
Axibo	Axi
Axipo	Axi
Axipu	Axi
Ayi	
Ayizi	
Ayo	Mulao
Aynu	Ainu
Aza (#1)	Ani
Aza (#2)	Puwa
Aza (#3)	Polouo
Azar (#1)	Ani
Azar (#2)	Puwa
Azar (#3)	Asahei
Azar (#4)	Daizhan
Azar (#5)	Digao
Azar (#6)	Labapo
Azarpuo	Puwa
Azhe	
Azhepuo	Azhe
Azi	Zaiwa
Azong	

B

Name:	See:
Ba	Tujia
Ba-e	Mang
Baheng, Liping	
Baheng, Sanjiang	
Bahengmai	Baheng, Sanjiang
Bai	
Baierzi	Qixingmin
Bai Hmong	Hmong Daw
Baihong	
Baihua	Han Chinese, Cantonese
Baihuo	Bai
Baiku	Baonuo
Baiku Yao	Baonuo
Bai, Lijiang	Bei
Bailili	Gaisu, Southern
Bailisu	Gaisu, Southern
Bai Lolo	Sanie
Bai Long	Longjia
Bailuo	Luoluopo, Southeastern
Baima	
Bai Miao (#1)	Hmong Daw
Bai Miao (#2)	Horned Miao
Baini	Bai
Baipu	Zuoke
Bai Yi	
Baiyi (#1)	Luoluopo, Central
Baiyi (#2)	Bai Yi
Baiyi (#3)	Gepo, Eastern
Baiyi (#4)	Sanie
Baiyi (#5)	Tushu
Baiyi (#6)	Depo
Baiyi (#7)	Gese
Baiyi (#8)	Nosu, Mangbu
Baiyiren	Gepo, Western
Baiyizhe	Depo
Baizi	Bai
Baju	Pumi
Baka	Boka
Bakurat	Ami
Ban (#1)	Ban Yao
Ban (#2)	Lami
Bana	Pana
Bang	Bulang
Ban Mien	Ban Yao
Ban Yao	
Bao'an	Bonan
Baonan	Bonan
Baonuo	
Bapai	Zaomin
Baraog	Wa
Baraoke	Wa
Bargu	Buriat
Basket-Carrying Yao (#1)	Dongnu
Basket-Carrying Yao (#2)	Bunuo
Batanglu	Paiwan
Bawang Rong-Ke	Ergong
Baxing Yao (#1)	Baheng, Liping
Baxing Yao (#2)	Baheng, Sanjiang
Be	Lingao
Bee Yo	Biyo
Bei	
Beidalao	
Beidongnuo	
Beijinghua	Han Chinese, Mandarin
Beilong Yao	Nunu
Beilou Yao (#1)	Dongnu
Beilou Yao (#2)	Bunuo
Beiquba Naxi	Naheng
Bela	
Ben	
Bendi	Li, Bendi
Bendi Lolo	Pubiao
Bengi-Boga'er	Lhoba, Bogar
Benglong	De'ang, Pale
Ben Ren	Ben
Bhotia	Tibetan, Central
Bi	Biyo
Biantou Miao	Hmong Shuad

Name:	See:
Biao Chao	Biao-Jiao Mien
Biao-Jiao Mien	
Biaoman	Biao Mien
Biao Mien	
Biao Mien, Shikou	
Biao Min	Biao Mien
Biao Mon	Biao Mien
Big Black Yi (#1)	Neisu, Da Hei
Big Black Yi (#2)	Wopu
Big Flowery Miao	A-Hmao
Bijie Yi	Nosu, Shuixi
Bio	Biyo
Biseka	Tujia
Bisu	
Bit	
Biyao	Biyo
Biyo	
Biyue	Biyo
Bizeka	Tujia
Bizika	Tujia
Black Hmong (#1)	Hmong Bua
Black Hmong (#2)	Hmong Dlex Nchab
Black Karen	Riang
Black Lisu	Lipo, Eastern
Black Miao (#1)	Hmong Bua
Black Miao (#2)	Hmu, Northern
Black Nosu	Nosu, Shuixi
Black Tai	Tai Dam
Black Trouser Yao	Numao
Black Yang	Riang
Black Yi (#1)	Nosu, Shengzha
Black Yi (#2)	Nasu, Eastern
Black Yi (#3)	Neisu, Da Hei
Black Yi (#4)	Neisu, Xiao Hei
Black Yi (#5)	Suodi
Black Yi (#6)	Nosu, Xiaoliangshan
Black Yi (#7)	Nosu, Mangbu
Black Yi (#8)	Luoluopo, Central
Blang	Bulang
Bli	Li, Ha
Blue Miao	Hmong Njua
Bo	Qixingmin
Boat People	Han Chinese, Dan
Boga'er	Lhoba, Bogar
Bogol	
Boguol	Bogol
Bo-i	Bouyei
Boka	
Bokar	Lhoba, Bogar
Bo Kho Pa	Pula
Bola	Bela
Bolotse	Bolozi
Bolotsze	Bolozi
Bolozi	
Bolyu	Palyu
Bonan	
Bonan, Tongren	
Bonglung	De'ang, Pale
Boo Ko	Baihong
Boo Yi	Nosu, Butuo
Bopa	Ergong
Boren	Qixingmin
Bou-Shuung	Zhuang, Northern
Bou-Tsuung	Zhuang, Northern
Bouyei	
Boyu	Tibetan, Boyu

Name:	See:
Brogpa	Amdo, Hbrogpa
Brugchu	Tibetan, Zhugqu
Bubukun	Bunun
Bu Dai	Tulao
Budai	Tulao
Buddhist Bonan	Bonan, Tongren
Budo	
Bu Dou	Budo
Budu	Budo
Buerzi	Ersu
Buffalo Dung Hmong	Hua Miao
Bugan	
Bui	Bouyei
Buko	Budo
Buku	Baihong
Bula	Bela
Bulang	
Bulei	De'ang, Pale
Buman	Bouyei
Bunan	
Bunan (#2)	Bunun
Bunao	Bunu
Bu-Nao	Bunu
Bunong	Buyang
Bunti	Bunun
Bunu	
Bunu, Baheng	Baheng, Sanjiang
Bunu, Bunao	Bunu
Bunu, Wunai	Wunai
Bunu, Younuo	Younuo
Bunum	Bunun
Bunun	
Bunuo	
Buoba	Minyak
Buozi	Zhaba
Buriat	
Buriat-Mongolian	Buriat
Burig	Purik
Burong	Buyang
Buryat	Buriat
Busha	Pusha
Butsang	Golog
Butu	Budo
Butuo Yi	Nosu, Butuo
Buxia	Bit
Buxin	Bit
Buxinhua	Bit
Buyang	
Buyayi	Bouyei
Buyuan	Jino, Buyuan
Buyui	Bouyei
Buyi	Bouyei
Buzhong	Bouyei

C

Name:	See:
Cai	
Caijia	Cai
Cai Jia Miao	Cai
Canglo Monba	Monba, Medog
Cangluo Monba	Monba, Medog
Cangva	Zhuang, Northern
Cantonese	Han Chinese, Cantonese
Cao	Mjuniang
Cao Lan	
Cao Miao	Mjuniang
Central Min	Han Chinese, Min Zhong

Name:	See:
Central Monba	Monba, Cona
Chabao	Jiarong, Chabao
Chaman	Mang
Changpao	
Changpao Yao	Changpao
Changpu	Zuoke
Changsha Yao	Beidongnuo
Changshu Hmong	Changshu Miao
Changshu Miao	
Chang Tang Nomads	Tibetan, Nghari
Chao Kong Men	Biao Mien
Chaoxian	Korean
Chashan	Lashi
Chashanhua	Lashi
Chashan Yao	Lakkia
Chedi	Lisu
Cheli	Lisu
Chesu	
Chesu (#2)	Lesu
Chesupuo	Chesu
Chia-jung	Jiarong
Chiang: Cimulin	Qiang, Cimulin
Chiang: Dajishan	Qiang, Dajishan
Chiang: Heihu	Qiang, Heihu
Chiang: Jiaochang	Qiang, Jiaochang
Chiang: Longxi	Qiang, Longxi
Chiang: Luhua	Qiang, Luhua
Chiang: Mawo	Qiang, Mawo
Chiang: Mianchi	Qiang, Mianchi
Chiang: Sanlong	Qiang, Sanlong
Chiang: Taoping	Qiang, Taoping
Chiang: Yadu	Qiang, Yadu
Chiarong	Jiarong
Chi Chu	Giay
Chientung Miao	Hmu, Northern
Chilao	Gelao
Chiming	Limin
Chin	Chin, Asho
Chin, Asho	
Chinese Jews	You Tai
Chinese Miao	Hmong Shuad
Chinese Muslim	Hui
Chinese Shan (#1)	Tai Mao
Chinese Shan (#2)	Tai Nua
Ching (#1)	Jing
Ching (#2)	Mo
Chingpaw	Jingpo
Chingpo	Jingpo
Chi-no	Jino
Chiutse	Rawang
Chomo	Groma
Chomo Tibetan	Groma
Chona	Tibetan, Jone
Chone	Tibetan, Jone
Chongtien	Tibetan, Zhongdian
Choni	Tibetan, Jone
Chopa	Rawang
Chou-ch'u Tibetan	Tibetan, Zhugqu
Chrame	
Chuanchun (#1)	Chuanlan
Chuanchun (#2)	Chuanqing
Ch'uan-chun-tsi	Chuanlan
Chuang	Zhuang, Northern
Chumbi Tibetan	Groma
Chuangqing	Chuanqing
Chuanlan	

Name:	See:
Chuanqing	
Chung (#1)	Lisu
Chung (#2)	Ya
Chung-Chia	Bouyei
Chung-tien Tibetan	Tibetan, Zhongdian
Chuo-mu Tibetan	Groma
Ch'utzu	Derung
Chwang	Zhuang, Northern
Cimulin	Qiang, Cimulin
Clear-Water Hmong	Hmong Dlex Nchab
Clear-Water Miao	Hmong Dlex Nchab
Color Waist Dai	Huayao Tai
Con	Angku
Cone	Tibetan, Jone
Cui Chu	Giay
Cun	
Cung	Ya
Cunhua	Cun
Cuona Monba	Monba, Cona

D

Name:	See:
Daban	Yerong
Daban Yao	Yerong
Dada	Tatar
Dadan	Tatar
Dafang Yi	Nosu, Shuixi
Daghur	Daur
Dagour	Daur
Dagur	Daur
Da Hei Yi (#1)	Neisu, Da Hei
Da Hei Yi (#2)	Wopu
Dahua Bei	A-Hmao
Da Hua Miao	A-Hmao
Dahur	Daur
Dai, Black	Tai Dam
Dai Kao	Tai Kao
Dai Kong	Tai Nua
Dai Le (#1)	Tai Mao
Dai Le (#2)	Tai Nua
Dai Loe (#1)	Tai Mao
Dai Loe (#2)	Tai Nua
Dai, Lu	Tai Lu
Dai Mo	Tai Mao
Dai Muslims	Paxi
Dai, Nua	Tai Nua
Dai Nuea	Tai Nua
Dai, Pong	Tai Pong
Dai, White	Tai Kao
Dai Ya	Ya
Daizhan	
Daizhan Aza	Daizhan
Daizhanpo	Daizhan
Da Jiao Ban	Chuanqing
Dajishan	Qiang, Dajishan
Dalang	Deng, Darang
Dali	Bai
Daliangshan Nosu	Nosu, Shengzha
Damu	Miguba
Dan	Han Chinese, Dan
Dang	Giay
Danjia	Han Chinese, Dan
Dao	Iu Mien
Daofuhua	Ergong
Daor	Daur
Daqishan Qiang	Qiang, Dajishan
Darang	De'ang, Pale

Name:	See:
Darong	Deng, Darang
Dashan	Jingpo
Dashanhua	Jingpo
Da Tou Long	Longjia
Daur	
Daur, Western	
Daur, Bogol	Bogol
Dawar	Daur
Dawo'er	Daur
Da Xiuzi	Chuanqing
Dbus	Tibetan, Central
Dbustsang	Tibetan, Central
De'ang, Pale	
De'ang Rumai	
De'ang Shwe	
Dehong	Tai Mao
Dehong Dai	Tai Mao
Deng, Darang	
Deng, Geman	
Deng Za	Za
Depo	
Deqen Naxi	Naxi, Northern
Deqin Tibetan	Tibetan, Deqen
Derung	
Di	Baima
Dianbao	
Diandongbei Miao	A-Hmao
Diao	
Diaoren	Diao
Diaozu	Diao
Dienbo	Dianbao
Digao	
Digao Aza	Digao
Digaopo	Digao
Dioi	Bouyei
Diso	Maru
Dli	Li, Ha
Do	Tai Dam
Dong Jia	Ga Mong
Dongjiahua	Ga Mong
Dong, Northern	
Dong, Southern	
Dongnu	
Dongshan Yao	Biao-Jiao Mien
Dongshan Yizu	Laluo, Jiantou
Dongxiang	
Dota	Duota
Dota Yi	Duota
Doupo	
Douxu	Ersu
Downhill Hmong (#1)	Hmong Dou
Downhill Hmong (#2)	Hua Miao
Drokpa	Tibetan, Nghari
Drokwa	Tibetan, Nghari
Drung	Derung
Dry-Land Dai	Han Tai
Dry Yi (#1)	Naluo
Dry Yi (#2)	Guopu
Duck-Raising Gedou	Ga Mong
Duck-Raising Miao	Ga Mong
Dulong	Derung
Dungan	Hui
Duoluo	
Duoluo Gelao	Duoluo
Duoni	Duota
Duota	

Name:	See:
Dzao Min	Zaomin

E

E	
East-Lower-Northern Yi	Nosu, Butuo
East Yugur	Yugur, Enger
Eastern East Guizhou Miao	Hmu, Eastern
Eastern Hmu	Hmu, Eastern
Eastern Jiarong	Jiarong, Situ
Eastern Jyarung	Jiarong, Situ
Eastern Lisu	Lipo, Eastern
Eastern Min	Han Chinese, Min Dong
Eastern Monba	Monba, Medog
Eastern Samaduo	Samadu, Eastern
Eastern Yogor	Yugur, Enger
East Guizhou Miao	Hmu, Northern
Eight-Clan Yao (#1)	Baheng, Liping
Eight-Clan Yao (#2)	Baheng, Sanjiang
Eka	
Ekaw	Akha
Eleuth	Olot
Elunchun	Oroqen
Eluosi	Russian
Elyut	Olot
Enger	Yugur, Enger
Eniba	Enipu
Enibo	Enipu
Enipu	
Enu	
Ergong	
Ersu	
Ersubuerzi	Ersu
Ersu Yi	Ersu
Er Yi	Neisu, Xiao Hei
Evenki	Ewenki, Solon
Ewenki, Aoluguya	Yakut
Ewenki, Yakut	Yakut
Ewenke	Ewenki, Solon
Ewenki, Chenbaehru	Ewenki, Tungus
Ewenki, Solon	
Ewenki, Tungus	

F

Fang Teo Ren	Chuanqing
Fish-Skin Tatars	Hezhen
Flower Dou Miao	Ge
Flower Gelao	Ge
Flowery Belt Dai	Huayao Tai
Flowery Belt Yi	Nisu, Xinping
Flowery Blue Yao	Kiong Nai
Flowery Miao	A-Hmao
Flowery Waist Dai	Huayao Tai
Flowery Waist Yi	Nisu, Xinping
Flowery Rooster Dai	Hongjin Tai
Flowery Root	Ge
Forest Miao	Hmong Vron
Foula	Lati
Fuchye	Nu
Fula	Lati
Fuma	
Fu Ma	Fuma
Fuyu Keerkezi	Khakas
Fuyu Kirgiz	Khakas

G

Gado	Kado

Name:	See:
Gahri	Bunan
Gaiji	
Gaijipo	Gaiji
Gaiqipo	Gaiji
Gaisu, Southern	
Gaisu, Western	
Gaisupuo	Gaisu, Southern
Gaisu Yi	Gaisu, Southern
Gam (#1)	Dong, Northern
Gam (#2)	Dong, Southern
Ga Mong	
Gan	Han Chinese, Gan
Gani (#1)	Nasu, Eastern
Gani (#2)	Naluo
Gantung	Rawang
Gan Yi (#1)	Nasu, Eastern
Gan Yi (#2)	Depo
Gan Yi (#3)	Naluo
Gan Yi (#4)	Guopu
Gan Yi (#5)	Aling
Ganyi	Nasu, Eastern
Gao	
Gao Gelao	Gao
Gaori	Hkauri
Gaoshan (#1)	Gesu
Gaoshan (#2)	Luoluopo, Central
Gaoshanzu (#1)	Lipo, Western
Gaoshanzu (#2)	Luoluopo
Gashai	Muda
Gatse	Golog
Gauri	Hkauri
Gazhuo	Mongol, Yunnan
Ge	
Ge (#2)	Ayizi
Gedang	Ge
Gedong	Ge
Gedou	Ge
Gedoudiu	Ge
Gedou Miao	Ge
Gedu	Ge
Gei	Li, Qi
Gejia	Ge
Ge Jia	Ge
Gejiaoren	Nanjingren
Gelao	
Gelo	Gelao
Ge Mong	Ga Mong
Gem Mun	Kim Mun
Gepo (#1)	Gepo, Eastern
Gepo (#2)	Gepo, Western
Gepo, Eastern	
Gepo, Western	
Gepu	Gepo, Eastern
Gepuo	Gepo, Eastern
Gese	
Gesitsa	Ergong
Gesu	
Gesu (#2)	Gese
Gesu Yi	Gesu
Getou	Ge
Gewu	Ge
Gha-Mu	
Ghao-Xong, Eastern	
Ghao-Xong, Western	
Ghara	Bunan
Giai	Giay

Name:	See:
Giang	Giay
Giay	
Gin	Jing
Gni	Sani
Gni-p'a	Sani
Gold	Hezhen
Golden Palaung	De'ang, Shwe
Goldi	Hezhen
Golog	
Golok	Golog
Gondla	Lahuli, Tinan
Gopu	Nasu, Eastern
Gou Er Long	Longjia
Gouzou	
Grass Miao	Mjuniang
Greater Neisu	Neisu, Da Hei
Great Flowery Miao	A-Hmao
Great Tai	Shan
Green Miao	Hmong Njua
Green Pu	Puwa
Green Yi	Nosu, Xiaoliangshan
Groma	
Gromo	Groma
Guabie Naxi	Naju
Guaigun	
Guangdong	Han Chinese, Cantonese
Guanhua	Han Chinese, Mandarin
Guanyingqiao	Jiarong, Huanyingqiao
Guiqiong	
Guizhong	Guiqiong
Gu Miao	Xi
Guo (#1)	Gepo, Eastern
Guo (#2)	Guopu
Guoke	Akha
Guoluo	Guopu
Guopu	
Guopu (#2)	Gepo, Eastern
Guoshan Yao (#1)	Iu Mien
Guoshan Yao (#2)	Iu Mien, Luoxiang
Guoyu	Han Chinese, Mandarin
Gupu	Gepo, Eastern
Guzu	Gepo, Eastern
Gwa-o	Mulao Jia
Gyantse	Tibetan, Gtsang
Gyarong	Jiarong
Gyarung	Jiarong
Gyirong	Kyerung

H

Name:	See:
Hagei	
Hagei Gelao	
Haixi Kazaks	Kazak, Qinghai
Hakei	Hagei
Hahl	Mongol, Khalka
Hakka	
Hakka, Hainan Island	
Hainan Cham	Utsat
Hainan Chinese	Han Chinese, Hainanese
Hainanese	Han Chinese, Hainanese
Hamunikan	Mongol, Khamnigan
Han Chinese, Cantonese	
Han Chinese, Dan	
Han Chinese, Gan	
Han Chinese, Hainanese	
Han Chinese, Hui'an	
Han Chinese, Huizhou	

Name:	See:
Han Chinese, Jin	
Han Chinese, Mandarin	
Han Chinese, Min Bei	
Han Chinese, Min Dong	
Han Chinese, Min Nan	
Han Chinese, Min Zhong	
Han Chinese, Pinghua	
Han Chinese, Puxian	
Han Chinese, Shaojiang	
Han Chinese, Shaozhou	
Han Chinese, Waxiang	
Han Chinese, Wu	
Han Chinese, Xiang	
Han Chinese, Xunpu	
Hanhi	Hani
Hani	
Hanluo	Luoluopo, Southeastern
Han Miao	Hmong Shuad
Han Tai	
Haoni	
Han-Paiyi	Tai Nua
Haw (#1)	Hani
Haw (#2)	Hui
Hazake	Kazak
Hbrugchu	Tibetan, Zhugqu
Hdzanggur	
Heche	Hezhen
Hedjen	Hezhen
Hei	Li, Qi
Heihu	Qiang, Heihu
Hei-hu Ch'iang	Qiang, Heihu
Heiku Yao	Numao
Heilongjiang Kirgiz	Khakas
Heilongjiang Olot	Olot
Heiluo	Luoluopo, Southeastern
Hei Miao (#1)	Hmong Bua
Hei Miao (#2)	Hmu, Northern
Heipo	Lipo, Eastern
Heitu	Li, Qi
Hei Yi (#1)	Nasu, Eastern
Hei Yi (#2)	Nosu, Shengzha
Hei Yi (#3)	Nisu, Yuanyang
Hei Yi (#4)	Nosu, Xiaoliangshan
Hei Yi (#5)	Nosu, Mangbu
Hei Yi (#6)	Luoluopo, Central
He Lisu	Lipo, Eastern
Hezhe	Hezhen
Hezhen	
Highland Yao	Iu Mien
Hinghua	Han Chinese, Puxian
Hinghua Min	Han Chinese, Puxian
Hkanung	Rawang
Hkauri	
Hli-khin	Mosuo
Hmnai	Wunai
Hm Nai	Wunai
Hmong, Central Huishui	Miao, Huishui (Central)
Hmong, Central Mashan	Miao, Mashan (Central)
Hmong, Eastern Huishui	Miao, Huishui (Eastern)
Hmong, Eastern Qiandong	Hmu, Eastern
Hmong, Eastern Xiangxi	Ghao-Xong, Eastern
Hmong, Luopohe	Miao, Luobohe
Hmong, Luzhai	Hmong Be
Hmong, Njua	
Hmong, Northeastern Dian	A-Hmao
Hmong, Northern Guiyang	Miao, Guiyang (Northern)
Hmong, Northern Huishui	Miao, Huishui (Northern)
Hmong, Northern Mashan	Miao, Mashan (Northern)
Hmong, Northern Qiandong	Hmu, Northern
Hmong, Northwestern Guiyang	Miao, Guiyang (Northwestern)
Hmong, South Central Guiyang	Miao, Guiyang (South-Central)
Hmong, Southern Guiyang	Miao, Guiyang (Southern)
Hmong, Southern Mashan	Miao, Mashan (Southern)
Hmong, Southern Qiandong	Hmu, Southern
Hmong, Southwestern Guiyang	Miao, Guiyang (Southwestern)
Hmong, Southwestern Huishui	Miao, Huishui (Southwestern)
Hmong, Western Mashan	Miao, Mashan (Western)
Hmong, Western Xiangxi	Ghao-Xong, Western
Hmong Bal Hout	Hmong Leng
Hmong Be	
Hmong Bel	Hua Miao
Hmong Bua	
Hmong Daw	
Hmong Dlex Nchab	
Hmong Dlo	Hmong Bua
Hmong Dlob	Hmong Dlex Nchab
Hmong Dou	
Hmong Dous	Hua Miao
Hmong Drout Raol	Hmong Be
Hmong Ghuad Dus	Hua Miao
Hmong La	Hmong Shuad
Hmong Leng	
Hmong Lens	Hmong Leng
Hmong Ndrou	Hua Miao
Hmong Nraug	Hua Miao
Hmong Nzhil	Hmong Be
Hmong Qua Mpa	Hmong Daw
Hmong Sa	Hmong Shuad
Hmong Shuad	
Hmong Si	Hmong Bua
Hmong Sib	Hmong Leng
Hmong Sou	Hua Miao
Hmong Soud	Horned Miao
Hmong Sua	Hmong Shuad
Hmong Vron	
Hmong Vron (#2)	Horned Miao
Hmu, Eastern	
Hmu, Northern	
Hmu, Southern	
Ho	Haoni
Hoche	Hezhen
Hokka	Hakka
Hokkien	Han Chinese, Min Nan
Hoklo	Han Chinese, Min Nan
Hokow	Queyu
Hol-Chih	Hezhen
Hon Ban	Cao Lan
Hongee	Naisu
Hongjin Tai	
Hongtou Miao	Hmong Leng
Hongxian Miao	Hmong Dou
Hong Yao	Younuo
Hongyi	Aluo
Hong Yi (#1)	Aluo
Hong Yi (#2)	Michi
Hong Yi (#3)	Naisu
Hong Yi (#4)	Lagou
Honi	Haoni

Name:	See:
Ho Nte	She
Hor	Ergong
Hor-ke	Ergong
Horpa	Ergong
Horn Miao	Horned Miao
Horned Miao	
Horse Tungus	Ewenki, Tungus
Hoton	Han Chinese, Mandarin
Hsiang	Han Chinese, Xiang
Hsiangcheng	Xiangcheng
Hsianghsi Miao	Ghao-Xong, Western
Hsiangtan	Xiangtang
Hsifan	Chrame
Hsiao Hwa Miao	Gha-Mu
Hu	
Huadou	Ge
Huagongji Dai	Hongjin Tai
Hua Hmong	Hua Miao
Hua Lan Yao	Kiong Nai
Hualo	Bugan
Hualuo	Luoluopo, Southeastern
Huami Yi	Azhe
Hua Miao	
Hua Miao (#2)	A-Hmao
Huang Yi	Doupo
Huayao Tai	
Huayao Yi	Nisu, Xinping
Hua Yao Yi	Nisu, Xinping
Huayi Yao	Flowery Shirt Yao
Huayuan Miao	Ghao-Xong, Western
Huazu	Bugan
Huguang	Laba
Huguangren	Laba
Hunan Yao	Iu Mien, Hunan
Huo Nte	She
Hui	
Hui'an	Han Chinese, Hui'an
Hui Chinese	Han Chinese, Huizhou
Huichou	Han Chinese, Huizhou
Huihe	Uygur
Huihui	Utsat
Huili Yi	Suodi
Huizhou	Han Chinese, Huizhou
Humai	De'ang, Rumai
Hunan	Han Chinese, Xiang
Hunanese	Han Chinese, Xiang
Huzhu	Tu
Hwa Lan Yao	Kiong Nai
Hwa Miao	A-Hmao
Hwayaodai	Huayao Tai
Hweichow	Han Chinese, Huizhou
I	
Idu	Lhoba, Yidu
Ikho	Akha
Ikor	Akha
Ilao	Gelao
Ili Turk	Tuerke
Ili Turki	Tuerke
Indonesian	
I-no	Nosu, Yinuo
Iu Mien	
Iu Mien, Changping	
Iu Mien, Hunan	
Iu Mien, Luoxiang	

Name:	See:
J	
Jang	Mosuo
Jao-jo	Zauzou
Japanese	
Jarong	Jiarong
Jazza	Golog
Jeu-g'oe	Akha
Jews	You Tai
Jiamao	Li, Jiamao
Jiamuhua	Ai-Cham
Jiangbe	Subei
Jiantou Lolo	Laluo, Jiantou
Jiantou Yi	Gepo, Eastern
Jiaochang	Qiang, Jiaochang
Jiaojiao Miao	Horned Miao
Jiaogongmian	Biao Mien
Jiarong, Chabao	
Jiarong, Guanyingqiao	
Jiarong, Shangzhai	
Jiarong, Sidabao	
Jiarong, Situ	
Jiasou	
Jim Mun	Kim Mun
Jin	Han Chinese, Jin
Jing	
Jingpaw	Jingpo
Jingpo	
Jingren	Qixingmin
Jinhua	Ai-Cham
Jinping Dai	Tai Dam
Jinyu	Han Chinese, Jin
Jino	
Jino, Buyuan	
Jinuo	Jino
Jiongnai	Kiong Nai
Jiongnaihua	Kiong Nai
Jiuren	Limin
Jone	Tibetan, Jone
Juchen	Hezhen
Juim Mun	Kim Mun
K	
Ka Bao	Pubiao
Ka Beo	Pubiao
Ka Biao	Pubiao
Ka Che	Keji
Kachin	Jingpo
Kadas	Paiwan
Kado	
Kadu	Kado
Kaduo	Mongol, Yunnan
Ka Dwo	Kado
Kai Pai	Pana
Kaixien	Ladakhi
Kala	Bulang
Kale-whan	Paiwan
Kalmyk	Oirat
Kalmyk-Oirat	Oirat
Kam (#1)	Dong, Northern
Kam (#2)	Dong, Southern
Kam (#3)	Khampa, Eastern
Kaman	Deng, Geman
Kamau	Li, Jiamao
Kamhmu	Khmu
Ka Mi	Kemei
Kammu	Khmu

Name:	See:
Kamnigan	Mongol, Khamnigan
Kamu	Khmu
Kan	Han Chinese, Gan
Kanao	Qanu
Kang (#1)	Tai Mao
Kang (#2)	Khampa, Eastern
Kang-i	Nasu, Eastern
Kanggan	Golog
Kangsar	Golog
Kao-jih	Hkauri
Kapiangan	Paiwan
Kar Bhote	Lhomi
Kara	Kirgiz
Katausan	Paiwan
Kathe Bhote	Lhomi
Kato	Kado
Katu	Kado
Kauri	Hkauri
Kawa	
Kazak	
Kazak, Qinghai	
Kazakh	Kazak
Kazax	Kazak
Ke (#1)	Hakka
Ke (#2)	Yizi
Kebi	Kemei
Kechia	Hakka
Ke'erkezi	Kirgiz
Keh Deo	Ge
Kehlao	Gelao
Keh-teo Miao	Ge
Kejia	Hakka
Keji	
Kejis	Keji
Kelao	Gelao
Keleo	Gelao
Kemei	
Kemeihua	Kemei
Kem Mun	Kim Mun
Kemu	Khmu
Keriya	
Keriya Uygurs	Keriya
Keqin	Jingpo
Keu	Ake
Kha	Khmu
Khabit	Bit
Khae	Lisu
Khakas	
Khakassian	Khakas
Khakhas	Khakas
Khako	Akha
Khalka	Mongol, Khalka
Kham	Khampa, Eastern
Khamba	Khampa, Eastern
Khamnigan (#1)	Ewenki, Tungus
Khamnigan (#2)	Mongol, Khamnigan
Khamnigan Evenki	Ewenki, Tungus
Khamnigan Ewenki	Ewenki, Tungus
Khamnigan Tungus	Ewenki, Tungus
Khampa	Tibetan, Zhongdian
Khampa, Eastern	
Khampa, Northern	
Khampa, Western	
Khams	Khampa, Eastern
Khams-Bhotia	Khampa, Eastern
Khams-Yal	Khampa, Eastern

Name:	See:
Khamu	Khmu
Khamuk	Khmu
Khanung	Derung
Khauri	Hkauri
Khi	Gelao
Khik	Tajik, Wakhi
Khmu	
Khomu	Khmu
Khotan	Hui
Khouen	Kuan
Khuen	Kuan
Khupang	Nu
Khween	Kuan
Khyang	Chin, Asho
Khyeng	Chin, Asho
Ki	Li, Qi
Kiakala	Kyakala
Kiakla	Kyakala
Kiang Nai	Kiong Nai
Kim Mun	
Kinh	Jing
Kiong Nai	
Kion Nai	Kiong Nai
Kiorr	Angku
Kirghiz	Kirgiz
Kirgiz	
Kiutze	Rawang
Kiutzu	Rawang
Kjang E	E
Kjutzu	Derung
Klan	Gao
Klao	Gao
Klau	Gao
Klo	Gelao
Ko	Akha
Koko Miao	Horned Miao
Kong	Tai Mao
Kong Ge	
Kong Geh	Kong Ge
Konkaling	Khampa, Eastern
Kon Keu	Kong Ge
Kontoi	Bulang
Kopu	Nasu, Eastern
Korean	
Krangku	Rawang
Kua-pie Naxi	Naju
Kuan	
Kuanhua	Kuan
Kubiao	Pubiao
Kucong	
Kudo	Kado
Kuei	Bouyei
Kui (#1)	Bouyei
Kui (#2)	Kucong
Kui Ge	Kong Ge
Kuman	Deng, Geman
Kuman Deng	Deng, Geman
Kun To	Zhuang, Southern
Kuo-lo	Guopu
Kutsung	Kucong
Kween	Kuan
Kwi	Kucong
Kwingsang	Nu
Kwinpang	Nu
Kyakala	
Kyang	Chin, Asho

Name:	See:
Kyerung	
Kyirong	Kyerung
L	
La (#1)	Tai Pong
La (#2)	Li, Ha
Laba	
Laba (#2)	Labapo
Laba Aza	Labapo
Laba Miao	Laba
Labapo	
Labbu	Bai
Labrang	Amdo, Rongmahbrogpa
Lachi	Lati
Lachikwaw	Lashi
Ladak	Ladakhi
Ladakh	Ladakhi
Ladakhi	
Ladaphi	Ladakhi
Ladhakhi	Ladakhi
Ladwags	Ladakhi
Laga	Laka
Lagou	
Lagou (#2)	Laka
Lagoupu	Lagou
Lahauli	Lahuli, Tinan
Lahouli	Lahuli, Tinan
Laho	Lahu
Lahu	
Lahuli	Lahuli, Tinan
Lahuli of Bunan	Bunan
Lahuli, Tinan	
Lahuna	Lahu
Lahu Na	Lahu
Lahu Shi	Kucong
Lahu Xi	Kucong
Lai (#1)	Li, Ha
Lai (#2)	Palyu
Laimo	Lemo
Lai Mo	Lemo
Lajia	Lakkia
Laka	
Laka (#2)	Lakkia
Lakia	Lakkia
Lakja	Lakkia
Lakkia	
Lakkja	Lakkia
Laku (#1)	Bela
Laku (#2)	Lahu
Lalaw	Nosu, Xiaoliangshan
Laloba (#1)	Laluo, Jiantou
Laloba (#2)	Laluo, Mishaba
Lalu (#1)	Lalu, Xinping
Lalu (#2)	Lalu, Yangliu
Lalu (#3)	Lalu, Xuzhang
Lalu (#4)	Laluo, Jiantou
Lalu (#5)	Laluo, Mishaba
Lalupo	Laluo, Mishaba
Lalu, Xinping	
Lalu, Xuzhang	
Lalu, Yangliu	
Laluo	Laluo, Jiantou
Laluo, Jiantou	
Laluo, Mishaba	
Lama	
Lami	
Lamsihoan	Ami
Landian	Kim Mun
Lang	Maru
Lang'e	Maru
Lan-San Chi	Cao Lan
Lansu	Maru
Lanten	Kim Mun
Lantien	Kim Mun
Lao	Gelao
Laobazi	Laba
Lao Han (#1)	Chuanlan
Lao Han (#2)	Chuanqing
Laomian	Bisu
Laopa	Laopang
Laopang	
Laopin	Bisu
Lao Terng	Khmu
La'ou Yuxi Mujiren	Muzi
Lao-wou (#1)	Luowu
Lao-wou (#2)	Lawu
Lao-wu	Lawu
Laowu	
Lapeitula	Puwa
Lapeitulapuo	Puwa
Laqua	Pubiao
Lashi	
Lashi-Maru	
Lasi	Lashi
Lati	
Laungaw	Maru
Lava	Lawa
Lavua	Lawa
Lawa	
Lawlaw	Nosu, Xiaoliangshan
Lawng (#1)	Maru
Lawng (#2)	Nung
Lawu	
Lawu (#2)	Awu, Southeastern
Lawu (#3)	Laowu
Le	Li, Ha
Lechi	Lashi
Lei-o	Mulao Jia
Leisu (#1)	Lesu
Leisu (#2)	Lisu
Leme	Bai
Lemo	
Leqi	Lashi
Leshuoopa	Lisu
Lesser Neisu	Neisu, Xiao Hei
Lesu	
Lesuo	Lisu
Letsi	Lashi
Lhao Vo	Maru
Lhardi	Golog
Lhasa	Tibetan, Central
Lhasa Tibetan	Tibetan, Central
Lhoba, Boga'er	Lhoba, Bogar
Lhoba, Bogar	
Lhoba, Yidu	
Lhoket	Lhomi
Lhomi	
Li	Lipo, Western
Li, Bendi	
Li, Ha	
Li, Jiamao	
Li, Meifu	

Name:	See:
Li, Qi	
Li-a	Lipo, Eastern
Liang'e Ren	Liwu
Light Hmong	Hmong Leng
Lihsaw	Lisu
Lijia	Limin
Li-li-sha	Paiwan
Limi	
Limin	
Limingzi	Limin
Limkou	Lingao
Limkow	Lingao
Lingao	
Linghua	
Lipa (#1)	Lisu
Lipa (#2)	Lipo, Western
Lipo, Dayao	Lipo, Western
Lipo, Eastern	
Lipo, Western	
Lipoo (#1)	Lipo, Eastern
Lipoo (#2)	Lipo, Western
Lipu	Lati
Lipuchio	Lati
Lipuke	Lati
Lipulio	Lati
Lipuo (#1)	Lipo, Eastern
Lipuo (#2)	Lipo, Western
Lipupi	Lati
Lipupo	Lati
Lipute	Lati
Liputio	Lati
Li Ren	Limin
Lisaw	Lisu
Lishaw	Lisu
Lishu	Lisu
Lissoo	Lisu
Lissu	Lisu
Lisu	
Lisu (#2)	Ersu
Lisu Taku	Lipo, Eastern
Liu	Liujia
Liude	
Liudepo	Liude
Liujia	
Liujiaren	Liujia
Liumi	Lami
Liwu	
Lizu (#1)	Lipo, Eastern
Lizu (#2)	Lipo, Western
Lodak	Ladakhi
Lodokhi	Ladakhi
Loe	Tai Nua
Lohe	Lahu
Lohei	Lahu
Loi	Li, Ha
Loisu	Lisu
Lolo (#1)	Luoluopo, Central
Lolo (#2)	Nosu, Shengzha
Lolo (#3)	Gaisu, Southern
Lolo (#4)	Nisu, Jianshui
Lolo (#5)	Nisu, Yuanyang
Lolo (#6)	Luoluopo, Western
Lolo (#7)	Luoluopo, Southeastern
Lolopo (#1)	Luoluopo, Central
Lolopo (#2)	Luoluopo, Western
Lomi	Naxi

Name:	See:
Long	
Long (#2)	Longjia
Long Comb Miao	Changshu Miao
Long-Horn Miao	Hmong Vron
Longjia	
Longjiazi	Nanjingren
Longming	Zhuang, Southern
Long-Shirt Yao	Beidongnuo
Longxi	Qiang, Longxi
Lopi	
Lop Nur	Uygur, Lop Nur
Lop Nur Turks	Uygur, Lop Nur
Lousu	Nasu, Wusa
Lou-wou	Luowu
Lowland Yao	Kim Mun
Lowu	Luowu
Lu	
Lu (#2)	Tai Lu
Lu (#3)	Nu
Lue	Tai Lu
Lugepo	Lu
Lu Ge Zi	Lu
Lugu Lake Mongols	Mongol, Sichuan
Luhua	Qiang, Luhua
Lu-k'ou	Lemo
Lulupu	Luoluopo, Central
Lu Miao	Hmong Njua
Lung-hsi Ch'iang	Qiang, Longxi
Lungming	Zhuang, Southern
Luo	Gepo, Western
Luolu	Luoluopo, Central
Luoluo (#1)	Gaisu, Southern
Luoluo (#2)	Luoluopo, Central
Luoluo (#3)	Nisu, Jianshui
Luoluo (#4)	Nisu, Yuanyang
Luoluopo, Central	
Luoluopo, Southeastern	
Luoluopo, Western	
Luoluopuo	Luoluopo, Central
Luopohe	Miao, Luobohe
Luopuo	Awu, Southeastern
Luoren	Gaisu, Western
Luowu	
Luowu (#2)	Alu
Luowu (#3)	Naisu
Luowu (#4)	Niesu, Central
Luozu (#1)	Gaisu, Southern
Luozu (#2)	Nisu, Jianshui
Lu Ren	Lu
Lushi	Mosuo
Lusu (#1)	Lisu
Lusu (#2)	Ersu
Lutze	Nu
Lutzu (#1)	Lisu
Lutzu (#2)	Nu
Luwa	Lawa
Luwu	Alu
Luzhai Miao	Hmong Be
Luzi	Nu
Luzu	
L'wa	Lawa
Ly	Tai Lu

M

Name:	See:
Mabe	Baihong
Machi	Lipo, Eastern

Name:	See:
Machipuo	Lipo, Eastern
Maganfang	Laluo, Jiantou
Magpie Miao	Miao, Chuan
Mahe	Baihong
Mahei	Baihong
Maingtha	Achang
Majia	Hakka
Mak	Mo
Malimasa	
Malu	Maru
Ma Mian Long	Longjia
Man (#1)	Iu Mien
Man (#2)	Kim Mun
Man (#3)	Manchu
Manbu	Mang
Man Cao Lan	Cao Lan
Manchia	Nosu, Shengzha
Manchou	Manchu
Manchu	
Manchurian Olot	Olot
Manchurian Solon	Ewenki, Solon
Mandarin	Han Chinese, Mandarin
Mang	
Mangbu Yi	Nosu, Mangbu
Mangoon	Hezhen
Mang-pu Yi	Nosu, Mangbu
Mang Ren	Mang
Mang U	Mang
Mangun	Hezhen
Manju	Manchu
Man Laqua	Pubiao
Manmet	
Man Met	Manmet
Manmi	Manmet
Manmit	Manmet
Mannai Olot	Olot
Man Ni	Cai
Manton	De'ang, Pale
Mantzu	Nosu, Shengzha
Manyak	
Mao (#1)	Aoka
Mao (#2)	Tai Mao
Mao Tai	Tai Mao
Maojia	Aoka
Maonan	
Ma Pa Seng	Baheng, Sanjiang
Maran	Ami
Marip	Jingpo
Maru	
Matu	Maru
Maw	Tai Mao
Mawo	Qiang, Mawo
Mawteik	Kado
Mbi	Bisu
Mbisu	Bisu
Mehua	Meng
Meifu	Li, Meifu
Mekong Tibetan	Tibetan, Deqen
Memba	Monba, Cona
Menba	Monba, Cona
Meng	
Meng (#2)	Mengwu
Menggu	Mongol
Menghua (#1)	Meng
Menghua (#2)	Laluo, Mishaba
Menghuazu	Laluo, Mishaba
Menghuaren	Eka
Menghwa	Meng
Mengwa	Meng
Mengwu	
Mengzu	Mongol
Menia	
Menpa	Monba, Cona
Mengwu	Awu, Southeastern
Meo Do (#1)	Ghao-Xong, Western
Meo Do (#2)	Hmong Daw
Meo Kao	Hmong Daw
Meo Lai	Baheng, Sanjiang
Mgolog	Golog
Mian	Iu Mien
Mianchi	Qiang, Mianchi
Miao, Baishi	
Miao, Big Flowery	A-Hmao
Miao, Black	Hmong Bua
Miao, Cao	Mjuniang
Miao, Chuan	
Miao, Enshi	
Miao, Green	Hmong Njua
Miao, Guiyang (Northern)	
Miao, Guiyang (Northwestern)	
Miao, Guiyang (South Central)	
Miao, Guiyang (Southern)	
Miao, Guiyang (Southwestern)	
Miao, Huishui (Central)	
Miao, Huishui (Eastern)	
Miao, Huishui (Northern)	
Miao, Huishui (Southwestern)	
Miao, Leng	Hmong Leng
Miao, Luobohe	
Miao, Lupanshui	
Miao, Luzhai	Hmong Be
Miao, Mashan (Central)	
Miao, Mashan (Northern)	
Miao, Mashan (Southern)	
Miao, Mashan (Western)	
Miao, Njua	Hmong Njua
Miao, Qa Nu	Qanu
Miao, Small Flowery	Gha-Mu
Miao, Xiangxi (Eastern)	Ghao-Xong, Eastern
Miao, Xiangxi (Western)	Ghao-Xong, Western
Mibisu	Bisu
Micha	
Micha: Nanjian	Micha
Michi	
Michia	Michi
Michipuo	Michi
Mien (#1)	Iu Mien
Mien (#2)	Iu Mien, Hunan
Mien (Guangxi-Yunnan)	Iu Mien
Mien-ch'ih Ch'iang	Qiang, Mianchi
Miguba	
Mijia	Michi
Mili	
Min Bei	Han Chinese, Min Bei
Min Chi	Michi
Min Qi	Michi
Minchia	Bai
Min Dong	Han Chinese, Min Dong
Ming	
Ming (#2)	Sani
Mingjia	Michi
Minglang	

Name:	See:
Mingzu	Ming
Minhe Tu	Mongour
Minkia	Bai
Min Nan	Han Chinese, Min Nan
Min Pei	Han Chinese, Min Bei
Minqi	Michi
Minya	Minyak
Minyak	
Minya Tibetans	Minyak
Miqi	Michi
Mi Qie Po	Michi
Miqipuo	Michi
Miri	Adi
Misabo	Laluo, Mishaba
Misan	Laluo, Mishaba
Misanru	Laluo, Mishaba
Misanxu	Laluo, Mishaba
Misapha	Laluo, Mishaba
Misapo	Laluo, Mishaba
Misaru	Laluo, Mishaba
Mishaba	Laluo, Mishaba
Misu	Bisu
Mitcha	Micha
Mixisu	
Miyao	Minyak
Mizu	Michi
M Ji	Muji
Mjiuniang	
Mngahris	Tibetan, Nghari
Mo	
Mo (#2)	Hmong Dou
Mochia	Mo
Mo-hsieh	Mosuo
Mohua	Mo
Mo Jia	Mo
Moifau	Li, Meifu
Moinba	Monba, Cona
Molao	Mulao
Momba	Monba, Cona
Mo Min	Mo
Mompa	Monba, Cona
Monba, Cona	
Monba, Medog	
Monchak	Tuva
Mong Do	Miao, White
Mongol	
Mongol, Alxa	
Mongol, Khalka	
Mongol, Khamnigan	
Mongol, Sichuan	
Mongol, Yunnan	
Mongolian	Mongol
Mongolian Huihui	Dongxiang
Mongolian Yugur	Yugur, Enger
Mongou	Mongour
Mongour	
Mongor	Mongour
Mongsa	Achang
Mongsha	Achang
Mong Trang	Miao, White
Monguor	Mongour
Monjak	Tuva
Monpa	Monba, Cona
Morlao	Mulao
Moso	Lahu
Mosso	Mosuo

Name:	See:
Mosuo	
Motuo Monba	Monba, Medog
Mou	Khmu
Mountain Dai	Han Tai
Mountain Hmong	Hmong Be
Mountain Lawa	Lawa
Mountain Speech Red Yao	Younuo
Moxie	Mosuo
Mozhihei	
Mu (#1)	Mulao
Mu (#2)	Naxi
Muda	
Mu Di Pa	Pula
Muhso	Lahu
Muji	
Muji (#2)	Muzi
Mujipo	Muji
Mujiren	Muzi
Mulam	Mulao
Mulao	
Mulao (#2)	Mulao Jia
Mulao Jia	
Mulao Miao	Mulao
Mulu	Maru
Muluo	Mulao
Munia	Menia
Munya	Minyak
Mushu Miao	Hmong Shuad
Muslim Mongols	Mongol, Alxa
Mussar	Lahu
Musso	Lahu
Mussuh	Lahu
Musu	Mosuo
Muta	Muda
Muya	Minyak
Muyak	Minyak
Muzi	
Myen	Iu Mien

N

Name:	See:
Naani	Hezhen
Nabazi	Laba
Nachi	Naxi
Naheng	
Nahsi	Naxi
Naisu	
Naju	
Nakhi	Naxi
Na Klao	Baonuo
Nalo	Naluo
Nalu	Naluo
Naluo	
Naluo (#2)	Naruo
Nama	Bai
Nameji	Namuyi
Namen	Lahu
Nam Hsan	De'ang, Pale
Namuyi	
Namuzi	Namuyi
Nanai	Hezhen
Nang Jing	Nanjingren
Nani	Hezhen
Nanjingren	
Nankingese	Nanjingren
Nao Gelao	Baonuo
Nao Klao	Baonuo

Name:	See:
Narou	Naruo
Naru	
Naru (#2)	Naju
Naruo	
Nasi	Naxi
Naso (#1)	Nosu, Shengzha
Naso (#2)	Nasu, Western
Nasu (#1)	Gepo, Eastern
Nasu (#2)	Neisu, Da Hei
Nasu (#3)	Neisu, Xiao Hei
Nasu (#4)	Nasu, Wusa
Nasu (#5)	Nasu, Panxian
Nasu, Eastern	
Nasu, Jinghong	
Nasu, Panxian	
Nasu, Southern	
Nasu, Western	
Nasu, Wusa	
Nasupo (#1)	Nasu, Jinghong
Nasupo (#2)	Nasu, Wusa
Nasupo (#3)	Nasu, Panxian
Nasupuo (#1)	Nasu, Eastern
Nasu Puo (#2)	Nasu, Western
Nasu Yi	Nasu, Western
Naxi	
Naxi, Northern	
Naza	
Nazaren	Naza
Nazasu	Naza
Neisu	
Neisu (#2)	Nisu, Jianshui
Neisu (#3)	Nisu, Xinping
Neisu (#4)	Nisu, Yuanyang
Neisu (#5)	Niesu, Central
Neisu, Da Hei	
Neisu, Xiao Hei	
Neisupo	Neisu, Da Hei
Ngacang	Achang
Ngac'ang	Achang
Ngai	Han Chinese, Dan
Ngambo	Amdo, Hbrogpa
Nganshuekuan	Tibetan, Deqen
Ngao Fon	Cun
Ngao Klao	Baonuo
Ngatsang	Achang
Ngawa	Golog
Nghari	Tibetan, Nghari
Ngharis	Tibetan, Nghari
Ngnai	Wunai
Ngochang	Achang
Ngolok	Golog
Ngura	Golog
Ngwe Palaung	De'ang, Pale
Nhang	Giay
Nhkum	Jingpo
Ni	Sani
Niang	Giay
Niesu, Central	
Niesu (#1)	Nisu, Jianshui
Niesu (#2)	Nisu, Xinping
Niesu (#3)	Nisu, Yuanyang
Niesupo (#1)	Neisu, Xiao Hei
Niesupo (#2)	Niesu, Central
Nihongo	Japanese
Nipo	Sani
Nisu (#1)	Neisu

Name:	See:
Nisu (#2)	Nisu, Jianshui
Nisu (#3)	Nisu, Xinping
Nisu (#4)	Nisu, Yuanyang
Nisu (#5)	Naisu
Nisu (#6)	Neisu, Xiao Hei
Nisu (#7)	Neisu, Da Hei
Nisu, Jianshui	
Nisu, Xinping	
Nisu, Yuanyang	
Nisupo (#1)	Nisu, Jianshui
Nisupo (#2)	Nisu, Yuanyang
Nisupo (#3)	Nosu, Xiaoliangshan
Nisupo (#4)	Doupo
Nisupuo	Nisu, Xinping
Niuweiba	Zuoke
Nong (#1)	Giay
Nong (#2)	Nung
Nongjiazi	Nanjingren
North Lolo	Nosu, Shengzha
Northeastern Jiarong	Jiarong, Chabao
Northeastern Mongolian	Buriat
Northeastern Yunnan Miao	A-Hmao
Northern Chinese	Han Chinese, Mandarin
Northern Hmu	Hmu, Northern
Northern Jiarong	Jiarong, Chabao
Northern Jyarung	Jiarong, Chabao
Northern Miao	Ghao-Xong, Western
Northern Min	Han Chinese, Min Bei
Northern Monba	Monba, Medog
Northern Mongolian	Buriat
Northern Tujia	Tujia
Northern Yi	Nosu, Shengzha
Nosu, Butuo	
Nosu, Mangbu	
Nosu, Shengzha	
Nosu, Shuixi	
Nosu, Tianba	
Nosu, Xiaoliangshan	
Nosu, Yinuo	
Nosupo	Nosu, Xiaoliangshan
Noutzu	Nu
Nu	
Nubra	
Nubran	Nubra
Numao	
Nu-Mhou	Numao
Nung	
Nung (#2)	Nu
Nung Rawang	Rawang
Nunu	
Nuosu (#1)	Nosu, Shengzha
Nuosu (#2)	Nisu, Yuanyang
Nuosu (#3)	Suodi
Nuosu (#4)	Nosu, Xiaoliangshan
Nuosu (#5)	Nosu, Mangbu
Nusu	Nu
Nu-tsu	Nu
Nutzu	Nu
Nuzi	Nu
Nuzu	Nu
Nyang	Giay
Nyarong	Tibetan, Deqen
Nyi	Nasu, Western

O

Name:	See:
Oirat	

Name:	See:
Olca	Hezhen
Olcha	Hezhen
Olchi	Hezhen
Olchis	Hezhen
Old Han (#1)	Chuanlan
Old Han (#2)	Chuanqing
Olet	Olot
Olonchun	Oroqen
Olossu	Russian
Olot	
Oleut	Olot
Onkor	Ongkor
Ongbe	Lingao
Ongkor	
Ongkor Solon	Ongkor
O-nu	Enu
Oold	Olot
Oran Toraja	Indonesian
Orochen	Oroqen
Oronchon	Oroqen
Oroqen	
Ouluo	Aluo
Ouni	Haoni
Ouzbek	Uzbek
Owenki	Ewenki
Ozbek	Uzbek

P

Name:	See:
Paddy-Field Miao	Hmong Shuad
Pagcah	Ami
Paheng	Baheng, Sanjiang
Pa Hng (#1)	Baheng, Liping
Pa Hng (#2)	Baheng, Sanjiang
Pai	Bai
Pai-hung	Baihong
Pai-i	Tai Lu
Paiuan	Paiwan
Paiwan	
Pai Yao	Zaomin
Paiyi	Tai Nua
Pala	Bela
Palaung Pale	De'ang, Pale
Palaung Rumai	De'ang, Rumai
Palaung Shwe	De'ang, Shwe
Palay	De'ang, Pale
Pale	De'ang, Pale
Palju	Palyu
Palyu	
Pana	
Panbei Yi	Nasu, Panxian
Pa Ngng	Baheng, Sanjiang
Pangtsah	Ami
P'an-hsien Yi	Nasu, Panxian
Panlong Yi	Nasu, Panxian
Pannan Yi	Nasu, Panxian
Panthay	Hui
Panxian Yi	Nasu, Panxian
Pan Yao (#1)	Iu Mien
Pan Yao (#2)	Iu Mien, Changping
Pan Yao (#3)	Iu Mien, Hunan
Pan Yao (#4)	Iu Mien, Luoxiang
Paoan	Bonan
Paongan	Bonan
Parauk	Wa
Pariok	Puroik
Pa Then	Baheng, Sanjiang
Pau Thin	Giay
Pawong	Ergong
Pawu	Baheng, Sanjiang
Paxi	
Payowan	Paiwan
Pe	Baima
Pe Miao	Miao, White
Peh Miao	Miao, White
Pei	Han Chinese, Mandarin
Pei-ch'u-paa Naxi	Naheng
Pei Tong Nuo	Beidongnuo
Pela	Bela
Penghua	Han Chinese, Pinghua
Penglung	De'ang, Pale
Pengwa	Han Chinese, Pinghua
Pengzi	
Penhwa	Han Chinese, Pinghua
Peppery Miao	Hmong Be
Persian	Tajik, Sarikoli
Phana	Pana
Phoke	Tibetan, Central
Phsin	Bit
Phsing	Bit
Phula	Pula
Phuman	Puman
Phyagphreng	Xiangcheng
Pimi	Pumi
Pin	Bisu
Ping	Han Chinese, Pinghua
Pingdi	
Pingding	Pingdi
Pingdi Yao	Pingdi
Pinghua	Han Chinese, Pinghua
Pingtou Lolo	Laluo, Mishaba
Pingtou Yi	Gepo, Eastern
Puto	Budo
Putu	Budo
Pinghwa	Han Chinese, Pinghua
Pingwu Tibetans	Baima
Pi-o	Biyo
Piongtoajeu	Pingdi
Piongtuojo	Pingdi
Pi-tse-k'a	Tujia
Pi-yueh	Biyo
Plang	Bulang
Pola (#1)	Bela
Pola (#2)	Poluo
Polo (#1)	Bela
Polo (#2)	Poluo
Po-lo-tzu	Bolozi
Poluo	
Pong	Tai Pong
Popei	
Potinhua	Han Chinese, Mandarin
Pou Nuo	Baonuo
Pouteng	Khmu
Praok	Wa
Primmi	Pumi
P'rome	Pumi
Prummi	Pumi
Pu (#1)	Puwa
Pu (#2)	Chuanqing
Pu (#3)	Poluo
Pu (#4)	Pula
Pubiao	
Pudu	Budo

Name:	See:
Pu-i	Bouyei
Pui	Bouyei
Pujai	Bouyei
Pu-Jui	Bouyei
Pula	
Pula (#2)	Bulang
Pula (#3)	Lati
Pula (#4)	Puwa
Pula (#5)	Ani
Pula (#6)	Asahei
Pula (#7)	Daizhan
Pula (#8)	Labapo
Pula (#9)	Poluo
Pulang	Bulang
Pulapo	Pula
Pulung	Buyang
P'um	Pumi
Puman	
P'uman	Puman
Pumi	
Pumi, Northern	Chrame
Pu Na	Giay
Pu Nam	Giay
Punglung	De'ang, Pale
Pu-No	Bunuo
Punong	Buyang
Pu Nong	Zhuang, Southern
Punti	Han Chinese, Cantonese
Punu	Bunu
Punung	Buyang
Pupeo	Pubiao
Pupo	Puwa
Pupula	Puwa
Pu Ren	Chuanqing
Puren	Puwa
Purig	Purik
Purigskad	Purik
Purik	
Purik Bhotia	Purik
Purik-pa	Purik
Puroik	
Pusha	
Puteik	Kado
Putian	Han Chinese, Puxian
Pu To	Zhuang, Southern
Putonghua	Han Chinese, Mandarin
Puwa	
Puwa (#2)	Pula
Pu-Xian	Han Chinese, Puxian
Puyi	Bouyei
Puyoi	Bouyei
Pu-yuan Chi-no	Jino, Buyuan
Puzu (#1)	Muji
Puzu (#2)	Puwa
Puzu (#3)	Poluo
Puzu (#4)	Pula
Pwi	Kawa

Q

Name:	See:
Qagcheng Tibetan	Xiangcheng
Qanu	
Qanu Miao	Qanu
Qa-o	Mulao Jia
Qau	Gao
Qau Gelao	Gao
Qi	Li, Qi
Qiakala	Kyakala
Qiandui	Li, Qi
Qiang, Cimulin	
Qiang, Dajishan	
Qiang, Heihu	
Qiang, Jiaochang	
Qiang, Longxi	
Qiang, Luhua	
Qiang, Mawo	
Qiang, Mianchi	
Qiang, Sanlong	
Qiang, Taoping	
Qiang, Yadu	
Qiang Yi	Qiangyi
Qiangyi	
Qianxi Yi	Nosu, Shuixi
Qin	Chin, Asho
Qinghai Bonan	Bonan, Tongren
Qing Miao (#1)	Hmong Vron
Qing Miao (#2)	Hmong Njua
Qingshui Miao	Hmong Dlex Nchab
Qingyi Miao	Aoka
Qiongwen	Han Chinese, Hainanese
Qisu	Chesu
Qisupuo	Chesu
Qiuce	Rawang
Qiungnai	Kiong Nai
Qixingmin	
Qotong	Han Chinese, Mandarin
Queyu	
Quinjiang	Bouyei

R

Name:	See:
Rangloi	Lahuli, Tinan
Rao	
Raojia	Rao
Raoruo	Zauzou
Rawang	
Red Hmong (#1)	Hmong Leng
Red Hmong (#2)	Miao, White
Red-Headed Hmong	Hmong Leng
Red-Headed Miao	Hmong Leng
Red Miao	Ghao-Xong, Western
Red Thread Miao	Hmong Dou
Red Top Miao	Hmong Dou
Red Yao	Younuo
Red Yi (#1)	Aluo
Red Yi (#2)	Michi
Red Yi (#3)	Naisu
Red Yi (#4)	Lagou
Rgyalathang	Tibetan, Zhongdian
Rgyarong	Jiarong
Riang	
Riang Liang	Riang
Rimong	Golog
River Gelao	Ge
River Miao	Miao, Chuan
Rongba	Amdo, Rongba
Rongmahbrogpa	Amdo, Rongmahbrogpa
Rongpa	Amdo, Rongba
Roumai	De'ang, Rumai
Rouruo	Zauzou
Rumai	De'ang, Rumai
Russ	Russian
Russian	
Russki	Russian

Name:	See:
S	
Sa	Giay
Sabari	Ami
Sagka	Tibetan, Gtsang
Sak	Kado
Sakha	Yakut
Sala	Salar
Salar	
Samadu, Eastern	
Samadu, Western	
Samaduo (#1)	Samadu, Eastern
Samaduo (#2)	Samadu, Western
Sa Man	Saman
Saman	
Samei	
Sameizu	Samei
Samin	Samei
Samobi	Paiwan
Samohai	Paiwan
Samon	Khmu
Samou	Samadu, Western
Sam Tao	Samtao
Samtao	
Samtau	Samtao
Samtuan	Samtao
San Chay	Cao Lan
San Chi	Cao Lan
San Da	Sanda
Sanda	
San Dao Hong	Nisu, Jianshui
Sangkong	Muda
Sani	
Sani (#2)	Samei
Sani (#3)	Minglang
Sanie	
Sanipo (#1)	Samei
Sanipo (#2)	Minglang
Sangla	Monba, Cona
Sanlong	Qiang, Sanlong
Sanpuo	Chesu
San Qiao	Sanqiao
Sanqiao	
Sansu	
Santa	Dongxiang
Sanya	Utsat
San Yi	Sani
Sanyie	Sanie
San Yi Puo	Sani
Saprek	Paiwan
Saragh	Yugur, Saragh
Saraygh	Yugur, Saragh
Sarig	Yugur, Saragh
Sarikoli	Tajik, Sarikoli
Sarikoly	Tajik, Sarikoli
Sari Yogur	Yugur, Saragh
Sarykoly	Tajik, Sarikoli
Sen Chun	Samtao
Se-Ni	Cai
Serwa	Sherpa
Serwang	Rawang
Sha	Shan
Shahrang	Golog
Shan	
Shangfeng Ren	Hua Miao
Shanghai	Han Chinese, Wu
Shanghainese	Han Chinese, Wu

Name:	See:
Shangzhai	Jiarong, Shangzhai
Shanha	She
Shanhua Hong Yao	Younuo
Shani	Sani
Shanie	Sanie
Shaniepu	Sanie
Shanshu	Lesu
Shansu (#1)	Lesu
Shansu (#2)	Sanie
Shanzi Yao	Kim Mun
Shaojiang	Han Chinese, Shaojiang
Shaozhou	Han Chinese, Shaozhou
Shaozhou Tuhua	Han Chinese, Shaozhou
Sharpa	Sherpa
Sharpa Bhotia	Sherpa
She	
Shengcha Yi	Nosu, Shengzha
Shengzha Yi	Nosu, Shengzha
Shenzhou	
Shenzhouren	Shenzhou
Shera Yugur	Yugur, Enger
Sher-feizu	Chuanqing
Sherpa	
Sher-tu	Chuanqing
Shi	Kucong
Shibe	Xibe
Shihing	Shixing
Shikou Yao	Biao Mien, Shikou
Shing Saapa	Lhomi
Shingsawa	Lhomi
Shira Yugur	Yugur, Enger
Shiye	Nanjingren
Shixing	
Sho	Chin, Asho
Shoa	Chin, Asho
Shughni	Tajik, Sarikoli
Shuhian	Shixing
Shuhin	Shixing
Shui	
Shui, Yunnan	
Shui Dai	Tai Lu
Shui Gelao	Rao
Shui-hsi Nosu	Nosu, Shuixi
Shuihu	Bouyei
Shuijia	Shui
Shui Nosu	Nasu, Western
Shui Pai-i	Tai Lu
Shuitian (#1)	Lopi
Shuitian (#2)	Mixisu
Shuitian (#3)	Popei
Shuitian (#4)	Naru
Shuitian Ren	Mixisu
Shuitianyizi	Popei
Shuitianzu	Mixisu
Shuixi	Nosu, Shuixi
Shuixi Yi	Nosu, Shuixi
Shuixi Miao	Hmong Shuad
Shui Yi (#1)	Popei
Shui Yi (#2)	Naruo
Shuiyi	Popei
Shuiyipuo	Popei
Shuiyizu	Popei
Shwe	De'ang, Shwe
Siang-Tan He-lou-jen	Xiangtang
Sibin	Xibe
Sibo	Xibe

Name:	See:
Sichuan Miao	Miao, Chuan
Sichuan Mongolians	Mongol, Sichuan
Sichuan Yi	Nosu, Shengzha
Sidabao	Jiarong, Sidabao
Si Jia	Xi
Silver Palaung	De'ang, Pale
Similu	Enu
Simolu	Enu
Si-mou-lou	Enu
Singfo	Jingpo
Singpo	Jingpo
Sipsongpanna Dai	Tai Lu
Sinkiang Daur	Daur, Western
Sinicized Miao	Hmong Shuad
Sinicized Yi	Michi
Sinkiang Solon	Ongkor
Siqi	Xiqi
Situ	Jiarong, Situ
Six Village Miao	Hmong Be
Small Black Yi	Neisu, Xiao Hei
Small Flowery Miao	Gha-Mu
Sogwo Arig	
Sogwo Arik	Sogwo Arig
Soisangyan	Han Chinese, Dan
Solon	Ewenki, Solon
Solon Evenki	Ewenki, Solon
Songjia	Lu
Song Ren	Cai
So-ti	Suodi
Soumi	Samei
Sou Miao	Mo
Southern Altai	Teleut
Southern East Guizhou Miao	Hmu (Southern)
Southern Lisu	Lisu
Southern Min	Han Chinese, Min Nan
Southern Monba	Monba, Cona
Southern Muji	Muzi
Southern Tuchia	Mozhihei
Southern Yi	Nasu, Southern
Spiti	Groma
Stimul	Paiwan
Striped Hmong	Miao, White
Striped-Arm Hmong	Miao, White
Suan	
Subei	
Subi	Subei
Sui	Shui
Suijia	Shui
Sui Li	Shui
Suipo	Shui
Suling	Puroik
Sulong	Puroik
Sulung	Puroik
Suod	Suodi
Suodi	
Suodi Nosu	Suodi
Suolun	Ewenki, Solon
Sushen	Hezhen

T

Name:	See:
Ta-ang	De'ang, Pale
Ta-ch'i-shan Ch'iang	Qiang, Dajishan
Tadzik	Tajik, Sarikoli
Ta'er	
Tagkah	Ami
Tagu	
Tagupo	Tagu
Taguren	Tagu
Tahu	Amdo, Rtahu
Ta Hua Miao	A-Hmao
Tahur	Daur
Ta Hwa Miao	A-Hmao
Tai	Li, Jiamao
Tai Blanc	Tai Kao
Tai Chuang	Zhuang, Northern
Tai Chung	Ya
Tai Cung	Ya
Tai D	Tai Kao
Tai Dam	
Tai Dehong	Tai Mao
Tai Do	Tai Dam
Tai Don	Tai Kao
Tai Hongjin	Hongjin Tai
Tai Kao	
Tai Kaw	Tai Kao
Tai Khao	Tai Kao
Tai Lai	Tai Kao
Tai Laka	Lakkia
Tai Lati	Lati
Tai Le (#1)	Tai Mao
Tai Le (#2)	Tai Nua
Tai-lo	Tho
Tai Loe (#1)	Tai Mao
Tai Loe (#2)	Tai Nua
Tai Long	Tai Mao
Tai Lu	
Tai Mao	
Tai Mo	Tai Mao
Tai Nua	
Tai Nuea (#1)	Tai Mao
Tai Nuea (#2)	Tai Nua
Tai Nung	Nung
Tai Noir	Tai Dam
Tai Pong	
Tai Shan	Shan
Tai Tho	Tho
Tai Ya	Ya
Tai Yay	Shan
Tajike	Tajik, Sarikoli
Tajiki	Tajik, Sarikoli
Tajik, Sarikoli	
Tajik, Wakhi	
Taklamakan	Uygur, Taklimakan
Taklimakan	Uygur, Taklimakan
Taku	Lipo, Eastern
Talu	
Talusu	Talu
Tamari	Paiwan
Tame Wa	Lawa
Tanah	Ami
Tanglang	
Tanglang Jiang	Tanglang
Tanka	Han Chinese, Dan
Taofu	Ergong
Taoping	Qiang, Taoping
T'ao-p'ing Ch'iang	Qiang, Taoping
Tarang	Deng, Darang
Taraon	Deng, Darang
Taron	Rawang
Tartar	Tatar
Tata'er	Tatar
Tatar	

Name:	See:
Tatze	Sogwo Arig
Tay	Tho
Tea Mountain Yao	Lakkia
Te-ch'in	Tibetan, Deqen
Telengut	Teleut
Teleut	
Ten	Yanghuang
T'en	Yanghuang
Thai Den	Tai Dam
Thai Nung	Nung
Thai Trang	Tai Kao
Thami	
That	Kado
Thauerh	Daur
Then	Yanghuang
Theng	Khmu
Thet	Kado
Tho	
Thu (#1)	Gelao
Thu (#2)	Tho
Thu Lao	Tulao
Tianba	Nosu, Tianba
Tianba Yi	Nosu, Tianba
Tianpao	Dianbao
Tibetan, Boyu	
Tibetan, Central	
Tibetan, Deqen	
Tibetan, Gtsang	
Tibetan, Jone	
Tibetan, Nghari	
Tibetan, Zhongdian	
Tibetan, Zhugqu	
Tielingute	Teleut
T'ien-pa Yi	Nosu, Tianba
Tienpao	Dianbao
Tibetan Muslims	Keji
Tienpo	Dianbao
Tinani	Lahuli, Tinan
To	Tho
Tomo	Groma
Tong (#1)	Baheng, Sanjiang
Tong (#2)	Dong, Northern
Tong (#3)	Dong, Southern
Tonggusi	Ewenki, Tungus
Tongjia	Dong, Southern
Tongkia	Dong, Northern
Tongoose	Ewenki, Tungus
Tongren	Bonan, Tongren
Torgot	Torgut
Torgut	
Tosu	Ersu
Trowoma	Groma
Trung	Derung
Tsang	Tibetan, Gtsang
Tsangla	Monba, Cona
Tsat	Utsat
Tshangla	Monba, Cona
Tsokhar	Golog
Tsuen	Cun
Tu	
Tu (#1)	Gesu
Tu (#2)	Luoluopo, Central
Tu (#3)	Lopi
Tu	Tusu
T'u	Zhuang, Northern
Tuchia	Tujia

Name:	See:
Tudja	Tujia
Tuerke	
Tujia	
Tujia (#2)	Lipo, Western
Tujia (#3)	Gepo, Western
Tujia (#4)	Lalu, Yangliu
Tujia, Southern	Mozhihei
Tulao	
Tulao (#2)	Gelao
Tulao (#3)	Limin
Tuli (#1)	Nisu, Xinping
Tuli (#2)	Lalu, Yangliu
Tuli (#3)	Lalu, Xuzhang
Tuli Yi	Nisu, Xinping
Tulung	Derung
Tuly	Nisu, Xinping
Tun	Chuanqing
Tung (#1)	Dong, Northern
Tung (#2)	Dong, Southern
Tung (#3)	Dongxiang
Tungan	Hui
Tungchia (#1)	Dong, Northern
Tungchia (#2)	Dong, Southern
Tung-Nu	Dongnu
Tungus	Ewenki, Tungus
Tungus Evenk	Ewenki, Tungus
Tunguz	Ewenki, Tungus
Tungjen (#1)	Dong, Northern
Tungjen (#2)	Dong, Southern
Tunghsiang	Dongxiang
Turen (#1)	Limin
Turen (#2)	Tusu
Turen (#3)	Laluo, Mishaba
Turk	Tuerke
Turkestan Daur	Daur, Western
Turkestan Solon	Ongkor
Turki Hwei Hwei	Salar
Turki Huihui	Salar
Turung	Derung
Tushu	
Tushupo	Tushu
Tusu	
Tusu (#2)	Tushu
Tusupo	Tusu
Tutiaozi	Laluo, Mishaba
Tuva	
Tuvin	Tuva
Tuwa	Tuva
Tuwo	
Tuzu	Tusu
Ty Dam	Tai Dam
Tz'u-mu-lin Ch'iang	Qiang, Cimulin

U

Name:	See:
U (#1)	Puman
U (#2)	Tibetan, Central
Udege Kyakala	Kyakala
Uighuir	Uygur
Uighur	Uygur
Uiguir	Uygur
Uigur	Uygur
Ulcha	Hezhen
Ulchi	Hezhen
Ulunchun	Oroqen
Ulych	Hezhen
Uni	Haoni

Name:	See:
Uryangkhai	Tuva
Usbaki	Uzbek
Uzbeki	Uzbek
Utsat	
Utset	Utsat
Uygur	
Uygur, Lop Nur	
Uygur Taklamakan	Uygur, Taklimakan
Uygur, Taklimakan	
Uygur, Yutian	
Uzbek	
V	
Va	Wa
Va Cuengh	Zhuang, Northern
Vakhan	Tajik, Wakhi
Variegated Miao	A-Hmao
Viet	Vietnamese
Vietnamese	
Vietnamese in China	Jing
Vo	Kawa
Vonun	Bunun
Vunum	Bunun
Vunun	Bunun
Vunung	Bunun
W	
Wa	
Waishu Miao	Hmong Shuad
Wakhani	Tajik, Wakhi
Wakhigi	Tajik, Wakhi
Wakut	Kawa
Wa-la	Puman
Wannan	Han Chinese, Huizhou
Wapuo	Puwa
Washing-Bone Miao	Lu
Water Yi	Popei
Waxianghua	Han Chinese, Waxiang
Wei	Tibetan, Central
Weilate	Oirat
Weiwuer	Uygur
Weizang	Tibetan, Central
Western Jiarong	Jiarong, Sidabao
Western Jyarung	Jiarong, Sidaba
Western Lawa	Lawa
Western Lolo	Luoluopo, Western
Western Mongol	Oirat
Western West Hunan Miao	Ghao-Xong, Western
West Hunan Miao	Ghao-Xong, Western
West Yugur	Yugur, Saragh
White Hmong	Miao, White
White Horse Tibetans	Baima
White Kalmuck	Teleut
White Lisu	Gaisu, Southern
White Lum	Hmong Daw
White Meo	Hmong Daw
White Miao (#1)	Hmong Daw
White Miao (#2)	Horned Miao
White Mongols	Tu
White Pants Yao	Baonuo
White Trouser Yao	Baonuo
White Yi (#1)	Luoluopo, Central
White Yi (#2)	Bai Yi
White Yi (#3)	Gepo, Eastern
White Yi (#4)	Sanie

Name:	See:
White Yi (#5)	Tushu
White Yi (#6)	Depo
White Yi (#7)	Gese
White Yi (#8)	Nosu, Mangbu
Wild Wa	Kawa
Wo	Yizi
Wogang	Han Chinese, Waxiang
Woni	
Woniu	Woni
Wopu	
Wopu (#1)	Neisu, Da Hei
Wopu (#2)	Neisu, Xiao Hei
Wu	Han Chinese, Wu
Wumeng	
Wumeng Yi	Wumeng
Wuming	Zhuang, Northern
Wunai	
Wusa	Nasu, Wusa
Wuse	E
Wusehua	E
Wutu	Wutun
Wutun	
Wutunhua	Wutun
Wuzibieke	Uzbek
X	
Xakas	Khakas
Xamang	Mang
Xamnigan	Mongol, Khamnigan
Xi	
Xiaerba	Sherpa
Xialusi	
Xiamahe Miao	Miao, Luobohe
Xiandao	
Xiangcheng	
Xianghua	Han Chinese, Waxiang
Xiangtan (#1)	Awu, Northern
Xiangtan (#2)	Xiangtang
Xiangtang	
Xiangtang (#2)	Lalu, Yangliu
Xiangtangpo	Xiangtang
Xianyou	Han Chinese, Puxian
Xiaoheiyi (#1)	Neisu, Xiao Hei
Xiaoheiyi (#2)	Nasu, Panxian
Xiao Hua Miao	Gha-Mu
Xiaoliangshan Nosu	Nosu, Xiaoliangshan
Xiaoliangshan Yi	Nosu, Xiaoliangshan
Xiaoshan	Zaiwa
Xiaoshanhua	Zaiwa
Xiarba	Sherpa
Xibe	
Xibe, Western	
Xibo	Xibe
Xiejing	Nanjingren
Xienan	Nanjingren
Xifan	Chrame
Xigatse Tibetan	Tibetan, Gtsang
Xigatze	Tibetan, Gtsang
Xi Jia	Xi
Xijia Miao	Xi
Xijima	
Ximahe Miao	Xi
Xinghua Min	Han Chinese, Puxian
Xinjiang Daur	Daur, Western
Xinjiang Ewenki	Ongkor
Xinjiang Mongol	Oirat

Xinjiang Xibe	Xibe, Western
Xinmin	Hakka
Xiqi	
Xiqi (#2)	Nasu, Da Hei
Xiqima	Xijima
Xishan Yi	Laluo, Mishaba
Xishuangbanna Dai	Tai Lu
Xiuba	
Xiuba Yi	Xiuba
Xiumoluo	Woni
Xiupo	Xiuba
Xumi	Shixing
Xumin	Han Chinese, Dan
Xunbu	Han Chinese, Xunpu
Xunpu	Han Chinese, Xunpu

Y

Ya	
Yadu	Qiang, Yadu
Yai	Giay
Yakut	
Ya Lu	Yugur, Saragh
Yanghuang	
Yanghwang	Yanghuang
Yanglam	Riang
Yang Sek	Riang
Yang Wan Kun	Riang
Yangya Gedou	Ga Mong
Yangya Miao	Ga Mong
Yani	Akha
Yao Bei Miao	Rao
Yaofuer	Yugur, Saragh
Yaojia	Rao
Yao Miao	Rao
Yao Min	Zaomin
Yaque Miao	Miao, Chuan
Ya-tu Ch'iang	Qiang, Yadu
Yau Min	Zaomin
Yaw Yen	Lisu
Yaw Yin	Lisu
Yayisai Enu	Enu
Yeche	Yiche
Yeh Jen	Lisu
Yellow Lahu	Kucong
Yellow Uighur	Yugur, Saragh
Yellow Yi	Doupo
Yenisei Tatar	Khakas
Yerong	
Yeyong	Yerong
Yiche	
Yi, Southern	Nasu, Southern
Yi, White	Bai Yi
Yi, Xiaoliangshan	Nosu, Xiaoliangshan
Yi, Yunnan	Nasu, Western
Yidu	Lhoba, Yidu
Yin	Riang
Yinuo	Nosu, Yinuo
Yinuo Yi	Nosu, Yinuo
Yipu	Yizi
Yiqin	Aling
Yiqing	Aling
Yiren	Yizi
Yisupuo	Nasu, Western
Yiu Mien	Iu Mien
Yizi	
Yizu	Nisu, Jianshui
Yogur	Yugur, Enger
Yohur	Yugur, Saragh
Yongchun	
Yongren Tai	Hongjin Tai
Yonzhi	
You	Tai Pong
Youle	Jino
Youmai	
Youmairen	Youmai
Youmian	Iu Mien
Younou	Younuo
Younuo	
You Tai	
Yuanhe	Uygur
Yue	Han Chinese, Cantonese
Yueh	Han Chinese, Cantonese
Yugar	Yugur, Enger
Yugu	Yugur, Enger
Yugur, Enger	
Yugur, Saragh	
Yuku	Yugur, Saragh
Yumian	Iu Mien
Yungchun	Yongchun
Yungshun	Yongchun
Yunnan Mongolians	Mongol, Yunnan
Yunnan Yi	Nasu, Western
Yunuo	Younuo
Yuno	Younuo
Yutian	Uygur, Yutian

Z

Za	
Zaba	Zhaba
Zaiwa	
Zang	Tibetan, Central
Zao Min	
Zauzou	
Zerwang	Rawang
Zhaba	
Zhaba (#2)	Queyu
Zhaboa	Zhaba
Zhangta	Xiandao
Zhanjia Ren	Hua Miao
Zhili	Naruo
Zhongjia	Bouyei
Zhouqu Tibetan	Tibetan, Zhugqu
Zhuang, Northern	
Zhuang, Southern	
Zhuomu Tibetan	Groma
Zhugqu	Tibetan, Zhugqu
Zhuoni Tibetan	Tibetan, Jone
Zuoke	

APPENDIX 3: Distribution of China's Peoples by Province

More than half of China's 490 ethnic groups are primarily found living in mountainous Yunnan and Guizhou provinces in southwest China. A staggering 200 groups have the majority of their members in Yunnan Province alone, although they have been crammed into just 26 official "nationalities" by the Chinese authorities. The table below allows the reader to compare the ethnolinguistic composition of China's provinces. The total number of groups living in the province is given, followed by the number of groups whose members are primarily located in that province. In Yunnan Province for example, there are a total of 234 groups, 200 of which are mostly concentrated within its borders. The fourth column lists the number of groups within that province that have more than 5% of their population as professing Christians. These could, comparatively-speaking, be considered "reached" by the gospel. The fifth column shows the percentage of groups in the province that are most unreached (i.e. less than 5% Christian). It is clear that, although Yunnan Province contains by far the highest number of reached groups, it still contains 170 unreached people groups within its borders. Overall, there is plenty of work to do!

Province:	Total Number of Groups in This Province:	Groups *Primarily* Located in This Province:	"Reached" Groups (>5% Christian):	"Unreached" Groups (<5% Christian):	% of Groups Unreached:
Yunnan 云南	234	200	30	170	85.0%
Guizhou 贵州	88	77	11	66	85.7%
Sichuan 四川	77	47	1	46	97.8%
Guangxi 广西	54	28	2	26	92.6%
Tibet 西藏	36	25	0	25	100.0%
Xinjiang 新疆	28	23	1	22	95.6%
Qinghai 青海	20	13	0	13	100.0%
Hainan Island 海南岛	19	13	1	12	92.3%
Fujian 福建	20	12	2	10	83.3%
Inner Mongolia 内蒙古	19	10	1	9	90.0%
Hunan 湖南	27	9	0	9	100.0%
Gansu 甘肃	17	9	0	9	100.0%
Heilongjiang 黑龙江	14	7	0	7	100.0%
Guangdong 广东	16	6	0	6	100.0%
Henan 河南	8	2	1	1	50.0%
Liaoning 辽宁	8	2	0	2	100.0%
Jiangxi 江西	13	1	0	0	100.0%

Province:	Total Number of Groups in This Province:	Groups *Primarily* Located in This Province:	"Reached" Groups (>5% Christian):	"Unreached" Groups (<5% Christian):	% of Groups Unreached:
Anhui 安徽	8	1	0	1	100.0%
Zhejiang 浙江	8	1	1	0	0.00%
Shanghai 上海	8	1	0	1	100.0%
Jilin 吉林	6	1	1	0	0.00%
Ningxia 宁夏	5	1	0	1	100.0%
Shanxi 山西	5	1	0	1	100.0%
Hubei 湖北	9	-	-	-	-
Beijing 北京	8	-	-	-	-
Hong Kong 香港	7	-	-	-	-
Hebei 河北	6	-	-	-	-
Shaanxi 陕西	6	-	-	-	-
Jiangsu 江苏	5	-	-	-	-
Tianjin 天津	5	-	-	-	-
Shandong 山东	4	-	-	-	-
Macau 澳门	3	-	-	-	-
TOTALS:		**490**	**52**	**438**	**89.4%**

APPENDIX 4:
Distribution of China's Peoples in Other Countries

Of the 490 people groups in China, 144 (29.4%) have communities located in other countries. China's peoples are found in at least 70 countries around the world, ranging from numerous minority groups in the southwest who spill over into neighboring Myanmar, Laos, Vietnam, and Thailand to a Uygur community in Morocco. In addition, many refugee communities of China's peoples have been accepted into Western nations and now live in places as diverse as the United States, France, Australia, Panama, South Africa, French Polynesia, Suriname, and Norway. (Note: The names listed below are the names used on the Profiles in this book. In some cases, the name used by a group in another country is different from that used in China.)

MYANMAR (46): Achang; Ake; Akha; Bela; Ben; Bisu; Bulang; Chin, Asho; De'ang, Pale; De'ang, Rumai; De'ang, Shwe; Deng, Darang; Deng, Geman; Derung; Han Chinese, Hui'an; Han Chinese, Mandarin; Hkauri; Hui; Iu Mien; Jingpo; Kado; Kawa; Khmu; Kong Ge; Kucong; Lahu; Lama; Laopang; Lashi; Lawa; Lisu; Maru; Miao, Chuan; Naxi; Nu; Rawang; Riang; Samtao; Shan; Tai Lu; Tai Mao; Thami; Tibetan, Deqen; Wa; Zaiwa

VIETNAM (40): Akha; Alu; Apu; Baheng, Sanjiang; Bouyei; Cao Lan; Dong, Southern; Gelao; Giay; Han Chinese, Cantonese; Han Chinese, Dan; Han Chinese, Hainanese; Han Chinese, Mandarin; Hani; Haoni; Hmong Bua; Hmong Daw; Hmong Leng; Hmong Njua; Hmong Shuad; Hua Miao; Iu Mien; Khmu; Kim Mun; Kucong; Lahu; Lami; Lati; Mang; Nung; Pubiao; Pula; Puwa; Shui; Tai Dam; Tai Kao; Tai Lu; Tho; Tulao; Vietnamese

LAOS (35): Ake; Akha; Alu; Angku; Bit; Biyo; Giay; Han Chinese, Mandarin; Han Chinese, Cantonese; Han Chinese, Hainanese; Han Chinese, Mandarin; Han Chinese, Min Nan; Hani; Hmong Daw; Hmong Leng; Hua Miao; Iu Mien; Kado; Kemei; Khmu; Kim Mun; Kuan; Kucong; Lahu; Nisu; Nung; Pana; Samtao; Tai Dam; Tai Kao; Tai Lu; Tai Mao; Tho; Vietnamese

THAILAND (29): Ake; Akha; Angku; Bisu; Bulang; De'ang, Pale; Hakka; Han Chinese, Cantonese; Han Chinese, Mandarin; Han Chinese, Min Dong; Han Chinese, Min Nan; Hmong Daw; Hmong Leng; Hua Miao; Hui; Iu Mien; Japanese; Jingpo; Khmu; Kucong; Lahu; Lawa; Lisu; Mang; Rawang; Shan; Tai Dam; Tai Lu; Ya

UNITED STATES (28): Hakka; Han Chinese, Cantonese; Han Chinese, Mandarin; Hmong Daw; Hmong Leng; Hua Miao; Indonesian; Iu Mien; Japanese; Khmu; Korean; Kuan; Kucong; Mongol; Nhang; Nosu, Shengzha; Nung; Oirat; Russian; Shan; Tai Dam; Tai Kao; Tai Lu; Tatar; Tho; Tibetan, Central; Uygur; Vietnamese

INDIA (25): Adi; Bunan; Deng, Darang; Deng, Geman; Groma; Jingpo; Khampa, Eastern; Ladakhi; Lahuli Tinan; Lhoba, Bogar; Lhoba, Yidu; Lhomi; Lisu; Monba, Cona; Monba, Medog; Miguba; Nubra; Purik; Puroik; Rawang; Sherpa; Thami; Tibetan, Central; Tibetan, Gtsang; Uygur

RUSSIA (20): Buriat; Daur; Ewenki, Solon; Ewenki, Tungus; Han Chinese, Mandarin; Hezhen; Kazak; Khakas; Korean; Manchu; Mongol; Mongol, Khalka; Mongol, Khamnigan; Oirat; Oroqen; Russian; Tatar; Teleut; Tuva; Yakut

MONGOLIA (14): Buriat; Ewenki, Solon; Ewenki, Tungus; Han Chinese, Mandarin; Hui; Japanese; Kazak; Mongol, Khalka; Mongol, Khamnigan; Oirat; Russian; Tuva; Uygur

TAIWAN (14): Ami; Bunun; Hakka; Han Chinese, Mandarin; Han Chinese, Min Nan; Hui; Iu Mien; Japanese; Mongol; Mongol, Khalka; Oirat; Paiwan; Tibetan, Central; Uygur

FRANCE (10): Giay; Hakka; Han Chinese, Cantonese; Han Chinese, Mandarin; Hmong Daw; Iu Mien; Tai Dam; Tho; Tibetan, Central

CANADA (9): Hakka; Han Chinese, Cantonese; Han Chinese, Hui'an; Han Chinese, Mandarin; Iu Mien; Japanese; Korean; Nung; Vietnamese

AUSTRALIA (9): Hakka; Han Chinese, Cantonese; Han Chinese, Mandarin; Iu Mien; Nung; Tai Dam; Tibetan, Central; Uygur; Vietnamese

GERMANY (9): Hakka; Han Chinese, Cantonese; Han Chinese, Mandarin; Japanese; Kazak; Korean; Oirat; Uygur; Vietnamese

KYRGYZSTAN (9): Hui; Kazak; Kirgiz; Korean; Mongol, Khalka; Russian; Tatar; Uygur; Uzbek

SINGAPORE (9): Hakka; Han Chinese, Cantonese; Han Chinese, Hui'an; Han Chinese, Mandarin; Han Chinese, Min Dong; Han Chinese, Min Nan; Han Chinese, Puxian; Indonesian; Japanese

MALAYSIA (8): Hakka; Han Chinese, Cantonese; Han Chinese, Hui'an; Han Chinese, Mandarin; Han Chinese, Min Bei; Han Chinese, Min Dong; Han Chinese, Min Nan; Han Chinese, Puxian

NEPAL (8): Khampa, Eastern; Kyerung; Lhomi; Sherpa; Thami; Tibetan, Central; Tibetan, Gtsang; Tibetan, Nghari

INDONESIA (7): Hakka; Han Chinese, Cantonese; Han Chinese, Mandarin; Han Chinese, Min Bei; Han Chinese, Min Dong; Indonesian; Uygur

KAZAKSTAN (7): Hui; Kazak; Korean; Russian; Tuerke; Uygur; Uzbek

UNITED KINGDOM (7): Hakka; Han Chinese, Cantonese; Han Chinese, Mandarin; Japanese; Nung; Tibetan, Central; Vietnamese

AFGHANISTAN (6): Kazak; Kirgiz; Tajik, Wakhi; Tatar; Uygur; Uzbek

UZBEKISTAN (6): Kazak; Kirgiz; Korean; Russian; Uygur; Uzbek

BRUNEI (5): Hakka; Han Chinese, Cantonese; Han Chinese, Mandarin; Han Chinese, Min Bei; Han Chinese, Min Dong

PHILIPPINES (5): Hakka; Han Chinese, Cantonese; Han Chinese, Hui'an; Han Chinese, Mandarin; Japanese

TAJIKISTAN (5): Kirgiz; Korean; Russian; Tajik, Wakhi; Uzbek

BRAZIL (4): Hakka; Han Chinese, Mandarin; Japanese; Korean

NETHERLANDS (4): Hakka; Han Chinese, Cantonese; Han Chinese, Mandarin; Indonesian

NEW ZEALAND (4): Hakka; Han Chinese, Cantonese; Han Chinese, Mandarin; Iu Mien

PAKISTAN (4): Purik, Tajik, Wakhi; Uygur; Uzbek

TURKEY (4): Kazak; Kirgiz; Tatar; Uygur

TURKMENISTAN (4): Kazak; Russian; Tatar; Uzbek

BHUTAN (3): Lhoba, Yidu; Monba, Cona; Tibetan, Central

PANAMA (3): Hakka; Han Chinese, Cantonese; Japanese

SAUDI ARABIA (3): Indonesian; Korean; Uygur

SOUTH AFRICA (3): Hakka; Han Chinese, Cantonese; Han Chinese, Mandarin

SWITZERLAND (3): Iu Mien; Tibetan, Central; Tibetan, Zhongdian

AZERBAIJIAN (2): Russian; Tatar

BYELARUS (2): Russian; Tatar

CAMBODIA (2): Vietnamese, Hakka

COSTA RICA (2): Han Chinese, Cantonese; Han Chinese, Mandarin

ESTONIA (2): Russian; Tatar

FRENCH POLYNESIA (2): Hakka; Han Chinese, Mandarin

IRAN (2): Kazak, Uygur

JAPAN (2): Japanese; Korean

KENYA (2): Hakka; Han Chinese, Mandarin

LATVIA (2): Russian; Tatar

LITHUANIA (2): Russian; Tatar

NORTH KOREA (2): Korean; Manchu

NORWAY (2): Tibetan, Central; Vietnamese

ARGENTINA (1): Japanese

ARMENIA (1): Russian

BANGLADESH (1): Chin, Asho

BULGARIA (1): Tatar

DENMARK (1): Iu Mien

DOMINICAN REPUBLIC (1): Japanese

FINLAND (1): Tatar

FRENCH GUIANA (1): Hmong Daw

JAMAICA (1): Hakka

MEXICO (1): Japanese

MOROCCO (1): Uygur

NAURU (1): Han Chinese, Cantonese

PARAGUAY (1): Japanese

PERU (1): Japanese

POLAND (1): Russian

ROMANIA (1): Tatar

SOUTH KOREA (1): Korean

SRI LANKA (1): Hakka

SURINAME (1): Hakka

TRINIDAD (1): Hakka

UNITED ARAB EMIRATES (1): Japanese

Notes

Introduction

1. Chinese Academy of Social Sciences (CASS), *Information China* (London: Pergamon Press, 1989), 3: 1248.
2. J. L. Cranmer-Byng (ed.), *An Embassy in China, Being the Journal Kept by Lord Macartney, 1793-94* (London: Longmans, 1962).
3. Archie R. Crouch, Steven Agoratus, Arthur Emerson and Debra E. Soled (eds.), *Christianity in China: A Scholar's Guide to Resources in the Libraries and Archives of the United States* (New York: M. E. Sharpe, 1989), xxxi.
4. Exodus 1:12 (*Holy Bible*, NIV).
5. Article 147 of the Chinese Penal Code.
6. Conrad Brandt, Benjamin Schwarz and John K. Fairbank, *A Documentary History of Chinese Communism* (New York: Antheneum, 1966), 217.
7. Gyatso Tenzin (Dalai Lama XIV), *My Land and My People* (New York: McGraw-Hill, 1962).
8. Zheng Lan, *Travels Through Xishuangbanna: China's Subtropical Home of Many Nationalities* (Beijing: Foreign Languages Press, 1981), 17.
9. Ralph R. Covell, *The Liberating Gospel in China: The Christian Faith Among China's Minority Peoples* (Michigan: Baker Books, 1994), 24.
10. Wolfgram Eberhard, *China's Minorities: Yesterday and Today* (Belmont: Wadsworth Publishing, 1982), 8.
11. Dennis Bloodworth, as cited in Covell, *The Liberating Gospel*, 18.
12. Paul Vial, "Deux mois chez les Miaotse" [Two Months Among the Miao], *Les Missions Catholiques*, no. 32 (1900): 434-35.
13. F. S. A. Bourne, as cited in Samuel R. Clarke, *Among the Tribes in South-West China* (London: Morgan & Scott, 1911), 1.
14. Wolfgram Eberhard, *Kultur und Siedelung der Randvolker Chinas*, as cited in Inez de Beauclair, *Tribal Cultures of Southwest China* (Taiwan: The Chinese Association for Folklore, 1974).
15. John Kuhn, *We Found a Hundred Tribes* (London: CIM, 1945), 8.
16. CASS, *Information China* 3: 1247.
17. Fei Xiaotong, "On the Question of Identification of Nationalities in China," *Chinese Social Sciences*, no. 1 (1980).
18. Sun Yatsen, *Memoires of a Chinese Revolutionary* (Taipei: China Cultural Service, 1953).
19. Colin Mackerras, *China's Minorities: Integration and Modernization in the Twentieth Century* (Hong Kong: Oxford University Press, 1994), 142-43.
20. CASS, *Information China* 3: 1281-82.
21. Australian Academy of the Humanities and Chinese Academy of Social Services (CASS), *Language Atlas of China* (*LAC*) (Hong Kong: Longman Group, 1987), A-3.
22. Fei Xiaotong, "Guan yu Wo Guo Minzu de Shi Bien Wenti," *Minzu Yi Shehui* (Beijing, 1981), 5, 26.
23. *Guizhou Nianjian 1985* (Guiyang: Guizhou Renmin Chubanshe, 1985), 340-41. The *Minzu Shibie Wenxian Ziliao Huibian, Minzu Yanjiu Cankao Ziliao* 15 (Guiyang: Guizhousheng Minzu Yanjiusuo, 1982), also states there are 80 unclassified groups in Guizhou, which contradicts Fei Xiaotong, "On Identification of Nationalities in China," which states there are only 30 unclassified groups in Guizhou.
24. Mackerras, *China's Minorities*, 143.
25. Martin Heijdra, "Who Were the Laka?: A Survey of Scriptures in the Minority Languages of Southwest China," *The East Asian Library Journal* 8, no. 1 (Spring 1998): 158.
26. Li Youyi, *Ethnology in China* (Griffith University Press, 1980), 10. Also see Lin Yuehua, "Zhongguo Xinan Diqu De Minzu Shibie" [Ethnic Studies in Southwest China], *Yunnan Shehui Kexue*, no. 2 (1984): 1.
27. Stevan Harrell, "Ethnicity and Kin Terms Among Two Kinds of Yi," in Chiao Chien and Nicholas Tapp, *Ethnicity and Ethnic Groups in China* (Hong Kong: The Chinese University of Hong Kong, 1989), 183.
28. *Yunnan Shaoshu Minzu* (Kunming, 1986), 627-28.
29. Hsu Itang [Xu Yitang], *Leibo Xiaolaingshan zhi Lomin* [A Report of the Lolo in Leibo, Xiaoliang Mountains] (Chengdu: University of Nanjing Institute of Chinese Cultural Studies, 1944).
30. Sir Reginald Fleming Johnston, *From Peking to Mandalay: A Journey from North China to Burma through Tibetan Ssuch'uan and Yunnan* (London: John Murray, 1908), 81.
31. Jamin Pelkey, "Yunnan's Myriad Yi: Profiles on the Peoples Classified as 'Yi' in Yunnan Province," unpublished report (May 1999): 3-5.
32. Joakim Enwall, *A Myth Become Reality: History and Development of the Miao Written Language* (Stockholm: Institute of Oriental Languages, 1996), 1: 14.
33. Ibid., 20.
34. Fei Xiaotong, "Fifty Years Investigation in the Yao Mountains," as cited by Jacques Lemoine and Chiao Chien in *The Yao of South China: Recent International Studies* (France: Pangu, 1991), 24.
35. Mackerras, *China's Minorities*, 143.
36. Zhang Tianlu, *Zhongguo Shaoshu Minzu de Ren Kou* (Liaoning: Renmin Chubanshe, 1987), 2.
37. "The Pumi People of China," report sent to the author by a Christian worker wishing to remain anonymous, 1995.
38. *Frontiers Focus* 4, no. 3.
39. See *Guizhou Tongji Nianjian 1992* (Beijing: Zhongguo Tongji Chubanshe, 1992), 117-23.
40. Guizhou Sheng Shaoshu Minzu Renkou Tongji Ziliao, *Minzu Yanjiu Cankao Ziliao*, no. 21, (Guiyang: Guizhou Minzu Yanjiuso, 1985), Preface.
41. Matthew 28:19 (*Holy Bible*, NIV).
42. Revelation 5:9 (*Holy Bible*, NIV).
43. Matthew 24:14 (*Holy Bible*, NIV).
44. Paul Hattaway, "The Yi of China," *New Zealand A-A-P Advocate*, no. 18 (New Zealand Adapt-a-People Programme, August 1996).
45. Covell, *The Liberating Gospel*, 219.
46. *Mission Frontiers* (April 1995).
47. Donald McGavran, *Understanding Church Growth* (Michigan: Eerdmans, 1970), 297-98.
48. Vicomte d'Ollone, *In Forbidden China: The d'Ollone Mission 1906-09, China-Tibet-Mongolia* (London: T. Fisher Unwin, 1912), 311.

Methodology and Terminology

1. Ralph D. Winter, "Unreached Peoples: Recent Developments in the Concept," *Mission Frontiers* (August-September 1989): 12.
2. Lawrence B. Radcliffe, "A Field Worker Speaks Out About the Rush to Reach All Peoples," *Mission Frontiers* 20, no.1-2 (January-February 1998), cited from the electronic edition.
3. Enwall, *A Myth Become Reality* 1: 41.
4. Patrick Johnstone, *Operation World* (Grand Rapids: Zondervan, 1993).
5. Ma Yin, *Questions and Answers about China's Minority Nationalities* (Beijing: New World Press, 1985), 3.
6. S. Robert Ramsey, *The Languages of China* (Princeton: Princeton University Press, 1987), 6-7.
7. David B. Barrett (ed.), *World Christian Encyclopedia* (New York: Oxford University Press, 1982), 110.
8. Patrick Johnstone, *Operation World* (England: STL Books and WEC Publications, 1987), 32.
9. Ralph D. Winter, "Unreached Peoples: What, Where, and Why?" in Patrick Sookhdeo (ed.), *New Frontiers in Mission* (Grand Rapids: Baker, 1987), 154, as cited in John Piper, *Let the Nations Be Glad: The Supremacy of God in Missions* (Grand Rapids: Baker, 1993), 206-207.
10. Taken from Enwall, *A Myth Become Reality* 1: 20.
11. Heijdra, "Who Were the Laka?" 159.
12. Enwall, *A Myth Become Reality* 1: 14.
13. Robert Storey (ed.), *China: a Travel Survival Kit* (Hawthorn, Australia: Lonely Planet Publications, 1994), 72.
14. Ibid., 75.
15. Ibid.
16. See Tony Lambert, *The Resurrection of the Chinese Church* (Illinois: OMF, 1994), 172-197.
17. Storey (ed.), *China*, 73.

Profiles

ACHANG

1. Robert Ramsey says that most Achang live in Myanmar. See Ramsey, *The Languages of China*, 278.
2. Unfortunately no research has been conducted into the various historical and cultural differences among the three Achang languages, so this study has been unable to include them as separate groups.
3. Jiangxi Educational Publishing, *Encyclopedic Dictionary of Chinese Linguistics* (*EDCL*) [*Zhongguo Yuyanxue Dacidian*] (Nanjing: Jiangxi Educational Publishing House, 1991), 554.
4. Grimes, Barbara F. (ed.), *Ethnologue: Languages of the World* (Dallas: Summer Institute of Linguistics, 1996, 13th ed.), 539.
5. Zhang Weiwen and Zeng Qingnan, *In Search of China's Minorities* (Beijing: New World Press, 1993), 217.
6. *China Prayer Letter and Ministry Report* (*CPLMR*), no. 119 (Hong Kong: China Ministries International, December 1991-February 1992).
7. Jonathon Chao (ed.), *The China Mission Handbook: A Portrait of China and Its Church* (Hong Kong: CCRC, 1989), 141.
8. *CPLMR*, no. 119 (December 1991-February 1992).
9. The 5,000 Achang who have been included in *Operation China* as *Achang, Husa* have been subtracted from the 1990 census figure of 27,708.
10. 90% of Achang live in Longchuan County and in the Zhedao and Dachang districts of Lianghe County. According to the 1990 census there were 7 counties or municipalities in China that recorded more than 500 Achang people. In descending order, they are: Longchuan 11,022; Lianghe 10,535; Yunlong 1,798; Luxi 1,530; Tengchong 1,054; Longling 782; Yingjiang 517.

ACHANG, HUSA

1. Xu Ye, "The Lingguan Route (II)," *China Tourism*, no. 120 (n.d.): 31.
2. Ibid.
3. Zhang Weiwen and Zeng, *In Search of China's Minorities*, 214.
4. Ibid.
5. Xu Ye, "The Lingguan Route," 31.

A CHE

1. The A Che were also mentioned in Wolfgram Eberhard, "Kultur und Siedlung der Randvolker Chinas," *T'oung Pao*, no. 36 (supplement, 1942).
2. Jamin Pelkey, "Initial Investigative Report on the Yi Peoples of Honghe Prefecture," unpublished report (February 1999): 8.

ADI

1. Bethany World Prayer Center, 1995 Joshua Project. There is little likelihood of there being such a high number of Adi in China. The Adi do not appear in Chinese government records. The vast county of Medog where the Adi live is the size of Holland, yet contains just 9,000 people of all nationalities. See He Guanghua, "The Lost Horizons of Medog," *China Reconstructs* (March 1995): 47-50. The *Lhoba, Bogar* group in China are known as *Bokar* in India and are considered a subgroup of the Adi; while the *Idu* (named *Lhoba, Yidu* in China) is considered a subgroup of Mishmi in India. It is possible these two Lhoba groups therefore constitute the majority of the Adi population in China.
2. He Guanghua, "The Lost Horizons of Medog," 47-50.
3. The 15 Adi subgroups in Arunachal Pradesh are: Ashing (959 people in the 1971 census, but due to reclassification their number was listed as only 66 in the 1981 census); Bokar (3,375 — 1981 census); Bori (1,884 — 1981 census); Gallong (8,999 — 1981 census); Karko (2,118 — 1971 census); Komkar (1,107 — 1981 census); Milang (2,595 — 1971 census; 706 — 1981 census); Minyong (25,259 — 1981 census); Padam (9,864 — 1971 census); Pailibo (1,190 — 1971 census); Pangi (1,317 — 1981 census); Pasi (1,944 — 1971 census); Ramo (818 — 1981 census); Shimong (3,140 — 1971 census); Tangam (84 — 1971 census). Except for the Bokar, it is not known which of these subgroups live in China.
4. Grimes, *Ethnologue* (1996), 540.
5. See Raghubir Singh, "A Rare Visit to a World Unto Itself," *National Geographic* (November 1988): 696.

ADU

1. *Huaning Xian Minzu Zhi* (1990), 45. This figure was estimated from information given in this source, but was not specifically stated.
2. Ibid.

A-HMAO

1. Wang Fushi and Mao Zongwu, *Renconstruction of Proto Miao-Yao* (Beijing: National Academy of Social Sciences, 1995).
2. The A-Hmao live in the following counties in Yunnan Province: Yiliang, Daguan, Zhaotong, Yongshan, Suijiang, Qiaojia, Wuding, Lufeng, Luquan, Chuxiong, Kunming, Anning, Qujing, Xundian and Xuanwei. Ibid.
3. The classification of the many different Miao groups is a confusing task. In the past, anthropologists often divided the groups according to their appearance and socio-cultural designations, such as *Black Miao, Cowrie-Shell Miao, Pointed Hat Miao*, etc. The Chinese now often list the various Miao groups according to their county or location. To complicate matters further, every linguistic survey seems to classify the Miao differently. My aim is to present the best overview of the ethnolinguistic make-up of the Miao possible at the present time. After much consideration, the classifications of Chinese linguist Wang Fushi and British linguist Michael Johnson have been mostly used. Johnson has recently forged a reputation as an expert on Miao linguistics, especially the Western (Chuanqiandian) Miao groups. The groups presented here are largely taken from Wang's descriptions in *Miaoyu Jianzhi*, and several of Johnson's manuscripts. This has resulted in some clumsy group names, such as the *Southwestern Guiyang Miao*, but at the present time the author considers Wang and Johnson's work the best available. It is hoped that in the near future thorough research will be undertaken to determine the true ethnolinguistic compilation of the Miao in China.
4. Wong How-Man, "Peoples of China's Far Provinces," *National Geographic* (March 1984): 308.
5. Enwall, *A Myth Become Reality* 1:14.
6. *The South China Morning Post* (Hong Kong, 1994).
7. Samuel Clarke, *Among the Tribes in South-West China*, 35.
8. In 1995 the Communist authorities restored Pollard's grave and that of another English missionary, Heber Goldsworthy. Their graves were declared a national monument.
9. Enwall, *A Myth Become Reality* 1:129.
10. Wong Tak Hing, "A Pilgrimage to the Mountains: A Visit to Miao Churches in Guizhou Province," *Bridge*, no. 24 (July-August 1987): 10.
11. For a comprehensive account of Communist plots to break up the A-Hmao church, see T'ien, *Peaks of Faith*, 90-100.
12. C. G. Edwards, "Kweichow Tribal Report," *The Field Bulletin of the China Inland Mission* (Shanghai, November 1948): 195.
13. Enwall, *A Myth Become Reality* 1:217.
14. Zhang Tan, *"Zhaimen" qian de Shimenkan: Jidujiao Wenhua Yu Chuan-Dian-Qian-Bian Miaozu Shehui* (Kunming: Yunnan Jiaoyu Chubanshe, 1992), 237.
15. Enwall, *A Myth Become Reality* 1:217.

AI-CHAM

1. Grimes, *Ethnologue* (1996), 540. The 1992 *Ethnologue* listed only "200 to 300 speakers" of Ai-Cham, but recent research has found the figure to be much higher. There were a total of 84,505 members of the Bouyei nationality (including the Ai-Cham) in Libo County according to the 1990 census.
2. For a comprehensive study of Ai-Cham, see Lin Jianxin, SIL, *Comparative Kadai: Linguistic Studies Beyond Tai* (Dallas: SIL *Publications in Linguistics* no. 86, 1988), 59-85.

AINU

1. Jiangxi Educational Publishing, *EDCL*, 580.
2. Grimes, *Ethnologue* (1988), 446.
3. Jiangxi Educational Publishing, *EDCL*, 580.
4. Ibid.
5. Grimes, *Ethnologue* (1996), 540.
6. Marco Polo, *The Book of Ser Marco Polo, the Venetian, Concerning the Kingdoms and Marvels of the East*, trans. Henry Yule (London: John Murray, 1903), 2: 183.
7. Arthur Moule and Paul Pelliot, *Marco Polo: The Description of the World* (London: Routledge & Sons, 1938), 2: 143.

AKE

1. An Chunyang and Liu Bohua (eds.), *Where the Dai People Live* (Beijing: Foreign Languages Press, 1985), 101.
2. Personal communication, December 1996. Another linguistic source claims Ake is "spoken by several thousand people living in Jinghong County," see James A. Matisoff, "Languages and Dialects of Tibeto-Burman," *STEDT Monograph II Series* (Berkeley: University of California, 1998).
3. An Chunyang and Liu (eds.), *Where the Dai People Live*, 83.
4. Vladimir Li, *Some Approaches to the Classification of Small Ethnic Groups in South China* (Prague: Institute of Oriental Studies, n.d.).
5. "The Ake (or Akeu) in Myanmar fled there from China. They said to me, 'We are not Akha', but when I compared their genealogies with the Akha genealogies they are basically the same... Their ancestral altars and offerings are not the same, since they show some influence from both the Han Chinese and Dai." Paul Lewis, personal communication, February 1999.
6. For a brief comparative discussion of Ake with some lexical terms and a phonetic inventory, see Li Yongsui and Wang Ersong (eds.), *Haniyn Jianzhi* (Beijing: Minzu Chubanshe, 1986).
7. Some Christian outreach has been conducted among the Ake in northern Thailand.

AKHA

1. According to the 1990 census there were 59,726 Hani in Menghai County; 54,429 in Jinghong County, and 40,241 in Mengla. The great majority of these people are Akha.
2. John Kuhn, *We Found a Hundred Tribes*, 9; Akha subgroups in China may include the Buli, Phusang, Luma, Mucchi, Nu-Quay, Oma and O'pa. The main clan of Akha in China is called *Jeu-g'oe*.
3. Paul Lewis, *Ethnographic Notes on the Akhas of Burma*, 787-89, as cited in Cornelia Ann Kammerer, "Customs and Christian Conversion among the Akha Highlanders of Burma and Thailand," *American Ethnologist* 17, no. 2 (May 1990): 282-83. Among many good linguistic studies of Akha are three articles by Inga-Lill Hansson: "A Phonological Comparison of Akha and Hani," *Linguistics of the Tibeto-Burman Area* 7, no. 1 (1982): 63-115; "A Comparison of Akha, Hani, Khantu and Pijo," *Linguistics of the Tibeto-Burman Area* 12, no. 1 (1989): 6-91; and "The Language of Akha in Ritual Texts," *Linguistics of the Tibeto-Burman Area* 14, no. 2 (1991): 55-67.
4. According to Henri Roux, "Deux Tribus de la Region de Phongsalay (Laos Septentrional)," *Ecole Francaise d'Extreme-Orient*, no. 24 (1924): 373-500, *Akha* means "intermediary". Roux says that 700 years ago the Akha

lived on the Cha Ten Plateau, between the Shan States and China. Wasps were devastating the country, and the Akha and Ho agreed that whoever would destroy them would have the right to rule the land. The Ho tricked the Akha and took control of the land, forcing the Akha to migrate southwards.

5. Research into the historical relationship between the Akha and Hani found the two groups shared an identical genealogical record for the first 20 to 22 generations. After that time the two groups broke off and became separate peoples. Significantly, the timing coincides with the Mongol invasion of Yunnan and the destruction of the Nanzhao Kingdom in AD 1252. See Leo Alting Von Geusau, "The Second Hani/Akha Culture Studies Conference, 12-18 May 1996," in *Chiang Mai Newsletter* 5, no. 10 (October 1996).
6. Paul and Elaine Lewis, *Peoples of the Golden Triangle* (New York: Thames & Hudson, 1984).
7. AMO, unpublished research, November 1996.
8. Personal communication, November 1997.

AKTO TURKMEN

1. Grimes, *Ethnologue* (1992), 529.
2. Marco Polo, *The Book of Ser Marco Polo.*
3. Grimes, *Ethnologue* (1996), 563.
4. Mackerras, *China's Minorities*, 174.

ALING

1. Pelkey, "Yunnan's Myriad Yi," 70.
2. Situ Xun, "A Feast for the Eyes: The Torch Festival," *China Tourism*, no. 94 (n.d.): 36.
3. Milton T. Stauffer (ed.), *The Christian Occupation of China* (Shanghai: China Consultation Committee, 1922), 349.

ALU

1. Pelkey, "Report on the Yi Peoples of Honghe Prefecture," 15.
2. Ma Yin, *China's Minority Nationalities* (Beijing: Foreign Language Press, 1989), 234.

ALUO

1. For a linguistic study of various Yi languages, including Aluo, see Robert Shafer, "Phonetique Historique des Langues Lolo," *T'oung Pao* 41, nos. 1-3 (1952): 191-229.
2. Bai Man, "Paying Tribute to Luo: A Yi Tribal Festival," *China Tourism*, no. 129 (March 1991): 49.
3. Ibid.
4. Ibid., 50.

AMDO, HBROGPA

1. This 1987 figure seems to disagree with that cited under Population in China. However, it includes the population of the Golog Tibetans (90,000 in 1982). The Golog people group are profiled separately and their number is subtracted from the larger figure (538,500) to arrive at a more realistic and specific population (448,500) for the Hbrogpa Amdo.
2. The Amdo groups live in Huangnan, Hainan, Haibei and Haixi Prefectures in *Qinghai* Province; Gannan Prefecture and Tianzhu County of southwestern *Gansu* Province and in parts of the Aba and Ganzhi Prefectures in northern *Sichuan* Province.
3. Chen Shuren, "Muni Gully: Wonderland of Nature," *China Tourism*, no. 110 (n.d.): 85.
4. *The Edge* 2, no. 3 (CB International, Fall 1997).
5. The Australian Academy and CASS, *LAC*, C-11, describes each of the four main Amdo languages as "vernaculars." Grimes describes them as dialects, but notes "those listed as dialects may not be intelligible with each other," see *Ethnologue* (1996), 540. In the author's opinion, after field surveys in 1995 and 1996, the four main identified Amdo languages are definitely mutually unintelligible, with dozens of additional dialects spoken across the vast Amdo region. The four main languages listed here can at best be described as the common trade languages spoken in four main geographical regions. There is a lack of reliable linguistic research conducted in the Amdo area. Detailed research could reveal many more mutually unintelligible languages spoken among the Amdo. Jackson Tianshin Sun, "Review of Zangmian Yu Yuyin Han Cohui [Tibeto-Burman Phonology and Vocabularies]", *Linguistics of the Tibeto-Burman Area*, 15, no. 2 (1992): 73-113, has studied and classified 23 Amdo dialects, including Golog varieties. Most of the names are based on locations. They are: *Amdo Sherpa* (spoken in the Ganaan Prefecture of Gansu Province; *Arig* (name of a village in Qilian County, Haibei Prefecture, Qinghai) [possibly the same as *Sogwo Arig*]; *Dawu* (Dawu County, Garze Prefecture, Sichuan); *Dunhua* (Xunhua County, Haidong Prefecture, Qinghai), *Gadê* (Gadê County, Golog Prefecture, Qinghai); *Gangca* (Gangca County, Haibei Prefecture, Qinghai); *Gonghe* (Gonghe County, Hainan Prefecture, Qinghai), *Guinan* (Guinan County, Hainan Prefecture, Qinghai); *Hualong* (Hualong Hui County, Haidong Prefecture, Qinghai), *Huangzhong* (Huangzhong County, Qinghai); *Jainca* (Huangnan Prefecture, Qinghai); *Jigzhi* (Jigzhi County, Golog Prefecture, Qinghai); *Labrang* (Xiahe County, Ganaan Prefecture, Gansu); *Ledu* (Ledu County, Haidong Prefecture, Qinghai); *Luqu* (Luqu County, Ganaan Prefecture, Gansu); *Maqu* (Maqu County, Ganaan Prefecture, Gansu); *Tianjun* (Tianjun County, Haixi Prefecture, Qinghai); *Tianzhu* (spoken in Wuwei District, Tianzhu County, Gansu); *Tongde* (Tongde County, Hainan Prefecture, Qinghai); *Tongren* (Tongren County, Huangnan Prefecture, Qinghai); *Zêkog* (Zêkog County, Huangnan Prefecture, Qinghai); *Zhaggo* (Zhaggo [Luhuo] County, Garze Prefecture, Sichuan); *Zoigê* (Zoigê County, Aba Prefecture, Sichuan).
6. Bradley, "East and South-East Asia," in Donald Laycock and Werner Winter (eds.), *A World of Language: Papers Presented to Professor S. A. Wurm on His 65th Birthday* (Canberra: The Australian National University, 1987), 170.
7. Vanya Kewley, *Tibet: Behind the Ice Curtain* (London: Grafton Books, 1990), 392.
8. There are several large Bon monasteries in the Gansu-Qinghai border area, including the towns of Tongren and Xiahe. Bon monks are allowed to marry, and circle temples in a counter-clockwise direction, unlike Tibetan Buddhists.
9. Covell, *The Liberating Gospel*, 80.
10. Dan Harrison, "Broken Vessels Called to Missions", in *The Great Commission Handbook* (Berry Publishing, 1994), 11.
11. *Pray for China* (Hong Kong: Christian Communications Ltd., April 1996).
12. Stauffer (ed.), *The Christian Occupation of China*, 281.
13. Ibid.
14. Douglas Allen, "Tibet: The Continuing Story," *China and the Church Today* (February 1986): 14-15. Even though this article states the believers were Amdo Tibetans, it is possible this event occurred among the Jone Tibetans in southern Gansu Province (see *Tibetan, Jone* Profile).

AMDO, RONGBA

1. Australian Academy and CASS, *LAC*, C-11.
2. It is important to note that even though the name 'Rongba' has socio-economic connotations, this group, and the other Amdo groups profiled, have been included because of linguistic differences. Some sectors of the missions world have produced lists of people based on socio-economic considerations "Racing car drivers in Toronto," "Hairdressers in San Francisco," etc.). This book attempts to deal only with those groups who are ethnically and/or linguistically different from each other.
3. *Beijing Review*, 27 June 1983.
4. Marku Tsering, *Sharing Christ in the Tibetan Buddhist World* (Pennsylvania: Tibet Press, 1988), 49.
5. Stauffer, *The Christian Occupation of China*, 281.

AMDO, RONGMAHBROGPA

1. Australian Academy and CASS, *LAC*, C-11.
2. Bradley, "East and South-East Asia," 170.
3. Joseph F. Rock, "Seeking the Mountains of Mystery," *National Geographic* (February 1930): 143-44. On a trip to Xiahe in 1995, the author observed there was still a simmering tension between the Amdo and Hui. The Amdo were incensed at plans of the Hui to build a large mosque, which would have been higher than the monastery roof. The Amdo threatened to smash the mosque to the ground if the Muslims proceeded with the construction.
4. Tsering, *Sharing Christ in the Tibetan Buddhist World*, 52.
5. Stauffer, *The Christian Occupation of China*, 281.

AMDO, RTAHU

1. Grimes, *Ethnologue* (1996), 540.
2. Bradley, "East and South-East Asia," 170.
3. Michael Buckley and Robert Strauss (eds.), *Tibet: a Travel Survival Kit* (Hawthorn, Australia: Lonely Planet Publications, 1986), 9.
4. Ibid., 25.
5. Stauffer, *The Christian Occupation of China*, 280.

AMI

1. Ralph Covell, *Pentecost of the Hills in Taiwan* (Pasadena: Hope Publishing House, 1998), 37.
2. Raleigh Farrell, "Taiwan Aboriginal Groups: Problems in Cultural and Linguistic Classification," *Academia Sinica: Institute of Ethnology Monograph*, no. 17 (1969): 53
3. See Suziki Shitz, *The Aborigines of Taiwan* (Taipei: Wu Lin Press, 1991).
4. File no. 54 (Pasadena, Ca: Institute of Chinese Studies.)
5. "A Trip to Lanyu Island." *China Tourism*, no. 80 (n.d.): 81.
6. Ke Ji, "The Amei People of Taiwan," *China Tourism*, no. 43 (n.d.): 52.
7. Covell, *Pentecost of the Hills in Taiwan*, 213.
8. Ibid., 215.
9. Ibid., 282.
10. Ibid., 217.
11. *CPLMR*, no. 119 (December 1991-February 1992).

ANGKU

1. Global Evangelization Movement (GEM), "World's Peoples Listed by Country, Part 1," report (1995).
2. According to linguist Frank Proschan 2,359 Kiorr live in northern Laos. S. A. Wurm and Shiro Hattori (eds.), *Language Atlas of the Pacific Area* (Canberra: The Australian Institute of the Humanities and the Japan Academy, 1981) list a 1981 figure of 1,000 Kiorr in Laos. The Kiorr are also known as the Con.
3. Grimes, *Ethnologue* (1988), 446.
4. de Beauclair, *Tribal Cultures of Southwest China*, 9.

ANI

1. *Kaiyuan Xian Zhi* [The Annals of Kaiyuan County] (1996), 618.
2. Marco Polo, *The Travels of Marco Polo: The Complete Yule-Cordier Edition* (New York: Dover Publications, 1903) 2: 54.
3. Pelkey, "Report on the Yi Peoples of Honghe Prefecture," 22.

AO BIAO

1. The combined population of the five Yao groups in the Dayaoshan is 36,000. Yang Tiande, "A Riot of Yao Color," *China Tourism*, no. 110 (n.d.): 85.
2. Xie Shixun, "Encounter with the Yao in Their Mountain Home," *China Tourism*, no. 73 (n.d.): 25.
3. Fei Xiaotong, "Fifty Years Investigation," 22-23.
4. Ibid., 27.
5. Ibid., 22-23.
6. Huang Yu, "Preliminary Study of the Yao 'King Ping's Charter'," in Lemoine and Chiao, *The Yao of South China*, 94-95.

AOKA

1. Jiangxi Educational Publishing, *EDCL*, 532. According to the 1990 census there were 121,045 Miao people living in Chengbu County, and 23,524 in Longsheng County. The Aoka are also located in surrounding areas.
2. Enwall, *A Myth Become Reality* 2:50.
3. "Miaoyu Fangyan he Chaungli Miaowen de Wenti" [The Dialects of the Miao Language and the Question of Miao Writing], *Zhongguo Kexueyuan Shaoshu Minzu Diaocha di'er Gongzuodui* (Guiyang, 1956): 59.
4. Ramsey, *The Languages of China*, 279.

A'OU

1. According to Zheng Guo-qiao, as cited in Stuart Milliken, "SIL China Nationalities and Languages Files" (Guangzhou, 1993).
2. Grimes, *Ethnologue* (1996), 548.
3. Jacob D. H. Lee (ed.), *China's 55 Ethnic Minorities* (Watson, Australia: YWAM Institute of Asian Studies, 1995), 14.

APU

1. Pelkey, "Report on the Yi Peoples of Honghe Prefecture," 17.
2. Alain Y. Dessaint, *Minorities in Southwestern China: An Introduction to the Yi (Lolo) and Related Peoples and an Annotated Bibliography* (New Haven: HRAF Press, 1980), 29-30.

ASAHEI

1. *Kaiyuan Xian Zhi*, 618.
2. Dessaint, *Minorities in Southwestern China*, 31.
3. Ibid.
4. Paul Vial, "Les Gni ou Gni-p'a: Tribu Lolottee du Yun-nan" [The Gni or Gni-p'a: A Lolo Tribe of Yunnan], *Les Missions Catholiques* 2, no. 26 (1893): 293.

ATI

1. The estimated 12,600 Ati of Huaning County live in the following areas: in and around Xiaozhai, Daxinzhai, and

Heiniubai villages of Huaxi District; some villages of Nuozu and Laotian Communities of Lufeng District; in and around Faguo, Mada, Zanle, Chongmai, and Dalu villages and communities of Chengjiao District; in and around Longmu, Tulaoyi, and Naguo villages of Xincheng District; Zele, Momian, and Xiaoguodu villages of Tonghongdian District; and in and around Zhongcun, Longtan, Yipu, Fagude, Daomakuai and Murui villages of Qinglong District. Jamin Pelkey, "Initial Investigative Report on the Yi Peoples of Yuxi Prefecture," unpublished report (November 1998): 7.
2. See *Zhongguo Shaoshu Minzu Yuyan Shiyong Qingkuang* (Beijing: Zhongguo Zangxue Chubanshe, 1994); and *Yiyu Jianzhi* (1985).
3. *Yuxi Diqu Minzu Xiang Qing Kuang* (1992), 145.

AWU, NORTHERN
1. Harrell, "Ethnicity and Kin Terms," 179.

AWU, SOUTHEASTERN
1. *Mile Xian Zhi* (1987), 689. This source uses 1984 population figures.
2. Perhaps the earliest mention of the Awu appears in Camille Sainson, *Nan-tchao Ye-che* (Paris: E. Leroux, 1904).
3. *Luxi Xian Zhi* (1992).

AXI
1. *Mile Xian Zhi*, 689. This book uses 1984 population figures.
2. Chu Fei, in *Jinshajiang Fengwu Waiji*, as cited in T'ien, *Peaks of Faith*, 147.
3. Ramsey, *The Languages of China*, 253. A linguistic study of Axi is included in Shafer, "Phonetique Historique des Langues Lolo."
4. An ancient Axi song includes these words: "Long, long ago in the Northwest — a place called 'Azhede' — there were Depu and Chepu; O, these were our ancestors, and that is where they lived." According to Jamin Pelkey, "The Axi claim they were the original inhabitants of the area around Lake Dian, ever since their ancestor 'Api' first settled there." See "Report on the Yi Peoples of Honghe Prefecture," 17.
5. Yao Aiyun, "Unique Dance of the Axi People," *China Today* (June 1996): 61-62.
6. Several Chinese articles on the Axi include Guang Weiran's *Axi Rende Ge* (Beijing: People's Literature Publishing Company, 1957), and Yuan Jiahua's two articles "The A-si Love Songs and the A-si Language," *Frontier Politics* 3 (Nan-k'ai State University, 1946), and *A-xi Shi Jia Ji Chi Yuyan* (Beijing: Chinese Scientific Institute, 1953).
7. Pelkey, "Report on the Yi Peoples of Honghe Prefecture," 7.
8. See Liétard's, "Le District des Lolos A-chi," *Les Missions Catholiques* 18, no. 11 (1904): 93-96.
9. Vial, "Les Gni ou Gni-p'a," 161.
10. The main Axi Catholic church in Mile was at Xiyi District. Six smaller churches were constructed in other parts of the county. Recently a Frenchman returned to Xiyi and contributed a large amount of money towards the construction of a church building for the Axi Catholics. Pelkey, "Report on the Yi Peoples of Honghe Prefecture," 20.

AYI
1. Jiangxi Educational Publishing, *EDCL*, 551.
2. Grimes, *Ethnologue* (1996), 540.
3. See Ma Yin, *China's Minority Nationalities*, 318.
4. *World Pulse*, 19 April 1996.

AYIZI
1. Pelkey, "Yunnan's Myriad Yi," 90.
2. Dessaint, *Minorities in Southwestern China*, 26.
3. Elliot R. Kendall, *Eyes of the Earth: The Diary of Samuel Pollard* (London: Cargate Press, 1954), 132.

AZHE
1. Pelkey, "Report on the Yi Peoples of Honghe Prefecture," 9.
2. *Mile Xian Zhi*, 689 (1984 figure).
3. Pelkey, "Report on the Yi Peoples of Honghe Prefecture," 9.
4. Ibid., 8.
5. Ibid., 9.

AZONG
1. Pelkey, "Yunnan's Myriad Yi," 21.
2. Ibid., 3-5.
3. Marco Polo, *The Travels of Marco Polo: Yule Cordier*, 53-54.

BAHENG, LIPING
1. Wang Fushi and Mao, *Renconstruction of Proto Miao-Yao.*
2. According to the 1990 census there were a total of 4,834 Yao people living in Liping County. The Baheng are therefore the dominant Yao group in Liping.

BAHENG, SANJIANG
1. Robert Cooper (ed.), *The Hmong* (Bangkok: Artasia Press, 1995), 54.
2. Dang Nghiem Van; Chu Thai Son and Luu Hung, *Ethnic Minorities in Vietnam* (Hanoi: The Gioi Publishers, 1993), 159.

BAI
1. This official 1990 census figure appears to disagree with that cited under Population in China. Since the larger figure (1,594,827) includes several groups (Nanjingren, Bei, Qixingmin, and Longia) which are profiled separately in *Operation China*, the combined number of these four groups is subtracted from the official figure to give the more realistic and specific population (1,442,627) for the Bai.
2. Robert Ramsey explains the enigma of the Bai language: "The language that they speak has not been shown to be related to any other. It has elements that look like Tibeto-Burman; others that look like Tai or Mon-Khmer; and some tantalizing ones that look like Chinese on several levels. But none of these prove a genetic affinity. Who then are the Bai?... In the PRC the Bai are classed as a Tibeto-Burman people, and their language is put into the Yi branch of that language family. This classification is premature. It is still not known what, if any, language family Bai belongs to, much less what branch." Ramsey, *The Languages of China*, 290.
3. According to the 1990 census there were 88 counties or municipalities in China that recorded more than 500 Bai people. In descending order, the largest are: Dali (Yunnan) 281,730; Eryuan (Yunnan) 198,196; Heqing (Yunnan) 138,397; Jianchuan (Yunnan) 137,689; Yunlong (Yunnan) 136,917; Sangzhi (Hunan) 92,755; Lanping (Yunnan) 81,243; Binchuan (Yunnan) 40,940; Dafang (Guizhou) 37,536.
4. According to Li Shao-ni, as cited in Milliken, "SIL China Nationalities and Languages Files."
5. Study by the Institute of Nationality Studies of the Chinese Academy of Social Sciences, 1982. "The Lemo sect distributed in the Nujiang area remained in the

society of primitive commune, and its Nama sect was in the feudal-serf social system." Jason Shaw, "Some Current Trends of Ethnology in China," 48, in Chiao and Tapp, *Ethnicity and Ethnic Groups in China.*

6. David Y. H. Wu, "Culture Change and Ethnic Identity Among Minorities in China," 16, in Chiao and Tapp, *Ethnicity and Ethnic Groups in China.*
7. John Kuhn, *We Found a Hundred Tribes*, 12.
8. David Wu, "Culture Change and Ethnic Identity," 15.
9. Martin M. C. Yang, "Peoples and Societies in Yunnan (Part I)," *Journal of Ethnology and Sociology,* no. 16 (Taipei, 1978): 21-112.
10. David Wu, "Culture Change and Ethnic Identity," 17.
11. Grimes, *Ethnologue* (1996), 541.
12. Huang Gouzhong, "Gengxin Hunyin Guannian Tigao Minzu Suzhi" [Changing the Consanguineous Marriages to Enhance the Quality of the Minority Nationalities]: 1-2, as cited in T'ien, *Peaks of Faith*, 2.
13. Himsey Hui, "The Bai," *China and the Church Today* (October 1985): 15.
14. "Ethnic Groups in Yunnan," *Bridge* (September-October 1990).
15. *CPLMR*, no. 119 (December 1991-February 1992).
16. See *World Pulse*, 19 April 1996.
17. John Kuhn, *We Found a Hundred Tribes*, 12-13.

BAIHONG

1. Shi Youyi (ed.), *Folkways of China's Minority Nationalities (Southwest)* (Chengdu: Huayi Publishing House, 1991), 30. According to the 1990 census there were 203,559 Hani in Mojiang County and 69,630 in Yuanjiang County. Many of these are Baihong.
2. Ibid.
3. The 1995 Joshua Project numbered 12,000 *Mahei* in China but this figure is undoubtedly too low.
4. T'ien, *Peaks of Faith*, 77.
5. Conner, "Midge's Musings," May 1997.
6. Bradley, "Language Planning for China's Minorities" in Laycock and Werner (eds.), *A World of Language.* Also see Julian K. Wheatley, "Comments on the 'Hani' Dialects of Loloish," *Linguistics of the Tibeto-Burman Area* 7, no. 1 (1982) 1-38; also Li Yongsui and Wang (eds.), *Haniyu Jianzhi.*
7. Wang Zhengfang, "We of the Hani Nationality," *China Reconstructs* (n.d.).
8. Von Geusau, "The Second Hani/Akha Culture Studies Conference."
9. Xie Shixun. "The Hanis of the Ailao Mountains," *China Tourism*, no. 79 (n.d.): 45.

BAIMA

1. The Baima people first came to attention in the March 1984 *National Geographic,* which estimated a population of 10,000 people.This figure is supported by researcher Midge Conner, who has traveled to the region several times and lists only 14 Baima villages. A recent visitor was told there were approximately 20,000 Baima. The 1991 Jiangxi Educational Publishing, *EDCL*, 538, and the 1996 Grimes *Ethnologue*, 541, on the other hand, list a Baima population of 110,000, and give their location simply as "Pingwu." This figure is not feasible with the population density of the area. The 1990 national census listed the following Tibetan populations (including the Baima) in the counties that contain Baima people: Nanping (13,623); Wenxian (5,857), and Pingwu (4,298).
2. Wong Chung Fai, "The Felt-Hatted Baima," *China Tourism*, no. 115 (n.d.): 31.
3. *Chronicles of the Northern Wei,* (AD 551-554).
4. Wong Chung Fai, "A Mountain Hamlet in Zhugqu," *China Tourism*, no. 115 (n.d.): 26.
5. CASS, *Information China* 3: 1249.
6. History tells how, during the Chao Dynasty (1028-257 BC), large numbers of Miao were banished to San Wei, a mountainous, remote area of southern Gansu. After a hundred years, the Miao were never mentioned again by Chinese historians. See Keith Quincy, *Hmong: A History of a People* (Cheney: Eastern Washington University Press, 1995), 40-41.
7. "The Baima have greatly contributed to the welfare of the giant pandas. They have sent more than 40 pandas to zoos across China, as well as zoos in Japan, England and France. 'Langlang', 'Jingjing', and 'Feifei' are Baima pandas." Asian Minorities Outreach, *The 50 Most Unreached People Groups of China and Tibet* (Chiang Mai: AMO Publishing, 1996), 4.
8. "A Day with the Baima," *China Today* (July 1991).

BAI YI

1. Samuel Clarke, *Among the Tribes in South-West China*, 135-36.
2. Wong How-Man, "Peoples of China's Far Provinces," 291.
3. Samuel Clarke, *Among the Tribes in South-West China*, 136.
4. Mrs. Ivan Allbutt, *China's Aboriginal Peoples* (London: CIM, 1941), 10.

BAN YAO

1. *Yunnan Nianjian 1986* (Kunming: Yunnan Nianjian Zazhishe), 454. There were a total of 37,500 Yao people living in Funing County, and 4,764 in Napo County, according to the 1990 census.
2. Song Enchang, "The Family Systems and Its Ethos Among the Yao of Yunnan," in Lemoine and Chiao, *The Yao of South China*, 231.

BAONUO

1. Nationalities Affairs Commission of Guangxi Zhuang Autonomous Region, *The Yao Nationality* (People's Publishing House, 1990), 44.
2. Kun Xin, "The White-Trousered Yao," *China Tourism*, no. 80 (n.d.): 60.
3. Ibid., 62.
4. Ibid.
5. Personal communication between a Libo government official and the author, 1995: The Baonuo's utter terror of all outsiders probably stems from their long history of being harassed and driven from their land by other races. In 1993 a Westerner, obviously not aware of the hostility of the Baonuo, scaled a mountain in Libo to visit them. As he entered the village he noticed the people running into their homes. A group of Baonuo, armed with large rocks and sticks, emerged from behind the trees and threatened to kill the visitor. He was fortunate to escape with his life. Most Baonuo are addicted to alcohol.

   Another visitor to the area reported the following in a personal communication with the author in 1998: "They'll do anything for money. Give them money, they'll buy booze, give them things they can use, they sell them and buy booze."

BEI

1. Stauffer, *The Christian Occupation of China*, 244.
2. Radcliffe, "A Field Worker Speaks Out."
3. David Wu, "Culture Change and Ethnic Identity," 16.

4. Peter Goulart, *The Forgotten Kingdom* (London: John Murray, 1957), 153.

BEIDALAO

1. Wang Fushi and Mao, *Renconstruction of Proto Miao-Yao.*
2. Ibid.
3. Ramsey, *The Languages of China*, 285.
4. Egon Von Eickstedt, *Rassendynamik von Ostasien* (Berlin: Walter de Gruyter, 1944), 174-75.

BEIDONGNUO

1. There were a total of 4,789 Yao people living in Libo County according to the 1990 census. This figure includes the members of other small Yao groups, such as the *Numao.*

BELA

1. Grimes, *Ethnologue* (1996), 541.
2. Jiangxi Educational Publishing, *EDCL*, 553-54.
3. Dwayne Graybill, personal communication, October 1997.
4. *China's Millions* (March 1898).
5. de Beauclair, *Tribal Cultures of Southwest China*, 9.
6. Yunnan Academy of Social Sciences (YASS) 220, Section 16; cited in T'ien, *Peaks of Faith*, 43.

BEN

1. John Kuhn, *We Found a Hundred Tribes.*
2. Grimes, *Ethnologue* (1996), 540.
3. V. Li, *Some Approaches to the Classification of Small Ethnic Groups.*
4. See Heijdra, "Who Were the Laka?" 156.
5. de Beauclair, *Tribal Cultures of Southwest China*, 9.
6. T'ien, *Peaks of Faith*, 47.
7. Ma Yin, *China's Minority Nationalities*, 310.

BIAO-JIAO MIEN

1. Pan Chengqian, "Yao Dialectology," in Lemoine and Chiao, *The Yao of South China*, 48.
2. Stauffer, *The Christian Occupation of China*, 216.

BIAO MIEN

1. Grimes, *Ethnologue* (1996), 541.
2. These are Iu Mien, Kim Mun, Biao Mien and Zaomin. See Pan Chengqian, as cited in Milliken, "SIL China Nationalities and Languages Files."
3. Jiangxi Educational Publishing, *EDCL*, 560-61.
4 Grimes, *Ethnologue* (1996), 541.
5. Pan Chengqian, "Yao Dialectology," 49. Also see David B. Solnit, "A Note on the Problematic Status of 'Shwa' in Biao Min Yao," *Linguistics of the Tibeto-Burman Area* 10, no. 2 (1987): 54-56; Solnit, "Some Evidence from Biao Min on the Initials of Proto-Mienic (Yao) and Proto-Hmong-Mien (Miao-Yao)," *Linguistics of the Tibeto-Burman Area* 19, no. 1 (1996): 1-18.
6. Gina Corrigan, *Odyssey Illustrated Guide to Guizhou* (Hong Kong: The Guidebook Company Ltd., 1995), 212.

BIAO MIEN, SHIKOU

1. Ralph A. Litzinger, "Making Histories: Contending Conceptions of the Yao Past," in Stevan Harrell (ed.), *Cultural Encounters on China's Ethnic Frontiers* (Seattle: University of Washington Press, 1995), 127.

BISU

1. Li Yongshui, as cited in Grimes, *Ethnologue* (1996), 541.
2. Dwayne Graybill, personal communication, 7 December 1996.
3. One Bisu woman in Thailand who recently became a Christian was taken away and forced to become a Buddhist nun in a temple. Kirk Person, personal communication, August 1997.

BIT

1. J.-O. Svantesson, as cited in Grimes, *Ethnologue* (1996), 541. This reference to Svantesson appears to have been from a personal communication between Grimes and Svantesson (1990), and not to a published article or book. Note, the 1991 Jiangxi Educational Publishing, *EDCL*, 594, lists only 200 *Buxin* (Bit) in China.
2. Linguist F. Proschan believes Bit is a Khmuic language, while J.-O. Svantesson believes it is Palaungic; 1990, personal communication with Barbara Grimes.
3. Elizabeth Perazic, "Little Laos: Next Door to Red China," *National Geographic* (January 1960): 57.
4. Vietnam News Agency, *Vietnam: Image of the Community of 54 Ethnic Groups* (Hanoi: The Ethnic Cultures Publishing House, 1996), 92.
5. William Clifton Dodd, *The Tai Race: Elder Brother of the Chinese* (Cedar Rapids: The Torch Press, 1923), 312.

BIYO

1. J.-O. Svantesson, 1990 personal communication, as cited in Grimes, *Ethnologue* (1996), 541.
2. Bradley, "Language Planning for China's Minorities."
3. Chun Cao, "The Hani Christians," *Bridge* (September-October 1990): 9.
4. Conner, "Midge's Musings," 3 May 1997.
5. See Li Yongsui and Wang (eds.), *Haniyu Jianzhi*, for a detailed word list and linguistic discussion of Biyo.
6. Dodd, *The Tai Race*, 84.
7. Chun Cao, "The Hani Christians," 9.
8. T'ien, *Peaks of Faith*, 98.
9. YASS 297, no. 3, as cited in T'ien, *Peaks of Faith*, 80.

BOGOL

1. Henry G. Schwartz, *The Minorities of Northern China: A Survey* (Western Washington University Press, Center for East Asian Studies, 1984), 119.
2. Sachiko Hatanaka, "Ethnicity and Culture Complex in the Northern Minorities," in Chiao and Tapp, *Ethnicity and Ethnic Groups in China*, 29.
3. *Mission Frontiers* (April 1995).
4. Hatanaka, "Ethnicity and Culture Complex," 29.
5. Schwartz, *The Minorities of Northern China*, 131.

BOKA

1. "The Boka live in south central Pingbian County, Honghe Prefecture, principally in the communities and villages of Dishuiceng District. Xile and Mawei communities of Baihe District also have many Boka. Another significant collection of Boka live in Heping District, Hongxiang community of northeastern Pingbian County. Pelkey, "Yunnan's Myriad Yi," 13.
2. Ibid., 14.
3. Pelkey, "Report on the Yi Peoples of Honghe Prefecture," 11.
4. Ibid., 12.

BOLOZI

1. Thomas F. Torrance, Jr., "Journal of My First Visit to Hong Kong, Chengdu and Wenchuan, April 22 to June 3, 1994," unpublished report (Edinburgh, 1994): 41.

2. David Crocket Graham, *The Customs and Religions of the Ch'iang* (Washington DC: Smithsonian Institute, 1958), 13-14.
3. Stauffer, *The Christian Occupation of China*, 225.

BONAN

1. Australian Academy and CASS, *LAC*, C-5. According to the 1990 census there was only one county or municipality in China that recorded more than 500 Bonan people. Jishishan County recorded 10,048 Bonan. This figure includes some members of the Bonan, Tongren group.
2. Schwartz, *The Minorities of Northern China*, 141.
3. Ibid., 139.
4. *Global Prayer Digest* (*GPD*) 15, no. 11 (November 1996).
5. Schwartz, *The Minorities of Northern China*, 46.
6. *CPLMR*, no. 119 (December 1991-February 1992).
7. Stauffer, *The Christian Occupation of China*, 266.

BONAN, TONGREN

1. *Mission Frontiers* (April 1995).
2. Buliash Todaeva, "Einige Besonderheiten der Paoan-Sprache," *Acta Orientalia Hungaricae*, no. 16 (1963): 175-97.
3. Schwartz, *The Minorities of Northern China*, 139.
4. Ibid.
5. Stauffer, *The Christian Occupation of China*, 266.
6. See Covell, *The Liberating Gospel*, 75.

BOUYEI

1. Linguist Jerold Edmonson, in *Languages of the Vietnam-China Borderlands*, University of Texas at Arlington, 1996, states the Giay of Vietnam speak a language identitcal to Bouyei. In China, the Giay have been officially included as part of the Zhuang nationality. The Bouyei of Ha Giang in Vietnam still speak their mother tongue, but those located in Lao Cai can now only speak Mandarin Chinese. See Dang; Chu and Luu, *Ethnic Minorities in Vietnam*, 139.
2. According to the 1990 census there were 58 counties or municipalities in China that recorded more than 500 Bouyei people. In descending order, the largest Bouyei populations are found in the counties: Dushan 162,569; Duyun 161,222; Wangmo 153,880; Luodian 144,706; Ceheng 135,406; Huishui 130,822; Zhenning 123,367; Anlong 123,070; Pingtang 122,998, and Zhenfeng 115,722.
3. Anthony Diller, "Tai Languages: Varieties and Subgroup Terms" (Canberra: ANU Faculty of Asian Studies, 1993).
4. "The Hidden Buyi People," prayer brochure (Pasadena: The Institute of Chinese Studies, n.d.).
5. John Kuhn, *We Found a Hundred Tribes*.
6. Samuel Clarke, *Among the Tribes in South-West China*, 107.
7. Grimes, *Ethnologue* (1992), 526, states "there are at least 40 dialects" of Bouyei. This is probably derived from the 1959 Bouyei linguistic survey, which surveyed 40 different places in Guizhou.
8. *Pray for China*, no. 127 (November-December 1995).
9. Ibid.
10. Dang; Chu and Luu, *Ethnic Minorities in Vietnam*, 139.
11. *Pray for China*, no. 127 (November-December 1995).
12. Samuel Clarke, *Among the Tribes in South-West China*, 140.
13. *CPLMR*, no. 119 (December 1991-February 1992).
14. Personal communication, July 1996.
15. *Qianxinan Buyizu Miaozu Zhihizhou Gaikuang* (1985), 67-68.
16. There has been some confusion regarding whether or not the Bouyei had Scripture portions translated into their language in 1904 by Samuel Clarke. Clarke labelled his work "Chungchia" which has led some to believe they were in a variety of Northern Zhuang rather than Bouyei. However, Clarke translated the portions in a village "barely five English miles from Guiyang," which is in Bouyei territory and not close to Northern Zhuang. See Heijdra, "Who Were the Laka?" 173. Although the work is now obsolete and cannot be read by the Bouyei, it may give help to future Bible translators among them.

BUDO

1. Xie Shixun, "The Hanis of the Ailao Mountains," 45.
2. Diller, "Tai Languages."
3. John Kuhn, *We Found a Hundred Tribes*.
4. Ma Yin, *China's Minority Nationalities*, 257.
5. H. A. Baker, *God in Kado Land* (Taiwan: The Adullam Reading Campaign, 1937), 147-48.
6. The Jensens were forced to leave China in 1949. Christine Jensen died soon after they returned to Denmark, but Axle Jensen lived to be 92 years old, and died in 1989. He wrote a book in Danish about their work in China, entitled *My Call to China*. Alfred Jensen, personal communication, Denmark, April 1998.

BUGAN

1. Li Jinfang, "Bugan: A New Mon-Khmer Language of Yunnan Province, China," *Mon-Khmer Studies*, no. 26 (1996): 135-60.
2. de Beauclair, *Tribal Cultures of Southwest China*, 9.
3. James and Marti Hefley, *China! Christian Martyrs of the 20th Century: an excerpt from 'By Their Blood'* (Michigan: Mott Media, 1978), 46.

BULANG

1. About 200 of the Bulang in Thailand are employed as gardeners in the suburbs of Bangkok.
2. According to the 1990 census there were 14 counties or municipalities in China that recorded more than 500 Bulang people. In descending order, the largest populations are found in: Menghai 27,755; Shuangjiang 11,725; Yongde 6,521; Lancang 6,503; Shidian 6,018; Yunxian 5,744, and Jinghong 4,834.
3. Several comprehensive studies into the Bulang language have been conducted in recent years, including Karen L. Block, "Discourse Grammar of First Person Narrative in Plang" (Arlington: University of Texas, 1994), xii, 168; Block, "What Makes a Story a Story in Plang?" *Mon-Khmer Studies*, no. 26 (1996): 357-85; and Debbie Paulsen, "A Phonological Reconstruction of Proto-Plang," *Mon-Khmer Studies* 18-19 (1992): 160-222.
4. Grimes, *Ethnologue* (1996), 783.
5. J.-O. Svantesson, 1990 personal communication, as cited in Grimes, *Ethnologue* (1992), 513.
6. *CPLMR*, no. 119 (December 1991-February 1992).
7. This official 1990 census figure appears to disagree with that cited under "Population in China." The larger figure (82,280) includes several groups (Angku, Kong Ge, Puman, and Samtao) which are profiled separately in *Operation China*. Therefore, their combined population is subtracted to give a more realistic and specific figure (61,900) for the Bulang.

BUNAN

1. GEM, "World's Peoples Listed By Country".

2. Grimes, *Ethnologue* (1996), 542.
3. GEM, "World's Peoples Listed By Country".
4. Grimes, *Ethnologue* (1996), 573.
5. Buckley and Strauss (eds.), *Tibet*, 249.

BUNU

1. Michael Johnson, personal communication, January 1998.
2. Bradley, "East and South-East Asia," 164.
3. Michael Johnson, "An Overview of Hmongic Languages and Linguistics (including updated 1996 research)," ms. (Chiang Mai, Thailand, 1995): 6.
4. "Yao Wedding Customs Traced Through Papercuts," *China Tourism*, no. 141 (March 1992): 86.
5. Huang Yu, "Preliminary Study of the Yao 'King Ping's Charter'," 94-95.
6. Ibid.
7. "The Yao of China and Southeast Asia," *Yao Update*, Irving, Texas.
8. This official 1982 census figure appears to conflict with the number cited under Population in China. The larger figure includes the 1982 populations of 11 subgroups of Bunu which are profiled separately in *Operation China*. Therefore, to arrive at a more realistic figure, their combined population is subtracted from 439,000 to give a population of 165,500 Bunu.

BUNUN

1. The author had a conversation with a Gaoshan in China in 1995. He claimed there were nine Gaoshan languages spoken in Fujian Province. No documentation has been cited to support this assertion.
2. *Chinese Around the World* (March 1995): 9.
3. Farrell, "Taiwan Aboriginal Groups," 34.
4. Covell, *Pentecost of the Hills in Taiwan*, 61.
5. Ho Ting-jui, *A Comparative Study of the Myths and Legends of Formosan Aborigines* (Taipei: Orient Cultural Service, 1971), 246-47.
6. *Chinese Around the World* (March 1995): 10.
7. Cliff Vost, *The Tribes of Taiwan* (Taiwan: Vision International, 1995).
8. Covell, *Pentecost of the Hills in Taiwan*, 17.
9. Farrell, "Taiwan Aboriginal Groups," 34.
10. Covell, *Pentecost of the Hills in Taiwan*, 222.
11. Ibid., 282.

BUNUO

1. Norma Diamond, "Defining the Miao," 105, in Harrell (ed.), *Cultural Encounters on China's Ethnic Frontiers*.

BURIAT

1. Slaviska Missionen, *Pray for Us*, prayer booklet (Stockholm, 1995).
2. Issachar Frontier Missions Research, *Mongolia Challenge Report: A Summary of Current Spiritual Needs and a Strategy for Response* (Seattle: Issachar, 1984), II, 2, i.
3. Ibid.
4. Juha Janhunen and Tapani Salminen, *UNESCO Red Book on Endangered Languages: Northeast Asia* (Helsinki, Finland: University of Helsinki, 1996).
5. Kang Jie, "The Buryats From Siberia," *China Tourism, no.* 83 (n.d.): 30.
6. William Swan, *Letters on Missions* (Boston: Perkins & Marvin, 1831), 179, as cited in Covell, *The Liberating Gospel*, 119.
7. Slaviska Missionen, *Pray for Us*.
8. Stauffer, *The Christian Occupation of China*, 273.
9. "Buriat-Mongolian Mission, Siberia," *The Evangelical Magazine and Missionary Chronicle*, no. 11 (July 1883): 328-31.
10. William Swan, *Missionary Magazine* (October 1937): 499-500.
11. Marshall Broomhall, *The Bible in China* (London: CIM, 1934), 128-29.

BUYANG

1. Liang Min, "The Buyang Language," in Jerold A. Edmonson, *Kadai: Discussions in Kadai and S. E. Asian Linguistics* (Arlington: University of Texas, 1990), 13.
2. V. Li, *Some Approaches to the Classification of Small Ethnic Groups*. Also see *Zhuangzu Jianshu* (Nanning: Guangxi Renmin Chubanshe, 1980), 9.
3. Dodd, *The Tai Race*, 94.
4. Liang Min, "The Buyang Language," 13.
5. Shaw, "Some Current Trends of Ethnology in China," 56.

CAI

1. *Minzu Shibie Wenxian Ziliao Huibian*, 28.
2. *Guizhou Nianjian 1985*, 340-41.

CAO LAN

1. GEM, "World Peoples Listed by Country." Wurm and Hattori, *Language Atlas of the Pacific Area* lists a total of 100,000 Cao Lan in both Vietnam and China. A 1986 figure places 77,000 in Vietnam. See Grimes, *Ethnologue* (1992), 523.
2. Bradley, "East and South-East Asia," 164.
3. Grimes, *Ethnologue* (1996), 566.
4. Diller, "Tai Languages."
5. Vietnam News Agency, *Vietnam*, 166.
6. Quincy, *Hmong*, 66-69.
7. Dang; Chu and Luu, *Ethnic Minorities in Vietnam*, 127.

CHANGPAO

1. See *Minzu Shibie Wenxian Ziliao Huibian*, 340-41.
2. Stauffer, *The Christian Occupation of China*, 175.
3. See *Guizhou Nianjian 1985*.

CHANGSHU MIAO

1. Corrigan, *Odyssey Illustrated Guide to Guizhou*, 60.
2. Michael Johnson, "Far Western Hmongic," ms. (Chiang Mai, Thailand, February 1998): 33.

CHESU

1. *Chuxiong Yizu Zizhizhou Zhi*, no. 1 (Beijing: Renmin Chubanshe, 1993), 361.
2. *Shuangbai Xian Zhi* (1996), 90.
3. Dun J. Li, *The Ageless Chinese: A History*, 140, as cited in Covell, *The Liberating Gospel*, 18.
4. Covell, *The Liberating Gospel*, 18.

CHIN, ASHO

1. Milliken, "SIL China Nationalities and Languages Files."
2. Grimes, *Ethnologue* (1996), 716.
3. Personal communication with Asho Chin in Yangon, Myanmar, April 1996.
4. Kuhn, *We Found a Hundred Tribes*, 19.
5. Johnstone, *Operation World*, 398, lists 916,000 Chin in Myanmar. Grimes, *Ethnologue* (1996), lists at least 369,000 Chin in India.

6. Sir George Scott, "Among the Hill Tribes of Burma: An Ethnological Thicket," *National Geographic* (March 1922): 301.
7. *Christian Mission* (Christian Aid Mission, January-February 1992).
8. Ibid.
9. *GPD* 7, no. 8 (August 1988).

CHRAME

1. Joseph F. Rock, "The Land of the Yellow Lama", *National Geographic* (April 1925): 467. There were a total of 34,616 "Tibetans" living in Muli County according to the 1990 census. The majority of these are Chrame people.
2. Torrance, Jr., "Journal of My First Visit."
3. Rock, "The Land of the Yellow Lama," 467.
4. Joseph F. Rock, "Konka Risumgongba: Holy Mountain of the Outlaws," *National Geographic* (July 1931): 1.
5. Ethno-historian Leo Moser writes, "As far back as the Shang times, the known world was conceived as a system of concentric circles or squares. At the center was the Shang capital. Surrounding it were the lands under the direct sovereignty of the Shang; surrounding these were a zone of feudal states... under a loose Shang hegemony; surrounding that were the outer states, in which semibarbarian or barbarian peoples resided. The barbarians were often called *sifang*, or '[people of the] four directions.'" Moser, *The Chinese Mosaic: The Peoples and Provinces of China* (Boulder: Westview Press, 1985), 23.
6. Harrell, "Ethnicity and Kin Terms," 181.
7. Rock, "The Land of the Yellow Lama," 477.
8. Ibid., 467.
9. Rock, "Konka Risumgongba," 19.
10. Ibid.
11. Ruxian Yan, "Marriage, Family and Social Progress of China's Minority Nationalities," in Chiao and Tapp, *Ethnicity and Ethnic Groups in China*, 87.
12. Rock, "The Land of the Yellow Lama," 477.

CHUANLAN

1. Fei Xiaotong, "Xin Zhongguo de Minzuxue Yanjiu yu Fazhan," in Lin Yuehua, *Minzuxue Yanjiu*.
2. V. Li, *Some Approaches to the Classification of Small Ethnic Groups*.
3. Samuel Clarke, *Among the Tribes in South-West China*, 10.
4. V. Li, *Some Approaches to the Classification of Small Ethnic Groups*.
5. Samuel Clarke, *Among the Tribes in South-West China*, 10.
6. "God's Presence Among the Miao," *Bridge*, no. 24 (July-August 1987): 4.
7. Ibid.

CHUANQING

1. *Minzu Shibie Wenxian Ziliao Huibian*, 68. In 1952, their population was given as "more than 200,000." Fei Xiaotong, "Xin Zhongguo de Minzuxue Yanjiu yu Fazhan."
2. Some sources state that the Chuanqing have been officially included in the Han nationality, however, this is not true. This misconception is based on the English translation of Fei Xiaotong's "Identification of Nationalities in China," 66-69, but the Chinese version of the same article simply says "we consider them Chinese," 167. Both the *Minzu Shibie Wenxian Ziliao Huibian*, 68-72, and the *Guizhou Nianjian 1985*, 341, say the Chuanqing remain the largest unclassified group in China.
3. Fei Xiaotong, "On Identification of Nationalities in China," 98-100.
4. *Frontiers Focus* 5, no. 2.
5. Samuel Clarke, *Among the Tribes in South-West China*, 9. One subgroup of the Chuanqing was known as the *Fang Teo Ren* ('Phoenix-Headed People') in reference to the hairdress of the women. Ibid., 10.
6. Moser, *The Chinese Mosaic*, 97.
7. *Minzu Shibie Wenxian Ziliao Huibian*, 68.
8. A recent figure for Catholics in Guizhou has not been published, but there were 100,000 before 1949. See *Bridge* (July-August 1987).

CUN

1. Bradley, "East And South-East Asia," 165.
2. Jiangxi Educational Publishing, *EDCL*, 569-70.
3. Grimes, *Ethnologue* (1996), 546.
4. Training Evangelistic Leadership, personal communication, June 1994.

DAIZHAN

1. Pelkey, "Yunnan's Myriad Yi," 30.
2. *Kaiyuan Xian Zhi* (1996), 618.
3. Samuel Clarke, *Among the Tribes in South-West China*, 115.
4. Roland Allen, *Missionary Methods: St Paul's or Ours* (London: World Dominion Press, 1912).

DAUR

1. According to the 1990 census there were 27 counties or municipalities in China that recorded more than 500 Daur people. In descending order, the largest populations are found in: Morindawa (Inner Mongolia) 26,289; Qiqihar (Heilongjiang) 21,748; Ewenki Banner (Inner Mongolia) 13,929; Elunchun (Inner Mongolia) 6,369; Fuyu (Heilongjiang) 5,932; and Zaluntun (Inner Mongolia) 4,810.
2. John F. Baddeley, *Russia, Mongolia, China* (New York, 1919), 428.
3. Ibid.
4. N. N. Poppe, *Dagurskoe Narechie* [The Daur Dialect] (Leningrad, 1930), 5.
5. Janhunen and Salminen, *UNESCO Red Book*.
6. The most comprehensive survey of the Daur language is Samuel E. Martin, *Dagur Mongolian Grammar. Texts and Lexicon Based on the Speech of Peter Onan* (Bloomington: Indiana University Press, 1961).
7. Schwartz, *The Minorities of Northern China*, 121.
8. Baddeley, *Russia, Mongolia, China* 2: 446.
9. Cheng Weidong, "Descendants of Hunters and Fairies: North China's Little-Known Daur People," *China Tourism*, no. 155 (May 1993): 33.
10. This official 1990 census figure for the total Daur population seems to be in conflict with that cited under Population in China. However, this larger figure (121,357) includes figures for the Western Daur (4,369) and the Bogol (1,000). This combined number is subtracted to give a more realistic and specific population (116,000) for the Daur.

DAUR, WESTERN

1. Edward Murray, "With the Nomads of Central Asia: A Summer's Sojourn in the Tekes Valley, Plateau Paradise of Mongol and Turkic Tribes," *National Geographic* (January 1936): 1.

2. Janhunen and Salminen, *UNESCO Red Book.*
3. *Zhongguo Shaoshu Minzu Jiankuang* 1: 28.
4. Cheng Weidong, "Descendants of Hunters and Fairies," 33.
5. Schwartz, *The Minorities of Northern China*, 131.

DE'ANG, PALE
1. Bradley, "East And South-East Asia," 159. According to the 1990 census there were a total of 8,153 De'ang people in Luxi County.
2. John Kuhn, *We Found a Hundred Tribes*, 14.
3. See Li Tseng Hsiu, "The Sacred Mission: An American Missionary Family in the Lahu and Wa Districts of Yunnan," thesis at Baylor University (Waco, Texas, 1987): 8.
4. See AMO, "The Palaung," *Newsletter*, no. 38 (March 1996).

DE'ANG, RUMAI
1. According to the 1990 census there were 980 De'ang people in Longchuan County and 955 in Ruili. This suggests the Rumai are also located in areas outside these two counties.
2. Carl F. Voegelin and Florence M. Voegelin, *Classification and Index of the World's Languages* (New York: Elsevier North Holland, 1977).
3. Zhang Weiwen and Zeng, *In Search of China's Minorities*, 228.
4. Ibid., 232.

DE'ANG, SHWE
1. Jiangxi Educational Publishing, *EDCL*, 593. According to the 1990 census there were 1,762 De'ang people in Zhenkang County and 955 in Baoshan. This suggests the De'ang Shwe are also located in areas outside these two counties.
2. Grimes, *Ethnologue* (1996), 558.
3. Although the De'ang believe themselves to be the brothers of the Karen, this is extremely unlikely as the Karen speak a Tibeto-Burman language, while the De'ang speak a Mon-Khmer language. However, both groups were among the original inhabitants of Myanmar, and lived alongside each other in the past. In the De'ang language they call the Karen *Dayang*. Some De'ang in Myanmar also call themselves *Dayang*.
4. *Unreached Peoples '79* (Colorado: David Cook Publishers, 1979).

DENG, DARANG
1. Australian Academy and CASS, *LAC*, C-10.
2. Jiangxi Educational Publishing, *EDCL*, 545.
3. *Zizang Shehui Jingji Tongji Nianjian* (Beijing: Zhongguo Tongji Chubanshe, 1989), 140-41.
4. CASS, *Information China* 3: 1249.
5. Mackerras, *China's Minorities,* 143.
6. See Sun Hongkai, Lu Shaozun, Zhang Jichuan and Ouyang Jueya, *The Languages of the Menba, Luoba and Deng Peoples* (Beijing: Chinese Social Science Publishing House, 1980).
7. Grimes, *Ethnologue* (1996), 546.
8. Rong Mei, "On the Sichuan-Tibet Highway," *China Tourism*, no. 74 (n.d.): 28.
9. Ibid.
10. *GPD* 18, no. 4 (April 1999).

DENG, GEMAN
1. Rong Mei, "On the Sichuan-Tibet Highway," 29.
2. Xu Yixi (ed.), *Headdresses of Chinese Minority Nationality Women* (Hong Kong: China Film Press, 1989), 49.

DEPO
1. *Chuxiong Yizu Zizhizhou Zhi*, 361.
2. Pelkey, "Yunnan's Myriad Yi," 69.

DERUNG
1. "The Drung," *Chinese Around the World* (July 1996).
2. Joseph F. Rock, "Through the Great River Trenches of Asia," *National Geographic* (August 1926): 181.
3. J.-O. Svantesson, 1990 personal communication, as cited in Grimes, *Ethnologue* (1992), 517.
4. Grimes, *Ethnologue* (1996), 722.
5. Ibid.
6. An interesting book about one man's determined attempts over a three-year period to visit the Derung, is Wade Brackenbury, *Yak Butter & Black Tea: A Journey Into Forbidden China* (Chapel Hill: Algonquin Books, 1997).
7. "The Drung," *Chinese Around the World* (July 1996).
8. Ibid.
9. The Morse family are well known for their exodus from China to Burma. See Eugene Morse, *Exodus to a Hidden Valley* (New York: Reader's Digest Press, 1974).
10. *CPLMR*, no. 119 (December 1991-February 1992). "I believe the lower figure to be more realistic," John Morse, personal communication, January 1998.
11. This official 1990 census figure appears to disagree with that cited under Population in China. Since the larger figure (5,816) also includes the Rawang people group, their number (500) is subtracted to give a more realistic and specific population figure (5,316) for the Derung.

DIANBAO
1. Australian Academy and CASS, *LAC,* C-7.
2. Diller, "Tai Languages."
3. Milliken, "SIL China Nationalities and Languages Files."
4. de Beauclair, *Tribal Cultures of South West China*, 9
5. Ibid.
6. See Li Fang-Gui, "The Songs of the T'ien-Pao, With a Phonological Sketch," *Academy Sinica: Bulletin of the Institute of Ethnology*, no. 30 (1970): 1-21.
7. Stauffer, *The Christian Occupation of China*, 350.

DIAO
1. See *Minzu Shibie Wenxian Ziliao Huibian.*
2. *Guizhou Nianjian 1985.*

DIGAO
1. Pelkey, "Yunnan's Myriad Yi," 29.
2. *Kaiyuan Xian Zhi* (1996), 618.
3. Marco Polo, *The Travels of Marco Polo: Yule-Cordier*, 53. The "great lake" referred to by Polo may be the lake near today's Xichang in southern Sichuan Province and home today of the Nosu Yi people.

DONG, NORTHERN
1. According to the 1990 census there were 63 counties or municipalities in China that recorded more than 500 Dong people. In descending order, the largest Dong populations (both Northern and Southern Dong) are in: Liping (*Guizhou*) 274,710; Tianzhu (*Guizhou*) 236,568; Xinhuang (*Hunan*) 180,429; Sanjiang (*Guangxi*) 171,925; Zhijiang (*Hunan*) 155,783; Huitong (*Hunan*) 154,849; Tongdao (*Hunan*) 147,879; Congjiang (*Guizhou*) 108,056 and Rongjiang (*Guizhou*) 97,496.

2. Milliken, "SIL China Nationalities and Languages Files."
3. See Wang Dewen, "A Comparative Study of Kam and Sui Initial Consonants," in SIL, *Comparative Kadai*, 129-41.
4. See Somsonge Burusphat, "Surface Indicators of Storyline in the Kam Origin Myth," *Mon-Khmer Studies*, no. 26 (1996): 339-55.
5. Gail Rossi, *The Dong People of China: A Hidden Civilization* (Singapore: Hagley & Hoyle, 1990), 5.
6. *CPLMR*, no. 119 (December 1991-February 1992).

DONG, SOUTHERN

1. See Zheng Guoqiao and Quam Yang, "The Sounds of Rongjiang Kam," in SIL, *Comparative Kadai*, 43-58.
2. Jerold Edmonson, as cited in Grimes, *Ethnologue* (1996), 546.
3. Ma Yin, *China's Minority Nationalities*, 356.
4. Kevin Sinclair, *The Forgotten Tribes of China* (Canada: Cupress, 1987), 97.
5. "We took two new Dong converts out of their village for intense Bible study for three weeks, and sent them back home. One month later, we brought the same two converts out for training. They told us the great news of the miracle of multiplication that was taking place in their village. Just in one short month they grew from two to 40 believers and have a house church in their village now." *Forward Momentum*, mission newsletter, February 1999.

DONGNU

1. Wang Fushi and Mao, *Reconstruction of Proto Miao-Yao*.

DONGXIANG

1. According to the 1990 census there were 28 counties or municipalities in China that recorded more than 500 Dongxiang people. In descending order, the largest Dongxiang populations are in: Dongxiang County (*Gansu*) 172,578; Guanghe (*Gansu*) 43,364; Hezhang (*Gansu*) 40,919; Linxia (*Gansu*) 21,710; Yining (*Xinjiang*) 20,885; Jishishan (*Gansu*) 15,287; and Huocheng (*Xinjiang*) 14,153. Other counties outside of Gansu with significant Dongxiang populations include Tacheng (*Xinjiang*) 2,560; Haiyuan (*Ningxia*) 2,381 and Gongliu (*Xinjiang*) 2,344. An additional 12 counties in Xinjiang contain more than 500 Dongxiang people.
2. Midge Conner, personal communication, October 1995.
3. Schwartz, *The Minorities of Northern China*, 101.
4. Ibid., 100. Today, the Yang clan in Yangzhijia claim to be descended from Tibetans. The Ma and the Mu clans are descended from Hui; and the Wang, Kang, Zhang, Gao, and Huang say they are descended from Han Chinese.
5. Ibid., 99.
6. *Zhongguo Shaoshu Minzu Jiankuang*, 5: 24-35.
7. *GPD* 10, no. 1 (January 1991).
8. See AMO, "The Dongxiang," *Newsletter*, no. 22 (August 1993).
9. Personal communication, August 1997.

DOUPO

1. Pelkey, "Yunnan's Myriad Yi," 85.
2. Ibid., 62.

DUOLUO

1. According to Zheng Guo-qiao, as cited in Milliken, "SIL China Nationalities and Languages Files."
2. de Beauclair, *Tribal Cultures of Southwest China*, 6.
3. Grimes, *Ethnologue* (1996), 548.
4. Samuel Clarke, *Among the Tribes in South-West China*, 14.
5. Ma Yin, *China's Minority Nationalities*, 365.
6. Ibid.

DUOTA

1. Hao Yaojun, "Carnival Mood Among the Hanis," *China Tourism*, no. 97 (n.d.): 60.
2. Ibid., 62.

E

1. Jiangxi Educational Publishing, *EDCL*, 570.
2. See Jerold A. Edmonson, "Fusion and Diffusion in E," in *Kadai*.
3. Jiangxi Educational Publishing, *EDCL*, 570-71.
4. Milliken, "*SIL China Nationalities and Languages* Files."
5. Jiangxi Educational Publishing, *EDCL*, 570-71.
6. Mrs Howard Taylor, *Guinness of Honan. By His Sister Mrs. Howard Taylor* (Philadelphia: CIM).

EKA

1. Pelkey, "Yunnan's Myriad Yi," 49.
2. d'Ollone, *In Forbidden China*, 173.
3. Pelkey, "Yunnan's Myriad Yi," 50.

ENIPU

1. *Weishan Yizu Huizu Zizhixian Zhi* (1993), 142-56.
2. Pelkey, "Yunnan's Myriad Yi," 59.
3. Paul Vial, "Les Lolos: Histoire, Religion, Moeurs, Langue, Ecriture" [The Lolos: History, Religion, Customs, Language, Writing], in *Etudes Sino-Orientales Part A* (Shanghai: Imprimerie de la Mission Catholique, 1898), Preface.
4. See Ma Changshou, "The Genealogical Table of the Lolos at Liangshan, Western Szechuan," *Bianjiang Yenjiu Luncong* 44, no. 4 (1942).
5. Dessaint, *Minorities in Southwestern China*, 227.

ENU

1. L. Gaide, "Notice Ethnographique sur les Principales Races Indigenes de la Chine Meridionale (Yun-nam en Particulier) et du Nord de l'Indo-Chine," *Annales d'Hygiene et de Medicine Coloniales*, no. 5 (1903).
2. John Kuhn, *We Found a Hundred Tribes*.
3. See Li Yongsui and Wang (eds.), *Haniyu Jianzhi*.
4. Matisoff, "Languages and Dialects of Tibeto-Burman."
5. Dwayne Graybill, personal communication, November 1996.
6. Ruth Tucker, *Guardians of the Great Commission* (Grand Rapids: Zondervan, 1988), 42.

ERGONG

1. See Sun Hongkai, "Chuanxi Minzu Zoulang Diqu de Yuyan" in *Xinan Minzu Yanjiu* (Chengdu: Sichuan Minzu Chubanshe, 1983). According to Jonathon Evans (personal communication, August 1999), Ergong (Horpa) speakers inhabit central and eastern Daofu County (Chengguan District, Wari, Xiajia and Muru townships of Wari District, Shazhong Township of Bamei District); and central and northwestern Danba County (Geshiza, Bianer, and Dandong townships of Dasang District, Donggu Township in Chuangu District, Bawang and Jinchuan townships of Jinchuan District) of Garze Prefecture, an area traditionally known as the five parts of Horpa territory. Scattered communities are also reported in adjacent Luhuo County (Renda Township of Xialatuo District) and Xinlong County (in Manqing, Zhuwo, and Duozhan townships of Hexi District).
2. See Jackson Sun, "Review of Zangmian Yu Yuyin Han

Cohui," 73-113; and Matisoff, "Languages and Dialects of Tibeto-Burman."

3. See B. H. Hodgson, "Sifán and Hórsók Vocabularies," *Journal of the Asiatic Society of Bengal*, no. 22 (1874); also Hodgson, "On the Tribes of Northern Tibet (Horyeul and Sokyeul) and of Sifan," in *Essays on the Languages, Literatures, and Religions of Nepal and Tibet* (London: Trubner & Co., 1874).The Ergong were also discussed by J. H. Edgar, "The Horpa of the Upper Nya or Yalung," *Journal of West China Border Research Society* (1932).
4. Sino-Tibetan Etymological Dictionary and Thesaurus (STEDT), *Description of the Sino-Tibetan Language Family* (Berkeley: University of California, Department of Linguists, 1996).
5. AMO, *The 50 Most Unreached People Groups of China and Tibet*, Preface.

ERSU

1. Jiangxi Educational Publishing, *EDCL*, 541-42.
2. See Jackson T. S. Sun (trans.), "Languages of the Ethnic Corridor in Western Sichuan," *Linguistics of the Tibeto-Burman Area* 13, no. 1 (Spring 1990): 2. The Ersu view themselves as related to other ethnic groups such as the Ergong and Chrame, along with whom they also wanted to be part of an official *Xifan* minority group.
3. Grimes, *Ethnologue* (1996), 547.
4. STEDT, *Description of the Sino-Tibetan Language Family*.
5. Audrey Muse, "A Profile of the Jiarong People of China," report, May 1996.

EWENKI, SOLON

1. According to Chao Ke, as cited in Milliken, "SIL China Nationalities and Languages Files."
2. According to the 1990 census there were 10 counties or municipalities in China that recorded more than 500 Ewenki people. These include Ewenki Banner (Inner Mongolia) 8,621; Morindawa (Inner Mongolia) 4,923; Elunchun (Inner Mongolia) 2,959; Arong (Inner Mongolia) 1,866; Nehe (Heilongjiang) 826, and Nenjiang (Heilongjiang) 609.
3. Ramsey, *The Languages of China*, 214.
4. See Igor Nedyalkov, "Evenki," *Topological Studies in Language*, no. 29 (Amsterdam, 1994): 1-34.
5. Hatanaka, "Ethnicity and Culture Complex," 29.
6. Schwartz, *The Minorities of Northern China*, 172.
7. Johannes Reimer, *Operation Soviet Union* (Fresno, CA: Logos, 1990).

EWENKI, TUNGUS

1. Janhunen and Salminen, *UNESCO Red Book*. According to the 1990 census there were a total of 1,867 Ewenki people living in the Chenbaehru Banner of Inner Mongolia.
2. Ibid.
3. Ibid.
4. "The Ewenkis," *Chinese Around the World* (June-July 1995): 9.
5. Ibid. See also *CPLMR*, no. 119 (December 1991-February 1992).
6. "The Ewenkis," 10.
7. Slaviska Missionen, *Pray for Us*.

FUMA

1. Training Evangelistic Leadership, personal communication, May 1994.
2. Stauffer, *The Christian Occupation of China*, 348.

GAIJI

1. Pelkey, "Yunnan's Myriad Yi," 49.
2. Ibid.
3. Pelkey, "Report on the Yi Peoples of Honghe Prefecture," 7. This information specifically refers to the Axi people, but the custom is also practiced by the Gaiji in some areas.

GAISU, SOUTHERN

1. Pelkey, "Report on the Yi Peoples of Honghe Prefecture," 9.
2. Ibid.

GAISU, WESTERN

1. Pelkey, "Yunnan's Myriad Yi," 47.

GA MONG

1. Chen Chao Qui, *Duyun Shi Minzu Zi* (Guizhou: Duyun Nationalities Affairs Publishing House, 1990), 171.
2. Ibid.
3. *Guizhou Nianjian 1997*. This new classification is ridiculous from an ethnolinguistic viewpoint. The Ga Mong speak a Western Hmongic language, but because they did not like being part of the Miao nationality it appears the government has compromised by putting them into the non-offensive She nationality, even though there are no historical or ethnolinguistic links between the Ga Mong and She to justify this.
4. Grimes, *Ethnologue* (1996), 549.
5. Graybill, personal communication, October 1997.
6. *Minzu Shibie Wenxian Ziliao Huibian*, 37.
7. Chen Chao, *Duyun Shi Minzu Zi*, 171.
8. Graybill, personal communication, October 1997.

GAO

1. According to Zheng Guo-qiao, as cited in Milliken, "SIL China Nationalities and Languages Files."
2. Ibid.
3. Samuel Clarke, *Among the Tribes in South-West China*, 13.
4. *Amity News Service*, January 1993.

GE

1. Wong How-Man, "Peoples of China's Far Provinces," 315.
2. Corrigan, *Odyssey Illustrated Guide to Guizhou*, 127.
3. A Hmong Daw Christian visited the Ge area in 1994. The Ge were amazed that he could speak their language and asked where he had learned to speak Ge. When he told them it was also his language, the Ge were offended and would not speak to him any more! Mike and Melissa Miao, personal communication, September 1997.
4. *The Book of a Thousand Tongues* (Detroit: Tower Books, 1971), 224.
5. Enwall, *A Myth Become Reality* 1: 159.
6. AMO, *The 50 Most Unreached People Groups of China and Tibet*, 14.
7. M. H. Hutton, "The New Testament for the Black Miao," *China's Millions* (November 1935): 205.
8. M. H. Hutton, "Fruit After Many Days," *China's Millions* (Australasian edition, August 1936): 137.
9. M. H. Hutton, "Steady Advancement," *China's Millions* (Australasian edition, August 1937): 124.
10. According to Pan Wenguang, as cited in Enwall, *A Myth Becomes Reality* 1: 159.

GELAO

1. This official 1990 census figure seems to disagree with that cited under Population in China. However, the larger figure (437,997) includes five ethnic groups (Gao, Yizi, Hagei, A'ou, and Duoluo) which are profiled separately in *Operation China*. Therefore, their combined population is subtracted to give a more realistic and specific figure (426,917) for the Gelao.
2. In 1982 China had still not fully recovered from the dark years of the Cultural Revolution of 1966-76. It was not fashionable to be identified as a minority nationality. By 1990, however, special medical and educational benefits, together with an allowance of two children per couple, suddenly meant that being a minority was advantageous. Thousands of people traced their genealogies back to find Gelao ancestry and were granted minority status.
3. According to the 1990 census there were 36 counties or municipalities in China that recorded more than 500 Gelao people. In descending order, the largest Gelao populations (all in Guizhou Province) are: Wuchuan County 135,139; Daozhen 104,173; Shiqian 86,297; Zheng'an 20,897; Lupanshui 8,218; Guanling 6,443; Zhijin 6,158, and Qianxi 6,111.
4. "The Gelos," *Chinese Around the World* (December 1995): 9.
5. Samuel Clarke, *Among the Tribes in South-West China*, 13.
6. Bradley, "East and South-East Asia."
7. Diller, "Tai Languages."
8. Grimes, *Ethnologue* (1992), 517.
9. "The Gelos," *Chinese Around the World* (December 1995): 9.
10. Samuel Clarke, *Among the Tribes in South-West China*, 13.
11. de Beauclair, *Tribal Cultures of Southwest China*, 6.
12. Samuel Clarke, *Among the Tribes in South-West China*, 15.
13. "The Gelos," *Chinese Around the World* (December 1995): 9.
14. Many sources have listed the existence of 1937 Scripture portions for the Gelao, but these were done in the Ge language of Guizhou Province, not in Gelao.

GEPO, EASTERN

1. There were 1,106 Gepo (Bai Yi) in Mile County according to the 1987 *Mile Xian Zhi*, 689 (1984 figure).
2. Pelkey, "Report on the Yi Peoples of Honghe Prefecture," 13-14.
3. Ibid., 13. "Chinese sources also mention further distinctions among the Gepo such as *Da Bai Yi* (Greater White Yi) and *Xiao Bai Yi* (Lesser White Yi). These names actually coincide with the *Pingtou* and *Jiantou* distinctions: *Da Bai Yi* being *Jiantou* and *Xiao Bai Yi* being *Pingtou*."
4. Ibid., 13.
5. Samuel Clarke, *Among the Tribes in South-West China*, 132.
6. "The Huize Church is Bleeding," *Bridge*, no. 55 (September-October 1992): 14. The article also reports that "74 incidents of people being illegally locked up, interrogated and cruelly beaten up occurred.... In order to destroy Christianity, they [local officials] made no bones to proclaim: 'Whoever arrests Rev. Wang Jiashui of this church will be rewarded: live 300¥, dead 400¥; for the head of evangelist He Chengzhou, live 150¥, dead 200¥."

GEPO, WESTERN

1. Pelkey, "Yunnan's Myriad Yi," 51.
2. d'Ollone, *In Forbidden China*, 32-33.

GESE

1. Pelkey, "Yunnan's Myriad Yi," 68.

GESU

1. *Chuxiong Yizu Zizhizhou Zhi*, 361.
2. Fei Xiaotong, "On Identification of Nationalities in China."
3. Ma Yin, *China's Minority Nationalities*, 234.
4. This festival is primarily a Western Lipo festival, but people from many other ethnic groups in the area also participate.

GHA-MU

1. Wang Fushi and Mao, *Renconstruction of Proto Miao-Yao.*
2. For a detailed account of Gha-Mu flood stories, see Samuel Clarke, *Among the Tribes in South-West China*, 43-59.
3. Zeng Xianyang, "Dancing for Love: The Tiaohuapo Festival," *China Tourism*, no. 117 (n.d.): 69-71.
4. Mike and Melissa Miao, "The Miao of China," unpublished prayer guide, Hong Kong, 1994.
5. Ibid.
6. *Miao Messenger* 5, no. 4 (Spring 1997). Also see Paul Lau, "A Visit to the Xiaohua Miao Minority," *China Tourism*, no. 143 (May 1992): 82-85, for an interesting account of Gha-Mu customs.
7. Among many strategies designed to destroy the Gha-Mu church, the Communists allocated Christians jobs in far-flung places in separate work units, knowing that their faith was strengthened by being together in fellowship. However, this backfired on the authorities, and the gospel spread much more widely than if the believers had been left together in one place. See T'ien, *Peaks of Faith*, 93.
8. Michael Johnson, personal communication, January 1998.

GHAO-XONG, EASTERN

1. According to the 1990 census the largest populations of Miao in Hunan Province were in Mayuang County (242,840), Suining (176,929), Huayuan (175,602), Fenghuang (168,784), Chengbu (121,045), Jishou City (92,750), Jingzhou (87,124), Yuanling (77,193), and Luxi (76,898). These figures include both the Eastern and Western Ghao-Xong, as well as a small number of Hmu.
2. There are Miao in Vietnam who call themselves *Red Miao* but they are not ethnolinguistically related to the Ghao-Xong in China. In addition, there is a group of Red Miao in Wangmo County, Guizhou, but they speak a Chuanqiandian (Western) Miao dialect.
3. Sinclair, *The Forgotten Tribes of China*, 30.
4. *The Liberating Gospel*, 104.
5. "West Hunan Itinerary," *China Tourism*, no. 36 (n.d.): 35.
6. Pan Chengqian, "Yao Dialectology," 62.
7. Miao, "The Miao of China."
8. Covell, *The Liberating Gospel*, 103.
9. Theopane Maguire, *Hunan Harvest* (Milwaukee: Bruce, 1946), viii-ix.

GHAO-XONG, WESTERN

1. Wang Fushi, *Miaoyu Jianzhi*, 103-04.
2. There is a small community of about 400 Western Ghao-Xong speakers in southwest Guizhou who had migrated from Songtao during the Qing Dynasty. The Chinese call

them *Hongzu* (Red Tribe). Today only older people can still speak their language; the younger people speak Bouyei and Chinese.

3. See Enwall, *A Myth Become Reality* 2:103-11.
4. *Shengzu Shilu* (1932) 16: 2-3.
5. Cen Yuying, *Qingding Pinding Guizhou Miaofei Jilue* (Imperial edition, 1884), 36, 40.
6. Wang Jia, "The Siyueba Festival at Jiwei," *China Tourism*, no. 107 (n.d.): 61.
7. Covell, *The Liberating Gospel*, 103.
8. The Western Ghao-Xong live in the following locations: *Hunan:* Huayuan, Fenghuang, Baojing, Jishou, Guzhang, Longshan, Xinhuang and Mayang counties; *Guizhou:* Songtao and Tongren counties; *SW Hubei*: Xuan'en County; SE *Sichuan:* Xiushan and Youyang counties; *Guangxi*: Hechi and Nandan counties.

GIAY

1. Wurm and Hattori, *Language Atlas of the Pacific Area.*
2. Edmonson, *Languages of the Vietnam-China Borderlands.* Edmonson says the Giay groups in Vietnam which his team studied came from Xingyi Bajie, Anlong Bakan, Anlong Leju, Caheng Naiyan, Zhengfeng Lurong, Wangmo Zhenxiang, and the Luodian Poqiu areas of China.
3. For a detailed description of the Giay language, see William J. Gedney, *Selected Papers on Comparative Tai Studies*, no. 29 (University of Michigan, Center for South and Southeast Asian Studies, 1989).
4. Diller, "Tai Languages."
5. Dang; Chu and Luu, *Ethnic Minorities in Vietnam*, 131.

GOLOG

1. Galen Rowell, "Nomads of China's West," *National Geographic* (February 1982): 244.
2. Mackerras, *China's Minorities,* 243.
3. Rock, "Seeking the Mountains of Mystery," 131.
4. Rowell, "Nomads of China's West," 244.
5. Grimes, *Ethnologue* (1992), 517.
6. Unfortunately, because the Golog rural areas are still virtually inaccessible to outsiders, no recent anthropological or linguistic research has been conducted there. The Golog still consist of numerous small ethnolinguistic or ethno-social groups. Joseph Rock, on his 1929 trip through the region (see "Seeking the Mountains of Mystery," 140-72) briefly mentions more than a dozen tribes, clans, and groups of Golog. These include the Lhardi tribe, the fearless Ngura nomads, the Amchok robber tribe, the Rimong tribe who is described as the most powerful Golog group, the Kangsar tribe who lived west of the Yellow River, the Kanggan, the Tsokhar tribe, a Golog tribe called the Ngawa who had their own king, the Gartse tribe, the Butsang, the Shahrang robber tribe living in the Ba valley, and a clan called the Jazza who are not a Golog tribe. Despite the upheavals in the 70-year period since this article was published, most or all of these groups still exist in their separate forms. Whether they still retain ethnolinguistic distinctions or now merely social distinctions is unknown. It is hoped research will permit the inclusion of some or all of these groups in future.
7. Rowell, "Nomads of China's West," 244.
8. Bai Yu, "Life in Baima, Near the Yellow River Source," *China Tourism*, no. 138 (December 1991): 57.
9. Rock, "Seeking the Mountains of Mystery," 131.
10. Ibid.
11. In late 1921 missionaries received the following letter from Kurung Tsering, the Head Lama at a monastery in Kokonor: "I, your humble servant, have seen several copies of the Scriptures and having read them carefully, they certainly made me believe in Christ. I understand a little of the outstanding principles and the doctrinal teaching of the One Son, but as to the Holy Spirit's nature and essence, and as to the origin of this religion, I am not at all clear, and it is therefore important that the doctrinal principles of this religion should be fully explained, so as to enlighten the unintelligent and people of small mental ability. The teaching of the science of medicine and astrology is also very important. It is therefore evident if we want this blessing openly manifested, we must believe in the religion of the only Son of God. Being in earnest I therefore pray you from my heart not to consider this letter lightly. With a hundred salutations!" Stauffer, *The Christian Occupation of China*, 282.

GOUZOU

1. See *Weining Yizu Huizu Miaozu Zizhixian Minzuzhi* (1997): 12-128.
2. d'Ollone, *In Forbidden China*, 133-34.
3. Samuel Clarke, *Among the Tribes in South-West China*, 121.
4. Grimes, *Ethnologue* (1996), 564.
5. Bradley, "Language Planning for China's Minorities."
6. *The History and Culture of the Nosu Yi people of the Liang Shan*, unpublished paper (Washington, 1995).
7. See Fei Xiaotong, "The Minority Peoples in Kweichow," *China Monthly Review* 121, no. 6 (1951). For some other early accounts of the Yi in Guizhou, see George Macdonald Home Playfair, "The Miaotzu of Kewichow and Yunnan From Chinese Sources," *China Review*, no. 5 (1876); also Sainson, *Nan-ychao Ye-che* (Paris: E. Leroux, 1904).
8. Samuel Clarke, *Among the Tribes in South-West China*, 132-33.
9. Ibid., 129.
10. *Weining Yizu Huizu Miaozu Zizhixian Minzuzhi*, 128.

GROMA

1. Grimes, *Ethnologue* (1996), 548. The Groma live in the Chomo (Yadong) County in Xigaze Prefecture.
2. Covell, *The Liberating Gospel*, 33.
3. Bethany World Prayer Center, 1995 Joshua Project.
4. Grimes, *Ethnologue* (1996), 548.
5. MARC, "Bhots in the State of Sikkim," *World Christianity: South Asia* (California: MARC Publications, n.d.).
6. Leslie Lyall, *A Passion for the Impossible* (Chicago: Moody Press, 1965), 158.
7. *DAWN Report*, no. 32 (November 1997): 6.

GUAIGUN

1. Pelkey, "Yunnan's Myriad Yi," 90.
2. Samuel Clarke, *Among the Tribes in South-West China*, 127.
3. Ibid., 127-28.

GUIQIONG

1. See Sun Hongkai, "Chuanxi Minzu Zoulang Diqu de Yuyan."
2. Dong Zhaofu, "Jiaowai Luhen" [Recollections of a Trip to the Frontiers], *Bianzheng Gonglun* (1930).
3. Sun Hongkai, "Chuanxi Minzu Zoulang Diqu de Yuyan."
4. Wu Wenhui and Zhu Jianhua, "Xikang Renkou Wenti, Shang," as cited in Mackerras, *China's Minorities*, 130.

5. Eileen Crossman, *Mountain Rain: A New Biography of James O. Fraser* (Singapore: OMF, 1982), 144.

GUOPU

1. d'Ollone, *In Forbidden China*, 107-08.
2. Jun Feng, "Rolling Uplands of Northwestern Guizhou," *China Tourism*, no. 111, (n.d.): 9.

HAGEI

1. According to Zheng Guo-qiao, as cited in Milliken, "SIL China Nationalities and Languages Files."
2. Samuel Clarke, *Among the Tribes in South-West China*, 13.
3. Corrigan, *Odyssey Illustrated Guide to Guizhou*, 215.
4. "The Church in Guangxi: Challenge to the Faithful," *Bridge*, no. 9 (January 1985).

HAKKA

1. Also in Thailand, French Polynesia, Panama, Surinam, USA, Brunei, South Africa, Jamaica, Sri Lanka, Philippines, Australia, New Zealand, Kenya, Netherlands, United Kingdom, France, Germany, Brazil, Trinidad, Canada and Cambodia.
2. The larger population figure (25,725,000) appears to disagree with that cited under Population in China. However, the 193,000 Hakka in Hong Kong (1993 Patrick Johnstone, *Operation World*) are added to this figure because of the 1997 hand-over of Hong Kong to China.
3. Further, 58,800 in Thailand (1984); 19,200 in French Polynesia (1987); 6,000 in Panama (1981); 6,000 in Surinam; 3,000 in Brunei (1979); also in numerous other countries (see n.1 above). Whole villages of Hakka people have recently been discovered in Siempang, northeast Cambodia.
4. Hakka population estimates for the year 2000 are *Guangdong* (8.1 million), *Jiangxi* (5.9 million), *Guangxi* (4.2 million), *Fujian* (2.6 million), *Hong Kong* (210,000), and *Hunan* (170,000).
5. Australian Academy and CASS, *LAC*, B-13.
6. CASS, *Information China* 3: 1249.
7. Stauffer, *The Christian Occupation of China*, 351.
8. Ibid., 352.
9. Ibid., 353.
10. See Ming, "A Young Woman Evangelist in a Booming Town," *Bridge*, no. 52 (March-April 1992): 12. For testimonies of Hakka Christians and other excellent Hakka information, see Jessie Gregory Lutz and Rolland Ray Lutz, *Hakka Chinese Confront Protestant Christianity 1850-1900: With the Autobiographies of Eight Hakka Christians, and Commentary* (Armonk, NY: M. E. Sharpe, 1998).
11. William Robson, *Griffith John: Founder of the Hankow Mission* (New York: Fleming H. Revell, c.1890), 47.

HAKKA, HAINAN ISLAND

1. Personal communication, July 1997.
2. See Stauffer, *The Christian Occupation of China*, 351.
3. Ibid.
4. Ibid., 146.

HAN CHINESE, CANTONESE

1. Also in Laos, Nauru, Costa Rica, Panama, New Zealand, Australia, Netherlands, United Kingdom.... Cantonese are located in most other western nations in the world.
2. The 1984 population figure (46,305,000) appears to disagree with that given under Population in China. However, this figure did not include the Cantonese living in Hong Kong and Macau. Because of Hong Kong's incorporation into China in 1997 and the hand-over of Macau in late 1999, their populations are added to the total population for Cantonese speakers in China. In addition, the figure for the Dan Chinese (3,150,000) is subtracted, since the Dan are profiled separately. This gives a more realistic number for the Cantonese of 48,945,000.
3. 20,000 in New Zealand; 6,000 in Philippines; 4,500 in Costa Rica; 3,500 in Brunei; 680 in Nauru, also in Laos. Total: 64 million.
4. Moser, *The Chinese Mosaic*, 17, 36.
5. Australian Academy and CASS, *LAC*, A-5.
6. Aby Zeid, *Achbar ul Sin wal Hind* [Observations Upon China and India], cited in John Foster, *Church of the T'ang Dynasty* (London: SPCK, 1939), 130.
7. Robson, *Griffith John*, 22.
8. Stauffer, *The Christian Occupation of China*, 161.
9. 200,000 is the highest estimate for all Protestants in Guangdong, both TSPM and underground church members. The highest other documented figure for Protestants is 160,000. *Guangdong Yearbook* (1992).
10. *Guangdong Yearbook* (1989).
11. Johnstone, *Operation World* (1993), 265, based on the figure of 8.5% Protestant and 4.8% Catholic. Johnstone also estimates some 9.2% of Macau's population to be Christian, the large majority being Roman Catholics.

HAN CHINESE, DAN

1. Eugene N. Anderson, Jr., *Essays on South China's Boat People* (Taipei: The Orient Cultural Service, 1972), 48.
2. Moser, *The Chinese Mosaic*, 219.
3. Ibid., 219-20.
4. Thousands of Dan in Hong Kong have been resettled in apartment blocks, although most are still engaged in activities relating to fishing. In Guangzhou, 60,000 Dan were forced to live in 15 apartment blocks, but still remain somewhat separate from other people.
5. Moser, *The Chinese Mosaic*, 220.
6. Barbara E. Ward, "A Hong Kong Fishing Village," *Journal of Oriental Studies* (January 1954): 201.

HAN CHINESE, GAN

1. Storey (ed.), *China*, 16.
2. Hefley, *China! Christian Martyrs of the 20th Century*, 32.
3. Ibid., 41.
4. Information is scant, but the TSPM estimates a total of 300,000 Protestants for the whole of Jiangxi Province, in addition to 10,000 Catholics. Huang Xianlin (ed.), *Zhongguo Renkou: Guangxi Fence* (Beijing: Zhongguo Caizheng Jingji Chubanshe, 1988).

HAN CHINESE, HAINANESE

1. Moser, *The Chinese Mosaic*, 197.
2. Storey (ed.), *China*, 16.
3. Ma Yin, *China's Minority Nationalities*, 406.
4. "The Church on Hainan Island: Past and Present," *Bridge*, no. 27 (January-February 1988): 4.
5. Ibid.
6. *Bridge* (June 1992).
7. *Bridge* (December 1989).

HAN CHINESE, HUI'AN

1. Lin Lai, "A Photo Safari Along the Fujian Coast," *China Tourism*, no. 87 (n.d.): 30. There were a total of 1,091,616 people recorded in Hui'an County according to the 1990 census.
2. Ibid., 31.

3. Wong Chung Fai, "The Lives of Hui'an Women," *China Tourism*, no. 117, (n.d.): 58.
4. Ibid., 54.
5. Ibid., 58-59, gives a brief report of a visit to a Hui'an Catholic Church.

HAN CHINESE, HUIZHOU

1. Australian Academy and CASS, *LAC*, B-11.
2. See Ping-Ti Ho, *Studies on the Population of China 1368-1953* (Cambridge, Mass: Harvard University Press, 1959), 240-44.
3. Moser, *The Chinese Mosaic*, 113.
4. Grimes, *Ethnologue* (1996), 544.
5. Moser, *The Chinese Mosaic*, 117.

HAN CHINESE, JIN

1. Australian Academy and CASS, *LAC*, B-7.
2. *Arnobii Disputationum adversus Gentes Libri Octo* (Rome, 1542).
3. Jes P. Asmussen, *Xuastvanift: Studies in Manichaeism* (Copenhagen: Munksgaard, 1965), 149. A Persian embassy reached the Wei Dynasty capital in north China, just outside the wall at Ta'tung, in AD 455.
4. A. de Gouvea, *Joznado Do Ancebispo Dom, Meneses*; French trans. J. B. Glen, *Historie Orientale, des Grans Progres de L'eglise Catholique, Apostolique et Romaine* (Anvers: Verdussen, 1609), 3-4.
5. Huang Xianlin (ed.), *Zhongguo Renkou*.
6. Tony Lambert, personal communication, May 1997.

HAN CHINESE, MANDARIN

1. Saeki, *The Nestorian Documents and Relics in China* (Tokyo: Maruzen, 1951), 57f, 456.
2. Samuel Hugh Moffet, *A History of Christianity in Asia* 1: *Beginnings to 1500* (San Francisco: Harper, 1992), 293.
3. Highest 1993 estimate by Amity Press. This figure includes estimates of all Christians, province-by-province, and not only of believers belonging to the TSPM church.
4. It has become fashionable for many mission organizations to quote figures of at least 90 million Christians in China, but these figures cannot be substantiated by systematic research.
5. The 1993 *Operation World* lists 58 million Protestants in China, of whom 47 million attend house meetings and 11 million attend the government-sanctioned Three-Self church. It also lists 8.7 million Catholics in China, making a total of 66.7 million believers.
6. The official 1990 census figure (701,116,436) appears to disagree with that cited under Population in China. However, this number includes the members of the Hui nationality, who are Mandarin-speaking Chinese Muslims. To arrive at a more realistic and specific population for the Mandarin Han Chinese, the 8,602,978 Hui (1990 census) are subtracted to give a figure of 692,188,658.
7. There are 62 dialects of Mandarin, grouped in 8 main dialect clusters: *Northeastern Mandarin* (82 million speakers in 1987): Jiaoning, Tongxi, Yanji, Zhaofu, Changjin, Nenke, Jiafu, Zhanhua; *Beijing* (18 million): Jingshi, Huaicheng, Chaofeng, Shike; *Jilu* (Beifang) (83.6 million): Laifu, Dingba, Tianjin, Jizun, Luanchang, Fulong, Zhaoshen, Xingheng, Liaotai, Canghui, Huangle, Yangshou, Juzhao, Zhanghuan; *Jiaoliao* (28.8 million): Qingzhou, Denglian, Gaihuan; *Zhongyuan* (169.4 million): Zhengcao, Cailu, Luoxu, Xinbeng, Pingyang, Jiangzhou, Xiezhou, Guanzhong, Qinlong, Longzhong, Nanjiang; *Lanyin* (11.7 million): Jincheng, Yinwu, Hexi, Tami; *Southwestern Mandarin* (200 million): Chengyu, Yaoli, Baolu, Qianbei, Kungui, Minjiang, Renfu, Yamian, Lichuan, Ebei, Wutian, Cenjiang, Qiannan, Guiliu, Changhe; *Jianghuai* (67.2 million): Hongchao, Tairu, Huangxiao.

HAN CHINESE, MIN BEI

1. Australian Academy and CASS, *LAC*, B-12.
2. Grimes, *Ethnologue* (1996), 545.
3. Ibid.
4. Storey (ed.), *China*, 19.
5. Eberhard, *China's Minorities*, 8.
6. James Legge, *The Notions of the Chinese Concerning God and Spirits* (Hong Kong: Hong Kong Register Office, 1852), 24-25, 28: The emperor also recited "To Thee, O mysteriously-working Maker, I look up in thought.... With the great ceremonies I reverently honor Thee. Thy servant, I am but a reed or willow; my heart is but that of an ant; yet have I received Thy favoring decree, appointing me to the government of the empire. I deeply cherish a sense of my ignorance and blindness, and am afraid, lest I prove unworthy of Thy great favours. Therefore will I observe all the rules and statutes, striving, insignificant as I am, to discharge my loyal duty. For distant here, I look up to Thy heavenly palace. Come in Thy precious chariot to the altar. Thy servant, I bow my head to the earth reverently, expecting Thine abundant grace.... O that Thou wouldest vouchsafe to accept our offerings, and regard us, while thus we worship Thee, whose goodness is inexhaustible!"
7. Moule and Pelliot, *Marco Polo*, 350.
8. The Min Bei Christians today prefer to use the standard Chinese Scriptures, rather than the 1934 translation in their own language.

HAN CHINESE, MIN DONG

1. Moser, *The Chinese Mosaic*, 31.
2. Legge, T*he Notions of the Chinese*.
3. Moule and Pelliot, *Marco Polo*, 347.
4. "Along the Fujian Coast," *Bridge* (January-February 1986): 4.

HAN CHINESE, MIN NAN

1. Grimes, *Ethnologue* (1996), 545.
2. James M. Hubbard, "Problems in China," *National Geographic* (August 1900): 297.
3. Moffet, *A History of Christianity in Asia*, 458.
4. Henry Yule and Henri Cordier, *Cathay And The Way Tither: Being A Collection*, 4 vols. (Delhi: Munshiram Manoharlal, 1998), 191-94.
5. "Along the Fujian Coast," *Bridge* (January-February 1986): 4.
6. Also in Indonesia, Philippines, Laos, Brunei.
7. This 1984 population figure appears to disagree with that cited under Population in China. However, because of the hand-over of Hong Kong to China in 1997, the 540,000 Min Nan speakers in Hong Kong are added to give a more realistic and specific population of 26,265,000.

HAN CHINESE, MIN ZHONG

1. J. E. Walker, "Shao-wu in Fuh-kien: A Country Station," *Chinese Recorder*, no. 9 (September-October 1878): 349.
2. Taken from website of the Revival Christian Church, Hong Kong,.
3. Hefley, *China! Christian Martyrs of the 20th Century*, 10.
4. John of Cara, "The Book of the Estate of the Great Kaan," trans. Henry Yule, *Cathay* 3: 100.

HAN CHINESE, PINGHUA

1. Australian Academy and CASS, *LAC*, B-14.
2. Ibid.
3. Dodd, *The Tai Race*, 148. Several excellent Chinese linguistic studies of the Pinghua language include Li Wei, "Guangxi Lingchuan Pinghua de Tedian," *Fangyuan*, no. 4, 251-54; and Zhang Junru, "Ji Guangxi Nanning Xinxu Pinghua," *Fangyuan*, 241-50.
4. Samuel Clarke, *Among the Tribes in South-West China*, 58-59.
5. Stauffer, *The Christian Occupation of China*, 148.
6. *Guangxi Yearbook* (1992).
7. Highest estimate for all Protestants by Amity Press, 1997.
8. *Guangxi Quqing* (1985).

HAN CHINESE, PUXIAN

1. Leo J. Moser says this is the result of a strong emphasis on sports in the local school system which dates back at least to 1878; *The Chinese Mosaic*, 173. At that time, according to Rao Fengqi, "champions of races were treated like scholars who had come in first in the imperial examinations. They were draped with red silk over their shoulders, flowers were pinned on their chests and they were given a parade through the streets." Rao Fengqi, "Why Does Putian County Produce So Many Athletes?" *China Reconstructs* (May 1983): 55-56.
2. Australian Academy and CASS, *LAC*, B-12.
3. Chronicon Ibn al-Athir (1160-1234), *History of the Mongols: Based on Eastern and Western Accounts of the Thirteenth and Fourteenth Centuries*, trans. B. Spuler (London: Routledge & Kegan Paul, 1972), 29.
4. Hefley, *China! Christian Martyrs of the 20th Century*, 10.
5. Moffet, *A History of Christianity in Asia*, 475.
6. "Along the Fujian Coast," *Bridge* (January-February 1986): 4.
7. "Of the Christians, about 20,000 adhere to the traditions of the True Jesus Church, while about 2,000 count themselves as members of the Little Flock. The old church building in Putian County gets used well. There are three Sunday services, each of which fills the 1,400-seat church.... More than 100 Christian meeting points in Putian have not yet been registered." "Putian Church: Different Traditions, New Developments," *Amity News Service*, June 1997.

HAN CHINESE, SHAOJIANG

1. Australian Academy and CASS, *LAC*, B-12.
2. Storey (ed.), *China*, 23.
3. William Marsden (trans.), *The Travels of Marco Polo* (New York: Dell, 1961), 300-01.
4. Moffet, *A History of Christianity in Asia*, 457.
5. Ibid.
6. Ibid.
7. Kenneth Scott Latourette, *A History of Christian Missions in China* (New York: Macmillan, 1929), 71.
8. Stauffer, *The Christian Occupation of China*, 458.

HAN CHINESE, SHAOZHOU

1. Australian Academy and CASS, *LAC*, B-13.
2. Ibid.
3. CASS, *Information China* 3: 1247.
4. Hefley, *China! Christian Martyrs of the 20th Century*, 13.
5. Ibid., 32.
6. Dr. George Ernest Morrison, *London Times*, 1900.

HAN CHINESE, WAXIANG

1. Grimes, *Ethnologue* (1996), 564.
2. Chen Qiguang, *Zhongguo Yuwen Gaiyao* (1990), 288-89. Also see Enwall, *A Myth Become Reality* 1: 59-72.
3. Robson, *Griffith John*, 22.

HAN CHINESE, WU

1. Australian Academy and CASS, *LAC*, B-9. Grimes, in *Ethnologue* (1996), 545, cites a 1984 figure of 77,175,000 Wu speakers.
2. *The Far Eastern Economic Review*, June 1997.
3. Moule and Pelliot, *Marco Polo*, 263. Polo calls Chinkiang *Quengianfu*.
4. Lambert, *The Resurrection of the Chinese Church*, 311.
5. Including 127,000 Protestants (*Bridge*, September-October 1993) and 120,000 Catholics (*Xinhua*, 21 March 1988).

HAN CHINESE, XIANG

1. Grimes, in *Ethnologue* (1996), 545, cites a 1984 figure of 36,015,000 Xiang speakers.
2. William Barclay Parsons, "Hunan: The Closed Province of China," *National Geographic* (October 1900): 393.
3. Enwall, *A Myth Become Reality* 1: 67.
4. Lin Shao-Yang, *A Chinese Appeal to Christendom* (1911).
5. *Eastern Express*, Hong Kong, 5 October 1995.
6. Robson, *Griffith John*, 60-61.
7. *Norwegian Missionary Society Handbook* (1993).
8. "Difficulties in Hunan Province," *Bridge*, no. 10 (March-April 1985): 3.

HAN CHINESE, XUNPU

1. Lin Jian and Chen Shizhe, "Fishing Village of Persistent Traditions," *China Tourism*, no. 114 (n.d.): 51.
2. Ibid.
3. Ibid.
4. Bai Yan, "The People and Their Lives in Modern Quanzhou," *China Tourism*, no. 140 (February 1992): 73.
5. Lin Jian and Chen, "Fishing Village of Persistent Traditions," 51.
6. Moffet, *A History of Christianity in Asia*, 458.
7. Lambert, *The Ressurection of the Chinese Church*, 147.
8. Ibid.

HANI

1. According to the 1990 census there were 32 counties or municipalities in China that recorded more than 500 Hani people. In descending order, the largest Hani populations are in: Mojiang 203,559; Honghe 181,330; Yuanyang 176,474; Luchun 155,473; Jinping 77,720; Yuanjiang 69,630; Menghai 59,726; Jinghong 54,429. Note: these figures do not refer only to the Hani ethnic group profiled here, but to the complete Hani nationality.
2. Of the groups included under the official "Hani" nationality in China, *Operation China* profiles the Akha, Baihong, Bisu, Biyo, Budo, Duota, Enu, Haoni, Kado, Lami, Meng, Muda, Neisu, Pana, Sansu, Woni, and Yiche separately.
3. *A Tour to the Mysterious Land of Yunnan* (Kunming: Yunnan Provincial Travel & Tourism Administration, n.d.), 129.
4. Bradley, "Language Planning for China's Minorities."
5. Milliken, "SIL China Nationalities and Languages Files."
6. Figures from the 1990 Chinese census.

7. CASS, *Information China* 3. The next worst rating were the Tibetans, at 40.7% The national average is 62.7%
8. Ibid. By contrast, the Manchu live an average of 72 years.
9. Bethany World Prayer Center, "The Hani" (1997).
10. Hani2000, "The Hani: Poorest of China's Poor," Unreached People Group Profile. "Initial work is underway on translating the New Testament into the Luchun (Dolnia) dialect of Hani. This dialect is the one chosen by the Chinese government to use for Hani writing." Paul Lewis, personal communication, February 1999.

HAN TAI
1. Zheng Lan, *Travels Through Xishuangbanna*, 4.
2. Asian Studies Institute, "The Dai People of Southeast Asia" (1996): 14.
3. Bethany World Prayer Center, "The Shan of Southeast Asia" (1997).
4. AMO, "The Black Tai," *Newsletter*, no. 36 (December 1995).
5. AMO, *The 50 Most Unreached People Groups of China and Tibet*, 8.
6. Asian Studies Institute, "The Dai People of Southeast Asia," 4.

HAONI
1. David Bradley, personal communication, January 1999. According to the 1990 census there were 203,559 *Hani* in Mojiang County and 69,630 in Yuanjiang County. Many of these are Haoni.
2. Bradley, "Language Planning for China's Minorities."
3. Wang Zhengfang, "We of the Hani Nationality."
4. T'ien, *Peaks of Faith*, 21.
5. *GPD* 1, no. 3 (March 1982).
6. T'ien, *Peaks of Faith*, 26.

HDZANGGUR
1. Rock, "Seeking the Mountains of Mystery," 162-63.
2. Ibid., 163.
3. Ibid., 162.

HEZHEN
1. 1,113 Hezhen live in Tongjiang County (Bacha and Jiejinkou townships), and near Sipai Village in Xilinzi Township of Raohe County. Some are scattered in several villages in Huachuan and Fujin counties, and 821 live in Jiamusi City.
2. Mackerras, *China's Minorities*, 122.
3. *GPD* 7, no. 5 (May 1988).
4. State Nationalities Affairs Commission, *China's Minority Peoples* (Beijing: China Pictorial Publishing House, 1995), 94.
5. See Owen Lattimore, "The Gold Tribe 'Fish-Skin Tatars' of the Lower Sungari," *Memoires of the American Anthropological Association*, no. 40 (Menasha, 1933).
6. Australian Academy and CASS, *LAC*, C-5.
7. Grimes, *Ethnologue* (1996), 558.
8. See Ivan A. Lopatin, *The Cult of the Dead Among the Natives of the Amur Basin* (The Hague: Mouton, 1960), 70-96.
9. Christian Mission to China and 10/40 Window, personal communication, South Korea, August 1997.

HKAURI
1. Matisoff, "Languages and Dialects of Tibeto-Burman."
2. Herman G. Tegenfeldt, *A Century of Growth: The Kachin Baptist Church of Burma* (Pasadena: William Carey Library, 1974), 22.
3. Ibid., 17.

HMONG BE
1. The Hmong Be are the first of many Hmong groups profiled in *Operation China*. The *Hmong* are only one branch of the Miao nationality in China. Some people outside China claim that *Hmong* should be the name used for all Miao people, but that is simply inaccurate. Only about 2 million of the 7.4 million Miao in 1990 called themselves *Hmong*. Because the Hmong are the westernmost Miao group in China, all of the Miao living in Southeast Asia (and subsequently, in Western nations around the world) are part of the Hmong group. Many of the diaspora Hmong strongly claim that *Hmong* should be used for all Miao peoples. They explain that the term *Miao* is derogatory. To those who have traveled through Miao areas in Guizhou, Hunan, and Guangxi, however, Hmong is not a suitable overall term for the Miao. The Miao in Hunan, for example, call themselves *Ghao-Xong*. Many Miao in eastern Guizhou use the autonym *Hmu*, while the Gha-Mu and A-Hmao use their respective autonyms. These other groups, numbering several million people, know nothing of the name *Hmong*. Subsequently, only those Western Miao groups who call themselves *Hmong* have been included under the heading of *Hmong* in *Operation China*. For further explanation of the usage of the names *Miao* versus *Hmong* see Enwall, *A Myth Become Reality* 1: 14-16.
2. Johnson, "Far Western Hmongic," 26.

HMONG BUA
1. Johnson, "Far Western Hmongic," 24.
2. Ibid.
3. Ibid., 23.
4. Tao Xiaoping, "Qianxi Chuannan Gongxian Miaozu Zhu Wenhua," *Miaoxue Yanjiu Lunwenji* (Guizhou: Bijie Diqu Miaoxue Hui, 1993).
5. Johnson, "Far Western Hmongic," 25.
6. See the Hmong Daw Profile for details.

HMONG DAW
1. Grimes, *Ethnologue* (1996), 549.
2. Sixty-three percent of the more than 100,000 Hmong (including Hmong Daw) in the United States were receiving unemployment benefits in 1987. There were Hmong in more than 30 states in the 1970's, but most have now migrated to states with the highest unemployment benefits: Wisconsin, Minnesota, and California. Quincy, *Hmong*, 22.
3. Johnson, "An Overview of Hmongic Languages," 13. There are other Miao/Hmong groups in southern China who call themselves *Hmong Daw*, such as the Chuan Miao, Hmong Shuad, and Horned Miao, but they do not speak the same language as the Hmong Daw in this Profile.
4. Ibid., 8.
5. T'ien, *Peaks of Faith*, 7.
6. Ibid., citing *Miaozu Jianshi* [A Short History of the Miao], ms. (Kunming, 1981): 13.
7. Even greater numbers of Hmong Daw are reported to have turned to Christ in northern Vietnam because of the broadcasts. They too have faced large-scale opposition from the Vietnamese authorities.
8. See AMO, "The White Miao," *Newsletter*, no. 39 (May 1996).
9. Gladstone Porteous, "Tribe After Tribe Being Reached,"

China's Millions (Australasian edition, February 1919): 14.

10. "Listeners in one particular Laotian Hmong village in the mid-1950's were responsive to Christian messages, but being illiterate, had no idea how to communicate with the Vientiane post office box given on the program. The chief of the village, therefore, sent a delegation down several days' walk to the capital, to the main post office, where they inquired if there was a religious man associated with a particular mail box. Postal officials did not understand the request and referred them instead to a member of the locally established religious hierarchy, who sent a representative back with the delegation, several days' walk return trip to the mountains. However, when the chief asked the representative to acquit himself in terms of his views, he was dissatisfied with the result and declared that it was 'not the same' as they had heard on the radio. He therefore apologized to the representative and sent him on his way back down the mountain. But the village were determined to make contact with the broadcaster. So, again a delegation went back, three days' walk, down the mountain to Vientiane, where they gave more details to the postal officials, who then decided these people must be referring to a foreigner who indeed had a mailbox. This missionary returned with the delegation, preached the gospel to the chief and his men, and all accepted Christ. As is quite ordinary in Hmong culture, the chief 'gave permission' to his village to become Christians, every one. And as a common response to a chief's suggestion, the whole village followed suit." *Miao Messenger* 6, no. 1 (Fall 1997).
11. The full Hmong Daw Bible was printed in late 1997. The New Testament was also revised. In 1995, 100 Hmong Daw Christian families living in Wenshan Prefecture were so exasperated with the police harassment and persecution that they packed up all their possessions and migrated 200 km to Xishuangbanna Prefecture, where they are able to worship in relative peace.
12. And Meo Do, Red Hmong, Mong Do, Mong Trang, Hmong Qua Mpa, Striped-Arm Hmong, Striped Hmong.
13. 200,000 Hmong Daw live in Wenshan Prefecture, Yunnan. They are primarily found in parts of Shizong, Wenshan, Yanshan, Qiubei, Maguan, Malipo, Guangnan, Funing, Xichou, Mengzi, Kaiyuan, Pingbian and Jinping counties in Yunnan Province. About 30,000 are located in Anlong, Ceheng and Luodian counties in the southwestern part of Guizhou. Hmong Daw communities can also be found in Longlin and Napo counties in western Guangxi.

HMONG DLEX NCHAB

1. Johnson, "Far Western Hmongic," 32.
2. Ibid., 33.
3. William Campbell, *Formosa Under the Dutch, Described From Contemporary Records with Explanatory Notes and a Bibliography of the Island* (London: Kegan Paul, Trench, Trubner, 1903), 510.
4. See AMO, "The White Miao."

HMONG DOU

1. Johnson, "Far Western Hmongic," 26.
2. Ibid.
3. Ibid.
4. J. R. Adam, "Pentecostal Blessing Among the Aborigines of West China," *China's Millions* (January 1907): 10-15.

HMONG LENG

1. Johnson, "Far Western Hmongic," 30.
2. Ibid., 31.
3. Ibid., 29.

HMONG NJUA

1. Johnson, "Far Western Hmongic," 32.
2. Ramsey, *The Languages of China*, 279.
3. Johnson, "Far Western Hmongic," 32.
4. Miao, "The Miao of China."
5. For a detailed account of the Hmong Njua religion, see Nusit Chindarsi, *The Religion of the Hmong Njua* (Bangkok: The Siam Society, 1976).
6. Far East Broadcasting Company (FEBC) issued the following detailed and fascinating description of the false Hmong messiah in Vietnam, dated 30 January 1998: "The false messiah's name is Yang Shong Meng. When he was born his hands, feet and side all bore scars like the Lord Jesus incurred from His time of suffering. When Yang Shong Meng was 30 years of age he began his ministry of sharing the gospel (his gospel). He is married and had four children. Not long after birth one died, leaving three remaining.

   "In 1989 he began teaching the Hmong who resided in North Vietnam to leave behind their wicked ways, not to steal and thieve, not to force litigation, not to drink liquor or alcohol. One must be a good person and follow his teaching solely in order to be in the truth, he taught. Also, because the Father loves the Hmong of North Vietnam, and because they have experienced more suffering than others, their Father God sent Yang Shong Meng into the world to teach about salvation from sin and how to be good, so that one day in the future they may be able to reside in heaven. There are many who have followed his teaching.

   "Six months after Yang Shong Meng began to teach the Vietnamese Hmong, they began to hear the gospel through FEBC radio broadcasts. It was during this time that the Hmong began to experience problems, because they didn't know whom to believe. In the end many began to listen to the gospel messages from FEBC and began to believe as we teach, but at present Yang Shong Meng still has an estimated following of 20,000 people.... He teaches that everyone must believe and do according to his teaching solely; one cannot follow the teachings of another. The OT and the NT are outdated because of their antiquity, so they are not helpful. He is the one whom the Father has sent from heaven to be born the saviour of the world. One must follow his teachings in order to be a true child of God and to live in heaven.

   "He builds rather large church buildings and always installs a cross over the door. If anybody would like to be able to read, this person must meet with Yang Shong Meng. Yang Shong Meng then instructs them to smoke a few bowls of opium, and then they really can read without even studying. He actually heals the sick and infirm. He has helped numerous persons with diseases. He teaches his followers that the FEBC broadcaster learns his teachings from Yang Shong Meng, and Yang Shong Meng accurately predicts the teachings on a day-to-day basis before they are broadcast. This has been documented.

   "In 1995-96 Vietnamese government officials incarcerated Yang Shong Meng. They were afraid that he might lead the Hmong in an uprising such as happened in 1960 when the Hmong went crazy after following a certain sorcerer, who had created his own Hmong alphabet and numerous problems. But even so Yang Shong Meng still has his own apostle named Paul who leads his followers at present. His teachings and his leadings has caused a tremendous amount of his followers to believe in the Lord Jesus as we ourselves teach. But even so, there is still a portion who believe Yang Shong Meng. There is also a group so confused that they do not know whom to believe."
7. The Hmong *Jesus* film translation is a combination of Hmong Njua and Hmong Daw. The character who played

Jesus speaks one dialect, the other cast members speak the other dialect. As a result, even speakers of the two Hmong varieties have difficulty understanding it, unless they have been previously exposed to both dialects.

HMONG SHUAD

1. Johnson, "Far Western Hmongic," 14.
2. The Hmong Shuad are located in Zhijin, Nayong, Dafang, Qianxi, Puding, Anshun, Ziyun, Zhenning, Guanling, Qinglong and Shuicheng counties of north-west Guizhou. In addition, 16,000 Hmong Shuad live in the Sanbao, Jichang, Bihen, Moji, Caizi, and Qingshan townships of Qinglong County, the Maluhe, Lihuan, and Zhenguyuan townships in the Longjiao District of Xingren County; and the Bocuan, Maoping, Guanziyao, Hongzhai, and Baisha townships in Pu'an County. Another 1,500 Hmong Shuad live in the Muzan, Sayu, Daba, and Logou townships of Anlong County. A small number are also found in Nashengjianshan of Xingyi County. In southeast Yunnan, the Hmong Shuad are located in Jinping County and in Wenshan Prefecture.
3. Johnson, "Far Western Hmongic," 14.
4. "An Overview of Hmongic Languages," 15.
5. Covell, *The Liberating Gospel,* 95.
6. Quincy, *Hmong*, 56.
7. Ibid., 85.

HMONG VRON

1. Corrigan, *Odyssey Illustrated Guide to Guizhou*, 88.
2. Harrison E. Salisbury, *The Long March: The Untold Story* (London: Macmillan, 1985).
3. Ouyang Changpei, "Visiting the Horn-Haired Miao People," *China Tourism*, no. 192 (July 1996): 66.

HMU, EASTERN

1. Wong How-Man, "Peoples of China's Far Provinces," 323.
2. Michael Johnson, personal communication, January 1988.
3. Johnson, "An Overview of Hmongic Languages," 6.
4. See Ramsey, *The Languages of China*, 279.
5. Miao, "The Miao of China."
6. In part, the legend, sung as a one-thousand-line poem, asks:

   "Who made the heaven and earth?
   Who made the insects?
   Who made men?
   Made male and made female?
   I who speak don't know.

   "Vang-vai (Heavenly King) made heaven and earth.
   Zie-ne made insects.
   Zie-ne made men and demons,
   Made male and made female.
   How is it you don't know?

   "Heavenly King is intelligent.
   Spat a lot of spittle in his hand,
   Clapped his hands with a noise,
   Produced heaven and earth.... "

   Samuel Clarke, *Among the Tribes in South-West China*, 41-42.
7. See Ivan Allbutt, "Black Miao Colonies," *China's Millions* (Australasian edition, October 1940): 154-55.
8. Scripture portions were translated into Eastern Hmu in 1928, but these are no longer available, and the script used is now obsolete.

HMU, NORTHERN

1. M. H. Hutton, "How the Message Came to the Black Miao," *China's Millions* (November 1937): 214.
2. Samuel Clarke, *Among the Tribes in South-West China*, 73-74.
3. Ibid., 139-71, for a detailed account of their work.
4. Hefley, *China! Christian Martyrs of the 20th Century*, 34.
5. "In Journeyings Amongst the Miao," *China's Millions* (June 1914): 47-48.
6. "Fruit After Many Days," 137.
7. Enwall, *A Myth Become Reality* 1: 216.

HMU, SOUTHERN

1. YASS 412, Section 20: 3, as cited in T'ien, *Peaks of Faith*, 11.
2. Miao, "The Miao of China."
3. William H. Hudspeth, *Stone Gateway and the Flowery Miao* (London: Cargate, 1937), 21-22.
4. Enwall, *A Myth Become Reality* 1: 90.
5. Ibid., 91.
6. "The Black Miao, of Kweichow," *China's Millions* (Australasian edition, October 1950): 106.

HONGJIN TAI

1. Luo Meizhen, as cited in Grimes, *Ethnologue* (1996), 561.
2. YASS 64, Section 9. There were a total of 6,234 Dai people in Wuding County and 1,777 in Huili County, Sichuan, according to the 1990 census.
3. Qian Sicong, "Baiyu Zhuan," in *Jingtai Yunnan Tujing Zhishu* (1455).
4. *Tengyue Tingzhi* [Gazette of Tengyue Prefecture] (1887), Chapter 11, Section 4.
5. *GPD* 10, no. 6 (June 1991).
6. Ibid.
7. Dodd, *The Tai Race*, 31-33.
8. Ibid., 45.

HORNED MIAO

1. Johnson, "Far Western Hmongic," 13.
2. Numerous Farwestern Miao groups in China call themselves *White Miao* but are not necessarily ethnolinguistically related.
3. Johnson, "Far Western Hmongic," 13.
4. Ibid.
5. Ibid.
6. Ibid., 14.

HU

1. Grimes, *Ethnologue* (1988), 449.
2. Jiangxi Educational Publishing, *EDCL*, 594.
3. A. J. Broomhall, *Hudson Taylor and China's Open Century* (Sevenoaks: Hodder & Stoughton and OMF, 1981) 4: 55.

HUA MIAO

1. Johnson, "Far Western Hmongic," 20.
2. Ibid.
3. Ibid.
4. Ibid.
5. Ibid., 27.

HUAYAO TAI

1. Asian Studies Institute, *The Dai People of Southeast Asia*, 17. According to the 1990 census there were a

total of 39,094 Dai people in Xinping County; 21,444 in Yuanjiang County. Most of these are Huayao Tai.

2. Personal communication with a Tai Lu, November 1997.
3. Stauffer, *The Christian Occupation of China,* 349. Also see Dodd, *The Tai Race.*
4. Xie Shixun, "The Floral-Belted Dais of the Red River," *China Tourism,* no. 78 (n.d.), 67.
5. See Li Ping, "The Flower Street Festival of the Dai," *China Tourism,* no. 165 (April 1994): 79-81.
6. Asian Studies Institute, "The Dai People of Southeast Asia," 2.

HUI

1. The official 1990 census figure (8,602,978) appears to disagree with that cited under Population in China. However, the populations of the Utsat (6,000) and the Keji (3,000) are subtracted from the 1990 census figure for the Hui, and these two groups are profiled separately. Also, because of the 1997 incorporation of Hong Kong back into the People's Republic of China, the 30,000 Hui in Hong Kong are added to the census figure. This gives a more realistic and specific population figure of 8,623,978 for the Hui.
2. *GPD* 9, no. 1 (January 1990). In Myanmar the Hui are known as *Panthay.*
3. Johnstone, *Operation World* (1993). In Kyrgyzstan and Kazakstan the Hui are known as *Dungan.*
4. In Mongolia the Hui are known as *Khotan.*
5. Also in *Sichuan*; *Inner Mongolia*; *Tianjin*; *Heilongjiang*; *Shaanxi*; *Jilin*; *Jiangsu*; *Shandong*; *Hubei*; *Hunan*; *Shanxi*; *Shanghai*; *Fujian*; *Guangxi*; *Guangdong*; *Zhejiang*; *Jiangxi*; and *Tibet*. There are also 30,000 Hui in the Hong Kong S.A.R. according to *Pray for the Hui* (prayer guide, n.p., 1998), 33.
6. CASS, *Information China* 3: 1248. According to the 1990 census there were 973 counties or municipalities in China that recorded more than 500 Hui people. In descending order, the counties with more than 100,000 Hui are: Tongxin (*Ningxia*) 220,464; Haiyuan (*Ningxia*) 204,543; Xiji (*Ningxia*) 188,158; Guyuan (*Ningxia*) 182,979; Zhangjiachuan (*Gansu*) 174,898; Beijing City 152,578; Wuzhong (*Ningxia*) 141,675; Minhe (*Qinghai*) 126,336; Guanghe (*Gansu*) 112,317; Tianjin City 107,163; Lingwu (*Ningxia*) 105,973; Kangle (*Gansu*) 104,861; Datong (*Qinghai*) 104,507; Pingliang (*Gansu*) 103,361; Linxia (*Gansu*) 102,455, and Hualong (*Qinghai*) 102,166.
7. "A four year drought, hail, frost and over-population in northwest Ningxia Province has resulted in an ambitious project to resettle 800,000 people from the mountainous cave villages to newly irrigated land near the Yellow River between 1997 and 2000." *Pray for China,* no. 138 (September-October 1997).
8. Quincy, *Hmong,* 58-59. There seems to be historical and cultural differences between the Hui in the southwest of China and those who migrated down the Silk Road and now live in Gansu, Qinghai, Ningxia, Xinjiang and other areas. Many Hui in southwest China even have different physical appearances from the northern Hui. The Hui in southwest China may have entered China through Southeast Asia and by sea, while the ancestors of the northern Hui migrated down the Silk Road from Central Asia.
9. Marshall Broomhall, *Islam in China: A Neglected Problem* (London: Morgan & Scott, 1910), 245.
10. Mrs. Howard Taylor, *The Call of China's Great North-West* (London: Religious Tract Society, n.d.), 157.
11. *GPD* 10, no. 1 (January 1991).
12. "There are 25-30 Hui believers." *Pray for China, no.* 138 (September-October 1997).
13. In a sense, because the identity of the Hui is completely wrapped up in their religion, there may never officially be a "Hui Christian." The two terms are contradictory. It is akin to saying a "Muslim Christian." The government counts all Chinese Muslims as members of the Hui nationality. If someone is not a Muslim they are not considered a Hui. Unfortunately, those few Hui who have found Christ have soon blended into Han Chinese culture and lost their ethnosocial identity as Hui.
14. Tony Lambert, "A Visit to Ningxia Province," *China Insight* (August-September 1993): 1-4.
15. Stauffer, *The Christian Occupation of China,* 249.
16. Covell, *The Liberating Gospel,* 66.
17. "In 1934, an American missionary known as Hai Chun Sheng bought 2.5 acres in Qinghai Province to use for outreach work. A cheap boarding house with seven rooms was built to facilitate contact with Muslims and four to six Muslim religious teachers received 'Scripture' study classes. In time, a handful of converts were baptized." *Pray for China,* no. 138 (September-October 1997).
18. AMO, "The Hui," *Newsletter,* no. 33 (June 1995). Many outsiders incorrectly presume that normal Chinese literature and cassettes will be sufficient to reach the Hui. This is not true. There are numerous words used by the Hui that are unique to them. They also find the Chinese Christian name for God (*Shangdi*) to be less than adequate to describe God's glory and greatness. Media outreach to the Hui needs to take into consideration these important differences.
19. "Goukou Church in Ningxia Province was a house meeting with five members ten years ago. Now there are more than 300 Christians, and they have built a church that seats 1,000, clearly anticipating rapid growth." *Pray for China,* no. 138 (September-October 1997).

INDONESIAN

1. Wei Kun, "The Gereja Batania," *Bridge,* no. 39 (January-February 1990): 16.
2. See Grimes, *Ethnologue* (1996), Indonesia: Sulawesi section.
3. Wei Kun, "The Gereja Batania," 16.
4. Ibid.
5. See Daniel, "Gereja Kemah Pertemuan: Second Indonesian Church in Hainan," *Bridge,* no. 53 (May-June 1992): 14-15.

IU MIEN

1. Nationalities Affairs Commission of Guangxi, *The Yao Nationality,* 14. According to the 1990 census there were 146 counties or municipalities in China that recorded more than 500 Yao people. The census figures did not distinguish between the different ethnic groups and languages among the Yao. In descending order, the largest Yao populations are in: Jianghua (*Hunan*) 210,944; Du'an (*Guangxi*) 137,812; Gongcheng (*Guangxi*)132,954; Fuchuan (*Guangxi*) 121,280; Dahua (*Guangxi*) 87,508; Liannan (*Guangdong*) 67,599; Jiangyong (*Hunan*) 62,647; Jinxiu (*Guangxi*) 48,825; Pingle (*Guangxi*) 47,665; Pingnan (*Guangxi*) 44,598; Bama (*Guangxi*) 38,983.
2. In the United States, 23,000 Iu Mien live in the San Francisco area, and Richmond, California. Some are located in Oregon, Washington, and two or three families in Alaska. The Iu Mien in America have struggled to adapt to American culture. Most older people cannot

speak any English at all, and the rate of unemployment is extremely high. Many Iu Mien youth are gang members.

3. Groff Weidman, "Landscaped Kwangsi: China's Province of Pictorial Art," *National Geographic* (December 1937): 709.
4. Australian Academy and CASS, *LAC*, C-8.
5. "The Metrical Structure of Yiu Mien Secular Songs," in Lemoine and Chiao, *The Yao of South China*, 370.
6. For a detailed study of cultural differences between the Iu Mien in China and the Iu Mien in Thailand, see Yao Shun An, "A Comparison of the Culture of the Yao People in China and Thailand," *Notes on Anthropology and Intercultural Community Work* 14 (1994): 16-25.
7. Lemoine and Chiao, *The Yao of South China*, 2.
8. This proclamation was issued for all Yao from generation to generation. Later rulers did not acknowledge the document, which led to oppression of the Yao who stubbornly refused to pay tax. The subsequent persecutions led to their wide dispersion across China.
9. Huang Yu, "Preliminary Study of the Yao 'King Ping's Charter,'" 103.
10. *CPLMR*, no. 119 (December 1991-February 1992).
11. Pelkey, "Report on the Yi Peoples of Honghe Prefecture," 22. Thorough research has revealed 4,100 Iu Mien Christians in the United States; 3,250 in Vietnam; 1,200 in Thailand; 120 in Laos; 75 in Canada; and 8 in Denmark.
12. The Iu Mien are found in the following counties: *Guangxi:* Yangshuo, Lingui, Guanyang, Longsheng, Yongfu, Luzhai, Gongcheng, Lipu, Mengshan, Pingle, Jinxiu, Yishan, Rong'an, Rongshui, Luocheng, Huanjiang, Shanglin, Laibing, Bose, Napo, Lingyun, Tianlin, Cangwu, Hexian, Fuchuan and Zhaoping counties; *Guangdong:* Yingde, Lechang, Shixing, Qujiang, Renhua, Wengyuan, Ruyuan, Liannan, Lianshan, Lianxian, Yangshan and Yangchun counties; *Yunnan:* Jinping, Honghe, Mengla, Malipo, Maguan, Guangnan, Funing, Hekou counties; *Guizhou:* Rongjiang, Congjiang, Luodian, Sandu, Danzhai, Leishan and Zhenfeng counties; *Jiangxi:* Quannan and Shanggao counties.
13. The Iu Mien Scriptures were translated primary for the Iu Mien living in Thailand and Laos. Most Iu Mien in China may not be able to understand the dialect. In addition, they would need to learn how to read the Roman script first, as the Yao New Testament employs the Roman alphabet.

IU MIEN, CHANGPING

1. Wang Fushi and Mao, *Reconstruction of Proto Miao-Yao.*
2. We Yuan, as cited in Richard Cushman, "Rebel Haunts and Lotus Huts: Problems in the Ethnohistory of the Yao," Ph.D. diss., Cornell University (1970): 36.
3. Yang Tiande, "A Riot of Yao Color," 86.
4. Ibid. In August 1984 representatives of various Yao groups met in Nanning, Guangxi. They agreed to unify the dates of the Pan Hu Festival and agreed to hold it on the 16th day of the 10th lunar month every year. Until then, the various branches of the Yao nationality had celebrated the festival at different times of the year.

IU MIEN, HUNAN

1. Wang Fushi and Mao, *Reconstruction of Proto Miao-Yao.*
2. Ibid.
3. Philip A. Kuhn, *Rebellion and Its Enemies in Late Imperial China: Militarization and Social Structure 1796-1864* (Cambridge, Mass.: Cambridge University Press, 1980), as cited by Ralph A. Litzinger, "Making Histories: Contending Conceptions of the Yao Past," 127.

IU MIEN, LUOXIANG

1. Wang Fushi and Mao, *Reconstruction of Proto Miao-Yao.*
2. Fei Xiaotong, "Fifty Years Investigation," 22-23.
3. Xie Shixun, "Encounter With the Yao," 100.
4. Yang Tiande, "A Riot of Yao Color," 87.

JAPANESE

1. The 1995 Joshua Project originally listed more than 400,000 Japanese in China. This high figure probably stems from the height of Japanese occupation of Manchuria in the 1930s.
2. "Exiles Come Home: War Displaced Japanese Return from China," *Christian Science Monitor* (1988).
3. Mackerras, *China's Minorities*, 121.
4. Hefley, *China! Christian Martyrs of the 20th Century*, 64.
5. 32,000 in Argentina, 20,000 in Singapore, 20,000 in Germany, 12,000 in Paraguay, 12,000 in United Kingdom, 10,000 in Taiwan, 1,500 in Dominican Republic, 1,300 in United Arab Emirates, 1,200 in Panama; also in Mongolia, Philippines, and Thailand. Total: 127.5 million.

JIARONG, CHABAO

1. Lin Xiangron, *Jiarongyu Yufa* (Chengdu: Sichuan Minzu Chubanshe, 1993), 412.
2. Muse, "A Profile of the Jiarong People of China."
3. Ibid.
4. Ibid.
5. Wu Wenhui and Zhu Jianhua, "Xikang Renkou Wenti, Shang," as cited in Mackerras, *China's Minorities,* 130.
6. Muse, "A Profile of the Jiarong People of China."
7. *Ascent to the Tribes: Pioneering in North Thailand* (London: OMF, 1968), 197-98.

JIARONG, GUANYINGQIAO

1. Jonathon Evans, personal communication, August 1999.
2. Ibid.

JIARONG, SHANGZHAI

1. Jonathon Evans, personal communication, August 1999.
2. Qu Aitang, "Jiarongyude Fangyan: Fangyan Huafen he Yuyan Shibie" [Jiarong Dialects: Issues in Dialect Subclassification and Language Recogniton], *Minzu Yuwen*, nos. 4 & 5 (1990).
3. Evans, personal communication, August 1999.
4. See Lin Xiangron, *Jiarongyu Yufa*, 526.
5. Fei Xiaotong, as cited in Jackson Sun (trans.), "Languages of the Ethnic Corridor in Western Sichuan," 1-2.

JIARONG, SIDABAO

1. Jonathon Evans, personal communication, August 1999.
2. Bradley, "East and South-East Asia," 168.
3. Evans, personal communication, August 1999.
4. Ge Jialin, "The Jiarong Tibetans Celebrate Their Harvest," *China Tourism*, no. 166 (May 1994): 58.
5. Muse, "A Profile of the Jiarong People of China."
6. Ibid.
7. Ibid.

JIARONG, SITU

1. Lin Xiangron, *Jiarongyu Yufa*, 411. The Hong Kong Association of Christian Missions lists a 1995 specific overall figure of 138,394 Jiarong (including the Situ Jiarong). J-O. Svantesson, in a personal communication,

1990, lists a figure of 100,000 speakers of Jiarong, as cited in Grimes, *Ethnologue* (1996), 551.

2. Jonathon Evans, personal communication, August 1999.
3. V. Li, *Some Approaches to the Classification of Small Ethnic Groups*.
4. Fei Xiatong, "Ethnic Identification in China," *Social Science in China*, no. 1 (January 1980): 147-62.
5. In recent years there have been numerous linguistic studies of the Jiarong languages. Some of these include Lin Xiangron, "Sound System of the Zhuo Keji (Ma'erkang) Dialect of Jiarong," *Yuyin Yanjiu*, no. 2 (1988); also Lin Xiangron, *Jiarongyu Yufa*; Ma Changshou, "Jiarong Minzu Shehui Shi," *Minzuxue Yanjiu Jikan*, no. 4 (1944); Qu Aitang, "Jiarongyu Gaikuang," *Minzu Yuwen*, no. 2 (1984) and "Jiarongyude Fangyan: Fangyan Huafen He Yuyan Shibie"; Yasuhiko Yashuda, *A Historical Study of the Jiarong Verb System* (Tokyo: Seishido, 1984); and Jackson Tianshin Sun, "Caodeng rGyalrong Phonology: A First Look," *Linguistics of the Tibeto-Burman Area* 17, no. 2 (1994).
6. See S. Y. Hu, "Ethnobotany of the Gia-rung Tribe," ms. (Yale: Yale Divinity School, n.d.).
7. Muse, "A Profile of the Jiarong People of China."

JIASOU

1. Pelkey, "Yunnan's Myriad Yi," 36.
2. Johnston, *From Peking to Mandalay*, 81.
3. Pelkey, "Yunnan's Myriad Yi," 36.

JING

1. According to the 1990 census 14,694 Jing live in Fangcheng County.
2. Ma Yin, *China's Minority Nationalities*, 397.
3. Bradley, "East and South-East Asia," 160.
4. Jun Su, "A Trip to the Three Islands Inhabited by the Jing People," *China Tourism*, no. 77 (n.d.), 38.
5. "He Will Not Break a Bruised Reed: Simon Church in Beihai," *Bridge*, no. 46 (March-April 1991): 10-11.

JINGPO

1. According to the 1990 census there were 8 counties or municipalities in China that recorded more than 500 Jingpo people. In descending order, they are: Longchuan 42,213; Yingjiang 36,211; Luxi 24,945; Ruili 10,554; Lianghe 1,230; Gengma 706; Tengchong 633; Wanding 558. Note: these figures refer to the Jingpo nationality, and not to the Jingpo ethnic group profiled in *Operation China*. These larger figures include the Zaiwa, Maru, Lashi, etc.
2. Johnstone, *Operation World* (1993), 398.
3. Ramsey, *The Languages of China*, 271-72.
4. Ma Yin, *China's Minority Nationalities*, 297.
5. Cai Jailin, "Jingpozu Lashi Chubu Diaocha," *Minzu Yanjiu Diaocha* 2 (Kunming, 1986): 126-27.
6. Sir George Scott, "Among the Hill Tribes of Burma," 301.
7. Tegenfeldt, *A Century of Growth*, 181.
8. YASS 220, Section 5.
9. Covell, *The Liberating Gospel*, 264.
10. *CPLMR*, no. 119 (December 1991-February 1992).

JINO

1. According to the 1990 census there were 2 counties or municipalities in China that recorded more than 500 Jino people. They are Jinghong (16,897), and Mengla (752).
2. Luo Yunzhi, "The Jinuo People's Sacrifice to the Rice God," *China Tourism*, no. 162 (January 1994): 73.
3. Zhang Weiwen and Zeng, *In Search of China's Minorities*, 240.
4. J. Chao (ed.), *The China Mission Handbook*, 161.
5. Personal communication, November 1997.
6. YWAM Macau, personal communication, June 1997.
7. This official 1990 census figure (18,021) appears to disagree with that cited under Population in China. However, it includes the population of 1,000 speakers of Buyuan Jino who are profiled separately in *Operation China*. Therefore, this figure is subtracted to arrive at a more realistic and specific population figure (17,021) for the Jino.

JINO, BUYUAN

1. Jiangxi Educational Publishing, *EDCL*, 552.
2. Zheng Lan, Travels Through Xishuangbanna, 9.
3. Bethany World Prayer Center, "The Jinuo of China," 1997.
4. *GPD* 11, no. 3 (March 1992).
5. *GPD* 12, no. 9 (September 1993).
6. Zhang Weiwen and Zeng, *In Search of China's Minorities*, 241.

KADO

1. According to the 1990 census there were 203,559 Hani in Mojiang County and 69,630 in Yuanjiang County. Many of these are Kado.
2. A high percentage of Kado are illiterate. When new bank notes were issued in the 1950s, "some Han merchants took advantage of the minority peoples' inability to read Chinese characters to cheat them on the exchange. It was reported that even the trade marks of socks were alleged to be bank notes." T'ien, *Peaks of Faith*, 77, fn. 46.
3. Grimes, *Ethnologue* (1996), 552.
4. "When a Hani believer, denounced as a 'despotic middle peasant', was slapped on the face by one of the spectators hired for the meeting, his fellow tribesmen wept bitterly on the spot. Even after prohibition, the Hani Christians protested unequivocally against using their church for accusation meetings against the landlords." See T'ien, *Peaks of Faith*, 77-78, fn. 46.
5. YASS 297, Section 16.
6. Baker wrote several detailed accounts of the work among the Kado. See *God in Kado Land*; *The Three Worlds* (Taiwan: The Adullam Reading Campaign, 1937) and "A Continued Account of God Working Among the Kado and Other Primitive Tribes in Yunnan Province, S. W. China," *Adullam News*, no. 36 (1937).
7. Mrs. Ivan Allbutt, *China's Aboriginal Peoples*, 11.
8. T'ien, *Peaks of Faith*, 85.
9. Ibid., 87.
10. YASS 288, Section 2-E; and YASS 297; cited in T'ien, *Peaks of Faith*, 43.
11. Ibid.
12. "Yunnan Duominzu Tese de Shaohuizhui Xiandaihua Wenti Yanju" [Research for Modernizing Multi-National Yunnan], 70, as cited in T'ien, *Peaks of Faith*, 123.

KAWA

1. J.-O. Svantesson, in a personal communication, as cited in Grimes, *Ethnologue* (1996), 563.
2. Identifying the Kawa in China is complicated because the Chinese used the term *Kawa* to refer to all Wa groups. *Kawa* means "Cut Wa" in reference to their former head-hunting practices. Today, most Kawa in China believe the name is derogatory and prefer to simply be called *Wa*. However, this group speaks a different language from the

other Wa groups in China and is not merely socio-historically distinct.

3. YASS 279, Section 8; cited in T'ien, *Peaks of Faith*, 21.
4. Tian Jizhou and Luo Zhiji, *Ximing Wazu Shehui Xingtai* (Kunming, 1980), 97, as cited in T'ien, *Peaks of Faith*, 20-21. In the 1980's, the Wa in Gouhe converted to Christianity. The past decimation of their community is still a sensitive issue, but in 1998 they indicated to a missionary that they were willing to take the gospel to the Kawa in Asai if God wanted them to.
5. T'ien, *Peaks of Faith*, 20.
6. Ibid., 21.
7. *CPLMR*, no. 119 (December 1991-February 1992).
8. T'ien, *Peaks of Faith*, 146.

KAZAK

1. This official 1990 census figure (1,111,718) appears to disagree with that cited under Population in China. However, it includes the 2,000 Kazaks in Qinghai who are an isolate language group. These are subtracted from the census figure to give a more realistic and specific population of 1,109,718 for the Kazak people group in China.
2. 491,637 (1964 census); 509,375 (1953 census).
3. 133,000 in Mongolia; 88,000 in Turkmenistan; 37,000 in Kyrgyzstan (1993 P. Johnstone); 3,000 in Iran; 2,000 in Afghanistan; 600 in Turkey (1982); and in Germany.
4. According to the 1990 census there were 45 counties or municipalities in China that recorded more than 500 Kazak people. In descending order, the largest are: Xinyuan 106,360; Zhaosu 59,334; Altai City 57,886; Nileke 57,296; Emin 55,191; Fuyun 51,070; Tekesi 48,816, and Tuoli 48,047. All of these are in Xinjiang.
5. Schwartz, *The Minorities of Northern China*, 19.
6. "Origin of the Names of China's Minority Nationalities," *China Tourism* 54 (n.d.): 75.
7. Schwartz, *The Minorities of Northern China*, 20.
8. Ibid.
9. Andrew D. W. Forbes, *Warlords and Muslims in Chinese Central Asia: A Political History of Republican Sinkiang 1911-1949* (Cambridge: Cambridge University Press, 1986), 17.
10. Sinclair, *The Forgotten Tribes of China*, 13.
11. *GPD* 2, no. 12 (December 1982).
12. *CPLMR*, no. 119 (December 1991-February 1992).
13. *Call to Prayer* (Colorado, August-September 1997).

KAZAK, QINGHAI

1. Wong How-Man, "Peoples of China's Far Provinces," 296.
2. Ibid.
3. See Milton J. Clark, "How the Kazaks Fled to Freedom," *National Geographic* (November 1954): 624.
4. *Reports of the British and Foreign Bible Society* (1922), 214.

KEJI

1. Jose Ignacio Cabezon, "Islam on the Roof of the World," *ARAMCO World* (January-February 1998): 17.
2. Buckley and Strauss (eds.), *Tibet*, 125.
3. *GPD* 10, no. 6 (June 1991).
4. Ibid.
5. Ibid.
6. Cabezon, "Islam on the Roof of the World," 19.
7. Ibid., 17.

KEMEI

1. Jiangxi Educational Publishing, *EDCL*, 594.
2. Dwayne Graybill, personal communication, December 1996.
3. Milliken, "SIL China Nationalities and Languages Files."
4. Jiangxi Educational Publishing, *EDCL*, 554.
5. Graybill, personal communication, December 1996.
6. Ibid.
7. Ibid.

KERIYA

1. "Keriya People in the Taklimakan Desert," *China Tourism*, no. 186 (January 1996): 56.
2. Ibid., 60.
3. Ibid., 57.

KHAKAS

1. Hu Zhenhua, "Heilongjiang Fuyu Xiande Kirgiz Zu Jiqi Yuyan Tedian," *Zhongyang Minzu Xueyuan Xuebao*, no. 35 (1983): 65-69.
2. Schwartz, *The Minorities of Northern China*, 32.
3. Reimer, *Operation Soviet Union*.
4. Grimes, *Ethnologue* (1996), 553.
5. Janhunen and Salminen, *UNESCO Red Book*.
6. Schwartz, *The Minorities of Northern China*, 29.
7. Hu Zhenhua, "Heilongjiang Fuyu Xiande Zu Jiqi Yuyan Tedian," 65.

KHAMPA, EASTERN

1. Rock, "Konka Risumgongba," 43.
2. Bradley, "East and South-East Asia," 170.
3. Grimes, *Ethnologue* (1996), 553.
4. Mackerras, *China's Minorities*, 71.
5. Buckley and Strauss (eds.), *Tibet*, 16. Throughout the 1960s Khampa rebels, from their base in Mustang, Nepal, continued to mount spasmodic attacks on the Chinese from across the border. This was ended only after Mao Zedong apparently personally threatened the King of Nepal.
6. Wang Duanyu, "Lama Jiao yu Zangzu Renkou," *Minzu Yanjiu* (1984): 46.
7. Tsering, *Sharing Christ in the Tibetan Buddhist World*, 86.
8. Covell, *The Liberating Gospel*, 50.
9. "Christianity and Tibet," *Pray for China Fellowship* (OMF International, April 1996).
10. Stauffer, *The Christian Occupation of China*, 278.

KHAMPA, NORTHERN

1. Australian Academy and CASS, *LAC*, C-11.
2. In recent years, severe winter storms have decimated the Northern Khampa. Tens of thousands of yaks and other animals have frozen to death, and hundreds of people killed by the cold or by the ensuing starvation. Various aid agencies have worked to allieviate the Northern Khampa's suffering.
3. Cited by Pamela Logan, *Lifestyle*, October-November 1994.
4. *The Edge* 2, no. 3 (Fall 1997).
5. Heinrich Harrer, *Seven Years in Tibet* (London: Pan Books, 1953), 94.

KHAMPA, WESTERN

1. Bradley, "East and South-East Asia," 170.
2. Cynthia Beall and Melvyn Goldstein, "The Remote World

of Tibet's Nomads," *National Geographic* (June 1989): 771.

3. Heinrich Harrer, *Return to Tibet* (Harmondsworth: Penguin, 1985), 24.
4. See David Plymire, *High Adventure in Tibet* (Springfield, Mo: Gospel Publishing House, 1959).
5. Stauffer, *The Christian Occupation of China*, 276.

KHMU

1. In the United States, small Khmu communities have formed in Santa Ana, California; Fort Worth, Texas; and Oklahoma City.
2. Jun Feng, "Xishuangbanna: Homeland of Minorities," *China Tourism*, no. 72 (n.d.): 36.
3. *China Reconstructs* (February 1988).
4. Perazic, "Little Laos," 57.
5. Jiangxi Educational Publishing, *EDCL*, 594.
6. "Though not Buddhists, the Khmu are entrusted with the Prabang (a statue of Buddha) during the Laotian New Year's celebration. The Prabang was brought to Laos when the first Lao chief came to the country from Cambodia. Thus, though the Laotian Buddhists are dominant in Laos and no longer follow animistic rituals, they recognize the fact that the Khmu tribe preceded them in the country by including them in their New Year's celebration." *GPD* 7, no. 9 (September 1988).
7. Quincy, *Hmong*, 71.
8. Vietnam News Agency, *Vietnam*, 98.
9. Jun Feng, "Xishuangbanna," 36.
10. AMO, "The Khmu," *Newsletter*, no. 47 (November 1997).
11. Ibid.
12. This official 1990 census figure (1,600) appears to disagree with that cited under Population in China. However, it includes 500 members of the Bit group who are profiled separately in *Operation China*. Therefore, the 500 are subtracted to give a more realistic and precise figure (1,100) for the Khmu.

KIM MUN

1. The Kim Mun live in the following locations: *Yunnan:* Malipo, Maguan, Xichou, Qiubei, Guangnan, Funing, Yanshan, Shizong, Hekou, Jiangcheng, Mojiang, Yuanyang, Jinping, Honghe, Luchun, Mengla and Jinghong counties; *Guangxi:* Xilin, Lingyun, Napo, Tianlin, Fengshan, Bama, Shangsi, Fengcheng, Lipu, Pingle, Jinxiu, Yongfu and Luzhai counties; *Hainan Island:* Qiongzhong, Baoting, Ledong, Qionghai, Tunchang, Wanning and Yaxian counties.
2. See Tadahiko Shintani and Yang Zhao, *The Mun Language of Hainan Island: Its Classified Lexicon* (Tokyo: Institute for the Study of Languages and Cultures of Asia and Africa, 1990). Ramsey states, "The ancestors of these 'Hainan Miao' were brought to the island in the sixteenth century by Chinese forces to help fight in their military campaigns against the Li. At that time the Chinese called them 'Miao' and that is still what they call them today." Ramsey, *The Languages of China*, 285-86.
3. Jiangxi Educational Publishing, *EDCL*, 561.
4. Xie Shixun, "Encounter With the Yao," 100.
5. "These Lanten are ingenious. Instead of hulling rice like the Siamese with two mill stones... the Lanten make a stream of water do the work. They have a mortar like the Lao and the pestle is at one end of a lever. But at the other end is a trough, into which pours a stream from a little height above. When the trough has become full enough to outweigh the ballast tied to the pestle and the trough dips down, the pestle raises; the trough then empties, and the ballast pulls the pestle down with some force into the rice in the mortar. Thus the canny Lanten harnesses the brook and makes it pound his paddy." Dodd, *The Tai Race*, 236.
6. "The raw materials used for making paper such as the roots of ferns and vine leaves can be found almost everywhere. The roots are first washed clean and then dried in the sun. Afterwards they are crushed and immersed in clean water for a long time till they start to rot. The vine leaves are also immersed in clean water for some time and then filtered out. The next step is to remove the roots, add the juice of the vine leaves and boil the mixture until it becomes a paste which is spread evenly on a net made of woven hemp with its four sides secured with planks on a specially built frame. When dried in the sun, a layer of paper forms on the net, and this can be removed and used... today it is used as window paper or pattern design paper for embroidery and shoe-making." He Huaibo, "The Primitive Paper-Making Technology of the Yao Nationality," *China Tourism*, no. 71 (n.d.): 59.
7. Song Enchang, "The Family Systems and it's Ethos," 231.
8. He Huaibo, "The Primitive Paper-Making Technology," 59.

KIONG NAI

1. Jiangxi Educational Publishing, *EDCL*, 559-60.
2. Yang Tiande, "A Riot of Yao Color," 85.
3. Xie Shixun, "Encounter With the Yao," 25.
4. Grimes, *Ethnologue* (1996), 543.
5. See David Strecker, "Some Comments on Benedict's Miao-Yao Enigma: the Na-e Language," *Linguistics of the Tibeto-Burman Area* 10, no. 2 (1987): 22-42.
6. Fei Xiaotong, "Fifty Years Investigation," 22-23.
7. Xie Shixun, "Encounter With the Yao," 31, 100.
8. Ibid., 100.

KIRGIZ

1. According to the 1990 census there were 19 counties or municipalities in Xinjiang that recorded more than 500 Kirgiz people. In descending order, the largest Kirgiz populations are: Akto 34,781; Wuqia 28,583; Aheqi 26,122; Atushi City 20,779, Tekesi 7,019.
2. "Origin of the Names of China's Minority Nationalities," *China Tourism*, no. 54 (n.d.): 75.
3. Hu Zhenhua, "Kirgiz yu Gaikuang," *Minzu Yuwen*, no. 14 (1982): 59.
4. Schwartz, *The Minorities of Northern China*, 29-30.
5. E. O. Reischauer and J. K. Fairbank, *East Asia: The Great Tradition* (Boston: Houghton Mifflin, 1958), 190.
6. C. Persson, "Christianity in the Tarim Basin," *Friends of Moslems* (April 1940): 20-21.
7. Covell, *The Liberating Gospel*, 172.
8. This official 1990 census figure (141,549) seems to disagree with the figure cited under Population in China. It includes the populations of the Akto Turkmen (2,000) and the Khakas (875). Therefore, the combined population of these two groups is subtracted from the 1990 census figure to arrive at a more realistic and specific number for the Kirgiz (138,600).
9. 70,151 (1964 census); 70,944 (1953 census).
10. The majority of Kirgiz live in Uqia, Akqi, Akto, and Atush counties. Others live in Uqturpan, Aksu, Yarkant, Tashkurgan, and Guma in southern *Xinjiang*; also Tekes, Monggolkure, Dorboljin, Bortaia, Jinghe, and Tokkuztara.

KONG GE

1. Robert Morse, unpublished study on the unidentified groups of Southwest China, 1991.
2. Luo Yunzhi, "The Aini People in Xishuangbanna," *China Tourism*, no. 179 (June 1995): 28.
3. Dwayne Graybill, personal communication, 7 December 1996. According to the 1990 census there were a total of 4,834 Bulang people, including the Kong Ge, in Jinghong County.
4. Luo Yunzhi, "The Aini People in Xishuangbanna," 28.
5. "The Kong Ge," *Asia For Christ*, no. 4 (September 1998).
6. Ibid.

KOREAN

1. *GPD* 4, no. 6 (June 1985). According to the 1990 census there were 158 counties or municipalities in China that recorded more than 500 Korean people. In descending order, the largest are: Longjin 183,990; Yanjishi 177,547; Helong 136,853; Hunchun 92,248; Wangqing 85,156; Tumen 70,278. All of these counties are in Jilin Province.
2. *Unreached Peoples '81* (Colorado: David Cook Publishers, 1981).
3. Schwartz, *The Minorities of Northern China*, 210.
4. Moffett, *A History of Christianity in Asia*, 297.
5. Storey (ed.), *China*, 19.
6. Ibid., 23.
7. Schwartz, *The Minorities of Northern China*, 207.
8. Ibid., 209.
9. Official government figures, 1990 census.
10. Moffett, *A History of Christianity in Asia*, 461.
11. Personal communication, August 1998.
12. *CPLMR*, no. 119 (December 1991-February 1992).
13. Information taken from the Amity Press website.
14. There are Korean communities also in Uzbekistan, Russia, Kazakstan, Saudi Arabia, Brazil, Canada, Kyrgyzstan, Germany, Tajikstan, and other countries.
15. 1,339,569 (1964 census); 1,120,405 (1953 census).
16. 103,000 in Kazakstan; 66,000 in Saudi Arabia; 60,000 in Brazil; 29,000 in Canada; 18,000 in Kyrgyzstan; 14,000 in Germany; 13,000 in Tajikistan; 4,000 in Guam; Total: 74.3 million (all figures from P. Johnstone, 1993).
17. 1,210,000 (46%) of all Koreans in China live in the Hyanbian Korean Autonomous County along the Tumen River; Yanji and Tumen cities; also Yanji, Helong, Antu, Hunchun, Wangquing and Dunhua counties in the Changbai Korean Autonomous Prefecture.

KUAN

1. Jiangxi Educational Publishing, *EDCL*, 594.
2. Bradley, "East And South-East Asia," 159.
3. Zheng Lan, *Travels Through Xishuangbanna*, 2-3.
4. *Amity News Service*, June 1996.

KUCONG

1. Grimes, *Ethnologue* (1996), 554.
2. *Pray for China*, no. 120 (1994).
3. "Kucong People in Yunnan," *China Tourism, no.* 18 (n.d.): 34.
4. *Yunnan Nianjian 1988*, 240.
5. James A. Matisoff, as cited in Grimes, *Ethnologue* (1996), 554.
6. The 1996 census listed 5,654 Kucong living in the southwest part of Xinping County. *Yuxi Nianjian* (1996).
7. "Kucong People in Yunnan," 34.
8. See Arthur D. and Pamela J. Cooper, "A Preliminary Phonology of the Banlan dialect of Lahu Shi," *Focus on Phonology: PYU Working Papers in Linguistics*, no. 1 (Chiang Mai, Thailand: Payap University Graduate Linguistics Department, 1996): 17-52.
9. Zheng Lan, *Travels Through Xishuangbanna*, 17.
10. YASS 349, Section 7, 70; cited in T'ien, *Peaks of Faith*, 143.
11. Zheng Lan, *Travels Through Xishuangbanna*, 17.
12. Jun Feng, "Xishuangbanna," 37.
13. T'ien, *Peaks of Faith*, 136. The Kucong in Burma first received the Gospel from William Young in 1903. "By May 1905, Young had baptized 1,623 converts, from both Lahu Shi [Kucong] and Lahu Na." Covell, *The Liberating Gospel*, 226.

KYAKALA

1. Janhunen and Salminen, *UNESCO Red Book*.
2. Storey (ed.), *China*, 743.
3. June Dreyer, *China's Forty Millions: Minority Nationalities and National Integration in the People's Republic of China* (Cambridge, Mass: Harvard University Press, 1976), 2.
4. Janhunen and Salminen, *UNESCO Red Book*.
5. Ibid.
6. Ibid.
7. Ibid.
8. Storey (ed.), *China*, 735.

KYERUNG

1. GEM, "World's Peoples Listed By Country."
2. Grimes, *Ethnologue* (1996), 729.
3. Ibid.

LABA

1. *Minzu Shibie Wenxian Ziliao Huibian*, 51.
2. Ibid.
3. The full list of unclassified groups from the 1982 census has never been released to the public in its entirety, but in recent years Chinese publications have begun to write about some of the groups. By collecting these articles, one is able to piece together something of the overall picture of Guizhou's unclassified groups.
4. *Guizhou Nianjian 1985*, 51.
5. Ibid.
6. Ibid.
7. Ibid.

LABAPO

1. Pelkey, "Report on the Yi Peoples of Honghe Prefecture," 14.
2. *Kaiyuan Xian Zhi*, 618.
3. See Augustine Henry, "The Lolos and Other Tribes of Western China," *Royal Anthropological Institute*, no. 33 (1903): 96-107.
4. Kenelm Burridge, "Missionaries and the Perception of Evil," in D. Whiteman (ed.), *Missionaries, Anthropologists, and Cultural Change* 1: *Studies in Third World Societies*, no. 25 (Williamsburg: College of William and Mary, 1985): 153.

LADAKHI

1. The Joshua Project originally listed a figure of 12,000 Ladakhi in China, which was also used in our book *The 50 Most Unreached People Groups in China and Tibet*.

Subsequent research, however, has shown this figure to be far too high. The Joshua Project also lowered their figure to 2,400 in China before the publication of their prayer profiles.

2. For an account of the Chinese invasion, see W. E. Garrett, "Mountain Top War in Remote Ladakh," *National Geographic* (May 1960).
3. Grimes, *Ethnologue* (1996), 586.
4. See Thomas J. Abercrombie, "Ladakh: The Last Shangri-La," *National Geographic* (March 1978): 332-59.
5. Hellmut de Terra, "On the World's Highest Plateaus," *National Geographic* (March 1931): 331-32.
6. Stauffer, *The Christian Occupation of China*, 278.
7. Ibid., 281.

LAGOU

1. Pelkey, "Yunnan's Myriad Yi," 70.
2. See *Weining Yizu Huizu Miaozu Zizhixian Minzuzhi*, 12-128.
3. Samuel Clarke, *Among the Tribes in South-West China*, 121.
4. Tian Huo, "The Colorful Peoples of the Wumeng Mountains," *China Tourism*, no. 111 (n.d.): 23.
5. *Weining Yizu Huizu Miaozu Zizhixian Minzuzhi*, 128.

LAHU

1. According to the 1990 census there were 24 counties or municipalities in China that recorded more than 500 Lahu people. In descending order, the largest are: Lancang 192,209; Menghai 36,209; Shuangjiang 31,734; Menglian 31,384; Gengma 16,170; Zhenyuan 14,249. All of these counties are in Yunnan Province.
2. T'ien, *Peaks of Faith*, 8.
3. James A. Matisoff, *The Grammar of Lahu* (Berkeley: University of California Press, 1973).
4. A Lahu dictionary exists. Institute for the Study of Human Issues, *Lahu-English Dictionary* (Philadelphia, n.d.).
5. T'ien, *Peaks of Faith*, 8.
6. "Stealing was customarily permitted when it was not committed in their own villages.... In some Lahu villages in Shuangjiang district, because of their miserable existence... stealing became an approved means of livelihood.... Consequently, villagers over the age of 25 had all become light-fingered. Some even achieved the record of stealing scores of cows from other villages." T'ien, *Peaks of Faith*, 15-16.
7. Harold Young, "To the Mountain Tops, A Study of the Lahu of Burma and Thailand," ms. (n.d.): 59. With the economy improving in recent years, the total annual sale of liquor in one Lahu district jumped from 100 tons in 1986 to 900 tons in 1987. *Renmin Ribao*, 21 June 1988.
8. Don Richardson, *Eternity in Their Hearts* (Ventura, Ca: Regal Books, 1981), 97-98.
9. Ibid., 98.
10. W. M. Young, "The Awakening of Keng Tung," *The Missionary Review of the World* (March 1906): 215. In recent years some scholars have critically reviewed Young's pioneer work. "William Young did not know the Lahu language or culture, and as a result he may have given interpretations of various things he saw from his own point of view.... The 'mass movements' Young wrote about were often extremely shallow, and based on misconceptions by the people. The Lahu thought if they had a bath (which they called baptism in Lahu) they would never die, and so when some who had been baptized later died the people were furious and said, 'We have been lied to', and would not allow Christian evangelists to stay overnight in their villages." Paul Lewis, personal communication, February 1999.
11. Niu Shao, "The Lahu Christians," *Bridge*, no. 43 (September-October 1990): 13.
12. *CPLMR*, no. 119 (December 1991-February 1992).
13. Niu Shao, "The Lahu Christians."
14. This official 1990 census figure (411,476) appears to disagree with that cited under Population in China. However, since the larger figure includes the Kucong and Laopang which are profiled separately in *Operation China*, their combined population is subtracted from the 1990 total to give a more realistic and specific population for the Lahu (369,400).
15. 191,241 (1964 census); 139,060 (1953 census)

LAHULI, TINAN

1. Voegelin and Voegelin, *Classification and Index of the World's Languages*.
2. Stauffer, *The Christian Occupation of China*, 278.
3. Bradley, "East and South-East Asia," 169.
4. Grimes, *Ethnologue* (1996), 587. One good linguistic study of the Lahauli languages is Jag Deva Singh, "Lahauli Verb Inflection," *Linguistics of the Tibeto-Burman Area* 12, no. 2 (1989): 41-49.
5. *GPD* 8, no. 7 (July 1989).
6. Ibid.
7. Covell, *The Liberating Gospel*, 57.

LAKA

1. An accurate population for the Laka is difficult to gauge due to the fact they are not officially recognized by the Chinese government and also because they are often grouped together under the Naluo. A 1930's report stated there were "more than one hundred Laka villages, with the largest having more than eighty households." See Heijdra, "Who Were the Laka?" 191.
2. Samuel Clarke, *Among the Tribes in South-West China*, 292.
3. The only known Chinese source that discusses the identity of the Laka is "Wuding Xian Diwuqu Minzu Guanxi Ji Zudian Guanxi De Diaocha," in *Zhongyang Fangwentuan Dierfentuan Yunnan Minzu Qingkuang Huiji*, 31-41.
4. "Jidujiao Zai Wudingqu de Qingkuang," in *Zhongyang Fangwentuan Dierfentuan Yunnan Minzu Qingkuang Huiji*, 16, as cited in Heijdra, "Who Were the Laka?" 169.
5. Lu Yi, "Yizu de Zucheng, Zhixi Ji qi Wenhua Tezheng," in Zuo Yutang and Tao Xueliang (eds.), *Bimo Wenhua Lun* (Kunming: Yunnan Renmin Chubanshe, 1993), 191-201.
6. Samuel Clarke, *Among the Tribes in South-West China*, 293.
7. Heijdra, "Who Were the Laka?" 169.
8. Ibid.
9. Samuel Clarke, *Among the Tribes in South-West China*, 301.
10. Covell, *The Liberating Gospel*, 278.

LAKKIA

1. Bradley, "East and South-East Asia," 166.
2. J.-O. Svantesson, personal communication, 1990, as cited in Grimes, *Ethnologue* (1996), 554.
3. Bradley, "East and South-East Asia," 166.
4. Diller, "Tai Languages."
5. Fei Xiaotong, "Fifty Years Investigation," 27.
6. Some Christian literature lists 1912 Scripture

translations for the Lakkia, but this is an error. The translations were done in the Laka language of northern Yunnan.

7. See David B. Solnit, "The Position of Lakkia Within Kadai," in SIL, *Comparative Kadai*, 219-38.
8. Grimes, *Ethnologue* (1996), 554.
9. Fei Xiaotong, "Fifty Years Investigation," 27.
10. Xie Shixun, "Encounter With the Yao," 26.
11. Stauffer, *The Christian Occupation of China*, 147.

LALU, XINPING

1. Pelkey, "Yunnan's Myriad Yi," 44.

LALU, XUZHANG

1. *Baoshan Xian Zhi* (1996), 706.
2. Ibid.
3. "Flowers and the Yi," *China Tourism*, no. 47 (n.d.): 76.
4. Samuel Clarke, *Among the Tribes in South-West China*, 133.

LALU, YANGLIU

1. Pelkey, "Yunnan's Myriad Yi," 43.
2. Dessaint, *Minorities in Southwestern China*, 170-71.

LALUO, JIANTOU

1. Pelkey, "Yunnan's Myriad Yi," 41.
2. Ibid.

LALUO, MISHABA

1. The Mishaba Laluo are found in the following counties of Yunnan: Fengqing (115,000), Yunxian (90,000), Nanjian (88,000), Weishan (78,000), Jingdong (50,000), Yongping (39,000), Yangbi (25,000), Bsoahan (20,000), Changning (19,000), Midu (18,000), Lincang (8,000), Gengma (6,000), Yongde (2,000), Cangyuan (1,500), Nanhua (1,500) and Shuangjiang (500). Pelkey, "Yunnan's Myriad Yi," 38.
2. Ibid., 39.
3. Ibid.

LAMA

1. Voegelin and Voegelin, *Classification and Index of the World's Languages*.
2. See Paul Popper, "Cane Bridges of Asia," *National Geographic* (August 1948): 243-50.
3. Ma Yin, *China's Minority Nationalities*, 317.
4. Henri Philippe Marie Prince d'Orleans, "From Yun-nan to British India," *Geographical Journal*, no. 7 (1896): 300-09.
5. Ma Yin, *China's Minority Nationalities*, 319.
6. Zhang Weiwen and Zeng, *In Search of China's Minorities*, 226.
7. Stauffer, *The Christian Occupation of China*, 463.

LAMI

1. Xia Jie, "The Long Dragon Banquet: The Lami Street Fest," *China Tourism*, no. 76 (n.d.): 77.
2. Pelkey, "Yunnan's Myriad Yi," 92.
3. See Von Geusau, "The Second Hani/Akha Culture Studies Conference."
4. Xia Jie, "The Long Dragon Banquet," 76.
5. Ibid.
6. Ibid., 78.

LAOPANG

1. GEM, "World's Peoples Listed By Country."
2. John Kuhn, *We Found a Hundred Tribes*.
3. Mundhenk, as cited in Grimes, *Ethnologue* (1996), 720.
4. Marcus L. Loane, *They Were Pilgrims* (Sydney, Australia: Angus & Robertson, 1970), 170.
5. Jane Hunter, *The Gospel of Gentility: American Women Missionaries in Turn-of-the-Century China* (Boston: Yale University Press, 1984), 19.
6. Zhang Weiwen and Zeng, *In Search of China's Minorities*, 313.
7. *CPLMR*, no. 119 (December 1991-February 1992).
8. Niu Shao, "The Lahu Christians," 13.
9. W. M. Young, "The Awakening of Keng Tung," 215.

LAOWU

1. Pelkey, "Report on the Yi Peoples of Honghe Prefecture," 14.
2. "The Laowu can be found in western Jinping County where they are suspected to live in the eastern parts of Laojizhai District (Pingzhai and Tuanjie communities) and the southwestern parts of Yingpan District (Shuitang and Taiyangzhai communities)." Pelkey, "Yunnan's Myriad Yi," 16.
3. Shaw, "Some Current Trends of Ethnology in China," 46.
4. de Beauclair, *Tribal Cultures of Southwest China*, 3.

LASHI

1. The 1995 Joshua Project listed an undocumented Lashi population of 37,000 in China, but this is too high. It is very difficult making an accurate estimate of the Lashi population in China due to the fact they are officially counted as part of the Jingpo nationality. Their numbers in China may also be lower than our figure. There were a total of 24,945 Jingpo people in Luxi County according to the 1990 census.
2. Ola Hanson, *The Kachins: Their Customs and Traditions* (Rangoon: American Baptist Mission Press, 1913), 21.
3. de Beauclair, *Tribal Cultures of Southwest China*, 9.
4. T'ien, *Peaks of Faith*, 16.

LATI

1. Liang Min, "The Lachi Language," in Edmonson (ed.), *Kadai*.
2. Diller, "Tai Languages."
3. Grimes, *Ethnologue* (1996), 555.

LAWA

1. Bradley, "East and South-East Asia," 160.
2. Linguistic research in Lawa in Thailand includes Jiranan Komonkitiskun, "Lawa Pronouns," *Mon-Khmer Studies* 21, (1992): 199-205.
3. Ma Yin, *China's Minority Nationalities*, 276-77.
4. Bethany World Prayer Center, "The Western Lawa of China" (1997).
5. T'ien, *Peaks of Faith*, 25.
6. Ibid., 31.

LAWU

1. Pelkey, "The Yi Peoples of Yuxi Prefecture," 7.
2. Perhaps the earliest mention of the Lawu appears in Sainson, *Nan-tchao Ye-che*.
3. Stevan Harrell, "The History of the History of the Yi," in Harrell (ed.), *Cultural Encounters on China's Ethnic Frontiers*, 85.
4. Vial, "Les Lolos," 38.

LEMO

1. Francis Kingdon Ward, *The Land of the Blue Poppy* (Cambridge: Cambridge University Press, 1913), 230.
2. Dwayne Graybill, personal communication, September 1997.
3. "Tremendous Success in Small Minority Area," *New China News Agency*, 25 November 1958.

LESU

1. *Chuxiong Yizu Zizhizhou Zhi*, 361. The Lesu inhabit 38 villages in Yuanjiang County, about 40 villages in Xinping County, six villages in Eshan County, and five villages in Shiping County of Honghe Prefecture, including Mosha Lang of Baoxiu District; Liumeini and Shiyatou villages of Daqiao District; and Sansu Village of Xincheng District.
2. Pelkey, "Report on the Yi Peoples of Honghe Prefecture," 19.
3. Shaw, "Some Current Trends of Ethnology in China," 46.
4. Pelkey, "Report on the Yi Peoples of Honghe Prefecture," 19.
5. Ibid.
6. Ibid. The Lesu have been vividly described as a people who practice "unsophisticated and jolly love-making. A marriage is a success by half, provided a lad and a girl go to the 'dancing around', care for each other, profess their mutual affection and get along swimmingly." *Yunnan Provincial Tourist Brochure* (Kunming, 1995).

LHOBA, BOGAR

1. He Guanghua, "The Lost Horizons of Medog," 47-50.
2. Australian Academy and CASS, *LAC*, C-10.
3. The figure of 200,000 Lhoba comes from Ma Yin, Questions and Answers about China's Minority Nationalities, 166-67. Ma mentions 200,000 Lhoba and 60,000 Monba in Tibet, which is undoubtedly a misprint. The table in the back of the same book lists 2,000 Lhoba and 6,000 Monba. No other research suggests such a high population for these groups. Unfortunately, much confusion has been caused as a result of references repeatedly quoting the misprint.
4. For a comprehensive commentary on the Bogar language, see Sun Hongkai et al., *The Languages of the Menba, Luoba and Deng Peoples.*
5. Ma Yin, *China's Minority Nationalities*, 224.
6. He Guanghua, "The Lost Horizons of Medog," 47-50.
7. "The Lhobas," *Chinese Around the World* (May 1995): 10.
8. Ibid.

LHOBA, YIDU

1. J.-O. Svantesson, 1990 personal communication, as cited in Grimes, *Ethnologue* (1996), listed 200,000 speakers of Lhoba in India, but we believe this figure refers to the Adi people, who speak a related language. Workers living in northeast India say there are either none, or a few people who call themselves *Lhoba* in India.
2. Ramsey, *The Languages of China*, 250.
3. Jiangxi Educational Publishing, *EDCL*, 546.
4. F. C. Wan, "Unforgettable Times With Our Lhoba Friends," *China Tourism*, no. 70 (n.d.): 103.
5. Ibid., 58.

LHOMI

1. Hildegard Diemberger, "Gangla Tshechu, Beyul Khenbalung," in C. Ramble and M. Brauen (eds.), *Anthropology of Tibet and the Himalaya* (Zurich: Ethnographic Museum of the University of Zurich, 1993), 60-69, states that Lhomi means "wild people of the south" but their name does not carry that connotation. *Lho* means "south" and *mi* "people." In fact, the Lhomi are not wild by nature at all, but are known for being sedate and peaceful.
2. See Olavi and Marja Vesalainen, "Lhomi Phonetic Summary" (Kathmandu: SIL and the Institute of Nepal and Asian Studies, 1976): 62; and "Clause Patterns in Lhomi," *Pacific Linguistics B*, no. 53 (Canberra: ANU, 1980): vii, 100.
3. Grimes, *Ethnologue* (1996), 729.
4. *GPD* 13, no. 5 (May 1994).
5. Ibid.

LI, BENDI

1. Australian Academy and CASS, *LAC*, C-14. According to the 1990 census there were 32 counties or municipalities in China that recorded more than 500 Li people. In descending order, the largest are: Ledong 155,144; Sanya City 152,277; Lingshui 147,789; Baisha 88,770; Qiongzhong 84,567; Baoting 84,122; Changjiang 67,880; Dongfang 63,501; Wanning 59,333; Tongshi City 55,471; Guanling (Guizhou) 55,105; Dan 40,165; Tunchang 11,654. Note: These figures refer to the total number of Li people. The census did not distinguish divisions among the Li. Because of considerable geographic overlap, it is impossible to estimate populations for each Li group based on the 1990 census. In addition, there are more than 8 more counties in Guizhou Province with more than 500 Li people; two in Guangxi; and one (Dianbai) in Guangdong.
2. Leonard Clark, "Among the Big Knot Lois of Hainan," *National Geographic* (September 1938): 408.
3. Samuel Clarke, *Among the Tribes in South-West China*, 20.
4. V. Li, *Some Approaches to the Classification of Small Ethnic Groups.* Also see Ramsey, *The Languages of China*, 247-48.
5. Bradley, "East And South-East Asia," 165.
6. Samuel Clarke, *Among the Tribes in South-West China*, 20.
7. Storey (ed.), *China*, 743.
8. Leonard Clark, "Among the Big Knot Lois of Hainan," 409.
9. *CPLMR*, no. 119 (December 1991-February 1992).

LI, HA

1. Leonard Clark, "Among the Big Knot Lois of Hainan," 410.
2. Grimes, *Ethnologue* (1992), 518.
3. See picture in Leonard Clark, "Among the Big Knot Lois of Hainan," 400.
4. Ibid., 408.
5. Ibid., 409.
6. Leung Sze Tai, "Christmas at the Foot of Five-Finger Mountain," *Bridge*, no. 27 (January-February 1988): 8.
7. The 1987 figure (450,000) appears to disagree with that cited under Population in China. However, this figure includes 60,000 members of the Cun nationality who are profiled separately in *Operation China*. Their population is subtracted from the larger figure to give a more realistic and specific figure for the Li Ha (390,000).

LI, JIAMAO

1. Australian Academy and CASS, *LAC*, C-14.
2. Ibid.

3. Jiangxi Educational Publishing, *EDCL*, 586.
4. Ibid.
5. Ma Yin, *China's Minority Nationalities*, 407.
6. "The Church on Hainan Island: Past and Present," *Bridge*, no. 27 (January-February 1988): 4.

LI, MEIFU

1. Australian Academy and CASS, *LAC*, C-14.
2. Ma Yin, *China's Minority Nationalities*, 406.
3. Ibid.
4. Zhang Weiwen and Zeng, *In Search of China's Minorities*, 313.
5. Leonard Clark, "Among the Big Knot Lois of Hainan," 411.
6. *Bridge* (May-June 1992) stated there were 37,000 Christians on Hainan Island. Since then the church has grown rapidly, including one church movement on northern Hainan which started approximately 550 house churches between 1992 and 2000.

LI, QI

1. Australian Academy and CASS, *LAC*, C-14.
2. Leonard Clark, "Among the Big Knot Lois of Hainan," 418.
3. Bradley, "East and South-East Asia," 165.
4. Leonard Clark, "Among the Big Knot Lois of Hainan," 411.
5. Ibid., 417-18.
6. Stauffer, *The Christian Occupation of China*, 162.
7. Leonard Clark, "Among the Big Knot Lois of Hainan," 418.
8. For a brief account of a Li church at Zhongcun Village, see Leung Sze Tai, "Christmas at the Foot of Five-Finger Mountain," 7-8.

LIMI

1. Pelkey, "Yunnan's Myriad Yi," 47.
2. John Kuhn, *We Found a Hundred Tribes*.
3. Pelkey, "Yunnan's Myriad Yi," 47.
4. For more specific cultural and religious information on the Limi see the *Yongde Xian Zhi* and the *Fengqing Xian Zhi*, 563.
5. Alan Burgess, *The Small Woman* (London: The Reprint Society, 1959), illus.

LIMIN

1. *Minzu Shibie Wenxian Ziliao Huibian*, 54.
2. *Guizhou Nianjian 1985.*

LINGAO

1. Storey (ed.), *China*, 289-90. The three main officials behind the scam were merely fired from their jobs and made to criticize their actions.
2. Australian Academy and CASS, *LAC*, C-14.
3. Bradley, "East and South-East Asia," 164.
4. Ibid., 163.
5. For information about the Lingao language, see M. Hashimoto, "The Be Language: A Classified Vocabulary of Its Linkow Dialect," *Institute for the Study of Languages and Cultures of Asia and Africa* (1980); and Mark Hansell, "The Relation of Be to Tai," in SIL, *Comparative Kadai*, 239-87.
6. Leonard Clark, "Among the Big Knot Lois of Hainan," 391.

7. "The Church on Hainan Island: Past and Present," *Bridge*, no. 27 (January-February 1988): 4.
8. Ibid.

LINGHUA

1. See Jiangxi Educational Publishing, *EDCL*, n.p.
2. Heijdra, "Who Were the Laka?" 162.
3. Ibid.
4. Stauffer, *The Christian Occupation of China*, 148.

LIPO, EASTERN

1. Robert Morse, "China's Peoples, One Fourth of Planet Earth," *North Burma Christian Mission Newsletter* (September 1990).
2. The Eastern Lipo were horrified when the government classified them as part of the Yi nationality in the 1950s. They had been slaves of the Yi for centuries. Because of this, the Eastern Lipo had deep resentment toward the Yi. The Eastern Lipo told the authorities they would accept inclusion under any minority group except the Yi. The government did not change their status until a compromise was reached in the 1960s or 1970s. The Eastern Lipo living in Yuanmou, Wuding and Luquan were reclassified as "Lisu" by the government, but only at district, county and prefecture levels. On a national level, the Eastern Lipo continue to be classified as Yi. To confuse matters, there are also "genuine" Lisu people living in the same areas. The Western Lipo, who have a completely different history and ethnicity, had no such objections to being classified as Yi. See 1996 *Chuxiong Zhou Nianjian.*
3. Linguist David Morse spoke Lisu to the Eastern Lipo and found they could understand him, but when they spoke back to him he could not understand them. David Morse, personal communication, November 1997
4. T'ien, *Peaks of Faith*, 140.
5. Samuel Clarke, *Among the Tribes in South-West China*, 289-90.
6. Ibid., 290.
7. Nicholls traveled to Japan in 1912 to oversee the printing of the Eastern Lipo and Naluo (Gani) Gospels. See Enwall, *A Myth Become Reality* 1: 116.
8. Stauffer, *The Christian Occupation of China*, 349.
9. *Yunnan Ribao*, October 4, 1978; cited in T'ien, *Peaks of Faith*, 111.
10. Mai Chenger, "Luquan Jidujian Qingkuang Diaocha" [Investigation of Christianity in Luquan District]: 2, as cited in T'ien, *Peaks of Faith*, 121.
11. Robert Morse, "China's Peoples, One-Fourth of Planet Earth." In the 1990's the "Crying Cult" swept through the Eastern Lipo churches. Believers were told that if they did not cry at the time they accepted Christ they had never truly repented. This heresy caused deep confusion and division among the Lipo Christians.

LIPO, WESTERN

1. Jamin Pelkey, personal communication, August 1998.
2. Pelkey, "Yunnan's Myriad Yi," 56.
3. YASS 340, Section 5; cited in T'ien, *Peaks of Faith*, 66.
4. Harrell, "Ethnicity and Kin Terms," 186.
5. Pelkey, "Yunnan's Myriad Yi," 56.

LISU

1. 270,628 (1964 census), and 317,465 (1953 census).
2. The Lisu in Yunnan are primarily located in the upper reaches of the Salween and Mekong (Lancang) Rivers. According to the 1990 census there were 41 counties or

municipalities in China that recorded more than 500 Lisu people. In descending order, the largest are: Lushui 84,593; Weixi 75,037; Lanping 60,215; Fugong 60,132; Yongsheng 45,068; Wuding 26,452; Lijiang 24,531 (all in Yunnan Province). In Sichuan, the largest Lisu communities are found in Dechang 4,845; Yanbian 4,401; Huidong 2,261; Panzhihua 1,767 and Miyi 1,620.
3. Sadao Mitsumori, *Biruma, Shan no Shizen to Minzoku* [The Land and Peoples of Burma and the Shan States] (Tokyo: Nihon Hyoronsha, 1945).
4. George Forrest, "The Land of the Crossbow," *National Geographic* (February 1910): 154.
5. *Lisuzu Jianshi* (Kunming, 1983), 39.
6. YASS 340, Section 5; cited in T'ien, *Peaks of Faith*, 66.
7. Phyllis Thompson, *To Each Her Post: The Inspiring Lives of Six Great Women in China* (London: Hodder & Stoughton, 1982), 151.
8. Forrest, "The Land of the Crossbow," 154.
9. A. B. Cooke, *Fish Four and the Lisu New Testament* (Philadelphia, 1947), 20.
10. Isobel Kuhn, *Nest Above Abyss* (Philadelphia: CIM, 1947), 5.
11. YASS 412, Section 20; cited in T'ien, *Peaks of Faith*, 73.
12. Hefley, *China! Christian Martyrs of the 20th Century*, 60.
13. *CPLMR*, no. 119 (December 1991-February 1992).

LIUDE
1. Pelkey, "Yunnan's Myriad Yi," 83.
2. Wu Si, "Yi Life in the Greater and Lesser Liangshan Mountains," *China Tourism*, no. 94 (n.d.): 19-20.
3. Ibid.

LIUJIA
1. See *Minzu Shibie Wenxian Ziliao Huibian*, 340-41.
2. *Guizhou Nianjian 1985*.

LIWU
1. Pelkey, "Yunnan's Myriad Yi," 82.
2. Samuel Clarke, *Among the Tribes in South-West China*, 130-31.

LONG
1. Pelkey, "Yunnan's Myriad Yi," 36.

LONGJIA
1. *Minzu Shibie Wenxian Ziliao Huibian*, 14.
2. Ibid.

LOPI
1. Harrell, "Ethnicity and Kin Terms," 186.
2. Ibid., 182.
3. de Beauclair, *Tribal Cultures of Southwest China*, 3.
4. Harrell, "Ethnicity and Kin Terms," 182.
5. Stevan Harrell, "Ethnicity, Local Interests, and the State: Yi Communities in Southwest China," *Comparative Studies in Society and History, An International Quarterly* XXXII (1990): 537. Perhaps the earliest mention of the Lopi appears in Sainson, *Nan-tchao Ye-che*.
6. Harrell, "Ethnicity and Kin Terms," 186. Also see Chen Zongxiang, "The Dual System and the Clans of the Li-su and Shui-t'ien Tribes," *Monumenta Serica*, no. 12 (1947).
7. Harrell, "Ethnicity, Local Interests, and the State," 537.
8. Ibid.
9. Bloodworth, as cited in Covell, *The Liberating Gospel*, 18.
10. Covell, *The Liberating Gospel*, 204.
11. Adrien Kaunay, *Histoire des Missions de Chine Mission du Setchoan*, vols. 1 & 2 (Paris: P. Tequi, 1920).

LU
1. *Minzu Shibie Wenxian Ziliao Huibian*, 52.
2. *Guizhou Nianjian 1985*, 340-41.
3. Ibid.
4. CASS, *Information China* 3: 1248.
5. *Minzu Shibie Wenxian Ziliao Huibian*, 52.

LUOLUOPO, CENTRAL
1. *Chuxiong Yizu Zizhizhou Zhi*, 361.
2. In a bid to avoid the derogatory connotations being applied to their name, most Luoluopo are content to identify themselves as Yi to outsiders. Luoluopo may also now be considered derogatory by this group, even though it is their autonym.
3. Jiangxi Educational Publishing, *EDCL*, 547. A linguistic study of various Yi languages, including Central Luoluopo, is Shafer, "Phonetique Historique des Langues Lolo," 191-229.
4. Some Central Luoluopo claim their ancestors were Chinese troops from places in eastern China such as Fujian and Zhejiang who were assigned to Yunnan Province many centuries ago. Not all Luoluopo claim this.
5. See Alfred Liétard, *Au Yun-Nan, Les Lolo p'o: Une Tribu des Aborigenes de la Chine Meridionale* (Munster: Aschendorff, 1913).
6. Liétard, "Notes sur les Dialectes Lo-Lo," *Ecole Francaise d'Extreme-Orient* 9, no. 3 (1909).

LUOLUOPO, SOUTHEASTERN
1. Pelkey, "Yunnan's Myriad Yi," 19.

LUOLUOPO, WESTERN
1. Pelkey, "Yunnan's Myriad Yi," 44.
2. Dessaint, *Minorities in Southwestern China*, 32.
3. Ibid.

LUOWU
1. Pelkey, "Yunnan's Myriad Yi," 67.
2. See Henry Rodolph Davies, *Yun-nan: The Link Between India and the Yangtze* (Cambridge: Cambridge University Press, 1909).
3. Aime-Francois Legendre, "Voyage d'exploration au Yunnan Central et Septentrional, Populations: Chinois et Aborigenes," *Societe d'Anthropologie de Paris, Bulletin et Memoires*, ser. 6:4, no. 5 (1913).
4. *Yuxi Diqu Minzu Xiang Qing Kuang*, 192-225.
5. *Chuxiong Xian Zhi* (1995), 145.
6. Ibid.
7. Ibid.

LUZU
1. Rock, "The Land of the Yellow Lama", 467.
2. Harrell, "Ethnicity and Kin Terms," 181.
3. See Jackson Sun, "Review of Zangmian Yu Yuyin Han Cohui," 73-113.
4. Ibid., 77.
5. Rock, "The Land of the Yellow Lama", 467.
6. Ruxian Yan, "Marriage, Family and Social Progress of China's Minority Nationalities," 87.

MALIMASA
1. Matisoff, "Languages and Dialects of Tibeto-Burman."

2. Rock, "Through the Great River Trenches of Asia," 161.
3. Personal communication, September 1997.
4. Grimes, *Ethnologue* (1996), 558.
5. Rock, "Through the Great River Trenches of Asia," 163.
6. For an account of their work see Christian Simonnet, *Thibet, Voyage au Bout de la Chretiente* (Paris: Editions du Monde Nouveau, 1949).
7. Zondervan Publishing, *Great Missionaries to China* (Grand Rapids, 1947), 111.
8. George Sweeting, *More than 2000 Great Quotes and Illustrations* (Texas: Word Publishing, 1985), 184.

MANCHU

1. 54% of all Manchu in China live in Liaoning Province (1990 census).
2. Sinclair, *The Forgotten Tribes of China*, 43.
3. Grimes, *Ethnologue* (1996), 556.
4. CASS, *Information China* 3: 1248. According to the 1990 census there were 419 counties or municipalities in China that recorded more than 500 Manchu people. In descending order, the largest are: Xiuyan (Liaoning) 436,235; Fengcheng (Liaoning) 428,617; Qinglong (Hubei) 336,080; Kaiyuan City (Liaoning) 326,145; Beizhen (Liaoning) 320,524; Xingcheng City (Liaoning) 265,255.
5. Schwartz, *The Minorities of Northern China*, 149.
6. Janhunen and Salminen, *UNESCO Red Book*.
7. Australian Academy and CASS, *LAC*, C-5.
8. Grimes, *Ethnologue* (1996), 556.
9. Midge Conner, in a personal communication, September 1995, says there is somewhat of a recent revival in the Manchu language, and it is even being taught to children in some schools in Heilongjiang.
10. Ramsey, *The Languages of China*, 216-17.
11. See Jerry Norman, *A Concise Manchu-English Lexicon* (Seattle: University of Washington Press, 1978); Norman and Paul Georg Von Mollendorf, *A Manchu Grammar With Analyzed Texts* (Shanghai: American Presbyterian Mission Press, 1892).
12. "Chinese records report that the Suzhen sent tribute to the kings of the Western Zhou in the eleventh century BC." Schwartz, *The Minorities of Northern China*, 145.
13. Stauffer, *The Christian Occupation of China*, 252.
14. Ibid.
15. Hefley, *China! Christian Martyrs of the 20th Century*, 35-37: "Chang Sen had been converted after being stricken blind in mid-life. Before his conversion he had been known as *Wu so pu wei te*, meaning 'one without a particle of good in him'. A gambler, woman-chaser and thief, he had driven his wife and only daughter from home. When he was stricken blind, neighbors said it was the judgment of the gods for his evil doing."

    On hearing rumours that the Boxer soldiers were coming to kill Chang, the local believers hid him in a cave. The soldiers arrived and soon they had "rounded up about fifty Christians for execution. 'You're fools to kill all these,' a resident told them. 'For every one you kill, ten will spring up while that man Chang Sen lives. Kill him and you will crush the foreign religion.' The Boxers promised to spare the fifty if someone would take them to Chang. No one volunteered. Finally when it appeared the Boxers would kill the fifty, one man slipped away and found Chang to tell him what was happening. 'I'll gladly die for them,' Chang offered.... He was bound by local authorities and taken to the temple of the god of war, and commanded to worship. 'I can only worship the One Living and True God,' he declared.... The blind evangelist was put in an open cart and driven to the cemetery outside the city wall.... When they reached the cemetery, he was shoved into a kneeling position. Three times he cried, 'Heavenly Father, receive my spirit.' Then the sword flashed, and his head tumbled to the ground. The Boxers refused to let the Christians bury his body. Instead, fearful of a report that Blind Chang would rise from the dead, they forced the believers to buy oil and burn the mangled remains.... The local Christians were thus spared persecution."
16. There are an estimated 600,000 Christians in Heilongjiang Province according to Tony Lambert, personal communication, May 1997. Even the official TSPM church acknowledges a figure of 400,000.
17. The official 1990 census figure (9,821,180) appears to disagree with that given under Population in China. However, this number includes the 2,000 members of the Kyakala who are profiled separately in *Operation China*. Therefore, their population is subtracted from the Manchu census population to arrive at the more realistic and specific figure of 9,819,180.
18. 2,695,675 (1964 census); 2,418,931 (1953 census).
19. Also in *Shanghai*; *Fujian*; *Jiangxi*; *Anhui*; and *Zhejiang*.
20. The Manchu script is now obsolete and all Manchu believers use the Chinese Bible.

MANG

1. YWAM COM, personal communication, May 1997.
2. Bradley, "East and South-East Asia," 160.
3. YWAM COM, personal communication, May 1997.
4. Dang; Chu and Luu, *Ethnic Minorities in Vietnam*, 100-01.

MANMET

1. Asian Studies Institute, "The Dai People of Southeast Asia," 19.

MANYAK

1. Rock, "The Land of the Yellow Lama," 447.
2. Hodgson, "Sifán and Hórsók Vocabularies."
3. Rock, "The Land of the Yellow Lama," 467.
4. Ibid.

MAONAN

1. The official 1990 census figure (71,968) seems to disagree with that cited under Population in China. However, the 32,000 Yanghuang are included in this number and this group is profiled separately in *Operation China*. Therefore, their number is subtracted from the 1990 census figure to give a more realistic and specific population of 40,000 for the Maonan.
2. According to the 1990 census there were seven counties or municipalities in China that recorded more than 500 Maonan people. In descending order, the largest are: Huanjiang 54,894; Hechi City 4,643; Du'an 3,283; Nandan 2,199; Yishan 1,447; Donglan 953.
3. State Nationalities Affairs Commission, *China's Minority Peoples*, 69.
4. Ma Yin, *China's Minority Nationalities*, 392.
5. Robert E. Speer, *Servants of the King: Young Peoples Missionary Movement of the United States and Canada* (1909), 103.
6. *CPLMR*, no. 119 (December 1991-February 1992).
7. "New Church for Maonan People," *Amity News Service*, June 1992.

MARU

1. The population of the Maru in China is difficult to

estimate due to the fact they are officially counted as part of the Jingpo nationality. There were a total of 24,947 Jingpo people living in Luxi County according to the 1990 census. Most of these are Maru.

2. Jiangxi Educational Publishing, *EDCL*, 553.
3. In 1995 a Maru scholar in Myanmar wrote a newspaper article claiming the Maru were the nation's original inhabitants. His house was subsequently burned to the ground.
4. *Pray for Myanmar*, no. 3 (Bangkok: Tribes and Nations Outreach, 1996).
5. Ibid.
6. One translation is being done by the Baptists, another by a missionary couple based on the Thailand-Myanmar border, and a third effort by the former Catholic priest who translated the New Testament currently in print. Tragically, the three ministries are not working together on the project. The former Catholic priest hoped to finish the Old Testament within five years' time. In January 1996, however, his home burned to the ground. The books he used to aid his translation work, and the special typewriter he owned which was designed to type the Maru characters, were destroyed. The whole book of Genesis and several chapters of the book of Exodus, which he had already completed, were burned.

MENG

1. Grimes, *Ethnologue* (1992), 523.
2. Yunnan Provincial Travel and Tourism Administration, *A Tour to the Mysterious Land of Yunnan*, 129.
3. Von Geusau, "The Second Hani/Akha Culture Studies Conference."
4. Mackerras, *China's Minorities*, 248.
5. Wang Zhengfang, "We of the Hani Nationality."
6. *A Tour to the Mysterious Land of Yunnan*, 129.
7. T'ien, *Peaks of Faith*, 29-30.

MENGWU

1. Pelkey, "Yunnan's Myriad Yi," 36.
2. Ibid., 35.

MENIA

1. Rock, "The Land of the Yellow Lama," 447.
2. Edward Baber, "Travels and Researches in Western China," *Royal Geographic Society Supplementary Papers*, no. 1 (1882).
3. See Jackson Sun, "Review of Zangmian Yu Yuyin Han Cohui," 73-113.
4. Rock, "The Land of the Yellow Lama," 465.

MIAO, BAISHI

1. According to the 1990 census there were a total of 108,968 Miao people living in Tianzhu County.

MIAO, CHUAN

1. Lang Weiwei, "Lun Sichuan Miaozu Renkou de Lishi Yanbian," *Guizhou Minzu Yanjiu* (February 1995). 62,000 Chuan Miao live in Yibin, and 55,000 in Luzhou.
2. Lang Wei, *Tianzhujiao, Jidujiao Zai Chuannan Miaozu Diqu Chuanbo Shulue* (1989), 24-27.
3. d'Ollone, *L'Ecriture des Miao tseu* (Paris: E. Leroux, 1912), 269-73.
4. See W. T. Herbert, "The 'Come Down From Heaven' Missionaries Among the Miao," *China's Millions* (Australasian edition, November 1923): 166.
5. Quincy, *Hmong*, 58.
6. Ibid.
7. F. Bird, "Let Us Go Into the Next Towns," *China's Millions* (Australasian edition, June 1931): 85. The best account of Chuan Miao customs and songs is David Crockett Graham's *Songs and Stories of the Chuan Miao* (Washington DC: Smithsonian Institute, 1954).
8. Enwall, *A Myth Become Reality* 1: 141.
9. E. B. Wright, "Summary Report of Work Among the River Miao," ms. (1946): 1.
10. Herbert, "The 'Come Down From Heaven' Missionaries," 165.
11. Herbert, "As Happy as a King," *China's Millions* (April 1922): 42.
12. Wright, "Summary Report of Work Among the River Miao," 1.
13. Ibid.

MIAO, ENSHI

1. Michael Johnson, personal communication, November 1998.

MIAO, GUIYANG (NORTHERN)

1. Wang Fushi and Mao, *Reconstruction of Proto Miao-Yao*.
2. Groff G. Weidman, "Landscaped Kwangsi," 710.
3. For an explanation of the usage of the names *Miao* versus *Hmong* see Enwall, *A Myth Become Reality* 1: 14-16.
4. Samuel Clarke, *Among the Tribes in South-West China*, 1.
5. *Frontiers Focus* 4 no. 3.
6. F. M. Savina, as cited in Quincy, *Hmong*, 18.
7. Miao, "The Miao of China."
8. Samuel Clarke, *Among the Tribes in South-West China*, 152.
9. Covell, *The Liberating Gospel*, 89.

MIAO, GUIYANG (NORTHWESTERN)

1. Li Yunbing, *Minzu Yuwen* (June 1993). For the other six unclassified groups, see the Qanu Profile, n. 3, in *Operation China*.

MIAO, GUIYANG (SOUTH CENTRAL)

1. Lois Hoadley Dick, *Isobel Kuhn: The Canadian Girl Who Felt God's Call to the Lisu People of China* (Minneapolis: Bethany, 1987), 15.

MIAO, GUIYANG (SOUTHERN)

1. Quincy, *Hmong*, 18.
2. Ibid., 18-20.
3. Ibid., 25.
4. Miao, "The Miao of China."
5. Wong Tak Hing, "A Pilgrimage to the Mountains," 9-10.

MIAO, GUIYANG (SOUTHWESTERN)

1. Stauffer, *The Christian Occupation of China*, 176.
2. Quincy, *Hmong*, 35.
3. Miao, "The Miao of China."
4. Samuel Pollard, *In Unknown China* (London, 1921), 101.

MIAO, HUISHUI (CENTRAL)

1. Australian Academy and CASS, *LAC*, C-9. According to the 1990 census there were 78,400 Miao people in Huishui County, and 37,678 in Changshun County. The census did not distinguish between different Miao ethnic groups and languages.
2. Lu Ciyun, *Lu Yunshi Zazhu* (1683).
3. *Baoqing Fuzhi, Juan 5*, as cited in Jiang Yongxing, *Miaowen Tanjiu* (1989), 114.

4. Miao, "The Miao of China."
5. W. H. Hudspeth, "A Miao Quarterly Meeting," *The West China Missionary News* (January 1917): 13.

MIAO, HUISHUI (EASTERN)

1. Chen Shiruo, "Miaojia Youle Wenzi," *Xin Hunan Bao*, 14 January 1957, as cited in Enwall, *A Myth Become Reality* 1: 57.
2. Shunsheng Ling & Yihfu Ruey, "A Report on the Investigation of the Miao of Western Hunan," *Academia Sinica* (Shanghai, 1947): 165-68.
3. Miao, "The Miao of China."
4. Norma Diamond, "The Miao and Poison: Interactions on China's Southwest Frontier," *Ethnology*, no. 27 (January 1988): 9.

MIAO, HUISHUI (NORTHERN)

1. Grimes, *Ethnologue* (1996), 549.
2. T'ien, *Peaks of Faith*, 6-7.
3. See Covell, *The Liberating Gospel*, 85.
4. Miao, "The Miao of China."
5. Ibid.

MIAO, HUISHUI (SOUTHWESTERN)

1. Grimes, *Ethnologue* (1996), 550.
2. Enwall, *A Myth Become Reality* 1: 14.
3. Samuel Clarke, *Among the Tribes in South-West China*, 39-40.
4. Miao, "The Miao of China."
5. Covell, *The Liberating Gospel*, 88.
6. Kendall, *Eyes of the Earth*, 88.

MIAO, LUOBOHE

1. Wong How-Man, "Peoples of China's Far Provinces," 323.
2. Enwall, *A Myth Become Reality* 1: 24.
3. Covell, *The Liberating Gospel*, 84-85.

MIAO, LUPANSHUI

1. Lupanshui is divided into three distinct administraive units by the government. According to the 1990 census the Lupanshui Luzhi Tequ contained 43,783 Miao people; the Lupanshui Panxian Tequ 18,887 Miao; and the Lupanshui Zhongshan Qu 7,381 Miao. Many of these Miao are Lupanshui Miao.

MIAO, MASHAN (CENTRAL)

1. Michael Johnson, personal communication, January 1998. Grimes, in *Ethnologue* (1996), 549, states there are 13 tones in Central Mashan. This number ranks the Mashan languages among the highest number of tones in the world, equaled only by some Dong dialects and some South American languages.
2. Yan Ruyu (ed.), *Miaofeng Beilan* [Recommendation for Repelling the Miao], Chapter 10, as cited in T'ien, *Peaks of Faith*, 6-7.
3. Miao, "The Miao of China."
4. Ibid.

MIAO, MASHAN (NORTHERN)

1. Wang Fushi and Mao, *Reconstruction of Proto Miao-Yao*.
2. Samuel Clarke, *Among the Tribes in South-West China*, 16.
3. John Kuhn, *We Found a Hundred Tribes*.
4. Grimes, *Ethnologue* (1996), 550.
5. Hudspeth, *Stone Gateway*, 16-18.

MIAO, MASHAN (SOUTHERN)

1. Wang Fushi, *Miaoyu Jianzhi*, 103-04. According to the 1990 census there was a total of 31,123 Miao people living in Wangmo County.
2. Samuel Clarke, *Among the Tribes in South-West China*, 2.
3. Michael Johnson, personal communication, July 1996.
4. Miao, "The Miao of China."

MIAO, MASHAN (WESTERN)

1. Qin Tianzhen (ed.), *Guizhou Shengzhi, Dilizhi Shangce* (Guiyang: Guizhou Renmin Chubanshe, 1985), 300.
2. *Pray for China*, no. 127 (November-December 1995).
3. Grimes, *Ethnologue* (1996), 551.
4. Miao, "The Miao of China."
5. Dodd, *The Tai Race*, 164.

MICHA

1. Pelkey, "Yunnan's Myriad Yi," 92.
2. Covell, *The Liberating Gospel*, 196.
3. d'Ollone, *In Forbidden China*.

MICHI

1. YASS 64, section 9; and YASS 67, section 10.
2. *Chuxiong Yizu Zizhizhou Zhi*, 361.
3. Harrell, "Ethnicity and Kin Terms," 183.
4. T'ien, *Peaks of Faith*, 140.
5. Harrell, "Ethnicity and Kin Terms."
6. T'ien, *Peaks of Faith*, 23.

MIGUBA

1. Jackson Sun, as cited in Matisoff, "Languages and Dialects of Tibeto-Burman."
2. K. S. Singh (ed.), *People of India: Arunachal Pradesh* XIV (Calcutta: Anthropological Survey of India, 1995), 57.

MILI

1. *Xinping Yizu Daizu Zhizhixian Gai Kuang* (Kunming: Yunnan Minzu Chubanshe, 1988).
2. *Zhenyuan Xian Zhi* (1992), 75.
3. Pelkey, "Yunnan's Myriad Yi," 46.

MING

1. Torrance, Jr., "Journal of My First Visit", 41.
2. "The Qiang," *Chinese Around the World* (October-November 1995), 11.

MINGLANG

1. YASS 64, section 9; and YASS 67, section 10, as cited in T'ien, *Peaks of Faith*, 142.
2. *GPD* 10, no. 6 (June 1991).

MINYAK

1. See Sun Hongkai, "Chuanxi Minzu Zoulang Diqu De Yuyan."
2. Rock, "Konka Risumgongba," 399.
3. Joseph F. Rock, "The Glories of the Minya Konka," *National Geographic* (October 1930): 411.
4. Although most people in China have never heard of the Minyak, there has been a surprisingly high amount of study of their language, starting in the 1850s, when B. H. Hodgson compiled a small lexicon of the language. See Hodgson, "Sifán and Hórsók Vocabularies." Other more recent Minya studies include Huang Bufan, "Muyayu," in Dai Qingxia et al., *Zangmianyu Shiwu Zhong* (Beijing: Yanshan Press, 1991); Sun Hongkai, "Qiangyu Zhishu Wenti Chutan," in *A Collection of Articles on the*

Nationality Languages (Xining: Qinghai University Press, 1982), and "Chuanxi Minzu Zoulang Diqu de Yuyan."
5. Jiangxi Educational Publishing, *EDCL*, 544.
6. See Sun Hongkai, "Chuanxi Minzu Zoulang Diqu de Yuyan."
7. Although groups like the Qiang, Minyak, Namuyi and Ergong all speak distinct languages today, there are strong cultural ties among people possessing these towers, as they feel the towers were built by their common ancestors.
8. Rock, "Konka Risumgongba," 411.
9. Ibid.
10. Ibid., 399.
11. Ibid.

MIXISU

1. d'Ollone, *In Forbidden China*, 135.
2. Samuel Clarke, *Among the Tribes in South-West China*, 255.

MJUNIANG

1. Jiangxi Educational Publishing, *EDCL*, 566.
2. Grimes, *Ethnologue* (1996), 543.
3. See Quincy, *Hmong*, 16-31.
4. Samuel Clarke, *Among the Tribes in South-West China*, 20.
5. Miao, "The Miao of China."

MO

1. *Minzu Shibie Wenxian Ziliao Huibian*, 60.
2. From the town of Dushan there are two roads leading south to Libo: the speedier valley road and the slower mountain road. Most minibuses making the three- or four-hour trip between the towns take the quicker route, shooting past Shui and Bouyei villages. The Mo people live in and around Jialiang, a town halfway around the mountain along the slower route.
3. Corrigan, *Odyssey Illustrated Guide to Guizhou*, 79.
4. *Guizhou Nianjian 1985.*
5. Australian Academy and CASS, *LAC*, C-7.
6. Several detailed studies of the Mo language include: Li Fang-Gui, "Notes on the Mak Language," *Academia Sinica, Institute of History and Philology, Series A*, no. 20 (1940); Tsutomu Rai, "Supplement to Li Fang-Gui's 'Notes on the Mak Language'," *Jimbun Kagaku Kigaku Kiyo, Ochanomizu Joshidaigaku*, no. 7 (1955), 19-61; and Ni Dabai, "Yangfeng Mak of Libo County," in SIL, *Comparative Kadai*, 87-106.
7. *Pray for China*, no. 127 (November-December 1995).
8. Samuel Clarke, *Among the Tribes in South-West China*, 140.
9. Training Evangelistic Leadership, personal communication, September 1996.
10. Robson, *Griffith John*, 34.

MONBA, CONA

1. Australian Academy and CASS, *LAC*, C-6. The 1990 census of China listed only 6,069 Monba people in Motuo County; 549 in Cona (Cuona) County; and 542 in Linzhi County. It is believed that many ethnic Monba people were officially counted as part of the Tibetan nationality, which explains the discrepancy in figures between government figures and linguistic figures for the Monba.
2. Bradley, "East and South-East Asia," 170.
3. Jiangxi Educational Publishing, *EDCL*, 538-39
4. Zhang Jianghua and Wu Congzhong, "Tibet's Menba Nationality," *China Reconstructs* (July 1979): 55.
5. Personal communication, May 1996.

MONBA, MEDOG

1. Australian Academy and CASS, *LAC*, C-6.
2. Bradley, "East and South-East Asia," 170.
3. He Guanghua, "The Lost Horizons of Medog," 47-50.
4. See Sun Hongkai et al., *The Languages of the Menba, Luoba and Deng Peoples*.
5. Bethany World Prayer Center, "The Men-Pa," 1997.
6. Zhang Weiwen and Zeng, *In Search of China's Minorities*, 139.

MONGOL

1. This official 1990 census figure (4,806,849) appears to disagree with that cited under Population in China. The lower figure (4,505,000) was arrived at after subtracting the figures for eight other groups profiled in *Operation China*: Torgut, Buriat, Olot, Tuva, Alxa Mongol, Khamnigan Mongol, Sichuan Mongol, and Yunnan Mongol. The result is a more realistic and specific population for the Mongol people group.
2. 1,965,766 (1964 census); 1,462,956 (1953 census).
3. CASS, *Information China* 3: 1248.
4. Ibid., 1249. According to the 1990 census there were 313 counties or municipalities in China that recorded more than 500 Mongol people. In descending order, the largest Mongol populations are in: Ke'erqin Zuoyizhongqi 333,436; Ke'erqin Zuoyihouqi 261,678; Tongliao City 188,192; Ke'erqin Youyizhongqi 184,347; Ke'erqin Youyiqianqi 161,183; Zalaite 151,927; Fuxin (Liaoning) 138,763; Naiman 130,019; Kalaqin 120,466. All of these are in the *Inner Mongolian Autonomous Region* unless otherwise stated.
5. Covell, *The Liberating Gospel*, 120.
6. Grimes, *Ethnologue* (1996), 557.
7. Plano Carpini, as cited in Moffett, *A History of Christianity in Asia*, 68.
8. John Stewart, *The Nestorian Missionary Enterprise: A Church on Fire* (Edinburgh: T. & T. Clarke, 1923), 159.
9. Ibid., 143-44.
10. Covell, *The Liberating Gospel*, 129.
11. Moule and Pelliot, *Marco Polo*, 79.
12. *CPLMR*, no. 119 (December 1991-February 1992).
13. This estimate comes from a source who wishes to remain anonymous. This source is better placed than anyone to gauge the true state of the Mongolian Church in China.
14. E-mail report, Germany, 19 January 1998. The main body of the report reads: "In 1985, in the city of Hohot, there were 2,000 mostly-Han believers meeting in two official churches and three home groups. By early 1998, the church in that city had grown to 150,000 (out of a population of 800,000), meeting in 41 official churches and 330 home groups. 6,000 of them are Mongolians.... What may be the overall number of Mongolian Christians in north China? I asked different people and the lowest estimate was 200,000. This is many more than we dared to expect before.... Most Christians in Inner Mongolia live in the eastern and north eastern parts. There are also Mongolian Christians in other church fellowships and home groups in distant places, the pastor named several Chinese provinces where there are Mongolian Christians."
15. Earlier this century, claims were often made of large numbers of Mongol believers in China, but these often

stemmed from a misunderstanding of the figures reported for Catholics in Inner Mongolia. In the early 1920s the Roman Catholic Church listed 105,695 baptized converts in Inner and Outer Mongolia, especially in the regions of Suwei Bashan, Alashan, and Olanbor (see Stauffer, *The Christian Occupation of China*, 274), and 200,000 Catholics by 1940 (J. Leyseen, *The Cross Over China's Wall* [Beijing: The Lazarist Church, 1941], 138). However, "the large majority of these were Han Chinese, and few were Mongolians," (Covell, *The Liberating Gospel*, 131]. The 1922 report is brought into focus with the note, "As far is known most of the work is on behalf of Chinese and little direct evangelistic activity is carried on among the Mongols," Stauffer, *The Christian Occupation of China*, 274.

MONGOL, ALXA

1. For an excellent account of a journey to the Alxa region, see Frederick R. Wulsin, "The Road to Wang Ye Fu," *National Geographic* (February 1926): 197-234.
2. Hasbagen, "Mongolians of Alxa in Western Inner Mongolia," *China Tourism,* no. 139 (January 1992): 39.
3. Ying Yang, "Alxa, Land of Camels," *China Tourism*, no. 113 (n.d.): 13.
4. Frontiers Canada, personal communication, June 1997.
5. Hasbagen, "Mongolians of Alxa," 30.
6. Ibid.
7. Ibid., 32.
8. Ying Yang, "Alxa, Land of Camels," 15.
9. Schwartz, *The Minorities of Northern China*, 99. Schwartz adds the other Muslim Mongol group migrated to Gansu and became today's Dongxiang minority.
10. Hasbagen, "Mongolians of Alxa," 39.
11. Ying Yang, "Alxa, Land of Camels," 9.
12. Hasbagen, "Mongolians of Alxa," 32.

MONGOL, KHALKA

1. Reimer, *Operation Soviet Union.*
2. Stauffer, *The Christian Occupation of China,* 268.
3. Grimes, *Ethnologue* (1996), 557. Some Mongolian experts would argue there are no significant linguistic or cultural differences between the Mongols in Mongolia and their cousins in China.
4. *GPD* 9, no. 2 (February 1990).
5. Rev. G. H. Bondfield, "Mongolia, a Neglected Mission Field," as cited in Stauffer, *The Christian Occupation of China*, 268.
6. Mrs. A. B. Magnuson, as cited in Hefley, *China! Christian Martyrs of the 20th Century*, 43.
7. Stauffer, *The Christian Occupation of China*, 266.
8. Broomhall, *The Bible in China,* 30-31.

MONGOL, KHAMNIGAN

1. Janhunen and Salminen, *UNESCO Red Book.*
2. Ibid.
3. Juha Janhunen, "On the Position of Khamnigan Mongol," *Journal de la Société Finno-Ougrienne,* no. 84 (Helsinki, 1992).
4. Juha Janhunen, "Material on Manchurian Khamnigan Mongol," *Castrenianumin Toimitteita*, no. 37 (Helsinki, 1990).
5. Issachar Frontier Missions Research, *Mongolia Challenge Report*, II,3,ii.

MONGOL, SICHUAN

1. One source says the Sichuan Mongols are ethno-historically Mosuo people. If that is true, their language today probably retains linguistic influence from Naxi. See Charles F. McKhann, "The Naxi and the Nationalities Question," in Harrell (ed.), *Cultural Encounters on China's Ethnic Frontiers*, 61.
2. Target Ministries, personal communication, Hong Kong, March 1997.
3. Ibid. "They have some vocabulary which has been passed down. I remember them saying their word for table was one such word."
4. Rock, "The Land of the Yellow Lama," 463.
5. Rock, "Konka Risumgongba," 26.
6. Target Ministries, personal communication, March 1997.
7. Ibid.
8. Ibid.

MONGOL, YUNNAN

1. *Yuxi Nianjian* (1997). *Yunnan Nianjian 1985*, 454, listed 8,800 Mongolians in Yunan Province. These include some of the group listed in *Operation China* as "Mongols, Sichuan."
2. *GPD* 11, no. 3 (March 1992).
3. Jiangxi Educational Publishing, *EDCL*, 552.
4. Grimes, *Ethnologue* (1996), 694.
5. Xian Yanyun, "In search of the Ancient Tea Caravan Route," *China Tourism,* no. 181 (August 1995): 31.
6. AMO, "The Yunnan Mongolians," *Newsletter*, no. 23 (October 1993).
7. Training Evangelistic Leadership, personal communication, September 1993.

MONGOUR

1. Australian Academy and CASS, *LAC*, C-2. There were a total of 38,005 members of the Tu nationality living in Minhe County according to the 1990 census. Most of these are ethnic Mongour, but some may be ethnic Tu.
2. Schwartz, *The Minorities of Northern China*, 109.
3. Zhaonasitu, as cited in Milliken, "SIL China Nationalities and Languages Files."
4. Ramsey, *The Languages of China*, 201.
5. Schwartz, *The Minorities of Northern China*, 109.
6. Ibid., 113-14.
7. Marjorie Medary, *Each One Take One: Frank Laubach, Friend to Millions* (New York: David McKay, 1954), 80-81.

MOSUO

1. Shi Youyi (ed.), *Folkways of China's Minority Nationalities*, 44.
2. Rock, "The Land of the Yellow Lama," 453.
3. A good account of Mosuo history can be found in McKhann, "The Naxi and the Nationalities Question," 54.
4. Matt Forney, "Total Recall," *Far Eastern Economic Review* (29 May 1997): 70.
5. Ibid. In 1997, only two shamans were still able to recite the entire text, but seven children were being trained to know the chants in order to retain the Mosuo culture.
6. See *Kindreds* 7, no. 2 (1996).
7. Personal communication, August 1997.

MOZHIHEI

1. Jiangxi Educational Publishing, *EDCL*, 556.
2. This extremely low figure suggests the two Tujia groups are, at best, only distantly related.
3. Bethany World Prayer Center, "The Tujia of China" (1997).

4. For a good overview of Tujia customs, see Hu Yue, "In Tujia Country," *China Tourism*, no. 103 (n.d.): 25-37.
5. Zhang Weiwen and Zeng, *In Search of China's Minorities*.
6. *Pray for China Fellowship* (November 1996).

MUDA
1. See James A. Matisoff, "Sangkong of Yunnan," *Linguistics of the Tibeto-Burman Area* 16, no. 2 (Fall 1993), 123-42.

MUJI
1. Henry, "The Lolos and Other Tribes of Western China," 96-107.
2. Pelkey, "Report on the Yi Peoples of Honghe Prefecture," 8.
3. Ibid.
4. *Gejiu Shi Minzu Zhi* (1990).

MULAO
1. According to the 1990 census there were 15 counties or municipalities in China that recorded more than 500 Mulao people. In descending order, the largest Mulao populations are in: Luocheng 195,927; Yishan 17,497; Liucheng 7,020; Xincheng 3,400; Liuzhou City 3,382; Du'an 2,580.
2. Grimes, *Ethnologue* (1996), 557.
3. de Beauclair, *Tribal Cultures of Southwest China,* 6.
4. Grimes, *Ethnologue* (1996), 557.
5. See Zheng Guoqiao, "The Influences of Han on the Mulam Language," in SIL, *Comparative Kadai*, 167-77.
6. Ma Yin, *China's Minority Nationalities,* 389.
7. *CPLMR*, no. 119 (December 1991-February 1992).
8. AMO, "The Mulao," *Newsletter*, no. 26 (April 1994).
9. *Amity News Service*, August 1997.

MULAO JIA
1. *Minzu Shibie Wenxian Ziliao Huibian*, 9.
2. See *Guizhou Nianjian 1994*, 201.
3. *Minzu Shibie Wenxian Ziliao Huibian*, 9.

MUZI
1. Pelkey, "Report on the Yi Peoples of Honghe Prefecture," 18.
2. Ibid., 17.
3. Ibid.
4. Ibid.
5. Ibid.
6. Ibid.

NAHENG
1. Stauffer, *The Christian Occupation of China*, 244.
2. See Matisoff, "Languages and Dialects of Tibeto-Burman."

NAISU
1. de Beauclair, *Tribal Cultures of Southwest China*, 8.

NAJU
1. Matisoff, "Languages and Dialects of Tibeto-Burman." Also see He Jiren and Jiang Zhuyi (eds.), *Naxiyu Jianzhi* (Beijing: Minzu Chubanshe, 1985).

NALUO
1. The 1993 *Chuxiong Yizu Zizhizhou Zhi*, 361, cites a 1957 figure of 8,522 Naluo living in Chuxiong Prefecture (which includes Wuding, Luquan and Yuanmou counties).
2. Paul Vial, *Dictionnaire Francais-Lolo, Dialect Gni: Tribu Situee dans les Sous-Prefectures de Lou Nan Tcheou, Lou Lean Tcheou, Gouang-si Tcheou, Province du Yunnan* [French-Lolo Dictionary, Gni dialect: A Tribe Located in the Sub-Prefectures of Lunan, Luliang and Guangxi counties, Yunnan Province] (Hong Kong: Imprimerie de la Societe des Missions Estrangeres, 1909), 81.

NAMUYI
1. See Sun Hongkai, "Chuanxi Minzu Zoulang Diqu de Yuyan."
2. A. Doak Barnett, *China On the Eve of Communist Takeover* (New York: Frederick A. Praeger, 1963), 228.
3. Rock, "Konka Risumgongba," 19.
4. Norman Grubb, *Christ in Congo Forests: The Story of the Heart of Africa Mission* (London: Lutterworth Press, 1945), 13.

NANJINGREN
1. *Minzu Shibie Wenxian Ziliao Huibian*. There were a total of only 15,896 Bai people in Bijie County according to the 1990 census. Dafang County in Guizhou contained 37,536 Bai, with sigificant numbers also in Lupanshui (16,829), Qianxi (13,061) and Zhijin (10,907).

NARU
1. Pelkey, "Yunnan's Myriad Yi," 83-84.
2. Ibid., 84.
3. Ibid.
4. Ibid., 62.
5. Ibid., 54.

NARUO
1. Personal communication, January 1998.
2. Robson, *Griffith John*, 52.

NASU, EASTERN
1. The Global Evangelization Movement listed 366,769 Kopu [Eastern Nasu] in 1995, but cite no sources for this figure. Jamin Pelkey, "Yunnan's Myriad Yi," 61, lists a population of only 141,600 Eastern Nasu people in Yunnan Province. These conflicting figures reflect some of the confusion that exists with the Eastern Nasu. In the past, missionaries usually refered to this group as the *Gani*. For now, we have used the higher GEM figure.
2. Samuel Clarke, *Among the Tribes in South-West China*, 293.
3. Ibid.
4. "Minority Churches in Yunnan," *Bridge* (May-June 1987): 11.
5. Samuel Clarke, *Among the Tribes in South-West China*, 301-02. The Eastern Nasu also sent evangelists to the Nosu in Sichuan around that time, but it seems their motives for going were mixed, and they met with no success. See T. Mulholland, "Amongst the Tribes," *China's Millions* (July 1932): 131.
6. The name of the Flowery Miao missionary was Yang Zhi; Enwall, *A Myth Become Reality* 1: 130.
7. Ibid., 116. Arthur Nicholls traveled to Japan in 1912 to oversee the printing. The Gospels arrived in China in 1913.
8. Mrs. Ivan Allbutt, *China's Aboriginal Peoples*, 11.
9. GEM, "World's Peoples Listed By Country". The highest concentration of Eastern Nasu believers are in Luquan County, followed by Wuding County and Yuanmou County.

NASU, JINGHONG
1. Pelkey, "Yunnan's Myriad Yi," 93.

2. Wu Si, "Yi Life in the Greater and Lesser Liangshan Mountains," 16.

NASU, PANXIAN

1. Pelkey, "Yunnan's Myriad Yi," 74.
2. Shi Songshan (ed.), *The Costumes and Ornaments of Chinese Yi Nationality Picture Album* (Beijing: Beijing Arts and Crafts Publishing House, 1989), 76.
3. "New Churches, Ordinations for Yi Christians," *Amity News Service*, April 1993.

NASU, SOUTHERN

1. Pelkey, "Yunnan's Myriad Yi," 19.
2. To show the differences between the different "Nasu" groups, when the Eastern Nasu gospel recording was played for the Southern Nasu, they "could not understand a word of it." Pelkey, "The Yi Peoples of Yuxi Prefecture," 5.
3. Pelkey, "Yunnan's Myriad Yi," 20.

NASU, WESTERN

1. Kang Enda, "The Yi Minority's Naked Leopard Dance," *China Tourism,* no. 172 (November 1994): 61.
2. Ibid., 60.
3. Ibid.
4. Ibid., 61.
5. *CPLMR*, no. 119 (December 1991-February 1992).

NASU, WUSA

1. Pelkey, "Yunnan's Myriad Yi," 71.
2. See *Weining Yizu Huizu Miaozu Zizhixian Minzuzhi*, 12-128.
3. Pelkey, "Yunnan's Myriad Yi," 71.
4. Kendall, *Eyes of the Earth*, 114-16.
5. Samuel Clarke, *Among the Tribes in South-West China*, 121.
6. *Weining Yizu Huizu Miaozu Zizhixian Minzuzhi,* 128. In Yiliang County of Yunnan Province a reported 709 "Yi" people in 225 families profess faith in Christ. See Pelkey, "Yunnan's Myriad Yi," 73.

NAXI

1. According to the 1990 census there were 20 counties or municipalities in China that recorded more than 500 Naxi people. In descending order, the largest populations are in: Lijiang 184,669; Zhongdian 21,613; Ninglang 18,087; Weixi 16,615; Yongsheng 8,483; Muli (Sichuan) 3,618; Kunming City 3,093; and Yanbian (Sichuan) 2,051. These figures do not only refer to the ethnic Naxi group profiled here, but also to the other groups considered part of the Naxi by the Chinese authorities.
2. de Beauclair, *Tribal Cultures of Southwest China,* 24.
3. State Nationalities Affairs Commission, *China's Minority Peoples*, 56.
4. Of the 20,000 Naxi manuscripts, 12,500 are in China (of which 6,000 still reside in Lijiang). The rest are scattered in libraries, museums, and private collections in Taiwan, Europe, and the United States.
5. There are three main dialects of Naxi, excluding the Mosuo language: The *Lijiang* dialect is spoken by 140,000 Naxi in Lijiang, Zhongdian, Weixi, Yongsheng, Deqen and Gongshan counties of Yunnan Province; *Dayanzhen* is spoken by about 30,000 Naxi living primarily in Dayazhen, Baishajie, Suhejie, Axi, Daoxinm and Daogutuo villages in Lijiang County; The *Baoshan* dialect is spoken by 10,000 Naxi living primarily in the Baoshan and Guoluo districts of Lijiang County.
6. *A Nakhi-English Encyclopedic Dictionary* (Rome: Instituto Italiano per il Medio ed Estremo Oriente, 1963). Recent linguist work has been done to produce a new Naxi dictionary.
7. "We were finishing our prayer meeting, praying God would shake the city up. We went into the town and ordered Naxi fried rice at one of our favorite restaurants. As the last bowl came to the table the lights flickered out for a moment, came back on again and then out for the last time for the next two weeks. Then I heard a roar a little like thunder coming from behind me. The ground began to shake and someone yelled, 'It's an earthquake!' I ran for the door but before I could get there I was thrown to the ground. I struggled to get up but just couldn't because the ground was shaking so violently.... Naxi people were screaming and running everywhere... later hundreds of people were jammed into a small cobbled square... some were frightened, some still in tears. Others were not coping at all.... The scenes that followed the next few days were emotional. There was mourning wherever we went. The Naxi people wear a white head dress when a family member dies." *China News*, Hong Kong, April 1996.
8. See Charles F. McKhann, "The Naxi and the Nationalities Question," 55.
9. "The Naxi" (Pasadena, Ca: Institute of Chinese Studies).
10. *GPD* 13, no. 9 (September 1994).
11. *Brigada Mission-Mobilizers Newsbrief*, June 1998.
12. The official 1990 census figure (278,009) appears to disagree with that cited under Population in China. However, the census figure includes the populations for the Mosuo, Northern Naxi, Malimasa, Naru, and the Naheng. These groups are profiled separately in *Operation China*, and their populations are subtracted from the census figure to give a more realistic and precise number (232,500) for the Naxi people group.

NAXI, NORTHERN

1. Personal communication, May 1999.

NAZA

1. Pelkey, "Yunnan's Myriad Yi," 82.
2. Samuel Clarke, *Among the Tribes in South-West China*, 126.

NEISU

1. Hani2000, "The Hani: Poorest of China's Poor."
2. T'ien, *Peaks of Faith*, 77.
3. Conner, "Midge's Musings," May 1997.
4. See YASS 297, section 3; cited in T'ien, *Peaks of Faith*, 79-80.

NEISU, DA HEI

1. Pelkey, "Yunnan's Myriad Yi," 64.
2. The 1987 *Mile Xian Zhi*, 689, listed a 1984 population of 1,746 Da Hei Yi (Greater Black Yi) people living in Mile County.
3. About 400 live in the Xiaopukan Village of Shemu Community in Dongshan District of Mile County. An estimated 1,600 also live in Niuping and Niaoyi communities of Wushan District in Mile. About 1,500 more Da Hei Neisu live in Wunaibai and Zhuxi villages of Baishui District in Luxi County. The 800 in Xilin (Lunan) County live in Gecha, Honglukou, Shizichang and Muzhuqing villages of Zhuqing District; and in Weihei and Muni villages of Xigaikou District. Another 1,800 live in Shizong and Luoping counties of Qujing Prefecture. A few reportedly live in Qiubei County in Wenshan Prefecture.

Pelkey, "Report on the Yi Peoples of Honghe Prefecture," 16.

4. Ibid. "Many peoples classified as 'Yi' by the Chinese government refer to themselves using such similar phonemes. Nisu, Niesu, Neisu, Naisu, Nasu, Nosu, and Nuosu, are all variations of Yi autonyms — each often denoting multiple and widely different people groups. Nevertheless, except in the case of the Naisu ('Red People') of east-central Chuxiong Prefecture, the meaning of these phonemically similar autonyms is identical: 'Black People.'"
5. Ibid.
6. Ibid.
7. Ibid.

NEISU, XIAO HEI

1. Pelkey, "Yunnan's Myriad Yi," 65.
2. Stevan Harrell, "The History of the History of the Yi," 63.
3. Pelkey, "Report on the Yi Peoples of Honghe Prefecture," 17.
4. Crabouillet, "Les Lolos," *Les Missions Catholiques* 5, no. 192 (1873), 71-72; no. 194 (1873), 94-95; and no. 195 (1873), 105-07.

NIESU, CENTRAL

1. Pelkey, "Yunnan's Myriad Yi," 58.
2. Ibid., 57-58. Even though this information specifically refers to the Western Lipo, the Central Niesu are believed to observe the same customs.

NISU, JIANSHUI

1. Pelkey, "Report on the Yi Peoples of Honghe Prefecture," 5.
2. Ibid. "Although the Nisu are the majority in the districts of Shilipu, Guopu and Caoba (in northeastern Mengzi County), their mother tongue is spoken by select individuals over 40 or 50 years of age. Concentrated in this basin for centuries, the Nisu chose to hold their ground when the Han Chinese shifted into the region. As a result, the 53,000 Nisu of Mengzi County have slowly lost their primal language, perhaps forever."
3. Ibid. "After successfully putting on the trousers, the groom is to wear them every day until his first child is born. When the child is born the pants become the baby's swaddling clothes."
4. Pelkey, "Report on the Yi Peoples of Honghe Prefecture," 20.
5. Ibid.
6. A 1989 Chinese study listed 53 Jianshui Nisu Christians in the Gaoda District of Tonghai County. *Yuxi Diqu Minzu Xiang Qing Kuang*, 145-46.

NISU, XINPING

1. Pelkey, "Yunnan's Myriad Yi," 9; and *Yuxi Diqu Minzu Zhi* (1992), 38.
2. "In the villages lived a handsome young man and a beautiful girl who loved each other but could find no happiness. They heard of a place where no devil could reach, an enchanting land of sunshine and abundance, happiness and freedom. They decided to search for this land to give a new life to their people.... After traveling through the dense forest and being swept over rapids, they found an open country. The light of their torch woke up the devil who stretched out his paws and captured them. With his magic, he killed the young man and locked the girl in a dungeon where she refused to be his wife. One night, while the devil was sleeping soundly, she escaped and fled to an old carpenter, whom she told the story. The old man told them that only a rooster could free the villages from their suffering. She left him, carrying the rooster that the old man had told her to take back to where the devil lived.... When the rooster crowed, the devil's heart was broken and he could no longer use his magic." Xu Yixi, *Headdresses of Chinese Minority Nationality Women*, 54.
3. Pelkey, "Report on the Yi Peoples of Honghe Prefecture," 10.
4. See Leslie T. Lyall, *A Passion for the Impossible*.
5. *Yuxi Diqu Minzu Xiang Qing Kuang*, 145-46.

NISU, YUANYANG

1. Pelkey, "Report on the Yi Peoples of Honghe Prefecture," 13.
2. Ibid., 6-7.
3. Ibid., 22. There are Yuanyang Nisu believers in Shangxincheng, Ganiang and Magai districts of Yuanyang County.

NOSU, BUTUO

1. Matisoff, "Languages and Dialects of Tibeto-Burman."
2. Dessaint, *Minorities in Southwestern China*, 13.

NOSU, MANGBU

1. Pelkey, "Yunnan's Myriad Yi," 67.
2. Ibid.
3. Kendall, *Eyes of the Earth*, 147.
4. Ibid., 90.

NOSU, SHENGZHA

1. "There are said to be 45 Liang Shan Nosu living in New York," "The History and Culture of the Nosu Yi people of the Liang Shan," unpublished paper (Washington, 1995).
2. Shi Songshan, *The Costumes and Ornaments of Chinese Yi Nationality Picture Album*, 36. According to the 1990 census the largest Nosu populations are found in Zhaojue County 196,236; Meigu 148,851; Yuexi 143,930; Yanyuan 124,923; Butuo 121,053; Xide 101,859.
3. Matisoff, "Languages and Dialects of Tibeto-Burman."
4. d'Ollone, *In Forbidden China*, 12.
5. *Yunnan Shaoshu Minzu*, 627-28.
6. CASS, *Information China* 3: 1258. Some of the Nosu subgroups may be the Ako, Asong, Behee, Buko, Butu, Dongchuan, Hwethom, Huang, Kangxiangyung, Khaskhong, Kiokio, Laichau, Luso, Miehlantze, Nobee, Nuoko, Pakishan, Peren, Phupha, Tsoko, Thongho, Ulu, Won. See Paul Hattaway, "The Yi of China," *A-A-P Advocate*, no. 18 (August 1996).
7. "Prior to 1950 the Nosu script's pronunciation of characters and the direction of writing "differed extensively from place to place." Bradley, "Language Planning for China's Minorities," 157.
8. Covell, *The Liberating Gospel*, 197.
9. AMO, "The Nosu," *Newsletter*, no. 46 (August 1997).
10. Corrigan, *Odyssey Illustrated Guide to Guizhou*, 207.
11. For an excellent explanation of this custom, see Samuel Clarke, *Among the Tribes in South-West China*, 112.
12. Covell, *The Liberating Gospel*, 202.
13. The first Protestant missionaries to travel through the Liangshan were George Nicholl and Charles Leaman in 1878. See A. J. Broomhall, "Assault on the Nine," in Broomhall, *Hudson Taylor and China's Open Century* 6: 122–26. The best account of pre-1949 missions work among the Nosu is Ralph Covell's *Mission Impossible:*

The Unreached Nosu on China's Frontier (Pasadena: Hope, 1990).

14. Covell, *The Liberating Gospel,* 219.
15. "18 cult leaders had traveled two days out of the mountains to consider the truths that had been presented to them. I determined to spend two days with them. By the end of the first day the conviction of the Holy Spirit was so strong that the two main leaders willingly stood up and publicly renounced their involvement in the cult and declared that they would return to every place and begin instructing all of the members to follow the Truth. They showed their sincerity by insisting that I baptize them, which I did for the eight key leaders.... And yet this is only the tip of the iceberg.... More than 12,000 conversions have resulted in the past year. And this among a people group which a few years ago had never had a church before!" *On Target* (Target Ministries, May-June 1997).

NOSU, SHUIXI

1. Pelkey, "Yunnan's Myriad Yi," 75.
2. Samuel Clarke, *Among the Tribes in South-West China,* 123-24.
3. Kendall, *Eyes of the Earth,* 128.

NOSU, TIANBA

1. Matisoff, "Languages and Dialects of Tibeto-Burman."
2. Dessaint, *Minorities in Southwestern China,* 31.
3. Covell, *The Liberating Gospel,* 208.

NOSU, XIAOLIANGSHAN

1. Bradley, "Language Planning for China's Minorities."
2. There were a total of 6,258 Yi people living in Lijiang County according to the 1990 census. This total includes the Tanglang group and possibly others. Most of the Xiaoliangshan Nosu around Lijiang are called *Green Yi* by the Chinese, because of the predominant color of their traditional dress and women's headdress.
3. Hsu Itang [Xu Yitang], *Leibo Xiaolaingshan Zhi Lomin* [A Report of the Lolo in Leibo, in the Xiaoliang Mountains] (Chengdu: University of Nanjing Institute of Chinese Cultural Studies, 1944).
4. See Roderick MacFarquhar, "The Minorities," *New Leader* 42, no. 23 (1959) and Pu Kuei-chung, "Yi Slaves of Xiaoliangshan Head for Socialism," *Guangming Ribao*, 9 September 1958.
5. Pelkey, "Yunnan's Myriad Yi," 79.
6. *A Primer on Islam and the Spiritual Needs of the Mohammedans of China* (Shanghai, 1919).

NOSU, YINUO

1. Shi Songshan, *The Costumes and Ornaments of Chinese Yi Nationality Picture Album,* 22.
2. Matisoff, "Languages and Dialects of Tibeto-Burman". Matisoff lists a population of "more than 300,000 speakers" of Yinuo Nosu.
3. "The History and Culture of the Nosu Yi people of the Liang Shan," unpublished paper, 1985.
4. Shi Songshan, *The Costumes and Ornaments of Chinese Yi Nationality Picture Album,* 22.
5. "The History and Culture of the Nosu Yi people of the Liang Shan."

NU

1. The official 1990 census figure (27,123) seems to disagree with that cited under Population in China. The census figure includes the Zauzou (2,500), Ayi (2,000), and Lama (1,000) who are profiled separately in *Operation China* and, therefore, are subtracted from the 1990 census figure for the Nu. This gives a more realistic and precise population figure (21,600) for the Nu.
2. According to the 1990 census there were 5 counties or municipalities in China that recorded more than 500 Nu people. In descending order, they are: Fugong 16,706; Gongshan 6,350; Lanping 1,879; Lushui 895; and Weixi 530. All are in Yunnan Province.
3. Jiangxi Educational Publishing, *EDCL,* 550.
4. Grimes, *Ethnologue* (1992), 517. There are three dialects of Nu in China. *Central Nu* is spoken by almost 4,000 people in Bijiang township, and in Zhizhiluo, Laomudeng, Miangu, Shawa and Zileng. *Northern Nu* has almost 2,000 speakers, living in the northern part of Bijiang County, including Wawa, Kongtong and Youduoluo. *Southern Nu* is spoken by a population of almost 3,000 in the southern part of Bijiang County, specifically in Guoke, Puluo, Tongping and Jiajia.
5. Xia Hu, *Nuqiu Bianai Xiangqing* (Kunming, 1912), 358.
6. Rock, "Through the Great River Trenches of Asia," 180-81.
7. Zhang Weiwen and Zeng, *In Search of China's Minorities,* 224.
8. *CPLMR*, no. 119 (December 1991-February 1992).
9. "Christianity and Tibet," *Pray for China Fellowship* (April 1996).
10. *China's Millions* (1943): 43.
11. T'ien, *Peaks of Faith,* 26.
12. The Morse family are well-known for their exodus from China to Burma. See Eugene Morse, *Exodus to a Hidden Valley.*
13. See the Tibetan, Deqen Profile in *Operation China.*

NUBRA

1. See "Keriya People in the Taklimakan Desert," *China Tourism*, no. 186 (January 1996).
2. Stauffer, *The Christian Occupation of China,* 278.
3. Cooperative Outreach of India, newsletter (1997).

NUMAO

1. There were a total of 4,789 Yao people living in Libo County according to the 1990 census. This figure includes the members of other small Yao groups, such as the Beidongnuo.

NUNG

1. There are Nung families in Philadelphia, Washington DC, and London, England. *GPD* 15, no. 11 (November 1996).
2. Samuel Clarke, *Among the Tribes in South-West China,* 93.
3. Diller, "Tai Languages."
4. Samuel Clarke, *Among the Tribes in South-West China,* 92-93.
5. Dodd, *The Tai Race,* 159.
6. de Beauclair, *Tribal Cultures of Southwest China,* 9.
7. Quincy, *Hmong,* 66-69.
8. *GPD* 15, no. 11 (November 1996).
9. *GPD* 9, no. 11 (November 1990).

NUNU

1. Vial, "Les Lolos," 38.

OIRAT

1. Issachar Frontier Missions Research, *Mongolia Challenge Report,* II,2,i.

2. Grimes, *Ethnologue* (1996), 557.
3. Australian Academy and CASS, *LAC*, C-3.
4. See Paula G. Rubel, *The Kalmyk Mongols: A Study in Continuity and Change* (Bloomington: Indiana University Publications, 1967).
5. Bethany World Prayer Center, "The Kalmyk-Oirat," 1997.
6. Murray, "With the Nomads of Central Asia," 48.
7. CASS, *Information China* 3: 1274.
8. Murray, "With the Nomads of Central Asia," 48.
9. Covell, *The Liberating Gospel,* 165.
10. Stauffer, *The Christian Occupation of China*, 273.
11. This official 1982 census figure (166,000) appears to disagree with that cited under Population in China. However, the 1982 census figure combined the populations of the closely related Oirat and Torgut. Since the Torgut are profiled separately in *Operation China,* their population is subtracted from the overall census figure. This arrives at a more realistic and specific figure (60,000) for the Oirat.
12. The *Jesus* film is available in Kalmyk, but it was translated for the Kalmyk living in Russia and contains many loanwords that are not used in China. The Oirat in China are not able to understand it.

OLOT

1. Janhunen and Salminen, *UNESCO Red Book.* According to the 1990 census there was a total of 2,599 Mongol people living in Fuyu County.
2. Ibid.
3. Grimes, *Ethnologue* (1996), 557.
4. Janhunen and Salminen, *UNESCO Red Book.*
5. Ibid.
6. The most competent scholar of Olot in China today is Hu Zhenhua of the Beijing Central Institute for Nationalities.
7. Janhunen and Salminen, *UNESCO Red Book.*

ONGKOR

1. Janhunen and Salminen, *UNESCO Red Book.*
2. She Lingyun, "Economic Construction in Xinjiang as a Means to Secure Peace," as cited in Linda Benson, *The Ili Rebellion: The Moslem Challenge to Chinese Authority in Xinjiang, 1944-1949* (New York: M. E. Sharpe, 1990), 29-32.
3. According to the 1990 census there were no members of the Ewenki nationality living in Yining County, so perhaps the Ongkor are now counted as Daur or Xibe.
4. Janhunen and Salminen, *UNESCO Red Book.*
5. See Bai Lan and Juha Janhunen, "On the Present State of the Ongkor Solon," *Journal de la Sociètè Fino-Ougrienne*, no. 84 (Helsinki, Finland, 1992).
6. "The Ewenkis," *Chinese Around the World* (June-July 1995): 10.

OROQEN

1. Schwartz, *The Minorities of Northern China*, 181.
2. Ibid., 187.
3. *CPLMR*, no. 119 (December 1991-February 1992).
4. Tianfu, "Hospitality Deep in the Daxingan Mountain Forests," *China Tourism*, no. 31 (n.d.): 54.
5. Hatanaka, "Ethnicity and Culture Complex," 29.
6. Schwartz, *The Minorities of Northern China*, 183.
7. See Qiu Pu, *The Oroqens: China's Nomadic Hunters* (Beijing: Foreign Languages Press, 1983).
8. See AMO, "The Oroqen," *Newsletter*, no. 45 (May 1997).

PAIWAN

1. Elaine Hui, "The Paiwan People of Taiwan," *China Tourism*, no. 82 (n.d.): 71.
2. File no. 54 (Pasadena, Ca: Institute of Chinese Studies).
3. Elaine Hui, "The Paiwan People of Taiwan," 70.
4. *Chinese Around the World* (March 1995): 9-10.
5. Covell, *Pentecost of the Hills in Taiwan,* 282.

PALYU

1. Grimes, *Ethnologue* (1996), 558.
2. Bradley, "East And South-East Asia," 160.
3. Jiangxi Educational Publishing, *EDCL*, 570.
4. Jerold A. Edmonson and Kenneth J. Gregerson, "Bolyu Tone in Vietic Perspective," *Mon-Khmer Studies*, no. 26 (1996), 117-33. Another linguistic study on the Palyu (Lai) language is Paul K. Benedict, "How to Tell Lai: an Exercise in Classification," *Linguistics of the Tibeto-Burman Area* 13, no. 2 (1990): 1-26.
5. See Benedict, "How to Tell Lai," 1.
6. Stauffer, *The Christian Occupation of China*, 153.

PANA

1. See AMO, *Faces of the Unreached in Laos: Southeast Asia's Forgotten Nation* (Chiang Mai: AMO Publishing, 1999), 85.

PAXI

1. Patrick Thornbury, *Minorities and Human Rights Law* (London: Minority Rights Group, 1987), 4.
2. According to the 1990 census Menghai County contained a total of 104,750 Dai people and only 1,595 Hui. If the Paxi have been included under the Hui, they would comprise most of the Hui in Menghai.

PENGZI

1. Pelkey, "Yunnan's Myriad Yi," 48.
2. d'Ollone, *In Forbidden China,* 173.

PINGDI

1. The exact population of the Pingdi is difficult to ascertain. The Jiangxi Educational Publishing, *EDCL* (1991), 532, lists "almost 1,000,000" speakers of the Pingdi language, half who are Yao and half who belong to the Han Chinese nationality. Nationalities Affairs Commission of Guangxi, *The Yao Nationality*, 14, states 10% of the Yao in Guangxi, i.e. only 123,000 people, are Pingdi Yao. Grimes, *Ethnologue* (1996), 551, lists the total number of speakers at 1,000,000.
2. Nationalities Affairs Commission of Guangxi, *The Yao Nationality*, 9.
3. See Heijdra, "Who Were the Laka?" 162.
4. Nationalities Affairs Commission of Guangxi, *The Yao Nationality*, 9.
5. Jiangxi Educational Publishing, *EDCL,* 532.
6. Bradley, "East And South-East Asia," 167.
7. Huang Yu, "Preliminary Study of the Yao 'King Ping's Charter," 94-95.
8. *GPD* 13, no. 2 (February 1984).

POLUO

1. Pelkey, "Yunnan's Myriad Yi," 23.
2. E. Myers Harrison, *Heroes of Faith on Pioneer Trails* (Chicago: Moody Bible Institute, 1945), 83.

POPEI

1. Jamin Pelkey, personal communication, January 1998.

2. Pelkey, "Yunnan's Myriad Yi," 59.
3. Ma Yin, *China's Minority Nationalities*, 234.

PUBIAO
1. Hoang Luong, as cited in Grimes, *Ethnologue* (1996), 802. Wurm and Hattori (eds.), *Language Atlas of the Pacific Area*, in 1981 listed 5,000 Pubiao in Vietnam, but more recent research confirms the much smaller number is accurate.
2. Heijdra, "Who Were the Laka?" 165.
3. Jiangxi Educational Publishing, *EDCL*, 570.
4. Zhang Junru, "The Pubiao Language," in Edmonson, *Kadai*, 23.
5. Bradley, "East and South-East Asia," 164.
6. Jiangxi Educational Publishing, *EDCL*, 570.
7. Liang Min, "On the Affiliation of the Ge-Yang branch of Kadai," in Edmonson, *Kadai*, 45.
8. Grimes, *Ethnologue* (1996), 555.
9. For a detailed study on the Pubiao language, see Zhang Junru, "The Pubiao Language."
10. Dang; Chu, and Luu, *Ethnic Minorities in Vietnam*, 172.

PULA
1. Pelkey, "Report on the Yi Peoples of Honghe Prefecture," 13.
2. The greatest concentration of Pula are in Yuanjiang and Honghe counties. Each county has 28 Pula villages.
3. One of the very few mentions of the Pula in Chinese literature is found in "Ma Cheng-ch'ang, Good Guide of the Pula People (Yi Nationality)", *New China News Agency*, 10 October 1960.
4. Henry, "The Lolos and Other Tribes of Western China," 96-107.
5. Ibid.
6. Pelkey, "Report on the Yi Peoples of Honghe Prefecture," 12.
7. Ibid., 12-13.

PUMAN
1. J.-O. Svantesson, "U," *Linguistics of the Tibeto-Burman Area* 11, no. 1 (1988), 64-133.
2. Bradley, "East and South-East Asia," 162.
3. Grimes, *Ethnologue* (1996), 563.
4. Jun Feng, "Xishuangbanna," 35.
5. Dodd, *The Tai Race*, 334.
6. W. Parkenham Walsh, *Modern Heroes of the Mission Field* (London: Hodder & Stoughton, 1982).

PUMI
1. According to the 1990 census there were 5 counties or municipalities in China that recorded more than 500 Pumi people. In descending order, the largest Pumi populations are in: Lanping 12,901; Ninglang 8,607; Lijiang 4,634; Weixi 1,245, and Yongsheng 863.
2. During the Hungwu reign (1368-1398) of the Ming Dynasty, official documents listed 600 households of the Pumi nationality in one region. Today, more than six centuries later the Pumi in that district have not increased and still number around 600 households. *Renmin Ribao*, 1 October 1988.
3. R. P. "The Pumi People of China," ms. (August 1995).
4. Ramsey, *The Languages of China*, 277.
5. *GPD* 11, no. 3 (March 1992).
6. Ma Yin, *China's Minority Nationalities*, 315.
7. Lucien Miller (ed.), *South of the Clouds: Tales from Yunnan* (Seattle: University of Washington Press, 1994).
8. AMO, "The Pumi," *Newsletter*, no. 31 (February 1995).
9. Personal communication, August 1997. Because of the tight police presence in this area, it appears little or no follow-up was able to be conducted among these new believers. It is possible they no longer profess to follow Christ.

PURIK
1. The Global Evangelization Movement lists a figure of 97,800 Purik in China, while the 1995 Joshua Project had a figure of 185,000 in China, and 685,000 in all countries. These figures are too high. In fact, some scholars doubt if there are any Purik in China at all.
2. *Unreached Peoples '81.*
3. Ibid.
4. Ibid.

PUROIK
1. Elizabeth M. Taylor, "A Review of the Social Basis for Sustainable Development in Arunachal Pradesh," ms. (n.d.).
2. See Jackson Sun, "Review of Zangmian Yu Yuyin Han Cohui," 80-81.

   The 1995 Joshua Project listed a figure of 49,000 *Sulung* in China, but this is undoubtedly too high. Many scholars do not acknowledge any Sulung/Puroik in Chinese territory at all.
3. K.S. Singh (ed.), *People of India*, 303.
4. Elizabeth Taylor, "A Review of the Social Basis for Sustainable Development."
5. See Stephen Fuchs, *The Aboriginal Tribes of India* (Madras: Macmillan Press, 1973).
6. Verrier Elwin, *A Philosophy for NEFA* (Itanagar: Directorate of Research, 1957), 154.
7. Elizabeth Taylor, "A Review of the Social Basis for Sustainable Development."
8. Ibid.
9. The Arunachal State Government strongly opposes missionary influence in Arunachal Pradesh. The 1971 census of Arunachal Pradesh lists 64% of the population as animists, 13% Buddhist, and 22% Hindu. Christians, Muslims, and Sikhs each have less than 1% of the population.
10. Elizabeth Taylor, "A Review of the Social Basis for Sustainable Development."

PUSHA
1. Shaw, "Some Current Trends of Ethnology in China," 56.
2. See *Zhuangzu Jianshu*, 9.
3. Australian Academy and CASS, *LAC*, C-7.
4. Crossman, *Mountain Rain*.

PUWA
1. Pelkey, "Report on the Yi Peoples of Honghe Prefecture," 9.
2. Ibid., 21. Catholic work also commenced among the Puwa in Dayakou Village in 1896. Through the years nine Puwa families believed and met in a church. Persecution affected the Puwa church in Mengzi, so that by 1950 none were reportedly still believers.
3. Pelkey, "Yunnan's Myriad Yi," 29.

QANU
1. Johnson, "An Overview of Hmongic Languages," 6.
2. There are several other ethnocultural Miao groups in the

area, all of whom speak mutually intelligible languages close to Northern Hmu. The Qanu are the only one of the several groups about whom there is information available.
3. Johnson, "An Overview of Hmongic Languages," 4.
4. The six unclassified groups have been listed after the names of the counties they inhabit: Pingtang (10,000), Luodian 1 (4,000), Dushan (4,000), Luodian 2 (4,000), Wangmo (3,000), and Wangmo Luodian (2,000).
5. Johnson, "An Overview of Hmongic Languages," 6.
6. Joseph Esquirol, *Dictionaire Kanao-Francois et Francois-Kanao* (Hong Kong, 1931).
7. Ge Zi, "Miaozu Wenzi Danshengle," as cited in Enwall, A *Myth Become Reality* 2: 57.
8. *Zhongguo Shaoshu Minzu Jiankuang Miaozu Yaozu Tujiazu Gelaozu* [Brief Account of the Conditions of the Minorities in China-Miao, Yao, Tujia, Gelao], as cited in Enwall, *A Myth Become Reality* 2: 3.

QIANG, CIMULIN

1. Liu Guangkun, *Maqo Qiangyu Yanjiu* (Chengdu: Sichuan Minzu Chubanshe, 1998). According to James Matisoff, the Cimulin Qiang have a "speaker population of about 9,000, primarily distributed in the vicinity of Cimulin in Xiaoheishui District; specifically, the villages of Ermulin, Rewo, Wumushu, Ciba, and Chinglanggou." Matisoff, "Languages and Dialects of Tibeto-Burman."
2. "The Stone, A Guardian of Life: The Qiang: Keeping a Unique Stone Culture," unpublished report (1998): 3.
3. Huang Bu-Fan (1987), 33, as cited in Milliken, "SIL China Nationalities and Languages Files."
4. J.-O. Svantesson, 1990 personal communication, as cited in Grimes, *Ethnologue* (1992), 526.
5. CASS, *Information China* 3: 1249.
6. AMO, "The Qiang," *Newsletter*, no. 27 (June 1994).
7. *CPLMR*, no. 119 (December 1991-February 1992).
8. Torrance, Jr., "Journal of My First Visit," 41.
9. AMO, *The 50 Most Unreached People Groups of China and Tibet*, 36.

QIANG, DAJISHAN

1. Liu Guangkun, *Maqo Qiangyu Yanjiu*. According to James Matisoff, the Dajishan Qiang take their name "from a village in Lixian County. Their primary distribution is in the vicinity of Xuecheng in southern Lixian County, including the villages of Xuecheng, Shangmeng, Xiameng, Xinglong, Lielie, Jiuzi, Putou, and Puxi. The village of Ganbao, to the west, is apparently a linguistic frontier." Matisoff, "Languages and Dialects of Tibeto-Burman."
2. de Beauclair, *Tribal Cultures of Southwest China*, 3.
3. The 1996 *Ethnologue*, 559-60, listed eight separate Qiang languages: Dzorgai, Kortse, Lofuchai, Northern Qiang, Pingfang, Southern Qiang, Thochu and Wagsod. No precise location or population information was listed. These names, however, are of little present-day linguistic value. Some of them are Tibetan-language place names and therefore cannot be located on any current maps of China. These eight language groups seem to be compiled from names used by different linguists dating back 150 years. For example, *Lofuchai* was a Southern Qiang dialect introduced by Wen Yu in the 1940s. He spelled it "Lopuchai." *Wasgod* was a Southern Qiang dialect also introduced by Wen Yu. The Chinese name for this dialect was *Wa Si* (Tile Temple), "probably a transliteration of a Tibetan name." *Dzorgai* was a Northern Qiang variety listed in 1912 by Vicomte d'Ollone, *Langues des Peuples non Chinois de la Chine* 6, no. 27-28 (Paris: E. Leroux, 1912). Dzorgai was probably a place name. *Kortse* was also introduced by d'Ollone in 1912, as was *Pingfang* (also spelt "Pinfang"). *Thochu* was first listed by Hodgson in 1874. He listed only about 30 words, which appear to be a Northern Qiang variety. The author thanks Jonathon Evans for the above information. *Operation China* uses the Qiang names and dialects that are currently used in China. However, the Qiang have yet to be comprehensively surveyed and there may be other mutually unintelligible dialects/languages among the Qiang that have not been documented. Linguistic sources over the years have listed numerous Qiang dialects. Most of the names reflect a location. They include Anzitou Qiang, Banpo Qiang, Dapuxi Qiang, Ershuizhai Qiang, Erwa Qiang, Gaodongshan Qiang, Heishui Qiang, Heping Qiang, Hniksu Qiang, Hou'erku Qiang, Jiashan Qiang, Jiuziying Qiang, Liping Qiang, Luobuzhai Qiang, Niushan Qiang, Puxi Qiang, Qingtuping Qiang, Ruodazhai Qiang, Seru Qiang, Suoqiaozhai Qiang, Tongshanzhai Qiang, Wasi Qiang, Weigu Qiang, Xiabaishui Qiang, Yanmen Qiang, and Zengtou Xiazhai Qiang.
4. James A. Matisoff, as cited in Grimes, *Ethnologue* (1996), 559.
5. David Graham, *Songs and Stories of the Ch'uan Miao*, 129
6. Jonathon Evans, personal communication, February 1999.
7. *GPD* 3, no. 6 (June 1984). The term *Qiang* was given to the various tribes that currently make up the official Qiang nationality in China by Chinese scholar Wen Yu in the 1940's. Before that time each group was known by their local name.
8. See Ge Lin, "The Qiang People and Their Ancient Castles," *China Tourism*, no. 59 (n.d.): 85.
9. Ibid., 30.
10. Torrance, Jr., "Journal of My First Visit," 41.

QIANG, HEIHU

1. There were 16,000 speakers of Heihu Qiang in 1990, according to Liu Guangkun, *Maqo Qiangyu Yanjiu*. According to James Matisoff, the Heihu Qiang are "distributed in the districts of Fengyi, Tumen, Shaba, and Xiaochang in Maoxian County; including the villages of Baixi, Sanlong, Huilong, Fanrong, Xingfu, Taiping, Weimen, Goukou, and Heihu, and the communes of Hongguang and Fengshou. Matisoff, "Languages and Dialects of Tibeto-Burman."
2. Ramsey, *The Languages of China*, 279.
3. Ibid., 274.
4. See Ge Lin, "The Qiang People and Their Ancient Castles," 26-30; 85.
5. "The Qiang," *Chinese Around the World* (October-November 1995): 11.
6. See Thomas F. Torrance, *The History, Customs and Religion of the Chi'ang, an Aboriginal people of West China* (Shanghai, 1920). Torrance also wrote *China's First Missionaries: Ancient Israelites*, which was reprinted in 1988. David Graham later gave very serious criticisms of the "Jewish" connection among the Qiang, and most serious scholars no longer accept Torrance's claims as valid. See Graham, *The Customs and Religions of the Ch'iang*, and *Folk Religion in Southwest China* (Washington DC: Smithsonian Institute, 1961). However, we have included several quotes from Torrance regarding his perceived connection between the Qiang and Jewish culture in these Qiang Profiles mostly because Torrance is the father of mission work among the Qiang and therefore his accounts of conversions among the Qiang are valuable, even though his conclusions regarding the origins of the Qiang have been discounted.

7. Thomas F. Torrance, Jr., "A Visit by Thomas F. Torrance to Chengdu, the Capital of Sichuan, and to Weichou and Chi'ang villages in Wenchuan County, the upper Min Valley, Sichuan, October 4-18, 1986," unpublished report (Edinburgh, 1986).
8. Torrance, Jr., "Journal of My First Visit," 1.

QIANG, JIAOCHANG

1. Liu Guangkun, *Maqo Qiangyu Yanjiu.*
2. "The Stone, A Guardian of Life," unpublished report (1988): 2.
3. William John Gill, *The River of Golden Sand* 1 (London: John Murray, 1880), 378. Gill's article was later published in Terrien de Lacouperie, *Languages of China Before the Chinese* (London, 1887).
4. "The Stone, A Guardian of Life," 15.

QIANG, LONGXI

1. There were 3,300 speakers of Longxi Qiang in 1990. Liu Guangkun, *Maqo Qiangyu Yanjiu.*
2. Jia Lin, "Over the Dadu River," 67.
3. Huang Bu-Fan, as cited in Milliken, "SIL China Nationalities and Languages Files."
4. Peace Books Company "The Qiangs: Worshippers of White Stones," in *Lifestyles of China's Ethnic Minorities* (Hong Kong: Peace Books, 1991).
5. Ge Lin, "The Qiang People and Their Ancient Castles," 30.
6. Torrance, Jr., "A Visit by Thomas F. Torrance to Chengdu."
7. Torrance, Jr., "Journal of My First Visit," 1.
8. Ibid., 41.

QIANG, LUHUA

1. Liu Guangkun, *Maqo Qiangyu Yanjiu.* According to James Matisoff, the Luhua Qiang "take their name from a village in Sichuan province, China. Speaker population of about 12,000, primarily distributed in the vicinity of Luhua in Heishui County; specifically, the villages of Sandagu, Shashiduo, Yang'er, Zegai, Ergulu, Shangyinshan, and Shangyangshan." Matisoff, "Languages and Dialects of Tibeto-Burman."
2. "The Stone, A Guardian of Life," unpublished report (1988): 4.
3. Ibid., 14.
4. Stauffer, *The Christian Occupation of China*, 277.

QIANG, MAWO

1. Liu Guangkun, *Maqo Qiangyu Yanjiu.* According to James Matisoff, the Mawo Qiang "take their name from a village in Sichuan province, China. Speaker population of about 15,000, primarily distributed in the vicinity of Mawo in Heishui County; specifically, the villages of Zhawo, Esi, Hongyan, Xi'er, Shuangliushu, Xiayinshan, and Xiayangshan." Matisoff, "Languages and Dialects of Tibeto-Burman."
2. Another source, "The Stone, A Guardian of Life," unpublished report (1988): 7-8, records a completely different legend about the origins of the Yun Yun shoes.... "When a Qiang man was traveling from the north to the south, he met a violent person... who fought with him. Although the Qiang man was unable to win in the beginning, on the second night of the battle he had a dream. In his dream, a god told him that the Qiang people needed to jump up so the clouds were under their feet and with the help of the white rock, they would be able to win the battle. After actually winning, they wore the cloud shoes to remember this important time in their history. The shoes also became a symbol of protection for the Qiang people and a good gift to express affection between a man and a woman."

QIANG, MIANCHI

1. Jia Lin, "Over the Dadu River," 68.
2. *GPD* 3, no. 6 (June 1984).
3. James A. Matisoff, as cited in Grimes, *Ethnologue* (1996), 559.
4. de Beauclair, *Tribal Cultures of Southwest China*, 3.
5. See W. B. Djang, "The Decline and Possible Future of a Great Race: The Ch'iang People," ms. (Yale: Yale Divinity School, 1948).
6. Zhang Weiwen and Zeng, *In Search of China's Minorities*, 144.
7. Ge Lin, "The Qiang People and Their Ancient Castles," 30.
8. Zhang Weiwen and Zeng, *In Search of China's Minorities*, 144.
9. Torrance, Jr., "Journal of My First Visit."
10. Ibid., 42.
11. Ibid., 7. Money was also given for the training costs of three Qiang church leaders to attend the government-sanctioned Sichuan Theological Seminary in Chengdu.
12. Ibid., 41.

QIANG, SANLONG

1. Liu Guangkun, *Maqo Qiangyu Yanjiu.*

QIANG, TAOPING

1. There were 4,900 speakers of Taoping Qiang in 1990. Liu Guangkun, *Maqo Qiangyu Yanjiu.*
2. Ma Yin, *China's Minority Nationalities*, 229.
3. Grimes, *Ethnologue* (1996), 560.
4. Wong How-Man, "Peoples of China's Far Provinces," 307.
5. Torrance, Jr., "Journal of My First Visit," 1.
6. Torrance, Jr., "A Visit by Thomas F. Torrance to Chengdu."

QIANG, YADU

1. Liu Guangkun, *Maqo Qiangyu Yanjiu.* According to James Matisoff, the Yadu Qiang "take their name from a village in Sichuan province, China. Speaker population of more than 10,000, primarily distributed in the vicinity of Wabuliangzi in southern Heishui County, and Chibusu in northern Maoxian County; specifically, the villages of Qugu, Heping, and Weicheng." Matisoff, "Languages and Dialects of Tibeto-Burman."

QIANGYI

1. Pelkey, "Yunnan's Myriad Yi," 51.
2. Ibid.
3. Ibid.

QIXINGMIN

1. *Minzu Shibie Wenxian Ziliao Huibian*, 56.
2. *Guizhou Nianjian 1985.*
3. *Minzu Shibie Wenxian Ziliao Huibian*, 56
4. See the Introduction to Zhang Jimin, "Lajiyu yu Gelaoyu de Guanxi," *Minzu Yuwen*, no. 3 (1992): 19-27.

QUEYU

1. Jiangxi Educational Publishing, *EDCL*, 543.
2. See Michael Peissel, *Cavaliers of Kham: The Secret War in Tibet* (London: Heinemann, 1972).

3. "Christianity and Tibet," *Pray for China Fellowship* (April 1996).
4. Ibid.
5. Stauffer, *The Christian Occupation of China*, 276.

RAO
1. Dwayne Graybill, personal communication, November 1997.
2. Chen Chao, *Duyun Shi Minzu Zi*, 159.
3. Ibid. The next largest are Piao (166), Longguantang (146), Hetou (134), and Pogiao (129).
4. *Pray for China*, no. 127 (November-December 1995).
5. See *Guizhou Nianjian 1992*, 218.
6. Graybill, personal communication.
7. Chen Chao, *Duyun Shi Minzu Zi*, 159.
8. Enwall, *A Myth Become Reality* 2: 50.
9. Ibid.
10. *Minzu Shibie Wenxian Ziliao Huibian*, 47.
11. *Pray for China*, no. 127 (November-December 1995).
12. Zwemer, *A Primer on Islam*.

RAWANG
1. Brackenbury, *Yak Butter & Black Tea*, 205.
2. John Morse, personal communication, January 1998.
3. Grimes, *Ethnologue* (1996), 722.
4. Morse, personal communication, January 1998.
5. "The Drung," *Chinese Around the World* (July 1996).
6. The Morse family's labors were not without hardship; the Rawang burned the Morse's house down several times in the early days in attempts to make them leave.
7. In recent years a growing number of Rawang youth have had opportunities to travel and make contact with the outside world. Some have become addicted to drugs and alcohol. Many Rawang churches are struggling, according to John Morse, personal communication, January 1998. On 18 March 1998 Joni Morse reported, "The number of evangelists laboring in the Lord's work among the Zerwang of China has now grown to twenty five families."
8. In 1996 several members of the Morse family, who are now based in northern Thailand, returned to the Rawang in Myanmar for the first time in 30 years. They attended a Rawang Christian convention at which 60,000 believers met for worship and fellowship. There were few dry eyes as the older Rawang thanked the missionaries for their love and commitment to bring the gospel to their people.

RIANG
1. J.-O. Svantesson, 1990 personal communication, as cited in Grimes, *Ethnologue* (1992), 526.
2. Grimes, *Ethnologue* (1996), 560. According to the 1990 census there were 1,762 De'ang people in Zhenkang County and 780 in Baoshan.
3. Ma Yin, *China's Minority Nationalities*, 324.
4. *GPD* 8, no. 9 (September 1989).
5. Ibid.

RUSSIAN
1. 1,342,000 in Byelarus; 916,000 in Kyrgyzstan; 905,000 in Latvia; 485,000 in Estonia; 390,000 in Azerbaijian; 388,000 in Tajikistan; 344,000 in Lithuania; 334,000 in Turkmenistan; 60,000 in Poland; 50,000 in Armenia, and 4,000 in Mongolia (all figures from P. Johnstone, 1993).
2. According to the 1990 census there were 5 counties or municipalities in China that recorded more than 500 Russian people. In descending order, the largest Russian populations are in: Urumqi City (*Xinjiang*) 2,173; E'ergun (*Inner Mongolia*) 2,071; Tacheng City (*Xinjiang*) 1,884; Yakeshi City (*Inner Mongolia*) 725; and Hailar City (*Inner Mongolia*) 628
3. Jiangxi Educational Publishing, *EDCL*, 596.
4. Sinclair, *The Forgotten Tribes of China*, 44.
5. Ma Yaojun, "Life of Chinese-Russian Descendants in Inner Mongolia," *China Tourism*, no. 83 (n.d.): 36-45.
6. C. Persson, "Christianity in the Tarim Basin," 20-21.
7. *CPLMR*, no. 119 (December 1991-February 1992).

SALAR
1. According to the 1990 census there were 9 counties or municipalities in China that recorded more than 500 Salar people. In descending order, the largest Salar populations are in: Xunhua (Qinghai) 60,418; Hualong (Qinghai) 9,653; Jishishan (Gansu) 5,392; Yining (Xinjiang) 1,447; Xining City (Qinghai) 1,262; Tongren (Qingjiang) 1,045
2. Ramsey, *The Languages of China*, 186.
3. Suzanne Kakuk, "Sur la Phonetique de la Langue Salare," *Acta Orientalia Hungaricae*, no. 15 (1962): 173.
4. AMO, *The 50 Most Unreached People Groups of China and Tibet*, 37.
5. *GPD* 10, no. 1 (January 1991).
6. Schwartz, *The Minorities of Northern China*, 40.
7. Other Salar uprisings occured in 1861, 1862, and 1895. At times the Salar were successful in resisting Chinese rule, but numerous towns were destroyed and thousands of Salar killed.
8. Ibid., 46. This date obviously conflicts with the Salar's story of their arrival in the region, which indicates they were already Muslims.
9. Ibid.
10. Stauffer, *The Christian Occupation of China*, 266.
11. Covell, *The Liberating Gospel*, 174.

SAMADU, EASTERN
1. Pelkey, "Yunnan's Myriad Yi," 77.
2. Samuel Clarke, *Among the Tribes in South-West China*, 129.

SAMADU, WESTERN
1. Pelkey, "Yunnan's Myriad Yi," 48.
2. Ibid.
3. David H. Adeney, *China, the Church's Long March* (Singapore: OMF, 1985).

SAMAN
1. Australian Academy and CASS, *LAC*, C-5.
2. Schwartz, *The Minorities of Northern China*, 145.
3. *China Tourism*, no. 158 (August 1993): 73.
4. Schwartz, *The Minorities of Northern China*, 147.
5. *China Tourism*, no. 158 (August 1993): 73.
6. Schwartz, *The Minorities of Northern China*, 153, 155.

SAMEI
1. Pelkey, "Yunnan's Myriad Yi," 75.
2. Grimes, *Ethnologue* (1996), 560.
3. Hong Mei, "A Closer Look at Beautiful Kunming," *China Tourism*, no. 47 (n.d.): 22.
4. Pelkey, "Yunnan's Myriad Yi," 75.
5. Ibid.
6. Grimes, *Ethnologue* (1996), 560.
7. Pelkey, "Yunnan's Myriad Yi," 76. For an extensive study on the Samei, see Xie Jianzhu, *The Samei People of*

Kunming's Eastern Suburbs (Hong Kong: Chinese University, n.d.).

8. Hong Mei, "A Closer Look at Beautiful Kunming."
9. Samuel Clarke, *Among the Tribes in South-West China*, ix.
10. *GPD* 10, no. 6 (June 1991).

SAMTAO

1. Grimes, *Ethnologue* (1996), 560.
2. Dodd, *The Tai Race*, 61.
3. Ibid.
4. Ibid., 213.

SANDA

1. Dwayne Graybill, personal communication, September 1996.
2. V. Li, *Some Approaches to the Classification of Small Ethnic Groups*.
3. Graybill, personal communication.
4. This is no doubt in reference to the banning of all religious activity during the Cultural Revolution (1966-76). Many tribal customs and rituals were forcibly discontinued and have not been observed with the same devotion since.
5. Richard F. Lovelace, *Dynamics of Spiritual Life: An Evangelical Theology of Renewal* (Downers Grove: Inter-Varsity Press, 1980).

SANI

1. *Lunan Xian Zhi* (1996).
2. A 1960 study listed only 26,870 Sani. Chu Fei, *Jinshajiang Fengwu Waiji* (Singapore, 1960), 12-13. A 1987 source listed 1,630 Sani living in Mile County. *Mile Xian Zhi*, 689 (1984 figure).
3. Bradley, "Language Planning for China's Minorities." Other Sani linguistic studies include Ma Xueliang's *Sani Yu 'Pzlp'slbzlfvl' Xiao Kao* (Chengdu: University of Nanjing Institute of Chinese Cultural Studies, 1940) and *Sani Yiyu Yanjiu* (Beijing: Chinese Scientific Institute, 1951); also Weera Ostapirat, "Sani's Fortis See-Saw and Initial Devoicing," *Linguistics of the Tibeto-Burman Area* 19, no. 1 (1996): 59-64.
4. Two cultural studies of the Sani are Gladys Yang's "'Ashma,' The Oldest Shani Ballad," *Chinese Literature*, no. 1 (1955); and Gladys Young, "Ashma (A Shani Ballad)," *Chinese Literature*, no. 3 (1955).
5. Xu Yixi, *Headdresses of Chinese Minority Nationality Women*, 54.
6. YASS 59, section 30; cited in T'ien, *Peaks of Faith*, 147.
7. Margaret Byrne Swain, "Père Vial and the Gni-p'a: Orientalist Scholarship and the Christian Project," in Harrell (ed.), *Cultural Encounters on China's Ethnic Frontiers*, 158.
8. "His struggle with the Han authorities became personally dangerous when the word went out among the Han that this priest had set himself up as the king of the Gni [Sani] and needed to be removed. After discovering the 'Mandarin's assassins' in his church late at night, Vial fought with them, receiving fourteen wounds, including damage to his right arm and a stab wound next to his heart. His followers dragged him back to his quarters, where he said to them: 'You see, I will die; it is because of you and in order to defend you that I voluntarily offer my life for you; always stay faithful to the religion that I have taught you.'" *Les Missions Catholiques* (1894, Current News section): 307-08.
9. Pelkey, "Report on the Yi Peoples of Honghe Prefecture," 23.

SANIE

1. Pelkey, "Yunnan's Myriad Yi," 76.
2. David Bradley; Maya Bradley and Li Longxiang, "The Sanyie of Kunming: a Case of Yi Language Death," paper published for the 30th International Conference on Sino-Tibetan Languages and Linguistics (1997).
3. Pelkey, "Yunnan's Myriad Yi," 77.
4. Ibid.

SANQIAO

1. See *Minzu Shibie Wenxian Ziliao Huibian*.
2. *Guizhou Nianjian 1985*.

SANSU

1. Henry, "The Lolos and Other Tribes of Western China," 96-107.
2. John Kuhn, *We Found a Hundred Tribes*, 10.
3. Von Geusau, "The Second Hani/Akha Culture Studies Conference."
4. Chun Cao, "The Hani Christians," 9.
5. John Kuhn, *We Found a Hundred Tribes*, 10.

SHAN

1. Shan communities in the United States are located along the West Coast; the Denver, Colorado area, and in Kansas City, Kansas.
2. Grimes, *Ethnologue* (1988), 457.
3. Diller, "Tai Languages."
4. *GPD* 14, no. 4 (April 1995).

SHE

1. Ramsey, *The Languages of China*, 285. In 1997 the central government surprisingly placed two people groups living in far-off Guizhou Province, the Ga Mong and the Xi, into the She nationality. These groups had previously been classified as Miao, but because they did not like the Miao, it appears they have been placed under She as a matter of compromise by the authorities. These two new groups have little or nothing in common with the She and should not be considered She people at all. According to the 1990 census there were 121 counties or municipalities in China that recorded more than 500 She people. In descending order, the largest She populations are in: Fu'an (*Fujian*) 58,002; Xiapu (*Fujian*) 37,892; Shanghang (*Fujian*) 30,699; Fuding (*Fujian*) 28,170; Ningdeshi (*Fujian*) 19,609; Lishui City (*Zhejiang*) 18,945, and Zhangpu (*Fujian*) 18,690
2. Bradley, "East and South-East Asia," 167.
3. Jiangxi Educational Publishing, *EDCL*, 561. The only remaining speakers of either variety are located in Guangdong Province. The Lianhua dialect or language is spoken in Huidong and Haifeng counties in the Lianhua mountains, while the Luofu dialect or language is still spoken in Buluo and Zengcheng counties. The combined total of speakers is only 1,000.
4. See Paul K. Benedict, "Miao-Yao Enigma: the Na-e Language," *Linguistics of the Tibeto-Burman Area* 9, no. 1 (1986): 89-90; and David Strecker, "Some Comments on Benedicts's Miao-Yao Enigma," 22-42.
5. Ma Yin, *China's Minority Nationalities*, 411.
6. Zhang Weiwen and Zeng, *In Search of China's Minorities*, 325.
7. *CPLMR*, no. 119 (December 1991-February 1992).

SHENZHOU

1. See *Minzu Shibie Wenxian Ziliao Huibia*.
2. *Guizhou Nianjian 1985*.

SHERPA

1. Xu Yixi, *Headdresses of Chinese Minority Nationality Women*, 49.
2. Grimes, *Ethnologue* (1996), 561.
3. Gu Shoukang, "The Sherpas: Hardy Folk of the Himalayas," *China Tourism*, no. 54 (n.d.): 10.
4. Bradley, "East and South-East Asia," 170.
5. There have been several comprehensive linguistic studies on the Sherpa language. See Austin Hale (ed.), "Collected Papers on Sherpa, Jirel," *Nepal Studies in Linguistics*, no. 2 (Kirtipur: SIL and the Institute of Nepal and Asian Studies, 1975): xii, 176; and Burkhard Schttelndreyer, "Narrative Discourse in Sherpa," *SIL Publications in Linguistics and Related Fields: Papers on Discourse*, no. 51 (Dallas: SIL, 1978): 248-66.
6. Bethany World Prayer Center, "The Helambu Sherpa of Nepal" (1997).
7. Ibid.
8. Gu Shoukang, "The Sherpas," 12.
9. See Jim Carrier, "Gatekeepers of the Himalaya," *National Geographic* (December 1992): 70-89.
10. Gu Shoukang, "The Sherpas," 12. The best account of Sherpa religious practices is Sherry B. Ortner, *Sherpas Through Their Rituals* (Cambridge: Cambridge University Press, 1978). Also see James F. Fisher and Sir Edmund Hillary, *Sherpas: Reflections on Change in Himalayan Nepal* (Berkeley: University of California Press, 1990).
11. Scott Anderson, personal communication in 1996.
12. Johnstone, *Operation World* (1993), 406.
13. The Sherpa in Nepal are allowed to trade across the border with the Sherpa in Tibet. A Sherpa Christian from Nepal, who died in 1997, was known to have shared the gospel with some of his associates in Tibet.

SHIXING

1. See Sun Hongkai, "Chuanxi Minzu Zoulang Diqu de Yuyan." For a recent account of the Shuilo River see Jon Bowermaster, "Rapid Descent: First Run Down the Shuilo River," *National Geographic* (November 1996): 116-29.
2. Rock, "Konka Risumgongba," 30.
3. Ibid.
4. STEDT, *Description of the Sino-Tibetan Language Family.*
5. Rock, "Konka Risumgongba," 30.
6. Ibid., 34.
7. Ibid.
8. Ibid.

SHUI

1. According to the 1990 census there were 28 counties or municipalities in China that recorded more than 500 Shui people. In descending order, the largest Shui populations are in: Sandu 164,855; Libo 30,041; Rongjiang 29,204; Duyun City 28,516; Dushan 23,619, and Danzhai 11,404.
2. Ramsey, *The Languages of China*, 245.
3. CASS, *Information China* 3: 1262.
4. *CPLMR*, no. 119 (December 1991-February 1992).
5. Personal communication, December 1997. In 1998, "God moved on their behalf in miracle-working power. They were able to share the gospel in further detail and pray for many sick. There was a five-year-old child in one village who had large welts and boils on his face who was healed after the worker prayed for him. In the presence of many witnesses in the village, the welts and boils left his face in just three days. There was another old man who had a disease in his legs for 20 years and was not able to walk because of it. Again, this brother prayed in faith believing for God's healing power to break through. Immediately after the prayer, the old man got up and walked. Because of this, many more in the village got saved, and the two workers were swamped every day with people requesting prayer for their sicknesses.... We are believing for a true people movement among the Shui." *Workers newsletter*, November 1998.
6. This official 1990 census figure (345,993) appears to disagree with that cited under Population in China. However, the population for the Shui in Yunnan (4,300) is subtracted from the total Shui 1990 census to give a more realistic and specific population for the Shui of 341,600. The Shui in Yunnan are profiled separately in *Operation China.*

SHUI, YUNNAN

1. The *Yunnan Nianjian* listed a 1985 population of just 4,300 Shui in Yunnan. *Yunnan Nianjian 1986*, 454.
2. See Wei Ch'ing-wen, "A Brief Description of the Sui Language," *Zhongguo Yuwen*, no. 138, October 1965, 400-12; and Li Fang-Gui, "A Preliminary Comparison of Three Sui Dialects," *Academia Sinica: Institute of History and Philology* (1951): 67-74.
3. Ma Yin, *China's Minority Nationalities,* 360.

SOGWO ARIG

1. According to the 1990 census there were 22,506 Mongols in He'nan County and only 320 in Tongde County. It is possible other ethnic Sogwo Arig in Tondge were counted as part of the Tibetan nationality.
2. Good pictures of the Sogwo Arig can be seen in Rock, "Seeking the Mountains of Mystery," 142.
3. d'Ollone, *In Forbidden China,* 283.

SUAN

1. Pelkey, "Yunnan's Myriad Yi," 48.
2. Kendall, *Eyes of the Earth*, 142.
3. d'Ollone, *In Forbidden China,* 173-74.

SUBEI

1. Xie Junmei, "Shanghai Lishi Shang Renkou de Bianqian," *Shehui Kexue* (March 1980): 112.
2. Mindy Gill, personal communication, March 1998.
3. Shanghai Municipal Council, *Report for the Year 1931 and Budget for the Year 1932* (Shanghai: Kelly & Walsh, 1932), 66.
4. Emily Honig, *Creating Chinese Ethnicity: Subei People in Shanghai, 1850-1980* (Boston: Yale University Press, 1992), 41.
5. Ibid., 56.
6. Ibid.
7. Ibid., 114.
8. Ibid., 121.
9. *Amity News Service*, June 1996.
10. *Xinhua*, 21 March 1988.

SUODI

1. Matisoff, "Languages and Dialects of Tibeto-Burman."
2. Pelkey, "Yunnan's Myriad Yi," 80.
3. Covell, *The Liberating Gospel*, 213.
4. Ibid., 204.
5. Ibid., 207.

TA'ER

1. Pelkey, "Yunnan's Myriad Yi," 83.

TAGU

1. Pelkey, "Yunnan's Myriad Yi," 82.
2. Kendall, *Eyes of the Earth*, 69.

TAI DAM

1. Bradley, "East And South-East Asia," 165.
2. Perazic, "Little Laos," 52.
3. Most of the 4,000 Tai Dam in the United States live in the Cedar Rapids, Iowa area. The state of Iowa sponsored their resettlement in the U. S. Approximately 100 Tai Dam in Iowa have become Christians.
4. A Tai Dam dictionary has been published by D. Fippinger and D. H. & F. Baccum.
5. For a comprehensive record of Dai legends, see Yan Wenbian; Zhang Pen and Gu Qing (eds.), *Dai Folk Legends* (Beijing: Foreign Languages Press, 1988).
6. Bethany World Prayer Center, "The Black Tai," 1997.
7. Personal communication, January 1996.
8. AMO, "The Black Tai."
9. The Tai Dam believers in Vietnam have encountered severe persecution since becoming Christians. The Vietnamese police traveled from house to house in the Dienbienphu area. Simply by seeing if a family had removed their spirit altar, they could tell if a family had become Christian or not. Leaders have been beaten and imprisoned.
10. The entire Tai Dam New Testament has almost been completed. Parts of the Old Testament are also available in Tai Dam, using the traditional Tai Dam script, as well as the Lao and Vietnamese orthographies.

TAI KAO

1. Some have estimated the Tai Kao population in China as high as 200,000; but this is inaccurate. Chinese sources do not list the Tai Kao at all, preferring to view the Dai nationality as a single ethnolinguistic group.
2. Bradley, "East And South-East Asia," 165.
3. de Beauclair, *Tribal Cultures of Southwest China*, 9.
4. *GPD* 10, no. 4 (April 1991).
5. Ibid.
6. Ibid.
7. Stauffer, *The Christian Occupation of China*, 350.

TAI LU

1. The 1986 population figure (550,000) appears to disagree with that cited under Population in China. However, this larger figure includes the populations for the Huayao Tai (55,000), Han Tai (50,000), and Paxi (1,000). These three groups are profiled separately and are subtracted from the 1986 figure. This gives the more realistic and specific population figure of 444,000.
2. J.-O. Svantesson, 1990 personal communication.
3. According to the 1990 census there were 115,971 Dai people in Jinghong County, 104,750 in Menghai; and 49,810 in Mengla. The majority of these are Tai Lu.
4. Diller, "Tai Languages."
5. "High minority birthrates and Han Chinese migration have brought incredibly swift and destructive changes to the Prefecture. Just one generation ago wild elephants, tigers, and bears roamed the primitive forests of Xishuangbanna. Today, youth in the region have a better chance of seeing one of these animals at the provincial zoo, as millions of acres of forests have been destroyed in the last half-century. The resulting soil erosion has made Xishuangbanna's rivers dry up and silt up, humidity and rainfall has decreased, and temperatures have become more extreme. In the early 1950s, over 60% of the area (which was home to 200,000 inhabitants) was covered in forests. A study in 1995 found that only 28% of the land is now forested, while the population has increased four-fold to 800,000 people." AMO, *The 50 Most Unreached People Groups of China and Tibet*, 8.
6. Dodd, *The Tai Race*, 188.
7. Ma Yin, *China's Minority Nationalities*, 262-63.
8. *GPD* 13, no. 4 (April 1994).
9. Zhu Liangwen, *The Dai (Or the Tai and their Architecture and Customs in South China)* (Kunming: The Science and Technology Press of Yunnan, 1992), 15. For a comprehensive study on religious practices among the Tai Lu, see T'ien Ju-K'ang, *Religious Cults of the Pai-i Along the Burma-Yunnan Border* (New York: Cornell University Monograph, 1986).
10. "God's Word to the Tai," newsletter (Spring 1996).
11. See AMO, "The Tai Lu," *Newsletter*, no. 44 (March 1997). Although finances were given to the government-sanctioned Amity Press in Nanjing for the printing of 2,000 Tai Lu New Testaments in 1992, only 1,000 were ever delivered. All attempts to discover the whereabouts of the other 1,000 have failed.

TAI MAO

1. Bradley, "East And South-East Asia," 164. According to the 1990 census there were 107,907 Dai people in Luxi County; 37,796 in Ruili; 30,506 in Lianghe, and 23,755 in Longchuan. The great majority of these are Tai Mao.
2. Grimes, *Ethnologue* (1992), 527.
3. Bradley, "East and South-East Asia," 164.
4. Zhu Liangwen, *The Dai.*
5. John Kuhn, *We Found a Hundred Tribes*, 5.
6. The Taiwanese Christians tried to follow up the new believers by letter. The letters were intercepted by the local authorities, who persecuted the new Tai Mao Christians.

TAI NUA

1. Bradley, "East And South-East Asia," 164.
2. Diller, "Tai Languages."
3. Bradley, "East and South-East Asia," 164.
4. Zhu Liangwen, *The Dai.*
5. *GPD* 14, no. 4 (April 1995).
6. Zhu Liangwen, *The Dai.*
7. Stauffer, *The Christian Occupation of China,* 241.

TAI PONG

1. The 1987 population figure appears to disagree with that cited under Population in China. This larger number includes the 34,000 Ya. However, the Ya are profiled separately in *Operation China* and their number is subtracted from the larger figure (100,000) to arrive at a more realistic and specific figure for the Tai Pong (66,000).
2. Diller, "Tai Languages." According to the 1990 census there were a total of 15,188 Dai people in Jinping County.
3. Bradley, "East and South-East Asia," 165.
4. Ibid.
5. *The Book of the Later Han Dynasty,* AD 25-220.
6. John Kuhn, *We Found a Hundred Tribes,* 9.

TAJIK, SARIKOLI

1. According to the 1990 census there were 6 counties or municipalities in China that recorded more than 500 Tajik people. In descending order, the largest Tajik populations

are in: Taxkorgan 20,794; Akto 3,953; Zepu 3,207; Shache 2,046; Yecheng 1,753; Pishan 912. These figures do not distinguish between the two Tajik language groups.

2. *CPLMR*, no. 119 (December 1991-February 1992).
3. Palmberg of the Swedish Missionary Society, as cited in Stauffer, *The Christian Occupation of China*, 276.
4. *Call to Prayer* (August-September 1997).

TAJIK, WAKHI

1. See Peter C. Backstrom, "'Wakhi,' Languages of Northern Areas," *National Institute of Pakistan Studies*, no. 2: *Sociolinguistic Survey of Northern Pakistan* (Islamabad: Quaid-i-Azam University, 1992): 57-74.
2. Milliken, "SIL China Nationalities and Languages Files."
3. Schwartz, *The Minorities of Northern China*, 217.
4. See John King, *Karakoram Highway: The High Road to China* (Hawthorn, Australia: Lonely Planet Publications, 1989).
5. Marco Polo, *The Book of Ser Marco Polo*.
6. Ke Ji, "The Colourful Tajiks," *China Tourism*, no. 42 (n.d.): 10-11.
7. Schwartz, *The Minorities of Northern China*, 220.

TALU

1. Pelkey, "Yunnan's Myriad Yi," 81.
2. Ibid., 78.
3. Samuel Clarke, *Among the Tribes in South-West China*, 134.

TANGLANG

1. Pelkey, "Yunnan's Myriad Yi," 87.
2. Stauffer, *The Christian Occupation of China*, 244.
3. Personal communication, January 1998.

TATAR

1. 2,294 (1964 census), and 6,929 (1953 census).
2. Also 39,000 in Turkmenistan; 28,000 in Azerbaijian; 26,000 in Turkey; 26,000 in Romania; 12,000 in Byelarus; 10,000 in USA; 10,000 in Bulgaria; 5,100 in Lithuania; 5,000 in Latvia; 4,000 in Estonia; 400 in Afghanistan; also in Turkey and Finland (all figures from P. Johnstone, 1993).
3. Australian Academy and CASS, *LAC*, C-5.
4. Jiangxi Educational Publishing, *EDCL*, 576.
5. Schwartz, *The Minorities of Northern China*, 72.
6. Chun Shizeng (ed.), *Chinese Nationalities* (Beijing: China Nationality Photography and Art Press, 1989), 92.
7. Ibid.
8. Covell, *The Liberating Gospel*, 165.

TELEUT

1. Janhunen and Salminen, *UNESCO Red Book*.
2. United Bible Society, 1993.
3. Janhunen and Salminen, *UNESCO Red Book*.
4. Ibid.
5. Ibid.

THAMI

1. Grimes, *Ethnologue* (1996), 734.
2. Gu Shoukang, "The Sherpas," 14.
3. "Pray for the Peoples of Nepal: A 30-day Prayer Guide for Different People Groups of Nepal," n.d.
4. Ibid.
5. Ibid.

6. *Sounds* (California: Gospel Recordings, Spring 1994).
7. *Advance*, newsletter (August 1997).

THO

1. Joshua Project 1995. Wurm and Hattori's 1981 *Language Atlas of the Pacific Area* lists a total of 2,000,000 Tho in both Vietnam and China. A 1984 figure places 870,000 in Vietnam. Grimes, *Ethnologue* (1986), 457. This implies a population of at least 1.13 million Tho in China.
2. Dodd, *The Tai Race*, 144.
3. Samuel Clarke, *Among the Tribes in South-West China*, 92-93.
4. Diller, "Tai Languages."
5. de Beauclair, *Tribal Cultures of Southwest China*, 9.
6. Quincy, *Hmong*, 68.
7. Dodd, *The Tai Race*, 132.
8. Ibid., 146.

TIBETAN, BOYU

1. Chen Yunguang and Zhang Heping, "Flower Gathering Festival at Boyu," *China Tourism*, no. 115 (n.d.): 20.
2. Ibid., 23.
3. Ibid.
4. Ibid.
5. Ibid., 20.
6. Ibid.
7. Ekvall's out-of-print book, *Gateway to Tibet*, recounts the missions history of this area.

TIBETAN, CENTRAL

1. 2,000 in Taiwan (1993 P. Johnstone); 1,500 in Switzerland; 352 in USA (1970 census); also in Norway, France, Australia, UK.
2. According to the 1990 census which did not distinguish between different Tibetan ethnic groups or languages as this book has, there were 186 counties or municipalities in China that recorded more than 500 Tibetan people. In descending order, the largest Tibetan populations are in: Lhasa City (*Tibet*) 96,431; Xiahe (*Gansu*) 86,671; Xigaze (*Tibet*) 76,246; Changdu (*Tibet*) 72,381; Mangkang (*Tibet*) 64,411; Nanmulin (*Tibet*) 61,014; Yushu (*Qinghai*) 59,630; Jiangda (*Tibet*) 59,585
3. Buckley and Strauss (eds.), *Tibet*, 23.
4. Our aim is to classify groups according to "mission significant" classifications, i.e. how far the gospel can penetrate from one people group to another without encountering cultural, linguistic, or other barriers. Using this criteria, the Tibetans are certainly a collection of more than a dozen different ethnolinguistic varieties. The Tibetans oppose such classifications, claiming that it weakens their unity as a race. They even argued for the inclusion of the Tu minority into the Tibetan nationality, despite the Tu speaking a Mongolian language and having a separate historical identity.
5. Bradley, "East and South-East Asia," 170.
6. William Carlsen, *Tibet: In Search of a Miracle* (New York: Nyack College, 1985), 37.
7. J. Dauvillier, "Temoignages Nouveaux sur le Christianisme Nestorien chez les Tibetans," in *Histoire et institutions des Eglise Orientales au Moyen Age* (London: Varioum Reprints 2, 1983), 165.
8. Anthony P. B. Lambert, "The Challenge of China's Minority Peoples," *Chinese Around the World* (April 1991).

TIBETAN, DEQEN

1. Grimes, *Ethnologue* (1996), 540, numbers 520,000 Atuence, a figure that has been used by the Joshua Project and other people group lists. However, the location given ("Yunnan-Tibet border") in no way supports such a large population. All Tibetans numbered only 101,500 in Yunnan Province in 1985 (*Yunnan Nianjian 1986*, 454). The regions across the borders in southern Tibet and southwest Sichuan, where the same language is spoken, are relatively sparsely populated. The 1987 Australian Academy and CASS, *LAC*, C-11, lists the Tibetan language in this area as Southern Kham, and gives a population of 134,300. This figure includes speakers from both the Deqen Tibetan (73,560) and the Zhongdian Tibetan (60,740) language groups. There were a total of 20,484 Tibetans living in Zayu County, Tibet, according to the 1990 census.
2. John Morse, personal communication, January 1998. In the early 1990s a dispute with the Myanmar authorities resulted in the rejection of Tibetans' citizenship that forced most Tibetans to go back across the border into China. Some have returned since then.
3. Tian Qui, "The Tibetans of Deqen," *China Tourism*, no. 108 (n.d.): 30.
4. Voegelin and Voegelin, *Classification and Index of the World's Languages* (1977).
5. Australian Academy and CASS, *LAC*, 1987, C-11.
6. For a detailed account of a Westerner's visit to the Deqen region, see Brackenbury, *Yak Butter & Black Tea*, 25-33.
7. See Lambert's "The Challenge of China's Minority Peoples," 9, and "Christianity and Tibet," *Pray for China Fellowship* (April 1996).
8. "A handful of the 700 church members are Naxi, the remainder are Tibetans. The church's Tibetan priest, who is only 27 years old, completed four year's study at the Catholic seminary in Beijing." Personal communication, 3 November 1997.
9. See Covell, *The Liberating Gospel*, 44-51.
10. Rock, "Through the Great River Trenches of Asia," 155.
11. Ibid, 164.
12. Stauffer, *The Christian Occupation of China*, 282.
13. Alex Buchan, "Catholic Church Hangs on in Tibet," *Compass Direct* (September 1998). According to the priest, "the Catholic community is very poor, nomadic, and has only had a church since 1986. Their knowledge of the faith is not strong." Of this total of 9,500 Catholics, about 7,500 are Deqen Tibetans and 2,000 are Zhongdian Tibetans.

TIBETAN, GTSANG

1. Cited in Buckley and Strauss (eds.), *Tibet*, 13.
2. Bradley, "East and South-East Asia," 170.
3. Tsering, *Sharing Christ in the Tibetan Buddhist World*, 75.

TIBETAN, JONE

1. Grimes, *Ethnologue* (1996), 546.
2. Joseph F. Rock, "Life Among the Lamas of Choni," *National Geographic* (November 1928), 572.
3. Ibid., 569.
4. Grimes, *Ethnologue* (1996), 546.
5. Rock, "Life Among the Lamas of Choni," 569.
6. Ibid.
7. Ibid., 576. When Rock visited there in 1928, he noticed that the gate to the Jone monastery bore an inscription by Emperor Kang Hsi (1710) in favor of Chih Lien, a Choni priest who had paid him a visit.
8. Ibid., 572.
9. Ibid., 576.
10. Stauffer, *The Christian Occupation of China*, 281.
11. *Global Chinese Ministries* (Colorado: OMF, March 1998).

TIBETAN, NGHARI

1. See Beall and Goldstein, "The Remote World of Tibet's Nomads," 752-81.
2. Bradley, "East and South-East Asia," 169.
3. Buckley and Strauss (eds.), *Tibet*, 141.
4. Tsering, *Sharing Christ in the Tibetan Buddhist World*, 78. Until recently, the church bell was held in a room in the basement of the Jokhang Temple in Lhasa, a sad reminder of the demise of Christianity from Tibet more than 250 years ago. In 1996 the bell was removed, possibly because so many foreigners were asking to see it.

TIBETAN, ZHONGDIAN

1. Tai Chi Yin, "Timeless Plateau: Zhongdian," *China Tourism*, no. 108 (n.d.): 24.
2. Ibid., 25.
3. See Krisadawan Hongladarom, "Rgylathang Tibetan of Yunnan: A Preliminary Report," *Linguistics of the Tibeto-Burman Area* 19, no. 2 (1996): 69.
4. Recent linguistic studies on the Zhongdian Tibetan language include Hongladarom, "Rgylathang Tibetan of Yunnan," 69-92; and Hpung Sarep, "Rgylathang Tibetan of Yunnan: A Preliminary Report," *Linguistics of the Tibeto-Burman Area* 19, no. 2 (1996): 93-184.
5. The Xiangcheng people who live across the Yunnan-Sichuan border to the north still retain many customs that are similar to the Qiang. The existence of the Xiangcheng supports the oral legend from Zhongdian.
6. Covell, *The Liberating Gospel*, 155.
7. Ibid., 51.

TIBETAN, ZHUGQU

1. According to the 1990 census there were a total of 36,870 Tibetan people living in Zhugqu County. This figure includes the Boyu Tibetans.
2. Wong Chung Fai, "A Mountain Hamlet in Zhugqu," 26.
3. Ibid.
4. Zheng Ming, "Mountain Ceremony of the Tibetans of Southern Gansu," *China Tourism*, no. 125 (November 1990): 56.
5. Ibid.
6. Ibid., 55. According to another legend, "Long, long ago a general commanding an army fighting away from home fell on the battle-field. The people of the locality associated him with the mountain on which he died, planting at its summit the arrows he carried with him, and started to venerate him as a god. Every year the rite was repeated to remember him and beg his protection."

TORGUT

1. Murray, "With the Nomads of Central Asia," 11.
2. Bethany World Prayer Center, "The Kalmyk-Oirat" (1997).
3. Issachar Frontier Missions Research, *Mongolia Challenge Report*, II, 2, i.
4. Moule and Pelliot, *Marco Polo*, 201.
5. Hefley, *China! Christian Martyrs of the 20th Century*, 18-19.
6. The *Jesus* film is available in Kalmyk, but it was translated for the Kalmyk living in Russia and contains

many loanwords that are not used in China. The Torgut in China are not able to understand it.

TU

1. This official 1990 census figure (191,624) seems to disagree with that cited under Population in China. However, the larger figure includes the Mongour (30,000) and the Wutun (2,000) who are profiled separately in *Operation China*. Therefore, the combined population is subtracted from the census figure to give a more realistic and specific number (159,624) for the Tu.
2. According to the 1990 census there were 21 counties or municipalities in China that recorded more than 500 Tu people. In descending order, the largest Tu populations are in: Huzhu (*Qinghai*) 57,147; Minhe (*Qinghai*) 38,005 [most of these are Mongour]; Datong (*Qinghai*) 34,753; Tianzhu (*Gansu*) 11,837; Tongren (*Qinghai*) 7,470 [some of these are Wutun]; Ledu (*Qinghai*) 6,587; Menyuan (*Qinghai*) 6,118.
3. *GPD* 10, no. 6 (June 1991).
4. Australian Academy and CASS, *LAC*, C-5.
5. Chun Shizeng (ed.), *Chinese Nationalities*, 54.
6. *GPD* 12, no. 9 (September 1993).
7. *CPLMR*, no. 119 (December 1991-February 1992).

TUERKE

1. Grimes, *Ethnologue* (1992), 519
2. Jiangxi Educational Publishing, *EDCL*, 576
3. Storey (ed.), *China*, 1007.
4. See Zhao Xiangru and Reinhold F. Hahn, "The Ili Turk People and Their Language," *Central Asiatic Journal*, no. 33 (1989); and Reinhold F. Hahn, "An Annotated Sample of Ili Turki," *Acta Orientalia Hungaricae*, no. 43 (1990).
5. Jiangxi Educational Publishing, *EDCL*, 576.
6. Zhao Xiangru and Hahn, "The Ili Turk People and Their Language."

TUJIA

1. According to a 1986 survey 1,486,698 Tujia lived in Hubei Province, 744,701 in Hunan Province, and 595,349 in Sichuan Province. Research based on the 1990 census placed 1,028,189 Tujia in Guizhou Province. Minority Research Associates, "The Tujia: A People of Song and Dance," unpublished paper. According to the 1990 census, there were 106 counties or municipalities in China that recorded more than 500 Tujia people. In descending order, the largest Tujia populations are in: Youyang (Sichuan) 356,363; Shimen (Hunan) 344,745; Lichuan City (Hebei) 293,663; Shizhu (Sichuan) 271,356; Youngshun (Hunan) 264,963; Dayong (Hunan) 255,677
2. Corrigan, *Odyssey Illustrated Guide to Guizhou*, 215.
3. Paul Vial, *De la Langue et de l'écriture indigènes au Yûnnân*, as cited in Enwall, *A Myth Become Reality* 1: 60.
4. According to the State Nationalities Affairs Commission, *China's Minority Peoples*, 42, *Bizika* means "aborigines."
5. Ma Yin, *China's Minority Nationalities*, 403.
6. Wong Chung Fai, "Xilankapu: Weaving With a Background of Centuries," *China Tourism*, no. 106 (n.d.): 63.
7. See Li Jie, "The Mysterious Ceremonies of Guizhou's Tujia Minority," *China Tourism*, no. 154 (April 1993): 26-36.
8. *CPLMR*, no. 119 (December 1991-February 1992).
9. Don Martin, "Spiritual Darkness Blinds 6 Million Tujia People," IMB News Stories, e-mail News Service, International Mission Board Southern Baptist Convention, 8 April 1999.
10. The *Jesus* film was being considered for translation into Tujia, but the ministry in charge of the project decided there were too few Tujia who can still understand their language to make it worthwhile. Even among those Tujia who still speak their language, many use Chinese as their first language and Tujia second.
11. This official 1990 census figure (5,704,223) seems to disagree with that cited under Population in China. However, it includes the 4,000 Mozhihei people. These 4,000 are subtracted from the larger number to arrive at a more specific and realistic population (5,700,223) for the Tujia people.

TULAO

1. For a linguistic overview of Tulao see Acharn Theraphan Khongkum's article in Jerold A. Edmondson and David B. Solnit, *Comparative Kadai: The Tai Branch* (Arlington: University of Texas, 1997).
2. Diller, "Tai Languages."

TUSHU

1. Pelkey, "Yunnan's Myriad Yi," 70.
2. Corrigan, *Odyssey Illustrated Guide to Guizhou*, 206.
3. *Weining Yizu Huizu Miaozu Zizhixian Minzuzhi*, 78.
4. Samuel Clarke, *Among the Tribes in South-West China*, 115.
5. Kendall, *Eyes of the Earth*, 24.
6. Ibid., 120.

TUSU

1. Pelkey, "Yunnan's Myriad Yi," 50.
2. Ibid.

TUVA

1. Australian Academy and CASS, *LAC*, C-5.
2. Janhunen and Salminen, *UNESCO Red Book*.
3. Ibid.
4. Australian Academy and CASS, *LAC*, C-5.
5. Grimes, *Ethnologue* (1996), 562.
6. *Frontiers Focus* 5, no. 2.
7. Xu Liqun, "By Motorbike Along China's Borders," *China Tourism*, no. 109 (n.d.): 32.
8. *Frontiers Focus* 5, no. 2.
9. *GPD* 15, no. 9 (September 1996).
10. *Call to Prayer* (November-December 1998). The Tuva Scriptures and *Jesus* film used by the Tuva in Russia are not understood by the Tuva in China.
11. *GPD* 15, no. 9 (September 1996).
12. Conner, "Midge's Musings," November-December 1995.

TUWO

1. Graybill, personal communication, October 1997.
2. Hefley, *China! Christian Martyrs of the 20th Century*, 19-20.

UTSAT

1. According to the 1990 census there were 4,918 Hui people in Sanya City.
2. Ramsey, *The Languages of China*, 168.
3. The claim was first made in P. K. Benedict, "A Cham Colony on the Island of Hainan," *Harvard Journal of Asiatic Studies*, no. 6 (1941): 129-34.
4. Ian Maddieson, "Tone in Utsat," in *Tonality in Austronesian Languages: Oceanic Linguistics Special Publication*, no. 24 (Honolulu: University of Hawaii Press, 1993), 75-89.

5. One Utsat man the author met in 1993 spoke Utsat, Mandarin, Cantonese, Hainanese, Malay, Arabic, and some English!

UYGUR

1. In 1953, 70% of the population of Xinjiang were Uygur, and only a very small number of Han Chinese were in the region. Benson, *The Ili Rebellion*, 29-32. The Chinese have since migrated into Xinjiang in massive numbers. In 1990 there were over 13 million people in Xinjiang, of whom only about seven million (54%) are Uygur. In 1996 alone, 57,000 Uygurs were arrested and 1,700 executed for separatist activities. *Call to Prayer* (October 1997).
2. The Uygur in Changde and Taoyuan counties of Hunan are "the descendants of 29 Uygur clans who migrated to China proper during the Mongolian world empire." Schwartz, *The Minorities of Northern China*, 1. They are now completely assimilated and are no longer able to speak Uygur.
3. Many of the Uygur in Guangzhou are involved in crime syndicates, especially drugs and prostitution.
4. Covell, *The Liberating Gospel*, 156.
5. Jiangxi Educational Publishing, *EDCL*, 574.
6. Schwartz, *The Minorities of Northern China*, 3.
7. "About 591, among Turkish prisoners captured and sent to Constantinople... some of the Turks were found with crosses tattooed on their foreheads. When asked what the crosses meant, they replied that Christians among them had said it would ward off the pestilence." *Theophylactus Simocatta*, v.10, and Theopanes, *Chronographia*, A.M. 6081, as cited in Moffett, *A History of Christianity in Asia*, 280.
8. Rene Grousett, *The Empire of the Steppes: A History of Central Asia*, trans. by N. Walford (New Brunswick: Rutgers University Press, 1970), 191.
9. Moffett, *A History of Christianity in Asia,* 400.
10. Kitab Books, newsletter, no. 10 (April 1996).
11. Covell, *The Liberating Gospel,* 167.
12. "The entire church was martyred. The faithful followers of Jesus were told to renounce their faith or die. One of them, a harmless-as-a-dove teenager Habil, politely refused. He knelt before the Lord and looked heavenward as a bullet ended Habil's life in this world....

    "In the late 1980s several Uygur Christians had soapy water publicly forced into their mouths in an attempt by the authorities to inwardly cleanse the new Christians from their 'defilement'. They were then forced to take a week-long crash course in the Koran during which they must recant their faith in Christ or face possible death." "30-Day Muslim Prayer Guide" (1996).
13. Hosanna Ministries, "Report on Xinjiang House Churches: Information for Prayer and Strategic Coordination" (Hong Kong, September 1997).
14. Ibid.
15. Ibid. One group of about 15 Uygur believers in Xinjiang are reported to have "interpersonal and doctrinal differences that threaten to divide them." *Call to Prayer* (November-December 1998). Just before *Operation China* went to press, the author was told by a leading Chinese housechurch leader of "a few thousand" Uygur converts in recent years, led to Christ by evangelists. Most of these Uygurs were convinced of the truths of the gospel when they experienced healing and supernatural signs and wonders. There was no opportunity to confirm this report before going to press.
16. *Call to Prayer* (August-September 1997). "The Uygur believers of Chung-ja, a small city in Kazakstan near the Chinese border, have planted two fellowships in the nearby towns of Ketmen and Shirin. Each congregation has about 30 believers." *Call to Prayer* (October 1997).
17. Several encouraging reports from Xinjiang were listed in *Pray for China* (September-October 1997): (a) "A keen 50-year old man is known to have visited various local mosques debating about Jesus with the religious leaders." (b) "A Muslim young man hurt his head while fighting and was taken to hospital since he was losing a lot of blood. The family was poor and could not afford to pay for treatment so took him home to prepare for his funeral. Then they remembered a neighbor who was a Han Christian who had explained about Jesus being a Savior. The neighbor preached and prayed with them and then as the young man prayed he realized that his wound had stopped bleeding. After a while he recovered and he and his family became Christians." (c) "In one Muslim village in Xinjiang Province, the *Jesus* video was shown. Various people in the village started asking 'Who is the true God?' after seeing the video. Later they met some Han Chinese Christians who explained the Christian faith and the village turned to Christ." (d) "An old man who regularly went to the mosque was one day taken ill.... At the same time he recalled hearing that Jesus was the one true God. As he thought about this he had a vision of Jesus and prayed to Him. After he left the mosque, he realized that he had recovered."
18. Small Uygur communities are also found in Taiwan, Australia, Turkey, Germany, India, Indonesia, Saudi Arabia, USA, Morocco, and possibly Iran.
19. This official 1990 census figure (7,214,431) appears to disagree with that cited under Population in China. It includes the populations of four other groups: Keriya, Taklimakan Uygur, Lop Nur Uygur, and Yutian Uygur. These are profiled separately in *Operation China* and so are subtracted from the census figure to give a more realistic and precise population (7,164,231) for the Uygur.
20. 3,996,311 (1964 census), and 2,775,622 (1953 census).
21. 1,000 in Australia; 500 in Turkey (1981); 200 in Taiwan (1997); small numbers in Germany, India, Indonesia, Saudi Arabia, USA, Morocco, and possibly Iran.
22. 80% of Uygur in Xinjiang live in the Hotan, Kashgar, Aksu and Korla regions that surround the Taklimakan desert.

UYGUR, LOP NUR

1. Australian Academy and CASS, *LAC*, C-4.
2. Marco Polo, *The Book of Ser Marco Polo.*
3. "Buried Cities and Shifting Sands: Onward to Dunhuang," *China Tourism*, no. 157 (July 1993): 61.
4. Ibid.
5. Marco Polo, *The Book of Ser Marco Polo.*
6. Ibid.

UYGUR, TAKLIMAKAN

1. "Lost Tribe Discovered," *China Today* (early 1990).
2. Ajiya, "The Taklimakan Desert," *China Tourism,* no. 70 (n.d.): 53.
3. Ibid.
4. "The Chinese estimate the Taklimakan holds 74 billion barrels of oil — three times the US oil reserves." Thomas B. Allen, "Xinjiang," *National Geographic* (March 1996): 42.
5. *South China Morning Post* (1990).
6. "Lost Tribe Discovered," *China Today.*
7. *South China Morning Post* (1990).
8. Ibid.

9. Ajiya, "The Taklimakan Desert," 55.
10. D. Twitchett and J. K. Fairbank (eds.), *The Cambridge History of China* 3: *Sui and T'ang China* (Cambridge: Cambridge University Press, 1979), 46-47.

UYGUR, YUTIAN

1. There were a total of 178,966 Uygur people in Yutian County (1990 census). Our estimate of how many belong to this ethnic group is conservative. The Yutian Uygur's population may be considerably higher.
2. Li Kai, "Xinjiang: Wonderland of Sight and Colours," *China Tourism*, no. 42 (n.d.): 27.
3. Rong Mei, "Jumi, Zhemotuona et Loulan, trois Anciens Royaumes," *China Tourism*, no. 82 (n.d.): 32.
4. Schwartz, *The Minorities of Northern China*, 5.
5. Rong Mei, "Jumi, Zhemotuona et Loulan," 32.
6. Li Kai, "Xinjiang," 27.
7. Mizra Haydar, *Tarikh-i-Rashidi*, as cited in Moffett, *A History of Christianity in Asia*, 492.
8. Hosanna Ministries, "Report on Xinjiang House Churches." In 1948 the Ling Gong Tuan church of Shandong Province received exactly the same vision, "but it is not clear if they led any Uygurs to Christ." In 1991 the underground churches of Henan Province also received the same vision, and have been sending evangelists into Xinjiang since.

UZBEK

1. 7,717 (1964 census), and 13,626 (1953 census).
2. Also 317,000 in Turkmenistan; 50,000 in Pakistan (refugees).
3. According to the 1990 census there were 9 counties or municipalities in China that recorded more than 500 Uzbek people. In descending order, the largest Uzbek populations are in: Yining City 3,447; Shache 1,344; Kashgar City 1,183; Urumqi City 1,179 and Mulei 1,149
4. Ramsey, *The Languages of China*, 185.
5. Australian Academy and CASS, *LAC*, C-5.
6. Jiger Janabel, *The Golden Horde and the Formation of the Ethnic Kazakhs* (The Center for the Study of the Eurasian Nomads, n.d).
7. *CPLMR*, no. 119 (December 1991-February 1992).
8. *Alliance Life*, 24 April 1996.
9. *Call to Prayer* (May-June 1997).

VIETNAMESE

1. Also in the United Kingdom, France, Netherlands, New Caledonia, China, Vanuatu, Martinique, Thailand, Philippines, New Zealand, Senegal, Cote d'Ivoire, and Finland.
2. 10,000 in France (1975); 8,000 in Netherlands; 5,000 in New Caledonia (1984); 770 in Vanuatu (1993); 330 in Martinique; also in Thailand, Philippines, New Zealand, Senegal, Cote d'Ivoire, Finland.
3. Xiao Yang, "Vietnamese Refugees in China," *Bridge*, no. 9 (January-February 1985): 22.
4. Ibid.
5. Personal communication with a Vietnamese refugee, Hong Kong, 1992.

WA

1. Johnstone, *Operation World* (1993), 398. According to the 1990 China census there were 18 counties or municipalities in China that recorded more than 500 Wa people. In descending order, the largest Wa populations are in: Cangyuan 124,850; Ximeng 56,706; Lancang 51,899; Gengma 37,133; Menglian 26,451; Yongde 19,060; Shuangjiang 11,888. Note: these figures refer to the total Wa nationality, which includes the Kawa, Lawa and Ben.
2. Covell, *The Liberating Gospel*, 224.
3. Bradley, "East and South-East Asia," 159-60. There are numerous linguistic articles dealing with the Wa languages and dialects. One of the best is Gerard Diffloth, "The Wa Languages," *Linguistics of the Tibeto-Burman Area* 5, no. 2 (1980): 1-182.
4. T'ien, *Peaks of Faith*, 20.
5. Tian Jizhou and Luo, *Ximing Wazu Shehui Xingtai*, 97.
6. YASS 270, section 21, no. 8.
7. Ibid., 270, section 7; cited in T'ien, *Peaks of Faith*, 17.
8. "God looked down from heaven and prepared the hearts of the Wa to receive the Gospel of His Son. An amazing testimony of God's love and power took place in northern Burma in 1906. Despite never having heard of Jesus, Wa 'prophets' began strongly speaking out messages similar to John the Baptist, telling the people to forsake their head-hunting and violence, and to prepare their hearts for the arrival of the True God. At that time a witch-doctor in a certain Wa village owned three white donkeys. He laid his hands on the middle donkey and told the village elders, 'If you follow this donkey it will lead you to the True God.' For weeks the elders followed the donkey a distance of 200 miles across remote terrain until one day it stopped outside the house of William Young, the American Baptist missionary who was working amongst the Lahu tribe. Young became the first to take the Gospel message to the Wa. Salvation swept many areas as hundreds of hearts already prepared by the Holy Spirit converted to Christ." AMO, *The 50 Most Unreached People Groups of China and Tibet*, 19. A slightly different version of the same event appears in Don Richardson, *Eternity in Their Hearts*, 102-04.
9. "Annual Report from Bana" (Valley Forge, Penn.: The American Baptist Archives Center, 12 April 1948): 148-151.
10. *CPLMR*, no. 119 (December 1991-February 1992).
11. The main reason for this nominalism is the Wa's illiteracy, resulting in few having a knowledge of the Scriptures, and a emphasis by the early missionaries on the necessity of attending church only, rather than a personal walk with Christ. Personal communication, August 1996.
12. The official 1990 census figure (351,974) appears to disagree with that cited under Population in China. However, this number also includes the Kawa, Lawa, and Ben ethnic groups, all of which are profiled separately in *Operation China* and have been subtracted from the census figure to give a more realistic and precise population (245,000) for the Wa.

WONI

1. Hani2000, "The Hani: Poorest of China's Poor."
2. Davies, *Yun-nan*, 365.
3. Bradley, "Language Planning for China's Minorities." An earlier linguistic study of Woni is Yuan Jiahua, "Woni yu Yinxi," *Xueyuan* 1, no. 12 (1948).
4. CASS, *Information China* 3: 1247.
5. Hani2000, "The Hani: Poorest of China's Poor."
6. Bethany World Prayer Center, "The Hani" (1997).
7. Dodd, *The Tai Race*, 84.
8. *CPLMR*, no. 119 (December 1991-February 1992).
9. Chun Cao, "The Hani Christians," 9.

WOPU

1. Pelkey, "Yunnan's Myriad Yi," 73.
2. Ibid., 64.

WUMENG

1. Pelkey, "Yunnan's Myriad Yi," 74.
2. Matisoff, "Languages and Dialects of Tibeto-Burman," lists the Wumeng in Yunnan Province only.
3. Samuel Clarke, *Among the Tribes in South-West China.*
4. Kendall, *Eyes of the Earth*, 100.

WUNAI

1. Bradley, "East and South-East Asia," 168.
2. Australian Academy and CASS, *LAC*, C-8.
3. Ma Yin, *China's Minority Nationalities,* 381.
4. David and Naomi Shibley, *The Smoke of a Thousand Villages and Other Stories of Real Life Heroes of the Faith* (Nashville: Thomas Nelson, 1989), 110.

WUTUN

1. Jiangxi Educational Publishing, *EDCL*, 556.
2. Grimes, *Ethnologue* (1996), 564.
3. Dwayne Graybill, personal communication, October 1996.
4. Ibid.
5. Ibid.
6. Ibid.

XI

1. Wang Fushi and Mao, *Reconstruction of Proto Miao-Yao.* Estimates of the population of the Xi in Chinese publications have varied widely, including figures of 10,000 and 50,000. See *Minzu Shibie Wenxian Ziliao Huibian*, and *Guizhou Nianjian 1985.* Earlier publications may have combined the Luobobe Miao with the Xi.
2. The author was told by a Xi village leader that in the 1950s, when the government was classifying minority groups, the head of the Kaili nationality affairs office was a Miao. The Miao man wanted as many members of the Miao minority as possible, and so included groups like the Xi, Ge, and Ga Mong as part of the Miao, much to their consternation.
3. *Guizhou Nianjian 1997.* This new classification is ridiculous from an ethnolinguistic viewpoint. The Xi speak a Western Hmongic language, but because they did not like being part of the Miao nationality, it appears the government has compromised by putting them into the She nationality, even though there are no historical or ethnolinguistic links between the Xi and She to justify this.
4. Enwall, *A Myth Become Reality* 1: 24.
5. Wang Fushi, *Miaoyu Jianzhi.*
6. Nuo Dao Qing, personal communication, August 1997.

XIALUSI

1. See *Minzu Shibie Wenxian Ziliao Huibian*, 340-41.
2. *Guizhou Nianjian 1985.*

XIANDAO

1. Dwayne Graybill, personal communication, November 1997. Grimes, *Ethnologue* (1996), 564, states the Xiandao live in parts of two villages (Xiandao and Meng'e) but the government built a new village in 1995 for the Xiandao, which combined the populations of the two previous villages.
2. de Beauclair, *Tribal Cultures of Southwest China*, 23.
3. Jiangxi Educational Publishing, *EDCL*, 554-55. Also see Milliken, "SIL China Nationalities and Languages Files."
4. Dwayne Graybill, unpublished report (November 1997).
5. The description of the disease suggests small-pox or chicken-pox, but the fact that the Xiandao have needed regular vaccinations for decades discounts that. Dwayne Graybill was shown the symptoms by the Xiandao, large red blotches found only on their faces. It is hoped people knowledgeable in field of medicine may soon visit the Xiandao and reveal the mystery behind their strange disease.
6. de Beauclair, *Tribal Cultures of Southwest China,* 9.
7. Graybill, personal communication, November 1997. This implies that he is a Communist Party member.

XIANGCHENG

1. There were a total of 22,325 people belonging to the Tibetan nationality in Xiangcheng, according to the 1990 census.
2. Xian Yanyun, "In Search of the Ancient Tea Caravan Route," 75.
3. Ibid.
4. Ibid.
5. Rock, "Konka Risumgongba," 17.

XIANGTANG

1. Pelkey, "Yunnan's Myriad Yi," 44-45.
2. *Luchun Xian Zhi* (1992).
3. John Kuhn, *We Found a Hundred Tribes.*
4. Gaide, "Notice Ethnographique sur les Principales Races," 449-94.
5. Pelkey, "Report on the Yi Peoples of Honghe Prefecture," 18.

XIBE

1. According to the 1990 census there were 27 counties or municipalities in Liaoning that recorded more than 500 Xibe people. In descending order, the largest Xibe populations are in: Shenyang City PQ 33,132; Kaiyuan City 18,335; Wafangdian City 12,000; Yixian 10,890; Shenyang City CC 7,156; Fengcheng 4,577
2. "Origin of the Names of China's Minority Nationalities," *China Tourism*, no.54 (n.d.): 75.
3. Zhao Zhan, "Xibe Zuyuan Kao" [The Origin of the Xibe], in *Zhongyang Minzu Xueshu Lunwen Xuanji* 2 (Beijing, 1980): 118.
4. Schwartz, *The Minorities of Northern China*, 169.
5. Ibid., 159.
6. Ibid., 164.
7. Amity Press, highest estimate for Protestants in Liaoning (1997).
8. *Zhongguo Shengshi Zizhiqu Ziliao Shouce* (Beijing, 1990).
9. This official 1990 census figure appears to disagree with that cited under Population in China. The larger figure (172,847) includes the 32,900 Western Xibe (1990 population estimate). Their number has been subtracted to give a more realistic and precise population of 139,950 for the Xibe.

XIBE, WESTERN

1. *Minzu Tuanjie*, no. 150 (1983): 10.
2. According to the 1990 census there were 7 counties or municipalities in Xinjiang that recorded more than 500 Xibe people. In descending order, the largest Western Xibe populations are in: Qapqal (Chanucha'er) 19,365; Urumqi City 2,675; Huocheng 2,658; Yining City 2,497; Gongliu 1,430; Tacheng City 1,111; Nileke 607.
3. Schwartz, *The Minorities of Northern China*, 165.

4. Ibid., 160.
5. Ke Ji, "Wonderful Xibe Archers," *China Tourism,* no. 42 (n.d.): 14-15.
6. Thomas Allen, "Xinjiang," 24.
7. Ke Ji, "Wonderful Xibe Archers," 15.
8. Conner, "Midge's Musings," May 1996.
9. John Pollock, *Victims of the Long March* (Waco: Word Books, 1970), 44.

XIJIMA
1. Pelkey, "Yunnan's Myriad Yi," 49.
2. Ibid.
3. Adeney, *China, the Church's Long March.*

XIQI
1. Pelkey, "Report on the Yi Peoples of Honghe Prefecture," 20.

XIUBA
1. Pelkey, "Report on the Yi Peoples of Honghe Prefecture," 18.
2. Li Chungsheng, "The Xiuba People," *China Pictorial* (August 1991): 42.
3. *Pingbian Miaozu Zizhixian Minzu Zhi* (1990).
4. Pelkey, "Report on the Yi Peoples of Honghe Prefecture," 18.
5. Li Chungsheng, "The Xiuba People," 42.
6. Pelkey, "Report on the Yi Peoples of Honghe Prefecture," 18.

YA
1. According to the 1990 census there were 21,444 Dai in Yuanjiang County, and 39,094 in Xinping County. Many of these are Ya.
2. The 1992 *Ethnologue*, 516, 530, lists Cung and Ya as separate languages in the same area, but they are the same people group. The 1996 *Ethnologue* does not list either language.
3. Jiangxi Educational Publishing, *EDCL,* 458.
4. Bradley, "East and South-East Asia," 165.
5. Diller, "Tai Languages."
6. Dodd, *The Tai Race*, 88.
7. Although the Tai Ya are listed as having Scripture portions translated by Mrs. W. C. Dodd in 1922, using the "Laotian Yuan" script, it is possible this refers to a different group than the Ya profiled here. William Dodd did travel among the Ya in China, however, but it is not known if he ever ministered to them.
8. Stauffer, *The Christian Occupation of China,* 236.

YAKUT
1. This is based on Chinese linguist Chao Ke's assertion that 6-7% of all Ewenki in China are Yakut. The 1990 census, however, listed only 420 Ewenki people living in the Ergun Banner, so the population of the Yakut in China may be lower than listed in this Profile.
2. Conner, "Midge's Musings," September 1996.
3. Taken from the Lena River Fleet website.
4. Conner, "Midge's Musings," September 1996.

YANGHUANG
1. *Minzu Shibie Wenxian Ziliao Huibian.*
2. Bradley, "East And South-East Asia," 164.
3. Australian Academy and CASS, *LAC,* C-7.
4. Several studies on the Yanghuang language are: F. K. Li, "Notes on the Ten (Yanghuang) Language," *Academia Sinica: Bulletin of the Institute of History and Philology,* no. 36 (1966): 419-26; no. 37 (1967): 1-45; and no. 40 (1969): 397-503; and F. K. Li "Notes on the T'en or Yanghwang Language: Introduction and Phonology," *Bulletin of the Museum of Far Eastern Antiquities*, no. 36 (1966): 419-26.
5. Grimes, *Ethnologue* (1996), 562.

YERONG
1. Liang Min, "The Buyang Language," in Edmonson, *Kadai,* 13. According to the 1990 census, Napo County contained a total population of 4,764 Yao people.
2. Ibid.
3. de Beauclair, *Tribal Cultures of Southwest China,* 5.
4. Fei Xiaotong, "Fifty Years Investigation," 24. These 300 appellations do not necessarily constitute ethnolinguistic identities. Most are Chinese descriptions given Yao peoples based on their style of clothing.
5. Fei Xiaotong, *Toward a People's Anthropology* (Beijing: New World Press, 1981), 97.
6. *Unreached Peoples '81.*

YICHE
1. "Yunnan's Yeche People," *China Pictorial* (August 1983): 37.
2. Wang Zhengfang, "We of the Hani Nationality."
3. Ou Yansheng, "The Yiche People's Kuzhazha Festival in the Ailao Mountains," *China Tourism,* no. 189 (April 1996): 63.
4. Bethany World Prayer Center, "The Hani" (1997).
5. T'ien, *Peaks of Faith*, 78.

YIZI
1. *Minzu Shibie Wenxian Ziliao Huibian*, 25.
2. *Guizhou Nianjian 1985.*
3. *Minzu Shibie Wenxian Ziliao Huibian*, 25.

YONGCHUN
1. Diller, "Tai Languages."
2. *Pray for China*, no. 135 (March-April 1997).
3. Zhang Weiwen and Zeng, *In Search of China's Minorities,* 283.
4. AMO, *Newsletter* (June 1992).

YONZHI
1. Rock, "Seeking the Mountains of Mystery," 173, 185.
2. Ibid., 173.
3. Ibid., 184.

YOUMAI
1. See *Minzu Shibie Wenxian Ziliao Huibian.*
2. *Guizhou Nianjian 1985.*

YOUNUO
1. Bradley, "East and South-East Asia," 168. Grimes, *Ethnologue* (1996), 543, lists a 1994 population of 30,000 Younuo. This is probably taken from the Australian Academy and CASS, *LAC,* C-8, which states "there are possibly as many as 30,000 speakers of each of these dialects."
2. Michael Johnson, personal communication, January 1997.
3. Dodd, *The Tai Race*, 352.

YOU TAI

1. Michael McCabe, "The Jews of China," *San Jose Mercury News*, 17 November 1984.
2. There have been several books written about the Chinese Jews. One of the most recent is D. Leslie, *The Survival of the Chinese Jews: The Jewish Community of Kaifeng* (Leiden: Brill, 1972).
3. Ibid.
4. Nancy Ryan, "Jews in the Far East Have Rich and Varied Roots," *Chicago Tribune*, 23 January 1987.
5. Moule and Pelliot, *Marco Polo*, 143.
6. Matteo Ricci, *Opera storiche del P. Matteo Ricci*, as cited in Arhur Christopher Moule, *Christians in China Before the Year 1550* (London: SPCK, 1930), 1-g.
7. Ibid., n.p.
8. McCabe, "The Jews of China."
9. "National and International Religion Report," 29 April 1996.
10. *GPD* 12, no. 9 (September 1993).
11. Ryan, "Jews in the Far East Have Rich and Varied Roots."
12. McCabe, "The Jews of China."
13. These scrolls and prayer books are now located in libraries in Israel and North America.
14. "In 1845, James Finn, author of a book about Chinese Jews, wrote a letter in Hebrew to the Jews of Kaifeng. He asked a number of questions regarding their way of life, their style of prayer, their origin and the holidays they celebrated. Twenty-five years later, in 1870, he received a reply, written in Chinese, indicating they no longer knew any Hebrew. The letter was full of despair. It said, in part: 'During the past 40 or 50 years, our religion has been but imperfectly transmitted, and although the canonical writings are still extant, there is no one who understands so much as a word of them.... Morning and night with tears in our eyes and with offerings of incense, we implore God that our religion may flourish again.'" McCabe, "The Jews of China." Also see Oliver Bainbridge, "The Chinese Jews," *National Geographic* (October 1907): 627.

YUGUR, ENGER

1. According to the 1990 census there were just two counties or municipalities in China that recorded more than 500 Yugur people. 8,813 were listed in Sunan County and 2,275 in Jiuquan City. The census did not distinguish between the two Yugur groups.
2. Schwartz, *The Minorities of Northern China*, 61.
3. Ibid., 57.
4. P. M. Scott, "Some Mongol Nestorian Crosses," *The Chinese Recorder* (February 1930): 104-08, and (November 1930): 704-06.
5. Moule and Pelliot, *Marco Polo*, 150.

YUGUR, SARAGH

1. Schwartz, *The Minorities of Northern China*, 60.
2. Ibid., 59.
3. Ma Yin, *China's Minority Nationalities,* 130.
4. Zhang Weiwen and Zeng, *In Search of China's Minorities*, 74.
5. Personal communication, August 1997.
6. See AMO, *The 50 Most Unreached People Groups of China and Tibet,* 48.

ZA

1. Sun Hongkai, "On Nationality and the Recognition of Tibeto-Burman Languages," *Linguistics of the Tibeto-Burman Area* 15, no. 2 (Fall 1992): 7-8.

ZAIWA

1. Grimes, *Ethnologue* (1996), 565.
2. *Jingpo Yuyan Jianzhi (Zaiwa)* (Beijing: Nationalities Publishing House, 1984), 1.
3. Wei Kun, "The Jingpo Christians," *Bridge*, no. 43 (September-October 1990): 16. Ola Hanson, *The Kachins*, 21, describes the Zaiwa as a "group that arose by intermarriage between the Maru and the Laphai clans of Jingphaw."
4. Recent linguistic studies on the Zaiwa language include Mark Wannemacher, "The Interaction of Tone, Phonation Type and Glottal Features in Zaiwa," *Focus on Phonology: PYU Working Papers in Linguistics*, no. 1 (Chiang Mai, Thailand: Payap University, 1996): 1-16; and Wannemacher, "Zaiwa Syllable Structure," *Focus on Phonology* (1996): 119-125.
5. T'ien, *Peaks of Faith*, 145.
6. *Jingpozu Shehui Lishi Diaozha* 2 (Kunming: Yunnanrenmin, 1982), 161.
7. YASS 253, section 8; cited in T'ien, *Peaks of Faith,* 51.
8. Ibid.
9. William James Sherlock Carrapiett, *The Kachin Tribes of Burma* (Rangoon: Government Printing and Stationery, 1929).
10. YASS 254, section 2; cited in T'ien, *Peaks of Faith*, 16-17.
11. Francis and Jennie Fitzwilliam of CIM commenced work among the Zaiwa in 1935.
12. *Dehong Daizu Jingpozu Zizhizhou Diaocha Gaikuang* (Mongshi: Dehong Minzu Publishing House, 1986), 99; cited in T'ien, *Peaks of Faith*, 144.
13. *GPD* 11, no. 3 (March 1992).

ZAOMIN

1. Other sources number "about 50,000" Zaomin. Pan Chengqian, "Yao Dialectology," 48.
2. "The word 'Pai' originally meant a tribe.... The Yaos of Liannan thus call themselves Ba Pai Yao [in Chinese] (Ba Pai means the eight largest, leading tribes). Within each pai everyone wears dress of the same style, which is, however, quite different from that of the other pai tribes." Hua Nian, "Odd Customs in a Mountain Village," *China Tourism*, no. 84 (n.d.): 31.
3. Zee Yunyang, "A Comparison of Ba Pai and Guoshan Yao Tones," in Lemoine and Chiao, *The Yao of South China*, 71.
4. Jiann Hsieh, "Pai Yao's Ethnicity Through Their Own Document: A Preliminary Study of a Pai Yao Religious Book," in Chiao and Tapp, *Ethnicity and Ethnic Groups in China*, 226.
5. Ibid.
6. Pan, "Yao Dialectology," 49.
7. Zee Yunyang, "A Comparison of Ba Pai and Guoshan Yao Tones," 72.
8. Li Mo, "The Ancient Distribution of the Yao in Guangdong," in Lemoine and Chiao, *The Yao of South China*, 145.
9. Sinclair, *The Forgotten Tribes of China*, 30.
10. Chiao Chien, "Principles of the Pai Yao Kinship," in Lemoine and Chiao, *The Yao of South China*, 197.
11. Xu Wenqing, "Myths and Legends of the Lian Nan Ba P Yao," in Lemoine and Chiao, *The Yao of South China*, 406.
12. Ibid.

13. Some of the Zaomin songs include verses such as:

"You, the deceased,
When you lived in this world,
you had slashed and burned the forest of the hills,
you burned thousands of worms, ants, bamboos and trees to death.
Do you confess your sin or not?"
....
"You, the deceased,
When you lived in this world,
you had used a bigger dou (peck) to measure grains in but a smaller one to measure grains out.
Do you confess your sins or not?"

Song-Gui Shu [Book for Driving Away Ghosts], 244-45, as cited in Jiann Hsieh, "Pai Yao's Ethnicity Through Their Own Document."
"Other kinds of behavior regarded as sins include killing living creatures, destroying bamboos and trees, profaning deities, beating and scolding people, mistreating cattle, indulging in an easy and wantoning life, or enticing another's husband or wife into adultery;" Jiann Hsieh, "Pai Yao's Ethnicity Through Their Own Document," 221.

14. "Churches in Northern Guangdong," *Bridge*, no. 33 (January-February 1989): 11.
15. Ibid., 12.
16. See AMO, *The 50 Most Unreached People Groups of China and Tibet,* 17.

ZAUZOU

1. Jiangxi Educational Publishing, *EDCL*, 551.
2. Rock, "Through the Great River Trenches of Asia," 178.
3. J.-O. Svantesson, 1990 personal communication, as cited in Grimes, *Ethnologue* (1996), 565. Also see Graham Thurgood, "Zauzou: A New Lolo-Burmese Language," *Linguistics of the Tibeto-Burman Area* 9, no. 2 (1986): 90.
4. Ma Yin, *China's Minority Nationalities*, 318.
5. Zhang Weiwen and Zeng, *In Search of China's Minorities,* 225.
6. YASS 281, section 1; and YASS 345, section 4, as cited in T'ien, *Peaks of Faith*, 71.

ZHABA

1. Sun Hongkai, "Chuanxi Minzu Zoulang Diqu de Yuyan." A later source listed only 7,700 Zhaba. See Jiangxi Educational Publishing, *EDCL* (1991), 542. The Zhaba are not the same as the Queyu, some of whom also call themselves Zhaba. The Queyu have here been profiled separately.
2. Storey (ed.), *China*, 839.
3. STEDT, *Description of the Sino-Tibetan Language Family.*
4. Marco Polo, *The Travels of Marco Polo: Yule-Cordier*, 44.
5. Wang Duanyu, "Lama Jiao Yu Zangzu Renkou," 46.
6. Isobel Kuhn, *Ascent to the Tribes*, 54.

ZHUANG, NORTHERN

The Zhuang in Shaanxi live in Zuoshi County. Only a few old people are reported to still speak Zhuang. According to the 1990 census there were 208 counties or ıunicipalities in China that recorded more than 500 ıang people. In descending order, the largest Zhuang ·lations are in: Yongning 756,283; Laibin 566,303; 541,907; Wuming 531,668; Du'an 438,683; 415,929; Guigang City 402,166; Tiandeng 3; Pingguo 376,737; Nanning City 368,816, and ı 363,047. All of these are in Guangxi. The census did not distinguish between Northern and Southern Zhuang.

2. *Frontiers Focus* 4, no. 3.
3. According to Ramsey, "In their first surveys of the minorities, Communist researchers found many more millions of Zhuang than had ever been known to exist. Zhuang families and clans were brought protesting out of the Chinese closet. In one study of 152 clans... not a single family admitted to a Southern [minority] origin. Those with the surname Zhao claimed Chinese ancestry that stemmed from the palace retinue of the Song court. Those with the surname Wei said that their genealogical lineage went back to the son of the great Han general Han Xing; when the father was executed, they explained, the son had fled south and, in order to conceal his identity, had deleted the left half of the character of his surname Han, leaving a different character pronounced Wei. Yet is spite such imaginative attempts to conceal their identity, these Southern families were all registered as Zhuang." *The Languages of China,* 167, 235.
4. See Ibid., 242-43.
5. Bradley, "East and South-East Asia," 164.
6. *Pray for China*, no. 135 (March-April 1997).
7. Personal communication, December 1997.
8. Sinclair, *The Forgotten Tribes of China,* 30.
9. Huang Xianlin (ed.), *Zhongguo Renkou*, 52.
10. *Pray for China*, no. 135 (March-April 1997).
11. According to a report in *DAWN Friday Fax*, 1 January 1999, "Five years ago, a YWAM missionary met an old man on her first visit to a Zhuang village in southwestern China.... Because the missionary could not speak the Zhuang dialect, she could only communicate with the old man using Chinese symbols. They started a 'silent conversation', and after a while, the old man indicated his desire to become a Christian. When the missionary returned to Hong Kong, she found a letter from the old man asking her to return to tell him more about the Christian faith. She did, and discovered that he had already gathered 11 friends whom he told about Christianity. At a later visit, there were already 30, and she found a church of 500 on her most recent visit."
12. 13,388,118 (1982); 8,386,140 (1964); and 6,611,455 (1953)

ZHUANG, SOUTHERN

1. Australian Academy and CASS, *LAC*, C-13.
2. Bradley, "East and South-East Asia," 164.
3. CASS, *Information China* 3: 1249.
4. Stauffer, *The Christian Occupation of China*, 151.
5. This 1990 population figure of 4,000,000 appears to disagree with that cited under Population in China. However, it includes the Giay, Tho, Nung, Cao Lan, and Buyang ethnic groups which are profiled separately in *Operation China*. Therefore, these populations are subtracted from the larger figure which gives a more realistic and precise population of 3,515,000 for the Southern Zhuang.

ZUOKE

1. Pelkey, "Yunnan's Myriad Yi," 36-37.
2. Ibid., 37.
3. Lu Jinyu, "Historical and Cultural Selections from Wenshan Prefecture." This is available at the Wenshan Prefectural Library.

Appendix 1: Other Possible Groups

1. All of these tribes are mentioned in d'Ollone, *In Forbidden China*, 311.
2. Grimes, *Ethnologue* (1996), 715.
3. V. Li, *Some Approaches to the Classification of Small Ethnic Groups.*
4. Marshall Broomhall, "Some Tribes of South-West China," *International Review of Missions* 6, no. 22 (1917)
5. Australian Academy and CASS, *LAC*, C-3.
6. Janhunen and Salminen, *UNESCO Red Book.*
7. Matisoff, "Languages and Dialects of Tibeto-Burman."
8. John Kuhn, *We Found a Hundred Tribes.*
9. Ibid., 19.
10. Dwayne Graybill, personal communication, November 1996.
11. V. Li, *Some Approaches to the Classification of Small Ethnic Groups.*
12. Xie Shixun. "The Hanis of the Ailao Mountains," 45.
13. John Kuhn, *We Found a Hundred Tribes.*
14. Hermann von Wissmann, "Sud-Yunnan als Teilraum Sudostasiens," *Schriften zur Geoplolitik Heft*, no. 22 (Berlin, 1943).
15. John Kuhn, *We Found a Hundred Tribes*, 19.
16. de Beauclair, *Tribal Cultures of Southwest China*, 23.
17. John Kuhn, *We Found a Hundred Tribes*, 19.
18. Ibid.
19. V. Li, *Some Approaches to the Classification of Small Ethnic Groups.*
20. John Kuhn, *We Found a Hundred Tribes*, 19.
21. d'Ollone, *Langues des Peuples non Chinois de la Chine.*
22. Grimes, *Ethnologue* (1996), 717.
23. John Kuhn, *We Found a Hundred Tribes.*
24. Ibid., 19.
25. Ibid.
26. Ibid.
27. Graybill, personal communication, October 1997.
28. Fan Yitian, "Tantan Jiang Bian Guzong" [A Talk About the River Guzong], *Yunnan Ban Yuekan*, no. 3 (1931).
29. John Kuhn, *We Found a Hundred Tribes.*
30. Ibid.
31. Ibid.
32. V. Li, *Some Approaches to the Classification of Small Ethnic Groups.*
33. Plymire, *High Adventure in Tibet*, 66-68.
34. John Kuhn, *We Found a Hundred Tribes.*
35. Bradley, "East and South-East Asia," 164.
36. Grimes, *Ethnologue* (1992), India section.
37. Bradley, "East and South-East Asia," 160.
38. Diller, "Tai Languages."
39. Grimes, *Ethnologue* (1996), 802.
40. de Beauclair, *Tribal Cultures of Southwest China*, 23.
41. GEM, "World's Peoples Listed By Country."
42. Diller, "Tai Languages."
43. de Beauclair, *Tribal Cultures of Southwest China*, 22.
44. Fred Carey, "A Trip to the Chinese Shan States," *Geographical Journal* 14, no. 4 (1899).
45. T'ien, *Peaks of Faith*, 23.
46. Gaide, "Notice Ethnographique sur les Principales Races."
47. Diller, "Tai Languages."
48. GEM, "World's Peoples Listed By Country."
49. Graybill, personal communication, November 1996.
50. John Kuhn, *We Found a Hundred Tribes.*
51. Wu Zhouming, "The Ancient Trail in Sichuan," *China Tourism*, no. 59 (n.d.), 84.
52. Grimes, *Ethnologue* (1992), 518.
53. See Enwall, *A Myth Become Reality*, 1: 29.
54. John Kuhn, *We Found a Hundred Tribes.*
55. Grimes, *Ethnologue* (1992) , 523.
56. Bradley, "East and South-East Asia," 160.
57. d'Ollone, *Langues des Peuples non Chinois de la Chine.*
58. Gu Shoukang, "The Sherpas: Hardy Folk of the Himalayas," 14.
59. John Kuhn, *We Found a Hundred Tribes.*
60. Grimes, *Ethnologue* (1992) , 525.
61. Xie Shixun. "The Hanis of the Ailao Mountains," 45.
62. AMO, *Faces of the Unreached in Laos*, 84.
63. Grimes, *Ethnologue* (1996), 559.
64. John Kuhn, *We Found a Hundred Tribes*, 14.
65. Gaide, "Notice Ethnographique sur les Principales Races."
66. Matisoff, "Languages and Dialects of Tibeto-Burman."
67. Diller, "Tai Languages."
68. Henry, "The Lolos and Other Tribes of Western China."
69. Baker, *God in Kado Land*, 53.
70. AMO, *Faces of the Unreached in Laos*, 94.
71. Taken from the Joshua 2000 Project website.
72. Peter Goulart, *The Princes of the Black Bone: Life in the Tibetan Borderland* (London, 1958), 21.
73. See Graham, *The Customs and Religions of the Ch'iang*, 21.
74. Diller, "Tai Languages."
75. de Beauclair, *Tribal Cultures of Southwest China*, 23.
76. John Kuhn, *We Found a Hundred Tribes.*
77. Grimes, *Ethnologue* (1992), 527.
78. Bradley, "East And South-East Asia," 169.
79. Matisoff, "Languages and Dialects of Tibeto-Burman."
80. John Kuhn, *We Found a Hundred Tribes.*
81. Grimes, *Ethnologue* (1996), 699.
82. Andre Migot, "Recherches sur les Dialectes Tibetains du Si-Kang (Province de Khams)," *BEFEO* 48, no. 2 (1957): 417-562.
83. Carey, "A Trip to the Chinese Shan States."
84. See Rock, "Life Among the Lamas of Choni," 570, 606.
85. Robert Shafer, "Classification of the Sino-Tibetan Languages," *Word*, no. 11 (1955): 94-111.
86. Grimes, *Ethnologue* (1988), 458.
87. Jacques Lemoine, "Ethnicity, Culture and Development Among Some Minorities of the People's Republic of China," in Chiao and Tapp, *Ethnicity and Ethnic Groups in China*, 8.
88. Carey, "A Trip to the Chinese Shan States."
89. Thomas F. (Jr.) Torrance, "Journal of My First Visit," 41.
90. Ji Xichen, *Liangshan Yizu di Feiyue* [The Liangshan Yi

Tribe's Great Leap Forward] (Beijing: General Science Publishers, 1958).

91. Fei Xiaotong (ed.) et al., *Three Types of Rural Economy in Yunnan* (New York: Institute of Pacific Relations, 1943).
92. John Kuhn, *We Found a Hundred Tribes*, 19.
93. Cited by Dessaint, *Minorities in Southwestern China*, 1953.
94. Hsu Itang, *Les trois Grandes Races de la Province du Yunnan* (Paris: Adrien-Maisonneuve, 1932).
95. Alfred Liétard, *Les trois Grandes Races de la Province d Yunnan* (Paris: Adrien-Maisonneuve, 1932)
96. See R. Hein Geldern, "Die Asiatiche Herkunft der Sudamer ikanischen Metalltechmik" [The Asiatic Origin of the South American Metallurgy], *Paideuma* (May 1954).
97. Hermann von Wissmann, "Sud-Yunnan als Teilraum Sudostasiens," (Berlin: Schriften zur Geopolitik Heft 22, 1943).
98. de Beauclair, *Tribal Cultures of Southwest China*, 7.
99. Suo Wen Jing, "Hani Zu," *Minzu Huaba*, n.11 (1962).
100. GEM, "World's Peoples Listed By Country," report.
101. John Kuhn, *We Found a Hundred Tribes.*
102. Hua Nian, "Odd Customs in a Mountain Village."
103. Matisoff, "Languages and Dialects of Tibeto-Burman."

Journals and Magazines

A-A-P Advocate (New Zealand Adopt-a-People Programme)
Acta Asiatica
Acta Orientalia Hungaricae
AD 2025 Global Monitor
Adullam News
Alliance Life (Christian & Missionary Alliance)
American Anthropologist
American Ethnologist
American Oriental Society Journal
Anglican Theological Review
Annales d'Hygiene et de Medicine Coloniales
Anthropological Linguistics
Anthropological Institute of Great Britian and Ireland
Anthropology
Anthropos
Annual Reports of the British and Foreign Bible Society
Annual Reports of the Presbyterian Church (USA)
ARAMCO World
Asia for Christ
Asiaweek
Asian Minorities Outreach *Newsletter*
Asian Report
Asian Survey
Behavior Science Notes
Baptist Missionary Magazine
Beijing Review (formerly *Peking Review*)
Bianjiang Yenjiu Luncong [Frontier Studies]
Bianzheng Gonglun [Frontier Affairs]
Bible Society Record
Bridge — Church Life in China Today
British Association for the Advancement of Science Report
Bulletin de la Societe Linguistique de Paris
Bulletin of Chinese Studies
Bulletin of Concerned Asian Scholars
Bulletin of the Department of Anthropology
Bulletin of the Institute of Ethnology
Bulletin of the Institute of History and Philology
Bulletin of the John Rylands Library
Bulletin of the Museum of Far Eastern Antiquities
Bulletin of the School of Oriental and Asian Studies
Bulletin of the School of Oriental and African Studies
Burma Research Society
Call to Prayer (Turkish World Outreach)
Castrenianumin Toimitteita
Catholic Life
Central Asiatic Journal
Chiang Mai Newsletter
China and the Church Today
China At War
China's Millions
China Exchange News
China Insight
China Journal
China Journal of Science and Arts
China Magazine
China Monthly Review
China News Analysis
China Now
China Pictorial
China Prayer Update (Antioch Missions)
China Quarterly
China Reconstructs
China Review
China Today
China Tourism
China Year Book
Chinese Around the World
Chinese Literature
Chinese Recorder
Christian Mission (Christian Aid Mission)
Christian Science Monitor
CIM Report
Comparative Studies in Society and History
Compass Direct
Current Trends in Linguistics
DAWN Report
Dili Zazhi [Geographical Magazine]
Eastern Horizon
East of Asia
Ecole Francaise d'Extreme-Orient
Etudes Sino-Orientales [Sino-Oriental Studies]
Ethnologica
Ethnology
Fangyuan [Neighborhood]
Far Eastern Economic Review
Focus on Phonology
Freedomways
Friends of Moslems
Friends of Turkey
Frontiers Focus
Geographical Journal
Geographical Review
Global Prayer Digest
Guangming Ribao [Bright Light Daily (newspaper)]
Guizhou Minzu Yanjiu [Guizhou Province Nationality Research]
Harvard Journal of Asiatic Studies
Hmong-Australia Society Newsletter
Indo-China Issues
International Bulletin of Missionary Research
International Journal of Frontier Missions
International Journal of the Sociology of Language
International Review of Missions
Journal de la Société Finno-Ougrienne
Journal of American Folklore
Journal of Chinese Linguistics
Journal of Contemporary Asia
Journal of Ethnology and Sociology
Journal of Language and Culture
Journal of Oriental Studies
Journal of Sociology and Anthropology
Journal of the American Oriental Society
Journal of the Anthropological Institute
Journal of the Anglo-Mongolian Society
Journal of the British Institute of Persian Studies
Journal of the Central Asian Society
Journal of the North-China Branch of the Royal Asiatic Society
Journal of the Royal Asiatic Society
Journal of the Siam Society
Journal of the Society of Oriental Research
Journal of the West China Border Research Society
Journal of West China Research Society
Kailash, A Journal of Himalayan Studies
Kindreds (Tribes & Nations Outreach)
Kangzang Qian Bang [Xikang-Tibet Pioneer]
Language
Les Missions Catholiques
Lingua
Linguistics of the Tibeto-Burman Area
Memoires of the American Anthropological Association
Miao Messenger

Minzu Gongzuo [Labor of the Nationalities]
Minzu Huabao [Nationalities Pictorial]
Minzu Tuanjie [Unity of the Nationalities]
Minzu Wenhua [Culture of the Nationalities]
Minzu Xuebao [Nationality Collegiate Journal]
Minzuxue Yanjiu Jikan [Collected Papers on Minority Studies Research]
Minzu Yanjiu [Nationality Research]
Minzu Yuwen [Nationality Languages]
Mission Frontiers
Missions Update
Mon-Khmer Studies
Monumenta Serica
Muslim World
National and International Religion Report
National Geographic
Nepal Studies in Linguistics
New Leader
North Burma Christian Mission Newsletter
North China Branch of the Royal Asiatic Society
On Target (newsletter of Target Ministries)
Open Doors
Pacific Affairs
Pacific Linguistics
Paideuma
Philology
People's China
Pray for China (newsletter of Christian Communications Ltd., Hong Kong)
Pray for Myanmar (Tribes & Nations Outreach)
Pray for China Fellowship (OMF International)
Publication of the Frontier Peoples' Culture Department
Reformed Bulletin of Missions
Renmin Ribao [The People's Daily]
Royal Anthropological Society
Royal Geographic Society
SCAN — Society of Central Asian News
Shaoshu Minzu Yuwen Lunji [Minority Language Research and Theories]
Shehui Kexue [Social Sciences]
Sinologica
Sounds (Gospel Recordings)
Southeast Asia Chronicle
Southeast Asian Journal of Social Science
Studia Serica
Thai-Yunnan Project Newsletter
The China Quarterly
The East Asian Library Journal
The Edge (newsletter of CBInternational)
The Field Bulletin of the China Inland Mission
The Kingdom Overseas
The Missionary Review of the World
The United Methodist Magazine
The Voice of the Martyrs
Tianshan Yuegan
Tibetan Review
Tonan Ajia Kenkyu [Southeast Asian Studies]
Topological Studies in Language
T'oung Pao
Trends in Linguistics
Voice of Eastern Turkestan
Wenhua Jianshe [Cultural Reconstruction]
West China Missionary News
West China Research Society
Workers
World Pulse
World Christianity (MARC Publications)
Xinan Minzu Xueyuan Xuebao [Southwest Minorities Institute Journal]
Xinhua (a Chinese daily newspaper)
Xizang Yanjiu [Tibetan Studies]
Xueyuan [Source of Knowledge]
Yao Update
Yunnan Ban Yuekan [Yunnan Bi-Monthly]
Yunnan Minzu Yuwen [Nationality Languages of Yunnan]
Yunnan Shehui Kexue [Yunnan Social Sciences]
Zhongguo Minzushi Yanjiu [Research on the History of China's Nationalities]
Zhongguo Shaoshu Minzu [China's Minority Nationalities]
Zhongguo Yuwen [China's Languages]
Zhongguo Zangxue [Tibetology in China]
Zhongyang Fangwentuan DierfentuanYunnan Minzu Qingkuang Huiji [A Collection of the State of Affairs of Yunnan's Nationalities from the Second Sector of the Chinese Local Culture Division]
Zhongyang Minzu Xueyuan Xuebao [Zhongyang Minorities Institute Journal]

Archives

American Baptist Archives (Valley Forge, Pennsylvania)
China Inland Mission Archives (Billy Graham Center, Illinois)
Methodist Missionary Society Archives
Yunnan Academy of Social Sciences (Kunming, Yunnan)
Yunnan Ethnic Research Institute (Kunming, Yunnan)
Yunnan Provincial Archives (Kunming, Yunnan)

Bibliography of Chinese-Language Publications

Baoshan Xian Zhi [The Annals of Baoshan County]. 1996.

Cai Jailin. "Jingpozu Lashi Chubu Diaocha" [A Study of Lashi Among the Jingpo]. *Minzu Yanjiu Diaocha* [Minority Investigative Research] 2. Kunming, 1986.

Cen Yuying. *Qingding Pinding Guizhou Miaofei Jilue* [Documents Concerning the Pacification of Guizhou Miao Bandits]. Imperial Edition, 1884.

Chang Hongen, ed. *Lahuyu Jianzhi* [The Concise Annals of the Lahu Language]. Beijing: Minzu Chubanshe, 1986.

Chen Chao Qui. *Duyun Shi Minzu Zi* [A Study of the Minorities of Duyun]. Guizhou: Duyun Nationalities Affairs Publishing House, 1990.

Chen Dingxiu. "Qian Xinan Miaozu Gaishu" [Primary Account of the Miao of the Southwest]. *Guizhou Minzu Yanjiu (Jikan)* [Collected Papers on Guizhou Minorities Research]1 (1991).

Chenger, Mai. "Luquan Jidujian Qingkuang Diaocha" [Investigation of Christianity in Luquan District]. Report, Kunming, 1988.

Chengjiang Xian Nianjian [The Chengjiang County Annual]. 1995.

Chen Qiguang. *Zhongguo Yuwen Gaiyao* [An Outline of China's Languages]. 1990.

Chen Shilin; Bian Shiming, and Li Xiuqing, eds. *Yiyu Jianzhi* [The Concise Annals of the Yi Language]. Beijing: Minzu Chubanshe, 1984.

Chen Shirou. "Miaojia Youle Wenzi" [The Miao Have Got Writing]. *Xin Hunan Bao* [New Hunan Daily], 14 January 1957.

Chen Yin. "Lahu Zu" [The Lahu Nationality]. *Minzu Tuanjie* 4 (1964).

Chen Zongxiang. "Luolo de Zongjiao" [The Religion of the Lolo]. *Bianzheng Gonglun* 7, no. 2 (1948).

China Tibetan Studies Press. *Zaoqi Chuanjiaoshi Jin Zang Huodong Shi* [History of Early Missionary Activity in Tibet]. Beijing, 1992.

Chu Fei. *Jinshajiang Fengwu Waiji* [Personal Narration of the Scenery of the Golden Sand River]. Singapore, 1960.

Chuxiong Xian Zhi [The Annals of Chuxiong County]. 1995, 1996.

Chuxiong Yizu Zizhizhou Zhi, no. 1. Beijing: Renmin Chubanshe, 1993.

Chuxiong Zhu Nian Jian [Annals of Chuxiong Prefecture]. 1996.

Dai Qingxia; Xu Shouchun, and Gao Xikui. *Lisuyu Jianzhi* [The Concise Annals of the Lisu Language]. Beijing: Minzu Chubanshe, 1986.

Dai Qingxia et al. *Zangmianyu Shiwu Zhong* [Fifteen Tibeto-Burman Languages]. Beijing: Yanshan Press, 1991.

Dehong Dai Zu Jingpo Zu Zizhizhou Diaozha Kaikuang [A Study of the Dehong Dai and Jingpo Autonomous Prefecture]. Mangshi, 1986.

Deng Zhi-fu. "Sichuan Xinan Zhi Yuzu" [The Foreign Tribes of Southwest Sichuan]. *Chengdu Daxue Shixue Zazhi* [Chengdu University Historical Magazine], no. 2 (1930).

Dong Zhaofu. "Jiaowai Luhen" [Recollections of a Trip to the Frontiers], *Bianzheng Gonglun* (1930).

Duoerji Detai. "Chuanxi Zangqu Geshizahua Dongci de Rencheng Han Shu Fanchou" [The Categories of Person and Number in the Geshiza Speech in the Tibetan Area of Western Sichuan]. *Xinan Minzu Xueyuan Xuebao*, no. 3 (1993)

________ "Chuanxibei Zangqu Geshizahua Yinxi Fenxi" [An Analysis of the Sound System of the Geshiza Speech in the Tibetan Area of Northwestern Sichuan]. *Yunnan Minzu Yuwen* 1 (1995).

Duyun Shi Minzu Zi [A Study of the Minorities of Duyun]. Guizhou: Duyun Nationalities Affairs Publishing House, 1990.

Eshan Huabao [Eshan Pictorial]. n.d.

Fang Guoyu. *Yizu Shi Gao*. Chengdu: Sichuan Minzu Chubanshe, 1984.

Fan Yitian. "Tantan Jiang Bian Guzong" [A Talk About the River Guzong]. *Yunnan Ban Yuekan* 3 (1931).

Fei Xiaotong [Fei Hsiao Tung]. "Guan yu Wo Guo Minzu de Shi Bien Wenti" [On the Question of Ethnic Identification in China]. In *Minzu Yi Shehui* [The Societal Nationality](Beijing: Renmin Chubanshe, 1981).

________ "Xin Zhongguo de Minzuxue Yanjiu yu Fazhan" [Studies in and Development of Ethnography in New China]. In Lin Yuehua, *Minzuxue Yanjiu*.

Fengqing Xian Shi [The Annals of Fengqing County].

Fu Miaoji. *Zhong Guo Shaoshu Min Zu Yuyan Jianzhi Congshu (57 Zhong)* [Collected Works on Chinese Minority Languages (57 Volumes)]. Beijing, 1980–1986.

Gejiu Shi Minzu Zhi [The Annals of the Minority Nationalities of Gejiu County]. 1990.

Ge Zi. "Miaozu Wenzi Danshengle" [The Miao Writing is Born]. *Xin Qian Ribao* [New Guizhou Daily], 14 November 1956.

Guang Weiran. *Axi Rende Ge* [The Songs of the Axi]. Beijing: People's Literature Publishing Company, 1957.

Guangxi Quqing. 1985.

Guizhou Nianjian [Guizhou Annual]. Guiyang: Guizhou Renmin Chubanshe, 1985, 1991, 1992, 1994.

Guizhou Sheng Jidujiao Lishi Zilian [History of Christianity in Guizhou Province]. Guiyang, 1958.

Guizhou Sheng 1990 Nian Renkou Pucha Ziliao (Dianzi Jisuanji Huizong) [1990 Guizhou Provincial Census Data (Collected by Electronic Computer)] 1. Beijing: Zhongguo Tongji Chubanshe, 1993.

Guizhou Sheng Shaoshu Minzu Renkou Tongji Ziliao [Statistical Data on the Population of the Minority Nationalities of Guizhou Province]. Guiyang: Guizhou Minzu Yanjiusuo, 1985.

Guizhou Shengzhi, Dilizhi Shangce [Guizhou Provincial Annals, Geography Annals] 1. Guiyang, 1985.

Guizhou Tongji Nianjian [Guizhou Statistical Annual] 1992. Beijing: Zhongguo Tongji Chubanshe, 1992.

He Jiashan, ed. *Gelaoyu Jianzhi* [Concise Annals of the Gelao Language]. Beijing: Minzu Chubanshe, 1983.

He Jiren, and Jiang Zhuyi, eds. *Naxizu Jianzhi (Naxiyu)* [Concise Annals of the Naxi People and their Language]. Beijing: Minzu Chubanshe, 1985.

Hekou Xian Zhi [The Annals of Hekou County]. 1994.

Honghe Huabao [Honghe Pictorial]. 1987.

Honghe Zhou Zhi, Di Yi Juan [The Annals of Honghe Prefecture] 1. 1997.

Honghe Zhou Nianjian. [Honghe Prefecture Annual]. 1991, 1995, 1996, 1997.

Honghe Zhou Yizu Minjian Tiaoyao [Yi Folkdances of Honghe Prefecture]. 1992.

Honghe Zhou Zhi Diyi Juan [The Annals of Honghe Prefecture] 1. 1997.

Huang Bufan. "Chuanxi Zangqu de Yuyan Guanxi" [Linguistic Relationships in the Tibetan Area of Western Sichuan]. *Zhongguo Zangxue*, no. 3 (1988).

________ "Daofuyu" [The Daofu Language]. In Dai Qingxia et al. *Zangmianyu Shiwu Zhong*.

________ "Muyayu" [The Muya Language]. In Dai Qingxia et al. *Zangmianyu Shiwu Zhong*.

_______ "Qiangyuzhi" [The Qiangic Branch]. In Ma Xueliang, ed. *Hanzahngyu Gailun.*
Huang Gouzhong. "Genxin Hunyin Guannian Tigao Minzu Suzhi" [Changing the Consanguineous Marriages to Enhance the Quality of the Minority Nationalities]. Report, 1988.
Huang Xianlin, ed. *Zhongguo Renkou: Guangxi Fence* [China's Population: Guangxi Volume]. Beijing: Zhongguo Caizheng Jingji Chubanshe, 1988.
Huaning Xian Minzu Zhi [The Annals of the Minorities of Huaning County]. 1990.
Hu Zhenhua. "Heilongjiang Fuyu Xiande Kirgiz Zu Jiqi Yuyan Tedian" [The Kirgiz of Fuyu County, Heilongjiang, and Their Language]. *Zhongyang Minzu Xueyuan Xuebao*, no. 35 (1983).
_______ "Kirgiz yu Gaikuang" [A Survey of the Kirgiz Language]. *Minzu Yuwen*, no.14 (1982).
Jiangchuan Xian Zhi [The Annals of Jiangchuan County]. n.d.
Jiang Dingliang. *Xinan Bian Jiang Minzu Luncong* [Articles on the Border Tribes in the Southwest]. Guangzhou: Haiju University Press, 1948.
Jiang Wenhan. *Zhongguo Gudai Jidu Jiao Ji Kaifeng Youtai Ren* [Ancient Christianity in China and the Jews of Kaifeng]. Shanghai: Zhi Shi Press, 1982.
Jiang Yongxing. *Miaowen Tianjiu* [Filling in the Missing Research on Miao Writing]. 1989.
Jiangxi Educational Publishing House. *Zhongguo Yuyanxue Dacidian* [Encyclopedic Dictionary of Chinese Linguistics]. Nanjing: 1991.
Jiangchuan Xian Nianjian [The Jiangchuan County Annual]. 1993.
Jianshui Xian Zhi [The Annals of Jianshui County]. 1994.
Jingpozu Shehui Lishi Diaozha [Historical and Ethnic Studies of the Jingpo Nationality]. Kunming: 1982.
Jingpo Yuyan Hjianzhi (Zaiwa) [A Short Account of the Jingpo (Zaiwa) Language]. Beijing: Nationalities Publishing House, 1984.
Jinping Xian Zhi [The Annals of Jinping County]. 1994.
Ji Xichen. *Liangshan Yizu Di Feiyue* [The Liangshan Yi Tribe's Great Leap Forward]. Beijing: General Science Publishers, 1958.
Jun De. "Chuannan Ma bian Yiren Zhi Gaikuang" [The General Condition of the Yi in the Ma Border Region of Southern Sichuan]. *Kangzang Qian Bang* 2, no. 9 (1935).
Kaiyuan Xian Zhi [The Annals of Kaiyuan County]. 1996.
Kunming Minzu Min Su He Zongjiao Diaocha [Studies of the Religious Practices of Minorities in Kunming]. Kunming, 1983.
Lang Wei. *Tianzhujiao, Jidujiao Zai Chuannan Miaozu Diqu Chuanbo Shulue* [Study on the Spread of Catholicism and Christianity in Miao Regions of Southern Sichuan]. 1989.
Lang Weiwei. "Lun Sichuan Miaozu Renkou de Lishi Yanbian" [Historical Development of the Miao of Sichuan]. *Guizhou Minzu Yanjiu* (February 1995).
Lei Bolun. "Lolo ren Minfeng Tuzhi" [The Customs and Environment of the Lolo]. *Dili Zazhi* 12, no. 1 (1921).
Lei Jinliu. "Yunnan Jijiang Lolo de Zu Xian Congbai" [Ancestral Worship Among the Lolo of the Jijiang Area in Yunnan]. *Bianzheng Gonglun* 3, no. 9 (1944).
Li Can. "Yunnan Bianchu de Liangzhong Miaozu Baiyi yu Yeren" [Two Miao groups, the White Yi and Ye or Wild Men, of the Yunnan Border Areas]. *Wenhua Jianshe* [Cultural Reconstruction] 3, no. 7 (1937).
Li Wei. "Guangxi Lingchuan Pinghua de Tedian" [The Characteristics of Pinghua in Lingchuan, Guangxi]. *Fangyuan*, no. 4.
Li Yongsui and Wang Ersong, eds. *Haniyu Jianzhi* [The Concise Annals of the Hani Language]. Beijing: Minzu Chubanshe, 1986.
Li Yunbing. *Minzu Yuwen* [Nationality Writings] (June 1993).
Lin Mingjun. "Chuan Miao de Gaikuang" [A Survey of the Chuan Miao]. In *Minguo Nianjian Miaozu Lunwenji* [Minguo Annual Miao Theses].
Lin Xiangron. *Jiarongyu Yufa* [Jiarong Grammar]. Chengdu: Sichuan Minzu Chubanshe, 1993.
Lin Yuehua. *Minzuxue Yanjiu* [Studies in Ethnography]. Beijing: Zhongguo Shehui Kexue Chubanshe, 1985.
_______ "Zhongguo Xinan Diqu de Minzu Shibie" [Ethnic Studies in Southwest China]. *Yunnan Shehui Kexue*, no. 2 (1984).
Ling Bing. *Zhong Mian Tai Yin Bian Minqin* [The Customs of Border Peoples of China, Myanmar, Thailand and India]. Hong Kong: World Book Store, 1938.
Ling Chunsheng. "Minzu de Dili Fenbu" [The Geographical Distribution of Nationalities]. *Minzu Yanjiu Jikan* [Collected Papers on Nationality Research] 5, n.d.
Lisuzu Jianshi [A Short History of the Lisu]. Kunming, 1983.
Liu Guangkun. *Maqo Qiangyu Yanjiu* [Research on the Mawo Dialect of Qiang]. Chengdu: Sichuan Minzu Chubanshe, 1998.
Liu Lu, ed. *Jingpozu Yuyan Jianzhi (Jingpoyu)* [Concise Annals of theJingpo People and their Language]. Beijing: Minzu Chubanshe, 1984.
Luchun Xian Zhi [The Annals of Luchun County]. 1992.
Lunan Xian Zhi [The Annals of Lunan County]. 1996.
Luo Meizhen. "Lun Fangyan: Jian tan Daiyu Fangyan de Huafen." *Minzu Yuwen*, no. 3 (1993).
Lu Shaozun, Pumiyu Jianzhi [A Concise Description of the Pumi Language]. Beijing: Minzu Chubanshe, 1983.
Luxi Xian Zhi [The Annals of Luxi County]. 1992.
Ma Changshou. "Jiarong Minzu Shehui Shi" [Ethno-History of the Jiarong]. *Minzuxue Yanjiu Jikan*, no. 4 (1944).
Mao Zongwu; Meng Zhaoji, and Zheng Zongze, eds. *Yaozu Yuyan Jianzhi* [Concise Annals of the Yao People and their Language]. Beijing: Minzu Chubanshe, 1982.
Ma Xueliang. *Sani Yiyu Yanjiu* [A Study of Sani, a Yi dialect]. Beijing: Chinese Scientific Institute, 1951.
_______ *Sani yu 'Pzlp'slbzlfvl' Xiao Kao* [A Brief Examination of the Sani Language]. Chengdu: University of Nanjing Institute of Chinese Cultural Studies, 1940.
_______, ed. *Hanzahngyu Gailun* [Introduction to Sino-Tibetan Languages]. Beijing: Beijing University Press, 1991.
Mengzi Xian Zhi [The Annals of Mengzi County]. 1995.
Mile Xian Zhi [The Annals of Mile County]. 1987.
Mile Yizu Lishi Wenhua Kong Yuan [Discovering the Source of the History and Culture of the Yi in Mile County]. 1995.
Minzu Shibie Wenxian Ziliao Huibian, Minzu Yanjiu Cankao Ziliao [Compilation of the Classified Nationality Literature in Nationality Research Reference Material] 15. Guiyang: Guizhousheng Minzu Yanjiusuo, 1982.
Ni Dabai. *Dong-Tai yu Gailun* [Studies on the Dong and Tai Languages]. Beijing: Zhongyang Minzu Xueyuan Chubanshe, 1990.
Pingbian Miaozu Zizhixian Minzu Zhi [The Annals of the Pingbian Miao Autonomous County]. 1990.
Qian Sicong. "Baiyu Zhuan" [Bibliography of Hundreds of Aboriginals]. *Jingtai Yunnan Tujing Zhishu* [Topography of Yunnan Compiled in the Jingtai Dynasty: 1450–1456].
Qianxibei Miaozu Yixu Shehui Lishi Zonghe Diaocha [The Summation of Historical and Social Investigation on the Far Northwestern Miao]. Guiyang: Guizhou Renmin Chubanshe, 1986.
Qianxinan Buyizu Miaozu Zhihizhou Gaikuang [Survey of the Qianxinan Bouyei and Miao Autonomous Prefecture]. 1985.
Qin Tianzhen, ed. "Guizhou Shengzhi, Dilizhi Shangce" [Guizhou Provincial Geography Annals 1]. Guiyang: Guizhou Renmin Chubanshe, 1985.
Qu Aitang. "Jiarongyu Gaikuang" [Outline of the Jiarong Language]. *Minzu Yuwen*, no. 2 (1984).
_______ "Jiarongyude Fangyan: Fangyan Huafen he Yuyan Shibie" [Jiarong Dialects: Issues in Dialect Subclassification and Language Recogniton]. *Minzu Yuwen*, nos. 4 & 5 (1990).

Shengzu Shilu [The Veritable Record of Emperor Shenzu Renhuangdi]. 1932.
Shen Xu, and Liu Zhi. *Zhongguo Xinan yu Dongnanya de Kuajing Minzu* [China's Southwestern and Southeastern "Kuajing" Peoples]. Kunming: Yunnan Minzu Chubanshe, 1988.
Shiping Xian Zhi [The Annals of Shiping County]. 1990.
Shuangbai Xian Nianjian [The Shuangbai County Annual]. 1996.
Shuangbai Xian Zhi [The Annals of Shuangbai County]. 1996.
Song Enchang. *Zhongguo Shaoshu Minzu Zongjiao* [The Religion of China's Minorities]. Kunming: Yunnan Renmin Chubanshe, 1985.
Song Guangyu. *Huanan Bianjiang Minzu Tulu* [The Peoples' Dirt Roads in Huanan and Bianjiang]. Taipei: Zhongyang Tushuguan, 1991.
Sun Hongkai. *Qiangyu Jianzhi* [A Brief Description of the Qiang Language]. Beijing: Minzu Chubanshe, 1981.
________ "Chuanxi Minzu Zoulang Diqu de Yuyan" [The Languages of the Ethnic Corridor in Western Sichuan]. In *Xinan Minzu Yanjiu*. Chengdu: Sichuan Minzu Chubanshe, 1983.
________ "Liujiang Liuyu de Minzu Yuyan ji qi Xishu Fenlei" [The Languages of the Nationalities in the Six Rivers Valley and Their Language Family Classification]. *Minzu Xuebao*, no. 3 (1983).
________ "Qiangyu Zhishu Wenti Chutan" [Initial Research Into the Genetic Affiliations of the Qiangic Languages]. In *A Collection of Articles on the Nationality Languages*. Xining: Qinghai University Press, 1982.
Suo Wen Jing. "Hani Zu" [The Hani People]. *Minzu Huabao*, no. 11 (1962).
Tang Zhenzong. *Zhongguo Shaoshu Minzu Di Xin Mianmao* [The New Appearance of China's National Minorities]. Beijing, 1953.
Tao Xiaoping. "Qianxi Chuannan Gongxian Miaozu Zhu Wenhua" [Elementary Analysis of the Bamboo Culture of the Miao of Gong County, Sichuan]. *Miaoxue Yanjiu Lunwenji* [Articles on Miao Research]. Guizhou: Bijie Diqu Miaoxue Hui, 1993.
Tao Yunkui. "Jige Yunnan Zangmian Yuxi di Juangshi Gushui" [Creation Myths of Some Tibeto-Burman peoples in Yunnan Province]. *Bianjiang Yenjiu Luncong*, no. 45 (1945).
Tian Jizhou, and Luo Zhiji. *Ximing Wazu Shehui Xingtai* [The Social Structure of the Wa Minority in Ximing]. Kunming, 1980.
Wang Duanyu. "Lama Jiao yu Zangzu Renkou" [Lamaism and the Population of the Tibetans]. *Minzu Yanji* (1984).
Wang Fushi. *Miaoyu Jianzhi* [A Sketch of the Miao Language]. Beijing: Nationalities Publishing House, 1985.
Wa Zu Shehui Lishi Diaozha [Historical and Ethnic Studies of the Wa Nationality]. Kunming: 1984.
Wei Qingwen, and Tan Guosheng, eds. *Zhuangyu Jianzh* [Concise Annals of the Zhuang Language]. Beijing: Minzu Chubanshe, 1980.
Weining Yizu Huizu Miaozu Zizhixian Minzuzhi [The Annals of the Minority Nationalities of the Weining Yi, Hui and Miao Autonomous County]. 1997.
Weishan Yizu Huizu Zizhixian Zhi [The Annals of the Weishan Yi and Hui Autonomous County]. 1993.
Wen Yu. "Chuan Xi Qiangyu Zhi Chubu Fenxi" [A Tentative Classification of the Ch'iang Languages in Northwestern Sichuan]. *Studia Serica*, no. 2 (1941).
________ "Lifan Hou'erku Qiangyu Yinxi" [Phonology of the Qiang Language, Hou'erku Dialect]. *Studia Serica*, no. 4 (1945).
________ "Lun Heishui Qiangyu Zhong Zhi Final Plosives" [The Final Plosives in the Heishui Dialect of the Ch'iang Language]. *Studia Serica*, no. 1 (Chengdu, 1940).
________ "Wenchuan Lofuzhai Qiangyu Yinxi" [Phonology of the Qiang Language, Lofuzhai Dialect]. *Studia Serica* 3, no. 2 (1943).
________ "Wenchuan Wasi Zu Qiangyu Yinxi" [Phonology of the Qiang Language, Wasi Dialect]. *Bulletin of Chinese Studies*, no. 3 (1941).
Wu Wenhui, and Zhu Jianhua. "Xikang Renkou Wenti, Shang" [Zikang Population Problems 1]. *Bianzheng Gonglun* III.
Xia Hu. *Nuqiu Bianai Xiangqing*. Kunming, 1912.
Xie Junmei. "Shanghai Lishi Shang Renkou de Bianqian" [Historical Changes in the Population of Shanghai]. *Shehui Kexue* (March 1980)
Yimen Xian Gaikuang [A Brief Account of Yimen County]. n.d.
Xinping Yizu Daizu Zhizhixian Gaikuang [A Collection of Literary and Historical Selections from Xinping Yi-Dai Autonomous County] 1. Kunming: Yunnan Minzu Chubanshe, 1988.
Xi Wang Zhi Lincang [Hope for the Countryside of Lincang]. 1993.
Xu Yitang [Hsu Itang]. *Leibo Xiaolaingshan Zhi Lomin* [A Report of the Lolo in Leibo, in the Xiaoliang Mountains]. Chengdu: University of Nanjing Institute of Chinese Cultural Studies, 1944.
Yang Hanxian. *Jidujiao Zai Dian-Qian-Chuan Jiaojing Yidai Miaozu Diqu Shilue*. Guiyang: Guizhousheng Minzu Yanjiusuo, n.d.
Yan Ruyu, ed. *Miaofeng Beilan* [Recommendation for Repelling the Miao]. 1820.
Yiyu Jianzhi [The Simplified Annals of the Yi Language]. 1985.
Yongde Xian Zhi [The Annals of Yongde County].
Yuan Jiahua. *A-xi Shi Jia Ji Chi Yuyan* [The Axi Language and Folksongs]. Beijing: Chinese Scientific Institute, 1953.
________ "Ershan Woni yu Chutan" [The Woni Language of Ershan]. *Publication of the Frontier Peoples' Culture Department* 4 (1947).
________ "Woni yu Yinxi" [Woni pronunciation]. *Xueyuan* 1, no. 12 (1948).
Yuanjiang Xian Zhi [The Annals of Yuanjiang County]. 1993, 1994.
Yuanyang Xian Minzu Zhi [The Annals of the Nationalities of Yuanyang County]. 1994.
Yu Cuirong, and Luo Meizhen, eds. *Daiyu Jianzhi*. Beijing: Minzu Chubanshe, 1980.
Yunnan Miao Zu Yaozu Sheihui Lishi Diaozha [Historical and Ethnic Studies of the Miao and Yao Nationalities in Yunnan]. Kunming, 1982.
Yunnan Minzu Min Su He Zongjiao Diaocha [Studies of the Religious Practices of Minorities in Yunnan]. Kunming: 1985.
Yunnan Nianjian [Yunnan Annual]. Kunming: Yunnan Nianjian Zazhishe, 1985, 1986, 1988.
Yunnan Shaoshu Minzu (Xiudingben) [Yunnan's Minorities]. Kunming: Yunnan Renmin Chubanshe, 1983.
Yunnan Sheng Lunan Yizu Zizhixian Wenshi Yanjiushi [Yunnan Province Lunan Yi Autonomous County Historical and Cultural Research Center]. *Yi-Han Jianming Cidian* [Yi-Han Dictionary]. Kunming: Yunnan Minzu Chubanshe, 1984.
Yunnan Sheng Zhi Juan Wushijiu Shaoshuminzu Yuyan Wenzi Zhi [The Annals of Yunnan Province 59: The Annals of Minority Languages and Writings]. 1998.
Yunnan Yuxi Xiongdi Minzu [Minority Brothers of Yuxi, Yunnan]. n.d.
Yuxi Diqu Minzu Xiang Qing Kuang [The Conditions of Yuxi Prefecture's Minority Districts]. 1992.
Yuxi Diqu Minzu Zhi [The Annals of the Nationalities in Yuxi Prefecture]. 1992.
Yuxi Diqu Zhi Diyi Juan [The Annals of Yuxi Prefecture] 1. 1994.
Yuxi Nianjian [Yuxi Prefecture Annual]. 1990, 1997.
Zhang Jimin, "Lajiyu yu Gelaoyu de Guanxi" [The Relationship between the Gelao and Laji Languages]. *Minzu Yuwen*, no. 3 (1992).
Zhang Junru. "Ji Guangxi Nanning Xinxu Pinghua" [A Sketch of the Xinxu Pinghua of Nanning, Guangxi]. *Fangyuan*.

Zhang Tan. *'Zhaimen' Qian de Shimenkan: Jidujiao Wenhua yu Chuan-Dian-Qian-bian Miaozu Shehu* [The Stone Threshold in Front of the Narrow Gate: Christian Culture and the Miao Society of the Sichuan-Yunnan-guizhou Border Regions]. Kunming: Yunnan Jiaoyu Chubanshe, 1992.

Zhang Tianlu. *Zhongguo Shaoshu Minzu de Ren Kou* [Population of China's Minority Nationalities]. Liaoning: Renmin Chubanshe, 1987.

Zhao Zhan. "Xibe Zuyuan Kao" [The Origin of the Xibe]. In *Zhongyang Minzu Xueshu Lunwen Xuanji* 2. Beijing, 1980.

Zhenyuan Gaikuang [A Brief Account of Zhenyuan County]. 1992.

Zhenyuan Xian Zhi [The Annals of Zhenyuan County. 1992.

Zhongguo Dabaike Quanshu: Minzu [China Becomes Known: Nationalities]. Beijing: Zhongguo Dabaike Quanshu Chubanshe, 1986.

Zhongguo Gui Zhu [China Returns]. 3 Vols. Beijing: Zhongguo Shehui Kexue Chubanshe, 1987.

Zhongguo Kexueyuan Shaoshu Minzu Diaocha Di'er Gongzuodui [Second Work Group on Minorities Research of the Academia Sinica]. Guiyang, 1956.

Zhongguo Minzu Jiaoyu Luncong [Articles on the Education of China's Minority Nationalities]. Beijing: Zhongyang Minzu Xueyuan Chubanshe, 1988.

Zhongguo Minzu Renkou Ziliao: 1990 Nian Renkou Pucha Shuju [China Nationalities Population Data: 1990 Census Statistics]. Beijing: Zhongguo Tongji Chubanshe, 1994.

Zhongguo Minzu Yuyan Lunweiji [Collection of Articles on China's Minority Languages]. Chengdu: Sichuan Minzu Chubanshe, 1986.

Zhongguo Shaoshu Minzu Jiankuang [An Overview Survey of China's Minority Nationalities].

Zhongguo Shaoshu Minzu Shangyu Yanjiu Lunji [Chinese Minority Language Research and Theorems]. Beijing: NPH, 1990.

Zhongguo Shaoshu Minzu Wenzi [Chinese Minority Scripts]. Beijing: Zhongguo Zangxue Chubanshe, 1992.

Zhongguo Shaoshu Minzu Yuyan [Chinese Minority Languages]. Chengdu: Sichuan Minzu Chubanshe, 1987.

Zhongguo Shaoshu Minzu Yuyan Shiyong Qingkuang [The Conditions of the Usage of China's Minority Languages]. Beijing: Zhongguo Zangxue Chubanshe, 1994.

Zhongguo Shengshi Zuzhiqu Ziliao Shouce. Beijing, 1990

Zhongguo Yuwen Gaiyao [Outline of China's Languages and Writing]. Beijing: Zhongguo Minzu Xueyuan Chubanshe, 1990.

Zhongyang Fangwentuan Dierfentuan Yunnan Minzu Qingkuang Huiji. Kunming: Yunnan Minzu Chubanshe, 1986.

Zhou Zhizhi, and Yan Qixiang, eds. *Wayu Jianzhi* [Concise Annals of the Wa Language]. Beijing: Minzu Chubanshe, 1984.

Zhuangzu Jianshu [A Brief History of the Zhuang]. Nanning: Guangxi Renmin Chubanshe, 1980.

Zhu Jingyu, and Li Jiaquan. *Shaoshu Minzu Secai Yuyan Jiemi: Cong Tuteng Fuhao Dao Shehui Fuhao* [Minority Color and Language Connections: From Totem Symbols to Social Symbols]. Kunming: Yunnan Minzu Chubanshe, 1993.

Zhu Wenxu. "Liangshan Yizu Nuli Shehui Xingshici de Ciyuan Jiegou yu Dengji Fenhua" [The Slavery Society of the Liangshan Yi People and its Formal Word Origin Processes and Divisions]. *Minzu Yuwen*, no. 1 (1987).

Zizang Shehui Jingji Tongji Nianjian. Beijing: Zhongguo Tongji Chubanshe, 1989.

Zou Qiyu, and Miao Wenjun, eds. *Zhongguo Renkou: Yunnan Fence* [China's Population: Yunnan]. Beijing: Zhongguo Caizheng Jingji Chubanshe, 1989.

Zuo Yutang, and Tao Xueliang, eds. *Bimo Wenhua Lun* [Cultural Theories on Witchdoctors]. Kunming: Yunnan Renmin Chubanshe, 1993.

General Bibliography

Note: The author has attempted to be as exhaustive as possible. Sources are listed though some are now out of print, others are available in China only, and a few have incomplete bibliographic details.

Abercrombie, Thomas J. "Ladakh: The Last Shangri-La." *National Geographic*, March 1978.

Adam, J. R. "Pentecostal Blessing Among the Aborigines of West China." *China's Millions*, January 1907.

Adeney, David H. *China, the Church's Long March*. Singapore: OMF, 1985.

Ainscough, Thomas M. *Notes From a Frontier*. Shanghai: Kelly & Walsh, 1915.

Ajiya. "The Taklimakan Desert." *China Tourism*, no. 70, n.d.

Akiner, Shirin. *Islamic Peoples of the Soviet Union*. London: Kegan Paul, 1983.

Allbutt, Ivan. "Black Miao Colonies." *China's Millions* (Australasian edition), October 1940.

_______ "The Black Miao, of Kewichow." *China's Millions*, October 1950.

Allbutt, Mrs Ivan. *China's Aboriginal Peoples*. London: CIM, 1941.

Allen, Charles. *A Mountain in Tibet*. London: Futura, 1982.

Allen, Douglas. "Tibet: The Continuing Story." *China and the Church Today*, February 1986.

Allen, Roland. *Missionary Methods: St. Paul's or Ours?* London: World Dominion Press, 1912.

Allen, Thomas B. "Xinjiang." *National Geographic*, March 1996.

Alley, Rewi. *Folk Poems from China's Minorities*. Beijing: New World Press, 1982.

Allworth, Edward A. *The Modern Uzbek — From the 14th Century to the Present*. Stanford: Hoover Institution Press, 1990.

Almazan, Edgar Rolando. *The Hidden Zhuang: A People of the Soil*. Georgia: Toccoa Falls College, 1991.

Amundsen, Edward. *In the Land of the Lamas: The Story of Trashilhamo, a Tibetan Lassie*. London: Marshall Brothers, 1910.

An Chunyang, and Liu Bohua, eds. *Where the Dai People Live*. Beijing: Foreign Languages Press, 1985.

Anderson, Eugene N, Jr. *Essays on South China's Boat People*. Taipei: The Orient Cultural Service, 1972.

Anderson, John. *Mandalay to Momien: A Narrative of Two Expeditions to Western China of 1868 and 1875 Under Colonel Edward B. Sladen and Colonel Horace Browne*. London: Macmillan, 1876.

_______ *A Report of the Expedition to Western Yunnan via Bhamo*. Calcutta: Office of the Superintendent of Government Printing, 1871.

Andrew, F. Findlay. *The Crescent in Northwest China*. London: The Religious Tract Society, 1921.

Andrews, Peter Alford, ed. *Ethnic Groups in the Republic of Turkey*. Germany: Wiesbaden, 1989.

Antisdel, C. B. "Lahoo Narration of Creation." *Burma Research Society Journal* 1, no. 1 (1911).

_______ "Lahoo Traditions, Continued." *Burma Research Society Journal* 1, no. 2 (1911).

Asia for Christ. "The Kong Ge." No. 4, September 1998.

_______ "The Tajik." No. 3, March 1998.

Asian Analyst Supplements Agency. *National Minorities in China*. n.p., 1969.

Asian Minorities Outreach. *Faces of the Unreached in Laos: Southeast Asia's Forgotten Nation*. Chiang Mai, Thailand: AMO Publishing, 1999.

_______ *The 50 Most Unreached People Groups of China and Tibet*. Chiang Mai, Thailand: AMO Publishing, 1996.

_______ *The Peoples of Vietnam*. Chiang Mai, Thailand: AMO Publishing, 1998.

_______ "The Akha." *Newsletter*, no. 41, September 1996.

_______ "The Amdo Tibetans." *Newsletter*, no. 40, July 1996.

_______ "The Black Tai." *Newsletter*, no. 36, December 1995.

_______ "The Chrame." *Newsletter*, no. 51, December 1998.

_______ "The Dongxiang." *Newsletter*, no. 22, August 1993.

_______ "The Hui." *Newsletter*, no. 33, June 1995.

_______ "The Jino." *Newsletter*, no. 35, October 1995.

_______ "The Khmu." *Newsletter*, no. 47, November 1997.

_______ "The Ladakhis." *Newsletter*, no. 55, December 1999.

_______ "The Lisu." *Newsletter*, no. 24, December 1993.

_______ "The Luoluopo." *Newsletter*, no. 54, August-September 1999.

_______ "The Miao." *Newsletter*, no. 28, August 1994.

_______ "The Mo. " *Newsletter*, no. 32, April 1995.

_______ "The Mulao." *Newsletter*, no. 26, April 1994.

_______ "The Naxi." *Newsletter*, no. 20, April 1993.

_______ "The Nisu (Xinping)." *Newsletter*, no. 57, May 2000.

_______ "The Nosu." *Newsletter*, no. 46, August 1997.

_______ "The Oroqen." *Newsletter*, no. 45, May 1997.

_______ "The Palaung." *Newsletter*, no. 38, March 1996.

_______ "The Pumi." *Newsletter*, no. 31, February 1995.

_______ "The Qiang." *Newsletter*, no. 27, June 1994.

_______ "The Salar." *Newsletter*, no. 25, February 1994.

_______ "The Shui" *Newsletter*, no. 34, August 1995.

_______ "The Tai Lu." *Newsletter*, no. 44, March 1997.

_______ "The Tajik." *Newsletter*, no. 50, September 1998.

_______ "The Tibetans." *Newsletter*, no. 30, December 1994.

_______ "The Wa." *Newsletter*, no. 37, February 1996.

_______ "The White Miao." *Newsletter*, no. 39, May 1996.

_______ "The Yao." *Newsletter*, no. 21, June 1993.

_______ "The Yi Peoples." *Newsletter*, no. 53, May-June 1999.

_______ "The Yunnan Mongolians." *Newsletter*, no. 23, October 1993.

Asian Studies Institute. "The Dai People of Southeast Asia." Unpublished report, 1996.

Asmussen, Jes P. *Xuastvanift: Studies in Manichaeism*. Copenhagen: Munksgaard, 1965.

Atiya, Azis S. *A History of Eastern Christianity*. London: Methuen, 1968.

Austin, Alvyn J. *Saving China: Canadian Missionaries in the Middle Kingdom 1888-1959*. Toronto: University of Toronto Press, 1986.

Australian Academy of the Humanities and the Chinese Academy of Social Sciences (CASS). *Language Atlas of China*. Hong Kong: Longman Group, 1987.

Avedon, John. *In Exile from the Land of Snows*. New York: Alfred A. Knopf, 1984.

Awasty, Indira. *Between Sikkim and Bhutan*. Delhi: B. R. Publishing, 1978.

Ayer, J. C. *Source-Book for Ancient Church History*. New York: Scribner, 1913.

Baber, Edward Colborne. "Travels and Researches in Western China." *Royal Geographic Society Supplementary Papers*, no. 1 (1882).

Backstrom, Peter B. "'Wakhi,' Languages of Northern Areas." *National Institute of Pakistan Studies*, no. 2:

Sociolinguistic Survey of Northern Pakistan (Islamabad: Quaid-I-Azam University, 1992).
Backus, Charles. *The Nan-Chao Kingdom and T'ang China's Southwestern Frontier.* Cambridge: Cambridge University Press, 1981.
Baddeley, John F. *Russia, Mongolia, China.* New York, 1919.
Bailey, T. Grahame. *Linguistic Studies from the Himalayas.* London: The Royal Asiatic Society, 1915.
Bainbridge, Oliver. "The Chinese Jews." *National Geographic,* October 1907.
Bai Lan, and Juha Janhunen. "On the Present State of the Ongkor Solon." *Journal de la Société Fino-Ougrienne,* no. 84 (1992).
Bai Man. "Paying Tribute to Luo: A Yi Tribal Festival." *China Tourism,* no. 129, March 1991.
Bai Yan. "The People and Their Lives in Modern Quanzhou." *China Tourism,* no. 140, February 1992.
Bai Yu. "Life in Baima, Near the Yellow River Source." *China Tourism,* no. 138, December 1991.
Bai Ziran, ed. *A Happy People: The Miaos.* Beijing: Foreign Languages Press, 1988.
Baker, H. A. *Beyond the Veil.* Shanghai, 1941.
_______ *God in Kado Land.* Taiwan: The Adullam Reading Campaign, 1937.
_______ *The Three Worlds.* Taiwan: The Adullam Reading Campaign, 1937.
_______ "A Continued Account of God Working Among the Kado and Other Primitive Tribes in Yunnan Province, S. W. China." *Adullam News,* no. 36 (1939).
Banister, Judith. *China's Changing Population.* Stanford: Stanford University Press, 1987.
Barfield, Thomas J. *The Central Asian Arabs of Afghanistan.* Arlington: University of Texas Press, 1981.
_______ *The Perilous Frontier: Nomadic Empires in China.* New York: Basil Blackwell, 1989.
Barnett, A. Doak. *China On the Eve of Communist Takeover.* New York: Frederick A. Praeger, 1963.
Barrett, David B., ed. *World Christian Encyclopedia.* New York: Oxford University Press, 1982.
Barthold, Wilheim V. *Four Studies on the History of Central Asia.* Leiden: E. J. Brill, 1956.
_______ *Turkestan Down to the Mongol Invasion.* Leiden: E. J. Brill, 1963.
Ba Te. "Lahoo Folklore: The Hunt for the Beeswax." *Burma Research Society Journal* 2, no. 1 (1912).
_______ "A Marriage Custom Among the Akhas and the Myinchas." *Burma Research Society Journal* 16 (1926).
Bawden, Charles R. *The Modern History of Mongolia.* London: Weidenfeld & Nicholson, 1968.
_______ *Shamans, Lamas and Evangelicals.* London: Routledge & Kegan Paul, 1985.
Bechert, Heinz, and Richard Gombrich. *The World of Buddhism.* London: Thames & Hudson, 1984.
Beckingham, C. F. *The Achievements of Prester John: An Inaugural Lecture.* London: School of Oriental and African Studies; 1966.
Beall, Cynthia, and Melvyn Goldstein. "The Remote World of Tibet's Nomads." *National Geographic,* June 1989.
Bell, Sir Charles. *The People of Tibet.* Oxford: Clarendon Press, 1928.
_______ *Tibet, Past and Present.* Oxford: Clarendon Press, 1924.
Benedict, Paul K. *Austro-Thai: Language and Culture With a Glossary of Roots.* New Haven: HRAF Press, 1975.
_______ "A Cham Colony on the Island of Hainan." *Harvard Journal of Asiatic Studies,* no. 6 (1941).
_______ "How to Tell Lai: an Exercise in Classification." *Linguistics of the Tibeto-Burman Area* 13, no. 2 (1990).
_______ "Languages and Literatures of Indochina." *Far Eastern Quarterly* 6, no. 4 (1947).
_______ "Miao-Yao Enigma: the Na-e Language." *Linguistics of the Tibeto-Burman Area* 9, no. 1 (1986).
_______ "The Perils of Reconstruction: The Case of Proto Yao." *Linguistics of the Tibeto-Burman Area* 17, no. 2 (1994).
Benson, Linda. *The Ili Rebellion: The Moslem Challenge to Chinese Authority in Xinjiang,* 1944-1949. New York: M. E. Sharpe, 1990.
Bernatzik, Hugo Adolf. *Akha and Miao.* New Haven, 1970.
Bethany World Prayer Center, Joshua Project 2000. "The Black Tai" (1997).
_______ "The Chiang of China" (1997).
_______ "The Hani" (1997).
_______ "The Helambu Sherpa of Nepal" (1997).
_______ "The Jinuo of China" (1997).
_______ "The Kalmyk-Oirat" (1997).
_______ "The Men-pa" (1997).
_______ "The Shan of Southeast Asia" (1997).
_______ "The Tujia of China" (1997).
_______ "The Western Lawa of China" (1997).
Beyer, Stephan V. *The Classical Tibetan Language.* Albany: State University of New York Press, 1992.
Bigandet, Paul A. *An Outline of the History of the Catholic Burmese Mission from the Year 1720 to 1887.* Rangoon: Hanthawaddy Press, 1887.
Bird, F. "Let Us Go Into the Next Towns." *China's Millions,* June 1931.
Birnbaum, Norman. "Communist China's Policy Toward Her Minority Nationalities, 1950-1965." Doctoral diss., St. John's University, New York, 1970.
Bista, Dor Bahadur. *The People of Nepal.* Kathmandu: Ratna Pustak Bhandar, 1972.
Block, Karen L. "Discourse Grammar of First Person Narrative in Plang." Paper, University of Texas (Arlington, 1994).
_______ "What Makes a Story in Plang?" *Mon-Khmer Studies,* no. 26 (1996).
Bondfield, G. H. "Mongolia, a Neglected Mission Field." In Stauffer, *The Christian Occupation of China.*
Boon Chuey Srisavasdi. *The Hill Tribes of Siam.* Bangkok: Khun Aroon, 1963.
Booz, Patrick R. *Yunnan: Southwest China's Little-Known Land of Eternal Spring.* Illinois: Passport Books, 1987.
Bosshardt, Rudolph A. *The Restraining Hand.* London: 1936.
Bourne, Frederick Samuel Augustus. *China: by Mr. F. S. A. Bourne of a Journey in South-Western China.* London: His Majesty's Stationery Office, 1888.
Bowermaster, Jon. "Rapid Descent: First Run Down the Shuilo River." *National Geographic,* November 1996.
Boyle, John A. Successors of *Genghis Khan: Translated from the Persian of Rashid al-Din.* New York: Columbia University Press, 1971.
Brackenbury, Wade. *Yak Butter & Black Tea: A Journey Into Forbidden China.* Chapel Hill: Algonquin Books, 1997.
Bradley, David. "East and South-East Asia." In Laycock and Werner (eds.), *A World of Language.*
_______ "Language Planning for China's Minorities: The Yi Branch." In Laycock and Werner (eds.), *A World of Language.*
_______ "Pronouns in Burmese-Lolo." *Linguistics of the Tibeto-Burman Area* 16, no. 1, Spring 1993.
_______ "Tibeto-Burman Languages of PDR Lao." *Linguistics of the Tibeto-Burman Area* 19, no. 1 (1996).
_______ Maya Bradley, and Li Longxiang. "The Sanyie of Kunming: a Case of Yi Language Death." Paper published for the 30th International Conference on Sino-Tibetan Languages and Linguistics (Berkeley: University of California, 1997).
Brandt, Conrad; Benjamin Schwartz, and John K. Fairbank. *A Documentary History of Chinese Communism.* New York: Antheneum, 1966.
Bridgman, E. C. "Sketches on the Miau-tze." *North China Branch of the Royal Asiatic Society,* no. 3 (1859).
Brokelmann, Carl. *History of the Islamic Peoples.* New York: Capricorn, 1960.

Broomhall, A. James. *Hudson Taylor and China's Open Century.* Sevenoaks: Hodder & Stoughton and OMF, 1981.

_______ *Strong Man's Prey.* London: CIM, 1953.

_______ *Strong Tower.* London: CIM, 1947.

Broomhall, Marshall. *The Bible in China.* London: CIM, 1934.

_______ *The Chinese Empire: A General and Missionary Survey.* London: Morgan & Scott, 1907.

_______ *Islam in China: A Neglected Problem.* London: Morgan & Scott, 1910.

_______ *The Jubilee Story of the China Inland Mission.* Philadelphia: CIM, 1915.

_______ *Some a Hundredfold: The Life and Work of James R. Adam Among the Tribes of Southwest China.* London: CIM, 1916.

_______ "Some Tribes of South-West China." *International Review of Missions* 6, no. 22 (1917).

Brown, Thompson G. *China Mission Handbook* 1910-33. Shanghai, 1934.

_______ *Christianity in the People's Republic of China.* Atlanta, n.d.

Browne, Lawrence E. *The Eclipse of Christianity in Asia from the Time of Muhammed till the fourteenth Century.* Cambridge: Cambridge University Press, 1933.

Bruk, Solomon Il'ich. *Peoples of China, Mongolian People's Republic, and Korea.* Washington: U.S. Joint Publications Research Service, no. 1710, 1959.

_______ "Distribution of National Minorities in the People's Republic of China." In Stephen P. Dunn and Ethel Dunn (eds.), *Introduction to Soviet Ethnography* 2 (Berkeley: Highgate Road Social Science Research Station, 1958).

Bruksasri, Wanat, and John McKinnon, eds. *The Highlanders of Thailand.* Kuala Lumpur: Oxford University Press, 1983.

Buchan, Alex. "Catholic Church Hangs on in Tibet." *Compass Direct*, September 1998.

Buchanan, Claudius. *Christian Researches in Asia: With Notices of the Translation of the Scriptures into the Oriental Languages.* Boston: Armstrong & Cornhill, 1811.

Buckley, Michael, and Robert Strauss, eds. *Tibet: a Travel Survival Kit.* Hawthorn, Australia: Lonely Planet Publications, 1986.

Budge, Ernest A. W. *The Monks of Kublai Khan Emperor of China.* London: Religious Tract Society, 1928.

Bull, Geoffrey T. *When Iron Gates Yield.* London: Hodder & Stoughton, 1955.

Burgess, Alan. *The Small Woman.* London: The Reprint Society, 1959.

Burkitt, F. C. *Early Eastern Christianity Outside the Roman Empire.* London: Murray, 1904.

Burridge, Kenelm. "Missionaries and the Perception of Evil." In Whiteman, D. (ed.), *Missionaries, Anthropologists, and Cultural Change* 1: *Studies in Third World Societies*, no. 25 (Williamsburg: College of William and Mary, 1985).

Burusphat, Somsonge. "Surface Indicators of Storyline in the Kam Origin Myth." *Mon-Khmer Studies*, no. 26 (1996).

Butler, Jacqueline. *Yao Design.* Bangkok: The Siam Society, 1970.

Butler, John. *A Sketch of Assam With Some Account of Hill Tribes, by An Officer.* London: Smith, Elder & Co., 1847.

Cabezon, Jose Ignacio. "Islam on the Roof of the World." *ARAMCO World*, January-February 1998.

Cable, Mildred. *George Hunter: Apostle of Turkestan.* London: CIM, 1948.

Campbell, William. *Formosa Under the Dutch, Described From Contemporary Records with Explanatory Notes and a Bibliography of the Island.* London: Kegan Paul, Trench, Trubner, 1903.

Carey, Fred. "A Trip to the Chinese Shan States." *Geographical Journal* 14, no. 4 (1899).

Carey, William. *Adventures in Tibet.* Chicago: Student Missionary Campaign Library, 1901.

Carlsen, William. *Tibet: In Search of a Miracle.* New York: Nyack College, 1985.

Carrapiett, William James Sherlock. *The Kachin Tribes of Burma.* Rangoon: Government Printing and Stationery, 1929.

Carrier, Jim. "Gatekeepers of the Himalaya." *National Geographic*, December 1992.

Central Institute of Indian Languages. *Distribution of Languages in India in States and Union Territories.* Mysore, 1973.

Chan Hok-Lam, and William T. De Bary, eds. *Yuan Thought: Chinese Thought and Religion Under the Mongols.* New York: Columbia University Press, 1982.

Chang Chi-Jen [Zhang Ji-ren]. "The Minority Groups of China and Chinese Political Expansion into Southeast Asia." Manuscript, University of Michigan, 1956.

Chang Jen-Kai [Zhang Ren-Gai]. "The Minority Races of South Szechuen." *China Monthly Review* 122, no. 4 (1952).

Chang Kun. "A Comparative Study of the Southern Ch'iang Dialects." *Monumenta Serica*, no. 26 (1967).

Chang Sen [Zhang Sen]. "China's National Minority Areas Prosper." *Peking Review* 26, no. 21 (1959).

Chang Weipang [Zhao Weibang]. "A Lolo Legend Concerning the Origin of the Torch Festival." *Studia Serica* 9, no. 2 (1950).

Chao, Jonathon, ed. *The China Mission Handbook: A Portrait of China and its Church.* Hong Kong: CCRC, 1989.

Chao, R. Y. *Aspects of Chinese Sociolinguistics.* Cambridge: Stanford University Press, 1943.

_______ *Mandarin Primer.* Cambridge: Harvard University Press, 1948.

Charbonnier, Jean. *Guide to the Catholic Church in China 1989.* Singapore: China Catholic Communication, 1990.

Chattopadhyaya, Alaka. *Atisa and Tibet.* Delhi: Motilal Banarsidass, 1967.

Chazee, Laurent. *Atlas des ethnies et des sous-ethnies du Laos.* Vientiane: Laurent Chazee, 1995.

_______ *The Peoples of Laos: Rural and Ehtnic Diversities.* Bangkok: White Lotus Press, 1999.

Ch'en, Kenneth K. S. *Buddhism in China: A Historical Survey.* Princeton: Princeton University Press, 1964.

Ch'en Yuan. *Western and Central Asians in China Under the Mongols.* Berkeley: University of California, 1969.

Chen, Jack. *The Sinkiang Story.* New York: Macmillan, 1977.

Chen Shuren. "Muni Gully: Wonderland of Nature." *China Tourism*, no. 110, n.d.

Cheng Weidong. "Descendants of Hunters and Fairies: North China's Little-Known Daur People." *China Tourism*, no. 155, May 1993.

Chen Yunguang, and Zhang Heping. "Flower Gathering Festival at Boyu." *China Tourism*, no. 115, n.d.

Chen Zongxiang. "The Dual System and the Clans of the Li-su and Shui-t'ien Tribes." *Monumenta Serica*, no. 12 (1947).

Cheng Te-k'un, and Liang Ch'ao-t'ao [Zheng Dekun and Liang Zhaotao]. "An Introduction to the Southwestern Peoples of China." *West China Union University Museum Guidebook*, no. 7 (Chengdu, 1945).

Chesneaux, Jean. *Peasant Revolts in China, 1840-1949.* London: Thames & Hudson, 1973.

Chiao Chien. "Principles of the Pai Yao Kinship." In Lemoine and Chiao (eds.), *The Yao of South China.*

_______, and Nicholas Tapp, eds. *Ethnicity and Ethnic Groups in China.* Hong Kong: The Chinese University of Hong Kong, 1989.

China At War. "The Lolos of Sikang." Vol. 7, no. 5 (1941).

China Inland Mission. *Anping Kwei: China and the Gospel, An Illustrated Report.* London: CIM, 1914.

_______ *Anshunfu: China and the Gospel, An Illustrated Report.* London: CIM, 1906; 1907; 1911; 1912; 1913.

_______ *Kweichow: China and the Gospel, An Illustrated Report.* London: CIM, 1916; 1929.

_______ *Panghai: China and the Gospel, An Illustrated Report.* London: CIM, 1907; 1911.

_______ *Sapushan: China and the Gospel, An Illustrated Report.* London: CIM, 1910; 1912; 1914.
China Pictorial Publications. *Minority Peoples in China.* Beijing: China Pictorial Publications, 1987.
Chindasari, Nusit. *The Religion of the Hmong Njua.* Bangkok: The Siam Society, 1976.
Chinese Academy of Social Sciences (CASS). *Information China.* London: Pergamon Press, 1989.
Choedon, Yeshi, and Norbu Dawa. *Tibet.* London: Tiger Books, 1997.
Chopra, P. N. *Sikkim.* New Delhi: S. Chand, 1979.
Chou Tse-yu [Zhou Zeyou]. "The Lisu People Along the Nuchiang River." *China Pictorial*, no. 5 (1963).
Chronicon Ibn al-Athir. *History of the Mongols: Based on Eastern and Western Accounts of the Thirteenth and Fourteenth Centuries.* Translated by B. Spuler. London: Routledge & Kegan Paul, 1972.
Chun Cao. "The Hani Christians." *Bridge*, September-October 1990.
Chun Shizeng, ed. *Chinese Nationalities.* Beijing: China Nationality Photography & Art Press, 1989.
Chu Thai Son, ed. *Vietnam: a Multicultural Mosaic.* Hanoi: Foreign Languages Publishing House, 1991.
Clandney, Dru C. *Muslim Chinese: Ethnic Nationalism in the People's Republic of China.* Council on East Asian Studies, Harvard University Press, 1991.
Clark, Leonard. "Among the Big Knot Lois of Hainan." *National Geographic*, September 1938.
Clark, Milton J. "How the Kazaks Fled to Freedom." *National Geographic*, November 1954.
Clarke, G. W. *Kweichow and Yunnan Provinces.* Shanghai, 1894.
Clarke, Samuel R. *Among the Tribes in South-West China.* London: Morgan & Scott, 1911.
Cochrane, Wilbur Willis. *The Shans* 1. Rangoon: Government Printing Press, 1915.
Coehlo, V. H. *Sikkim and Bhutan.* New Delhi: Indraprastha Press, 1967.
Cohen, Paul A. *China and Christianity: The Missionary Movement and the Growth of Chinese Antiforeignism, 1860-1870.* Cambridge: Harvard University Press, 1963.
Cole, Johnnetta B. *Come Wind, Come Weather: The Story of Year 1950.* London: CIM, 1950.
_______ *The Contested Highway: Part of the Story of C.I.M. in 1942.* London: CIM, 1952.
Colquhoun, Archibald Ross. *Across Chryse, Being the Narrative of a Journey of Exploration Through the South China Border Lands from Canton to Mandalay.* 2 Vols. London: Sampson Low, Marston, Searle & Rivington, 1883.
_______ *Amongst the Shans.* London: Field & Tuer, 1885.
_______ "On the Aboriginal and Other Tribes of Yunnan and the Shan Country." *Anthropological Institute of Great Britian and Ireland* 13, no. 1 (1884).
Cook, T. "The Independent Lolo of South-west Szechwan." *West China Border Research Society*, no. 8 (1936).
Cooke, A. B. *Fish Four and the Lisu New Testament.* Philadelphia: 1947.
_______ *Honey Two of the Lisu-Land.* London, 1932.
Coon, Carelton. *The Living Races of Man.* New York: Alfred A. Knopf, 1965.
Cooper, Arthur D., and Pamela, J. "A Preliminary Phonology of the Banlan dialect of Lahu Shi." *Focus on Phonology: PYU Working Papers in Linguistics*, no. 1 (Chiang Mai, Thailand: Payap University Graduate Linguistics Department, 1996).
Cooper, Robert, ed. *The Hmong.* Bangkok: Artasia Press, 1995.
Constable, Nicole. *Guest People: Hakka Identity in China and Abroad.* Seattle: University of Washington, 1996.
Corrigan, Gina. Odysey *Illustrated Guide to Guizhou.* Hong Kong: The Guidebook Company, 1995.
Couling, Charlotte Eliza. *The Luminous Religion: A Study of Nestorian Christianity in China.* London: Carey, 1925.
Covell, Ralph. *The Challenge of Independent Nosuland.* Chicago: Conservative Baptist Foreign Mission Society, 1947.
_______ *The Liberating Gospel in China: The Christian Faith Among China's Minority Peoples.* Grand Rapids: Baker Books, 1995.
_______ *Mission Impossible: The Unreached Nosu on China's Frontier.* Pasadena: Hope Press, 1990.
_______ *Pentecost of the Hills in Taiwan.* Pasadena: Hope Publishing, 1998.
Crabouillet. "Les Lolos." *Les Missions Catholiques* 5, nos. 192, 194, 195 (1873).
Cranmer-Byng, J. L., ed. *An Embassy in China, Being the Journal Kept by Lord Macartney, 1793-94.* London: Longmans, 1962.
Crossman, Eileen. *Mountain Rain: A New Biography of James O. Fraser.* Singapore: OMF, 1982.
Crouch, Archie R.; Steven Agoratyus; Arthur Emerson, and Debra E. Soled, eds. *Christianity in China: A Scholars' Guide to Resources in the Libraries and Archives of the United States.* New York: M. E. Sharpe, 1989.
Cultural Palace of Nationalities. *Clothings and Ornaments of China's Miao People.* Beijing: The Nationality Press, 1985.
Cunningham, E. R.; G. Kilborn Leslie, et al. *The Nosu Tribes of Western Szechwan: Notes on the County and Its Peoples and on the Diseases of the Region.* Shanghai: Henry Lister Institute, 1933.
Cushman, Richard. "Rebel Haunts and Lotus Huts: Problems in the Ethnohistory of the Yao." Ph.D. diss., Cornell University, 1970.
d'Ollone, Henri Marie Gustave Vicomte. *L'Ecriture des Miao tseu.* Paris: E. Leroux, 1912.
_______ *In Forbidden China: The d'Ollone Mission 1906-09, China-Tibet-Mongolia.* London: T. Fisher Unwin, 1912.
_______ *Langues des Peuples non Chinois de la Chine* 6, nos. 27-28. Paris: E. Leroux, 1912.
d'Orleans, Henri Philippe Marie Prince. "From Yun-nan to British India." *Geographical Journal*, no. 7 (1896).
Dang Nghiem Van; Chu Thai Son, and Luu Hung. *Ethnic Minorities in Vietnam.* Hanoi: The Gioi Publishers, 1993.
Daniel. "Gereja Kemah Pertemuan: Second Indonesian Church in Hainan." *Bridge*, no. 53, May-June 1992.
Das, Sarat Chandra. *Journey to Lhasa and Central Tibet.* London: Murray, 1902.
Dauvillier, J. "Temoignages Nouveaux sur le Christianisme Nestorien chez les Tibetans." In *Histoire et institutions des Eglise Orientales au Moyen Age* (London: Varioum Reprints 2, 1983).
Davies, Henry Rodolph. *Yun-nan: The Link Between India and the Yangtze.* Cambridge: Cambridge University Press, 1909.
Dawson, Christopher. *The Mongol Mission: Narratives and Letters of the Franciscan Missionaries in Mongolia in the 13th and 14th Century.* New York: Sheed & Ward, 1955.
de Beauclair, Inez. *An Introduction to the Southwestern Peoples of China.* Chengdu: West China Union University, 1945.
_______ *Tribal Cultures of Southwest China.* Taiwan: The Chinese Association for Folklore, 1974.
_______ "Culture Traits of Non-Chinese Tribes in Kweichow Province, Southwest China." *Sinologica* 5, no. 1 (1956).
_______ "Ethnic Groups." In Hellmut Wilheim (ed.), *A General Handbook of China* (New Haven: HRAF Press Monograph No. 55, 1956).
De Fillipi, Fillipo. *An Account of Tibet: The Travels of Ippolito Desideri of Pistola, 1712 to 1727.* London: George Routledge & Sons, 1932.
De Francis, John. *The Chinese Language.* Honolulu: University of Hawaii Press, 1984.
Demko, George J. *The Russian Colonization of Kazakhstan, 1896-1916.* Bloomington: Indiana University Press, 1969.

De Rachewiltz, Igor. *Papal Envoys to the Great Khans*. London: Faber & Faber, 1971.
Dessaint, Alain Y. *Minorities in Southwestern China: An Introduction to the Yi (Lolo) and Related Peoples and an Annotated Bibliography*. New Haven: HRAF Press, 1980.
De Terra, Hellmut. "On the World's Highest Plateaus." *National Geographic*, March 1931.
Deuri, R. K. *The Sulungs*. Shillong: Research Department of the Government of Arunachal Pradesh, 1983.
Diamond, Norma. "Defining the Miao." In Harrell (ed.), *Cultural Encounters on China's Ethnic Frontiers*.
_______ "The Miao and Poison: Interactions on China's Southwest Frontier." *Ethnology*, no. 27, January 1988.
Diao, Richard. "The National Minorities and their Relations with the Chinese Communist Regime." In Peter Kunstadter (ed.), *Southeast Asian Tribes, Minorities and Nations*.
Dick, Lois Hoadley. *Isobel Kuhn: The Canadian Girl Who Felt God's Call to the Lisu People of China*. Minnesota: Bethany House, 1987.
Diemberger, Hildegard. "Gangla Tshechu, Beyul Khenbalung." In C. Ramble and M. Brauen (eds.), *International Seminar on the Anthropology of Tibet and the Himalaya* (Zurich: Ethnographic Museum of the University of Zurich, 1993).
Diffloth, Gerard. "The Wa Languages." *Linguistics of the Tibeto-Burman Area* 5, no. 2 (1980).
Dikkoter, Frank. *The Discourse of Race in Modern China*. London: Hurst & Company, 1992.
Diller, Anthony. "Tai Languages: Varieties and Subgroup Terms." (Canberra: Faculty of Asian Studies, Australian National University, 1993).
Djang, W. B. "The Decline and Possible Future of a Great Race: The Ch'iang People." Manuscript, Yale Divinity School, Yale, 1948.
Dodd, William Clifton. *The Tai Race: Elder Brother of the Chinese*. Cedar Rapids: The Torch Press, 1923.
Dommen, Arthur. *Laos: Keystone of Indochina*. Boulder: Westview Press, 1985.
Dowling, Bruce T., and Douglas P. Olney, eds. *The Hmong in the West*. University of Minnesota Press, 1982.
Doyle, Edward, and Samuel Lipsman. *The Vietnam Experience: Setting the Stage*. Boston: Boston Publishing Co., 1981.
Dreyer, June Elizabeth Tuefel. *China's Forty Millions: Minority Nationalities and National Integration in the People's Republic of China*. Cambridge, Mass: Harvard University Press, 1976.
Duchesne, Louis. *Early History of the Christian Church* 2 & 3. London: Murray, 1912.
Dupree, Louis. *Afghanistan*. Princeton: Princeton University Press, 1980.
Dyen, Isidore. *The Lexicostatistical Classification of the Austronesian Languages*. New Haven: Yale University Press, 1963.
Eberhard, Wolfgram. *China's Minorities: Yesterday and Today*. Belmont: Wadsworth Publishers, 1982.
_______ *A History of China*. Los Angeles: University Press, 1960.
_______ *The Local Cultures of South and East Asia*. Leiden: Brill, 1968.
_______ "Kultur und Siedlung der Randvolker Chinas." *T'oung Pao*, no. 36 (supplement, 1942).
Edgar, J. H. *High Altitudes: Missionary Problems in Kham or Eastern Tibet*. Chengdu: Canadian Mission Press, n.d.
_______ "The Ancient Yong and Possible Survivals in Szechwan." *Journal of West China Research Society*, no. 6 (1933).
_______ "The Horpa of the Upper Nya or Yalung." *Journal of West China Border Research Society* (1932).
Edmonson, Jerold A., ed. *Kadai: Discussions in Kadai and S. E. Asian Linguistics*. Arlington: University of Texas, 1990.
_______ *Languages of the Vietnam-China Borderlands*. Arlington: University of Texas, 1996.
_______, and David B. Solnit. *Comparative Kadai: The Tai Branch* (Arlington: University of Texas, 1997).
_______, and Kenneth J. Gregerson. "Bolyu Tone in Vietic Perspective." *Mon-Khmer Studies*, no. 26 (1996).
Edwards, C. G. "Kweichow Tribal Report." *The Field Bulletin of the China Inland Mission*, November 1948.
Ekvall, Robert L. *Gateway to Tibet*. Harrisburg: Christian Publications, 1938.
_______ *Religious Observances in Tibet*. Chicago: University of Chicago Press, 1964.
Elias, Norbert. *A History of the Moghuls of Central Asia*. Translated by E. Dennison Ross. London: Curzon Press, 1895.
Elwin, Verrier. *India's North-East Frontier in the Nineteenth Century*. London: Oxford University Press, 1959.
_______ *A Philosophy for NEFA*. Itanagar: Directorate of Research, 1957.
Embree, John Fee, and Lilia Ota Dotson. *Bibliography of the Peoples and Cultures of Mainland Southeast Asia*. New York: Russel & Russel, 1972.
Embree, John Fee, and William Leroy Thomas. *Ethnic Groups of Northern Southeast Asia*. New Haven: Yale University, 1950.
Enriquez, Colin Metcalf Dallas. *Races of Burma*. Delhi: Indian Government Manager of Publications, 1924.
_______ "The Yawyins or Lisu." *Burma Research Society*, no. 11 (1921).
Enwall, Joakim, ed. *Hmong Writing Systems in Vietnam: A Case Study of Vietnam's Minority Language Policy*. Stockholm: Center for Pacific Asia Studies at Stockholm University, 1995.
_______ *A Myth Become Reality: History and Development of the Miao Written Language* 1. Stockholm: Institute of Oriental Languages, 1996.
_______ *A Myth Become Reality: History and Development of the Miao Written Language* 2. Stockholm: Institute of Oriental Languages, 1997.
_______ "In Search of the Entering Tone: The Importance of Sichuanese Tones for Understanding the Tone Marking System of the Sichuan Hmong Pollard Script." In *Outstretched Leaves on His Bamboo Staff: Studies in Honour of Goran Malmqvist on His Seventieth Birthday*. Stockholm: Association of Oriental Studies, 1994.
Esquirol, Joseph. *Dictionaire Kanao-Francois et Francois-Kanao*. Hong Kong, 1931.
Ethnic Cultures Publishing House. *Vietnam: Image of the Community of 54 Ethnic Groups*. Vietnam News Agency, 1996.
Evans-Pritchard, Sir Edward E. *Peoples of the Earth* 13. London: Tom Stacey, 1973.
_______ *Theories of Primitive Religion*. Oxford: Oxford University Press, 1965.
Far Eastern and Russian Institute. *A Regional Handbook on the Inner Mongolia Autonomous Region*. New Haven: HRAF Press, 1956.
Farrell, Raleigh. "Taiwan Aboriginal Groups: Problems in Cultural and Linguistic Classification." *Academia Sinica Monograph*, no. 17 (Institue of Ethnology, 1969).
Fei Xiaotong [Fei Hsiao Tung]. *Toward a People's Anthropology*. Beijing: New World Press, 1981.
_______ "China Minorities Nationalities." *Far Eastern Economic Review* 13, no. 3 (1952).
_______ "Fifty Years Investigation in the Yao Mountains." In Lemoine and Chiao, *The Yao of South China*.
_______ "The Minority Peoples in Kweichow." *China Monthly Review* 121, no. 6 (1951).
_______ "On the Question of Identification of Nationalities in China." *Chinese Social Sciences*, no. 1 (1980).
_______, ed.; Li Yu-I, and Chang Tse-i. *Three Types of Rural Economy in Yunnan*. New York: Institute of Pacific Relations, 1943.

_______, and Lin Yuehua. "A Study of the Social Nature of the Minority Nationalities." *Renmin Ribao* 14 (August 1956).

Feng Hanyi, and John Knight Shryock. "The Historical Origins of the Lolo." *Harvard Journal of Asiatic Studies*, no. 3 (1938).

Fergusson, W. N. *Adventure, Sport and Travel on the Tibetan Steppes*. London: Constable & Company, 1911.

_______ "The Tribes of North-Western Se-chuan." *Geographical Journal* 32, no. 6 (1910).

Fisher, James F., and Sir Edmund Hillary. *Sherpas: Reflections on Change in Himalayan Nepal*. Berkeley: University of California Press, 1990.

Fitzgerald, Charles Patrick. *The Empress Wu*. Taiwan: Rainbow Bridge, 1968.

_______ *Son of Heaven*. Cambridge: Cambridge University Press, 1933.

_______ *The Tower of Five Glories: A Study of the Min Chia of Ta Li, Yunnan*. London: Cresset, 1941.

Fletcher, Joseph F. *Studies on Chinese and Islamic Inner Asia*. Hampshire: Variorum Press, 1995.

Foning, A. R. *Lepcha: My Vanishing Tribe*. New Delhi: Sterling, 1987.

Forbes, Andrew D. W. *Warlords and Muslims in Chinese Central Asia*. London: Cambridge University Press, 1986.

Forney, Matt. "Total Recall." *Far Eastern Economic Review*, 29 May 1997.

Forrest, George. "Journey on Upper Salwin: October-December 1905." *Geographical Journal*, no. 32 (1908).

_______ "The Land of the Crossbow." *National Geographic*, February 1910.

Foster, John. *The Church of the T'ang Dynasty*. London: SPCK, 1939.

Franck, Harry A. *Roving Through Southern China*. New York: The Century Company, 1925.

Franke, Wolfgang. *A Century of Chinese Revolution: 1851-1949*. New York: Harper Torchbooks, 1970.

_______ *China and the West, The Cultural Encounter: Thirteenth to Twentieth Centuries*. New York: Harper & Row, 1967.

Freeman, Michael. *Hilltribes of Thailand*. Bangkok: Asia Books, 1989.

Fuchs, Stephen. *The Aboriginal Tribes of India*. Madras: Macmillan Press, 1973.

Fu Miaoji. *Tibeto-Burman Sounds and Vocabulary*. Beijing: Zhongguo Shihui Kexue Chubanshe, 1991.

_______ "Written Languages for China's Minorities." *People's China*, no. 3 (1957).

Gaide, L. "Notice Ethnographique sur les Principales Races Indigenes de la Chine Meridionale (Yun-nam en Particulier) et du Nord de l'Indo-Chine." *Annales d'Hygiene et de Medicine Coloniales*, no. 5 (1903).

Gao, Shou-shi. "The Lagu of Yunnan." *Minzu Huabao*, no. 3 (1960).

Garrett, W. E. "Mountain Top War in Remote Ladakh." *National Geographic*, May 1960.

Geddes, William Robert. *Migrants of the Mountains: The Cultural Ecology of the Blue Miao (Hmong Njua) of Thailand*. Oxford: Clarendon Press, 1976.

Ge Jialin. "The Jiarong Tibetans Celebrate Their Harvest." *China Tourism*, no. 166, May 1994.

Geldern, R. Hein. R. "Die Asiatiche Herkunft der Sudamerikanischen Metalltechmik" [The Asiatic Origin of the South American Metallurgy]. *Paideuma* (May 1954).

Ge Lin. "The Qiang People and Their Ancient Castles." *China Tourism*, no.59, n.d.

Gernet, Jacques. *A History of Chinese Civilization*. Cambridge: Cambridge University Press, 1982.

Gilhodes, C. *The Kachins: Religion and Customs*. Calcutta: Catholic Orphan Press, 1922.

Gill, Linda Hoyle. *Portraits of China*. Honolulu: University of Hawaii Press, 1989.

Gill, William John. *The River of Golden Sand*. London: John Murray, 1880.

Gilmour, James. *Among the Mongols*. London: The Religious Tract Society, 1882.

Ginsburgs, George, and Michael Mathos. *Communist China and Tibet: The First Dozen Years*. The Hague: Martinus Nijhoff, 1964.

Gjessing, Gutorm. "Chinese Anthropology and New China's Policy Towards Her Minorities." *Acta Sociologica* 2, no. 1 (1957).

Global Evangelization Movement. "World's Peoples Listed by Country." Unpublished report, 1995.

Goforth, Jonathon. *By My Spirit*. London: Marshall, Morgan & Scott, 1915.

Goulart, Peter. *The Forgotten Kingdom*. London: John Murray, 1957.

_______ *The Princes of the Black Bone: Life in the Tibetan Borderland*. London, 1958.

Graham, David Crockett. *The Customs and Religions of the Ch'iang*. Washington DC: Smithsonian Institute, 1958.

_______ *Folk Religion in Southwest China*. Washington DC: Smithsonian Institute, 1961.

_______ *Songs and Stories of the Ch'uan Miao*. Washington DC: Smithsonian Institute, 1954.

_______ "The Lolo of Szechuan Province." *American Anthropologist*, no. 32 (1930).

_______ "The Lolos of Szechwan." *West China Branch of the Royal Asiatic Society*, no. 3 (1926).

_______ "A Lolo Story: 'The Great God of O-Li-Bi-Zih' by Lin Kuang-tien." *Journal of American Folklore*, no. 68 (1955).

Graham, Shirley. "Minority Peoples of China." *Freedomways* 1, no. 1 (1961).

Gregory, John. W., and C.J. Gregory. *To the Alps of Chinese Tibet*. Philadelphia: J. B. Lippincott, 1924.

Grimes, Barbara F. (ed.). *Ethnologue: Languages of the World*. Dallas: SIL, 1988, 11th edition; 1992, 12th edition; 1996, 13th edition.

Grist, William Alexander. *Samuel Pollard: Pioneer Missionary in China*. London: Cassell, n.d.

Grousett, Rene. *The Empire of the Steppes: A History of Central Asia*. Translated by N. Walford. New Brunswick: Rutgers University Press, 1970.

Grubb, Norman. *Christ in Congo Forests: The Story of the Heart of African Missions*. London: Lutterworth Press, 1945.

Grunfeld, A. Tom. *The Making of Modern Tibet*. London: M. E. Sharpe, 1987.

Grunfeld, Frederick V. *Wayfarers of the Thai Forest: The Akha*. Amsterdam: Time-Life Books, 1982.

Gryaznov, Mikhail. *The Ancient Civilizations of Southern Siberia*. New York: Cowles Publishing, 1969.

Guiness, M. Geraldine. *The Story of the China Inland Mission*. 2 Vols. London: Morgan & Scott, 1900.

Gu Shoukang. "The Sherpas: Hardy Folk of the Himalayas." *China Tourism*, no. 54, n.d.

Gyatso, Kelsang. *Buddhism in the Tibetan Tradition: A Guide*. London: Routledge & Kegan Paul, 1984.

Hahn, Reinhold F. "An Annotated Sample of Ili Turki." *Acta Orientalia Hungaricae*, no. 43 (1990).

Hale, Austin (ed.) "Collected Papers on Sherpa, Jirel." *Nepal Studies in Linguistics*, no. 2 (Kirtipur: SIL and Institute of Nepal and Asian Studies, 1975).

Hall, John. *The Yunnan Provincial Faction (1937-39)*. Canberra, 1976.

Hani2000. "The Hani: Poorest of China's Poor." Unreached people group profile.

Hansell, Mark. "The Relation of Be to Tai." In SIL, *Comparative Kadai*.

Hanson, Ola. *The Kachins: Their Customs and Traditions*. Rangoon: American Baptist Mission Press, 1913.

_______ *Missionary Pioneers Among the Kachins*. New York: American Baptist Foreign Missionary Society, 1922.

_______ "Among the Kachin Hills." *Baptist Missionary Magazine*, no. 74 (1895).

_______ "Among the Kachins." *Baptist Missionary Magazine*, no. 83 (1903).
_______ "The Kachin Religion." *Baptist Missionary Magazine*, no. 76 (1896).
Hansson, Inga-Lill. "A Comparison of Akha, Hani, Khantu and Pijo." *Linguistics of the Tibeto-Burman Area* 12, no. 1 (1989).
_______ "The Language of Akha in Ritual Texts." *Linguistics of the Tibeto-Burman Area* 14, no. 2 (1991).
_______ "A Phonological Comparison of Akha and Hani." *Linguistics of the Tibeto-Burman Area* 7, no. 1 (1982).
Hao Yaojun. "Carnival Mood Among the Hanis." *China Tourism*, no. 97, n.d.
Harrell, Stevan (ed.). *Cultural Encounters on China's Ethnic Frontiers*. Seattle: University of Washington, 1995.
_______ "Ethnicity and Kin Terms Among Two Kinds of Yi." In Chiao and Tapp (eds.), *Ethnicity and Ethnic Groups in China*.
_______ "Ethnicity, Local Interests, and the State: Yi Communities in Southwest China." *Comparative Studies in Society and History, An International Quarterly*, no. 32 (1990).
_______ "The History of the History of the Yi." In Harrell (ed.), *Cultural Encounters on China's Ethnic Frontiers*.
Harrer, Heinrich. *Ladakh*. Innsbruck: Penguin Verlag, 1978.
_______ *Return to Tibet*. Harmondsworth: Penguin, 1985.
_______ *Seven Years in Tibet*. London: Pan Books, 1953.
Harrison, Dan. "Broken Vessels Called to Missions." In *The Great Commission Handbook* (Evanston, Ill: Berry Publishing Services, 1994).
Harrison, E. Myers. *Heroes of Faith on Pioneer Trails*. Chicago: Moody Bible Institute, 1945.
Hasbagen, "Mongolians of Alxa in Western Inner Mongolia." *China Tourism*, no. 139, January 1992.
Hashimoto, M. "The Be Language: A Classified Vocabulary of Its Linkow Dialect." *Institute for the Study of Languages and Cultures of Asia and Africa* (1980).
Hatanaka, Sachiko. "Ethnicity and Culture Complex in the Northern Minorities." In Chiao and Tapp (eds.), *Ethnicity and Ethnic Groups in China*.
Hattaway, Paul. *China's Unreached Cities* 1: *A Prayer Guide for 52 of China's Least Evangelized Cities*. Chiang Mai, Thailand: AMO Publishing, 1999.
_______ "The Yi of China." *A-A-P Advocate*, August 1996.
Haudricourt, A. G. "La Langue Lakkia." *Bulletin de la Societe Linguistique de Paris* 62, no. 1 (1967).
Hayase, Yasuko, and Seiko Kawamata. *Population Statistics of China*. Tokyo: Institute of Developing Economics, 1990.
Hayes, Ernest H. *Sam Pollard of Yunnan*. London: Livingstone, 1928.
Heberer, Thomas. *China and its National Minorities: Autonomy or Assimilation?* New York: M. E. Sharpe, 1989.
Hefley, James, and Marti. *China! Christian Martyrs of the 20th Century: an excerpt from 'By Their Blood'*. Michigan: Mott Media, 1978.
He Guanghua. "The Lost Horizons of Medog." *China Reconstructs*, March 1995.
He Huaibo. "The Primitive Paper-Making Technology of the Yao Nationality." *China Tourism*, no. 71, n.d.
Heijdra, Martin. "Who Were the Laka?: A Survey of Scriptures in the Minority Languages of Southwest China." *The East Asian Library Journal* 8, no. 1 (Spring 1998).
Heissig, Walther. *The Religions of Mongolia*. Berkeley: University of California Press, 1980.
Hendricks, Glenn L.; Bruce T. Dowling, and Amos S. Deinard, eds. *The Hmong in Transition*. New York: Center for Migration Studies, 1986.
Henry, Augustine. "The Lolos and Other Tribes of Western China." *Royal Anthropological Institute*, no. 33 (1903).
_______ "On The Lolos and Other Tribes in Western China." Report of the British Association for the Advancement of Science (1902).
Herbert, W. T. "As Happy as a King." *China's Millions*, April 1922.
_______ "The 'Come Down From Heaven' Missionaries Among the Miao." *China's Millions*, November 1923.
Hicks, C. E. "The No Su People of the Neighborhood of Chao-tung in Yunnan." *Chinese Recorder and Missionary Journal* 41, no. 3 (1910).
Hinton, Harold C. "The *National Minorities in China*." *Far Eastern Economic Review* 19, no. 11 (1955)
Hirth, F. *China and the Roman Orient, Researches into Their Ancient and Medieval Relations as Reprinted in Old Chinese Records*. Leipzig: Hirth, Kelly & Walsh, 1885.
Hodgson, B. H. "On the Tribes of Northern Tibet (Horyeul and Sokyeul) and of Sifan." In *Essays on the Languages, Literatures, and Religions of Nepal and Tibet* (London: Trubner, 1874).
_______ "Sifán and Hórsók Vocabularies." *Journal of the Asiatic Society of Bengal*, no. 22 (1874).
Hogberg, L. E. *The Mission Field in Russia and Chinese Turkestan*. Stockholm, 1910.
Hongladarom, Krisadawan. "Rgylathang Tibetan of Yunnan: A Preliminary Report." *Linguistics of the Tibeto-Burman Area* 19, no. 2 (1996).
Hong Mei. "A Closer Look at Beautiful Kunming." *China Tourism*, no. 47, n.d.
Honig, Emily. *Creating Chinese Ethnicity: Subei People in Shanghai, 1850-1980*. Boston: Yale University Press, 1992.
Hosanna Ministries. "Report on Xinjiang House Churches: Information for Prayer and Strategic Coordination." Hong Kong, September 1997.
Ho Ting-jui. *A Comparative Study of the Myths and Legends of the Formosan Aborigines*. Taipei: Orient Cultural Service, 1971.
Howorth, Henry H. *History of the Mongols from the Ninth to the Nineteenth Centuries*. 5 Vols. Originally 1876; Reprinted Taiwan: Ch'eng Wen, 1970.
Hsieh, Jiann. "Pai Yao's Ethnicity Through Their Own Document: A Preliminary Study of a Pai Yao Religious Book." In Chiao and Tapp (eds.), *Ethnicity and Ethnic Groups in China*.
Hsu Hung-pao [Xu Hongbao]. "The Lisus of the Nu River." *China Reconstructs* 14, no. 6 (1965).
Hsu Itang [Xu Yitang]. *Les trois Grandes Races de la Province du Yunnan*. Paris: Adrien-Maisonneuve, 1932.
Hu, S. Y. "Ethnobotany of the Gia-rung Tribe." Manuscript, Yale Divinity School, n.d.
Hu Yue, "In Tujia Country." *China Tourism*, no. 103, n.d.
Huang Baoshan. *Snowy Mountains and Grasslands: Travels in Northwestern Sichuan*. Beijing: Foreign Languages Press, 1990.
Huang Chang-lu. "How the Minorities in Yunnan Change." *Peking Review* 24, no. 17 (1958).
Huang Shoubao. *Ethnic Costumes from Guizhou*. Beijing: Foreign Languages Press, 1987.
Huang Xing. "On Writing Systems for China's Minorities Created by Foreign Missionaries." *International Journal of the Sociology of Language*, no. 97 (1992).
Huang Yu. "Preliminary Study of the Yao 'King Ping's Charter'." In Lemoine and Chiao (eds.), *The Yao of South China*.
Hua Nian. "Odd Customs in a Mountain Village." *China Tourism*, no. 84, n.d.
Hubbard, James M. "Problems in China." *National Geographic*, August 1900.
Huc, Abbe. *Christianity in China, Tartary and Thibet*. London: Brown, Green, Longmans & Roberts, 1857.
Hudden, Alfred C. *Head-Hunters*. London, 1932.
Hudspeth, W. H. *Stone Gateway and the Flowery Miao*. London: Cargate, 1937.
_______ "A Miao Quarterly Meeting." *The West China Missionary News*, January 1917.

Huffman, Franklin E. *Bibliography and Index of Mainland Southeast Asian Languages and Linguistics.* New Haven: Yale University Press, 1986.
Hugoniot, Richard D., ed. *A Biographical Index of the Lesser Known Languages and Dialects of India and Nepal.* Waxhaw: SIL, 1970.
Hui, Elaine. "The Paiwan People of Taiwan." *China Tourism,* no. 82, n.d.
Hui, Himsey. "The Bai." *China and the Church Today,* October 1985.
Hultvall, John. *Mission and Revolution in Central Asia: The Swedish Missions in East Turkestan 1892-1938.* Stockholm, 1981.
Hunter, Jane. *The Gospel of Gentility: American Women Missionary in Turn-of-the-Century China.* Boston: Yale University Press, 1984.
Hutton, M. H. "Fruit After Many Days." *China's Millions,* August 1936.
_______ "How the Message Came to the Black Miao." *China's Millions,* November 1937.
_______ "In Journeyings Among the Miao." *China's Millions,* June 1914.
_______ "The New Testament for the Black Miao." *China's Millions,* November 1935.
_______ "Steady Advancement." *China's Millions,* August 1937.
Institute for the Study of Human Issues. *Laku-English Dictionary.* Philadelphia, n.d.
Israeli, Raphael. *Muslims in China: A Study in Cultural Confrontation.* London: Curzon Press, 1980.
Issachar Frontier Missions Research. *Mongolia Challenge Report: A Summary of Current Spiritual Needs and a Strategy for Response.* Seattle: Issachar, 1984.
Jagchid, Sechin, and Paul Hyer. *Mongolia's Culture and Society.* Boulder: Westview, 1979.
Jamieson, C. E. "The Aborigines of West China." *China Journal of Science and Arts* 1, no. 4 (1923).
Janabel, Jiger. *The Golden Horde and the Formation of the Ethnic Kazakhs.* The Center for the Study of the Eurasian Nomads, n.d.
Janhunen, Juha. "Material on Manchurian Khamnigan Mongol." *Castrenianumin Toimitteita,* no. 37 (1990).
_______ "On the Position of Khamnigan Mongol." *Journal de la Société Finno-Ougrienne,* no. 84 (1992).
_______, and Tapani Salminen. *UNESCO Red Book on Endangered Languages: Northeast Asia.* Finland: University of Helsinki, 1996; quotes from this book has been taken from the UNESCO internet site.
Jarring, Gunnar. *Materials to the Knowledge of Eastern Turki.* Lund, 1946.
_______ *Matters of Ethnological Interest in Swedish Missionary Reports from Southern Sinkiang.* Lund, 1979.
Jia Lin. "Over the Dadu River." *China Tourism,* no. 60, n.d.
Jiangxi Educational Publishing. *Encyclopedic Dictionary of Chinese Linguistics (EDCL)* [Zhongguo Yuyanxue Dacidian]. Nanjing: Jiangxi Educational Publishing House, 1991.
Jiann Hsieh. "Pai Yao's ethnicity Through Their Own Document: A Preliminary Study of a Pai Yao Religious Book." In Chiao and Tapp, *Ethnicity and Ethnic Groups in China.*
Jeffrey, J. H. *Khams.* Devon: Arthur H. Stockwell, 1974.
Johnson, Michael. "Far Western Hmongic." Research manuscript, Thailand, February 1998.
_______ "An Overview of Hmongic Languages and Linguistics (including updated 1996 research)." Research manuscript, Thailand, 1995.
Johnston, Sir Reginald Fleming. *From Peking to Mandalay: A Journey from North China to Burma through Tibetan Ssuch'uan and Yunnan.* London: John Murray, 1908.
Johnstone, Patrick. *Operation World.* England: STL Books and WEC Publications, 1987.
_______ *Operation World.* Grand Rapids: Zondervan, 1993.
Jun Feng. "Rolling Uplands of Northwestern Guizhou." *China Tourism,* no. 111, n.d.
_______ "Xishuangbanna: Homeland of Minorities." *China Tourism,* no. 72, n.d.
Jun Su. "A Trip to the Three Islands Inhabited by the Jing People." *China Tourism,* no. 77, n.d.
Kakuk, Suzanne. "Sur la Phonetique de la Langue̹ Salare." *Acta Orientalia Hungaricae,* no. 15 (1962).
Kammerer, Cornelia Ann. "Customs and Christian Conversion Among the Akha Highlanders of Burma and Thailand." *American Ethnologist* 17, no. 2 (May 1990).
Kandre, Peter. "Autonomy and Integration of Social Systems: The Iu Mien ('Yao' or 'Man') Mountain Population and their Neighbors." In Peter Kunstadter (ed.), *Southeast Asian Tribes, Minorities and Nations.*
Kang Enda. "The Yi Minority's Naked Leopard Dance." *China Tourism,* no. 172, November 1994.
Kang Jie. "The Buryats From Siberia." *China Tourism,* no. 83, n.d.
Kansakar, Tej R. "Multilingualism and the Language Situation in Nepal." *Linguistics of the Tibeto-Burman Area* 19, no. 2 (1996).
Karnow, Stanley. *Vietnam: A History.* New York: The Viking Press, 1983.
Katzner, Kenneth. *The Languages of the World.* New York: Funk & Wagnalls, 1977.
Kaunay, Adrien. *Histoire des Missions de Chine Mission du Setchoan.* Paris: P. Tequi, 1920.
Keen, F. G. B. *The Meo of Northwest Thailand. Wellington,* New Zealand: R. E. Owen, 1966.
Ke Ji. "The Amei People of Taiwan." *China Tourism,* no. 43, n.d.
_______ "The Colourful Tajiks." *China Tourism,* no. 42, n.d.
_______ "Wonderful Xibe Archers." *China Tourism,* no. 42, n.d.
Kendall, Elliot R. *Beyond the Clouds: The Story of Samuel Pollard of South-west China.* London: Cargate Press, 1947.
_______ *Eyes of the Earth: The Diary of Samuel Pollard.* London: Cargate Press, 1954.
Kewley, Vanya. *Tibet: Behind the Ice Curtain.* London: Grafton Books, 1990.
Ke Xiangfeng. "Marriage Among the Independent Lolos of Western China." *American Journal of Sociology,* no. 54 (1949).
Khongkum, Acharn Theraphan. "The Thu Lao." In Edmonson and Solnit (eds.), *Comparative Kadai.*
King, John, ed. *Karakoram Highway: The High Road to China.* Hawthorn, Australia: Lonely Planet Publications, 1989.
Kingsmill, Thomas W. "Han Wu Tu, and the Aboriginal Tribes on the Southwestern Frontier of China." *China Review,* no. 25 (1900).
Kloss, Heinz, and Grant D. McConnell. *Linguistic Composition of the Nations of the World 1: Central and Western South Asia.* Quebec: International Center for Research and Bilingualism, 1974.
Komonkitiskun, Jiranan. "Lawa Pronouns." *Mon-Khmer Studies* 21 (1992).
Kotturan, George. *The Himalayan Gateway: History and Culture of Sikkim.* New Delhi: Sterling, 1983.
Krader, Lawrence. *Peoples of Central Asia.* Indiana University Press, 1971.
_______ *Social Organization of the Mongol Turkic Pastoral Nomads.* The Hague: Mouton, 1963.
Kuhn, Isobel. *Ascent to the Tribes: Pioneering in North Thailand.* London: OMF, 1968.
_______ *In the Arena.* Chicago: Moody Press, 1958.
_______ *Nest Above Abyss.* Philadelphia: CIM, 1947.
_______ *Second Mile People.* Kent: OMF, 1982.
_______ *Stones of Fire.* Chicago: Moody Press, 1960.
Kuhn, John. *We Found a Hundred Tribes.* London: CIM, 1945.

Kuhn, Philip A. *Rebellion and Its Enemies in Late Imperial China: Militarization and Social Structure 1796-1864.* Cambridge, Mass.: Cambridge University Press, 1980.

Kung Tien Min. *Christianity in the T'ang Dynasty.* Hong Kong: Council on Christian Literature for Overseas Chinese, 1960.

Kunstadter, Peter, ed. *South East Asia Tribes, Minorities and Nations.* 2 Vols. Princeton: Princeton University Press, 1967.

Kun Xin. "The White-Trousered Yao." *China Tourism*, no. 80, n.d.

Kwanten, Luc Herman M. *Imperial Nomads: A History of Central Asia, 500-1500.* Philadelphia: University of Pennsylvania Press, 1979.

Lacouperie, Terrien de. *Languages of China Before the Chinese.* London, 1887.

Lam Ping-Fai, Robert, ed. *Ethnic Costumes of the Miao People in China.* Hong Kong: Urban Council, 1985.

Lamb, Harold. *Genghis Khan: Emperor of All Men.* New York: McBride, 1927.

Lambert, Tony. *The Resurrection of the Chinese Church.* Illinois: OMF, 1994.

_______ "The Challenge of China's Minority Peoples." *Chinese Around the World*, April 1991.

_______ "Christianity and Tibet." *Pray for China Fellowship*, 1996.

_______ "A Visit to Ningxia Province." *China Insight*, August-September 1993.

Langlois, John D., ed. *China Under Mongol Rule.* Princeton: Princeton University Press, 1981.

Larson, Frans August. Larson, *Duke of Mongolia.* Boston: Little, Brown & Co., 1930.

_______ *On Tramp Among the Mongols.* Boston: Little, Brown & Co., n.d.

Latourette, Kenneth Scott. *The Chinese: Their History and Culture.* New York: Macmillan, 1941.

_______ *A History of Christian Missions in China.* New York: Macmillan, 1929.

_______ *A History of the Expansion of Christianity.* 7 Vols. New York: Harper, 1937.

Lattimore, Owen. *Mongolian Folktales and Stories.* Ulan Bator: State Publishing House, 1979.

_______ "Byroads and Backwoods of Manchuria." *National Geographic*, January 1932.

_______ "The Gold Tribe 'FIsh-Skin Tatars' of the Lower Sungari." *Memoires of the American Anthropological Association*, no. 40 (1933).

Lau, Paul. "A Visit to the Xiaohua Miao Minority." *China Tourism*, no. 143, May 1992.

Laufer, Berthold. "The Si-hia Language, a Study in Indo-Chinese Philology." *Toung Pao* 17, no. 2 (1944).

Law, Gail. *Chinese Churches Handbook.* Hong Kong: Chinese Coordination Centre for World Evangelism, 1982.

Laycock, Donald C., and Werner Winter, eds. *A World of Language: Papers Presented to Professor S. A. Wurm on His 65th Birthday.* Canberra: The Australian National University, 1987.

Lazzarotto, Angelo S. *The Catholic Church in Post-Mao China.* Hong Kong: The Holy Spirit Study Center, 1983.

Leach, Edmund. *Political Systems of Highland Burma: A Study of Kachin Social Structure.* London: Bell, 1954.

Learner, Frank Doggett. *Rusty Hinges: A Story of Closed Doors Beginning to Open in North-East Tibet.* London: CIM, 1933.

Le Bar, Frank M.; Gerald C. Hickey, and John K. Musgrave. *Ethnic Groups of Insular Southeast Asia.* New Haven: HRAF Press, 1972.

_______ *Ethnic Groups of Mainland Southeast Asia.* New Haven: HRAF Press, 1964.

Le Bar, Frank, and Adrienne Suddard, eds. *Laos: Its People, Its Society, Its Culture.* New Haven: HRAF Press, 1960.

Lee, Chae-Jin. *China's Korean Minority: The Politics of Ethnic Education.* Colorado: Westview Press, 1986.

Lee, Jacob D. H., ed. *China's 55 Ethnic Minorities.* Watson, Australia: YWAM Institute of Asian Studies, 1995.

Lee Shiu-Keung. *The Cross and the Lotus.* Hong Kong: Christian Study Center on Chinese Religion and Culture, 1971.

Legendre, Aime-Francois. "The Lolos of Kientchang, Western China." Smithsonian Institution Annual Report, 1910.

_______ "Voyage d'exploration au Yunnan Central et Septentrional, Populations: Chinois et Aborigenes." *Societe d'Anthropologie de Paris, Bulletin et Memoires*, Series 6:4, no. 5 (1913).

Legge, James. *The Nestorian Monument of Hsi-an Fu in Shen-Hsi, China.* London: Trubner, 1888.

_______ *The Notions of the Chinese Concerning God and Spirits.* Hong Kong: Hong Kong Register Office, 1852.

Lehman, Winfred P., ed. *Language and Linguistics in the People's Republic of China.* Austin: University of Texas Press, 1975.

Lei Hongan. *Traditional Religious Beliefs of the Minority Nationalities.* Kunming: Yunnan Ethnic Research Institute, 1984.

Lemoine, Jacques. "Ethnicity, Culture and Development Among Some Minorities of the People's Republic of China." In Chiao and Tapp (eds.), *Ethnicity and Ethnic Groups in China.*

Lemoine, Jacques, and Chiao Chien, eds. *The Yao of South China: Recent International Studies.* France: Pangu, 1991.

Leslie, Donald. *The Survival of the Chinese Jews: The Jewish Community of Kaifeng.* Leiden: E. J. Brill, 1972.

Leslie, Dald Daniel. *Islam in Traditional China.* Canberra, Australia: Canberra College of Advanced Education, 1986.

Leung Sze Tai. "Christmas at the Foot of Five-Finger Mountain." *Bridge*, no. 27, January-February 1988.

Levine, Nancy E. *The Dynamics of Polyandry, Kinship, Domesticity, and Population on the Tibetan Border.* Chicago: University of Chicago Press, 1988.

Lewis, Paul W. *Ethnographic Notes on the Akha of Burma.* 4 Vols. New Haven: HRAF Press, 1968-70.

_______ "The Rice Theme in the Akha Culture." *Journal of Sociology and Anthropology* 2, no. 2 (Thailand: Chiang Mai University, 1969).

_______ "The Role and Function of the Akha Village Priest." *Behavior Science Notes* 3, no. 4 (1968).

_______, and Elaine Lewis. *Peoples of the Golden Triangle.* New York: Thames & Hudson, 1984.

Leyseen, J. *The Cross Over China's Wall.* Beijing: The Lazarist Church, 1941.

Liang Ming. "The Buyang Language." In Edmonson, *Kadai.*

_______ "The Lachi Language." In Edmonson, *Kadai.*

_______ "On the Affiliation of the Ge-Yang branch of Kadai." In Edmonson, *Kadai.*

_______ "The Origins of the Kam-Sui Peoples." *Zhongguo Minzushi Yanjiu* (1987).

Li Cai. "Xinjiang: Wonderland of Sight and Colours." *China Tourism*, no. 42, n.d.

Li Chi. *The Formation of the Chinese People: An Anthropological Inquiry.* New York: Russell & Russell, 1928.

Li Chungsheng. "The Xiuba People." *China Pictorial*, August 1991.

Li, Dun J. *The Ageless Chinese: A History.* New York: Charles Scribner's Sons, 1978.

Li Fang-Gui. *A Handbook of Comparative Tai.* Honolulu: University of Hawaii Press, 1977.

_______ "Notes on the Mak Language." *Academia Sinica Monographs Series A*, no. 20 (Institute of History and Philology, 1940).

_______ "A Preliminary Comparison of Three Sui Dialects." *Academia Sinica* (Institute of History and Philology, 1951).

_______ "The Songs of the T'ien-Pao, With a Phonological Sketch." *Academia Sinica: Bulletin of the Institute of Ethnology*, no. 30 (1970).

Li, F. K. "Notes on the Ten (Yanghuang) Language." *Academia Sinica: Bulletin of the Institute of History and Philology*, nos. 36 (1966), 37 (1967), 40 (1969).

_______ "Notes on the T'en or Yanghwang Language: Introduction and Phonology." *Bulletin of the Museum of Far Eastern Antiquities*, no. 36 (1966).

Li Jie. "The Mysterious Ceremonies of Guizhou's Tujia Minority." *China Tourism*, no. 154, April 1993.

Li Jinfang. "Bugan: A New Mon-Khmer Language of Yunnan Province, China." *Mon-Khmer Studies*, no. 26 (1996).

Li Kai. "Xinjiang: Wonderland of Sight and Colours." *China Tourism*, no. 42, n.d.

Li Mo. "The Ancient Distribution of the Yao in Guangdong." In Lemoine and Chiao (eds.), *The Yao of South China*.

Li Ping. "The Flower Street Festival of the Dai." *China Tourism*, no. 165, April 1994.

Li Shulan, ed. *Panorama of Guangxi Tourist Areas*. Guangxi: Lijiang Publishing House, n.d.

Li Teng Hsiu. "The Sacred Mission: An American Missionary Family in the Lahu and Wa Districts of Yunnan." Thesis, Baylor University, Texas, 1987.

Li, Vladimir. *Some Approaches to the Classification of Small Ethnic Groups in South China*. Prague: Institute of Oriental Studies, n.d.

Li Youyi. *Ethnology in China*. Griffith University Press, 1980.

Lieu, Samuel N. C. *Manichaeism in the Late Roman Empire and Medieval China*. Tubingen, 1992.

_______ *The Religion of Light: An Introduction to the History of Manichaeism in China*. Centre of Asian Studies, University of Hong Kong, 1979.

Liétard, Alfred. *Au Yun-Nan, Les Lolo p'o: Une Tribu des Aborigenes de la Chine Meridionale*. Munster: Aschendorff, 1913.

Les trois Grandes Races de la Province du Yunnan. Paris: Adrien-Maisonneuve, 1904.

_______ "Le District des Lolos A-chi." *Les Missions Catholiques*, no. 36 (1904).

_______ "Notes sur les Dialectes Lo-Lo." *Ecole Francaise d'Extreme-Orient* 9, no. 3 (1909).

Lin Jian, and Chen Shizhe. "Fishing Village of Persistent Traditions." *China Tourism*, no. 114, n.d.

Lin Jianxin. "An Investigation of the Ai-Cham Language." in SIL, *Comparative Kadai*.

Lin Lai. "A Photo Safari Along the Fujian Coast." *China Tourism*, no. 87, n.d.

Lin Shao-Yang. *A Chinese Appeal to Christendom* (1900).

Lin Xiangron. "Sound System of the Zhou Keji (Ma'erkang) Dialect of Jiarong." *Yuyin Yanjiu*, no. 2 (1988).

Lin Yuehua [Lin Yaohua]. *The Lolo of Liang Shan*. New Haven: HRAF Press, 1980.

_______ "A Brief Account of Yenching Expedition to the Lolo Community." *West China Border Research Society Journal Series A*, no. 15 (1944).

_______ "Kinship System of the Lolo." *Harvard Journal of Asiatic Studies*, no. 9 (1946).

_______ "The Miao-Man Peoples of Kweichow." *Harvard Journal of Asiatic Studies* 5, no. 3 (January 1941).

Litzinger, Ralph A. "Making Histories: Contending Conceptions of the Yao Past." In Harrell (ed.), *Cultural Encounters on China's Ethnic Frontiers*.

Livo, Norma J., and Dia Cha. *Folk Stories of the Hmong*. Libraries Unlimited, 1991.

Loane, Marcus L. *The Story of the China Inland Mission in Australia and New Zealand 1890-1964*. Australia: CIM, 1965.

_______ *They Were Pilgrims*. Sydney: Angus & Robertson, 1970.

Lopatin, Ivan A. *The Cult of the Dead Among the Natives of the Amur Basin*. The Hague: Mouton, 1960.

Loup, Robert. *Martyr in Tibet: The Heroic Life and Death of Father Maurice Tourney, St. Bernard Missionary to Tibet*. New York: David McKay Co., 1956.

Lovelace, Richard F. *Dynamics of Spiritual Life: An Evangelical Theology of Revival*. Downers Grove: Inter-Varsity Press, 1980.

Lovett, Richard. *James Gilmour and His Boys*. London: Religious Tract Society, 1894.

_______ *James Gilmour of Mongolia*. London: Religious Tract Society, 1893.

Lowis, C. C. *Tribes of Burma*. Rangoon: Government Printing, 1910.

Luke, H. C. *Mosul and Its Minorities*. London: M. Hopkinson, 1925.

Luo Yunzhi. "The Aini People in Xishuangbanna." *China Tourism*, no. 179, June 1995.

_______ "The Jinuo People's Sacrifice to the Rice God." *China Tourism*, no. 162, January 1994.

Lupas, Liana, and Erroll F. Rhodes. *Scriptures of the World: A Compilation of the 2,018 Languages in Which at Least One Book of the Bible Has Been Published Since the Bible Was First Printed by Johann Gutenberg*. Reading: United Bible Societies, 1993.

Lutz, Jessie Gregory, and Roland Ray Lutz. *Hakka Chinese Confront Protestant Christianity 1850-1900: With the Autobiographies of Eight Hakka Christians, and Commentary*. Armonk, N.Y.: M.E. Sharpe, 1998.

Lyall, Leslie T. *A Passion for the Impossible: The China Inland Mission 1865-1965*. Chicago: Moody Press, 1965.

MacFarquhar, Roderick. "The Minorities." *New Leader* 42, no. 23 (1959).

MacGillivray, D., ed. *A Century of Missions in China 1807-1907*. Shanghai: Christian Literature Society for China, 1907.

MacGowan, J. *The Imperial History of China*. Shanghai: American Presbyterian Mission Press, 1906.

Mackerras, Colin. *China's Minorities: Integration and Modernization in the Twentieth Century*. Hong Kong: Oxford University Press, 1994.

_______ *The Uighur Empire According to the T'ang Dynastic Histories: A Study in Sino-Uighur Relations 774-840*. Canberra: Australian National University, 1988.

MacLean, Arthur John, and William Henry Browne. *The Catholicos of the East and His People*. London: SPCK, 1892.

Ma Changshou. "The Genealogical Table of the Lolos at Liangshan, Western Szechuan." *Bianjiang Yenjiu Luncong* 44, no. 4 (1942).

Maddieson, Ian. "Tone in Utsat." In *Tonality in Austronesian Languages: Oceanic Linguistics Special Publication*, no. 24 (Honolulu: University of Hawaii Press, 1993).

Maguire, Theopane. *Hunan Harvest*. Milwaukee: Bruce, 1946.

Major Statistics of the 1982 Census. Beijing: People's Republic of China State Statistics Bureau, October 1982.

Ma Nai Hui, and Su Jun Hui, eds. *China's Minority Nationalities*. Beijing: China Nationalities Photographic Art Publishing, 1988.

Marsden, William, trans. *The Travels of Marco Polo*. New York: Dell, 1961.

Martin, Samuel. *Dagur Mongolian Grammar: Texts and Lexicon Based on the Speech of Peter Onan*. Bloomington: Indiana University Press, 1961.

Matisoff, James A. *The Grammar of Lahu*. Berkeley: University of California Press, 1973.

_______ "Languages and Dialects of Tibeto-Burman." *STEDT Monograph II Series* (Berkeley: University of California, 1998).

_______ "Sangkong of Yunnan, Secondary 'Verb Pronominalization in Southern Loloish'." *Linguistics of the Tibeto-Burman Area* 16, no. 2 (1993).

Ma Xueliang. "Minority Languages of China." *China Reconstructs* 3, no. 3 (1954).

_______ "My Research Career." *Linguistics of the Tibeto-Burman Area* 12, no. 1 (1989).

_______ "New Script for China's Minorities." *China Reconstructs* 4, no. 2 (1955).
_______ "New Scripts for China's Minorities." *China Reconstructs* 11, no. 8 (1962).
Ma Yaojun. "Life of Chinese-Russian Descendants in Inner Mongolia." *China Tourism*, no. 83, n.d.
Ma Yin. *China's Minority Nationalities*. Beijing: Foreign Languages Press, 1989.
_______ *Questions and Answers about China's Minority Nationalities*. Beijing: New World Press, 1985.
McCabe, Michael. "The Jews of China." *San Jose Mercury News*, 17 November 1984.
McGavran, Donald. *Understanding Church Growth*. Michigan: Eerdmans, 1970.
McGilvary, Daniel. *A Half Century Among the Siamese and the Lao*. New York: Fleming H. Revell, 1912.
McKhann, Charles F. "The Naxi and the Nationalities Question." In Harrell (ed.), *Cultural Encounters on China's Ethnic Frontiers*.
McKinnon, John, and W. Bhrukrasri, eds. *Highlanders of Thailand*. Kuala Lumpur: Oxford University Press, 1983.
Medary, Marjorie. *Each One Take One: Frank Laubach, Friend to Millions*. New York: David McKay, 1954.
Mehra, G. N. *Bhutan*. New Delhi: Vikas, 1974.
Menges, K. H. *The Turkic Language and Peoples*. Wisbaden: Otto Harrassowitz, 1968.
Metford, Beatrix. *Where China Meets Burma*. London: Blackie & Son, 1935.
Miao, Mike, and Melissa Miao. "The Miao of China." Prayer guide, Hong Kong, 1994.
Mickey, Margaret P. *A Bibliography of South and Southwest China, With Special Reference to the Non-Chinese Peoples and their Relation to the Peoples of Adjacent Areas: Works in Western Languages*. New York: Viking Fund, 1948.
Miller, Lucien, ed.; Guo Xu, trans. *South of the Clouds: tales from Yunnan*. Seattle: University of Washington Press, 1994.
Milliken, Stuart. "SIL China Nationalities and Languages Files." Unpublished research paper, Guangzhou, 1993.
Minford, John, trans. *Favourite Folktales of China*. Beijing: New World Press, 1983.
Ming. "A Young Woman Evangelist in a Booming Town." *Bridge*, no. 52, March-April 1992.
Ming Yin. *United and Equal: The Progress of China's Minority Nationalities*. Beijing: Foreign Languages Press, 1977.
Mitsumori, Sadao. *Biruma, Shan no Shizen to Minzoku* [The Land and Peoples of Burma and the Shan States]. Tokyo: Nihon Hyoronsha, 1945.
Moffett, Samuel Hugh. *A History of Christianity in Asia* 1: *Beginnings to 1500*. San Francisco: Harper, 1992.
Moody, Edward H. *Sam Pollard*. London: Oliphants, n.d.
Morse, Eugene. *Exodus to a Hidden Valley*. New York: Reader's Digest Press, 1974.
Morse, Robert. "China's Peoples, One Fourth of Planet Earth." *North Burma Christian Mission Newsletter*, September 1990.
_______ "A study of the unidentified groups of Southwest China." Unpublished research, Chiang Mai, Thailand, 1991.
Morton, W. Scott. *China: Its History and Culture*. New York: McGraw Hill, 1980.
Moseley, Christopher, and R. E. Asher, eds. *Atlas of the World's Languages*. London: Routledge, 1994.
Moseley, George V. H., III. *The Consolidation of the South China Frontier*. Berkeley: University of California Press, 1973.
_______ *The Party and the National Question in China*. London: Harvard University Press, 1967.
_______ "Voices in the Minority." *Far Eastern Economic Review* 55, no. 9 (1967).
Moser, Leo J. *The Chinese Mosaic: The Peoples and Provinces of China*. Boulder: Westview Press, 1985.
Moses, L., and S.A. Halkovic. *Introduction to Mongolian History and Culture*. Bloomington: University of Indiana Press, n.d.
Mottin, J. *The History of the Hmong (Meo)*. Bangkok: Rung Ruang Ratana Printing, 1980.
Moule, Arthur Christopher. *Christians in China Before the Year 1550*. London: SPCK, 1930.
_______, and Paul Pelliot. *Marco Polo: The Description of the World*. 2 Vols. London: Routledge, 1938.
Mulholland, T. "Amongst the Tribes." *China's Millions*, July 1932.
Murray, Edward. "With the Nomads of Central Asia: A Summer's Sojourn in the Tekes Valley, Plateau Paradise of Mongol and Turkic Tribes." *National Geographic*, January 1936.
Muse, Audrey. "A Profile on the Jiarong People of China." Report, May 1996.
Myrdal, Jan. *The Silk Road: A Journey from the High Pamirs and Ili through Sinkiang and Kansu*. New York: Pantheon Books, 1979.
Nagano, Yasuhiko. *A Historical Study of the Jiarong Verb System*. Tokyo: Seishido, 1984.
Nairne, W. P. *Gilmour of the Mongols*. London: Hodder & Stoughton, 1924.
Nationalities Affairs Commission of Guangxi Zhuang Autonomous Region. *The Yao Nationality*. Nanning: People's Publishing House, 1990.
Nedyalkov, Igor. "Evenki." *Topological Studies in Language*, no. 29 (1994).
Neill, Stephen. *A History of Christian Missions*. New York: Penguin, 1964.
Neterowicz, Eva M. *The Tragedy of Tibet*. Washington DC: The Council for Social and Economic Studies, 1989.
New World Press. *Xinjiang, the Land and the People*. Beijing: New World Press, 1989.
_______ *Yunnan Travelogue: 100 Days in Southwest China*. Beijing: New World Press, 1983.
Ni Dabai, "Yangfeng Mak of Libo County." in SIL, *Comparative Kadai*.
Nida, Eugene A., and William A. Smalley. *Introducing Animism*. New York: Friendship Press, 1959.
Nishida, Tatsuo. "Bisugo no Keito" [The Lineage of the Bisu]. *Tonan Ajia Kenkyu* 4, no. 3 (1966).
_______ "Bisugo no Kenkyu: Taikoku Hokubu ni Okeru Bisuzoku no Gengo no Yobiteki Kenkyu" [A Preliminary Study of the Bisu Language]. *Tonan Ajia Kenkyu* 4, no. 1 (1966).
Niu Shao. "The Lahu Christians." *Bridge*, no. 43, September-October 1990.
Norbu, Dawa. *Red Star Over Tibet*. New Delhi: Sterling, 1987.
Norbu, Thubten Jigme, and Colin M. Turnbull. *Tibet: Its History, Religion and People*. New York: Penguin Books, 1987.
Norman, Jerry. *Chinese*. Cambridge: Cambridge University Press, 1988.
_______ *A Concise Manchu-English Lexicon*. Seattle: University of Washington Press, 1978.
Norman, Jerry, and Paul Georg Von Mollendorf. *A Manchu Grammar With Analyzed Texts*. Shanghai: American Presbyterian Mission Press, 1892.
North China Daily News & Herald. Directory of Protestant Missions in China 1934. Shangai, 1934.
North, Eric M. *The Book of a Thousand Tongues*. New York: American Bible Society, 1938; Detroit: Tower Books, 1971.
Ortner, Sherry B. *Sherpas Through Their Rituals*. Cambridge: Cambridge University Press, 1978.
Ou Yansheng. "The Yiche People's Kuzhazha Festival in the Ailao Mountains." *China Tourism*, no. 189, April 1996.
Ouyang Changpei, "Visiting the Horn-Haired Miao People." *China Tourism*, no. 192, July 1996.
Page, Homer. *The Little World of Laos*. New York: Charles Scribbner's Sons, 1959.

Pan Chengqian. "Yao Dialectology." In Lemoine and Chiao, *The Yao of South China.*
Parker, E. H. *A Thousand Years of the Tatars.* London: Kegan Paul, Trench & Trubner, 1895.
Parkin, Robert. *A Guide to Austroasiatic Speakers and Their Languages: Oceanic Linguistics Special Publication*, no. 23 (University of Hawaii Press, 1991).
Parsons, Hy. "Aborigines in West China." *Missionary Review of the World* 54, no. 2 (1931).
Parsons, William Barclay. "Hunan: The Closed Province of China." *National Geographic*, October 1900.
Patterson, George. *Requiem for Tibet.* London: Aurem, 1990.
Paulsen, Debbie. "A Phonological Reconstruction of Proto-Plang." *Mon-Khmer Studies* 18-19 (1992).
Peace Books Company. *Life Styles of China's Ethnic Minorities.* Hong Kong, 1991.
Peissel, Michael. *Cavaliers of Kham: The Secret War in Tibet.* London: Heinemann, 1972.
Pelkey, Jamin R. "Initial Investigative Report on the Yi Peoples of Yuxi Prefecture." Unpublished report, Thailand, November 1998.
_______ "Initial Investigative Report on the Yi Peoples of Honghe Prefecture." Unpublished report, Thailand, February 1999.
_______ "Yunnan's Myriad Yi: Profiles on the Peoples Classified as 'Yi' in Yunnan Province." Unpublished report, Thailand, May 1999.
Perazic, Elizabeth. "Little Laos: Next Door to Red China." *National Geographic*, January 1960.
Persson, C. "Christianity in the Tarim Basin." *Friends of Moslems*, April 1940.
Philipps, E. D. *The Royal Hordes: Nomad People of the Steppes.* London: Thames & Hudson, 1965.
Pickens, Claude L. Jr. *Annotated Bibliography of Literature on Moslems in China.* Hankow: Society of the Friends of the Muslims in China, 1950.
Ping-Ti Ho. *Studies on the Population of China 1368-1953.* Cambridge, Mass: Harvard University Press, 1959.
Piper, John. *Let the Nations Be Glad: The Supremacy of God in Missions.* Grand Rapids: Baker, 1993.
Playfair, George Macdonald Home. "The Miaotzu of Kewichow and Yunnan From Chinese Sources." *China Review*, no. 5 (1876).
Plymire, David. *High Adventure in Tibet.* Springfield: Gospel Publishing House, 1959.
Pollard, Samuel. *In Unknown China.* London: Seeley, Service & Co., 1921.
_______ *The Story of the Miao.* London: Henry Hooks, 1919.
_______ *Tight Corner in China.* London: Andrew Crombie, 1921.
Pollard, Walter. *The Life of Sam Pollard in China: An Account of the Intrepid Life of Adventure, Danger, Toil and Travel of a Missionary in The Far and Little Known Interior of the Vast Chinese Empire.* London: Seeley, Service & Co., 1928.
Pollak, Michael. *Mandarins, Jews and Missionaries: The Jewish Experience in the Chinese Empire.* Philadelphia: Jewish Publication Society of America, 1980.
Pollock, John C. *A Foreign Devil in China: The Story of Dr. L. Nelson Bell, An American Surgeon in China.* Grand Rapids: Zondervan, 1971.
_______ *Hudson Taylor and Maria.* New York: McGraw-Hill, 1962.
_______ *Victims of the Long March.* Waco: Word Books, 1970.
Polo, Marco. *The Book of Ser Marco Polo, the Venetian, Concerning the Kingdoms and Marvels of the East.* 2 Vols. Translated by Henry Yule. London: John Murray, 1903.
_______ *The Travels of Marco Polo.* New York: Penguin, 1958.
_______ *The Travels of Marco Polo: The Complete Yule-Cordier Edition.* New York: Dover Publications, 1903.
Poppe, Nicholas. *Mongolian Language Handbook.* Washington: Center for Applied Linguistics, 1970.
Poppe, N. N. *Dagurskoe Narechie* [The Daur Dialect]. Leningrad, 1930.
Popper, Paul. "Cane Bridges of Asia." *National Geographic*, August 1948.
Population Census Office of the State Council. *The Population Atlas of China.* Hong Kong: Oxford University Press, 1987.
Porteous, Gladstone. "Tribe After Tribe Being Reached." *China's Millions* (Australasian edition), February 1919.
Prawdin, Michael. *The Mongol Empire: Its Rise and Legacy.* London: Allen & Unwin, 1940.
Pray for the Hui. Prayer Guide, n.p., 1998.
Pruen, Mrs. *The Provinces of Western China.* London: CIM, 1906.
Pu Kuei-chung. "Yi Slaves of Xiaoliangshan Head for Socialism." *Guangming Ribao*, 9 September 1958.
Pulleybank, E. G. *The Chinese and their Neighbors in Prehistoric and Early Historic Times.* Berkeley: University of California Press, 1983.
Purnell, Herbert C. "The Metrical Structure of Yiu Mien Secular Songs." In Lemoine and Chiao, *The Yao of South China.*
Qiu Pu. *The Oroqens: China's Nomadic Hunters.* Beijing: Foreign Languages Press, 1983.
Quincy, Keith. *Hmong: A History of a People.* Cheney: Eastern Washington University Press, 1995.
Radcliffe, Lawrence B. "A Field Worker Speaks Out About the Rush to Reach All Peoples." *Mission Frontiers* 20, nos. 1&2, January-February 1998.
Ramsey, S. Robert. *The Languages of China.* Princeton: Princeton University Press, 1987.
Rao Fengqi. "Why Does Putian County Produce So Many Athletes?" *China Reconstructs*, May 1983.
Raqquete, Gustav. "Eastern Turkestan as a Mission Field." *International Review of Foreign Missions* 14 (1925).
Rattenbury, Harold B. *Advance in Southwest China.* London: Methodist Missionary Society, 1943.
Reimer, Johannes. *Operation Soviet Union.* Fresno, CA: Logos, 1990.
Reischauer, Edwin O., and J. K. Fairbank. *East Asia: The Great Tradition.* Boston: Houghton Mifflin, 1958.
Richardson, Don. *Eternity in Their Hearts.* California: Regal Books, 1981.
Richardson, Hugh E. *Tibet and Its History.* London: Oxford University Press, 1962.
Rijnhart, Susie Carson. *With the Tibetans in Tent and Temple.* Chicago: Fleming H. Revell, 1901.
Rizvi, Janet. *Ladakh: Crossroads of High Asia.* Delhi: Oxford, 1983.
Robinson, Joan. "National Minorities in Yunnan." *Eastern Horizon* 14, no. 4 (1975).
Robson, William. *Griffith John: Founder of the Hankow Mission.* New York: Fleming H. Revell, c.1890.
Rock, Joseph F. C. *The Ancient Nakhi Kingdom of Southwest China.* 2 Vols. Cambridge: Harvard University Press, 1947.
_______ "The Glories of the Minya Konka." *National Geographic*, October 1930.
_______ "Konka Risumgongba: Holy Mountain of the Outlaws." *National Geographic*, July 1931.
_______ "The Land of the Yellow Lama." *National Geographic*, April 1925.
_______ "Life Among the Lamas of Choni." *National Geographic*, November 1928.
_______ "Seeking the Mountains of Mystery." *National Geographic*, February 1930.
_______ "Through the Great River Trenches of Asia." *National Geographic*, August 1926.
Rockhill, William Woodville. *The Journey of William of Rubruck to the Eastern Parts, 1253-55, With Two Accounts of the Earlier Journey of John of Pian de Carpine.* London: Hakluyt Society, 1900.
_______ *The Land of the Lamas.* New York: Century Company, 1891.

Rong Mei. "Jumi, Zhemotuona et Loulan, trois Anciens Royaumes." *China Tourism*, no. 82, n.d.

________ "On the Sichuan-Tibet Highway." *China Tourism*, no.74, n.d.

Rorak, Gloria. "Life Among the Lahu." *Catholic Life*, November 1969.

Rose, Archibald. "The Reaches of the Upper Salween." *Geographical Journal* 34, no. 6 (1909).

________, and J. Coggin Brown. "Lisu (Yawyin) Tribes of the China-Burma Frontier." *Royal Asiatic Society of Bengal*, no. 3 (1911).

Rossabi, Morris. *China Among Equals: The Middle Kingdom and Its Neighbors, Tenth-Fourteenth Centuries.* Berkeley: University of California Press, 1983.

________ *Khubilai Khan: His Life and Times.* Berkeley: University of California Press, 1988.

Rossi, Gail. *The Dong People of China: A Hidden Civilization.* Singapore: Hagley & Hoyle, 1990.

Roux, Henri. "Deux Tribus de la Region de Phongsalay (Laos Septentrional)." *Ecole Francaise d'Extreme-Orient*, no. 24 (1924).

Rowell, Galen. "Nomads of China's West." *National Geographic*, February 1982.

Rubel, Paula G. *The Kalmyk Mongols: A Study in Continuity and Change.* Bloomington: Indiana University Publications, 1967.

Ruxian Yan. "Marriage, Family and Social Progress of China's Minority Nationalities." In Chiao and Tapp, *Ethnicity and Ethnic Groups in China.*

Ryan, Nancy, "Jews in the Far East Have Rich and Varied Roots." *Chicago Tribune*, 23 January 1987.

Saeki, P. Yoshiro. *The Nestorian Documents and Relics in China.* Tokyo: Maruzen, 1951.

Sainson, Camille. *Nan-ychao Ye-che.* Paris: E. Leroux, 1904.

Saklani, Girija. *The Uprooted Tibetans in India.* New Delhi: Cosmo, 1984.

Sallisbury, Harrison E. *The Long March: The Untold Story.* London: Macmillan, 1985.

Samolin, William. *East Turkistan to the Twelfth Century: A Brief Political Survey.* The Hague: Mouton, 1964.

Sarep, Hpung. "Rgylathang Tibetan of Yunnan: A Preliminary Report." *Linguistics of the Tibeto-Burman Area* 19, no. 2 (1996).

Saunders, J. J. *The History of the Mongol Conquests.* London: Routledge & Kegan Paul, 1971.

Savina, F. M. *Histoire des Miao.* Hong Kong: Société des Missions Etrangeres des Paris, 1930.

Schein, Louisa. "The Miao in Contemporary China: A Preliminary Overview." In Hendricks et al. (eds.), *The Hmong in Transition* (New York: Center for Migration Studies, 1986).

Schmidlin, Joseph. *Catholic Mission History.* Illinois: Mission Press, 1933.

Schram, Louis M. J. *The Monquors of the Kansu-Tibetan Frontier, Part I: Their Origin, History and Social Organization.* Philadelphia: American Philios. Society, 1954.

________ *The Monquors of the Kansu-Tibetan Frontier, Part III: Records of the Monquor Clans.* Philadelphia: American Philios. Society, 1961.

Schttelndreyer, Burkhard. "Narrative Discourse in Sherpa." In *SIL Publications in Linguistics and Related Fields: Papers on Discourse*, no. 51 (Dallas: SIL, 1978).

Schwartz, Henry G. *The Minorities of Northern China: a Survey.* Bellingham: Western Washington University Press, 1984.

Scott, Sir George. "Among the Hill Tribes of Burma: An Ethnological Thicket." *National Geographic*, March 1922.

Scott, P. M. "Some Mongol Nestorian Crosses." *The Chinese Recorder*, February & November 1930.

Sebok, Thomas A. ed. *Linguistics in East Asia and Southeast Asia 2: Current Trends in Linguistics.* The Hague: Mouton, 1967.

Serruys, Henry. "Early Mongols and the Catholic Church." *Neue Zeitschrift fur Missionswissenschaft* (1963).

Shafer, Robert. *Introduction to Sino-Tibetan.* Wiesbaden: Otto Harrassowitz, 1974.

________ "Classification of the Sino-Tibetan Languages." *Word*, no. 11 (1955).

________ "Phonetique Historique des Langues Lolo." *T'oung Pao* 41, no. 1-3 (1952).

Shanghai Municipal Council. *Report for the Year 1931 and Budget for the Year 1932.* Shanghai: Kelly & Walsh, 1932.

Shaw, Jason. "Some Current Trends of Ethnology in China." In Chiao and Tapp, *Ethnicity and Ethnic Groups in China.*

She Lingyun. "Economic Construction in Xinjiang as a Means to Secure Peace." *Tianshan Yuegan*, no. 1 (15 October 1947).

Shibley, David, and Naomi. *The Smoke of a Thousand Villages and Other Stories of Real Life Heroes of the Faith.* Nashville: Thomas Nelson, 1989.

Shi Songshan, ed. *The Costumes and Ornaments of Chinese Yi Nationality Picture Album.* Beijing: Beijing Arts and Crafts Publishing House, 1989.

Shi Youyi, ed. *Folkways of China's Minority Nationalities (Southwest).* Chengdu: Huayi Publishing House, 1991.

Shintani, Tadahiko, and Yang Zhao. *The Mun Language of Hainan Island: Its Classified Lexicon.* Tokyo: Institute for the Study of Languages and Cultures of Asia and Africa, 1990.

Shiratori, Yoshiro. *Visual Ethnography: The Hill Tribes of South East Asia.* Japan: Kodansha, 1978.

Shitz, Suziki. *The Aboriginies of Taiwan.* Taipei: Wu Lin Press, 1991.

Shunsheng Ling, and Yihfu Ruey. "A Report on the Investigation of the Miao of Western Hunan." *Academia Sinica* (Shanghai, 1947).

Sinclair, Kevin. *The Forgotten Tribes of China.* Canada: Cupress, 1987.

Singh, Jag Deva. "Lahauli Verb Inflection." *Linguistics of the Tibeto-Burman Area* 12, no. 2 (1989).

Singh, K. S., ed. *People of India: An Introduction* 1: *Calcutta: Anthropological Survey of India.* New Delhi: Oxford University Press, 1992.

________ *People of India: Arunachal Pradesh* XIV. Calcutta: Anthropological Survey of India, 1995.

Singh, Nagendra. *Bhutan: A Kingdom in the Himalayas.* New Delhi: Thomson, 1972.

Singh, Raghubir. "A Rare Visit to a World Unto Itself." *National Geographic*, November 1988.

Sino-Tibetan Etymological Dictionary and Thesaurus (STEDT). *Description of the Sino-Tibetan Language Family.* Berkeley: University of California, Department of Linguistics, 1996.

Sinor, Denis. *Inner Asia: a Syllabus — The Uighurs.* Bloomington: Indiana University Press, 1971.

Situ Xun, "A Feast for the Eyes: The Torch Festival." *China Tourism*, no. 94, n.d.

Skipton, R. Kennedy. "Hill Peoples of Yunnan-China." In Evans-Pritchard (ed.), *Peoples of the Earth* 13.

Slaviska Missionen. *Folkboken: Folkgrupperna I OSS, Baltikum och Kina.* Sweden, 1998.

________ *Pray for Us.* Prayer booklet, Sweden, 1995.

Snellgrove, David, and Hugh Richardson. *A Cultural History of Tibet.* Colorado: Prajna Press, 1980.

Solnit, David B. "A Note on the Problematic Status of 'Shwa' in Biao Min Yao." *Linguistics of the Tibeto-Burman Area* 10, no. 2 (1987).

________ "The Position of Lakkia Within Kaddai." In SIL, *Comparative Kadai.*

________ "Some Evidence from Biao Min on the Initials of Proto-Mienic (Yao) and Proto-Hmong-Mien (Miao-Yao)." *Linguistics of the Tibeto-Burman Area* 19, no. 1 (1996).

Song Enchang. "The Family Systems and Its Ethos Among the Yao of Yunnan." In Lemoine and Chiao, *The Yao of South China.*
Speer, Robert E. *Servants of the King: Young Peoples Missionary Movement of the United States and Canada.* 1909.
Spillett, Hubert W., comp. *A Catalogue of Scriptures in the Languages of China and the Republic of China.* London: British & Foreign Bible Society, 1975.
Spuler, Berthold. *The Mongols in History.* New York: Praeger, 1972.
_______ *The Muslim World, Part II: The Mongol Period.* Leiden: E. J. Brill, 1960.
State Nationalities Affairs Commission. *China's Minority Peoples.* Beijing: China Pictorial Publishing House, 1995.
Stauffer, Milton T., ed. *The Christian Occupation of China.* Shanghai: China Consultation Committee, 1922.
Stein, Sir Aurel. *On Ancient Central Asian Tracks.* London: Macmillan, 1933.
Stein, R. A. *Tibetan Civilization.* London: Faber & Faber, 1972.
Stevens, K. Mark, and G. E. Wehrfritz. *Southwest China: Off the Beaten Track.* London: Collins, 1988.
Stewart, John. *The Nestorian Missionary Enterprise: A Church on Fire.* Edinburgh: T. & T. Clarke, 1923.
Storey, Robert et al., eds. *China: a Travel Survival Kit.* Hawthorn, Australia: Lonely Planet Publications, 1994.
Stover, Leo, and Takeno Stover. *China: An Anthropological Perspective.* Pacific Pallisades: Goodyear Publishing, 1976.
Strecker, David. "The Hmong-Mien Languages." *Linguistics of the Tibeto-Burman Area* 10, no. 2 (1987).
_______ "Some Comments on Benedict's Miao-Yao Enigma: The Na-e Languages." *Linguistics of the Tibeto-Burman Area* 10, no. 2 (1987).
Stevenson, Henry Noel Cochrane. "The Hill Peoples of Burma." *Burma Pamphlets*, no. 6 (London: Longmans, 1944).
Stevenson, Paul Huston. "The Chinese-Tibetan Borderland and Its Peoples." *China Journal*, no. 6 (1927).
_______ "Notes on the Human Geography of the Chinese-Tibetan Borderland." *Geographical Review*, no. 22 (1932).
Summer Institute of Linguistics. *Comparative Kadai: Linguistic Studies Beyond Tai. Publications in Linguistics*, no. 86 (Dallas, 1988).
Sun Hongkai. "A Brief Account of My Research Work, With an Appended Bibliography." *Linguistics of the Tibeto-Burman Area* 10, no. 1 (1987).
_______ "Languages of the Ethnic Corridor in Western Sichuan." *Linguistics of the Tibeto-Burman Area* 13, no. 1 (1990).
_______ "Notes on Anong, a New Language." *Linguistics of the Tibeto-Burman Area* 11, no. 1 (1988).
_______ "On Nationality and Recognition of Tibeto-Burman Languages." *Linguistics of the Tibeto-Burman Area* 15, no. 2 (1992).
_______ "A Preliminary Investigation into the Relationship Between Qiong Long and the Languages of the Qiang Branch of Tibeto-Burman." *Linguistics of the Tibeto-Burman Area* 12, no. 1 (1989).
_______; Lu Shaozun; Zhang Jichuan, and Ouyang Jueya. *The Languages of the Menba, Luoba and Deng Peoples.* Beijing: Chinese Social Science Publishing House, 1980.
Sun, Jackson Tianshin. "Caodeng Gyalrong Phonology: A First Look." *Linguistics of the Tibeto-Burman Area* 17, no. 2 (1994).
_______ "Review of Zangmian Yu Yuyin Han Cohui" [Tibeto-Burman Phonology and Vocabularies]. *Linguistics of the Tibeto-Burman Area* 15, no. 2 (1992).
Sun Yatsen. *Memoires of a Chinese Revolutionary.* Taipei: China Cultural Service, 1953.
Sutton, S. B. *In China's Border Provinces: The Turbulent Career of Joseph Rock, Botanist and Explorer.* New York: Hastings House, 1974.
Svantesson, Jan-Olof. "U." *Linguistics of the Tibeto-Burman Area* 11, no. 1 (1988).
Swan, William. *Letters on Missions.* Boston: Perkins & Marvin, 1831.
Swain, Margaret, Byrne. "Pere Vial and the Gni-p'a: Orientalist Scholarship and the Christian Project." In Harrell (ed.), *Cultural Encounters on China's Ethnic Frontiers.*
Sweeting, George. *More Than 2000 Great Quotes and Illustrations.* Texas: Word Publishing, 1985.
Taggart, Frederick. *Rome and China: A Study in Correlations in Historical Events.* Berkeley: University of California Press, 1939.
Tai Chi Yin. "Timeless Plateau: Zhongdian." *China Tourism*, no. 108, n.d.
Tapp, Nicholas. *Sovereignty and Independence: The White Hmong of Thailand.* Singapore: Oxford University Press, 1990.
Taylor, Elizabeth M. "A Review of the Social Basis for Sustainable Development in Arunachal Pradesh." Manuscript, n.d.
Taylor, Howard. *Behind the Ranges: Fraser of Lisuland, S. W. China.* Redhill, London: Lutterworth Press and CIM, 1944.
_______ *Hudson Taylor and the China Inland Mission.* London: CIM, 1931.
Taylor, Mrs Howard. *The Call of China's Great Northwest.* London: Religious Tract Society, n.d.
_______ *Guinness of Honan. By His Sister Mrs. Howard Taylor.* Philadelphia: CIM.
Taylor, J. Hudson. *After Thirty Years: Three Decades of China Inland Mission.* London, 1898.
Tegenfeldt, Herman G. *A Century of Growth: The Kachin Baptist Church of Burma.* Pasadena: William Carey Library, 1974.
Teichman, Eric. *Travels of a Consular Officer in Eastern Tibet.* London: Cambridge University Press, 1922.
Tenzin, Gyatso (Dalai Lama XIV). *My Land and My People.* New York: McGraw-Hill, 1962.
Thomas, David D. *Mon-Khmer Subgroupings in Vietnam.* The Hague: Mouton, 1966.
Thompson, H. Gordon. "From Yunnan-fu to Peking Along the Tibetan and Mongolian Borders." *Geographical Journal*, no. 67 (1926).
Thompson, Phyllis. *China: The Reluctant Exodus.* Sevenoaks, Kent: Hodder & Stoughton, 1979.
_______ *King of the Lisu.* London: CIM, 1956.
_______ *To Each Her Post: The Inspiring Lives of Six Great Women in China.* London: Hodder & Stoughton, 1982.
Thornbury, Patrick. *Minorities and Human Rights Law.* London: Minority Rights Group, 1987.
Thurgood, Graham. "Zauzou: A New Lolo-Burmese Language." *Linguistics of the Tibeto-Burman Area* 9, no. 2 (1986).
Tianfu. "Hospitality Deep in the Daxingan Mountain Forests." *China Tourism*, no. 31, n.d.
Tian Huo. "The Colourful Peoples of the Wumeng Mountains." *China Tourism*, no. 111, n.d.
Tian Liangeng. "Yi Peoples of the Lesser Liang-shan Make Rapid Transition to Socialism." *Renmin Ribao*, 14 June 14 1959.
Tian Qui. "The Tibetans of Deqen." *China Tourism*, no. 108, n.d.
T'ien Ju-K'ang. *Peaks of Faith: Protestant Mission in Revolutionary China.* Leiden: E. J. Brill, 1993.
_______ *Religious Cults of the Pai-i Along the Burma-Yunnan Border.* New York: Cornell University Monograph, 1986.
Tiley, Chodag. *Tibet, the Land and the People.* Beijing: New World Press, 1988.
Todaeva, Buliash. "Einige Besonderheiten der Paoan-Sprache." *Acta Orientalia Hungaricae*, no. 16 (1963).
Torrance, Thomas. *China's First Missionaries: Ancient Israelities.* Chicago: Daniel Shaw, 1988 reprint.
_______ *The History, Customs and Religion of the Chi'ang, an Aboriginal people of West China.* Shanghai: 1920.

_______ "Notes on the West China Aboriginal Tribes." *West China Border Research Society*, no. 5 (1932).
Torrance, Thomas F. (Jr.). "Journal of My First Visit to Hong Kong, Chengdu and Wenchuan, April 22 to June 3, 1994." Report, Edinburgh, 1994.
_______ "A Visit by Thomas F. Torrance to Chengdu, the Capital of Sichuan, and to Weichou and Chi'ang villages in Wenchuan County, the upper Min Valley, Sichuan, October 4-18, 1986." Report, Edinburgh, 1986.
Tsering, Marku. *Sharing Christ in the Tibetan Buddhist World*. Pennsylvania: Tibet Press, 1988.
Tsutomo Rai. "Supplement to Li Fang-Gui's 'Notes on the Mak Language'." *Jimbun Kagaku Kigaku Kiyo, Ochanomizu Joshidaigaku*, no. 7 (1955).
Tucci, Giuseppe. *The Religions of Tibet*. Berkeley: University of California Press, 1980.
Tucker, Ruth A. *From Jerusalem to Irian Jaya: A Biographical History of Christian Missions*. Grand Rapids: Zondervan, 1983.
_______ *Guardians of the Great Commission*. Grand Rapids: Zondervan, 1988.
Twitchett, D., and J. K. Fairbank, eds. *The Cambridge History of China: Sui and T'ang China*. Cambridge: Cambridge University Press 3, 1979.
Upcraft, W. M. "The Wild Men of Szechuan." *Chinese Recorder*, October 1892.
Van Dyck, Howard. *William Christie: Apostle to Tibet*. Harrisburg: Christian Publications, 1956.
Vannicelli, Luigi O. F. M. *La Religione dei Lolo, Contributo allo Studio Etnologico delle Religioni dell'estremo Oriente*. Milan: Catholic University Publications, 1944.
Vesalainen, Olavi, and Marja. "Clause Patterns in Lhomi." *Pacific Linguistics B*, no. 53 (1980).
_______ "Lhomi Phonetic Summary." (Kathmandu: SIL and the Institute of Nepal and Asian Studies, 1976).
Vial, Paul. *Dictionnaire Francais-Lolo, dialect Gni: Tribu situee dans les sous-prefectures de Lou Nan Tcheou, Lou Lean Tcheou, Gouang-si Tcheou, Province du Yunnan* [French-Lolo Dictionary, Gni dialect: A Tribe Located in the Sub-Prefectures of Lunan, Luliang and Guangxi counties, Yunnan Province]. Hong Kong: Imprimerie de la Societe des Missions Estrangeres, 1909.
_______ *De la Langue et de l'écriture indigènes au Yûn-Nân*. Paris: E. Leroux, 1890.
_______ "Le Gni ou Gni-p'a: tribu Lolottee du Yunnan" [The Gni or Gni-p'a: A Lolo Tribe of Yunnan], *Les Missions Catholiques* 2, no.26 (1893).
_______ "Les Lolos: Histoire, Religion, Moeurs, Langue, Ecriture" [The Lolos: History, Religion, Customs, Language, Writing]. *Etudes Sino-Orientales* [Sino-Oriental Studies] *Part A*. Shangai: Impremerie de la Missions Catholique, 1898.
Vietnam News Agency. *Vietnam: Image of the Community of 54 Ethnic Groups*. The Ethnic Publishing House, 1996.
Vine, Aubrey R. *The Nestorian Churches: a Concise History of Nestorian Christianity in Asia from the Persian Schism to the Modern Assyrians*. London: Independent Press, 1937.
Voegelin, Carl F., and Florence M. Voegelin. *Classification and Index of the World's Languages*. New York: Elsevier North Holland, 1977.
Von Eickstedt, Egon. *Rassendynamik von Ostasien*. Berlin: Walter de Gruyter, 1944.
Von Fuerer-Haimendorf, Christoph. *The Sherpas of Nepal*. London: John Murray, 1964.
_______ *Tribes of India: The Struggle for Survival*. Delhi: Oxford University Press, 1985.
Von Geusau, Leo Alting. "The Second Hani/Akha Culture Studies Conference, 12-18 May 1996." *Chiang Mai Newsletter*, October 1996.
Vost, Cliff. *The Tribes of Taiwan*. Taiwan: Vision International, 1995.
Waddell, L. Austine. *The Buddhism and Lamaism of Tibet*. New Delhi: Heritage, 1979.
Walker, Anthony R. *Lahu Nyi (Red Lahu) Village Society and Economy in North Thailand*. 2 Vols. Chiang Mai, Thailand: Tribal Research Center, 1977.
_______ *Studies of Ethnic Minority Peoples, in Contributions to Southeast Asian Ethnography*. Singapore: Double-Six Press, 1982.
Walker, J. E. "Shao-wu in Fuh-kien: A Country Station." *Chinese Recorder*, no. 9, September-October 1878.
Walsh, W. Parkenham. *Modern Heroes of the Mission Field*. London: Hodder & Stoughton, 1982.
Wan, F. C. "Unforgettable Times With Our Lhoba Friends." *China Tourism*, no. 70, n.d.
Wang Chang Fu. *The Culture and Customs of the Yi people of the Liang Shan*. Chengdu: Sichuan National Publishing House, 1994.
Wang Dewen. "A Comparative Study of Kam and Sui Initial Consonants." In SIL, *Comparative Kadai*.
Wang Fushi, and Mao Zongwu. *Renconstruction of Proto Miao-Yao*. Beijing: National Academy of Social Sciences, 1995.
Wang Jia. "The Siyueba Festival at Jiwei." *China Tourism*, no. 107, n.d.
Wang, Mary T. "A Remote Tribe in West China." *China Magazine* 16, no. 5 (1946).
Wang Zhengfang. "We of the Hani Nationality." *China Reconstructs*, n.d.
Wannemacher, Mark. "The Interaction of Tone, Phonation Type and Glottal Features in Zaiwa." *Focus on Phonology: PYU Working Papers in Linguistics*, no. 1 (Chiang Mai, Thailand: Payap University Graduate Linguistics Department, 1996).
_______ "Zaiwa Syllable Structure." *Focus on Phonology* (1996).
Ward, Barbara E. "A Hong Kong Fishing Village." *Journal of Oriental Studies* (January 1954).
Ward, Francis Kingdon. *From China to Hkamti Long*. London: Edward Arnold, 1924.
_______ *The Land of the Blue Poppy*. Cambridge: Cambridge University Press, 1913.
_______ *The Mystery Rivers of Tibet*. London: Seeley, Service & Co., 1923.
Weekes, Richard V., ed. *Muslim Peoples: A World Ethnographic Survey*. London: Aldwych Press, 1984.
Weera Ostapirat. "Sani's Fortis See-Saw and Initial Devoicing." *Linguistics of the Tibeto-Burman Area* 19, no. 1 (1996).
Wei Ch'ing-wen. "A Brief Description of the Sui Language." *Zhongguo Yuwen*, no. 138 (October 1965).
Weidman, Groff G. "Landscaped Kwangsi: China's Province of Pictorial Art." *National Geographic*, December 1937.
Wei Kun. "The Gereja Batania." *Bridge*, no. 39, January-February 1990.
_______ "The Jingpo Christians." *Bridge*, no. 43, September-October 1990.
Weins, Harold J. *China's March into the Tropics*. Hamden, CT: Shoe String Press, 1954.
Wen Yu. "The Personal Endings of the Verb in the Jyarung Language as Spoken at Paslok." *Studia Serica* 1, no. 4 (1940).
Wessels, C. *Early Jesuit Travelers in Central Asia 1603-1721*. The Hague: Martinus Nijhoff, 1924.
Wheatley, Julian K. "Comments on the 'Hani' Dialects of Loloish."*Linguistics of the Tibeto-Burman Area* 7, no. 1 (1982).
White, John Claude. *Sikkim and Bhutan: Twenty-One Years on the Northeast Frontier (1887-1908)*. Delhi: Vivek, 1971.
Wingate, Rachel O. *The Steep Ascent: The Story of the Christian Church in Turkestan*. British & Foreign Bible Society, n.d.
_______ "A Mission of Friendship to the Muslims of Turkestan." *Muslim World*, January 1959.
Winnington, Alan. *The Slaves of the Cool Mountains: The Ancient Social Conditions and Changes Now in Progress on the Remote South-Western Borders of China*. London: Lawrence & Wishart, 1959.

Winter, Ralph D. "Unreached Peoples: Recent Developments in the Concept." *Mission Frontiers* (August-September 1989).

_______ "Unreached Peoples: What, Where, and Why?" In Patrick Sookhedo (ed.), *New Frontiers in Mission* (Grand Rapids: Baker, 1987).

Wolfenden, S. N. *Outlines of Tibeto-Burman Linguistic Morphology*. London: Royal Asiatic Society, 1929.

_______ "Concerning the Variation of Final Consonants in the Word Families of Tibetan, Kachin, and Chinese." *Journal of the Royal Asiatic Society* (1937).

Wong Chung Fai. "The Felt-Hatted Baima." *China Tourism*, no. 115, n.d.

_______ "The Lives of Hui'an Women." *China Tourism*, no. 117, n.d.

_______ "A Mountain Hamlet in Zhugqu." *China Tourism*, no. 115, n.d.

_______ "Xilankapu: Weaving With a Background of Centuries." *China Tourism*, no. 106, n.d.

Wong How-Man. "Peoples of China's Far Provinces." *National Geographic*, March 1984.

Wong Tak Hing. "A Pilgrimage to the Mountains: A Visit to Miao Churches in Guizhou Province." *Bridge*, no. 24, July-August 1987.

Wright, A. *Buddhism in Chinese History*. Stanford: Stanford University Press, 1959.

Wright, Arthur F., and Dennis Twitchett, eds. *Perspectives on the T'ang*. Taiwan: Rainbow Ridge, 1973.

Wright, E. B. "Summary Report of Work Among the River Miao." 1946.

Wu, Aitchen K. *Turkistan Tumult*. London: Methuen, 1940.

Wu, David Y. H. "Culture Change and Ethnic Identity Among Minorities in China." In Chiao and Tapp, *Ethnicity and Ethnic Groups in China*.

Wulsin, Frederick R. "The Road to Wang Ye Fu." *National Geographic*, February 1926.

Wurm, Stephen A., ed. *Atlas of the World's Languages in Danger of Disappearing*. Paris: UNESCO, 1996.

Wurm, Stephen A., and Shiro Hattori, eds. *Language Atlas of the Pacific Area*. Canberra : Australian Academy of the Humanities in collaboration with the Japan Academy, 1981-83.

Wu Si. "Yi Life in the Greater and Lesser Liangshan Mountains." *China Tourism*, no. 94, n.d.

Wu Zhouming. "The Ancient Trail in Sichuan." *China Tourism*, no. 59, n.d.

Xia Jie. "The Long Dragon Banquet: The Lami Street Fest." *China Tourism*, no. 76, n.d.

Xian Yanyun. "In Search of the Ancient Tea Caravan Route." *China Tourism*, no. 181, August 1995.

Xiao Yang. "Vietnamese Refugees in China." *Bridge*, no. 9, January-February 1985.

Xie Jianzhu. *The Samei People of Kunming's Eastern Suburbs*. Hong Kong: Chinese University, n.d.

Xie Shixun. "Encounter With the Yao in their Mountain Home." *China Tourism*, no. 73, n.d.

_______ "The Floral-Belted Dais of the Red River." *China Tourism*, no. 78, n.d.

_______ "The Hanis of the Ailao Mountains." *China Tourism*, no. 79, n.d.

Xu Lang, ed. *Guiyang*. Beijing: New World Press, 1989.

Xu Liqun. "By Motorbike Along China's Borders." *China Tourism*, no. 109, n.d.

Xu Wenqing. "Myths and Legends of the Lian Nan Ba Pai Yao." In Lemoine and Chiao, *The Yao of South China*.

Xu Ye. "The Lingguan Route (II)." *China Tourism*, no. 120, n.d.

Xu Yixi, ed. *Headdresses of Chinese Minority Nationality Women*. Hong Kong: China Film Press, 1989.

Yang, Gladys, trans. "Ashma (A Shani Ballad)." *Chinese Literature*, no. 3 (1955).

_______ "'Ashma,' The Oldest Shani Ballad." *Chinese Literature*, no. 1 (1955).

Yang, Martin M. C. "Peoples and Societies in Yunnan (Part I)." *Journal of Ethnology and Sociology*, no. 16 (Taipei, 1978).

Yang Tiande. "A Riot of Yao Color." *China Tourism*, no. 110, n.d.

Yan Wenbian; Zhang Pen, and Gu Qing, eds. *Dai Folk Legends*. Beijing: Foreign Languages Press, 1988.

Yao Aiyun. "Unique Dance of the Axi People." *China Today*, June 1996.

Yao Shun An. "A Comparison of the Culture of the Yao People in China and Thailand." *Notes on Anthropology and Intercultural Community Work* 14 (1994).

Yashuda, Yasuhiko. *A Historical Study of the Jiarong Verb System*. Tokyo: Seishido, 1984.

Ying Yang. "Alxa, Land of Camels." *China Tourism*, no. 113, n.d.

Young, Harold. "To the Mountain Tops: A Study of the Lahu of Burma and Thailand." n.d.

Young, John M. L. *By Foot to China: Mission of the Church of the East*. Tokyo: Radio Press, 1984.

Young, W. M. "The Awakening of Keng Tung." *The Missionary Review of the World*, March 1906.

Younghusband, Sir Francis. *India and Tibet*. London: John Murray, 1910.

Yuan Jiahua. "The A-si Love Songs and the A-si Language." *Frontier Politics* 3 (Nan-k'ai State University, 1946).

Yule, Henry, and Henri Cordier. *Cathay And The Way Thither: Being A Collection Of Medieval Notices Of China*. 4 Vols. Tokyo: Kyoyekishosha, 1866; Reprinted Delhi: Munshiram Manoharlal.

Yunnan Provincial Travel & Tourism Administration. *A Tour to the Mysterious Land of Yunnan*. Kunming, n.d.

Zee Yunyang. "A Comparison of Ba Pai and Guoshan Yao Tones." In Lemoine and Chiao, *The Yao of South China*.

Zeng Xianyang. "Dancing for Love: The Tiaohuapo Festival." *China Tourism*, no. 117, n.d.

Zhang Jianghua, and Wu Congzhong. "Tibet's Menba Nationality." *China Reconstructs*, July 1979.

Zhang Junru. "The Pubiao Language." In Edmonson, *Kadai*.

Zhang Weiwen, and Zeng Qingnan. *In Search of China's Minorities*. Beijing: New World Press, 1993.

Zhao Xiangru, and Reinhold F. Hahn. "The Ili Turk People and Their Language." *Central Asiatic Journal*, no. 33 (1989).

Zheng Guoqiao. "The Influences of Han on the Mulam Language." In SIL, *Comparative Kadai*.

Zheng Guoqiao, and Quam Yang. "The Sounds of Rongjiang Kam." In SIL, *Comparative Kadai*.

Zheng Lan. *Travels Through Xishuangbanna: China's Subtropical Home of Many Nationalities*. Beijing: Foreign Languages Press, 1981.

Zheng Ming. "Mountain Ceremony of the Tibetans of Southern Gansu." *China Tourism*, no. 125, November 1990.

Zheng Peng. *Our Beautiful Xishuangbanna*. Shenzhen: Meiguang Colour Printing, n.d.

Zhong Dakun, ed. *The Yi Nationality of the Liang Shan Mountains*. Beijing: The People's Fine Arts Publishing House, 1992.

Zhu Liangwen. *The Dai (Or the Tai and their Architecture and Customs in South China)*. Kunming: The Science and Technology Press of Yunnan, 1992.

Zide, Norman H., ed. *Studies in Comparative Austroasiatic Linguistics*. The Hague, Netherlands, 1966.

Zondervan Publishing. *Great Missionaries to China*. Grand Rapids: Zondervan, 1947.

Zwalf, W. *Heritage of Tibet*. London: British Museum, 1981.

Zwemer, Samuel. *A Primer on Islam and the Spiritual Needs of the Mohammedans of China*. Shanghai, 1919.

General Index

Ethnolinguistic groups profiled in the text are displayed in bold. Titles of publications, and page references to color photo sections, are in italic. Alternate names for people groups are listed in Appendix 2 and have not all been included in this Index.

D

E

F

G

I

J

M

N

O

P

Q

R

S

T

X

Y

Z

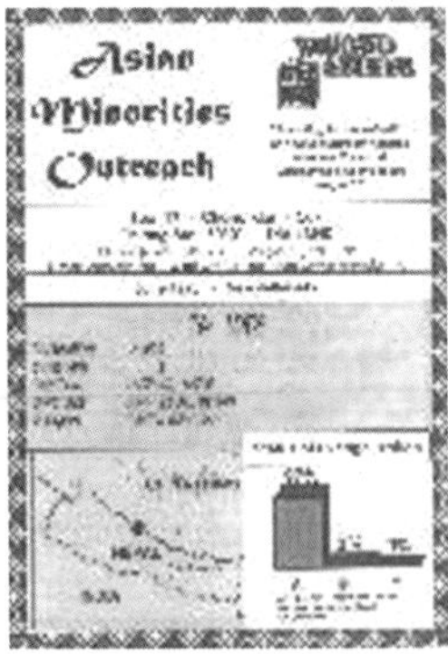

The Asian Minorities Outreach (AMO) *Newsletter* containing people-group profiles is sent free of charge to Christians around the world for the purpose of raising awareness, prayer, and financial support for outreach among the most unreached ethnic groups of Asia. The *Newsletter* is available from AMO in Thailand only. Please contact the Chiang Mai AMO address below with any ministry information requests or to receive the *Newsletter.*

The following books by Paul Hattaway can be ordered from the stockists listed below. Order from the address nearest to you – prices include postage within the specified geographical area.

The Peoples of Vietnam **examines the unique and varied cultures of Vietnam. It encourages caring Christians around the world to pray in an informed way for all the peoples of Vietnam**

- 114 pp -
ISBN 974-85301-6-7
$12.00 / £8.00

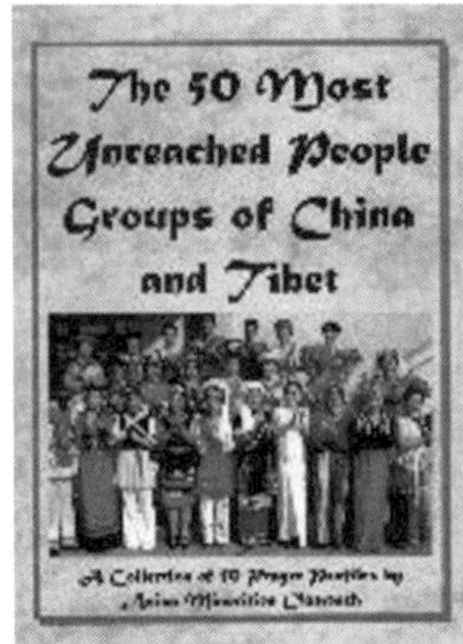

Thousands of people around the world have used *The 50 Most Unreached People Groups of China and Tibet* to pray and intercede for the needy peoples of China and Tibet, and new workers have been mobilized for this harvest field

- 110 pp -
ISBN 974-85307-0-1
$10.00 / £7.00

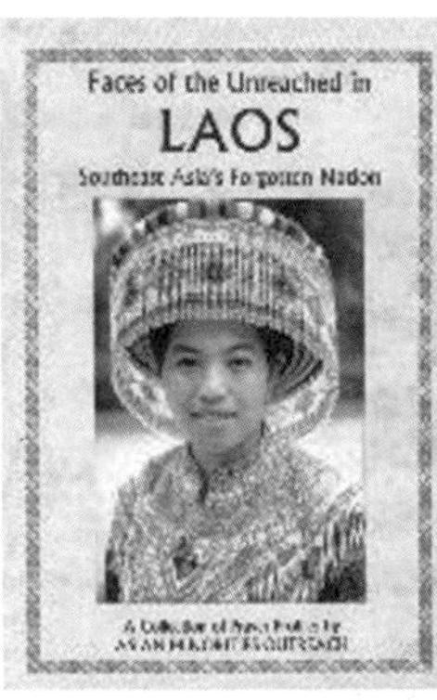

For centuries land-locked Laos has been the forgotten nation of Southeast Asia – by politicians, explorers, and missionaries alike. *Faces of the Unreached in Laos: Southeast Asia's Forgotten Nation* is the first known book that attempts to profile all the peoples of Laos in order to encourage prayer, awareness, and outreach to these 138 needy groups

- 158pp - ISBN 974-85302-7-2; $15.00 / £10.00

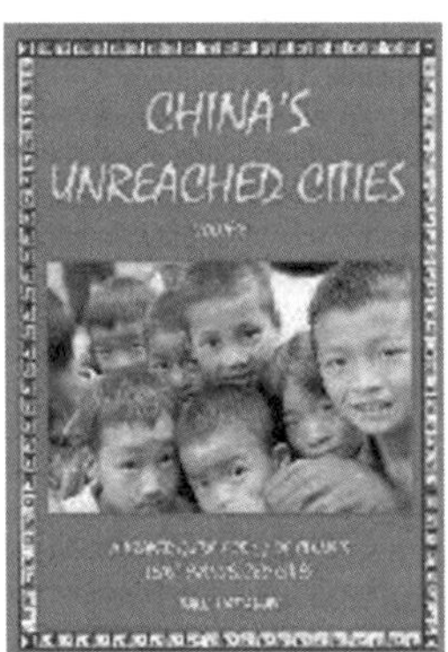

Jim Nickel, President of the Institute of Chinese Studies, explains the significance of *China's Unreached Cities*: "We must reach the cities because that is where the people are.... By the year 2010 it is estimated that half of China's population will live in urban areas – up from 28% in 1994." The cities of China, as you will discover in the pages of this book, are largely unevangelized. Reaching them with the gospel of Jesus Christ is a daunting task, but it must be done

- 124pp - ISBN 97485302-8-8; $13.00 / £8.00

The complete set of four titles can be ordered @ $39.00 / £26.00.

Australasia and Asia:
Asian Minorities Outreach
Box 17
Chang Klan P.O.
Chiang Mai, 50101
Thailand

e-mail: amo@xc.org
website:www.antioch.com.sg/mission/asianmo/

North America:
Asian Minorities Outreach
P.O. Box 901
Palestine
TX 75802
U.S.A.

UK, Europe, and Africa:
Piquant
P.O. Box 83
Carlisle
CA3 9GR
United Kingdom

e-mail: amo@piquant.net
website: www.piquant.net